The Rise and Development
of Western Civilization

The Rise and Development of Western Civilization

VOLUME I
Second Edition

JOHN L. STIPP
Knox College

C. WARREN HOLLISTER
University of California, Santa Barbara

ALLEN W. DIRRIM
San Fernando Valley State College

John Wiley & Sons, Inc., New York · London · Sydney · Toronto

FRONTISPIECE: *Athens in the time of Hadrian. The Granger Collection.*

Copyright © 1967, 1972 by John Wiley & Sons, Inc.

All rights reserved. Published simultaneously in Canada.

No part of this book may be reproduced by any means, nor transmitted, nor translated into a machine language without the written permission of the publisher.

Library of Congress Catalogue Card Number: 76-171915

ISBN 0-471-82613-8 Cloth   ISBN 0-471-82620-0 Paper

Printed in the United States of America.

10 9 8 7 6 5 4 3 2 1

To our parents

Preface to the Second Edition

Textbooks, like any academic endeavor, periodically need re-examination. A college generation has passed since publication of the first edition of *The Rise and Development of Western Civilization*, and some recasting is in order. Although the book's fundamental structure and substance have not been radically altered, necessary changes have been made.

One change has involved the occasional shifting or clarification of emphases. In volume 1, for example, the original section on the late Roman Empire too easily gave the impression, despite contrary cautionary remarks, of a sudden collapse of that empire. In this edition material has been added to underscore the innovative sanctions and alterations of Diocletian and Constantine. Similarly, significant parts of the complex of chapters dealing with post-medieval and early modern times have been reworked. The same treatment, where needed, is given to material in volume 2. There, for example, exposition of the background of the Russian Communist Revolution underemphasized the role of precommunist theoreticians and revolutionaries; accordingly, a fairly substantial section of new matter has been included. On the other hand, some material has been deleted where its inclusion has come to seem unnecessary in a survey account of Western civilization; an example of this kind of change is the excision of the section on the New Deal.

Many comments sent in by users of one or both volumes have motivated other changes. Examples of the latter are the addition of a section on the nature and use of history, the reordering of the sequence of units of Crete and Greece, and the addition of new maps. There is neither point to, nor practicability in, listing exhaustive details of the range of suggestions; but reference should be made here to the citation, in the *Acknowledgments* section, of some critic-reviewers whose comments and suggestions have been especially helpful. The authors will be pardoned if they also express their understandable gratification to those respondents who plainly and sometimes very forcefully asserted that any wholesale tinkering with the text would almost certainly spoil it for them.

Naturally, major events and developments that have occurred since the appearance of the first edition are given attention in this one. To make room for such new material several units have been abridged.

But despite all the additions, changes, deletions, and other modifications, the book retains its original nature and purpose. It seeks now, as it did in the original edition, to present the basic characteristics of our heritage thematically and graphically.

October, 1971

JOHN L. STIPP
ALLEN W. DIRRIM
C. WARREN HOLLISTER

Preface to the First Edition

Several assumptions underlie this account of the rise and development of Western civilization. One is that the modern college student possesses a quickened intellectual curiosity. Given a reasonably comprehensive body of data, he may be trusted to reach responsible judgments on his own. Another—only seemingly contradictory to the first—is that he needs some guidelines to keep him on the main paths; otherwise he may easily get lost in a forest of facts. The present work deliberately focuses attention on pivotal decisions and developments. Where they are encountered, the tempo slows to allow treatment in depth. Where they are not present, the narrative passes over details mainly of interest only to the specialist. For the most part, the problems which invite this kind of study are problems whose nature or "solution" bears upon our own times.

A third premise, closely related to the second, rests in the belief that historical trends or movements deserve emphasis over separate, particular events. Of course this does not mean neglect of the latter; the pages of this volume actually contain almost a distressing amplitude of them. The point is that a sustained effort is made to present them so that they reveal the larger concerns of man and the spirit of the times that envelopes them.

A fourth assumption is that no meaningful understanding of the various facets of human experience—religion, politics, literature, economics, art, philosophy, science—can come from studying them in isolation. Repeatedly the literature or art of a particular "period" is considered in intimate connection with political and economic activity, as in, for example, the section entitled "School of Hellas: Form." Here Sophocles and his work are seen not only as wonders of the world of drama, but as important forces involved in the creation of a political and military organization which shaped much of the history of the Greek people then and for a long time afterward.

Finally, encompassing these beliefs is a fundamental faith that the collective memory of man which we call history is not an academic —and sometimes dispensable—discipline in essence, but a requisite for the enlargement of man. The eminent historian, Carl Becker, phrased this faith in compelling words:

"The value of history is, indeed, not scientific but moral: by liberalizing the mind, by deepening the sympathies, by fortifying the will, it enables us to control, not society, but ourselves—a much more important thing; it prepares us to live more humanely in the present and to meet rather than to foretell the future."

The results of recent research, published in articles and monographic and general works, have been used throughout. Naturally they have modified a number of opinions and conclusions once firmly held. But a critical, and at times stubborn, insistence that new findings prove to be more than merely new has saved, it is hoped, both writers and readers from misunderstanding in the name of new understanding. At all times we have stood ready, where it seemed necessary, to report that from the available evidence no conclusions could be reached, however important the event or object under study. On a few occasions we have had to confess that from the evidence it seemed that no conclusions were ever likely to be reached. On the whole, however, we are left with the feeling that the material in the pages that follow offers opportunities enough, for those who want to know, to learn where Western man has been and how he got where he is. Any lesser purpose seems hardly worthwhile.

June, 1966

JOHN L. STIPP
ALLEN W. DIRRIM
C. WARREN HOLLISTER

Acknowledgments

We wish to express appreciation to a number of fellow historians who have carefully read portions of the manuscript and made many helpful suggestions. They are not, of course, to be held accountable for any errors of fact or interpretation, for which we bear sole responsibility.

    Klaus Baer, University of California (Berkeley)
    R. Davis Bitton, University of California (Santa Barbara)
    William J. Bouwsma, University of California (Berkeley)
    Gene A. Brucker, University of California (Berkeley)
    Sidney A. Burrell, Boston University
    Mortimer Chambers, University of California (Los Angeles)
    Ann D. Kilmer, University of California (Berkeley)
    Gordon Leff, University of Manchester
    William G. Sinnigen, Hunter College

In preparing the present edition we have profited from wide-ranging comments sent in from many users of the text whose classroom experience with it give to their suggestions a special weight and influence. Of this group we should like to give particular credit to the following:

    Alfred Andrea, University of Vermont
    Robert P. Barnes, Central Washington State College
    Miles W. Campbell, New Mexico State University
    Samuel E. Dicks, Kansas State Teachers College
    Lee N. Layport, Jr., Santa Ana College, California
    Edith C. Tatnall, Metropolitan State College, Denver, Colorado
    Warren L. Vinz, Boise State College, Idaho

We also wish to express our collective debt to Jere Donovan of *Time Magazine,* whose maps have made portions of this work instructive beyond the power of words. We are deeply obliged to our chief editor, Carl E. Beers, for his careful over-all supervision of this new edition. We further wish to express our appreciation to Arthur Vergara for his in-depth editing and to Marjorie Graham for her valuable help in the selection and arrangements of illustrations and maps. For his encouragement and guidance throughout the long period of gestation of the original edition, William L. Gum deserves our continuing appreciation. Each of us is under special obligation to particular individuals. We should like to express this obligation in the following separate statements.

Grateful acknowledgments are made to: Elizabeth B. Wilson for critically reading most of the material of the first six chapters of volume 1 and for making countless helpful suggestions; my wife, Cleo, not only for patient understanding throughout, but for skillful help in preparation of portions of the manuscript; Jo Ann Ooiman, typist extraordinary and, more importantly, perceptive critic; Mark Lawrence and other members of the Seymour Library staff for their inestimable assistance; and Mary Mangieri and Kathy Freise for their competent handling of seemingly endless typing chores.

J.L.S.

Contents

Prologue

A. The Study of History — 1
   DEFINITIONS — 1
   THE PURPOSE OF STUDYING HISTORY — 3

B. The Emergence of Man — 5
   THE GENESIS OF MAN — 5
   PRELITERATE CULTURE — 7

CHAPTER I
The Birth of Civilization

A. Egypt: Sphinx and Falcon — 17
   PRE-DYNASTIC HISTORY — 17
   FOUNDING OF THE FIRST DYNASTY — 20
   THE OLD KINGDOM — 22
   TIME OF TROUBLES—THE FIRST INTERMEDIATE PERIOD — 33
   THE MIDDLE KINGDOM — 34
   RELIGIOUS VENTURING — 34
   THE SECOND INTERMEDIATE PERIOD—THE HYKSOS INVASION — 36
   IMPERIAL EGYPT — 37

B. Mesopotamia: The First Eden — 45
   SUMERIAN AND AKKADIAN SETTLEMENTS — 45
   POLITICS AND CULTURE — 49
   ECONOMIC CONDITIONS — 57
   PAX BABYLONICA — 58

CHAPTER II
Small States, Empires, and the Hebrews

A. The "Catalysts": Mitanni, Hatti, Phoenicia, Aramaea, and Lydia — 65

HURRIAN CULTURE	66
THE HITTITE EMPIRE	67
THE PHOENICIANS—MIDDLEMEN OF THE NEAR EAST	68
ARAMAEANS AND LYDIANS	69
B. The Fusion of the Ancient Near East: The Empires of Assyria, Chaldea, Persia	70
THE ASSYRIANS	70
THE CHALDEANS	76
THE PERSIANS	78
C. The Hebrews—Chosen of Yahweh	83
EARLY HISTORY	83
THE EXODUS: WANDERING AND NATIONHOOD	87
POLITICAL DECLINE, SPIRITUAL ADVANCE; PROPHECIES FULFILLED	89
A NEW VISION	92

CHAPTER III

Aegean and Greek Civilizations

A. Crete	99
CRETAN CIVILIZATION	99
B. The Greek Way: Phoenix	106
MYCENAEAN HEGEMONY	106
THE IONIAN RENAISSANCE	110
ATHENIAN SOCIETY	117
SPARTAN SOCIETY	122
COLONIZATION AND CLASS STRUGGLE	126
PRELUDE TO GLORY: GREEK SOCIETY, 600–500 B.C.	130
NATURE AND SIGNIFICANCE OF THE PERSIAN WARS	136

CHAPTER IV

The Greek Way: From Polis to Cosmopolis

A. The Golden Age	145
THE SCHOOL OF HELLAS: MIND	145
THE SCHOOL OF HELLAS: WORD	154
THE SCHOOL OF HELLAS: FORM	161
B. The Age of Empire	170
POWER POLITICS, SOCIAL LAG, AND THE PELOPONNESIAN WAR	170
ARMS AND THE MAN: THE ALEXANDRIAN EMPIRE	174
THE DEPARTURE FROM THE GOLDEN MEAN: HELLENISTIC SOCIETY	177

CHAPTER V
The Roman World: The Republic

- A. Genesis and Early Development of Roman Culture — 195
  - EARLY SETTLEMENTS AND CULTURE — 195
  - THE VITAL CENTER OF LATIUM: EMERGENT ROME — 199
  - POLITICS AND CULTURE OF THE EARLY REPUBLIC — 200
  - THE IMPERIAL IMPULSE: THE PUNIC WARS — 209
  - THE DECLINE OF THE REPUBLIC — 213
  - THE LITERATURE OF THE REPUBLIC — 215
  - THE CONQUEST OF THE EAST — 217
- B. Roman Culture in a Time of Troubles — 220
  - A CENTURY OF STRUGGLE: 145–31 B.C. — 220
  - LITERATURE IN THE CENTURY OF STRUGGLE — 236

CHAPTER VI
The Roman World: Empire and the Christian Community

- A. The Empire — 247
  - THE ESTABLISHMENT OF THE PRINCIPATE — 247
  - LITERATURE AND CULTURE OF THE GOLDEN AGE — 253
  - PAX ROMANA—IMPERIAL ROME — 265
  - THE CULTURE OF THE SILVER AGE — 273
  - THE DISINTEGRATION OF THE ROMAN WORLD — 285
- B. The Christian Community — 290
  - ORIGINS OF THE CHRISTIAN FAITH — 290
  - THE SPREAD OF THE FAITH — 295
  - TRIALS AND TRIUMPH — 302

CHAPTER VII
Rome's Three Heirs: Byzantium, Western Europe, Islam

- A. Background: The Christian Empire — 307
  - THE MOOD OF THE LATE EMPIRE — 307
  - THE LATIN DOCTORS — 310
  - THE GERMANIC BARBARIANS — 313
- B. Byzantium — 319
  - BYZANTINE STATE AND CULTURE — 319
  - REIGN OF JUSTINIAN — 326
  - RETRENCHMENT AND REVIVAL — 327
- C. The West — 331
  - POLITICAL, ECONOMIC, AND CULTURAL DECLINE — 331
  - WESTERN EUROPE IN THE SIXTH AND SEVENTH CENTURIES — 333

D. Islam 340
- BACKGROUND AND ORIGINS 340
- ISLAMIC RELIGION: DYNASTIC DEVELOPMENTS 342
- EARLY CALIPHS; CIVIL WAR 343
- UMAYYAD AND ABBASID DYNASTIES 344

CHAPTER VIII
Carolingian Europe and the New Invasions

A. The Rise of the Carolingian Empire 353
- THE SIGNIFICANCE OF THE CAROLINGIAN RENAISSANCE 353
- AGRICULTURAL TECHNOLOGY 354
- POLITICAL AND RELIGIOUS DEVELOPMENTS 355
- THE FRANCO-PAPAL ALLIANCE 360
- CHARLEMAGNE'S EMPIRE 365

B. The New Invasions 372
- THE LATER CAROLINGIANS 373
- SARACENS, MAGYARS, VIKINGS 375

C. Europe Survives the Siege 380
- RESPONSE TO THE INVASIONS: ENGLAND 380
- RESPONSE TO THE INVASIONS: FRENCH FEUDALISM 383
- RESPONSE TO INVASIONS: GERMANY 387
- EUROPE ON THE EVE OF THE HIGH MIDDLE AGES 391

CHAPTER IX
The High Middle Ages: Economic, Territorial, and Religious Frontiers

A. Economic Frontiers 399
- THE HIGH MIDDLE AGES: PERIODIZATION, CHARACTERISTICS 399
- TOWNS AND COMMERCE 400
- DECLINE OF FEUDALISM 404
- EVOLUTION OF AGRARIAN LIFE 405

B. Territorial Frontiers 406
- EUROPEAN EXPANSION 406
- SPAIN 407
- SOUTHERN ITALY AND SICILY 408
- THE CRUSADES 413
- THE GERMAN EASTWARD EXPANSION 419

C. Religious Frontiers 421
- THE CHURCH IN THE HIGH MIDDLE AGES 421
- THE CRISIS IN BENEDICTINISM 423
- THE NEW MONASTICISM 424
- HERESIES AND THE INQUISITION 427
- MENDICANTISM 429
- THE PASSING OF THE HIGH MIDDLE AGES 436

CHAPTER X
Church and State in the High Middle Ages

A. *Empire and Papacy*	439
THE BACKGROUND OF THE STRUGGLE	439
THE INVESTITURE CONTROVERSY	443
THE AGE OF FREDERICK BARBAROSSA	448
THE DECLINE OF THE MEDIEVAL EMPIRE	458
THE PAPACY AFTER INNOCENT III	459
B. *England in the High Middle Ages*	462
THE ANGLO-NORMAN MONARCHY	462
HENRY II	467
RICHARD AND JOHN	472
HENRY III AND EDWARD I	475
C. *France in the High Middle Ages*	482
THE CAPETIANS	482
PHILIP AUGUSTUS, LOUIS VIII, AND ST. LOUIS	484
PHILIP THE FAIR 1285–1314	487

CHAPTER XI
Literature, Art, and Thought in the High Middle Ages

A. *The Dynamics of High Medieval Culture: Literature and Art*	493
LITERATURE	494
ARCHITECTURE AND SCULPTURE	501
B. *The Dynamics of High Medieval Culture: Education, Medicine, and Law*	508
THE RISE OF UNIVERSITIES	508
MEDICINE AND LAW	510
C. *The Dynamics of High Medieval Culture: Philosophy and Science*	513
PHILOSOPHY	513
SCIENCE	528
CONCLUSION	530

CHAPTER XII
The Renaissance: 1300—ca. 1520

A. *The Meaning of Renaissance*	533
WHY WE USE THE WORD *Renaissance*	533
B. *Cultural and Artistic Developments*	535
LETTERS AND LEARNING	535
THE FINE ARTS	553

  C. Socioeconomic, Political, and Religious Developments   566
   ECONOMIC AND SOCIAL TRENDS   566
   THE COURSE OF POLITICS   573
   CRISIS IN THE CHURCH   591
   THE LEGACY OF "THE RENAISSANCE STYLE"   599

CHAPTER XIII

The Confessional Age: The Reformation of the Sixteenth Century

  A. The Protestant Reformation   605
   THE GERMAN REFORMATION   607
   THE SHATTERING OF REFORMATION UNITY   618
   ENGLAND SECEDES FROM ROME   623
   THE CALVINIST REFORM   628
  B. The Humanist between Confessional Fronts   635
  C. The Catholic Reformation   638
  D. Eastern Europe and the Reformation   647
  E. The Reformation and the Modern World   650

CHAPTER XIV

The Century of Crises: 1560–1660

  A. Empires and Mercantilism   661
   EUROPE'S TERRITORIAL EXPANSION   661
   THE COURSE OF ECONOMIC CHANGE   667
  B. Spain and the Religious Wars   678
   THE DOMINANCE OF THE SPANISH HABSBURGS   678
   ELIZABETHAN ENGLAND   689
   FRENCH CIVIL AND RELIGIOUS WARS   692
  C. Four Decades of War and Revolution: 1618–1660   697
   THE ERA OF THE THIRTY YEARS' WAR   697
   STUART ENGLAND   708
  D. The Art and Literature of Crisis   715
   THE AGE OF THE BAROQUE   715
  E. The Roots of Crisis   723
   RELIGIOUS, MILITARY, AND ECONOMIC TURMOIL   723
   RENAISSANCE COURTS   724
   WITCHCRAFT: TRADITION REAFFIRMED   725
   ABSOLUTISM AND THE SEARCH FOR SECURITY   725
 Illustration Credits   730
 Index   733

List of Maps

MAPS BY
J. DONOVAN

Ancient Egypt	19
Mesopotamia, "The Land Between The Rivers"	47
Migrations into Akkad-Sumer	48
The Aramaean "Trade Empire"	70
Assyrian Empire, c. 650 B.C.	71
Chaldean Empire, c. 550 B.C.	77
Persian Empire, c. 500 B.C.	78
Palestine, 1200 B.C.	84
Migrations, First Wave	100
Migrations, Second Wave	100
Migrations and Settlements in the Ancient Near East	105
The Peloponnesus	116
Early Greek Settlements	116
Ancient Greece	116
Alexander's Empire, 323 B.C.	176
Hellenistic Kingdoms in the Third Century B.C.	177
Early Migrations into Italian Peninsula, Sicily, and Carthage Tarramarans	199
Some Roads of Ancient Rome	209
Roman Provinces During the Reign of Augustus	252
Roman Empire, c. A.D. 100	268
Movement of Germanic Tribes to c. A.D. 450	287
The Germanic Invasions	315
Europe at Clovis's Death, A.D. 511	318
Conquests of Justinian	327
Europe, c. 600	334
The Islamic Empire	344
The Carolingian Empire	364
Partition of the Empire, Treaty of Verdun, 843	374
Invasions, 9th & 10th Centuries	378
England	381
The Holy Roman Empire in 962	389
Reconquest of Spain	407
The Crusader States	415
German Settlements to the East, 800–1400	420
The Holy Roman Empire in 1190	452
Angevin Empire in 1154	469
Growth of the French Royal Domain	485
Italy, c. 1490	575
Spain at the Time of Ferdinand and Isabella	577
France after the Hundred Years' War	581
The Empire and Central Europe, c. 1490	587
Expansion of Muscovy to 1533	589
The Ottoman Advance	590
The Holy Roman Empire, c. 1520	607
Europe in 1526	621
Religions, 1560	640
Explorations and Colonial Empires, c. 1450–c. 1600	668
Division of the Netherlands, 1579–1609	686
Religious and Political Divisions of France, 1585–1598	695
Central Europe after 1648	703
Revolts against Philip IV	706
Sweden's Baltic Empire	709
English Civil Wars	713

Historians are not the only tellers of the story of man. Besides the scholar—and perhaps beyond him—there is the artist, working in many media, telling the story directly.

It would be impossible, in the compass of a few pages, to capture anything but a hint of man's artistic heritage. Still, the pictures that follow show man at his most revealing; for whereas in the arts he has also treated the objects of his love, hate, and worship, here man poses for himself. Thus the pictures that make up this study, which ranges over centuries, are humanity's changing—but always recognizable—self-portrait.

TOP: *Woman milling grain;* BOTTOM: *cook with goose. Limestone figures from Saqqara, 5th Dynasty (25th c. B.C.)*

FEDERICO BORROMEO–SCALA

Standard of Ur. *Wood panel inlaid in shell and lapis lazuli. From Ur, ca. 2500 B.C.* TRUSTEES OF THE BRITISH MUSEUM, LONDON

Ladies in Blue. *Fresco from palace at Knossos, 17th c.* B.C. HERAKLION MUSEUM

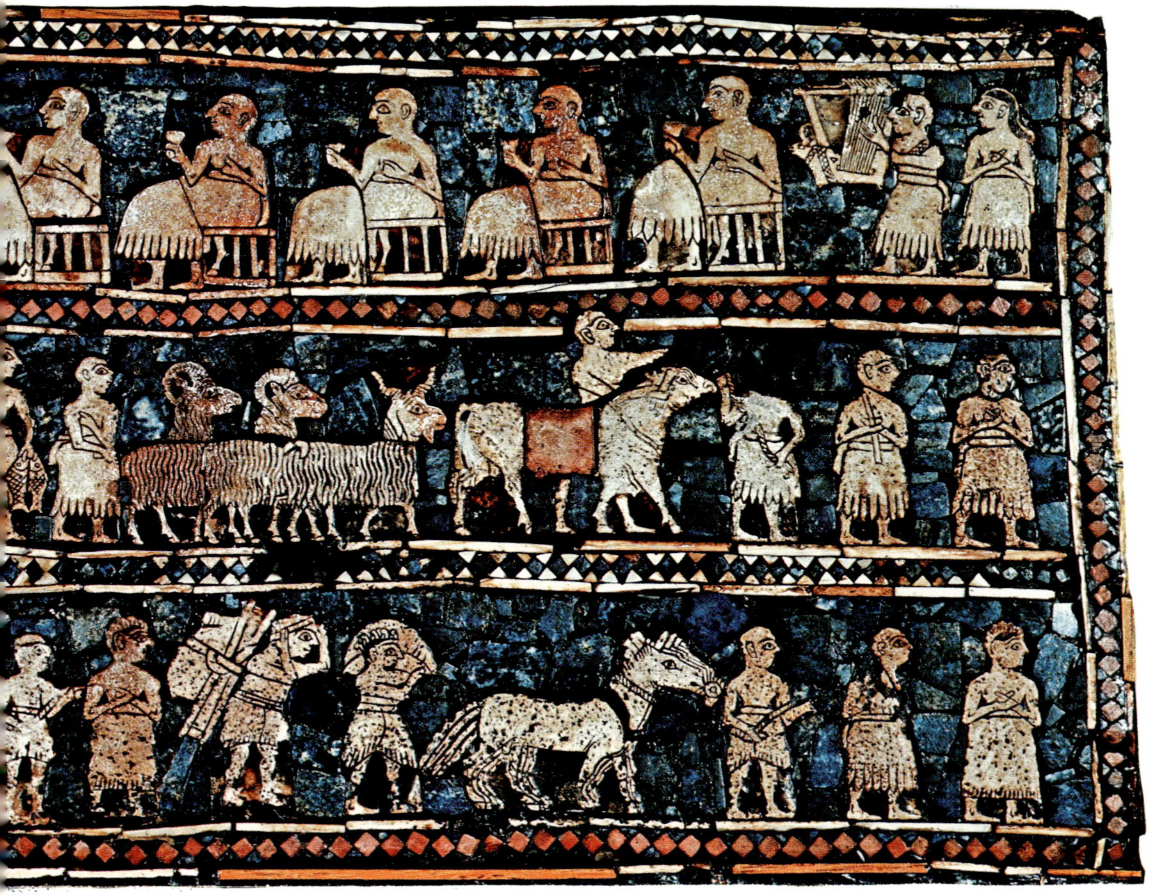

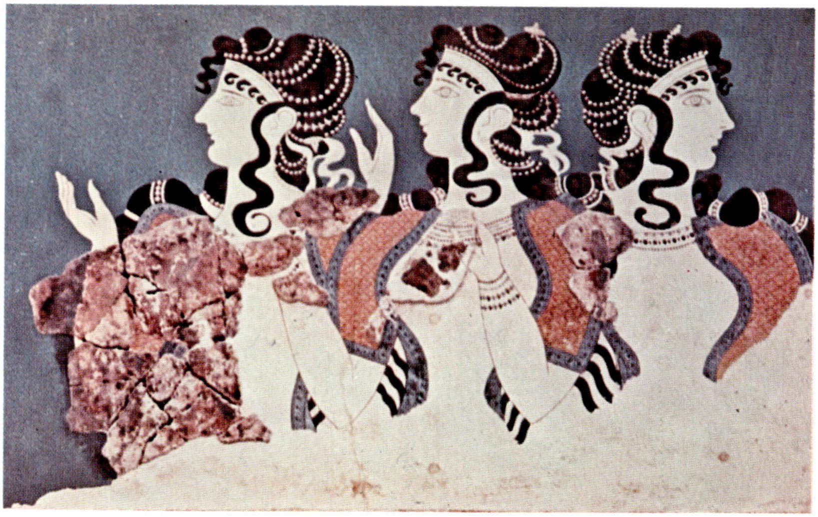

The Death of Penthesilea. Vase painting, ca. 460 B.C.

ANTIKENSAMMLUNGEN, MUNICH

OPPOSITE: *Pugilist. Bronze sculpture in Museo delle Terme, ca. 50 B.C.*

EUROPEAN ART COLOR SLIDES

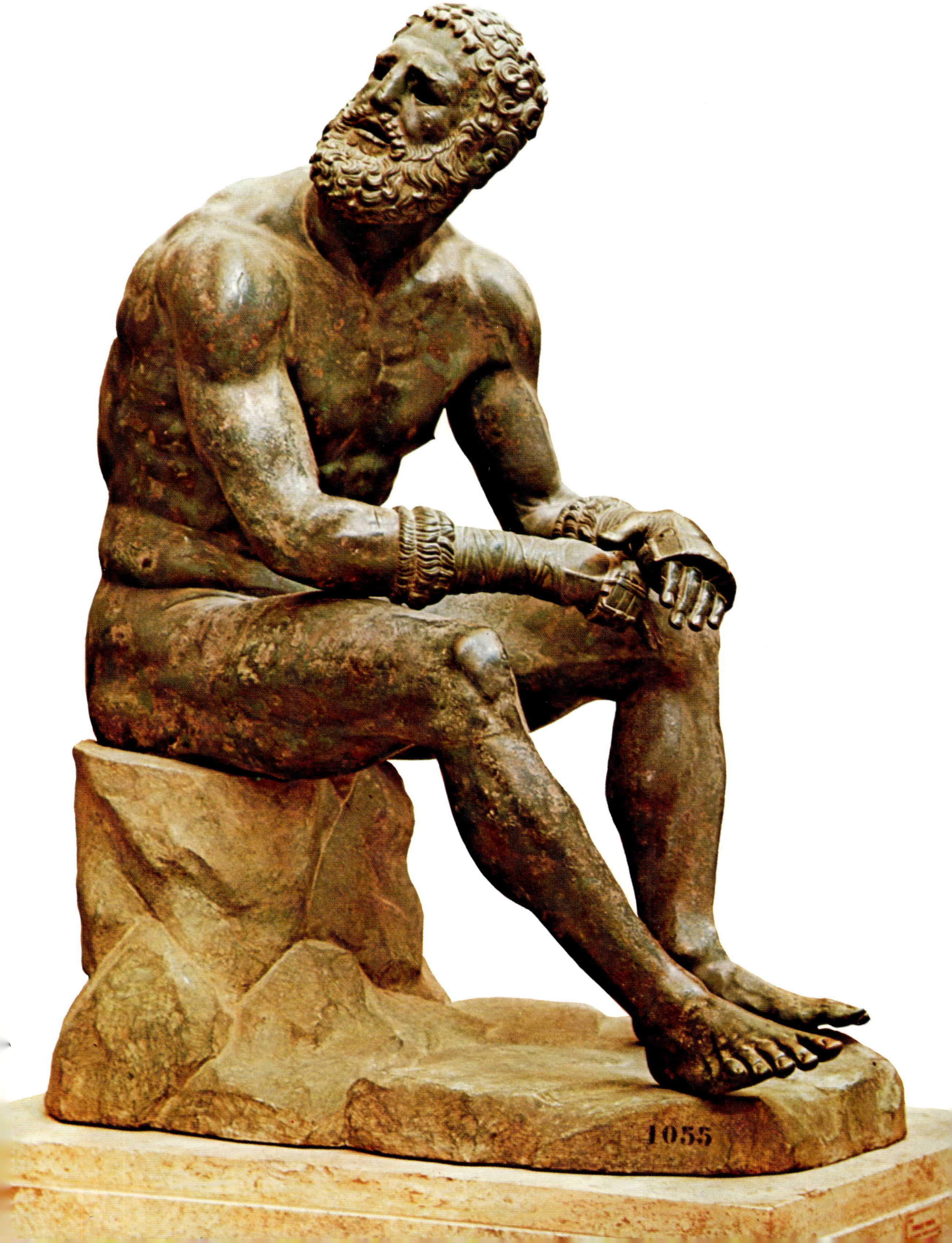
1055

Fishing scene. Mural from Tomb of Hunting and Fishing at Tarquinia, ca. 520 B.C.　　SCALA

OPPOSITE ABOVE: *Dioscourides of Samos (ca. 3d c. B.C.): Strolling musicians. Mosaic from Villa of Cicero, Pompei.*　　SCALA

OPPOSITE: *Gladiators in combat. Floor mosaic from Torrenova, 4th c. A.D.*
EDITORIAL PHOTOCOLOR ARCHIVES

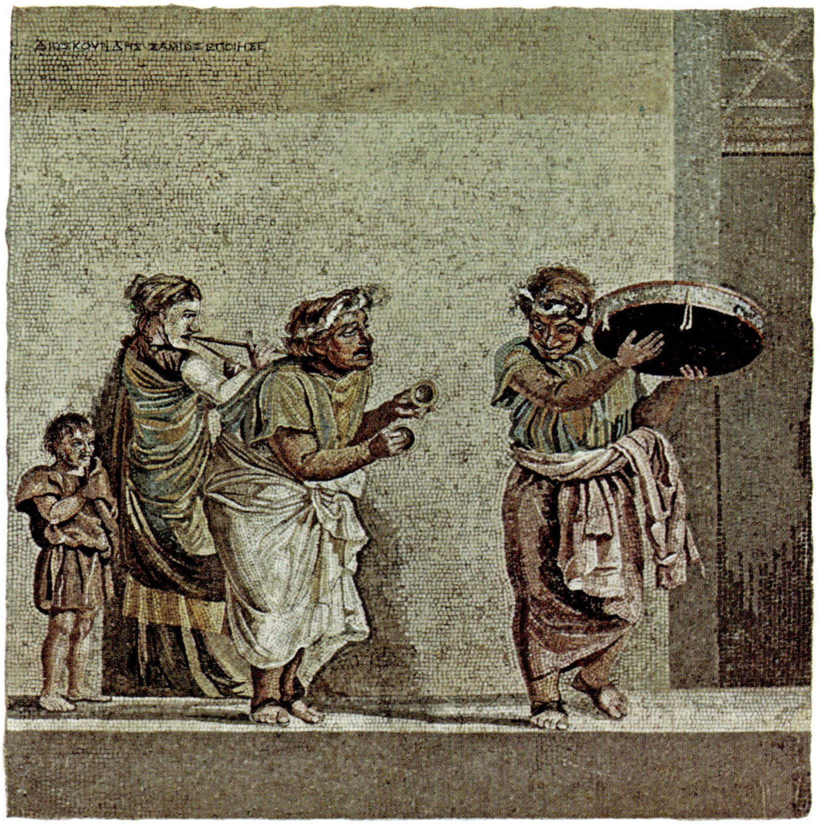
ΔΙΟΣΚΟΥΡΙΔΗΣ ΣΑΜΙΟΣ ΕΠΟΙΗΣΕ

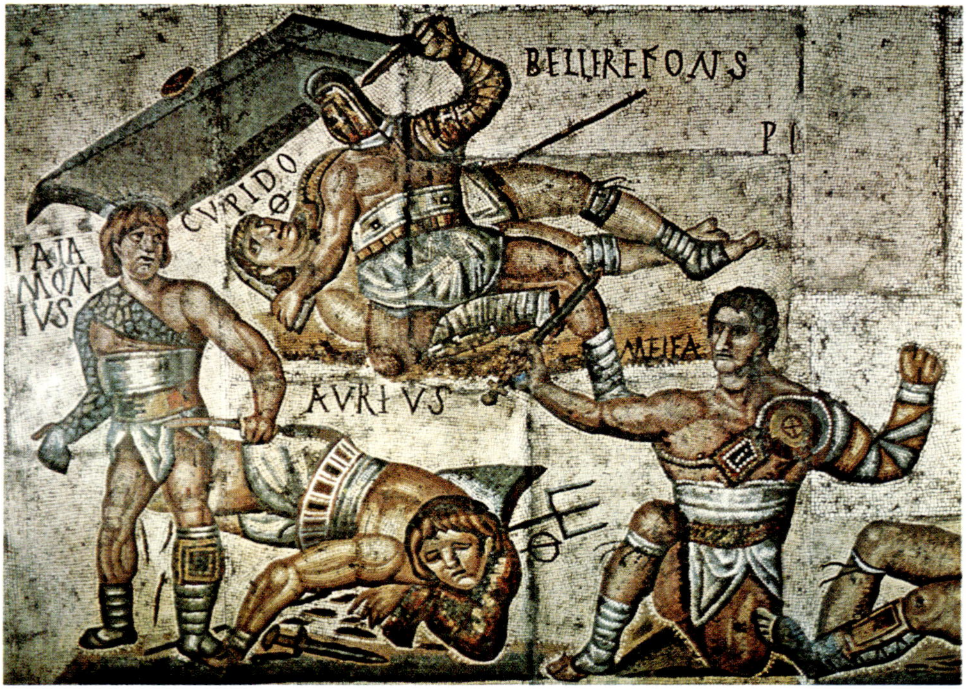
BELLEREFONS
CVPIDO
AVRIVS

Constantine IV Concedes the Privileges to Reparto. Mosaic from San Apollinare in Classe, Ravenna, ca. 550.

SCALA

RIGHT: *Christian prince subduing heretic. Carolingian ivory. Museo Nazionale del Bargello, 9th c.*
EDITORIAL PHOTOCOLOR ARCHIVES

BELOW: *Bayeux Tapestry. Detail showing Saxon foot soldiers confronting Norman cavalry. Town Hall, Bayeux, France, ca. 1075.* SCALA

Ambrogio Lorenzetti (1300?–1348): Good Government. *Detail of fresco from the Palazzo Pubblico, Siena.*

SCALA

OPPOSITE: *Atelier Bouccicand Master (ca. 1410): Army of Titus destroying Jerusalem. Miniature from Boccacio's* Du Cas des Nobles Hommes et Femmes.

ROBERT S. CRANDALL FROM THE GRANGER COLLECTION

Ce xviii Chapitre contient le cas de la destruction de la cité de Jherusalem et du peuple des Juifs. Et commence ou latin. Adhuc quidem aministracione et C.

E qui estoye pensif et esmaye et par desdaing couroucie contre les hommes gloutons. Je te noye mon visaige et ma pensee devers la charoingne du glouton empereur aulus vitelius

qui dedens les ondes du tybre flottoit plus et plus. Et ainsi comme je tour noye, ma pensee et mon visaige contre la charoingne de vitelius je vy si grant nombre de maleureux qui par troupeaulx acouroient vers moy que je ne cuide pas que nature mere de toutes choses en eut tant engendre. Tous ces hommes acourans devers moy disoient quilz descendirent jadis du noble et saint patriarche jacob le prix du peuple dysrael. Ilz gemissoient tous ilz estoient couvers de douloureuses

TOP: *Grape harvesting;* BOTTOM: *farmer plowing fields. Historiated initials from manuscript, 15th c.*　　　　　　　　　　　　EDITORIAL PHOTOCOLOR ARCHIVES

TOP: *Fruit and vegetable market;* BOTTOM: *tailor shop. Frescoes from Castello d'Issogne, Val d'Aosta, late 15th c.*   EDITORIAL PHOTOCOLOR ARCHIVES

Benozzo Gozzoli (1420–1498): **Procession of the Magi.** *Detail showing Lorenzo the Magnificent, fresco from Palazzo Medici Riccardi, Florence.*

Quentin Massys (1466?–1530): Contract of Marriage. *São Paulo Museum of Art.*
ROBERT S. CRANDALL FROM THE GRANGER COLLECTION

Emanuel de Witte (1617?–1692): Interior of the Old Church at Amsterdam. Mauritshuis, The Hague.

SCALA

Prologue

A. The Study of History — DEFINITIONS

The term *history* has two meanings. One refers to everything that has happened since the beginning of the world to the breath you exhaled a second ago. The other denotes a written account, critically designed and carefully researched, of selected happenings. A particular example of the first is the birth, life experiences, and death of Abraham Lincoln; an example of the second is Benjamin Thomas's biography, *Abraham Lincoln.*

Some historians try to make the distinction between these meanings as slight as possible. They argue that if the facts are carefully enough and exhaustively enough researched, and if they are plainly laid "end on end," they tend to explain themselves. Other historians view such accounts more as annals or "chronologies" than as histories. They insist that, far from revealing self-evident truth, facts by themselves may—and more often than not do—bewilder the reader, or invite contradictory understandings, or both. To them, the capstone of the historian's achievement is judicious interpretation. The German historian Leopold von Ranke summed up the essence of the first approach when he urged those who would best honor the Muse of History to "extinguish the self." Supporting the second view, Professor Fritz Stern has said that "from beginning to end the historian's person is involved in his work." Perhaps the distinction in meaning is most succinctly expressed in a comparison of the German word for history, *Geschichte,* with the English and French equivalents, which derive from the Greek word *histor* ($\H{\iota}\sigma\tau\omega\rho$): the first signifies "happening," the second "knowing." Still other historians, although recognizing and respecting the positions held by the proponents of either school, prefer to avoid what they regard as the extremes of each while employing the advantages of both as they see them. A good example of "let the facts speak for themselves" historiography is

H. L. Osgood's volumes on American colonial history. Almost any sample reading in Arnold Toynbee's *A Study of History* will provide a taste of interpretative writing. As for a third, or hybrid, category, perhaps the book you are reading fits into it.

Occasionally the question is still asked: "Is History a science?" It is not. Science deals with rather precisely measured quantities and forces. To the extent that any study is a true science, its content or subject matter is verifiable either by laboratory tests, or mathematical "proofs," or both. Historical data simply do not lend themselves to this kind of treatment. We cannot have a rerun of Lincoln's Gettysburg address to arrive at definitive answers to such questions as what its reception by the audience was and whether the speaker stressed the word *people,* as some historians claim, or the prepositions in the famous phrase that comes near the end of the speech. And even if such a rerun were possible we would still need to use our own evaluative judgment in dealing with the precise purposes Lincoln had in mind in making the remarks at all, and the effect that he hoped or expected they would produce.

This does not mean, of course, that historians are not bound by rather strict standards of professional practice and by a body of relatively exact methodological procedures. For example, a historian examining a document new to him—and documents, for better or worse, constitute the bulk of historical data—must occasionally determine whether it is genuine or forged. To do this he employs, sometimes using the works of others, the techniques of external criticism. One of these, if the document in question is purportedly part of an official record, is *diplomatics,* or the study of conventional form and handwriting. If a seal is involved, a special discipline—*sigillography*—may be used. Other disciplines are turned to as need requires, such as *philology* (when texts differ and tests for authentic meaning are necessary; for example, the meaning of many ancient Hebrew words is uncertain, and scholars turn to other languages, such as Old Babylonian, to try to determine exactly or at least approximately, what these words signify), *lexicography,* and *genealogy.* Once satisfied that the document under study is genuine, the historian puts another question: granted its authenticity, is it a *reliable* account of the event or events that it deals with? Consider this simple example: you attend, let us say, a World Series baseball game. Later serious charges are made that certain players of one team "threw" the game. You set down your account of what you witnessed and send it to the commissioner, who files it with stacks of related data. Later he examines the testimony he has gathered, including your summary account. By various checks he determines that you were actually in attendance and are indeed the author of the document. But what is it worth? Do you know enough about baseball to justify your remarks and observations? If you do, what assurance has he that you are not one of those implicated in the felony and are not trying to muddy the waters; or that you are not a crank who desires publicity? Let us further suppose that you die before these questions can be put directly to you. Then the commissioner-turned-historian must study your letter for signs of reliability. If a number of your statements happen to be at sharp variance with the official records, your letter will probably be put aside. Or if your prose is purely purple and pejorative, little credence can be given to it. On the other hand, if your statements seem judicious in temper and in close accord with the collected data, they will probably be marked for serious consideration. This is what the historian means by "internal criticism." There are, of course, many other methodological usages included in the historian's practice of his art.

Here the important point is simply that historiography, like architecture or medicine, is just that—an art.

THE PURPOSE OF STUDYING HISTORY

Historians give different answers to the question "Why study history?" Some say merely that, for whatever reason, human beings have an insatiable curiosity that the reading of history helps to satisfy. Others believe, or profess to believe, that historical studies stimulate mental activity, much as it was once argued that logical abilities developed by the study of mathematics carried over into other disciplines. A few historians even confess that they write almost exclusively for other historians. In ancient times many just as frankly stated their didactic purpose—as, for example, Livy, who in effect claimed that his detailed history of Rome was mainly designed to develop man's moral sense. In our own times some European and American historians have said the same; a notable example in this country is Carl Becker.

This study has as its basic purpose the presentation of Western civilization's major "happenings" so that they add up, for those who will provide the necessary catalyst of their own thought, to a significantly extended memory of where man has been and, consequently, to a more sensitive understanding of where he is now. If you say, "But surely man can live without knowing his own or any other people's history," you are of course right; most persons in fact do. But to the extent that human life is uninformed, it tends to be provincial, insensitive, and shallow. Although the particular circumstances are different, the same is true of individuals who suffer from amnesia. Put yourself in this hypothetical situation: as you leave this room you are suddenly stricken with a complete loss of memory. You do not know your name, where you are, where you live, where you are going, who are your friends, etc. Let us further suppose that this unhappy condition persists throughout your life. You find a new job, and new friends, and you make your way. But it is a hauntingly "cut-off," circumscribed way. Persons who, for whatever reasons, are not concerned about the collective memory we call history are often similarly cut off from understanding the larger nature and nuances of both their individual and communal lives. An example or two will illustrate this.

Many adults of this decade—perhaps most—feel growing apprehension over the widening gulf that separates their world from the world of youth. They see some young people adopting attitudes that dismay them, drug habits that frighten them, clothes that offend them, and manners that irritate them—the list could go on, perhaps endlessly. Their apprehension is real but, if the evidence of common conversation and general reading may be relied upon, it is derived from neither sound perception nor any understanding of what is and has been. These people need the illumination of historic light (though certainly not only this). They need to learn that what youth is doing today is not a harbinger of the apocalypse. Athenian youth of the fifth century B.C.—to cite one historic precedent—let their hair grow, cultivated beards, refused to wash, abandoned domestic conventions, and repudiated adult culture in general. They believed that their prosperous, sophist society had wasted its cultural capital, had abandoned itself to flagrant hedonism cloaked by pious hypocrisies, and was embarked on the violent adventures of power politics. One famous protestor, Diogenes, lived in a tub and, we are told, developed the habit of roaming Athenian streets with his lantern "looking for an honest man." One need not suppose that everyone should become an instant expert on ancient Greek society to observe that the more advanced our understanding of, and familiarity with, this and similar historic "scenes," the better our prospects of sensing and effectively dealing with current generation-gap phenomena.

Another example: for many years troubles and tensions have marked relations between the capitalist and communist worlds. Sometimes tensions are relaxed, and we speak of a "thaw" in the Cold War. Sooner or later the thaw yields to a refreeze as new crises develop—Cuba, Vietnam, the Middle East, and others. No American or Russian leader wants panic buttons pushed; but both the Kremlin and the White House are eternally at the ready for the eventuality of crisis confrontation passing beyond mere confrontation. For many Americans each week, month, and year brings renewal of the haunting threat of communist world domination. Undoubtedly, many Russians—certainly all in high official positions—share fears that are shaped by the crisis–confrontation syndrome. Fortunately, both sides show persisting determination not to loose the nuclear doom that either could loose. Significantly, ten years of hot wars in Korea and Vietnam have been fought with conventional weapons. But if all nuclear bombs everywhere were destroyed tomorrow and no new ones created, the capitalist–communist conflict would remain. Millions of Americans are seemingly convinced that sooner or later the communist devil must be destroyed; presumably millions of communists feel the same way about capitalist devils. Here again the human record informs, to the extent that it is sensitively consulted and judiciously used, the decision-making processes we are struggling with today. Among a number of historic "cases" open to such study, one particularly stands out. In 1517 a protesting priest touched off a religious controversy that divided most Western peoples into two warring camps. For many years the conflict widened and deepened. Protestants viewed the pope and Catholic officials as the devil's own; Catholics saw Lutherans, Presbyterians, and other religious protestors as satanic destroyers of souls that God yearned to save. Neither side believed conscience and coexistence were compatible. Both desired to see the world purged of the other. A century and a half of hot and cold wars finally persuaded them that they were, after all, wrong, and that the bloody conflict that neither could win had to be stopped. No one who knows the historic facts would pretend that there are significant or even slight similarities between the Protestant/Catholic–capitalist/communist crusades. But the main points at issue, the depth and the dimensions of the struggle, are more than similar; they are of one kind, or cultural piece. For those, then, who are able to tap this part of the collective memory that is History, the pieces of the current Cold War puzzle, as well as choices among alternative policies and actions, certainly come into sharper and clearer focus.

This is the kind of "use of History" that one eminent American historian subscribed to when he said that "the value of history is [that] it prepares us to live more humanely in the present and meet rather than foretell the future." These plain words speak to the basic purpose of this account of the rise and development of Western civilization.

B. The Emergence of Man

THE GENESIS OF MAN

Man stands small amid the immensities and mysteries of the universe. Above him stretch measureless space and countless heavenly bodies. Among these bodies our solar system is part of a galaxy so vast that approximately 200 million years are required for it to revolve about its axis. And there are millions of galaxies, some of them larger than our "Milky Way." Underfoot, the Earth abounds in complexities. Its crust, a mere 30 or 40 miles thick, has been barely scratched; its 4000 miles of mantle and core are subjects more of conjecture than of verifiable description.

The mere mention of these immensities and complexities is enough to suggest how wrong man once was to view everything in anthropomorphic terms; but it may also serve to place him in a perspective that reveals power and promise. If we confess that astronomically man is an infinitesimally small speck, we should not overlook the corollary that man is the astronomer. Likewise, if we are tempted to think of the works of man as puny and passing, we should make sure that we are weighing them in a realistic time scale. One earth scientist, for example, has pointed out that if "the 4.5 billion year age of the earth is thought of as one year, the 500 million years of fossil record is equivalent to about forty days. The time of humans, assuming that it is about one million years, would amount to less than two hours, and that of modern man, giving him fifty thousand years, is a little more than five minutes."[1] Another account carries the comparison further: " . . . the Pyramids of Egypt were built two minutes ago; Caesar was murdered fifty seconds ago! By this same schedule, the American republic has existed for less than five seconds." Viewed in this light, the human condition, so often in our times the object of gloomy prophecies, takes on a new aspect. If in "two hours" man can develop from a slouching hominid to an Einstein and a Gandhi, the hours and days ahead may not seem too foreboding.

Early Hominids

There is disagreement among anthropologists concerning the age of man, either as hominid (subman) or as *Homo sapiens* (thinking man). The first hominid appeared perhaps 3,000,000 years ago; modern *Homo sapiens* developed perhaps about 50,000 years ago. These dates, more than any others, seem representative of the views of modern prehistorians and anthropologists. But new finds in the

---

[1] Ruth Moore, *The Earth We Live On* (New York: Alfred A. Knopf, 1956), p. 406 fn. Current estimates of hominid history are closer to three million years.

Cautionary Remarks About Table I (Facing Page)

The purpose of the chart on the opposite page is to provide an overall time sense of geological and human evolutionary development during the past three million years. Unfortunately, there is no consensus among paleontologists, anthropologists, and geologists on some elemental matters; for example, when the Pleistocene Era began, how many glaciations took place (ranging from four to twenty), when the first manlike creatures appeared, and what terms should be used to describe the various kinds of early men (as well as their "homo" characteristics).

It should be noted too that on such a small chart much more must be left out than can be included. No mention is made, for example, of *Meganthropus,* or of fossils of the *Paranthropus* type beyond those cited at the bottom right of the chart, or of Steinheim, Fontéchevade, and many other hominids.

In the most recent edition of his *Prehistoric Men* (1967), Professor Robert Braidwood points out that at the present time anthropologists and prehistorians have some seemingly solid justification for dividing the record of human evolution into three parts or stages: (1) the earliest, the *Australopithecine-Habiline,* whose stone tools and other found artifacts seem to be associable with the skeletal remains; (2) the *Homo erectus* stage, which ranges from Java Man to Steinheim and Fontéchevade Man (some time before Neanderthal Man); and (3) the *Presapiens,* Neanderthalas, and finally Cro-Magnon Man. Braidwood believes that the first-stage "creatures" may soon be accepted as "men." He is sure the second- and third-stage beings are "tool-making humans."

TABLE I

	Geologic Ages	Cultural Stages	Glacial Record	Evolution of Man
PRESENT	Holocene	Civilization Food-Producing (Neolithic Age)	Post-Fourth Glacial Age	
10,000				
25,000			FOURTH ICE AGE	GRIMALDI MAN
50,000			(There was an interglacial interval of about 10,000 years within this glacial period.)	CRO-MAGNON MAN (*Homo sapiens*)
			THIRD INTERGLACIAL AGE (ended about 80,000 years ago)	NEANDERTHAL MAN
100,000	AGE	(Paleolithic Age)		
150,000			THIRD ICE AGE	
200,000				
250,000				
300,000		FOOD-GATHERING AND COLLECTING STAGE	SECOND INTERGLACIAL AGE	
350,000				
400,000				
450,000			SECOND ICE AGE	Peking Man (*Sinanthropus*) HEIDELBERG MAN
500,000	PLEISTOCENE			
1,000,000			FIRST INTERGLACIAL AGE (ended 800,000 years ago)	
3,000,000			FIRST ICE AGE	Java Man (*Pithecanthropus Erectus*) *Zinjanthropus boise* HOMO HABILIS AUSTRALOPITHECUS AFRICANUS

(left axis: ↑ expanded scale ↓ from PRESENT to ~50,000; ↑ compressed scale ↓ to 1,000,000; ↑ much compressed scale ↓ to 3,000,000)

many diggings scattered across the world may at any time require serious revision of what seems now to represent a consensus of views. The force and importance of this qualification can best be understood by reference to an actual example of the uncertainties that beset the current work of experts. Recently *Current Anthropology* published an article entitled "The Pleistocene Epoch and the Evolution of Man," by Cesare Emiliani, an eminent geologist. Among other things, Emiliani holds that "cannibalism may have played a very important role during (the earliest) and later stages of human development." He also asserts that we must assume that different kinds or species of "men" developed because from "each large, polytypic [i.e., of several or many types] stock, a small population became separated, evolved independently, and spread to compete with, and eventually to replace, the original stock." Another hypothesis concerns Neanderthal men who, he says, appear "to have been particularly subject to deforming arthritis and, perhaps, because of their larger sinus cavities, to cold, flu, and other diseases associated with cold weather. If so, modern man replaced them more because of a physiological advantage than by warfare or other means." Approximately 25 other authorities were asked to read and comment on Emiliani's paper. Many of them, with due academic respect, attacked it outright, and not one could find any real evidence to support the cannibal thesis (so strong, indeed, was the attack on this point that, in his reply, Emiliani said that he should have discussed "cultural" cannibalism as well as "nutritional" cannibalism). A number of his critics also denied the thesis of "speciation through separation," one countering that modern views on speciation and evolution simply do not "require geographic isolation for phyletic evolution. . . . One species can change into another by evolution in the same continuously occupied area." The reference to the possible cause of Neanderthal Man's demise also ran into strong contention, one reviewer pointing out that since Neanderthals were cold-adapted and had "borne through" several millennia of rough weather, "it seems curious that their disappearance is explicable by a sudden ineffectiveness of such a favorable adaptation."

Such scholarly buffetings and about-faces warn us of the futility of either demanding or accepting "definitive" answers to our very natural questions about the evolution of man. Given this caution, we may briefly note some tentative judgments that seem fairly sound at the present writing.

The cranial capacities of *Zinjanthropus boisie* and *Australopithecus africanus* hardly exceeded that of present day chimpanzees (for the dates of all early "men" referred to here, see Table I). On the other hand, their spines were sufficiently erect to allow them to walk in a manner suggesting human locomotion. But for reasons presently unknown they seemed unable to make further progress toward "Homohood"; some 1,500,000 to 500,000 years ago they gave way to three more advanced species, commonly called Java Man, Heidelberg Man, and Peking Man. All walked fairly upright and all possessed cranial cavities larger than those of their predecessors. Heidelberg Man was the first hominid to possess definitely human teeth. Peking Man lived in caves, learned to make fire, and used crude stone tools.

Neanderthal Man appeared at the beginning of the last ice age, that is, about 80,000 years ago. Because he had such a thick skull and had not assumed the wholly erect position that he might, as a latecomer, have been expected to reach, some authorities consider him a regressive development, or perhaps an anthropological blind alley.

The Emergence of Homo sapiens

Apparently Neanderthal Man yielded to modern man in two ways: by extermination and by absorption. Some evidence seems to indicate that our male direct ancestor, Cro-Magnon Man (for Africans, Grimaldi Man?) whose spine was fully erect and whose brain was actually larger than ours, intermarried to some extent with female Neanderthalas. In any event, about 25,000 to 50,000 years ago modern man, as we know him today, came to dominate all related *homo* forms, and finally to eliminate them.

Thus evolved present-day *Homo sapiens*. The record, as we have seen, is disappointingly spotty; and the authorities sharply disagree in their reading of it. At present we have no satisfactory way of choosing among the various schools of thought that date the appearance of "wise man," *Homo sapiens*. Did he first appear about 500,000 years ago or not until some 450,000 or so years later? We cannot be sure. Moreover, the same expert will sometimes seemingly contradict himself. For example, von Koenigswald declares *Homo sapiens* to be about 150,000 years old. He also holds that "sapiens" art first developed about 60,000 years ago. We are left to wonder why, if *sapiens* has existed for so long, it took him nearly 100,000 years to express himself in artistic form. On the other hand, we should appreciate how much paleontologists and anthropologists have done with what little there is. It has been estimated that a surface perhaps no larger than a card table could hold all the available important hominid fossils (excluding Neanderthal finds). From this precious little a prodigious amount has been learned. And only a beginning, of course, has been made.

What were the basic characteristics of the new man? With other Primates, he had an opposable thumb; that is, he could manipulate thumb in conjunction with fingers in such a way that his hand became a tool user. But no other Primate had the two features that made modern *sapiens* the "sharer of creativity" that he became—an erect spine and, especially, a reflective thinking apparatus. The erect spine enabled him to go about "on two" instead of four, thus freeing his hands for tool making and tool using. But it was man's reflective thinking apparatus that gave substantial meaning to his existence. Other animals think, but not reflectively. No cow, for instance, reflects, as she chews her cud, on the particular joy that will be hers when the spring rains come and the grass grows greener (or if she does, our total human experience becomes considerably unreliable). The cow, of course, is aware; but she is not aware that she is aware. Of all living creatures only man possesses this attribute.

As we conclude our rapid survey of the birth of *Homo sapiens* we may be tempted to fret over his lowly beginnings and to feel that his evolution by "natural selection"—that is, by possessing inherited characteristics that favored survival—reduces human life to a thing of chance and purposelessness. The famous anthropologist, Ernest Hooton, pertinently answers this dolorous query: "We need not," he says, "give man and his ancestors the credit of developing their own intelligence, but if a human being is not a manifestation of an intelligent design, there is no such thing as intelligence."[2]

PRELITERATE CULTURE

Food-gatherers

As paleontologists and anthropologists study the fossil remains of man in an ef-

---

[2] Quoted in Gustav H. R. von Koenigswald, *Meeting Prehistoric Man*, translated by M. Bullock (New York: Harper & Row, Publishers, 1956), pp. 52–53.

fort to reconstruct his primitive physical history, archeologists and social anthropologists try to reconstruct his preliterate cultural history by examining the artifacts (buildings, utensils, tools, weapons, etc.) and nonartifactual materials (bones, grains, shells, etc.) that he left behind. Although they have been at it for scarcely more than a century, their work has already sketched the fundamental aspects of earliest human existence. Generally, they distinguish between three stages of societal development: the planned food-gathering stage; the pre-civilized food-producing stage; and the civilized food-producing stage (see Table II, p. 13).

For perhaps nearly three million years—from his emergence into the hominid category—man was fundamentally a gatherer or collector of food. This is not to imply that his whole time and energy were spent in foodgathering or that the basic significance of his experiences lay in economic activity. Still, the evidence is clear that this parasitic existence molded a substantial portion of the pattern of early man's motivational life.

He lived in groups, but the groups were quite small (for that matter, it must be understood that hominids *in toto* were few). One of our early ancestors, Peking Man, learned the miracle of firemaking, one of the greatest discoveries in human history. Plentiful archeological evidence shows that these forebears of ours—scattered across parts of Europe, Africa and Asia—used various crude tools of stone, bone, and antler; probably wood was employed too, but of course this material, by its nature, left no remains for study. During the long period of the last European glacier homes were built in caves (where caves existed; otherwise in the vast open spaces) from which forays went forth for the purpose of slaying the bison and other large game that roamed the tundras bordering the European icesheet.

It is certain that very early hominids formulated and consistently practiced burial rites. The significance of these rites is a matter of dispute among prehistory specialists—some infer religious meaning, others deny this, holding rather that fear of bad fortune probably gave rise to these customs. One prominent authority, Henri Frankfort, holds that "from the first, man possessed creative imagination, and we have to reckon with this in considering social cohesion. . . . Their art proves that their relation with their game was not a mere matter of killing and devouring, and that their parties were kept together, not merely by common need, but also by imagination, religious conceptions, made explicit, not in doctrine, but in acts."[3] Another authority insists, "even the rude Neanderthaler had an ideology."

As we have seen, during the very late years of the food-gathering stage modern man appeared. Already the trend toward racial differentiation may have set in, although the various cultures identified by archeologists and social anthropologists do not necessarily bear a race-culture relationship; in other words, the same basic complex of customs might be created and experienced by differing races, such as the sub-Sahara Negroes and the Eastern European Caucasians.* It is thought that both clothes and homes were made of the

---

[3] *The Birth of Civilization in the Near East* (Garden City, N.Y.: Doubleday & Co., Anchor Books, 1956), p. 28.

* It used to be thought that Grimaldi man, who appeared about the same time as Cro-Magnon man, was the progenitor of the black man, as Cro-Magnon man was of the white. Authorities have become very wary of this identification, reasonably insisting that "bones do *not* indicate skin color." Professor Grahame Clark has spoken perceptively to this question: ". . . pigmentation must have been to some extent adaptive: thus in the Old World blond, fair-skinned people tend to go with a cool, cloudy habitat; brunettes with the strong sunlight and bright skies of climates like that of the Mediterranean area; the darkest skinned with the hottest, nonforested region (for example, the savanna of Africa); and those

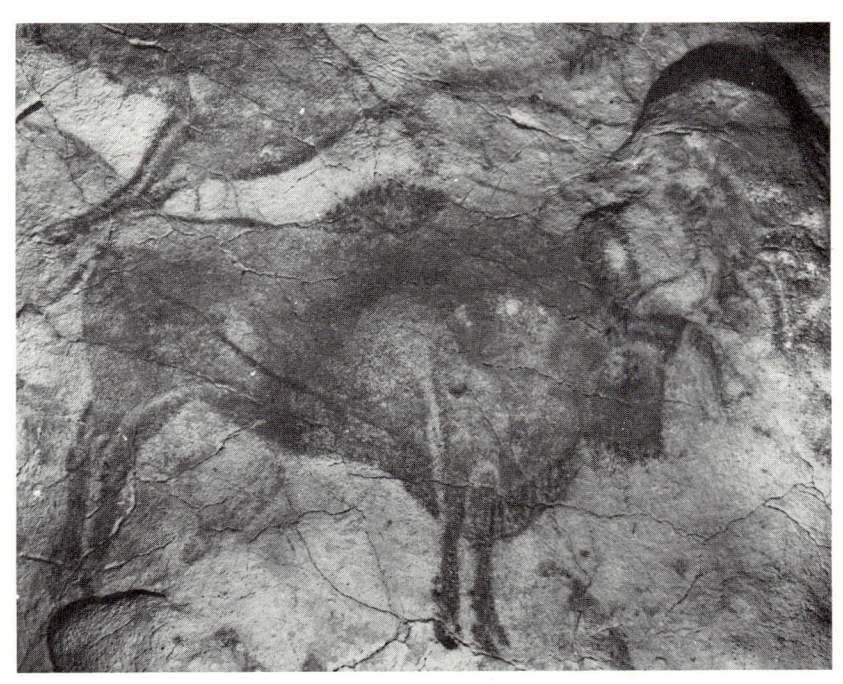

Cro-Magnon art (ca. 20,000 B.C.): wall painting of a bison from the Altamira caves.

skins of animals. During this period—that is, about 25,000 years ago—the atl-atl (a bone or wood device with attached thongs at its end, designed to accelerate the speed and force of a stone or spear projected from it) was conceived and effectively used. At this time, too, hunting drives were organized. For these forays the men of a settlement or "station" would form two bands of hunters. One would seek out the game, the other would lie in ambush to fall upon whatever prey was chased into the trap. These were tremendous achievements, for now man could gather food in amounts not possible before. As a consequence, the human population increased and societal life became correspondingly more complex, thus demanding of man cooperative efforts, which in turn stimulated further practical and ideological inventions.

Probably as a magical means of ensuring good hunting, Cro-Magnon man and his immediate successors developed art forms and techniques that present-day artists frankly call beautiful by the latter's own standards. The first style of painting —perhaps around 40,000 B.C.—concentrated solely on animal scenes. Later, bison and other animal forms were represented on the ceilings and walls of caves, usually in such a way as to suggest the mastery of man over beasts. For example, in one cave in Spain there are drawings of deer being forced by one group of hunters

---

with yellowish skin and crinkly hair with the tropical rain-forests of Africa and Southeast Asia. Again, there are sound reasons for linking width of nasal aperture with climate, since it is a function of the nose to mitigate the temperature of the air before it is drawn into the lungs; it is therefore not at all surprising to observe the narrow nostrils of the Eskimo or even the North European, the medium ones of the Mediterranean or the broad ones of the Negro."
World Prehistory (Cambridge: Cambridge University Press, 1961), p. 24.

B. The Emergence of Man

toward another group, the latter firing arrows at the trapped animals.

By this time the last great ocean of ice that had—some 70,000 years earlier—spread over great areas of Europe and Asia, affecting not only their own climates and conditions of living, but those of Africa (and the Americas) as well, had shrunk to almost the vanishing point. As a result of this retreat of cold weather, a much changed flora and fauna developed. For example, in northern Africa a "drying out" took place that turned "the plateaux from grassland into steppe and ultimately into desert, and making [more inhabitable] the valleys of the great rivers [such as the Nile in Africa and the Tigris and Euphrates in Asia]." *

In Europe forests sprang up and man was confronted with a series of new and bewildering environments. In response to these challenges he relied heavily on the newly developed bow and arrow. Along with the ice, mammoths, bison, and oxen vanished; thus man was forced to concentrate on the smaller, swifter animals that took the place of the retreating or vanishing big game. The domestication of other animals, particularly sheep, goats, and oxen occurred soon after the domestication of dogs.

Food-producers

In Europe the food-gathering stage lasted until 4000 B.C. and later. But as early as ca. 9000 B.C. an agricultural revolution took place in Asia (and Africa?) that swiftly led men into ways we call civilized (See Table II). The central feature of this cataclysmic event was the discovery, possibly by woman, that wild grain—barley and wheat especially—which was used to supplement early man's meat diet, contained seeds that, when deposited in the earth, produced more grain. Thereafter man gradually replaced his chasing and *collecting* habits (although not altogether, of course) with *food-producing* practices. It is this that Gordon Childe refers to when he speaks of "that revolution whereby man ceased to be merely parasitic and, with the adoption of agriculture and stock raising, became a creator emancipated from the whim of his environment."[4] Indeed it is not an exaggeration to say that this revolution was as destiny-laden as the industrial revolution that occurred some 10,000 years later.

So man left savagery and entered barbarism. It is not known whether this triumph over environment stimulated man—or, again, more probably woman—to still another epochal discovery, but in any case it was during this period that pottery was invented. At this point in their development human beings caused a chemical change to take place in plastic clay, a change that resulted in a durable utensil that could be used for a number of purposes, but particularly for storing food and drink. Moreover not only were more efficient tools produced—the polished stone ax-head, for example—but a new thrust of creative designing was applied to the concept of *tools to make tools* (although from as early as ca. 35,000 B.C. burins had been used as tool-making tools).

With the agricultural revolution came the settlement of sizable villages and, later, towns, for the domestication of plants meant that man's wandering days were over (but of course this was not true for all men; nomads are still roaming certain regions of the earth), and he could settle down and produce food and the materials for clothing instead of chasing

---

* Frankfort, op. cit., p. 29. The bracketed words *more inhabitable* have been added to correct Professor Frankfort's statement, which was valid enough at the time, but which no longer holds in the light of discoveries made since his death in 1954. Frankfort's original statement affirmed by implication the total uninhabitability of the river valleys before the great "drying out."

[4] *New Light on the Most Ancient Near East,* 4th ed. (New York: Praeger Publishers, 1968), pp. 1–2.

TABLE II

From Caves to Cities*

All dates B.C.

Date	Development	Region
3000	formal political state, writing, monumentality in art—"civilization"	Mesopotamia
3500	incipient urbanization; "political" organization of communities	
4500	systematized farming; appearance of market towns; migration into valley areas	
7500	permanent villages appear	Hilly flanks north and east of Mesopotamia and in Syria-Palestine
ca. 10,000	incipient agriculture developed; intensification of planned food-collection	
ca. 30,000	food-gathering yielding to "planned collection" of food	
ca. 3,000,000	cave-dwelling hunters, fishers; random food-gathering	Food-gathering Near East

*Adapted from a chart originally constructed by Professor Robert J. Braidwood.

about after them. Within a relatively short period—perhaps several thousand years—improved grains, the possible use of manure for fertilizer, plows, hoes, and sickles (the latter set with flint as a cutting edge), techniques of breadmaking, and, it may be added, the brewing of beer, were developed by the new farmer-villager. The towns were still small—although Jericho (modern Tell es-Sultan), founded some 9000 years ago and now believed by some experts to be the first "city" in human history, probably had considerably more than the ten to twenty households of the usual precivilization village. As the revolution resulted in a distinct increase in population, urbanism was clearly not far off—no further, actually, than man's solution of two problems that kept primitive society primitive: unceasing war, and lack of adequate food reserves. The time required to establish a food-producing (Neolithic) culture—in portions of Asia and, somewhat later, in northeast Africa—was brief compared to the long millennia of the food-gathering age; but its accomplishments were tremendous. In the Nile and Tigris-Euphrates valleys man was ready to effect the "urban revolution" and establish what we call, with whatever reservations, *civilization*.

13   B. The Emergence of Man

Selected Readings

A. The Study of History

Butterfield, Herbert. *Man on His Past.* Boston: Beacon Press, 1966.

In almost everything that he writes Butterfield has a way of holding one's interest. Here see especially chapter 3 for a quick breakthrough into what historians can say about their art as it is developed by a distinguished practitioner of it (in this case, Leopold von Ranke).

*Geyl, Peter. *Debates With Historians.* New York: World Publishing Company, Meridian Books, 1966.

Compare Geyl's view of Ranke in chapter 1 with Acton's in Butterfield (cited above). Perhaps most interesting to American students is the author's critical analysis of the writings of some American Civil War historians (chap. 12).

*Koht, Halvd. *Driving Forces in History.* New York: Atheneum Publishers, 1968.

In this brief work a famous Norwegian historian discusses what he considers to be the moving forces of history—such as religion, economics, war, science—in two ways: how they are constituted (i.e., their substance) and how particular historians have treated them.

*Stern, Fritz, ed. *The Varieties of History.* New York: World Publishing Company, Meridian Books, 1964.

A collection of essays on 30 historians, from Voltaire to Jacques Burzun, in less than 400 pages. Each chapter has a clear, descriptive title pointing to some area of investigation or interest: "History as Biography," "Historical Materialism," "History as a Science," "Historical Relativism," etc. If only one work on historiography is used, this could well be that one.

B. The Emergence of Man

Abstracts with Programs for 1969. Part 7. Boulder: The Geological Society of America, 1970.

This collection of abstracts will hold interest only for the student who has a special interest in what earth scientists are currently doing. Approximately six of the abstracts and graphs deal, in a rather complicated manner, with the attempt to determine the age of the Pleistocene Age.

Braidwood, Robert J. *Prehistoric Men.* 7th ed. New York: William Morrow and Co., 1967.

In this edition of his small classic, Professor Braidwood has taken care to change only those parts affected by more recent research. This book, primarily addressed to the nonspecialist, is both eminently readable and worth reading. Some prehistorians do not agree with certain of Braidwood's conclusions, but the reader is given fair warning of their controversial nature.

*Childe, Gordon. *New Light on the Most Ancient Near East.* 4th ed. New York: Praeger Publishers, 1968.

A standard work that any serious student of the genesis of civilization should read. The author's argument for the "urban revolution" has been challenged in recent years, as has his retention of the traditional thesis that basic cultural patterns are spread by migrant groups.

*Childe, Gordon. *What Happened in History*. Baltimore: Penguin Books, 1957.

> *A general and highly readable account of human development from earliest times through the decline and fall of the ancient world.*

Clark, Grahame. *World Prehistory*. 2d ed. Cambridge: Cambridge University Press, 1969.

> *This updated study of preliterate hominid history (although a few sections include the earliest phases of literate life) is well worth reading; it is lucid, scholarly, and—for a short work (about 300 pages)—remarkably comprehensive. Undergraduate students of Western civilization will find particularly useful the first chapter, on "Man's Place in Nature," as well as the sixth and seventh chapters, on "The Foundations of European Civilization."*

Clark, Grahame, and Piggott, Stuart. *Prehistoric Societies*. New York: Alfred A. Knopf, 1965.

> *An attempt by two trained scholars to present the data of the specialists to lay readers. Its theme leaves the current of pessimistic evaluations of human development. It frankly aims at restoring "a little confidence not only in man's capacity to endure the frequent catastrophes of human existence but also in his intellectual abilities."*

Coon, Carlton S. *The Story of Man*. New York: Alfred A. Knopf, 1962.

> *This book presents a reliable account of what anthropologists have discovered about the development of man from his hominid origins through his emergence as a reflectively thinking creature. Except for the author's use of contemporary primitive societies as guides for interpreting some anthropological data, this work is probably more generally accepted by scholars in the field than any other.*

Engle, Shirley H. *New Perspectives in World History*. New York: National Council for Social Studies, 1964.

> *A collection of essays by various specialists. For a good brief account of how man evolved from lower animal life, and for details of new hominid findings, see chapter 6.*

Harding, G. Lankester. *The Antiquities of Jordan*. Rev. ed. New York: Praeger Publishers, 1967.

> *Chapter 2 offers an interesting overview of the prehistoric and historic development of Jordan, ranging from the earliest records (from about 8000 B.C.) to the conquest of Jordan by the Muhammedans in the seventh century. Especially fascinating are the parallel accounts of Israel's invasion of the land as they are found in archaeological artifacts and in the Old Testament.*

*Hawkes, Jacquetta, and Wooley, Sir Leonard. *Prehistory and the Beginnings of Civilization*. London: George Allen and Unwin, 1963.

> *This is the first volume of UNESCO's grand design to bring out a multivolumed history of the cultural and scientific development of mankind. Because of its long period of preparation, some of the volume's conclusions became outdated before it went to press.*

>The extensive notes placed at the end of each chapter are a mixed blessing for the nonspecialist. Some are more useful than the textual comment to which they refer; others are simply uncalled for or, at worst, an encumbrance. The reader has to fend for himself as best he can.

Leakey, L. S. B. *The Progress and Evolution of Man in Africa.* London: Oxford University Press, 1961.

>This small book can be read in one sitting. It seeks in one chapter to trace and place the evolution of Africa's earliest "near men." The other chapter (actually the first; both were originally lectures delivered to English university audiences) presents a lively argument for a greater understanding of African culture.

* Marek, Kurt W. [C. W. Ceram]. *The March of Archeology.* New York: Alfred A. Knopf, 1958.

>Still probably the best introductory account of what the work of the archaeologist is really all about. The author is overmodest in claiming that his book "is not basically a scientific but a literary work." In addition to a clear textual presentation there is an abundance of "visual aids"—almost every page is illustrated by either a halftone or a color plate, an illuminating chart, or a helpful chronological table.

Parkes, Henry B. *Gods and Men: The Origin of Western Culture.* New York: Alfred A. Knopf, 1959.

>Special emphasis is given to Hellenic concepts and Judeo-Christian beliefs. The author disdains the "objective" approach in his study of our cultural heritage. In a very real sense he is an advocate of a way of life.

Verhoogen, John et al. *The Earth.* New York: Holt, Rinehart & Winston, 1970.

>This book is a detailed, often technical account of the evolution and nature of our planet. The authors try to present the material in a plain and direct way, but often this is not possible. However certain portions may be read with profit by those who may have no grounding in the study of geology: chapter 1 ("The Earth as a Whole"); chapter 4 ("Time and Geology"); and chapter 14 ("Some Aspects of the Chemical Evolution of the Earth"). An earlier, more popularized account may well be used in conjunction with this volume: Ruth Moore, **The Earth We Live On** (*New York: Alfred A. Knopf, 1956*).

Asterisk (*) denotes paperback.

CHAPTER I
The Birth of Civilization

A. Egypt: Sphinx and Falcon

PRE-DYNASTIC HISTORY
Settlement of the Valley

The fundamental features of Egypt's long history are reasonably clear, but unfortunately we cannot say the same for Egypt's formative, predynastic culture.* Disciplined conjectures of specialists point to late Neolithic peoples moving into the Nile region, probably from the south or the east, some 6000 or 7000 years ago. The valley itself was still too swampy, even in its upper reaches, to permit immediate settlement. On the other hand, beyond the lush strip on either side of the valley stretched forbidding deserts. Nature and the venturous human spirit, however, combined to produce a compromise. Flanking spurs, neither swamp nor desert, fringed the life-bearing river, and here the Badarians and the later Nagadians (as archaeologists have designated these early migrants) settled. The encounter with the Nile had begun.

The momentous change from food-gathering to food-producing probably occurred along the raised flanks of the Fertile Crescent, from which new agricultural practices were introduced into Egypt, possibly by migrants from Asia. Or, for the Egyptians, the change may have taken place in their own valley. One noted Egyptologist, John A. Wilson, has ventured this speculation: "The animals of the upland, including man, were . . . herded down to the river bank, pursuing plant food and pursuing each other. A much closer juxtaposition meant great acquaintance; man found that it was advan-

---

* Traditionally the history of Egypt has been divided into dynasties—periods of ruling houses. About 300 B.C. an Egyptian priest-historian, Manetho, set up this frame of reference. The Manethonian account has often been proved unreliable in certain particulars by Egyptologists, especially in the last half-century. But the dynastic pattern remains for the most part sufficiently sound to allow its continued use.

tageous to keep certain animals close at hand for his future food supply; he found that certain plants could be teased into great productivity for his feeding and the feeding of those animals which he was holding beside him."

Commerce and Culture

Trade connections with Mediterranean peoples had probably not yet been established, although informal commercial relations may have been maintained with people from Arabia. A likely supposition is that goods were transported across the *wadis* (dry channels in the desert, formerly streams) to Red Sea "ports" and thence by water to nearby settlements.

Artifacts found in graves and settlement sites prove that the Nile dwellers were advanced in the manufacture of flint tools, the materials for which they quarried systematically. Houses or huts of the scattered villages were round with the foundations, at least, of mud. The inhabitants were small in stature, the males averaging about 5½ feet, the females perhaps 5 or 6 inches less. The Asiatic origin of their grains and animals may provide a clue to the question of their original habitat, although migration from South Africa cannot be ruled out. Almost certainly they were not descendants of the Paleolithic groups that roamed over North Africa before the last glaciation.

The religion of the Nile dwellers was characterized by worship of a host of gods and goddesses, both human and animal. A female figurine of the earliest period shows a fertility goddess cupping her breasts in her hands, perhaps an early form of the later goddess Hathor of the "House of Horus." Some of the other figures combined human and animal features. Probably the worship of Horus, the falcon god who later came to play a central role in the religio-political life of Egypt, was introduced by invading conquerors (from the Arabian peninsula?) who suddenly debouched into the valley of the upper Nile about 500 years after the Badarians and early Nagadians had settled on the river's spurs.

The "New Egyptians" and Their Culture

These newcomers, of uncertain origin, almost at once effected important changes in the prevailing culture. Their vases, for example, reflected an esthetic sense different from that of the indigenous groups they absorbed.

The invaders gradually spread north and south from the point at which they entered the Nile Valley (near Nagade; see map, p. 19), absorbing or displacing the earlier inhabitants. And since in the north the old cultures maintained themselves, there thus developed a Lower Egypt and an Upper Egypt, the demographic pattern of which gave rise to the appellation "Land of Two Lands."*

From investigation of their cemeteries and community ruins, we know that a substantial population increase occurred in the south. This was probably both cause and consequence of the developing mastery of the flood waters of the Nile. As identification and control of the life-giving annual flooding progressed, a greater food supply resulted. This encouraged a population increase, which, in its turn, stimulated the conception and execution of larger drainage and irrigation projects.

Local communities (*nomes*, in later terminology), formed about their clan leaders and animal-god totems, slowly evolved group practices and social sanctions. In ways that, from lack of evidence, are yet impossible to trace, each of the "Lands"

---

* "Lower" is northern Egypt, "Upper," southern. The terminology reflects the topography of the land: the northern delta region is a lowland region; the south is irregularly elevated.

18   The Birth of Civilization

gravitated toward the establishment of a central authority. Thus in the several centuries before 3000 B.C. there came into being the twin kingdoms of the Nile, equipped with bureaucratic systems, owing allegiance to central authority, and poised, quite unconsciously, on the brink of history.

Sumerian Contributions

Egyptologists are inclined to believe that the decisive thrust into literate life came from Sumeria. There the creation of writing as well as other marks of civilization had already been achieved. Presumably the invention of writing was marked by two stages: in the first, pictures of objects were drawn—man, tree, boat; in the second, the *rebus principle** was used to convey notions not easily communicable by picture drawing. Since the very earliest Egyptian writing of which we have any record already included the second stage, it is not easy to avoid the assumption that the Egyptians took over both the idea and principles of written expression from Sumerian originals. Among the borrowings were the cylinder seal and the monumental style of architecture, a style that, as we shall see, was so perfected by the Egyptians as to constitute a lasting mark of their genius.

Geographic Isolation

No substantial evidence indicates that the Mesopotamian "conquest" was other than cultural or that the Two Kingdoms were subjugated by Sumerian legions. Geographic conditions certainly discount the likelihood of military invasion. The habitable canyon of Upper and Lower Egypt is bounded by cataracts and hills,

* The use of symbols for the phonetic value of the objects depicted. For instance, the mouth (*ro* in Egyptian) for the consonant *r*.

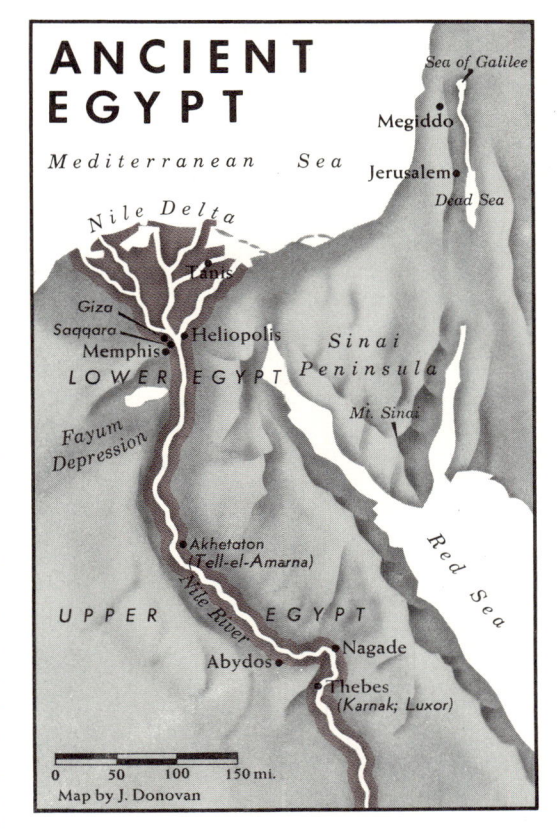

cliffs, and deserts. In the delta region, swamps, marshes, canals, and lakes discouraged invasion from the north. And Egypt was further isolated from the Fertile Crescent areas in Asia by the exceedingly difficult terrain of the Sinai Peninsula on the northeast (where, later, fleeing Hebrews were to wander for "40 years").

Reference to this isolation should not, however, deceive us into thinking of the land of the Two Kingdoms as hermetically sealed. Obviously this was not the case, for otherwise cultural infiltration (probably initiated by trade or Sumerian search for gold mines in the desert between Egypt and the Red Sea) would not have occurred. Overemphasis on the concept of the "sealed tube" might also lead us to imagine a homogeneity of habits and tastes along the ranging valley. This was certainly not the case. Throughout the

A. Egypt: Sphinx and Falcon

TABLE I

Chronological Periods of Egyptian History

All dates B.C.

ca. 5000 – 3100

BADARIANS AND NAGADIANS MOVE INTO VALLEY (FROM ASIA?)
    establishment of a food-producing economy
    worship of most of the traditional Egyptian gods introduced

"NEW EGYPTIANS" INVADE AND SETTLE VALLEY
    borrowings from Sumeria:
        writing
        monumental architecture
    population clusters in North and South
    steady urbanization of Egyptian culture
    formation of central authority in Upper (and Lower?) Egypt

ca. 3100 – ca. 2700

FOUNDING OF FIRST DYNASTY
    the "Two Lands" united by Menes
    copper mines in Sinai and Nubia worked
DEVELOPMENT OF ADMINISTRATION
GENERAL CONSOLIDATION AND ORGANIZATION OF CULTURAL GAINS

ca. 2700 – ca. 2200

OLD KINGDOM
    artistic surgence
    isolationist self-consciousness
    highly centralized political theocracy
    rise of nomarchies in the provinces
    wisdom literature first appears

---

whole of its thousands of years of prehistory and history Egypt remained, however paradoxical the phrase, The Land of Two Lands.

Egypt's Thrust into History

We have seen that for well over a thousand years Egyptians were unconsciously preparing themselves for what turned out to be a rather sudden and somewhat dramatic spiraling into historic life. Before we examine that history, we might ponder certain questions posed by an Egyptologist who probed behind the results of the urban revolution and the Mesopotamian catalyst in search of the mysterious, compulsive inner urge toward change that must be present before any spiritual change can be effected. What were the inner forces that lifted the Egyptian toward a new life? Were they not based on a *natural* desire to break with conventions that confine the self within a rigid mold? Did he not imperatively reach out for the new? Is it not likely that the Mesopotamian stimulus, far from inducing slavish copying, prompted a creative response?[1]

FOUNDING OF THE FIRST DYNASTY

The founding of the First Dynasty involved a physical phenomenon that rested

[1] John A. Wilson, *The Burden of Egypt* (Chicago: The University of Chicago Press, 1951), pp. 40–42 (later published as a Phoenix paperback under the title *The Culture of Ancient Egypt*).

TABLE I (cont'd)
Chronological Periods of Egyptian History

ca. 2200 – ca. 2050

FIRST INTERMEDIATE PERIOD
  collapse of centralized authority
  nomarchical chaos
  literary flowering
  "democratization of the hereafter"

ca. 2050 – ca. 1800

MIDDLE KINGDOM
  redevelopment of political cohesion
  refinement of arts
  economy prosperity
  first really large-scale irrigation project (the Fayum, see map, p. 19)

ca. 1800 – ca. 1570

HYKSOS INVASION—SECOND INTERMEDIATE PERIOD
  foreign rule

ca. 1570 – ca. 1100

EMPIRE (NEW KINGDOM)
  independence and unity reestablished
  conquest of other lands; period when "Egypt ruled the East"
  foreign influence in religion, culture
  Amarna period
  at end: decline of economy, power, political and private morality
    settlement of foreigners (especially Libyans) in Egypt, who
    gradually began to dominate the army

on a metaphysical assumption. Both archaeological and historical evidence clearly point to a conquest of Lower Egypt by a king from Upper Egypt around 3100 B.C. Although the unity thus created suffered later disruptions, they were temporary. For approximately 2000 years Egypt towered in the Ancient East, truly a colossus (See Table I).

The Physical Conquest

The physical conquest was effected by "Menes." (Specialists are still uncertain of the actual identity of the unifying pharaoh. But if Menes was not the unifier he was the first ruler to evoke the Egyptian concept of kingship.) From his native town of Thinis, near Abydos, he moved his forces some 300 miles down the Nile, subjugating the Lower Kingdom's nomes as he went. To serve as a permanent base of operations and administration, a new city, which we know as Memphis, was built; in Egyptian accounts it was referred to merely as the White Walls. Here the boundaries of the two kingdoms met, so that the choice of the site was probably symbolic as well as strategic. Evidence indicates that the struggle for unification was long-lasting, continuing throughout most of the First Dynasty. The period of cultural consolidation was equally protracted, extending over three or four centuries. But by about 2700 B.C. national dynastic control was a physical reality.

The Metaphysical Assumption

By this time, too, the metaphysical assumption had become firmly fixed. Its essence is simplicity itself: the king (

21   A. Egypt: Sphinx and Falcon

King Narmer's palette (ca. 3000 B.C.) shows this Upper Egyptian pharaoh bringing the northern "Land" under his subjection. Narmer is one of several southern pharaohs whose combined efforts unified Egypt.

this belief. Egypt was, indeed, the gift of the Nile, that magic ribbon of water that made the land a livable one; yet Egyptians knew that their land was *two*. Here was a mystery of the gods, paramount in their national life but permanently beyond their comprehension. Only a god could reconcile the conflicting forces of the universe, including the contrasts of the Two Lands (by the end of Egyptian civilization the phrase "Two Lands" was understood to mean not Egypt but the world).

Moreover, the Egyptians were given neither to ventures in mysticism nor to what we would call scientific inquiry. As patient pragmatists, they were willing to try different means for gaining their ends. To them, all matter and motion were of the divine substance. They sensed, therefore, no essential difference in the several components of the universe. They ranged naturally from the world of men to the realm of the gods, and thus readily accepted the idea of the pharaoh as actually a god living on earth in order to rule Egypt.

THE OLD KINGDOM

Supremacy of the Pharaoh and the Rise of Nomarchies

In the five centuries of the Old Kingdom elaborate institutions were created, many of which, for better or worse, were to endure across the next 2000 years. Legally, the pharaoh was the state. His word was law, and his commands were unquestionably obeyed. As a god he owned the country. Theoretically the land and all its produce were rightfully his; in practice this meant that the state, then as now, had the right to tax, draft, and confiscate. Naturally the pharaoh needed subordinates to help him administer the manifold duties of government. Originally the chief of these came from his family and circle of noble friends. Later a kind of civil service system was worked out that recruited tal-

pharaoh, a word originally referring to the palace in which the king lived) was a god—not, it must be noted, a delegate or regent of the gods, but a god himself. By about 2500 B.C. the notion had become so widely accepted that pharaohs made bold to designate themselves as sons of the chief god, Re. In our scientific and democratic times, of course, such an idea is so patently unthinkable that a schoolchild would reject it; and, further, would probably reject the contention that human beings ever could have seriously believed it. Yet the Egyptians did. The pharaoh was god; even more, "he, as god, *was* the state." A discussion of how this dogma came to be accepted would lead us beyond the scope of our study, but we may note one scholar's observation that geographic conditions and the Egyptian state of mind probably led to the formulation and acceptance of

22   The Birth of Civilization

Not all of the pharaoh's tax collectors, often village headmen, were scrupulous in accounting for their collections. The above scene depicts the "trial" of four such delinquents.

ent wherever it could be found (although usually it was from among the children of officials); in this very limited sense popular participation in government was introduced.

Taxes were levied by the pharaoh and his advisors and brought into the treasury by his staff of tax collectors (symbolically there were two treasuries, one for each land). Each of the "two lands" was divided into approximately 20 nomes, or provinces, ruled by nomarchs selected by the pharaoh. The provincial governors in turn appointed hosts of lesser officials such as treasury and military officers and scribes, who periodically submitted reports on affairs in their nomes. By Dynasty V (see Table I) these nomarchs were successful in persuading the pharaoh to make their offices hereditary. Thereafter their influence steadily increased, especially in the south. Eventually they sought, sometimes successfully, to usurp royal power when times of trouble beset the god-kings.

Trade and Agriculture

Throughout the period of the Old Kingdom a developing foreign trade flourished, especially with the areas later called Syria, Nubia, and Somaliland. Numerous accounts tell us of the importation of cedar, ivory, ebony, gums, resins, and myrrh. Sometimes these accounts were written to make it seem that the importations were tributes from conquered peoples. But this is hardly likely, for other records speak of Egyptian products, especially manufactured goods, going in the other direction.

The basic strength of Egypt's economy, however, then and for the long centuries to follow, lay in agriculture. Emmer, barley, and cattle formed the bulk of the produce. The god-king and his family lived on taxes and revenues from public domains as, to a smaller extent, did his hierarchy of officials. Bare subsistence was the average citizen's lot, although recent evidence indicates that some farmers and craftsmen maintained a relatively high standard of living. From the peasants' toil about one-third to one-half went to the state and to the landlord. In times of famine large-scale starvation and death were suffered. From bas-relief scenes and from other evidence we must conclude that he reacted to his cruel lot as later American slaves and Russian serfs reacted to theirs. Unable to escape oppressively burdensome tasks and almost subhuman status, he sang through his chores

A. Egypt: Sphinx and Falcon

to lift his spirits, used guile where he could, and for the rest bent under and bore his burdens. Besides lords and peasants there was a multitude of priests, scribes, architects, and artisans; but data concerning them are scanty.

Women and Marriage

Although Old Kingdom society was essentially man-centered and man-dominated, women were not regarded as chattels. Like men they could own and control property; and occasionally they might become officials. But perhaps the best notion of their status, at least during the Old Kingdom period, can be obtained from this excerpt from the writing of an Egyptian of that period:

If thou art a man of standing, thou shouldst found thy household and love thy wife as is fitting. Fill her belly, clothe her back. Ointment is the prescription for her body. Make her heart glad as long as thou livest. She is a profitable field for her lord. Thou shouldst not contend with her at law, and keep her far from gaining control. . . .[2]

The pharaoh possessed a number of concubines; among those who could afford it, polygamy was commonly practiced. Since succession to the throne was provided in large part through matriarchal channels, the habit of brother-sister marriage early developed as a kind of accession insurance, a custom continued down to Roman times. But, contrary to popular belief, no one but royalty practiced it. On the other hand, first-cousin marriages were not only permitted but favored.

Science

Science as we know it today did not exist. Nowhere does the record indicate interest in knowing in order to know, in abstract thought, or in leading what the Greeks called the "examined life." In a narrow sense Egyptian thought was utilitarian; when he found it useful, the Egyptian pursued knowledge assiduously and his achievements were remarkable.

Early in the Third Dynasty a solar calendar was devised. This had been preceded by two other calendars: the first was constructed to mark the rhythmic flow of the Nile—inundation, seed time, harvest; the second was based on the waxing and waning of the moon, to regulate social, religious, and civil celebrations. Neither calendar satisfied the long-run administrative needs of the complex state apparatus. The Nile could not be counted on to flood precisely at the same point in the season, and lunar months could not be synchronized with a changing "river" calendar. By patient, tedious observation and calculation Egyptian officials discovered the 365-day average lapse between the commencement of the inundation periods. This average, set up as a standard unit of time, could then be geared to the wheeling movement of a fixed star, thus yielding a dependable frame of reference.

The patterns of star clusters and the position of individual units within them were discovered early; instruments were devised to observe the cyclic movements of heavenly bodies in order to tell the time at night. But neither the interest, the instruments, nor the mathematical knowledge needed to merge these movements into a comprehensive, systematic cosmological account was present.

In mathematics, the Egyptian early devised a numbering system with which he was able to reckon complicated sums and deal with quantitative differentials. He worked out some of the fundamental propositions of geometric progression, and his understanding of geometry gave him a working knowledge of the simpler properties of such figures as he needed to plan the construction of houses, temples, and pyramids.

[2] James B. Pritchard, ed., *Ancient Near Eastern Texts* (Princeton: Princeton University Press, 1955), p. 413.

Egyptian medicine was a mixture of reasonably accurate knowledge based on observation and practice and plain unadulterated magic. When we consider the Egyptian's strong abiding emphasis on the work of unseen forces in all realms of life, large and small, it is surprising how much reliable medical knowledge he assembled. The centrality of the function of the heart in the complex of body processes was well known, although physicians failed to understand the full nature of the circulatory system. The kinds, positions, and functions of the bones were learned early. In a surviving papyrus extensive passages deal with the highly effective treatment of fractures. On the other hand, however, much medical lore included fantastic incantations designed to propitiate, exorcise, or otherwise effectively deal with evil spirits.

Writing

Earlier reference was made to Egypt's borrowing the idea and principles of written language from Mesopotamia. Both were creatively reworked. Very soon Egyptian scribes discovered the principle of phonetic writing; for example, "⬚, the picture of a house, received the value $p + r$ because the Egyptian word for house was *por*, whence—the vowels being felt of as little account—the hieroglyph ⬚ was adopted for writing of a number of words, for example *pire* 'to go forth' which possessed the sounds $p + r$ in that order."[3] It is evident that when a phonetically used sign stood for a word of one consonant only (Alan Gardiner, an Egyptian-language specialist, gives as an example ◯, *ro*—mouth) the Egyptian stood on the verge of alphabet making. That he did not take this imaginative leap—as Phoenician scribes, profiting from this development, later did—hardly detracts from this solid achievement.

Moreover, Egyptian copyists, busy with the expanding affairs of the growing nation, soon found any kind of pictographic writing too cumbersome for rapid, easy use. So they adopted the practice of indicating only the barest outline of each picture or phonetic symbol, thus inventing a cursive script that we call *hieratic*. As writing became a more widespread practice, especially in the Empire period (though it remained throughout the whole of Egyptian history the property of the minority), it tended to become more cursive. Out of this cursive eventually developed the so-called *demotic* script (in the seventh century B.C.) which, from about 700 B.C. on, became the writing of those engaged in business.

Literature and Art

In the literature of all periods both hieroglyphic (for inscriptions and certain religious texts) and hieratic (on papyrus) styles were used. The literary remains of the Old Kingdom, however, apart from rituals and mortuary texts, are too scant in volume to provide a basis for critical judgment. In the First Intermediate Period and the Middle Kingdom a grand flourishing of wisdom literature, stories, poems, and songs occurred. But with the establishment of the Empire a steady decline set in. A typical text of the earliest period is found in the many rituals for the dead. The following excerpt is from one such text, written about 2400 B.C. The opening and close of each paragraph were intended to instruct the votary in actions to be performed as "the words are spoken":

Words to be spoken: "O Osiris King Neferka-Re, take to thyself the eye of Horus. Lift thou it to thy face." A lifting of bread and beer. Lifting before his face. Words to be spoken. "Lift thy face, O Osiris. Lift thy face, O this King Neferka-Re, whose state of glory had departed [to

---

[3] Stephen R. K. Glanville, *Legacy of Egypt* (Oxford: Oxford University Press, 1942), p. 64.

A. Egypt: Sphinx and Falcon

This basalt slab, inscribed by Egyptian priests in the Hellenistic period, was found by troops of Napoleon in 1799. It contains an inscription written in hieroglyphs, demotic script, and Greek. With this key, scholars were able to decipher hieroglyphic writing and to bring much of Egypt's life into history.

the other world]. Lift thy face, O this King Nefer-ka-Re, honored and keen, that thou mayst look at that which came forth from thee, . . . Wash thyself, O King Nefer-ka-Re. Open thy mouth with the Eye of Horus. Thou callest thy *ka,* like Osiris, that it may protect thee from all wrath of the dead. O King Nefer-ka-Re, receive thou this bread, which is the Eye of Horus." Laid on the ground before him.[4]

[4] Pritchard, op. cit., p. 325.

The artists of the Old Kingdom established canons of style and form that were to endure for nearly three millennia. They sought the essence of the Old Kingdom's overall view of life, mastered the techniques to make it manifest, and produced artistic creations that the modern world is only now beginning to appreciate. Of the sculptors, Breasted quotes the classical archaeologist Charles Perrot as saying, "It must be acknowledged that they produced works which are not to be surpassed in their way by the greatest portraits of modern Europe."

Architecture and Sculpture

It is commonly acknowledged that Egyptian architects employed mass as no people before or since. The tombs and temples of the Old Kingdom are enduring wonders. The largest of the pyramid tombs, built by Khufu—whose Greek name, Cheops, is perhaps more familiar to us—is properly known simply as the Great Pyramid. Well over two million huge blocks of stone (some weighing 15 tons) were required to give it the form and substance its creators desired. Covering an area of 13 acres, it rose to a height of 480 feet, more than one-third that of the Empire State Building (it is now about 30 feet less in height, medieval vandals having destroyed the top). Each side measured 755 feet, with a difference of only 7.9 inches between the shortest and the longest. Elaborate corridors and chambers were an integral part of the structural design; especially noteworthy were the Grand Gallery and the King's Chamber. The former is 153 feet long and 28 feet high. Its polished limestone walls reach to an impressive height of 7½ feet. Seven courses rise above that level, each overlapping by several inches that upon which it rests, thus constituting an expansive corbeled vault. The King's Chamber, made altogether of granite, has a ceiling constructed of nine slabs, each weighing more than four tons. A temple causeway from the valley, and the valley temple, were part of the whole complex.[5]

Beyond superb handling of mass, Egyptian designers solved the architectural problem of space by the invention of the column, the arch, and the dome, although the latter two were not much employed.

[5] See I. E. S. Edwards, *The Pyramids of Egypt* (Baltimore: Penguin Books, 1961).

Later, Greek architects were to follow Egyptian models in fashioning their own chaste Doric columns.

Sculptors worked both in the round and in relief, but, again, in neither was it their aim to evoke an esthetic or intellectual response. Rather, their purpose was to facilitate the subject's transition from this world to the next and at the same time to eternalize his earthly life.* Consequently it was the custom, maintained for many centuries, to set the carefully wrought statues—many of them (like the sitting figure of Khafre) rightfully belonging in the category of masterpieces—in the tomb chapels and mortuary temples of the pharaohs and nobles. In work depicting the form and features of royalty and nobility a style was early set and substantially maintained (save for the brief Amarna period) that was characterized by impassive calm and enduring nobility calculated to suggest, and perhaps even in part to effect, the eternal existence of the subject. Some authorities conjecture that when the

* But we should recall that until a century or two ago no art was created for the sole purpose of being viewed as a "work of art."

An Old Kingdom scribe, probably a minor official in the employ of a nome bureaucrat.

A. Egypt: Sphinx and Falcon

Contrary to a commonly held belief, much Egyptian art was natural and free-flowing. These geese, for example, could have been modeled from their counterparts in any contemporary American setting.

latter was a pharaoh the ongoing life of the state was intimately involved, since in Egyptian theology the two were one. Occasionally even high officials were shown in a more work-a-day pose and depicted realistically. One example of such realism is seen in the famous figure of the "Louvre scribe," so convincingly vivacious that it is hard to think of it as a lifeless stone figure carved in the distant days of some Second Dynasty pharaoh.

In both architecture and sculpture visible remains of the artist's work are numerous, thanks to the medium as well as to the dry climate and protecting sands. Unfortunately the works of Egypt's painters have not fared so well. A number of paintings remain that indicate that while this discipline did not altogether escape stylization, it was affected less by it than were the others. Perhaps this was because paint is a freer medium than stone, easier and quicker to use; and because the painter's subject was often taken not from royal or noble life but from the worlds of the lower animals and of plant life. Shown in the illustration, for example, is an almost perfect example of naturalism. The geese are real, posturing as real geese posture still. Anatomical structure is naturalistic; lines are graceful and sure.

Religion

Thus the arts flourished in the Old Kingdom. Sometimes they were performed by members of the upper classes for their own delectation; often in the service of religion. We need now to examine that religion, its catholic touch, its demanding and ultimately smothering embrace.

Because of the central position of the tomb in Egyptian life, we are naturally inclined to regard the Egyptians as a people morbidly preoccupied with death. Precisely the opposite was true. Egyptians found life zestful and unendingly rewarding. The security they enjoyed, once the goal of political and cultural consolidation was achieved by the leaders of the early dynasties, contributed in large measure to this attitude. Thanks to the geographic position of the Valley Kingdom, foreign invasions were few and, except for the Hyksos episode (see p. 36f.), inconsequential. Civil disruption did occur, but only infrequently. A benign climate warmed and brightened the land, while the unfailing rhythm of the mysterious Nile heightened the sense of security and anticipation. From the vantage point of their valley it seemed to the Egyptians that the whole universe conspired for good—their good. This thesis is not meant, of course, to deny or to play down the vicissitudes of life that beset this, as every other, people—sickness and suffering, extended periods of want, famine, class cruelties, oppressions large and small; it argues merely against the common notion that Egypt was a land of the dead where the goal was the grave.

In short, the Egyptian paid much attention to death because he so much loved life. The pious European ascetic of medieval times might seek death as an escape from the sin and suffering of this world, and as a prelude to eternal spiritual bliss. But the Egyptian wooed this life; he was anything but spiritual. He wished to continue beyond death the life he currently lived, and all his embalmings and tombs and theological constructs were designed simply with this in view. It was almost impossible for the Egyptian to think in metaphysical terms. True, he spoke of *ba,* the soul; and of a *ka,* a kind of generalized and superior personality. But both were envisioned as ongoing, glorified magnifications of his earthly being, fundamentally physical. Very definitely, Egyptian religion was a religion of life.

In the system of religious beliefs as it was originally established, only the pharaoh enjoyed immortality by intrinsic right. Very soon this doctrine was modified, by royal fiat, to include his family and such members of the nobility as he designated. (Later, as we shall see, a religious development in the First Intermediate Period broadened the "scope of the saved" to include the middle classes; still later, to all who lived by *ma'at* and who managed to obtain from the priests the requisite rites and incantations. The concept *ma'at* is defined on p. 34.) But at all times the daily ongoing life of the masses was dependent on the eternal existence of the ruler. Hence it was imperative that everything be done, especially as related to the construction and maintenance of the ruler's pyramid-tomb, to give assurance that this immortality was not endangered. In this sense every individual lived in the pharaoh.*

Except for a brief period, to be considered presently, the main outlines of the theological framework constructed in these early times remained constant throughout the entire history of ancient Egypt; although, unlike the later Jews, the Egyptians were unsuccessful in efforts to make their system philosophically sound and logically consistent. Early in the history of the Old Kingdom, probably during the First Dynasty, a first step was made toward evolving a metaphysical explanation of creation that approached the Judaeo-Christian view of creation as seen in the account in Genesis and the Logos doctrine elaborated in later Greek philosophy and made central in the fourth gospel of the New Testament. In one of the many different Egyptian explanations of creation (which appear to a modern mind quite contradictory, but which did not appear so to an Egyptian) the creator Ptah:

> made all and brought the gods into being . . . everything came forth from him, nourishment and provisions, the offerings of the gods, and every good thing. Thus it was discovered and understood that his strength is greater than (that of the other) gods. And so Ptah was satisfied [or, so Ptah rested], after he had made everything, as well as all the divine order. He had formed the gods, he had made cities, he had founded nomes, he had put the gods in their shrines, he had established their offerings, he had founded their shrines, . . . he had made their bodies like that (with which) their hearts were satisfied. So the gods entered into their bodies of every (kind of) wood, of every (kind of) stone, of every (kind of) clay, or anything which might grow upon him, in which they had taken form. So all the gods, as well as their *ka*'s gathered themselves to him, content and associated with the Lord of the Two Lands.[6]

Here the god Ptah conceives the elements of the universe with his mind ("heart") and brings them into being by his commanding speech ("tongue"). Thus, at the beginning of Egyptian history, there was an approach to the Logos Doc-

---

* One scholar offers a qualified dissent: "I wonder if there is really more to pyramid building than that the king, like everyone else, wanted an appropriate setting for the next life—and could afford it."

[6] Pritchard, op. cit., p. 5.

trine.* However, this explanation of creation, in which a divine being created altogether through intellect and will, never became the basis of a metaphysical theology. It was submerged by the more normal myth-oriented theological systems of ancient Egypt.

According to Memphite theology Ptah created the original Ennead, the first nine gods. In Heliopolitan doctrine Atum (or, in still another theological complex, Re, who later came to be known as Re-Atum and was eventually linked with Amon of Thebes as Amon-Re) was the sun god who by self-insemination gave birth to Shu, god of air, and Tefnut, goddess of moisture. From the union of these two came Geb, god of earth, and Nut, goddess of the sky, who, in turn, bore four children: Osiris, who married his sister Isis, and Seth, who similarly was both brother and husband of Nephthys. Originally Geb gave Upper Egypt to Seth and Lower Egypt to Osiris but, later changing his mind, made Osiris ruler of the united Kingdom. Out of this judgment a feud developed, quite understandably, between Seth and his brother, who seemed to have been unduly favored. According to the mythological account, Seth slew Osiris, cut his body into pieces, and strewed the parts up and down the valley. Osiris's bereaved wife then betook herself upon a prolonged journey that culminated in the finding and gathering together of the dismembered parts of her husband's body. With this restoration Osiris became god of the dead, or, in paradoxical Egyptian thought, the god of the eternally living. Later he came to be associated with the grain, or bread, of Egypt and hence with the Nile.

Geography and climate conspired to emphasize the primacy of three gods—Re, Osiris, and Horus. The blazing Egyptian sun dominated cloudless skies and, in a sense, the whole realm; thus it was natural that the sun god should take a commanding position in the first community of the gods. Similarly, the vital, rhythmic flow of the grain-producing Nile occasioned perennial appeals to Osiris. Although present evidence does not permit the statement of it as a fact, it may reasonably be conjectured that Egyptians thought of the eternal winds of the desert, ridden by the high-flying falcon, as enveloping the whole life of the "now," epit-

---

* The specific biblical reference is to the opening sentence of the Gospel of John, which reads: "In the beginning was the Word [Logos], and the Word was with God, and the Word was God."

As a river people, the Egyptians naturally thought of the boat as necessary equipment for the next life. This particular model bark was found in an Old Kingdom tomb.

omized by Horus, the pharaoh-god whose emblem was the falcon. Re was thought of as making his daily journey across the sky from east to west in a boat, a vehicle naturally suggesting itself to a river people. Each night he was rowed back through the Underworld, to reappear triumphantly the next morning. Thus a cycle of birth, death, and rebirth daily impressed itself upon the land, symbolizing and reenforcing belief in the eternality of life. In the same way the legend of Osiris's death and resurrection gave assurance that endless todays were linked forever with endless tomorrows, especially as this same god was the pharaoh who "lived in death" as well as the god of endlessly recurring harvests.

The details of this complex of religion and cosmology varied from region to region and period to period, sometimes in important respects. Consequently, it happened that on occasion the Egyptian would be confronted with differing, even contradictory, explanations and rituals. But it must be repeated (while also allowing for Crane Brinton's injunction against believing that Egyptian religious thought and life were bound in "frozen uniformity") that in its main features and "psychic weighting" the system remained basically unaltered throughout the whole of ancient Egypt's history. Religious symbols in the tombs of the late Saitic pharaohs (in the 600s B.C.), for example, were remarkably similar to those of the First Dynasty more than 2000 years earlier, and had much the same meaning.

The theology constructed and elaborated in the Old Kingdom made a place for moral and ethical conduct but did not give it primacy: the individual was urged to be honest, just, dutiful, and considerate but chiefly for narrowly selfish ends. That is, the injunctions against immoral behavior were laid down for the sake of practical expediency—a kind of honesty-is-the-best-policy approach—and to propitiate the gods, themselves almost invariably practical-minded.

Step Pyramid at Saqqara.

Pyramids

In the Memphite theology, chaos—that is, that which existed before Ptah created all things—was of a watery nature. To establish a place from which he could operate to bring phenomena into existence Ptah raised an island from the formless waters, called the Primeval Hill. It is thought by some Egyptologists that the pyramids of the god-kings were symbolic of this raised island. Frankfort believes that the idea was introduced by Zoser (or Djoser, a pharaoh of the Third Dynasty) who "changed the superstructure of the royal tomb from the [original] flat, oblong mound, the mastaba . . . and realized the equation of his resting place with the fountain-head of emerging life, the Primeval Hill, by giving his tomb the shape of a step pyramid, a three dimensional form . . . of the hieroglyphic for the Hill. The kings of the Fourth Dynasty substituted the true pyramid, which was the specific Heliopolitan form of the Primeval Hill. . . ."[7] Some authorities, on the other hand, believe that the pyramidal form symbolized the god-king's intermediate station between eternal and temporal existence. In any

[7] *Kingship and the Gods* (Chicago: The University of Chicago Press, 1948), p. 153.

A. Egypt: Sphinx and Falcon

The pyramids of Mycerinus (Menkure), Chephren, and Khufu (Cheops). These Fourth-Dynasty representations of the "primeval hill" symbolized the eternal life of the pharaoh and thus of his people.

case, the pyramid-tombs of the pharaohs epitomized the link between gods and man, between the now and the hereafter, serving as the specific instrument by which the pharaoh-god Horus became the god Osiris.

As time passed, more and more of Egypt's wealth went into the construction of these massive structures and into the building and maintenance of the temples that served them. Statistics of pyramidal dimensions, given in square feet, clearly reflect this trend: the base of Zoser's tomb, approximately 400; one of Seneferu's, in the next dynasty, 620; of Khufu's or Cheops's, 756; and of Khafre's, or Chephren's, 708. Although monumentality was less emphasized in the Fifth and Sixth Dynasties, pyramids were still built on the grand scale. So great were the labors required in the building of these colossal monuments that typically a pharaoh began construction of his tomb immediately upon his accession to the throne. Although in recent years some students have tended to belittle both the kind and degree of labor involved, the evidence seems stronger for the original thesis. Herodotus, the Greek historian, reports a story current in the fifth century B.C. that insists that Khufu's pyramid required the labor of more than 100,000 men for nearly 20 years. Sir William M. F. Petrie, a modern British Egyptologist, has confirmed the reasonableness of these figures.

Decline of the Old Kingdom

In fact pyramid construction increasingly came to absorb the bulk of the energy, thought, and wealth of the whole nation. By the end of the Sixth Dynasty (around 2200 B.C.) a gradually deepening crisis reached its climax. Although the valley was rich in resources, it could not supply the needs of its inhabitants under an economy so given to unproductive uses. As the national economy declined, its principal units—estates of the nobles—became more restrictively self-contained. Moreover, as the affairs of the Old Kingdom became more complex and large-proportioned, the authority of the local governor—the nome leader—increased. It is natural to assume that with this increase in power came an increase in the appetite for power. In any case, the evidence is clear that by approximately 2200 B.C. central authority had become seriously weakened and the powers of the nome leaders correspondingly greater.

Thus, in spite of the elaborate theological underpinning that had subsumed the tremendous political, economic, and social achievements of this pioneering civilization across one half millennium, the Old Kingdom almost literally crumbled under the slowly crushing weight of its divine rulers' tombs. Egyptian civilization was not to perish; indeed it was to rise to greater heights. But a time of troubles had come to the valley, and, if the paraphrase be permitted, the voice of destruction was heard in the land. The lights had dimmed; the first act of the Egyptian drama was over.

TIME OF TROUBLES—THE FIRST INTERMEDIATE PERIOD

The interlude between the fading of the Old Kingdom and the flourishing of the Middle Kingdom is called the First Intermediate Period. It lasted about 200 years.

During this period the land of the Two Kingdoms, now split into a hodgepodge of contending nomarchies, was characterized by a kind of feudal anarchy. Although records show the existence of what were called the Seventh and Eighth Dynasties, their pharaohs were shadowy figures. Individual nome leaders exercised what control they could over their local areas. During the Ninth Dynasty of Herakleopolis nomarchs fought each other in Middle and Upper Egypt for control of the Valley. In the meantime, numerous Asians from the Fertile Crescent had filtered into the defenseless delta. Eventually a new dynasty arose in Thebes (the Eleventh) and consolidated its position in the southern part of Upper Egypt. For about three generations the Theban kings of the Eleventh Dynasty fought the Herakleopolitan Tenth and its vassal nomarchs in middle Egypt and succeeded once more in bringing unity and order to Egypt; the invaders were either expelled from the land or absorbed into the population.

A scribe of these troubled times has left an account of the bewildering and anarchic conditions that is worth quoting in part:

Why really the Nile is in flood, (but) no one plows for himself, (because) every man says: "We do not know what may happen to the land!"

Why, really, women are dried up, and none can conceive. Khnum ["the potter god (who) shaped infants on his wheel"] cannot fashion (mortals) because of the state of the land. . . .

Why really, the land spins as a potter's wheel does. The robber is (now) the possessor of riches. . . .

[Why] really, the desert is (spread) throughout the land. The nomes are destroyed. Barbarians from outside have come to Egypt. . . . There are really no people anywhere. . . .

Why really, laughter has disappeared, and is [no longer] made. It is wailing that pervades the land, mixed with lamentation. . . .

Why really, all maid-servants make free with their tongues. When the mistresses speak, it is burdensome to the servants. . . .

Behold now, it has come to a point where (men) rebel against the auraeus ["the deified snake which was the guardian of a temple or palace"]. the . . . [?] of Re, which makes the Two lands peaceful. . . .

Behold, the owners of robes are (now) in rags. (But) he who never wove for himself is now the owner of fine linen. . . .

Behold, not an office is in its (proper) place, like a stampeded herd which has no herdsman. . . .

So Lower Egypt weeps. The storehouse of the king is a (mere) come-and-get-it for everybody, and the entire palace is without its taxes. . . .[8]

Thus there appeared in the land a spirit of doubt and dismay, of disbelief in gods and men, and a corresponding tendency to live a life of abandon and sensationalism, reminding us of our own century's Jazz Age, with its theme of "Runnin' Wild!"

But Egypt's confidence and optimism were clouded, not killed; eventually the dynast of a Theban house successfully brought an end to the chaos and restored unity to the land.

THE MIDDLE KINGDOM

The new nation that slowly formed is called by modern historians the Middle Kingdom to distinguish it from the Old Kingdom and the Empire (or New Kingdom) that followed it after still another interlude of darkness. But the aptness of the designation goes somewhat beyond chronological classification. The Twelfth Dynasty, which encompassed most of the three-century span of the Middle Kingdom, was characterized by several rulers who felt a heightened sense of responsibility for the way they used their power. Although the new pharaohs (usually taking the name of either Amenemhet or Senusert*) continued to act and speak as though they believed in their absolute divinities, they tolerated some provincial decision-making. Thus there developed a kind of semifeudalism that, while still providing strong central authority in the North and South, allowed local governors in Middle Egypt a large measure of self-regulation.

Ethical Concerns

A surviving document of this period clearly marks the difference between the old concept and the new, for it depicts Amenemhet I confessing to his son the mistakes that he, as ruler, has made. In the Old Kingdom such an admission would have been unthinkable. As Wilson has phrased it, the confession was the "sorrowful plea of a fallible human." In his *Burden of Egypt* this author has titled a chapter dealing with the Middle Kingdom "The King as the Good Shepherd," to distinguish the new concept of rulership from the old idea of the pharaoh as a god without worry. Throne names taken by a number of this dynasty's pharaohs reflect this concern. The throne name of Amenemhet II, for example, was "He Who Takes Pleasure in Ma'at," while that of Senusert II was "He Who Makes Ma'at Appear."[9] The concern is evident as we gain understanding of the term *ma'at*. Although the meaning of this term changed from time to time, denoting, for example, *justice* to Egyptians of the Twelfth Dynasty, but *absolute truth* to the people in Akhanaton's reign (about 500 years later), it basically implied the essence of the *good* aspects and manifestations of life. The god-king was ma'at, as was the daughter of Re and the life-giving Nile, as well as many other concrete things. But subsuming all was a cosmic force that partook of eternal harmony and "rightness."

RELIGIOUS VENTURING

In religious thought the Egyptian of this time was in a transitional state between dynamism, animism, pantheism, and

[8] Pritchard, op. cit., pp. 441–43 passim.
* Sesostris is the Greek version of the latter name.
[9] Wilson, op. cit., p. 133.

34   The Birth of Civilization

monotheism. By 2000 B.C. the Nile dweller, although somewhat cautiously, had come to probe the meaning of his traditional belief in God as force and God as many. Documentary evidence reveals a sage declaring, "Generation passes generation among men, and the god, who knows (men's) characters, has hidden himself. (But) there is none who can withstand the Lord of the Hand. . . ." It is possible that the religious philosopher was beginning to suspect that one pulsing power made up the universe. If so, he was indeed close to pantheism. Or, as Frankfort has pointed out, "A step in the direction of personalizing God might have led him to true monotheism." And an indication of how close the times came to investing religion with ethical concern appears in an excerpt from the "king's instructions," noted above, an excerpt that could easily pass for a line from the writings of one of the later Hebrew prophets: "More acceptable is the character of one upright of heart than the ox of the evildoer."* Here the inner moral worth of the individual is weighted more heavily than oblations, incantations, and sacrifices. But in actual fact neither the road to pantheism nor the road to ethical (or any other kind of) monotheism was taken by the Middle Kingdom Egyptian.

The "Affluent Society"

In this period the copper mines of Mount Sinai were systematically worked and tin was added to the refined ore, so that the Bronze Age began. Trading was carried on with peoples of the eastern Mediterranean shore as well as with sea peoples to the north and Nubians to the south. One of the most ambitious projects carried out by the kings of Dynasty XII was the conversion of portions of the Fayum depression (see map, p. 19) into a large flood-control area to serve the needs of Lower Egypt. In addition, certain areas adjacent to the Fayum were brought under cultivation for the first time. Political as well as economic changes were effected, for the dual program was of a nature so ramifying and complex that large-scale cooperation of many settlements was required, thus knitting together many hitherto semi-isolated communities.

Although economic affluence was still restricted to official classes, some amelioration of the lot of workers and peasants seems to have occurred; and some laborers became artisans or independent small farmers. In short, the change in the standard of values, reflected in politics, religion, and social relations, bore meaningfully on economic conditions.

The arts flourished, and even the crafts achieved a distinction of rare quality. The exquisite jewelry that belonged to the royal princesses reveals the dexterity and subtle craftsmanship of Egyptian workmen. Fortunately for us, many treasures of the Dahshur necropolis escaped the attention of tomb robbers; otherwise we might never have known of the artistic capabilities of the Middle Kingdom craftsmen.

Above all, the writers of the period excelled in their creations, ranging feelingly and subtly over many subjects. Some of the tales were of such heroic proportions and continuing worth that they have influenced modern literature. In architecture, pyramids became less mountainous; some sculptured works were cast in a less massive mold. Altogether, the artistic sensitivities of the valley people were given ample scope for creative expression.

So for more than a hundred years the reunited Two Lands gave promise of a new freedom in political, moral, intellectual, and esthetic ventures. Although periodic raids reached into the outside world, in the main the nation pursued the arts of peace. For a while it seemed as though the

---

* Compare, for example, Micah's sentiments, where he denounces ritualistic sacrifice and asks, "What doth the Lord require of thee but to love mercy, do justly, and walk humbly with thy God?"

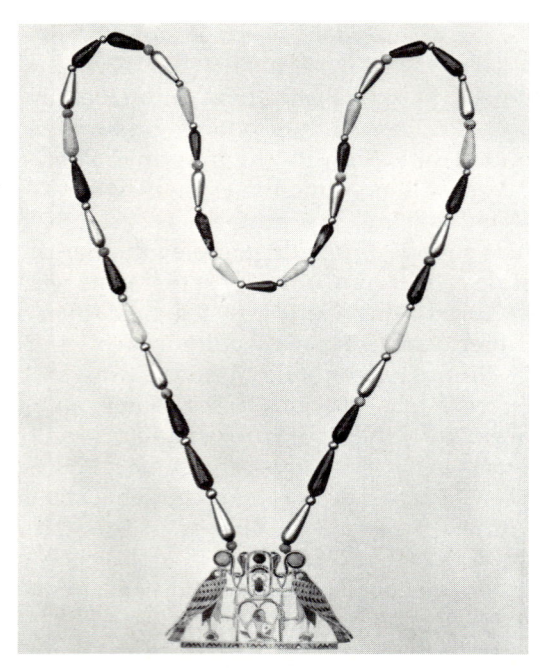

This Twelfth-Dynasty necklace belonged to Princess Sit Hat-Hor Yunet. Its beads and pectoral are of gold, carnelian, lapis lazuli, and green feldspar.

collective genius of the human spirit might flower into the chaste grandeur of true sophistication. But the challenge was too great. The Middle Kingdom began to show signs of inability to "survive national prosperity and the renewal of materialism." Provincial privileges, fed by parochial pride, threatened to weaken the fabric of national life. Sesostris III arrested the development by eliminating the powerful nomarchs of Middle Egypt, who suddenly disappeared in his time. But the drift toward political particularism was resumed at his death. It is significant that throughout the years remaining before the arrival of the Hyksos many kings ruled, none for long, and none related to the other. The real rulers were the Pharaoh's highest officers, who, the evidence seems to indicate, were all members of one family who inherited the office and managed the country. The second act of the Egyptian drama was over; the Middle Kingdom had had its opportunity—and its day.

THE SECOND INTERMEDIATE PERIOD—THE HYKSOS INVASION

Evidence indicates that before the Hyksos—a term signifying "rulers of foreign lands"—swept into Egypt from the Palestine area, change was the order of the day in much of the Fertile Crescent, especially along the foothills of the Zagros mountains north and west of the Tigris River. We have just noted the Egyptian failure to respond aggressively and imaginatively to challenge. Outside Egypt movements of peoples were taking place on a scale that caused serious cultural dislocation. For example, at the same time that invaders from the north were subjugating the Nile kingdom, the Kassites* were flooding over larger areas of the Tigris-Euphrates Valley. Probably these ranging invaders came from regions north and east of the Caucasus mountains, but surer identification must wait upon further research.

Even more remains to be learned about the Hyksos. Documentary evidence of a reliable nature is almost completely lacking.† Consequently this portion of Egyptian history is briefly told. We know that the invaders swept down into the valley ca. 1670 B.C., bringing with them advanced fighting equipment (the composite bow, for example) with which they were eventually able to subjugate most of Egypt.

The capital was moved to Tanis in the delta region, into which flowed booty and tribute from all parts of the kingdom.‡ Since Egyptian culture was superior to that brought in by the "barbarians," the newcomers took over what they could un-

* See chap. 2, p. 70.
† For an account of the Hyksos see R. N. Engberg, *The Hyksos Reconsidered*. It is, unfortunately, quite outdated; but there is as yet no other work in English.
‡ Tanis is the Egyptian name; the Hyksos called it Avaris. It is the modern San el Hagar.

The Birth of Civilization

derstand and use. This, it developed, was not a little; indeed, before they were expelled they had become almost completely Egyptianized. If the arts did not flourish under the new rulers, they at least did not markedly decline. A number of scientific observations recorded by Egyptian scribes were recopied and presumably studied. And a reasonable order and justice seemed to prevail throughout a large part of the nation. Still, in the main, civilization marked time in the valley.

Ejection of the Hyksos

Sometime around 1600 B.C. signs of serious restiveness appeared. As in the First, so in the Second Intermediate Period Thebes served as the nucleus of opposition and of unifying activity. Although most of the high officials seemed satisfied with the status quo, royalty was not. The struggle to oust the invaders was begun by Sekeneure Ta'o II and continued by Kamos, whose premature death gave the movement's leadership to his brother Ahmose, who, in his eleventh reigning year, finally succeeded in capturing Tanis. Even this triumph was not enough. For more than a hundred years the sacred land had suffered foreign rule. If left at the delta's edge, might not the foreign hosts return? So they were pursued to Sharuhen, near the first Palestinian settlements, which the Egyptians took after a three-year siege. Once again the Two Kingdoms were one; once again Egypt was the Valley of the Gods. Still, haunting questions remained: Might not history repeat itself? Might not the sacred valley again suffer profane violation at the hands of new barbarians?

IMPERIAL EGYPT

The Resort to Conquest

The Amenhoteps and Thutmoses (four of each) of the Eighteenth Dynasty thought that they knew the answer: the conquest and occupation of other lands. In the beginning the reasoning was deceptively simple. Foreign invaders had come from the north. If a buffer state were created there, Egypt would be secure. So the region immediately adjacent to the delta was brought under control. But this only raised the question of *its* future security? As added insurance, Egyptian legions conquered areas farther north. Before Ahmose—first of the Eighteenth Dynasty rulers—had died, Egypt's new borders had been extended to about 70 miles from Jerusalem. As we shall see, a long pause then followed while the Land of the Two Lands was reknit internally. Thereafter the imperialist impulse drove all before it until checked by Mitannian troops along the great bend of the Euphrates—all, that is, in Palestine, Phoenicia, and almost the whole of Syria.

Centuries before, pharaohs had probed the northland. But those thrusts were sporadic and more in the nature of raids than attempts to build an empire. What, then, explained the present great drive? Documentary evidence does not spell out the answer. But the inference seems clear. The shock of foreign invasion, the build-up of vengeful patriotism, the victorious sweep of "foreign devils" from the land had all worked a change in Egypt's image of itself and of the world about. One may perhaps liken the psychological shift somewhat to that experienced by Japan in the latter half of the nineteenth century. For ages Japan had been an island kingdom, turned within itself, unaware or only contemptuously aware of the world around it. "Opened" by Americans in the 1850s, it suddenly sensed the power and potential hostility of the outer world and "awakened" to its own latent powers and demanding needs; within a century's span it was in control of a large portion of Southeast Asia.

Ahmose's two successors drove south to conquer Nubia (to Egyptians, the land of "Kush") and checked Libyan raids in the west. But the long century of Hyksos rule had wrought too many disruptive changes to give the valley-people's kings time or energy for external adventures. The land of the gods had been scarred and profaned; a time of healing and reconstruction was required. Under Hatshepsut (1486–1468 B.C.) thorough national renovation was effected. New buildings and temples were constructed, cults reestablished, and the offended gods propitiated. Within a generation Egypt seemed to be itself again.

Hatshepsut's successor, Thutmose III, spent the next three decades creating an empire such as the ancient world had never seen. In Egyptian nomenclature the region of present-day Palestine and the coastland of Phoenicia was called Djahi; that lying between Beiruit and Damascus, Coelesyria; the lands to the north, so far as the Euphrates, Retenu. In none of these areas was there a strongly consolidated state; rather, each was made up of many small communities endlessly quarreling among themselves. The retreating Hyksos, it is true, had formed a loosely organized confederation in parts of Palestine, which, led by the king of Kadesh, tried to stand against the advancing Egyptians. They took their stand at Megiddo (see map, p. 19), east of the Sea of Galilee. To get at them the legions of pharaoh had to file through a narrow pass and at great risk debouch into the valley of Esdraelon. Why the Kadesh chieftain allowed them to negotiate this route without harassment is unknown. The two armies fell upon each other in the open plain, where in a one-day battle the northern forces were completely routed. Had the booty they left behind not been so tempting they might have been destroyed before escaping behind the protective walls of Megiddo. Even so, complete capitulation was only postponed, for after a seven-month siege by the Egyptians they were starved into surrender. According to a contemporary Egyptian account:

Then that fallen one [the chief of Kadesh], together with the chiefs who were with him, caused all their children to come forth to my majesty with many products of gold and silver, all their horses with their trappings, their great chariots of gold and silver with their painted equipment, all their battle armor, their bows, their arrows, and all their implements of war—those things, indeed, with which they had come to fight against my majesty. And now they brought them as tribute to my majesty while they stood on their walls giving praise to my majesty in order that the breath of life might be given to them.

Then my majesty caused them to swear an oath, saying: "Never again will we do evil against Menkheperre [praenomen of Thutmose III]—may he live forever—our lord, in our lifetime, for we have witnessed his power. Let him only give breath to us according to his desire. . . ."

Then my majesty allowed to them the road to their cities, and they went, all of them, on donkeys. For I had taken their horses, and I carried off their citizens to Egypt and their property likewise.[10]

Thereafter Thutmose III undertook the subjugation of all the peoples of Coelesyria and Retenu. In two campaigns the conquering Pharaoh burned and battled his way to the Euphrates. Although rebellions broke out from time to time, necessitating reconquest, the Near East from Sharuhen to Naharin, and from the Mediterranean coast to the Euphrates River, ultimately acknowledged the overlordship of the living Horus. So fearfully renowned had he and his rampaging forces become that the conquest of Nubia, to the south, was accomplished with hardly a struggle.

For well over a century the vast empire stood out as the greatest political and military force in the Near East. But it should

---

[10] George Steindorff and Keith C. Seele, *When Egypt Ruled the East* (Chicago: The University of Chicago Press, 1942), p. 55.

be noted that the glue of this massive conglomerate was Egyptian soldiers, both "regular" and garrison troops. Should they be weakened by persisting and growing pressures from the conquered, or by big changes in Egypt's domestic situation, or both, the days of the empire would be numbered. Later we shall see that external attacks and internal dissension did, indeed, number those days.

The "New" Egypt

A steady stream of wealth flowed into Egypt from the conquered lands—cattle and slaves, gold and silver, coniferous woods (particularly the "cedars of Lebanon"), and vases of alabaster, wines and oils, grains and furniture—the list is endless. A great amount of this "tribute" went to the god Amon and his priests. Temples were erected and priests supplied to attend them. The new wealth was also used to pay and provision mercenary troops. Much, too, was spent on the rapidly multiplying personnel recruited to staff the ever-growing civil bureaucracy. On the other hand, little trickled down to the masses. Actually, in one sense their lot became worse, for whereas formerly a degree of social mobility marked Egyptian life, in most of the Empire period a sharp class cleavage existed.*

Indeed, a general change, reaching far beyond class cleavage, came over Egyptian life. Although at no time in its history, including the Empire period, did urbanization as we know it today develop, a cosmopolitan air settled over the land. On the surface the hold of tradition seemed strong; but change and a desire for the new infiltrated the multiple interstices of the whole society. Changes ranged from such simple innovations as random tree-planting in landscape gardening (in place of "orderly rows of trees planted in careful balance") to a reformulation of the spirit of the people. The old, secure "folk society" was gone. And with its going, alarms and fears beset ordinary citizens and officials alike. None knew when new invaders might threaten again. The bureaucratic apparatus was expanded, and military preparations were increased; but such security measures apparently made the people feel only more insecure. On the other hand, imperial power and wealth encouraged a restless search for new experiences, giving to the land something of the atmosphere of our own nineteenth-century "Gilded Age."

During the latter part of the Eighteenth and a substantial portion of the Nineteenth dynasties (roughly the 300 years from 1550 to 1250 B.C.) artists of the Empire period responded to the quickened pulse of the new life. At Thebes (Karnak) and Luxor (its suburb), colossal colonnaded halls, courts, temples, obelisks, and statuary "produced an impression both of gorgeous detail and overwhelming grandeur of which the sombre ruins . . . impressive as they are, offer little hint at the present day." In literature new genres appeared. Especially noteworthy was the evolution of a delicate love poetry. The following is a fair sample of the new form:

> *Seven days from yesterday I have not*
> *   seen my beloved*
> *And sickness hath crept over me,*
> *And I am become heavy in my limbs*
> *And am unmindful of mine own body.*
> *If the master-physicians come to me,*
> *My heart hath no comfort of their*
> *   remedies,*
> *And the magicians, no resource is in*
> *   them,*
> *My malady is not diagnosed.*
> . . . .

---

* "That high value set upon the individual Egyptian, down to the ordinary peasant, in the early Middle Kingdom was a thing of the distant past. Under the Empire the peasant was only an indistinguishable element in the mass of Egyptians organized and retrained for national unified effort." Wilson, op. cit., p. 186.

Nefertiti.

> *Better for me is my beloved than any
> remedies....
> My salvation is when she enters from
> without,
> When I see her, then am I well;
> Opens she her eye, my limbs are young
> again....
> And when I embrace her, she banishes
> evil
> And it passes from me for seven days.* [11]

The Religious Revolution

In religion a curious paradox developed. Outwardly the forms and symbols were the same as they had always been. A citizen of the Old Kingdom, returning to the expansive Empire, would have found himself at home in almost any temple of the land. But the "true believer" of Old Kingdom days, to say nothing of the probing seeker of the Middle Kingdom period, was gone. True, temples and priests multiplied as never before. But the rites were practiced mechanically, without conviction; and dependence on sheer magic and the power of incantations deepened. Two thousand years of civilized life had failed to produce an enriched and enlightened metaphysic.

After two centuries of imperial grandeur, military conquest, territorial expansion, and moral and religious deterioration, a religiously grounded reaction set in. The revolution, esthetically seeded in the reign of Amenhotep III (1413—1377 B.C.), erupted suddenly following the accession to the throne of Amenhotep IV (Akhenaton, 1377 B.C.). He and his sister-wife—the beautiful Nefertiti—were profoundly dissatisfied with the spiritual foundations of the Empire. The close association of Amon-Re with the imperial banners, the rituals of that god's growing army of priests (who were, moreover, part of the control group that today would be called the power elite), hypocritical abuse of ma'at—these and other developments caused the king and his consort to throw off the yoke of tradition and attempt to create a new cult concentrated on a single god—an exceedingly un-Egyptian enterprise.

Repudiating Amon-Re and his ubiquitous priests, the young pharaoh, whom Breasted has called the first *individual* in history, dropped his original throne name, Ahmenhotep, ("Amon is satisfied") in favor of Akhenaton ("Beneficial to the Aton"). From Thebes the machinery of government was moved to a new site about midway between Thebes and Memphis, especially chosen as ground for the new capital (the modern Tel el Amarna).

Central in Akhenaton's system was his worship—and through him that of all Egyptians—of the Aton whose representative he was. He stressed natural living.

[11] Alan H. Gardiner, "Writing and Literature," in Glanville, op. cit., p. 77.

For example, the Pharaoh directed royal artists and sculptors to give up the stylized patterns of the past and to portray him as he was—and all others as they were. Since the king's own physique was rather unusual—sloping shoulders, heavy hips, a distinct pot belly—the direction was at least courageous. In an attempt to erase the memory of Amon and the other gods, Akhenaton ordered references to them chiseled out of all the monuments in the land.

The new religion emphasized the central sway of one god who ruled not only Egypt but the whole world. Every land, according to the famous "Hymn to the Aton," was filled with the god's beauty, which extended "to the outermost limits of all that thou hast made." Every man was put in his own place; every people was provided with its own language; all were distinguished from one another by the color of their skin, as well as by their speech. For Egypt there was the life-giving Nile; but the Aton had caused "Niles in the heaven" to water the soils of other peoples, and thus give them opportunity to sow and to reap and to live. To administer the practices of the new religion Akhenaton created his own hierarchy of priests, who saw to it that Aton was never represented in human or animal form, but always as the life-giving sun. Magical incantations disappeared, to be replaced by prayers to the Aton. No longer were tomb walls decorated with representations of various lifetime activities of the one entombed. Rather, all paintings and relief works centered on worship scenes glorifying Aton and his pharaoh-son. Whether these drastic changes betokened a developing monotheism is debatable. Some specialists, such as Breasted and Frankfort, have argued that they did; others, particularly Wilson, believe that they point not to monotheism but to syncretism or monolatry. In any case, the changes were basic.

Amon-Re's priests, to say nothing of the bewildered average Egyptian whose

Akhenaton and his family worshipping the Aton.

whole way of life was outraged by such large-scale innovations, resented the loss of position, security, and the familiar conditions of the old life. Within a few years a strong reaction set in. There is reason to believe that the pharaoh himself was toying with some kind of compromise solution when, after a decade of strenuous effort to convert his people, he died, leaving his young son-in-law, Tutankhamon, to deal with the growing unrest. Still a boy, Tutankhamon and his regents quickly yielded to public and government pressures. Within a short time the governmental apparatus was returned to Thebes and Memphis, and the revolution was over. (Our stress has been on the

A. Egypt: Sphinx and Falcon

TABLE II

Chronology of Periods, Dynasties, and Pharaohs*

With certain exceptions, dates (911 B.C.) are given in rounded figures. Before 2000 B.C. a margin of 100 years or so should be allowed; after 2000 B.C. the margin may be reduced within a range of 50 to 5 years. Not all pharaohs are included.

PREDYNASTIC PERIOD	ca. 5000 to 3100
DYNASTIES I AND II	3100–2700
OLD KINGDOM	2700–2200
Dynasty III	2700–2650
Zoser	2700
Dynasty IV	2650–2500
Seneferu	2650
Khufu (Cheops) "Pyramid Age"	2630
Khafre	2600
....	....
Dynasty V	2550–2400
Dynasty VI	2400–2250
FIRST INTERMEDIATE PERIOD	2250–2225
Dynasties VII and VIII	2225–2155
Dynasties IX, X, and XI (period of confused claims to throne)	2115–2000
MIDDLE KINGDOM	2050–1780
Dynasty XII	1990–1780
Amenemhet I	1990–1960
Senusert I	1970–1926
Amenemhet II	1929–1894
Senusert II	1897–1878
Amenemhet III	1840–1792

religious motivation of Akhenaton's innovations. Some scholars believe that Akhenaton was less concerned with religious reform than with breaking the power of Amon's priests.)

The few years remaining to the Eighteenth Dynasty (1360—1320 B.C.) were spent reestablishing the old regime and consolidating the remaining empire in Asia. On the surface, at least, Egypt had returned to her ancient ways.

Imperial Ventures Renewed

To the early pharaohs of the succeeding Nineteenth Dynasty it seemed that the Empire of Thutmose III could and should be reconquered. Consequently Egyptian legions marched again. Under Seti I (ca. 1300 B.C.) a large part of Palestine was brought under subjugation and the frontier extended into Syria. Here, however, a new threat loomed. For some time a new people, the Hittites, had been consolidating their strength in southeastern Anatolia (see chap. 2). Egypt's new push for power and imperial glory coincided with similar Hittite ambitions. In the first skirmishes that followed, the Egyptians came off the victors. Thereafter, however, a long, drawn-out tug developed that seriously sapped the strength of both contestants. In an effort to deal a decisive blow to the northern "barbarians" Ramses II led a large army against them (ca. 1285

TABLE II (cont'd)

Chronology of Periods, Dynasties, and Pharaohs*

SECOND INTERMEDIATE PERIOD	1780–1550
Kamose	1585
EMPIRE	1570–1090
Dynasty XVIII	1570–1320
Ahmose I	1570–1545
Amenhotep I	1545–1525
Thutmose I	1525–1495
....	....
Thutmose III (conqueror of Palestine and Syria)	1490–1436
Hatshepsut	1486–1468
Amenhotep II	1436–1413
....	....
Amenhotep III	1403–1366
Amenhotep IV—Akhenaton (Ikhnaton)	1377–1360
Tutankhamon	1360–1351
....	......
Haremhab	1347–1319
Dynasty XIX	1319–1205
Ramses I	1319–1318
Seti I	1318–1304
Ramses II (period of Exodus of Jews?)	1304–1238
....	......
Dynasty XX	1200–1090
POST-EMPIRE PERIOD	1090–664
Dynasties XXI to XXV	1090–664
SAITE PERIOD	664–525
PERSIAN CONQUEST	525
CONQUEST BY ALEXANDER THE GREAT	332

*A somewhat modified version of the chronology in Wilson, op. cit., pp. vii–viii.

B.C.). Things did not turn out well. For one thing, Hittite strength had grown disproportionate to Egypt's. For another, the new expedition was none too wisely led. Hoping to drive the increasingly aggressive Hittites from their stronghold of Kadesh (in Syria), Ramses blunderingly led his armies into a trap. Although he personally escaped death and capture—indeed, he returned home to boast of a great victory—the Hittites were not driven back, and the Egyptians, for all their pharaoh's boasting, had to abandon plans of conquering all of Syria.

Eventually both states recognized the need to come to some kind of terms. The Hittites might have beat down the one-time masters of the East had they only Egypt to contend with; but by the thirteenth century, as we shall see, various "Sea Peoples" were forcing their way into the narrow corridor and areas adjacent to it. These continuing attacks drained off a substantial portion of Hatti's war potential. About 1280 B.C. an alliance was concluded that called for each to recognize a vaguely defined neutralized zone in Syria, to help the other if attacked by a third major power, and to exchange what today we would call "displaced persons." The lengthy document was written in the international language of the day, Akkadian cuneiform, and appropriately attested to by a host of divine witnesses. All the evidence—and there is a considerable amount of it—points to the treaty's lasting effects. Neither side ever again sent its forces against the other; reciprocal aid was extended; and a highly publicized state marriage set a special seal on the arrangements (when a young Hittite princess was made wife of the not-so-young Ramses II). But it could not save Hatti from the steadily stepped-up assaults of the Sea Peoples and the Assyrians. By the end of the thirteenth century she was overrun and occupied, leaving Egypt alone before the gathering hosts.

"The Empty Years"

About 1200 B.C. a prince of one of the "northern barbarian" states battered his way into Egypt. According to the plaintive terms of an Egyptian document, the Syrian conqueror "set the entire land as tributary before him. One joined his companion so that their property might not be plundered. They treated the gods like the people, and no offerings were presented in the temples."[12] Under Ramses III the foreigners were driven out, and imperial glory faintly beckoned again. The Sea Peoples were repulsed, and Palestine was retaken. But the elan of Egypt was weak, and its people were tired. Under Ramses IV all foreign territories were lost forever. With the flow of tribute stopped, economic hard times beset the land: goods became scarce, prices rose, and inflation spread throughout the valley. To make things worse, iron had by now become the dominant metal; Egypt had no iron mines nor the means of purchasing iron products. Thus stricken, the nation degenerated into a jungle of warring nomes hacking away at each other, and at ever bolder invaders. Libyan chieftains carved out provinces in the west; Ethiopian princes drove down from the south and for a while set up a ruling dynasty (the Twenty-fifth, 712—664 B.C.). In the later years of their ascendancy Assyrian conquerors overran Lower Egypt and dictated internal and external affairs under puppet pharaohs. The wings of Horus, the falcon god who once had ridden triumphantly the high winds of imperial conquest, drooped in defeat.

Even so, the end was not yet. In the seventh century Assyria was forced by threats from the north to withdraw from her garrison sites. A prince from Sais, in Lower Egypt, founded a new dynasty (the Twenty-sixth, 664–525). Once again the land was united; once again the future seemed bright. Trade flourished, especially with the Greek city-states, and with communities along the Phoenician coast. Foreign powers, busy holding each other in check, left the Land of Two Lands alone and in peace. But it was a peace of cultural stasis, of spiritual retrogression. Apprehensive of the new and seemingly cowed by its challenges, Saite Egypt reached back into the past for security and serenity. Old and Middle Kingdom customs, literary genres, and art forms became rigid and sacrosanct models.

Such posturing before the mirror of history could not hope to develop meaningful growth or even to maintain itself; any storm, from within or without, would destroy it. For modern readers Cleopatra's Egypt evokes a certain sense of excitement and curiosity. In reality the scenes of her day were sterile and empty—and had been for a half millennium before her. The storm came in 525 B.C. when the Persians swept down into the valley and exploited the land. In 332 B.C. Alexander the Great repeated the process as, with melancholy monotony, did the Romans, the Moslems, and, in the century before ours, the British. The Hebrew prophet Isaiah, concerned over his own people turning from the Lord to seek refuge in military alliances, looked to Egypt as a lesson and warned in the voice of Jehovah: "And I will set the Egyptians against the Egyptians: and they shall fight everyone

---

[12] Wilson, op. cit., p. 257.

against his brother, and everyone against his neighbor. . . . And the spirit of Egypt shall fail in the midst thereof."

The long drama of seemingly serene unchangeableness, as symbolized by the Sphinx, and of the paradoxical impulse of movement and aggrandizement, as represented by the Falcon, was over.

Now could the mournful dirge of an earlier time of troubles speak again to a stricken people. "Why really, laughter has disappeared, and is [no longer] made. It is wailing that prevades the land, mixed with lamentation."

B. Mesopotamia: The First Eden

SUMERIAN AND AKKADIAN SETTLEMENTS

"History begins in Sumer."* In the valley cradled by the Tigris and Euphrates rivers writing was invented, complex commercial concepts and techniques were created, and a sophisticated municipal order was established. Here, in short, the original model of the civilized community was set up (see map, p. 47).

With these inestimable achievements to their credit the Mesopotamian peoples deserve systematic and detailed study. Unfortunately, in an introductory study such as ours this is hardly possible. For one thing, the remains of these civilizations, although quantitatively impressive, pose many problems as yet unsolvable by archaeologists, philologists, and historians. Some will probably never be solved. For another, "Mesopotamia," unlike Egypt, Greece, Rome, Spain, etc., does not designate a particular political, ethnic, or language group. Rather, it signifies a congeries of peoples and areas: Sumerians, Akkadians, Babylonians (Amorites), Assyrians, and others (see Table III), in addition to lands stretching from the Persian Gulf to the upper reaches of the Tigris-Euphrates Valley. Also, chronic political instability, mass migratory activity, and endless wars lasting more than three millennia blur historical focus.

For these reasons it is not feasible to organize this section according to the pattern used for the Egyptians and for most of the other peoples that we shall study. We shall briefly survey the political highlights of the early Mesopotamian peoples, therefore, and give our major attention to cultural developments.

Soil, Cities, and Strife

Geography does not wholly determine political developments but it strongly influences them. Ancient Sumer contained about 25,000 square miles of territory; Akkad, even less. Yet these tiny

---

* Therefore logically the section on Egypt should have followed rather than preceded this section. But because Egyptian history is so much of one piece (besides beginning so soon after that of Mesopotamia) the advantages of pedagogy were allowed to overrule logic.

TABLE III
Major Periods of Mesopotamian History, 4500–1100

(All dates B.C. and only approximate)

4500–3500*	UBADIANS ("Proto-Euphrateans") origins unknown; conjecture: infiltration of Semites from west and north, non-Semites from east; fusion
3500–3000	SUMERIANS—Protoliterate Period origins uncertain; from Caspian Sea area? entered valley from Elam? mixed with "native" peoples
3000–2350	SUMERIANS—Early Dynastic Period first Dynasty of Kish, about 3000 first Dynasty of Ur, about 2700 King Lugal-Zuggesi of Lagash, about 2400
2350–2150	AKKADIANS—Sargonid Period Sargon the Great, about 2350 Akkadian ascendance, 2350–2150
2150–1900	SUMERIANS resurgence under Gudea of Lagash, about 2100
1900–1500	BABYLONIANS (Amorites) Hammurabi (for dates see fn. p. 59)
1500–1100	KASSITES Invaded from east; no development of inherited culture

* Some authorities believe that the first settlements were made about 1000 years earlier. Compare Samuel Kramer, *The Sumerians* (Chicago: The University of Chicago Press, 1963), p. 40.

---

portions of land offered economic allurements that vaster surrounding stretches could not match. Like the Nile, the two rivers bounding this region flooded annually, leaving heavy and fertile silt deposits after each inundation. By almost any standard of agricultural productivity this part of Mesopotamia was a land to be prized. When compared with the hilly and desert regions around it, it was virtually a paradise.*

It must not be supposed, however, that the valley lands alone were habitable. Evidence clearly indicates the presence (ca. 8000 B.C.?) of numerous cave dwellings located along the hilly flanks of the "Crescent." Their inhabitants used tools of stone, bone, and flint; except for the dog, they had not as yet domesticated animals. They hunted and fished for a living; artifactual remains clearly indicate that wild grain crops were harvested to supplement their meat diet. Some 2000 years later (the archaeological record provides no clue to the interim period) the so-called Neolithic revolution—better understood as the agricultural revolution—had been accomplished. Remains show foundations of mud-walled houses, the inhabitants of which cultivated the soil and kept a number of domesticated animals—the horse, ox, sheep-goat, pig. Shortly thereafter an advanced phase of village life devel-

* Indeed, the Garden of Eden, conceived in the folk-memory of the ancients, was situated here.

46   The Birth of Civilization

oped "marked by the remains of towns of some size and the appearance of buildings which can only be temples."[13] The inhabitants of these towns gradually moved into the valley and outward from an east-west axis.

One group of migrants settled along the Gulf coast, naming the area Sumer, (see map, p. 47). Although scholars agree that the Sumerians were not Semites or Indo-Europeans, they are quite uncertain of the ethnic family the Sumerians belonged to. Almost certainly "Mediterraneanoid"—short, long headed, black haired—they probably entered the valley from the east (from Elam?) sometime during the fifth millennium B.C. Ur, Lagash, Eridu, and Nina were some of their many coastal settlements (now located about 150 miles inland; silt deposits, averaging over two miles a century, have accounted for the Gulf's diminished dimensions). Somewhat later, a Semitic people settled farther up the valley near Akkad (Agade), south of present-day Baghdad.

For more than a thousand years—from about 4000 B.C. to approximately 2850 B.C.—Sumerian cities multiplied in number and advanced in cultural development. At no time during this long period, however, was a confederacy established or "national" unity encouraged. As with the later Greeks and the still later Renaissance Italians, Sumerians rooted their most significant values in the local, independent community. One might think that Egyptian experience would have been repeated, for irrigation and canal-building activities were as necessary in Mesopotamia as in Egypt and would seem to call for the same kind of continuing, cooperative enterprise. But the opposite was true. Jealous guardianship of water rights and agrocommercial advantages led each city to be wary of its neighbors, so that a mosaic of small units rather than an enduring nation resulted.

The periodic flooding of the Tigris and Euphrates rivers accounted, as we have seen, for an abundance of highly productive soil. Occasionally, however, serious overflooding occurred, which resulted in great loss of life and property. Around 2900 B.C. the valley was deluged by raging waters 16 feet in depth. Not only whole cities, but clusters of them, were destroyed. Subsequently Mesopotamians came to believe that the gods, disgusted with the faults and frailties of humankind, had sent the flood to destroy their recalcitrant children (the biblical account of Noah

[13] Robert J. Braidwood, *The Near East and the Foundations for Civilization* (Eugene, Oreg.: Oregon State System of Higher Education, 1952), p. 33. This is a short authoritative account of the incubation period of Western civilization. See also Carl H. Kraeling and Robert M. Adams, eds., *City Invincible* (Symposium on Urbanization and Cultural Development in the Ancient Near East) (Chicago: University of Chicago Press, 1958, 1960).

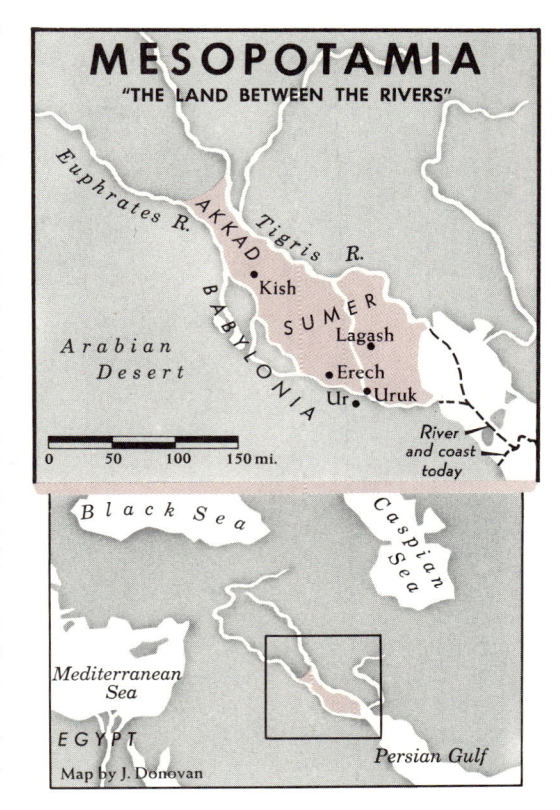

B. Mesopotamia: the First Eden

Bronze head of an Akkadian ruler (ca. 2250 B.C.). The empty eye sockets were once inlaid with precious stones. The curled beard and pleated hair are Sumerian stylistic conventions.

and the Ark is doubtless rooted in such calamities).

Not long after this catastrophe Sumerian city-states succeeded in establishing control over the northern Akkadian communities. This hegemony lasted for about 400 years, surely more than enough time to fashion a state. But instead of unity, greater disunity resulted. Soon, too, original primitive democracy gave way to royal despotism and pitiless exploitation of the peasants. This apparently left the people with neither the heart nor the vision to embark on the challenging task of state making. Equally important, neither the city-states nor their royal masters could leave off indulging particularist ambitions. Exaggerating for emphasis, one may say that everybody fought everybody else most of the time. True, one king, Lugal-Zaggesi of Lagash (ca. 2400 B.C.), succeeded for a time in bringing the greater part of Sumer-Akkad under his rule. But before lasting consolidation could be effected, the Akkadians found a leader to shake off "alien" domination.

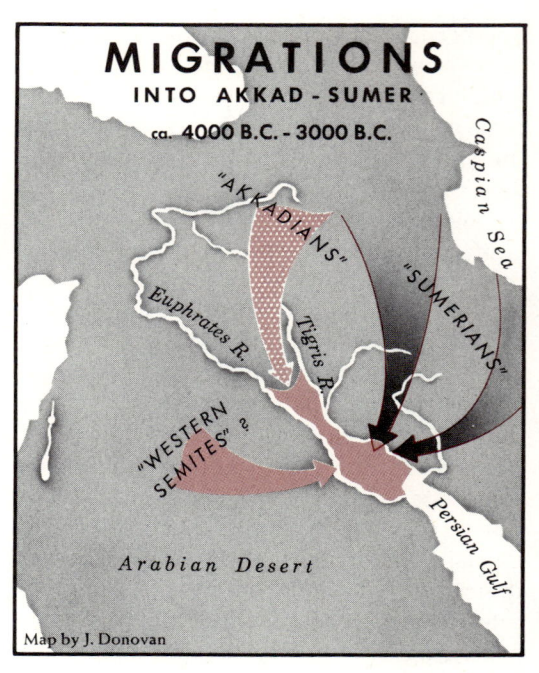

Under this extraordinarily energetic king—the fabled Sargon the Great—the Akkadians moved against Sumer, which now paid for its prolonged political follies by being brought under complete Semitic domination (this was in 2350 B.C., which one scholar has designated "the earliest computed date in history"). Once again opportunities of unification were offered. Although differing in ethnic backgrounds, Sumer and Akkad had much in common. For two millennia the latter had absorbed Sumerian culture so completely that the two peoples had become almost one in language, arts, religion, and general social habits. Indeed, none of the various invading peoples throughout almost 3000 years of history succeeded in changing the basic pattern of Sumerian-Mesopotamian culture—all were assimilated into it.

Despite such affinities Sumerian communities chafed under "foreign" control

48 The Birth of Civilization

and finally succeeded, around 2150 B.C., in destroying the power of the ranging empire. Thereafter for nearly two centuries (except for one passing interlude) the old pattern of intercity strife was monotonously and fatally repeated. When a new, vigorous people—the Amorites (Babylonians)—struck eastward from their Syrian base around 1900 B.C., they found a tired and divided land unable to stand against them. "Having wasted its youth in fratricidal wars, Sumer in its old age died for lack of blood." Politically it never experienced a resurrection.

POLITICS AND CULTURE

Genesis of Oriental Despotism

But culturally no rebirth was needed, for in patterns of civilized living the Mesopotamians were pioneers throughout the ages. Before taking up their achievements, however, we need to note briefly the nature and development of the individual community's political life.

Unlike many of modern times, the earliest cities of Mesopotamia did not evolve from rural beginnings. Instead evidence shows urban establishments existing from the time that the first migrants entered the valley. Because they were deeply motivated religiously, Mesopotamians quite naturally associated their city-state with a god or goddess; but there was more to this than mere association, for the city was considered a temple-community owned by a divine ruler. Acting as surrogates for the god were elders selected by the community by reason of their standing and good judgment. In a very real sense, therefore, these earliest, or protoliterate, cities were theocracies in theory and primitive democracies in practice. For nearly a thousand years this seemingly dichotomous sociopolitical structure prevailed.

Our records are too incomplete to say when the change to monarchy occurred. Very probably an intervening oligarchic form developed when an aristocratic class siphoned off the people's power and ruled in the name of the local god. By 2800 B.C. we find kingship firmly established; thereafter the monarch's power steadily increased until it became absolute. Probably the endemic wars made the trend toward centralized authority inevitable. In any case, oriental despotism had by this time become a permanent fixture of Mesopotamian life. Although in many cities councils of elders still met, their duties were perfunctory and more or less ritualistic.

Religious Attitudes

For their city god and the higher gods of the pantheon the valley people felt close and abiding concern. Man-made troubles were always threatening; but the unpredictable habits of the natural elements gave rise to even profounder feelings of insecurity and tension. As was earlier noted, raging waters and overflowing river and canal banks could and did work indescribable havoc. On the other hand, devastating droughts occurred from time to time. Often in some and occasionally in all areas the intense summer heat prostrated multitudes. Thus beset by human and natural violence, Mesopotamia wrought its achievements in a deeply disturbed atmosphere.

Hence religious concern was characterized by elaborate efforts to propitiate the gods, to beguile them with offerings and ceremonial practices in the hope that at least a modicum of good fortune and tranquility might be experienced. In protoliterate times Sumerians were content with god-concepts quite vague and unorganized. Later there developed an involved system of religious thought marked by a hierarchy of divine beings, temple worship, and elaborate liturgical practices, all subsumed under certain commonly accepted metaphysical postulates.

Of the latter, outstanding was the belief that human life was eternally shaped by an overarching fate that was basically indifferent to the hopes and wants of mankind, and, indeed, of the gods and their (occasionally, at least) rewarding response. But one could never be sure. A second assumption, seemingly in contradiction to the first, held that the lowly human being was given a divine word or hint now and then that might enable him to pattern his life in a purposeful and more satisfying manner. It is probably going too far to associate this "word" closely with the later Platonic or Christian doctrine of the *Logos* (see Sec. B and chap. 6). Still, there is some relation. To the Mesopotamians thunder from the heavens signified the intention of the gods to communicate—for good or for ill—with man. If, by liturgical or other appropriate ceremonies, man prepared himself to receive the word, he might have some share—however humble—in the shaping of events.

Besides such metaphysical venturing, Sumerians and others of the region established a definite hierarchy of gods, thus creating mankind's first systematic polytheistic religion. In this system cosmogony—description of the creation of the universe—played an important part. In the beginning, according to the most ancient Sumerian writings (for the most part coming down to us through Semitic sources), were Apsu, primeval god of fresh water, and Tiamat, primeval goddess of salt water. Their coming together (at the delta of the Tigris-Euphrates?) produced An, who, overthrowing his father, became sky-god and brought order out of chaos; En-lil, god of the wind, or storm god; Tammuz, god of vegetation; Ea, god of water; Inanna, queen-of-heaven goddess of love and fertility; Ningirsu, god of the spring rains; and many others. Later peoples, through a kind of creative borrowing, modeled their own gods after these. The Egyptian Osiris, for example, bears a marked resemblance to Tammuz. The Semitic Ishtar is Inanna under another name. En-lil is clearly similar to the later Roman Jupiter. And the Great Mother, of the classical world, may be likened to Tiamat and Inanna.

Literature

Naturally, religious and cosmogonic speculations played a large part in Mesopotamian literary creations. In the myth *Inanna's Descent to the Nether World* vague reassurance was given to Sumerian mortals that Heaven might prevail over Hell.

In the *Creation Epic,* composed about 2000 B.C., unknown Babylonian authors drew upon earlier Sumerian legends to explain how the world was brought into being:

> *When on high the heaven had not been named,*
> *Firm ground below had not been called by name,*
> *Naught but primordial Apsu, their begetter,*
> *(And) . . . Tiamat, she who bore them all,*
> *Their waters commingling as a single body;*
> *No reed but had been matted, no marsh land had appeared,*
> *When no gods whatever had been brought into being,*
> *Uncalled by name, their destinies undetermined—*
> *Then it was that the gods were formed within* [*Apsu and Tiamat*]. . . .

The epic then goes on to relate the creation of the gods and their parents' subsequent dissatisfaction with them. Marduk, son of Anu, took it upon himself to chasten his fellow gods, but not out of regard for Apsu or Tiamat, whom he regarded as the fundamental obstacles in the way of establishing order.

> *He crossed the heavens and surveyed the regions. . . .*
> *He constructed stations for the great gods,*
> *Fixing their astral likenesses as constellations.*
> *He determined the year by designating the zones:*
> *He set up three constellations for each of the twelve months. . . .*
> *Opening his heart, he addressed Ea*
> *To impart the plan he had conceived in his heart:*
> *"Blood I will mass and cause bones to be.*
> *I will establish a savage, 'man' shall be his name. . . .*
> *May food offerings be borne for . . . [men's] gods and goddesses.*
> *Without fail let them support their gods!*
> *Their lands let them improve, build their shrines,*
> *Let [all human beings] wait on their gods."* [14]

Secular as well as religious interests were made the subjects of creative literary activity. The justly famous *Epic of Gilgamesh*, originally sketched by the Sumerians, was thoroughly reworked by the Akkadians and finally shaped in the form we know it by the Babylonians. Its theme is one that has haunted humanity across the ages: what is mankind's ultimate destiny?

As the long poem opens, Gilgamesh, King of Erech, is embarrassing his subjects by his many and varied debaucheries. The gods, in answer to Erechite prayers, propose that the mother-goddess create a disciplining foil to Gilgamesh. So Enkidu is born, simple of heart, strong of limb. He is to humble the riotous Gilgamesh. To do so Enkidu must undergo experiences which will give him human understanding and values. The humanizing agent is an Erechite courtesan who gently guides him in the arts of erotic love. Through this experience Enkidu sheds his brute nature and gains worldly wisdom.

Eventually Enkidu and Gilgamesh join in combat. Neither, however, vanquishes the other and the struggle is renounced for friendship. Thereafter both set out on a series of adventures. Huwawa, fearsome guardian of a great cedar forest, is conquered and slain. Ishtar, goddess of love, invites Gilgamesh's attentions; when he spurns her she sends the Bull of Heaven to destroy Erech. The two heroes, however, kill the divine avenger, bringing down the wrath of the gods. Enkidu falls ill and dies and Gilgamesh, bereft of his great friend, realizes for the first time something of the meaning of death.

> *For Enkidu, his friend, Gilgamesh*
> *Weeps bitterly, as he ranges over the steppe:*
> *When I die, shall I be like Enkidu?*
> *Woe has entered my belly,*
> *Fearing death I roam over the steppe!* [15]

Learning that a certain fabled Mesopotamian hero of the Flood may possess the secret of eternal life, Gilgamesh sets out to find him. The quest is long but rewarding. The hero takes compassion on Gilgamesh and reveals the identity of a particular, isolated plant that both restores life and assures unending life to whoever eats of it. After many adventures Gilgamesh finds the plant. Now his pessimism vanishes, and all is bright again. In his exuberant mood he decides to bathe in a nearby cool well. While he is in the water a serpent scents the plant, finds it, and carries it away. Discovering his new and now truly final loss, Gilgamesh "sits down and weeps, his tears running over his face." Thus the epic both mirrored and fed the deep and dark suspicions of the Mesopotamians—life might tease and beckon, but invariably it ends in nothingness.

---

[14] Pritchard, op. cit., pp. 60–69 passim.

[15] Pritchard, op. cit., p. 88.

Not all Mesopotamian literature was of epic proportions. Here, for example, is a delicate lyrical verse, thought by one Sumerologist to be the first love song ever written:

> Bridegroom, dear to my heart,
> Goodly is your beauty, honeysweet,
> Lion, dear to my heart,
> Goodly is your beauty, honeysweet.
>
> You have captivated me, let me stand tremblingly before you,
> Bridegroom, I would be taken by you to the bedchamber,
> You have captivated me, let me stand tremblingly before you,
> Lion, I would be taken by you to thy bedchamber.
>
> Bridegroom, let me caress you,
> In the bedchamber, honey filled,
> Let us enjoy your goodly beauty,
> Lion, let me caress you,
> My precious caress is more savory than honey.
>
> Bridegroom, you have taken your pleasure of me,
> Tell my mother, she will give you delicacies,
> My father, he will give you gifts.
>
> Your spirit, I know where to cheer your spirit,
> Bridegroom, sleep in our house until dawn,
> Your heart, I know where to gladden your heart,
> Lion, sleep in our house until dawn. . . .[16]

Besides epic tales and lyrical verses Sumero-Akkadian writings took many other forms: historical texts, hymns and prayers, incantations, legal texts, letters, "lamentations," scholarly disputations, scientific compendia, economic texts, and—the largest body of all,—the "omen" texts (a Semitic contribution).

Here the invincible might of the royal adventurer Gilgamesh is represented by the hero's calm clutching of a lion to his untroubled breast.

[16] Kramer, op. cit., pp. 213–14.

52   The Birth of Civilization

Language

In recent years archaeologists have dug up, pieced together, and translated so many tablets that we may be tempted to conclude that we now have a sound and extensive knowledge of Mesopotamian literature. Unhappily this is not quite the case. For example, although the selections quoted above seem to run smoothly and to make good sense, there are still authorities who sharply disagree among themselves over both form and interpretation of some sections.

One reason for continuing uncertainty among specialists (especially concerning Summerian literature) is the poor state of preservation of some of the materials. More importantly, the Sumerian polyphonic system lends itself more easily to transliteration than to translation; that is, although we are often able to read the signs, we cannot always derive suitable meanings from them. This difficulty, in turn, is partly rooted in the fact that Sumerians invented written language; it fails, therefore, to fall into any of the recognized broad language categories (for example, Hamitic, Semitic, Indo-European, Ural-Altic, Caucasic, etc.).

From the beginning, it appears, they used both pictograms and arbitrary (syllabic) phonetic symbols.* It is important for us to keep in mind this concurrent usage, otherwise we may easily and erroneously conclude that Sumerian script evolved simply by gradual adaptation from pictures or images. Originally (when a straight stick was used to scratch or draw the signs) the sign for sun, or day was ⊗; later, when scribes came to adopt the space-saving habit of turning all signs 90 degrees, it became ◯ and still later, in early Babylonian (when the triangular stylus producing wedge shapes was developed), and finally, in Assyrian (when all signs became simplified), it became thus it is true that in some instances images served as the starting point. But in many they did not. Completely arbitrary symbols were often employed, as for example ⊗ which signified "sheep." Moreover, phonetic values were very soon substituted for some notion-signs. At first the drawing of an arrow simply meant that weapon. Originally the vocal sound for arrow approximated "ti," which happened also to be the sound for "life." It thus became relatively easy to transmute the image-sign into a phonetic symbol, and to let the drawing for arrow represent either. In order to keep the two meanings apart, another sign was placed before it—a determinative, meaning "wood-object", when the drawing meant "arrow"; when

Blackstone tablet showing early Sumerian pictograms.

---

* Unlike the Egyptians, Mesopotamians did not have papyrus resources available. Clay tablets were easy to make, however, and on them they inscribed their signs using a wedge-shaped stylus. From the impression thus made we call their writing cuneiform, after the Latin word *cuneus* ("wedge").

B. Mesopotamia: the First Eden

"life," the sign stood by itself.[17] In this way the reproduction of phonetic symbols began.

Architecture and Sculpture

The invention of language and the creation of living literature—some of which remains a part of our present heritage—bespoke talents of an order that naturally found expression in other forms of artistic endeavor. Predominant among these was architecture. Because little stone of any kind and almost no marble were available, Mesopotamian builders were forced to use sun-dried brick. Such a medium is not conducive to a grand flowering of architectural talents, particularly when the architects know that their handiwork will probably suffer disintegration within a relatively short time. Consequently we have no Karnak parallels in this Asian valley. Even so, those remains that we do have are impressive.

Those of Uruk (modern Warka), for example, indicate an original structure measuring some 150 by 175 feet; those of Ur measure 130 by 190 feet. Some rose to a height of about 50 feet, a few much higher. Although they did not compare in size to the great pyramids of Egypt, they were nonetheless successful experiments in massive architecture. For the most part Mesopotamian "monumental architecture" consisted of palaces or temples. In the latter case special care was taken to achieve impressiveness, for community welfare depended on the favor of the gods. To court and keep that favor almost any extravagance was justified. The temple-towers, called *ziggurats*, were almost invariably of conventional shape and construction. Generally they rested on carefully chosen elevated sites. Superimposed on the base was a series of terraces culminating in the sanctuary, the whole constituting a stepped tower. In the sanctuary were a niche for statuary and an altar, the latter attended by priests whose quarters were often provided on one of the lower terraces. To break the drab expanse of brick wall, varied patterns of recesses and buttresses were commonly employed. The arch and vault were used sparingly. Because the walls were necessarily very thick, supporting columns were unnecessary. Most of these temple-towers have long since crumbled. Among those surviving,—as ruins—are the fabled ziggurats of Ur and Babylon, the latter celebrated in Biblical literature as the tower of Babel.

In contrast to the monumentality of its architecture, Mesopotamian sculpture, except later relief, was faltering in conception and awkward in workmanship. Extant remains, mostly statuettes, show a highly stylized approach in general and anatomical distortion in particular. Lack of suitable working materials no doubt accounted in part for acceptance of inferior standards (although some stone materials such as diorite were imported). But religious motivation was probably more important. Scrupulous and continuous attendance upon the gods and their wants was considered necessary. Since the priests and other officials could not spend all of their time in the sanctuary, sculptured models were substituted, for which artistic perfection was not required. It was customary, also, to bury statues in tombs rather than subject them to public display, a practice scarcely calculated to refine the canons of artistic performance.

Sculpture in relief, however, was boldly and skillfully executed, especially in the later Akkadian and Babylonian periods. Martial and hunting scenes were favorite subjects. Often the sculptor portrayed a mighty warrior-king leading his hosts into the thick of battle. The dead enemy, arrow-pierced, lay under the heels or chariot wheels of the conquering legions.

---

[17] See Frankfort, op. cit., p. 55 fn., on which this brief exposition is based.

These were probably models of priestly attendants of the shrines of Sumerian gods. The depiction of alert devotion was a prime objective of Sumerian sculptors.

Or a king is portrayed receiving tribute and homage from the defeated foe. In hunting scenes the king or a nobleman is shown shooting at close range an arrow into a lion or other wild beast or sometimes actually holding off a rearing animal with one hand while with the other he drives a lance into the exposed breast. Other favorite carved reliefs featured the winged bull or the lion with human head.

But it was in the cylinder seal that Mesopotamian art came into mature flowering. Used chiefly as signatures or official stamps, the seals ranged in subject matter from simple geometric designs to complicated displays of ritualistic acts. Again, animal and hunting scenes were favorites. The stone or metal seal was rolled over damp clay, impressing upon it the incised design. Since the cylinder's surface offered little available space, the artist was challenged to the utmost to combine detail with distinctness. Thousands of impressions recovered by archaeologists prove how successfully he met the challenge. Typical examples are shown in the above illustration.

Science

In the arts Mesopotamians were both imaginative creators and talented craftsmen. Does the record show comparable achievements in science? Much depends on how we define the term. If we mean a body of verifiable data collected and assessed in an objective, orderly

Sumerian cylinder seal and impression (ca. 1900 B.C.) showing a worshipper being presented by a divine sponsor to a great god seated on an elegant throne.

manner (that is, by means of what today we call "the scientific method"), then we may say flatly that science was unknown to these early people. However if we define its essence as measurement, the answer is quite different, for the Mesopotamians invented its basic concepts and techniques. As we have seen, the Egyptians came close to determining the true span of the solar year; but this was merely a refinement of earlier pioneering by Sumerians, who long before had calculated a 360-day year. The number of days in the month they determined by lunar reckoning. The resulting calendrical hiatus they closed by simply adding an extra month periodically, thus bringing the cycle of 12 lunar months of 29 or 30 days each into rough agreement with the solar year.

Undoubtedly their interest in weather and seasons, itself based on a deeper concern for a steady supply of foodstuffs, motivated them to observe closely the movements of heavenly bodies. But another influence was more important: Mesopotamian cosmology postulated a direct relationship between human affairs and divine activities. If men could gain some understanding of the ways of the gods they might be able to predict and shape events to come, at least in a vague and general way. The gods themselves, of course, could never actually be seen. But the intimate association of some of them with certain celestial bodies permitted an indirect observation of their habits and, it was hoped, their purposes. In this way astrology was born. Across many centuries this pseudoscience built up a corpus of data that ultimately served as the foundation for the true science of astronomy.

Five of the planets were identified and joined with the sun and moon to give further substance to Mesopotamian belief in the sacred properties of the number seven. From this may have come the division of the week into seven days. And because the Mesopotamians found 12s more easy to work with than 10s—although they also used the decimal system—they fixed upon 12 double hours as the day's span.

By the beginning of the second millenium Mesopotamians had become so adept in the theory and practice of numeration that they were as able as modern man in problems of multiplication. They constructed tables with multipliers for integers up to 20 and by decades above 20. Fractions and large numbers were handled with ease. Problems of various kinds—the areas of circles and squares, calculations needed to excavate artificial waterways, etc.—were solved by application of intricate geometric formulations, including the propositions and proofs of what later came to be called the Pythagorean theorem. The Table IV from a school text illustrates the computation involved in determining the area of square fields.[18]

In the same way that the gods influenced overall human behavior it was believed that demons affected the behavior and health of particular parts of the body. Mesopotamian medicine, in short, was mostly magic—but not altogether. We now know, for example, that as early as ca. 2200 B.C. Sumerian physicians had identified a number of chemical properties and

[18] Kramer, op. cit., pp. 93–94.

The Birth of Civilization

TABLE IV

Sumerian Computational Symbols Used in Measuring Fields[a]

This table is intended to help in the computation of the area of square fields. The first column (left) gives the length of the side (sag) measured in gar-du (1 gar-du = 6 yards approx.). The second column (middle) gives the length of the other side, stating that it is equal (sá) to the first side. The third column (right) gives the area measured in iku (1 iku = 100 gar-du^2). Thus to obtain the area in gar-du^2, multiply the results given in the third column by 100.

Notice that a special set of number signs is used in surface measurements:

◯ = 1080 iku   ◈ = 180 iku   ○ = 18 iku

$$600 \text{ sag gar-du} \times 600 \text{ sá} = 1080 \times 3 + 180 \times 2 = 3600 \text{ iku}$$
$$(60 \times 9)(60 \times 9) = 1080 \times 2 + 180 \times 4 + 18 \times 2 = 2916 \text{ iku}$$
$$(60 \times 8)(60 \times 8) = 1080 \times 2 + 180 \times 8 = 2304 \text{ iku}$$
$$(60 \times 7)(60 \times 7) = 1080 + 180 \times 3 + 18 \times 8 = 1764 \text{ iku}$$
$$(60 \times 6)(60 \times 6) = 1080 + 180 + 18 \times 2 = 1269 \text{ iku}$$
$$(60 \times 5)(60 \times 5) = 180 \times 5 = 900 \text{ iku}$$
$$(60 \times 4)(60 \times 4) = 180 \times 3 + 18 \times 2 = 576 \text{ iku}$$
$$(60 \times 3)(60 \times 3) = 180 + 18 \times 8 = 324 \text{ iku}$$
$$(60 \times 2)(60 \times 2) = 18 \times 8 = 144 \text{ iku}$$

etc.

[a] From Kramer, op. cit., pp. 93–94.

---

processes. In a medical text of this period we note that potassium nitrate was included in certain prescriptions. Other medicinals required for their concoction an understanding of fairly complicated separating processes. Recovered tablets list diseases, symptoms, and treatments with an orderliness (although often not with factual accuracy) that compares favorably with modern texts. How such scientific beginnings in the medical arts could be rooted in an almost universal dependence on magical lore is a question that we must pass over here.

ECONOMIC CONDITIONS
Economic Structure

The blend of magic and medicine is perhaps easier to understand, however, than the peculiar threading together of religio-politico-economic interests that characterized the valley civilization. In a general assessment of these interests two paradoxes are involved. As we have seen, even the original city-states showed no signs of having gradually evolved from a rural background. Their urban character was further marked by the clear division of labor among artisans and traders, professional people, priests, and officials. Yet they were not cities as we think of cities today. For example, modern citizens of Detroit are almost wholly engaged in industry, commerce, business; in no sense can they be thought of as even part-time farmers. The contrast between their way of living and that of the typical rural regions of south-central Michigan is quite distinct. No such contrast is evident in the Sumerian city-state and surrounding areas. Here townspeople cultivated the land during the growing seasons and the rest of the time kept shop, so to speak, quite in the manner, as one writer has pointed out, of the burghers of medieval Europe. "In the Fourteenth Century the English town was still a rural and agricultural community as well as a center of industry and commerce. . . . In 1388 it was laid down by Parliamentary Statute that in harvest-time journeymen and apprentices should be called upon to lay aside their crafts and should be compelled to cut, gather, and bring in the corn; mayors, bailiffs, and constables were to see this done."[19] The Mesopotamian city was, amidst its flourishing commerce, a farming community.

The second paradox is grounded in beliefs and practices dealing with property rights. In recognition of this fact the king--called *ensi* (chief "tenant farmer" of the deity who owned the city)—set aside, at the decree of the priests, certain areas as a sacred community, the produce of which was used exclusively for purposes of worship. Here were built the temple, always the city's most elaborate structure; dwellings and offices of the priests; and paraphernalia for the annual festivals held in honor of the divine landlord. Thus propitiated, the god gave over the remaining land for private use. Hence there resulted a mixed economy: under a system that has been called theocratic socialism, collective labor was used on all the temple lands; for the rest, private enterprise prevailed.

Class Structure

Three classes made up the general body of society—the ruling king, priests, and noblemen; free peasants, artisans, and professional people; and slaves. The last, men captured in war together with their women and children, worked as laborers on dikes, canals, and other public property, as menials in business, and as domestics in the homes of the wealthy. Most peasants were tenants who, in return for their toil, received subsistence portions of the land's produce. Artisans were but little better off; the metal they worked, the cloth they wove, and the pottery they shaped were bought up by traders at low prices often fixed by royal decree. Merchants, on the other hand, fared well. As the Near East's first civilized society, Mesopotamia early developed elaborate commercial connections with its less advanced neighbors; and then, as now, the middleman accumulated greater profits than either producer or wage-earning consumer. Thousands of clay tablets uncovered by archaeologists—bills of sale, letters of credit, promissory notes, and the like—attest to both the range and volume of trade and the profits made by traders. Even so, the greatest wealth was owned by royalty, nobility, and the priests.

PAX BABYLONICA

Legal System

In the early years of the second millennium B.C., political dominance passed to conquering Semitic tribes pressing in from the west, (see p. 49). Originally called Amorites by the valley people (after Amurru—land to the west; roughly, mod-

---

[19] Quoted by Henri Frankfort, *The Birth of Civilization in the Near East* (Bloomington, Ind.: Indiana University Press, 1954), p. 58.

ern Syria), the conquerors made Babylon their capital. Eventually, under Hammurabi* and his successors, they ruled an empire embracing Sumer, Akkad, and a number of surrounding countries. For some three centuries the newcomers brought stability, peace, and unity to the land. Under this *Pax Babylonica* both consolidation and spatial expansion of Sumero-Akkadian culture were effected. Especially significant was Babylonia's nurturing of the valley's achievements in literature and law.

For example, the Sumerian forerunners of the Gilgamesh saga were reworked so masterfully in the *Epic of Gilgamesh* that in some respects a new creation was produced. Certain episodes and motifs, of course, were retained, but Babylonian writers refashioned the central theme so thoroughly that we are justified in likening the borrowing to the kind later employed by Virgil, Molière, and Shakespeare. The new rulers were equally gifted in refining and codifying statutory enactments. The famous Code of Hammurabi, for example, mirrors in detail the social milieu of his time. The prologue extols the king as a "devout, god-fearing prince" whose reign is dedicated to the preservation of justice, the destruction of the wicked, the protection of the weak, and the provision "in abundance [of] all sorts of things" for his people. Thereafter some 300 laws set forth behavioral do's and don'ts, followed by an epilogue in which the king warns his successors not to "distort my words" or to "alter my statutes."

Customs regarding marriage and divorce, family life, and sexual practices are clearly reflected in the Code:

If a man has taken a wife and has not executed a marriage contract, that woman is not a wife.

Upper part of the stele inscribed with Hammurabi's Code; Hammurabi is confronting the sun-god.

If a man's wife be caught lying with another, they shall be strangled and cast into the water. If the wife's husband would save his wife, the king can save his servant.

If a man has ravished another's betrothed wife, who is a virgin, while still living in her father's house, and has been caught in the act, that man shall be put to death, the woman shall go free.

If a man's wife, living in her husband's home, has persisted in going out, has acted the fool, has belittled her husband, he shall prosecute her. If her husband has said, "I divorce her," she shall go her way; he shall give her nothing as her price of divorce.

If her husband has said, "I will not divorce her," he may take another woman to wife; the wife shall live as a slave in her husband's house.

Widows and children are carefully provided for:

If a widow, whose children are minors, has made up her mind to marry another, she may not do so without the consent of the judges,

---

* Authorities are far from agreement on the dates of Hammurabi's reign. Once the middle 1900s B.C. seemed to represent a consensus; later it was post-dated some 200 years. Now some again favor the earlier date.

who shall investigate the condition of her former husband's estate. They shall entrust her former husband's estate to her later husband and to her, and they shall have them testify that they will look after the estate and also rear the young children, without ever selling the household goods.

The state sought to guarantee, by law, good workmanship and fair wages and prices:

If a builder constructs a house for a man, and has not made his work sound, and the house falls, causing the death of the owner, that builder shall be put to death.

If a surgeon performs an operation with a bronze lancet on a patrician for a serious injury, and causes his death . . . his hands shall be cut off.

If a man hires a cattle-herder, he shall pay him six *Gur* [a "triple barrel," about 300 quarts] of grain per year.

Note the Code's recognition of class discrimination:

If a man has knocked out the eye of a patrician, his eye shall be knocked out.

If a man has knocked out the eye of a plebeian, he shall pay one mina of silver.

On compulsory military service:

If a soldier or warrant-officer has been detailed on the king's service, and has not gone, or has hired a substitute in his place, that soldier or warrant-officer shall be put to death. . . .

If [military officers] have obtained a soldier by conscription and have accepted and sent on the king's service a hired substitute [those officers] shall be put to death.

On debtor-relief:

If a man has incurred a debt and a storm has flooded his field or carried away the crop, or the corn has not grown because of drought, in that year he shall not pay his creditor. Further, he shall post-date his bond and shall not pay interest on that debt.[20]

Decline

Blanketed by the Code's many provisions and ruled by a succession of gifted dynasts, Babylonian society enjoyed a period of unity, peace, and prosperity. In the meantime, however, two new peoples had established themselves in areas flanking the valley, which soon, of course, became for them a tempting prize. In the late 1600s Hittite and Kassite raiders plundered outposts around the periphery of the Babylonian Empire. Ultimately Hittite forces veered to the south, concentrating on Syria, Palestine, and Egyptian territories along the eastern rim of the Mediterranean and its hinterland. But the westward push of Kassite hordes continued. Under this ceaseless pressure the empire gradually gave way until, around 1500 B.C., it crumbled completely, recovering only under a new conqueror's rule.

For 2000 years Mesopotamia and Egypt had shared control of the ancient Near East. Now the balance of power was destroyed, and a new era, dominated by other forces and peoples—the "catalysts of history"—emerged.

[20] See C. H. W. Johns, *Babylonian and Assyrian Laws, Contracts, and Letters* (New York: Charles Scribner's Sons, 1904), pp. 44–67, passim.

Selected Readings

A. Egypt: Sphinx and Falcon

Baumgartel, Elsie J. *The Cultures of Prehistoric Egypt.* London: Oxford University Press, 1955.

This is the most satisfactory, indeed almost the only study of Egyptian society before the rule of the dynasts. It considers these questions: who were the earliest post-Paleolithic inhabitants; what parts of Egypt were settled; what environmental conditions favored and hindered settlement; what were the religious and economic habits of the settlers; what were the relations between the peoples of Upper and Lower Egypt?

Breasted, James A. *A History of Egypt.* New York: Charles Scribner's Sons, 1912.

This pioneering, comprehensive work on the civilization of Egypt is still very useful. Probably no other historian of this civilization offers the student such penetrating insights and profound understanding; but it should be used with the works of Wilson, and Steindorff and Seele, cited below.

Covensky, Milton. *The Ancient Near Eastern Tradition.* New York: Harper & Row, Publishers, 1966.

This 100-page account of early Near Eastern civilizations is particularly worthwhile for students who have gained a reasonable competence in the factual content of this area and time and who find need for a plainly written overview.

Desroches-Noblecourt, Christine. *Tutankhamen.* New York: New York Graphic Society, 1963.

A great deal more than the short life of Tutankhamen is set forth in this 300-page book: imperial palace politics, social habits, sartorial customs, and royal family feuds, for example. In addition many plates and drawings, most of them reproductions of tomb findings, give a sense of immediacy beyond the power of words. Walkari's book, cited below, is particularly fascinating when read in conjunction with this work.

*Edwards, I. E. S. *The Pyramids of Egypt,* Baltimore: Pelican Books, 1961.

This is a revised edition of the original and not a reprint. It is sound, interestingly written, and comprehensive.

Frankfort, Henri. *Kingship and the Gods.* Chicago: The University of Chicago Press, 1948.

Easily the best work on this subject. The duties of the king are described in detail as are the devices and ceremonies of royal succession and the relationship of kingship and divine powers. Egyptian views and practices are described in the first half of the book, Mesopotamian in the second.

Glanville, R. K. *The Legacy of Egypt.* London: Oxford University Press, 1942.

A series of articles by specialists. The essays consider such items as mechanical and technical processes in ancient Egypt, science and medicine, and calendars and chronology. They are dated but still worthwhile.

Janson, H. W. *History of Art.* Englewood Cliffs, N.J.: Prentice-Hall, 1962.

This lavish and enlightening display of Egyptian art (pp. 35–49) should be used with Pritchard's texts, cited below.

Kees, Hermann. *Ancient Egypt.* Chicago: The University of Chicago Press, 1961.

Using the works of Wilson and Breasted cited here, one may pass over parts one and two of this book. Part three describes in detail particular cities and areas such as Memphis, Abydos, Amarna, the Delta region, and the Fayum.

Montet, Pierre. *Eternal Egypt.* Translated by Doreen Weightman. London: Weidenfeld and Nicholson, 1964.

An internationally known Egyptologist here presents in 300 pages a lucid, readable account of Egyptian life. Its topical arrangement makes it especially attractive when used with Breasted's work which, of course, it updates.

Moscati, Sabatino. *The Face of the Ancient Orient.* Chicago: The University of Chicago Press, 1960.

An interpretative study of the fundamental characteristics of the civilizations of the ancient Near East. The author presents the main features of the "components": Sumerians, Babylonians, Assyrians, Egyptians; describes the catalytic effect on these features of various small states; and discusses the grand synthesis effected by Persia. Generous and pertinent selections from original source materials give flavor and weight to this valuable study.

Pritchard, James B., ed. *Ancient Near Eastern Texts.* Princeton: Princeton University Press, 1955.

A collection of myths, epics, legal and historical texts, descriptions of festivals, hymns, prayers, wisdom literature, songs, poems, and letters. Some manuscripts are fragmentary; but in general the collection gives a sense of identification no historical narrative could possibly impart. The organization is faulty; but the table of contents is so detailed that it somewhat compensates for the misarrangement of the items, many of which are of great interest and significance.

Steindorff, G., and Seele, Kenneth. *When Egypt Ruled the East,* 2d ed. Chicago: The University of Chicago Press, 1956.

After very brief introductory material on the early periods the authors present a detailed account of Egypt under Thutmose III and his successors. For this portion of Egyptian history the book is really an updating of Breasted's work.

* Wilson, John A. *The Culture of Ancient Egypt.* Chicago: The University of Chicago Press, 1956.

This is a reprint of his The Burden of Egypt, in which the author is interested primarily in interpreting data rather than recording it. As an evaluative study of the Egyptian mentality and pattern of values it has no serious competitor.

For a good fictional account of Egypt in the days of the empire see M. T. Walkari, The Egyptian. *The novel is based on an Egyptian source, "The Story of Sinuhe."*

B. Mesopotamia

Braidwood, Robert J. *The Near East and the Foundations for Civilization.* Eugene, Oreg.: Oregon State System of Higher Education, 1952.

> *A series of lectures that challenge Childe's theory of the urban revolution as the catalyst of civilization, as well as the traditional chronological and terminological frame of reference for prehistoric times. A highly stimulating work. Some of it is now outdated by the author's own further study, but it remains a valuable source of information and interpretation.*

*Childe, Gordon. *New Light on the Most Ancient Near East.* 4th ed. New York: Praeger Publishers, 1968. (See notation in Selected Readings for Prologue.) See chapters 6, 7, 8, and 10. See also Childe's *What Happened in History* (Baltimore: Penguin Books, 1957), chap. 5.

*Kramer, Samuel. *History Begins at Sumer.* Garden City, N.Y.: Doubleday & Co., Anchor Books, 1959.

> *Twenty-seven "firsts" in history, among them the first schools, legal precedent, "farmer's almanac," animal fables, tale of resurrection, literary borrowing, and love song.*

Kramer, Samuel. *The Sumerians.* Chicago: The University of Chicago Press, 1963.

> *Dean of Sumerologists, Professor Kramer has packed in these 350 pages an abundance of findings and opinions about ancient Sumerians. The first 300 pages cover archaeology, kings, the Sumerian city, religion, literature and education, and the Sumerian "character." The last 50 pages (appendices) deal with Sumerian writing and language, votive inscriptions, date formulas, letters, and a "farmer's almanac."*

*Moscati, Sabatino. *The Face of the Ancient Orient.* (See notation under A, above.) See chapters 1–3.

Oppenheim, A. Leo. *Ancient Mesopotamia.* Chicago: The University of Chicago Press, 1964.

> *Two warnings: despite the title, Sumeria is omitted; and despite the author's aim at writing for the general reader, the book is not at all easy to read, chiefly because of his conceptual and organizational preferences. Still the general reader, with sufficient effort and patience, will find in this book a complex of facts and an overall view of the "Mesopotamian" past seldom encountered in other texts.*

Pritchard, James B., ed. *Ancient Near Eastern Texts* (See notation under A, above). See pp. 37–120; 217–19; 265–69; 331–46; 382–93; 425–27; 434–41; 455–67.

Pritchard, James B., ed. *The Ancient Near East in Pictures.* Princeton: Princeton University Press, 1954.

> *A selection of halftones presenting "people and their dress," "daily life," writing, and religious scenes and figures. The second half of the book is made up of detailed notes describing the pictures.*

* Asterisk (*) denotes paperback.

CHAPTER II
Small States, Empires, and the Hebrews

A. The "Catalysts": Mitanni, Hatti, Phoenicia, Aramaea, and Lydia

In the early years of our century a pioneering Egyptologist, J. H. Breasted, coined the phrase "Fertile Crescent" to denote and delimit the rich, crop-yielding portions of the Ancient Near East. It is an apt phrase. Many peoples, it is true, roamed other regions—swamp, desert, mountain, steppe. But only in the Crescent did man find conditions that invited transition from barbarism to civilization.

Here, for some 20 centuries, the two valley peoples and their Aegean offshoot cultivated at once the good earth and their own native talents. They created intricate governmental structures, urban life, elaborate religious concepts and practices, sophisticated literature, law codes, and advanced forms of art and architecture. Naturally such achievements and the conditions nurturing them acted as a magnet upon peripheral groups. Another attractive force was the partial disintegration of the fabric of civilization that occurred at the end of the Old Babylonian period. Sometime during the eighteenth or seventeenth century B.C. (depending on which chronology is used; see p. 59, fn.) the successors of Hammurabi lost a large measure of the politico-military control that the early Babylonian rulers had exercised. For more than a hundred or so years a kind of dark age—marked by the disappearance of documentation—spread over the land. When documents next appear they show the presence of new ethnic groups of so-called Indo-Europeans. ("Indo-Europeans" here refers to the Hurrians, Hittites, and Lydians. Generally the phrase is used as a label to designate about a dozen ethno-language groups. Some are now extinct—such as the Anatolian group which includes the three peoples mentioned above—but most are not: Germanic, Italic, and Slavic, for example.) Inscriptions dated ca. 1450 and administrative directives dated ca. 1550 have been found. As early as 2000 B.C. some of the "outsiders" were raiding, or infiltrating into, the Mesopotamian and Aegean Edens. Some, such as the Indo-European Hittites and the Hurrians, came from the highlands of the northwest or northeast. Others, particularly the Semitic Hebrews and Aramaeans, trekked north from the desert stretches of Arabia. Later still others drove down from the Balkan peninsula or across the Aegean Sea, such as Lydians, Phrygians, Philistines.

Thus genesis and exodus combined to close one era and open another as the original civilizations entered into decline and migrant streams, pressing into the favored lands, absorbed their advanced ways of living. Out of these lands the components of civilization flowed into all of western Asia, touching finally the coastal region where they formed a base for the birth of western culture.

Some of the many bearers of these cultural components that we must briefly note are the Mitannians (or later Hurrians), Hittites, Phoenicians, Aramaeans, and Lydians.* Others, such as the Mysians, Arzawans, Cilicians, and Carians, must be passed over because of limits of space and the relatively minor role that they played in shaping events of their own or later times.

HURRIAN CULTURE

Of the Hurrians it has been said that we know too much to ignore them completely and too little to write their history. Originating, as far back as present authorities can trace them, in the area around Lake Van (see map, p. 70), they made their first migrations sometime before the end of the third millennium, settling in the valley's northern region. After conquering, and then peacefully coexisting with, the indigenous population—with whom they freely intermarried—they assumed control of a number of adjacent city-states. About 1500 B.C. they consolidated these into the kingdom of Mitanni (a "nation" of basically Hurrian population, with an unknown Indo-European ruling class as superstructure).

From their first contacts (as early as the Sargonic period, ca. 2300 B.C.) the Hurrians absorbed Mesopotamian culture, fusing it with their own customs, religions, and traditions. The hierarchy of their gods came to include Sumero-Babylonian divinities as well as such Indo-Aryan deities as Indra and Mithras. Like the Babylonians before them, they borrowed from Sumerian literature as well as created their own stories.

Too little is known of their art and architecture to justify even tentative evaluation. Nor have we, as yet, come upon legal texts that provide us with an understanding of their socioeconomic institutions, although we can learn much of them and their "family law" as especially reflected in the tablets from Niozi, a place where Hurrian-Assyrian association flourished. Thanks to the great archival finds at Tell-el-Amarna† we are on somewhat firmer ground concerning their relations with other peoples. We know that they (as Mitannians) had become, around 1400 B.C., one of the greater second-rank powers. In token of this power status several Egyptian rulers arranged marriages between themselves and the daughters of Mitannian kings. Cuneiform tablets found at Amarna (indicating, incidentally, that Babylonian-Akkadian had become the international language of diplomacy) show, too, that Egypt and Mitanni were occasionally allied against common enemies. This was especially true of the Hittites, with whom they engaged in a great power struggle about 1350 B.C.

---

* In his *Face of the Ancient Orient* (see Selected Readings, this chapter) Sabatino Moscati argues that these states of the Near East performed a "release of culture" function that made possible the grand syntheses effected by certain large empires. We acknowledge our debt to him for this and several other ideas developed in this section; compare, for example, p. 80, fn.

† A collection of letters and tablets found in 1887.

THE HITTITE EMPIRE

The Old Empire

Long before their conquest of Mitanni the Hittites had established themselves in northern Anatolia in the great bend of the Halys River (see map, p. 70). We do not know their point of origin and the exact time of their migrations. The evidence suggests what one authority has called "a repeated and prolonged penetration" from the Black Sea area, at about the same time that the Amorites moved into Sumer and Akkad (ca. 2000 B.C.?). Almost certainly these invading Indo-European-speaking tribes intermarried with indigenous peoples and, after a century or so, succeeded in setting up a cluster of city-states.

In this early period the government was made up of a council of nobles and an elective king. One of the latter, Labarnas (ca. 1680—ca. 1650 B.C.), sent out military forces from his capital city, Hattusas (modern Boghazkoy), and eventually created what we have come to call the Old Empire, comprising a large part of the Anatolian peninsula.

Outstanding among the features of this empire was its "federalist" character. Conquest was not followed by ruthless subjugation, wholesale killings, or dispersion. Rather the records show that a surprisingly advanced concept of international law was applied to the conquered lands; they were encouraged to sign treaties with the victor in which mutual rights and obligations were set forth, although naturally the conquerors' advantages outweighed those of the conquered. Following its consolidation of Anatolian dominance, Hatti turned south to Amurru (Syria) and adjacent lands. For a time its fortunes fluctuated, due principally to rising ambitions among the nobles to usurp royal power. In the 1500s a strong king forced through constitutional reforms that gave the monarch the right to name his successor. Thereafter the southward push was resumed, finally culminating in the extension of Hittite hegemony to the Syrian border. There Egyptian legions stood against the challenging power.

The New Empire

It is probably at this juncture that the New Empire emerged, characterized by the complete destruction of remaining noble prerogatives and by extensive plans to deal with the Egyptian threat. Under Suppilulimas I (1375–1335 B.C.), the Hammurabi of the Hittites, the Hittite Empire absorbed the Hurrians and took over a number of Amurru's border towns. Egyptians and Hittites had clashed before, but now they engaged in a long series of encounters that ultimately sapped the strength of both. In 1296 B.C., at Kadesh on the Orontes, armies of the two empires met in an extended battle that proved that neither could conquer the other. Even worse, it became clear that each state, by its endless fighting, had bled itself weak beyond recovery. Less than a half-century later the marauding Sea Peoples poured into Anatolia and the Palestinian region, scattering the imperial forces of both powers. By 1200 B.C. the Hittite Empire, as a Near Eastern power-state, had disappeared from history.

Despite their control of a substantial portion of Asia Minor for nearly a millennium, the Hittites never succeeded in creating a civilization after the manner of the Egyptians and Mesopotamians. That is, they failed to make of the cultural elements that they had absorbed an organic whole, a meaningful ethos. But if their history lacked a central theme, their institutions clearly reflected what has been called the principle of federalism, a strong and prevailing tendency to borrow from others. Sometimes these borrowings were synthesized into a predominantly Hittite practice or institution. More often they were simply loosely grouped together. In religion, for example, all their neighbors' gods were honored. Thus we find Anu and Ea worshipped along with Ishtar and their own Telipinus, the latter (the incarnation of a one-time king) behaving remarkably like Osiris. Whereas other mountain peoples had one storm god, the Hittites tolerantly included in their pantheon a variety, each representing the deity of an ethnic group, or even subgroup. Somehow all were loosely linked together under the sun goddess of Arinna and her consort, the Weather-god of Heaven. In further conformity to the principle of tolerant eclecticism, the ceremonies and liturgies of various peoples were brought together into a loose commingling.

In short, most of the salient features of Hittite civilization were derivative in origin and generally inferior to the cultures of those from whom they freely borrowed. But a degree of genius was clearly reflected in their skillful juxtaposing of many seemingly disparate elements. Superior sensitivity and talent, too, were shown in their construction of legal texts. Here they brought a humane touch unmatched by any earlier society (and many later ones), for in Hittite justice the law of retaliation—"an eye for an eye"—was repudiated in favor of the principle of reparation. But if other advances were made, our knowledge of them must await new archaeological finds.

THE PHOENICIANS— MIDDLEMEN OF THE NEAR EAST

Marauding expeditions of the Sea Peoples—a variety of peoples from the Balkan and eastern Mediterranean areas who moved about in this period from motivations very little understood at present—climaxed the collapse of the fading Hittite and Egyptian empires around 1200 B.C. In the resulting power void, several of the so-called smaller states were able to achieve independence. They were thus allowed to mature talents that brought satisfaction to themselves and that continued, long after their brief period of sovereignty had passed, to influence the wider world.

Among these peoples were the Phoenicians, a branch of the Canaanites that had early settled along the eastern Mediterranean coast (see map, p. 70). Since Egyptian records speak of the pharaoh's legions subduing Phoenician city-states in the sixteenth century B.C., we may reasonably conclude that the more important ones, such as Tyre, Sidon, Byblos, and Acco, had established themselves many years earlier.

Originally the rich soil of the Lebanon coastal plains encouraged an agrarian culture; but steady growth of population stimulated the communities to turn to the sea. Harbors (many now silted up) were numerous. Moreover, extensive cedar forests covering the Lebanon spurs provided an abundance of shipbuilding materials, resin as well as timber. Also, "in the Egyptian vessels which entered their harbors they found a model for their own craft."

Under these influences the Phoenicians ventured into the Mediterranean and eventually became the greatest sea merchants of ancient times. Their own waters yielded a shellfish whose secretion provided a dye that made Tyrian purple a universal trade name. From eastern nomadic tribes they obtained wool, which they wove into garments and carpets. From Africa came ebony and ivory. Metalware was manufactured from Cyprus's copper and Cornwall's tin. Spices and perfumes were imported from Arabia. And always and from everywhere Phoenicians purchased or stole slaves to supply a market that finally ringed the whole Mediterranean basin.

Although trade rather than colonization was their chief interest, the Phoenicians planted a number of settlements ranging from Cyprus to Spain. Of these new states Carthage, settled in the northern tip of what is now Tunisia (ca. 725 B.C.), became the most prominent. Ultimately it became the chief commercial power of the western Mediterranean world.

As the Near East's middleman, the Phoenician merchant naturally tended to develop efficient systems of contract-making and accounting. From this economic prod—as well as from the long centuries of language-making dating from earliest Egypto-Sumerian times*—he fashioned a series of symbols that came to be adopted by those with whom he traded. These symbols, representing neither pictures, ideas, nor phonetic syllables, were arbitrary signs denoting consonantal sounds, 22 in all. In this way was born (ca. 1400 B.C.) the alphabet that we use today (except for vowel signs later added by the Greeks).

ARAMAEANS AND LYDIANS

In the meantime another "small people," the Aramaeans, had taken advantage of the decline of the river powers to develop a culture and pattern of life of their own. Although archaeologists have yet to do much more digging before we can speak authoritatively of their culture, we know that the Aramaeans, like the Phoenicians, were a Semitic people who migrated early from the desert regions of Arabia into the middle land.

Their chief state was Aram. Its capital, Damascus, was strategically located, as were virtually all Aramaean cities, along the main caravan routes running from Mesopotamia to Egypt (see map, p. 70). As a consequence this people became, by about 1000 B.C., the foremost inland traders of the ancient Orient. From the Phoenicians they borrowed alphabetic writing and spread it wherever their trade carried them. Sometime after the beginning of the first millennium B.C. the Aramaean language had become so popular that it dominated all other systems of speech and writing in the Near East. By Jesus' day it had supplanted them so thoroughly that the son of Joseph, "of the seed of David," Hebrew born and raised, spoke Aramaic, not Hebrew. A portion of this far-ranging people migrated to southern Mesopotamia, around Babylon, where they took the name "Chaldeans."

Equally spotty is the record of another people of this era, the Lydians. Since, to date, none of their literature has been recovered, we must go to the accounts of others, chiefly the Greeks. Probably the original Lydians migrated around 1200 B.C. from the Balkan area into west central Asia Minor, where they intermarried with native peoples (see map, p. 70).

With Hittite power spent, the newcomers, like other migrants of the period, were able to consolidate tribal groups into a loose confederacy. It seems likely that by about 700 B.C. they had formed a kingdom whose boundaries had gradually expanded westward until they reached the sea and eastward as far as the Halys River. Within a century or so Lydia was recognized as the strongest power in Asia Minor.

Although precious metals had long been used as a medium of exchange, no earlier people had thought of minting coins that bore the official stamp of its government. Appearing in the eighth or seventh century B.C., this Lydian innovation naturally stimulated international trade. By the reign of the famous King

---

* And including, most importantly, the formulation of an "abecedary" by the western Semitic forerunners of the Phoenicians, the "Ugartians" (early Canaanites). The "Ras Shamrah" tablets, named after the ancient village in whose ruins they were found (ca. 1930), revealed true alphabetic writing. The 30 signs that made it up were the direct precursors of our own alphabet.

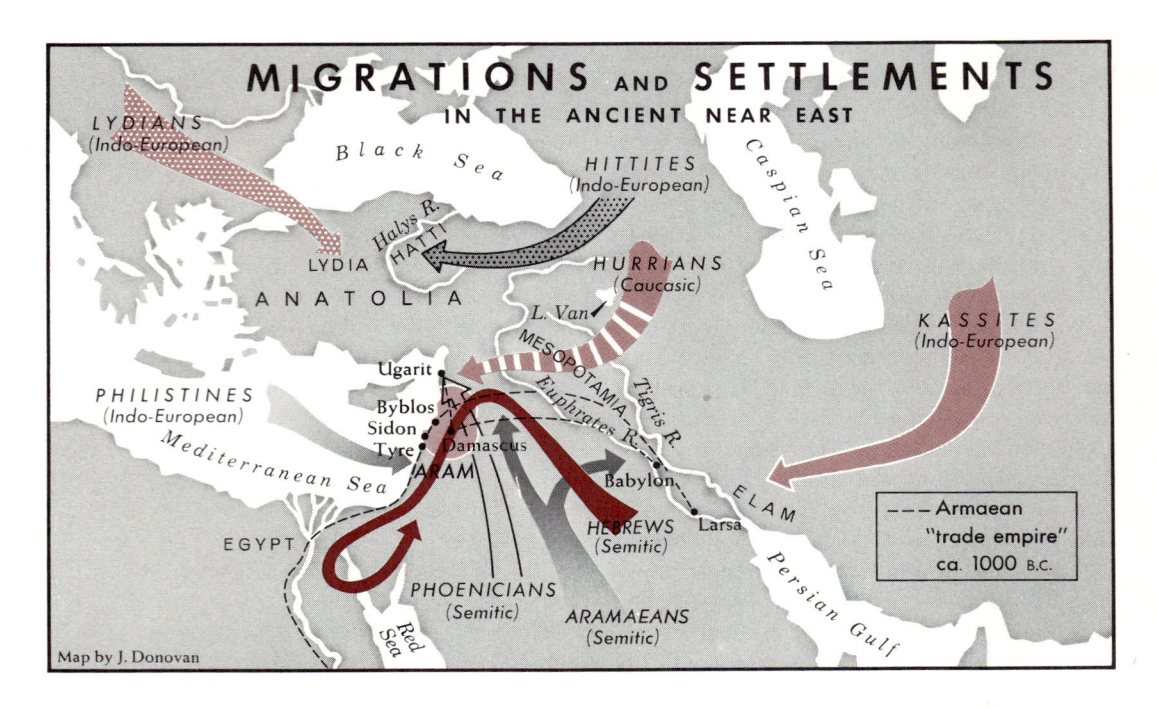

MIGRATIONS AND SETTLEMENTS IN THE ANCIENT NEAR EAST

Croesus (569–546 B.C.) Lydia had become renowned for its wealth. Even more significant was its role as cultural mediator between East and West. For example, the philosophic and cosmological speculations of certain Ionians such as Thales, Anaximenes, and Anaximander (speculations that initiated the Greek venture in rational thought) rested partially upon Lydian absorption and transmission of Eastern lore.

At the height of its power, about 550 B.C., the Lydian empire controlled most of the western half of the plateau, including the Greek settlements along the coast. Under the tolerant Croesus the Greeks were allowed to retain their local traditions and governmental forms; were recognized, even, as already possessing a superior culture. So a beneficent reciprocal relationship was established. The Greeks had much to learn from the ancient East; their clearly superior talents could serve a wider world. Lydia thus served as both bridge and buffer between the old and the new.

B. The Fusion of the Ancient Near East: The Empires of Assyria, Chaldea, Persia

THE ASSYRIANS

Viewed from the perspective of our own times the history of the ancient Near East may be divided into three major epochs: the genesis and growth of the valley civilizations; their decline and the rise of numerous small states that fed upon, developed, and spread their achievements; and the effecting of a climactic cultural synthesis wrought by the newly formed empires of Assyria, Chaldea, and Persia.

Small States, Empires, and the Hebrews

Actually the Assyrians, a Semitic people originating in the desert lands, entered Mesopotamia long before the rise of the small states. Archaeological remains indicate that they had settled in the northern region of the valley around 2800 B.C., anticipating the Amorite invasion farther south by many centuries. For nearly two millennia they lived in a restricted area of the highland country, fighting to wrest subsistence from the sullen soil and rugged terrain and, periodically, fighting against neighboring tribes competing for choicer lands and booty. By about 1900 B.C. they had established a number of merchant colonies in Anatolia. Periodically they were subjected to foreign rule—for example, to the Sumerians (ca. 2500 B.C.) and Babylonians (ca. 1800 B.C.). Such rule was cast off in the mid-eighteenth century B.C. under the leadership of King Shamshi-Adad I, a contemporary of Hammurabi (according to those who accept the "short" chronology) and a man of similar talents. For more than a thousand years thereafter Assyrians wore no foreign yoke, rather bringing others into submission to them.

From the Akkadians and Babylonians the Assyrians borrowed writing and other cultural tools and techniques. For example, their Assyrian legal code was but a modification of the Code of Hammurabi. The Gilgamesh epic was taken over and made their own, with certain names and episodes changed to suit their own ethos and local conditions. If their later history may serve as a clue, the Assyrians would have liked to take much more—no less, indeed, than the lands and cities and peoples of all Sumer-Akkad and Babylonia. We must suppose that for centuries they looked down upon the riches of the south with envy and impelling desire, for the contrast between this lush land and their own barren stretches was great and surely hard to bear. But strong and flourishing cultures had preempted the Crescent. Assyrian ambitions, nurtured by a hardy environment and whetted by the vision of plenty, had necessarily to wait upon a time more propitious for ventures in conquest.

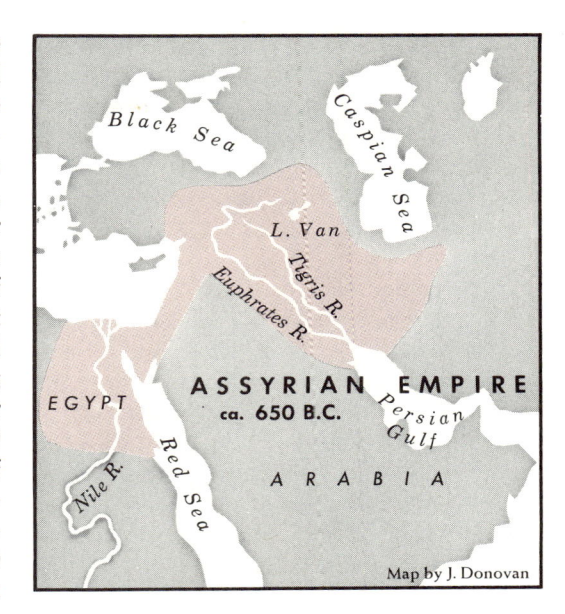

Not long after 1200 B.C. this time came. The great empires and cultures had collapsed, notably the Egyptian and Hittite; even the rough Kassite grip on Sumer had relaxed. As we have seen, many small states had set themselves up as independent peoples, threading together the cultural strands of the whole ancient Near East and, for a while, enjoying the fruits of local autonomy and international intercourse. But only for a while. For in Assyria visions of booty and empire had come to warrior kings eager to lead their legions into the valley below, into Anatolia and Palestine and even, as it turned out, into the hitherto unconquerable Land of the Two Lands.

Assyrian Conquests

The first thrust was made by Tiglath-pileser I (ca. 1076 B.C.). Driving westward and to the north, Assyrian spearmen and archers conquered old Hurrian and Hittite settlements, stopping only when they had reached the Great Sea. Recovered documents inform us of the aggressive spirit that moved this people to conquests such as the East had never before witnessed. In one account we read these words of the proud conqueror:

> With the help of Assur, my lord, I gathered my chariots and my troops. I looked not behind me. Mount Kashiari, a difficult region, I traversed. With their twenty-thousand warriors and their five kings, I fought in the land of Kutmuhi and I defeated them. The corpses of their warriors I hurled down in a destructive battle like the Storm [god]. Their blood I caused to flow in the valley and on the high places of the mountains. I cut off their heads and outside their cities, like heaps of grain, I piled them up. Their spoil, their goods, and their possessions, in countless numbers I brought out.[1]

It is true that Tiglath-pileser's immediate successors were not able to maintain the conqueror's pace; during the 1000s and 900s Aramaeans and others held their own, and even cut into Assyrian gains. But under Ashurnasirpal II (883–859 B.C.) Assyrian might swept forward again. Save for a temporary faltering in the eighth century, the relentless push by loot-hungry kings continued until most of the Orient, from the Persian Gulf to the Lake Van region, then westward to Phoenicia and southward into Egypt, was dominated by the surrogates of the great god Assur (see map, p. 71).

In 722 B.C. under Sargon II (722–705 B.C.) Israel's ten tribes were conquered and dispersed (the "ten lost tribes"). Shortly before, Damascus had been captured and its people deported. In 689 B.C. Sennacherib sacked and burned Babylon. Egypt's turn was next, succumbing under the hammer blows of Esarhaddon and Ashurbanipal (626 B.C.).

[1] Daniel D. Luckenbill, *Ancient Records of Assyria and Babylonia,* vol. 1 (Chicago: The University of Chicago Press, 1926), p. 74.

The last of the great Assyrian rulers, Ashurbanipal was as proud of his learning as of his conquests. As a token of this gentler passion he established a royal library at Nineveh made up of many thousands of cuneiform tablets containing literary, historical, religious, and scientific works of inestimable value. Much of what we now know of this period and area comes from this source. Besides collecting "books" the king donated large sums to foster the arts, especially architecture and sculpture. But we may question whether the basic impulses that motivated his overall behavior were esthetically sensitive and genteel. Included in his art collection, for example, is a relief scene showing him reclining in the palace gardens at dinner with his queen. Attendants stand behind each, gently fanning the air; court musicians pluck strings and pipe under the fanlike coniferous tree. The tableau bespeaks appealing tranquillity; but closer scrutiny brings into focus the severed head of an enemy chieftain dangling from a branch of one of the trees conveniently situated in the king's direct line of vision.

The Collapse of the Empire

Ashurbanipal's successors were unable to hold the empire together. For nearly two centuries much of the Near East had lain under the heavy hand of the cruelest conqueror of ancient times. By terror the Assyrians had subdued scores of people and by terror they had sought to keep them from any thought of rebellion. But terror as an instrument of imperial policy has its limits, and by the seventh century B.C. the burden of mass misery had passed beyond the bearable. When, therefore, the Chaldeans and Medes to the south dared to raise the banner of revolt, nation after nation joined in the attack. Within a dozen years the empire had collapsed. Some notion of the fury of the oppressed peoples can be gauged by the treatment

Small States, Empires, and the Hebrews

meted out to Nineveh, capital and symbol of Assyrian might. Capture and sacking did not suffice. Building by building, stone by stone, the city was dismantled so that not even a charred skeleton remained. The ground itself was slashed and churned by shards. Finally a solemn malediction was pronounced over it, calling upon the gods to curse this infamous spot for eternity.

Some 250 years before, an Assyrian warrior-king had exulted:

The land of Kubbu I traversed, and I went down into the midst of the cities of the lands of Ashsha and Kirki which are before the land of Hatti. The cities of Umalia and Hiraw, strongholds which lie in the midst of the land of Adani, I captured. I slew many of the inhabitants thereof, and their spoil in countless quantities I carried off. The cities I destroyed, I devastated. . . . Unto the city of Uda, the stronghold of Lapturi, the son of Thbrisi, I drew nigh. I stormed the city; with mines, siege engines, and battering rams I took the city. [More than] 1400 . . . of their fighting men I put to the sword, 580 men I captured alive, 3000 prisoners I brought out. The living men, I impaled on stakes round his city, of the others I put out the eyes.[2]

For a nation that had placed its faith wholly in preparedness and terror, its sudden destruction must have seemed incomprehensible except as a freak whim of the gods. To others it was not so surprising. The Jewish prophet Nahum, probably a contemporary of Ashurbanipal, was sure he knew of the coming calamity and etched his vision in bold, bitter strophes:

> Woe to the bloody city,
>   completely false, full of booty!
>   no limit to the plunder there!
> Crack of whip . . . rattle of wheel,
>   rearing steed, somersaulting horse.
>   and jolting chariot!

[2] Luckenbill, op. cit., pp. 167–69.

> and flashing sword and glittering spear,
>   heaps of slain and no end of the
>   corpses! . . .
> Behold I have caught you, says the
>   Lord. . . .
>   and I will throw your skirts upon
>   your face
> and I will show nations your nakedness
>   and kingdoms your shame. . . .
> Your shepherds sleep [O king of Assyria],
>   your nobles slumber.
> Your people are scattered . . . with
>   none to gather them.
> Your hurt will not heal, your wound is
>   festered.
> All who hear the news of you clap their
>   hands over you,
> for over whom has not passed your evil
>   continually?[3]

Assyrian Culture: Architecture and Sculpture

So Assyria died as it had lived, by the sword. But not all of its energy and imagination were devoted to battles. In architecture its achievements are impressive. Although there was much borrowing from the Babylonians, Assyrian builders came to define a form and feeling of their own. Because stone was available in northern Mesopotamia, true columns were used as functional units, particularly in the *bit khilani*, a structure featuring a large forecourt. Palaces were of spacious dimensions, sometimes housing hundreds of rooms grouped about multiple courtyards. Temples and temple towers, often many-storied, contained sanctuaries where priests of Assur, Ishtar, Nabu and other gods and goddesses offered up sacrifices, prayers, and petitions. Brick, it is true, was used more often than stone in constructing both palaces and temples. However, the exceptions amply proved that Assyrian architects were the equal of

[3] *The Interpreter's Bible,* 12 vols. (Nashville: Abingdon Press, 1956), 6:956.

B. The Fusion of the Ancient Near East

their Egyptian counterparts and distinctly superior to those of any earlier Mesopotamian society.

In sculpture the valley influence is clearly evident. Human figures were stylistically represented, stiff and impersonal. Animal statuary, on the other hand, revealed the sculptor's flair for movement and realistic treatment of details. A favorite subject was colossal winged bulls with human heads. Often such statues were embedded in the walls of palace gates, thus giving the artist opportunity to combine carving in the round with relief. Great stelae and soaring obelisks were erected to commemorate the achievements of warrior-kings. Often the obelisks were covered with cuneiform inscriptions that have proved as worthwhile to the modern Assyriologist as to the ancient annalist or, for that matter, to the tourist. Relief-work on palaces and other public buildings usually depicted scenes of the chase or battle.

Religion and Literature

Assyria's abiding passion for conquest and plunder might suggest an indifference to religious concerns. Quite the opposite was true. Hundreds of recovered tablets describe in great length ceremonial practices designed to propitiate Assur, their chief divinity, and Ishtar, commonly designated "my lady," or "lady of Nineveh." Sacred days and seasons were numerous when Assyrians, under the ministrations of their priests, prayed and petitioned for divine favor and protection. As might be expected, strength and power rather than ethical behavior were given first place in the Assyrian hierarchy of values. But purely human strength and courage, *sans* divine aid, were regarded as a contradiction of terms, a concept without fruitful meaning.

Assyrian writers borrowed liberally from early Mesopotamian literature, pro-

This relief scene shows Ashur-bani-pal on a lion hunt. This last of the great Assyrian conquerors liked to boast of his educational and cultural achievements. But his palace adornments, of which this is a typical example, reveal the true spirit and interests that moved him and all other Assyrian rulers.

ducing epics and myths that dealt with the creation of life and the mystery of death in much the same way as did their predecessors. Because they are so similar it would be wearisome to examine the newer versions. But we should remember that much of what we know of the best ancient Near Eastern literature depends on these derivative accounts.

Original Contributions of the Assyrians

In general, then, Assyrian institutional life was imitative and adaptive, but not altogether so. Two developments in particular were marked by invention and originality. War has characterized human existence from its beginning. But Assyria revolutionized this fearful art, chiefly through the application of technology and terror. Iron weapons and armor, for example, were used on a scale hitherto unknown. Permanent professional armies replaced militia. To break up the massed war chariots of enemy formations, a new type of cavalry was created equipped with superior arms and infused with a spirit not dissimilar to that of the Japanese Samurai. This cavalry's swift thrusts through enemy ranks—in effect and for that time somewhat analogous to Nazi tank tactics in World War II—scattered opposing forces into disorganized groups that were then surrounded and annihilated. Siege operations usually involved heavy losses, to reduce which the Assyrians perfected the construction and use of large battering rams. They also perfected the technique of underground mining for battle tactics, employing it with such success that often the seemingly most impregnable fortress was demolished with astonishing dispatch.

Terror and war, of course, go together; but Assyria was the first state to apply terror consistently and thoroughly as an instrument of national policy. As a result more than one city-state, learning that the dread legions were in its vicinity, sent out emissaries, not to negotiate, but to notify the conqueror of its willingness to surrender unconditionally in the (often) vain hope of escaping mass annihilation and deportation. Subsequent to the fall of Assyria, other peoples copied the technical innovations of the warrior state, although most were temperamentally either unable or unwilling to use all-out terror as an instrument of aggression.

For all their raw savagery the Assyrians were not so stupid as to seek the complete destruction of all the lands and peoples they conquered. Numerically an insignificant nation, they realized that their imperial dreams depended on the exploitation of the lands and products, the muscles and minds, of many peoples. So with the same efficiency that marked their destructive ways they set about putting together the greatest empire the world had yet seen—indeed, the first true empire.*

The basic imperial pattern was simple. Peoples that had for one reason or another escaped the full fury of Assyrian conquest (for example, the Hebrews of Judah) were made tributary states and required to make annual payments in goods or coin or both. Others were allowed to keep their princes whose rule, however, was placed under the supervision of governors sent out from Nineveh. The remaining states were annexed outright. As the needs of empire multiplied, naturally the bureaucratic apparatus expanded. By about 700

---

* The word *empire* has been used in reference to the enterprises of earlier peoples—Egyptians, Akkadians, Cretans, Babylonians, Hittites. But all of these earlier efforts were on a relatively small scale. Neither Egypt nor Crete nor Hatti was able to extend its dominion into the lands of the Tigris-Euphrates Valley; except for limited periods (for example, the Sargonic), Akkadia and Babylonia restricted their expansion to the areas of this valley. In short, they were empires dominating particular regions of the Near East. Assyria linked valley to valley and both to southern Anatolia.

This colossal winged bull with human head, a favorite subject of Assyrian sculptors, is from one of the gates of the Citadel of Sargon II (ca. 725 B.C.). Altogether, the gate was made up of four of these giant guardian demons.

B.C. most of the ancient Near East thus found itself bound together under the sway of an iron-willed dominant minority.

The Assyrian policy of ruthlessly deporting and resettling foreign populations of course inflicted traumatic experiences on the conquered. But it also exploited to the full the earlier catalytic functions of the smaller states. In this sense it tremendously stimulated the diffusion of culture, helped to break down narrow, provincial views and introduced, although in embryonic form, the concept of one world. However mean and inhumane his motivation, man ventured here, at this time and in this place, his first attempt to create the ecumenical state.

THE CHALDEANS

Less than a century later a greater and even more significant consolidation of lands and states was effected by the Persians, but before considering this new synthesis we must briefly note the precipitous rise and fall of the Chaldean empire. We have already seen that the Chaldeans and Medes spearheaded spreading revolts that brought down Assyria.

76 Small States, Empires, and the Hebrews

Around 600 B.C. its sprawling empire was divided up, Media taking the eastern portion, Chaldea the western.

The remote origins of the Chaldeans are not known. A Semitic people of the desert (late Aramaean tribes?) they settled in and around Babylon which, long before the fall of Assyria, they had rebuilt on a grand scale. Allied with Cyaxares of Media, their king, Nabopolassar, led them in the attack on Nineveh and, after its fall, garrisoned the lands from the valley to the sea. At his death his son Nebuchadnezzar inherited a fair-sized empire and a taste for further conquest. During the next half-century (605–561 B.C.) he extended Chaldean rule, defeating the Egyptians at Carchemish and rebellious tribes in the Hatti country and captured Jerusalem, from which he sent thousands of Jews into captivity to Babylon (see map, right). But not all of Nebuchadnezzar's energies were spent in battle. Interested in beautifying Babylon, he erected magnificent temples and palaces and even, to please his Median queen, who missed the mountains of her homeland, constructed for her a many-tiered ziggurat.

His death in 561 B.C. brought on a six-year interval of royal infighting among contenders for his throne, which culminated in the accession of Nabonidus. As it turned out, this king was much more interested in sight-seeing and antiquarian lore than in statecraft. A large part of his reign was spent in Arabia where, it seems, he occupied himself with the reconstruction of the ancient ruins of a religious community dedicated to Sin, the moon-god. Naturally this irritated the priestly caste back in his home country, where the great gods Marduk and Nabu were supreme. Added to the dissension that developed between Babylon's priests and their wayward ruler was dissatisfaction with the king's son, Belshazzar, who acted as his father's regent in Babylon. To Belshazzar royal power meant mainly license to satisfy his very pronounced leanings toward a life of debauchery—elaborate and endless banquets and drinking bouts, a well-supplied harem, and a general gratification of whatever senses might remain responsive to titillating stimulation.

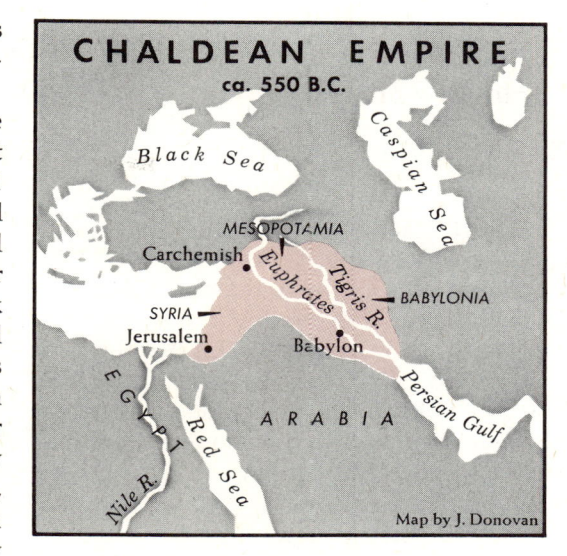

Such conditions, persisting over an extended period, hardly presaged a bright future for the empire. Already a new people, the Persians, had usurped the power of Media in the east (550 B.C.), had marched into Anatolia and conquered the rich Lydian kingdom (546 B.C.), and were looking for new ventures in aggrandizement. In 538 B.C. they sent their legions against Babylon. So far had internal strife and royal degeneracy developed that the city surrendered without a struggle, and the Chaldean empire whimpered out. As a scribe of Cyrus, the Persian conqueror, put it, "All the inhabitants of Babylon . . . as well as the entire country of Sumer and Akkad, princes and governors . . . bowed to him . . . and kissed his feet."[4]

[4] James B. Pritchard, ed., *Ancient Near Eastern Texts* (Princeton: Princeton University Press, 1955), p. 316.

B. The Fusion of the Ancient Near East

THE PERSIANS

Beginnings

The Persians were an Indo-European people whose roots go back to the third millennium B.C. and to regions east of the Caspian Sea. They were of the same stock as those who, around 2000 B.C., migrated westward, finally sifting down into the Aegean and Italian peninsulas, and those who trekked in the opposite direction, settling eventually in India. By the time of the Kassite invasion (ca. 1600 B.C.) several tribes, probably fleeing from the domination of their cousins, the Medes, had set up a loose confederacy at the head of the Persian Gulf. For the next thousand years they increased in population, absorbed Mesopotamian culture, and welded it to their own complex of customs, ideologies, and expansionist dreams.

Imperial Achievements

Around the middle of the sixth century B.C., as we have noted, these dreams began to take on reality as Cyrus led his forces to victory over Medes, Lydians, and Chaldeans. In scarcely more than a decade he had subjugated the whole of Anatolia (including the Greeks on the coastal fringe) and the Syro-Palestinian corridor, and then turning east, had established Persian hegemony as far as the Indus River. Before his death in 529 B.C. he had created the greatest empire the world had yet known, and had laid plans for its further expansion (see map, below).

For unknown reasons the reign of his successor, Cambyses (529–521 B.C.), was cut short, but not before he had conquered Egypt and joined it to the sprawling state. In 521 B.C. Cyrus's son-in-law, the great Darius (521–485 B.C.), became king and continued his predecessor's conquering ways. Aryan states in northwest India were added to the empire. Turning west, the Great King invaded Europe, where he subjugated Thrace and established overlordship of Macedonia. Perhaps this is as far as Darius would have ventured, for by this time (490s B.C.) his domain was so huge that even the prodigious energies of the Persians were strained to maintain it as a going concern. Or perhaps, as some historians believe, the empire builder had marked the Greek city-states and the Aegean peninsula as his next project. In any case, it is certain that the Greeks themselves were too apprehensive of the aggressor's growing power to await events passively. In the next chapter we shall consider the nature and significance of the Persian Wars. Here we need only note that at Marathon, in 490 B.C., the Persians suffered a great defeat at the hands of the Greeks, and a decade later they received an even more decisive one.

But the Afro-Asian empire remained intact and for nearly 200 years served to mix and merge the many Oriental heritages

PERSIAN EMPIRE ca. 500 B.C.

Map by J. Donovan

into a true amalgam. Before considering the characteristics of this synthesis we may inquire how such an achievement could have been effected by a new people living on the periphery of the civilized world.

Probably the most important influence was a negative one. Some 3000 years earlier Mesopotamian peoples had shaped mankind's first civilization, creating writing, literary forms, religions, and advanced economic and political systems. All the evidence points to the melancholy fact that by the sixth century B.C. these once venturing peoples were tired. The weight of centuries of static institutions bore heavily upon them. Innovation had yielded to convention, vision to nostalgia, the promise of tomorrow to the cult of antiquity. In short, the ancient Near East had lapsed into spiritual and institutional senility.

Beneficent Aspects of Persian Rule

Iranian (Persian) leaders, on the other hand, were alive with hope and a sense of expectancy. From Cyrus to Artaxerxes I (d. 424 B.C.) they dreamed imperial dreams and so successfully translated them into reality that by the latter's reign Persian rule extended from the Himalayas to the Adriatic, from the Caucasus to the Indian Ocean. But military vigor and venturesomeness were not the sole determinants of the cultural synthesis that was effected. What marked and made Persian hegemony so outstanding was enlightened policies and refined administrative procedures. Among the former was the principle that non-Iranian peoples should not merely be allowed, but encouraged, to retain and develop their own pattern of culture. Yahwism, for example, was recognized as the official religion of the Hebrews, and the Jews in Babylon were permitted to return to Palestine. Other peoples were similarly treated. This substitution of tolerance for monolithic structuring, of catholic sympathy for vindictive parochialism, laid strong foundations for the construction of a universal state.

To administer the new ecumenical community Cyrus and his successors divided it into 20 satrapies (provinces) ruled over by a governor whose official title was "protector of the Kingdom." Basic laws, applicable throughout the empire, were determined by the king. Within the framework of these laws provincial codes were drawn up by the local governors and their advisors, many of whom were natives of the region. To make sure that the governor neither abused the royal system of justice nor conspired to set himself up as an autonomous ruler, the king created a corps of "king's messengers" whose business it was to make annual inspection of provincial affairs. Since distances within the empire were so great, an elaborate system of roads was laid out to facilitate rapid exchange of news and reports and, of course, the efficient dispatch of military units to trouble spots.

The Persian Amalgam

For nearly two centuries, under the aegis of the "King of Kings" and his bureaucratic apparatus, a multitude of Near Eastern institutions, tongues, habits, and outlooks was diffused and, to a degree, blended into a cosmopolitan civilization. To a reflective citizen of the times it might have appeared that the river of life had, across the millennia, drawn from the streams of every age to issue into one channeled current. Or, to change the figure of speech, that the Crescent had acted as a magnet, drawing into itself, and refining, the energies, visions, and talents of the surrounding desert and mountain peoples. As one modern authority has put it:

In the Audience Hall of his palace in Persepolis, whose remains are shown here, Darius the Great staged grand receptions and court spectacles, designed to impress Persians and subject peoples alike with the grandeur and power of the King of Kings. The capitals of the massive columns were made up of the head and shoulders of bulls and other animals, an unprecedented architectural feature.

... ancient Oriental history may be regarded as a synthesis. The component elements, the reagents, are the civilizations of the valleys, Egypt, and Mesopotamia, which are historically the first to establish their states and continue to have essential independence for many centuries. The substances that determine or assist the process of synthesis, the catalysts, are the peoples of the mountains and of the desert, who bring about the conjunction of the opposed forces, leading first to equilibrium, then to the domination of one side. The last of the catalysts produces the synthesis.[5]

[5] Sabatino Moscati, *The Face of the Ancient Orient* (Chicago: The University of Chicago Press, 1960), p. 294.

In art this synthesis was particularly marked. Old Babylonian forms merged with those of Assyria and Chaldea to reflect the universality of the empire of empires. Colored bricks, for example, were used in the time of Hammurabi and before. On the Persian palace at Susa, well over a thousand years later, we find a frieze made up of colored bricks, depicting scenes that clearly suggest the later art forms of Assyria, in particular the typical winged animal with human head. Darius himself, as we find in a royal inscription, called attention to the many sources drawn upon to construct one of his palaces—Lebanon for cedars, Car-

80   Small States, Empires, and the Hebrews

mania for *yaka* wood, Bactria for gold, Egypt for silver and ebony, and Assyria, Ionia, Media, and Chaldea for laborers and artisans.

In the same way language served at once as an instrument to absorb and diffuse culture. To issue royal orders, transact business, commemorate significant events, tell tales, and to canonize and spread their sacred scriptures the Persians employed three languages and two scripts. For decrees, commemorative inscriptions, and like pronouncements a cuneiform script was used, its syllabary probably invented by the Medes. To give direction to complicated administrative affairs, imperial officials wrote on a different material and used a language without a syllabary. Hieroglyphics were used by those engaged in the conduct of Egyptian affairs.

Zoroastrianism

Paradoxically one of the most significant and lasting influences of Persian culture, its religion, had in its original form little of the imitative or eclectic. Its founder, Zoroaster (Zarathustra), probably lived in the seventh or sixth century B.C. For reasons and under conditions unknown to us, this prophet took it upon himself to recreate the ancient religious lore of his people. Early Aryan (that is, Iranian) faiths held that the world was ruled by many spirits, some good, some evil. Of the good the greatest were Ahura, the divine creator, and Mazdah, the spirit of wisdom. Lesser deities were called *devas* if kindly, *daevas* if evil. From the lore of this religion Zoroaster created a monotheistic faith in which Ahura and Mazdah were merged into the Creating Word. Existing before the world was formed, the Word brought all forms of life into being. Over all brooded the Holy Spirit of Ahura Mazdah boding good for species of every kind, particularly for Man. That man might, through struggle, appreciate more meaningfully and win the intended goodness, a twin of the Holy Spirit, Ahriman—the Evil One—was created by Ahura. Thenceforth all life became a contest, between truth and error, light and dark, good and evil.

Zoroaster dismissed the various *devas* and *daevas* as chimeras, conjured out of human fears and insecurity. Nor did he allow place for statuary, elaborate rituals, or a priestly caste. Any person seeking the good and the true could find them. Similarly anyone, if he wished, could reject them or pervert them into evil. At death the virtuous passed on into the eternal bliss of heaven. Practitioners of evil, on the other hand, descended into the everlasting torment of hell. Later this doctrine was modified to hold that a great climacteric final day of judgment would come when the creator's Holy Spirit would weigh all souls in the balance and grant everlasting life to those who had followed the Righteous Way, and visit destruction upon those who had turned aside from it.

The *Gathas*, Zoroaster's collected work, contain certain key words and phrases, which are repeated over and over: the Holy One, Good Thought, Righteousness, Piety, Salvation. The ethical content of its teachings combined with its monotheistic character to place Zoroastrianism far in advance of the religious concepts and practices of any other peoples of its time (except, as we shall see, the Hebrews). In fact, the new faith was so far beyond its milieu that, like Akhenatonism, it failed to receive ready acceptance by the masses. It is not surprising, therefore, that at Zoroaster's death his teachings underwent changes designed to minimize its abstractions and to emphasize symbols, sacrifice, liturgy, and priestly mediation. Before long the ancient Aryan fertility goddess, Anahita, was returned to the pantheon as was Mithra, god of light. Thus in time Zoroastrianism, originally a reforming protest against polytheism and empty formalism, took on characteristics of the paganism it had sought to supplant. Even so, then and thereafter many disciplined and devout minds "found in [Zoroaster's] doctrines something so new, so fresh, so bracing that his influence may be detected in the majority of the later religious movements. It is no accident that the *Gathas* of Zoroaster sound so much like the first New Testament."[6]

Astronomy

As was true of all early religions, so with the later, corrupted, form of Zoroastrianism there was linked an intensive study of heavenly phenomena. But now astrology showed unmistakable signs of yielding to disciplined reason. Before the Persians, the Chaldeans had divided the heavens into the 12 signs of the zodiac. Even earlier, as we have seen, the solar year, the lunar month, and the division of the day into 24 hours had been worked out by priests and astrologers. Now Persian savants, collecting, collating, and refining previous studies, produced a corpus of data not significantly added to until the Copernican revolution. In the fifth and fourth centuries B.C. astronomical observations were combined with mathematical calculations to ascertain and systematically formulate the cycles of the planets, major movements of the stars, eclipses of sun and moon, and the length of the seasons. Although much of this learning was still yoked with religio-astrological lore and used to predict events in the lives of individuals and nations, this could not fundamentally detract from the soaring achievements of ancient astronomy, "the one science the Orient gave the West full grown."

The Amalgam Dissolved

Added, then, to this synthesis of ancient eastern culture were Persia's own contributions to religion and science. By about 500 B.C., 3000 years of civilized refinements to the art of living had been brought by this empire to a grand flowering. Judged by this performance, the Iranian promise was bright; but both performance and promise failed. The facts themselves are simple: in the early fifth century B.C. the empire challenged the Greeks and was defeated; about 150 years later it lay in ruins, bestrode by a Macedonian conqueror. In this brace of centuries an amazing breakthrough in politics, philosophy, art, and science had occurred; but these achievements were the Greeks'. The old world had lost its vision and lay moribund. But it is unlikely that the facts, so simply stated, will soon or ever yield the secret of their causative impulses. Why did the Persian amalgam dissolve? Why did not the Iranians, instead of their Greek cousins, achieve the breakthrough to a new vision of life? One can conjecture that the material power and glory of imperial dominion sapped their spiritual élan. Or that the weight of 3000 years of tradition smothered their spirit; or that both of these influences combined perhaps with unknown others, robbed the Persians—at their moment of victory—of the most meaningful achievement: the development of the beautiful and the good. Whatever the hypothesis, the fact remains: the East had spent its genius. Henceforth the West would mold and fashion afresh the creative forces of life.

---

[6] Arthur T. Olmstead, *History of the Persian Empire* (Chicago: The University of Chicago Press, 1948).

C. The Hebrews— Chosen of Yahweh

Chronologically the Hebrews should have been considered in our earlier study of the so-called smaller states. They are taken up here because their history is intricately and fundamentally connected with the development of Western man, which we shall examine next.

Originally the term *Hebrew* (from *Habiru; Ibri*) meant "transient," "nomad," "wanderer." As such it was applied to many groups of peoples who roamed throughout the Near East during the millennium 2000–1000 B.C., non-Semitic as well as Semitic. In the earlier centuries the word was invariably used to denote drifters, alien nobodies. Later it denoted certain Semitic groups without homeland ties. In our own day it is used to designate the biblical Jews and their descendants—a confusing practice, since long before the Bible was written the Jews had given up the name Hebrews in favor of Israelites; but popular reference makes use of the older term virtually mandatory.

EARLY HISTORY

Migrations and Pastoral Life

The origins and migrations of the Hebrews are difficult to pin down. Abraham was probably their first patriarchal leader. Conjecture places his birth in the region of Ur during the reign of Hammurabi, and from there he migrated to Harran, along the upper reaches of the Euphrates, where the Hurrians dwelt. When a number of the latter migrated to Palestine, Abraham and a portion of his tribe accompanied them. In this peaceful, nondramatic manner the first Hebrews entered the Promised Land.

Since the more productive regions of Palestine were already settled—the littoral of the eastern Mediterranean and the valley of the Jordan—the wanderers had to be content with the hilly central portion. And for the most part they were content. Settled here and there in small units, with grazing their chief occupation, the Hebrews established a pattern of life that was satisfying although primitive. Heads of families—patriarchs such as Isaac, Jacob, and Joseph—ruled over their tribes with paternal devotion. Pastoral life constituted the common economic bond.

The Covenant and Monolatry

But far outweighing this material condition as a unifying element was the covenant concept originally shaped, according to biblical tradition, by Abraham. In essence the covenant was a reciprocal promise: first, Abraham undertook to commit himself and his peo-

PALESTINE 1200 B.C.

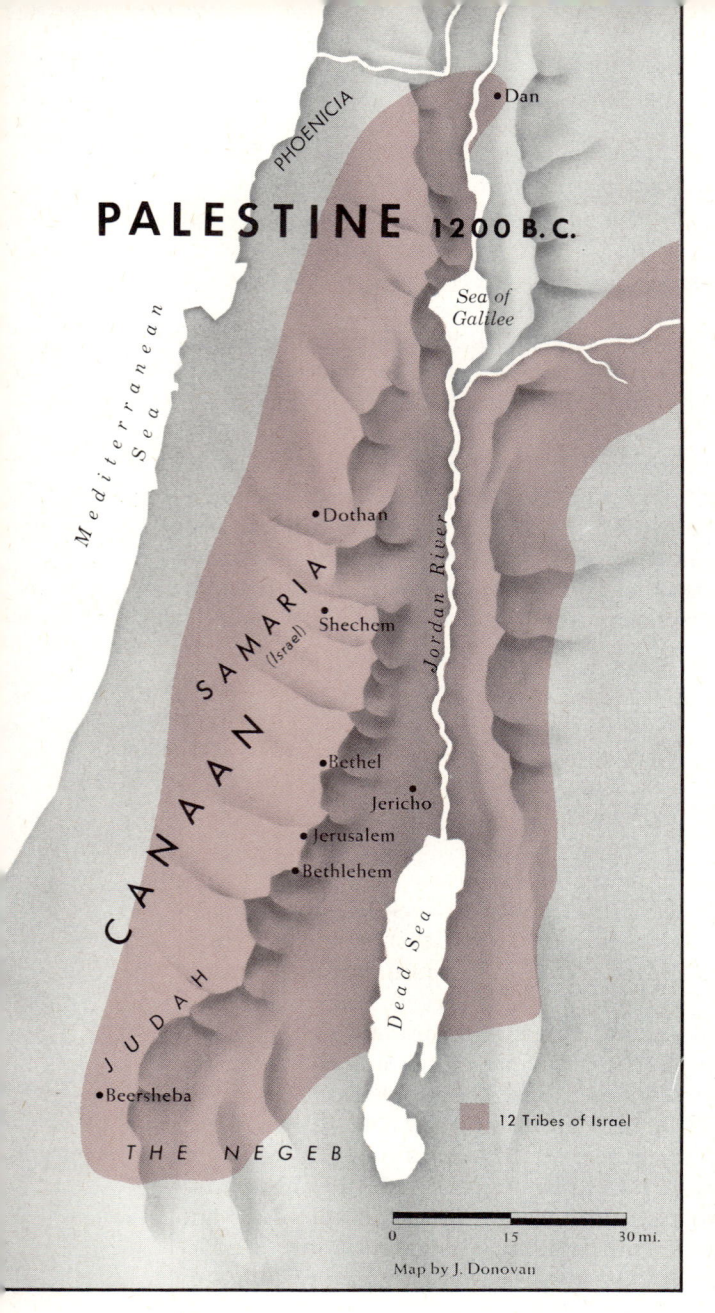

Map by J. Donovan

This commitment should not, however, be understood to imply a monotheistic faith. Yahweh was "God of Abraham," not of the universe. Canaanite tribes had their Baals; Egyptians had their Re, Osiris, Amun; Aegeans had still other gods; and so on. These early Hebrews are rightly called monolatrists—believers in one *tribal* god. But even so, the Hebrew advance is significant. Except for the reformers of the Akhenaton period in Egypt, no people before the biblical Hebrews had either sufficiently refined insights or sufficient faith and daring to accept the dictum that "there must not be to you other gods against my face."*

Dedicated though they were to the way of Yahweh, these early Jews did not hesitate to question, and at times challenge, the designs of their Lord, even when they had anything but a strong case. For example, when Aaron seduced his people into worshiping a golden calf, the Lord in indignation said to Moses

> . . . your people which you brought out of the land of Egypt have corrupted themselves. They have quickly turned aside from the way which I commanded them . . . they are a stiff-necked people. Now therefore let me alone that I may work vengeance upon them and destroy them. . . . Moses replied, Lord, why does your wrath wax hot against your people whom you have brought forth from the land of Egypt with great power and with a mighty hand? Will not the Egyptians say, the Lord of these people tricked them out of our land in order to slay them in the mountains? Turn away from your fierce wrath and repent of this evil against your

ple to one god, Yahweh (*El* or *Elohim*, the original Hebrew word for God), beside whom there should be no other. In return Yahweh promised to protect and develop one people, the Hebrews of the house of Abraham.

---

* A number of scholars have claimed otherwise, an example of which is found in W. F. Albright's article in *The American Scholar* 7 (1938): 138 and in his *Archaeology of Palestine and the Bible*, New York, 1932, p. 163, cited in T. H. Meek, *Hebrew Origins* (New York: Harper & Row, Publishers, Harper Torchbooks, 1960), p. 205.

Small States, Empires, and the Hebrews

people. Remember Abraham, Isaac, and Israel, your servants, whose seed you swore you would multiply as the stars of the heavens. And the Lord repented of the evil which he thought to do to his people.[7]

Material Quests: the Eisodus

The searching quest for God and his truth was accompanied by an equally restless probing for more mundane satisfactions, chief of which was economic well-being. The region of central Palestine afforded subsistence and even a modest measure of abundance; but occasional poor seasons and the natural tendency of man to better his lot impelled some Hebrews to trek farther south, particularly into the fabled land of Egypt.

Typical of this sporadic migrant movement was Abraham's visit to, and Isaac's sojourn in, what the Bible calls the land of Goshen, the delta area of the Nile. When their ethnic cousins, the Hyksos, conquered Egypt (see p. 36) other Jewish groups poured in. Some individuals among them, such as Joseph, actually achieved positions of considerable power. Others became minor officials, and all enjoyed advantages that went with their close association with the conquerors. For several generations this *Eisodus* ("going into") continued, quite naturally influencing Jewish habits and thoughts as the superior culture of Egypt made itself felt. No one, of course, can say how Hebrew history would have developed had this situation continued indefinitely. But one may conjecture that had this happened the religious genius of the Hebrews would have died aborning. For it was exodus and wandering, not eisodus and settlement, that really shaped that genius.

Oppression in Egypt

As noted in chapter 1, differences among the Egyptians soon dissolved in the humiliation of foreign rule, prompting a great patriotic rally. Measured in terms of Egypt's long history the day of the invaders was brief indeed. By 1550 B.C. Egypt was itself again, at least in the repossession of national unity and political sovereignty. It will be recalled, too, that under a new dynasty Egypt went on, after ousting its foreign rulers, to conquer all of Palestine and much of Syria, thus bringing the many Jews living there under its domination. Of course Hebrews who remained in the delta region also felt Egypt's wrath. As the Old Testament has it: "Now there arose a new king over Egypt, who did not know Joseph. . . . [The Egyptians] therefore . . . set taskmasters over them to afflict them with heavy burdens . . . and made their living bitter with hard service, in mortar and brick, and of all kinds of work in the field. . . ."[8]

Egyptian control over Palestine weakened in the fourteenth century. Taking advantage of their opportunity, wandering Hebrews from the Trans-Jordan area crossed the river. There, alternately conquering and infiltrating peacefully, they established new settlements among the Canaanites and among other Hebrew tribes. Although this is probably the period when Joshua conquered Jericho (perhaps ca. 1320 B.C.), conquest was less typical of Jewish expansion than was peaceful migration.

But if Egypt's hold was weakened it was not entirely broken. Intermittent punitive expeditions raided Hebrew communities and sent many inhabitants to Egypt as prisoner-slaves. As oppression increased, these captives and their descendants natu-

---

[7] Adapted from F. C. Cook, ed., *The Holy Bible*. 10 vols. (New York: Charles Scribner's Sons, 1881), 1:407–8.

[8] Exod. 1:8–14 passim.

rally yearned for a deliverer who would lead them out of the land of bondage and, it was hoped, into a land that they could call their own. Such a leader did appear about 1200 B.C. But before we consider the dramatic exodus led by Moses brief attention must be given to Hebrew life in the half-millennium after Abraham.

Palestinian Life before the Exodus

During this long period three clusters of Jewish settlements were established in Palestine (or Canaan). One was in the north, where a number of Abraham's people lingered when their leader pushed farther south. Shechem and Dothan subsequently became centers of this cluster (see map, p. 84 for these and other locations referred to). Another was in central Palestine, around Bethel. A third was formed to the south, in the Negev, particularly around Beersheba.

It appears that after the conquest of Jericho Joshua turned north to Shechem, where he organized many of the Hebrews into an amphictyony (confederacy with strong religious bonds). In the book of Joshua (24:20 f.) we learn that he said to his people:

If you forsake the Lord, and serve strange gods then he will turn and do you hurt, and consume you, after the good he has done you. And the people said to Joshua, "No; but we will serve the Lord." And Joshua then said to the people, "You are witnesses against yourselves that you have chosen the Lord, to serve him." And they said, "We are witnesses." "Now therefore," he said, "put away the foreign gods which are among you, and incline your heart unto the Lord God of Israel." And the people said to Joshua, "The Lord our God we will serve, and his voice we will obey." So Joshua made a covenant with the people that day, and made them a statute and an ordinance in Shechem. . . . And Israel served the Lord all the days of Joshua, and all the days of the elders who outlived Joshua. . . .[9]

At this place and in this time *Israel* was born; but as yet it embraced only the tribes of the north.

In a similar way Hebrews who had settled in the central and southern portions of Palestine were urged by their "judges" (leaders) to resist the temptation to bow down to local gods, forsaking Yahweh. In the main the response was similar to that of their kinsmen in the north. From many references in the Old Testament, however, we know that periods of backsliding were not uncommon. After all, wherever the Jews settled in Palestine neighboring tribes greatly outnumbered them. Moreover, because the migrations and conquests occurred at different times and in rather widely separated areas, no secure feeling of unity had developed. It is not altogether strange, therefore, that for most of this early period the concept "God of the Hebrews" was slow to form. Even then it only imperfectly influenced the daily life of the Jews.

Much of this, however, was soon to change. For one thing, the long years of grinding servitude in Egypt had made many Hebrews willing to risk almost anything to escape the pharaoh's rule. For another, Egypt had by the end of the thirteenth century become so weakened from its wars with the Sea Peoples and so torn with internal dissension that the risk seemed not too great. Finally, there was at hand an inspired man of vision who was determined to lead his people out of bondage. In short, the Eisodus of Abraham, of Jacob, and of Joseph was now to issue in an Exodus under Moses.

[9] Adapted from Cook, op. cit., 2:113–14.

The Exodus and the Egyptians drowning in the Red Sea; copy of a mural from the Dura-Europos Synagogue painted on the site, 1933–35.

THE EXODUS: WANDERING AND NATIONHOOD

Moses and the Wilderness Experience

The great venture was set in motion around 1195 B.C. Along some route (which authorities are unable to agree upon) Moses led his people across the Red Sea (or "Reed Sea") into the Sinai Peninsula. For a generation or longer—the biblical account reckons it as 40 years—a number of Hebrew tribes—Levites, Reubenites, and others—sought both to unify themselves and to push their way northward, where they hoped to found a permanent homeland.

The task was not easy. Hard desert experiences led many to question their decision to leave Egypt, where, although unfree, they at least had plenty to eat. Scriptures record that Moses "heard the people weep throughout their families, every man at the door of his tent." Moreover, various tribal elders schemed to usurp Moses' authority. One such was Aaron, who encouraged his people to forsake Yahweh and bow down before a golden calf. At times Moses himself felt the odds to be too great: "And Moses said unto the Lord, wherefore hast thou afflicted thy servant? . . . I am unable to bear this people alone, because it is too heavy for me" (Numbers: 11:11–14).

Over these seemingly endless dissensions and doubts, however, Moses' faith and vision prevailed. With patient understanding, with clear and sometimes sharp exhortation, and by personal example he led his people not into a promised land—others were to do that—but into a new covenant destined slowly to replace the earlier tribal covenants of Abraham, Isaac, and Jacob. It was this experience that was to make the Jews a unique people and ultimately to shape some of the most basic features of Western life. Under the triple impact of the exodus, long wanderings, and the genius of Moses' leadership, these southern Hebrews formed themselves into a nation. More important, they dedicated themselves to one God—Yahweh. Thus out of historic conditions and inner resources there came for the Jews a revelation; and out of this revelation, an abiding faith.

To symbolize the new nation's common devotion to one god a tabernacle—"Tent of Meeting"—was constructed (portable, as required by a people on the march). In return for his continuing guidance and protection Yahweh demanded of his chosen people a pattern of behavior compatible with his nature. Research has made it abundantly clear that the details of this pattern were not at the time spelled out as clearly as they appear in the two decalogues of Exodus (20:2–17; 34:17–26, commonly called the Ten Commandments). But it is equally clear that the main features of the code were shaped by Moses and accepted by his people: "Thou shalt have no other Gods before me . . . ; thou shalt not take the name of the Lord thy God in vain . . . ; honor thy father and mother . . . ; thou shalt not kill; thou shalt not commit adultery . . . ; thou shalt not bear false witness"; etc. Quite probably, too, a wooden chest (the Ark) was built to enshrine the sacred commands. In this way, then, Hebrew *ethical monolatry* was born and a hinge of Western civilization forged.

Conquest of Canaan

But the newly formed, God-centered people were as yet without a homeland. True, the land of Canaan (or, more correctly, a part of it) had been infiltrated by their ancestors. Against this fact, however, was actual and longstanding control of the land by the Egyptians and the Canaanites, the latter a complex of peoples (including the Phoenicians) of Semitic origins. It was into this area—"Canaan Land"—that the successors of Moses led the Israelites in the belief that Yahweh had singled it out for their possession.

The conquest was neither quick nor complete. From ca. 1165 to ca. 1050 B.C. Israelite judges—religious and military leaders—pitted their armies against Canaanite garrisons, now winning battles, now losing them. Probably they would have had fewer successes had not the land been under invasion at the same time by another migrating people, the Philistines, one of the Sea Peoples. It is from them that the name Palestine derives (see map, p. 70). Under this double thrust Canaanite control collapsed. By about 1050 B.C. the two conquerors stood poised against each other.

Two circumstances favored the Israelites. For several centuries their tribal groups, as we have seen, had settled in the region. Many of them now joined their kinsmen against the Sea People. Also, to gain the strength that combined efforts bring, they agreed to unite under a single king, Saul (ca. 1020 B.C.). Under these conditions the Philistines were routed and confined to a small area along the Mediterranean coast. God's Chosen had found their home.

The New Nation: Saul, David, Solomon

Saul's reign, however, was a troubled one, ending in his suicide. Shortly thereafter David, his young rival, assumed the throne. Under David, Israelite gains were consolidated and extended until the new nation became something of a power. On David's death, around 960 B.C., his son Solomon was acclaimed king. His 40-year reign raised Israel's prestige to the greatest temporal heights it was ever to achieve. From Dan to Beersheba and from the coast to the Jordan River, Palestine blazed in martial and material splendor. Trade and mining brought extraordinary prosperity. To symbolize the permanence and majesty of Israel's position Solomon built a great temple, in the Holy of Holies of which the Ark was enshrined.

POLITICAL DECLINE, SPIRITUAL ADVANCE; PROPHECIES FULFILLED

Causes of Decline

But outward splendor belied Israel's inner life. In the nearly 300-year span from the Exodus to the death of Solomon, the one-time flaming fire of devotion to Yahweh had faded into a flicker of formal incense-burning. Delivered from Egyptian bondage, successfully led out of the wilderness, victoriously established in the land of Canaan, many of the Jewish people became indifferent to the strict demands of the New Covenant. In short, apostasy fed on material success. Others—descendants of those who had not made the trek to Egypt—had always been sympathetic to the Canaanite worship of Baal. By Solomon's time the religious prod, source of this people's genius, had been blunted and converted into a perfunctory, even soothing, pat.

Accompanying, and in part causing, decline in the life of the spirit was the play of power politics. Small as it was, the new nation for a brief moment achieved hegemony over the Palestinian corridor. The heady delights of this experience led it into new ventures that soon entangled it with other nations of like ambitions. As it happened, at this time there occurred a recrudescent flash of Egyptian imperialism. Even more threatening was the rise of Assyrian power. Caught thus between the pincers of a (temporarily) revived Egypt in the south and a rampant Assyria in the north, the imperial glory of tiny Israel abruptly and permanently faded.

Another influence fostering decline was the complex of differences separating northern Jews and their southern kinsmen. Long settled in Palestine, the former had quite naturally absorbed many Canaanite social and religious habits. In addition they were superior to the Jews of the Exodus in both numbers and affluence. As Professor Meek has bluntly expressed it, "only for a brief period were they [the northern and southern Jews]

When the Hebrews settled in "Canaan Land" they tended to absorb social and religious customs of the Canaanites and Phoenicians. Worship of the god Baal, represented here, affronted Hebrew judges and prophets, who warned of Yahweh's wrath to come.

C. The Hebrews—Chosen of Yahweh

ever united and then not very closely, when they were engaged in a common cause against a common foe, the Philistines. As soon as this pressure was removed in the time of David, their differences quickly reappeared."[10] The death of Solomon (a southerner whose reign, moreover, was marked by excessive taxation borne especially by the people of the north) proved a good excuse for a separation long brewing. Around 925 B.C. the ten northern tribes seceded and set themselves up as an independent nation, which they called Israel. The remaining southern tribes constituted what came to be called the kingdom of Judah.*

Corrupted spiritually, sundered politically, and lying athwart one of the main trade and military routes connecting three continents, the two little states could hardly survive for long. Around 722 B.C. Assyria conquered and destroyed Israel, so completely dispersing its people that thereafter they were known as the "ten lost tribes." Something over a century later the Chaldeans, under their conquering King Nebuchadnezzar, overran Judah, sacked Jerusalem, destroyed the Temple, and took many citizens captive to Babylon. Jewish life seemed ended.

Politically it was ended. True, the kingdom of Judah was reestablished after the Persian conquest of Chaldea (539 B.C.; see p. 79). It remained, however, subservient to the Persians; and with their collapse and the subsequent rise of Hellenistic empires, even its qualified autonomy was lost. But spiritually the issue was quite different. In the realm of religious experience, where its genius lay, this harassed people made a most remarkable advance.

Elijah and Elisha

The foundations of this advance were laid before the Jews suffered their humiliations of defeat and dispersal. Such prophets as Elijah and Elisha, for example, clearly sensed the catastrophic drift that affairs were taking. They boldly confronted even kings, pointing out the backsliding of the times and declaring in the name of Yahweh, "Behold, I will bring evil upon you, and will take away your prosperity." Such plain speaking naturally bothered rulers whose equivocal position forced them to consider it a kind of subversive activity. An instance of this is cited in 1 Kings, chapter 18, when the Israelite king, Ahab (ca. 870 B.C.), confronted Elijah personally. ". . . and when Ahab saw Elijah he said to him, 'are you the troubler of Israel?' And Elijah said, 'I have not troubled Israel, but you have, and your father's house before you, in that you have forsaken the Lord's commandments and have followed the Baal's.'" Following this direct exchange the prophet spoke to an assembly of citizens: "Addressing the people, Elijah said, 'How long will you falter between two faiths? If Yahweh is your God, follow him, but if Baal, then follow him.' But to this the people would not answer."[11]

Amos and Hosea

A century later the equally forthright Amos surveyed conditions and felt overwhelming disgust at the growing tendency to substitute empty ceremony for

---

[10] Theophile James Meek, *Hebrew Origins* (New York: Harper & Row, Publishers, Harper Torchbooks, 1960), p. 47.

* From which "Jew" is derived. The terminology applicable to the Jews is somewhat complicated. Originally Jewish as well as a number of other tribes were called Hebrews. From about 1000 B.C. the northern kingdom was called Israel, and the southern Judah. Later the northern group, or what was left of it, took the name Samaria, after its chief city. By Jesus' day Judeans considered themselves exclusively the Jewish people; references to their northern kinsmen—Samaritans—were consistently of a derogatory nature (hence the power of the Christian parable of the Good Samaritan).

[11] Adapted from Cook, op. cit., 2:590–91.

90 Small States, Empires, and the Hebrews

moral behavior. In the fifth chapter of the book that bears his name the prophet has the Lord declare: "I hate, I despise your feast days, and I will not smell of the sacrifices of your solemn assemblies. Though you offer me burnt offerings, I will not accept them, neither will I pay any attention to your peace offerings of fatted beasts. Take away from me the noise of your songs; I will not listen to the melody of your viols. Rather let judgment run down as waters, and righteousness as a mighty stream."

Economic injustices of the times provoked the prophet to such sharp warnings as (in chap. 6): "Woe to them that lie down upon beds of ivory, and stretch themselves upon their couches, and eat the lambs out of the flock. . . . that chant to the sound of the viol, and invent to themselves instruments of music, like David; that drink wine in bowls, and anoint themselves with expensive ointments, but are not grieved for the affliction of Joseph."

Another prophet of this period, Hosea, used the vivid imagery of sexual infidelity to warn Israelites of the sin of idolatry that they were committing, and the price that they would pay for it. Likening Yahweh to a husband and Israel to a faithless wife, Hosea (in 2:2ff.) has the Lord admonishing his children thus:

Plead with your mother, plead; for she is not my wife, neither am I her husband [since Israel, by worshiping Baal and other gods, had broken the tie with Yahweh]. Let her therefore put away her whoredoms out of my sight, and her adulteries from between her breasts. Otherwise I shall strip her naked, and set her as in the day she was born, and make her a wilderness, and set her like a dry land, and slay her with thirst [a triple allusion to the birth of Israel in the wilderness, the parching dryness of the barren land, and the death that comes from inability or blind unwillingness to escape from it]. And I will not have any mercy upon her children, for they are the children of whoredoms. For their mother has played the harlot . . . saying, I will go after my lovers, [who] give me my bread and my water, my wool and my flax, my oil and my drink [referring to Israel's willingness to adjust to the ways of the world—particularly Baal worship—in order to gain and increase materials goods].

Therefore, behold, I will hedge up [her] way with thorns, and make a wall, that she shall not find her path [Yahweh intervenes to make it impossible for Israel permanently to continue her infidelities?]. And she shall follow after her lovers, but she shall not overtake them; she shall seek them but not find them. Then shall she say, I will go and return to my first husband, for it was better then with me than now. [There follows now the penalty which Israel must pay for her transgressions.] But she does not know that it was I who gave her corn and oil and multiplied her silver and gold. Therefore will I . . . take away my corn thereof, and my wine in the season thereof, and . . . my wool and my flax which I gave her to cover her nakedness. . . . And I will visit upon her the days of the Baals, when she burned incense to them, and when she decked herself with earrings and jewels, and went after her lovers and forgot me.[12]

First Isaiah and Micah

In the same way Yahweh's prophets in the south spoke of the people of Judah. (Outstanding among the southern prophets was "Isaiah," a term used to refer to what biblical authorities are sure is really two persons, possibly three. The first of the series of two or three wrote before the Babylonian Captivity; the other or others after it.) The first Isaiah (30:8ff.) reports these words of the Lord:

Now go, write it before them on a tablet, and note it in a book, that it may be a witness forever: That this is a rebellious people, lying children who will not hear the word of the Lord;

[12] Adapted from Cook, op. cit., 6:419–22. Bracketed matter added.

who say to the seers, See not, and to the prophets, Prophesy not right things unto us; speak unto us smooth things; prophesy illusions; get out of the way, turn away from the path, speaking no more to us of the Holy One of Israel.

Wherefore thus says the Holy One of Israel: Because you despise my word, and trust in oppression and perverseness, and stay therein, therefore this iniquity shall be to you as a breach in a high wall, whose breaking comes suddenly in an instant. And [the Lord] shall break it as the potter's vessel is broken into pieces. He shall not spare, so that there shall not be found in the bursting of it a sherd to take fire from the hearth, or to take water from a cistern. For thus says the Lord God, the Holy One of Israel: In returning the rest you shall be saved; in quietness and confidence shall be your strength. But you would not, but said rather: No, for we shall flee upon horses. Therefore you shall flee. And you say, we will ride upon swift steeds. Therefore they who pursue you shall be swift. One thousand shall flee at the threat of one . . . till you be left as a beacon upon the top of a mountain, and as an ensign upon a hill. [13]

Isaiah's contemporary, the prophet Micah, spoke in the same manner, in the name of Yahweh:

O my people, what have I done to you? How have I wearied you? Tell me. For I brought you up out of the land of Egypt and broke the shackles of your bondage—that you may know the righteousness of the Lord. [Now you may say:] Wherewith shall I come before the Lord, and bow myself before the high God? Shall I come with burnt offerings, with calves a year old? Will the Lord be pleased with thousands of rams, or with ten thousands of rivers of oil? Shall I sacrifice my first born for my transgressions, the fruit of my body for the sin of my soul? O man, he has shown you what is good; for what does the Lord require of you but to do justly, to love mercy, and to walk humbly with your God? [14]

A NEW VISION

Jeremiah and Second Isaiah

At the time, the adjurations of the prophets went unheeded. The northern kingdom fell under the fury of the Assyrian legions; later Chaldea conquered the southern kingdom. Nonetheless the words burned deeply in the Jewish conscience. Later they served to create an attitude of God-centeredness that made the Hebrews not only a unique people but a light for many nations in the ages that followed. For if the ninth- and eighth-century prophets did not construct ethical monotheism, they substantially prepared the way for it; and in the sixth century their southern colleagues perfected it.

Preeminent in this creative achievement were the labors of Jeremiah and the second Isaiah. In their statements we find reflected the full essence of ethical monotheism. For example, in Jeremiah:

Come back, O backsliding children, says the Lord, for I am married unto you, and I will take you, one of a city and two of a family, and I will bring you to Zion. And I will give you pastors according to my heart, who shall feed you with knowledge and understanding. And it shall come to pass . . . in those days that people will not ask after the ark of the covenant [merely a thing of wood]. They shall call Jerusalem the throne of the Lord, and all the nations shall be gathered unto it, in the name of the Lord. . . . [15]

And in Isaiah, as he speaks in the Lord's name:

---

[13] Cook, op. cit., 5:189–90.

[14] Ibid, 6:629–30.

[15] Cook, op. cit., 5:344–45, an adaptation of Jer. 3:14–17.

Let all the end of the earth look to one to be saved, for I am God and there is none else. I have sworn in righteousness that unto me every knee shall bend; every tongue shall swear. People shall say, surely in the Lord have we righteousness and strength. To him all men shall come.[16]

This triumphant call may seem inconsonant with the actual conditions of the times. Jerusalem had been sacked, the Temple destroyed, the people themselves (though not all of them) taken captive into a strange land. Earlier their nation had suffered disruption, and their northern kinsmen had been dispersed. How, then, could a triumphant note be struck?

Changing Concepts of the Universe and History

In the exilic period, despair was rejected out of the Jew's response to a new prophetic and priestly vision. Fundamentally it developed from a fresh assaying of the nature of the world and the meaning of history. For centuries the Hebrews had been content to think of Yahweh as their God who had led them to the Promised Land of peace and plenty. Other regions, other peoples, other gods, to say nothing of the cosmos in its entirety, interested them very little. Yahweh had covenanted with them; that was enough. Now, captives in a foreign land, surrounded by strange institutions and practices (*after*, it must be kept in mind, the experiences and implications of the Exodus), the Jews were forced to rethink their previous cosmology, if it could be called that, and the meaning of historic existence.

From this reevaluation the world took on for them greater and more varied dimensions. Jerusalem did not disappear from, or cease to be important in, their hopes; but it no longer constituted the only meaningful part of the universe. In the same way, their understanding of the significance of historic existence changed. In scarcely more than a century Israel and Judah had been conquered and dispersed. How, then, were they a chosen people? What was the meaning of the Covenant—or of life itself?

Out of the torment of such frank probing came new appreciations and a larger faith. One of the results of this probing, as we have seen, was the fashioning of pure ethical monotheism. Yahweh was not just their God, but the merciful Father of all peoples. Beyond this concept, grand as it was, other understandings developed. Since their peoplehood had been destroyed, the idea of collective moral responsibility was untenable. In its place arose the idea of individual responsibility. One of the greatest of the exilic prophets, Ezekiel, boldly declared in Yahweh's name:

What do you mean by using this proverb of the land of Israel: "The fathers have eaten sour grapes and set their children's teeth on edge?" As I live, . . . you shall never again have occasion to use this proverb. . . . Behold, all souls are mine; as the soul of a father, so also the soul of the son is mine; and the soul that sinneth shall die. But if a man be just and right . . . he shall surely live.[17]

Quite understandably this shift to individual responsibility resulted in reducing the emphasis on political nationalism and its religious significance. It would be going too far to say that the Jews forgot their homeland, or their mystical faith in the high places of Palestine. Nonetheless, salvation no longer rested merely in God-given national sovereignty. Rather it was founded in the Law now made more rigid and elaborate. In short, a spiritual rather than a purely geographical homeland was envisioned. A new order of religious of-

---

[16] Ibid., pp. 246–47, an adaptation of Isa. 45:22–24.

[17] Adapted from Cook, op. cit., 6:78.

ficials, the Scribes, marked out in legalistic detail the features of the new Promised Land.

New Concepts of God and Man: Job

Equally important was a new insight gained concerning man's understanding of the ways of God. As the Jews reflected on the miseries that had befallen them they naturally came to ask how a just god could so treat his chosen people. True, more than once they had fallen into backsliding; but always they had returned and repented, seeking forgiveness. Was Yahweh really a god of mercy and compassion? Or had their faith from the time of Abraham been one long elaboration of delusion? Were the good rewarded and the evil punished; or was life shaped by blind chance, by forces indifferent to human welfare?

The vivid drama we call the Book of Job came out of this doleful pondering. It provided believing Jews (and later, Christians) with an answer that seemed, however grim, to be consonant with divine nature and human misery. Briefly the answer was this: such questions are not true questions; finite man has not the right so to interrogate his infinite creator. God, although present in every living second of every life, is also far removed from man, transcendent, altogether holy. "My thoughts are not your thoughts, saith the Lord." Man may indeed propose, but God disposes; it is not for us to demand explanations. What seems to be fortuitous, unjust, or even malicious must be accepted in a faith larger than our reasoning can ever make sense of. And with this man must be content. If one objects, "how can human beings live sensibly and rationally without eternally putting questions?" Job implicitly replies, certainly man must question, but the questions and hoped-for answers must lie within the scope of human understanding. Man has not formed his faith out of nothing, but rather out of actual, meaningful experience. It is unreasonable to frame questions which deny the reality of this experience. So long as you are man, do not play God.

Zoroastrian Influences

It is difficult to believe that such profound and extensive changes in religious thought came from Jewish experience and introspection alone. Earlier we noted the development of Zoroastrianism in Persia, a development that soon spread into many parts of Mesopotamia, including Babylon. Certain influences from this religion, with which the Jews rubbed elbows for so long, almost surely made themselves felt. For example, the doctrine of death and judgment—eschatology—figures little if at all in the religious thought of the Jews before the captivity. During and after this period it came to play a substantial part in their thought. Since Zoroastrianism emphasized this doctrine, one must believe that the Hebrews borrowed from their captors. Thus we find second Isaiah speaking of the Last Day, when "the glory of the Lord shall be revealed, and all flesh shall see it together." When we come to study the rise and development of Christianity, this and other loan ideas will be considered more fully.

Climaxing the eschatological content of the Hebrew's exilic faith (although not itself deriving altogether from Babylonian influences) is the idea of the suffering servant who finally reconciles sinful man to his sinless creator. Pre-exilic and exilic experiences not only had taught the Jews that Yahweh was not alone theirs, but the world's God; it confirmed their conviction that they were a chosen people. But "chosen" took on added significance. Now it meant that by virtue of both their special insights and their sufferings, the Jews were to serve as the vehicle of universal redemption. Singled out by Yahweh as his special servants, the Hebrews were privileged to apprehend before all other peoples the Lord's majesty and love. But by the same token they were destined to experience hardships and sufferings by which they—and vicariously through them, all mankind—ultimately would be saved.

The Messianic Promise

Finally, some of the prophets came to believe that one person rather than the whole nation would mediate salvation for mankind. One suffering servant, "of the seed of David," would take unto himself all the sins of mankind and atone for them. In other words, he would be a Messiah, once

> despised and rejected of men, a man of sorrows and acquainted with grief. And we hid, as it were, our faces from him; and he was despised, and we esteemed him not. Surely he has borne our griefs and carried our sorrows . . . he was wounded for our transgressions and bruised for our iniquities. The whole of our chastisement is upon him, and by his stripes we are healed.[18]

But there were other leaders who rejected the notion of a "personal savior" either for themselves or for their people. They continued to believe that Yahweh's word, given first to them, but destined ultimately to reach all mankind under a refashioned Hebrew tutelage, would redeem every sinful creature who cherished it.

Released from captivity when the Persians conquered Chaldea, most of the Jews in exile returned to Palestine. With them they took their reformed religion and entrusted its administration to the Pharisees, their priestly caste. A few centuries after their return one group of this chosen people believed that in Jesus their deliverer had appeared, and Christianity was born. Most, however, continued either to look to the future for their Redeemer or to counsel faithful observance of the Covenant's terms against the day when the Lord's will and way prevailed universally. For them and their coreligionists today the Redeemer is still the Promised One.

[18] Adapted from Cook, op. cit., 5:267–68.

Selected Readings

Frye, Richard N. *The Heritage of Persia.* London: Weidenfeld and Nicholson, 1962.

> *The first three chapters constitute one of the most useful summaries in English of the origin, political development, and economic and religious life of the greatest empire of pre-Alexandrian ancient times.*

*Gaster, Theodor H. *The Dead Sea Scrolls.* Garden City, N.Y.: Doubleday & Co., Anchor Books, 1956.

> *Although now somewhat outdated by more recent studies, this book is the best single source for undergraduate study of the famous scrolls. Nine-tenths of it is devoted to the scrolls themselves and notes explaining and interpreting particular passages. The 30-page introduction is marked by scholarly insights, bold interpretation, and good humor.*

Harden, Donald. *The Phoenicians.* New York: Frederick A. Praeger, Publishers, 1962.

> *One of the multivolumed series* Ancient Peoples and Places. *Its topical treatment of Phoenician history includes consideration of the homeland of the Phoenicians, their colonies, religion, towns, industry, and art.*

The Interpreter's Bible. Vol. 1. Nashville: Abingdon Press, 1952.

> *The section entitled "The Old Testament World," by William F. Albright, contains a summary account of the ancient Near East from prehistoric man to Alexander's conquest of the Persian Empire. Much of it is now outdated, but the work is still valuable, for it is studded with excerpts from ancient sources as they bear upon historical interpretation. The section "The History of Israel," by Theodore H. Robinson, is both simply and soundly written.*

*Meek, Theophile James. *Hebrew Origins.* New York: Harper & Row, Publishers, Harper Torchbooks, 1960.

> *A scholarly account, although in places somewhat controversial, of the beginnings of the Hebrew people, law, conception of God, priesthood, prophecy, and monotheism.*

Moscati, Sabatino. *The Face of the Ancient Orient.* Chicago: The University of Chicago Press, 1960.

> *Chapters 5 and 6 give concise, informative, and well-written accounts of the Hittites, Hurrians, Canaanites, and Arameans. Generous excerpts from ancient sources clearly outline the values and habits of these peoples.*

Moscati, Sabatino. *The World of the Phoenicians.* Translated by Alastair Hamilton. London: Weidenfeld and Nicolson, 1965.

> *An account of Phoenician civilization from the invasion of the "Sea Peoples" (about 1200 B.C.) to the advent of Hellenism. As a product of careful scholarship and vivid presentation it is rewarding in its entirety. If a limited time is to be given to it, probably the best chapters to read are those on art (4 and 11). Here one finds a set of illustrations combined with textual explanation that make this people and their times—as well as the peoples they had commercial and social intercourse with—stand out clearly and "in the round."*

Mylonas, George E. *Mycenae and the Mycenaean Age.* Princeton: Princeton University Press, 1966.

> *This is an updating of the author's earlier* Ancient Mycenae, the Capital City of Agamemnon *(1957). After 233 pages of text on Mycenean citadels, grave circles, shrines, the author's view of the meaning of Mycenaean culture, and a 20-page epilogue on "The End of An Age," the reader is treated to about 40 pages of excellent illustrations. A useful two-page chronology immediately follows the epilogue.*

Olmstead, Arthur T. *History of the Persian Empire.* Chicago: The University of Chicago Press, 1948.

> *The standard English work on the ancient Persians. Although somewhat out of date, its full treatment of almost every element of this civilization makes it required reading for anyone who would become closely informed on affairs of the Achaemenid world.*

Oppenheim, A. Leo. *Ancient Mesopotamia.* Chicago: The University of Chicago Press, 1964.
> *Chapter 3 contains essays on Babylonian and Assyrian history*

*Orlinsky, Harry M. *Ancient Israel.* Ithaca, N.Y.: Cornell University Press, New York, ca. 1954.
> *A summary history of the Israelites from their origins to the post-exilic period. Especially interesting when used in conjunction with Meek's book.*

Parkes, Henry B. *Gods and Men: The Origin of Western Culture.* New York: Alfred A. Knopf, 1959.
> *Chapter 4 is good for an overall view of Near Eastern imperialism.*

Pritchard, James B., ed. *Ancient Near Eastern Texts.* Princeton: Princeton University Press, 1955.
> *See especially pp. 120–159 (Hittite and Ugaritic myths, epics, and legends), 199–207 (Hittite treaties), 274–301 (assorted Assyrian documents), 499–506 (Canaanite and Aramaic inscriptions).*

*Smith College Studies in History. *A Land Called Crete.* Northampton, Mass.: Smith College, 1967.
> *Five essays, of which the last three are especially worthwhile: one on changing opinions concerning Minoan influence on the mainland, another on the decline and death of Mycenean culture, and the last on Homer and the Dark Ages.*

Asterisk (*) denotes paperback.

CHAPTER III
Aegean and Greek Civilizations

A. Crete — CRETAN CIVILIZATION

Pivotally situated vis-à-vis three continents, blessed with a mild, salubrious climate, and large enough to hold a sizable population, Crete was ideally endowed to cradle one of the early civilizations of the ancient Near East. But it was not until our own century that archaeologists uncovered evidences of its extraordinary achievements. Even now, after the diligent labor of two generations of scholars, our understanding of its nature and significance is provokingly fragmentary.

From the absence of paleolithic artifacts we must conclude that the first migrants came to the island only some six or seven thousand years ago; we cannot be sure from where, nor what routes were used. For about 2000 years the settlers enjoyed and suffered experiences common to other food-gathering societies. From caves they graduated to round adobe huts and then, for some, to squarish houses of unworked stone. Like other peoples of this period they used tools of stone or bone. In later centuries they imported obsidian from neighboring islands from which they shaped hard cutting instruments and arrowheads. Throughout this early period they practiced little agriculture, relying upon hunting, fishing, and stockraising for their livelihood. Their pottery, although polished, was crudely formed as were the many statuettes they modeled to represent fertility goddesses and other divine beings.

Cultural Achievements

After 3000 B.C. a series of migrations, the causes of which are little understood, reshuffled populations in many parts of the Near East. Various tribes from the Balkans, it seems, moved south into the Greek mainland. Farther south and east other groups, of Mediterra-

founded, Cyprus was inhabited, and various Syrian cities formed trade connections with Egypt. Moreover copper was discovered, an achievement that soon marked, for this region, the end of "neolithic" culture. For Crete the overall consequence of these developments was an upward civilizing thrust that eventually set it off as one of the most advanced regions of the ancient world. Pottery decorations reflected a refined and subtle sense of line and color; stone and ivory carvings showed an acutely sensitive taste. Many tombs, yielding their secrets in recent years, contained precious objects of art and other items denoting an advanced standard of living. Pictographic writing, herald of a later linear script, was introduced, inspired perhaps by Egyptian hieroglyphics. Other evidence clearly indicates that Anatolian influences bore heavily upon receptive Cretan culture.

In the following millennium, which, as we have seen, witnessed the flowering and fading of the Old Kingdom in Egypt and the rise and decline of Sumer and Akkad in Mesopotamia, Crete sustained a steady advance in the arts that civilize. Further "immigration explosions" pushed new groups from Asia and Europe into northern and central Greece and the offshore islands to the southeast (see map, left). Other groups made new settlements along the western fringe of Asia Minor. The resulting increase in volume and tempo of trade naturally benefited Crete, where, because of its location, many lanes of commerce tended to converge; moreover the introduction of bronze further improved its position. Tin, the alloy which when combined with copper produces bronze, was chiefly obtainable from the farther north and west—from the Cornish tip of England, from Gaul and Spain, and from western Italy—although some was got from peoples in the Caucasus regions. Lying between the sources of supply on the one hand and markets on

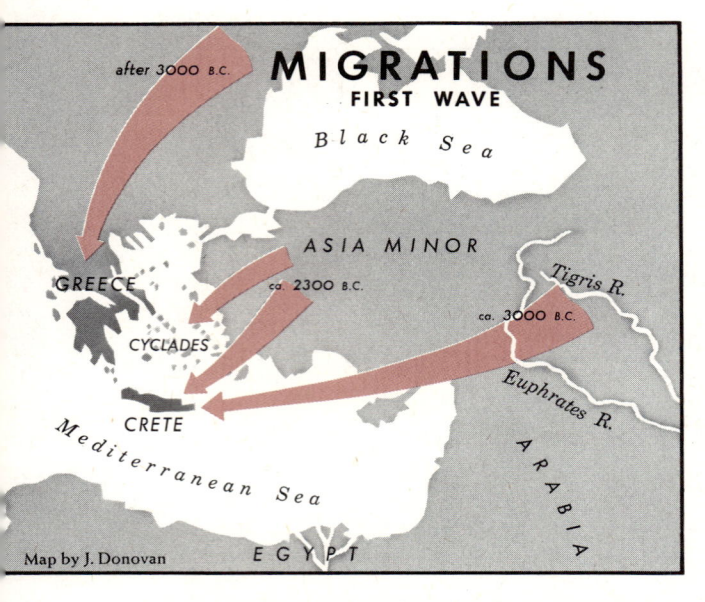

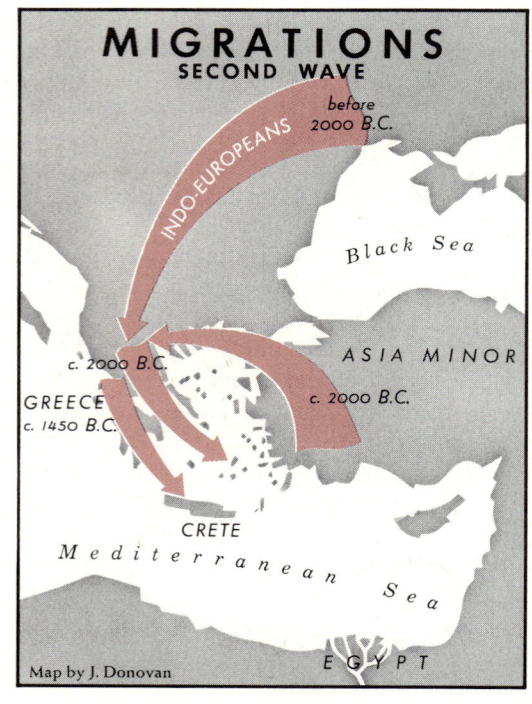

nean stock, migrated to Crete, the peninsula, and its islands to the east (the Cyclades; see map, above). The first settlements at Hissarlik (later Troy) were

100   Aegean and Greek Civilizations

the other, Crete became both an exchange center and a producing workshop. Thus nurtured by commerce and the cultural forces that flow with it the Cretans became, by 2000 B.C., the dominant sea people of the Mediterranean world.

For centuries thereafter the nature and achievements of their civilization were rivaled only by the Hittites and Old Babylonians and surpassed, if at all, by the resurgent Egyptians (during the Middle Kingdom and Empire periods). Whether or not Crete's capital city, Knossos, is "the parent city of Western civilization" is doubtful. But the claim suggests something of the enduring significance of this civilization. The apex of its development was reached about 1700 B.C. and was sustained for nearly 300 years. Then, about 1450 B.C., Mainland Mycenaeans, as these early Greeks are called, conquered the island and brought to an end the independent, autonomous Cretan society that had flourished for well over a thousand years. Sources supporting this view will be given in a later section dealing with Mycenaean society.

Palace Political System

In their own right and because collectively they constituted an important link between the old world of the Near East and the new Western world to be patterned by the Greeks, the chief features of this society are worth examining.

Of the governmental apparatus of earliest Cretan society not much is known. For the first thousand years, it is supposed, the population was grouped into clans, each dominated by its elders. Among the clans there seems to have been no close association. Later two cities—Knossos on the northern rim of the island and Phaistos on the southern—seem to have vied for cultural (and political?) predominance. Eventually Knossos triumphed. For a while (shortly before 1700 B.C.) it appeared that the triumph might be short-lived, for achaeological finds clearly show the almost complete destruction of the city's palace buildings. About a generation later, however, a new and grander palace complex (including the legendary Labyrinth?) was constructed under the supervision of a new dynasty established, perhaps, by Minos.* Within a remarkably short time a ramifying bureaucratic system emerged that provided centralized controls hitherto lacking. Doubtless many cities retained a modicum of self-government; but there can be little doubt that local chieftains were subservient to the central government when the latter did not appoint royal governors in their places.

The king gradually gathered into his hands not only political power but also dominant religious authority. To these power categories still a third was added, for available evidence makes it plain that the rulers soon became the country's foremost entrepreneurs. They owned the large workshops that produced such articles as porcelain ware, beautiful—and expensive—pottery, and various commodities wrought from precious metals, often embellished by exquisite jewel inlays. Thus by the seventeenth century an effective political system, at once close-knit and wide-ranging, dominated by the palace and centered in Knossos undergirded a substantial portion, if not all, of Cretan society.

Economic and Religious Life

Economic support for this system—as well as for the general societal fabric—

* We do not know whether Minos was the personal name of the first king of this dynasty or whether it was his title. In any case, this word and its variant forms are commonly used by archaeologists to designate Cretan society generally.

Cretan Snake Goddess.

came from agriculture and trade in agricultural products. The wooden plow, the bronze sickle, and the extensively found *pithoi* (grain receptacles) amply testify to common and continuing cultivation of the soil. But great wealth, such as was needed to support the kingdom's advanced urban culture, was channeled through the ports and landing quays that circled the island. Important exports were oil (from the ubiquitous olive), wine, luxury items from the workshops of metalsmiths and ceramic factories, finely wrought tools, and weapons produced by armorers unexcelled throughout the Near East. In exchange the Cretans imported foodstuffs, ivory, and heavy stone from Egypt; porphyry, amber, and obsidian from nearby islands and the mainland; tin from the farther west, and various luxury items from Asia Minor and Mesopotamia.

Because of agriculture's dominant role in the economy, it generated both the basic force and the dominant forms of this society's religious life. The central figure in Cretan religion was the Mother Goddess, creator and sustainer of all life. Extant figurines emphasize her lifegiving breasts, cupped in her hands, or resting on her folded arms, or bare and thrust forward. One signet relief shows her seated under a sacred tree, breasts supported with one hand, while with the other hand she holds aloft a floral symbol, receiving offerings from two women and a young girl. In other scenes she is shown holding coiled snakes; or between rampant lions; as "Our Lady of the Sea"; or in the form of a bird. Although supreme, she was not the only divinity. Lesser male gods were worshiped, especially one whom, according to the conjecture of some authorities, the later Greeks called Zeus. Whether the later Zeus or not, he was given noble anthropomorphic features. Sometimes he was represented as an animal, particularly the bull, and at other times as a man, when he was invariably and quite naturally Minos. Occasionally he assumed the features of both and hence became the Minotaur who, according to later Greek legend, demanded from time to time the sacrifice, in his elaborate Labyrinth, of specially chosen Greek men and maidens. In Greek mythology the Mother Goddess tended to merge into Hera or Demeter; sometimes with the Eileithyiae, goddesses of childbirth. Other Greek amalgams of earlier Cretan folk faith included Ariadne, who successfully supervised Theseus's journey through the labyrinth, and Dionysos, son of Zeus.

For many centuries ritualistic worship of the goddesses and gods took place in natural settings—on hilltops, or on "slopes from which fruitful waters splashed," or in caves. Sacrifice of animals, especially bulls and boars, constituted the central rite. Others included the parade of acolytes and worshipers before priestesses who received offerings and bestowed benedictions on behalf of the goddesses whose surrogates they were. Later, men took part in the cult rites, but never on a par with women. Holy festivals, some of which were later taken over by the Greeks, celebrated special occasions such as the vernal equinox and the harvesting of the olive crop. On such occasions religious dances and long processionals marked the Cretan effort to propitiate divine powers and invoke their aid. As with the festive days, some of these liturgical exercises were later incorporated into Greek religious practices.

Humane Character of Cretan Society

Cretan society, then, conformed to the general pattern of all ancient societies: religion subsumed and supported it (quite normally without possessing any real ethical content). In certain other respects, however, it differed from the common pattern. In contrast to Asian and African societies, for example, it did not fortify its cities or maintain large armies. It is true that its efficient and well-equipped navy controlled the sea. But even here commerce and self-defense were prime considerations rather than imperial aggrandizement, although by 1770 B.C. Crete probably possessed an empire of sorts. The place of women also set it apart. We have already noted their prominence in religious affairs; in other activities they played an active part, quite in contrast to the habits of the average home-hidden female of ancient times. Of course women did the work of the home. But they felt—and were—free to leave it for other pursuits as their interests and means might prompt. They participated, for example, in the hunt, in chariot races, and in acrobatic exhibitions, particularly as bull-leapers and occasionally as pugilists.* Although the archaeological evidence is slight, from what there is we may suppose that woman's legal position was strong. Her position in the home certainly was.

Moreover, Cretan life in general seemed to be relatively free of constraint and class-stratification. Certainly we cannot claim that Cretan civilization was characterized by substantial economic and political equality. There were the very rich and the very poor; but it seems that the contrasts were less sharp than in other Near Eastern societies. And one may speculate that the Cretans enjoyed a sense of "release of energy" to a degree unmatched by any people before the Greeks.

Art

Conditions of openness and creative energy are reflected in Cretan art, which, although derivative, excelled that of any of its contemporaries. In Egypt and Mesopotamia the artistic genius of man abundantly showed itself, but it was devoted almost exclusively to the glorification of rulers and gods. For the Cretans "art extends to everything and to all men. . . . At table they want jugs and cups of graceful form adorned with brilliant painting or fine engraving. They like to see about them the play of oblique light in their rooms, and, on the walls, the lively images of all that pleases them in nature and increases their joy of life."[1]

Diggings reveal, particularly at Hagia Triada, the refined sensitivity and master craftsmanship that enabled the Cretans to paint large mural scenes that capture the

---

* For a fuller description of feminine life in Cretan society see Gustave Glotz, *The Aegean Civilization* (New York: Alfred A. Knopf, 1925), pp. 142–45, from which the above statements are drawn.

[1] *Ibid.*, pp. 303–4.

Chieftain Vase.

Octopus Vase.

élan of life. Multihued flowers and plants frame the movements of animal and human figures caught in arresting postures—bounding rabbit, crouching wildcat, treading bull; dancing women and kneeling priestess. Other compositions, especially in the palace at Knossos, vividly portray the activities and atmosphere of court life or grandly reproduce the majestic Minos. Perspective was never really mastered, and almost to the end the island artists retained certain Egyptian stylistic conventions (for example, frontal shoulders atop a body turned sidewise). But, overall, Cretan art was adaptable and esthetically satisfying.

In contrast to the masters of fresco painting, with their grand designs, Cretan sculptors almost invariably produced creations of diminutive dimensions. Whether working with relief or in the round the typical artist turned out objects that for delicacy, imaginative treatment, and technical craftsmanship, were hardly equaled in the ancient world. A good example in relief is the Chieftain Vase. Here a king is represented receiving homage from a vassal accompanied by troops. Circumscribed by the severe space limitations of an object just over three inches high with a circumference diminishing from top to bottom, the artist managed to portray the full significance of the ceremony. At the same time, he could work in such intricate detail as the king's "triple necklace reaching from shoulder to shoulder." A civilization must necessarily have long since passed its adolescence before such a masterpiece of artistic conception and execution can be produced. Other sculptures depict animal scenes such as the wild goat with its young and representations of men and beasts. But it was in the ceramic arts that Cretan genius found its fullest expression. By 1800 B.C. potter-painters were turning out ware exquisite in symmetry, line, and color. Rich

Aegean and Greek Civilizations

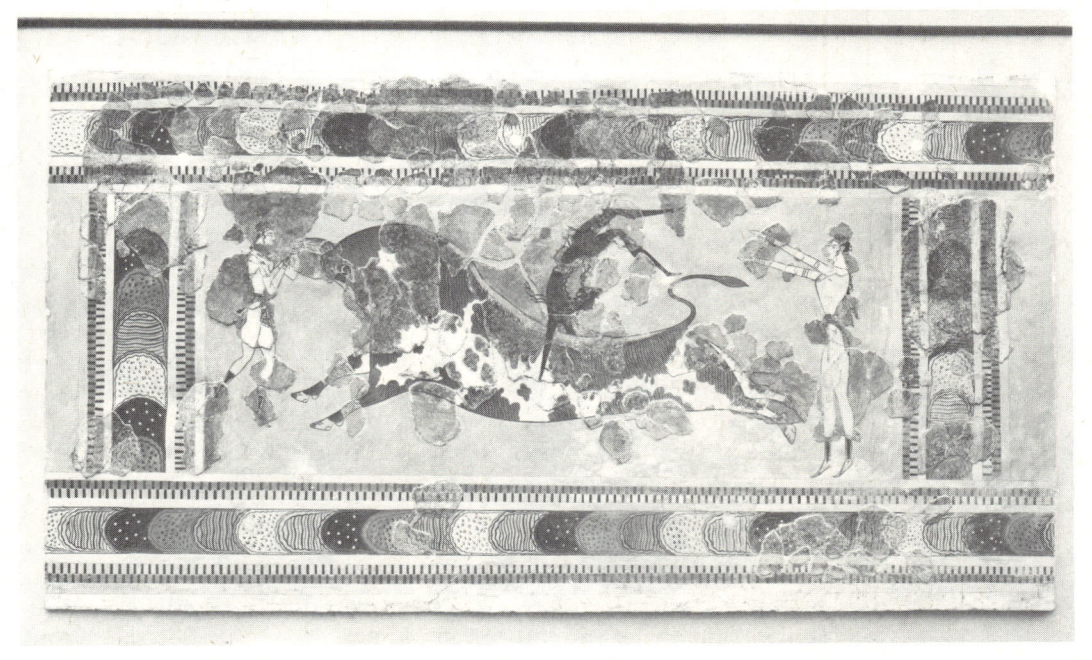

The Toreador Fresco from Knossos

contrasting colors were combined with sinuous spirals to decorate vases whose swelling curves were at once voluptuously bold and demurely alluring. One could almost say that the Cretan vase, in its disciplined exuberance and refined élan, symbolized the essence of Cretan civilization.

Language and Literature

So much can be said of Cretan art because many examples of it have been unearthed in the island and throughout the Aegean world. Unfortunately the same cannot be said of this people's language and literature. Indeed, to date no remains of its literature and little of its language have been found. It is true that many seals, stones, and jars show inscribed characters, hieroglyphs or ideograms suggesting Egyptian (or Anatolian?) influence. But so far no one has been able to read them. In addition, excavations have brought to light two scripts, labeled by Sir Arthur Evans simply as Linear A and Linear B. The latter, discussed in the section treating of Mycenaean civilization, has been deciphered and found by many authorities to be archaic Greek. Linear A is certainly Cretan, but no cryptographer has yet succeeded in forcing it to yield its secrets. We know that it was used at least as early as 1700 B.C. (and the hieroglyphs, of course, still earlier). Linear B (if we accept the predominant expert opinion) was adapted from it for use by Mycenaeans when those early Greeks invaded, and for a while ruled, the island kingdom (ca. 1400–ca. 1200 B.C.).* But we cannot safely go beyond these few and relatively barren facts. The next chapter in Cretan history must await another triumph by the philologist.

* See p. 108.

105   A. Crete

B. The Greek Way: Phoenix

MYCENAEAN HEGEMONY

The Coming of the Greeks

As we have seen, Cretan civilization shaped and sustained its greatest glories in the period ca. 1750—ca. 1450. Not long before, an Indo-European-speaking people had pushed probing settlements into the northern portion of the Peloponnese, mixed with the native population, and gave increasing indications of making its presence felt in the wider Aegean world. The Greeks had arrived.

Because our civilization traces many of its roots to the Greeks we have given long and close study to this people (who eventually came to call their land *Hellas* and themselves *Hellenes*). We are tempted to think of them as a special breed. Certainly to some they appear as a race of giants whose magical genius sparked into existence, out of practically nothing, a brave new world compounded of political democracy, profound philosophic constructs, the scientific attitude, and a unique and unsurpassed art and literature. The actual historic record does indeed confirm brilliant achievements in all these fields; but the further grand and sweeping generalizations it must leave to the panegyrist. As accepted by most historians, the record is silent, for instance, on the question of a "special breed." Nor can we say with confidence who the "original" Greeks were, or from where they came. As for creating out of the void, they did nothing of the kind. We know, for example, that the Mycenaeans borrowed generously from the whole Aegean world, including the Syro-Palestinian coastal civilizations, and particularly from the Cretans. The classical Greeks did indeed, as this statement implies, work great changes in their Mycenaean heritage; but it is important to keep in mind the distinction between cultivating a heritage and creating a way of life *de novo*.

So we need, at the outset, to place the creative genius of the classical Greeks in historical perspective, lest their later glory blind us to the way of truth they themselves so stubbornly cherished.

Ionian Greek culture of the seventh and sixth centuries B.C. reflects the interaction between East and West. Epic poetry arose among the Greeks of Asia at a time when European Greece was narrowly provincial and relatively inarticulate. We must overcome our long habit of attributing systematic, rational thought, and orderly classification of data to the Greeks alone and reconsider our notion that the achievements of the Egyptians and Babylonians had been wrought more or less haphazardly. These generalizations imply that somehow the Greeks were a unique people. They were not. They were different, they were gifted; but they were not superhuman. What may make them seem so is essentially a matter of their appearance in time; they came into history when conditions were ripe for their talents.[2]

[2] T. S. Brown, *Ancient Greece* (New York: Free Press, 1965), p. 5.

"The glory that was Greece" is solid in its own right; it does not need the fancy ideas and the fancier phrases of the rabid Hellenophile.

Whoever they were and from wherever they came, the original Mycenaeans—sometimes called Achaeans, the first of a series of "waves," to be followed by Dorian tribes—were a primitive people (see map, p. 116). When they came down into the peninsula they were illiterate, unsophisticated in their religious concepts, crude in artistic skills, uninformed in the arts of husbandry, and suspicious of the sea that lapped around them. But they were bold and energetic, eager to learn.[3]

[3] Compare Hammond, op. cit., p. 39.

Absorption of Cretan Culture

Accepting the twentieth century B.C. as the period of their emergence into the peninsula, we may say that they spent the first three centuries acclimatizing themselves to their physical and cultural environment (see chart, above). From the indigenous population with whom they mingled they learned the peasant's craft. Climate, soil, and terrain did not encourage grain cultivation, so they became, as did those before them, cultivators of the vine and the olive tree. From Cretan seamen and settlers they learned of the sea routes and ports of the Aegean world and how to construct and maneuver ships. Either by peaceful trade or—more commonly in the early centuries—by piratical

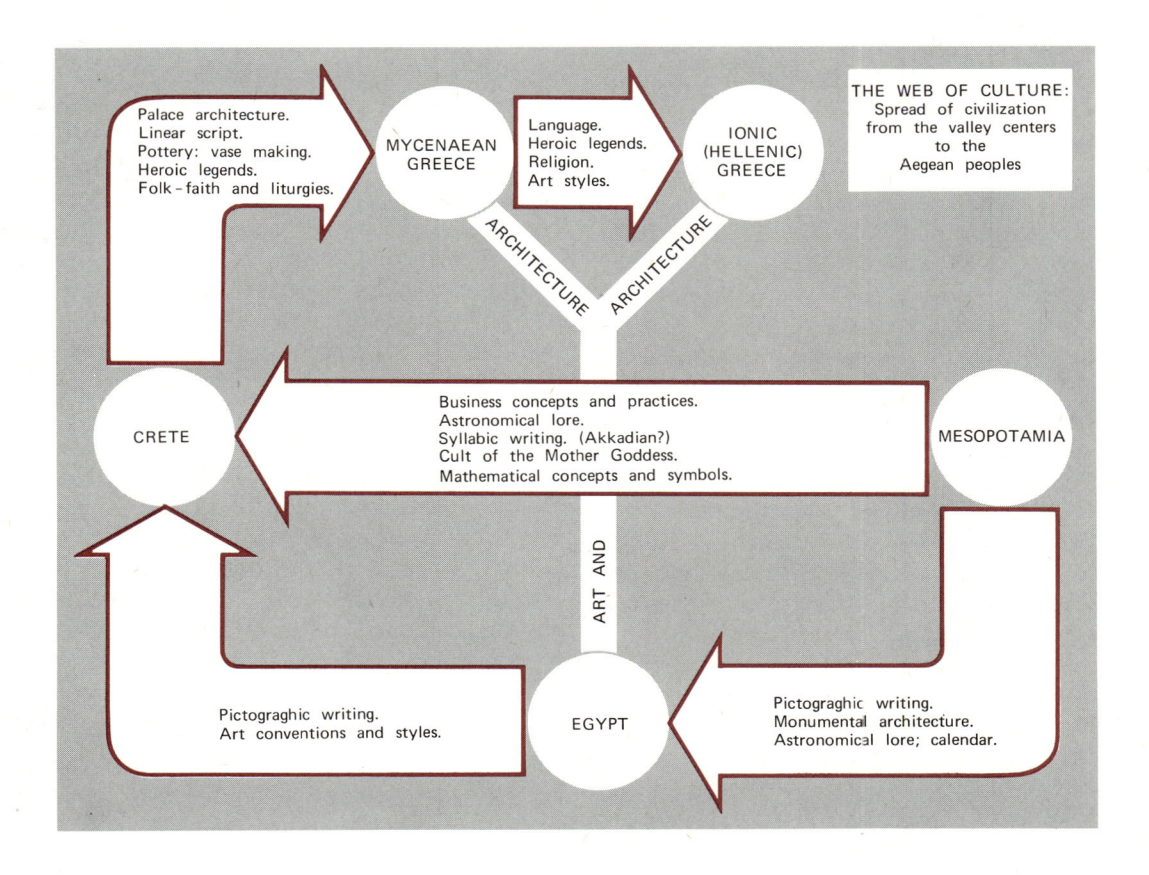

THE WEB OF CULTURE:
Spread of civilization from the valley centers to the Aegean peoples

MYCENAEAN GREECE
- Palace architecture.
- Linear script.
- Pottery: vase making.
- Heroic legends.
- Folk-faith and liturgies.

IONIC (HELLENIC) GREECE
- Language.
- Heroic legends.
- Religion.
- Art styles.

ARCHITECTURE

CRETE

- Business concepts and practices.
- Astronomical lore.
- Syllabic writing. (Akkadian?)
- Cult of the Mother Goddess.
- Mathematical concepts and symbols.

MESOPOTAMIA

ART AND

EGYPT
- Pictograghic writing.
- Art conventions and styles.

- Pictograghic writing.
- Monumental architecture.
- Astronomical lore; calendar.

B. The Greek Way: Phoenix

raids they obtained grain and other necessities from more favored peoples around them, particularly those scattered along the southern littoral of the Black Sea and from the states of western Asia Minor. By 1600 B.C. they had made the Peloponnesus their own, fashioned a viable economy, and formed numerous politically well-organized urban centers (for example, Mycenae, Tiryns, and Pylos).

In this period Cretan civilization had reached its peak. For the next 200 years (ca. 1650—ca. 1450) Greek cities frankly and fully exposed themselves to the influences of this civilization. If, centuries later, the Western world went to the School of Hellas, it but followed a precedent set by the Greeks themselves. They learned the arts of vase and pottery making, ivory carving, and fresco painting. They copied the bureaucratic patterns set by Crete and Hatti to make their own religious institutions effective.

Although the matter is still not definitively resolved, it appears that Cretan scribes taught the Greeks how to write. But the newcomers preferred, naturally, to write in their own language. For many years archaeologists believed that certain tablets found at Knossos by Sir Arthur Evans in 1900 were inscribed with Minoan signs. They called the writing "Linear B." Nearly four decades later many similar tablets were found on the mainland, first at Pylos and later at a number of other sites of ancient Mycenaean cities. Scholars' suspicions that the writing was not Minoan were strengthened when Michael Ventris, an amateur cryptographer, successfully deciphered the script in 1952 and declared it to be an early form of Greek writing. Evidence indicates that the new written language was constructed around 1400 B.C.

Meanwhile Mycenaean seamen and merchants had learned the craft of maritime commerce so well that by the fifteenth century they had usurped the position held by their teachers. Henceforth, until the 1100s Greek ships and Greek traders were predominant in the Mediterranean. In short, their energetic, steady advance in material power and cultural refinement apparently led them to challenge, around 1450 B.C., the whole structure of the Cretan thalassocracy. Archaeological and philological evidence may point to Mycenaean control of Knossos itself around this time, in which case the challenge was successful.

The next two centuries (ca. 1400—ca. 1200 B.C.) marked the full flowering of Mycenaean culture. Magnificent many-roomed palaces were built and richly furnished. Walls of the more important rooms as well as of the traditional great hall (megaron) were often covered with frescoed murals. Some basic structural forms were borrowed from Crete, as was the plain round column with its base slightly smaller than its top, where a large circular capital rested. Elaborate beehive tombs (designated *tholos* tombs) housed royal remains. "So excellent was the construction of one of the latest (built around 1330 B.C.), the corbel dome of the so-called 'Tomb of Agamemnon,' . . . that this chamber has survived intact to the present day. To stand within this chamber and peer into the dim heights of its vaults . . . is an impressive experience. The technical skill and excellence of workmanship . . . make it one of the outstanding architectural achievements of antiquity."[4]

Reference has already been made to the Mycenaean use of loan-gods. But it should not be supposed that the Greek religious fabric was of a piece with the Cretan. It is true that in both of these the Mother Goddess was supreme, but already male divinities—Zeus and Poseidon, for example—were showing challenging strength. Dionysos (and

[4] J. Walter Graham, "Mycenaean Architecture," *Archeology* 13, no. 1 (Spring 1960): 48–49. The date of the construction of this tomb lies more probably in the thirteenth than the fourteenth century.

perhaps Apollo) appeared early. Increasingly, too, Mycenaean religious thought tended to move the gods closer to man—or man closer to the gods (a tendency that, in classical Greece, became a fixed pattern).

The Hellenic practice of establishing colonies along the rim of the Mediterranean derived from Mycenaean precedent. The Ahhijava people, for example (in the Levant?), were settlers from the Mycenaean mainland, so large and powerful that they have been called "a power second only to Egypt and the Hittites."

Decline of Mycenaean Civilization

Probably the political and cultural center of this early Greek civilization was the city of Mycenae itself. Evidence suggests that its king exercised a kind of control—how loose or strong we cannot say—over other princes such as those ruling in Pylos, Knossos, Athens, and Argolis. Under his leadership various military campaigns were conducted, including, quite probably, the attack on Troy around 1220 B.C. In all likelihood the main objective of the attack was control over trade routes along the western coast of Asia Minor. For long the Acheans had made substantial profits from commercial relations with peoples of coastal Asia. One region in the central area, however, had been excluded by reason of Hittite dominance. When Hittite strength ebbed in the late thirteenth century B.C., two contestants vied for "business rights" in the region—the Achaeans and "Trojans." Quite likely it was this economic motivation—and not the abduction of a mainland queen—that caused a Mycenaean king to rally his princes for a showdown. In the war that followed Troy was destroyed and with it, presumably, the restrictions to commerce. But the Greek victory was an empty one, for within a generation or so Mycenaean civilization underwent rapid deterioration.

What caused the flourishing Mycenaean culture to fade so quickly and so completely? Here again the experts disagree. Four events—perhaps combining fortuitously—seem to bear major responsibility. One was a series of devastating intercity wars. Authorities do not know what precipitated this particularly catastrophic fighting. Many cities were wholly or partially laid waste. Also, in the 1200s certain "Sea Peoples," whose original homes were probably in the Balkan and eastern Mediterranean areas, conducted widespread raids throughout the Aegean world. Some hired out as mercenaries for various states then involved in disastrous wars, particularly the Hittites, Egyptians, and Phoenicians. Their sea raids and later land migrations throughout this area, especially in Asia Minor and Palestine, created pressures that caused other groups in turn to move about and themselves become "Sea Peoples."

The resulting vacuum brought anarchy into the region. As a consequence, orderly commercial relations, on which the prosperity of the Aegean world by now depended, were destroyed. Quite naturally the web of Mycenaean civilization was torn and weakened.

Shortly thereafter (in the late 1100s and throughout the 1000s) a fourth disruptive force thrust its way into the sundering Aegean world. For reasons again unknown, a crude but vigorous tribe of Greeks from the northwest, the Dorians, spilled into the Mycenaean and Cretan lands, conquering and destroying as they came. Caught between destructive pressures from both the East and the West, and visited by economic stagnation and international chaos, Mycenaean civilization collapsed. To escape from poverty and invaders alike many mainland Greeks migrated eastward: to Attica (where, according to probably reliable tradition, Athens was spared invasion); to the south-central fringe of Asia Minor; to the islands lying off it. Eventually these mass migrations to, and resettlements in, what came to be called Ionia contributed to the shaping of classic Hellenic civilization. In the meantime, however, many generations of Aegean peoples retrogressed into a shadowy world of subsistence living, little literary activity, and dimming memories. In this way a new Dark Age, not unlike that out of which it had emerged 1000 years before, blacked out Mycenaean civilization.

THE IONIAN RENAISSANCE

People and Places

But this so-called darkness was compounded of dawn as well as of dusk. For the new settlements based their transplanted, cruder life on past, although currently diminished, achievements and on dim but persistent memories of earlier glories. Moreover the disintegration of the Hittite state gave almost unlimited opportunities for creative reconstruction to the bewildered refugees who streamed into the political vacuum. The burden of ancient, binding customs was shed. Although admittedly far-fetched, the analogy of Puritan America is worth considering: migrating Englishmen in the seventeenth century of our era left their homes and settled in a land so institutionally unencumbered that they could raise, almost as they pleased, their City of God. In much the same way refugee Greeks settled in an area so far from the centers of oriental despotism—although not so far that the fingers of culture could not reach them—that they were free to construct, eventually, their own City of Man.

Each dialect-tribe selected that portion of the coastal fringe which the logic of geography dictated. Many Mycenaeans (Achaeans) joined with the Aeloians to settle the region between the Hellespont and Ionian coastal settlements; some associated themselves with pioneering Ionians in treks either to the Cyclades or to the coast directly to the east. Aeolians, from Thessaly and Boeotia, settled along the northern strip from Troy to Smyrna, while those Dorians who did not choose to remain in their newly-won Laconian base occupied areas along the southern coast (see map, p. 116). Hellenic history* thus began, "in the night of the eleventh, tenth, and ninth centuries," not in Hellas but in Asia Minor. (Athens, which for unknown reasons seems not to have been overrun by invaders, is an important exception to this generalization.)

Almost certainly these displaced Greeks, and for that matter the mainlanders from whom they parted, had no notion of the glories to come. Although the art of writing may not have been forgotten, it was so little used that, until Homer, we have virtually no literate records. For several generations at least, pottery decorations also reflected cultural retrogression: the intricate and skillful designs in Cretan and Mycenaean times from plant and animal life were but crudely imitated. The record is too scanty to give more than a general picture, but as such it tends to show scattered and insecure migrant groups feeling out new lands and neighbors. From these they sought social and psychic satisfactions towards which their traditions and genius pointed.

Conditions prevailing for the next several centuries invited a cultural renaissance. After the decline of the Hittites and Egyptians there existed no great power capable of securing domination over the newcomers. Moreover their nearest neighbor of substantial size, Lydia (from

---

* As distinguished from the earlier Mycenaean phase of Greek history. The Greeks, it may be added, did not call themselves by this name (which comes from a later Roman designation). Sometime around 1000–900 B.C. they took to referring to themselves as Hellenes, and their collective lands as Hellas. Before this they probably called themselves Achaeans.

ca. 800 on), stood as a buffer between them and potential aggressors. In addition to serving as a shield this state made significant cultural contributions to the coastal colonies: coinage, art motifs, and astronomical data. Other peoples, especially the Phoenicians, siphoned off the lore of older Mesopotamian cultures and, through trade and travel, fed it into Greek life. They also taught the fringe communities new secrets of the sea as an exploitable avenue of commerce and colonization. Most importantly, they developed alphabetic writing, which the Greeks eventually adapted to their own language (chiefly by adding vowels).

For nearly a half-millennium (ca. 1050—ca. 550 B.C.)—until an aggressive Persian empire emerged—the Greeks thus enjoyed advantages that allowed them to fashion the fabric of a revitalized civilization. Nor were mainland Greeks unaffected by these developments. For throughout most of this period Athens, as well as other cities in western Greece (especially Ionian and Aeolean cities), maintained close and continuing relations with their Asian brothers.

The spade of the archaeologist will one day undoubtedly turn up sufficient evidence to fill in the details of the Ionian renaissance. Until then, however, we must rely mainly on Homer's two epic masterpieces, the *Iliad* and the *Odyssey*. We know that the material of both poems had a long oral tradition before being given literate, artistic expression (probably about 750 B.C.)* Mycenaean minstrels sang of manlike gods and godlike men, weaving historic fact into heroic legend. Athena's winning ways with Odysseus, the ambitions, conflicts, and conquests of mighty lords, and, later, the story of Achaean (Mycenaean) destruction of haughty

---

* The Homeric questions—Was there really such a poet? and if so did he write the Greek epics?—are too confused and too irrelevant to be considered here. Scholarly consensus tends to confirm Homer's historicity and his authorship of the *Iliad*. Most scholars believe that another poet, or other poets, wrote the *Odyssey*. Here the phrase "Homeric poems" is used as convenient rhetoric.

Warrior Vase from Mycenae. This detail depicts soldiers going off to war; their helmets are similar to those described by Homer.

B. The Greek Way: Phoenix

Troy—these and other themes, sifted and refined by generations of critical acclaim, were organized and given unity by the genius of Homer. There can be no doubt that much of the eighth-century Homeric epics quite faithfully described late Mycenaean society. For example we read in the Odyssey:

And Meriones gave Odysseus bow and quiver and a sword, and on his head set a helmet made of leather, and with many a thong was it stiffly wrought within, while without the white teeth of a boar of flashing tusks were arranged thick set on either side, well and cunningly, and in the midst was fixed a cap of felt.

No such headgear as Homer thus describes was used in his own times. But "just such a helmet was discovered in a tholos tomb of Dendra in the Argolid."[5] Homer also describes bronze weapons, war chariots, and gold cups of a certain style that were not common in his own day, when iron had come into use. Moreover the poet refers to flourishing cities that by the eighth century B.C. were but dust and ashes.

Political Organization

Political organization was composed of a loose but viable societal structure of which the family was the basis. Throughout a good part of the eleventh century B.C. it was in many cases the core if not the whole of the village. As the genealogical chain lengthened, clusters of blood-related families came to constitute the clan, which, in its turn, formed one part of the tribe. Lands conquered by the ever-fighting communities were plotted into estates by the king and distributed by lot to families who could cultivate their allotments but could not dispose of them.

[5] J. B. Bury, *A History of Greece* (London: The Macmillan Co., 1959), p. 51.

From the *Iliad* and the *Odyssey* we can discern the outlines of early political developments that eventually led, in the Periclean age, to the patterns perfected by Athens and Sparta. We learn that the citizen-body—the Assembly (originally a military institution)—periodically met to indicate by its acclaim or silence its attitude toward propositions which, affecting the general populace, were presented to it by the king. It is true that the ruler was not bound by this expression of citizen opinion. But then, as now, a lack of community morale could render nugatory arbitrary dictation; so that that king was rash indeed who continually ignored popular sentiment. It is, for example, difficult to imagine Agamemnon going ahead with plans for the attack on Troy had he not had active support from his citizens (that is, the soldiers) of Mycenae and allied communities. To advise him on policy the king relied on a council of elders made up of prominent members of the most powerful clans. These favored aristocrats were the real political power in the budding city-state; from about 850 B.C. on (to ca. 600 B.C.), they gradually edged out the king completely. (In Sparta and a number of other Dorian cities this pattern was not followed; the contrasting systems, as they finally developed, are discussed on pp. 117–126.)

Religion

Into the socioeconomic warp of Greek life the woof of religion was closely threaded. Much has been made, and should be, of the man-centered nature of Greek society. But it is a careless assessment of that society which leads to the conclusion that the Greeks were godless humanists. By the middle of the sixth century and increasingly in the fifth century B.C. inspired poets (who, contrary to Hebrew and Roman experience, shaped the national religion) pictured human life as bounded by divine justice. Around 545 B.C. Theognis, by his very questioning of this justice, revealed how central to Greek thought the concept was:

Dear Zeus! I marvel at thee, Thou art lord of all, alone having honor and great power; well knowest thou the heart and mind of every man alive; and Thy might, O King, is above all things. How then is it, son of Cronos, that thy mind can bear to hold the wicked and the righteous in the same esteem, whether a man's mind be turned to temperateness, or, unrighteous works persuading, to wanton outrage.*

In the period immediately preceding the Ionian renaissance, as earlier, the gods were conceived as more interested in acts of propitiation than in human efforts to live the good life. But it would be a mistake to think of them as given over wholly to capricious frolicking, unconcerned with human endeavor. In the *Iliad* they are revealed as intimately involved in the plans and activities of both the attackers and defenders of Troy. Zeus, it is true, was neutral, but Hera, his consort, was forever intervening on behalf of the Achaeans, while his son Apollo was as busy on the other side. Although in a different way and to a different degree from the Hebrews, the Greeks were a god-conscious people.

In the beginning their religion was probably based on the simple, human recognition of "Otherness" in life.† Like other peoples, the Greeks encountered frustration and hurt and emptiness; and when they did, they sought surcease or help from the elemental force or forces that had brought forth creation. Gradually they constructed a complex of religious concepts designed to allow them to live in happiness and in harmony with the necessities of existence, that which would benevolently link them with the "Other."

In this effort they borrowed symbols and ideas from various peoples, particularly the Cretans. But to borrowing they added insights and inspirations of their own. By the time of the period that we are now considering (500s B.C.), the fundamental features of their religion had developed somewhat as follows. In the beginning there was chaos out of which *moira* (destiny or fate) brought order. Although the Greeks were, across the centuries, to modify many other features and articles of their religious faith, this concept remained basic and inviolate. It clearly indicates the rationalistic bent of Greek religious thought. The gods may act by whim; mortal men may be foolish or wise; but neither gods nor mortals could alter the basic structure and slant of the Cosmos (the Greek word for order). This, of course, did not mean that men could not probe the secrets of the universe. Indeed, an abiding cosmic imperative ordained this very probing, the aim of which was always to bring man and order into alignment and a harmonious relationship. Such an attitude and such probing, as one scholar has pointed out, necessarily invited man "to contend with the Angel." The call of the heroic haunted the Greek and prompted him toward self-realization and self-enlargement. From this nagging prod came his greatest achievements. But from it, too, came brokenness and tragedy, for the line between enlargement and aggrandizement is hard to draw and still harder to honor in the actual give and take of life. Part of the price of the achievement of power is resistance to the temptation to abuse it, to confuse the created with the creator, and hence to arrogate to the human self superhuman attributes. From wisdom, later acquired, such great Greek tragedians

---

* Quoted by André Bonnard, *Greek Civilization*, 3 vols. (London: George Allen & Unwin, 1957–61), 1:149. If the authorities who assign the date ca. 500 B.C. to Job are right, it is interesting to note how parallel, in this instance at least, were the current religious concepts of the Hebrew and the Greek.

† That is, a force, or forces, beyond, and greater than, the "natural" phenomena of this world. Compare Bonnard, op. cit., 1:133.

This is one of the finest "black figure" paintings of the archaic period. The artist, using the black silhouette technique, shows Achilles, that busy warrior, slaying Penthesilea. Both figures are set off with exquisite engraved detail.

as Aeschylus, Sophocles, and Euripides spent their genius in laboring this theme —the delusions of *hubris* (pride) and the sufferings endured from the inevitable visitation of *nemesis* (retributive justice.)

The Homeric Gods

In the centuries that cradled the Ionian renaissance, however, this subtle refinement of religious thought had not yet developed. The *Iliad* hymns the praises of the aristocratic warrior-hero, the *Odyssey* those of a hero's conquest of the sea and its perils and the obstacles separating man from country and home. In both the gods are present and prominent: Zeus, son of Cronos, whom he deposed as the "Sky-God"; his sister and wife, Hera; Poseidon, god of the sea; Hades, ruler of the underworld, and his consort Persephone (Core); Demeter, goddess of fruitfulness; Apollo, "Archer-King" and patron of poetry and music; Athena, "Patroness of the Arts and Crafts" and goddess of wisdom; Aphrodite, goddess of love (and mother of Aeneas, mythical founder of Rome); Ares, god of war; Artemis, goddess of the chase; Hephaestus, god of fire and "Master of Crafts"; and Eileithyia, goddess of childbirth (sometimes referred to in the plural).

These and other gods made up the pantheon of divinities that ruled over the Homeric Greeks. Recognized by all Hellenes, whether in Asia Minor, the Cyclades, or the mainland, they served to impart a feeling of unity, of national identity. It should be pointed out, however, that each village, large or small, had its own local god who often played a more prominent part in the villager's life than the major figures named above. The community or clan chief acted also as chief priest, so that no strict hierarchy of religious officers ever evolved. Nor did dogma or official creed develop. Thus in religious as well as in secular affairs the Greek propensity for independent inquiry was encouraged.

Political Particularism

Out of the darkness of their times of troubles there emerged (by the 800s and 700s B.C.) the pattern of a resurgent Greek society. By this time Greeks of the Asian coastal fringe islands and mainland, fed by the experiences, observations, and in-

In this detail an artist is shown painting a garment on the god Hercules. The artist is using a technique called encaustic, which involves daubing on colored wax that is later heated to a high temperature.

ventions of the old societies of the East, had knit together the basic elements of a new civilization. Reborn commercial contacts also stimulated cultural reconstruction. Contributing to it further was the Greeks' creative response to their (once) new milieu and to their own ancient traditions and folk-memories.

Undergirding this emerging civilization was a growing realization that they were a "peculiar people." They might and did admire other peoples, especially the Egyptians, Lydians, and Phoenicians. Or they might look down upon ethnic groups (such as the Cimmerians from the Caucasus region, who had not developed the advanced tastes and insights that they themselves enjoyed). But whether others were admired or scorned, all were called "barbarians," that is, peoples whose speech was cacaphonic noises—"bar-bar-bar"—to their ears; or, more simply, as the outer world of non-Greeks.

But if new glories beckoned, new ills beset them too, interlaced with the ancient and abiding evil of political particularism. For in spite of the dawning consciousness of ethnic and linguistic bonds and of a common core of traditions, the Greek city-states found then, as later, the obstacle of disunity too great to overcome. Geography at least partly accounts for this fatal tendency to reject genuine and lasting union. The Greek mainland is a maze of mountains the ranges of which (unlike our American ranges) follow no simple pattern but instead crisscross the whole peninsula. Settlements were necessarily made in scattered pockets cut off from one another. Here the *poleis* (plural of *polis*, "city-state") developed, each nurturing a parochial pride that sharpened the paradox of their common Greekness. Athens, Sparta, Corinth, Thebes, to name but four of the hundreds of city-communities, could indeed arrange joint proj-

B. The Greek Way: Phoenix

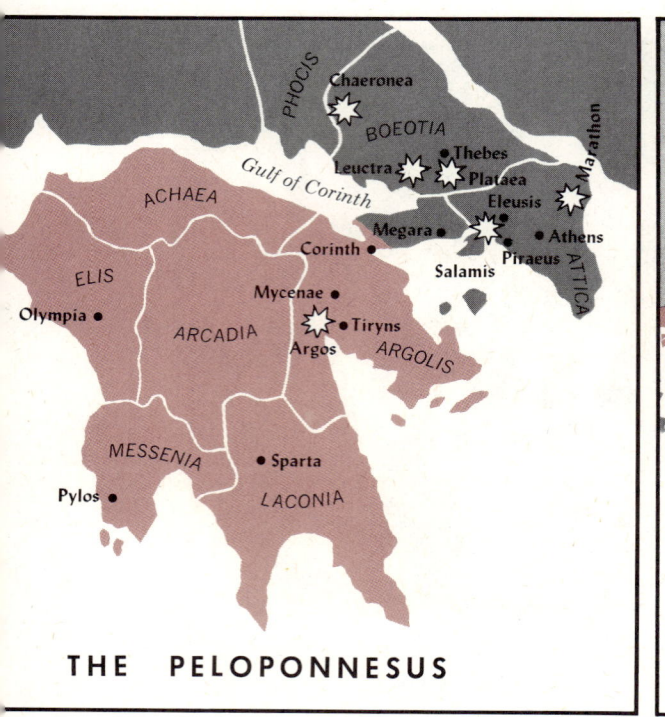

THE PELOPONNESUS

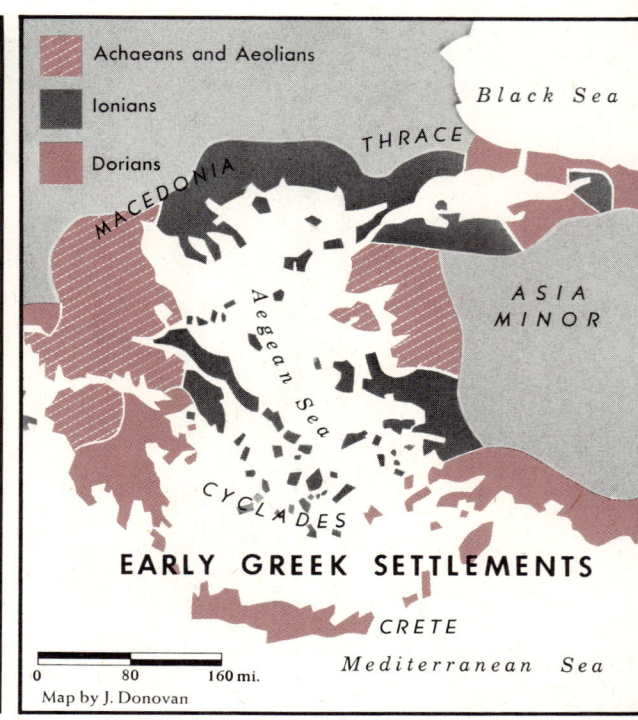

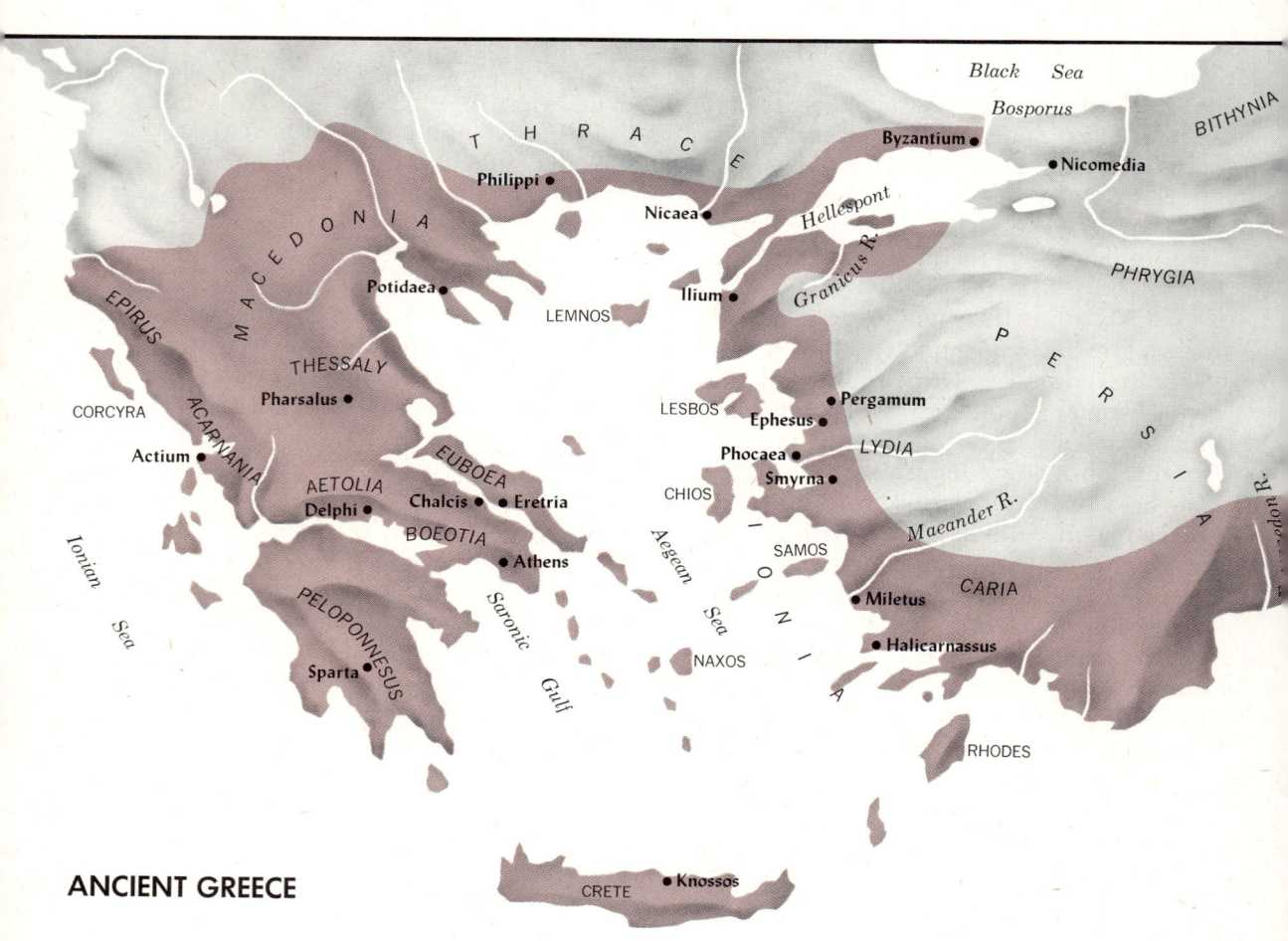

EARLY GREEK SETTLEMENTS

- Achaeans and Aeolians
- Ionians
- Dorians

Map by J. Donovan

ANCIENT GREECE

ects such as the Olympic games (instituted in 776 B.C.) or the religious festivals at Delphi. In the face of great danger from abroad they could merge military units in common defense, as in the Persian Wars—but even then, only with the greatest reluctance, and only temporarily. To examine in detail the great divergence among the Greek states, as well as to consider their intrinsic significance, we now turn to the development of two states that stood out above all others—Athens and Sparta.

ATHENIAN SOCIETY

Long before the Persian Wars the Athenian community had revealed the promise of coming greatness. It will be remembered that it had been spared the fierce thrusts of the Dorian invasion (in the eleventh century B.C.). By that time, too, it had probably spread beyond its original site, nestling in the valley of three mountains and protected westward by the sea, to include a fair part of the Attic sub-peninsula. The natural advantages of the original polis certainly made it easy for its early kings to absorb surrounding villages and to grow in outward strength and inner substance. But we must guard against the temptation to conclude, as we consider the later flowering of the Greek, and particularly the Athenian, genius that the conscious ultimate aim was the creation of a Greek nation-state, or the shaping of "one great community of enlightenment and beauty." At no time in the whole of Greek history did either such aim influence the course of events.

Social Factors: Economic and Political

Even so, for a very long time the lot of the average Athenian was a hard one. Attic soil in many regions was thin and had over the centuries wasted away; in some areas it was tillable only at the barest subsistence level. Moreover the better soil had long since been preempted by leaders of the stronger clans—by the Eupatridae, the aristocratic "beautiful and good." With good bottom land—the Plain—thus out of reach, the commoners retreated to the hill country to scratch for themselves what living they could. Some, commanding more energy and talent than others, abandoned agriculture altogether and took to the sea as sailors or traders; others, in time, turned to artisan crafts. Ultimately there developed in this way three social classes: the aristocrats of the Plain, the peasants and laborers of the Hills, and the commercialists and artisans of the Coast.

Like many another polis, Athens by the seventh century B.C. had substituted the rule of the landed few for monarchy. Technically, all citizens, save for the lowest class, had the franchise and could theoretically help shape national policy as members of the Assembly, or *Ecclesia*. In actual practice the latter was powerless before the wealth, prestige, and talents of the landlords. The Council of Areopagus, with its members selected from the lords, in reality made all law and policy. Executive officers, called *archons* (originally three, later nine), administered priestly, judicial, and military affairs.

Around 630 B.C. an abortive attempt by a certain Cylon to set up a tyranny* favorable to the commoners failed. The common people were still too ignorant, too gullible, and too insecure to form an effective followership. To forestall the evolution of such a movement the aristocrats in 621 B.C. appointed one of their own class, Draco, to set down the law in writing—an obvious move of appeasement. The Draconian codification may appear to modern eyes as a sorry sop indeed to the grievance of the little man.

---
* For an explanation of this much misunderstood title and office, see page 129.

One item, for example, provided the death penalty for cabbage stealing; others were of such severity that "Draconian" came later to describe all harsh, retributive legislation. Nonetheless an advance had been made. Severe though it was, the law was at least known and beyond capricious whim. Moreover clans were denied the right to inflict punishment on members of other clans suspected of capital crimes.

Solonian Reforms

Even so, little had been done to meet the rising restiveness of the yeomen, traders, and artisans.* The yeoman, unable to compete with the great landlord, necessarily assumed an increasingly heavy mortgage burden. The landless laborers drifted into slavery as they found themselves unable to pay off—at increasingly high interest rates—their inevitable borrowings. And the artisan suffered hardship when more and more of his markets and profits came under manipulation by the governing agrarian class. But once more Athenian aristocrats, prodded by moderates arguing that reform would forestall revolution, saved some of their power by agreeing to share it. In 594 B.C. Solon, aristocrat by birth, wealthy merchant by profession, and poet by avocation, was asked to revise the city's constitution.

His archonship proved a turning point in Athenian history. The rule of the masses, he believed, would invite anarchy; the continued exploitative rule of the landed few, bloody chaos. He therefore chose a middle course. Tempering rather than destroying class distinctions, he decreed the abolition of slavery for debt. Since the law was made retroactive, the debts of thousands were canceled. He further set bounds to the size of estates,

* But it should not be thought that traders and artisans constituted important classes in Athens at this time.

making land by sale available to many. To bring down commodity prices he decreed the prohibition of agricultural exports, olive oil alone an exception. Coinage reform was effected as were measures designed to improve trade. Foreign artisans were granted easier access to citizenship. To the *Thetes*—the lowest citizen class—he opened membership in the Ecclesia. Perhaps most significantly, he created the *Heliaea*, popular courts whose members were chosen by lot. With this innovation the commonest of the commoners could participate in the actual administration of justice. Another decree made any retiring magistrate accusable before the popular courts and thus amenable during his administrative career to a measure of popular control.

In addition a new body—the Council of Four Hundred—was created to prepare legislation for submission to the Ecclesia. For membership in the former, comprising 100 representatives from each of the four tribes, all citizens except the Thetes were eligible. Thus the stature of that citadel of noble control, the Areopagus, was considerably diminished. The new power bloc was now made up of the wealthy; in short, timocracy was substituted for the aristocratic rule of the well born. To modern Americans this may not seem much of an enlargement of the political good life. To Athenians it was a substantial enlargement of that life. A man can make money; he cannot make ancestors.

Obviously the ruling happy few were dealt a severe blow by these reforms. Whenever and however it could, the Plain faction sabotaged the new regime. And those of the Hill also felt aggrieved, insisting that the reforms had not gone far enough. Nor was the Coast altogether satisfied. The nobles, they felt, had been let off too lightly while the commoners had been granted undue advantages. So the new constitution, although undoubtedly preparing the way for more democratic

118   Aegean and Greek Civilizations

institutions in the future, left so many groups dissatisfied that a season of turmoil blighted the nation. The Coast people, steadily growing in economic power as trade and manufacturing prospered, especially resented those (few) aristocratic controls that the Solonian reforms had left intact. A modern American analogue may be found in the ongoing contest waged between cosmopolitan areas such as New York and Chicago and their rural hinterlands. The Hill people too expressed growing discontent with their alleviated but still rather desperate plight. In short, Athens's day of the "tyrant" had come.

Pisistratus

Twice before finally establishing himself in power, a new leader, Pisistratus, made attempts to capture political control (in 560 and 559 B.C.). Each time the Plain and the Coast forgot their differences long enough to combine against him. But in 546 B.C. "the peoples' champion," himself an aristocrat, came back to stay until his death nearly twenty years later. Highly gifted in the art of persuasion, well endowed with leadership qualities and supported enthusiastically by the commoners, Pisistratus wrought important changes in the Athenian way of life. Recalcitrant nobles were sent packing, their confiscated estates distributed among the Hillsmen. Loans to newly settled commoners were made easy and interest rates held down, resulting in a genuine measure of agricultural stability. Athenian trade was given added impetus by the seizure and occupation of Sigeum, an Anatolian port close to the Hellespont that dominated a large share of East-West commerce.

With both the nobility and the rich merchant class held firmly in check, the more democratic features of the Solonian constitution were given new emphasis. Although Pisistratus's candidates invariably seemed to win key political positions (reminding us, perhaps, of the consistent success of officially endorsed candidates in the Soviet Union today), the *demos*—the people—were increasingly reminded that they were the real power of the state. This steady emphasis, fructifying the principle that when an image is strongly presented over a long period of time the odds are great that semblance becomes substance, helped eventually to produce a really democratic life.

Unsatisfied with mere politico-economic reforms, far-reaching though they were, Pisistratus labored to increase Athenian appreciation of the city's spiritual genius and the growing esteem many Hellenes held for it. To this end he fostered the *Panathenaea,* an elaborate festival designed to glorify the polis's protective goddess Athena. Music, athletic contests, and competitive recitations were features of this celebration, to which contestants from all over Hellas were invited. Pisistratus himself established rules for the declaiming of poetry. He also brought to Athens, from a nearby village, the festival of Dionysos. Dramatic works were exhibited at this festival, with emphasis given to the performances of tragedies. (It was from the latter, indeed, that the forms and themes of classic Greek tragedy later developed.) Moreover, recognizing the natural affinity between the Asian Ionian and his Attic counterpart, Pisistratus deliberately fostered the cult of Apollo—a god beloved by all Hellenes—whose principal base had long been established on the island of Delos, lying midway between the mainland and the coast of Asia Minor. Thus by the sixth century B.C. it became easy and natural for Greeks to look on Athens as the spiritual center of the whole Ionian world.

In such ways Pisistratus sought to enlarge the scope and significance both of the individual's existence and of the Athenian role in Greek life. But when he died, in 528 B.C., another time of troubles plagued his people. Pisistratus's successors were more interested in self-aggrandizement than in political and cultural progress.* The populace again grew restive, and, exploiting this situation, the aristocrats made another attempt to reinstate oligarchic rule. For aid they appealed to Sparta, no lover of democracy and long apprehensive of Athenian achievements. For a number of years intrigues and the violence that flowed out of them wracked the nation until it appeared to many that their hard-won gains would disappear in the turmoil of chronic civil strife.

But the taste of democracy and individual responsibility was hard to forget. The commoners were able now, as they had not been a generation before, to discern and discount aristocratic double-talk. They were ready, too, to recognize a leadership that pointed the way to popular sovereignty. The slowly absorbed inheritance of ancient Near Eastern cultures, the centuries-long conditioning of the soil and the sea, the hard lessons of class struggle, the beckoning memories of the Pisistratid interlude—all now shaped a response that could, under the guidance of an able and dedicated leader, flower into a larger life.

Cleisthenes

In 507 B.C. Cleisthenes, by birth an aristocrat, by late (and reluctant) persuasion a democrat, offered himself as that leader, and the commoners accepted him enthusiastically. The reforms that followed were thoroughgoing. The new leader understood that if democracy was to abide, the clan system had to be rooted out of the fabric of Athenian politics. So long as the old classes were left intact—that is, grouped into the four traditional tribes—so would an aristocratic seedbed remain to produce new champions of the old order. So Cleisthenes began with this.

In place of the four tribes he substituted ten geographic divisions that comprised noncontiguous areas in the hill, plain and coastal regions. The people of these areas were thus fused into artificially created districts. The reformation destroyed not only the old tribal divisions but, of course, the provincial clan loyalties rooted in them. What remained of the old blood associations became, in essence, social and religious groups without political power. The old *demes* clannish "townships" remained, indeed constituted the chief local political units. But since they were scattered throughout the ten new geographic tribes, their blood power and economic hegemony were broken.

The Areopagus, or Council of Elders—ancient citadel of aristocratic power—was not abolished. But its remaining prerogatives were transferred to a new Council of Five Hundred,† formed of 50 democratically selected representatives from each of the ten divisions. Among its duties was the preparation of legislation for the Ecclesia, now a power in fact as well as in theory. The members of the latter became truly sovereign since they no longer felt the threat of aristocratic discipline if they disapproved a suggested law. Naturally, the Ecclesia could not remain in continuous session, and since policies occasionally had to be decided upon when it was not sitting, the new council—itself too large for permanent session—appointed from each tribe on a rotating basis a Committee of Fifty to deal with such needs.

The *archons*—judicial, religious, political, and military administrators—continued to be elected by, and held responsible to, the Ecclesia. But within a generation the military archon (the *polemarch*) and many of his administrators had yielded most of their power to new of-

---

* But compare Thucydides *The Peloponnesian War* 6. 54.

† This now superseded the Solonian Council of Four Hundred.

Outline of Athenian Political Structure

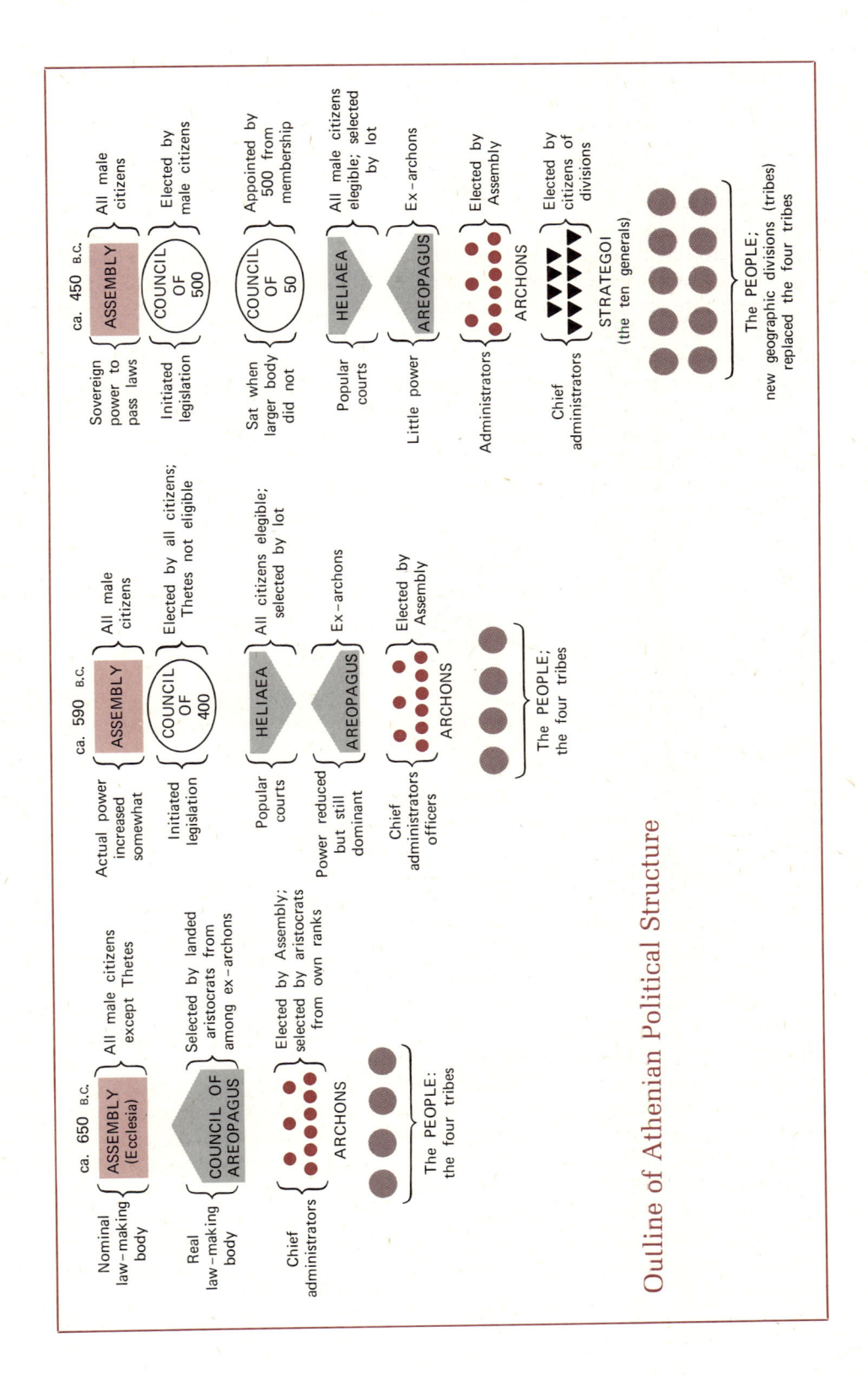

ca. 650 B.C.

- Nominal law-making body: **ASSEMBLY (Ecclesia)** — All male citizens except Thetes
- Real law-making body: **COUNCIL OF AREOPAGUS** — Selected by landed aristocrats from among ex-archons
- Chief administrators: **ARCHONS** — Elected by Assembly; selected by aristocrats from own ranks
- The PEOPLE: the four tribes

ca. 590 B.C.

- **ASSEMBLY** — All male citizens; Actual power increased somewhat
- **COUNCIL OF 400** — Elected by all citizens; Thetes not eligible; Initiated legislation
- **HELIAEA** — All citizens eligible; selected by lot; Popular courts
- **AREOPAGUS** — Ex-archons; Power reduced but still dominant
- **ARCHONS** — Elected by Assembly; Chief administrators officers
- The PEOPLE: the four tribes

ca. 450 B.C.

- **ASSEMBLY** — All male citizens; Sovereign power to pass laws
- **COUNCIL OF 500** — Elected by male citizens; Initiated legislation
- **COUNCIL OF 50** — Appointed by 500 from membership; Sat when larger body did not
- **HELIAEA** — All male citizens elegible; selected by lot; Popular courts
- **AREOPAGUS** — Ex-archons; Little power
- **ARCHONS** — Elected by Assembly; Administrators
- **STRATEGOI** (the ten generals) — Elected by citizens of divisions; Chief administrators
- The PEOPLE: new geographic divisions (tribes) replaced the four tribes

121

ficers, the *Strategoi*. This metamorphosis arose out of two developments. Eventually the archons came to be chosen by lot from a panel selected by the Ecclesia. This practice quite naturally led to a dilution of the quality of such officers. Moreover they were limited to only a year's tenure without eligibility of reselection. Under Cleisthenes each tribe elected its own general, the Strategos noted above. Time and experience proved the latter, more carefully selected and eligible for reelection, to be of distinctly greater competence. Hence the ten generals came to be entrusted with affairs quite beyond their military commands and soon became the state's chief administrators. Logically enough the president of the Strategoi eventually functioned, although without specific legal sanction, as a kind of prime minister. It was in this capacity that Pericles, elected Strategos some 30 times, shaped policies during the great age that bears his name (see chart, p. 121).

Also, whether introduced by Cleisthenes or by some later statesman, there came into use (ca. 485 B.C.) the institution called *ostrakismos* (ostracism). Periodically the Ecclesia gave the citizenry an opportunity to decide whether any, and if so who, among its politicians ought for the state's safety to be sent into exile. Paradoxically, it also served on (rare) occasion to enhance the exiled statesman's reputation. For example, the Athenian assessor who drew up the first tax system for the Delian League—Aristides "the just"; (see p. 170 fn.),—subsequently lost favor with his fellow citizens and was exiled for the maximum period, ten years. Before the period was over, however, sad second thoughts caused Athenians to recall him. Although ostrakismos did not at all take the place of party responsibility—which really never existed in all Athenian history—it did somewhat serve to keep ambitious statesmen from overreaching themselves.

By the early 400s B.C., then, Athens had achieved a substantial degree of democracy. Its laws were sanctioned by the whole (male, free) citizenry and administered and interpreted by democratically selected representatives. Under such leaders as Themistocles, Cimon, Ephialtes, and Pericles, the Attic city-state emerged in the period ca. 480—ca. 430 B.C. as a kind of wonder society. In the south and west Sparta tried several times in the early part of this period to stay Athenian advance, but on each occasion Sparta and its allies received serious setbacks. The art, philosophy, and literature of the age—the Periclean age—we shall presently consider. Altogether, Athenian glory shone so luminously that its citizens themselves were sometimes hard put to take it in.

Despite its power and glory, Athens was, and remained, but a part of Greece. Many another city-state, it is true, came willingly or through coercion under its control. But many did not; paramount among those who stood apart from, and often against, the Attic commonwealth was Sparta.

SPARTAN SOCIETY

Settlement and Conquest

Not much of this community's early history is known. The original Spartans were Dorians who, in the eleventh century, flooded down into the Peloponnesus and settled in a region that they came to call Laconia (or Lacedaemone). From the beginning their view of life and their habits set them off from Achaeans and related Aeolian tribes. We should not, however, wring too much out of this statement. As "Spartans" they "did not live within a charmed circle, exempt from the ebb and flow of contemporary life . . . they shared much the same structure of life" as that of other Greeks.[6] Nor should we think of them as a people set apart by blood or unique genetic qualities. Nevertheless their society showed certain characteristics—strongly and for a long time—which set it apart from most other Greek societies. Although it is true, for example, that many Greek peoples were conservative and rather crude, still Spartans stand out in Hellenic history as proud exemplars of these traits.

Hellenes generally, as we have seen, soon took to the sea, to be molded and shaped by it and by the intercourse that it invited. Spartans too were at first enthusiastic exploiters of marine trade avenues. But, unlike Athens, their interest in the sea declined as they established themselves in the rich Eurotas Valley, took over the choice lands, and imposed upon conquered peoples a distinct and distressing serfdom. In time a number of the valley villages grouped themselves together into a sprawling city-state, which, as Sparta, ultimately brought the whole Laconian plain into one or another form of subservience.

By the eighth century B.C. their numbers had increased beyond the land's productivity, fertile as it was. Other city-states met a similar challenge by turning to trade or colonization or both. Sparta's response was annexation of more alien territory—with fateful results. To the west lay Messenia, broad in expanse and rich of soil; and to this inviting region Sparta turned for living space. The conquest proved far more difficult than the invaders had anticipated. Indeed, if the scanty records are to be relied upon, a full score of years (ca. 737—ca. 715 B.C.) was needed before the conquerors were finally able to divide the land among their own nobility and force the sullen Messenians into serfdom. Even then their hold was anything but strong. For many years the conquered chafed under the yoke and plotted for freedom. Around the middle of the seventh century B.C. they rose in a fierce and long continued revolt (ca. 640—ca. 620 B.C.) that taxed the Spartans to the limit of their resources.

In the end they were able to reimpose control, but the bloody interlude fundamentally changed their way of life. Down to about 650 B.C. the Spartan community had been touched by, and had responded to, the same esthetic impulses that had marked Greek genius elsewhere. Their work in ivories, for example—as early, perhaps, as the ninth century—clearly shows a delicate and refined artistic talent and taste. Poetry and drama, dancing and festivals, had gladdened their days and lifted their spirits. But Sparta, unlike much of Greece as it evolved toward modern manners and outlooks, stubbornly perpetuated traditional habits and attitudes. The long, drawn-out Messenian rebellion led Spartans to believe that perpetual readiness for war was imperative if they were to keep their dominant position in the subpeninsula. There was neither leisure nor incentive for cultivating the arts and refinements that distinguished other Greeks.

Government

So to keep the Messenian serf forever in his place—and for that matter their own—and to prevent another uprising, which might the next time overwhelm the small body of elite nobility, the Spartan aristocrats now turned their community into a garrison state. Every Greek community, then and later, relied on military force to serve its interests when they seemed threatened, as states still do. But under the constitutional "reforms" of Lycurgus* the

---

[6] Chester G. Starr, "The Credibility of Early Spartan History," *Historia* 14, no. 3 (1965): 269.

* Whether Lycurgus was an actual historical figure is unimportant. The new constitution *is* historic, and the Spartans did live under its provisions.

whole of Sparta was turned into a permanent armed camp.

Dating from the village mergers that had made Sparta a city-state, two kings—probably representing the two strongest tribes—had shared royal power. But except during times of war the real power lay in the *Gerousia,* or Council of Elders, made up of representatives of the leading clans. Ostensibly the *Apella*—or Assembly, made up of all citizens—could disapprove laws framed by the council. But the Elder elite exercised almost sovereign powers. The Lycurgan constitution recognized all three of these institutions. In addition it raised from obscurity the *Ephorate,* made up of five nobles who presided over the Apella and exercised judicial functions. It also created the *Crypteia,* or secret police, with functions soon to be described. In effect, the Lycurgan "reforms" froze the class structure and provided instruments to guarantee its perpetuity.

Class Structure and Economic Life

With the final conquest of Messenia, Sparta's serf population (*helots*) came to outnumber the citizen population some fifteen to one. The mere arithmetic of the situation was frightening to the Spartan masters. A fair American analogue may be found in the antebellum South where, in some states, Negro slaves so outnumbered their masters that the latter lived in real and unending fear of servile insurrection. To ensure the military strength necessary to cope with such an uprising, all Spartan children were subjected at birth to physical examination. Babies showing deformities or structural weaknesses were dispatched at once (as often were female infants regardless of their physical condition). Those who later developed deficiencies rendering them unfit for military service were segregated into a kind of second-class citizenship.

Spartan soldier draped in a cloak; his helmet, of the Corinthian type, protects both face and head.

To keep the Helot population permanently cowed, the Ephors annually declared war on them and sent out the Crypteia to do its work. This consisted of routine—and wanton—slaying of such numbers of serfs as would serve to keep the masses in proper subjection. To keep, on the other hand, Spartan war youth in prime condition a fantastic regimen was developed. At the age of seven each young Spartan was taken from his home and directed to join a Youth Pack. There he was subjected to rigorous discipline; for example, going "barefoot in winter . . . clad in a single cloak." In order to develop cunning and daring he was encouraged to forage about the countryside stealing produce from farms to supplement his Pack fare which, for this purpose, was deliberately kept to a bare subsistence level. Successful foraging earned merits which might point to Pack leadership. Detection of his crimes, on the other hand, brought condemnation and demerits. Annually the Packs convened at the Artemis shrine to undergo the ordeal of whipping, when the bravest proved themselves by standing up under the lash after others had fallen or fled. After 12 years of Pack life the Spartan youth was assigned to a barracks where he underwent ten years of drill and general military training. During this period marriage was permitted, even encouraged; but the regimen called for the warrior husband to steal away from barracks for only brief liaisons with his wife.* From the age of 30 to 60 the Spartiate male was enrolled in the regular armed forces, where he participated in endless maneuvers interspersed with campaigns against recalcitrant allies or foreign foes.

Although Spartan nobles were allowed to own private property, much of the land was worked under supervision of the state.[7] Helots, of course, worked the fields, giving to designated nobles a stated portion of each year's yield, illogically demanded in bad times as well as good. Thus members of the warrior caste were assured economic security, although they were prohibited from exploiting the land for personal profit. Under the Lycurgan constitution male citizens were denied the opportunity of engaging in commerce, even when they had reached retirement age. Further, to discourage trade, gold and silver were prohibited (until the 300s B.C.) as media of exchange; in their place cumbersome iron pieces were used.

However such restrictions did not hold for citizens of those city-states that ringed Sparta and had been brought under her hegemony. These "people round about" (*Perioikoi*) were free to engage in any activity they chose; it was therefore among this group that traders and artisans were found. Noninterference even extended to their social and political institutions. Three things only were demanded of them—annual tribute, armed contingents, and acquiescence in Spartan direction of their foreign affairs. On the negative side they were denied Spartan citizenship and even the right to marry Spartan women.

Spartan Hegemony

In this way Sparta, by the fifth century B.C., came to dominate the whole of the Peloponnesus. At the core of its state was the warrior caste. Tilling the soil—and also conscripted for battle when exigencies so demanded—were the toiling

---

* Upon occasion the state sanctioned "breeding leaves" when the soldiers, single or married, were given permission to mate with whatever women were handy, providing only that the latter were Spartan citizens. The marital status of either partner was regarded as immaterial. Compare Bury, op. cit., p. 133, who says of Spartan women, "They were, proverbially, ready to sacrifice their maternal instincts to the welfare of their country. Such was the spirit of the place." Such was the spirit of Nazi Germany too. Himmler, for example, specifically directed his SS elite to breed with whatever good Aryan women they could find; for this purpose leaves were granted even when *Festung Europa* was being encircled by Allied troops.

[7] Bury, op. cit., p. 131.

Helots. Round about, the Perioikoi supplied tools and weapons. States too large or too far away for Perioikoi status were grouped, under Sparta's firm leadership, in the Peloponnesian League. This League, which rivaled the Athenian-led Delian League (see p. 170) included almost all of the flourishing city-states of the Peloponnesus, such as Corinth, Sicyon, Megara, and Tegea. For a brief period even Athens was forced to join the League. With the internal affairs of these League members Sparta interfered not at all; indeed several came to consider themselves rivals of the leader (Corinth, for example). But until the 300s B.C., when the whole Hellenic world crumbled in the violence and aftermath of the Peloponnesian War, none cared to push its claims too far.*

For this position of power, of course, Sparta paid a heavy price. A single war, or even a series of wars, may conceivably stimulate the esthetic talents and impulses of a people; but when war becomes a total and permanent way of life, cultural horizons close down. So it was with Sparta. In all of Greece its warriors were regarded with fear and respect. Its monolithic structure was even admired, eventually, by such philosophers as Plato and Aristotle. But out of such a community come no poets or dramatists, no sculptors or gifted architects, no political theorists or creative thinkers. The garrison state may produce a cultural iron age; it can never give birth to a golden age. And in the end even its warriors may fail as, indeed, did Sparta's.

COLONIZATION AND CLASS STRUGGLE

Power of the Aristocracy

In considering the disparate societies of Athens and Sparta we have bypassed certain developments of Greek society generally. Throughout most of the mainland and Asian coastal regions the "beautiful and the good," as the aristocrats called themselves, had established control by the late 700s. The qualities they prized above all others were blood and land. Possessing these, they believed they had both the right and the duty to oversee the affairs of society.

However under this aristocratic rule the lot of the little man steadily and grievously worsened. Such conditions, of course, were common enough in the ancient cultures of the Fertile Crescent, where binding custom and political despotism had crusted over free play of the human spirit. There the commoner and the slave—the "unbeautiful"—had long since accepted their status as ordained by fate. The Asian coastal fringe and Greece, however, were far enough removed from these lands to constitute a pioneer region. And pioneers are notoriously sensitive to humiliations fostered by static, class-stratified societies. So the little man fought back, occasionally enlisting the aid of the wealthier—but also underprivileged—merchants and artisans, with results that we shall presently examine.

Some notion of the spirit of the times may be obtained from the *Works and Days* of Hesiod (ca. 725 B.C.). The poet's father, it seems, had left his home in Asia Minor to settle in Boeotia (an example of reversal of the migration trend of several hundred years before?) where he hoped to find a way out of his poverty. The piece of land he was able to acquire was diligently worked and with his death duly passed on to his sons Perses and Hesiod. The former received the fairer portion of the estate, a circumstance that undoubtedly contributed to the bitterness that shows through much of the poet's work. In his *Works and Days* he describes five ages of mankind. The first was a golden age, free of evil. The following silver age was "less noble by far." Men of the third period were even more degenerate—"They ate no bread,

---

* There were two exceptions—Argos and Achaea—but neither was able to dominate the League or at any time seriously to threaten Sparta's leadership.

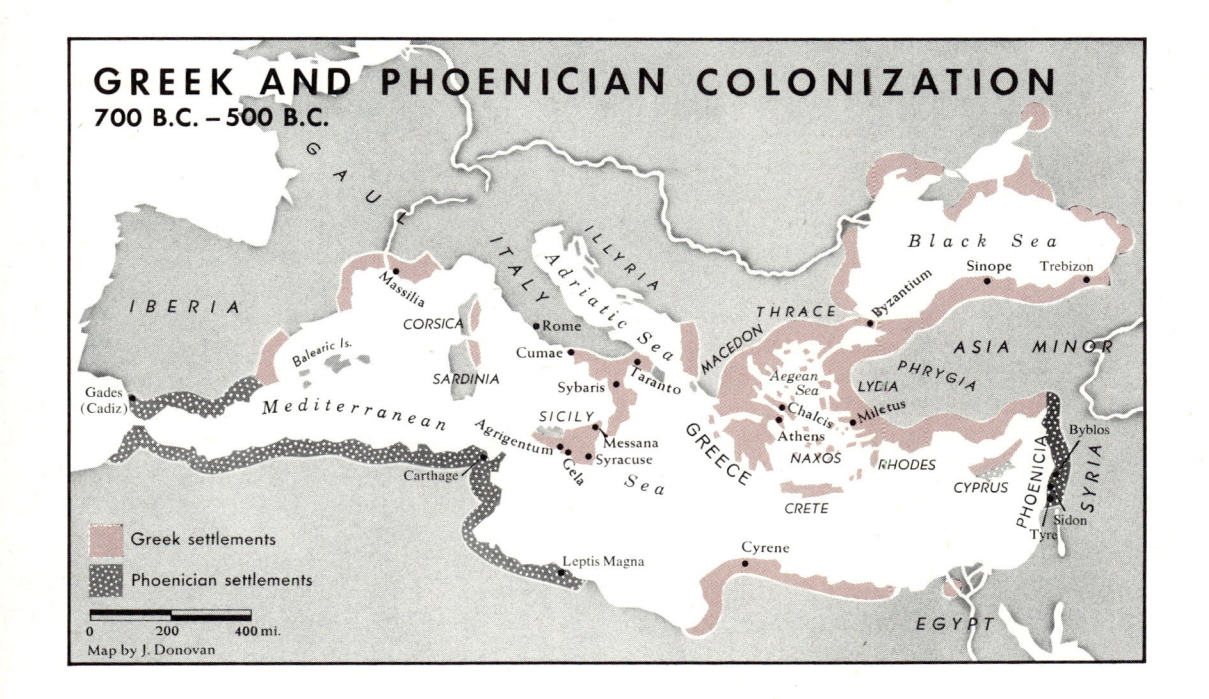

GREEK AND PHOENICIAN COLONIZATION
700 B.C. – 500 B.C.

but were hard of heart like adamant, fearful men who were finally destroyed by their own hands and passed to the dark house of chill Hades, and left no name." Grown temporarily more merciful, Zeus created a fourth race, some of whom fought and destroyed the Trojans and thereafter lived "untouched by sorrow in the islands along the shore of deep swirling ocean." But the fifth generation was so steeped in misery that the poet lamented that he had not "died before or been born afterwards. For now truly is a race of iron, and men who never rest from labour and sorrow by day and from perishing by night; and the gods shall lay sore trouble upon them."[8]

Colonization

In a sense these sufferings constituted the pangs of a new Hellenic birth of freedom, part of the glory to come. But many commoners—led by lesser nobles edged out of positions of power by their own elite—preferred the risks of a new land to what seemed the permanent insecurities of their homeland. Thus there developed (ca. 750—ca. 550 B.C.) what is called the Greek age of colonization (see map, above). Originally the pioneers sought expansion in the Anatolian hinterland, but Phrygia and Lydia stopped such attempts before they were well started. Colonization efforts in Cyprus and Syria were precluded by a stubborn Phoenician veto. Therefore other areas had to be settled. Miletus, for example (probably the strongest Greek community in Asia Minor), sent colonists to Trebizond and other Black Sea areas; Megarans founded Byzantium; and the Euboean cities of Chalcis and Eretria colonized Thrace (until halted by the Persians in the 500s B.C.). Chalcis was especially active, turning west as well as to the north and east, establishing Cumae (ca. 750 B.C.) some 100 miles south of Rome, from

[8] Hugh G. Evelyn-White, *Hesiod, Homeric Hymns, and Homerica.* (New York: G. P. Putnam's Sons, 1920), p. 11 ff.

B. The Greek Way: Phoenix

which restless pioneers moved on to found Naples. Other Chalcidians settled colonies in Sicily, such as Naxos and Messana. Greeks from the island of Rhodes colonized Gela in Sicily, which sent an offshoot to Agrigentum (ca. 580 B.C.). On the southern tip of the Italian peninsula Achaeans located at Sybaris, Spartans at Taras (Taranto). Other Greeks ventured farther west, colonizing Massilia (Marseilles) on the present French Riviera. In northern Africa Dorians established a flourishing settlement at Cyrene. Thus by the early sixth century B.C. migrant Greeks had ringed the Mediterranean with carbon copies of their home poleis.

Unlike the Phoenicians the Greeks were interested not only in commercial ventures but in establishing communities.* They took with them, of course, their language, habits, and customs (much as pioneering Puritans and Cavaliers were to do when they settled the Atlantic seaboard of the New World more than 2000 years later). Far from discouraging emigration, most of the home communities facilitated such efforts in every way they could; for the freer they became of potential malcontents the more they could rest secure—or hoped they could—in their own privileged positions. Once established, the Greek colonists made their way not only as enterprising merchants and independent yeomen but also as cultural links that bound the barbarian hinterland to the developing genius of the Ionian way of life. So effective were they as diffusionists that by Roman times Sicily and much of southern Italy was called, simply and quite appropriately, Magna Graecia.

Commercial Class

But if the stay-at-home aristocrats hoped, with commoners moving out, to avoid a democratic day of reckoning they were soon disillusioned. For one thing, and paradoxically, by breaking old family ties and thereby enhancing the position and place of the individual, the migrations actually gave impetus to the democratic impulse in the home communities. For another, increasing commercial relations led to a relatively rapid acceptance of coined money as a medium of exchange. Until about 640 B.C. when the officially stamped coin was invented (by the Lydians), commerce had been forced to employ such media of exchange as goods themselves, that is, barter, or pieces of gold and silver validated by weight rather than by the official seal of a government. During the seventh century B.C. the new invention steadily advanced in general acceptance, making possible a systematic accumulation of capital. "Henceforth value was placed not on blue blood, but on what a man was and what he had." In short, a commercial class grew in numbers and affluence, and would soon, in its efforts to wrest control from the landed gentry, make plain its willingness to join hands with other commoners.

These economic developments led to a third influence weakening aristocratic control. The new quasi-business class could now afford the military equipment formerly the distinguishing mark of the landed elite. It must be understood that there was no such class consciousness as developed later in Western history. The new factor in seventh-century Greece was the presence of money in new hands. Thus the defense of the city-state became as much the responsibility of nonaristocrats as of the nobility. Sensitive to the political implications of the new situation the trading class now began to challenge tradition—and to back up its challenge with the power of the purse and threats of a military strike. Well might the highly conservative poet Alcaeus (a contemporary of the gifted Sappho) complain that the aristocratically piloted ship of state was in grave danger of foundering:

* But we should not overlook the Phoenician settlements in Carthage and Cadiz.

I cannot understand how the winds are set against each other. Now from this side and now from that the waves roll. We between them run with the wind in our black ship driven hard pressed and laboring under the giant storms. All around the mast-step washes the sea we shipped. You can see through the sails already while there are opening rents within it. . . .[9]

Perhaps one aspect of the "giant storms" that Alcaeus, as a conservative aristocrat, found hard to understand was the development of the institution of "tyranny." For modern students the term is an unfortunate one. It easily brings to mind a Mussolini, a Hitler, a Stalin. In ancient times *tyrannis* designated a leader who had seized power from a legitimate ruler. The overthrown ruler was as likely—indeed, far more likely—to have played what we today think of as the tyrant's role than the usurper. Originally the tyrant was essentially a reliever of oppression. Alcaeus was himself (as a type) an excellent example of a prime mover of the "giant storms" he so deplored. For he and his aristocratic colleagues had badly bungled affairs of state by stubbornly refusing to recognize the deserved rights of those not in their charmed circle. As one authority has put it, the poet was "obsessed by his own troubles, but his troubles and so his poems were mainly political; an embittered aristocrat, his attitude goes far to explain why his world was breaking up around him."* By the sixth century B.C. not only the newly rich merchant—who in any case was not then a numerous breed —but the inquiring commoner had learned what not to endure. Often, as we saw in the section on Athens, the succoring tyrant was a renegade aristocrat (as in our own times was Franklin D. Roosevelt). But

Terracotta statuette of a barber trimming a man's hair.

the phenomenon was not peculiar to Athens; it could occur in any part of the Greek world. Before formal constitutional government was introduced, it often did.

Finally, the adaptation of the Phoenician alphabet to the Greek language (sometime after 800 B.C.) gave winged power to ideas hitherto crippled and cramped by awkward and inadequate syllabaries. The creative talents of the Greek, freedom biased, could now sing eloquently of woes not to be borne, of dimly remembered glories of the past, and of a way of life—the "examined life"— that would surpass them all. Thus by the eighth century B.C. a new Greek world, Hellas, emerged from the long night of the "second dark age," probing the promise of man and eventually laying, in large part, the foundations on which our own Western society was built. Before turning to a detailed study of the golden age that flowered and faded in the fifth and fourth centuries we need to take an overall view of the general state of society as it existed

[9] Moses Hadas, ed., *The Greek Poets* (New York: Random House, The Modern Library, 1953), p. 186.

* See A. Andrews, *The Greek Tyrants* (London: Hutchinson & Co., Hutchinson University Library, 1956), p. 19.

in the late 600s and 500s and briefly to consider the Persian Wars, which helped to bring the Great Age into being.

PRELUDE TO GLORY: GREEK SOCIETY, 600–500 B.C.

Religion and Morality

Some changes took place in Greek religion that are worth noting. Stesichorus, a lyric poet living in Sicily (ca. 600 B.C.), is credited with modifying the ancient Atrean legend that told of Clytemnestra's murder of her husband, Agamemnon, and of her own death at the hands of her son. Stesichorus made of this a moral tale, a version that Aeschylus and other later tragedians used as a model. In addition to this new emphasis on morality the Greeks began to show a curiosity about the afterlife and a "desire for personal contact with the supernatural."*

Out of these concerns were born several important religious movements. One was the Orphic cult, named after the poet-priest Orpheus. Into the popular religion its leaders wove a metaphysic that sought to relate man to the powers of the underworld. It also initiated a complex system of rites and practices designed not only to give man a place in the next life but to regulate his behavior in this one. Here for the first time appears Greek sensitivity to individual guilt and its atonement, to the soul as a spiritual and superior component of man's being, and to suffering as a requisite of salvation.

Another was the Eleusinian cult—so called after Eleusis, a city near Athens—where certain ceremonies came annually to be held. From olden times had come the story of Hades' abduction of Demeter's daughter, Persephone, "The Maiden of the Grain." Appealing in deep grief to Zeus, Demeter begged for her daughter's return. To this appeal Zeus had responded, ordering Hades to restore the maiden. But the god of the underworld proved stubborn and a bargain was finally struck: Persephone (Core) would remain with Hades four months of the year, returning to the world of life for the other eight months. According to one interpretation of the legend, the latter period coincided with the first fall plantings and ran through the harvesting and threshing of the grain in June. Across the centuries, however, this folk-myth of the year's seasons and man's dependence on them took on metaphysical overtones. In this new elaboration man has his season of life and growth, nurtured by Mother Earth. Upon his death he is buried and in his turn "nourishes the plants of the earth." After a season the renourished earth brings forth another harvest of grain to sustain the living who, in due time, return to the earth, which is thus again enabled to produce another harvest—and so on endlessly. Originally this life-death cycle bespoke a relationship between Earth and human generations. Later it came to symbolize individual immortality. Finally, the doctrines of the Eleusinian cult came to promise a blessed afterlife.

Speculative Philosophy

Greek religion, then, came to deal, however partially and indirectly, with basic spiritual postulates later developed by Western society. Much more direct and profound was the Greek venture into philosophy, begun as early as 600 B.C.

Before considering its basic features, however, we must note this paradox: much of Greek rationalistic philosophy was based on traditional religious constructs. As we have seen, Greek religion postulated a basic order that preceded in

---

* But it should not be understood that the "new emphasis on morality" was closely comparable, either in kind or degree, to that developed by the Hebrews at about the same time. Compare Starr, op. cit., pp. 238–46.

time, as well as surpassed in power, all gods and the divine powers associated with them. Within this order, and created by it, particular gods were appointed to rule over its component parts—Hades in the underworld, Zeus in the sky, Poseidon in the sea, etc. Although nothing closely approaching the Judeo-Christian ethic was associated with either the gods or the specific forces over which they ruled, still "a moral or sacred character still clung to the world itself, that system of provinces within which the [gods] had sprung up and developed."[10] The first Greek philosophers, as we shall see, eliminated superhuman gods; but they retained much of the religious character of the natural world. "In other words, when Anaximander thought he was getting to close quarters with Nature, this Nature was not simply the outer world presented to us through our senses, but a *representation* of the outer world [or *Moira*], actually more primitive than the [gods] themselves"—a representation "taken over by philosophy from religion, not independently deduced from observation of this world and its natural processes."[11]

Interested originally in astronomy, Thales of Miletus, called "the father of Greek, and thereby of European, philosophy and science," came to probe the question of the origin of the world of materiality. His deliberations led him to conclude that despite the various shapes and seemingly diverse natures of the phenomena about him, all partook of, and evolved from, a single substance. The fact that he finally fixed on water as that substance should not detract from the magnitude of his philosophic achievements. For none before him had sought a principle, grounded in reason and shaped by systematic thought, which would link together the "joints of existence" and reveal a fund-

[10] Francis MacDonald Cornford, *From Religion to Philosophy* (London: Edward Arnold, 1912), p. 42.
[11] Ibid., p. 43.

amentally universal cause. This quasi-scientific approach to the explanation of cosmological riddles opened a long era of brilliant speculation.

Anaximander (fl. 575 B.C.), Thales' student, agreed with his master on the abstract principle of causation but argued that a "boundless mass," not water, was the primordial force out of which all things came and into which all things returned. He also introduced the notion—later elaborated by Pythagoras—that every particular phenomenon took its being from the influence of an opposite tendency. And he may be said to have anticipated Darwin in that he developed the theory that humankind derived from a lower form of animal life. Associated with him is another Ionian, Anaximenes, who held that although a basic force did indeed give form and life to all things, this form was neither water nor "the Unlimited," but air. Its expansion and contraction, he supposed, created phenomenal differences that separated each being from another and gave each its identity.

Impelled by the developing Greek impulse to reason out the nature and purposes of existence, still another Ionian, Hecataeus (ca. 525 B.C.), sharply attacked what he considered the naive misunderstandings of the poets of the Homeric cycle. It was ridiculous, he held, to attribute the great exploits of their Mycenaean forbears—for example, the conquest of Troy—to divine relationships and intervention. Achilles was probably the bastard son of a Greek maid; certainly he was not the offspring of a sea nymph; nor Aeneas, of Aphrodite. All phenomena, he believed, were explicable not by reference to the poetry of religion but by careful observation and relentless, searching thought.

An Ionian migrant to southern Italy, Xenophanes (ca. 525 B.C.), followed Anaximander in his insistence that all attributes are reducible to one substance. Like Hecataeus he was contemptuous of the Homeric "old-time religion." There was indeed, in his view, a god; even a number of lesser gods. But the latter were not to be thought of as inflated mortals, nor the former a magnified Zeus. Rather Xenophanes reasoned that the cosmos itself, in its entirety, was the body of god; the lesser gods were what we might call natural forces. With this understanding, he argued, we must begin. Otherwise we conceive of god in our own image, an error that the lower animals avoid only because they lack the power of reflective thought; with it, to the fish of the sea, god would surely take the form of a large fish, to the mountain goat, the form of a goat, etc. In the same manner he assailed mystical cults of the Orphic order, whose priests, he charged, had concocted a mystique only for the purpose of exploiting and controlling the naturally superstitious common citizen.

In a subtly conceived synthesis the mystical elements of the Orphic cult were combined with the new trend toward rationalism by Pythagoras (ca. 530 B.C.), another Greek migrant to southern Italy. Pythagoras taught that numbers were the stuff of creation. From his study of what might be called the physics of music he concluded that tonal pitch was strictly and absolutely related to measurable physical properties. The length of the lyre string, for example, determined the tone that its plucking would bring forth. He thus postulated the thesis that all phenomena are reducible to number combinations (a concept that still finds expression in such a common remark as I've got your number). Out of his researches and those of his followers came a body of data some of which stands today and some of which pointed the way to subsequently refined understandings. An example of the former is the well-known Pythagorean theorem that the square of the hypotenuse of a right triangle is equal to the sum of the squares of the other two sides. An example of the latter is the observation regarding the shape of the earth and other astronomical calculations, which "led to a considerable step, taken by [Pythagoras's] followers, in the direction of the Copernican system— the distinction of real and apparent motions.[12] From the theory of numbers— which to him were reality itself and not merely symbols of reality—he developed a religio-ethical system that partook of Orphic practices. For the Pythagoreans, to put it crudely, heaven was harmony. To achieve harmonious perfection human beings must learn, through a discipline colored by asceticism, to cancel out life's "mathematical" incongruities. To this end Pythagoras established a religious brotherhood dedicated to the perfection of virtue "that is the harmonious equilibrium of the soul's aspirations and practices."[13]

But in the main, Greek philosophic thought was reason-based. Particularly important was the seminal thought of Parmenides and Heraclitus. Parmenides (b. 514? B.C.) followed Xenophanes in holding that total existence is one basic being, without beginning or end, unchanging forever. The changes that men think they experience are illusions created by the false promptings of our senses. The way to truth is found by logic and reason alone. Properly used, they reveal the encompassing unity of all phenomena and, contrariwise, the sham of apparent pluralism. Heraclitus (fl. 500 B.C.), on the other hand, denied the reality of permanence. All things, according to him, are in a state of flux. Nothing *is,* everything is *becoming*— "you cannot step into the same stream twice." (Our modern debate on the nature of reality—process or substance—repeats some arguments that derive from the premises of these ancient philosophers.)

We have sampled enough of the workings of the Greek mind to see how, even in this early period, they radically differed from those of other minds. Search-

[12] Bury, op. cit., p. 317.
[13] Hadas, op. cit., p. 176.

ing questions, of course, had been put by older peoples—Sumerians, Egyptians, Babylonians, Hebrews. But never before had the mind that framed them been oriented as was the Greek mind. The Egyptian, for example, pondered deeply on the godhood of the pharaoh, how to symbolize in stone the falcon spirit, or how to guarantee in the next life the happiness of this one. Hebrew prophets and patriarchs were, in a remarkable number of instances, profound and creative, but always with the single purpose of learning how to bring themselves and their people into a right relationship with Yahweh. But the Greeks probed out of an almost compulsive curiosity to learn the secrets of the physical universe, the facts of the world about them, the nature of man, and the interrelations of society that would most meaningfully develop man's nature. In short, by their continuous and rationalistic examination of life they shaped the scientific attitude.

Literary Development

Such philosophic ventures did not, of course, exhaust the Greek genius. We have already noted the literary works of Theognis, Alcaeus, and Stesichorus. Early in the seventh century B.C. Archilochus of Paros declared his independence from the heroic hexameter and, indeed, from the whole Homeric school of thought. To express his views of the nature of the "inner" community, which seemed to him more important than mulling over the deeds of mythical giants, he invented a new genre—the lyric poem. Typical of his use of it—and as well of the Greek search for the Golden Mean—is this excerpt:

> *Tossed on a sea of troubles,*
>   *Soul, my soul*
>   *Thyself do thou control. . . .*
> *Rejoice in joyous thing—nor*
>   *overmuch*

> *Let grief thy bosom touch*
> *Midst evil, and still bear in mind*
> *How changeful are the ways of human*
>   *kind.*[14]

Simonides of Amorgos used the new meter to give vent to his rather dour views on the worth of women. Alcamaean adapted it to festive occasions when choral groups sang the poet's hopes and woes. And Sappho (ca. 600 B.C.), acknowledged as "the greatest woman poet of antiquity," employed it to frame such passionate lines as these:

> *. . . should I but see thee*
>   *a moment,*
>   *Straight is my voice hushed;*
> *Yea, my tongue is broken, and through*
>   *and through me*
> *'Neath the flesh impalpable fire runs*
>   *tingling;*
> *Nothing see my eyes, and a noise*
>   *of roaring*
>   *Waves in my ear sounds;*
> *Sweat runs down in rivers, a tremor*
>   *seizes*
> *All of my limbs, and paler than grass in*
>   *autumn,*
> *Caught by pains of menacing death,*
>   *I falter,*
>   *Lost in the love-trance.*[15]

In the mid-sixth century B.C. Thespis of Athens introduced a dramatic element destined to flower into that wondrous creation we call Greek tragedy. Hitherto many Greek city-states, to celebrate their god-given well-being or to plead for it, had set aside certain days for public performances. Commonly a chorus, dancing in stately steps to flute music, would chant praises or imprecations to one of the greater gods (such as Dionysos, who was more often hymned as a nature god than as the god of wine). Across the years these festivals grew increasingly impressive.

[14] Hadas, op. cit., pp. 183–84.
[15] Ibid.

133   B. The Greek Way: Phoenix

A typical example of "black figure" painting. On the reddish clay, black figures were painted in silhouette. As on this vase, the lacelike details were scratched in with a fine-pointed instrument.

Large male choruses, bedecked in the skins of goats and swaying in dithyrambic fervor, evoked vicarious experiences of weal or woe among their massed audiences. Often the leader would chant a line, dirgelike or eulogistic, which would call for choral response. Into the metrical sweep of these strophic-antistrophic choric odes Thespis introduced the independent reciter of lines. This actor, almost always impersonating a god, would sound a warning or a note of prophecy, setting off a choral response of lamentation or jubilation. In this way Greek drama was born.

Art; Everyday Life

The imaginative leaps in literature were marked by similar advances in art, especially pottery making and sculpture. The fetching prearchaic geometric designs yielded to a new style. Geometric patterns were still used, but now they were juxtaposed with graceful animals and live human forms to make the vase's beauty outreach its utilitarian function. This "orientalizing ware" (so-called from obvious borrowing of naturalistic styles from the Near East) exhibited an exuberant spirit that gave full play to emotional expression. Techniques as well as motifs changed. The "simple outlining of the decoration gave way in many workshops to solid black-figure painting. This was picked out and enriched by the use of supplementary color (white, red, and purple) and of incision to render more specific detail than Geometric patterns had ever deemed necessary."[16] In sculpture the artist reproduced the vigor and verve of young men and women.

It should not, of course, be supposed that these seventh- and sixth-century developments in religion, philosophy, literature, and art consumed all the waking hours of the average Greek. Then, as now, the bread-and-butter aspects of life occupied most of man's attention and energy. For the average Greek a new day meant but return to the field where olives were beaten from the trees; or where ploughing was resumed; or to the threshing floor where chaff was winnowed from the grain; or to the grape pit where his bare feet trod out the juice of wine-to-be. Commoners who were not yeomen farmers or shepherds were artisans—pottery makers, iron-workers, merchants, sailors, or, occasionally, gold-

[16] C. G. Starr, *A History of the Ancient World* (New York: Oxford University Press, 1965), p. 229.

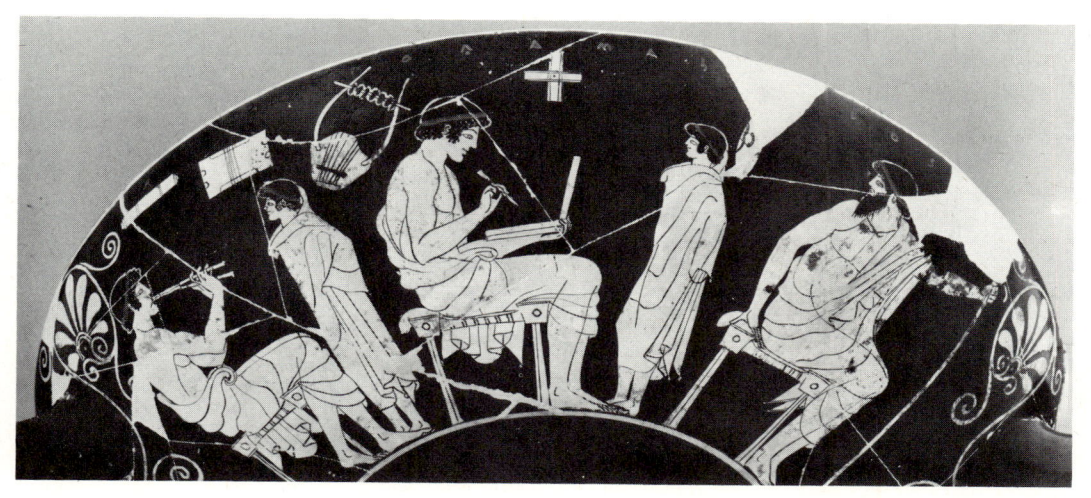

In this classroom scene two students (standing) learn musical and writing arts from their teachers. The bearded man seated on the right is a slave who escorts the boys to and from school.

and silversmiths. Increasingly slaves were used for the most menial tasks, especially work in the mines, or, if they were literate, as managers, clerks, and tutors for the sons of wealthy landowners and traders. Boys attended grammar school, where music and rhetoric were taught. Girls stayed at home with their mothers, where they learned the arts of home craft and their position as a woman, which was distinctly and frankly inferior to man's.

Athletics; the Elan of the Greek Way

Athletic activities played a large part in the life of the Greek male. Games and contests were featured at various seasons in almost every polis, culminating in elaborate annual tournaments in some cities. Moreover every four years a week was set aside for a great socioreligious festival—the Olympic games. Work and fighting ceased while contestants from all over the Greek world gathered at Olympus to display their prowess in foot and chariot races, the javelin throw, boxing bouts, and jousting. And every three years the literati gathered at Delphi to compete in dramatic and musical contests. These great gatherings, held in the third and fourth years of each Olympiad, gave the Greeks unexampled opportunities to practice the educational trinity they preached: the disciplined synchronization of body, mind, and soul; and, incidentally, the only meaningful national unity they were ever to know.

In short, by about 550 B.C. the Hellenic world had emerged from the long darkness inaugurated by the movements of the Sea Peoples and by the Dorian invasions. In their poleis, founded or resettled in a thousand places in the old Aegean world and far beyond it, they nurtured again the desire to "invite their souls." Free from threats in the west and, for many centuries, from the thralldom of smothering tradition in the east, they rediscovered a sense of security and the joy of living. When their monarchs proved recalcitrant and reactionary they overthrew them and set up aristocratic republics. When the new elite sought, in their turn, selfishly to perpetuate the rule of "the beautiful and

Detail from a Panathenaic amphora, showing a foot race.

the good," commoners either turned pioneers and colonized around the Mediterranean or girded themselves for another round in the class struggle. New miseries stimulated new energies. Dreaming Promethean dreams, the Greeks had found themselves again.

NATURE AND SIGNIFICANCE OF THE PERSIAN WARS

The Challenge of Persia

Eventually the dreams issued into a golden day, the so-called Periclean age. But not, as one would have supposed, in Ionian Asia, where first the light had dawned. For by the middle of the sixth century B.C. there had emerged, we will recall, the challenging Persian Empire. By then it had spread to the western limits of Asia Minor and engulfed the Greek world on its fringe. It is true that this world had accepted the Lydian overlordship a half-century earlier and seemed none the worse for it. But Lydian rule was quite nominal and, indeed, consistently respectful of the Greek genius. With the arrival of the Persians this nominal and tolerable state of dependency ended. Succeeding monarchs—Cyrus, Cambyses, and Darius (ca. 545—ca. 485)—grew increasingly impatient with Greek "recalcitrance." To ensure dominant control Darius finally established satraps who were directed to brook no nonsense. This foreshadowing of complete subjugation caused many coastal Greeks to flee to the farther west or to the mainland, thus reversing the migration pattern of the tenth and ninth centuries.

Naturally the mainland Greeks looked askance at the rolling Persian tide and asked themselves where it would end and whether Greece itself would not one day be washed under. Coupled with this fear was fraternal sympathy for their Asian kin. Even so, when Darius overplayed his hand in attempting to subjugate certain areas in Europe along the Danube and suffered a sound defeat, only Athens and Eretria gave ready aid to the Ionians who rose in revolt. In 499 B.C. 20 Athenian ships sailed against the Persian conquerors. But Oriental might was not thus easily broken. Within a few years the revolt had been put down, and as a warning against

136   Aegean and Greek Civilizations

PERSIAN WARS 490-479 B.C.

such misbehavior in the future the great center of Ionian culture, Miletus, was sacked and put to the torch.

Greeks and Persians alike now girded themselves for a showdown. To punish Athens (technically its vassal) for its bold interference, Persia made ready a punitive expedition under Mardonius. With Athens humbled, the "pacification" of Greece could follow and thus put a permanent end to Ionian uprisings. For its part Athens sounded a general alarm and asked for a united front, warning other Greek communities that *its* doom spelled doom for *all*. The appeal, however, evoked little response from the rest of Greece, and when the blow fell, Athens, almost alone, stood up to it.[17]

[17] Compare N. G. L. Hammond, *A History of Greece to 332* B.C., Oxford: The Clarendon Press, 1959), pp. 208–9.

Marathon

After a period of elaborate preparations the Persians, under Darius, believed themselves ready for the encounter. In 490 B.C. a large contingent of troops—cavalry, archers, and spearmen—sailed into the Bay of Marathon (see map, above), about 20 miles northeast of Athens. Landing a large portion of his troops below Marathon between the stretches of marshy land, Datis (to whom Darius entrusted execution of the invasion plans) faced the Athenians encamped among the foothills. With this contingent he planned to crush the Greek *hoplites* (heavily armed infantrymen) while sending the rest of his forces southward around the bay to march directly against Athens. Apparently this strategy was based upon Darius's conviction that his numerical superiority would win the day at Marathon while fifth-column activities in Athens (that it was hoped would develop out of the fierce factional struggle then going on in the city) would make easy his capture of this proud polis. In principle the plan was plausible enough. Certainly the Greeks were greatly outnumbered; certainly defeat 20 miles from home would leave their city an easy prey even without the defection of traitors.

Circumstances combined, however, to render the plausible quite impracticable. For one thing, it seems that the cavalry units were included in the second group. This resulted in Persian inability to swiftly envelop the flanks of the Greek army (itself without cavalry) when the latter advanced onto the plains of Marathon. For another, defense of the homeland often engenders a spirit and tenacity not easily equaled by an invader. In any case, in the ensuing battle Athenian infantrymen succeeded in driving the Persians into the sea. At this point a third development served to wreck Persian strategy completely. Sensing the destination and mission of the enemy convoy, Miltiades, the Athenian commander, called on his victorious but weary troops to march, at once and without rest, to the defense of their supposedly beleaguered city. Actually their forced march brought them into position before the Persian ships could disembark their troops; seeing the futility of an attempted landing, Datis called off the attack and returned home.

The effect of this double victory over the vaunted Persian hordes was tremendous. All Hellas rejoiced at the miracle of Marathon. To the Greek world Athens appeared as a city apart, a polis of heroic stature whose victories gave a sharp impetus to the Hellenic leadership that it was then shaping.*

---

* Compare Hammond, op. cit., p. 217, and Starr, op. cit., p. 285. Ancient rivalries, however, did not dissolve in the glow of Hellenic pride. Within a short time city-state was again conspiring against city-state. And it was Sparta, not Athens, that shaped the League that stood against the Persians in their second attempt to conquer Greece. But even so, there remained what might be thought of as an emotional afterglow; so that Greek cities, while continuing to seek to undermine, from time to time, each other's power and position, especially Athens's, could at the same time salute the genius that gave rise to such power and position. So fearfully and wonderfully made is man.

Second Persian Invasion

But the Persians were not discouraged. Darius laid new plans to conquer these western upstarts; when he died in 485 B.C. Xerxes, his son, pushed these plans with all the vigor of his aggressive sire. Taking advantage of the stubborn particularism that seemed second nature to the Greeks, he concluded diplomatic bargains with Argos, Thebes, and Thessaly, promising them a prominent position in the new Greece that would rise under Persian hegemony. A new army of some 200,000 was organized and a new fleet readied. Instead of a direct attack across the sea Xerxes planned to cross the Hellespont (on pontoon bridges), deploy his forces in friendly Thessaly, and drive down into the heart of Greece with Athens and Sparta as special targets.

Well understanding the ordeal ahead, Athens, following the advice of Themistocles, its most gifted leader, concentrated on the construction of a large navy. Jealous and bickering city-states were urged to submerge rivalries in the face of this new and graver threat from the east. Under the rallying force of a determined Sparta about 30 city-states, including Megara, Corinth, Phocis, and Aegina, formed a defensive Panhellenic League, in which supreme military command was given to Sparta. When Xerxes began his march in 480 B.C. the Greeks were probably as ready as ever they had been or were to be for ac-

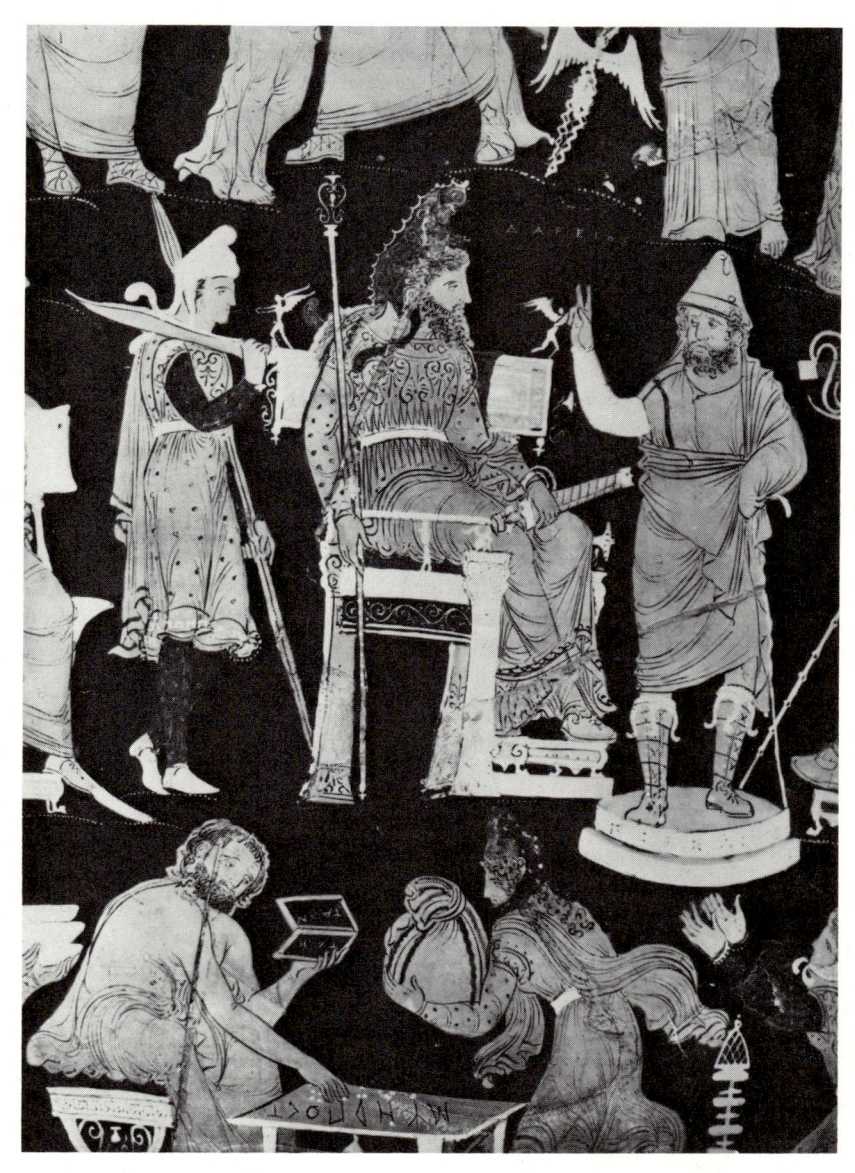

Here Darius sits in royal splendor listening to his military advisers brief him on the feasibility of the invasion of Greece. The artist, almost three generations removed from the event, evidently thought that the king's exalted position deserved whatever creative license he was capable of, so that there are gods and goddesses above and tribute bearers below.

tion in a common enterprise. Which is to say that not even a majority of citizens supported the League's purposes.

Thermopylae

Northern Greece was quickly overrun. Indeed, Greek strategy had allowed for this in the face of Thessalonian defection. Real defense was to begin in the central region around Thermopylae. Here, under strong Spartan leadership, Greeks met Persians and stood them off until, through treachery, the latter learned of a route that enabled them to skirt the pass of Thermopylae and attack the heroic defenders from the rear. Thus surprised (and vastly outnumbered) the latter fought to the end under which, the circumstances, could only mean complete annihilation. The Persians then poured into Attica as a flood, and city after city capitulated. Athens itself was captured and burned, and the way seemed open for the conquest of the Peloponnesus.

Salamis and Plataea

An attack on the isthmus was mounted as the fleet made ready to land troops in the rear of the defenders with the hope of duplicating the Thermopylae triumph. But at this point the foresight and wisdom of Themistocles decided the issue. The Greek navy, well equipped and daringly led, maneuvered the Persian armada into a fight in the Bay of Salamis, just off the Athenian coast. There the Persians suffered a decisive defeat. With half his fleet destroyed and bereft of supplies and logistical requisites, Xerxes was placed in a serious dilemma. To stay with his stranded army would not only invite disaster but encourage fresh revolts among restive Ionians along the Asian coast. To withdraw his forces northward and back across the pontoon bridge would save his army but lose the war. The Persian king's decision was both reasonable and fatal. Leaving the army under the command of an able general, Mardonius, to try a stand at Plataea (see map, p. 137), Xerxes hastened back to Asia Minor to superintend the containment of Ionian rebellion and to assemble, so far as he could, a relieving navy.

Heartened by success, the Greeks, in the spring of 479 B.C., inflicted a crushing defeat on Mardonius's army. Similarly encouraged Ionian Greeks joined their mainland brothers in a battle off Miletus—at Cape Mycale—where Persian forces were again routed. Thereafter the coastal cities vied with one another in ridding themselves of their Persian overlords. For the second time in hardly more than a decade the mighty Persian Empire had been humbled.

Effects of Greek Victories

It is customary to argue that Greek victories at Marathon, Salamis, and Plataea held back the Persian flood and saved Europe from drowning in the murky sea of Oriental despotism. The European way of life, it is claimed, was thus given a chance to root itself in the Greek ethos and eventually to flower in disciplined thought, democracy, and vaulting esthetic expression.[*] It is difficult to believe that the events of this decade—roughly, 490–480 B.C.—did indeed constitute such a huge page of history. More reasonable, perhaps, is the assumption that man's creative genius is neither doomed nor endangered by discrete events even of the proportions described above. It is, in short, hard to accept the argument that

[*] One of the most extreme formulations of this opinion is to be found in C. P. Rodocanachi, *Athens and the Greek Miracle,* Beacon Press, Boston, 1951; we read on p. 186: "Everything on which our civilization lives to this day may be said . . . to have been potentially implied in the intellectual, moral and social achievements of Athens in the fifth century B.C."

Europe would have died aborning had the hosts of Xerxes won the day. Nevertheless these events were of high significance. Two great Hellenic communities were, at a crucial juncture of their development, spared Eastern domination; were allowed, rather, to create their own image—or, in the case of Sparta, to maintain the institutions that it had already developed—as their native talents dictated. If the objection is raised that the Spartan image turned out to be a rather sorry thing, it must also be conceded that the Athenian way of life came to shape some of the basic features of later European society (and ultimately our own). We need not go the whole way with those historians who link the birth of freedom with this Greek victory. But we may reasonably hold that without that victory the creative development of Western man's mind and Western institutions would have been seriously retarded. If the Persian Wars did not create Western man, they nevertheless unquestionably permitted an early flowering of Hellenic society.

Selected Readings

A. Crete

Bury, J. B. *A History of Greece*. Revised by Russell Meiggs. London: The Macmillan Co., 1959.

Chapter 2 views Cretan life more or less in the manner of Hammond, cited below.

Clark, Grahame. *World Prehistory*. 2d ed. Cambridge: Cambridge University Press, 1969.

See chapter 6.

Evans, Arthur. *The Palace of Minos*. 6 vols. London: The Macmillan Co., 1921–36.

This elaborate work, by the "discoverer" of Minoan civilization, is exhaustive in factual material and now highly controversial in his interpretation of it. For years his thesis that Crete was the "cradle of Western civilization" was accepted by many scholars. Since 1960 this view has been seriously challenged by Leonard Palmer and others (for Palmer see below).

Hammond, N. G. L. *A History of Greece to 322 B.C.* Oxford: Oxford University Press, 1959.

In Book 1, pp. 19–35, Professor Hammond cites the sources of knowledge for this civilization, deals generally with the origins of Minoan culture, and refers briefly to Mycenaean Linear Script tablets found at Knossos. His views are disputed by a number of other scholars, notably C. G. Starr, cited below.

Palmer, Leonard R. *Mycenaeans and Minoans*. New York: Alfred A. Knopf, 1962.

In this book Professor Palmer presents evidence to refute Evans's contention that Crete fundamentally influenced its northern neighbors in the Peloponnesus. See especially Chapters 6 and 7. Palmer's chief argument concerns the stratigraphy of the Linear B findings at Pylos.

Starr, C. G. "The Myth of the Cretan Thalassocracy." *Historia* III (1955), pp. 283–91.

See also Starr, A History of the Ancient World *(New York: Oxford Uni-*

versity Press, 1965), pp. 104—8; The Origins of Greek Civilization (New York: Alfred A. Knopf, 1961), pp. 36–39.

* A good fictional account of ancient Cretan life is found in Mary Renault, *The King Must Die* (New York: Pantheon Books, 1958).

B. The Greek Way: Phoenix

* Andrews, A. *Greek Tyrants.* New York: Harper & Row, Publishers, Harper Torchbooks, 1963.

    A competent, thorough analysis of these much misunderstood statesmen.

Bonnard, André. *Greek Civilization.* 3 vols. London: George Allen & Unwin, 1957–61.

    Although both translators and a number of other scholars dissociate themselves from Bonnard's controversial approach and interpretations, these volumes nevertheless make up one of the most meaningful studies of Greek culture to be published in our times when used with such standard works as those of Bury, Hammond, and Starr cited below.

Bowra, C. M. *The Greek Experience.* London: Weidenfeld and Nicholson, 1957.

    Topical treatment of Greek religion, the polis, philosophy, art, literature, and, in chapter 5, the "good life."

Bury, J. B. *A History of Greece to the Death of Alexander the Great.* London: The Macmillan Co., 1959.

    Professor Meigg's updating of this classic study assures its continuing reputation as one of the most significant works on Greek history. If only one work were to be read this would be it.

Dodds, E. R. *The Greeks and the Irrational.* Berkeley and Los Angeles: University of California Press, 1951.

    This should be required reading for those who still hold that Hellenic civilization and rational living are synonymous.

Ehrenberg, Victor. *The Greek State.* New York: Barnes & Noble, 1960.

    A sociopolitical analysis of the polis. One of the most authoritative brief accounts available of the life and problems of the Greek citizen.

Ehrenberg, Victor. *Society and Civilization in Greece and Rome.* Cambridge, Mass.: Harvard University Press, 1964.

    The first three essays are interpretative lectures on Homeric Greece, the Archaic age, and "the Athenian century." They deal, in part, with the impact of things on thought, the significance of social customs and habits, and the relationship between poetry and "education."

Finley, M. I. *The Ancient Greeks.* New York: The Viking Press, 1963.

    A delightful and informative essay—a "personal analysis"—of certain cultural aspects of Greek civilization. Especially useful when read with Bury, Hammond, or Starr.

Hale, William Harlan. *The Horizon Book of Ancient Greece.* New York: American Heritage Publishing Co., 1965.

    A fascinating account written for popular reading. The illustrations are superb; the maps are strikingly graphic; the text, although not always con-

sistent with the findings of scholarly research, is imaginatively organized and highly readable.

Hammond, N. G. L. *A History of Greece to 322 B.C.* Oxford: Oxford University Press, 1959.

A close second to Bury's work. Professor Hammond takes some positions sharply challenged by some other (mostly American) scholars, especially in the first 100 pages. Here it is useful to compare Starr's The Origins of Greek Civilization *(noted below).*

* Homer, *The Iliad and The Odyssey.* Translated by E. V. Rieu. Baltimore: Penguin Books, 1950.

No reading, however extensive, about the heroic age can substitute for "Homer's" own accounts of it. These translations are perhaps the best.

* Kitto, H. D. F. *The Greeks.* Baltimore: Penguin Books, 1951.

Many of Kitto's interpretations are as subjectively arrived at as are Bonnard's. The book is not a narrative history of the Greek people so much as an evaluative essay of certain aspects of their culture—for example, the Greeks as warriors and thinkers.

Muller, Herbert J. *Freedom in the Ancient World.* New York: Harper & Row, Publishers, 1961.

Chapters 6–8 should be read with Toynbee's work (cited below). Both works have the same basic approach; the comparable and contrasting emphases should stimulate the reader's own imaginative reconstruction of the Hellenic genius.

Palmer, Leonard R. *Mycenaeans and Minoans,* New York: Alfred A. Knopf, 1962.

Professor Palmer seeks to interpret the script deciphered by Ventris; in doing so he challenges the basic thesis of Evans's Palace of Minos. *This can be profitably read in conjunction with Miss Vermeule's work (cited below).*

Parkes, Henry B. *Gods and Men: The Origin of Western Culture.* New York: Alfred A. Knopf, 1959.

Pages 147–304 treat of Hellenic and Hellenistic culture from the standpoint of one mainly interested in examining "social myths" and the "spiritual" core of civilized mores.

Robinson, Cyril E. *Hellas: A Short History of Ancient Greece.* Boston: Beacon Press, 1955.

If Bury, Hammond, or Starr is not read, this work should be. It is sound in scholarship, balanced in interpretations, and readable.

Starr, Chester G. *The Origins of Greek Civilization.* New York: Alfred A. Knopf, 1961.

This book contains an abundance of facts describing early Greek culture, down to the period of colonization. However the data serve sometimes to cloud, rather than clarify, some concepts.

Toynbee, Arnold J. *Hellenism.* New York: Oxford University Press, 1959.

A philosophic approach to the problem of Greek humanism and its bearing on the rise and decline of Greek culture.

Ventris, Michael, and Chadwick, John. *Documents in Mycenaean Greek.* Cambridge: Cambridge University Press, 1956.

Much of the language is technical; still the lay reader can feel some excitement as he is led stage by stage through the maze of cryptography and philological venturing that resulted in cracking the once (and still somewhat) baffling Linear B script.

Vermeule, Emily. *Greece in the Bronze Age.* Chicago: The University of Chicago Press, 1964.

An up-to-date, highly readable, and controversial account of Mycenaean history. All aspects of Mycenaean culture are included: politics, economics, art, religion, palace life, language, shaft graves. This is especially worthwhile when read in conjunction with Palmer and Webster.

Webster, T. B. L. *From Mycenae to Homer.* London: Methuen & Co., 1958.

A detailed and scholarly study of Mycenaean art and poetry. The last chapter connects the Mycenaean heritage to Greek culture in Homeric times.

Asterisk (*) denotes paperback.

CHAPTER IV
The Greek Way: from Polis to Cosmopolis

A. The Golden Age — THE SCHOOL OF HELLAS: MIND

Athenian Culture: Philosophy

Across the Saronic Gulf, scarcely 100 miles from Sparta, lay Athens. But it was a way of life more than a body of water that separated them. For while Sparta was making itself into the soldier-master of the Peloponnesus, Athens was setting itself up as the "School of Hellas."* It is true that the latter did not neglect the sword, even in the end dying by it.† But for a glorious day, whose afterglow is still felt, the Attic city cultivated the genius of the human mind and spirit.

Anaxagoras

We have already seen how, in Ionia, the Milesian school of philosophers prefigured the inquiring mind. From Ionia Anaxagoras (born ca. 500 B.C.) brought this mind to Athens and made it the center of philosophic speculation. To him the essence of each discrete phenomenon was organically connected with all phenomena.

---

* A word of caution. The phrase "School of Hellas" is Periclean rhetoric that can easily mislead. That Athens stood preeminent in political, intellectual, and artistic achievements is beyond dispute; that it consciously and systematically planned to "tutor" its fellow Hellenes is not. Indeed, the available evidence—and there is much of it—tends to contradict Pericles' proud boast. Rather it reveals an Athenian elite (as distinguished from rank-and-file citizens) motivated by parochial pride and exploitative self-aggrandizement. A "school" the polis did indeed become, but certainly not by deliberate design.

†For a half-century after the Persian Wars, Athens anomalously devoted its talents to cultural creativity and aggressive imperialism. At the same time that it produced literature, philosophy, and art unsurpassed by earlier peoples (and, in the opinion of most scholars, rarely surpassed since), it also methodically and effectively destroyed the freedom and creative responsiveness of many of the surrounding poleis.

145

The particular shape and nature of objects, animate and inanimate, were formed by an all-encompassing mind (*nous*), which, while molding and activating all things, stood wholly and perfectly beyond them. Motion, created by the nous, set the phenomenal mass into turbulence out of which came combinations resulting in definite objects. In this way Anaxagoras explained the world of things as the senses experience them. But the philosopher distrusted human senses, holding them to be but crude perceivers of reality. For him man's reflective apparatus alone could pierce (but not influence) reality's secret.

Empedocles

Empedocles (ca. 490–430 B.C.) was a man of many trades and master of most of them—physician, rhetorician, poet, politician. But it was as philosopher that his talents were used with the most lasting effect. In his view all life was composed of four god-forces: fire, air, water, earth. The flux of life, powered by the polar influences of love and disaffection, unendingly brought these forces into combination and juxtaposition. From the workings of the principle of disaffection, or repulsion, were created the sun and moon, sea and earth, and all other seemingly opposed phenomena. On the other hand, the principle of love accounted for the harmonious features of all organic beings. Especially important (and rather paradoxical) was his theory that the interplay of antithetical forces culled out the weak and the ill-adapted; in short, what today we would call the principle of the survival of the fittest.

Democritus

His contemporary, Democritus (fl. 425 B.C.), propounded a seminal notion that was destined to languish two and a half millennia before bearing fruitful development—the atomic theory. According to this Thracian philosopher all matter was reducible to minute solid corpuscles moving about in infinite void, "the first really atheistic doctrine in the ancient Greek world." All flora and fauna were, in his view, explicable by investigation and understanding of the laws of attraction and combination. Essentially—that is, in their *essence*—man and mud were identical; only by the manner in which atoms combined were they different. Not only was the individual atom identical with every other, it was also indestructible. Its appearance (in combinations perceived by man) could change, but its basic being existed in eternity. Thus Democritus anticipated, besides the atomic theory, the first law of thermodynamics which holds that the fundamental stuff of life can never be destroyed. Nor, of course, could something come out of nothing. Thus Democritus taught that "in the beginning" there were atoms and void. The heavier atoms, falling at a faster rate, caught up with the lighter and came into forcible contact with them; some were thus thrown upward and others sideways. A circular motion was thereby created that resulted in a variety of combinational possibilities, which in turn resulted in the creation of a number of world bodies. In this way the universe was created. In like manner all phenomena were brought into existence, including human beings. Strangely enough for a materialist, Democritus posited the existence of the soul, holding it to be a combination—the most subtle of all—of psychic and corporeal atoms. He argued that the highest expression of existence in human life was found in pleasure; *not*, it should be noted, in sensual satisfaction, but "soul pleasure." Perfection was manifested in serenity, itself attained by the avoidance of both overmuch and overlittle exploitation of atom-laden rational experiences. Thus was the principle of *sophrosyne*—balance, the "golden mean"—expressed early in philosophy.

Protagoras

Democritus's distinguished older contemporary (although possibly his pupil) was Protagoras (ca. 481–411 B.C.), architect of the Sophist school of thought, Pericles' tutor, and friend to two of Athens's most gifted dramatists, Sophocles and Euripides. Protagoras, although not unmindful of the importance of cosmological probing, was primarily interested in the human response to man's phenomenal environment. Bypassing arguments over the nature of ultimate reality, he sought to place men meaningfully in actual existence. This first of the philosophical humanists thus argued that "man is the measure of all things." Outer phenomena exist, but only man can *reflect* on these phenomena; only man is aware that he is aware. Man is more significant than other beings because he can and does manipulate his environment to enhance the superior quality of his being. Hence the "meanings" of all other things are (for man) what he judges them to be.

Since none but the smallest fragments of Protagoras's writings are extant we do not really know how he developed his thesis. Conceivably he could have argued that human beings, differing in perceptions and apprehensions, could and do erect a variety of value systems. If this is what he meant, then he must be understood to hold that there are no absolute truths—that individuals or communities may construct standards satisfying and meaningful to them but quite "untrue" for other individuals or communities. On the other hand, he may have held that human apperception and belief have a common built-in rudder. In this case relativism has virtually no place in his system of thought. A much-quoted remark, found in one fragment of his writings and often referred to as proof of his relativist position, may actually point in the other direction: "I cannot say whether the gods exist or not, or, if they do, what they are like. Many things hinder us from knowing; principally the obscurity of the subject and the shortness of human life." From this we may conjecture that where phenomena are not so "obscure," man may *know*. Such knowledge, of course, implicitly affirms the absolute existence of phenomena. Accordingly, if man does possess a built-in rudder, then intelligent and consistent thought must necessarily lead to the apprehension of absolute meanings and values. But we do not possess nearly enough of his original writings to say which view he actually held.

Sophism

Of Protagoras's many pupils (of whom Socrates was one) a number developed ramifying lines of thought that collectively came to be known as Sophism—the thought of the "wise ones." For several reasons this variegated philosophy attained, for a short time, a wide popularity. One reason was Protagoras's own ambiguity, which invited a multitude of reactions. Another was the growing suspicion of philosophic absolutism felt by Greeks as earlier rival and contradictory systems (Heraclitus vs. Parmenides, for example) struggled for recognition as the only "right way." Also, by about 460 B.C. the demands of pure democracy clearly called for rhetorical and dialectical skills that only professional logicians could teach. Finally, Athens's increasing wealth accentuated natural tendencies to find solutions in compromise and expediency.

For a while the city was overrun with

Socrates.

rhetoricians and dialecticians who offered to teach the culturally handicapped, often at a stiff price, not only how to articulate their views but how to discover the fundamental "truths" underlying them. From these conditions of doubt, need, and greed rose the practice of sophistry. Almost certainly a number of the practitioners were sincere seekers after truth. Gorgias, for example, was no fee-splitting logician casing the market for the newly affluent or would-be intellectuals. His view that man can never really *know* anything and that virtue is dependent on milieu and moment may seem defeatist and dour, but there can be little doubt that it came from sincere and prolonged inquiry and perhaps great insight. The same may be said for Hippias, who held that morality was mere convention; or Thrasymachus, who argued against natural rights of any kind. But other sophists sold their dialectical wares in a robust seller's market, holding one day this position, another day the opposite, and sometimes the propriety of both—or neither. Soon Athens became dotted with what one scholar calls think-shops that gladly sold what the buyer demanded. Thus in the world of ideas and attitudes everything became relative, amorphous, chameleon like.

Socrates

Out of this morass of intellectual hucksterism came Socrates (469–399 B.C.) preaching the validity of definable verities. Unlike his fee-conscious and prose-conscious contemporaries he wrote nothing and taught without charge. To Socrates the Sophists had become "intoxicated with the exuberance of their own verbosity." For him, truth existed, eternal and absolute. But it could not be found by fancy speech or clever formulae. The path to truth was rather by honest and disciplined examination of the incongruous and seemingly contradictory. An example might run like this: A holds that democracy produces the good society, B that it results in evil. Which is true, if either; or to what extent may both be right? A may ask B what evil democracy produces; B responds with two statements. A is forced to grant the validity of the first statement, but points out a fallacy in the second. B replies that for reasons a, b, and c the remaining statement seems true. A then shows how a cannot be true if the first statement, agreed to by both is sound; and that b and c depend upon a. Upon reflection B concedes that the second statement cannot, after all, stand. And so the dialectic goes on until the husks of error, half-truth, and prejudice are peeled away revealing the kernel of absolute truth. Neither A nor B may particularly like the truth that is thus uncovered. But granting honesty and intelligence—prerequisites of the Socratic method—both accept the result. Its evaluation and application, however, invite varying and again contradictory views, when once more the dialectic is set to work.

Curiously, the man who held that the virtues existed and were knowable, for himself claimed no knowledge except knowing that he did not know. But only *his* method of inquiry, he insisted, could produce knowledge. He made his dialectic thoroughly familiar to other Athenian philosophers and, through them, to their students, and ultimately to all the great thinkers of the Western world. With it he questioned everything, even the most sacred and seemingly secure institutions. In the end the state, finding his ceaseless prodding unbearable, put him to death; but not before some of the most gifted minds of his age had become converted to his way. Paradoxically, some of them—for example Plato—later denounced the very individualism that the Socratic method fostered. But the revolution in thought had by then been effected and, like all revolutions, was irreversible.

Almost certainly, however, it was not because Socrates taught a particular method of inquiry that he was condemned to death. A generation before, in his famous funeral oration, Pericles had boasted of the same liberty and genius of the inquiring mind. But between that time and the execution of Socrates Athens had bled itself to death in the sanguinary Peloponnesian War. The comparative suddenness and completeness of the catastrophe had stunned its citizens and led them to look for a scapegoat. Socrates, with his incessant probing and doubting, seemed a convenient victim.

Plato

As the violent end of Athenian democracy shaped the final act of Socrates' life, so this tragic death and the turbulence of the times influenced the basic form of Plato's thought. "Democracy was no longer advancing, progressive, creative, as it had been in the middle of the fifth century. Its inevitable expansion had invited the inevitable cataclysm, and Plato lived in the pause that preceded a great new advance."[1] For our present purpose it is more important to emphasize the cataclysm than the pause. The cultural scars that marked his times impressed Plato deeply. He surveyed the society about him and concluded that the democratic impulse and all that it implied and involved were the root of the error and evil of his day.* The democratic doctrine declared that every free, male, adult citizen was as capable as any other of envisioning the good life and of creating and executing such polity as would foster its development. To Plato experience and the times seemed clearly to prove false this doctrine and the metaphysic that cradled it. Democracy postulated the thesis that every citizen, simply by exercising the prerogatives of citizenship, could develop wisdom and the will to create the good. Plato's philosophy finally came to rest on the premise that only the gifted few could see the light of wisdom and lead a limited number of others to virtuous ways.

Of fundamental importance in Plato's political thought is the concept of the tripartite nature of man. Some human beings are given the gift of profound, intuitive insight; these are the men of *reason*. Others possess a *power of will* that enables them to execute the plans of the men of reason. The masses are devoid of both high reason and powerful will. Motivated mainly by the *impulse to acquire material gain,* they are designed by nature

---

[1] Alban Dewes Winspear, *The Genesis of Plato's Thought,* 2d ed. (New York: S. A. Russell, 1956), p. 163.

* This is an oversimplification. Space does not permit consideration of Plato's family connections and friends, all of them aristocratic. For an extensive examination of such influence on Plato's thought, see Winspear, op. cit., chap. 6.

to produce and distribute the material goods of life.

Accordingly, the ideal society is a graded, hierarchical structure where the ruler is the wise man (or men) whose policies, executed by the men of will, confer unending blessings on the whole realm. A Platonic fable, seeking to emphasize this threefold structure of society, depicts the philosopher as the Man who compacts with the soldier-administrator Lion to discipline and keep in check the Many-Headed Beast, the masses. In this regimen the last learn to know the value of obedience, the men of will develop the courage and initiative that maintain and protect the state, while the creative ruler ceaselessly probes the secrets of universal justice.

Necessarily, then, the ruler is the only possessor of knowledge that Plato, like Socrates, equates with virtue. The soldier-administrator, under the tutelage of the leader, may probe past and present conditions and form *opinions*. When based on serious and disciplined study, such opinions are not merely useful in the life of the republic but actually indispensable. They do not, however, touch eternal truth. Rather they result from keen perception of the changing shadow world. The acquiring masses, busy with the bread-and-butter business of life, do not even form clear perceptions of the shadows. For the most part they live in a state of the Great Unknowing, recognizing meaning only in superficial phenomena or through directives given to them by their superiors.

Subserving this premised political structure was an elaborate metaphysic dealing with the nature of reality, of which only the barest outline may be given here. According to this metaphysic reality resides and subsists wholly in Ideas (in Plato's thought, *idea* meant what we today would more likely call essence). In the beginning God, out of a desire to share his goodness and being, created many ethereal forms of truth: humankind, vegetation, the animal kingdom, inanimate objects, fire, water, etc. But to invest these forms with a species of sovereignty —not to do so would be but to play with sharing—God, out of void and time, created a corporeal world of concrete objects, or instances. Thus there were two worlds—spiritual forms, where actual and whole truth existed, and the world of "parallel shadows" out of which might come, man willing, the journey to the world of reality. This is man's destiny: to travel, if he will, from the seeming to the real. Or, if he will not, to pass from shadows to hell; that is, from convertible error to inconvertible and eternal error.

To be specific, Plato argued that in this corporeal world it is impossible for any human being to know, let us say, a real river. Man's perceptual sense, it is true, may discern the banked water and its flowing course. But such constitute only an imperfect instance of the Idea (or essence) of *riverness*. Similarly, it is impossible for perfect justice to manifest itself or exist in the world in which we live. A specific act may partake of the essence of justice—for example, the appreciative returning of a borrowed object. But this act, or instance, can in no way embrace the totality of the essence of justice.

To enhance the partial apprehension or experience of justice—or of riverness— man must resort to intuitive thought. The latter is fostered and quickened by disciplined practice of the dialectical method of inquiry. However, such enhanced apprehension does not, as one might suppose, involve genuine learning. For learning implies acquiring, and acquiring, *adding to*. But all truth, that is, reality, has been given once for all; it can neither be augmented nor diminished. What man commonly believes to be learning is really intuitive *recollection* of the perfect reality from which he and all other corporeal things were, as it were, split off in the act of creation.

Most human beings never become conscious of the shadowiness of the world in which they live. Their experiences, although of the stuff of shadows, seem very real. But the disciplined thinker can divine the hollowness of both himself and the phenomena around him. By use of the dialectic he may grope his way out of the shadow realm into the light of higher understanding. Here he sees what *is* in contrast to what merely *seems to be*. But if he is true to the beckoning urge, he will not be content merely to find the light and bask in its glow. Rather he will return to the "cave of shadows" to aid such others as are willing and able to break their chains and discover reality. Here preeminently is the philosopher-king at work. Those who follow him are saved; those who refuse to leave their cave world are doomed.

Plato's ethic-metaphysic thus sought to delineate and explain the Good Society, as his political philosophy set forth the means to achieve it. Like Socrates, he reacted strongly against the Sophist school, which, as we have seen, tended to deny the verities. He inveighed against the earlier cosmologists who had postulated a material, mechanistic universe. And he eloquently denounced the democratic impulse, which, he believed, had brought Hellas to the brink of ruin. For Plato reality was spiritual, not material. Absolute and eternal elements joined to make up the Good Life, sustained by a God-designed overall harmony.

Most of the later years of Plato's life (ca. 365–347 B.C.) were spent conducting classes in the school he set up in Athens—the Academy.* If it is an exaggeration to say that the "whole of modern philosophy [is] a footnote to Plato," it is fair enough to hold that, with the exception of Aristotle, no single ancient thinker has exerted so much influence on speculative thought as this Athenian aristocrat, and that "his insistence that man's reach should exceed his grasp . . . [has] been an inspiration to the intellectual life [of Western man] for over twenty-three hundred years."[2]

---

* The name derives from *Academia,* a god, in whose honor a grove was named in which Plato and his students met.

Aristotle

For many decades the elaborate synthesis of Plato's thought was mulled over and taught at the Academy, which continued to attract hundreds of students from all around the Mediterranean basin. Among them was Aristotle (389–323 B.C.), destined to become as influential with later generations as his master. According to traditional chronology Aristotle belongs rather to the Hellenistic age than to the Hellenic, which ended around 400 B.C. But logically he may be considered here, since his philosophy, although reaching maturity a generation or two after the fall of Athens, is more the intellectual culmination of the Periclean than the Alexandrian age.

Born some 200 miles to the north and east of Athens (in Stagira, hence his cognomen "the Stagirite"), Aristotle found in that city the atmosphere of learning for which he yearned and in Plato the master he was seeking. But his own genius was too vaulting to be confined by another's. After Plato's death he founded a school of his own in Athens—the Lyceum—and there spent the rest of his life remodeling the mansion of philosophy.

But if he altered the Platonic structure he did not destroy it. Like Plato he believed that the essence of reality is found in ideas, which he called "forms" (we would think of them as universals). Unlike his master, however, he did not believe reality resided exclusively in ideas. On the contrary, he held that it was also found in the substance, or matter, that the forms prefigured. Thus, for example, a particular tree, although modeled by the universal of "treeness," partook of reality as truly as the idea that shaped it.

Again, like Plato he believed that all reality is purposive; that all being, in short, rests in teleological design. But here

---

[2] Vincent M. Scramuzza and Paul L. MacKendrick, *The Ancient World* (New York: Holt, Rinehart & Winston, 1958), p. 341.

too parallelism yielded to divergence. For although Plato postulated a world of reality and a world of chimera, he understood them to be linked by a double connection—by God's thrust into the shadows and man's reach out and up from them. On the other hand Aristotle, rather paradoxically, denied the doctrine of duality while asserting that of the "unmoved mover"—that God "began" all and was total being without ever to any degree being involved in the phenomenon of "becoming" in this world.

For Aristotle, then, the individual man was real. Man's purpose—true of all forms of life—was to realize his potentials, which, since man's genius lay in his unique reflective thinking apparatus, meant to think; ultimately, indeed, to experience a life of pure thought.

But if man is to know himself he must necessarily know the nature and relationship of all other phenomena that are also real—rain, bees, trees, etc. Such understanding, Aristotle believed, could result only and exclusively from the use of a particular mode of inquiry. He called it *logic;* our phrase today would be "the scientific method." A basic element of this mode of inquiry was what he called the syllogism, a species of deductive reasoning in which there are set up major and minor premises that lead by necessity to an inescapable conclusion. A simple example would be: all human beings breathe; John is a human being; therefore John breathes.*

With this intellectual tool and its refinement Aristotle set himself the chore of learning all the secrets of nature and life. That he naturally failed to achieve this fantastic goal is less significant than the pioneering paths he blazed for others to

* So apparently simple a concept may be thought of as having always existed or as existing necessarily from earliest times. Yet the closest anyone had come to conceiving the syllogism before Aristotle was Anaxagoras, who got as far as recognition of the *unsoundness* of such a proposition as: all human beings breathe; X breathes; therefore X is a human being.

Aristotle.

The Greek Way: from Polis to Cosmopolis

follow. For he not only gathered and collated an enormous mass of data in a number of disciplines but he created the disciplines themselves. His *Politics* exemplifies this. Before his time, from "Menes" through Solon and Plato, many minds had grappled with the nature and function of political organization. But none had identified and explicated the scientific principles that subsume civic life. To accomplish this Aristotle collected more than 150 Greek constitutions, subjecting their aims and provisions to scientific scrutiny. From this labor he adduced fundamental political propositions that have continued to serve state-makers and politicians to our own day.

In the same way he created disciplines in the life sciences. His *History of Animals* sets up classifications, never before attempted, of various species. To effect this categorization he resorted again to long continued observation and critical analysis. In this work he drew a distinction between vertebrate and invertebrate animals (although he did not use these terms), assigning each species to its appropriate category. He likewise distinguished anatomical elements that constitute "wholes" (such as the eye) from other "parts," which permeate the entire unit (for example, flesh or blood). Similarly, he grouped and classified the plant world, probably being aided in this task by receiving an almost endless stream of specimens from scholars who accompanied the far-ranging armies of his former pupil, Alexander.

Almost no field of study escaped his patient exploration. In his *Poetics* he examined the nature and purpose of literary creation. Art, he held, although it partakes of the nature and purpose of the good towards which all creation is drawn, is distinguishable from the good by its primary concern with the beautiful. Whereas "the moral good shows us the highest end in its Becoming . . . the beautiful exhibits it in its perfection, as it is when no more hindrances are to be surmounted."[3] No creation is valid art, according to Aristotle, unless it evokes pleasure that comes from the harmonious union of the true (or the probable) and the good. There is thus nothing of "art for art's sake" in the Aristotelian doctrine. He makes this quite specific in his discussion of tragedy. The latter, as exemplified in, say, *Agamemnon* or *Oedipus Rex*, must deal with characters who suffer because, although they seek the good, they are involved in evil. Their heroic suffering touches in the spectator his passions of pity and fear. The fermentation and flow of these passions serve finally to exorcise from his own being its feelings of guilt and inadequacy and to bring, through vicarious purgation, psychic health and satisfactions.

Throughout his teaching there is woven the dictum of "nothing too much." In politics he advocates the rule of the middle class. In ethics he stresses the notion that ascetic selflessness negates the power potentials of man as surely as the madness that comes from extreme egocentrism. In short, his whole thought was predicated upon the Greek ideal of sophrosyne—the golden mean.

By his death in 323 B.C. Aristotle had brought into being the sciences of logic, physics, biology, psychology (in its incipient form), and ethics. Moreover he had refashioned Platonic metaphysics and created the canons of artistic expression. Critics who labor his many errors and false judgments—and there are very many of both—quite miss the point. We know now that Darwin erred and, on more than one occasion, formulated serious misjudgments; yet no informed person would care to denigrate the Darwinian contribution. It is in this perspective that Aristotle's achievements should be judged. Indeed his place looms larger today than when he strode the walk of the Lyceum.

[3] Johann Edward Gromann, *A History of Philosophy*, translated by W. S. Hough, 4th ed., 3 vols. (London: George Allen & Unwin, 1922), 1:174.

THE SCHOOL OF HELLAS: WORD

Athenian Literature

It is hardly an accident that, while Sparta was busy nurturing its martial spirit, producing disciplined warriors but no thinkers or literati or artists, Athens, thrall to no garrison state rule, should respond to the intellectual stimulus, beckoning from Ionia, to become the School of Hellas. Here, as we have seen, democracy (limited, to be sure) first took root and form. Here philosophy reached maturity. Here science was born. Scarcely less significant than Athens's political, speculative, and scientific achievements were its expressions of literary and artistic life.

One scholar has said that Greek tragedy was "nothing but the poetical response of the Athenian people to the historical pressures which made it what it was: the defender of democracy (however narrow its substructure may have been) and of the citizens' liberty."[4] This is a large "nothing but." For Greek tragedy encompassed, in its way, almost all of the basic purposes that were the concern of Greek philosophy.

It is a mistake, therefore, to assume that the great Greek tragedians, Aeschylus, Sophocles, and Euripides, used their creative gifts to embroider heroic legends with existentialist fantasies. On the contrary, each was a faithful votary of the muse of history. No more sound, either, is the commonly held view that their works proclaim the inexorable doom of man. As a matter of fact it is toward hope—not despair—that they point. Nor is such pointing mere literary window dressing. All these dramatists were concerned with real human behavior. They were, indeed,

[4] André Bonnard, *Greek Civilization*, 3 vols. (London: George Allen & Unwin, 1957–61), 1:13.

didactically motivated—interested not in the notion that "the play's the thing" but in conveying a message. They were advocates pleading a case, earnestly hopeful that their pleading would not be in vain. Only with this understanding may we profitably examine their creations.

We have already seen how, in earlier days, the Eupatridae mercilessly exploited the underprivileged and made their life a kind of hell. Here were the historic conditions that first impelled the Greek dramatist to tragic response, as they impelled the masses and their tyrant leaders to political struggle. Not long after came a new threat, from the East, when again the Greeks stood to the test and, at Marathon and Salamis, threw back the aggressor. From both, extended trials, suffering, degradation, and violent death came as intimate and abiding companions. Although from each period the Greek world emerged victorious, the demanding experience prompted grave questioning. Whence came the evils that they suffered? Were there such things as cosmic justice and harmony? Were the gods indifferent to human fate, or—even worse—was Fate itself fashioned to preclude the human achievement of permanent goodness and happiness? These questions and their logical implications lie at the root of the dramatic confrontations that Greek writers made to their times of troubles.

Aeschylus

Of the approximately 70 plays written by Aeschylus (525–456 B.C.) more than 60 are lost. The extant few, however, are masterpieces that have served to shape and inspire the works of most subsequent tragedians. Of these perhaps the *Oresteia*, a trilogy made up of *Agamemnon*, the *Choephori* ("Libation bearers"), ("Benevolent spirits"), and the *Eumenides*, best serves the purposes of our study. In all three the dramatist's basic theme is the relation of human endeavor to destiny. In each his aim is to align earthly struggle and suffering with divine harmony and justice.

Agamemnon deals with murder, injustice, and impiety. As the early myths tell us, the Mycenaean king finally succeeds in storming and sacking the city of Troy and rescuing the adulteress Helen. Enamored of Cassandra, daughter of the Trojan king, he brings her with him on his return home. Long ago his own wife, Clytemnestra, took a paramour of her own, the vain and cowardly Aegisthus. To make sure that she would have advance warning of her husband's return the queen has arranged for flares to be lit from city to city to signal the fall of Troy and the stages of the king's homeward trek. Thus prepared, she makes a great show of affection when Agamemnon enters his capital, showering upon him extravagant tokens of wifely devotion. But almost within the hour of his entrance into the palace that he had not seen for ten years she hacks him to death with an axe and boldly proclaims her deed to the populace. In justification she reminds the people of Agamemnon's wanton slaying of their daughter, Iphigenia, in propitiation of the supposed wrath of the gods, and points to her husband's flaunting a mistress in her face. The drama ends in this mélange of murder and vicious intrigue.

Vengeance is the theme of the *Choephori,* whose chief characters are Orestes and his sister Electra, offspring of the doomed Agamemnon and his murderous spouse. For a decade Electra has been humiliated by the spectacle of her faithless mother openly cavorting with the caddish Aegisthus. The murder of her father naturally increases her longing for revenge. At this point the god Apollo intervenes, laying upon Orestes the command to destroy his mother. Although he is made as miserable as his sister over his mother's behavior, he recoils from such a mandate; but men cannot stand against the gods, and in the end he murders both Clytemnestra and her lover.

Now while this crime had been commanded by a god in the name of justice—because the son must avenge the father and there is no law but this family law which allows for the punishment of Clytemnestra—the same crime will, also in the name of justice, be prosecuted by the deities of vengeance, the Furies, who will demand the death of Orestes. Thus the chain of crime and vengeance seems as though it may be endless.[5]

But in *The Eumenides* a reconciliation among the gods and between them and humankind is effected. In this third portion of the trilogy the Furies haunt and harass Orestes ceaselessly. Before they destroy him, however, the goddess Athena intervenes and proposes a solution. Let the citizens of Athens make up a jury; let the evidence on both sides be presented; and let the verdict decide Orestes' fate. So a panel of his fellow Hellenes sit in judgment and hear the arguments for and against him (with, appropriately, the god Apollo as counsel for the defendant). With evidence in and jury polled, Orestes is declared guilty by exactly one-half the panel and innocent by the other half. At this juncture Athena appears and casts the deciding vote for acquittal. The vicious chain is broken. Moreover the goddess worked a divine miracle by transforming the vengeance-hungry Furies into benign spirits—the Eumenides. In this fashion both divine and human justice and harmony were established.

So ultimately the tragic trilogy bespoke man's promise, not doom. As the scenes progress the spectators not only experience vicarious release—the "catharsis" celebrated by Aristotle in his critique of Attic poetry—but are given instruction in living the life of the golden mean.

[5] Ibid., p. 168.

155   A. The Golden Age

Throughout the drama the middle way between *hubris* and *nemesis* is labored. Agamemnon is portrayed as a justly established ruler, but also as yielding to vainglory in setting forth on the Trojan venture. Electra is shown as properly sensitive to the voice of conscience, but meanly motivated in her vengeful response. Orestes appears as a son understandably stricken and affronted by his mother's crass and brutal behavior, but too easily overpersuaded to correct one wrong by committing another.

Moreover the drama faithfully portrays the fatal attraction one misstep may hold for a second, and that for a third and a fourth and so on. Agamemnon, in yielding to the desire to avenge Helen (a willing victim, it should be noted) by waging war against the Trojans, found it difficult to withstand the cruel command to sacrifice his own daughter in order that the avenging fleet could sail. His integrity thus compromised, he could himself commit adultery in the name of challenging it. And on his return, when Clytemnestra spread the purple carpet before him—which, he well knew, was rightly trod by the gods alone—his far and repeated straying from the path of piety and disciplined living allowed—indeed impelled—him to commit this final blasphemy. Throughout he was given opportunities of wrenching himself from his drift to destruction; but, of course, after each misstep the return became progressively more difficult.

Sophocles and Euripides

Thus Aeschylus, responding to the challenge of his times, sought to probe the larger meanings and purposes of life, the nature of justice and destiny, and the relationship between the human and the divine.* A generation later Sophocles (495–406 B.C.) took up the same theme and produced works that some critics hold in even higher esteem than those of his predecessor. *Oedipus Rex, Oedipus at Colonus, Antigone,* and *Electra* are four of the many tragedies he wrote (though of all only seven are extant). Where Aeschylus modified traditional dramatic form by adding another person to the one actor and chorus, Sophocles presented his audience with chorus and three actors, thus allowing a more subtle and complex development of plot. His contemporary, Euripides (480–406 B.C.), concentrated on the secular and interpersonal conflicts of mundane existence (as in his *Medea, Hippolytus,* and *Iphigenia at Aulis*). These works moved Sophocles to remark that "he painted men as they ought to be while Euripides painted them as they are," a remark that pointed to "the most important change wrought by the last of the great tragedians in the Greek drama."[6]

The later works of Sophocles and Euripides clearly depicted the deterioration of Athenian life that we shall note in the following section. Athenian progress in democratic and material achievements offered in actual life the same temptations of power and glory that were underscored in Attic tragedy. And Athens, the proud polis—just like Agamemnon and Oedipus—yielded to them, as we shall see, with the same fatal results that befell the heroes of Aeschylus and Sophocles.

Aristophanes

Somewhat ironically the dramatist whose characters most vividly bring alive the spirit of this period was Aristophanes, no tragedian but a writer of comedies. Within his life span (ca. 450–389 B.C.)

---

* For a full and rewarding examination of the Aeschylean genius and its impact see Bonnard, op. cit., vol. 1, chap. 9, on which the above is patterned.

[6] George Howe and G. S. Harrer, eds., *Greek Literature in Translation* (New York: Harper & Row, Publishers, 1924) p. 284.

156   The Greek Way: from Polis to Cosmopolis

Oedipus ponders the riddle of the Sphinx.

Athens both achieved its peak and began its downward plunge. In the new milieu of violence and spreading chaos Aristophanes sought with the scorn of his biting satire to expose the fatal drift affairs had taken. In *The Acharnians* and *Lysistrata* he caricatured both the person of the warrior and the spirit of war. The "hero" of *The Acharnians* is an ignorant peasant who, realizing that leaders and people alike have fallen victim to war-madness while loudly proclaiming desire for peace, preposterously makes peace for himself and proceeds to live accordingly. Athenians were invited to laugh at the ludicrous episodes that followed—and also to realize on their way home from the play that they had been laughing at themselves. *Lysistrata,* a wry, bawdy drama, revolves about circumstances that follow when the war-weary women of Greece declare a "love-strike" against their strutting martial spouses.

Other targets of his lampooning wit were democratic demagogues (*The Knights*), those of his own craft whom he considered bowed down with their own weightiness (*The Frogs*, aimed at Euripides, no less!), and the sophists, of whom Aristophanes considered Socrates the pompous master wordmonger (*The Clouds*). With his death a century of classic drama closed.

Lyric and Epic Poetry

Of lyric and epic poetry of this period there is not much to examine, since tragic drama seemed to absorb the Greek genius.

157   A. The Golden Age

But at least one lyricist, Pindar (ca. 515–ca. 435 B.C.), wrote verse graced by an enduring nobility. To Pindar the gods' greatest gift to man was heroic action, particularly as it exhibited itself in athletic contests and war. But to earn a hero's reward the athlete or warrior must identify himself with the community, particularly the aristocratic portion that nurtured him; otherwise his talents would be wasted in mere vainglory. A fair sample of his many odes follows:

> *If any man be fortunate in the glory of games*
> *or strength of riches, and yet check down bitter excess in his heart,*
> *it is his to be wrapped in the praise of his city's men.*
> *Great prowess descends upon mortals, Zeus, from you; the prosperity of the worshipful lives long;*
> *but those whose hearts are aslant, with them it stays not long to wax or blossom.*
> *In requital for great things done we must praise the noble in song,*
> *and in our acclamation lift them high with the gentle Graces.*
> *It is Melissos' destiny for twofold success to turn*
> *his heart toward the sweetness of satisfaction.*
> *In the glades of Isthmos he was given garlands, and in the folds of the valley*
> *of the deep-breasted lion he made Thelus* to be acclaimed*
> *by conquering in the chariot race. He refutes not the*
> *virtue in men's blood engendered. Know that, of old, Kleonymos was famed for chariots;*
> *And they of his mother's side, akin to the children of Labdakos,*
> *advanced laboring their wealth on the four-horsed car.*

* Pindar's home city.

> *But time, in the turning-over of days, works change for better or worse; the unwounded are God's children.*[7]

History

The Greek genius in drama was matched in prose by the creation of a new discipline, history. Essentially, history is rational inquiry into the record of human events. By this definition all, or almost all, that man spoke or wrote about past human behavior, hopes, fears, etc., before Herodotus is not history, however valuable or interesting it may be. We have read excerpts of Mesopotamian accounts about the creation of man and about human developments of various kinds. We have read portions of such accounts written by other pre-Greek writers. But these are not history in the particular sense in which we are using it here because those writers did not inquire in order to know, and because they dealt more with superhuman than with human affairs. Many of these accounts are elementary theology rather than history; many are recitals of legendary heroics. It should be repeated that many were of high worth. But they were not history.

In the fifth century B.C. the Greek mind, following in the tradition of knowledge seeking established a century earlier, turned to the question, "What are the past events that have given rise to certain current events?" Here the discipline was born; here was the question *before* the answer; indeed, *for* the answer. Here was rational probing into the *human* past.

Acclaimed by later generations as the Father of History, Herodotus (ca. 484–ca. 428 B.C.) spent the early years of his life traveling over a large portion of the civilized world known to him—the Greek mainland and islands, Asia Minor (he was

[7] Richmond Lattimore, trans., *The Odes of Pindar* (Chicago: University of Chicago Press, 1947), p. 135.

born and raised in Halicarnassus), Mesopotamia, Crete, and Egypt. Everywhere he went he probed with a prodigious energy and curiosity, collecting data of all kinds: on geography, genealogy, political and social institutions, historic annals, and folklore.

Sometime in the 450s B.C. he began to compose his account of the Persian Wars. To Herodotus these wars constituted an epochal turning point in human affairs. They demonstrated the superiority of the Greek way over that of all other peoples, although Persian virtues and values as well as those of other nations were liberally included in his story. His great work begins with a prologue in which the historian's purpose is stated: to immortalize the legacy of the past; to describe the clash of great cultures; to teach men that life is a connected whole, not a hodge-podge of discrete events. The first two-thirds of the history is taken up with the background of the Great Wars—the rise and fall of Lydia; the origins of the Greeks; the growth of Media; Persian invasions and conquests; the Ionian revolt. Thereafter he relates in ample detail the struggle between the Greeks and the Persians, concluding with an epilogue that treats of the liberation of Ionia and the return to the mainland.

It may be argued that if Herodotus had been Persian rather than Greek, his history would have shown the superiority of the Persian way; or that he may have had an inkling of his conclusion before he had finished his probing or had even begun it. Whatever the merit or lack of merit in either argument, neither one makes very much difference. For Herodotus *did* have genuine curiosity and genuine questions; he *did* labor long and hard for answers; and he *did* confine his work to human affairs. Whatever the faith with which he followed his own concept and method of inquiry (and most modern historians would grade him well on both counts), the more important fact is his creation of them.

His successor, Thucydides, was less catholic in his interests but more precise in his method. He sought to discover the course and significance of the Peloponnesian War, in which for a while he himself participated. He tried to divest himself of bias the better to learn stark truth. He disciplined himself to put aside impinging interests that might cloud his understanding of whatever answers he might find to his main question. The most famous portions of his history may seem to the modern student examples of how history should not be written. They are speeches—long speeches—which by Thucydides' own admission were put together by himself. But the substance of the speeches was not invented. This historian spent many years in close study of sources, both written and oral, subjecting these data to checking and rechecking. And at all times, it should be said again, he sought to stay outside of the material. He began with no thesis; he shrank from no information that was personally offensive. Thus from such study he learned an amplitude of facts about both events and the men who were involved in them. Only then, according to his own assertion, did he "put into the mouth of the speaker the sentiments proper to the occasion, expressed as I thought he would be likely to express them." If modern historians dare not use this particular part of the Thucydidean method, they do not unduly berate him for using it.* Indeed, it is because he was so insistent on maintaining an impartial spirit and on critically examining accounts that might and often did contain error and deception that he is called the creator of "scientific" history. Yet he was no devotee of the notion that the facts explain themselves. When he felt the need, he gave himself to interpretation without apology. A sample of this in-

---

* Thucydides did not, of course, invent this genre of expression. It was a commonplace technique of exposition in all ancient literatures and was surely used by minstrels before writing was invented.

159   A. The Golden Age

terpretative writing is given in a later portion of this chapter.

After Thucydides historiography markedly declined. In the whole of the fourth century only one name stands out. Although not to be compared with either Herodotus or Thucydides, Xenophon (434?–355 B.C.) made a significant contribution to man's "collective memory." He is best known for his *Anabasis*, a dramatic account of the attempt of a pretender to the throne to gain, with the aid of Greek mercenaries (including Xenophon himself), supreme power in Persia. More important (although far from reliable in many instances) is his *Hellenics*, a history of the Peloponnesian War that picks up where Thucydides left off. In order both to illustrate the condition of the Athenian polis in the closing years of the war and to allow a taste of Xenophon's style, a portion of this work is excerpted. It deals with an event of 404 B.C., when the arch conservatives of Athens had temporarily regained power under the rule of "The Thirty." The conservative leader was Critias, who was determined to suffer no moderation of the reactionaries' program, which had been challenged by his more liberal colleague Theramenes. As Xenophon tells the story:

Now the Thirty were elected as soon as the long walls . . . had been demolished: but though elected for the purpose of drawing up a code of laws by which they should regulate their affairs they continually deferred drawing up and promulgating those laws, but appointed a council, and the other offices, according to their own pleasure. Then they arrested, and brought to trial for their lives . . . those whom all knew to have lived in the time of the democracy by laying false information [against those, that is, who had agitated for the continued rule of democracy] and to have been a pest to the better type of men . . . they arrested whom they pleased; no longer those only who were ill-disposed and [of] little worth, but now such as they thought to bear least patiently being brushed aside. . . . Critias . . . was headlong in putting many to death . . . while Theramenes was opposed to it. Critias [finally bringing the latter to trial] rose and spoke as follows. "Gentlemen of the council, if any of you think that more are being put to death than the occasion requires, let him reflect, that when forms of government are changed, these things in all cases happen. . . . We . . . knowing that democracy is a hateful form of government to such men as me and you, and knowing also that the Lacedaemonians [that is, Spartans], who have been our preservers, the people would never be friendly, whereas the aristocracy would always continue faithful to them, are, in accordance with the wishes of the Lacedaemonians, establishing this form of government. And if we find anyone opposed to the oligarchy, as far as we can see, we put him out of the way. . . . Now then we find this Theramenes here by all means at his command to be ruining both us and you." [In reply Theramenes cited his long record of service to Athens and concluded with this challenge:] "If . . . you can, Critias, on what occasion, in concert with the popular or tyrannical party, I attempted to deprive the good and honorable of a share in government, mention it. . . ." [After this] . . . Critias, perceiving if he left it to the council to decide on his [opponent's] case by vote, he would escape, and thinking that life would not be worth having, he went up to the Thirty and had some conversation with them. After this he went out and ordered the men with daggers to present themselves openly before the council, at the bar of the house. . . . [Then] the herald of the Thirty ordered the Eleven to come for Theramenes; and when they had entered with the officers, led by Satyrus the boldest and most shameful of the number, Critias said, "We will deliver up to you this Theramenes here, condemned according to law: do ye, Eleven, seize and lead him off to the proper place, and do your duty with him."[8]

[8] J. S. Watson and Henry Dale, *The "Hellenics"* (London: G. Bell & Sons, 1882), pp. 326–35 passim.

THE SCHOOL OF HELLAS: FORM

Sculpture and Architecture

Before its decline into grandiose sophistry the afflatus of the Hellenic world worked its wonders in other artistic disciplines, particularly sculpture and architecture. Already by the early fifth century Greek talent had achieved a monumental breakthrough in the plastic arts. By this time it had effected a marriage of imagination and technique that produced works characterized by exquisite tension between the real and the ideal. Before we sample these masterpieces, however, we should note that they were paid for by several centuries of apprenticeship. In the *Hera of Samos,* which resembles more a "[tree] trunk which is turning into a woman than the image of the divine being," the Greek mind, although showing promise of the flowering to come, was still tied to the rigid patterns of the past. Even so, as early as the Pisistratids a steady advance in media had been made—from wood and limestone to marble and bronze.

An example in the latter medium is the *Delphic Charioteer* (ca. 475 B.C.). Already it shows the approaching breakthrough, in its realistic treatment of posture and especially of the hands and feet, as does the marble *Calf-bearer.* It is true that the awkward and restrictive "laws of frontality" were still being honored, but their days were clearly numbered. Indeed, within a single generation, by what one authority has called a kind of sudden artistic mutation, Greek art shed its archaic features and assumed classic dimensions.

Dramatically heralding the new art are the works of Myron (480–445 B.C.), especially his famous *Discobulus* and the *Marsyas with Athena* (of which only Roman copies are extant). In the *Discobulus* Myron portrays a discus thrower at the climax of his windup, at the moment when disciplined energy and muscles tauten the whole body for release. "With this statue Myron transports us into a world of action in which movement has suddenly become sovereign, and man knows the intoxication of strength restrained by balance. In this sense he is the founder of statuary, as Aeschylus, his contemporary, is the inventor of dramatic action. Both of them are exploring the limits of human strength."[9] To call this "realism" is true, but it is not the whole truth. For at this point Greek art proclaims man as Titan, as possessor of strengths and will, which, in the words of a contemporary Hebrew psalmist, mark him as "a little lower than the angels."

Myron's contemporary, Phidias (490–417 B.C.), approached perfection in demonstrating the Greek conception of the ultimate relationship between the human and the divine. Called by a Greek traveler and geographer of Roman times the "maker of gods," Phidias portrayed the divine in human form, suggesting simultaneously the closeness of the gods to men and human potentials for making "what is" into "what ought to be." In his colossal Olympian *Zeus* the artist managed to evoke in spectators (according to ancient writers) at once a sense of awesome majesty and benign concern for humanity. In the famous *Lemnian Athena* Phidias again humanized divinity while inviting man to let his reach exceed his grasp. The later years of his life were spent supervising the decoration of the Parthenon, himself designing and executing an undetermined number of its reliefs as well as the huge *Athena* that was its esthetic center. Nearly 100 *metopes* (panels), each over a yard square, told the story of legendary crises: battles between the Amazons and Greeks, between half-human heroes

---
[9] Bonnard, op. cit., 1:46.

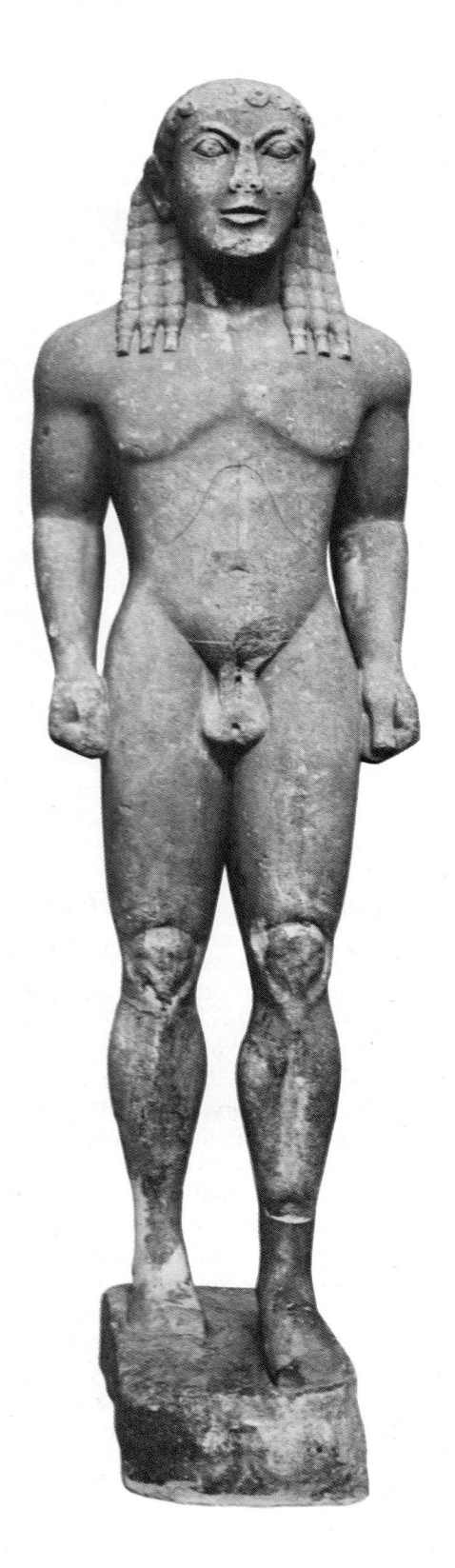

LEFT:
Biton, early sixth-century figure, clearly indicates the Greek sculptor's debt to his Cretan and Egyptian mentors.

BELOW:
Hera of Samos. This draped figure reveals how closely Greek sculptors of the early sixth century were bound to stylized Egyptian conventions.

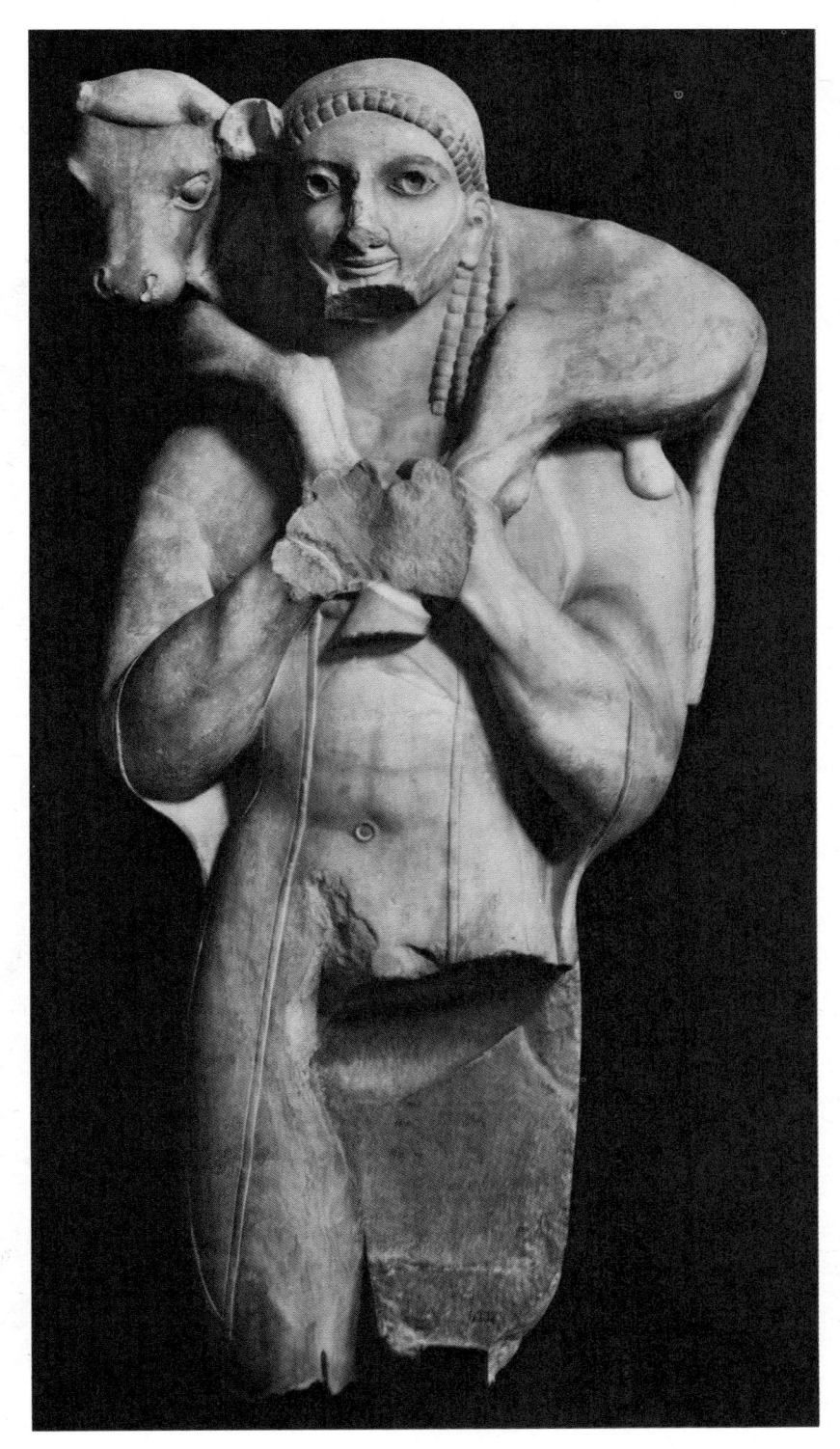

The Calf-Bearer, a sixth-century votive statue.

Roman copy of Doryphorus, by Polyclitus (ca. 430 B.C.).

Diadumenus, by Polyclitus.

Hermes, by Praxiteles. The hand of the missing right arm held a bunch of grapes for which the infant Dionysos is reaching.

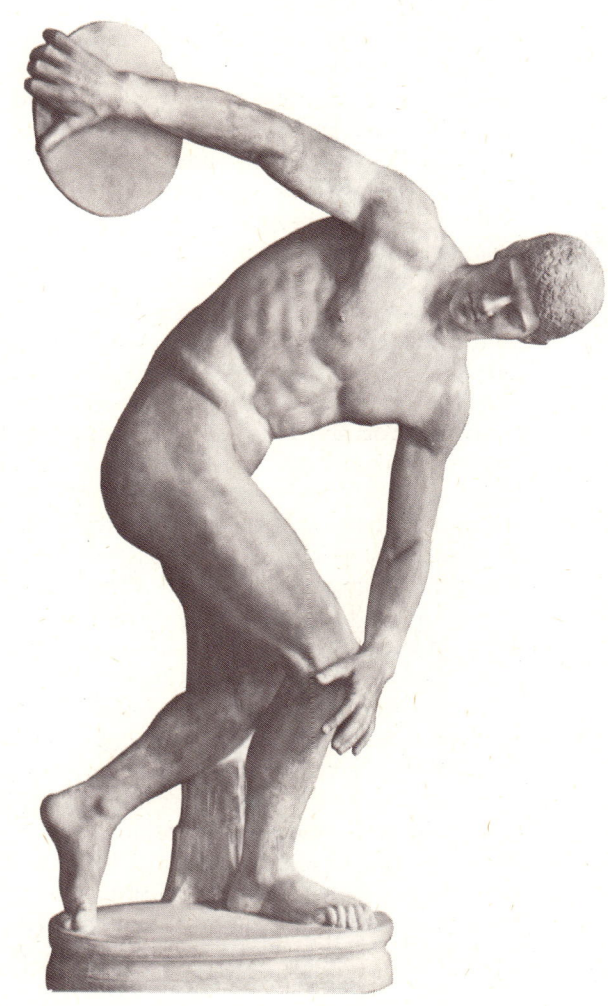

Discobulus. This Roman copy of a work by Myron (ca. 455 B.C.) is a measure of the growth of Greek genius in the century since the Calf-Bearer.

and the gods, between Centaurs and Lapithae (a mythical people of Thessaly), and between Agamemnon's warriors and Hector's Trojans, "all representing the eternal pattern of conflict and conquest." The east and west pediments depicted the birth of the city's protecting goddess and her struggle with the sea god Poseidon. Encircling the inner walls (*cella*) was a continuous frieze portraying the Panathenaic Procession, a festival held every four years to celebrate Athena's power and benevolent spirit.

The culmination of this classical religio-humanistic impulse, this supremely creative effort to build the world of man according to the model of the world of the gods, is found in the statues of Polyclitus (fl. 452–415 B.C.). We have seen how Myron brought life to bronze. In Polyclitus's *Doryphorous* (lance-bearer) and *Diadumenus* (victorious athlete) we move beyond masterly expression of the moment of action to equally masterly representation of *man becoming* or, more broadly, "the conception of a society that is becoming more than itself." The human body is portrayed in anatomical faithfulness: the muscles are bunched in the right places as the weight of the body is thrown slightly on the right foot, with the heel and instep of the left foot lifted from the ground, suggesting, in all, the posing of *life* rather than a passing burst of energy. In the *Diadumenus* the facial expression reflects the double mystery of the union of mind-body and man-god. It is easy (as well as dangerous, of course) to imagine the emotional response of mid-fifth century Hellenes as they beheld the works of this sculptor. Here, they may well have felt, is what we are and what we may become, conscious of the reality around us and sensitive to the spirit that beckons us god-ward. So impressed were Polyclitus's contemporaries with his *Doryphorous* that they called it simply the *canon*—the standard and measure, as they believed, of plastic art for eternity.

A century later, behind an artificially prettied facade, the glory that was Greece lay in shambles. But so strong had been the creative thrust that even in the fourth century's managed chaos its force was still felt. In this period a number of works were produced by Praxiteles (fl. ca. 370–330 B.C.), the most famous of which is *Hermes.* Here the god is portrayed with the child Dionysos in his arms, half-teasingly offering the infant a bunch of grapes. The touch of the master is as clear and abundant as in the great works of the preceding century, although the tendency of the Hellenistic world to go the way of the flesh—that is, to indulge in what is called naturalism—is already manifest in the purely human features of the god.*

The heights reached by Greek sculpture in the fifth century B.C. were matched by those achieved in architecture. Indeed, these were usually united in the same artistic effort. The most conspicuous example of this union of esthetic disciplines is the Parthenon, temple of the virgin goddess Athena. As early as the Pisistratid period the great natural elevation abutting Athens to the north—the Acropolis—had been envisioned as a site for temple construction, and such construction had actually been started. In the sack of Athens during the Great Wars, however, the Persians had destroyed these beginnings. A generation after Salamis the work was taken up afresh, this time under the general supervision of Pericles. His aim was to create a work of art that would serve not only as an offering of thanks to the city's protecting goddess but also as a symbol of the vaulting spirit of Athens. In addition, he hoped it would serve as a spiritual rallying center for all of Hellas. Co-operating with him in both the planning and the execution of this enterprise were

---

* This description of the works of the Greek masters gives the impression that we possess all or most of them. Unfortunately this is not true. Our knowledge of many of them comes from ancient writings and from numerous copies made by the Romans.

Phidias, Sophocles (who between writing chores on the *Antigone* sandwiched in service as chairman of the Financial Commission of the Delian League), and Athens's great architects, Ictinus and Callicrates. For 15 years (447–432 B.C.) this politico-esthetic brain trust devoted a great part of its collective energy to the building of that temple, called by some the most nearly perfect structure ever reared by man.

In its basic design the Parthenon is simplicity itself: a double-columned rectangular building with a colonnaded portico on each end—"a marble poem." The columns are of the chaste Doric design. To give the effect of symmetrical solidity the four treadways are of unequal dimensions. The first is almost imperceptibly smaller than the second, the second than the third, the third than the fourth, so that "as seen from a distance the . . . upper step does not give the impression of sinking under the weight of the edifice." Indeed, the whole embodies a number of such deliberate and subtly calculated disproportions and imbalances. The step surfaces, for example, are given a slight swelling toward the center in order to offset the optical illusion of concavity that would otherwise result. The same is true of the floor; and the "columns, besides the usual upward taper, have a delicate convex curve. The outside ones lean inward. The refinements correct the inadequacy of the human eye. But for them the building would seem to bulge at the top and its horizontal lines to sag. . . . The Athenian worshipper, stirred by the outward grandeur of the Parthenon and its sculptured story, was stirred even more when he beheld . . . the goddess within her shrine, dwarfing the spectator in her vast majesty, magnificently robed as befitted one radiating the power and beauty appropriate to the daughter of Zeus. . . ."[10]

Before the century ended three other buildings adorned the Acropolis. Designed by Mnesicles, the Propylaea, occupying the westernmost portion of the Acropolis and serving as its gateway, combined the more slender Ionic column with the Doric. Its five entrances invited assorted throngs, religious processionals, individual worshippers, and ordinary sightseers. To the southwest Callicrates erected a miniature shrine to the city's great protectress, the *Athena Nike,* containing his delightfully informal representation of the goddess tying her sandal. Several hundred feet beyond it rose the two-level Erechtheum, an elegant Ionic structure; female figures, the Caryatids, supported the roof of one porch.

Although it would be absurdly wrong to say that the construction of the Erechtheum (completed ca. 405 B.C.) marked the last artistic triumph of the Hellenic world, it is accurate enough to hold that by then that world had seen its greatest architectural triumphs.

From reliable manuscript sources we know that painting was also a highly developed art. But almost all surviving examples are the examples found on pottery. Many of them are in red, or in red or black, although all of the fundamental colors were used. Prolific Attic vase painters ranged through many themes such as female figures in various poses, sometimes running; soldiers donning helmets and other war gear; mythological heroes and heroines; and landscape scenes. Undoubtedly a number of both themes and techniques were taken from the pure painting of the period (400s B.C.), especially from murals and other large works of Polygnotos and Mikon, Greece's two master artists of that century.

Hellas's Golden Age was relatively shortlived, encompassing scarcely two generations. But for posterity perhaps a portion of the famous remark made in another context by Winston Churchill aptly applies—never was so much owed by so many to so few.

---

[10] Scramuzza, op. cit., pp. 225–53.

A view of one side and one colonnaded portico of the Parthenon. Even the ruins of today suggest the chaste grandeur of this once "marble poem."

On the western edge of the Acropolis the Propylaea, pictured here together with the Temple of Athena Nike, was the great gateway through which Athenians and visiting tourists passed to see the other marble marvels of the city's proud showpiece.

RIGHT:
Nike, from the Temple of Athena Nike, by Callicrates.

BELOW:
Erechtheum, with Caryatids.

B. The Age of Empire — POWER POLITICS, SOCIAL LAG, AND THE PELOPONNESIAN WAR

Politics: Rivalries and Alliances

The battle of Plataea had freed Greece from the Persian threat. But how long would security last? Would not the great Eastern horde mount a third attack? And if it did, could the miracle of 479 be repeated?

In spite of the ambiguity of the situation, almost immediately after Plataea the Greek weakness for particularism again showed itself. Each city-state returned, or tried to return, to the world of its own polis. Except for the period of the Persian Wars, Sparta had long looked on Athens as an evil second only to the Persian "barbarians," a feeling fully reciprocated by the Athenians. Argos, Corinth, and Thebes, among others, feared both city-states and sought ways to counter their power.

Nevertheless Athens was able to persuade a number of other communities to join in a naval confederation (478 B.C.) to guard the peninsula and free the Ionians still under Persian rule.* This Delian Confederacy—so-called from locating the common treasury and council on the island of Delos—did succeed in keeping the Persians Asia-bound. But for the allies the price was high. From the beginning Athens made it clear that it intended to call the tune, demanding ships or their equivalent in money as it saw fit.† Two states that declined to join (Scyros and Carystus) were promptly conquered and made subject to Athenian rule. Naxos, wishing to withdraw, was occupied. When Xerxes showed signs of regathering his forces for another offensive he was attacked and decisively beaten before he could leave Asian waters. Following this victory (Eurymedon, 468 B.C.) Athenian ambitions knew no limits. Thasos, off the Thracian coast, was overrun in 465 B.C. A few years later both the league council and the treasury were moved from Delos to Athens. By then the defensive alliance, which eventually came to number some 470 cities, had been turned into an Athenian empire.

By this time the democrats under the leadership of Pericles had taken most of their power from the conservative Areopagites. They had also begun reconstruction of the temples and other buildings on the Acropolis, whose glories, they hoped, would serve not only as the "school of Hellas" but as the symbol of

---

* Originally the allies had invited Sparta to head a protective league. It was only after Sparta refused that they turned to Athens, some reluctantly.

† The original assessment was carried out with little or no friction, due to the reputation of Aristides who was chosen as the assessor. Throughout the peninsula the character of this statesman was recognized as above reproach. His original decisions were indeed scrupulously fair and just.

Athenian supremacy. From the steadily increased levies abundant wealth was at hand together with, as we have seen, almost a plethora of intellectual and artistic talents. And unification of the poleis into a Greek confederacy was long overdue.

With what can only be called tribute money the great Attic city did indeed adorn the Acropolis; but creation of a confederated Hellas was quite another matter. For one thing, certain decisions of the government, dominated now for a generation by Pericles and his subordinates, made the city suspect. In the period 454–451 B.C. pay for public service, especially court service (in the *Heliaea*), was instituted. Also a new law was passed restricting citizenship to those who could claim both parents as citizens of Athens. On the surface neither law seemed reprehensible. If the poorer commoner was to exercise his office-holding privileges he must be compensated. And since *metics* (residents of foreign birth) and other foreigners increasingly made up a substantial portion of the population, the Athenian genius seemed threatened. But in the long run state pay tended to make many an Athenian a kind of idle, professional citizen. And citizenship restrictions kept much fresh political talent from participating in the democratic development of Athenian life.

Moreover two wars, in the 450s and 440s B.C., found Athens again at grips with Persia in the east and with Sparta in the west. The treaties that concluded them were fair enough. But the martial appetite, it seems, grew with feeding; in any case, the peace treaties marked only a lull. At the same time the war experiences coarsened the spirit of the people. For example, in 440 B.C. Miletus was attacked without any legal sanction, its walls torn down, its warships seized, and an indemnity of more than one million dollars imposed. And in 416 B.C., bluntly asserting the "law of nature," Athens destroyed Melos, murdering all men of military age and enslaving the others.

The Peloponnesian War

Thus constituted, with imperial designs motivated by hubris, in proud ignorance of the nemesis to come, Athens cast about for more worlds to conquer. To the east Persia temporarily lay powerless. But to the west Sparta and her allies seemed an intolerable challenge. It is true that during the period 445–431 B.C. a treaty of peace kept the rivals on nominally good terms. But, according to Thucydides, each side during that period was actually readying itself for a showdown. In 431 B.C. it came, desired by both but precipitated by Athens.

In a survey such as this it is not possible to consider the details of wars, temporary truces, individual battles, and factional strife. To the student who has a special interest in the bitter and prolonged military struggle between Athens and Sparta, Thucydides is available. In his classic work may be found an extended analysis of the motivations and aspirations of each side, the war's tortuously complex course, and its conclusion and significance. Here we may only note that it lasted, with interruptions, for nearly 30 years; nurtured rapacity and violence in the Greek soul; accentuated the drift from religious faith to sophist philosophy; mutilated what many had prized as the democratic way of life; and increased the natural and fatal Greek tendency to exalt polis over people. To illustrate the degeneration of the Greek way of life a few brief excerpts from Thucydides may be cited:

. . . all of Greece was in turmoil, the Athenians being called in everywhere by the democratic leaders and the Spartans by the oligarchs. . . . During peace and prosperity cities and individuals alike, through not meeting unbearable conditions, have more amiable sentiments; but war, depriving them of their everyday well-being, is a violent teacher, molding the tempers of the majority to resemble their present circumstances. And thereafter the cities were torn by revolution, those where it occurred late through a knowledge of earlier revolutions greatly surpassed them in new refinements, showing excessive ingenuity both in bringing them about and in making reprisals. They even took pleasure in altering the usual meaning of words to describe their actions. Hare-brained recklessness was denominated as loyal bravery, the hesitation of a reasonable man as veiled cowardice, moderation as camouflage for unmanliness and great wisdom as inability to act. . . . The violent man was always believed while anyone who opposed him was subject to distrust. The man who succeeded in a plot was felt to be clever and the one who found it out in advance to be even more so. But anyone who suggested ways of avoiding the necessity of a conspiracy was said to be ruining his party and cringing in the face of the enemy. The man who successfully carried out some dastardly enterprise was praised, and so was he who incited someone else who had previously had no such intention. Also, blood ties came to be less binding than those of party, since men would dare anything for the party and without any excuse. . . . Their trust in one another was not so much strengthened by divine law as it was by their breaking the laws together. Reasonable proposals from their opponents were accepted only as a precautionary measure, if they had obtained the advantage not in a generous spirit. . . . It was more satisfying to take revenge on account of the oath, not only because it was safer than acting in the open, but also because winning through treachery was admired as an act of superior intelligence. . . . The cause of all these things was the pursuit of power, for personal profit or out of vanity, which caused furious rivalries. Leaders of both parties in the cities resorted to high-sounding phrases, advocating the equality of all citizens before the law, or the moderation of a government of the rich. . . . Grasping for power, either by a rigged vote or by violence, they were prepared to sate their desires with immediate victory. . . .

In this way every form of viciousness arose out of the revolutionary disturbances in Greece, and that simplicity in which honor plays so large a part was laughed out of existence, while the division into opposing ideological camps brought about general distrust. There was no word strong enough, no oath terrible enough to reconcile them, for when they found themselves on top there was no one who did not take precautions against injury in the future, since their conviction that it was useless to depend upon oaths made it impossible to trust anyone.[11]

In a loose sense the long struggle may be called a kind of world war. Not only were almost all of the major Greek cities involved at one time or another; but Athens and Sparta alternately courted and received Persian aid and thus invited the ancient enemy of both to fish anew in their troubled waters. To the north, rising Macedonia, neither Greek nor barbarian, lent diplomatic support now to this side, now to that. Westward, colonies of the mother cities felt the lapping waves of fury and became embroiled in the martial tempest, particularly Corinthian Syracuse. And Carthage, poised on the tip of modern Tunisia, did what it could to weaken the efforts of any and all who might threaten its command of the Great Sea's (Mediterranean) western lanes of commerce. In a much closer sense the 30-year conflict was also a class war. Oligarchs fought democrats for control of particular city-states, "the Athenians being called in everywhere by the democratic leaders and the Spartans by the oligarchs." A typical example of the intimate relationship between the struggles for imperial power

[11] Thucydides *History of the Peloponnesian War* 3. 82–83 passim; from Truesdell S. Brown, ed., *Ancient Greece* (New York: Free Press of Glencoe, 1965), pp. 150–52.

and class domination is revealed by Thucydides in his account of the tug of war between Athens and Sparta for Corcyra (modern Corfu, off the coast of Albania). In an effort to escape destruction, Corcyraean elders adopted a policy of neutrality and sent a delegation of envoys to Athens to explain their action.

On their arrival the Athenians arrested the envoys for fomenting revolution, and the others, whom they had corrupted, they removed to Aegina for safekeeping. Meanwhile, when a Corinthian trireme reached Corcyra with envoys from Sparta, the men now controlling the government attacked the democrats and defeated them in a battle. When night came on the democrats fled to the acropolis and the heights of the city, and established themselves there in force. They also held the Hyllaic harbor. Their opponents seized the market place, where most of them lived, and the harbor nearest it which faced the mainland.

The next day there was light skirmishing while each side sent around to the countryside to summon the slaves, promising them their freedom. Most of the slaves allied themselves with the democrats, but on the other side 800 mercenaries were brought over from the mainland to help.

After a day had passed there was another battle, and the democrats won, having the advantage of a strong position and great numbers. Their wives boldly took a hand, hurling pottery from the houses and enduring the rage of battle despite their sex. The rout came late in the day, when the oligarchs now afraid the democrats might proceed unopposed to the arsenal and then destroy them, set fire to the dwellings and rooming houses around the market place to head off an attack. They did not spare their own property nor that of anyone else, so that quantities of merchandise were burned and the entire city might have been destroyed if a wind had sprung up to carry the flames on through. With this the fighting ended, and both sides spent the night peacefully on the alert. Following the democratic victory the Corinthian vessel slipped out to sea, and most of the mercenaries succeeded in making their escape to the mainland.[12]

In 404 B.C. the once invincible Athens capitulated to the Peloponnesian power that it had goaded into war. But Sparta no more than Athens could create a lasting empire. Most of the next 100 years were taken up with assorted civil and foreign wars. Thebes, Corinth, and Argos periodically enjoyed a passing dominance. Occasionally Sparta and Athens would again show signs of establishing hegemony as Persia threw its purchased weight to one side or the other. Internally, as during the original struggle, oligarchies and democracies were torn down and propped up with startling speed and impermanence. Wealth, strength, hope, and vision—all were battered in the seemingly endless melee of intraparty and international strife.

Individualism; the Rise of Rhetoric

It should not be supposed, of course, that the end of the Peloponnesian War marked the end of the Greek civilization. Man is a resilient creature. Hubris may indeed lead to nemesis; but nemesis does not mean the obliteration of man's genius. However battered, that genius showed itself in Greek life after the long night of war.

We have already noted the rise of sophism in the fifth century. Its emphasis on the critical attitude shaped a value that Greek thinkers nurtured then and for generations thereafter—the worth of the individual *as* individual. At the very beginning of the fourth century Socrates, according to Plato's account, stated the credo in its simplest terms when he said that no man, from whatever authority, could separate him from his own intellect and conscience. In the turbulent decades that fol-

[12] Thucydides 3. 72–74.

lowed, this spirit of "man by himself" infected society at almost every level. "Men [were] brooked less easily by the ties of state, of the Olympian religion, or of the old patriarchal family. In philosophy they sought personal ethical guidance and reassurance; in literature and art they favored a more emotional, realistic approach."[13] Later we shall critically examine some of the more extreme traits that grew out of the new emphasis on individualism. But that it contributed to a more meaningful encounter with life cannot be denied.

Besides a new emphasis on individualism sophism also gave rise to the art of rhetoric. By the fourth century literacy was no longer confined to the gifted few. True, the Greek multitude was still untutored; but the reading public had grown substantially. The critical issues of the times also invited "dialogue." And out of these circumstances there developed a school of expression that gave to the spoken and written word unparalleled attractiveness and persuasiveness. The man who gave classic form to this new venture in communication was Isocrates (ca. 436–338 B.C.). Himself no orator, he prepared speeches to be read by various managers of public affairs or of public enlightenment. He raised to an art the composing of sentences, the choice of words, the evocation of images. "His studied and elaborate style included elements such as the balance of clauses in antithesis, the use of clauses of the same length, the use of words of the same sound at the same positions in different clauses, and the refusal to place a word beginning with a vowel after a word ending in a vowel."[14] Perhaps it is not an exaggeration to say that after Isocrates the expression of Greek thought was never the same. Later, as we shall see, many Roman writers and orators formed their own works on this model and themselves served as models for the orators and the literature of subsequent ages. Unfortunately, the rhetoric of Isocrates, Demosthenes (see below), and others of such caliber was debased by a host of copiers more interested in superficial effect than in true articulation of serious thought. Indeed, so popular did this prostitution of the true art become that thereafter "rhetorical" was used to describe artificial, pretty speech.

ARMS AND THE MAN: THE ALEXANDRIAN EMPIRE

Rise of Macedonia

In the early years of the fourth century Macedonia, growing in strength and ambition as the once proud poleis of the south killed off one another, looked to the spreading chaos with mounting interest and, by 350 B.C., considered the time ripe for some adventuring of its own. Sensing this new danger, a Greek orator and statesman, Demosthenes, delivered in the Athenian assembly a series of prophetic warnings (the famous Philippics). But sustained vigor and purpose had been drained from Greece. At Chaeronea in 338 B.C., rough and rude warriors of the northern kingdom rode down the forces of the stricken cities. The peninsula lay prostrate before a new conqueror. Later the fabric of Greek civilization, threaded with various patterns from the East, would clothe a new Western society; but for the present it was a garment rent. The glory of classical Greece had departed.*

---

[13] Chester G. Starr, *A History of the Ancient World* (New York: Oxford University Press, 1965), p. 391.

[14] Ralph Turner, *The Great Cultural Traditions* (New York: McGraw-Hill Book Co., 1941), p. 627.

* In our study of the Roman world in the following chapter we shall see that in 338 B.C. Rome dissolved the Latin League and soon thereafter consolidated its control of the Italian peninsula. Never before or since in human history have signs clearly heralding the death of one great civilization and the birth of another been so dramatically juxtaposed within the space of a single year.

Shortly after the battle of Chaeronea its victor, Philip II, died (336 B.C.). To the Greeks, anxious to throw off the new Macedonian yoke and also to resume their own intercity fighting, the death of this fearsome warlord from the north seemed a gift from Apollo. But they were soon disillusioned. For Philip's successor, Alexander III (356–323 B.C.), had plans of his own and, although but a stripling of 20 years, ample ability to realize them.

Alexander the Great

In 335 B.C. Alexander turned to the north, where strong Balkan tribes had shown signs of breaching the frontier of civilization. Within the year he had defeated both the Getae and Triballi, brought the Celts of the region into alliance, cowed the Scyths, and reestablished Macedonian hegemony in Thrace. Soon a wish-fathered rumor that Alexander had been slain in the campaign reached the Greeks. Thebes at once rose in revolt. To make clear once and for all who was master, Alexander descended by forced marches upon the rebel city and overwhelmed its defenders. Acting as "agent" for a terrified Greek league, he leveled it to the ground, sparing only the temples and Pindar's house. All of its inhabitants, young and old, were sold into slavery and its outlying lands distributed to nearby cities. The lesson was not wasted on the rest of Greece.

The remainder of his brief life—barely a dozen years—was spent in the subjugation of Egypt and western Asia. This fantastic saga has been retold many times and cannot be detailed here. It must suffice to note that in the battles of Granicus River, 334 B.C., and Issus, 333 B.C. (see map, p. 176), Persian forces under Darius III were defeated, permitting Alexander to move south and wrest Egypt from Persian control. From here the conqueror turned east, where, at Gaugamela in 331 B.C., he routed the hosts of Darius for the third time. Thereafter he conquered with monotonous regularity whatever kingdoms and armies stood between him and India. Even the latter was invaded; but his troops had had enough, and Alexander was forced to turn back. Before he could ready new plans for the conquest of

Demosthenes, eloquent prophet of doom.

B. The Age of Empire

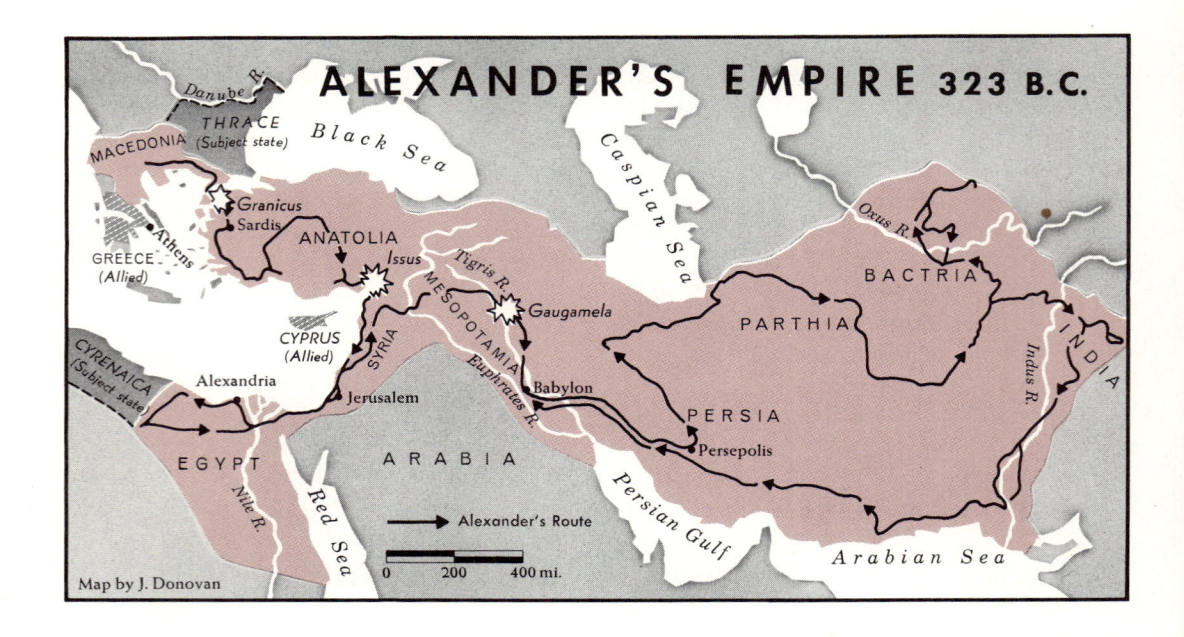

Arabia, bypassed in his rush to the east, he fell ill in Babylon and died in the summer of 323 B.C. At his death he left an empire that sprawled from the Adriatic Sea to the Indus River.

It is difficult to conjecture what impact East and West might have had on each other as a result of this forced and artificial union had Alexander been conqueror only; but he was much more than this. Added to his vaulting martial ambitions was a seemingly genuine desire to merge Greeks and Persians into one people, one vast community. To effect it he encouraged mass intermarriage (himself setting the example). To this end, too, he founded some 20 cities scattered from the Nile to the Indus, settled by Macedonians and Greeks. Liberally equipped with libraries and other cultural paraphernalia, and administered by commissions made up of both Asians and Europeans, these population centers invited a blending of eastern and western ways. The grand community, of course, never materialized. But important changes were wrought nevertheless. Language and law moved east. By the time of the birth of Christ, *koine*, a common version of classic Greek, was used by Asians and Europeans alike, as were (although not universally) many principles of Greek legal procedure.[15] On the other hand the Macedonian type of government, monarchy, was so strongly supported by Oriental custom that Greek democracy and oligarchy both gradually yielded to it. It can be argued, of course, that both East and West (especially the latter), wearied by burdens of wars, would have changed, Alexandrian thrust or not. But the thrust is history and must be duly recorded.

Division of Alexander's Empire

With Alexander's death in 323 B.C. a long struggle for imperial control began among his leading generals and in the end the empire was partitioned. Macedonia, with its hegemony over a number of Greek cities, was taken over by Antigonus (and his successors, the Philips and

[15] See M. Rostovtzeff, *The Social and Economic History of the Hellenistic World,* 3 vols. (Oxford: Oxford University Press, 1941), 2:1068–69.

176   The Greek Way: from Polis to Cosmopolis

HELLENISTIC KINGDOMS
IN THE THIRD CENTURY B.C.

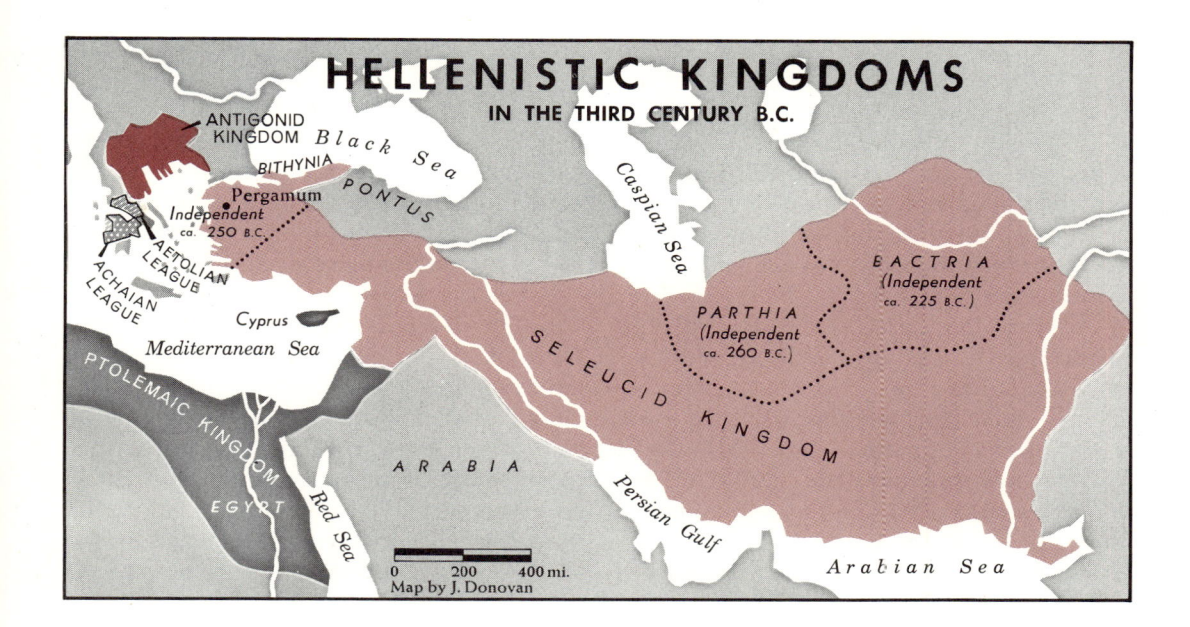

others). Much of Asia Minor and most of Syria and Mesopotamia fell to Seleucus (some of whose successors were the several Antiochuses). Ptolemy, another Macedonian war lord, carved out an empire made up of Egypt, Palestine, and part of Syria. Most of India, never conquered by Alexander, continued to maintain its independent existence. In northwestern Asia Minor along the littoral of the Black Sea, Pontus, ruled by a local dynasty, resisted Seleucid attacks. Later, Attalus Philadelphus freed Pergamum from Seleucid rule, as did various local leaders in other sections of the empire. In Greece proper two new leagues, the Aetolian and Achaean, preserved in their respective spheres a kind of home rule. (For delineation of these areas see map, above; it should especially be noted that neither Attica nor Lacedaemonia were part of these leagues).

Although the faint promise of peace initially held out by the partition never materialized, it should not be concluded that unending violence disrupted life in the cities. As a matter of fact most post-Alexandrian communities enjoyed an orderly existence either under royal bureaucratic officials or, more commonly, under their own semiautonomous (or at least locally based and controlled) municipal officers. Still, if intercity life was relatively stable and peaceful, interdynastic relations were not. But wars and violence, endemic as they were, were not all that marked the Hellenistic period. Gradually there came into being a new spirit, changed economic and social conditions, new philosophies and literature, different approaches to science and art, and new religions.

THE DEPARTURE FROM THE GOLDEN MEAN: HELLENISTIC SOCIETY

From Polis to Cosmopolis

From 430 until about 145 B.C., by which time a large part of the Hellenistic world had come under Roman rule, internecine wars drained the poleis of their energy and wealth. Most of them were eventually absorbed into one or another of the larger empires. In the process much of the *élan*

177   B. The Age of Empire

that had given the Greek his genius was lost. Where there had been *polis*-man there was now *personal*-man, uprooted, disoriented, insecure. Essentially this is what the vaunted individualism of Hellenistic times came to mean. Concurrently, with the disappearance of the city-state and the creeping merger of East and West, *ecumene*-consciousness evolved, for with the city no longer the Greek's world, the world became his city. *Polis* became *cosmopolis*. To the modern student individualism and cosmopolitanism connote progress in human sophistication. To some extent this reasoning holds for Hellenistic man, but to a greater degree it does not. True, the world was wider; but the old order and the old signposts were gone. And if the meeting of East and West, the merging of city with city, made the Greek less provincial, it also made him less Greek. The old ideal of sophrosyne faded before the frameless discontents of the people and the scrambling of the nouveaux riches for materialistic power and glory. Even criticism of the new spirit was given a kind of amused tolerance: "When Apemantus the Cynic invaded the feast of Timon of Athens to denounce waste and worldliness, he was welcomed by the *bons vivants* as a kind of sauce to the fatted calf."

Social Conditions

Perhaps in an effort to create a cultural microcosm that would substitute for the city, many Greeks, both in the homeland and those abroad, established clubs whose officers bore titles resembling those of polis officials. Neither political nor professional in nature, the clubs were designed to afford an outlet for the Greek spirit that had flowered in the city-state. Basically they functioned as recreational and social associations whose members—typically of the times, often a mixture of Greek and "barbarian"—found in the brotherhoods a sense of community that was lacking in the macrocosm of the new ecumene. In a sense the associations were a kind of graduate school for gentlemen, with membership open to those who had gone through the grammar, poetry, rhetoric, and physical education courses offered in the numerous private schools.

There is even some evidence that here and there women joined in such associations. If they did—and there is positive evidence of one in Alexandria—this would seem to argue an advance in the status of women. Strengthening this thesis is the prominent role that at least a few women played in political affairs. In both Macedonia and Egypt royal control was shared occasionally by such outstanding individuals as Olympias and the famous line of Cleopatras. But on the other hand evidence is strong that most women of the time—the wife of the typical burgher, artisan, or peasant—remained as underprivileged as her Hellenic sisters. Female infants, for example, continued to be abandoned. Those who were allowed to survive lived, as Tarn has phrased it, on a different and lower level from that of men even though informal "relations between the sexes became less cramped and more rational." And the record clearly shows that female slaves outnumbered bondsmen, especially among the "house-born."

Economic Conditions

If the status of women underwent little change, the same cannot be said of economic conditions. To be sure, mainland Greeks continued to experience grinding poverty, save for speculators and favored tradesmen. But in Asia Minor, Mesopotamia, and Egypt boom times were nurtured by the Alexandrian amalgam. For one thing, Alexander's plans to explore little-known lands were carried out, at least in part, by the dynasts who succeeded him. The first Seleucus, for example, probed areas of the Persian Gulf and settled colonies in the region. Later the coasts of Arabia and Upper Egypt were explored and trading opportunities exploited. To the north the hinterland of the Caspian Sea attracted both settlers and merchants. And although India remained strong enough to repel invaders, envoys and traders were allowed beyond the Indus River who eventually gave the Hellenistic world a vastly expanded understanding of this mysterious land.

Quite naturally, the creation of large empires and continued exploration stimulated trade. Throughout most of this period two great routes served to expedite both the exchange of goods and the diffusion of culture. The most important route was the sea-lane that ran from the delta of the Indus across the Indian Ocean, up the Persian Gulf, overland to Antioch and thence to all parts of the Western world. The second, or southern, route connected India with southern Arabia (see map, p. 177). Through these great arteries flowed goods of all kinds: gold and silver, quicksilver, (important in the manufacture of vermilion), grains, wines, oil, fruits and nuts, sugar, linen and other textiles, papyrus, glassware, marble, ebony and other rare woods, ivory, diamonds and other precious stones, spices, frankincense, and an unending stream of slaves.

To serve this trade many cities were founded or enlarged; for example, Antioch, Seleucia, Ephesus, and the many Alexandrias. In other words, the old producing centers turned into transit-trade centers. This, of course, meant the aggrandizement of the merchant bourgeois class; but not this class alone. In Egypt especially, but also in Asia, monarchs were not only rulers but often the chief entrepreneurs. The huge fortunes amassed by merchants and kings gave the general impression of great prosperity (save for mainland Greece). But it is important to note that this affluence did not seep down to the commoners; so that in contrast to, for example, fifth-century Athenians the masses of Greece, Egypt, and Asia were separated from the wealthy few by an ominous and ever-widening gulf.

Hellenistic Philosophy

In response to these changed socioeconomic conditions and the development of a different spirit and outlook, Hellenistic philosophers labored to provide a rationale that would give sense and purpose to their new world. Their way had already been prepared by the *Cynics*.* The welter of wars and the courting of hubris made a mockery of the doctrine of sophrosyne once so persuasively preached by Greek philosophers, dramatists, and artists. So in the early post-Periclean age there arose a school of thought, or better, a way of life, dedicated to renunciation of the false values and perverted practices that had dissolved the way of the golden mean. Led by Antisthenes (ca. 450–366 B.C.) and his disciples, Cynicism peeled away the pretensions of conventional life and called for a return to primitive virtue. Especially attacked were the prerogatives of wealth, race, and caste, which, in the eyes of the Cynics, made life a jungle of jealousies, a desolate wasteland where "ignorant armies clash by night." Everything invited their bitter denunciation: the foolish and fatal pride of the polis; the demeaning distinction between Greek and barbarian, master and slave, man and woman; the madness that status seekers confused with glory; the continued erection of elaborate temples while the shrine in the soul was

---

* The word suggests to the modern student something rather different from the original connotation, which was derived from the Greek word for dog. In their contempt for current customs and behavior these practical philosophers cast off the garment of convention and revelled in primitivism. Many adopted the very simplest kind of garb, some even disdaining physical cleanliness—hence their designation as "dog people."

prostituted; the catering to the appetite for things rather than thought; and the fondness for finely spun theoretical speculation as the ancient world slowly crumbled into chaos.

Related to Cynicism but differing from it in at least one important respect were the teachings of the *Skeptics*. Introduced by Timon, an associate of Alexander the Great, the doctrine of the unknowability of anything and all things came into a brief flowering in the third century B.C. The Skeptics argued that the consistency with which the greatest thinkers—as, for example, Heraclitus and Parmenides—eternally contradicted one another proved the impossibility of attainment of true knowledge. The search for the true and the good should frankly yield to cultivated indifference to the ineffable mystery of life and death. In this way man could shelter, perhaps, at least a modicum of serenity in his harassed soul. But since the day-to-day experience of human existence has an immediacy and concreteness that cannot be ignored (to say nothing of the mysterious prod within man that compels him to seek answers to his questions and bring order into his life), the philosophy of the Skeptics failed to attract wide acceptance.

Of incomparably greater influence, then and thereafter, were the teachings of Zeno (late fourth and early third century B.C.). A Phoenician who had come to Athens, which was still regarded as the school of Hellas, Zeno gathered about him on the Painted Porch (the Stoa, hence the name *Stoics* for his followers) a group of students disillusioned of the worth of Platonism and Aristotelianism and especially unsatisfied with the offerings of Cynicism and Skepticism. Zeno was fundamentally interested in what we would today call the human situation. But since man is a creature he cannot be understood apart from his creator. So Zeno began with a theological postulate: God was the fiery ether out of which all things came, in which all things rest, and to which all things return. By necessity there is therefore a spark of the divine in man; all are God's children and brothers one to another. Thus the Stoics taught, in the words of Plutarch, that "there should not be different City-States, each distinguished from the rest by its own peculiar system of justice: *all* men should be fellow citizens; and there should be one life and one order, as a flock pasturing together, which feeds together by a common law."

According to this philosophy man's basic response to the conditions of life is to seek the true and the good, as prompted by the divine impulse within him. So motivated, he will come, through reason, to an understanding of the nature of his Creator, of himself, and of his relationship to all things, giving him power to achieve the good and endure the evil. Although such understanding comes only through individual effort, Stoicism, in contrast to Cynicism and Epicureanism, by no means preached the doctrine of the essential solitude of man or of man's need to retire to the cultivation of his own garden; rather, quite the opposite. Since all are brothers, all are involved in a common life. Hence each is bound by duty and conscience to probe life unceasingly for that which is worthy and purposed by God for all. Being sons of God, men will seek to build the heavenly kingdom. Being finite, they will err and sin. For the Stoic, the good was to be sought and lived in humble appreciation of the Creator's grace. By this same grace man must learn to tolerate the results of human error and sin. Later we shall see how this philosophy came to influence profoundly both the Roman world and Christian doctrine.

But in Zeno's own time and that of his disciples *Epicureanism* had a more immediate influence. Like Zeno, Epicurus (341–270 B.C.) subordinated all interests to ethical considerations. Unlike him, he repudiated pantheism and elaborated a system of mechanistic materialism. With Democritus, Epicurus argued that the essence of all things is atoms which combine by chance to produce objects, "dissolving if unfit, persisting as individuals and species if fit. . . ." There is no God, or, if there is, he is wholly unrelated, by reason of his necessary perfection, to imperfect objects including, of course, man. All religions therefore are superstitions that stand between man and the goal of human life, which is the achievement of inner tranquillity. To the extent that man places his trust in religious myth he neglects reason and reason's method of comprehending the universe. All about man is discord and discord's products—endless possibilities of harassment and disturbances. Only the disciplined mind can bring order to the world of sensation in which we live. Necessarily this order is inner and personal.

By insisting on the need for the individual to create his own spiritual world, tolerant and tranquil, Epicureanism came by some to be considered as a kind of salvation through disciplined selfishness. Actually, however, Epicurus based his teachings on the doctrine of sacrificial altruism. If he will, man may through reason transmute selfish drives into compassion; indeed, he must since reason links all men to one another. And no man, conscious of this and faithful in the use of his talents, can fail to understand that personal serenity is incompatible with indifference to the inner well-being of others. On the other hand Epicureanism, in its concentration on the creation of the inner citadel of security, disavowed all interest in public affairs. As the conditions of Hellenistic life became more hectic and man more concerned with material things, this way of life became, in the hands of dilettante philosophers, almost diametrically opposite to that of its original nature and form. It became, in short, the refuge of debauchees, who used it to justify their own escapist attitude of "eat, drink and be merry, for tomorrow we die." As we shall see when we examine the literature of the Roman world, the best exposition of its true nature was presented in Lucretius's famous *De Rerum Natura* (Concerning the Nature of Things).

Science

More compelling for the Hellenistic world than the pull of philosophy was the attraction of science. The ecumene created by Alexander, the continuing explorations after his death, and the materialistic approach prompted by, among other motivations, commerce and industry tended to incline the Greek mind toward observation, measurement, and analysis of natural phenomena (although interest in the occult and in religion did not die out).

The tendency of the Hellenistic Greek toward scientific inquiry was given focus, especially in astronomy, by the lore of Babylonia, where the disciplined use of recorded astronomical observations had its origin. Kidinnu and his predecessor, Aristarchus of Samos (ca. 310–230 B.C.) postulated the startling thesis that the earth orbits the sun and not vice versa. This suggestion, as Tarn points out, "should have been epoch-making." But the theory died at birth, for Aristarchus made the orbits of the planets circular rather than elliptical and geometricians of the day had no difficulty in conclusively proving that the sun could not rest in the center of a circle. Had Aristarchus been able to make the imaginative leap to elliptical movements, thus firmly establishing the heliocentric theory, it is quite possible that the Christian Fathers would have incorporated it—as they later did the geocentric theory—into their theology, obviating much of the catastrophic wrench that followed the demonstrations of Copernicus and Galileo some 2000 years later. As it was, other Hellenistic scientists, particularly Claudius Ptolemy (ca. A.D. 150) rejected the idea and persuasively argued the geocentric thesis.

Similarly leaning upon Babylonian lore, Hipparchus (fl. 161–126 B.C.) charted the heavens, positioning no less than 805 fixed stars. It is thought that he may also have discovered the regular movement of the sun across the equator, thus establishing the pattern of the progression of the seasons. The moon's distance from the earth and its diameter were calculated with approximate accuracy. In the next century Posidonius (fl. ca. 100 B.C.) came close to determining the distance and diameter of the sun, accomplishments again unfortunately ignored by Ptolemy.

Because of the close relationship of the methods and processes of mathematics to philosophy, Hellenistic intellectuals were particularly attracted to it. Since the system of notation was as yet unformed, the Greeks developed geometry rather than algebra. Compiling and systematizing the advances made in this field, Euclid (ca. 300 B.C.) produced a textbook that served students down to our own century. Archimedes of Syracuse (ca. 287–212), although professing to believe that knowledge was gained only for its own sake, was as much at home with applied mathematics and its derivatives as with theory. For example, when his friend and close relative Hiero, king of Syracuse, asked him to determine whether a certain royal crown was pure gold or contained some silver, as he suspected, Archimedes mulled over the problem for days. The key to the solution came to him in his bath. The displacement of water by his body suggested to him the idea of measuring the displacement of water by both gold and silver objects. In this way he hit upon the law of specific gravity.

Similarly motivated was Archimedes' discovery of the laws of leverage. When Rome was planning an attack against Syracuse Hiero again applied to the mathematician for help. In this case the problem was how to launch the *Syracusia*, a war vessel of far greater than normal tonnage. Working out the laws governing the mechanics of the pulley, Archimedes devised an instrument that permitted him, unaided by any force beyond his own muscular strength, to launch the outsized ship. His *On Plane Equilibria or Center of Gravity of Planes* laid the foundation of theoretical mechanics, as his *On Floating Bodies* created the study of hydrostatics, a branch of physics dealing with the pressure and equilibrium of liquids. He also "calculated the limits for the value of π . . . [and] laid the foundations of the calculus of the infinite."

In geography Eratosthenes (ca. 275–195 B.C.) not only extended the use of the parallels of latitude and the meridians of longitude but succeeded in measuring within a remarkably small margin of error (less than 200 miles) the circumference of the earth. Anticipating Vasco da Gama by about 1700 years, he argued that one could sail from Spain to India by rounding Africa.* He correctly guessed that all the oceans flow into one another and constructed the best maps that the ancient world produced.

Hippocrates (ca. 470–370 B.C.), father of the science of medicine, developed the canon and basic practices of the healing arts. He believed that symptoms could be effectively treated only if case histories were kept and consulted. So he introduced the practice of keeping a detailed account of a particular illness, its response to treatment, and the seeming permanence of the cure, or seeming causes of the disease's resistance to treatment.† But he was not satisfied with mere technical competence. Just as important, he believed, was the social and moral standard of values held by the physician. Out of this concern he

---

* And anticipating Eratosthenes were the Phoenicians who, according to Herodotus, had turned the trick in reverse.

† He also unhappily introduced a theory of disease the influence of which bedeviled patient and practitioner alike for centuries: that all bodily disorders originate in a malfunctioning of one or more of the four "humors"—yellow bile, black bile, blood, and phlegm.

drew up an oath that has lasted to our day. In it the promise is made that the practitioner will be governed solely by the needs of the patient, not by fees; that (implicitly) he will not practice mercy killing; and that all statements made by patient to doctor will be kept in strict confidence.

Perhaps the greatest name in medical science after Hippocrates was Herophilus (early third century B.C.). From vivisection of animals and dissection of cadavers Herophilus was able to explain many features of the nervous system. He pointed out the connection between the brain and the spinal cord, taught that the function of the arteries is to carry blood, not air, and came close to discovering the circulation of the blood (an achievement, we may note, that had to await the passing of another 20 centuries).

Another medical pioneer was Erasistratus, of Chios (200s B.C.). Particularly important were his singling out the distinction between sensory and motor nerves, and his study of cranial convolutions. On the practical side may be mentioned his devising of the catheter.

Literature and the Fine Arts

The steady advance in science was not matched by similar achievements in literature. Not that writers were scarce or that their production was limited; in fact, the age was drenched with a flood of literary works. New and efficient means of processing the papyrus reed supported the steadily rising rate of literacy. Also, public libraries sprang up in many cities, for example in Rhodes, Pergamum, Antioch, and Alexandria. At one time the library at Alexandria could boast of a collection of nearly a million rolls. Here, too, the Ptolemys set up and maintained a museum—the first in history—where devotees of the muses spent their lives in genteel practice of the arts. But little of this tremendous output of creative energy has survived the test of the ages (or for that matter has survived in physical form, so that much of what we know of it comes from later references).

Still, despite so little remaining from so much, Hellenistic literature did make a lasting mark on Western culture. In part this is due to its borrowings from Hellenic works, in part to the amiable genius of its one great dramatist—Menander—and finally to Roman zeal in borrowing, indeed often copying, the best that the later Greek world produced.

Aratus of Soli wrote, among dozens of other works, a long poem detailing the positions and clusters of the stars. Of itself it is scarcely worth mentioning, but somehow its hexameters intrigued, some two centuries later, the great Virgil, who used it as a kind of model for his *Georgics*. Even more influential was the epigram invented by Antimachus and developed, among others, by Callimachus (ca. 310–245 B.C.). Later we shall note the use made of it by the Roman versifier Martial; here we may sample it both to appreciate its original form and to mark the distance Hellenistic poets had traveled from the lofty themes of their Hellenic masters.

> *Sleep on, Conopion, and care not for*
> *Thy lover sleepless on thy frigid porch.*
> *Sleep on, ungentle one, nor heed a love*
> *Unpitied even in thy careless dreams.*
> *Thy neighbors sigh; bereft of pity,*
>   *though,*
> *Thy artful sleep. But greying hair will*
>   *yet*
> *Remind Conopion of all these things.*
> . . . .
>
> *Callignotus vowed to Ionis that*
> *No man or woman would he ever hold*
> *More dear than she. This oath he*
>   *swore.*
>   *But what*
> *They say is true—immortals' ears*
> *Are not for lovers' oaths. And now his*
>   *flame*

B. The Age of Empire

This relief shows Menander, master playwrite of Hellenistic times, inspecting masks to be worn by actors who will make, we must suppose he is hoping, his characters literally come to life.

    *Is—yes!—a man, while poor Ionis
        shares
With the Megarians a limboed love.*[16]

Besides the epigram other poetic forms were devised by Hellenistic writers, particularly the idyll and the pastoral. But their virtues ran to perfection of structure and pretty turns of speech rather than to probing insights expressed in disciplined, unpretentious form. Equally mediocre, or worse, were the tragedies produced by dramatists who sought the profound and found, at best, only the precious. Of all their works—and Tarn points out that they were "manufactured in quantities"— not one of worth remains. In comedy the record is better, although by about 250 B.C. this esthetic vein had petered out. But the New Comedy bore little resemblance, either in structure or content, to the Aristophanean model. For one thing, the chorus disappeared. For another, the content tended to deal almost exclusively with manners. The plot, moreover, was usually a mélange of impossible coincidences, mistaken identities, and contrived endings. Some understanding of the new comedy can be gained from the following excerpt from Menander's only extant play, the *Dyskolos* (translated by Gilbert Highet under the title *The Curmudgeon*). The scene is laid in the Athenian countryside. The god Pan instructs the audience in what to expect. The following gives a fair notion of

---

[16] These are epigrams 64 and 27 from Callimachus's collection. Adapted from prose, *Callimachus, Lycophron, Aratus,* Loeb Classical Library (New York, 1921), pp. 181, 155.

184   The Greek Way: from Polis to Cosmopolis

the interests labored by writers of the New Comedy:[17]

[Enter Pan, from his sacred cave.]
Pan: Imagine this to be the Athenian countryside—that place called Phyle—and the grotto here behind me a local sanctuary for these hardrock farmers who live in Phyle: this is a very famous shrine. The farm you see here on the right is owned and worked by a man called Cnemon. He hates all his fellow-men. He treats them all like a curmudgeon. He loathes people. Loathes people? Why, though he is well into middle age, never in all his life has he said an agreeable word, not one. He's never given anyone "Good morning," except to Pan (that's me), his neighbor—when he's forced to pass my shrine; and then he's sorry he opened his mouth, I'm sure of that. Well, though he's such a character, he married a wife! He chose a woman lately widowed, whose first husband had died not very long before, leaving her with one son, still almost a baby. But he quarreled with his new wife the whole day long, and went on bickering afterwards nearly the whole night, and lived a wretched life. Then a daughter was born. This made him worse. His wife suffered unspeakably, found her existence full of hard labor and sourness, and left him. She went away to find a home with her son—the son of her first marriage. He has a tiny farm, only a field or two, here in the neighborhood close by; and there he just contrives to scratch a living for his mother, and himself, and a single faithful servant left him by his father. The boy is now in his teens, but has a mind far more mature than youth of his age: for we progress through learning to face difficulties. Meanwhile, the old man lives alone with just his daughter and one old servant-woman: carrying logs, digging, always digging and slaving, and—starting with his neighbors and his own wife, right down as far as the walls of Athens—hating the whole world, each and every one. The girl has grown to be just what he's made her, ignorant but innocent of evil. She is quite devoted to my sisters here, the Nymphs: she honors them sedulously; and so she has persuaded us to show some favor to her. There is a youth, who has a wealthy father, a landowner in this place, with enormous estates worth many thousands: he is a young man about town. Well, he came out to hunt with his servant and his dogs, and he happened to stop off at this place, by pure chance. I used my power as a god. He fell in love with the girl. There are the main facts. Now you shall see the story worked out in detail, if you like. I hope you will. For here I think I see, coming towards us now, the young man in love, with his friend and boon companion, deep in conversation about his love affair. [Exit Pan into his grotto.]

As we shall see, many Roman writers leaned heavily upon Menander and other writers of the New Comedy. From them came both the models and the inspiration that shaped the plays of other and later western writers including Molière and Shakespeare.

Finally it may be noted that, characteristically, Hellenistic man had a strong penchant for digests of both Hellenic and his own literature. Much as today many Americans concentrate their readings on digests of books, so Hellenistic readers demanded and were given copious digests of all kinds of literary, philosophic, and scientific writings. Other works in popular demand were romantic and historical novels.

History

Our chief authority for the development of events during the half-century after Alexander's death is Hieronymus (ca. 250 B.C.), who was both politician and historian. Besides serving as a source for Plutarch in the writing of his *Lives,* the works of Hieronymus helped later historians to put flesh on the skeletal outline of this period. Following him, Polybius (ca. 198–117 B.C.) produced a narrative of

[17] Gilbert Highet, ed. and trans., "The Curmudgeon by Menander," *Horizon* 1, no. 6 (July 1959): 81.

events from about 230 to about 145 B.C. A Greek captured by the Romans, he became almost a Roman himself, much admired by his contemporaries and much used by subsequent historians. Upon him we depend for a great deal of what we know of the second and third Punic Wars and of the story of Rome's conquest of the Mediterranean world. Although strongly biased in favor of the Romans, he nonetheless dealt justly with Hannibal and generally tried to find and present the truth as his abilities and sources allowed. By modern historians he is often ranked second only to Thucydides.

The Plastic Arts

In whatever medium of expression, style always reflects the spirit of a people. So the new spirit of Hellenistic man evoked a new style in the plastic arts, as in all others. It would be folly to hold that Hellas, even in its golden period, perfectly practiced the sophrosyne that it preached. Still, Hellas conceptualized, idealized, and seriously tried to live by it. In Hellenistic times this was not so. With the Peloponnesian War and the Alexandrian conquests came a new world, larger in dimensions, smaller in hopes, psychically restless, impatient of all faiths. It was eager to probe and to find, if it could, the *real* for what increasingly it came to regard as the grand illusions of the golden days. With such feelings and outlook it was inevitable that art styles of the Hellenistic world would be different from those of the Hellenic world. For modern man it is easy, if he is an ardent admirer of the Greek genius of the fifth century B.C., to look on its successor as degenerate or prettily precious or both. But it is also easy to overlook the terms of existence of an age, and therefore to do injustice to their artistic expression. Judged by those terms the Hellenistic practitioner of the plastic arts possessed his own genius.

Sculpture and architecture—we cannot speak of painting and music, since almost no remains are extant—clearly reflected the new mood, the new spirit. The trend toward realism, the *what is* in contrast to the *what ought to be*, is perhaps best exemplified in the famous head of Euthydemus, a Bactrian king (ca. 200 B.C.). He is of the earth—earthy; "in his sun-helmet, his eyes squinting against the desert sun, his nose beaked like an eagle, his mouth hard and cynical . . . the type of empire builder of all ages." Other subjects were often equally mundane—Negroes of the Sudan, fishermen, naked beggars, old women. Another genre included the crippled, dwarfs, and gnomes. The passion for naturalism reached its apogee (or nadir) in the great altar frieze at Pergamum. Commissioned by King Eumenes II to celebrate a great Pergamenian victory over northern barbarians, the frieze is a kind of carnival of raw naturalism. Covering 450 feet, it is alive with action and passion, civilizations pitted against each other, giants battling gods to the death, all executed with such finesse in the portrayal of ferocity and violence that later the Christian writer of the book of *Revelation* referred to the whole as "Satan's throne." Famous, too, is the *Laocoon,* depicting father and sons caught in the coils of entwining serpents. The expressions of horror and pain in this work are detailed with almost unbearable realism.

Other works of the period, executed by artists whose technical skills equaled and eventually surpassed those of their Hellenic masters, were of quite another appeal. The *Capuan Venus,* dating from about 300 B.C., is a Hellenistic artist's effort to bring to life the compelling force of victorious Aphrodite. That the artist succeeded is further proved by the many copies that were turned out (including the famous *Venus de Milo*?) in the Roman period and later. The *Nike of Samothrace* (ca. 250 B.C.?) shows Victory alighting from a flight. Housed in the Louvre, it evokes, even in its present mutilated form, an emotional response that testifies to the sculptor's genius. Equally arresting is the *Sleeping Hermaphrodite,* in which the artist combined to a remarkable degree romantic sensualism and austere classicism.

For the most part architects were content to use models of the Hellenic and Eastern past. Although faith in Olympian gods had faded, numerous temples in their honor continued to be erected. For example, at Didyma, off the coast of Asia Minor, an imposing temple was dedicated to Apollo, even larger and more elaborate than that god's shrine on the Acropolis. As in the other arts Hellenistic departure from the golden mean is plainly evident, the Didyma temple's frontal columns typically forsaking the chaste Doric model, and the whole showing a strong Egyptian influence. In time the ornate and eventually gingerbread Corinthian column replaced both the Doric and Ionian styles. Secular basilicas—the form of which was copied by builders of the first Christian churches—gained popularity in the second and first centuries B.C., being used mostly for marketing purposes or to house bureaus and offices of city officials.

Religion

As philosophy, literature, and the arts underwent change in the post-Alexandrian world, so too did religion. We have already noted that with the decline of the city-state the gods of Greece faded into fuzzy myth. Alexander indeed conquered the East, but the conquest "was by the sword alone, not the spirit." The essential weakness of the Greek was his sense of being cut adrift. The protective Athena was gone; gone, too, as sources of spiritual renewal, were the powers of Zeus and Apollo. As for the philosophic systems of Zeno and Epicurus, the average person could not master their intricacies and did not try. A new religion was needed. The East offered not one, but many, including magic, Babylonian astrology, and the various mystery cults. In the following chapter brief reference will be made to the cult of the Phrygian Great Mother, a cult that flourished in the centuries preceding the advent of Christ. Here particular attention must be given to a mystery religion that attracted an even greater number of votaries, the cult of the goddess Isis.

To the lost little man—and woman—of Hellenistic times, Isis appeared as the supreme savior. Through the loss of her husband-brother Serapis (the hellenized Osiris) she knew the sorrows of humankind. Through her boundless will and infinite mercy she had conquered death in the restoration of Serapis and thus promised everlasting life to all believers. Here was a message the Hellenistic mortal was waiting for. The old familiar world had dissolved; the new was frameless and chaotic. To the rootless masses Isis offered salvation for eternity, and they turned to her in ever increasing numbers. "When finally Christianity triumphed, and Zeus and Apollo, Serapis and the star-gods, were hurled from their seats Isis alone in some sense survived the universal fall; the cult of the Virgin had been introduced before the Serapeum* was sacked, and Isis' devotees passed quietly over to the worship of another Mother—how quietly sometimes may be seen from this, that various instances are said to be known of her statue afterwards serving as images of the Madonna."[18]

In 430 B.C., as the Peloponnesian War opened, Pericles had lauded Athens as the School of Hellas. Three centuries later both the School and Hellas lay prostrate. Peace and order were to come, but it was not the Hellenes who were to make the one or construct the other; for by this time the Roman world had absorbed the Greek Way. Another chapter in the development of Western civilization had opened.

* A temple dedicated to the pagan trinity of Isis, Serapis, and Anubis.

[18] W. W. Tarn, *Hellenistic Civilization,* 3d ed. (London: Edward Arnold, 1952), pp. 359–60.

A detail from the famous Pergamum Altar. Here Athena is subduing the winged giant Alcyoneus and is about to be given a crown of victory by the winged goddess on the right.

Euthydemus, a Bactrian king (ca. 200 B.C.).

Old Market Woman, a striking example of the raw realism of Hellenistic art.

RIGHT:
Capuan Venus (ca. 300 B.C).

BELOW:
Sleeping Hermaphrodite.

Nike of Samothrace.

Selected Readings

Many of the books cited in chapter 3 may be consulted for various topics of this chapter. Particularly pertinent are: Bury, *A History of Greece;* Hammond, *A History of Greece to 332* B.C.; Finley, *The Ancient Greeks;* Kitto, *The Greeks;* Robinson, *Hellas;* Parkes, *Gods and Men;* Toynbee, *Hellenism;* Muller, *Freedom in the Ancient World;* Bowra, *The Greek Experience;* and Dodds, *The Greeks and the Irrational.* In addition, the following works are recommended.

Bonnard, André. *Greek Civilization.* 3 vols. London: George Allen & Unwin, 1957–61.
> *Provocative—and often controversial—views and evaluations of all of the chief figures discussed in this chapter.*

Bowra, C. M. *Sophoclean Tragedy.* London: Oxford University Press, 1944.
> *Compare with Bonnard, vol. 2, chap. 4.*

Cary, Max. *History of the Greek World from 323 to 146* B.C. 2d ed. London: Methuen & Co., 1951.
> *A scholarly standard work, well conceived and well written.*

*Cornford, F. M. *Before and After Socrates.* Cambridge: Cambridge University Press, Cambridge Paperbacks, 1960.
> *One of the most stimulating and enlightening discussions of the development of human inquiry.*

*Cornford, F. M. *The Origin of Attic Comedy.* New York: Doubleday & Co., Anchor Books, 1961.
> *Like Dodds, Cornford stresses the deep, and to him decisive, strain of irrationality that he believes is found under the deceptive layer of rational thought and behavior so often mistaken for the true Greek "way." In the final chapter he discusses Greek comedy as a derivative of Greek tragedy.*

Ehrenberg, Victor. *The People of Aristophanes.* London: Basil Blackwell, 1951.
> *A fascinating account of Greek social life in the comedies. Farmers, traders, slaves, neighbors, citizens—these and others are given flesh and character.*

*Jaeger, Werner. *Aristotle.* New York: Oxford University Press, Oxford Paperbacks, 1962.
> *This is probably the most reliable account of the views of, and the method of inquiry used by, Aristotle.*

Martin, Seymour G. et al. *A History of Philosophic Thought.* New York: F. S. Crofts & Co., 1947.
> *A useful survey of the principal roads taken by seekers of the "why" and the "what" of human existence.*

Rostovtzeff, M. I. *Social and Economic History of the Hellenistic World.* 3 vols. Oxford: Oxford University Press, 1941.
> *This detailed study is comprehensive in coverage and cogent in argument. Although it is outdated—as well as controversial in some areas—it is still worth careful reading.*

Tarn, W. W., and Griffith, G. T. *Hellenistic Civilizations.* New York: St. Martin's Press, 1952.

Probably the best general account. Tarn died before certain important researches were completed, but Professor Griffith has competently woven them into the earlier text.

Winspear, A. D. *The Genesis of Plato's Thought.* 2d ed. New York: S. A. Russell, 1956.

A plainly written exposition of the ideas and values that still form much of the content of philosophic thought.

For good translations of all the major works of Greek philosophers, poets, and historians consult appropriate titles in the Loeb Classical Library.

Asterisk (*) denotes paperback.

CHAPTER V

The Roman World: the Republic

A. Genesis and Early Development of Roman Culture

EARLY SETTLEMENTS AND CULTURE

Earliest Migrations

The founding of the city of Rome about 650 B.C.* had been preceded by many millennia of human movement and endeavor in the narrow, bootlike Italian peninsula. Archaeologists have found human remains that go back well over 100,000 years. Recovered stone tools indicate the presence throughout the peninsula of early human societies. Cave paintings, similar to those found in Spain and France, point to the flourishing of paleolithic *Homo sapiens* culture. But bones, caves, cave paintings, and rude tools are about all that remain, much too little to allow a meaningful reconstruction of that life.

The descendants established a communal life characterized by the use of pottery and refined stone implements. Prehistorians used to call these descendants "Ligurians" (after remains that were first found in Liguria, a region in northwest Italy). The term, however, does not have much meaning. Since we know almost nothing of the racial origins of their forebears, we cannot of course know much of theirs. We are ignorant also of their language patterns. We cannot even use the term to designate in general the numerous autochthonous tribes that, long before neolithic times, had filtered into the plains and had fanned out in every direction.

Some time after ca. 2300 B.C. migrant groups poured into the peninsula and mixed with the native population. The earliest of these groups came over the Alpine passes from Switzerland. They settled in northern Italy, where they built dwellings on piles driven into the soft earth shoring the lakes. Their agrarian culture is at-

---

* Here "founding" denotes the consolidation of several village-towns settled much earlier.

tested by numerous archaeological finds such as plowshares, milling stones, and sickles. At about the same time another migrant band (originally from Spain) came down into the peninsula from southern Germany. These "Bell Beaker" people (named after their bell-shaped beer tankards) were rough and rowdy wanderers who came to settle in various regions in northern Italy, where they established trade connections with neighboring tribes.

A third wave, the *Terramaricoli* (so designated from the black, bitter earth on which they later built their pile-raised huts) settled in the Po Valley around 1700 B.C. Archaeological evidence suggests that they came from the Danube basin, probably from the vicinity of present-day Hungary. Their farming techniques were advanced as were, indeed, their culture patterns generally. If they did not introduce the use of bronze, they certainly made it a common feature of Italian culture. Their pottery ware was distinguished for its burnished decorations. They were probably innovators, too, in the use of the horse as a draft animal.

Around 900 B.C. another band of invaders settled in Latium and Etruria. Later a number of them migrated to the north, around Bologna; they are called Villanovans, after a village near Bologna where their remains were first found. Authorities dispute their place of origin. Recent evidence indicates that they were a Balkan people who crossed the Adriatic, lived for a while on lands east of the Apennines, then crossed the mountains to settle, eventually, in Latium and Etruria. To Italy's by now burgeoning culture they contributed the use of iron. It is possible (but certainly not yet proved) that they were more influential than other migrant groups in establishing Indo-European dialects in the peninsula. Probably it is safe to say that through their common intermarriage with the Terramaricoli and the "Ligurians" they helped to provide the main ethnic base for the general complex of Italic peoples (of which the most important were the Umbrians, the Samnites, and the Latins).

Thus by around the beginning of the first millennium B.C. the peninsula had been settled from end to end by either indigenous tribes or migrants or by the descendants of the fusion of these two groups. The economy was of course agrarian, although loose commercial relations were maintained among tribal communities and, in Umbria at least, an ironmongering industry had developed. Linguistically, a complex of tongues prevailed despite the common, fundamentally Indo-European, pattern. The Umbrians and the Samnites, for example, spoke different dialects, while that of the Latins differed markedly from both. None of the peoples in this long formative period had a written language. Their political organizations were of a decidedly amorphous kind. Village-states, clan-oriented, were dominated by leaders of local *gentes* (a kind of extended family). The village-states, in turn, were often associated with each other in *pagi*, or cantons—territories approximately as large as the smaller counties of present-day England. Normally the *pagus*, although formally governed by a body—the folk moot—of all free citizens, was ruled by the elite of the land-owning class.

The religions of the Italic peoples were as different from one another as their various dialects and modes of cantonal life. Local earth and river gods were placated by farmers anxious for good harvests and good fortune generally. Only one element was common to all—the mediator between household and the manifold animistic forces was the *paterfamilias*, the oldest male of a family group (to whom, it should be added, complete authority over every aspect of life had from earliest times been entrusted). Although war as a way of life was subscribed to by probably none of the Italici, conflicts were endemic as the folk-groups jostled one another in their ceaseless search for living space and defensible boundaries. In art their talents were undeveloped except for the Villanovans; they had no written language. Human ingenuity and industry had shaped a culture in the Italian peninsula, but it was clearly inferior to the ancient societies to the east. Adventuring bands from the Aegean world had settled in Sicily a thousand years before, but continuing relations had failed to develop, and the western frontier lagged far behind the East. (See map, opposite.)

Greeks and Etruscans

Sometime after 800 B.C., however, enduring contact was established as a result of two population movements. Eruptive political and military events sent a new wave of migrants (whom the Romans came to call *Etruscans*) to the "new west."* And population pressures, combined with commercial expansion, produced a Greek exodus to southern Italy and to Sicily.

On the eve of these new fateful invasions an equally significant development occurred in Latium without which their impact would certainly have had quite different consequences. The plains of Latium lie in a pocket some 25 miles wide and about 60 miles long, south and east of the angle formed by the Tyrrhenian Sea and the Tiber River. So active were the many volcanoes in this region and so swampy and malaria-infested the land that natives and migrants alike shunned it. Not until about the ninth century B.C. when volcanic activity had largely ceased and the soil had become fertile and tillable did this neglected pocket draw settlers. Then migrant groups began to test its subsistence possibilities, merging finally into a melange of some 40 tribe-complexes, of which one took the name *Romans*.* For many years they practiced a primitive agricultural economy, which kept them alive but culturally below the level of their neighbors. Living in small villages, each more or less sufficient to itself, they occasionally grouped themselves for religious purposes into cult bodies, which, however, had neither continuity nor recognizable features. It would have been difficult to have convinced any, including the Romans, that destiny was beckoning one of them to supreme rule over the Western world.

Hardly had the Latins emerged from their period of ethnic incubation when the Eastern invaders settled along the Italian coast, flanking them north and south. From about 800 to about 700 B.C. the Etruscans spread out in Latium and Campania (later in the Po Valley), conquering as they went. The Greeks were, in the main, content to trade with other peoples, although among themselves they practiced the same intramural fighting that, as we have seen, prevented their political consolidation in the East. It was probably this fatal fascination with self-destruction that prevented them from coming into eventual control of the peninsula, for their cultural achievements were unquestionably superior to those of either the Italici or the Etruscans. Even so, they (probably) gave the Etruscans their al-

---

* The problem of Etruscan origins has been argued since Herodotus and Dionysius of Halicarnassus first posed it. Some modern authorities hold that these people are descendants of the Lake-Dwellers; some, that they migrated from Lydia or an adjacent area in Asia Minor (accepted in the present account); others, that the autochthonous neolithic tribes constituted their ethnic base; still others, that a fusion of migrants from the East and autochthonous neolithic tribes gave birth to this people.

The most recent extended account of these theses is Howard H. Scullard, *The Etruscan Cities and Rome*, (Ithaca, N.Y.: Cornell University Press, 1967), chap. 2, "Who Were the Etruscans?" The evidence is used with scholarly care, and the author refuses to give what might be called the "final word." The book is interestingly written and is the best single account.

* It should be noted that some archaeologists dispute this reading of the evidence.

A. Genesis and Early Development of Roman Culture

phabet, which the latter subsequently passed on to the Romans. Moreover the Greeks "introduced into Italy the cultivation of the vine and the olive . . . and so took the first steps by which the country was converted into the 'garden of Europe.'" And of course their widespread commercial contacts effectively served as agents of cultural diffusion.

Far more immediately important than Greek influence, however, was that of the Etruscans, who stimulated the prepared potentials of the Latins in a variety of ways. They established regular trade routes with the Gauls and other Indo-Europeans to the north; excelled in the production of realistic statuary in terracotta; set the style in house construction; introduced expert workmanship in metals, especially gold, and popularized Greek design and decoration in pottery. Although the phrase "scientific farming" cannot be used to describe Etruscan development of the economy, their elaborate and effective drainage systems augmented agricultural output. Of yet greater significance was their influence on urbanization. It is probably not an exaggeration to say that the Etruscans found the Romans semitribal villagers and left them fairly sophisticated city-dwellers. Possibly a combination of circumstances worked this transformation. Almost surely and quite naturally one circumstance was the introduction of civic forms already developed by the Etruscans; another quite possibly was a Roman urge to strengthen themselves against the day when they could wrest control from their tutors[1]

By the seventh century population pressure and economic opportunities prompted Etruscan merchants (and later craftsmen) to settle in the Roman villages. Eventually they brought into these back-

[1] See Howard H. Scullard, *A History of the Roman World, 753 to 146 B.C.*, 3d ed. (London: Methuen & Co., 1963), chap. 2, for a detailed account of Etruscan "tutoring."

Etruscan sarcophagus. These figures of man and wife, done in multicolored terracotta, suggest a gaiety or, at least, benign contentment strangely out of keeping with the accoutrements of a tomb.

198   The Roman World: the Republic

EARLY MIGRATIONS
INTO ITALIAN PENINSULA, SICILY, AND CARTHAGE

Map by J. Donovan

endless wars among communities and dynasts, erosion of local patriotism, growing cosmopolitanism, and the spread and intricate complication of commercial connections. The combination of these conditions made the Mediterranean world chaotic while at the same time it invited the imperial promptings of a new power, should one arise while such conditions continued. Eventually the Romans sensed and responded (although in the beginning dimly and haphazardly) to these cues. But the emergence and consolidation of their power was a slow and, in the beginning, unlikely development. Numerically they were insignificant; chronologically they were late-comers; culturally they were anything but advanced.

The desire to understand why it was the Romans rather than the Samnites or Umbrians or another Italic people who accomplished the unification of Italy is reasonable enough but difficult to satisfy. Rome's location in the center of western Italy is surely part of the answer. Being so situated, Rome could build and control roads running north and south, thus gaining both economic and military advantages. The seven hills, which as a cluster constituted the locale of what eventually became the city of Rome, afforded further military advantages. Another advantage was Rome's location near the Tiber. Saltbeds near the mouth of the Tiber attracted many miners and merchants. But since the most convenient trails leading to them were eventually dominated by the Etruscans, the miners and merchants took to using Rome as a bridge to get to and from the saltbeds. "Thus Rome became a bridge town, a road center, a salt market, and a magnet of trade and population."[2] But it is hardly answer enough. In our own early history the geographic location and advantages of New

ward settlements most of their own arts and industries. Possibly the very name of the city was given to it by the Rumulo, thought to be the first Etruscan family to settle in Rome. There is no doubt that subsequent Etruscan leaders, especially the Tarquins, ruled Rome as elective kings. But their dominion, of whatever kind, was short-lived. Their city-states could no more form a permanent union than could those of the Greeks. Around the end of the sixth century they were battered so badly by Latin tribes and Syracusan Greeks that their dominance was broken. Roman leaders, naturally welcoming the event, set up political housekeeping for themselves in what is commonly called the Revolution of 509.

THE VITAL CENTER OF LATIUM: EMERGENT ROME

Why Rome?

In the preceding chapter we noted that late Hellenistic times were marked by

---

[2] Fritz M. Heichelheim and Cedric Yeo, *A History of the Roman People,* (Englewood Cliffs, N.J.: Prentice-Hall, 1961), p. 51.

199 A. Genesis and Early Development of Roman Culture

York City and Philadelphia far surpassed those of any New England communities; yet the latter rather than the former took the lead in helping to create the federal union. If the question revolved about the ejection of the Etruscans the answer would not be difficult. By the sixth century Rome and its neighboring towns were flanked by ambitious Etruscans, Greeks, and raiding hill tribes. Fully to gain and preserve their own autonomy, particularly against the warlike proclivities of the Etruscans, the natives were driven to extreme military measures. As occupants of the area closest to the Etruscan threat, the Romans must have felt this military imperative more keenly than the other Latin tribes. It is reasonable to suppose that with the failure of the Etruscans to effect consolidated rule the primary responsibility for ejecting them devolved on Rome. This, of course, is quite another matter from the unification of Italy. To say that Roman character accounts for it is to say very little. Whence came Roman character? It is true that age-long tradition had hallowed certain basic virtues—family solidarity, sober industry, respect for authority, and devotion to the idea of order. However, the Romans were not alone in these virtues.

In any case, by what the Romans came to think of as a great revolutionary thrust —which many modern historians consider rather a prolonged evolutionary development—they assumed the posture of leadership. But the following of other peoples did not develop automatically. For one thing, no one knew when resubjugation of Latium might be attempted, for the Etruscans were only defeated, not destroyed; for many years they continued to keep nostalgic account of doings in the rich Latin plains. For another, most of the other neighboring towns did not relish the prospect of Roman rule. Moreover other Italic tribes, notably the Sabines, Aequi, and Volsci, had territorial ambitions of their own. Even so, the emergence of Italy as a people and as a power is essentially the story of the rise of Rome.

Fragmentary Nature of Source Material

Unfortunately the story of republican Rome is based on meager evidence, at least for its first hundred years. It is true that with the coming of the Etruscans and Greeks writing had been introduced. The Greeks, however, never ruled Rome, and the Etruscan records are still undeciphered. By the time Roman history began to be assembled in literary form— in the second century B.C.—folk myth and fanciful invention had become so interwoven with the extant documentary material that it was hard to separate fact from fiction. It is certain that the traditional story of Rome's founding and rise, repeatedly told by later historians and attractively portrayed by Virgil, has nuclei of fact; it is equally certain that it is, in the main, false. The first serious work on Roman history that has survived, compiled by the Greek Polybius, was not published until about 150 B.C. Livy, probably the greatest name among Roman historians, did not complete his work until the Republican period was ended. Scattered throughout the earlier years were the records of a number of annalists, but annals and history are different even when the former are fully and accurately kept which in this case they were not. Thus the Republic's early history must be sketched in general and tentative terms.

POLITICS AND CULTURE OF THE EARLY REPUBLIC

Territorial Expansion

Four broad themes predominate: territorial expansion; the development of political institutions; class struggle between the patricians and plebeians; and the unplanned, fatal drift into imperial conquest (i.e., beyond the peninsula). After driving out its foreign rulers Rome faced the problem of dealing with raiding marauders from the east and south. Rome's solution of the problem was to set a pattern for most of its later conquests, a pattern marked by winning an ally to defeat a common foe followed by subjugation of the ally. At various times in the early fifth century B.C. the Sabines, Aequi, and Volsci harassed Latium by their fierce excursions into the plains. In order to stay these "thieving, covetous hillsmen" Rome and its Latin allies banded together as closely as their own conflicting interests allowed. For years they won and lost battles in the see-saw contest. Finally, in the latter half of the fifth century B.C. Roman leaders reorganized their armed forces, mounted new attacks against the raiders, and drove them back into the hills. But the peace was soon broken when the citizens of Veii, simply by being rich, powerful, and Etruscan, acted as a magnet on the metal of Roman ambition. For several years Roman troops, supported by levies from the cities of the Latin League, relentlessly pressed against the river stronghold. So vigorous was the resistance that for a time it appeared that Rome would suffer defeat and Etruscan dominance would reemerge. Eventually the stubborn Roman assaults proved more than the Veitians could stand and they were forced to capitulate. As was now their practice, the Romans settled their own colonists on choice portions of the land. Some colonists so rewarded were newly recruited peasant-soldiers.

Within a decade, however, catastrophe befell the rising power. Restless Gauls, raiding far beyond their borders to the north, drove into central Italy and surprised the Romans who, in the battle of Allia (ca. 390 B.C.), suffered complete rout. For a while the Celtic hordes occupied Rome, leaving only when a sizable indemnity was paid. This humiliating experience taught the Romans a lesson they long remembered. Now more than ever, the ruling aristocracy found it necessary to yield to demands put forward by the commoners as the latter became an increasingly indispensable reservoir of military strength. Encouraged by the apparent vulnerability of their erstwhile conquerors, the Aequi and Volscians resumed their attacks on Rome, which (with the grudging help of the other Latin cities, who feared the hill people above all others) rallied and inflicted on them lasting defeat. Once again Roman colonists were settled in conquered territory; and for added protection permanent garrisons were set up among the defeated tribes.

As a result of these conquests Roman territory now spread out over 300 square miles. Clearly, so far as peninsular affairs were concerned, the city-state was beginning to feel the tug of manifest destiny. The significance of this development was not, of course, lost on the members of the Latin League. They had little choice, when many dangers threatened, but to follow Rome's lead and authority. But in normal times they insisted on running their own affairs. To Rome such an attitude seemed unreasonable and dangerous. Anticipating a conflict, it besought an alliance with the Samnites to the east and south, who, respectful of Roman power and ever fearful of their own neighbors, accepted the offer. Thus strengthened, Rome maneuvered its one-time allies into declaring war and proceeded, by 338 B.C., to reduce them to a politically subordinate position. In the settlement that followed the genius of the rising new state showed itself at its best. Instead of humiliating terms, citizens of the Latin towns were offered privileges of an economic and social nature that were substantially the same as those enjoyed by the Romans. Indeed, citizenship rights were granted to those migrants who chose to move into Roman territory and establish residence. Of course, in return

A. Genesis and Early Development of Roman Culture

Rome required certain concessions, particularly the right to raise Latin levies when needed.

It would be tedious to recount the remaining and repetitious details of Roman conquest and consolidation. By about 325 B.C. the Gauls were ready for new raiding adventures. Understanding how such thrusts might serve them, and believing that it was now or never, the Samnites attempted to crush the growing power of Rome. But Rome's sense of order and genius for political organization together with its former policy of showing leniency toward the conquered now kept the cities of the Latin League from attacking it. Presumably they sensed that a Samnite victory could not provide the conditions requisite for a reasonably stable life. In any case, they joined forces against the Samnites and allowed Rome to dictate another peace.

By this time only the Greeks remained outside the Roman orbit. In 282 B.C. they besought Pyrrhus, a warrior king from the Greek mainland, to join them and lead their combined forces. The Romans, encouraging the Sicilian Carthaginians in the belief that cooperation against outside military adventures would serve both well, fought a seven-year war that ended in complete subjugation of the Greek settlements in Italy. Once more the process of colonization and garrisoning was repeated. By 275 B.C. nearly the whole of the peninsula was confederated under one rule, and the Republic extended from the Po Valley to the Mediterranean Sea. From Rome, its vital center where an intricate system of government had developed, came a general, overall policy for the entire land.

Political Institutions

In the beginning this system of government had been, in concept and practice, quite simple. The citizen body was originally made up of three tribes whose main business was to contribute needed revenues and military levies. Each tribe was divided into ten *curiae,* artificial units created to determine local policy and admission into the citizen body. When these units met together they were known as the *Comitia Curiata,* or Assembly. In their turn the *curiae* were made up of groups of families, called *gentes.* Quite naturally the citizen-body was divided into the few highborn landed aristocrats (*patricians,* after *patres,* "fathers") and the many poor *plebeians* (from *plebes,* "commoners"). But wealth, although very important, did not constitute the only or even primary factor distinguishing the two classes. Rather the line was fundamentally drawn on the basis of blood lines and social connections. As the wealthy families established themselves and extended their holdings, many plebeians exchanged their precarious economic condition for a more secure one by voluntarily attaching themselves to noble families. These commoners, called *clientes* ("clients"), naturally tended to go along with whatever program the patricians favored.

After the Revolution of 509 the Assembly, dominated by the patricians, abandoned monarchy as a form of government. Two leaders—called *consuls*—were selected from among the most outstanding nobles to administer the affairs of state. In this period their power was complete except that persons suffering sentences of death or exile might appeal to the Assembly. Advising the consuls was the Senate, originally made up of patricians nominated by the consuls, which soon came to exercise the right of virtually selecting its own nominators. Since the consuls, elected for only one year, normally became members of the Senate upon the expiration of their terms, the government early became a closed corporation of aristocracy. In theory the Senate could neither initiate nor pass laws. Suggested legislation was brought by the consuls (or dictator, referred to presently) to the Assembly, which, without debate, either confirmed or rejected it. But in practice senators had much to do with lawmaking. Commonly the consuls sought the Senate's advice before introducing legislation; indeed it was only in the Senate that full and free debate on policy occurred. Since both senators and consuls were patricians (until about 400 B.C.), and since the Senate was a continuing body, mainly made up of experienced ex-magistrates, its advice more often than not was accepted. Further, it is likely that considerable legislation was actually, although informally, initiated by senators, who always had easy access to the consuls. Naturally, as the Republic grew in size, population, and complexity, the two consuls were unable to attend personally to all necessary duties. Hence in the century following the Revolution of 509 additional magistracies were added.

Almost from the beginning religious affairs were supervised by a *Pontifex Maximus* and his priestly associates who performed the ceremonies requisite to continued rapport between the Romans and their gods. Soon elected *aediles* were entrusted with overseeing the more pedestrian affairs of day-to-day life such as food and water supplies and, occasionally, judicial settlement of minor nonpolitical offenses. Around the middle of the fifth century two *censors* were elected (normally every five years, for a period of eighteen months) to perform important functions that will be described shortly when reference is made to a change that occurred in the organization of the Assembly. A short time later, in 420 B.C., originally two, and ultimately eight, *quaestors* were selected by the Assembly to handle financial affairs. In the next century (366 B.C.) two *praetors* came to be elected to assist the consuls, particularly when the latter were out on their frequent military expeditions. To these responsibilities authority over important judicial cases came to be added. By the middle of the next century the number of *praetors* was increased to six; some became promagistrates governing provinces. A number of aides, assistants, and clerks completed the administrative apparatus of the state save for one very important emergency office. Normally the consuls performed their functions harmoniously enough (often dividing the year into six months, work for each, the better to avoid serious conflict). But when, as happened on occasion, their policies and implementing measures ran headlong into each other and chaos threatened, or when the state was gravely menaced by foreign foes and the consuls seemed unequal to the emergency, a dictator was appointed. His tenure, however, was strictly limited to six months and, until the latter days of the Republic, was unrenewable, an arrangement obviously calculated to ensure the permanent hegemony of the senatorial order, which did not want a dictator to become a king.

From military necessities the Assembly lost most of its power around the middle of the fifth century, when foreign foes were pressing hard on the state. Feeling the need of army reorganization so as to make its legions tactically more maneuverable, Rome divided its adult population (according to wealth) into five groups; each group, in turn, was subdivided into companies of 100 men, or *centuriae*. The necessary enumeration of the population was entrusted to two new officials—census-takers, or censors—who drew up the official list of male citizens and decided to which group each citizen belonged.* "The procedure of the censors was to call up in the first place all citizens,

---

* The officials subsequently were given the power to withdraw citizenship and office-holding privileges from those deemed unworthy This power was used with such consistent discretion and restraint that the office of censorship came to be regarded as the highest honor a Roman citizen could attain.

A. Genesis and Early Development of Roman Culture

in order to give their names and furnish details of property, and after completion of the catalogue to summon all those liable for service to an inspection parade, which was held in military array on the *Campus Martius,* the mustering ground of the Roman army. At this convention the citizens were marshalled in their appropriate 'centuries,' and the assembly accordingly received the name of *Comitia Centuriata.*"[3] Since its meetings were fairly regular and its membership embraced the total male citizen body, the new organization soon took on a political cast. As men passed fighting age (46) they were grouped into *seniores* and, while retaining their full voting and other citizen rights, were assigned, as need arose, to garrison duty only. By about 425 B.C. the new *Centuriate Assembly* came to supersede the Comitia Curiata, although technically the latter continued in existence, functioning for the most part as a religious body.

Class Struggle: Patricians versus Plebeians

In spite of the disproportionate weight given the vote of the wealthy in the "centuries," the plebes gained advantages as compared to their former condition by reason of their use of the military strike (discussed below). Their appetite grown with this feeding, they increasingly resented patrician conservatism. This period marks, then, the beginning of the long struggle of the commoners for first-class citizenship. Going on concurrently with the fight for consolidation, this "conflict of the orders" potentially held even greater good than unification, if a liberal, republican society is reckoned a supreme good. That it prized and lost this goal is at once Rome's glory and shame.

[3] Max Cary, *A History of Rome Down to the Age of Constantine,* 2d. ed. rev. (London: Methuen & Co., 1954), p. 8.

The glory began in 494 B.C. (or 449 B.C.?—authorities dispute the date of this first secession) when, heavily in debt and threatened with wholesale slavery (which normally followed failure to maintain solvency), the commoners were called upon by their patrician rulers to rally for another struggle against another foe. This time the plebes rebelled; but not by a violent show of force. They simply made a mass pilgrimage to their sacred mount, the Aventine, and after deliberation formed a state (extra-legally, of course) of their own. Paralleling the Curiate Assembly dominated by the patricians they set up their own *Concilium Plebis* (hereafter referred to as the Tribal Assembly, or *Comitia Tributa*), a popular body that elected two, later ten, *tribunes* whose duty it was to intervene for them when patrician rule became harsh or extreme. Naturally the patricians resented this recalcitrance; but in the face of endless pressures from foes and the very real need for plebeian help they yielded. Probably they supposed that this subversive development could be undone at their leisure. Such leisure, however, they came rarely to find, and the military strike set a precedent and a practice that ultimately, although briefly, created a state with strong democratic potentials.

In essence a veto power was exercised by the tribunes. They listened to appeals by commoners convicted of crimes carrying the penalty of exile or death, and if in their joint or individual opinion justice had miscarried, they forbade execution of the sentence. Two circumstances lent power and permanence to their vetoes: the sacred vow of the whole plebeian order to take vengeance should any of their tribunes suffer violence, and the tribunes' judicious and temperate use of their power. Another demand proved so reasonable that the patricians found themselves unable to oppose it, imbued as they were from long habit of devotion to duty and to responsibility. This demand called for a written expression of the "sense of the community"—the unwritten laws of custom. In 451 B.C. specially elected *Decemvirs* set themselves to this task, completing it the next year. The result was the famous Law of Twelve Tables, which codified all existing laws and spelled out the political, social, and economic rights and duties of all Roman citizens. Henceforth the plebes knew where stood (although they often complained, with increasing success, of particularly harsh provisions of the Tables).

Not infrequently modifications of the code were effected by another plebeian innovation, the *Plebiscita.* In addition to electing Tribunes, the Comitia Tributa from time to time expressed the legislative wishes of the commoners. Although these plebiscites did not have the binding effect of law, they served as prods inducing the Centuriate Assembly to take cognizance of plebeian needs. And later, as we shall see, they took on legal force as well as precedence over the Senate's opinion and advice.

The middle of the fifth century was a busy period for the plebeians. In 449 B.C. the Horatian Laws widened the scope of their powers still further. These laws filled a lacuna in the Tables that had failed to include the plebeian right of appeal; and they possibly sanctioned the calling of the Centuriate Assembly into session by the tribunes who might propose laws on their own authority.

Before long the two orders clashed over yet another issue, eligibility to the consulship. Although the contest went on for some 80 years, its outcome was never really in doubt; for by then Rome had come to depend heavily on plebeian arms. In 367 B.C. the Licinian-Sextian Laws granted the plebeian demand. Henceforth "middle-class" commoners—called *novi homines,* ("new men")—could and did become consuls and other magistrates. This betokened a still more significant development. Since by now the magistrates almost automatically became, at the end of their year's term, members of the Senate, that august body came to be made up of citizens of both orders. It would be wrong to conclude, however, that this constituted a decisive democratic advance. In actual fact the plebeian leaven oftener than not was more affected than the patrician lump it was intended to change, especially since by an earlier law of 445 B.C. plebeians were granted the privilege of marrying into patrician families. "If plebeians won office and passed into the Senate, they were apt to acquire the conservative attitudes of their fellow-senators; even if they persisted as champions of democracy, they were a small minority in a powerfully conservative body. The officeholding aristocracy, both patrician and plebeian, was not greatly interested in helping small farmers, who were more than ever in distress, and were being absorbed by the *Latifundia,* the great estates," particularly after the fateful Punic Wars.[4]

Nevertheless the commoners' surge, which continued throughout the fourth century, was real and of substantial proportions. Shortly after the gains effected by the Licinian-Sextian legislation the plebes won the mandate by which at least one of the consulships had to be filled by a plebeian. Further, the Tribal Assembly was granted the right to legislate for all citizens, not just plebeians. At first this right was qualified by a provision requiring Senate approval. But in 287 B.C. the Hortensian Law was passed making this approval automatic. Rome had become, in form, a democracy. Commoners and patricians alike voted laws into existence; members from either order were eligible for all magistracies; and the senatorial veto, invariably conservative, was legally eliminated. Two hundred and twenty-two years after the Revolution, Italy had be-

---

[4] William Chase Greene, *The Achievement of Rome* (Cambridge, Mass.: Harvard University Press, 1938), p. 199.

TABLE I
Political Structure of the Roman Republic

EARLY REPUBLIC

CONSUL / CONSUL — Initiated legislation; chief magistrates

ASSEMBLIES
Comitia Curiata
Comitia Centuriata — Elected consuls; approved or disapproved legislation; appointed magistrates. (After mid-400s, Centuriata is dominant body)

SENATE — "Advised" Assemblies and Consuls; actual, though not nominal, law-making body; called into session by consuls (or dictator)

THE PEOPLE (originally three tribes; later the number was increased)

MAGISTRATES: AEDILES, PONTIFEX MAXIMUS, QUAESTORS, DICTATOR, CENSORS, PRAETORS

BY EARLY THIRD CENTURY

Initiated legislation; chief magistrates — CONSUL

Approved or disapproved legislation; elected consuls — Assembly Comitia Centuriata — Consuls; at least one from plebeian class

Comitia Curiata — By now possessed no political power

TRIBUNES — "Protectors of the common people"; initiated legislation; could veto any law; chief magistrates

Comitia Tributa — Approved or disapproved legislation; elected tribunes; elected only by plebeians

SENATE

THE PEOPLE (These circles are symbolic only; by 241 B.C. there were 35 tribes)

MAGISTRATES: AEDILES, PONTIFEX MAXIMUS, QUAESTORS, DICTATOR, CENSORS, PRAETORS

206 The Roman World: the Republic

come confederated; and a substantial portion of its people lived under a nonautocratic form of government (see Table I). No other people of ancient times could claim such an achievement.

Genesis of Roman Literature

From meager sources scholars can thus piece together the broad political developments of the early Republic. But these sources hardly avail for a satisfactory account of Rome's nonpolitical life—social, religious, and literary experiences and patterns. As we have seen, written language came late to the Italici. Its early forms, quite understandably, were employed for more pedestrian uses than grand epics and stirring prose creations. Still, in "banquet" ballads, epitaphs, and *annales* the beginnings of a literature appear. Undoubtedly the ballads embodied many early folk myths so intricately embroidered by later writers. Among these myths was the story of Coriolanus, whose dramatic exploits inspired a host of literati from Plutarch to Shakespeare.

Other folk myths include an elaborate account of how Rome's legendary founder, Romulus, urged his men to join him in a daring venture to find for themselves the kind of women who would provide Rome with heroic sons. The vigor and grace of the maidens of a tribe to the east powerfully attracted them. A dramatic raid involving romantic derring-do was brought off successfully, and hence there arose the legend of the "Rape of the Sabines." Other familiar myths tell of the gallant courage of "Horatio at the Bridge," where single-handedly a Roman soldier saved Rome from the invading Etruscans, and of the "geese that saved the city from the Gauls." But none of these tales was given formal, rhetorical expression until late in the Republican period, so slow was the literary life of Rome to develop.

Early Roman Religion

On the other hand Roman religious life was shaped in the mists of early prehistoric times. From the beginning it was marked by a sense of awe and sober effort to learn and live the will of the spirits—numia—which figured existence and gave animation, for good or ill, to all things. Twin foci, the field and the home, were central in the spatial and functional framework of the spiritual life developed by the Romans. As farmers they had a deep and abiding reverence for nature and her vital, mysterious ways and for nature's greatest gift, the family and home. The will of the numina worked in all things: soil, river, wind, rain, threshold, hearth, storeroom. The earliest religious festivities celebrated features of rural life—"the Saturnalia, or sowing, the Robigalia, for the aversion of mildew, the Consualia, for the storing of the harvest"; or they honored "household deities which consecrated the various parts of the house—Ianus [Janus], spirit of the door; Vesta, spirit of the hearth; the Penates, spirits of the storerooms . . . all of whose good will may be kept by the offering of appropriate gifts at the appropriate time."

In the home the chief religious functionary was the paterfamilias, and the chief object of worship was his genius, or protecting spirit. If the genius of the head of the family was ill disposed toward that head the whole family suffered; if well disposed, all members of the family were favored. In the early days of the Republic, before a degree of urbanization was effected and before an intricate state cult had developed, the paterfamilias, standing in awe of his genius and soberly performing the rites necessary for health and good fortune, was the vital center of all family life. In public affairs special officers, the *pontifex maximus* and his priests, propitiated the gods and ascertained, by such practices as interpretation of the formation of flights of birds and examination of the entrails of animals, whether the time was right (or the auspices good) for an official state action or ceremony. Meetings of the Assemblies, for example, were invariably preceded by such searching for signs; if the priests' findings were negative, the assemblies postponed or canceled their deliberations.

Although there was no true hierarchy, some gods were recognized as having significance beyond a particular place and specific function. Especially was this true of Jupiter (or Jove), who, while thought of as the sky-god, was understood to symbolize the highest powers of all the gods. Under his vaulting domain all creatures lived and in his name men made their most solemn pledges. "Mars . . . another god to develop early . . . started as an agricultural numen, perhaps the averter of disease and bad weather, but soon became also the averter of violence." Through the head of the family or the priest prayers to these and other gods were addressed, often together with sacrificial offerings. Early Roman religion thus permeated every facet of life—social, economic, and political. It is true that ethical content was lacking. Romans reverently understood that powers greater than themselves existed, but this understanding expressed itself in propitiatory prayers and sacrifices rather than in ethical behavior. Absent, too, were emotionalism and belief in an afterlife beyond a meaningless, shadowy existence. These deficiencies were felt and dealt with, but not until the society of Republican Rome had undergone the havoc of the Punic Wars and had, by about 100 B.C., merged its character with that of the East.

Fine and Applied Arts

Equally undeveloped were Roman art and architecture, save for fresco painting and some temple building. Patrician houses, although ample in size, were pedestrian in both interior and exterior design, while the houses of the masses were, after 500 years of community life, no better than the temporary sod houses of the American frontier West. Except for wax images, found often in homes as an expression of family reverence for the dead, native sculpture was nonexistent; the sculpture done was the work of Etruscans and migrant Greeks. In certain practical arts, on the other hand, Roman genius early showed itself. From the fifth

A section of the remains of the Flaminian Way, which crossed the Apennines to connect Italy's western and eastern coasts.

208 The Roman World: the Republic

century through the years of the Empire such a great system of roads was constructed as the world had never seen before, nor, in some respects, since. Across the mountainous terrain of the peninsula the Romans flung out roads in all directions. The famed Appian Way, begun by Appius Claudius in the late fourth century, stretched ultimately from Rome to Brundisium, some 300 miles to the south and east. The Flaminian Way, running another 300 miles northward, connected Rome with the eastern coast of present-day Venezia (see map, opposite). They and all the other important throughways were constructed in such a manner that they bore, with little repair, the tramp of legions, the grinding wear of commercial and military wagons, and the pounding of cavalry for periods not of years but of centuries; parts of some, indeed, are still in existence. With the same skill the Romans constructed gigantic aqueducts that provided Rome and other cities with clear mountain water. Some of these, too, are still intact. Much of Rome's culture was derivative (although more so in the Empire than in the Republic). But in the practical arts Rome had no equal in ancient, and few in modern, times.

Economically Rome was the same agrarian society in, say, 250 B.C. that it had been 500 years before. After the Punic Wars, it is true, the capital of the Republic became to a very limited extent a sort of middleman receiving goods that it did not produce and distributing them at a profit. But this was the business of the economic elite only. The masses, from early Etruscan times, were obliged to give unremitting toil to the land. Much of the produce went to their masters, who were either Etruscan or Roman landowners with large holdings. This is not to say that commoners were not themselves landowners; actually, more often than not they were. Always, however, the economic tune was called by the landed nobles.

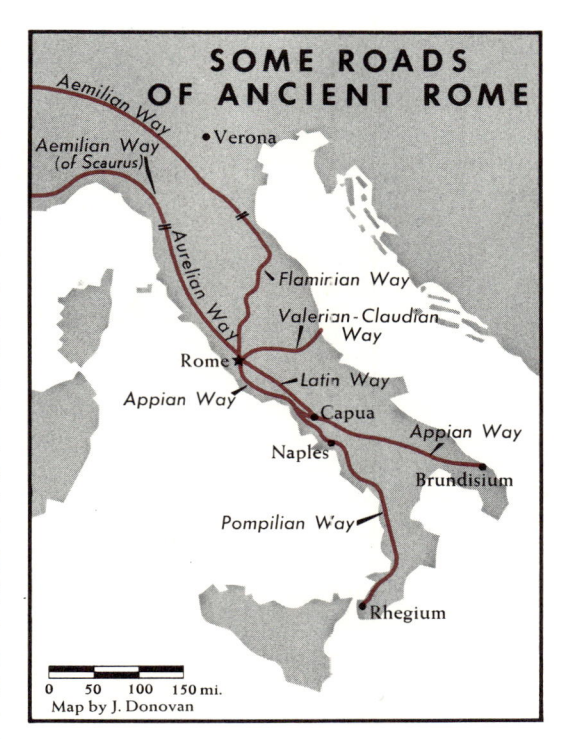

THE IMPERIAL IMPULSE: THE PUNIC WARS

Carthage Challenged

Unlike Rome, Carthage—founded in the eighth century B.C. by venturing Phoenicians—had early concentrated on trading activities. By 275 B.C. this state had become the master merchant of the western Mediterranean, controlling almost all the important ports of call except a few held by such Greek centers as Messina (Messana) and Syracuse, in Sicily. With this general situation Rome had no particular quarrel. Roman ships, it is true, were forbidden to carry from Carthaginian ports. But Rome had long been content to allow Carthage, or any other state with such ambitions, to dominate maritime commercial activity. With Italy unified under Roman control it was likely, of course, that Rome might want to come to

209   A. *Genesis and Early Development of Roman Culture*

some understanding with the Punic power across the straits; for by that time the economic requirements of a large Republic called for something more than the simple agrarian economy of early days. Conceivably a workable arrangement could have been peacefully negotiated by diplomacy, with Carthaginian imperial ambitions recognized in return for mercantile concessions to Rome, together with assurances that Sicily would not be used as a springboard for aggression against Rome. This possibility, however, was precluded by an adventitious series of events that initially gave no hint of the vast consequences to follow. These events we must now consider.

Some time in the early part of the third century a ruffian band of Greek mercenaries, demobilized by Rome after the Pyrrhic wars, migrated to Messina, a trading city in Sicily just off the toe of the Italian boot. Within a short time they had taken over the town and used it thereafter as a base for various piratical and marauding raids. Both to eliminate this disturbance and to extend their territory, Greeks of the nearby city-state of Syracuse sent off an expeditionary force. The Messina pirates, now divided into factional groups, sought help, some appealing to Carthage, some to Rome. Always eager to fish in troubled waters, especially when a strategically located trading center was involved (and more particularly since it already controlled the western half of the island) Carthage promptly sent aid. Rome's response was tardy and equivocal, with both Senate and Assembly expressing little interest. But the current consuls sensed a serious threat to Rome's confederate allies in southern Italy if Carthage moved into Messina. They therefore prevailed on the Assembly to assent to the dispatch of a succoring column. Before this show of force the small Punic contingent hastily withdrew. Thus Roman legions for the first time since the founding of the city set foot on soil beyond the peninsula and, in 264 B.C., casually challenged the greatest empire in the western Mediterranean. They could not know the hinge of history they had forged.

Relief of a warship with legionaries, from Temple of Fortuna Primagenia.

210   The Roman World: the Republic

The First Punic War

Accepting the challenge, Carthage readied a large force at Agrigentum, on the southern coast of Sicily. In reply, Roman commanders swiftly drove their columns southward, laid seige to the Carthaginian base and, in 262 B.C., captured and sacked the city. But one defeat did not bring Carthage to Roman terms. Instead the Punic power readied new and larger forces. At this point Rome realized the scope of the encounter. If Messina was to be preserved from Carthaginian control, the whole island must be swept clear of Carthaginian troops. More than this, the surrounding sea-lanes must be dominated by the Roman navy, which was then practically nonexistent. So a large commitment of land troops and the creation of a strong navy were requisites for Roman victory. Within two years a fleet of more than 150 ships had been constructed and equipped, a remarkable achievement that later historians were to make into a much-embellished legend.

In 260 B.C. the new Roman fleet encountered a Punic squadron off Mylae, near Messina. In the ensuing battle the Carthaginians lost 50 ships and their reputation as the master of western Mediterranean waters. After landing troops at Mylae the Romans fanned out along the coast, overrunning a number of harbor cities. Attempts to subjugate Sardinia and Corsica proved abortive. But in the waters off Ecnomus (near modern Licata in southern Sicily) Roman galleys in 256 B.C. again defeated a strong Carthaginian complement and secured a case for the invasion of Carthage itself. Under Atilius Regulus thrusting legions came within a mile of the capital city before being halted. Had Rome followed its old practice of offering liberal terms to a defeated foe, it is likely that the war would have ended here. But Regulus demanded impossible terms, provoking Carthaginian leaders to call for a grand rally. In the valley of the Bagradas, inspired Punic troops aided by Greek mercenaries first drove back and then routed the invaders. Roman galleys, bearing troops intending to deliver the final blow, were forced to turn back with such straggling survivors as they could hastily pick up.

Driven by a desire for revenge and sustained by the dogged spirit that had brought victory in its long struggle to pacify and consolidate Italy, Rome now called on its own people and on its allies for a new and greater effort. Within a year it succeeded in outfitting an even greater fleet. With this it transported a newly assembled army to Panormus (Palermo) where in naval and land engagements it defeated strong Carthaginian forces. Moving west along the coast, the invaders then laid siege to Lilybaeum (Marsala). But here Punic troops proved superior, and once more Rome was checked. Even worse, at about the same time (249 B.C.) the new fleet was all but destroyed off Drepana (Trepani), on the western tip of Sicily. This double disaster, following what had seemed once again to be a decisive victory, rocked Rome. For the next seven years a kind of informal armistice was observed by both sides, punctuated by occasional Punic raids to keep the Romans off balance.

By 242 the Romans had recovered their nerve, and with new ships and new levies they returned to the attack. This time they succeeded in reducing both Lilybaeum and Drepana, and the weary Carthaginians at last sued for peace, taking what terms they could get. These were short and harsh—the surrender to Rome of all Sicily (save for a few scattered Greek cities that had been Roman allies) and the payment of a huge indemnity. Thus in 241 B.C. the first Punic War ended and a new imperial power was established in the west. Contrary to its usual practice, Rome extended neither citizenship nor partnership to the people of the conquered island. Instead the Senate, now risen to dominance over the popular assemblies by reason of both its continuing tenure and the extended period of emergency, sent out a governor to rule as Rome decreed. Similar rule was instituted in Corsica and Sardinia, which Carthage was forced to yield to the new empire in 238 B.C.

Although the victor, Rome was almost as exhausted by the long and terrible ordeal as the defeated foe. Gaulish hordes, encouraged by Roman exhaustion, again swept down from the Po Valley. Initial successes encouraged them to attempt permanent conquest, and for the next ten years Roman resources were drained to the limit. Probably the deciding factor was the loyalty of Italian allies, who, even had they not long since become convinced of the beneficence of Roman order, feared above all things the yoke of the Celtic barbarian. By 222 B.C. the invaders were finally conquered and all of northern Italy from the Apennines to the Alps was annexed by Rome.

The Second Punic War

But the severest test was still to come. In the 20 years following its defeat Carthage made an amazing comeback under the aggressive leadership of Hamilcar, a gifted general and statesman, and under his even more talented son, Hannibal. Stripped of its island possessions in the war with Rome, Carthage turned to Spain for imperial recovery. By 220 B.C it was master of most of the Iberian peninsula. Rome's concern over the resurgence of Punic power led it to fear for its own new power status. Carthage, for its part, was determined to brook no Roman veto in the peninsula. When that veto seemed to materialize, as Rome interfered with Punic expansion in 218 B.C., Carthage badgered Rome into declaring war.

In the Second Punic War the initiative was taken by Hannibal. He performed a kind of military miracle when he led his forces, which included elephant-trains, across southern France and down through the Alpine passes in the snows of late autumn. In northwest Italy Publius Scipio, consular commander of the Roman army (and father of the later famous Scipio Africanus), was the first to taste of the many bitter defeats that Hannibal was to inflict. Stinging under their own recent rout and heartened by new hope of reversing fortune, the Gauls jubilantly joined the fray. By the next year the invaders were in Etruria where, at Lake Trasimene, they smashed another Roman army under Flaminius. The road to Rome now seemed open. But the city's strong defenses and Hannibal's lack of an adequate supply base to support a long siege led the aggressive general to bypass it and head south. Under a dictator, Q. Fabius Maximus,* a new policy of delaying actions was adopted that gave little opportunity for Hannibal to display his genius. But the Comitia Tributa, growing impatient with indecisive guerilla warfare, overruled the Senate and appointed two new commanders eager for battle. On the open plains of Apulia, near Cannae, the two armies met head-on. The result was the greatest catastrophe the Republic had yet suffered. With the loss of but 6000 men Hannibal cut the Roman legions to pieces. When Capua, in Campanis, went over to the invader, King Philip of Macedonia, who had been carefully watching events, indicated that he was ready to take up where Pyrrhus had left off.

But Roman doggedness again showed

---

* From this general and his policy of harassment rather than frontal assault has come the phrase "Fabian tactics."

itself. Young boys and even bondsmen were pressed into service; Fabian tactics were again resorted to. Its judgment vindicated, the Senate thereafter made decisions without further challenge. By clever diplomatic maneuvering it stirred up Philip's enemies in Greece to keep that monarch fully occupied at home. In 207 B.C. Roman forces met and defeated a large Carthaginian contingent under Hasdrubal (the battle of the Metaurus River); and Hannibal was forced to begin a series of retreats. The Senate had earlier sent new legions to Spain; under the Scipios they eventually won complete control of the peninsula. The Senate also maintained a large navy that served both to supply Roman troops in Spain and to break up enemy communications.

In Italy some of the newly raised forces reconquered Capua, while others continued to harass the weary Hannibal. When Philip once again showed signs of changing his mind, Roman troops were landed in Greece. Although they did not bring him to heel, they found allies (especially Pergamum, in Asia Minor) who once more kept the ambitious monarch too busy to venture abroad. In the meantime from newly won Spain the younger Scipio mounted a massive assault against Carthage itself. To meet this attack Hannibal was now forced to return home. In 202 B.C., at Zama, about 50 miles south of Carthage, the two armies met in the final battle of the war. There the forces of the once invincible Punic commander suffered a defeat greater than they had inflicted on the Romans at Cannae. In the following year Carthage gave up the struggle and accepted a Roman peace much harsher than the first—payment of an enormous indemnity and cession of the whole of its European empire. About 50 years later the remaining stub of the great Carthaginian state was rooted out in the third, brief and vicious, Punic War (149–146 B.C.).

THE DECLINE OF THE REPUBLIC

Political and Economic Changes

But if the victor gained imperial grandeur it lost republican glory. For the Rome that emerged from the Punic Wars was quite different from the Rome that had so casually entered into them. The old Rome was basically an ethnic unit; although all were not citizens, few were subjects, and still fewer slaves. Although its political structure had been shaped perhaps as much by improvisation as by deliberate plan, it was nevertheless well suited to the developing needs of the Italian people. On the other hand, the imperial necessities of the new Rome were glaringly inconsonant with the services offered by a republican constitution.

Equally significant was the change that occurred in class structure. Two generations of yeoman farmers had been taken from the fields and, under terms of service sometimes running to 20 years, fed into the armed forces. In many instances the unhusbanded farms were sold to the ever-growing army of speculators. In this way the newly rich developed large estates—*latifundia*—worked by slaves provided by the seemingly endless wars. The returning landless yeomen increasingly drifted to the cities, particularly Rome. There they constituted an unemployed mob eager to exchange their votes for promises of governmental largess. To curry favor with this uprooted, restless multitude, candidates for office promised greater and greater benefits, which usually took the form of doles and contrived amusement—the famous "bread and circuses."

In these circumstances a permanent proletariat formed. Its endless demands further debased political officialdom, which, across the war years, had already grown alarmingly corrupt. Rome's more extensive involvement in commerce (which naturally followed the ebbing of Punic hegemony), its increased profits from conquest, and financial and land speculation combined to give rise to a new class, the *Equites.* The main interest of this middle-class order was, very simply, to make money. Its members cared nothing for democratic development, nor for republican order, nor for any order at all save as it prevented turmoil that interfered with business. Though they did not enjoy the social prestige and perquisites of the old landed aristocracy, they ranked substantially above the yeomen and artisans. They were, in short, an evolving middle class.

The Militarization of Roman Life

Quite naturally modifications of the old Roman way went beyond political and economic changes. It is hardly reasonable to suppose that the long years of fighting, which subordinated normal civic privileges and responsibilities to wartime exigencies, could fail to affect the spirit and habits of the Roman people. Although always ready to fight when they believed their interests were threatened, they had never practiced violence as a way of life. But the Punic Wars were "marked by many brutalities, the Romans in particular being guilty of indiscriminate plundering and massacre in the towns recovered by them." It is difficult to believe that a coarsening of the spirit did not result. A related sign of the deterioration of the republican way of life was manifest in the tendency of field commanders to flout senatorial directives, flattered as they were by the subservience of the conquered and emboldened as they were by the power of their own fiat. With growing frequency these leaders ventured on forays not only without, but sometimes even contrary to, the Senate's dictum, hinting at a practice that would eventually turn the later Empire into an outright military autocracy.

Religious Changes

Changes also occurred in religious attitudes and practices. We have already noted early Roman faith in religious sanctions, which, although tenuous, embraced all fundamental features of life. For example, we have seen how the paterfamilias acted as priest for the family, propitiating the gods and bespeaking their help. Although an ethical code formed no intergral part of such worship, it was marked by a very strong moral sense. Not only the head but all members of the family remained conscious of their dependence on forces beyond themselves. Out of this consciousness developed the well-known Roman traits of reverence for authority and earnest application of skills and talents. But once the city-state had come to embrace most of Italy, national gods and their priests necessarily grew in importance. To such predominance had the new state religion grown by the third century B.C. that it preempted much of the attention formerly given to the gods of the household. Hereafter substance tended to yield to symbol and form. This in turn encouraged the devising of exploitative practices by an officialdom increasingly more interested in manipulating the masses than in fostering true religious attitudes and habits. Out of the void of this barren state cult many Roman citizens, of the masses and classes alike, sought new paths to spiritual security.

As it turned out, guides were at hand. With the emergence of Rome as the controlling Mediterranean power many people from the East, particularly Greece, migrated westward. Naturally they brought with them their own religious practices.

Thus from the early second century on there came to be established in Rome the so-called mystery religions—the worship of Cybele, the Great Mother; the cult of Isis; and varieties of proto-Gnosticism (see p. 243) and Zoroastrianism. In all of these new systems intense emotionalism, long absent from Western religion, marked the search for individual salvation; a search destined, for the Romans at least, to go largely unrewarded until the advent and flowering of Christianity, for which these religions helped to prepare the way.

Thus the great Roman victory at Zama in 202 B.C. marked more than the end of a war. It signified the end of an age. Gifted Republican leaders, as we shall see, would try to save the Republic; but they would fail. Empire and world rule beckoned.

THE LITERATURE OF THE REPUBLIC

Reworking of the Greek Heritage

It has been said that the stupendous national victory of the First Punic War produced a psychic upsurge that created an impressive Roman literature. This judgment, although sweeping, seems sound. About 240 B.C. a liberated Greek slave, Livius Andronicus, translated the *Odyssey* into Latin. The birth of Roman literature may be dated from this event. There is more than anomaly in the statement. Of course, translation is not creation. But, for one thing, the latinized version of the *Odyssey* served as a textbook for generations of Roman writers (including Horace). More importantly, it introduced Romans both to the grand epic and to the possibilities that lay in working the mines of classical literature.

Thereafter Roman poets, dramatists, and prose writers unashamedly—indeed, often proudly—borrowed both form and substance from the Greeks. Found, too, in the *Odyssey* were a number of basic promptings, inherently congenial to the Roman character, that came to shape Latin literature: solemn pride in national achievement, the desire to praise the power of *virtus*, and the urge to identify and enlarge the attributes of human dignity. On the other hand, the new literature differed from its classic model in at least three respects. Unlike their masters, Roman writers never tired of conjoining word and act, revealing their pragmatic bent, nor of using their genius to exhort, thus manifesting their moral, often didactic, purpose. Ultimately, too, they came to patronize, perforce, a different audience and spirit. For where the Greek literati wrote for elite and hoi polloi alike, their Roman pupils soon came to cater almost exclusively to the Roman aristocracy. In the early works of Naevius and Ennius this tendency was less pronounced; but the bias was there.

Naevius, a contemporary of Andronicus, is best known for his *Bellum Punicum*, a long verse history of the First Punic War. Probing the misty regions of legend for material to serve as prologue for his main theme, he celebrated the supposed connection between the fabled Troy and his own city, thereby providing "sketches in the rough for what became polished scenes in Virgil." Although he drew on Greek literature for both plots and techniques, he protested Hellenism's creeping dilettantism, which seemed to threaten old Roman strengths, as when he cautioned:

> *If you would return to virtue, you must shun depravity—*
> *Fatherland and father follow, more than foreign infamy.*

Despite "producing the first national epic Italy had ever known," Naevius did little to refine the crudities of his native language. This task was begun, quite self-consciously, by a contemporary, Quintus Ennius, who is sometimes called the father of Latin poetry. Scorning religious sanctions, Quintus Ennius threaded his work with Epicurean humanism, sometimes holding the gods to be one-time heroes promoted to divinity, sometimes broadly hinting that whatever their nature or origin they had no meaningful connection with human affairs. Believing himself, perhaps half seriously, to be the reincarnation of Homer, he devoted most of his life to writing, in Homeric hexameter, the story of Rome's genesis and rise to mastery of the (then) Western world. This work, known as the *Annales,* was received with great favor, catering to Rome's growing consciousness of its unfolding genius and destiny. Although it was not until the Augustan Age, some 200 years away, that a perfected form of the Latin hexameter was shaped, Ennius pointed the way to that golden day. Besides his monumental *Annales* several lesser works were produced, including epigrams (one glorifying himself), encomiums on the current great (Scipio Africanus, for example), and fables pointing up sound morality.

But not all of Rome's writers were concerned with morality and destiny. Indeed the most famous of them, T. Maccius Plautus (ca. 254–184 B.C.), concentrated on the trivial. His forte was elegant comedies of manners. So extraordinary were his talents, so sensitive his reaction to a war-weary people's "rebound toward relaxation," that, despite his obvious borrowing from Menander and other Hellenistic writers, his comedies effectively and faithfully portray his own Roman world of transition. More than 20 of his plays have survived, most of which deal with assorted roisterers, wenches, knaves, gentle ladies with a variety of prices, braggarts, liars, and thieves of every talent. His pieces not only served the tastes of his times, but were so deftly and appealingly done that they became a rich quarrying ground for masters of a later age. One of them, *Menaechmi,* the plot of which was lifted from a Greek play, in its turn served as a model for Shakespeare's *Comedy of Errors;* another, *Amphitruo,* for Molière's *Amphitrion.*

The last of the great dramatists of this period, Terence (P. Terentius Afer, ca. 195–139 B.C.), followed Plautus in dealing with the manners of society and in his copious borrowing from the Greeks. But his setting and style were different. He did not bother to give a Roman gloss to his borrowed material; the spirit of Athens illumined every scene. Where Plautus used broad humor, even slapstick, Terence probed the foibles of the new society with gentle irony and the smile of understanding. Brought as a slave to Rome he became the pet of aristocracy, especially that branch of it which looked to Hellenic culture for the glory that would crown Rome's new position. But if he avoided some of his predecessor's literary gaucheries, he did so at the expense of verve and exuberance. Indeed he ended by almost refining the élan out of life.

Of the six plays that survive perhaps his last, *Adelphoe,* was his best. Here he combined "polished repression" with drollness to contrast effectively the experiences of life that come from the exercise of genteel moderation as against those that evolve out of extravagant, over-energetic derring-do. But in all his works his chief emphasis was on the light that shone from the East. Athena beckoned, and he devoted his literary charm to win for her his backwoods countrymen. His gentle, implicit refrain was, "Go East." And when he died (appropriately in Greece) in 139 B.C., he must have known that his wooing would be remembered. For then the march of Empire to the East had become reality.

THE CONQUEST OF THE EAST

Origin of Roman Involvement in Eastern Affairs

Within two generations after Zama, Rome controlled directly or indirectly the greater part of the old Alexandrian Empire—all of Greece, most of the present-day Balkans, a substantial portion of Asia Minor, and Egypt (as "protector"). (See Table II.) This *what* of history can be validly documented, as can most of its *how*. But when we come to the important *why*, our sources are incomplete and confusing. Perhaps we must be satisfied with these bare clues: Rome had learned to distrust the word of Philip of Macedonia and somewhat to fear his aggressive policy of expansion to the south and particularly to the west (especially as such designs might touch Ilyria). Rome's new position of power attracted the attention of small states in the East, the more so as they feared the increasingly expansive designs of the great empire-builders. By this time, too, Rome (however consciously or unconsciously) had begun to think of itself in relation to "lesser" powers and peoples in vague but developing terms of patron and clients.

In the preceding chapter we noted the breaking up of Alexander's empire after the emperor's death in 323 B.C. At the close of the second Punic War, more than a hundred years later, Philip V ruled Macedonia; Antiochus III, Syria and a portion of Asia Minor; and Ptolemy V ruled Egypt. Besides these larger divisions there were a number of independent states such as Rhodes, Pontus, and Pergamum; numerous "free cities" (for example, Sparta and Athens); and, in the Greek peninsula, two federations of states, the Aetolian League in the central-south and the Achaean League in the Peloponnese.

Philip was eager to refashion the old, expansive Macedonian Empire. With Rome engaged in a death struggle (as he hoped) with Carthage, he believed that the time had come to reach an understanding with Antiochus, an understanding that would allow them to divide the lands of the Ptolemies and to pick up whatever else was available. Whether or not such a bargain was ever consummated (and scholars are inclined to be doubtful), Philip plunged at once into a series of wars with his neighbors. His early successes naturally caused consternation among the smaller states. Soon several of them, joined by Egypt, appealed to Rome for help.

By this time Carthage had been forced into surrender, and Rome's armies were available for other expeditions if Romans had a mind so to use them. But many Romans, like Cato, were not of this mind; in particular, the centuriate assembly opposed the venture. A majority of the Senate, however, found the suggestion appealing and urged the Assembly to reconsider. Once again, in trying to un-

TABLE II
Chronology of Military Events 282 to 64 B.C.

Text Reference, pp:	Major Wars	B.C.
202	War with Pyrrhus	282–272
211	First Punic War	262–241
212	Second Punic War	218–201
212	First Macedonian War	215–205
218	Second Macedonian War	200–197
218	Third Macedonian War	171–168
213	Third Punic War	149–146
219	Fourth Macedonian War	149–149
224	Jugurthine War	111–105
225	The Social War	91–88
226	First Mithridatic War	88–84
228	Second Mithridatic War	83–81
229	Servile War (Spartacus)	73–71
230	Third Mithridatic War	74–64

Section of a sculptured frieze from a pillar erected to memorialize Paullus's victory over Perseus at Pydna. Ironically, the pillar was erected in a Greek city, Delphi, to commemorate a Greek defeat.

derstand how that body was won over, conjecture must be relied on. Since Philip had once shown a tendency to fish in troubled Italian waters it was arguable that unless he were put down, once and for all, Rome could never feel really secure. It is certainly true that many of the aristocrats, such as Scipio and Flaminius, had long been ardent philhellenists. It is reasonable to suppose that the Equites, having made their fortune in the last war, were not altogether averse to another. Probably, too, some nobles sniffed glory and profits. In any case the Assembly reversed its decision, although without enthusiasm. In 200 B.C. a new Macedonian war opened and Roman legions marched again in the name of freedom and order.

Roman Conquests

If there were eager Roman leaders who thought in terms of a glorious summer campaign, they were soon disillusioned. For the next half-century Rome learned hard lessons in the "school of Athens." Not that Roman legions had lost their winning ways. Without exception all of the major military engagements fought throughout this long period resulted in smashing Italian victories. In 197 B.C. at Cynoscephalae, for example, Flamininus easily conquered the oversanguine Philip and ended the war in one season of fighting. In 196 he proudly announced to the hysterically grateful Greeks that they were now free to live their own lives. Eight years later, at Magnesia, the famed Scipio Africanus, in a Roman response to a second appeal from the Greeks, defeated Antiochus, who, with Philip checked, had thought circumstances propitious for regathering the pieces of the once great Seleucid Empire. In 171 B.C. Perseus, son of Philip, renewed his father's fight (the third Macedonian War). At Pydna (168 B.C.) he received from Aemilius Paulus the same kind of trouncing his sire had received from Flamininus.

Establishment of Roman Control

The Roman problem seemed to be not how to win wars but rather how to secure peace. Here again some kind of judgment concerning motivation must be made; otherwise the hectic comings and goings of Rome's leaders and legions, the alarums and passions of Greek and Asian allies and enemies (and they often and bewilderingly reversed positions) amount to no more than sound and fury.

We have noted that after Cynoscephalae Flamininus declared the Greeks free and took his legions home. No sooner had the liberator gone, however, than the liberated fell upon each other, ending up not only castigating Rome for allowing such discord to develop, but inviting Antiochus to move in. With the return of the legions and the defeat of the Syrian monarch, the same tableau was reenacted—again Roman troops withdrew, and again another aggressor (rejuvenated Macedonia) took to the field. The process seemed both pointless and unending. It might appear, therefore, that after Pydna Rome had taken the only sensible course when it divided Macedonia into four separate states, forbade all but one to have armies, and served notice to the East that hereafter breakers of the peace would be held to a strict accountability.

But other parts of the record make it difficult to be satisfied with this seemingly reasonable conclusion. Judgments are finally made on actual behavior rather than on announced intentions, even when the latter are made in complete honesty. And on this basis Rome's record is open to serious question. For example, the much-heralded freedom announced so ceremoniously by Flamininus in 196 B.C. was, after all, *declared,* not self-realized. Granted the Greeks showed no disposition to achieve any other kind; still, such is not real freedom. Also, the record is plain that Rome by deliberate policy fostered the already strong Greek tendency toward divisiveness and particularism. In addition, it steadfastly refused to allow any state—for example the Syrian empire of Antiochus—to develop the stature that Rome itself had developed. Moreover, after Pydna, Macedonians were forced to pay indemnities so huge that Rome soon decreed that her own citizens need no longer pay direct taxes. It can hardly be denied that such behavior gave clear indication that the Romans were coming to understand that imperialism paid well. After this same war, moreover, Roman commanders rounded up some 150,000 Macedonians and Greeks and sold them as slaves in the West. As one more example of what the record shows, 21 years after the "settlement" of Pydna the Romans, their patience used up after another bout of recalcitrance among the Greeks, sacked and burned the city of Corinth (even as that year they were destroying the city of Carthage). As a final warning of what could be expected if Greeks continued to fail to learn the virtues of orderly management of their affairs, all of Corinth's citizens were sold into slavery.*

By the middle of the second century, then, Rome had indeed "gone East." By that time it had become so deeply and inextricably involved in the turbulence of that part of the Mediterranean world that unless it resigned itself to living with turmoil, it seemed imperative to impose outright domination. Rome would hardly choose turmoil; so it had to be domination. Ironically, at the very time that it succeeded in imposing order abroad Rome lost it at home. To this highly un-Roman phase of Roman history we must now turn.

* A modern parallel that suggests itself, though in much milder form, is the treatment of certain Latin American states by the United States before the latter adopted its "good neighbor" policy.

A. Genesis and Early Development of Roman Culture

B. Roman Culture in a Time of Troubles

A CENTURY OF STRUGGLE: 145–31 B.C.

The Maldistribution of Wealth

The century following the destruction of Corinth and Carthage—that is, ca. 145–31 B.C.—was throughout a time of troubles. Economic conditions were especially confused. Had an economic census been taken it probably would have shown a tremendous leap over previous years in what today would be called gross national income. We have already noted the development of large estates, the growing influx of slaves and tribute, the emergence of Rome as the exchange center of the Mediterranean world, and the rise of a moneyed class. All this economic bustle and stir, however, only meant that the rich were getting richer. The masses, whether they remained on the farm or went to the cities for nonexistent jobs, lived on the near side of starvation. As the latifundia waxed, yeoman holdings correspondingly waned, so that increasingly the little farmer was forced either to try to compete on unequal terms—an obvious impossibility—or give up rural life altogether. To use a borrowed phrase, a Grand Barbecue was being held to which the

A stooped farmer takes his cow to town; in the background are a number of roadside shrines.

220   The Roman World: the Republic

proletariat were not invited. Naturally the plebes' misery and resentment sought political channels for expression and redress. Just as naturally the beneficiaries under the status quo opposed any suggestion of change. So the makings of a new class struggle were at hand.

The Disintegration of Commoners' Gains

Had these conditions existed before the Punic Wars (a none-too-realistic reference, since the wars produced the conditions) popular remedial resources would have been available, particularly the tribunes and the Tribal Assembly. Technically, they still were; but the long, terrible years of fighting had changed the substance, if not the form, of Roman politics. For one thing, the Senate had again become supreme. Also, under the relentless pressures of the Hannibalic war the safeguard of annual consular elections could no longer be relied on. Only consuls could command. To be effective they could hardly be regulated by the calendar, otherwise a change of command could occur in the middle of a campaign (this, it is true, had happened before; but there had not been Hannibals before). By the same token, all other decisions, whether of a political or economic nature, must, during these tumultuous times, come from a body enjoying continuity and talent; which, again, meant the Senate.

Moreover, even before the wars a significant change had taken place in the *tribunate,* a change that definitely pointed to "the degradation of the democratic dogma." Originally the voice of the sacrosanct tribune was literally the voice of the people. But with the intermarriage occurring between the classes, the tribunes tended to become "integrated into the new patricio-plebeian senatorial oligarchy" (and with the establishment of policy by assassination, soon to develop, certainly not sacrosanct). Thus by 200 B.C. the supreme representatives of the plebeians had themselves joined the elite. There seemed no one and no place for the commoner to turn to. Nevertheless, many came to believe that conditions were so bad that little could be lost by a fight to improve them.

The Warning of Cato

A generation earlier M. Porcius Cato, prototype of the "noble Roman," had sensed the dangers of a coming day of pseudosophistication and prosperity. He believed greatness rested upon the ancient virtues: family loyalty, industrious and reverent cultivation of the soil, increasing nurture of the citizen's sense of social and civic responsibility, and devotion to tested tradition. Fearing the effects of the easy wealth and swollen power that Romans were beginning to taste, Cato had lashed out against the life of luxury. He attacked both the tendency to regard money as the nexus of human relationships and the prostitution of political power for personal gain—in short, all practices that he thought had developed as a result of the Hellenization of Roman society. (A broad category indeed. As censor he once expelled a senator from office for publicly kissing his wife.) To his contemporaries he seemed "a survival into Rome's age of prosperity of a typical product of the earlier period of narrow resources." Still it must be admitted that much of what he said about the "ordered society and unity of the heroic age of the Republic" would have been well worth heeding.

Trouble from within Rome: the Gracchi

Shortly after Cato's death the first of two concerted efforts was made to stay the destructive course events were taking. The attempted revolution—for it amounted to that—was fathered, paradoxically, by a representative of an old noble plebeian family. Believing that the crux of Rome's troubles lay in the gentry's monopoly of land—particularly as it compounded the problem of what to do with the proletarian mobs in the capital city—Tiberius Sempronius Gracchus stood for election as tribune (133 B.C.) on a platform calling for a rather radical redistribution of the public land. Naturally the Senate immediately and vigorously objected.

In circumstances that the wars had made normal, the political machine of the nobility should have had little difficulty in ensuring Gracchus's defeat. For more than a century the Senate had made war and peace, directed military campaigns, manipulated the magistrates, usurped almost complete judicial powers—in short, had acted as the oligarchic dictatorship that it was. True, commoners could vote, but only in Rome, which long since had become a kept city. One important feature was new: by the last quarter of the second century the equestrian order, the Equites, had created a machine of their own. It is true that both the "knights" and the nobles were capitalists with interests that usually drew them together when the masses became restive. But as entrepreneurs the Equites had grievances of their own. That the nobles had preempted all the high political offices did not particularly bother them; as bankers, brokers, traders, tax collectors, and such, they had little time or inclination for politics as a profession. But occasionally landed and entrepreneurial interests clashed. Then the Equites found it convenient to draw a little closer to the "forgotten men." In the years just preceding the Gracchan revolt the Senate had thought it necessary to defeat a certain measure promoted by the business class. The two machines, therefore, were not working together in 133 B.C. when the great challenge was made. This situation, combined with the appeal of Gracchus's platform and oratory and the desperate temper of the masses, accounted for an overwhelming popular victory.

At his first opportunity Tiberius introduced a bill authorizing the redistribution of public lands. The Assembly, for once disregarding the Senate's advice, prepared to pass it. Before a vote could be taken, however, the Senate induced (bribed is the more accurate word) another tribune to veto the bill's formal presentation. At this point the Gracchan movement clearly showed its revolutionary nature. Arguing that the people's will had been thwarted by an unworthy political maneuver, Tiberius asked the Assembly to unseat his colleague. The Assembly promptly did and, just as promptly, enacted the land bill into law. At once the Senate charged Tiberius with violating the constitution—as he had —and made preparation to assert its will.

Nevertheless a commission was set up to execute the act's provisions and actually did make considerable progress in carrying them out. Eventually some 75,000 yeomen were settled on rented tracts taken from the public domain. When his one-year term as a tribune expired, Tiberius, contrary to custom (which forbade tribunes to succeed themselves), announced his candidacy for reelection. By this time the city was seething with plots and counterplots. During the campaign gangs fought gangs as the proletariat, aided by the Equites, sought to keep its champion in power. In the rioting Tiberius was killed. "This was practically the first bloodshed in Rome's long record of political struggles. The peaceful record of the past was almost matchless in political history. But this day established a precedent which was to be followed more than once, and for which the Senators of a later day were to pay a heavy price."[5]

[5] Tenney Frank, *History of Rome* (Jonathan Cape, London: 1923), p. 198.

The Senate immediately appointed a judicial commission that ruthlessly purged the Gracchan followers of their more prominent spokesmen and set about to restore the former order. Fearing new proletarian uprisings, the nobles grudgingly allowed the agricultural commission to continue its work. But they soon felt sufficiently confident to repeal the authorizing law, and the new settlements on the land stopped. Once again a cry went up and once again a Gracchus—Gaius, the former tribune's brother—offered himself as the people's leader. His program appealed to many of the "little" people—and to some not so little. It included governmental regulation of grain prices, which of course appealed to the urban masses, who often found the gap between what they had and what they needed to pay for their daily bread too great to close. It included also what today we would call public works—the building of wharves and warehouses in Rome to take up the slack of unemployment. When this—as most of the other items in his program—was enacted into law the patricians suffered a severe political blow. For they had long made it a practice to use the unemployed as a reservoir of voters to bribe at election times. Another group that supported Gaius was the Equites. For them the young statesman offered the auctioning off of contracts to tax-collecting agencies, which of course meant handsome profits for interested equestrians. He also promised to remake the jury system so that its members were no longer drawn from the nobility but from an updated list of the Equites, thus obviating the aristocratic bias that increasingly cropped up in suits involving the commercial class. He further proposed full citizenship for all Latins, with the current rights of the latter to be granted to the non-Latin Italians. These were clearly necessary reforms if Italy was to become a true nation (analogous, perhaps, to the attitude taken by the federal government toward our western territories in the late 18th and early 19th centuries). Here, however, Gaius ran afoul of his own followers in Rome who were too jealous of their status as citizens to see it given to others.

Although twice elected to the tribunate, Gaius made scarcely more headway than his brother. And he met the same fate in 121 B.C., when a consular bodyguard, acting on the Senate's order, charged a meeting he was haranguing and demanded his surrender and appearance before a judicial commission. Rather than accept purging at the hands of the Senate he took his own life. The triumphant nobles proceeded to round up as many of the fallen leader's lieutenants as they could for the peremptory treatment that was now becoming a part of the normal political pattern.

To cope as it had with the second Gracchus the Senate devised a practice that set a dangerous precedent commonly followed thereafter. To justify sending troops to apprehend the democratic leader the Senate passed what came to be called the *senatus consultum ultimum,* the "last decree." This decree declared martial law and gave the consul absolute power to do what he thought was necessary to preserve the state. Once again a rough parallel may be found in modern times. Article 48 of the Weimar constitution gave the German president the power to suspend constitutional guarantees when the safety of the state was threatened. Hindenburg's free use of this power in 1931–32 set the precedent for Hitler's virtual abrogation of the constitution in the following years and for the subsequent Nazi dictatorship. If the political machine of the landed nobles could at any time issue a "last decree" proscribing political opponents, obviously the practice would not be forgotten by other groups that might later succeed in wresting power from the Senate. Nor was it forgotten. "Unfortunately the Senate learned only pride from its victory; but the struggle had formulated the issue so clearly that the class war was sure to return. When it did it was the selfish military ruler who took advantage of the contest and overwhelmed both the contestants."[6]

Probably few Romans in ca. 120 B.C. took occasion quietly to sit down and assess the fundamental troubles that were steadily drawing them into chaos, a chaos that ultimately seemed to sanction autocracy as the only way out. Had they done so, the appraisal might have looked like this:

Extreme maldistribution of wealth had given luxury to the few and bare subsistence to the masses.

The steady, century-old crumbling of constitutional guarantees had added large political grievances to economic distress.

Refusal to extend citizenship to ethnic kin while managing their political lives was inexorably leading to a violent reckoning—the "social war."

The incessant and constantly growing need to protect far-flung frontiers had necessarily created permanent large standing armies and given militarists increasingly greater powers.

In short, the Roman "republic" was in the throes of class struggle, enduring depression (for the many), bitter sectional rivalry, and large-scale imperio-militarist ventures that added up behind the grand imperial facade to mounting distress, disorder, and despair.

Trouble from Outside Rome: Africa

For a while after the failure of the Gracchan revolution the Senate seemed to have regained supremacy. Throughout the next several years it busied itself nullifying popular legislation and making free use of the *senatus consultum ultimum*. But since such a program had almost nothing to do with existing problems except to aggravate them, it is not surprising that the Senate's respite was brief.

The new trouble began in Africa. West of Carthage lay Numidia, a Roman protectorate. In 118 B.C. its ruler died, and rival princes claimed the throne. One, Jugurtha, soon gained supremacy. His cousin Adherbal at once appealed to Rome. Still in the process of consolidating its recovered power, the Senate found the plea an annoyance and sought a compromise. To this end it sent a commission to Jugurtha that did work out a settlement, giving divided portions of the kingdom to each claimant. The commission had hardly returned, however, before Jugurtha, asserting that his cousin was plotting to unite the principalities and have him murdered, sent his army marching. For the second time Adherbal appeared before the Roman Senate and demanded help. Once again a commission was sent and a compromise arranged. Jugurtha continued to play this game until he tired of it, whereupon he murdered Adherbal together with a band of Italian traders who happened to be with him.

Furious Romans now demanded that the Senate bring an end to a ridiculous situation that was seriously compromising Roman prestige. Senatorial bungling continued, however, until the opposition—or Populares, as the anti-aristocratic party* was coming to be called—seemed in a position to exploit the affair successfully. To end the embarrassing impasse the Senate dispatched an army to Africa. In the war that followed, Jugurtha—helped by insurgents in Spain—put up a struggle that seemed beyond the power of the legions to handle.

---

[6] Ibid., p. 210.

* The phrase must not be understood in its modern political sense. At no time in the ancient period did parties exist as we know them today.

Career of Marius

This was not the only embarrassment plaguing the Senate. Barbarians from the north—Cimbri (from present-day Belgium) and Teutons, from beyond the Danube—were harassing Roman outposts and creating a serious nuisance. Moreover at home the Equites, angered over the inability of the Senate to avenge the murder of the Italian traders and doubtful whether the senators were really concerned, moved closer to the popular party. In these circumstances the Populares took heart and endorsed the consular candidacy of Gaius Marius, a republican general who had made a name for himself in Africa. Backed by the equestrian order and strongly supported by the tribunes, Marius was overwhelmingly elected.

As consul he introduced a measure that he hoped would make his campaign against Jugurtha brief and successful. But its consequences turned out to be much more significant than the defeat of an African chieftain. His proposal called for supplementation of the draft militia system by recruitment of a volunteer, client army; and the frightened Assembly readily enacted the bill into law. A few years later Rome was to get its fill of professional armies; but current conditions seemed to warrant the innovation.

Thus equipped—and considerably aided by the skillful diplomacy of L. Cornelius Sulla, his young quaestor—Marius quickly brought Jugurtha to surrender. The country now possessed another province and a new hero. From Africa the victor set out at once to deal with the threatening Cimbri and Teutons. There, in three years of hard fighting, he completely annihilated the barbarian armies. Clearly the Populares had found a redoubtable champion. They made the most of their discovery.

Exploiting the military glory of the popular chieftain, various other leaders worked diligently to further discredit and weaken the Senate. Two of them, C. Servilius Glaucia and L. Apulius Saturninus, were elected tribunes with a program calculated to bring them prestige and power. They pushed through a new grain law that provided for the sale of grain at submarket prices to needy citizens. Another law gave Marius's veterans generous land settlements in Africa. Still another proposed further grants in Narbonensis—a province in southern Gaul lying between the Alps and the Pyrenees—and the founding of new colonies in Sicily, Achaea, and Macedonia. But the last proposal, though it finally carried, displeased many Romans, who objected to a provision that gave Marius the right to grant citizenship to colonial settlers. Marius deemed it prudent to dissociate himself from Glaucia and Saturninus when the tribunes showed an alarming taste for violence. Glaucia, for example, electioneering for the consulship in 99 B.C., coldly arranged the murder of his conservative opponent. With popular favor veering away from the extremists, the Senate passed its formidable "last decree" and ordered Marius, consul again (now for the sixth time), to execute it. In his bungling attempt to avoid the Senate's directive Marius failed to afford proper protective custody to his prisoners, who suffered lynching at the hands of an excited Roman mob. The aftermath of this shabby series of events returned the aristocratic party to power.

The Social War

But the Senate, regrettably consistent, continued to ignore the fundamental economic and political problems in favor of partisan advantage. One nobleman, Livius Drusus, did attempt to make the country face the Italian question and to bring his party to terms with the Equites. Elected tribune in 91 B.C. he favored a bill giving citizenship to Rome's Italian allies and another that would admit 300 Equites to the Senate. But senators peremptorily refused to widen the circle of the select few; and all parties, as might have been expected, opposed enfranchising the Italians. On the latter point Drusus proved obdurate. Not only had he promised this justice to Italian and Latin leaders; apparently he had gone so far as to sanction a march on Rome if legal measures failed. When word of this alleged plot became known, nobles, Equites, and commoners alike denounced Drusus as a dangerous traitor. In the heat and passion of this new controversy he was assassinated.

Repeatedly rebuffed in their peaceful attempts to gain citizenship, and with their most powerful advocate murdered, the Italians now answered violence with violence. In 90 B.C. the long dreaded "social war" became a frightful reality. Picentes, Samnites, Umbrians, Etrurians, and citizens of other second-class states sent their combined armies against Rome. At the head of its legions Rome placed its old warrior Marius (who was glad to get back into action again) and his one-time quaestor, Sulla. But the Italians had fought too long under Roman generals not to have mastered the military tactics that had won Rome its victories. When Marius's troops in the north and Sulla's in the south ran into serious trouble, the Senate saw its hope for any early victory fading. Moreover a new threat had developed in the East. Mithridates, king of Pontus, had begun to manifest Alexandrian ambitions. Indeed, at the very time that the Italians were repulsing Marius's and Sulla's legions, the forces of Mithridates were romping through Asia Minor and pointing themselves towards Greece. Under these circumstances Rome finally offered citizenship to all Italians who would lay down their arms within 60 days; so the social war ended in an Italian victory.

The Power of the Professional Army

The Senate now gave full attention to Mithridates and readied its legions for another pacification of the East. Because the booty would be great both Marius and Sulla wanted the command. Between the Jugurthine and social wars the one-time comrades had come to take polar positions on political questions. Sulla had aligned himself with the conservatives (now sometimes called *Optimates*) Marius remained the stalwart hope of the Populares. Both political and personal feelings, therefore, were involved in the rivalry.

The Senate naturally chose Sulla, who at once mobilized his legions, themselves eager for a rich, plundering foray. Embittered at what they considered a gratuitous insult to the savior of Rome, Marius and his followers sought to reverse the decision. As it happened, one of the conservative tribunes had been trying for some time to push through the Assembly a project that his own party had consistently blocked. He now agreed to work for a change in command in return for support from the Populares. What have been termed "election thugs" were freely used in the confused and stormy balloting, and by the use of these tactics the decision was reversed.

Answering violence with violence, the daring Sulla promptly led his legions against Rome and overthrew the divided and wavering government. The professional—and personal—army thus entered Roman history. From this time—88 B.C.—until the collapse of the Empire some 500 years later, it was to constitute the fundamental sanction, however camouflaged, of the Roman state. Sulla's coup d'etat "demonstrated the fact that in the city-state of Rome, where the life of the government resided within the walls of one city, any unscrupulous general who commanded an army loyal to himself

Sulla.

Marius, champion of the Populares.

could at will make himself the autocrat at Rome. . . . Henceforth demagogues were destined to make use of the discovery, a discovery which eventually pointed the way to Caesar's dictatorship and the Empire."[7]

With Mithridates already consolidating his gains in Asia Minor Sulla had no time to set the Roman house in sound, conservative order. Under the banner of his legions he did succeed in forcing the Assembly to commit suicide: at his dictation it passed a law making senatorial consent a prerequisite for the enactment of all legislation, thus abrogating the democratic gains of the ancient Hortensian Law. But further "reforms" would have to await his return.

Dictatorship of Marius

Upon Sulla's departure the "democratic" party, led by L. Cornelius Cinna and at once joined by Marius with his still loyal army, overthrew the conservative government and established a nightmare regime. It is possible that the troubled, hectic times had unsettled Marius's mind, for his actions at this point

[7] Ibid., p. 234.

B. Roman Culture in a Time of Troubles

Pompey the Great.

by his orgy of hate, but Cinna and Marius's son carried on.

Meanwhile in Asia Sulla slowly but convincingly settled accounts with Mithridates. By the terms of the settlement the province of "Asia" was returned to Rome, other states were given back to native rulers under Roman protection, and Mithridates agreed to pay a sizable indemnity. Sending ahead blunt warnings that he would spare no one who stood in his way, Sulla returned to the hectic city and once more stormed and captured it. Some of the generals sent out to intercept him joined him. Among these were Cn. Pompeius, soon to be styled Pompey the Great, and Marcus Crassus, who later, with Pompey and Julius Caesar, formed the First Triumvirate.

Dictatorship of Sulla

Now it was the turn of the "White Terror"; the same savage scenes were repeated. Thousands were persecuted, captured, and executed, some after prolonged torture. In several instances whole towns were destroyed. Later Cicero wrote that he "saw the severed heads of ["renegade"] senators displayed in the streets of Rome." The office of dictator, long since fallen into disuse, was revived; and Sulla, filling it, set himself the task of writing a new constitution. By its provisions the Senate was made the ultimate legislative authority. Tribunes were forbidden to hold any other magistracy, nor could they call the people into meeting. Juries were selected exclusively from the ranks of the Senate. And the grain laws, dating from Gracchan days, were repealed. This was, indeed, conservatism revisited.

So long as Sulla lived his constitution structured Roman life. Factional disputes and imperial disturbances were held in check. For five years (83–79 B.C.) the

were those of a mad butcher.[8] Systematically the ranks of the nobility were decimated. For centuries certain aristocratic families had constituted the government's reservoir of talent; within a matter of weeks a number of these families were wrecked by the vengeful, one-time hero. One may liken what then occurred in Rome to events in France during the Reign of Terror, or in Germany during Hitler's blood bath of 1934, or in Stalin's purges. Marius died within a year (86 B.C.), perhaps worn out

[8] Compare Heichelheim, op. cit., p. 200.

228   The Roman World: the Republic

Roman world may not have breathed the air of freedom or enjoyed economic justice, but its life, such as it was, was lived in peace. In 78 B.C. the great dictator died (a year after he had voluntarily retired from public life) and his elaborate edifice of order collapsed. Once more the way was open for ambitious generals to fight their way to wealth and fame. Of Romans imbued with the old devotion to duty and to the traditional virtues there seemed almost none, save for the gentle Cicero. Rome was to recover and proudly enter a new era of grandeur; but for still another half-century it was, like a stubborn but battered prizefighter, out on its feet.

Pompey and Crassus

The last act of the long drama of the Roman Republic opened with a strange and sanguine struggle between Pompey the Great and his erstwhile collaborator Julius Caesar; and ended, when they had passed from the scene, with an even stranger and sharper struggle between Caesar's chief protagonists, Mark Antony and the younger Octavian (soon to be called Augustus).

After Sulla's death the most conspicuous figure in Roman life was Pompey. His fame rested on a series of impressive military victories stretching from the defeat of Sertorius in Spain to the final crushing of Mithridates in Asia Minor. Sertorius, fleeing to Spain when Sulla came to power, had built up a strong popular following with the intention of returning to Rome and reestablishing the old constitution. To bring an end to this threat the Senate sent Pompey to relieve the original commander, who, in several years of fighting, seemed unable to make appreciable headway. Pompey gladly responded. Once there, he learned what his predecessor had been up against. The inhabitants of Spain, long mulcted by greedy Roman governors, found Sertorius's tolerant and honest regime worthy of support. Moreover, a number of diehard Marians had migrated to Spain, from which they hoped the general would lead a march on Rome. Nevertheless Pompey persevered and after five years of strenuous fighting succeeded in crushing Sertorius and imposing peace on the peninsula.

In the meantime a new crisis flared at home. Since the Hannibalic War, slaves had come to make up an increasingly large portion of Rome's population. Increasingly, too, their lot had grown unbearable. In 73 B.C., under the leadership of a ferocious slave-gladiator, Spartacus, a rebellion broke out that for two years brought back many of the vicissitudes of Hannibal's invasion. To deal with these marauding "armies" the Senate appointed M. Licinius Crassus commander of a large legionary force. Although more interested in money and political power than in fighting, Crassus set about his task with skill and determination. Final victory, however, seemed to elude him. Impatient with his slow progress and impressed with Pompey's victories, the Senate, in 71 B.C., dropped Crassus in favor of Rome's new hero. Before the year was out the insurrection was put down. Pompey's stock accordingly rose even higher, although many understood that his quick victory was made possible only by Crassus's undramatic but punishing efforts. In the next year (70 B.C.) Rome elected each to the consulship.

Although neither trusted the other, both saw the advantages of working together. In addition to his military glory, and largely because of it, Pompey now received the acclaim of the popular party. True, he had gone to Spain as the Senate's agent; but he had made it clear that a Sullan regime should never again be tolerated. On the question of how to avoid this (to mention only the negative aspect of the problem) Pompey was silent. The truth was that Pompey had no workable political program, simply because he had no political talent—a deficiency which, unfortunately, his military prowess tended to obscure. Crassus, on the other hand, had something of Talleyrand's touch. Moreover he was the richest man in Rome. So the two traveled in cautious tandem, the power and the glory of the one combining with the cunning and wealth of the other to the temporary benefit of both.

Under their consulship three important laws were passed. The tribunician power, destroyed by Sulla, was restored. This naturally gratified the plebeians (although they had long since lost the disciplined will to make use of it). Jury lists were again drawn from the ranks of the Equites (although not from their ranks alone), mollifying this bourgeois order. And to expedite the purging from the Senate of many members appointed by Sulla, the office of censor was reintroduced. Naturally the Senate fought all three measures. But Pompey's legions and Crassus's money prevailed, helped by the oratory of Cicero and the subtle machinations of Julius Caesar, then 30 years old and already impatient with destiny.

Their year's term expiring, both Pompey and Crassus retired to private life, alert for whatever new opportunities might develop. For Pompey the waiting was brief. The chronic turbulence of Rome's internal affairs had allowed Mediterranean pirates practically to take over the sea and some of its peripheral areas. To deal with this growing menace a tribune friendly to Pompey sponsored a bill in 67 B.C. that gave the great commander extraordinary powers to equip a fleet and to do whatever was necessary to clear the seas. Ever ready to prove his prowess, Pompey responded to the challenge with such energy and dispatch that within the year piratical forays had been completely eliminated.

In the East, however, affairs had again deteriorated. Sulla, it will be remembered, had foreshortened his struggle against Mithridates in order to crush the Marian uprising. By 74 B.C. the Pontic king felt free to make another attempt to master the East. Rome had sent an able general to meet the new threat; but fighting had dragged on for eight years with little Roman success. Now Pompey was directed to end the Mithridatic threat once and for all. New legions and near plenary powers (authorized by the *Lex Manilia*, which gave Pompey power equal to that of the provincial governors in Asia and without time limit, thus establishing yet another precedent pointing toward the creation of an authoritarian state) were granted the willing leader. For the next four years he tested his strength against the oriental monarch. In the end Roman might again prevailed; and with Mithridates's death in 62 B.C. Asia Minor once more enjoyed a Roman peace.

Political Intrigues

In the meantime Pompey's colleagues back home were busy with schemes of their own. In 68 B.C. Julius Caesar, with the help of Crassus, was elected quaestor and attached to the praetorian office in Spain. There he carefully observed the management of provincial affairs. Elected upon his return to the office of aedile, he borrowed further sums from Crassus to stage extravaganzas for the Roman populace. The name of Caesar was beginning to take on a magic glow. But what really counted, he well knew, was a personal army. To gain this he ventured to persuade the Senate to send him to Egypt, where, he solemnly declared, a fraudulent king was ruling. The king's predecessor, he insisted, had willed the kingdom to Rome, and Rome ought to claim its legacy.

But his inability to produce the will and the Senate's weariness with imperial problems that were already pressing thwarted this grandiose plan. He contented himself, therefore, with election to the office of Pontifex Maximus. Capitalizing on his growing popularity, he successfully offered himself the next year for the praetorship, which made him eligible to return to Spain in 61 B.C. as governor.

Others were busy with plans and projects of their own, particularly one Sergius Catilina ("Catiline"). A man of inordinate ambition unchecked by scruples, Catiline had twice run for the consulship without success, being once beaten by Cicero, who regarded him as a dangerous man on horseback. In 62 B.C. he recklessly plotted to overthrow the government and make himself dictator. Once again Cicero thwarted him, exposing the conspiracy before the Senate in orations that have become famous. Evidence is rather strong that in one way or another both Crassus and Caesar were involved in Catiline's earlier bids for office, although neither supported him in his wild schemes to seize power by force.

Although it might seem to have become the normal pattern, the hectic scramble for power this time held special significance. For several years all Rome had been asking what Pompey would do when he returned from the East. Precedent seemed to make the answer obvious; those with political ambitions therefore felt harassed and hurried. But the great general surprised everybody by disbanding his army when, trailing countless trophies of triumph behind him, he entered the city in 62 B.C. He asked only two things of the government—confirmation of all his settlements in the East, and land to his veterans as he had promised. But the Senate refused both. It had not forgotten his brusque treatment of the aristocracy when he was consul; and his demobilization of the army gave them courage.

The Rise of Julius Caesar

At this juncture the vaulting ambitions of Caesar, Crassus, and Pompey brought them into a strange partnership. Long since Crassus had marked Pompey as his chief enemy. Nor could Caesar see himself as master until the great general was somehow eliminated. For his part, Pompey despised Crassus and considered Caesar an annoying upstart. But each professed to be the people's champion; and each was opposed by the stubborn Senate, which now seemed to have found in Cicero a new if somewhat strange (to it) leader. Under these circumstances, and at the initiative of Caesar, the three pooled their resources and formed what is known as the First Triumvirate. Backed by Crassus's wealth and Pompey's prestige, Caesar was elected consul in 59 B.C. Honoring terms of the bargains, he pushed through a bill legalizing Pompey's Asian settlements and another granting land to his veterans. Legislation favorable to the equestrian order pleased Crassus, their spokesman. For himself Caesar secured, shortly after his retirement as consul, the proconsulship of Cisalpine Gaul (and Illyricum) for a period of five years. The partnership creaked, but it worked.

In 58 B.C. Caesar departed for Gaul, where he hoped to build up an army strong enough to support him in whatever designs future circumstances might suggest. The years of the proconsulship won fame for Caesar and the whole of Gaul for Rome. On the other hand neither Crassus nor Pompey was able to manage so well. Pompey had revived Caesar's old scheme—now strenuously opposed by him—to invade and annex Egypt; but both aristocratic and popular enthusiasm was lacking. With equal lack of success Crassus had schemed to win for himself a provincial governorship. When, therefore, Caesar suggested renewing the compact for another five years and promised

Julius Caesar. This is probably a faithful likeness, since it was copied from his death mask.

to support both partners for consulships, with provinces to follow, they agreed. In fact, mutual suspicions and recriminations had by now all but destroyed what little substance there had been in the original agreement.

With the death of Crassus in 53 B.C. and the election of Pompey as sole consul the following year, the triumvirate came to an end. Now Pompey and Caesar openly faced each other in the battle for Rome. Yet it is doubtful whether Pompey's heart was really in the struggle. Probably what he desired above all else was not mastery over the Republic but recognition as its "first citizen." Strong evidence indicates that he would have liked to quietly enjoy this role of *princeps* for the rest of his life.* But for Caesar, prestige, although precious, was not enough. He yearned for power and grand achievement. The years in Gaul had schooled him in both the techniques of battle and the arts of statecraft. They had touched his genius and given him a vision of a remade society. He saw in the shambles of Rome the inevitable product of imperial power and grandeur cracking the ancient mold of republican life. A new structure was required, and he firmly believed that fate had singled him out as its architect.

In 49 B.C., therefore, with Gaul finally pacified and his second term as proconsul drawing to a close, Caesar announced his intention of returning to Rome to seek election as consul. Both Pompey and the Optimates, having more than an inkling of Caesar's ambition, feared above all just this. To thwart him the Senate, asserting that the proconsul was planning a coup d'etat, passed the fateful senatus consultum ultimum and authorized Pompey to take whatever action was needed. Two of Caesar's friends, Mark Antony and Cassius, had, in their capacity as tribunes, tried to prevent passage of the Senate's decree. Failing this, they fled to Caesar's camp and warned him of the menacing action. The balked leader had a choice: he could bow to the decree, hope to conciliate Pompey and the Senate, and wait for a more propitious moment. Or he could, against ancient law, move his troops across the proconsular boundary—in this case the river Rubicon—and march on Rome. He promptly elected to scorn the decree and ordered his troops to march.

In the civil war that followed the popular party rallied under Caesar's banner. Pompey, taking a number of frightened

---

* For a different view of Pompey and his ambitions see Ronald Syme, *Roman Revolution* (London: Oxford University Press, 1960).

232   The Roman World: the Republic

senators with him, fled to Greece, where he hoped to recruit troops untouched by Caesar's magic. In Rome Caesar took time to secure his position. Elected consul, he at once had legislation passed that relieved pressing economic problems. Another law gave citizenship to Roman settlers in the Po Valley. New—naturally pro-Caesarian —senators were appointed; and fresh legions were raised. In a brief Spanish campaign he destroyed forces loyal to the Optimates. With the home front and its hinterland secured he then set off for Greece, where, at Pharsalus (48 B.C.), the two armies met. The encounter was a brief one. Pompey led an army larger than Caesar's, reinforced, moreover, by strong cavalry units. But Caesar's troops had been taught and toughened by ten years of fierce and almost continuous combat with the barbarian hordes of Gaul. His army utterly routed, Pompey fled to Egypt, where he hoped to enlist that country's help. As it happened, Ptolemy was himself engaged in a civil war against Cleopatra, his sister and the coruler of Egypt. In the intrigues that followed, Pompey was assassinated; but by that time most of his legions had joined Caesar.

To prevent Egypt from later serving as a base of operations against him, Caesar not only attempted to heal the breach between the royal contestants but also to win them as allies. With Ptolemy he was unsuccessful, eventually becoming involved with him in a brief war, in which the ruler lost his life. Cleopatra proved more amenable to his approach, and was soon set up as Egypt's sole sovereign under Rome's protection. (Not all of the affairs between the two, it might be added, were confined to the business of statecraft.) For several years mopping-up operations were required elsewhere—in Asia Minor, Numidia, Spain. With these last remnants of opposition crushed (45 B.C.), Caesar indeed "bestrode the world like a colossus."

Caesar's Appraisal of the Times

Before considering the political ordering that Caesar brought to the chaos of his times we need to note a fact of fundamental importance. Subsuming his various plans and projects was a correct reading of Roman history missed by his predecessors; a reading that led him clearly to understand that with the Punic Wars the age of the Republic had ended and a new age, the essence of which was the Empire-state, had come into existence. To meet the imperative demands of the new age, new institutions were necessary. The Senate was a body of many minds and many factions; unlike Caesar, it scorned the record of the past. The Assembly was made up of an even greater number of minds, also divided, and with less talent. Moreover, the long years of bread and circuses had shunted the Assembly's old dynamic drive away from the goal of creative sovereignty into the blind alley of demanding dependence. Nor did either body understand, much less desire to remedy, the complicated and corrupt political conditions persisting in the provinces, conditions created and exploited by inexperienced and greed-motivated governors. Although perhaps not perfectly, these things Caesar understood; and he acted accordingly and energetically.

Believing that effective permanent government could not rest on vindictive cruelty, he deliberately adopted an attitude of leniency and tolerance. Defeated enemies he conciliated, frequently offering them offices in the government they had sought to overthrow. Brutus, who later planned his murder, was an ironic example of this forgiveness. Proscription itself was proscribed. This attitude alone went far toward bringing back to the restless, turbulent populace the hope that humanitarian purpose might again guide human endeavor. It gave promise in place of menace, in short, for Rome's tomorrows.

Calendar Reform

Caesar's political accounting was large in scope and left unfinished by his assassination. The calendar, which, because of its anachronistic condition, prevented effective execution of public and private business, was given early attention. The old calendar of 355 days required the intercalation of one month biennially; and then it was only imperfectly aligned astronomically. Because of the incessant confusion, this intercalation had been neglected for almost 10 years. Under Caesar's supervision a committee of experts, advised by a prominent astronomer brought in from Alexandria, added (in 46 B.C.) 67 days between the last day of November and the first of December. It also distributed ten additional days over the other months and provided for the permanent intercalation of one day every four years to allow for the hiatus of the remaining one-quarter of a day. Save for a slight correction authorized by Pope Gregory in the sixteenth century, this Julian calendar (which is now called Gregorian) has served to our own times.

Reform Laws

To rid Rome of the rabble that for years had offered its support to the highest bidder and had made a mockery of stable government, Caesar decreed several wisely conceived laws. One, fostering a back-to-the-land movement, required all large landholders to reduce the number of their slaves in favor of a like number of freemen. Another forced capitalists to invest at least one-half of their wealth in land. A third abolished the multitude of social clubs (little Tammanys) which gave constant encouragement to demagoguery.

To take up the slack of urban unemployment until his laws could be given effect, Caesar set in motion an extensive program of public works (a kind of Roman PWA). He ordered road and canal building, harbor improvement, rechanneling of the Tiber, drainage of the Pontine marshes (completed by Mussolini in our own century), and the construction of temples and other public edifices. Strict laws against crime were passed, backed by energetic enforcement. Caesar's sumptuary decrees—involving heavy fines for ostentatious display and luxurious living—while not particularly effective served to remind Romans of the natural relationship of simple living to the maintenance of a stable society. Left in the planning stage was a project designed to bring all existing laws, municipal and imperial, into harmony, and to supplement them with such rules as would allow effective administration of the empire.

All of this, Caesar well knew, required the creation of an autocracy. Not wanting "to lend dignity to old republican offices," he refused the Senate's offer of a ten-year consulship. But when the Senate then voted him the dictatorship for life he promptly accepted it. Subsequently he combined in his person the functions—indeed the titles as well—of consul, tribune, "prefect of morals" and pontifex maximus. Before his planned departure for Parthia, where he hoped to win new imperial victories, he was given the added power of naming the two consuls and one-half of the magistracies.

In the main these revolutionary changes met with popular acclaim. The depth and sweep of his program and the magic of his touch promised an end at last to the long years of anarchy and turbulence. To many Romans he seemed a kind of divine savior; and Caesar, sensing the mood, capitalized on it if, indeed, he did not motivate it by the creation of a new goddess, Venus Genetrix, which linked divinity with his own *gens*. Soon the Senate, caught up in this current of emotionalism, voted that a statue of Caesar be given a place among the statues of the gods when they were paraded before the games.

Opposition to Caesar

But if a subservient Senate and enthusiastic crowds acclaimed Caesar as lord and savior, a stubborn minority of old-line republicans fumed in bitter and impotent rage. Brutus and Cassius tried to rally their countrymen against the looming autocracy. Added to their passionate opposition against plots to subvert the Republic was strong personal animus against the arrogant behavior of Caesar. Earlier we noted Caesar's practice of clemency. But this calculated approach to the creation and maintenance of political stability did not, strangely enough, suggest to the dictator the expediency of moderating, in the interests of conciliation, the egomania that made him insufferable even to some of his would-be admirers and supporters. Among his republican opponents, naturally, it raised emotions to a turbulent pitch. When Caesar's laws and agents made their campaign too dangerous they turned to the one remaining weapon, assassination. To Brutus and other representatives of the old order, tyrannicide, far from being a crime, was considered the highest form patriotism could take. Thus as Caesar swept from power to power, and especially as he came to show signs of restoring the hated monarchy and becoming a new Alexander, the conspirators made ready for their own "last decree."

Caesar planned to leave for the East immediately after the Ides of March. The conspirators feared he would there proclaim himself god-emperor. So the Republic, if it was to be saved, must be saved at once. Thus it was that on March 15, 44 B.C., avenging daggers struck down the conqueror. It is difficult to see how Brutus and his colleagues could have hoped to be hailed as saviors. Rome was reveling in Caesar as savior. Moreover the city was crowded with the commander's troops. Perhaps the conspirators hoped that with Caesar dead his magic spell would dissolve. Perhaps they hoped that a chastened Rome would set itself the task of restoring peace and order according to the tenets of the republican faith. Cicero, who had not been privy to the assassins' plot, rejoiced in Caesar's death, saying that for all true republicans it opened the way for "one hope, that the Roman people will at last show themselves worthy of their ancestors." But that he could have believed and voiced such a sentiment is a fair measure of the light grip that by then he and other dissidents had on reality.

The assassination of Caesar plunged the Roman world again into factional strife and confusion. Antony, strangely spared by the assassins, originally assumed a moderate position in order to see which group would prove stronger. He did not have long to wait. The mobs in Rome cried out against the murder of their idol; and Caesar's troops showed no inclination to yield their power to a bickering Senate. Under these circumstances Antony moved easily into the posture of Caesar's avenger.

By his will Caesar had designated his grandnephew, Octavian, as his heir and adopted son. At the time of Caesar's death the young man (then 18 years old) was in Athens studying under a tutor. Within the month he appeared in Rome to claim his inheritance. Antony, hardly in a position to repudiate a Caesar while himself fighting under that name, grudgingly made room for him. Throughout the rest of the year hectic jockeying for position continued. Marcus Brutus fled to Greece, where he set about raising an army. Decimus Brutus, a relative, watched and waited in Gaul. Antony and Octavian, after sparring cautiously, formed a loose combination against these and other republican forces. The next year Antony defeated Decimus Brutus* and was maneuvered by Octavian, now officially

---

* But not before Antony's own forces had been routed earlier by troops sent against him by the Senate.

bearing Caesar's name, into agreeing to a working partnership that soon came to include, purely for reasons of expediency, M. Aemilius Lepidus, a faithful henchman of Caesar. Thus was born the Second Triumvirate. To consolidate their position the new rulers now loosed proscriptive terrors unequaled in the city's bloody history. Listed for slaughter were 300 Senators and 2000 Equites. "Soldiers hunted out marked persons, cut off their heads and brought them in, receiving gold for each head." Even the great Cicero was not spared; for several days, by Antony's order, the head of the one-time savior of the Republic was prominently displayed in the city. With the opposition thus cowed the triumvirs assigned areas of the Empire to each other, ostensibly for purposes of pacification. Antony took the East, Octavian the West, and Lepidus (soon to be dropped), Africa.

In 42 B.C Antony and Octavian defeated the forces of Marcus Brutus at Philippi. Perhaps each suspected that the next and final contest must be between themselves. Established in the East, Antony soon came to play the part of an oriental monarch under the heady tutelage of Cleopatra, who found Caesar's lieutenant as attractive and useful as his captain. While Octavian was busy at home establishing order and encouraging the return of prosperity Antony made Cleopatra "Queen of Kings" and finally designated his two sons, born of Cleopatra, as future rulers of certain eastern provinces. When this became known (32 B.C.) Octavian had little trouble persuading the Senate to declare war (nominally against Egypt), and the issue was joined. The next year, at Actium, the two armies met in what turned out to be an easy victory for Octavian; soon thereafter Antony took his own life. With favorable precedent to guide her Cleopatra coyly invited the victor to a conference. But this time her charms were of no avail; and preferring death to a Roman prison, she followed Antony in suicide.

Once more the Roman world had a master; but this time the old pattern was not to be repeated. With Octavian, Rome had come of imperial age.

LITERATURE IN THE CENTURY OF STRUGGLE

Military and political decisions and events constituted the chief forces that worked the pivotal change marking Roman history from about 150 B.C. to the demise of the Republic. But of course literary, philosophical, religious, and economic developments inevitably were part of that history, too. In literature the works of five writers are especially worthy of notice.

Lucretius

T. Lucretius Carus's *De Rerum Natura* was written in the years of agony that characterized the onset of the civil wars. The age, as we have seen, was unsettled by a haunting fear of tomorrow's senseless violence. It suffered from the agony of the dissolution of old frames of reference, from blind groping in a widening void, and from the desperately eager conversion of many to the inviting hopes of alien and esoteric faiths. These and other wracking features of his period stirred Lucretius and set him on his quest for the balm of abiding truth. His search led him to the philosophy of Epicurus where, he came to believe, the final answers lay. Thereafter he became a man with a message. *De Rerum Natura* ("Concerning the nature of things") is, therefore, actually a homiletical exercise designed to save man from his wretched superstitions and harassments.

Undergirding and feeding this wretchedness, Lucretius believed, were twin evils—religion and man's fear of death. Let man rid himself not only of false gods but of all gods; then let him explore the natural world and learn its secrets. From this bold venture in reason two rewards would be his: serenity that allows acceptance of blind, purposeless life; and welcome rapport with death.

At the outset of his long work (of six books, about 700 lines) he hymns his master, Epicurus, as a man of Greece who

> . . . first dared to raise his mortal eyes against
> [crude creed and myth]
> And even stand and fight.
> And him no fables of gods could daunt,
> Nor heaven with lightening flash or thunderbolt dismay.
> But only stirred the more the valorous splendor of his mind.
> He longed to be the first to crack the cramping bonds of nature.
> And so his splendid strength of soul prevailed.
> Outside he went, beyond the flaming ramparts of the world
> And ranged the infinite whole in mind and thought's imagining.
> And from his mental voyages to us brought back,
> Like conqueror crowned in victory, the news of Nature's laws
> Of what could come to be and what could not,
> The code that binds each thing, its deep-set boundary stone.
> And so religion in its turn is trampled under foot and trodden down,
> And man is made like god by one man's victory.[9]

Encouraging his readers to resist any guilt feelings that they might have in daring to read such unorthodox lines, Lucretius gives an example of the real sin that religion provokes. He cites the fate of Iphigenia, innocent of all guile, as she is cruelly sacrificed to the gods by her own father.

> Think how at Aulis, Grecian chiefs, picked leaders of mankind,
> Stained altars of the chaste and huntress queen
> With maiden's blood in obscene rite and wanton sacrifice.*
> And she, poor girl, the fillets on her maiden locks
> Adorning either cheek,
> Saw father stand by sacral stone, stedfast but sombre;
> The slaves of sacrifice with swords concealed
> To spare a father's natural sympathy,
> The clansfolk weeping at the doleful spectacle;
> In tongueless terror down she fell and swooned.
> Poor girl, it could not help at all at such a time
> That she had long ere this been first to call him father.
> For borne aloft in rough men's hands, poor trembling girl,
> Not tenderly like bride in husband's grasp
> (To altar led the escort not to wedlock's home),
> No wedding hymn, but funeral chant, accompanied her
> Who chastely died by wanton act
> Just when love's consummation should be hers.
> And so she died,
> A sad and sacrificial victim at a father's blow,
> That jealous god by butchery propitiate

---

[9] This and the following selections from Lucretius are from Alban Dewes Winspear, *The Roman Part of Science, Lucretius: "De Rerum Natura"* (New York: The Harbor Press, 1956), pp. 5–7, 129.

* When the Greek fleet was delayed by contrary winds at Aulis, the soothsayer Calchas announced that the goddess Artemis had been offended and could be propitiated only by the sacrifice of the child of one of the leaders. Agamemnon summoned his daughter Iphigenia, under pretense of marrying her to Achilles, and had her slain to appease the offended goddess.

> *Might grant auspicious voyage to the fleet.*
> *That is religion, these its monstrous acts.*

Nor need men fear death. There are no gods to punish for eternity. Death brings only the balm of sleep. Men may and do lament the passing of joyous experiences of life:

> *Grow stiff with cold when sleeping under weight of ponderous slab?*
> *Or feel oppressed and ground by weight of earth above?*
> *"No more," they say, "no more can joyful home fires welcome you,*
> *Nor loyal comely wife,*
> *Nor children be the first to share a father's kiss*
> *And touch the heart in joyful well-springs of content."*
> *"No more," they say, "can you be prosperous and guard your own."*
> *"Poor wretch," they say, "how wretchedly*
> *Has death's accursed single day snatched life's best gifts."*

To which Lucretius gives answer:

> *But this they do not say "You'll want these things no more."*

With superstition and false fears overcome man may, if he will, reach the heights of serene contemplation. But to gain these heights he must probe nature's secrets. The burden of the long poem is an exposition of nature's being and ways, all advanced according to the "scientific" determination of Democritus and the Garden philosophy of Epicurus. Not many Romans, of course, had either the wit or the will to follow the Lucretian abstractions. But the intellectual elite was attracted to, and influenced by, the spell of his compelling hexameters. Cicero referred to the poem's "many flashes of genius"; and Virgil, among others, imitated the poet's style while rejecting his philosophy.

Catullus

If Lucretius had, as a few critics have insisted, something to do with shaping the work of Catullus (ca. 84-54 B.C.) the evidence for it is none too plain. Whereas Lucretius sorrowed over the ignorant state of mankind and laboriously worked out a plan of salvation, Catullus sang of himself, especially of the waxing and waning of his love life. Where Lucretius wrote in the measured, solemn manner of the old Romans, Catullus, affected by the new fashions of the Alexandrine school, scorned archaic syntax, vocabulary, and often meter in favor of the sweetly passionate dicta of the Eastern literary cult. Even their interpretations of the essence of Epicurean philosophy differed. Lucretius found in it solace of mind; Catullus, satiation of the senses. Although Catullus wrote a few longer works, his genius lay in exploiting a Latinized elegiac form, the brief lines of which seared the reader's emotions as a hot brand. His chief subject was his love for "Lesbia," who in real life was Clodia Pulchra, one of Rome's famous courtesans. He met her as a young man newly come to the city and immediately fell under the spell of the charms he spent the rest of his brief life celebrating. The following passages indicate the stormy course the affair took.

> *Let's live, my Lesbia, and love*
> *And care no chit for ancient's spite.*
> *Whereas their setting sun returns,*
> *Our flashing meteor briefly burns*
> *And fades into an endless night.*
>
> *Give me a thousand kisses—add*
> *A hundred, then a thousand more,*
> *Another hundred add, and still*

*Another thousand yet before
A hundred once again until,
Confused by countless thousands, we
Confess we've lost what score there be,
Confounding Envy's power to bead
Our mingled kisses to its need.*[10]

. . . .

*My Lesbia, this love of mine you own
Exceeds the measure of the much-loved few,
No love could be more fondly faithful than
This foolish, guileless love I give to you.
Your very faults, my Lesbia, bewitch
My soul and give it blissful stress.
I own that be you faithless or sincere
I cannot love you more, my love, or less.*

. . .

*I hate, I love. Forebear to ask me to explain.
I only know I feel the wondrous pain*

. . . .

*Ah, mad Catullus, sigh no more these sighs.
Confess what's lost; recall the skies
Of yesternight whose balm your girl, by leave,
Enhanced with favors given and received.*

*Then blushing yes became a distant no
And you do well to recognize it so.
Be obdurate, disdaining now to plead
Surcease from suffering; leave her to her need.*

*My girl, farewell; Catullus now is set
In stony hardness 'gainst his thankless pet.
But you, my Lesbia, can you stand the slight*

*When not a lover comes to spend the night?
Or who will woo? Whose name now linked with thine?
Whose lips receive the love bites that were mine?
Catullus, now! Refuse thou thus to pine!*

Caesar

Catullus's contemporary, Julius Caesar (100–44 B.C.), was, as we have seen, more the maker of history than its mirror, although he wrote far more and better than one would suppose a busy warrior could. His literary efforts were broad in scope: orations, essays (on astronomy and grammar, for example), epigrams, drama (still another *Oedipus*), love poems, as well as his ten books of commentaries. Save for a few of the orations and, of course, the commentaries, all have been lost. His orations were marked by directness and studied simplicity. Although the Alexandrine school was too precious for him, nevertheless he did not care to use the polished, rolling periods of Cicero. Caesar's severe approach is even more marked in his seven books of commentaries *On the Gallic Wars*, and in his three books *On the Civil War*. It has been said that his memoirs have no superior as military narratives. In his *Gallic Wars* he went out of his way to eliminate the first person singular and instead referred to himself in the third person; by deliberate calculation, it has been charged, he sought in this way to throw himself into even greater relief. The work is a marvel of compact, austere prose. This is all the more remarkable when we recall that it was essentially an electioneering tract. He knew that his enemies in the Senate were waiting for an opportunity to reveal him as a swashbuckling adventurer plotting to play fast and loose with the constitution. His *Gallic Wars* were aimed at countering their argu-

---

[10] These and the following selections from Catullus are adapted from John Nott, trans., *The Poems of Catullus*, 2 vols. (London, 1795), 1:15–19, 23–27; 2:119–21, 137.

ments before they could be advanced. But for us his work is significant not as a campaign document or even for the unadorned grace of its forthright style, but for its rich record of the pacification of Gaul. Unfortunately, so much cannot be said for the worth of his history of the civil war, an uncompleted work that contains little of value that less prejudiced sources do not offer.

Cicero

Far surpassing Caesar in literary talent (though except in his own eyes, in few other ways) was Marcus Tullius Cicero (106-43 B.C.), after Caesar the most renowned of ancient Romans. There is hardly a form of literary expression that he left untried—poetry, philosophic essays, letters, works on grammar and rhetoric, theological treatises and, preeminently, orations. Of the latter, 57 survive, the most famous being the two *Philippics,*—his passionate indictments of the character and design of Caesar's colleague, Mark Antony. On these especially, and to a lesser extent on his similar diatribes against Catiline, rest his fame as the ancient world's greatest orator after Demosthenes. For the latter orations he earned the title "savior of his country." From the former came not only lasting acclaim but, tragically for him, his own death warrant; for as we have seen, Antony had found it impossible to forgive the powerful and damning strictures of his eloquent adversary.

Beyond his own creations he produced two books on the principles and the history of the art of persuasion—*De Oratore* and *Brutus,* both serving as textbooks until the end of the Middle Ages. Although in no sense works of original thought, his volumes on philosophy, especially his *Academica* and *Paradoxia*, were landmarks in the development of the Roman mind. In the *Academica* he provided his countrymen with their first systematic exposition of Greek philosophy, treating in detail the Epicurean, Stoic, and Academic systems. In the *Paradoxia* he ingeniously expounded on what seemed to be contradictions in Stoic principles. Perhaps even more importantly, in these works he creatively modified and enriched the Latin language, so that thereafter Roman scholars could express in their own language the shadings and subtleties of Hellenic literature. To a less degree he did the same for literary criticism. Although hardly equal to the task, his *De Natura Deorum* sought to answer Lucretius's defense of Epicureanism. His poetry, written in the early years of his career, can only be described as expert versification. Surpassing all, especially in their power to evoke both the spirit and features of his age, are his letters, about 800 of which have survived. To our own day they remain the most important single source of historical data dealing with the last days of the Republic.

Sallust

The foremost historian of the period, indeed saluted by Martial as Rome's first real historian, was Sallust (C. Sallustius Crispus, 86–35 B.C.). A partisan of Caesar's and a one-time tribune, Sallust retired to private life after Caesar's death and devoted the remaining nine years of his life to writing. His two major works were *Bellum Catilinarium,* in which he described the political maze of that politician's conspiracy, and *Bellum Jugurthinum,* a narration and interpretation of Rome's war with Jugurtha. In the first work his aim, on Thucydides' history of the Pelo- of Caesar's rule with that which succeeded it. His second work was based, in broad aim, on Thucydides' history of the Peloponnesian War. In this volume he set the pattern that Roman historians would use as a model. Until then annalists, with their bare, dry laying of facts end on end, had served exclusively as Clio's servants; nor did Caesar's fetching prose attempt more than an unadorned recital of fact. Sallust endeavored to read the meaning of the facts, to discover motives, to discern trends and movements. Moreover, imitating Thucydides, he undertook the characterization of prominent personages, formulating long speeches for them to deliver. These "quotations" of course were invented, but only in the sense that Thucydides invented his characters' speeches; that is, after judicious assessment of the leader's personality and response to contemporary conditions. A sample may be taken from *Bellum Jugurthinum* to demonstrate his technique. On a particular occasion Marius, the great popular champion, called a meeting of the people to explain why the Populares, and particularly he as its leader, should be entrusted with prosecution of the Jugurthine War—and for that matter with Roman affairs generally. Sallust has him speaking thus:

I am unable to display [as the aristocrats are forever doing] . . . the busts, triumphs, or consulships of my ancestors; but should circumstances require it, I can show lances, standards, collars, and other military honors; [including] scars upon my breast; this is my nobility, not transmitted by inheritance as theirs to them; but what I have acquired by numerous hardships and dangers. My language is not studied; to that I attach little importance. Merit unadorned is its own sufficient evidence. [The aristocrats] require art, to conceal by eloquence their shameful deeds. Neither have I learned the literature of Greece. . . . But I have been educated in the accomplishments most serviceable to the state: to disable an enemy; to watch on my post; to fear nothing but dishonor; to endure equally heat and cold; to sleep on the ground . . . with such instructions will I train my soldiers. . . . By these and similar means, your ancestors distinguished themselves and the republic, upon whom, our aristocracy depending, though differing in principles, disparage us who are their rivals, and claim from you all preferments, not upon their qualifications but as a right. . . . Their forefathers have left them all they could leave: their wealth, their rank, and their own illustrious memories. Merit they neither could nor did transmit. . . . They call me mean and unrefined; because I cannot, with sufficient elegance, furnish an entertainment, and keep no jester or cook at higher wages than a land steward; all which I am free to admit; for, I have understood from my father and other venerable men, that refinement is suited to women, toil to men; that to all honorable men more fame than wealth should belong; that arms and not domestic luxuries, should be their pride. Why, then, cannot they always do what is their delight . . . indulge in gallantry and wine—spend their old age in the revelry wherein they passed their youth, devoted to the appetites and the most sensual of the passions; and leave the toil and the dust and other such scenes to us, to whom these are more welcome than the banquet.[11]

Philosophy and Religion

Our study of the literature of this period suggests the trends taken by philosophic and religious thought, which were also derived from the Greeks. By the time of Augustus, Epicureanism and Stoicism were competing on equal terms. The great systems of the Academies, on the other hand, had gone into eclipse. They had opened brilliantly with the promise that the play of man's mind would lead to the discovery of all truth. But by Augustan times Neoplatonists and Neoaristotelians had despaired of such a grand achievement. Reacting against this failure, most philosophic speculation was inclined to subsume its activity with implicit acknowledgment that first causes were beyond human ken. For the Epicurean this did not mean averting attention from

[11] Henry Owgan, *The Histories of Caius Crispus Sallust* . . . (Dublin: William B. Kelly, 1869), pp. 131-32.

This wall painting portrays some of the liturgical exercises of the popular cult of Isis.

nature and its ways; as we have seen, for Lucretius it meant precisely the opposite. But the underlying assumption was that while man's mind could and should seek causal connection of events—should forever peck away at the *how*—the basic *why*, or even *what*, was unanswerable. The philosopher's task, therefore, was to seek the partial truth that could be discovered and to fit man's life into it. With this Stoicism agreed, adding the argument of duty. For the Stoic, contemplation for the sake of contemplation was useless, even foolish. He therefore criticized the Epicurean not only for allowing his thought to run to hedonistic seed but, as much, for neglecting the "disciplined doing" which naturally followed a true understanding of the laws of nature.

But to the average person neither Epicureanism nor Stoicism afforded satisfaction. Most persons, then as now, could not grasp philosophy's abstractions or follow its cogently reasoned arguments. Moreover their lot was often so miserable and destitute of promise that they were hardly likely to subscribe to any system that predicated the acceptance of "things as they are." In addition, masses and intellectuals alike found it impossible, in the actual conditions of life, to hold in eternal abeyance the *why* of existence and the related question of man's destiny after death. Long since, faith in the ancient religion had dimmed. To the state cult, especially as it was nurtured by Augustus and his successors, citizens gave lip service, but more as a political symbol than as a way of life. Out of these promptings the average Roman displayed an increasing willingness to explore the new religions that filtered in from the East. These often spoke to the individual and his demanding needs, promising spiritual satisfactions both in this and in the next world.

During the trying days of the Hannibalic War the old Roman gods had seemingly proved unworthy of continued supplication and worship. It was at this time that the cult of Cybele (the Great Mother) made its appearance. The Great Mother was a nature goddess whose benevolent spirit inclined her to listen and attend to the wants of every man. These she could readily understand because, as the legend proclaimed, her son was human, not divine; and the steady devotion of Attis, the son, to his mother evoked in her a compassionate concern that was centered on mercy and that promised redemption. Accompanying these articles of faith, mystical rituals and liturgical devices invited emotional responses that served as an effective release from the tensions and fears of life. After Hannibal's defeat the Great Mother cult suffered an eclipse. But when several centuries later the Empire began to crack and fall apart, its devotees became numerous.

Another mystery religion, Isis worship, flourished in the late years of the Republic. We are familiar with its chief features from our study of Egyptian civilization. Brought to Rome, it underwent some modifications. Serapis became the remote supreme god, "while Isis herself became a gentle queen of the living and the dead." As they were of the cult of the Great Mother, songs, liturgies, and an elaborate priesthood were important features of this religion.

During the war between Pompey and Caesar, Mithraism attracted many followers in Rome. Its influence, especially as it bore on the rise and development of Christianity,* will be considered later. Much of the impetus given to this and other mystery religions came originally from the hordes of migrants pouring in from regions of the ancient Near East, where "religion of the spirit" had its birth. By the second century A.D. these faiths had become, together with Christianity, an integral part of the religious life of the West.

Economic Conditions

Such profound changes marked Roman life during the 200 years from Hannibal to Octavian; but not *every* aspect of life. The economic system and its practices remained essentially unaltered. For most Italians agriculture continued to serve as the main source of livelihood. It is true that under the prodding of the elder Cato new techniques and practices had developed. But the husbandman of Rome at the dawn of the Empire period planted, cultivated, and harvested much as had his forefathers.

The exigencies and opportunities of imperial dominion brought into prominence the equestrian order and created an influential bourgeois class. But much of the trading was still carried on by Greeks whether they lived in Italy, Africa, or in the East. Consequently Italians remained indifferent to tariff policies and regulatory measures, giving them almost no official or sustained attention until the time of Diocletian. This tends to puzzle the modern student who is used to thinking of national development in terms of class struggle, duty schedules, money and banking policies, governmental regulation of business, and the like. But we need to

---

* A relationship reversed by some modern historians.

B. Roman Culture in a Time of Troubles

keep in mind that in the period we are considering a huge slave supply made genuine class struggle impossible, save for an occasional servile revolt. It even ruled out such common proletarian protests as strikes. For the most part factories were small and locally owned. There were great centers of industry, to be sure, but not in Italy. In the main the equestrian order controlled banking and hence dominated what we would call the real estate business.

But if the basic structure of the economic system remained unaltered, the overall effects produced by it remarkably changed the society it sustained. Particularly significant was the mushrooming of cities, both in size and number. Wealth, although inequitably distributed, increased at such a rate that the age may be called one of luxury. Roman political control made the whole Mediterranean world one great free-trade area. Commerce accordingly flourished, further encouraged by the Roman-built network of roads. The two centuries of the *Pax Romana* that followed witnessed a still greater augmentation of the "gross national product," so that the advent of Octavian heralded an era not only of peace but also of unprecedented prosperity. And the nature of the new state that Octavian set up, the salient features of which we may now examine, guaranteed that these gains would outlive the generation that so rapturously hailed them.

Selected Readings

Boak, A. E. R., and Sinnigen, William G. *A History of Rome to* A.D. *565.* 5th ed. New York: The Macmillan Co., 1965.

Any text that survives nearly a half-century of reading is worthy of attention. This one is up-to-date, well balanced in scope (about one-half of it is devoted to pre-Empire periods), and, within the limits imposed by a narrative of some 500 pages, comprehensive. If the works of Cary, Geer, or Heichelheim, cited below, are not used, this one should be.

*Carcopino, Jerome. *Daily Life in Ancient Rome.* New Haven: Yale University Press, 1940.

A highly readable account of the routine activities and common attitudes of Roman citizens.

Cary, Max. *A History of Rome Down to the Age of Constantine.* 2d rev. ed. London: Methuen & Co., 1954.

Another standard text, more readable than Boak and Sinnigen's; it is somewhat out of date, although certainly not so much as to cause it to be passed over lightly.

*Cowell, F. R. *Cicero and the Roman Republic.* Baltimore: Penguin Books, 1948.

The best book by far on the last hundred years of the Republic. It is exceptionally well organized and exceptionally well written. Unique "Isotype" charts are used to clarify and vivify sequential developments

Earl, Donald. *The Moral and Political Tradition of Rome.* Ithaca: Cornell University Press, 1967.

The first two chapters—"Morality and Politics" and "The New Men"—are particularly recommended, as is the early part of chapter 3, ("The New

Order"), *for a clarifying discussion of Roman* nobilitas, fides, *and* virtus. *The author holds that these terms are beyond translation; but he makes good his purpose—to spell them out in interesting detail by concentrating his attention "on the moral and political tradition of Rome as interpreted by major authors at important stages of Roman history."*

Geer, Russell M. *Classical Civilization—Rome.* Englewood Cliffs, N.J.: Prentice-Hall, 1941.

Although even more back-dated than Cary's, this work is still worth reading. Textbooks rarely achieve a "classic" status, but this one is an exception. The author has an extraordinary feel for what should be stressed as well as an unusual talent for clear expression. This book treats "cultural" interests more fully and meaningfully than does any of the other three texts cited.

Heichelheim, Fritz M., and Yeo, Cedric A. *A History of the Roman People.* Englewood Cliffs, N.J.: Prentice-Hall, 1962.

This work incorporates the findings of recent research. The chapters on Italian prehistory and the Etruscans are particularly worthwhile. Some interpretations are controversial and somewhat faulted by a species of pedantry.

Homo, Léon. *Roman Political Institutions from City to State.* New York: Barnes & Noble, 1962.

A sociohistorical study of the "necessities" of Roman life that shaped Rome's political structure from pre-Etruscan times to the late Empire.

Marsh, Frank B. *A History of the Roman World from 146 to 30* B.C. 2d ed. London: Methuen & Co., 1953.

For those who like an amplitude of detail this work on Rome's tumultuous century of change from Republic to Empire is good solid reading. The notes by Professor Scullard, who readied the second edition for the press, are especially valuable.

Mommsen, Theodore. *The History of Rome.* Translated by W. P. Dickinson. London: J. M. Dent & Sons, Everyman's Library 1911.

This multivolumed classic will probably continue to be read long after many of the other works cited, valuable as they are, have had their day. For those with sufficient leisure and learning who like to lose themselves in the full sweep of the Republic's 500-year history, this great work will continue to offer impelling charm despite its early date and its sometimes tendentious character.

But even Mommsen's work does not allow the savoring of the life of Republican Rome as does a first-hand reading of the works of Caesar, Cicero, and Catullus, available in many modern translations and in a variety of paperbacks.

Pareti, Luigi et al. *The Ancient World.* Vol. 2. London: George Allen & Unwin, 1965.

This elaborate work (underwritten by UNESCO) is made up of three parts (each a separate volume). The first describes the ancient world from 1200 B.C. *to 500* B.C.; *the second to the advent of Christ; the third to* A.D. *500. In the main it incorporates the latest findings of historical research; but in* dealing with some topics (such as the Etruscans) it is stubbornly out of date. Its organization, like that of its companion volume, is seriously flawed. Events are treated topically at the expense of clear sequential development. Also, as in the first volume, some of the footnotes are unusually enlightening and important; others are quite out of place and often unnecessary.

Pulgram, Ernst. *The Tongues of Italy.* Cambridge, Mass.: Harvard University Press, 1958.

A unique attempt to correlate linguistic and nonlinguistic facets of Italian history. For our purposes the sections entitled "Prehistoric Background," "The Indo-Europeanization of Italy," and "The Latinization of Italy" are particularly worthwhile.

Richardson, Emeline. *The Etruscans.* Chicago: The University of Chicago Press, 1964.

Probably the best work on Etruscan origins, art, language, and religion. If the reader's interest is whetted, an extensive topical bibliography may be consulted.

Rostovtzeff, M. J. *History of the Ancient World.* Oxford: Oxford University Press, 1927.

Rather out-of-date and opinionated, but still worth consulting if used in conjunction with one or more of the other works cited.

Scullard, Howard H. *A History of the Roman World, 753 to 146* B.C. 3d ed. London: Methuen & Co., 1963.

The best single general account of Roman history down to the "century of troubles." Professor Scullard lets the reader know what other scholars think about an event or development and at the same time expresses his own judgment (somewhat oversubtly at times, it must be admitted). He presents evidence the reader needs without losing either himself or the reader in the mass of details.

Starr, Chester G. *A History of the Ancient World.* New York: Oxford University Press, 1965.

Mainly concerned with political and economic developments, chapters 21–32 give the reader a generally sound understanding of Rome's emergence, expansion, Republican institutions, imperial sway, and eventual decline. This work is especially recommended for its utilization of recent research. Its style makes for easy reading.

*Syme, Ronald. *Roman Revolution.* London: Oxford University Press, 1960.

A scholarly, often controversial, and sometimes puckish account of the forces at work in the remaking of Roman political life and outlook after the Punic Wars.

Asterisk (*) denotes paperback.

CHAPTER VI
The Roman World: Empire and the Christian Community

A. The Empire

THE ESTABLISHMENT OF THE PRINCIPATE

From Chaos to Order

For 200 years the Romans had lived in a hectic world of change. What began as a scrape with the Carthaginians had turned into a struggle for empire, from which the Romans had emerged both triumphant and bewildered. The brave new world into which they had stumbled excited and flattered them. From an undistinguished tribe nestling in the hills along the Tiber they had somehow become masters of the Mediterranean world. But in the process old prizes were lost. In a sense they had become alienated from themselves. The Republican surge had faltered and failed. The yeoman farmer still existed, but precariously, his old central position in the state swept away before the servile flood. Old religions, old family customs, the old spirit—all were profoundly changed. For more than a hundred years civil violence had wracked and torn the corpus of Roman society until it was scarcely recognizable as a society with a future.

These things the Romans experienced rather than understood. They yearned for a way out of disorder, a way that would somehow save the Republic, keep the Empire, and end the chaos. But if the Romans failed to understand their times and themselves, Octavian understood both very well. And if he lacked, as he did, a ready-made solution, he had what perhaps was better: the genius to sense the spirit of the times, to take a step and test its worth, then another and another, until gradually a program evolved that seemed best to fit the Roman facts of life. These things he knew: that there must be peace; that Empire existed; that it was incompatible with the Republic that it had succeeded; that his tradition-bound people wanted to eat their Republican cake and to keep their Empire; and that his job was to produce a policy that would weld reality with memory and illusion. It is difficult to believe, of course, that the more perceptive Romans did not understand what was going on. History is not innocent of periods in which man deliberately deceives himself in order to do something that one part of him clearly condemns. It may be that the new "Golden Age" was such a period.

Augustus

We do not know whether Octavian (soon to be styled Augustus) himself knew how well he worked. Probably he did not, for there is nothing in his record that suggests the brilliant flashes of insight and introspective analysis of his famous great-uncle. In many ways he resembled America's founding father. Like Washington he possessed an almost unerring judgment of the fit and the proper, of the unglamorous but achievable, of the workable compromise and the techniques needed to effect it, and of when to show courage and when to prefer caution. But if he did not have at his command the resources of a superman's mystique, he knew how to learn from Caesar's malpractice of such magic. As clearly as his predecessor he understood that the Republic was finished. But unlike Caesar, he knew that this was the last thing his countrymen would admit. The "Revolution of 509" had hallowed it; the long "struggle of the orders" had revealed its rich potentials. And now it was gone. But to say so was a kind of suicide. Needed was a formula that somehow kept illusion and yet coped with reality. To working out precisely such a formula Octavian devoted the next 15 years.

Part of his success lay in the almost instantaneous recognition by the public of his basic motivation. Although ambitious, he was driven by a tenacious desire to serve the public weal. He could scheme, but unlike Crassus he was not interested in politics as a game; nor was he touched with Caesar's megalomania. Although he received more than his share of material goods (reserving the whole wealth of Egypt as his private income), he was not out for booty. Although he deliberately and successfully set out to make himself an absolute ruler, he was not basically interested in power per se. And although he accepted and used an awesome array of titles, he was not glory-mad. Fundamentally he was interested in saving the Roman world from destruction, and the Roman world well understood this. It sensed further that great glories lay ahead; perhaps even the restoration of the Golden Age of the early Republic.* And as the repose of peace and the glory of Empire continued and developed decade after decade the sense grew into a conviction: the miracle of restoration had indeed come to pass.

Princeps

Returning in triumph from Egypt, Augustus found the people ready to give him permanent dictatorial powers.† But remembering the fate that befell his great-uncle, he let it appear that he asked for nothing. He knew, of course, that the Empire called for some form of absolutism. But he understood also that ancient aspi-

---

* So much in all truth must be said of what seem to be the historic facts. Still, the overall impression may mislead. Left out of this recital of facts are these value questions: Could not the Romans have found resources within themselves to sense the incompatibility of imperial glory and republican *virtus*? Could they not, by great effort, have become tutor rather than ruling lord of the West? Could not such a "liberal Republic" have avoided both the glossy glory and the eventual decay that marked and finally mocked the "grandeur that was Rome"?

† Technically this was illegal, since the title "dictator" had been abolished after Caesar's death.

rations and Republican memories were not dead. He had somehow to foster a faith that was at once unrealizable and necessary if the active cooperation of the orders, without which he could do nothing, was to be gained. In short, a redefinition of the state was called for that sanctioned absolutism without seeming to do so. To achieve this definition Augustus resorted to a bold and dramatic, almost melodramatic, coup. On January 13, 27 B.C. he appeared before the Senate and humbly asked to be relieved of all the powers, legal and extralegal, that had been granted him over the previous decade. Peace was won; order had been achieved. It was time, he said, for the Republic to be restored to its rightful rulers, the Senate and the Assemblies. For himself he asked only that he be given surcease from responsibilities and a chance to enjoy life as a private citizen, if the senators in their wisdom would allow this.

At once a tumult of protests broke out. So promptly and overwhelmingly did the demonstration occur that it is naive to suppose that it was spontaneous. Obviously his followers had been given their cues. But, equally obvious was the real concern that lay behind the demonstration. Clearly, without Augustus violence would break out afresh. Rome had had its fill of factionalism and anarchy. His task, Romans insisted, was far from complete. Peace and order had been achieved. Now let their champion remain to nurture them. Bowing to this popular demand Augustus humbly agreed to stay at his post, accepting as legal powers all those that he had surrendered and more.

Throughout the drama the emperor was careful to see that all the forms and practices of the old Roman constitution were faithfully observed. Nonetheless he found himself again elected to the consulship and in a position to effect whatever legislative changes he felt were necessary. Even more important, he "consented" to assume responsibility for a number of

Augustus. He brought order out of chaos and pointed his people toward imperial glory. He also interred the Republic.

provinces. As it turned out, these were the provinces in which the most powerful armies were quartered. The fact that his offices were limited in tenure mattered little since his prestige and wise rule made his reelection automatic. The time soon came, indeed, when his prestige allowed him to give up the consulship altogether, although of course those who thereafter held the offices were his nominees. Soon the tribunician sacrosanctity that had been granted him in 30 B.C. was widened in scope. Ultimately he achieved complete legislative power, quite apart from his control of the consuls. Thus he was in essence supreme commander of the arm-

249   A. The Empire

ies, chief lawmaker,* and, as personal "owner" as well as ruler of Egypt, independently wealthy.

But it must be repeated, on the surface this was not at all plain. Nothing belonged to Augustus that the Senate and the people had not voted him. To the rule of the Senate, moreover, certain (pacified) provinces were given. Senate meetings were regularly held; and Augustus sat with the rest, although as *princeps senatus* (that is, first among equals). All of his legislation was submitted for approval to the senators (whose ranks had been purged of the "new family" members and reduced in number to 600). Whatever the reality behind it, the facade of Roman life was again Republican.

Peace and Prosperity

To signify the coming of a reign of peace Augustus, in 28 (?) B.C., closed the temple of Janus. Moreover he reduced by half the size of the armed forces, settling his discharged veterans on land in Italy or in the provinces (land paid for out of his own exchequer, not confiscated as had so often been the practice in the past). As a stopgap until his plans could become effective he spent lavish sums in Rome to entertain the unemployed. He also inau-

---

* Technically the assemblies were, and long remained, the supreme lawmakers; but only technically. Often Augustus yielded a point to them. But when legislation believed by Augustus to be of real importance was under discussion both the *princeps* and the assemblies knew who would make the decision.

Roman ships dominated the Mediterranean Sea after Carthage was destroyed. Here, in this mosaic, is a merchant ship at harbor in Ostia, near Rome. A slave is carrying oil aboard.

250   The Roman World: Empire; Christian Community

gurated a gigantic building program that gave the economy a much-needed stimulus. Construction of various kinds of public edifices was begun, new roads were planned and laid, and some 80 new temples were erected. Drawing on the riches of his Egyptian "bank," he embarked on an extensive program of what might today be called federal subsidization, designed to succor the hard-pressed senatorial class. As business revived, the equites rejoiced to find their profits growing ever larger. A decline in the interest rate reflected the stabilization of the economy and helped the peasant, eternally in debt, to share in the overall prosperity. Thus all classes, although unevenly, made material gains in the new period of peace and plenty.

Nor were the provinces, which, of course, formed the predominant bulk of the Empire, neglected. Indeed in some respects they benefited the most. During the preceding century and a half they had become dependents of Rome. Many of them had been exploited and despoiled by rapacious governors who had come for their year of misrule and had left with private fortunes. To them the Republic meant not so much glory and order as corruption and legal pillage. So when Augustus instituted a new system characterized by career officials supervised by the emperor himself, the provinces hailed the new ruler as a veritable god. Indeed in the East his image was worshiped, and shrines were dedicated to his genius.*

The princeps, as he preferred to be called, made a strenuous effort to revive ancient religious habits and to resurrect the old concept of the family and of family morality. New temples were heavily subsidized. Sumptuary laws (which proved none too effective) were passed to regulate conduct. To dramatize the coming of the new Golden Age, Augustus arranged a grand celebration, in 17 B.C., of the seventh centenary (rather arbitrarily calculated) of the founding of Rome. For three days the capital was given over to festivities, crowned by a solemn and impressive march through the city of a chorus of young boys and girls chanting a triumphal ode composed by Horace.†

Thus Rome seemed finally to have found itself. After its violent time of troubles it was at peace. A measure of prosperity was enjoyed. An order that gave signs of enduring had been established. The future seemed bright, prefigured by the hope and vision, albeit dim, of the progressive enlargement of man. During the 30 years that still remained of Augustus's rule, golden hopes seemed to take on flesh, to form and to shape themselves into reality.

The Price of Paternalism

But the illusion of the glorious Republic regained was after all only an illusion. The Republic in actual fact had not been restored but interred. Behind the show of partnership lay one-man rule—autocracy. Augustus had jerked the state back from the abyss of chaos and corruption; and the state was grateful. As a benevolent autocrat he had imposed order and a kind of well-being. What, though, would happen under another absolutist ruler who happened not to be benevolent? And even assuming, which one certainly could not, that all of Rome's future autocrats would be benevolent—what then? Could the vision of the progressive enhancement of individualism tolerate permanent paternalism of any sort?

Moreover, social mobility was seriously restricted by finely calculated legislation. Manumission of slaves was made difficult. The freedman was encouraged to be satisfied with his lot by the creation for him

---

* For a geographical survey of the provinces at the time of Augustus see map, p. 252.

† See p. 259.

ROMAN PROVINCES
DURING THE REIGN OF AUGUSTUS

Imperial Provinces
Senatorial Provinces

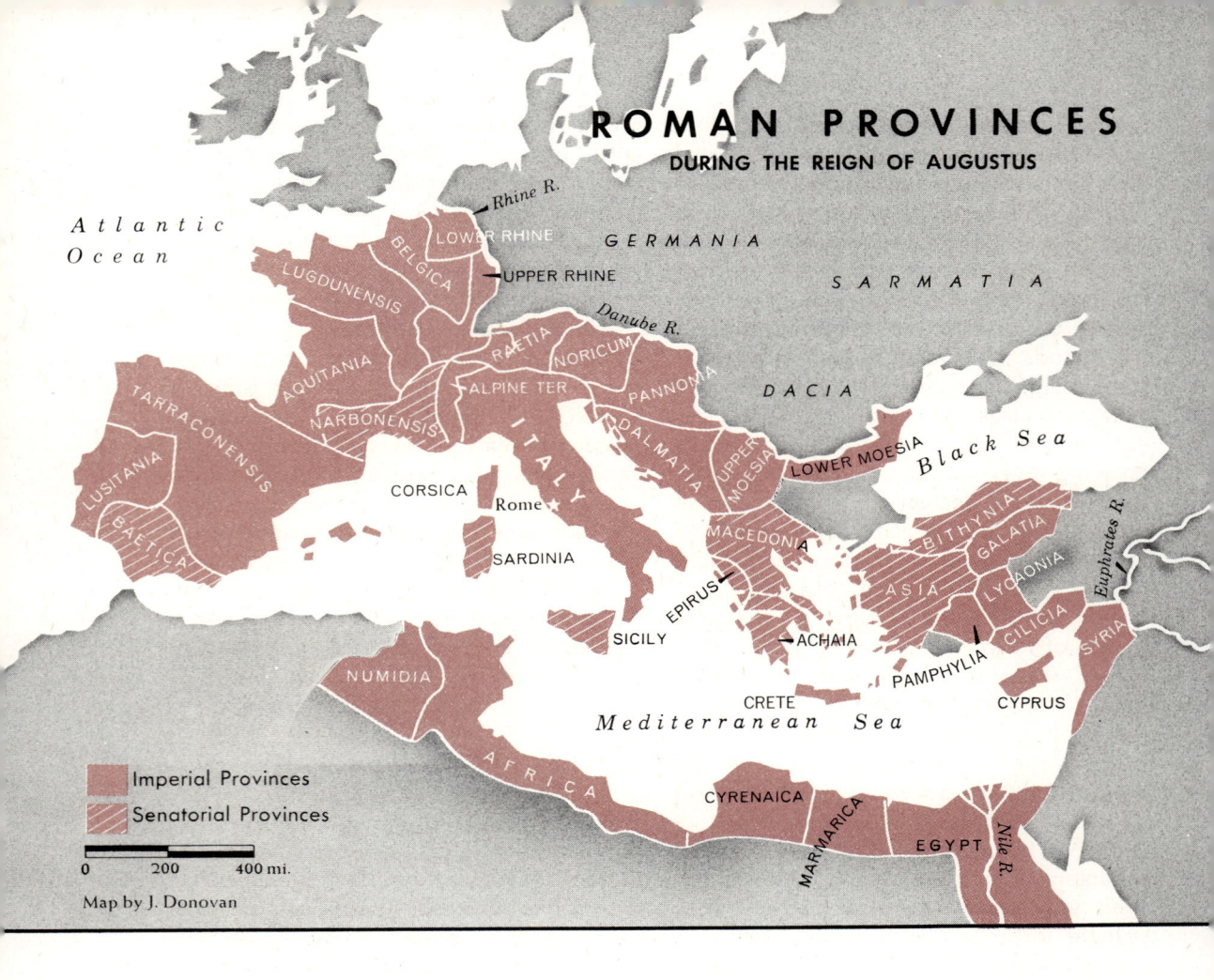

Map by J. Donovan

of an honorary society, the *Augustales,* an organization of priestly officers dedicated to service in the cult of the Genius of Augustus. Intermarriage between yeomen and equestrian orders was discouraged. Both Equites and senators were given distinct symbols to wear, setting them off from the other orders.

Beyond this, the morale of the senatorial class steadily deteriorated. Increasingly, younger members of this order, knowing they were never to exercise real responsibility and power in governing the state, tended to drift into bored acquiescence. The equestrians, the upper bourgeoisie, became, as their wealth increased under preferred treatment, more and more the victims and exemplars of that crass culture which extravagant riches so often promote. In short, as the state grew in grandeur, the dignity and inner worth of man seemed to shrink in significance, although the full impact of these developments was long in making itself felt.

If history were merely past politics, we should next move on to the succession of emperors and political events that followed the establishment of the Principate. From our habit of thinking so largely in these terms, such a progression seems reasonable enough. But to do so would be to confuse structure for substance. The stuff of human vision, of dream and desire, is expressed in literature and art, in philosophy and religion, rather than in politics. Especially was this true of the Augustan

252   The Roman World: Empire; Christian Community

Age, the so-called new Golden Age of Rome. Indeed, except as we turn to these developments, we can only superficially understand either the Augustan program or the cultural forces that simultaneously shaped it and were shaped by it.

LITERATURE AND CULTURE OF THE GOLDEN AGE

Of all the achievements of the Golden Age (paradoxically, not only rooted in the preceding years of struggle but culminating before the imperial period was well begun) one of the greatest was its literary production. Many of the creations of its literary titans—Virgil, Horace, Ovid, Livy—were masterworks that have lived. Save for that of the Greeks and certain portions of the Old Testament, no literature in ancient times matched it in stylistic grace and brilliance, in profundity and subtlety of thought.

Virgil

Sallust's death in 35 B.C. marked the end of what some have called the Ciceronian prelude to the Golden Age. By this time a new and greater constellation of literati had appeared. The greatest of these was Publius Vergilius Maro (70–19 B.C.). Virgil's* life spanned the interval of transition from chaos to order. He has rightly been called both priest and prophet of the new day. Indeed, in a way he was its creator, sharing the honors with Augustus, his friend and patron. Although it is especially true of his greatest poem, the *Aeneid*, his aim in all his works was to glorify the Italian land and its people, Empire and emperor, and to herald the coming age.

* Technically, the correct spelling is Vergil. Traditional usage is followed here.

His earliest work—ten poems (*Eclogues*, or *Bucolics*)—is much his slightest. In some of these verses he tested his developing talents on the often-told stories of classical Greece. But even here we find his main theme given expression (although the verses were mainly meant to evoke the charms of pastoral life). At the time that Virgil wrote the poem quoted below Augustus was showing every sign of grooming his young son-in-law, Marcellus, as his successor, a choice much applauded by the Romans. The poet used this projected purpose (which never materialized) as a point from which to take off in celebration of Rome's present glory and the greater glory to come.

> *The cycle of great epochs starts anew*
> *And Virgin Astraea evokes Saturnian*
>   *sway.*
> *From heaven now new progeny is sent.*
> *O chaste Lucina, to this infant boy*
> *Whose reign shall see the age of iron*
>   *yield*
> *And all over the world a golden age*
>   *begin*
> *Be thou propitious—now Apollo reigns*
> *He shall partake of god-like life, shall*
>   *see*
> *Commingled with the gods great men;*
>   *himself*
> *By gods be seen, and by his father's*
>   *virtues**
> *In peace shall rule the world. . . .*
> *Harmonious in the order, the Fates,*
>   *long since fixed,*
> *Will cause their spindles thus to sing,*
>   *"Run on,*
> *Ye ages, thus." Dear offspring of the*
>   *gods,*
> *Illustrious son of Jove, set forward on*
> *Thy way to signal honors, now the*
>   *time*

* Reference to Augustus. The relationship was somewhat complicated. Marcellus was nephew to Augustus as well as, later, his son-in-law. Had he lived to succeed Augustus he would have become his adopted son.

253 A. The Empire

Is come. . . .
   See how all things rejoice at this
New age. Oh that my life should last until
It hath sufficed to sing thy deeds.[1]

The *Georgics,* a long poem of four books, was suggested by Maecenas, the emperor's gifted political adviser and Virgil's personal friend and benefactor. Like the *Eclogues,* the verses deal with the calm grandeur of Italy's pastoral life (in addition to suggestions on practical farming). Notice how Virgil woos his countrymen with scenes suggestive of the "good old days," which he believed needed to be brought back if the golden age were truly to return.

The plowman beats the plowshare on the forge,
Or makes his vats of tree-trunks hollowed out,
Brands his cattle, numbers his piles of grain,
Sharpens fence posts or pitchforks, prepares
Umbrian trellises for the slow vine.
Then you may weave the baskets of bramble twigs
Or dip your bleating flock in the clean stream.
Often the farmer loads his little mule
With olive oil or apples, and brings home
A grindstone or a block of pitch from market.

And some will stay up late beside the fire
On winter nights, whittling torches, while
The housewife runs the shuttle through the loom
And comforts the long labor with her singing;

Or at the stove she simmers the new wine,
Skimming the froth with leaves. Oh idle time!
In that hale season, all their worries past,
Farmers arrange convivialities—
As after laden ships have reached home port,
The happy sailors load the prow with garlands.[2]

But Virgil's fame rests on the *Aeneid,* a long epic poem justly counted one of the world's greatest masterpieces. The poet's aim in this work, to which he devoted the last ten years of his life, was to provide his countrymen with a kind of spiritual foundation of the new age that he envisioned. He conceived his task as this: to reveal the Roman genius, to evoke the first Golden Age (destroyed sometime after the Punic Wars), to liken it to the Augustan Age, and to silhouette the outlines of the Empire's coming grandeur. His method was partly historical. Using Homer as a model and borrowing freely from him, Virgil chose Aeneas, a warrior from the heroic age of Troy, as the central figure of his poem. As the poet has it, Aeneas—sired by a Trojan prince out of Venus—and a band of his followers fled from the doomed city to embark upon a long series of adventures before settling in Latium. There the hero wooed Lavinia, daughter of the king, and from this union came Rome's founders. According to Virgil, therefore, his countrymen were the product of this merger of Trojan and Latin blood.

Blessing this project was Venus; opposing it, Juno. Most of the mighty adventures recounted in the poem occur as consequences of this divine contest. The Aeneid opens with a simple statement of the poet's theme:

---

[1] Adapted from a prose translation. T. A. Buckley, ed., *The Works of Virgil* (New York: Harper and Brothers, 1855), pp. 11–13.

[2] L. R. Lind, ed., *Latin Poetry in Verse Translation* (Boston: Houghton Mifflin Company, 1957), p. 75.

Of arms I sing and the man, that hero who
Exiled by fate from fallen Troy besought
The darkling shores of far off Italy.
Much was he tossed on sea and land by powers
Above, by savage Juno's cruel rage;
Much, too, he suffered in the toils of war
Until, in final victory he birthed
A city, god-bequeathed, in Latium,
From whence the Latin progeny, from whence
The Alban fathers and the lofty walls of Rome.[3]

The denouement is foretold in an early book when Jupiter, in answer to a protest from Venus that his stubborn spouse is playing havoc with fated events, assures her that

. . . Romulus, exulting in the strength
Of that she wolf who was his constant nurse,
Shall rule as sovereign over Latium
And build in honor of his father, Mars,
A city for his people who shall take
From thence the name of Romans for their own.
According to my will no limits nor
Duration for the empire they shall found
Shall mark its sway. Dominion without end
I give to it. And frantic Juno, now
Afret with sullen fear, disturbing seas
And earth and skies, will one day change her ways
And join with me to favor over all
One people, Romans, lords of all the world,
A nation of the gown. Such is my will.[4]

Virgil then begins his long recounting of the adventures and vicissitudes that befall Aeneas and his band after they flee Troy. As their ships near Carthage, Juno sends a storm that fails to wreak the havoc she had planned. They suffer shipwreck but are taken in by Dido, queen of Carthage, and given refuge. Presently Aeneas finds himself tempted to settle in the land, especially after Dido clearly indicates that she would not be displeased. In the first throes of the love that she comes to feel for him the beautiful queen is in anguish over fear that her affection does dishonor to the memory of her husband, whose death had plunged her into deep grief. In her torment she turns to her sister and makes confession:

My sister Anna, terrifying dreams
Distract my mind. What think you of this great,
This wondrous man who comes to our abode?
How graceful he appears; in manly mien
And fortitude and warlike deeds how great!

Were I not fixed and steadfast in my vow
No man to join in wedded bonds again,
Since my first love by death has left me mocked,
Were I not thoroughly tired of marriage bed
And nuptial torch, to this one frailty
I might perhaps give way. . . . I recognize
The symptoms of my former flame.

To which Anna answers beguilingly:

O dearer to your sister than the light,
Will you persist in mournful solitude
To waste your young desires—to know no dear
Delights of children, nor rewards of love?
Think you that ashes and shrouded dead

[3] Buckley, op. cit., p. 103.
[4] Ibid., p. 113.

255   A. The Empire

> *Can care for that? . . .*
> 　　*Will you resist a flame*
> *Which you approve? . . .*
> *Thus by such speech she fanned the fire of love*
> *In Dido's breast and buoyed her wavering mind*
> *With hope, her scruples banishing.*[5]

So Dido wooed Aeneas, who returned her love. But Jove, not to be thwarted by this miscarriage of his plans, sends Mercury to bring Aeneas to his senses.

> *No sooner had his winged feet the shores*
> *Of Libya touched, he found Aeneas hard*
> *At tasks—here rearing towers, there raising up*
> *New structures—; while bedecked with gifts*
> *From Dido's ample stores, with Tyrian cloak*
> *Deep purple hued with intertwining thread*
> *Of gold, and at his side a sword beset*
> *With yellow jasper. . . .*

Mercury at once upbraids the erring hero:

> 　　*How is it now*
> *You set yourself to lay foundations for*
> *A stately Carthage and, fond slave you are,*
> *To raise a state for Dido, blind, alas,*
> *To your own kingdom and its near concerns?*
> *The sovereign of the gods who rules all by*
> *His nod sends me with this command—if now*
> *You seek no glory for yourself, have due*
> *Regard for young Ascanius* and for*

[5] Ibid., pp. 176–77.

* Aeneas's son; Julus and Ascanius are the same person.

> *The hopes of Iulus, thine own heir for whom*
> *Is destined all of Italy, and more—*
> *Expansive Roman lands.*[6]

Thus prodded by the gods, and realizing that he had come close to allowing personal feelings to interfere with the working out of plans that destiny had ordained for his people, Aeneas gave orders to his companions to prepare for the journey to Italy; Dido was not to be told. The lovesick queen soon divined his intentions, however, and here gives vent to her profound and passionate grief:

> *And did you hope, deceiving one, to hide*
> *From me this wicked purpose, and to steal*
> *Away in silence from my coasts? Will not*
> *Our love, nor your once plighted faith, nor death*
> *That Dido must prefer if you depart*
> *Detain you? . . .*
> 　　*Will you leave me and our love?*
> *If ever you saw charms in me, I beg*
> *You pity now a falling race; if yet*
> *Can prayers avail, I pray you do not leave.*
> *For your sake have I sacrificed my shame*
> *And what was hallowed, virtuous name—*
> *To whom do you abandon Dido, you,*
> *My guest, since name of husband you disdain?*
> *Could I bear a child before you leave,*
> *A young Aeneas playing in my hall,*
> *To stay your image in his face and form*
> *I should not feel so captive and forlorn.*

But Aeneas, putting duty before love—and shame—"held his eyes unmoved." Preparations for the journey continued, openly now below the Queen's towers.

[6] Ibid., p. 183.

Weeping at the sight, Dido implores her sister to plead one last hour for her.

> *In suppliant terms, O Anna, thus*
>   *bespeak*
> *The haughty foe: I never counseled*
>   *with*
> *The Greeks against the Trojan race, or*
>   *sent*
> *A fleet to Troy; nor did I ever violate*
> *The ashes of Aeneas' father. Why does*
> *He now refuse to listen to my heart?*
>   *Where does*
> *He go? O see if he will grant to his*
> *Unhappy lover one last plea—to stay*
> *His flight until the winds blow fair. I*
>   *plead*
> *No more for that once-promised*
>   *wedlock which*
> *He spurns, nor that he would deprive*
>   *himself*
> *Of that fair Latin land, but only this—*
> *One moment more, a respite from the*
>   *pain*
> *Abiding, till, subdued by fate, I learn*
> *How woe to face. This final favor I*
>   *beseech*
> *When, if he grant it me, I'll see him*
>   *gone*
> *And be with death content.*[7]

But even this "one moment" Aeneas, although "feeling deep pangs in his mighty chest," refused, in the name of duty. Unable to move him, Dido took her own life rather than live the rest of it in misery and shame. And so, with deep feelings of guilt, Aeneas set out for the land he was destined to conquer. Upon landing in Italy he was transported to the world of the shades. At this point in the poem Virgil expounds on the doctrine of reincarnation. Aeneas is shown the ghosts of those who had lived in the first Golden Age and is told which are destined for a second life on earth. His guide is the ghost of his dead father, Anchises. Among others is pointed out to him one who is to be Aeneas's own son, by Lavinia; then others of his descendants. Then—

> *This way now turn your eyes and view*
>   *this line—*
> *These be your Romans.*
>   *This is Caesar; there*
> *The race of Iulus who shall one day rise*
> *To spacious axle of the sky. This, this*
> *Is one whom you have heard is*
>   *promised you—*
> *Augustus Caesar, offspring of a god*
> *Who shall evoke again a golden age*
> *In Saturn, those lands where Saturn*
>   *reigned,*
> *And shall extend his Empire to the east,*
> *To lands beyond the Zodiac. . . .*

Other ghosts are pointed out, including those of Julius Caesar and Pompey:

> *Those ghosts whom you observe in*
>   *equal arms*
> *To shine, in perfect friendship*
>   *now. . . .*
> *But ah, what battles and what havoc*
>   *will*
> *They raise when once they gain the*
>   *light*
> *Of life. . . .*

Cato, the Gracchi, the Scipios, and Fabius are also pointed out. Then, in a touching passage, Virgil speaks of the young Marcellus, once slated to succeed the great emperor but who died before he reached his majority. It is said that when Virgil read these lines to Augustus and Octavia, the latter fainted. Aeneas asks his father:

> *What youth is he, O father, who thus*
>   *walks*
> *Beside the hero; son, perhaps or of*
> *The line of his descendants? What a*
>   *noise*
> *Attendants make around him!*
>   *How much like*

[7] Ibid., pp. 184–85, 188

257   A. The Empire

*The other! Then his father,
    through his tears,*
*Began: Seek not, my son, to know the
    deep*
Disaster of thy kind. Him will the Fates
*Show on the earth, nor suffer long to
    live.*
*Oh gods, these gifts you gave to him!
    Seemed they*
*Too powerful in your eyes for durance
    long?*

*No youth shall raise the Latin fathers'
    hopes*
So high in all the Trojan lines as he.
Nor ever shall the land of Romulus
So glory in a son as great.
    Ah piety!
Ah, faith of ancient times![8]

Much of the remainder of the poem centers on the long struggle between Aeneas's Trojans and the Latin armies led by Turnus. In the end Aeneas slays Turnus, and victors merge with vanquished to form a new imperial people.

Horace

Where Virgil's genius lay in the grand epic, that of his contemporary and friend, Quintus Horatius Flaccus (65–8 B.C.), is found in lyrics that sing praises of the homeland. Born of lowly parentage (his father was a freedman), Horace nonetheless was given a sound education. After his early years of schooling at Rome he went to Athens for "graduate" study in the liberal arts. While there he learned of the assassination of Julius Caesar. Shortly thereafter, when Brutus fled to Greece to raise an army against Caesar's defenders, the future poet laureate of the Augustan Empire allowed himself to be enrolled in the ranks of the Republicans. He fought—and fled—at Philippi, losing, as a consequence, not only status at home but also what little property his father had left him. Returning under the general amnesty he worked quietly for a time at clerical chores. His early verse attracted Virgil's attention and they soon became close friends. Through Virgil the one-time Republican was introduced to Maecenas, Augustus's chief adviser. Subsequently Horace met, and became intimate with, the emperor himself. By this time he had come to see the promise of the Augustan age. Although he turned down an offer to become the emperor's private secretary, he thereafter proved a strong supporter of the regime.

His great period of productivity (ca. 35–13 B.C.) saw the publication of two books of *Satires,* a number of *Epodes* ("refrains"), four books of *Odes,* and two of *Epistles.* The *Satires* might be called conversation pieces in verse. Their content included jibes at contemporary figures and comments on current social issues and political problems. They are by no means his best work. The *Epodes* "resemble the *Satires* in their frequent polemical character, the *Odes* in the lyric form in which they were cast." The latter two works, some excerpts from which we shall sample, marked Horace as a poet of the first rank. His *Epistles,* informal verse essays on matters of day-to-day concern, were similar to the *Satires.*

If Virgil was the prophet of the new age, Horace was its moralist, if the term may be used without its sometimes prudish and narrow connotation. This is clearly evident in the concern over the state of society found in his verses, especially those written immediately after his return to Italy from Greece. It is clear, too, in his dawning realization of the significance of the Augustan effort, and in his subsequent calm and mellow meditations on the good life. Rejecting alike Lucretian and Catullan Epicureanism, Horace finally came to infuse his work with a humane Stoicism, lightly overlaid with perfunctory obeisance to traditional and state religion.

---

[8] Ibid., pp. 247–50 passim.

Back in Italy after the fiasco at Philippi, the poet looked at things around him and did not like what he saw:

> Ah, Rome, what scars, what crimes,
>   what brothers slain!
> What shame have these coarse times
>   dared to disdain?
> What evil have we left untried, our
>   youth
> Not sampled, careless of Saturnian
>   truth?
> What altars spared in quest of passing
>   gain? [9]
> . . . .
> Our times, in sin prolific, first
> The marriage-bed with taint have
>   cursed,
> And family and home;
> This is the fountain-head of all
> The sorrows and the ills that fall
> On Romans and on Rome.
>
> The ripening virgin joys to learn
> In the Ionic dance to turn
> And bend with plastic limb;
> Still but a child, with evil gleams,
> Incestuous loves, unhallowed dreams,
> Before her fancy swim.
>
> Straight, in her husband's wassail hours,
> She seeks more youthful paramours,
> And little sees, on whom
> She may her lawless joys bestow
> By stealth, when all the lamps burn
>   low,
> And darkness shrouds the room.
>
> Yea, she will on a summons fly,
> Nor is her spouse unconscious why,
> To some rich broker's arms,
> Or some sea captain's fresh from
>   Spain,
> With wealth to buy her shame, and gain
> Her mercenary charm. [10]

[9] Adapted from a prose translation by C. E. Bennett in his *Horace, The Odes and Epodes* (London: William Heinemann, 1918), p. 85.

[10] Louis Untermeyer, ed., *Q. Horatius Flaccus, Odes and Epodes* (New York: Limited Editions Club, 1961), p. 183.

But Horace's finely tempered spirit soon caught the signals of the Augustan trend. Within a few years his tune had changed and hope was strongly hymned.

> Safe plods the steer among the rural
>   fields;
> The rural fields Ceres and Plenty bless;
> The wing'd ships fly through
>   unmolested seas;
>   Honor's fine dread of shame
> Returns; no lusts pollute the modest
>   home;
> License is tamed by manners as by
>   laws;
> Nor reads the husband in his infant's
>   face
>   A likeness not his own.
> . . . .
> Live, O good chief, Rome's feast-days
>   to prolong!
> This is our orison at sober morn,
> Our prayer with wine-dews on the lip,
>   when sinks
>   Beneath the sea, the sun. [11]

When Augustus decreed a gigantic three-day celebration to mark the beginning of the new era (17 B.C.), he requested Horace to write a song for children to sing as they paraded through Rome. Sample verses from the Carmen Saeculare follow:

> After a hundred years and ten are told,
>   Again may these three days of fair
>   delights
> Come round with songs and pastimes
>   as of old,
>   As many pleasant nights.
> And you, ye Fates, who evermore
>   declare
> The truth pronounced, the voice of
>   destiny,
> Grant that the future equal good may
>   bear
>   To past prosperity.
> Grant to our youth, ye gods, all mortal
>   health,

[11] Untermeyer, op. cit., pp. 279, 281.

A. The Empire

Although executed long after Horace's time, this milking scene would have pleased the poet, whose odes and epodes gravely hymned just such goatherds and pastoral activities.

To our declining years, ye gods, grant rest,
And may the race of Romulus in wealth,
Fame, offspring, all be blest.[12]

Although the following lines were written earlier (and were concluded with a quip, deleted here, which plainly indicates a tongue-in-cheek approach to the subject), they bespeak the pastoral calm in which Horace came to delight in his later years, when all seemed right with the new Roman world.

How happy in his low degree,
How rich in humble poverty is he

[12] Christopher Hughes, *The Odes, Epodes, Carmen Saecularae* . . . (London: Longmans, Green, Reader and Dyer, 1867), p. 324 ff.

Who leads a quiet country life,
Discharged of business, void of strife. . . .
Nor trumpets summon him to war,
Nor drums disturb his morning sleep,
Nor knows he merchants' gainful care,
Nor fears the dangers of the deep. . . .
When beauteous Autumn rears his head,
He joys to pull the ripened pear
And clustering grapes with purple spread.
Sometimes beneath an ancient oak,
Or on the matted grass he lies:
No god of sleep he need invoke. . . .
The jolly shepherd smiles to see
His flocks returning from the plains;
The farmer is as pleased as he
To view his oxen, sweating smoke,

Bear on their necks the loosened yoke:
To look upon his menial crew
That sit around his cheerful hearth,
And bodies spent in toil renew
With wholesome food and country
   mirth.[13]

The poetic genius of Horace thus served, as did Virgil's, not only to signal the dawn of a new age but in part to create it. Hope was high, the ship of state steady under the firm (if heavy) hand of Augustus, and the imperial realms compassed almost the whole of the Mediterranean world. The Golden Age, it seemed, had indeed returned.

Ovid

The third great poet of this age, P. Ovidius Naso (43 B.C.–A.D. 18), unlike his two colleagues, was remarkably indifferent to the national renaissance and imperial glory of which his times gave promise. Ovid's genius, indeed, rested on him but lightly. That he had genius was recognized by his contemporaries and is confirmed by posterity. His mastery of the elegiac form, his delicate phrasings, his incisive handling of antithetical themes, the natural grace of his most casual verse amply demonstrate his native talents. But, for whatever reason, he did not choose to exploit them. He neither plumbed the depths of the individual psyche nor reached for the grand epic theme. The potential profundity of his genius shunned microcosm and macrocosm alike. He preferred, as another has expressed it, to be the sophisticated voice of the smart set of Rome. Almost invariably his treatment of whatever subject matter is marked by the urbane touch, the casual approach. He spoke as Rome's great literary *bon vivant*. Whereas Catullus wrote movingly out of genuine ecstacy or suffering, Ovid wrote of love wittily and naughtily. In short, he

[13] Untermeyer, op. cit., pp. 321–27 passim.

Perseus rescuing Andromeda; this scene is the subject of one of Ovid's Metamorphoses.

manipulated the theme as a sort of professional paramour.

His earliest work, the *Amores*, constituting some 50 elegies, has as its subject, as the title indicates, the story of love. Clearly no Lesbia inspired them. Rather they are a kind of clinical examination of the wondrous vagaries of Cupid's mysterious ways. The opening elegy laments the existence of Aurora, goddess of the dawn, who forever brings cessation to love-sweets of the night. Another treats of a lover's lament over having, in a fit of temper, dared to strike his mistress. Withal there is no binding theme, unless ringing the changes on all the sensations and thoughts roused by the erotic impulse is such a theme.

A. The Empire

In his *Heroides* Ovid attempts the difficult task of analyzing the complex of feminine emotions when touched by love. In form they are verse letters from goddesses or "legendary ladies." In one, for example, Briseis, a slave girl, writes to Achilles—who loved and left—pleading for his lost affection.

> *If you have decided for a return to your*
>   *ancestral mansion,*
> *I am no heavy burden for your*
>   *fleet;*
> *I shall go as a captive with conqueror,*
>   *not as a wife with her husband;*
> *My hands are trained to work*
>   *with wool.*[14]

Although not his best work, the *Ars Amatoria* ("The art of love") is one of his best known. Ovid explains in libidinous detail the techniques a successful lover must master. So contrary did it run to the effort that Augustus was contemporaneously making to reinstill the ancient Roman virtues that most authorities believe it played no small part in Ovid's subsequent banishment from Rome. Probably his best work went into the *Metamorphoses* ("The changeling shapes"). Here he came close to depth analysis of the opposing influences in life that shade the everlasting yea into its everlasting nay. In one of these stories—they have been likened to a kind of Roman *Arabian Nights*—Narcissus, born of god and nymph, finds his beauty captivating all, himself especially. When asked by his parents how long a life their beautiful child would have, an oracle had replied, "Until he knows himself." One day he went to a clear stream for a drink and saw his body perfectly reflected. With this wondrous creature he at once fell in love and pondered how he could win the beauty for himself. His ultimate discovery that the image was his own person destroyed him, for in thus identifying himself, he paradoxically estranged himself: How could a wooer be the wooed?

Published after his death, Ovid's *Fasti*—the Roman calendar—dwells on the origin and meaning of religious and civil holidays. Typical themes are the festival of Janus, the beginning of spring, the rites of Diana on the Aventine hill, and the rekindling of the fire of Vesta. He intended to dedicate the work to Augustus as a lure to tempt his banisher into changing his mind. But Augustus died too soon for this, and Ovid knew better than to appeal to the hardened heart of Tiberius, the new emperor. The poet died at the age of 60, still in exile and still lamenting, in none too inspired lines, his sad fate.

Livy

In prose one great name stands out, Titus Livius (ca. 59 B.C.–A.C. 17). For 40 years he labored on a project hardly less stupendous in scope than that of Virgil—nothing less than the history of Rome from its founding to his own times. The accomplishment of this huge task itself made history. Through it Livy promoted, as did Virgil in the *Aeneid,* a developing sense of nationalism. Much as did Horace in his *Odes,* he made his countrymen conscious of the moral virtues that reputedly gave Rome its early strength. In this sense he too was both harbinger and creator of the new Golden Age.

But this is not to suggest that his history is not subject to serious criticism. For one thing, he was not a researcher as modern historians use the term. He leaned heavily on secondary sources even when, as on a number of occasions, he had access to the primary materials from which others had drawn. When he did use documents he frequently failed to give samples of their exact wording, which would have imparted to the reader a livelier sense of the

---

[14] H. F. Frankel, *Ovid: A Poet Between Two Worlds* (Berkeley and Los Angeles: University of California Press, 1945), p. 14.

times. In his early books (the whole work ran to 142 books, of which, unfortunately, only 35 are extant) he relied too much on legend. His judgment, when the evidence was more complete and complex, was not always as discriminating as it should have been. And throughout, his chauvinism is clearly apparent. He was as much interested in history as literary art as in history as "objective" inquiry—in itself a good thing except where, as was often the case with him, such interest carries one away. Finally, his understanding of the intricate complexity of his subject left much to be desired. In these and other ways his history is faulty and must be read with caution.

But on the other hand, it is not altogether fair to judge an ancient historian by modern standards. And it must be added that he did not deliberately twist evidence to make it fit his story, although he certainly embellished it. Further, literary art of itself deserves a place, and a rather high place, in all worthy historical writing. Finally, it must be admitted that without Livy most later historical works on Republican Rome would dwindle to a shadowy sketch. Indeed, a contemporary authority has argued that if the 107 lost books were found, hardly a page of Roman history as written by modern historians would escape revision.

Livy's aim is clearly set forth in the opening pages of his work. If, he says, the reader is "in good earnest" to apply himself to the Romans, he will make a special effort

. . . to consider these points: what their life and manners were; through what men and by what measures, both in peace and in war, they got their empire and extended it; then, as discipline gradually declined, let him follow in his thoughts their morals, at first as slightly giving way, then how they sank more and more, then began to fall headlong, until he reaches the present times [that is, in the time of Augustus], when we can neither endure our cultural ailments nor their cures. This is what is particularly salutary and useful in the study of history, that you behold instances of every kind of conduct displayed as on a conspicuous monument; that you may then select for yourself and for your country that which you may imitate; as well as also note what is shameful in the undertaking, and shameful in the result, which you may avoid.[15]

Livy thus declares himself to be a moral historian, uninterested in the fact for its own sake, and frankly didactic, as were most of the poets of his age. The extended quotation given below permits personal assessment of his style and, to a degree, his method. It is taken from Book I, where the author is describing the conflict between "national," family, and personal interests involved in the famous Coriolanus affair. Coriolanus, a legendary warrior, had shown great valor in the Romans' war against the Volscians. But when the commoners made demands inconsistent with what he thought to be good order, the warrior left his state and family and joined his former enemies, leading them, finally, against Rome itself. At this point, writes Livy,

A great number of women waited on Veturnia, Coriolanus' mother, and Volumnia, his wife; whether by advice of the senate or instigated by their own fears is not said. But they certainly prevailed with Veturnia, a very old lady, and Volumnia, carrying her two sons by Coriolanus with her, to walk to the enemy's camp and try if the tears and progress of the women would defend the city, since the men were no longer able to do it by arms. When they had reached the camp, word was carried to Coriolanus that a great train of ladies had come to wait upon him. Since neither the majesty of a public deputation, nor the respect due to religion and the priesthood had been capable of moving him, he thought he would be proof

[15] Titus Livius, *The History of Rome*, trans. D. Spillan, 2 vols. (New York: Harper and Brothers, 1879), 1:15–16 (slightly modified).

against the tears of a troop of women. One of his acquaintances, however, identified Veturnia who, disconsolate, was standing between her daughter-in-law and her grandchildren. "If my eyes do not deceive me," he said to Coriolanus, "your mother, wife and children are here." Coriolanus threw himself from his tribunal, almost out of his senses, and ran full of anguish to embrace his mother. "Wait," she said, assuming an air of resentment rather than entreaty, "let me know whether I speak to a son or to an enemy. Am I considered your mother or your captive? Have I lived so long only first to see you banished, then the enemy of your country? Are you capable of ravaging the land that gave you birth and brought you up in its bosom? However violent are your thirst for resentment and for revenge, did not the sight of these plains (of Latium) disarm your rage? And when you came within sight of Rome, did you not then think within yourself, those walls which I am about to attack contain all that is dear to me in the world—my house, my household goods, my mother, wife, children! Also, had I not been a mother, Rome would not now be besieged. Had I not had a son, I should have died free, in a free country. But I can suffer nothing now that is not more shameful for you than miserable for me; nor can my misery, however great at present, be long continued. Think of these infants, who if you persist, must suffer an untimely death, or a long servitude." His wife and children then saluted him. The tears and lamentations of all the Roman ladies at length softened Coriolanus. He embraced his family and dismissed them. Soon after he decamped and marched his army back from the city. According to some accounts the Volsci were so exasperated at his withdrawing the legions from the Roman territory that they put him to death. Others give a defferent account of the matter. Fabius, by far the most ancient author extant, declares that he lived to a great old age, and mentioned a saying of his in the decline of his life, "That banishment was in all cases unbearable, but especially to an old man."

The men were not jealous of the encomiums bestowed upon their women. Such was their unselfishness that none endeavored to detract from the glory of another. To preserve the remembrance of so singular an event by a public monument, they built and dedicated a temple to Female Fortune.[16]

Livy's *History* was published serially, as he finished and polished the work section by section. It received wide acclaim during his lifetime. Augustus himself professed, probably quite sincerely, great admiration for the work. Although manifesting imperial leanings, it proclaimed with compelling artistry the virtues of the Republican society that Augustus purportedly was striving so hard to reestablish.

Literary Decline

We have now read enough of the literature of the Golden Age to sense that the grand phrase was not a misnomer. Two further observations remain. It is easy to equate chronologically the Golden Age of Roman literature with the famous *Pax Romana*. This, however, is a mistake. If, not too arbitrarily, we date the latter period from 30 B.C. to the end of the reign of Marcus Aurelius in A.D. 180, we see that although the great literature falls within this epoch, it does so but barely. Lucretius, Catullus, Caesar, Cicero, Sallust—all lived and died before that period. Even Virgil, Horace, Ovid, and Livy had produced their major works before the Age of Peace was well begun. The Golden Age of literature, therefore, does not coincide with the Imperial Age. Indeed, the years of the latter witnessed a distinct falling away from the established standards. It was, we should note, the Silver Age that belonged to the Empire; and even it, as we shall see, failed to sustain itself for more than half that period.

[16] William Gordon, *Titus Livius' Roman History* . . . (Edinburgh: Bell and Bradford et al., 1809), pp. 165–66 (slightly modified).

This decline suggests a second observation. The *promise* of the Augustan reforms undoubtedly stirred the creators of the literature that we have surveyed. But actual *practice* belied the glorious auspices. There is, for example, no Cicero in the Augustan and succeeding ages. This is hardly an accident. Authoritarian regimes do not encourage genuine oratory, for this comes only from unfettered thought freely expressed. Artificially bedecked declarations, pretty and precious, there were; but no stirring works of challenge. When, in one instance, an orator did dare to say what he thought about Augustus and his new regime, his books and speeches were publicly banned and the offending protestor was sent into exile. When, too, a few recalcitrant judges gave decisions adverse to Augustus's decrees, the princeps promptly stipulated that thereafter no acceptable legal advice or opinion could be given except under terms laid down by Augustus himself. Thus under the New Order, which did indeed bring peace and the rule of law, creative imagination—that is, freedom—was stifled and ultimately sacrificed. Under such conditions one does not expect "golden literature" to flourish, nor did it.

PAX ROMANA— IMPERIAL ROME

Tiberius

A pressing problem for Augustus in his later years was the question of a successor. For one thing, how was he to be chosen? To leave the choice to the Senate would only invite a return of factionalism and violence. Even less eligible to make such a decision was the popular Assembly, for the people had long since drifted away from a sense of participation and responsibility in matters of high statecraft; besides, by this time it had become in the main merely a nominal power. For Augustus to nominate his own successor would be tantamount to proclaiming the dictatorship that he had been at such pains to conceal. Still, in the end this is what he did. Rather reluctantly (earlier designees having died) he selected his stepson Tiberius, eldest child of his third wife. By way of preparation for the succession Augustus, in his declining years, gave over power to Tiberius until the latter came to share full authority. Accordingly, when the emperor died in A.D. 14, the Senate lost no time in proclaiming the new princeps and called upon army and people to swear personal allegiance to him. Thus a pattern of succession was set that served for the next half-century, the period of the so-called Julio-Claudian line (A.D. 14–68).

The apprehensions Augustus had begun to feel in his later years proved only too well grounded. Tiberius, who ruled from A.D. 14 until his death in A.D. 37, was an able administrator but haughty and tactless, lacking almost completely the knack that Augustus had of getting on with people. Well trained and determined in purpose, he faithfully followed Augustan policies, winning the enthusiastic support of the people in the provinces. At home he fared less well. The Senate chafed under a system that increasingly made clear its own subservient position. The Roman masses objected to Tiberius's program of economy, which for them meant fewer circuses and smaller doles. Plebeians generally resented an imperial edict that frankly recognized that the people no longer elected the magistrates. Even the army, long his supporter, turned sour when he pared down the budget for military expenditures. Friction developed between Drusus, the emperor's son, and Germanicus, a nephew whom Augustus had forced Tiberius to designate as his successor. When Germanicus suddenly died, the emperor was suspected of murdering him, although the available evidence does not support this suspicion. A few years later Drusus was poisoned. When Tiberius learned that one of his once most trusted lieutenants had ordered the murder (motivated by imperial ambitions of his own), he gave himself over to vicious temper tantrums. The last years of his reign were marked by absolute tyranny. When he died in 37 he was cordially hated by everyone.

Violence Revisited

For some years following Tiberius's death the morale so carefully fostered by Augustus was badly shaken. Of the six emperors of this period, all died by murder or suicide. Tiberius's great-nephew Gaius (better known by his nickname Caligula—"Little Boots") occupied himself during his three-year reign with incest, assassinations, and assorted cruelties. Officers of his own Praetorian Guard finally slew him and forced the Senate, which briefly toyed with the possibility of restoring the old Republic, to proclaim his uncle, Claudius, as the new princeps. In 54 Claudius was assassinated at his wife's orders so that Nero, her son by an earlier marriage, might become ruler. One of Nero's early decisions—although delayed in execution—was to get rid of his mother, whom he rightly suspected of having ambitions to be the power behind the throne. Fourteen years later Nero himself fell victim to the violence he spent his tenure cultivating. Within one year, 68–69 (the "Year of the Four Emperors") Galba, Otho, and Vitellius likewise met violent deaths.

Imperial Order

In spite of this outburst of imperial gangsterism the Empire held together, indeed flourished. Troops posted along its borders kept the "barbarians" from attempting more than occasional raids. With the soldiers came Roman culture, which the conquered lands gradually absorbed. From time to time the scholar and his paraphernalia accompanied the soldier, so that books and learning edged their way northward with conquest. Soon amid the general peace and prosperity cities came to vie with one another for regional honors and glory. Public buildings of all kinds were erected: government offices, public baths, temples. Private dwellings of the rich were constructed on a grand scale and handsomely furnished and decorated. Hellenistic culture, siphoned off and modified by Roman colonists, took root and

Much of the glory that was Rome was based on slave labor. Here a high crane, operated by slaves, performs its functions. The scene is from a tomb relief.

laid the foundation for the later medieval civilization from which our own has developed.

Throughout this period, too, signs appeared of the spread of new faiths, doubtless developing from the westward flow of religious ideas carried by devotees of the mystery cults and by neo-Pythagoreans; and of ethical monotheism, carried by refugee Hebrews, and by those who had come into contact with the earliest Christian missionaries. Although numerically the most insignificant, the last were especially zealous. The crucifixion of Jesus had occurred in Tiberius's reign. Scarcely 20 years later Peter and Paul were effectively spreading the new gospel in lands along the northern rim of the Mediterranean basin. Three of the Christian gospels were composed during this period and, presumably, soon came to be read in the newly formed congregations whose members were eager to carry the "good news" to the whole world.

In the provinces a new breed of citizen was emerging. Many of the discharged legionaries stayed on in the regions they had guarded, often as husbands of native women. Since they were Roman citizens their settlement in the provinces meant that Roman law and Roman civic sense came to merge with foreign habits and folkways. Members of auxiliary units, upon their discharge, were often granted citizenship rights. To be a Roman thus came to mean something quite different from what it had meant in the days of the old Republic.

Vespasian

The situation in Rome itself, however, was far too serious to continue without placing in jeopardy the whole realm. In the capital the important question was, Would the new emperor preserve the Principate, or would he openly acknowledge the "secret" of the army's power and frankly set up a military autocracy? He chose to follow the Augustan pattern, a decision that, coupled with his very real abilities, saved the Pax Romana from untimely collapse.

Vespasian (69–79; his full name was Titus Flavius Vespasianus, from which he and his successors are called Flavians) was in no way related to the Julio-Claudians. Strictly speaking he was not even a Roman, but a native of the Sabine country. A man of strong will, ready to use whatever tactics a situation seemed to call for, experienced in military and administrative affairs, he assumed the throne in 69 with a confidence that soon proved itself in practical results. Within a half-dozen years he had reestablished order in the capital, reorganized the Empire's finances, reconstituted the personnel of the Senate, and made provision for his son, Titus, to succeed him. During his regime he

TABLE I
Roman Rulers: 27 B.C.–A.D. 180

JULIO-CLAUDIAN LINE

Augustus	27 B.C.–A.D. 14
Tiberius	14–37
Caligula	37–41
Claudius	41–54
Nero	54–68

"THE YEAR OF THE FOUR EMPERORS"

Galba; Otho; Vitellius; Vespasian	68–69

FLAVIAN LINE

Vespasian	69–79
Titus	79–81
Domitian	81–96

"THE FIVE GOOD EMPERORS"

Nerva	96–98
Trajan	98–117
Hadrian	117–138
Antoninus Pius	138–161
Marcus Aurelius	161(147)–180

ROMAN EMPIRE ca. A.D. 100

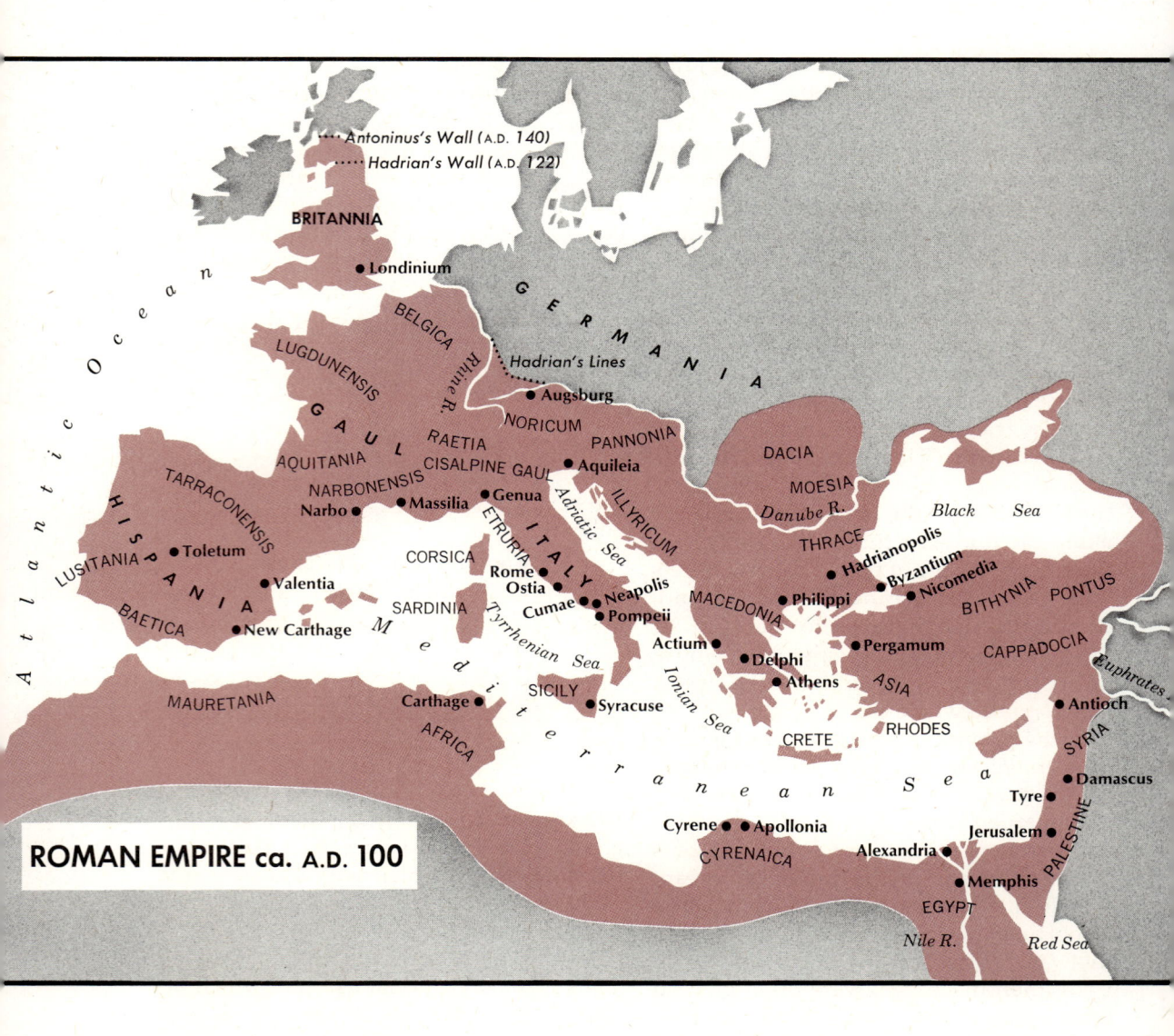

founded new colonies and gave "Latin rights" to all freemen in Spain. Vacant civil service posts were filled by competent administrators. Professional informers—the hated *delatores*—were sent packing. Accordingly, morale among both public officials and private citizens markedly improved. To placate the eternal Roman mob and win favor in the city generally, Vespasian ordered the construction of a superamphitheater (the famed Colosseum), where games and exhibitions were staged on a scale never before attempted.

The "Five Good Emperors": Trajan

For a quarter-century the Flavian restoration healed the wounds of the Caligula–Nero epoch, yielding in 96 to Nerva, the first of the "five good emperors."* Thus from the death of Vitellius in 69 to the end of the Pax Romana in 180 citizens of the Empire enjoyed all the benefits that benevolent paternalism could bestow.

* The last Flavian, Domitian, instituted a reign of terror in the last years of his rule; but this was an exception, and fortunately a brief one.

"The five"—Nerva (96–98); Trajan (98–117); Hadrian (117–138); Antoninus Pius (138–161); and Marcus Aurelius (161–180)—were humane and gifted statesmen who brought almost perfect execution to the system worked out by Augustus. If in the end they failed, that failure came from the nature of autocracy, which the so-called Principate masked but could not essentially alter; that is, it came from the Augustan attempt to "will the impossible, making inevitable the impracticable."

The advent of Trajan (98) signaled the trend toward cosmopolitanism that came to characterize life in the later Empire. The Julio-Claudians were Romans, members of two of the city's oldest and most honored families. Vespasian, although not Roman, was at least Italian. But Trajan was neither, having been born in Spain of stock that had separated from its Italian roots 300 years before. To him Aeneas and the Roman gods were merely interesting legends, of little consequence as part of a political rationale designed to meet

Praetorians, sometimes makers of emperors.

269   A. The Empire

problems of statecraft. During his reign the commonwealth's most distant boundaries were reached. Dacia—modern Rumania—was added, as were generous (overgenerous, for they had soon to be relinquished) portions of the ancient Near East—Armenia and Mesopotamian Parthia. In both old and new provinces new roads were built on a grand scale. Naturally, many were constructed primarily to serve military needs, but not a few were built to expedite travel and commerce.

With Roman peace, Roman law, and Roman roads serving it, commerce naturally continued its prosperous ways. And as the sprawling Empire thus became an ever-expanding free-trade area, correspondingly and causally it served as a cultural magnetic field. As such it attracted and fused Eastern and Western religions, philosophies, laws, and the forms and substance of literature and art. Steady development of this cosmopolitan trend depended on the Empire's remaining a manageable unit. Trajan's successors diligently worked to effect this. Hadrian went so far as to construct permanent limits along the Danube and in England (Hadrian's Wall)—a clear indication that imperial boundaries had been set.

Hadrian

Under Hadrian, Trajan's successor, the cosmopolitan trend was consciously and actively encouraged. Particularly significant was the continuing development of law and jurisprudence. Here the Roman was at home; here, for once, he was creator. We have seen how in the early days the Romans codified law in the Twelve Tables. Subsequently new statutory enactments were added. But the genius of Roman law lay more in interpretation and the place given to precedent than in static legislation. Legislation, the letter of the law as it applied to Roman citizens (the *ius civile*), existed and was sufficiently detailed. But the interpreters of this law, the praetors and the *juris prudentes*,* often modified it as they applied it to various kinds of concrete cases.

Moreover, the web of commercial life bound Roman and non-Roman in an intimate association that law and equity served to regulate. The Roman solution was to set up a general imperial system of contractual relationships. These were based on provisions of the ius civile, which either were, or could be, made applicable by imperial edict or judicial interpretation. This wider body of law, progressive in principle and embracing the whole state and not just the Roman part of it, was called the *ius gentium.*

Gradual denationalization was, of course, implicit in this process. Consequently Roman law had become, by the end of the fourth century, universal law. Of still wider scope, although more amorphous and only indirectly applied, was that body of general principles dealing with fundamental human rights—the *ius naturale.* Long since, philosophers and moralists had set forth certain ideas concerning the good life. Imperial jurisprudence came to recognize these as worthy maxims, even if they were not always practicable. In effect, then, this natural law served as the ideal towards which positive law pointed.

Hadrian's contributions were real and substantial. A number of his judgments came to be embodied in the corpus of Roman law. He collected and collated previous imperial pronouncements that bore on his own decisions; under him the appointment of praetorian prefects was made with due regard for legal talent (originally praetorian prefects were commanders of the elite imperial guard; later

---

* Unofficial jurists whose training and native abilities gave their opinions something of the authority attaching today to the decisions of official members of our higher courts.

they were given important judicial and administrative duties).

Antoninus

This progress of developing law, of general peace and prosperity, and of the cosmopolitanization of the imperial state continued in the 23-year reign of Antoninus Pius, Hadrian's successor. Indeed, this period marked the apogee of the Pax Romana. Antoninus well deserved the title "pius", bestowed upon him by Senate and people. Save for Marcus Aurelius he was the most sensitive, gentle, humane ruler in the whole of Roman history. Accordingly his subjects could not praise him enough. Many had been the exaggerated praises composed by skillful rhetoricians showered on emperors in the past, even on such debased rulers as Caligula and Nero. But they had been calculated panegyrics motivated by favor-seeking and greed. The laudations of Antoninus were sincere. Aristides the Sophist, for example, "describes the state of the Roman Empire in terms of glowing admiration. The richness and happiness of the countries of the Empire testify to the excellence of Roman government. Everywhere towns have been founded or restored and a place of honor has been reserved for Hellenic culture. The Roman World is administered as a single household which enjoys a perpetual holiday, and is safeguarded from external aggression by the discipline of the Roman army."[17] Even the Senate, long the ark of anti-imperial sentiment, found in rule and ruler only praiseworthy features. The Mediterranean civilization seemed at last to have achieved permanent political stability. One ruler, one state, and one law combined to produce and sustain an age of peace and plenty.

[17] H. M. D. Parker, *The History of Rome*, 2d ed. New York: Barnes & Noble, 1958), p. 38.

Marcus Aurelius

Associated with Antoninus during the last 14 years of his reign was his adopted son, Marcus Aurelius. During these years the younger man's nobility of character had clearly shown itself, and the Empire's peoples confidently looked forward to a continuation of good times. If Plato had been alive at Marcus's accession he might well have believed that in the new ruler his ideal of philosopher-king had been realized. In a sense he would have been right. The new ruler personified to a remarkable degree "the virtues that had been Rome's glory." Preeminently he embodied the essence of *pietas*. By nature and training a philosopher, he ruled not for glory but rather reluctantly from a sense of duty. His gentle and compassionate stoicism is reflected in his book of devotions that we know as the *Meditations*. In them we sense a quality akin to that which motivated the founders of the world's great religions. He admonished man to "see that the godhead within thee have the guardianship of . . . one who has taken his post like a soldier, who awaits the bugle that shall sound his recall in all readiness to obey." Like Christ he taught that:

It is peculiar to man to love even those who do wrong. And this happens, if when they do wrong, it occurs to thee that they are kinsmen, and that they do wrong through ignorance and unintentionally, and that soon both of you will die; and above all, that the wrong-doer has done thee no harm, for he has not made thy ruling faculty worse than it was before.[18]

The End of the Pax Romana

Despite Marcus's genuine devotion to duty, and his noble character, his reign marked the end of the great Roman peace.

[18] *The Thoughts of the Emperor M. Aurelius Antoninus*, trans. George Long (New York and London: G. P. Putnam's Sons, n. d.), pp. 194–95.

Almost the whole period of his rule (161–180) was spent conducting military campaigns. Various portions of the provinces of Germany and Raetia were invaded by tribes from the north. Rebellion broke out in Britain; in the East a whole spate of wars developed. At the same time Rome suffered from one of the most disastrous plagues of its history. And to these troubles were added the harassments of famine. For nearly a score of years Marcus jumped from one trouble spot to another. Not infrequently he was forced to return to the same area when it was discovered that pacification had not been complete. It is true that at his death the frontiers still held; but the signs were ominous. Teutonic tribes to the north had been repulsed; but they were still there, still active, and were to grow bolder. Financial strains were so severe that in one period the emperor had been forced to auction off family jewels and other valuables to meet military expenses. The felicities of the age had somehow and quite suddenly vanished. "It was as though a mysterious night descended on the bright day."

If, as one authority has warned, "to speak of a 'decay' of the Roman empire at this period would be premature," it is nevertheless necessary to note the static spirit of the times which blanketed the whole period of the "good emperors," and which passed for contentment. Actually the glossy, brilliant external features of the age masked an inner decay, an imperceptive willingness to expend the cultural capital that the Augustan solution and its hopeful reception had built up. However well-intentioned the rulers were, they made no move to introduce, or to allow others to introduce, political innovations pointing toward a more independent citizenship, or even decentralized control. No program was devised to reduce the gap between the wealthy few and the impoverished many. No thought was given to the great despoiling of the human soul that the institution of slavery necessarily effected. If the Empire was surrounded by *limites* that retarded invasions, it was also encompassed by psychic *limites* that held back the free play of man's creative powers and needs.

At Marcus's death in 180 the succession passed to his son Commodus who was almost the complete antithesis of his father. The Empire, in fact, witnessed a reenactment of the scenes of Nero's reign. Court favorites were given the highest civil and military positions. Thus released from responsibilities the new emperor gave himself over to the grossest debaucheries. Many of his palace days and nights were spent in open carousing with mistresses and "pretty boys." The demure mask of the Principate that most of his predecessors had been careful to keep in place slipped in his careless hands. All who cared to look could see the imperial power in its raw state. The praetorian prefect became a kind of Oriental vizier. Alien Eastern gods were lavishly worshiped in court circles. Just before his death the young Emperor proclaimed a new trinity —Isis, Serapis, and himself. The Senate, alternately cowed and bribed, offered no opposition. As for the Roman mob, it wildly hailed an emperor who dramatically entered the arena to slay bears and panthers before the thrill-hungry crowds that packed the amphitheater. Either this tragicomedy or the machinery of imperial government had to give way. In 192 desperate conspirators arranged for his athletic trainer to strangle the mad ruler in his bath. Thus ingloriously the Antonine line petered out.

The year 192, like the year 69, was one of four emperors. For 87 days Pertinax, who had been Commodus's city prefect, wore the purple. But when he disciplined the Guards who had elevated him to the throne, they cut off his head and paraded it through the city, meanwhile offering his place to the highest bidder. A wealthy senator, M. Didius Julianus, purchased the crown and wore it uneasily for a few weeks. But restive troops along the Danube had other plans. Their favorite was Septimius Severus, who, after a citizen-soldier had obligingly assassinated Julianus, rode into the city to be proclaimed by legionaries and Senate alike.*

Under Septimius (Punic born and reared) and his immediate successors order was restored and the Empire entered its third century intact. But it was a very different empire from the Augustan dream. Living frankly now on the sufferance of the soldiers, it would last only so long as military strength lasted. The Golden Age, heralded by Virgil, planned by Augustus, and winsomely developed by the Antonines, was over. It is true that the Empire was to survive for many years; but not in faith and hope. The vision was gone. If the Virgilian vision is thought of as pointing to a release of purposeful energy it had, in fact, long since faded—possibly as early as the Neronian period. For at no time thereafter did Roman civilization show those creative scars which mark the struggle of a dynamic society.

THE CULTURE OF THE SILVER AGE

This reduction of the heroic tension is clearly reflected in the literature of the period, significantly called the Silver Age. Contrary to the less peaceful regimes preceding it, the Principate had severely curtailed liberty of expression. The growing material comforts of the times had created a superficial contentment which tended to drug any Ciceronian impulse that might have challenged the imperial censorship. This combination of coercion and self-induced atrophy of the will resulted in a literature that, while often elegant, was rarely inspired or inspiring. When not precious or pedantic it was often bitterly captious. And almost always, whether bourgeois or bitter, it feared its tomorrows. The foibles of the present or the glories of the past were safer.

Literature: Seneca and Pliny

Seneca (3 B.C.—A.D. 65), for a while Nero's adviser, produced nine tragedies and numerous prose essays. The former were brilliantly written but smacked of the contrived display so characteristic of Silver Age literature. Drenched in blood and violence, they caught passing attention; but they are regarded today only as interesting museum pieces. His philosophical essays have fared better. In them he preached benevolent Stoicism as a cure for the psychic malaise of his society. If he was suspected of not practicing what he preached, still, the rhetorical force that marked his presentation of Stoic benignity has made his dialogues live.

No less polished, and just as suavely constructed, are the letters of Pliny the Younger (62–113). Most of them were written with an eye to publication and hence lack the spontaneity and unconscious self-revelation of Cicero's correspondence. But Pliny's touch is so urbane and his ability to turn the winsome phrase so masterly that his letters attract in spite of their artificial flavor. Of special importance for us is the wealth of historical data found in much of his correspondence. As governor of Bithynia during Trajan's reign, Pliny wrote endless inquiries to his master concerning the administrative and social problems that demanded his attention. Through these letters we get a close and detailed picture of one segment of provincial life, and of imperial administration in action. The following excerpt reveals Pliny's puzzlement over the correct treatment to be accorded to a new religious sect.

It is my invariable rule, Sir, to refer to you in all matters where I feel doubtful. . . . Having

---

* Actually, three other claimants were put forward by different sets of troops; Septimius had to spend several years putting down his rivals.

never been present at any trials concerning those who profess Christianity, I am unacquainted not only of the nature of the crimes, or the measure of their punishment, but how far it is proper to enter into an examination concerning them . . . whether repentance entitles them to a pardon; or if a man has been once a Christian, it avails nothing to desist from his error; whether the very profession of Christianity, unattended by any criminal act, or only the crimes themselves inherent in the profession are punishable; on all these points I am in great doubt. In the meantime the method I have observed towards those who have been brought before me as Christians is this: I asked them whether they were Christians; if they admitted it, I repeated the question twice, and threatened them with punishment; if they persisted, I ordered them to be punished; for I was persuaded, whatever the nature of their opinions might be, a contumacious and inflexible obstinancy certainly deserved correction. . . . it appears to be a matter highly deserving your consideration, more especially as great numbers must be involved in the danger of these prosecutions, which have already extended, and are still likely to extend, to persons of all ranks and ages, and even of both sexes. In fact this contagious superstition is not confined to the cities only, but has spread its infection among the neighboring villages and country. Nevertheless, it still seems possible to restrain its progress . . . it is easy to conjecture what numbers might be reclaimed if a general pardon were granted to those who shall repent their error.[19]

Juvenal and Martial

The mood of the post-Augustan Age found satire its most acceptable mode of expression. Among the many practitioners of this pungent if often oblique form of critical assessment, Juvenal was preeminent (ca. 50–130). His themes were the decadent state of society, the exploitive idiosyncracies of man, the dry-crust literature of his day, the almost complete depravity of women (he was a bachelor), the defense mechanisms that shield human conduct, and the like. Very much like him in style although less appealing as a human being was Martial (40–104), whose epigrams have made him as quotable as Pope. Beyond the virtuosity of his rhetorical genius there is almost nothing lovely about the man. Because Domitian found his flattery pleasant Martial paid the dictator the most ridiculous public attention. But when the tyrant was assassinated and Rome made it clear how despised he was, Martial quickly faced about and heaped calumny upon his one time benefactor. Everything and everybody became grist for his mill. At times he was the indignant champion of virtue, as when he wrote:

Till nightfall you lunch, till nightfall, Turgidius, you dine, and with all sorts of wine day and night you reek. And although you are careful of your person, you are unwilling to take a wife; your unwillingness says: 'A chaste life pleases me.' Turgidius, you lie; this is not a chaste life. Would you have me tell you what is a chaste life? Moderation.[20]

But (more in character) he also wrote, "Aper is abstemious, sober; so what is that to me? A slave I praise so, not a friend." And, "Do you wonder, Aulus, that our good friend Pabullius is so often taken in? A good man is always a greenhorn."

Suetonius and Tacitus

Among the biographers of the period none achieved the eminence of Suetonius, whose *Lives of the Caesars* has furnished

---

[19] F. C. T. Bosouquet, ed., *The Letters of Caius Plinius Caecilius Secundus* . . . (London: George Bell and Sons, 1878), pp. 393–95.

[20] Martial, *Epigrams,* Loeb Classical Library, trans. W. C. A. Kerr, 2 vols. (London, 1920), 2:531, 355, 341. "Aper" is a pun on the word for pig.

many historians with delectable anecdotes. Scorning the flourish of so many of his contemporaries Suetonius set down in factual, unadorned fashion the findings of his tireless research. Unfortunately he seemed unable to discriminate between the significant and the trivial, so that we find him accepting court gossip as enthusiastically as the data of the archival material with which he worked. As a matter of fact, his impish habit of retailing scandal of all sorts cost him his job as court scribe. But since he was so close to court circles his works, in spite of the dross that encumbers them, remain of value.

Far surpassing him, and indeed all others of the Silver Age, is Tacitus (ca. 55–120), whose fame rests on a much broader base than as the depicter of German tribal habits and folkways. Little is known of his personal life. Active in political affairs (he served one term as consul), Tacitus wrote from the perspective of the "old Roman." His diligent research and his supreme gifts of expression combined to make his histories worthy of the most careful study. It is true that they do not suggest some of the advantages that the Empire undoubtedly brought to the Mediterranean world. But his Republican bias is so open and obvious that the reader has little difficulty in keeping it in calculation. His most important works are the *Annales*, which detail the events of Roman history during the period of the Julio-Claudian emperors; the *Historiae*, which carry the story down through Domitian; the *Germania*, our most important single source on primitive Teutonic culture; and *Agricola*, which, as the biography of his father-in-law (governor of the province of Britain), gives an early account of that frontier region.

Plutarch and Aristides

A contemporary of Tacitus and a native of Greece, Plutarch (46?–120) has put a host of later historians in his debt. His first work was a series of lives of outstanding Greek political figures. Finding these sketches so well received he paralleled them with their Roman counterparts. These *Lives* have long played a disproportionately large role in shaping the schoolboy's notions of Roman political character.

A fellow Greek, but of a later generation, Aelius Aristides (115–185) produced a number of grave and graceful essays on the general state of society of the Roman world of his time. They are both literature and sociological documents.

Medicine and Astronomy

Although not as literature, the works of two Hellenized provincials may be noted. Galen of Pergamum (131–201) devoted most of his life (apart from his duties as personal physician to three of Rome's emperors) to compiling the "scientific" medical lore of his day. The monumental treatise that he published remained the standard textbook for the next thousand years. Ptolemy (ca. 150), an Alexandrian scholar, did similar services for astronomy and geography. The Ptolemaic theory of the constitution of the heavens was accepted as late as the seventeenth century, when Galileo was brought to his knees for challenging it.

Architecture

If the trend in literature during the post-Augustan years was downward, developments in architecture moved in the opposite direction. Authorities still argue whether the architectural triumph of the Flavian and Antonine periods reflected native Roman genius or skillful discipleship. Certainly the three Greek orders of the column were directly taken over by the Romans. And the pediment of the

Detail from the Arch of Titus showing soldiers bearing loot from Palestine.

Arch of Constantine.

Roman soldiers, roughing up prisoners (while succoring their own wounded), press forward in this "stage set." Dozens of these "sets" make up the spiral bands of Trajan's Column.

Column of Trajan.

This gigantic amphitheatre, long called the Colosseum, was built by Vespasian to impress the Roman masses. Its bloody "games" thrilled countless spectators and shamed some, including Seneca.

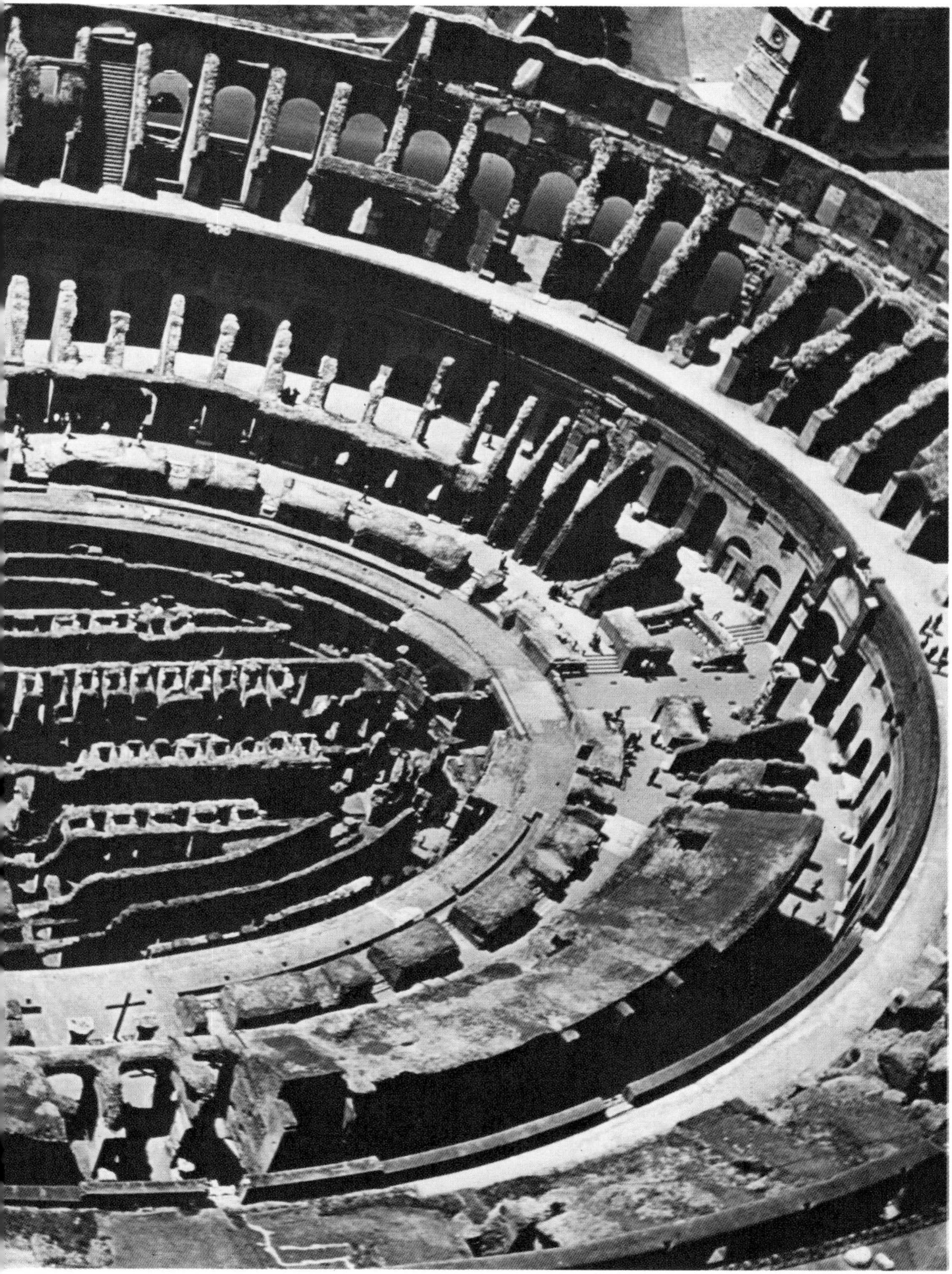

An engraving showing the interior of the Pantheon.

Ruins of the Baths of Caracalla.

Pantheon would have looked quite at home in Periclean Athens. But the Romans were not mere copyists. After a period of tutelage they adapted Hellenistic form to Roman spirit so masterfully that the argument about creativity loses much of its point.

The architectural efforts of the Greeks—and particularly the Athenians—were directed toward the construction of buildings designed to glorify the polis and to provide settings for meaningful living. In one degree or another probably these aims also characterized Roman efforts. But glorification of the imperial impulse was certainly the predominant theme. From Augustus on, Rome was deliberately made into a showpiece; and provincial "Romes" tried hard to keep pace with the mother city. It is not without significance that the most outstanding examples of Roman originality in this discipline were the triumphal arch and the commemorative column.

A good example of the former is the Arch of Titus, begun by Vespasian to memorialize Titus's triumph over the Jews. In this massive monument the imperial mood is dramatically expressed. Masterly reliefs on both outer and inner walls of the arch tell the story of this victory. There is the long procession of booty-bearing figures, booty that included the sacred trumpets and the seven-branched candelabrum. Titus looms large as the invincible conqueror, a kind of god, crowned by Victory. The whole work, in short, stirs in the spectator the restless urge to share in the celebration. The even more elaborate Arch of Constantine bespeaks the same exultant pride (although the craftsmanship is second-rate). Impressive columns served a like purpose. The Column of Trajan, made of costly marble, reaches a height of 100 feet, topped by a statue of the conqueror; spiraling scenes of his victories over the Dacians make up the intricate sculptured relief.

Since Roman taste ran less to theater than to grand exhibitions, Greek models were again modified. To cater to the Roman yen for spectacles, huge "bowls" were constructed; notably the Amphitheatrum Flavianum, truly deserving of the name given it in medieval days—the Colosseum.* Its facade, the features of which are well known to almost everybody, was probably modeled on that of the Theater of Pompey. But behind the facade are examples of bold, original, skillfully executed structural design. To sustain the burden of a capacity crowd (perhaps 75,000), the barrel vault was abandoned in favor of a new technique—cross, or groined, vaulting. Another innovation was the triple-entrance hall, dominated by nave and aisles that lost width as they fed their way into the yawning depths. Intricate underground stalls and passageways honeycombed the substructures. From these areas issued the wild beasts and gladiators that brought the cheering multitudes to their feet. To give the Romans a holiday they would not soon forget, Vespasian decreed 100 days of games to celebrate its opening. Much of this glorified stadium still stands, its ruins attracting modern tourists as its bloody spectacles drew Roman crowds 2000 years ago.

The same bold use of cross vaulting permitted architects to construct magnificent *thermae*, or baths. Dozens of them were built in Rome. Hardly an Italian or provincial community dared call itself a city without at least one public bath. Those built by Caracalla and Diocletian were the most famous. One of them could accommodate 3000 bathers; the other was so sumptuously constructed and appointed that Caracalla is scarcely remembered for anything else. The soaring magnificence of its main hall was framed and supported by a series of groined vaults, affording

* Actually derived from its proximity to a huge statue.

A. The Empire

ABOVE: *Marcus Aurelius.*

ABOVE LEFT: *Hadrian.*

LEFT: *Domitian.*

vast space unbroken by supporting columns.† Some rooms were provided with steam baths; others allowed bathers the titillation of hot, warm, and cold sprays. Recreation and games rooms, as well as gossip corners, were elegantly furnished.

Despite the Augustan impetus given to religion, temples in the Empire period received less attention than in Republican days. Sometimes, almost as an afterthought, they were adjoined to the baths. The most famous example of temple architecture is the Pantheon, rebuilt by Hadrian on the site of the Pantheon of Agrippa erected by Augustus. Its Grecian facade is composed of rearing columns supporting a typical pediment. The central chamber is an enormous room which "has a perfection of form and a restful sense of space that is without equal in the whole world." The dome is of concrete, without vaulted support. At the top is a 20-foot opening through which sunlight could filter to light up the whole. Many official palaces, governmental offices, and palatial private homes were constructed in the Flavian-Antonine period. By the end of the second century Rome could justly claim that it yielded in splendor to no city of the fabled East.

Sculpture

Reference has already been made to the relief work that profusely adorned arches, columns, and public buildings. Sculptors worked in the round as well. Some of the statuary of this period, particularly of the emperors, rivaled the best efforts of the Greeks. It is true that the Roman penchant for both realistic detail and sumptuous ornamentation ruled out true expression of classic idealism. But any other kind of art would have been un-Roman; what was lost in classic artistry was made up in historical documentation. "The grim smile on Vespasian's dour but not uncongenial countenance, the boyish openness of Titus's face, the hard intellectual cast of Domitian's eyes and forehead, the searching glance of Hadrian and the almost mask-like passivity of M. Aurelius—all these distinguishing features are reproduced to the life."[21] The spiraling relief recited history no less than did the pen of Livy and Tacitus (the campaigns of the Dacian and Danubian wars, for example), often filling gaps left by written accounts long since lost. In all, of course, the theme of empire was dominant.

Economic Conditions

Imperial stirrings which gave rise to the construction of arches, columns, amphitheaters and other edifices stimulated economic development as well as esthetic impulses. Aping though not matching the grand public projects, private buildings such as villas and baths, constructed by wealthy families, reached unprecedented sumptuousness. Military roads, fanning out in all directions, served commerce no less than military security as they linked up widespread trading centers. By the time of the Antonines the volume of goods produced and distributed throughout western Europe reached a level as high as any reached across the next 1000 years. Limited commerce was even carried on with portions of the Far East.

The working classes, however, did not partake proportionately in the Empire's affluence. It can be argued that so much prosperity must have offered some material comforts to the servile order, and no doubt it did. But existing evidence suggests that although the mass of slaves received adequate nourishment they lived in the meanest circumstances. And since

---

† Copied by the architects of the one-time Pennsylvania Station in New York City.

[21] Max A. Cary, *A History of Rome Down to the Age of Constantine* (London: Methuen & Co., 1954), pp. 686–87.

By the third century the Empire's economy was in a bad way. This tomb relief scene of a banker and two of Rome's toiling poor accurately portrays the economic gap that separated the rich few from the harassed masses.

their numbers were so great, they naturally kept down the wage level of the free worker so that he too lived at a bare subsistence level. Under Nerva and his successors the *alimenta*—what today might be called a farm relief program—provided easy loans to free farmers, the interest from which was used as grants to needy families. This program bettered the lot of thousands of citizens; but the very need for such a system makes obvious the serious maldistribution of wealth.

In the early part of the third century general economic conditions suffered a serious decline. This was mainly due to three causes. As wealth accumulated in the hands of the new nobility and the equestrian order, extensive investment in real estate, an old Roman habit, was given free play. A large portion of working capital was thus drained from other enterprises. Also, with the end of Roman conquest the Empire, having no new provinces to exploit, was thrown back on its own resources. Potentially such resources were ample enough, but the habit of exploiting new territories rather than applying intensive efforts to opportunities in the old rendered them less remunerative. Finally, from the reign of Marcus Aurelius on, border raids increased in number and scope until there existed what can only be called a permanent state of invasion. Thus, from the end of the second century on, more and more of the Roman world's wealth was diverted into the imperial exchequer to meet the constantly mounting costs of war. In the end, taxes for military purposes soared to such figures that both confidence in the regime and business incentive were killed. In short, as the third century opened, *civilization* slowly yielded to *militarization*.

THE DISINTEGRATION OF THE ROMAN WORLD

"Pamper the Army and Despise the Rest"

Technically the Principate continued in existence throughout most of the third century. But in actuality the accession of Septimius Severus (193–211) marked its end. For the new ruler frankly acknowledged the army as the force that held the Empire together. His reported advice to his sons epitomizes the change: "Pamper the army and despise the rest." Among the precautions taken by the new ruler was the disbanding of the Praetorian Guard, hitherto made up almost exclusively of Italians, and the creation of a new one open to soldiers from the provinces. This went far to break the power of the political generals in Rome who so often had made and unmade emperors.

Under Septimius both size and pay of the army were substantially increased, aggravating the already heavy tax burden. Because the emperor showed promise of preventing a recurrence of the terrible events of 69, probably most citizens were willing enough to pay the stiff price that stability seemed to demand. But had they wanted to protest no effective means were at hand. The assemblies had long since fallen into disuse. For 200 years the Senate had been a kept body. Now under Septimius it was all but abolished. Twenty-nine of its recalcitrant members were executed; the right of senators to be tried in their own assembly was taken from them; many administrative posts, hitherto held by senators, were now assigned to equestrians.

The death of Septimius in 211 made way for Caracalla (211–17), who carried on the policies of his father, though without his intelligence and discipline. During his brief reign he decreed citizenship for all free persons in the Empire (212). And he constructed elaborate baths which became forever associated with his name. For the rest he took up where Nero had left off; and he met the same fate. Several others of the Severi tried to recapture the firm grip of Septimius but without success. From 235 to 285 the Empire can only be described as a shambles. In this period 26 emperors were put up and pulled down by plundering armies. Warfare along the borders became endemic. Everywhere barbarian forces stabbed at the imperial frontiers and infiltrated the regions of their breakthroughs in Italy, Spain, and Gaul. In the East, Mesopotamia and Syria suffered incursions by Persian invaders. Serious plagues broke out, devastating whole regions. To appease the bewildered and panic-stricken populace, emperors occasionally ordered a round of Christian persecutions. At times, various provinces broke away from the Empire and set themselves up as independent political units, or as loosely organized confederations. An especially significant symptom of the decay of Roman power was the decision of Aurelianus, emperor from 270 to 275, to build a protecting wall around Rome. Once world conqueror, the mighty city had itself become an object of foreign aggression.

Economic and Administrative Problems

The structure and processes of imperial administration were likewise in a perilous state. The trend toward centralized, absolute control necessitated the creation of a vast army of bureaucrats, many of whom, like their counterparts everywhere in all ages, cultivated opportunities of perpetuating and enlarging their enclaves of power, and of fattening themselves on whatever graft they could devise. Often the resources of towns were drained by junketing visits of bureaucratic VIPs, and the forced provisioning of military contingents. In their turn, townsmen passed on to the peasants the bulk of the tax burden. In addition, secret police filtered into all the provinces and, as one historian of the period has bluntly put it, "took a leading part in terrorizing the subjects."

Many farmers, unable to sustain the onerous tax burden, simply left their fields for other means of livelihood. Often this meant futile job hunting in towns and cities or the turning to outright brigandage. An important side-effect of the abandonment of farms by the "little people" was, not surprisingly, an increase in the number of large estates—*latifundia*—as landholding noblemen and sharp speculators took over deserted farm lands. Naturally, this only further widened the gap between the prosperous few and the impoverished masses.

In an effort to restore some measure of economic stability, emperors resorted to certain extreme actions and devices that we will soon take note of. It is hard to believe that the wiser of the imperial advisors took many of their own suggestions seriously; but perhaps the very desperateness of the times and the pall of impending disaster served to sanction wild remedies.

As economic conditions steadily deteriorated, tax revenues naturally fell far below the levels required to meet even minimum imperial needs. At this point rulers turned to currency debasement as a way out of immediate collapse.

Temporary Recovery under Diocletian and Constantine

By the end of the third century, conditions had become so chaotic that all classes, including the normally rampaging legions, sensed the need to submit to whatever authority showed promise of creating firm order. In 284 Gaius Diocletianus, an ex-freedman from Dalmatia, ousted the current emperor and set about establishing that authority. Essentially it rested on an unusual variety of the "divide and rule" principle. Clearly understanding that the sprawling empire could no longer be governed from one base, Diocletian established two courts, one in the East headed by himself, and another in the West, which he entrusted, under his general supervision, to a loyal lieutenant, M. Aurelius Maximianus. Each held the title "Augustus." Each was assisted by a "Caesar," a kind of deputy Augustus, who, under the new imperial structure, was to become regional emperor when his superior died.

To promote administrative effectiveness Diocletian made use of an advisory council, the *consilium principis,* made up of leading nobles and other propertied persons from the privileged classes. He also increased on a vast scale bureaucratic offices throughout the provinces. The number of provinces was likewise increased by reducing the size of each, in order to ensure closer administration of local affairs. Superimposed on this multiunit system were six Eastern and six Western "dioceses," each governed by an official appointed by the emperor (later the number of dioceses varied from reign to reign).

As we have already seen, many citizens left their overtaxed farms, their seemingly pointless official duties, their ravaged homesteads to move randomly over the countryside, seeking some measure of solace and security. To prevent complete social collapse, emperors felt forced to issue "stay" decrees, forbidding citizens to leave their homes, farms, or jobs. Municipal administration eventually sank to an unbelievable condition in which citizens were drafted to fill offices and forced to remain at their thankless tasks under pain of death. Such measures, originally considered emergency and temporary, came to be systematized and made permanent by Diocletian and his successor, Constantine.

Naturally, command of the army remained the emperor's first concern, for without this, administrative competence and reforms meant little. Because citizens had lost faith in the Roman world as they had long known it, they could not be relied on for the Empire's defense. In short, the hard core of imperial military might was now made up of mercenary barbarian contingents part of which were formed into a large mobile expeditionary force, whose chief business was to protect the frontiers. Detachments were used to guard the emperor and to maintain internal peace.*

The mutually agreed-upon abdication in 305 of Diocletian and Maximianus was followed by a period of violent fighting among the succeeding Augusti and their Caesar-designats. In 313 Constantine and Licinius defeated their rivals and reestablished the East-West diarchic pattern. Ten years later Licinius was forced into exile and Constantine became sole ruler of the Empire. Most of the administrative and military policies and practices initiated by Diocletian—adding up to a species of planned economy under political absolutism—were preserved by the new emperor.

But Constantine recognized that conditions required more than mere preservation of his predecessor's reforms. For many years, as we have seen, barbarians from the north and east had probed along the far-flung lines of the Empire's frontiers. Large numbers of Goths, Alemanni, Franks, Saxons, Vandals, Burgundians, and Lombards—themselves pushed by

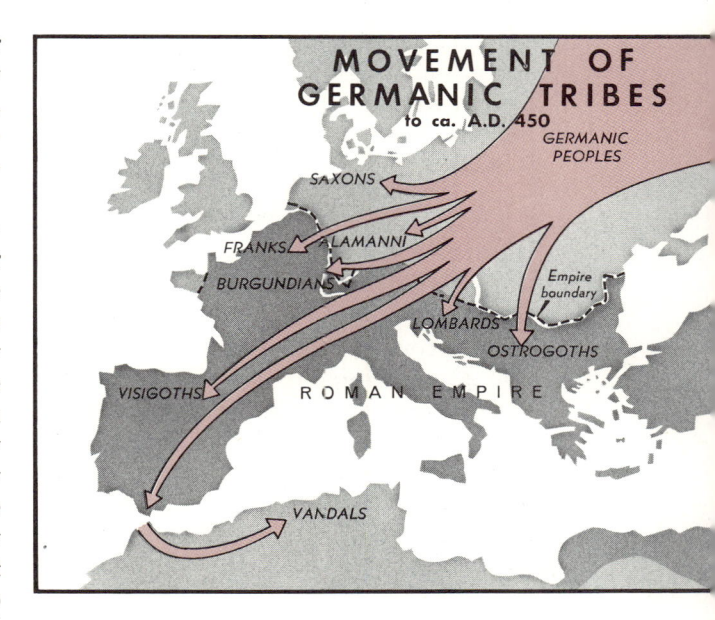

* Every Roman male citizen was still required by law to serve in the army. But the law was invoked only in emergencies or, more commonly, to raise bounty money.

MOVEMENT OF GERMANIC TRIBES to ca. A.D. 450

Eurasian tribes moving in from the east—savagely sharpened and boldly enlarged the scope of their attacks. (For the groupings and movements of the Germanic tribes see map, this page. For a more detailed account of the invasions and their influence in shaping a new society in the West, see pp. 313–316.) By Constantine's time their thrusts had become so harassing that he decided that the Empire's governmental machinery was safer in the East. Accordingly, he moved his court to the ancient Greek city of Byzantium (renamed Constantinople in 330).

Even more consequential was Constantine's acceptance of Christianity, which by then had become the dominant religion in the Western portion of the Empire. Whether the emperor's conversion was genuine or a matter of political expediency or a combination of both is debatable and, in the larger view, relatively unimportant. Far more significant was his recognition that the centuries-old bond between ruler and ruled—the mythical connection of princeps and people as it was originally established by Augustus—was irretrievably lost, and that the only available sanc-

A. The Empire

tion to replace it was the new and rapidly spreading religion. Thereafter state and church worked in ever closer union until, in 392, Christianity was made the official religion.

Weaknesses of the "Reformed" Empire

The reforms of Diocletian and Constantine unquestionably saved the Empire from falling apart in the early fourth century. They could not, however, save it from eventual collapse, for their remedies partook too closely of the diseases that they sought to cure. To combat the discontent and restiveness that result from the militarization of any society they created yet more legions. For a while these rough barbarian mercenaries secured peace, but it was a prisonlike peace wholly inconsonant with purposes that invite and enlarge humane living. Likewise, the elaborate, centrally controlled bureaucracy that mushroomed throughout the Roman world in the fourth and fifth centuries enforced municipal law and imposed internal order. But again, the kind of sanction used—fundamentally marked by exploitative and corrupt coercion—was the source of its own eventual dissolution. To meet the ever-rising costs of maintaining the burgeoning hosts of military and bureaucratic personnel, taxes were steadily increased. Since they were largely passed on to the already nearly pauperized peasantry, neither they nor the peasants had much of a future. In short, the reforms of Diocletian and Constantine, as one specialist has put it, both postponed and accelerated the Empire's collapse.

Barbarian Invasions

With Constantine's death in 337 internal dissension broke out afresh amid, of course, raids and invasions of the ubiquitous Germans. From here on the Empire went into steady and sharp decline. In 378 the Goths defeated imperial troops in the battle of Adrianople. The next year a new emperor, Theodosius (379–95), pacified the invaders by allowing them to settle within the Empire. Upon his death the Empire was divided into its western and eastern divisions; Arcadius (395–408) succeeded to power in Constantinople, and Honorius (393–424) in Rome. The latter's long term was a troubled one. The usual plots and factional struggles, while bad enough, were not the chief worry, for by this time the pressure of the German tribes was irresistible. In 410 the Visigoths, under their able chieftain Alaric, attacked Rome and looted the city for three days. Buildings and temples suffered relatively little damage, but Roman morale was crushed. In 452 a marauding army of Huns and their allies, led by Attila, again threatened Rome which somehow was reprieved by the daring intervention of Pope Leo I. In the next century Justinian (527–65) reunited the two portions of the Empire in what, presumably, he thought was a permanent settlement. It was not. Even had the reunion endured the empire would have been Byzantine, not Roman. The strength and grandeur of Rome had long since faded. Whatever the beliefs and nostalgic yearnings of Westerners of the fifth century, the Roman World had passed into history. (A more detailed account of the Germanic invasions and their influence in shaping a new society in the West is reserved for the opening section of the following chapter; the map on p. 287 is intended to convey only a general graphic sense of the "Barbarian" breakthrough into Europe.)

The Fall of Rome

The phrase "fall of Rome" has ill served many generations of undergraduate students of Roman history. It suggests a precipitate collapse, a sudden change from a sophisticated way of life to a primitive existence. Actually there was nothing sudden about the disintegration of the Roman world. It began during the reign of the illustrious Marcus Aurelius, nearly 300 years before the ousting of the last "Roman" ruler in 476 and the triumph of the "barbarian" chieftains. At times, for example in the mid-300s, rampaging violence and spreading anarchy did indeed seem to mark the end of the world that the Romans had built. But, as we have seen, strong men and strong measures periodically checked the forces of decline and decay. The path was downward to be sure, but its course was too gradual and too long to warrant any judgment connoting sudden change. As late as the fifth century some very intelligent and sensitive observers put into the historic record what we must accept as their honest evaluations of conditions, evaluations that, far from hinting of collapse, emphasized the eternality of Roman power and glory. They were wrong, but their accounts are yet further proof that the Roman world was a long time dying.

A summary view of Roman history such as ours usually ends with a consideration of the question *why* Rome "fell." Scholars agree there is no single answer; some insist that there are no satisfying multiple answers. But the question has a haunting insistence that cannot be denied. In the present study attention, from time to time, has been deliberately focused on particular decisions and developments that suggest the outlines of a judgment. Hence if the facts presented have been of sufficient scope and pertinence, if their organization has lent itself to reasonably clear understanding, and if the occasional interpretative comment has been rooted in the logic of fact, then there is no need for further consideration of the question.

It is only fair, however, to list representative samples of the more commonly argued theses. The first answer was framed by the ancients themselves. Contemporary pagans insisted that Rome fell because Romans deserted their ancient deities for the Christian God. In their view the Empire had only received the divine wrath that it had invited. Against this St. Augustine, in *The City of God*, held that anarchy, violence, and chaos had often been visited on ancient empires; and that, anyway, man's true home was heaven, not Rome. In medieval times emphasis was laid on moral decay. Still later the old pagan argument was given a new turn: the triumph of Christianity had both watered down the Roman will to conquer and rule, and had turned Roman purposes and hopes from this world to the next. At all times many have seen the collapse as merely the result of inexorable barbarian pressures. The twentieth century has added economic arguments, particularly those stressing loss of fertility of the soil, and the debasement of monies by emperors from the third century on. Another case has been made on biological grounds. From the second century B.C., this argument runs, slaves and other migrants flooded into the peninsula from all parts of the Mediterranean world, particularly from the East. Across the centuries the incidence of intermarriage rose until the native vigor of the original Roman stock had been crossbred out of existence. (The latter argument, it might be added, has little support among historians.) If Everyman, as Professor Carl Becker has affirmed, is indeed his own historian, the implicit arguments of this chapter as well as those just listed may or may not find their way into the individual reader's own assessment. But judgment of some kind is inescapable.

The Roman Legacy

In similar case is the question, what is the Roman legacy? Again, if the narrative text has served intended purposes, an extensive enumeration of Rome's contributions is supererogatory. But here too a summary review is in order. In language the debt is obvious. Almost all tongues of western Europe and the Western Hemisphere either were derived from Latin or were substantially shaped by it. Roman law is still the basis of Western jurisprudence. No less important is the idea of the world state. For hundreds of years a large portion of the human race lived under one government and one law. The memory and meaning of that experience lives in, and influences, our own day—else we are hard put to explain such a contemporary experiment as the United Nations and its forerunner, the League of Nations. A final contribution is of still greater import. The Pax Romana failed to achieve the Augustan dream. But it gave Rome time and opportunity to form itself into a cultural sponge which could and did absorb the endowments and treasures of Hellenistic civilization, treasures which in turn were passed on to the medieval world and thence to our own. However dubious one may be of the phrase "the grandeur that was Rome," these achievements stand.

B. The Christian Community

ORIGINS OF THE CHRISTIAN FAITH

Roots of Christianity

As the Augustan dream of world empire faded with passing centuries the Christian vision of another kingdom took on form and features. Rome, the city of man, ruled for a time; but the City of God would endure forever. In this faith Western civilization made a new turning.

The vital center of the new religion is Jesus Christ. But its setting and formative elements reach far back into pre-Christian times. A thousand years before Jesus a God-centered Jewish nation was founded. Yet earlier, Hebrew leaders and judges had implanted in their countrymen the conviction that Yahweh had chosen them as his people. The covenant was clear and binding: in return for abiding faithfulness, God would richly bless them and, in the fullness of time, give them custodianship of his eternal kingdom.

But the straight way of the Lord was hard to keep, and more than once his Chosen had turned from it. Invariably catastrophe had followed—dispersion of the Ten Tribes, Babylonian Captivity, Macedonian conquest and, in the last years of the pre-Christian era, seemingly endless harassment as Alexander's successors used the Holy Land as a pivotal area for imperial conquest. A climax was reached in 168 B.C. when a Seleucid emperor, Antiochus IV, outlawed Judaism. To dramatize his decree he profaned the Temple by ordering the erection within its holy precincts of an altar to Zeus. The Jewish reaction is clearly described by the writer of one of the apocryphal books of Hebrew scriptures:

In those days, arose Mattathias . . . a priest . . . [who] spoke with a loud voice [saying], Though all the nations that are under [Antiochus's] dominion obey him, and fall away every one from the religion of their fathers, and give consent to his commandments: yet will I and my sons and my brethren walk in the covenant of our fathers. God forbid that we should forsake the law and the ordinances. . . . Then many sought after justice and judgment, went down into the wilderness to dwell there: both they and their children, and their wives, and their cattle; because afflictions increased sore upon them. . . . Then came there unto [Mattathias] a company of Assideans, who were mighty men of Israel, even all such as were voluntarily devoted unto the law. Also all they that fled from persecution joined themselves unto them, and were a stay unto them. So they joined their forces, and smote sinful men in their anger and wicked men in their wrath.[22]

This Maccabean revolt, as it came to be called, was successful, regaining for the Jews not only their right to worship Yahweh but political independence as well. Unfortunately their new kings turned out to be as rapacious and godless as their foreign oppressors. In disgust and desperation a segment of the more pious Hebrews, the Assideans (or Hassidim), withdrew to the desert stretches east of Jerusalem. There, about 135 B.C., they established a number of religious communities under the rule of their own priests. Of the hopes and habits of these puritan Hebrews the newly discovered Dead Sea Scrolls have revealed much. Exilic Hebrews had been extraordinarily influenced by Persian religious ideas. So it was only natural that the Assideans came to combine strict orthodox observance of the Law with certain Zoroastrian beliefs. Among these were the struggle between the sons of light and the sons of darkness, the coming of a Right Teacher who would prepare the way for an anointed one, and a final day of judgment, when the Messiah would usher in the eternal Kingdom of God.

Apocalyptic Hopes

As a matter of fact a number of Gentiles throughout the Mediterranean world held similar apocalyptic beliefs. The times too long had been out of joint. There had been too many wars and too much wickedness. Surely the end of history was at hand when the forces of creation would rescue the elect, destroy the world, and inaugurate a reign of heavenly peace. Such hopes, however, were hard to hold to within the framework of current patterns of religious thought. For the educated, Greek philosophy had undercut these patterns; for the masses, they seemed barren and unprofitable.

Now and then from the prevailing wilderness of discontent and disillusion a voice would cry out in both warning and hope. One such was the strident call of John the Baptist (flourished ca. A.D. 25) who urgently preached the need for men to repent, against the day of the coming Kingdom. Intended for the whole world, John's Assidean-tinged message actually reached only into scattered Jewish communities. But where it was heard its impact was strong. The Lord, he declared, was interested not in elaborate liturgy but righteous living. Let those whose hearts were dark with sin repent and prepare for the coming of the Eternal Day. The substance of regeneration—inner purification—should be outwardly symbolized by the rite of baptism. But let men not wait, lest the day of the Lord overtake them before they had loosed the bonds of the Evil One. Soon bands of disciples formed to preach the word of the Baptist, spreading it west to the sea and north into Galilee. Among those quickened by the message was Jesus of Nazareth.

---

[22] 1 Macc. 2:1–44 passim.

291   B. The Christian Community

Life and Teachings of Jesus

Contemporary references to the life and import of Jesus and to the formation of primitive Christian societies are almost wholly restricted to those found in Christian scriptures. In Mark, probably the first Gospel to be written, we learn that after John the Baptist was imprisoned by Herod, Jesus went forth proclaiming, "The time has come; the Kingdom of God is upon you; repent and believe the Gospel."[23]

For however long his ministry lasted—one, two, or three years—this was its burden. Although he rarely made specific reference to Satan, the Evil One, he constantly emphasized the conflict between the true and the false, and its imminent resolution. Perhaps his many miracles of healing and of controlling the forces of nature are best understood in this light: the force of evil was great indeed, but the power of God was greater; and in the end God would prevail. This is not, of course, to imply Jesus's indifference to human want and suffering. On the contrary, his whole mission was motivated by compassion. Explicitly and implicitly he affirmed that God is love, ineffably merciful and total. Whether the Sermon on the Mount as we find it in Matthew is a summary of his teachings or a literal recording of a specific event matters little. It epitomizes Jesus's concept of the meaning of existence:

> *How blest are those who hunger and
>   thirst to see right prevail;
>   they shall be satisfied.
> How blest are those who show mercy;
>   mercy shall be shown to them.
> How blest are those whose hearts
>   are pure; they shall see God.
> How blest are the peacemakers;
>   God shall call them his sons.*

[23] From *The New English Bible,* New Testament (Oxford and Cambridge university presses, 1961), p. 58.

And again:

"You have learned that [our forefathers] were told, 'Love your neighbor, hate your enemy.' But what I tell you is this: Love your enemies and pray for your persecutors; only so can you be the children of your heavenly Father. . . . You must therefore be all goodness, just as your heavenly Father is all good."

The Lord's prayer reflects this same tension. The Father's name is to be hallowed, not Satan's. His kingdom will come, not the Evil One's. We are to seek God's help in resisting the Devil's lures: "And do not bring us to the test, But save us from the evil one."[24]

There can be little doubt that Jesus believed the end of the world at hand; that his divine mission was to proclaim the good news (that is, "Gospel") of the coming Kingdom; and that his purpose was to prepare for its advent. Theologians differ on the question whether Jesus, during his life on earth, understood that his suffering and death constituted vicarious atonement for man's sins, the reconciliation of God and man (although, of course, this soon came to be, and remains still, the cardinal truth of orthodox Christianity).

Early in his ministry he chose 12 men, the Apostles, to help him spread the good news. With them he went about the countryside preaching and performing miracles. Most of his time was spent with the common people; as the friend, as Luke has it, "of tax collectors and sinners." More than once he was chided for living too much with the wayward and lowly. Often he seemed to go out of his way to reprove men of wealth and position. Such men, we must suppose he believed, had succumbed to worldly temptations. To the

[24] Ibid., pp. 8, 10–11 passim.

rich young man who earnestly sought of him how he was to be saved, Jesus finally advised the giving away of all his wealth. On another occasion he plainly said, "How difficult it is for a rich man to enter the kingdom of heaven."

But his sharpest strictures were directed against his own religious leaders. They had become, he felt, corrupted by privilege and power, more interested in forms and legalisms than true spiritual guidance. "Ye tithe mint and cummin, and neglect the weightier matters." He likened them to gleaming coffins of death, "whited sepulchers." Naturally these leaders, drawn mostly from the *Sadducees* and *Pharisees,* viewed unfavorably such a man and such a message.

Jewish Reactions

For years the Sadducees had held high priestly offices. From them were recruited the majority of the Sanhedrin, Judah's supreme legislative and judicial body (functioning, of course, under Roman supervision). Conservative in all things, they rejected whatever was not rooted in the ages such as the doctrine of resurrection and the existence of angels. Both concepts were late in becoming a part of Jewish thought; hence both were, to them, unorthodox additions to the ancient Law. They differed from other sects, also, in holding that man possessed absolute free will. To this elite group Jesus and his teachings seemed heterodox and dangerous.

The Pharisees (and the most learned among them, the *Scribes*) were the chief spiritual leaders of the Jews. To the written Law they added tradition, and conceived themselves to be the most reliable interpreters of both. Filling the chief offices of the synagogues, they came into direct and intimate contact with the people. Modern readers of the New Testament often derive from it a somewhat distorted picture of these leaders. It is true that they often were officious and hypocritical. But unlike the Sadducees, they made genuine efforts to keep the ancient Law alive and meaningful by incorporating into or adding to it concepts and practices consonant with changing times. That they sometimes overreached themselves is undeniable. But their basic intention and function should not be overlooked, nor their courageous work in saving for their people the corpus of the Jewish faith after the destruction of Jerusalem in A.D. 70. In an effort to balance our usually one-sided view it has been argued that

The Pharisees were the only guides and teachers who had a word for the people; and they, and none other, saved from the ruin of the Jewish nation all that could be saved, and spoke to the stricken hearts of their countrymen the words of comfort and hope. The Judaism which has come down through the centuries is essentially Pharisaism.[25]

Nonetheless, the charges leveled against them by Jesus and the Gospel writers were not without substance. Often they *were* interested more in the letter of the Law than in the spirit. At the dawn of the Christian era they often *did* lack vision and nerve; and they could be unbearably stuffy.

In contrast to them was another, smaller sect called the Essenes. No mention is made of them by New Testament writers (because they were so close to the way of life preached by Jesus and his followers?). But secular sources yield some information about their beliefs and practices. For them the true faith was that proclaimed by the prophets. Long since, they believed, these had become corrupted by the doctors of the Law. Wealth and worldly power were bad per se and should be renounced in favor of the ascetic life. Prayer, work, and worship, in preparation

[25] R. T. Herford, *The Pharisees* (London: George Allen and Unwin, 1924), p. 52.

B. The Christian Community

for the Day of the Lord, almost exclusively occupied their time and directed their energies.

Except for the emphasis on asceticism, these were essentially the ideas stressed by Jesus. Within a short time his message and what were regarded as his miracles had attracted a large following; too large, as it turned out, for the Sadducees and the Pharisees. To them John the Baptist and Jesus were only two of a lengthening series of prophets who excited and agitated the Jewish people. They stirred up unrest, subverted priestly authority, and made the great Roman rulers uneasy. Especially serious was the latter concern. Many of the multitudes acclaiming Jesus clearly understood him to be the herald of the New Jerusalem. Unchecked, this subversive movement could only result in harsh Roman countermeasures.

To prevent this the Sanhedrin finally acted. Using one of the new prophet's own disciples, the betrayer Judas, the high court arrested Jesus and brought him to trial, charging blasphemy. Witnesses were brought to testify that the prisoner had made claims for himself that only God could make. As Mark relates it,

> Then the High Priest stood up in his place and questioned Jesus: "Have you no answer to the charges that these witnesses bring against you?" But he kept silence; he made no reply. Again the High Priest questioned him: "Are you the Messiah, the Son of the Blessed One?" Jesus said, "I am; and you will see the Son of Man seated on the right hand of God and coming with the clouds of heaven." Then the High Priest tore his robes and said, "Need we call further witnesses? You have heard the blasphemy. What is your opinion?" Their judgement was unanimous: that he was guilty and should be put to death.[26]

Under Roman law the Sanhedrin could not execute a sentence of death. But it could make petition to the local Roman governor, Pontius Pilate. At first Pilate, satisfied that the accused was not guilty of serious subversion, was inclined to let Jesus off with mild punishment. But the priests and officials were insistent. To pacify them Pilate acquiesced, and thus Jesus's life and ministry were brought to an end.

Collapse and Revival of the Faith

At once the movement seemed to collapse. Many of Jesus's followers had already left him after he made it clear, just before his death, that he was not interested in reestablishing the old Jewish kingdom. Others took his death as proof that the Sanhedrin had been right; another false Messiah had fooled them for a while. Even the eleven remaining Apostles were cast down—one of them, Peter, going so far as to deny he had ever known Jesus. Seemingly another subversive minor movement had had its brief hour and was no more.

But soon the Apostles and others of the disciples regained their courage and faith. For them Jesus had brought a new vision not to be dimmed. That this vision shone brightly is historically demonstrable. Without it the great risks and sufferings gladly accepted by those who, then and long after, lived by the sign of the cross cannot be explained. But what exactly this vision was, what its features and form were, no historian can say. A conjecture may run thus: Jewish understanding of the nature of Yahweh had developed, it is true, far beyond the concept of dread Sovereign—indeed, to that of kindly Father. But never before had Jews seen Godliness walking the earth, incarnate in man. They had long known what it meant to be God's Chosen People; but to be direct sharers of the Holy Spirit was as ecstatically new as it was past understanding.

[26] *The New English Bible*, op. cit., p. 87.

Moreover, the gentle love-force emanating from their teacher still moved and enthralled his followers; life could never again be the same. Finally, the crucified one was reported to have risen from his tomb and to have appeared to some of his disciples before his ascension into heaven. Like a fanned flame their spirit flared again. Exaltation replaced despair. Many of his words, ambiguous at the time he spoke them, took on startling significance.

The Son of Man is now to be given up into the power of men, and they will kill him; and three days after being killed he will rise again. . . . Heaven and earth will pass away; my words will never pass away. But about that day or that hour no one knows, not even the angels in heaven, not even the Son; only the Father. . . . Keep awake, then, for you do not know when the master of the house is coming.[27]

So the little band of believers, led by the shamed and chastened Peter, rallied their forces and their hopes. In the synagogue of Jerusalem they naturally formed a group apart. For most Jews the Messiah was still the promised one. For the disciples the Messiah had come, conquered death, ascended to heaven, and would return to establish the eternal Kingdom of God. Their task was to continue to purify themselves, call others to repentance, and generally to prepare for the Day of the Lord. Some Jews, partly persuaded by the Apostles' teachings, asked what they should do. As recorded in Acts (2:38–39) Peter was prompt and incisive in response:

Repent . . . and be baptized, every one of you, in the name of Jesus the Messiah for the forgiveness of your sins; and you will receive the gift of the Holy Spirit. For the promise is to you, and to your children, and to all who are far away, every one whom the Lord our God may call.[28]

THE SPREAD OF THE FAITH

The Work of Peter and Paul

Peter's reference to the Holy Spirit was probably prompted by the Pentecostal "miracle of tongues." On that day, as

[27] Ibid., pp. 74, 83–84.

[28] Ibid. p. 200.

295   B. The Christian Community

Peter and Paul, the two Jews probably most responsible for taking the "good news" to the Gentiles.

reported in Acts, there came to the believers "tongues like the flames of fire," which caused a great commotion among the population. Suddenly Jesus's followers seemed able, according to the writer of the book of Acts, to praise God and to prophesy in the language of many of the foreign residents of Jerusalem—Romans, Parthians, Medes, Egyptians, Arabians. In explanation of the phenomenon Peter pointed out that God had promised that a portion of his Spirit would be given to man in the last days. Jesus, past herald and present savior, had brought about the fulfillment of that promise. All who wanted to be saved could be saved. Thereupon, according to Acts (2:41), "those who accepted his word were baptized, and some three thousand were added to their number that day."

In the meantime communities of believers beyond Jerusalem had been established. To care for families of Christian hellenized Jews, seven deacons had been appointed in the home church. After one of their number, Stephen, had been stoned to death by some fanatical Pharisees, the rest fled the city. Following this scattering, numerous congregations were formed throughout the land: in Samaria, Caesarea, Joppa, certain Galilean towns, and as far north as Damascus and Antioch (see map, p. 295).

In Damascus there shortly occurred an event of special significance. One of the most vigorous of the new sect's opponents—by his own words "a Pharisee of Pharisees"—was Saul of Tarsus. He had witnessed the lynching of Stephen at Jerusalem and had busied himself harassing Christians in various cities. The congregation at Damascus attracting his attention, he set out for that city. But his plans strangely miscarried. En route to the city he was struck by a blinding vision of the risen Messiah. As later recorded, Paul (as he soon came to be called) "heard a voice speaking to him, 'Saul, Saul, why are you persecuting me?' 'Who are you, Lord?' he asked. 'I am Jesus whom you are persecuting,' was the reply. 'But stand up now and go into the city and you will there be told what you must do.'" In Damascus Paul met with Christians who baptized him, whereupon "without delay he proclaimed Jesus in the synagogue, declaring that he is the Son of God."[29]

The conversion of Paul marked a turning point in Christian history. Hitherto Gentiles had, for the most part, been excluded from the disciples' teachings. Believing that his special task was to evangelize the Roman Empire, Paul set out on a number of missionary journeys that eventually encompassed most of the Mediterranean world. Galatia, Phrygia, "Asia,"* Macedonia, Greece, Italy, and possibly Spain heard his preaching and felt the effects of his organizing genius. By the time of his death (ca. 65) the Christian church had become established in communities ranging from one end of the Great Sea to the other; and where it had originally been Jewish it was now almost wholly Gentile. Others, such as Peter and Philip, were partly responsible for this metamorphosis, but Paul was its chief agent.

Nor was this, great as it was, his only influence. For the religion that took root in the Empire was markedly different from that preached along the byways of Galilee. By his own avowal Jesus had come not to destroy the Law but to fulfill it. But for Paul the Law was of little consequence. Jesus had said "repent and be saved." To Paul repentance of sins was no longer enough. One must experience and acknowledge an abiding faith in Christ Jesus as both Messiah and Redeemer.

Again, Jesus gave not the slightest hint that he intended to found a church. Paul on the other hand not only spoke of a new church but was its principal creator. Furthermore, although Jesus several times referred to his coming death and resurrection, neither formed the crux of his message. With Paul, Christ crucified and risen became the central article of faith.

"World" Evangelism: Development and Difficulties

By the end of the first century of our era nearly 50 churches bore witness to the newer, Pauline, Christianity. In most of them exhorters, elders, and deacons preached the word and cared for the witnesses. In some, bishops presided over affairs of the congregation. By then, too, it had become apparent that the second coming of Christ was not to be expected on the morrow. Hence a closer concern came to be felt for the establishment of enduring institutions and for increased efforts to evangelize the world.

For the latter the time was ripe. Throughout the Mediterranean world, as we have seen, faith in the ancient religions had waned. Moreover the democratic hopes of ancient Greece and the yearnings of the commoners of Republican Rome lay buried under the brutalizing effects of centuries of imperialist wars and growing authoritarian Roman rule. The world thus held few allurements for the common man; his dissolving faith offered little hope for another chance beyond the grave. He was, in short, materially and spiritually prepared for the "good news" of Christianity. Since the new religion recognized the spiritual equality of the sexes, women especially were drawn to it. In addition, the willing martyrdom of many believers proved an impelling force. Few devotees of the official cults or mystery religions were ready to lay down their lives for their convic-

---

[29] *The New Testament in Modern English,* trans. J. B. Phillips (New York: The Macmillan Co., 1958), pp. 262–63.

* The reference here is to a Roman province in western Anatolia.

tions. Many Christians, beginning with St. Stephen, gladly did, causing one early Church Father to declare that "the blood of the martyrs is the seed of the church." Finally, the readiness of Christian leaders to incorporate into their creed and worship ideas from other religions, where these appeared compatible with the central message of Christianity, added an appeal for those seeking salvation yet loath to part from familiar religious habits.

The multiplication of congregations, scattered over wide areas, naturally created doctrinal and organizational problems. All Christians, it is true, believed in Jesus as Lord and Savior. But interpretations and practices were far from uniform. In Jerusalem, for example, leaders of the Church emphasized Jewish law and tradition, insisting in particular on circumcision. On the other hand many converts in Antioch were so thoroughly hellenized that the mother church felt called on to send Paul to them lest Jewish roots be lost (although, as we know, quite the opposite result occurred). Farther west, Christians, accustomed to Roman law and procedure, invested their beliefs and practices with a legalism and organizational structure quite at variance with patterns developing in Asia Minor and Palestine.

Formulation of Christian Doctrine

Even more important was the growing divergence of doctrinal beliefs, which was almost inevitable. The New Testament was not yet in existence; the only Bible these early Christians knew was the body of canonical Jewish scriptures. Necessarily the experiences of the members of the new congregations had to serve as guides to right interpretation and understanding. But since the particulars of these experiences differed from congregation to congregation, doctrinal beliefs—expressions of such experiences—naturally lacked uniformity.

One example of such variation of beliefs concerned the nature of the Savior. Certain churches in Asia Minor came to hold that Jesus was, to use theological terminology, Very God, but not Very Man. To them the Savior, that is, God, took on the appearance of earthly reality, but not its substance. This concept doubtless grew out of Gnostic doctrine. Gnosticism had developed, probably out of Zoroastrianism, some time before the advent of Jesus. Devotees of this religion believed in the existence of two worlds, the good and the evil. In their view God was, in the beginning, pure spirit and pure goodness. Desiring to share his nature, he permitted another world (or, in Gnostic phraseology, an emanation) to develop out of himself. From this second creation another evolved and then still others until our own world came into existence. But by this time God's nature, his pure spirit and goodness, had become so corrupted that the latest emanation constituted a world quite apart from its original essence. In this way, according to Gnosticism, evil was born.

Accordingly all "earth children"—physical creatures worlds removed from God—were born in sin. If they would, however, they could return to primeval goodness. The road back to God was long and difficult but possible by reasons of the existence of "the Primal Man . . . the man who existed [by God's grace] before the world, the prophet who goes through the world in various forms and finally [according to later Gnostic Christians] reveals himself in Christ." To many early Christians seeking redemption from sin by a good God, such divine knowledge (which is what "gnosticism" means) was welcome. It explained how evil could exist in the world coevally with a good God. It threw light on St. John the Evangelist's affirmation that "in the beginning was the

Word, and the Word was with God, and the Word was God."* And it clarified, for them, the redemptive role of the Savior.

Most Christians, however, found such teachings utterly unacceptable. If Christ only *seemed* to be real, that is, true man, his human suffering necessarily was unreal. It followed that atonement was likewise unreal and hence man was left in sin, unsaved. They also vigorously protested the Gnostic Christians' disregard for the Old Testament. To Gnostic Christians the latter was patently valueless since "it portrayed Yahweh as immoral, or at least amoral; for them one could choose either morality or the Jewish scriptures but not both." They chose morality, and in the place of the Old Testament they increasingly tended to substitute Paul's letters to the churches, Luke's Gospel and its supplement, the book of Acts. To non-Gnostic Christians this was cutting the vine from the roots, and they called for a cleansing in the Church to prevent "deceitful schemers" from killing the Word.

So disputes multiplied. Left unchecked, these doctrinal differences could have resulted in the complete fragmentation of the Church. On the other hand, reconciliation of contrary interpretations was quite impossible in the absence of an agreed-upon body of writings that set forth the true scheme of salvation. (Even with such, of course, varying interpretations were possible; but this is another question.) Therefore Church authorities set themselves to the task of determining what was revealed truth and what was not.

It was a difficult chore. Paul and his colleagues, it was true, had written many epistles to the early churches. But they certainly did not intend their letters to be taken as inspired scripture. Rather, they sought to admonish erring communities, point out pitfalls, sustain flagging spirits, or counteract the effects of what they considered false teachings or immoral behavior. For their part, the Gospel writers were mainly interested in committing oral Christian history and teachings to permanent written form. But churches found both letters and Gospels so useful and enlightening that they adopted the habit of reading from them at divine services. By the end of the second century this habit, combining with the necessity to combat centrifugal doctrinal tendencies, led the Church Fathers to determine which were truly inspired writings and which were not. The selection came to include thirteen Pauline letters, seven "catholic," or general, epistles, the tract called The Hebrews, the book of Revelation, the Acts of the Apostles, and accounts of the Gospel according to Matthew, Mark, Luke, and John. Confirmed by Church councils across the next 200 years, they came to be considered and called the New Testament, as divinely inspired as the Old.*

Persecution of the New Faith

In the meantime a new difficulty beset the spreading faith. So long as Christian communities were small and scattered Roman authorities paid them little heed. But already within a generation after Christ's death they had established themselves in Rome and in other metropolitan areas where they quickly attracted unfavorable attention. Almost invariably they tended to denounce this world as transitory, unreal, and evil. Naturally such a negative attitude was resented by the gen-

---

* An affirmation that identifies Jesus with God and that affirms, therefore, the preexistence of Jesus.

* Again, it is hard to avoid oversimplification. Actually, some early Christian communities preferred one or more other letters or gospels to those named above. It was not until ca. 700 that complete agreement was reached among the main body of Christians. Even as late as the sixteenth century a council of Church Fathers deemed it necessary to reaffirm the canonicity of several New Testament writings.

B. The Christian Community

eral populace. In the eyes of the latter, the Christians themselves were most unrealistic. They denied concrete facts that both experience and reason supported. They refused to cooperate in the joint enterprise of day-to-day living. And they were forever decrying enjoyment of physical satisfactions that all normal, sensible human beings sought. Moreover, they met in secret, practicing allegedly unholy and sacrilegious ceremonies. Before long the charge of cannibalism came to be leveled against them; for what was their "holy meal" but the eating of human flesh and the drinking of human blood? Finally, they categorically refused to acknowledge any lord but their own, even when officials made it plain that rejection of required "loyalty ceremonies" clearly proved dissentients to be subversive enemies of the state.

It is hardly surprising, therefore, that they soon became objects of persecution. As early as the writing of the work commonly known as the "Epistle to the Hebrews" (ca. A.D. 100) we find Christians commiserating one another and adjuring all to keep the faith.

"Remember the days gone by, when, newly enlightened, you met the challenge of great sufferings and stood firm. Some of you were abused and tormented to make a public show, while others stood loyally by those who were so treated."[30]

The "public show" may refer to the first great persecution in A.D. 64 under Nero, when the emperor, to quiet Roman mobs distraught over a great fire that destroyed much of their capital city, blamed Christians for the deed and had hundreds of them arrested. According to Tacitus they were, after their conviction,

covered with wild beasts' skins and torn to death by dogs; or they were fastened on crosses, and when the daylight failed, were burned to serve as lamps by night. Nero had offered his Gardens for the spectacle, and gave an exhibition in his Circus, mixing with the crowd in the habit of a charioteer. . . .[31]

Under Domitian (d.96) persecution seemed to center on the ranks of the so-called upper classes, some admittedly doubtful evidence pointing, for example, to the execution of two relatives of the emperor himself. The book of Revelation, probably written at this time, is almost entirely concerned with the struggle going on between Rome—"the mother of whores"—and the Church. In the second century three prominent Christian leaders, among many nameless fellow-sufferers, were martyred: Ignatius, bishop of Antioch; Polycarp, bishop of Smyrna; and Justin Martyr, one of early Christendom's profoundest philosophers. Not all Roman emperors, it is true, were active persecutors of the new faith; many were indifferent, some were backhandedly sympathetic. But the steadily growing power of the Church, the desperation of city mobs as the Empire slowly declined, and the fierce resolves of the later emperors to stamp out seditious heresy brought to Christians continuing and heightened tribulations.

Christian Apologetics

To answer mounting criticism and to blunt the thrust of growing persecution a number of Christian intellectuals began to publish explanations ("apologies") of their faith and practice. An early and typical example is Justin Martyr (ca. 100–165), who, around 150, wrote his first *Apology*. In it he explained that Christian congregations met on the first day of the week to offer thanks to God for his merciful

[30] *The New English Bible*, op. cit., p. 384.

[31] Tacitus, *The Annals*, 4 vols. (Cambridge, Mass.: Harvard University Press, Loeb Classical Library, 1937), 4:285.

bounties, to express love for each other (symbolized in the "Kiss of Love") and to confirm and enlarge their common faith. He took care to make clear that the holy meal was made up of prepared bread and water "mingled with wine." What he called the "memoirs of the apostles" were read from, together with portions of the writings of the prophets. After the offering of prayers members were asked to consider the material needs of fellow Christians. "The rich among us come to the aid of the poor, and we always stand together." The collection of offerings concluded the service after which the communicants dispersed to their homes.

Following Justin other apologists published works designed to prove their faith, combat heresies, and regularize church ceremonies. Irenaeus (125–202), Bishop of Lyons, composed a comprehensive work —*Against Heresies*—which served for centuries as a model of its kind. In it he not only pointed out which beliefs and practices were false but systematized the presentation of orthodox teachings. He made it clear that God's special grace was given to the Apostles through the laying on of hands and, through the Apostles, to the ever-renewed body of clergymen. He listed the canonical books of the New Testament and, at the same time, insisted that the Old Testament was divinely inspired and hence a basic part of Christian scriptures. Certain fundamental practices, such as baptism, were categorized and explained.

Church Organization; Petrine Doctrine

In a further effort to guard against outside attack as well as to guarantee internal harmony the early Fathers set about effecting a general order and system of Church government. Even during apostolic times, as we have seen, a nuclear organization had evolved. To instruct the faithful and to administer approved rites, *presbyters* (priests) were needed. To carry out necessary charitable functions others, called *deacons,* were called upon to serve. Over all activities some administrative agent was needed; hence arose the office of *episcopos*—"overseer," or bishop. By the middle of the second century most churches were organized in this fashion. Since bishops exercised general supervision of all church affairs they soon came to a predominant position of authority. When questions arose over correct doctrine or behavior, or when united action was needed to stand against a hostile pagan group, most Christians looked to the bishop for leadership; and most bishops readily accepted this responsibility. Later, as congregations multiplied and clustered in given areas one particular "overseer" within each area came to exercise authority over the others. For the most part these areas were closely modeled after the Roman province or diocese. Of all the provinces of the Empire, that which had Rome as its capital was regarded as the seat of ultimate authority. Quite naturally many early Christians turned to the Roman diocese—or "see," as the religious province was called—for guidance. Particularly was this true of the majority of the bishops whose dioceses were in western Europe, but also of some eastern bishops.

In addition, a particular scriptural passage gave further weight to the concept of the supremacy of the Roman bishop. In the Gospel according to Matthew (16: 18–20) Jesus said to Peter "You are Peter, the Rock; and on this rock I will build my church, and the forces of death will never overpower it. I will give you the keys of the kingdom of Heaven; and what you forbid on earth shall be forbidden in heaven, and what you allow on earth shall be allowed in heaven." Asserting that Peter had founded the Church at Rome, many bishops and other ecclesiastical officials thus held that this Apostle and his successors constituted authority to which all important religious questions must be referred for final settlement. It is true that in the early centuries other diocesan leaders disputed this dictum. And most of the Eastern churches (or Orthodox churches) came finally to repudiate it. But in the West this view prevailed and the bishop of Rome, from about the fourth century on, became the Holy Father (*papa,* that is, pope) and head of the visible Church.

Rise of Christian Monasticism

Not all Christians, however, were satisfied with this institutionalization of their faith. To them the world and its ways were pure evil. The Church, in allowing itself to become a part of the world, partook of its evil even when clearly stressing its own redemptive role. Rather what was needed, they felt, was a complete renunciation of the way of the flesh, including marriage and the gratification of sensual appetites. Christians, they argued, could not have it both ways. If earthly existence is basically a struggle between Satan and God, the true believer, by tolerating, or worse, adjusting to, the material world, in reality succumbs to Satan and forfeits his place in the Body of Christ. Only complete renunciation could bring salvation.

Very early in Christian history, therefore, some members of the faith, acting singly, practiced the ascetic life. In 285 St. Anthony gave general advice to a number of ascetics, who continued the practice of living individual, hermit lives. In the next century St. Basil, of Caesarea, established a communal order that emphasized manual labor and scriptural study rather than physical self-harassment. By this time the ascetic ideal had taken root in the West, where both individual and communal asceticism were practiced. In 529 St. Benedict made a significant and lasting contribution to this way of life. At Monte Cassino, near Naples, he set up a community dedicated to celibacy, poverty, and obedience to its leader (abbot). Thereafter the movement spread until monasteries dotted every area of western Europe.

At first the Church regarded this development with apprehension. How could the Christian flock be shepherded and enlarged if its leaders withdrew from it? Moreover most communicants were clearly unable to hold to the ideals of celibacy and poverty. On the other hand, could priests and bishops denounce a way of life practiced by Jesus and Paul (who made themselves very clear on these matters; for example, Paul: "To the unmarried and widows I say it is well for them to remain single as I do. But if they cannot exercise self-control, they should marry"; and Jesus: "You cannot serve God and Mammon.*"). Eventually a workable compromise was reached. Monastic ideals admittedly represented the highest demands of the faith. For the few men who could so live the Church would officially recognize their commitments and exercise general supervision over their communities. For the rest—the vast majority—it would continue to offer a ministry that, although looking to their ultimate salvation, demanded less of weak mortals.

TRIALS AND TRIUMPH

Continuing Threats to Christian Unity

By the fourth century Christianity had spread its faith and its institutions over most of the ancient world, steadily growing stronger as the Roman Empire declined. As we have seen, under Constantine it was given official status and support. Several generations later Theodosius made it the sole legal religion (392). From a feeble esoteric sect it had become

---

* Reference to Paul: 1 Cor. 7:8; reference to Jesus: Luke 16: 10.

an ecumenical faith. Pagan victory altars had yielded to the cross. Soon its leaders would wield more power than claimants to the imperial throne. Even so, dangers from within and without made its future not altogether certain. For many years theologians had been unable to agree, for example, on the nature of the God they worshiped. The Apostles had spoken of Father, Son, and Holy Spirit. Was God One or Three? Many (especially Eastern) ecclesiastics were inclined to hold the Second and Third persons of the Trinity as unequal in nature and power to God the Father. On the other hand, some insisted on the unhumanness of Jesus; or, in creedal language, that the Christ was Very God but not Very Man. In 325 at Nicea (near Constantinople) a great gathering of churchmen met to deal with this question. Leading the forces arguing that the Second and Third persons were inferior to the Creator was Arius, a presbyter of North Africa. Against him were arrayed Athanasius, bishop of Alexandria, and his followers, who insisted that all were of one substance—that One was Three and Three were One. Eventually the Trinitarians won the council to their position and the mystery of the Trinity became both the foundation of the orthodox creed and an important force in unifying Christian believers. But for a time the question threatened to split the Church asunder.†

Mithraism

Even more menacing than Arianism and other heretical doctrines were rival religions, especially Mithraism and Manichaeism. The former, older than Christianity, was an offshoot of Zoroastrianism. Its central figure, Mithras, was worshiped as the god whose principal mission was to overcome the leader of the sons of darkness and to bring man to a perfect understanding of the power and majesty of Ahura Mazda. By the first century B.C. a number of mystery cults, centering their worship on Mithras as the divine mediator between God and Man, flourished in the East. Several of them reached Rome at about the same time as Christianity. For well over two centuries they vied with it for popular acceptance. Like Christianity, Mithraism laid emphasis on strict moral behavior, preached a day of judgment when the good would win heaven and the evil suffer the fires of hell, and looked to a divine savior for atonement of human sins. Authorities still cannot agree on the question who borrowed from whom. But it is certain that both religions shared common observances and practices—Sunday as the holy day of the week; December 25th as the date of their savior's birth (here the evidence seems clear that Christianity borrowed from Mithraism); the use of holy water; and participation in a common sacred meal that offered sustaining grace to believers. It was probably the conversion of Constantine to Christianity that assured the latter its seal of victory over the Mithraic faith, at least at so early a date.

Manichaeism

But while one rival was entering decline, another, Manichaeism, was posing a new and even greater challenge. Like Mithraism, it was rooted in Zoroastrian sources. Born in the third century, Mani, its founder, combined certain Mesopotamian religious beliefs with those of eastern Christianity to produce a faith which, for a while, seemed destined to conquer not only the Near Orient but the West as well. Even such a Christian stalwart as St. Augustine had been a staunch Manichaean before his conversion. Indeed for a while, particularly in the fifth century, it

---

† But not all Christians then or now could accept the doctrine. Modern dissenters are called Unitarians.

303   B. The Christian Community

appeared likely that intellectuals, and the philosophically minded generally, would carry the new religion to a dominant position in the Empire. In essence Manichaeism postulated the existence of two kingdoms—the world of Light and the world of Darkness. For a time God ruled the world of Light in pure love and justice. But Satan, born of Darkness, came to envy God's world and to desire it for his evil rule. To counter Satan God created Primal Man. But the Evil One overcame the appointed savior so that God was forced to set himself directly in combat with the spirit of darkness. The god of evil was defeated, but not before the world of light had become streaked with satanic shadows. Thus mortal man is a compound of both good and evil with his ultimate salvation depending upon the thorough cleansing of himself of Satan's spirit. To help him achieve this purity God has sent inspired prophets into the world to sustain and counsel all those who would discipline themselves for such mentorship. Included among these prophets were Abraham, Noah, and Jesus. But the last and greatest was Mani, who revealed to man the full measure of salvation.

Similar to Christianity in its ethical content, and like it promising eternal life for the saved, Manichaeism attracted to itself thousands of the declining Empire's weary and distraught subjects. Outlawed by emperors, made anathema by popes, for a time it spread despite (and, like Christianity, probably in part because of) persecution. But though it lingered on, in one form or another, into the Middle Ages—Albigensianism for example, was largely shaped by it—by the eighth or ninth century Manichaeism had lost most of its followers to Christianity. The latter's special concern for the unlearned masses and the steady support given it by imperial officials probably combined with the Christian faith's intrinsic strengths to effect its victory over this and various other competitors.

Donatism

Another variation in Christian belief and practice was formed by two leaders who happened to have the same name—Donatus. Their teachings (in the 300s) were grounded in the conviction that only thoroughly pure Christians—saints on earth—should constitute the body of the Church. Otherwise, they believed, backsliders would influence others to play fast and loose with the tenets of salvation until the Church became a mere "come and get it" for pious hypocrites and weak-willed sinners. They particularly emphasized the need for priests to be saintly in their lives since, they argued, unpure priests could not validly administer the sacraments. Throughout most of the fourth century Donatism spread widely, especially in North Africa. However, under increasing pressure from Church councils and the secular power of the Constantine state, it gave way until, with the coming of the Islamic tide in the seventh century, it disappeared almost completely.

Final Triumph of Christianity

In spite, then, of persecution, serious internal differences, and rival faiths, Christianity emerged as the dominant religion of the Mediterranean world. And since it had so intimately woven itself into the religiosocial life of this world it became, when Rome fell,* the one universal institution round which the Empire's disoriented subjects could rally in their desperate struggle to survive the collapse of Western civilization. The further account of how society created and stabilized a new order under the aegis of the Church will be taken up in the next chapter.

* The reference, of course, is to the Western empire, not the Eastern (which survived for another thousand years).

Selected Readings

A. The Empire

A number of titles suggested in the bibliography for chapter 5 are useful for this chapter also, especially part 3 of Pareti, *The Ancient World;* Boak and Sinnigen; *A History of Rome to* A.D. *565;* Heichelheim and Yeo, *A History of the Roman People.*

Badian, Ernst. *Roman Imperialism in the Late Republic,* 2d ed. Ithaca, N.Y.: Cornell University Press, 1968.

> This short book of less than 100 pages is one of the most devastating accounts of human greed to be found in any library of Roman life. Almost no Roman "great" emerges great, including Cicero.

Charlesworth, Martin P. *The Roman Empire.* London: Oxford University Press, 1958.

> Into its 200 pages is packed a surprising abundance of facts touching on, among other subjects, work and taxes, the army and navy, the person and position of the emperor, education, art, and "relaxation."

Crook, John. *Law and Life of Rome.* Ithaca, N.Y.: Cornell University Press, 1967.

> Although the author takes pains to point out that his book is "not quite about Roman law" and not "quite a book about Roman social and economic life," it actually deals very interestingly with both. If you want to know what married life was like in the Rome of the late Republic and Principate, or what life meant to slaves, or how commerce was carried on, or how the machinery of law worked, or what the citizen's actual relation to the state was, this is the book to read.

Gelzer, Matthais. *The Roman Nobility.* Translated by Robin Seager. New York: Barnes & Noble, 1969.

> "A full and reliable introduction to the social and political structure of the Roman republic" is one claim the translator makes for Gelzer's classical study of the Roman world. If long use by specialists is a mark of the book's "fullness and reliability," the claim is soundly made. In any case, it seems (at least for the Republican years of the Roman world) a definitive account of the Equestrian and Senatorial orders, the concept of nobility, the function of the consuls, and relationships "based on personal connection."

Gibbon, Edward. *The Decline and Fall of the Roman Empire.* New York: Washington Square Press, 1936 (edited and abridged).

> Despite new evidence and several generations of attack, this work remains a classic exposition of the history of this fateful period.

Larsen, J. A. O. *Representative Government in Greek and Roman History.* University of California Press, 1955.

> Although a little given to the use of technical language, the author presents a readable account of provincial assemblies and how they were transformed during the late Empire period from their original modes of functioning.

Rowell, Henry Thompson. *Rome in the Augustan Age.* Norman, Okla.: University of Oklahoma Press, 1962.

> In this book of some 200 pages there are good sections on religion, morals,

ideas, city life, and Augustus's rise to power. Especially valuable for undergraduate reading is the chapter on the New Order. No other book so succinctly and satisfactorily explains the Augustan blueprint for the new "Golden Age."

Waddy, Lawrence. *Pax Romana and the World Peace.* London: Chapman & Hall, 1950.

An interpretative study of why Rome became a great ruling state and why it faltered and finally failed. The author often suggests parallels with our own times.

Use should be made of appropriate titles in the Loeb Classical Library, especially for the works of Virgil, Horace, Livy, and Ovid.

B. The Christian Community

Gough, Michael. *The Early Christians.* London: Thames and Hudson, 1961.

A brief work based in the main on archaeological evidence. After a short historical sketch of the first three centuries of Christianity, it is concerned with a consideration of the first six centuries of Christian art and architecture.

Guignebert, Charles. *Ancient, Medieval and Modern Christianity.* New Hyde Park, N.Y.: University Books, 1961.

Originally published in 1921 and 1927, this work is written from the standpoint of a non-Churchman. Orthodox Christians will find it offensive; most readers, whether Christian or not, will find it fascinating as a polemical tour de force.

Hutchinson, Paul, and Garrison, Winfred E. *Twenty Centuries of Christianity.* New York: Harcourt Brace Jovanovich, 1959.

Most of this book was written by Garrison, whose basic outlook is that of a liberal Christian. It is sound in scholarship and readable in style.

Kershner, Frederick. *Pioneers of Christian Thought.* Indianapolis: The Bobbs-Merrill Co., 1930.

One of the most useful guides through the labyrinth of early Christian theology. The author's style is lucid, his organization simple and effective, his general outlook liberal. The reader will be surprised to discover how much "heresy" has found its way into both dogma and creed of orthodox Christianity.

Loisy, Alfred. *The Birth of the Christian Religion.* Translated by L. P. Jacks. London: George Allen & Unwin, 1948.

An interesting attempt by a noted scholar to set forth the genesis and early development of Christianity without miracles and the often special pleading of the theologian-historian.

Asterisk (*) denotes paperback.

CHAPTER VII
Rome's Three Heirs: Byzantium, Western Europe, Islam

A. Background
The Christian Empire

THE MOOD OF THE LATE EMPIRE

During the three centuries following the end of the Roman imperial line in the West in 476, the Mediterranean world underwent a profound transformation. Where once a single state had encompassed the far-flung lands of the Mediterranean basin, now three distinct civilizations were established on the ruins of the old Empire. These three—Byzantium, western Europe, and Islam—differed sharply from one another in style and outlook; all had broken appreciably from the traditions of Old Rome. Yet each, although to a different degree, was a product of the Greco-Roman past. Although no longer Roman, each was deeply indebted to the legacy of classical antiquity. The rise of these three great cultures out of the seedbed of the late-Roman state is the subject of this chapter.

Intensification of Otherworldly Outlooks

Each of Rome's three heirs was animated by a powerful transcendental faith. Each, in its own way, was shaped by the intense religious experience of the late Empire itself. Accordingly, our examination of these three successor civilizations must begin with a fuller study than has been possible thus far of the Roman Empire's Christian phase, that is, of the crucial decades between Constantine's conversion and the fall of the Western empire, when Church and Caesar worked in tandem toward the Christianization of the ancient world.

As Rome grew old, the allegiance of its people gradually shifted from the traditional gods of hearth, field, and city, to potent transcendental deities of the Orient such as Isis, Mithras, and the Great Mother, who promised the priceless gifts of personal redemption and eternal life. Even in the buoyant years of the "five good emperors," imperial culture and prosperity had failed to affect a vast, wretched substratum of the population. And as the peace of the second century gave way to the turbulence and disintegration of the third, an ever-increasing portion of the Empire's inhabitants were reduced to a state of grinding poverty and futility. To men such as these the shining dreams of classical humanism—an ordered universe, an ideal republic, a good life—were cruel illusions. For them, the world was not enough, and the salvation cults became their one hope.

The older pagan cults of Jupiter, Minerva, and the other deities of the classical pantheon survived the turmoil of the third century but only in profoundly altered form. They, too, were transformed by the great transcendental upsurge of the age. For during the third century all that was vital in the traditional pagan cults was incorporated into a vast philosophical scheme known as Neoplatonism. One of the most influential philosophers of the Roman era, Plotinus, taught this doctrine of one god, infinite, unknowable, and unapproachable except through a mystical experience. Plotinus's god was the ultimate source of all things, physical and spiritual. All existence was conceived as a vast hierarchy radiating outward from God, like concentric ripples in a pond, diminishing in excellence and significance in proportion to its distance from the divine source. Human reason, which the Greeks had earlier exalted, was now reduced to impotence, for the nexus of reality was an unknowable god that lay beyond reason's scope.

Despite their mystical doctrine of monotheism, the Neoplatonists allowed a place in their system for the manifold deities of paganism. The pagan gods were interpreted as symbols of the Neoplatonic god—cruel symbols, but useful nevertheless. The pagan pantheon, so radically unsuited to the deepening mood of otherworldliness, was now galvanized and given new relevance by the overarching structure of Neoplatonic philosophy. So it was that the deities of Old Rome came to participate increasingly in the new trend toward mysticism and monotheism. The distinction between Jupiter and Mithras was steadily fading.

Christianity and the Empire

It was in this atmosphere of mysticism and the supernatural that Christianity won its final victories. By Constantine's time the age of questing rationalism and fallible, anthropomorphic deities had long passed, and with the emperor's conversion and his subsequent victory at Milvian Bridge the triumph of Christianity over its mystical rivals was all but assured.

The Christians were deeply grateful to Constantine, their first imperial convert. But had they possessed the broad, retrospective view available to the modern historian they might have expressed a kind of gratitude also toward Diocletian, their last imperial persecutor. For the ruthless, authoritarian measures by which Diocletian and Constantine revived the faltering Empire had the effect of postponing imperial collapse in the West for nearly two centuries, and the Christians put this borrowed time to good use. Indeed, Constantine's new capital of Constantinople provided the foundation for the Christian Byzantine Empire, which endured for a millennium. Had Rome collapsed at the end of the third century—had there been no experience of a Christian Roman Empire—the subsequent history of Europe, North Africa, and Western Asia would have been substantially altered.

The fourth-century empire witnessed mass conversions to Christianity under the benevolent support of Christian emperors. From a vigorous, dedicated minority sect, Christianity expanded during the fourth century to become the dominant religion of the Mediterranean world. No longer persecuted and disreputable, Christianity became official, conventional, respectable. And of course it lost much of its former spiritual force in the process. Moreover, total victory was accompanied by a new surge of internal dissension. The fourth century was an age of bitter doctrinal struggle, and here, too, the Christian emperors played a commanding role. It was only with strong imperial support that Arianism, the most powerful of the fourth-century heresies, lost its hold on the inhabitants of the empire. Theodosius I (378–95) condemned the Arians and broke their power, making orthodox Christianity the official religion of the Roman state. Indeed, Theodosius proscribed paganism itself, and the old gods of Rome, deprived of imperial sanction, gradually passed into memory.

Orthodox Christianity now dominated the empire; yet old heresies lingered on and vigorous new ones arose.* And although Arianism was dying in the empire by the late fourth century, it survived among the Germanic peoples along the frontiers. These barbarians had been converted by Arian missionaries around the middle of the century, at a time when Arianism was still strong in the empire, and the persecutions of the orthodox emperor Theodosius had no effect on the faith of the Germanic tribes. Consequently, when in time the barbarians built their successor states on the debris of the Western empire they were divided from their Roman subjects not only by culture but also by the bitter antagonisms that have traditionally separated rival versions of the Christian faith.

Christianity gained much from Constantine's conversion but it also lost much.

* See pp. 304–5.

The post-Constantine Church was less fervent, less dedicated than before; it was also less independent. For the gratitude of Christians toward Constantine almost reached the point of adulation. He was regarded as a thirteenth Apostle, as the master of all churches, as a monarch whose office was commissioned by God. His regal presence dominated the great ecumenical Council of Nicaea in 325, and it was at his bidding that the council denounced Arianism. In the decades that followed, the Arian-orthodox struggle swayed back and forth according to the inclinations of the emperors. First the Arian leaders were condemned to exile, then the orthodox, until at length, late in the fourth century, Arianism subsided under the pressure of the sternly orthodox emperor Theodosius I. Good Catholics rejoiced when Theodosius banned Arianism, but they might well have been apprehensive of a situation in which such crucial matters of faith depending upon imperial fiat.

A situation of this sort is traditionally called "caesaropapism." It arises from a political structure in which church and state are both controlled by a single individual—a "caesar-pope." Caesaropapism was a significant characteristic of the Christian Empire, and in the East it became a fundamental ingredient in the organization of the Byzantine state throughout its age-long history. For a thousand years church and state tended to merge under the encompassing authority of the emperor at Constantinople. His subjects regarded him not merely as a Caesar but as the supreme ruler of a Christian state (or rather, in the eyes of the Eastern Romans, *the* Christian state). As such, he was usually able to depend on the fervent support of his Christian subjects, and their support gave the Eastern empire the strength to endure. On the other hand, the Eastern emperor's orthodoxy evoked a spirit of uncompromising hostility in districts where heterodox views held sway.

The fusion of Christian and classical traditions is illustrated in the New Testament themes cast on the bronze doors of this fifth-century church.

The religious dissaffection of these districts—most notably Egypt and Syria—facilitated their absorption into the Arab world during the opening stages of the seventh-century Islamic conquests.

Dominant in the East, caesaropapism failed in the West. For the fifth century brought renewed turbulence and, ultimately, political catastrophe to the Western empire; Western Christians began to doubt the wisdom of placing all their hope in the imperium. Gradually they came to realize that the disintegration of the empire did not mean the end of the world or the collapse of the Church. Eastern Christians might indeed regard their empire as the Ark of Christ, but those in the West wisely refused to bind themselves to a sinking ship. Accordingly, the Western Church slowly began to assert its independence of imperial authority thereby laying the foundation for the church-state tension that became such a dominant theme in the evolution of European civilization.

THE LATIN DOCTORS

The conversion of Constantine was merely one event in the long and significant process of fusion between Christianity and Greco-Roman civilization. We have already seen this process at work among the early Christian apologists who sought to present their faith in the intellectually respectable context of Greek philosophy. The classical-Christian synthesis was carried still further by great third-century theologians such as Origen of Alexandria, who produced a masterful fusion of Christian doctrine and Platonic philosophy. The process reached its climax in the Western empire during the later fourth and early fifth centuries with the work of three Christian intellectuals, Ambrose, Jerome, and Augustine, who have come to be regarded as "Doctors of the Latin Church." Working at a time when the Christianization of the empire was proceeding apace, yet before the intellectual vigor of classical antiquity had faded, these three scholar-saints applied all the sophisticated wisdom of their fine classical educations to the elucidation of the Christian faith. Nearly seven centuries were to pass before western Europe regained the intellectual level of late Antiquity, and the writings of these three Latin Doctors therefore exerted a powerful influence on the thought of the succeeding ages.

Ambrose and Jerome

Although Ambrose, Jerome, and Augustine made their chief impact in the realm of intellectual history, all three were deeply involved in the political and ecclesiastical affairs of their day. Ambrose (ca. 340–97) was bishop of Milan, a great city of northern Italy that in the later fourth century replaced Rome as the imperial capital in the West. He was a superb administrator, a powerful orator, and a vigorous opponent of Arianism. Thoroughly grounded in the literary and philosophical traditions of Greco-Roman civilization, he enriched his Christian writings by drawing heavily on Plato, Cicero, Virgil, and other great figures of the pagan past. And as one of the first champions of ecclesiastical independence of the authority of the Christian Empire he stood at the fountainhead of the church-state controversy that was to affect western Europe for more than a millennium. For when the powerful orthodox emperor Theodosius I, massacred the rebellious inhabitants of Thessalonica, Ambrose excommunicated him from the Church of Milan, forcing Theodosius to humble himself and beg forgiveness. The emperor's public repentance set a momentous precedent for the principle of ecclesiastical supremacy in matters of faith and morals—a precedent that would not be forgotten by churchmen of later centuries.

Jerome (ca. 340–420) was the most scholarly of the three Latin Doctors. A restless, troubled man, he roamed widely through the empire, living at Rome for a time, then fleeing the worldly city to found a monastery in Bethlehem. Jerome's monks in Bethlehem devoted themselves to the copying of manuscripts, a task that was to be taken up by countless monks in centuries to come and which, in the long run, resulted in the preservation of countless works of Greco-Roman antiquity which would otherwise have vanished. The modern world owes a great debt to Jerome and his successors for performing this humble but essential labor.

Jerome himself was torn by doubts as to the propriety of a Christian immersing himself in pagan literature. On one occasion Jesus appeared to him in a dream and banished him from paradise with the words, "You are a Ciceronian, not a Christian." For a time thereafter Jerome renounced all pagan learning, but he was much too devoted to the charms of classical literature to persevere in this harsh resolve. In the end he seems to have concluded that Greco-Roman letters might properly be used in the service of the Christian faith.

Jerome's supreme achievement lay in the field of scriptural commentary and translation. It was he who produced the definitive Latin translation of the Bible from its original Hebrew and Greek—the so-called Latin Vulgate Bible, which many Catholics still use. By preparing a trustworthy Latin text of the fundamental Christian book, he made a notable contribution to the civilization of western Europe.

Augustine

Augustine of Hippo (354–430) was the towering intellect of his age. His achievements exceeded those of Ambrose, the ecclesiastical statesman, and Jerome, the scholar. For Augustine too was a statesman and a scholar, and he was a great philosopher as well. As bishop in the important North African city of Hippo he was deeply immersed in affairs of his day, and his writings were produced in response to vital contemporary issues. Augustine's thought combines profundity and immediacy—the abstract and the human. In his *Confessions* he describes his own intellectual and moral Odyssey through paganism and Manichaeism into Christian orthodoxy. He writes with the hope that others, lost as he once was, might be led by God to the spiritual haven of the Church.

Augustine wrote voluminously against the various pagan and heretical doctrines that threatened Christian orthodoxy in his age. Out of these diverse writings there emerged a lofty system of speculative thought that served as the intellectual foundation for medieval philosophy and theology. Like so many of his predecessors and contemporaries he worked toward the synthesis of classical and Christian thought, but more than any before him he succeeded in welding the two cultures into one. He was disturbed, as Jerome was, by the danger of pagan thought to the Christian soul. But, like Jerome, he concluded that although a good Christian ought not to *enjoy* pagan culture he might properly *use* it for Christian ends. Accordingly, Augustine used the philosophy of Plato and the Neoplatonists as a basis for a new and thoroughly Christian philosophical scheme. As the thirteenth-century philosopher Thomas Aquinas said, "Whenever Augustine, who was imbued with the philosophy of the Platonists, found in their teaching anything consistent with faith, he adopted it; those things which he found contrary to faith, he amended."

Thus, Augustine stressed the Platonic notion of ideas and archetypes as the models of tangible things, but instead of placing his archetypes in some abstract "heaven," as Plato did, he placed them in the mind of God. For Augustine, the Platonic archetypes were "divine ideas." These ideas constituted the highest form of reality—the only true knowledge—and the human mind had access to the archetypes through a form of God's grace which Augustine called "divine illumination." Augustine was much too good a Christian to fall into the Zoroastrian notion that matter was worthless of that the human body was evil. But by emphasizing the superiority of ideas over particulars he was led to the conclusion that the material world was less important—less real—than the spiritual world. He concluded that man's body was a prison for his soul, and that the soul's escape from its material body was the chief goal of the Christian life. And he insisted that man, corrupted by the original sin of Adam's fall, was incapable of escaping the prison of his body except through God's grace. Hence, man could not earn his own way into heaven; he was predestined to salvation or damnation by the will of God.

These and other doctrines were developed in the process of Augustine's long struggle against the heretical sects that flourished in his age. In the course of his arguments he examined many of the central problems that have occupied theologians ever since—the nature of the Trinity, the existence of evil in a world created and governed by an omnipotent God, the special power and authority of the priesthood, the compatibility of free will and predestination.

When pagan critics ascribed the Visigothic sack of Rome in 410 to Rome's desertion of her former gods, Augustine met the challenge by writing his profoundly influential *City of God** which set forth a complete Christian philosophy of history. Human development was interpreted not in economic or political terms but in moral terms. Kingdoms and empires rise, prosper, and decline according to a divine plan, ordained from the beginning, yet forever beyond human comprehension. But even though the pattern of history must always elude us, we do know this: that God is not interested in the fate of tribes and empires except insofar as they affect the destiny of individual men—that the chief business of history is the salvation of human souls. And the salvation of souls depends not on the victories of Caesar but on the grace of God. Accordingly, true history has less to do with the struggles of states than with the struggle between good and evil that rages within each state and within each soul. The human race is divided into two distinct groups not Romans and barbar-

* See p. 292.

ians as the pagan writers would have it, but those who live in God's grace and those who do not. The former are members of the "City of God," the latter belong to the "City of Evil". The two cities are hopelessly intertwined in this life, but their members will be separated at death by eternal salvation or damnation. The divine plan for human history therefore has one fundamental purpose: the growth and welfare of the City of God. As for the city of Rome, perhaps, in the long run, its decline will be beneficial—perhaps even irrelevant!

The Romans had never excelled in the realm of speculative thought, but with the Christian Augustine, Roman philosophy came into its own at last. He was the empire's greatest philosopher and, indeed, one of the two or three foremost minds in the history of Christianity. His theory of the two cities, although often simplified or reinterpreted in later generations, influenced Western thought and politics for a thousand years. His Christian Platonism dominated medieval philosophy until the mid-twelfth century and remains a signigicant theme in religious thought to this day. His distinction between the ordained priesthood and the laity has always been basic to Catholic theology. And his emphasis on divine grace and predestination was to be a crucial source of inspiration to the Protestant leaders of the sixteenth century.

As a consequence of Augustine's work, together with that of his great contemporaries, Ambrose and Jerome, Christian culture was firmly established on classical foundations. At Augustine's death in 430 the classical-Christian fusion was essentially complete. The strength of the Greco-Roman tradition that underlies medieval Christianity and Western civilization owes much to the fact that these three Latin Fathers, and others like them, found it possible to be both Christians and Ciceronians.

THE GERMANIC BARBARIANS

Fusion of Classical, Christian, and Germanic Cultures

The civilization of medieval Europe built creatively upon a synthesis of three cultures: classical, Christian, and Germanic. The age of Ambrose, Jerome, and Augustine witnessed the virtual completion of the classical-Christian synthesis, but the impact of Germanic culture had only begun to be felt. It was not until approximately the eighth century that a fusion of classical-Christian and Germanic cultures was achieved, and only then can it be said that Western civilization was born. The intervening centuries, which are often called "The Dark Ages," provide a fascinating view of a new civilization in the process of formation. Throughout these turbulent years the classical-Christian tradition was preserved and fostered by the Church, while the Germanic tradition governed the political and social organization of the barbarian successor states that rose on the ruins of the Western empire. To be sure, the barbarians quickly accepted Christianity. Yet for centuries a cultural chasm separated the Church, with its classical-Christian heritage, from the Germanic kingdoms with their primitive, warlike culture. It is true, of course, that churchmen and aristocratic laymen tended, as time went on, to be drawn from the same social milieu. The Church of the Early Middle Ages was therefore able to preserve classical culture only in a simplified and corrupted form. But nevertheless it remained the great mission of the early medieval Church to civilize and Christianize the Germanic peoples.

One should be wary of generalizing too broadly on the subject of Germanic culture, for customs and institutions varied considerably from tribe to tribe. Agrarian peoples such as the Angles, Saxons, and Franks migrated slowly, but once settled, they were difficult to drive away. These three tribes were little influenced by Roman civilization and quite untouched by Christianity when they moved into the empire. Tribes such as the Visigoths, Ostrogoths, and Vandals, on the other hand, were more mobile and more rootless. All three had been converted to Arianism before they crossed the imperial frontiers, and had long been in touch with Roman culture. But whether agrarian or nomadic, the Germanic tribes all shared a common culture, and their political and social structures disclose significant similarities and parallels.

The *Germania*, written by the Roman historian Tacitus in A.D. 98, provides a sympathetic account of early Germanic institutions that is illuminating but not altogether trustworthy. It is not a dispassionate report, but rather a work of moral indignation written for the purpose of creating an edifying contrast between the "degenerate" Romans and the simple, unspoiled barbarians.* Tacitus's descriptions of Germanic political and military institutions and social customs are invaluable, but his eulogy of Germanic virtue and chastity is overdrawn. In reality, the barbarians were at least as prone to dishonesty, lechery, and drunkenness as their Roman contemporaries—perhaps more so.

The barbarians devoted themselves chiefly to tending herds, raising crops, and fighting wars. Each tribe was divided into numerous kindred groups or clans, which protected the welfare of their members by means of blood feuds. When a man was killed his clan would avenge him by declaring a feud against the killer and his clan. Since killings were common among the hot-tempered barbarians, the blood feuds constituted a dangerous threat to tribal cohesion. In order to reduce feuds the tribes developed a system of payments, known as *wergelds*, that might be rendered by the killer to the relatives of his victim to compensate for the killing and to appease their vengeance. The size of the wergeld depended on the social status of the victim. Smaller wergelds were established for lesser injuries such as cutting off a person's arm, leg, or finger, until in time the wergeld schedules came to cover every imaginable injury. Unfortunately the offender could not always be persuaded to pay a wergeld, nor would the victim or his clan always agree to accept it. Hence, even though the laws of the later Germanic kingdoms abounded in wergeld schedules, the blood feud was never entirely eliminated.

Tacitus describes another important unit within the tribe, entirely distinct from the kindred group, which was known as the *comitatus*. It was a war band in which the warriors and their chief were bound together in an honorable brotherhood by ties of fidelity and mutual respect. The chief of the comitatus was expected to set an example for his men in courage and military prowess. The followers were expected to fight bravely at their chief's side and, if the chief should be killed in battle, to avenge him by fighting to the death if need be. The heroic martial virtues of the comitatus, so characteristic of the Germanic outlook, persisted for centuries as the ideology of the medieval warrior nobility.

The members of a Germanic tribe, although subdivided into kindred groups and war bands, were bound together into a larger, tribal unit by their allegiance to a chieftain or king and by their recognition of a common body of customary law. The laws of the barbarian tribes were childish and irrational compared with those of the Roman Empire. Legal decisions often depended on whether the parties were able to adhere precisely to complex procedural formalities. An accused man was presumed guilty unless he could prove his innocence, and in many cases innocence

* See p. 281.

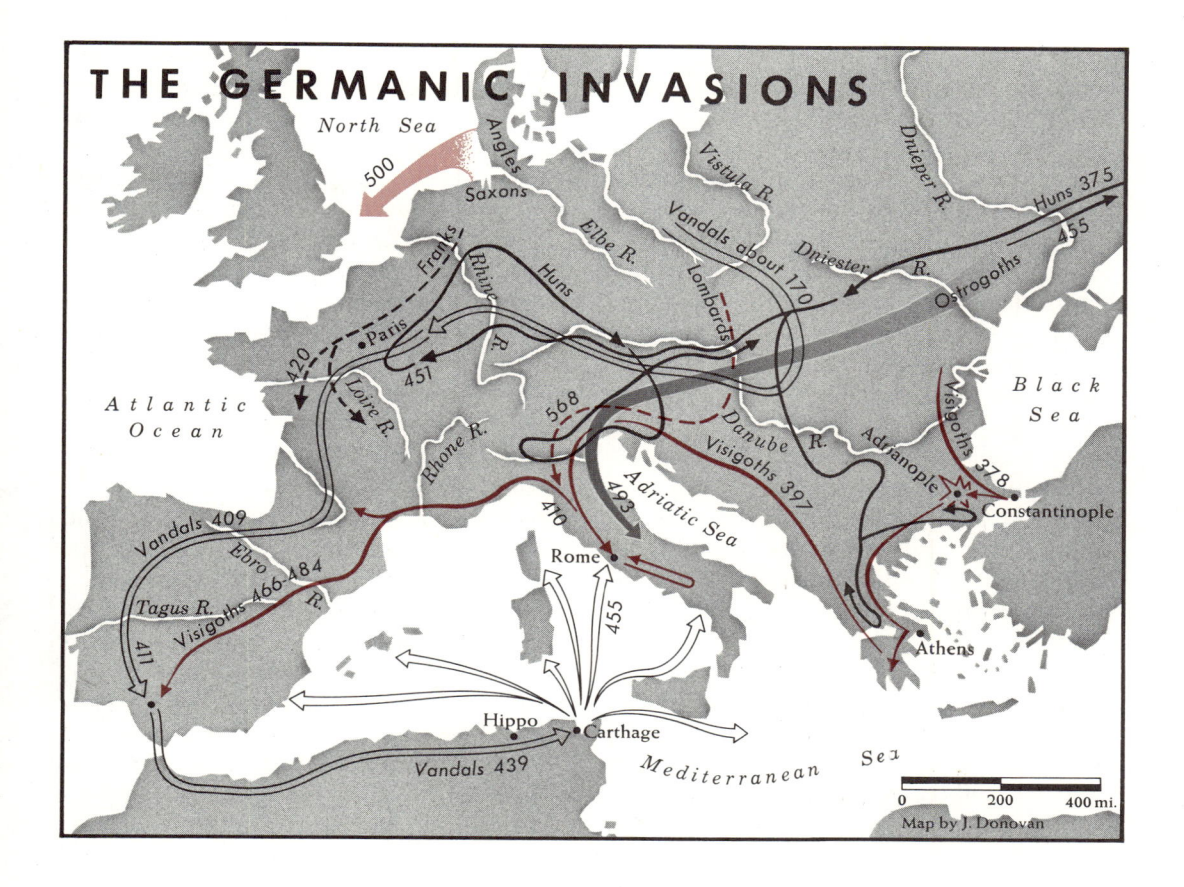

could be established only by the accused submitting to an "ordeal." He might, for example, be required to grasp a bar of red-hot iron and carry it some specified distance, or take a stone from the bottom of a boiling cauldron. If, after several days, his hand was healing properly, he was adjudged innocent. If his hand was infected, he was guilty. Similarly, he might be required to leap into a lake or pond. If he sank he was innocent; if he floated he was guilty; the pure waters would not "accept" a guilty man. Throughout the Early Middle Ages it was chiefly these Germanic customs rather than the majestic and sophisticated concepts of Roman law that governed jurisprudence in Western Europe. Roman law persisted in fragmentary or bastardized form, but not until the twelfth century did it undergo a fundamental revival in the West. And even then its victory over Germanic law was gradual and incomplete.

Yet Germanic law, crude though it was, made one crucial contribution to Western thought: implicit in the Germanic system was the concept that law arose from the immemorial customs of the people rather than from the will of the ruler. Since law transcended the royal authority, no king could be absolute. Many rulers of the Early Middle Ages put the customs of their people into writing, but few claimed the power to change old laws or create new ones. The constitutional principle of government under the law did not emerge clearly for centuries to come, but when it did appear at last, in the High Middle Ages, it was rooted in the traditions of Europe's Germanic past.

Scholars of the nineteenth century tended to dwell excessively on the seeds of constitutionalism and popular sovereignty that they thought they detected in the customs of the primitive Germanic peoples. Democracy, they suggested, originated in the German forests. Modern historians, on the other hand, have rightly stressed the prodigious gulf that separated German tribalism from Victorian constitutionalism. It should be evident that the veneration of customary "folk law" is not uniquely Germanic but is common to many primitive peoples. The significant fact is not that early Germanic kings were limited by customary law, but that the institution of limited monarchy endured and developed over the centuries of the Middle Ages.

By the time of the major fourth- and fifth-century barbarian invasions, relatively stable royal dynasties had emerged in most of the Germanic tribes. Often a dynasty must have begun with a particularly talented warrior supported by a large comitatus. But after a few generations his royal successors were claiming descent from a god. At the death of a king the assembly of a tribe normally chose as his successor the ablest member of his family. The custom of election persisted in most Germanic kingdoms well into the Middle Ages. During the fifth-century invasions it had the effect of preserving the dynasty while at the same time insuring that the tribe was led by an able warrior-king in an age when the western Roman Empire was often ruled by nincompoops.

Germanic Successor States

With the fifth-century invasions the Christian Empire came to an end in western Europe. In its place, by the century's close, a group of barbarian successor states was established. By the early years of the sixth century some of these states were beginning to achieve a degree of cohesion. Britian was then in the process of being overrun by groups of heathen Germanic peoples, known traditionally as the Angles, Saxons, and Jutes, whose conquests coalesced into several small kingdoms. Most of Spain was in the hands of the Arian Visigoths, whose kings found their power progressively eroded by a powerful, particularistic Visigothic nobility. A Vandal kingdom was established in North Africa whose Arian king and nobles made themselves hated by persecuting the indigenous orthodox Christians.

The two most powerful states in western Europe around 500 were Ostrogothic Italy and Frankish Gaul. By 493 Italy had fallen under the control of the Ostrogoths, led by an able and far-sighted king named Theodoric. The reign of Theodoric in Italy (493–526) brought peace and a degree of prosperity to the long-tormented peninsula. For although Theodoric and his people were Arians, he pursued a policy of toleration toward his indigenous orthodox subjects. Under Theodoric the Italian people began to build once again, erecting new public buildings and repairing roads and aqueducts. Indeed, the improvement in political and economic conditions gave rise to a minor intellectual revival in early sixth-century Italy that contributed significantly to the transmission of classical culture into the Middle Ages. Boethius, a competent philosopher and a high official in Theodoric's regime, produced thoughtful, original essays and Latin translations of important Greek philosophical works. These translations served as basic texts in western European schools for the next 500 years. Boethius's supreme work, *The Consolation of Philosophy*, was written at the end of his life when he had fallen from official favor and been placed in prison. This perceptive synthesis of Platonism and Stoicism, which lacks any mention of Christianity, proved to be one of the most widely read books in medieval Europe.

Boethius, shown here under the inspiration of the Muse, wrote his most famous work, The Consolation of Philosophy, *when he was imprisoned in Pavia for involvement in a plot to restore Byzantine rule to Italy.*

Another important scholar of Ostrogothic Italy was Theodoric's secretary, Cassiodorus, whose voluminous and flowery writings disclose a broad familiarity with classical culture. Cassiodorus spent the later years of his long life as abbot of a monastery named Vivarium, whose monks, following Jerome's example, devoted themselves to copying and preserving the great literary works of

EUROPE AT CLOVIS'S DEATH A.D. 511

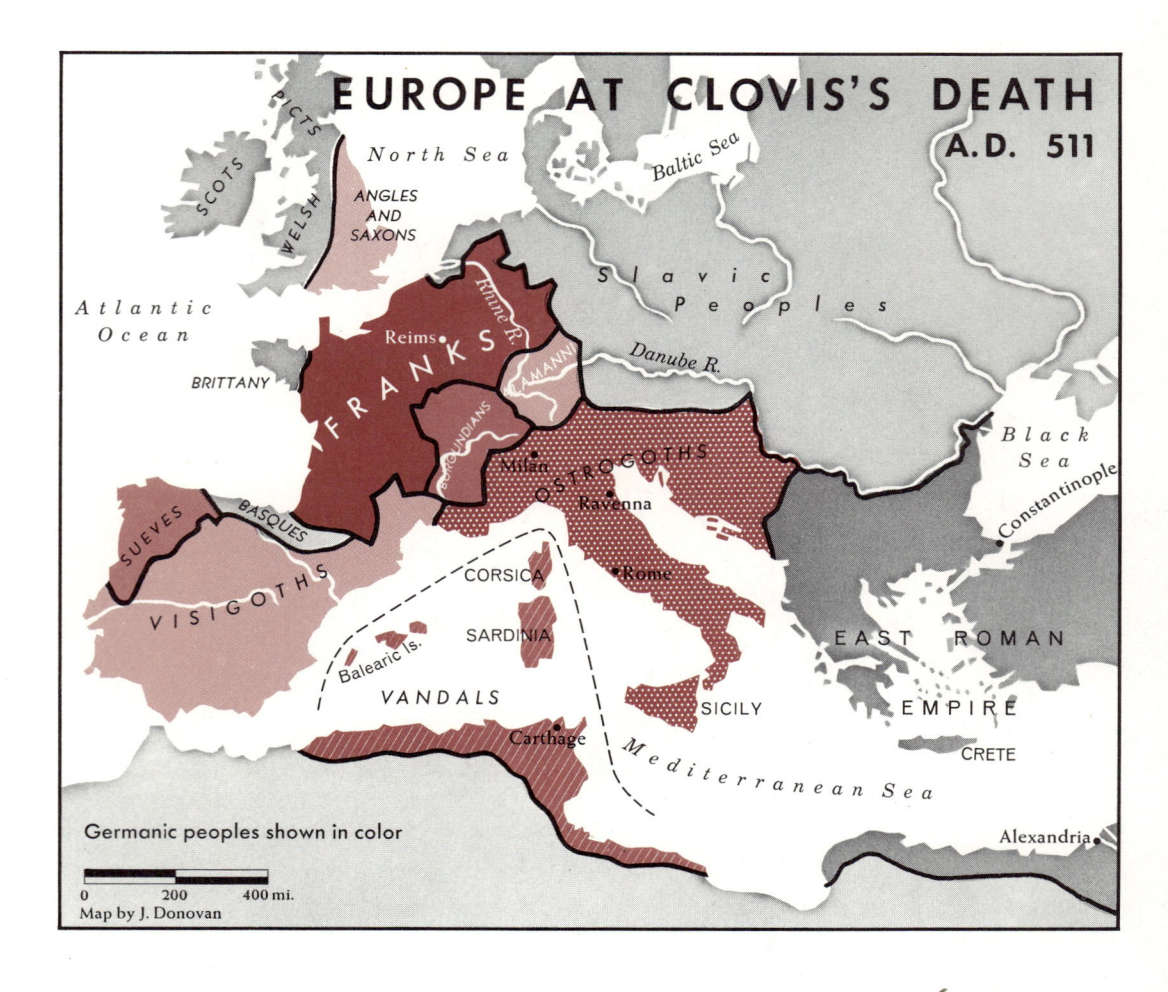

antiquity, both Christian and pagan. Cassiodorus's example was not lost on a younger contemporary of his, St. Benedict of Nursia, who stressed manuscript copying in the Benedictine monastic rule, thus inspiring countless generations of Western monks to carry on the good work.*
Frankish Gaul stands in sharp contrast to Ostrogothic Italy. Like the Ostrogoths, the Franks had a famous leader, a contemporary of Theodoric named Clovis (481–511), but whereas Theodoric was tolerant and civilized, Clovis was cruel, ruthless, and barbaric. Yet the Frankish kingdom of Gaul, conquered for the most part by Clovis, proved to be far more enduring than Ostrogothic Italy. For the Franks were good farmers as well as fierce warriors, and they established firm roots in the soil of Gaul. Clovis began his career not as an Arian but as a heathen, and in the course of his conquests he became a convert to orthodox Christianity, believing that the Christian God would aid him in his battles. The conversion of Clovis was doubtless a superficial one, yet it was enormously significant to the history of Europe. For when Clovis became a Christian his Frankish people followed him, thereby becoming the first major barbarian tribe to adopt the faith in its orthodox form. The conversion of Clovis doomed Arianism and foreshadowed the rise of

* See pp. 337–38.

Catholic France. Clovis himself remained a savage to the end of his days, but the Church came to regard him as a new Constantine and a stalwart champion of orthodoxy. With the passing of the centuries, the friendship between the Church and the Frankish crown became a fundamental and lasting element in the international political structure of medieval western Europe.

B. Byzantium

BYZANTINE STATE AND CULTURE

The Survival of the Eastern Empire At the death of Clovis in 511 the old Western empire had been transformed into a group of political fragments dominated by Germanic tribes—the Anglo-Saxon and Jutish states of Britain, Visigothic Spain, Vandal North Africa, Ostrogothic Italy, Frankish Gaul, and several smaller barbarian kingdoms. But the Eastern emperors, with their capital at Constantinople, retained control of an immense, crescent-shaped empire which girdled the eastern Mediterranean from the Balkans through Asia Minor, Syria, and Palestine, to Egypt. Why was it that the Eastern empire was able to survive the destructive forces that shattered the West?

To begin with, the Eastern empire had always been more populous than the West. It had led the Roman Empire from the beginning in industry and commerce, and its civilization was far older and more durable than that of the western provinces. Accordingly, the Western empire was considerably less devastating in the East.

Moreover, the Eastern empire enjoyed important strategic and geopolitical advantages. Its province of Asia Minor, protected from the barbarian incursions by invulnerable Constantinople, was a crucial reservoir of manpower for the East Roman army and was also a dependable source of imperial taxes. With the rich material and human resources of Asia Minor behind it, the Eastern capital at Constantinople held fast against the barbarian onslaught. This great city, dominating the passage between the Black Sea and the Mediterranean, secure behind its massive landward and seaward walls, was the economic and political heart of the Eastern empire. So long as the heart continued to beat, the empire endured. And over the centuries Constantinople's walls remained inviolate against the attacks of barbarians, Persians, and Muslims. Under the circumstances, it is quite understandable that the Germanic tribes should have preferred to carve out their states in the feebler and more vulnerable West.

It would be misleading, however, to assume that the prolonged survival of the Eastern empire was accompanied by a parallel survival of Roman civilization. The culture of classical antiquity was gradually transformed in the East, just as in the West, even though the line of Eastern emperors proceeded without significant interruption until 1453. Historians recognize this cultural transformation by giving a new name to the East Roman Empire of the Middle Ages. It is called the *Byzantine* Empire, after the Greek town of Byzantium, on whose site Constantinople was founded. When did East Roman civilization become Byzantine? There is no satisfactory answer, for the period of transition ran from the third century to the sixth, and even beyond.

Byzantine civilization represents a fusion of three elements: Roman government, Christian religion, and Greco-Oriental culture. From Rome, and most particularly from the authoritarian Empire of Diocletian and Constantine, Byzantium inherited its administrative system and its law. Byzantine autocracy was based on the political concepts of Diocletian and Constantine; Byzantine caesaropapism was a product of Constantine's Christian Empire. And the prevailing Byzantine mood, like the mood of the late Roman Empire, was one of defense—of self-preservation. To the Byzantines, their state was the ark of civilization in an ocean of barbarism—as the political embodiment of the Christian faith—and as such it had to be preserved at all costs. The appropriate virtues in such a state were entrenchment, not expansion; caution, not daring.

Bureaucrats, Armies, Heretics

This defensive, conservative mood is evident in both the Byzantine bureaucracy and the Byzantine army. The bureaucracy, huge and precedent-bound, abhorred the novel and seldom took risks. Resisting the policies of Byzantium's few vigorous and imaginative emperors, it gave cohesion to the state during the reigns of incompetents and thereby made its important contribution to the endurance of the empire. The army, small and highly trained, also clung to a policy of few risks. Its generals, often men of remarkable skill, usually pursued policies of cunning and caution. They knew only too well that the preservation of their empire might depend heavily on the survival of their armies.

The Byzantine emperors drew invaluable strength from the loyalty of their tax-ridden but fervent Christian subjects. The orthodox Christians within the empire regarded their ruler as more than a mere secular sovereign; he was God's vice-regent, the protector of the Holy Church, and as such he merited their unquestioned allegiance. Thus, Byzantine armies fought not merely for the Empire but for God. The Byzantine warrior was no mere soldier; he was a crusader. Christianity was a potent stimulus to patriotism, and the Byzantine emperors enjoyed popular support to a degree unknown in the pagan Rome of old.

But the emperor's central position in Byzantine Christianity was a source of weakness as well as of strength. Religious controversy was a matter of imperial concern, and heresy became a grave threat to the state. The fifth and sixth centuries were singularly rich in doctrinal disputes, and in the end these religious conflicts cost the empire dearly. The most widespread heresy of the age was Monophysitism, a doctrine that arose in Egypt and spread quickly into Syria and Palestine, creating a mood of hostility toward the orthodox emperors. The controversy between the orthodox and the Monophysites turned on the question whether Christ's humanity and divinity constituted two separate natures (as the orthodox said) or were fused together into one nature (Monophysitism). The Monophysite Christ possessed a single nature in which divinity tended to supersede humanity. Monophysitism has thus been seen as a step in the direction of Persian dualism—a return to the "spiritualism" of the ancient Near East, which tended to regard the physical world as evil. The dualism of evil matter versus good spirit conflicted with the orthodox Christian doctrine of God-made-flesh.

Monophysitism can also be viewed as a protest doctrine, upheld in districts that had been civilized long before the days of Roman rule, by peoples whose commitment to Greco-Roman culture was compromised by their own far older cultures. Even without Monophysitism, the inhabitants of Egypt and Syria might well have been expected to show separatist tendencies against embattled Byzantium, and Monophysitism, although far more than a mere excuse for rebellion, was nevertheless an appropriate vehicle for the antagonisms of Near Eastern peoples against a millennium of Greco-Roman domination.

The orthodox-Monophysite quarrel raged long and bitterly and constituted a dangerous threat to the unity of the Byzantine Empire. The emperors, convinced that doctrinal unity was essential to the preservation of their state, followed first one policy, then another, sometimes persecuting the Monophysites, sometimes favoring them, sometimes proposing compromise doctrinal formulas intended to satisfy everyone but in fact satisfying no one. Whatever policy the emperors might follow, the controversy remained an open wound in the body politic until the seventh century when the rich but disaffected Monophysite provinces were lost permanently to the expanding Islamic world. Only then, at the ecumenical Council of Constantinople in 680, did Byzantine orthodoxy win its definitive victory within the empire.

Byzantine Culture

Roman government, Christian religion, Greco-Oriental culture—these were the three pillars of Byzantine civilization. And all three were shaped, and to a degree transformed, by the experience of the fourth-century Christian Empire. As a consequence of that experience, Byzantium inherited Roman government in its late, authoritarian form. Byzantine Christianity was a direct outgrowth of the Christianity of the later Roman Empire—its theology tightened and defined by the Arian struggle, its priestly hierarchy overshadowed by the caesaropapism of the emperors. Just as Constantine had dominated the clergy at the Council of Nicaea in 325, so likewise did the Byzantine emperors, over the centuries, tend to dominate the patriarchs of Constantinople.

Byzantium's Greco-Oriental culture,

(Pp. 322–23) TOP, LEFT: *Sancta Sophia. This great church, converted into a mosque after the fall of Constantinople in 1453, was intended to epitomize the glory of Byzantine ecclesiastical architecture. Built between 532 and 537, it remains one of the great monuments of Justinian and Theodora. The spread of this architecture into Italy was impelled by the desire of Justinian to create ecclesiastical monuments to commemorate his rule. Among the more famous of these are the two Byzantine churches San Vitale and San Apollinare in Classe, at Ravenna, the last imperial capital of the Western empire.* BOTTOM, LEFT: *detail of mosaic from San Vitale depicting Justinian and his courtiers.* TOP, RIGHT: *section of mosaic, also from San Vitale, showing the empress Theodora and her attendants.* BOTTOM, RIGHT: *mosaic behind the altar of San Apollinare in Classe, which symbolically portrays the Transfiguration and the 12 Evangelists.*

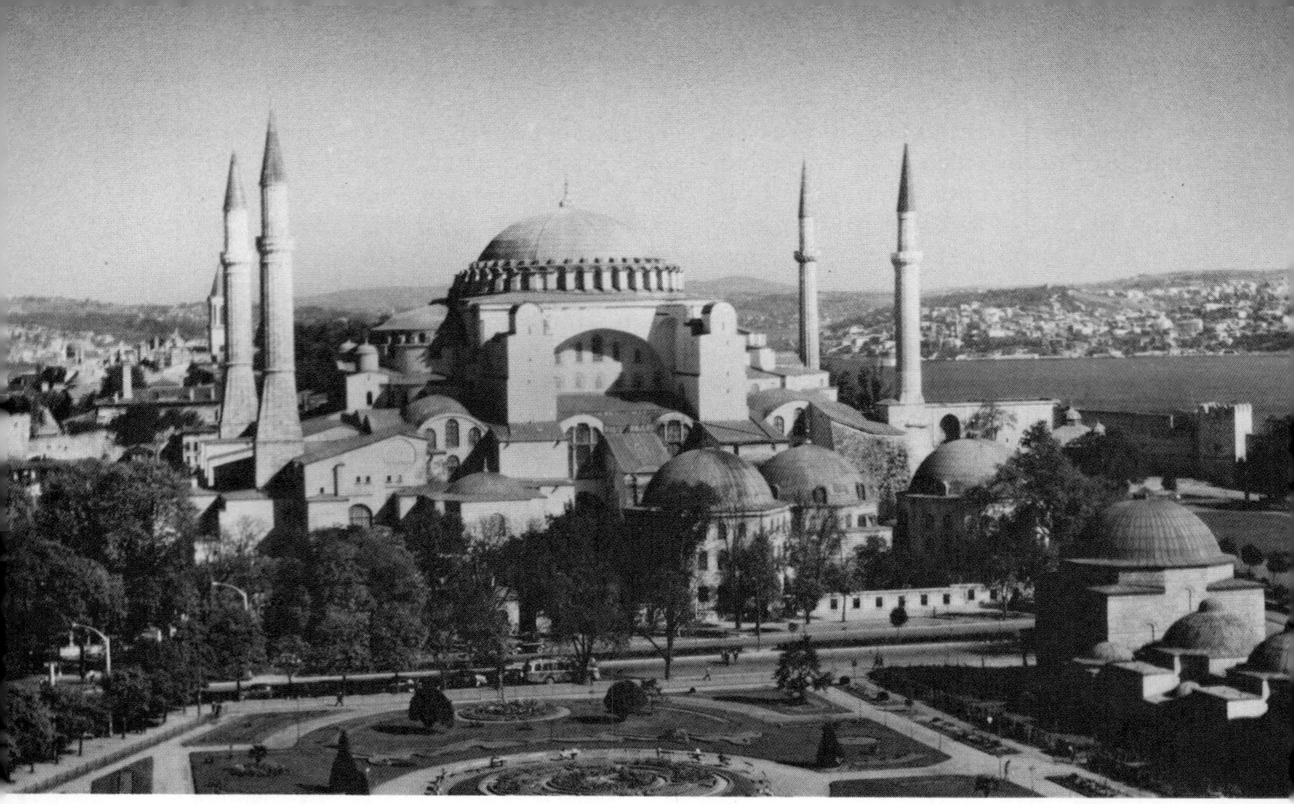

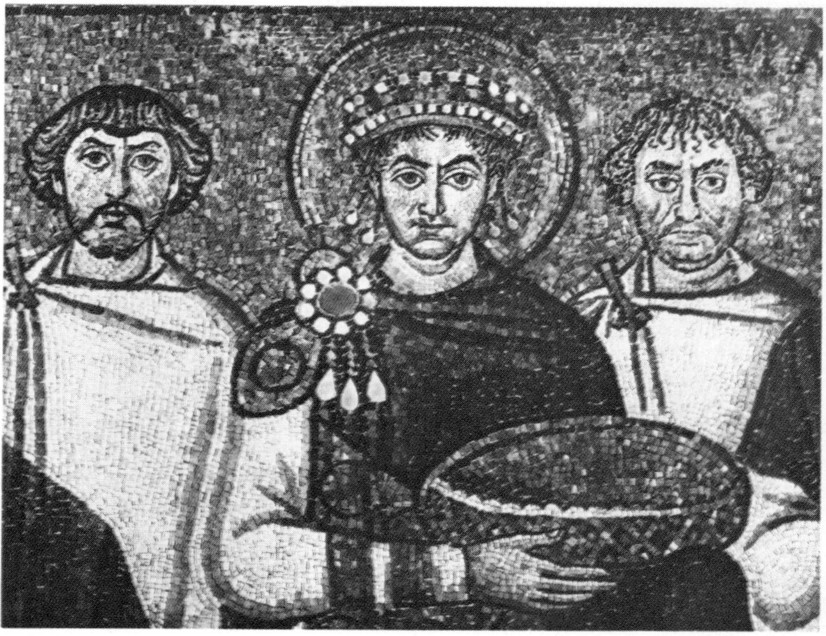

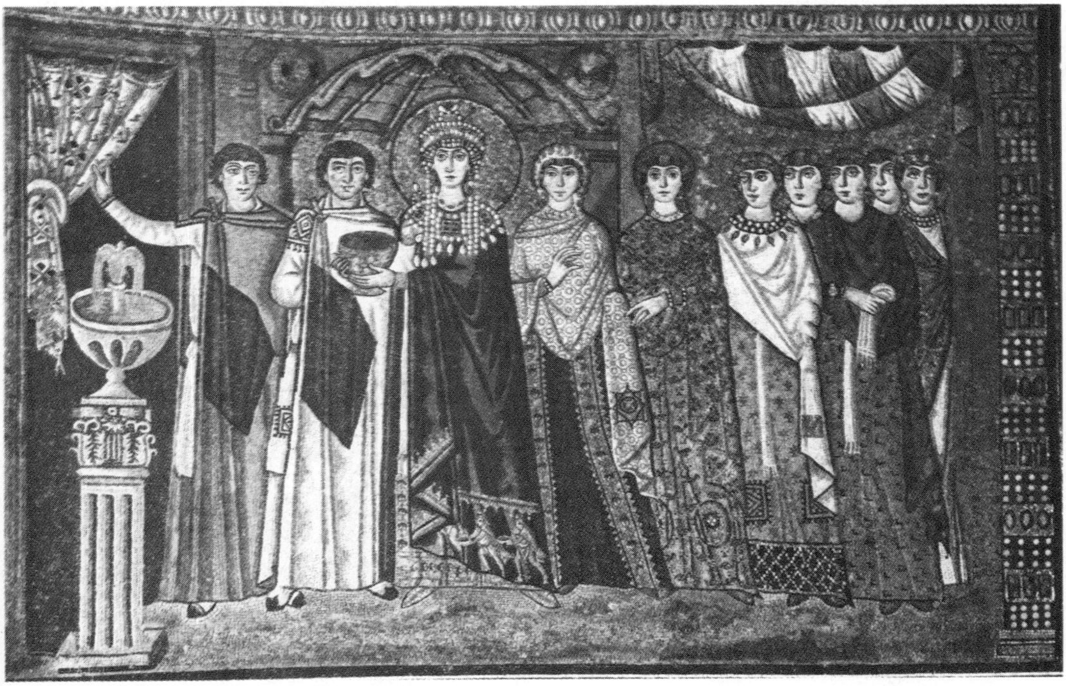

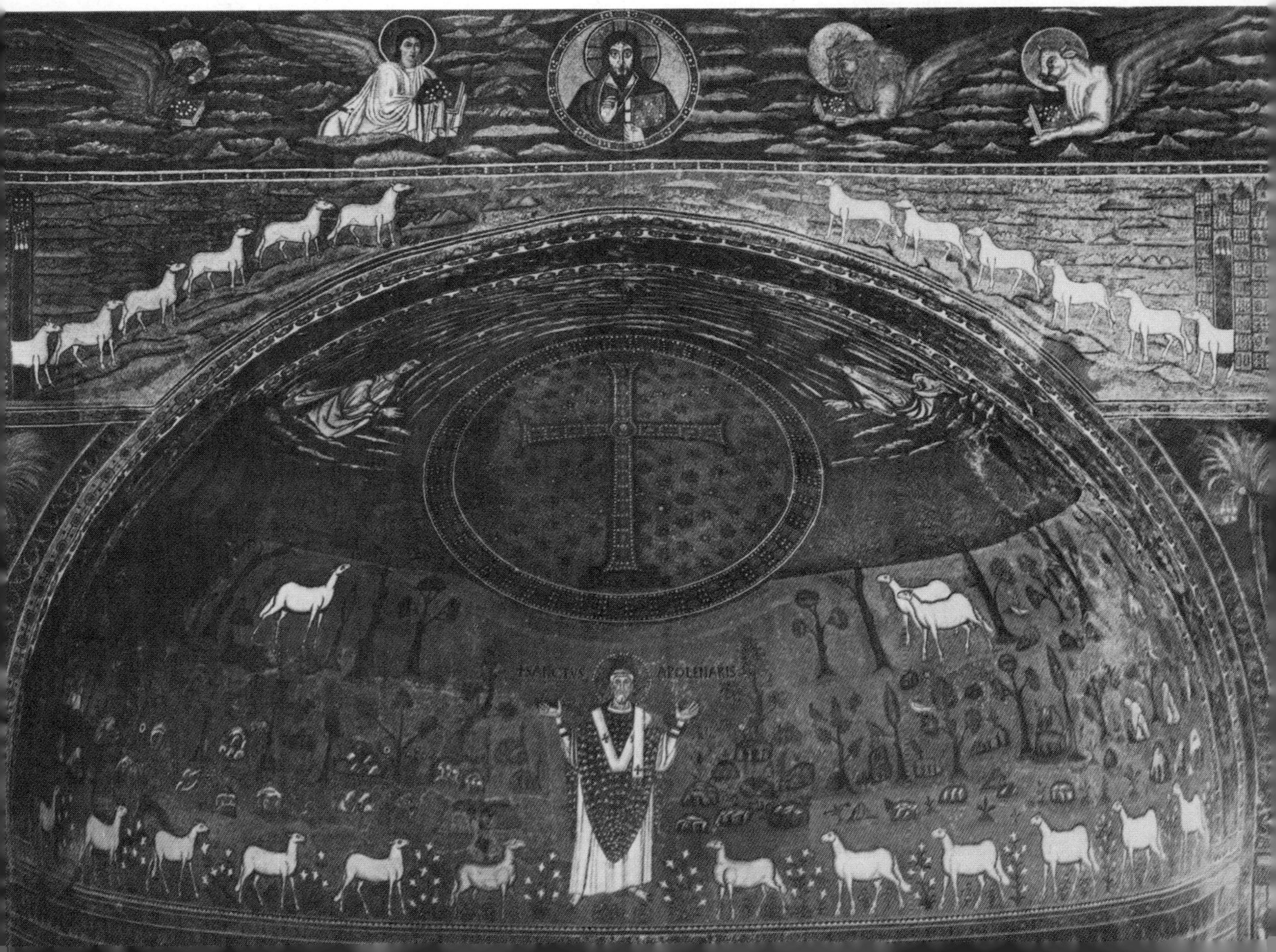
SANCTVS
APOLENARIS

too, was molded by the intellectual and cultural currents of the third, fourth, and fifth centuries. The Greek culture that Byzantium inherited was by no means the culture of Periclean Athens—with its sturdy, straightforward, superbly proportioned architecture, its deeply human drama, its bold flights into uncharted regions of speculative thought, and its controlled, tensely muscular sculpture. This tradition had undergone successive modifications in the Hellenistic age, during the Principate, and above all during the third- and fourth-century empire. The mood of otherworldliness that gradually seized Roman culture resulted in a momentous transformation of the classical spirit. There had always been a potent spiritual-mystical element in Greco-Roman culture, coexisting with the traditional classical concern with the earthly and the concrete. Now the mystical element grew far stronger. More and more of the better minds turned to religious symbolism, spiritual fulfillment, and individual salvation. Artists were less interested in portraying physical perfection, more interested in portraying sanctity. The new Christian art depicted slender, heavily robed figures with solemn faces and deep eyes. Techniques of perspective, which the artists of antiquity had developed to a fine degree, mattered less to the artists of the new age. Deemphasizing physical realism, the artist of the late empire adorned their works with rich, dazzling colors which stimulated in the beholder a sense of heavenly radiance and deep religious solemnity.

Such was the artistic tradition that By-

The extent to which the architecture of Byzantium continued to influence later generations even outside the Eastern empire may be seen in these two illustrations of the interior (p. 324) and exterior of St. Mark's, Venice. Begun in 1063, this cathedral of the Venetian patriarchs is one of the most ornate of all Byzantine churches.

zantium inherited. It conformed so perfectly to the Byzantine spirit that the artists of the Eastern empire were able to produce enduring masterpieces without ever departing far from its basic esthetic canons. Majestic churches arose in the Byzantine style—churches such as Sancta Sophia in Constantinople, St. Vitale in Ravenna, and St. Mark's in Venice—whose interiors shone with glistening mosaics portraying saints and statesmen, Christ and the Virgin, on backgrounds of gold. Here was an art vastly different from that of Greek antiquity, with different techniques and different goals, yet in its own way just as valid, just as successful, as the art of the Athenian golden age.

In the transcendental environment of Byzantium, Greek culture was significantly altered, yet Byzantine civilization remained Greek none the less. Greek was the language of most of its inhabitants, and, despite their deep commitment to the Christian faith, they never forgot their Greek heritage. Indeed, the transition from late Roman to Byzantine civilization is marked by an increasing dissociation from the Latin-Roman past and a height-

325   B. Byzantium

ened emphasis on the legacy of Hellenism. As time went on, Byzantine scholars forgot their Latin; Greek became the language of the imperial court. The Byzantine Church all but lost contact with the Roman pope. Greek philosophy and letters were studied with undying diligence by educated men who cherished their ties with the Hellenic past.

REIGN OF JUSTINIAN

Law, Art, and Religion

The first great creative surge of Byzantine civilization occurred during the reign of Justinian (527–65). In many respects Justinian stands as the last of the Roman emperors; in others, he was a Byzantine through and through. He spoke in the Latin tongue, and was haunted by the dream of reconquering the West and reviving the Roman Empire of old. It was under his direction that the vast heritage of Roman law was assembled into one coherent body. In all these respects he was a ruler in the great Roman tradition. On the other hand, his reign witnessed a Golden Age of Byzantine art and the climax of imperial autocracy and caesaropapism which typified Byzantine culture over the centuries that followed.

The spectacular achievements of Justinian's reign were a product not only of the genius of the emperor but also of the wise and cautious rule of his predecessors who endured the worst of the barbarian invasions, nurtured the financial resources of the Empire, and gradually accumulated a sizable surplus in the treasury. Justinian was also fortunate in the fact that the Germanic kingdoms of the West, which he had determined to conquer, were losing much of their early vigor. Theodoric, the great Ostrogothic king, died in 526, a year before Justinian ascended the Byzantine throne, and the Vandal monarchy of North Africa, once a cruel oppressor of its subject people, was now merely corrupt.

The opportunities were present, and Justinian was the man to seize them. He was a ruler of iron determination and boundless ambition, a prodigious administrator and organizer, and an able theologian. His tireless energy and daring represented a radical departure from Byzantine conservatism, but his vast plans, although largely successful in a limited sense, left the empire bankrupt and exhausted. He applied his theological knowledge to the difficult problem of reconciling the orthodox and the Monophysites, but his compromise formula was satisfactory to neither side. When a series of riots early in his reign resulted in the burning of much of Constantinople he lavished imperial funds on rebuilding the capital on an unprecedented scale. One product of his rebuilding program was the church of Sancta Sophia—Byzantium's greatest work of art. Gold, silver, ivory, and dazzling mosaics adorned its interior, and a vast dome seemed almost to float on air above it. The total effect was such as to stun even Justinian; he is said to have exclaimed on its completion, "Glory to God who has judged me worthy of accomplishing such a work as this! O Solomon, I have outdone thee!"

It was at Justinian's bidding that a talented group of legists set about to assemble the immense mass of legal precedents, juridical opinions, and imperial edicts that constituted the legacy of Roman law. These materials were arranged into a vast, systematic collection known as the *Corpus Juris Civilis*—the "body of civil law." Justinian's *Corpus* not only became the keystone of future Byzantine jurisprudence but also served as the vehicle in which Roman law returned to western Europe in the twelfth century to challenge the age-long domination of Germanic legal custom. The appearance of the *Corpus Juris Civilis* in the twelfth-century

West was of incalculable importance to the development of sophisticated and rational legal systems in the European states. Indeed, its effect is still very much apparent in the legal codes of modern nations. But the importance of the *Corpus Juris Civilis* extended even beyond this. In Justinian's hands, Roman law absorbed some of the autocratic flavor of the Byzantine state; in the late medieval and early modern West it became a factor in the rise of royal absolutism—a counterpoise to the limited-monarchy notions of Germanic legal tradition. The monarchs of late medieval and early modern Europe found much to admire in Justinian's precept that the highest law was the ruler's will.

The Reconquest of the West

Historians are prone to criticize Justinian for lavishing the limited resources of his empire on the chimerical policy of reconquering the West. In one sense they are quite correct: the reconquest did drain the treasury and prostrate the empire, and the victories of Justinian's western armies proved in time to be largely ephemeral. Yet Justinian, with his keen sense of the Roman imperial tradition, could not rest until he had made one all-out attempt to recover the lost western provinces and to reestablish imperial authority in the city of Rome. His armies, small but led by brilliant generals, conquered the worm-eaten Vandal kingdom of North Africa with astonishing ease in 533–54, and succeeded in wresting a long strip of the Spanish Mediterranean coast from the Visigoths. For 20 years his troops struggled against the Ostrogoths in Italy, crushing them at length in 555 but only after enormous effort and expense. The campaigns in Italy, which are known as the "Gothic Wars," devastated the Italian peninsula and left Rome itself in ruins. The Visigothic sack of 410 was nothing compared with the havoc wrought by Justinian's armies.

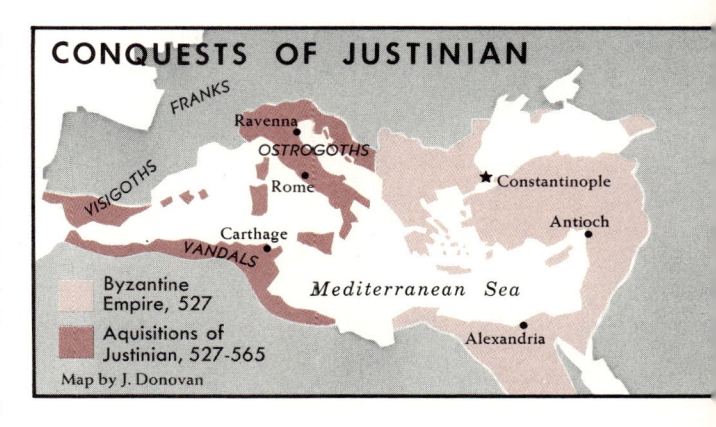

During the final decade of his reign Justinian ruled almost the entire Mediterranean coastline, but his vastly expanded empire was impoverished and bankrupt. A devastating outbreak of bubonic plague struck the empire in 541–43 and recurred sporadically over the succeeding decades, taking a fearful toll of human lives and crippling the Byzantine economy. But even without the plague Byzantium would have found it exceedingly difficult to hold its newly conquered territories. With his military attention focused westward, Justinian was powerless to prevent a great flood of Slavic peoples and Bulgars from ravaging the Balkans. When, in 561, the Avars settled on the Danube shore and proceeded to subjugate the Slavs and Bulgars, Byzantium found itself living in the shadow of a hostile and dangerous barbarian state. Justinian's greatest shortcoming was his inability to match ambitions to resources, and the huge empire that he bequeathed to his successors was exhausted and dangerously vulnerable.

RETRENCHMENT AND REVIVAL

The Loss of the West and the Crisis of Heraclius's Reign

The Byzantine Empire aspired to be Roman yet was destined by the realities of geopolitics to be Balkan and Near-Eastern. Justinian's western conquests were not enduring. In 568, three years after his death, a savage Germanic tribe known as the Lombards (Langobards, or Long Beards) burst into Italy, further devastating that troubled land and carving out an extensive kingdom in northern Italy centering on the Po Valley. Byzantium retained much of southern Italy and clung to Ravenna and other cities along the Adriatic coast, but its hold on Italy was badly shaken. Shortly afterward the Visigoths reconquered the Byzantine territories in southern Spain, and eventually, in the 690s, Byzantine North Africa—the former Vandal state—fell to the Muslims. In 751 the Lombards took Ravenna, and Byzantine power in Italy was reduced still further.

Justinian's successors were forced to abandon his ambitious policies and face the hard necessities of survival, turning their backs on the West to face more immediate threats from hostile peoples to the north and east. The Persian Empire pressed dangerously against Byzantium's eastern frontier, and the Avars, with their Bulgar and Slavic subjects, won control of most of the Balkans. The great crisis occurred during the reign of Emperor Heraclius (610–41) when Persian armies occupied Syria, Palestine, and Egypt and when, in 626, Constantinople just barely withstood a furious combined siege of Persians and Avars. Heraclius crushed the Persian army at last in 628 and recovered the lands that had been lost to Persia. He succeeded also in reestablishing imperial suzerainty over the Balkans. But no sooner had the Persians been defeated than the Muslim armies exploded out of Arabia to wrest Syria, Palestine, and Egypt from the empire and put Constantinople once again in grave danger. The Muslims besieged the city on several occasions, most notably in the great investment of 717–18, at which time the dogged Byzantine defense may have saved not only the empire but much of Eastern and Central Europe from being absorbed into the Arab world. The empire withstood the powerful northwestward thrust of Islam, retaining Constantinople, Anatolia, and an unsteady overlordship in the Balkan peninsula, thereby preserving the division of medieval western Eurasia into the three great cultures of Byzantium, Islam, and Western Christendom. The Christian kingdoms of the West were able to develop behind the shield of Constantinople's walls.

The Macedonian Emperors and the Conversion of the Slavs

Byzantium itself had won the time necessary for the gradual conquest and conversion of southeastern Europe. In the course of the seventh century it had lost such great urban cultural centers as Damascus, Alexandria, Antioch, and Carthage, with the result that the empire became far smaller and poorer, yet more homogeneous, more unified culturally, more completely centered on the one great city remaining: Constantinople. After several generations of retrenchment and consolidation Byzantium began to expand once again under the dynasty of "Macedonian" emperors (867–1056). A rich literary and artistic revival was accompanied by a series of important territorial conquests and by an evangelical surge that resulted in the conversion of countless Slavic peoples to Eastern Orthodox Christianity. Byzantium's political and religious expansion under the Macedonian emperors shaped the cultural development of Eastern Europe for the next millennium.

The Macedonians reconquered northern Syria for a time and pushed their Anatolian frontiers northeastward. But their most significant military accomplishment, in the long run, was the establishment of firm Byzantine rule over the Balkan Slavs and Bulgars. The greatest ruler of the dynasty, Basil II ("the Bulgar-slayer"; 976–1025) campaigned year after year in the Balkans demolishing a Bulgarian army in 1014 and eventually crushing all resistance to Byzantine imperial authority.

In the meantime, beginning in the middle years of the ninth century, the process of Byzantine religious conversion and acculturation among the peoples of southeastern Europe began in earnest. Missionaries such as Cyril and Methodius, "the Apostles to the Slavs," evangelized tirelessly among the south Slavs and Russians, drawing them into the orbit of Byzantine Christianity and culture. Cyril and Methodius, in the second half of the ninth century, invented the first Slavonic alphabet and employed it in the creation of a Slavic vernacular Bible and liturgy. Thus the Slavonic written language and the Slavonic Christian church came into being side by side. Ultimately, the evangelism of the Macedonian age brought the Balkans and Russia into the Orthodox church and into the sphere of Byzantine culture.

The Conversion of Russia

The age of the Macedonian emperors was concurrent with the rise of Russia— far beyond the political boundaries of the empire. Byzantium had always had economic and political interests on the northern shore of the Black Sea. In the ninth and tenth centuries trade flourished between the Black Sea and the Baltic, a trade that linked the Byzantine Empire with the vigorous commerce of the Viking world. Numerous Byzantine coin hoards dating from this era have been unearthed in Scandinavia, and Norsemen were widely employed as Byzantine mercenaries. Swedish Vikings probed deep into Russia in the ninth century and established a ruling dynasty in the Russian trading center of Novgorod, ruling over the native Slavic population and later intermarrying with it. In the tenth century a ruler of Novgorod captured the strategic Russian commercial town of Kiev, which became the nucleus of the first Russian state.

The Macedonian emperors at Constantinople took great pains to maintain warm diplomatic relations with Kievan Russia. Basil II received crucial military aid from Prince Vladimir of Kiev, having promised in return to give his own sister to Vladimir in marriage. The result of this marriage was nothing less than the conversion of Russia, Vladimir, on marrying his Byzantine princess, agreed to adopt Christianity. Kiev never submitted politically to the Byzantine emperors, but its people became spiritual subjects of the patriarch of Constantinople. In the course of the eleventh century, Kievan Russia disintegrated politically, and in the thirteenth century it was brought under the yoke of the Mongols, but its Christian-Byzantine culture survived these political disasters. In the fifteenth century, when the Byzantine Empire itself was demolished, the Christian princes of Moscow assumed the imperial title (caesar—czar). As Constantinople had been the "Second Rome," they intended Moscow to become the "Third Rome," and they asserted their dominion over both church and state much as their imperial "predecessors" at Constantinople had done. One scholar has even suggested that the present rulers of Russia, with their control of both the state and the Communist ideological apparatus, are carrying on the tradition of Byzantine caesaropapism in secularized form.

Military Disaster and Cultural Survival

The dynamisn and grandeur of the Macedonian age came to an end in the eleventh century with the passing of the Macedonian dynasty (1056) and the coming of a powerful new Asian tribe, the

Seljuk Turks. Only recently converted to Islam, the Seljuks had made a puppet of the Islamic caliph at Bagdad. In 1065 they wrested Armenia from the Byzantines, and when an imperial army attempted to drive them from Anatolia, it was annihilated at the epochal Battle of Manzikert in 1071.

Manzikert is one of the great turning points in Byzantine history. Even though the Seljuk Turks did not adequately follow up their great triumph, the disaster broke the Byzantine hold on Anatolia and thereby emasculated the empire. In the same fatal year of 1071 the Normans of southern Italy conquered the vital Byzantine Adriatic port of Bari, marking the virtual end of Byzantium's presence in the West. By now Western Christendom was acquiring the wealth and power of a great civilization, and prostrate Byzantium was forced to seek aid from the papacy and the Franks. The century of Manzikert ended with the First Crusade and the fall of Jerusalem (1099) not to Byzantine warriors but to French and Norman crusaders. Byzantium tottered on until the mid-fifteenth century, but it was never again the same. Its years of expansion were over, and its energies were thenceforth consumed in its struggle to endure.

Yet Byzantine culture survived the blow of Manzikert. Art and learning continued, and even at the very close of its long history, in 1453, Byzantium was in the midst of an impressive classical-humanist revival that made a significant impact on the Italian Renaissance.

To the end, Byzantium revered its classical heritage. As a custodian of Greco-Roman culture, the Eastern empire provided an invaluable service to the emerging civilization of western Europe. Roman law and Greek philosophy and letters were studied in Constantinople at a time when they were all but unknown in the West. The influence of Byzantine art on medieval Western Christendom was, in the words of a modern historian, "far-flung and everywhere beneficial: and whatever else the west disliked and despised about the east, its mosaics and enamels, its textiles and ivories, its pearl and onyx, its painting and its gold work were eagerly coveted and jealously guarded in western treasuries."[1]

Yet Byzantium's government was never able to transcend the stifling autocracy of the late Roman Empire or the fundamentally defensive mood that it implied. Byzantium's creative impulses were all too often stunted by its remorseless conservatism, and creative originality was less valued than the preservation of a priceless heritage.

Byzantium's lasting contribution to world history lies above all in its conversion of Russia and the Balkans. Eastern Orthodox Christianity is similar in basic doctrine to the traditional religions of western Europe, yet it differs in numerous important ways. The culture of Orthodox eastern Europe, deriving as it does from Byzantium, is more open to westernizing influences than, say, the culture of the Islamic or Hindu or Buddhist peoples. Eastern Europe today is westernized yet not fully Western. Its culture is similar, yet different; industrialized, but not fully at ease with parliamentary democracy on the Western pattern. Its historic traditions are varied and complex, but the tradition of Byzantium is not the least among them.

[1] Romily Jenkins, *Byzantium, The Imperial Centuries* (New York: Random House, Vintage Books, 1969), p. 385.

C. The West: POLITICAL, ECONOMIC, AND CULTURAL DECLINE

The ignorance and savagery of the early medieval West stand in sharp contrast to the urbanity or Byzantium. Yet western Europe had the inestimable advantage of a fresh start. It was inspired and enriched by the classical heritage, but not shackled by it.

Town and Country

In the aftermath of the Germanic invasions western Europe found itself cut adrift from the government of the Roman Empire. The Church survived to carry on much of the old classical legacy. But Germanic kings and nobles were generally incapable of preserving the political and economic institutions of the Roman past. Towns had been declining in western Europe ever since the third century; by 600 they were shrunken phantoms of what they once had been. North of the Alps the municipal governments of antiquity had disappeared without a trace. But many of the towns themselves managed to endure, after a fashion, as centers of ecclesiastical administration. They remained the headquarters of episcopal government and the sites of the bishops' cathedral churches. Many towns became important pilgrimage centers, for the more important cathedral churches possessed relics—portions of the bodies or clothing of departed saints—which were regarded as agents of spiritual and physical healing. The cathedral at Tours, for example, possessed the bones of the noted miracle-worker, St. Martin, which were said to heal any who touched them.

These episcopal centers played only a minor role in the culture and economy of the barbarian successor states. Far more important were the monastery, the peasant village, and the great farm or villa owned by some wealthy Roman or Germanic aristocrat and divided into small plots worked by semi-free tenant farmers. A small-scale luxury trade persisted, but by and large the economy of the sixth and seventh centuries was local and self-contained. Small agrarian communities produced most of their own needs, for their life was meager and their needs were few.

Except in Britian and northeastern Gaul the barbarians tended to become absorbed into the older indigenous population. Free Germanic farmers often descended into the ranks of the semi-servile *coloni*. But at the aristocratic level the pattern of life was set by the barbarian warrior nobility, and consequently the civility of the Roman villa gradually disappeared. The Roman and barbarian nobility were fused through intermarriage into one class—hard-bitten and warlike—far more Germanic then Roman.

Government; Intellectual Life

With the exception of Theodoric, the barbarian kings proved incapable of perpetuating the Roman administrative traditions which they inherited. They allowed the Roman tax system to break down; they permitted the privilege of minting coins to fall into private hands. The power and wealth of the state declined, not because the kings were generous but because they were ignorant. They lacked the slightest conception of responsible government and regarded their kingdoms as private estates to be exploited or alienated according to their whims. They made reckless gifts of land and public authority to nobles and churchmen and regarded what remained as their personal property, to be exploited for the sole purpose of their own enrichment. In brief, they succeeded in combining the worst features of anarchy and tyranny.

During the late Roman Empire western Europe had been ruthlessly overgoverned; now it was radically undergoverned. The Germanic monarchs did precisely nothing to enliven the economy or ameliorate the general impoverishment. The Church strove to fill the vacuum by dispensing charity and glamorizing the virtue of resignation, but it was ill-equipped to cope with the chaos of the barbarian West. Its organization was confined largely to the defunct towns and walled monasteries. Only gradually were rural parishes organized to meet the needs of the countryside. Not until after the eighth century did the country parish become a characteristic feature of the Western Church. In the meantime a peasant was fortunate if he saw a priest once a year. The monarchy and the Church, the two greatest landholders in the barbarian states, were better known among the peasantry as acquisitive landlords than as fountains of justice and divine grace. Rural life was harsh, brutish, and short, and the countryside was politically and spiritually adrift.

The intellectual life of the barbarian West was almost as backward as its political and economic life. The culture of old Rome was rotting, and the new civilization of western Europe had scarcely begun to develop. The intellectual level of the sixth and seventh centuries can best be appreciated by looking at a few leading scholars of the period. Bishop Gregory of Tours (d. 594), whose *History of the Franks* is our best source for the reigns of Clovis and his successors, must be counted one of the leading historians of his age. Yet Gregory's *History* is written in barbaric, ungrammatical Latin and is filled with outrageous and silly miracles. The world portrayed by Gregory of Tours was dominated by savage cruelty and naked force and beclouded by magic and superstitious fantasy. Both the story that he presents and the way in which he presents it attest to the radical decline of civilization in sixth-century Gaul.

Pope Gregory the Great (d. 604) was awarded a place alongside Ambrose, Jerome, and Augustine as one of the four Doctors of the Latin Church. But his writings, although marked by the profound practical wisdom and psychological insight of a potentially brilliant man, suffered from the cultural decadence of his age and are incomparably below the level of the fourth-century doctors in philosophical and scholarly sophistication. Pope Gregory's works had the effect of oversimplifying Augustinian theology and watering it down for the benefit of his own naive contemporaries. The lofty theological issues with which Augustine grappled are overshadowed in Pope Gregory's thought by a concentration on such secondary matters as angels, demons, and relics.

Bishop Isidore of Seville (d. 636) was known as the foremost intellectual of his generation. His most impressive work, the

Etymologies, was intended to be an encyclopedia of all knowledge. It was a valuable work for its time and was studied by many generations thereafter. But its value was vastly diminished by Isidore's lack of critical powers. He seems to have included every scrap of information that he could find, whether likely or unlikely, profound or absurd. It can perhaps be said that he was victimized by the credulity of the ancient writers on whom he depended, and left adrift by the weakness of the Roman scientific tradition. Nevertheless, as the greatest mind of his age he was astonishingly naive. On the subject of monsters, for example, he writes as follows:

The Cynocephali are so called because they have dogs' heads and their very barking betrays them as beasts rather than men. These are born in India. The Cyclopses, too, hail from India, and they are so named because they have a single eye in the midst of the forehead. . . . The Blemmyes, born in Lybia, are believed to be headless trunks, having mouth and eyes in the breast; others are born without necks, with eyes in the shoulders. . . . They say the Panotii in Sythia have ears of so large a size that they cover the whole body with them. . . . The race of the Sciopodes is said to live in Ethiopia. They have one leg apiece, and are of a marvelous swiftness, and . . . in summertime they lie on the ground on their backs and are shaded by the greatness of their feet.

Finally, in a burst of skepticism, Isidore concludes,

Other fabulous monstrosities of the human race are said to exist, but they do not; they are imaginary.

In fairness to Isidore it should be said that his treatment of monsters fails to show him to best advantage and that it was drawn from earlier materials dating from the ancient world. But he combined and synthesized these materials with an intellectual abandon typical of his age.

WESTERN EUROPE IN THE SIXTH AND SEVENTH CENTURIES

The century between 500 and 600 witnessed important changes in the political structure of Western Christendom. In 500 Theodoric's Ostrogothic regime dominated Italy, the Vandals ruled North Africa, the Visigoths governed Spain, Clovis and his Franks were conquering Gaul, and the Anglo-Saxons were beginning their settlements in Britain. A century later two of these states had been destroyed by Justinian's armies: North Africa was now Byzantine rather than Vandal, and the Ostrogothic kingdom of Italy had collapsed.

"Barbarian" Kingdoms

By 600 the Anglo-Saxon tribes had occupied much of Britain, enslaving many of the indigenous Celtic inhabitants and driving the rest into the western mountains of Wales or across the Channel to Brittany. Anglo-Saxon Britain was now a confused medley of small, independent heathen kingdoms in which the process of Christian conversion was just beginning.

Gaul in 600 was thoroughly dominated by the Franks under the cruel and incompetent successors of Clovis, founder of the *Merovingian* dynasty.* This dynasty followed the Germanic custom of dividing the kingdom among the sons of a deceased ruler. Often the sons would engage in bitter civil war until, as it sometimes happened, one of them emerged as sole

---

* Named after Clovis's half-mythical ancestor, Merovech.

monarch of the Franks. At his death, the kingdom would be divided among *his* sons, and the bitter comedy would be repeated. Merovingian government became more and more predatory and unenlightened, and the Frankish church became increasingly disorganized and corrupt.

Corruption was also paralyzing church and state in Visigothic Spain. The monarchy, which shed its Arianism and embraced Catholicism in 589, was able at length to reconquer its Mediterranean shore from feeble Byzantium (ca. 624). But the inept Visigothic kings allowed their power to slip little by little into the hands of a greedy and oppressive landed aristocracy. The worm-eaten regime was an easy prey for the conquering Moslems in the early 700s.

The century since Theodoric's reign had been a disastrous one for Italy. The horrors of Justinian's Gothic wars were followed by the invasion of the Lombards. By 600 the decimated peninsula was divided between the Byzantines in Ravenna and the south, and the Lombards in the north. The papacy, under nominal Byzantine jurisdiction, dominated the lands around Rome and sought to preserve its fragile independence by playing Lombard against Byzantine.

Creative Forces

Such was the condition of western Europe in 600. At first glance one can see little to hope for in the all-prevailing gloom. Yet this was the society out of which Western civilization was born. This was the formative epoch—the age of genesis—in which apparently minor trends would one day broaden into the powerful traditions that would govern the course of European history. Even in 600 there were glimmerings of light in the darkness. Classical culture still survived, if only in a sadly vulgarized form. Isidore of Seville was no Augustine, but he was far more than a mere barbarian. The Church, although tainted by the ignorance and corruption of its environment, still retained something of its power to inspire, to enlighten, and to civilize.

Far to the north, Ireland had been won for Christianity by St. Patrick in the fifth century; by 600 it had developed an astonishingly creative Celtic-Christian culture. Irish scholars were familiar with both Greek and Latin literature at a time when Greek was unknown elsewhere in the West. By the later seventh century Irish artists were producing magnificent manuscripts in a flowing, curvilinear Celtic style. Irish Christianity, isolated from the continental Church by the heathen Anglo-Saxon kingdoms, developed distinctive customs of its own. It was

334   Rome's Three Heirs: Byzantium, Western Europe, Islam

The spread of Celtic Christianity outward from Ireland in the sixth and seventh centuries is well illustrated by the **Lindisfarne Gospels.** *Lindisfarne was a Celtic monastic foundation in Northumbria whose monks had an enormous effect on the Christianization of northern England and Scotland.*

organized around the monastery rather than the diocese, and its leaders were abbots rather than bishops. Irish monks were famous for their learning, the austere holiness of their lives, and the vast scope of their missionary activities. They converted large portions of Scotland to their own form of Christianity and by the early 600s were conducting missionary activities on the continent itself.

Monasticism was the most dynamic and significant institution in the Early Middle Ages. The impulse toward monastic life is not peculiar to Christianity but is found in many religions—Buddhism and Judaism, to name but two. The Essenes, for example, whose cult may have produced the famous Dead Sea Scrolls, constituted a kind of Jewish monastic order. There have always been religious souls who longed to

335   C. The West

This Greco-Italian painting depicting the death of Ephraim (?) Syrus, a Syrian ecclesiastic, illustrates the Eastern origins of Christian monasticism. Around a pillar saint, monks in their cells work and pray.

withdraw from the world and devote their lives to uninterrupted communion with God, but among Christians this impulse was particularly strong. Monasticism came to be regarded as the most perfect form of Christian life—the consummate embodiment of Christ's own words: "And every man that has forsaken home, or brothers, or sisters, or father, or mother, or wife, or children, or lands for my name's sake, shall receive his reward a hundredfold, and obtain everlasting life."[2]

[2] Matt. 19: 29.

The impulse toward withdrawal and renunciation first affected Christianity in the later third century when the Egyptian St. Anthony retired to the desert to live the ascetic life of a godly hermit. In time the fame of his sanctity spread, and a colony of ascetics gathered around him to draw inspiration from his holiness. Saint Anthony thereupon organized a community of hermits who lived together but had no communication with one another, like apartment dwellers in a large American city. Similar hermit communities soon arose throughout Egypt and spread into other regions of the Empire. Hermit saints abounded in the fourth and fifth centuries. One of them, St. Simeon Stylites, achieved the necessary isolation by living atop a 60-foot pillar for thirty years, evoking widespread admiration and imitation.

In the meantime a more down-to-earth type of monasticism was developing. Beginning in early fourth-century Egypt and then expanding quickly throughout the Roman Empire, monastic communities, based on a cooperative rather than a hermit life, were attracting numerous fervent Christians who found insufficient challenge in the increasingly complacent post-Constantine Church. The holy individualism of the desert and pillar saints thus gave way to a more ordered monastic life. Still, the early communities remained loosely organized and continued to emphasize the ascetic practices of severe fastings, hair shirts, and purifying lashings, which had been pioneered by the hermits*

St. Benedict and His Rule

Benedict of Nursia (ca. 480–544) changed the course of Western monasticism, tempering its flamboyant holiness with common sense and realistic principles of organization. As a youth Benedict fled corrupt Rome and took up the hermit life in a cave near the ruins of Nero's country palace. In time word of his saintliness circulated and disciples gathered around him. As it turned out, Benedict was more than a mere ascetic; he was a man of keen psychological insight—a superb organizer who slowly learned from the varied experiences of his youth how the monastic life might best be lived. Born of a Roman aristocratic family, he brought to his task a practical genius and a sense of order and discipline that were typically Roman. He

* See pp. 303–4.

founded a number of monasteries which drew not only prospective saints but ordinary people as well—even the sons of wealthy Roman families. At length he established his great monastery of Monte Cassino atop a mountain midway between Rome and Naples. For centuries thereafter Monte Cassino was one of the chief centers of religious life in western Europe. It became a model monastery, governed by a comprehensive, practical, compassionate rule. In the midst of Justinian's Gothic Wars Benedict died, but his rule survived to inspire and transform western Europe.

Pope Gregory the Great described the Rule of St. Benedict as "conspicuous for its discretion." It provided for a busy, closely regulated life, simple but not ruthlessly ascetic. Benedictine monks were decently clothed, adequately fed, and seldom left to their own devices. Theirs was a life dedicated to God and to the attainment of personal sanctity, yet it was also a life that could be led by any dedicated Christian. It was rendered all the more attractive by the increasing brutality of the outside world. The monastic day was filled with carefully arranged activities: communal prayer, devotional reading, and work—field work, household work, manuscript copying—according to the needs of the monastery and the ability of the monk. The fundamental obligations were chastity, poverty, and obedience; the monk must be celibate; he must discard all personal possessions; he must obey his abbot. The abbot, elected by the monks for life, was unquestioned master of the monastery, but he was to consult the monks in all his decisions. He was strictly responsible to God and was instructed to govern justly in accordance with the Rule. He was cautioned not to sadden or "overdrive" his monks or give them cause for "just murmuring." Here especially is the quality of discretion to which Pope Gregory alludes and which doubtless has been the major factor in the Rule's success.

Contributions of the Benedictines

Within two centuries of Benedict's death the Rule had spread throughout Western Christendom. The result was not a vast hierarchical monastic organization but rather a host of individual, autonomous monasteries sharing a single Rule and way of life but administratively unrelated. Benedict had visualized his monasteries as spiritual sanctuaries into which pious men might withdraw from the world. But the chaotic and illiterate society of the barbarian West, desperately in need of the discipline and learning of the Benedictines, could not permit them to abdicate from secular affairs.

In reality, therefore, the Benedictines had an enormous impact on the world they renounced. Their schools produced the vast majority of literate Europeans during the Early Middle Ages. They served as a cultural bridge, transcribing and preserving the writings of Latin antiquity. They spearheaded the penetration of Christianity into the forests of heathen Germany and later into Scandinavia, Poland, and Hungary. They served as scribes and advisers to kings, and were drafted into high ecclesiastical offices. As recipients of gifts of land from pious donors over many generations they held and managed large estates which became models of intelligent agricultural organization and technological innovation. With the coming of feudalism Benedictine abbots became great vassals, responsible for political and legal administration and military recruitment over the large areas under their control. Above all, as islands of security and learning in an ocean of barbarism the Benedictine monasteries were the spiritual and intellectual centers of the developing classical-Christian-Germanic synthesis that underlay European civilization. To put it briefly, the activities of the Benedictine monks exerted a crucial influence on the civilizing of the barbarian West.

The Benedictines carried out their civilizing mission with the enthusiastic and invaluable support of the papacy. The alliance between these two institutions was consummated by the first Benedictines pope, Gregory the Great, who recognized immediately how effective the Benedictines might be in spreading the Catholic faith and extending papal leadership far and wide across Christendom.

We have already encountered Pope Gregory as a Dark Age scholar—a popularizer of Augustinian thought. His theology, although highly influential in subsequent centuries, failed to rise much above the intellectual level of his age. His real genius lay in his keen understanding of human nature and his ability as an administrator and organizer. His *Pastoral Care,* a treatise on the duties and obligations of a bishop, is a masterpiece of practical wisdom and common sense. It answered a great need of the times and became one of the most widely read books in the Middle Ages.

Gregory loved the monastic life and ascended the papal throne with genuine regret. On hearing of his election he went into hiding and had to be dragged into the Basilica of St. Peter to be consecrated. But once resigned to his new responsibilities, Gregory bent every energy to the extension of papal authority. He believed fervently that the pope, as successor of Peter, was the rightful ruler of the Church. He reorganized the financial structure of the papal estates and used the increased revenues for charitable works to ameliorate the wretched poverty of his age. His integrity, wisdom, and administrative ability won for him an almost regal position in Rome and central Italy, towering over the contemporary Lombards and Byzantines who were then struggling for control of the peninsula. The reform of the Frankish church was beyond his immediate powers. But he set in motion a process that would one day bring both France and Germany into the papal fold when he dispatched a group of Benedictine monks to convert heathen England.

The mission to England was led by the Benedictine St. Augustine (not to be confused with the great theologian and saint of an earlier day, Augustine of Hippo). In 597 Augustine and his followers arrived in the English kingdom of Kent and began their momentous work. England was then divided into a number of independent barbarian kingdoms of which Kent was momentarily the most powerful, and Augustine was assured a friendly reception by the fact that King Ethelbert of Kent had a Christian wife. The conversion progressed speedily, and on Whitsunday, 597, King Ethelbert and thousands of his subjects were baptized. The chief town of the realm—"Kent City," or Canterbury—became the headquarters of the new church, and Augustine himself became Canterbury's first archbishop.

During the decades that followed, the fortunes of English Benedictine Christianity rose and fell with the varying fortunes of the barbarian kingdoms. Kent declined after King Ethelbert's death, and by the mid-600s political power had shifted to the northernmost of the Anglo-Saxon states, Northumbria. This remote outpost became the scene of a deeply significant encounter between the two great creative forces of the age: Irish-Celtic Christianity moving southward from its monasteries in Scotland, and Roman-Benedictine Christianity moving northward from Kent.

Although the two movements shared a common faith, they had different cultural backgrounds, different notions of monastic life and ecclesiastical organization, and even different systems for calculating the date of Easter. At stake was England's future relationship with the continent and the papacy; a Celtic victory might well have resulted in the isolation of England from the main course of Western Christian development. But at the Synod of Whitby in 664, King Oswy of Northumbia decided in favor of Roman-Benedictine Christianity, and papal influence in England was assured. Five years later, in 669, the papacy sent the scholarly Theodore of Tarsus to assume the archbishop of Canterbury and reorganize the English church into a coherent hierarchical system. As a consequence of Northumbria's conversion and Archbishop Theodore's tireless efforts, England, only a century out of heathenism, became Europe's most vigorous and creative Christian society.

The Irish-Benedictine encounter in seventh-century Northumbria produced a significant cultural surge known as the Northumbrian Renaissance. The two traditions influenced and inspired one another to such an extent that the evolving civilization of the barbarian West reached its pinnacle in this remote land. Boldly executed illuminated manuscripts in the Celtic curvilinear style, a new script, a vigorous vernacular epic poetry, an impressive architecture—all contributed to the luster of Northumbrian civilization in the late 600s and the early 700s. This Northumbrian Renaissance centered in the great monasteries founded by Irish and Benedictine missionaries, particularly in the Benedictine monastery of Jarrow. Here the supreme scholar of the age, St. Bede the Venerable, spent his life.

Bede entered Jarrow as a child and remained there until his death in 735. The greatest of his many works, the *Ecclesiastical History of England,* displays a keen critical sense far superior to that of Bede's medieval predecessors and contemporaries. The *Ecclesiastical History,* our chief source for early English history, is the first major historical work to employ the modern chronological framework based on the Christian era (A.D.—Anno Domini). And Bede's chronological innovation reflects his deep sense of historical unity and purpose: the transformation of the world—particularly of England—through the spread of the Christian gospel and the monastic life. The *Ecclesiastical*

History reflects a remarkable cultural breadth and a penetrating mind and establishes Bede as the foremost Christian intellectual since Augustine.

By Bede's death in 735 the Northumbrian kings lost their political hegemony, and Northumbrian culture was beginning to fade. But the tradition of learning was carried from England back to the continent during the eighth century by a group of Anglo-Saxon Benedictine missionaries. In the 740s the English monk St. Boniface reformed the church in Frankland, infusing it with Benedictine idealism and binding it more closely to the papacy. Pope Gregory had now been in his grave for 140 years, but his spirit was still at work. St. Boniface and other English missionaries founded new Benedictine monasteries among the Germans east of the Rhine and began the long, difficult task of Christianizing and civilizing these savage peoples, just as Augustine and his monks had once Christianized heathen Kent. By the later 700s the cultural center of Christendom had shifted southward again from England to the rapidly rising empire of the Frankish leader Charlemagne, whose career will be traced in the next chapter. Significantly, the leading scholar in Charlemagne's kingdom was Alcuin, a Benedictine monk from Northumbria, a student of one of Bede's own disciples.

The Church and Western Civilization

The barbarian West differed from the Byzantine East in innumerable ways, the most obvious being its far lower level of civilization. But equally important is the fact that the Western Church was able to reject Byzantine caesaropapism and to develop more or less independently of the state. Church and state often worked hand in hand, yet the two were never merged as they were in Constantinople and, indeed, in most ancient civilizations. The early Christian West was marked by a profound dichotomy—a separation between cultural leadership which was ecclesiastical and monastic, and political power which was in the hands of the barbarian kings. This dualism underlay the fluidity and dynamism of Western culture. It produced a creative tension which tended toward change rather than crystallization, toward an uninterrupted series of cultural climaxes, and toward ever-new intellectual and spiritual configurations. Like Augustine's two cities, the heroic warrior culture of the Germanic states and the classical-Christian culture of church and monastery remained always in the process of fusion yet never completely fused. The interplay between these two worlds governed the development of medieval civilization.

D. Islam

BACKGROUND AND ORIGINS

Islam, Byzantium, and Western Christendom were Rome's three heirs, and of the three, Western Christendom remained for many centuries the most primitive and underdeveloped. Medieval Europe had much to learn from Islam and Byzantium, and its developing synthesis of classical, Christian, and Germanic traditions was shaped in many ways by its two neighboring civilizations. The influence of these neighbors was impeded, however, by Europe's profound hostility toward the "infidel" Muslims and the "effete, treacherous" Byzantines. In the eighth and ninth centuries western Europe's contacts with Islam were limited largely to the battlefield. Only after the turn of the millennium did the West begin to draw on the rich legacy of Muslim thought and culture.

Islam today is a distinctive culture and a living religion extending across an immense area in South Asia, the Middle East, and north Africa—from Indonesia to Pakistan to the Arab world of southwest Asia and Mediterranean Africa. This vast Islamic belt was created by a militant, compelling religion that burst into the world in seventh-century Arabia and spread outward with remarkable speed. In the first hundred years of its existence it shattered the Christian domination of the Mediterranean Basin, destroyed the Persian Empire, seized Byzantine's richest provinces, absorbed Spain, pressed deep into France, and expanded far into Southern Asia.

Arabian Setting; Muhammad

For countless centuries prior to the time of the prophet Muhammad (ca. 571–632), fierce nomadic tribes from the Arabian Peninsula (the modern Saudi Arabia) had repeatedly invaded the rich civilized districts of Palestine, Syria, and Mesopotamia to the north. As we noted in a previous chapter, many Semitic invaders of the Ancient Near East came originally from the Arabian Desert—the Amorites, the Chaldeans, the Canaanites, even the Hebrews.* These peoples quickly assimilated the ancient civilization of the Fertile Crescent and developed it in new, creative ways. But their kinsmen who stayed in Arabia remained primitive and disorganized.

In Muhammad's time most Arabians still clung to their nomadic ways and to their crude, polytheistic religion, but by then new civilizing influences were beginning to make themselves felt. A great caravan route running northward from southern Arabia served as an important link in a far-flung commercial network between the Far East and the Byzantine and Persian empires. Along this route cities developed to serve the caravans, and with city life came a modicum of civilization. Indeed, the greatest of these trading cities, Mecca, became a bustling commercial center which sent its own caravans northward and southward and grew wealthy on its middleman profits. As the tribal life of Mecca and other caravan cities began to give way to commercial life, new, foreign ideas challenged old ways and old viewpoints. It was in Mecca, around the year 571, that the prophet Muhammad was born.

At Muhammad's birth Emperor Justinian had been dead for six years. Muhammad's contemporaries include such men as Pope Gregory the Great and Bishop Isidore of Seville. When the Benedictine mission from Rome landed in Kent in 597 to begin the conversion of England, Muhammad was in his twenties, as yet quite unknown outside his own immediate circle.

The future architect of one of the world's great religions was born of a poor branch of Mecca's leading clan. With little formal education behind him, he became a caravan trader; as such, his travels brought him into close contact with Judaism, Christianity, and Persian Zoroastrianism. A high-strung, sensitive man with a powerful, winning personality, he underwent a mystical experience while in his late thirties and began to set forth his new faith by preaching and writing. He won little support in Mecca apart from his wife and relatives and a few converts from the underprivileged classes. The ruling businessmen of Mecca seemed immune to the teaching this low-born upstart. Perhaps they feared that his new religion would discredit the chief Meccan temple, the Ka'ba, which housed a sacred meteoritic

* See chap. 3.

stone and was a profitable center of pilgrimages. Their belief that Muhammad's faith would ruin Mecca's pilgrim business was an ironic miscalculation, but their hostility to the new teaching forced Muhammad to flee Mecca in 622 and settle in the town of Medina, 280 miles northward on the caravan route.

The flight to Medina, known among the Muslims as the Hegira, was a momentous turning point in the development of Islam and marks the beginning date of the Muslim calendar. Muhammad quickly won the inhabitants of Medina to his faith, and became the city's political chief as well as its religious leader. Indeed, under Muhammad's direction religious and civil authority were fused so that the sacred community was at once a state and a church. In this respect Muhammad's community at Medina foreshadowed the great Islamic state of later years.

The Medinans made war on Mecca, raiding its caravans and blockading its trade. In 630 Medina conquered Mecca and incorporated it into the sacred community. During the two remaining years of his life Muhammad, now an almost legendary figure in Arabia, received the voluntary submission of many tribes in the peninsula. By the time of his death in 632 he had united the Arabians as never before into a coherent political-religious group, well-organized, well-armed, and inspired by a powerful new monotheistic religion. The violent energies of these desert people were now channeled toward a single goal: the conquest and conversion of the world.

ISLAMIC RELIGION: DYNASTIC DEVELOPMENTS

Faith was the cement with which Muhammad unified Arabia. The new faith was called *Islam*, the Arabic word for "surrender." Muhammad taught that his followers must surrender to the will of Allah, the single, almighty God of the universe. Allah's attributes of love and mercy were overshadowed by those of power and majesty, and the greatest good was to submit to Allah's commands. Muhammad did not regard himself as divine but rather as the last and greatest of a long line of prophets of whom he was the "seal." Among his predecessors were Moses, the Old Testament prophets, and Jesus.

Koran; Religious Obligations

Islam respected the Old and New Testaments and was relatively tolerant toward Jews and Christians—the "people of the book." But the Muslims had a book of their own, the *Koran,* which superseded its predecessors and was believed to contain the pure essence of divine revelation. The Koran is the comprehensive body of Muhammad's writings, the bedrock of the Islamic faith: "All men and jinn in collaboration," so it was said, "could not produce its like." Muslims regard it as the word of Allah, *dictated* to Muhammad by the angel Gabriel from an original "uncreated" book located in heaven. Accordingly, its divine inspiration and authority extend not only to its precepts but also to its every letter (of which there are 323,621), making any translation a species of heresy. Every good Muslim must read the Koran in Arabic, and, as Islam spread, the Arabic language necessarily spread with it.

The Koran is perhaps the most widely read book ever written. More than a manual of worship, it was the text from which the non-Arabian Muslim learned his Arabic. And since it was the supreme authority not only in religion but also in law, science, and the humanities, it became the standard text in Muslim schools for every imaginable subject. Muhammad's genius is vividly illustrated by his success in adapting a primitive language such as seventh-century Arabic to the sophisticated religious, legal, and ethical concepts that one encounters in his sacred book.

Muhammad offered his followers the assurance of eternal salvation if they led upright, sober lives and followed the precepts of Islam. Above all, they were bound to a simple confession of faith: "There is no god but Allah, and Muhammad is his prophet." The good Muslim was also obliged to engage in ritualistic prayers and fasting, to journey as a pilgrim to Mecca at least once in his lifetime, and to work devoutly toward the welfare and expansion of the sacred community. Holy war was the supremely meritorious activity, for service to the faith was identical with service to the state. Public law in Islamic lands had a religious sanction, and the fusion of religion and politics which Muhammad created at Medina remained a fundamental characteristic of Islamic society. There was no Muslim priesthood, no Muslim "church" apart from the state; Muhammad's political successors, the caliphs, were defenders of the faith and guardians of the faithful. The creative tension between church and state which proved such a stimulus to medieval Europe was thus unknown in the Muslim world.

EARLY CALIPHS; CIVIL WAR

In the years immediately after Muhammad's death the explosive energy of the Arabs, harnessed at last by the teachings of the Prophet, broke upon the world. The spectacular conquests resulted in part from the youthful vigor of Islam, in part from the weakness and exhaustion of its enemies. Emperor Heraclius had just defeated the Persians, and both Byzantium and Persia were spent and enfeebled by their long and desperate conflict. And the Monophysites of Syria and Egypt remained deeply hostile to their orthodox Byzantine masters.

The Arabs entered these tired, embittered lands afire with religious zeal, lured by the wealth and luxuries of the civilized world. They had no master plan of conquest—most of their campaigns began as plundering expeditions—but their momentum grew with each unexpected victory. Moving into Byzantine Syria they annihilated a huge Byzantine army in 636, captured Damascus and Jerusalem, and by 640 had occupied the entire land, detaching it more or less permanently from Byzantine control. In 637 they inflicted an overwhelming defeat on the Persian army and entered the Persian capital of Ctesiphon, gazing in bewilderment at its opulence and wealth. Within another decade they had subdued all Persia and arrived at the borders of India. In later years they penetrated deeply into the Indian subcontinent and laid the foundations of the modern Muslim state of Pakistan. The Persians gradually adopted the Islamic faith and learned the Arabic language, thus preparing themselves for the great role which they would later play in Islamic politics and culture.

Meanwhile the Muslims were pushing westward into Egypt. They captured Alexandria in the 640s, thus absorbing into their cultural sphere the great metropolis that had been a center of Greek culture

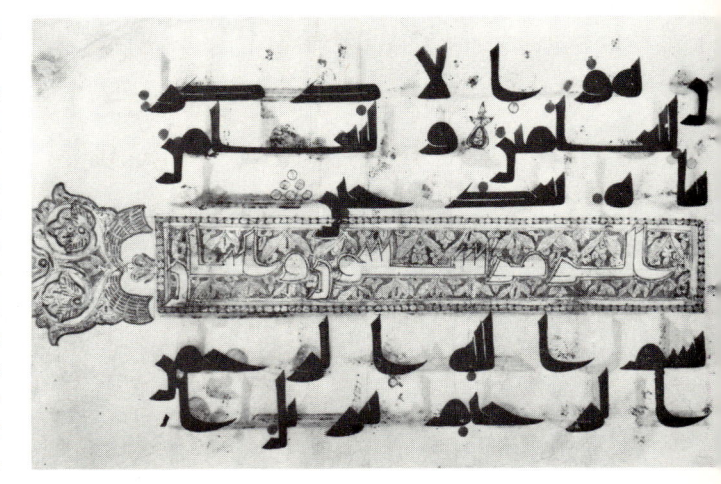

A leaf from an eighth- or ninth-century Koran.

THE ISLAMIC EMPIRE

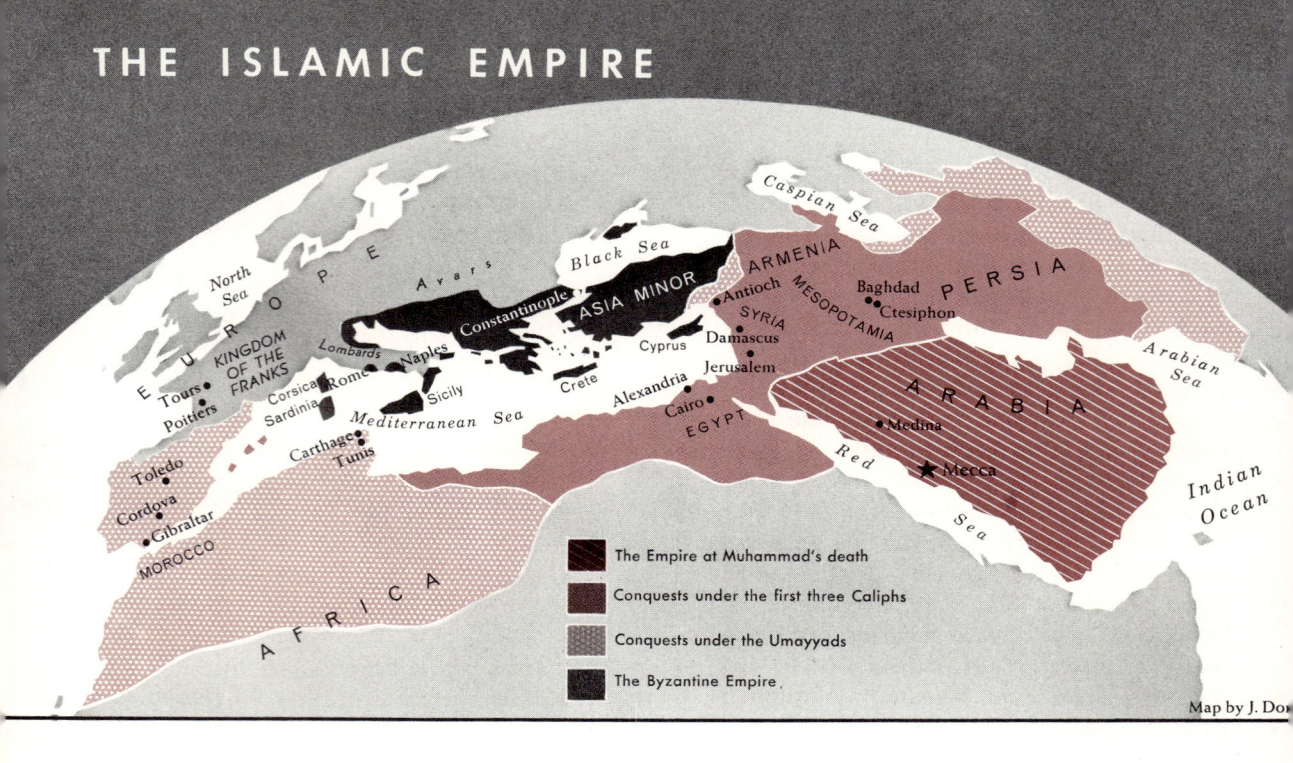

ever since the Hellenistic age. With Egypt and Syria in their hands they took to the sea, challenging the long-established Byzantine domination of the eastern Mediterranean. They took the island of Cyprus, raided ancient Rhodes, and in 655 won a major victory over the Byzantine fleet in the Battle of the Masts.

UMAYYAD AND ABBASID DYNASTIES

In 655 Islamic expansion ceased momentarily as the new empire became locked in a savage dynastic struggle. The succession to the caliphate was contested between the Umayyads, a leading family in the old Meccan commercial oligarchy, late to join the Islamic bandwagon but no less ambitious for all that, and Ali, the son-in-law of Muhammad himself. The Umayyad party rallied behind Muawiya, the dynamic Umayyad governor of Syria who was responsible for the recent buildup of Muslim sea power. Ali headed a faction that was to become exceedingly powerful in later centuries. His followers insisted that the caliph must be a direct descendant of the Prophet. As it happened, Muhammad had left no surviving sons and only one daughter, Fatima, who married the Prophet's cousin, Ali.

In 661 the Umayyad forces defeated Ali in battle, and Muawiya became the undisputed Caliph of Islam. Moving the Islamic capital to Damascus in Syria, he initiated an Umayyad dynasty of Caliphs that held power for nearly a century. But the legitimist faction that had once supported Ali persisted as a troublesome, dedicated minority, throwing its support behind various of the numerous descendants of Ali and Fatima. In time the political movement evolved into a heresy known as *Shi'ism* which held that the *true* caliphs—the descendants of Muhammad through Fatima and Ali—were sinless, infallible, and possessed of a body of secret knowledge not contained in the Koran. Shi'ism became an occult underground doctrine that occasionally rose to the surface in the

Rome's Three Heirs: Byzantium, Western Europe, Islam

form of civil insurrection. In the tenth century the Shi'ists gained control of Egypt and established a "Fatimid" dynasty of caliphs in Cairo. Shi'ism inspired an infamous band of Muslim desperadoes known as the "Assassins," who employed hashish as a means of producing ecstasy. The movement survives to this day in the Isma'ili sect led by the Agha Khan.

Umayyads

The intermission in the Muslim expansion ended with the Umayyad victory over Ali in 661. And even though the Islamic capital was now Damascus rather than Medina, the old Arabian aristocracy remained in firm control. Constantinople was now the chief military goal, but the great city on the Dardanelles repulsed a series of powerful Muslim attacks between 670 and 680. The Byzantine defense was aided by a remarkable secret weapon known as "Greek fire"—a liquid that ignited on exposure to air and could not be extinguished by water, but only by vinegar or sand. In 717-18 a great Arab fleet and army assaulted Constantinople in vain, and having expended all their energies and resources without success the Muslims abandoned their effort to take the city. Byzantium survived for another seven centuries, effectively barring inroads into southeastern Europe for the remainder of the Middle Ages.

In the meantime, however, Muslim armies were enjoying spectacular success in the West. From Egypt they moved westward along the North African coast into the old Vandal kingdom, now ruled by distant Byzantium. In 698 the Muslims took Carthage. In 711 they crossed the Straits of Gilbraltar into Spain and crushed the tottering Visigothic kingdom in a single blow, bringing the Spanish Christians under their dominion and driving the Christian princes into the fastness of the Pyrenees Mountains. Next the Muslims moved into southern Gaul and threatened the kingdom of the Merovingian Franks. In 732, exactly a century after the Prophet's death, the Muslims were halted at last on a battlefield between Tours and Poitiers by a Christian army led by the able Frankish warrior Charles Martel. The Christians at Tours were not the sort that one imagines when singing "Onward Christian Soldiers." They were semibarbarous Franks clad in wolfskins, their tangled hair hanging down to their shoulders. But they managed to halt the momentum of militant Islam in western Europe, just as the Byzantines had stopped it in the East.

The Muslim army at Tours was small and makeshift in comparison with the great Islamic force that had invested Constantinople in 717-18, but together these two battles brought an end to the era of major Islamic encroachments on the territories of the two Christian civilizations. The remainder of the middle ages witnessed continued Christian-Islamic warfare and some territorial change—most of Spain, for example, reverted to Christian control in the twelfth and thirteenth centuries—but Islam, Byzantium, and Western Christendom had achieved a relative equilibrium by the mid-eighth century and remained in balance for centuries to come.

Throughout the rest of the Middle Ages the three civilizations tended to expand not at one another's expense but away from each other—Byzantium into the Balkans and Russia, Islam into South Asia, and Western Christendom into Germany, Scandinavia, Hungary, and western Slavdom. The Crusades were, ultimately, only a minor exception to this generalization; the Christian reconquest of Spain and the Seljuk victory in Anatolia were much more important exceptions. But it was not until the fourteenth century, when the Islamic Ottomans swept into the Balkans, that the balance of the three power blocs began to tip.

345   D. Islam

The Golden Age of the Abbasids

In 750, seventeen years after the battle of Tours, the Umayyads were overthrown by a new dynasty, the Abbasids, Arabian in family background but with a program of greater political participation for the highly civilized conquered peoples, now converting in large numbers to Islam. It was above all the Islamized Persian aristocracy whom the Abbasids represented, and shortly after the victory of the new dynasty the capital was moved from Damascus to Baghdad on the Tigris, deep within the old Persian Empire, not far from the ruins of ancient Babylon. This move was accompanied by an eastward shift in Islam's orientation, which relieved some of the pressure against Constantinople and the West.

Baghdad, under the early Abbasids, became one of the world's great cities. It was the center of a vast commercial network spreading across the Islamic world and far beyond. Silks, spices, and fragrant woods flowed into its wharves from India, China, and the East Indies; furs, honey, and slaves were imported from Scandinavia, and gold, slaves, and ivory from tropical Africa. Baghdad was the nexus of a farflung banking system with branches in other cities across the Islamic world. A check could be drawn in Baghdad and cashed in Morocco, 4000 miles to the west. The Abbasid imperial palace, occupying fully a third of the city, contained innumerable apartments and public rooms, annexes for eunuchs, harems, and government officials, and a remarkable reception room known as the "hall of the tree," which contained on artificial tree of gold and silver on whose branches mechanical birds chirped and sang.

The wealth and culture of Baghdad reached its climax under the Abbasid caliph, Harun-al-Rashid (786–809), whose opulence and power quickly became legendary. Harun was accustomed to receiving tribute from the Byzantine Empire itself. When on one occasion the tribute was discontinued, he sent the following peremptory note to the emperor at Constantinople:

> In the name of God, the merciful, the compassionate.
> From Harun, the commander of the faithful, to Nicephorus, the dog of a Roman.
> Verily I have read thy letter, O son of an infidel mother. As for the answer, it shall be for thine eye to see, not for thine ear to hear.
> Salaam.

The letter was followed by a successful military campaign which forced the unlucky Byzantines to resume their tribute.

The era of Harun-al-Rashid was one of notable intellectual activity in which the learned traditions of Greece, Rome, Persia, and India were absorbed and synthesized. In Baghdad Harun's son and successor founded the House of Wisdom, which was at once a library, a university, and a translation center. Here and elsewhere Islamic scholars pushed their civilization far beyond the point it had reached under the Umayyads. Drawing from various traditions, Islamic culture had come of age with remarkable speed. At a time when Charlemagne was struggling desperately to civilize his semi-barbaric Franks, Harun reigned over glittering Baghdad.

The rise of the Abbasids marked the breakdown of the Arabian aristocracy's monopoly of political power. Now the government was run by a medley of races and peoples, often of humble origin. As one disgruntled aristocrat observed, "Sons of concubines have become so numerous amongst us; lead me to a land, O God, where I shall see no bastards."

The Abbasid government drew heavily from the administrative techniques of Byzantium and Persia. A sophisticated, complex bureaucracy ran the affairs of state from the capital at Baghdad and kept in touch with the provinces through a multitude of tax-gatherers, judges, couriers, and spies. The government was enlightened up to a point, although no more sensitive to the demands of social justice than other governments of its day. The Abbasid regime undertook extensive irrigation works, drained swamps, and thereby increased the amount of land under cultivation. But the status of the peasant and unskilled laborer was kept low by the competition of vast numbers of slaves. The brilliance of Abbasid culture had little effect on the underprivileged masses who, aside from their fervent Islamic faith, retained much the same primitive way of life that they had known for the last two millennia.

The Disintegration of the Abbasid Empire

The Abbasids were unable to maintain their power throughout the vast reaches of the Islamic empire. Communications were limited by the speed of sailing vessels and camels, and governors of remote provinces required sufficient independence and military strength to defend themselves from infidel attacks. Such local independence and power could easily ripen into full autonomy. The Abbasid revolution of 750 was followed by a long process of political disintegration as one province after another broke free of the control of the caliphs at Baghdad. Even in the palmy days of Harun-al-Rashid the extreme western provinces—Spain, Morocco, and Tunisia—were ruled by independent local dynasties. Spain, indeed, had never passed under Abbisid control but remained under the domination of Umayyad rulers. And by the later ninth century the trend toward disintegration was gaining strong momentum as Egypt, Syria, and eastern Persia (Iran) broke free of the Abbasids.

By then the Abbasid Caliphs were slowly losing their grip on their own government in Baghdad. Ambitious army commanders gradually usurped power, establishing control over the tax machinery and the other organs of government. In the later tenth and eleventh centuries the Fatimid caliphate of Cairo rose to great power, extending its authority to Syria and briefly occupying Baghdad itself (1056–57). Since about the mid-tenth century the Abbasid caliphs of Baghdad had been controlled by members of a local Persian aristocratic dynasty who took the title of "sultan" and ruled what was left of the Abbasid state. A century later, in 1055, the chief of the Seljuk Turks conquered Baghdad, assumed the title of "Grand Sultan," and then turned his forces against Byzantium with the devastating effects that we have already seen. Seljuk power declined in the twelfth century, to be followed by a period of further Islamic political disintegration concurrent with the Crusades. By the later twelfth century Islam recovered itself in Syria and Egypt, and in the course of the thirteenth century the crusaders were driven out. In that same century the emasculated Abbasid caliphate was destroyed. The Mongols took Baghdad in 1258, massacred a good part of its population (allegedly 800,000 people), and brought to an end the dynasty and the office that had ruled Baghdad, in fact or in name, for half a millennium.

The political troubles that the Abbasids endured from about 950 to 1258 were accompanied by a serious economic decline. Trade dried up, money became scarce, and Islamic rulers, whether in Baghdad, Cairo, or Damascus, were forced to reward their political underlings with land or revenue rights rather than wages. Thus imperialism gave way to localism, and wealth tended increasingly to be identified with land rather than with commerce. This led to further disintegration of the empire as petty officials became more involved in local matters than in the state.

The general unrest of the period encouraged waves of popular protest, both socioeconomic and religious. The Isma'ili sect, an outgrowth of the earlier legitimist faction, engaged in widespread terrorism and revolution. At the same time a mystical movement known as Sufism became immensely popular throughout the Islamic world. For centuries the Sufi movement, although never tightly coordinated, had provided the chief impetus to missionary work among the infidel. These Sufi mystics, often illiterate but always fervent, had achieved the conversion of millions of people in Africa, India, Indonesia, central Asia, and China. And it was they, rather than the orthodox religious scholars and lawyers, who could bring hope to the Muslim masses in times of trouble. Drawing from the Neoplatonic notion that reality rests in God alone, the Sufis sought mystical unity with the divine and stressed God's love over the orthodox emphasis on God's authority. The orthodox Islamic scholars contended vigorously against this mystical trend, but by the tenth century Sufism was the most powerful religious force among the people of Islam. It affects Islamic personal devotion to this day.

Islamic Culture: Conversion and Diffusion

Throughout the epoch of political disintegration the Muslim world remained united by a common tongue, a common culture, and a common faith. It continued to struggle vigorously with Byzantium for control of the Mediterranean and managed, at various times between the ninth and eleventh centuries, to occupy the key islands of Crete, Sicily, Sardinia, and Corsica. As early as the reign of Harun-al-Rashid most of the inhabitants of Syria, Egypt, and North Africa had converted to Islam, even though these lands had once supported enthusiastic and well-organized Christian churches. The Muslims did not ordinarily persecute the Christians; they merely taxed them. And it may well be that the prolonged tax burden was a more effective instrument of conversion than ruthless persecution would have been.

The brilliant intellectual awakening of Harun-al-Rashid's day continued unabated for another four centuries. The untutored Arab from the desert became the cultural heir of Greece, Rome, Persia, and India, and within less than two centuries of the Prophet's death Islamic culture had reached the level of a mature, sophisticated civilization. Its mercurial rise was a consequence of the Arabs' success in absorbing the great civilized traditions of their conquered peoples and employing these traditions in a cultural synthesis both new and unique. Islam borrowed, but never without digesting. What it drew from other civilizations it transmuted and made its own.

The political disintegration of the ninth and tenth centuries was accompanied by a diffusion of cultural activity throughout the Muslim world. During the tenth century, for example, Cordova, the capital of Umayyad Spain, acquired prodigious wealth and became the center of a brilliant cultural flowering. With a population of a half-million or more, Cordova was another Baghdad. No other city in western Europe could even remotely approach it in population, wealth, or municipal organization. Its magnificent mansions, mosques, aqueducts, and baths, its bustling markets and shops, its efficient police force and sanitation service, its street lights, and, above all, its splendid, sprawling palace, flashing with brightly colored tiles and surrounded by graceful minarets and sparkling fountains, made Cordova the wonder of the age.

All across the Islamic world, from Cordova to Baghdad and far to the east, Muslim scholars and artists were developing the legacies of past civilizations. Architects were molding Greco-Roman forms into a brilliant and distinctive new

Interior of the sanctuary of the mosque of Cordova. Begun in 786, this structure offers an excellent example of the horseshoe-shaped arch, a peculiarly Muslim architectural form.

style. Philosophers were studying and elaborating the writings of Plato and Aristotle despite the hostility of narrowly orthodox Islamic theologians. Physicians were expanding the ancient medical doctrines of Galen and his Greek predecessors, describing new symptoms and identifying new curative drugs. Astronomers were tightening the geocentric system of Ptolemy, preparing accurate tables of planetary motions, and giving Arabic names to the stars—names such as Altair, Deneb, and Aldebaran—which are used to this day. The renowned astronomer poet of eleventh-century Persia, Omar Khayyam, devised a calendar of singular accuracy. Muslim mathematicians borrowed creatively from both Greece and India. From the Greeks they learned geometry and trigonometry, and from the Hindus they appropriated the so-called Arabic numerals, the zero, and algebra, which were ultimately passed on to the West to revolutionize European mathematics.

Islamic literature produced no long, systematic masterpieces but excelled in short works of poetry and prose. The individual anecdote took precedence over the extended narrative. Muslim poets endeavored to perfect individual verses rather than create long, coherent poems. The quatrains of Omar Khayyam's *Rubaiyat* seem to have been arranged in alphabetical order rather than conforming to any overall plan. The chapters of the Koran itself, which had been left completely unorganized by Muhammad, were assembled by scholars under the Caliph Utman (644–56) in order of decreasing length with no attempt at structural unity. The enduring value of these works lies in the power and beauty of their individual chapters and verses.

Byzantium collapsed as a political force in the fifteenth century, although its religion and echoes of its culture persist in eastern Europe to this day. But Islam endures—as a political power, a great world religion, and a culture. The Arab conquests during the century after Muhammad changed the historical course of North Africa and southwest Asia decisively and permanently. The Arabs conquered their vast territories thrice over: with their armies, their faith, and their language. In the end, the term "Arab" applied to every Muslim from Morocco to Iraq, regardless of his ethnic background. Within its all-encompassing religious and linguistic framework, Arabic culture provided a new stimulus and a new orientation to the long-civilized peoples of former empires. With its manifold ingredients the rich Islamic heritage would one day provide invaluable nourishment to the voracious mind of the twelfth and thirteenth century West. Later, Islamic armies would bring Byzantium to an end and make Constantinople a Muslim city. Later still, in the sixteenth and seventeenth centuries, they would be at the gates of Vienna. Only in the nineteenth century did Islam become clearly subordinate to the West militarily and politically. And today there are signs that this subordination is at its end.

Selected Readings

*Augustine. *The City of God.* V. J. Bourke, ed. Garden City, N.Y.: Doubleday & Co., 1958.
   A skillful abridgment.

*Bark, William C. *Origins of the Medieval World.* Garden City, N.Y.: Doubleday & Co., 1960.
   A provocative work that challenges the view that Rome's fall was a disaster.

*Bede. *A History of the English Church and People.* Translated by Leo Shirley-Price. Baltimore: Penguin Books, 1955.
   A good translation of Bede's masterpiece.

Brown, Peter. *Augustine of Hippo: A Biography.* Berkeley and Los Angeles: University of California Press, 1969.
   A splendid recent study.

*Bury, J. B., *History of the Later Roman Empire.* 2 vols. New York: Dover Publications, 1957.
   The standard account, full and authoritative, by one of the distinguished historians of this century.

*Chambers, Mortimer, ed. *The Fall of Rome: Can It Be Explained?* New York: Holt, Rinehart & Winston, 1963.

> Well-chosen excerpts from historical writings dealing with the decline of Rome provide a compact, illuminating survey of historical opinion on the subject.

*Cochrane, C. N. *Christianity and Classical Culture*. New York: Oxford University Press, 1944.
> An intellectual tour de force, sympathetic to the rise of the mystical viewpoint.

*Dawson, Christopher. *The Making of Europe*. New York: World Publishing Co., Meridian Books, 1946.
> A thoughtful, sympathetic analysis of early medieval culture that emphasizes the central role of the Catholic faith.

Deanesly, Margaret. *A History of Early Medieval Europe: 476–911*. 2d ed. New York: Barnes & Noble, 1960.
> An excellent, accurate, and highly detailed text.

*Dill, Samuel. *Roman Society in the Last Century of the Western Empire*. New York: World Publishing Co., Meridian Books.
> A brilliant, older work, originally published in 1898.

*Gibb, H. A. R. *Mohammedanism: An Historical Survey*. 2d ed. New York: Oxford University Press, Galaxy Books, 1953.
> A skillful, compact summary of Islamic civilization.

*Gibbon, Edward. *The Triumph of Christendom in the Roman Empire*. New York: Harper & Row, Publishers, 1958.
> Chapters 15–20 of Gibbon's late-eighteenth-century masterpiece, *The Decline and Fall of the Roman Empire*. The entire work is available in a three-volume Modern Library edition.

Gregory of Tours. *History of the Franks*. Translated by O. M. Dalton. New York: Oxford University Press, 1927.
> The best contemporary account of early Merovingian Gaul.

*von Grunebaum, G. E. *Medieval Islam*. 2d ed. Chicago: The University of Chicago Press, 1963.
> A learned and original work; the best on the subject.

*Hitti, P. K. *History of the Arabs*. 6th ed. New York: St. Martin's Press, 1958.
> Broad, yet full; a monumental work. For a much shorter survey by the same author see *The Arabs: A Short History* (Chicago: Henry Regnery Co., Gateway Editions, 1956).

*Hussey, J. M. *The Byzantine World*. New York: Harper & Row, Publishers, 1961.
> A brief, skillful summary of Byzantine civilization.

*Jenkins, Romily. *Byzantium: The Imperial Centuries*. New York: Random House, Vintage Books, 1969.
> A fine, up-to-date account of the period from Heraclius to the battle of Manzikert, particularly valuable on the age of the Macedonian emperors.

351   Selected Readings

Laistner, M. L. W. *Thought and Letters in Western Europe*, A.D. 500–900. Rev. ed. London: Methuen & Co., 1936.
: The best intellectual history of the period.

Latouche, Robert. *The Birth of Western Economy,* New York: Barnes & Noble, 1960.
: A searching account of early medieval economic trends. The author particularly stresses the persisting importance of the small farm in the European countryside.

*Lewis, Archibald, *The Islamic World and the West,* A.D. 642–1492. New York: John Wiley & Sons, 1970.
: A thoughtful collection of essays by modern historians and original sources in English translation.

Lopez, Robert. *The Birth of Europe.* New York: M. Evans & Co., 1967.
: A treatment of the entire medieval period, filled with original insights, emphasizing social and economic history, and devoting much more attention to southern Europe than is usual in histories of the Middle Ages.

*Lot, Ferdinand. *The End of the Ancient World and the Beginnings of the Middle Ages,* New York: Harper & Row, Publishers, 1961.
: A masterly study that places stress on the economic factors in the decline. A valuable introduction by Glanville Downey summarizes recent scholarship on the problem of "decline and fall."

Ostrogorsky, George *History of the Byzantine State*. Rev. ed. New Brunswick, N.J.: Rutgers University Press, 1969.
: Longer and more detailed than the surveys by Hussey and Baynes and Moss (above), this is the best single-volume history of Byzantium.

Pirenne, Henri. *Mohammed and Charlemagne.* New York: World Publishing Co., Meridian Books, 1955.
: The firmest statement by the great Belgian scholar of his controversial thesis that Roman civilization persisted in the West until the eighth century. This book should be read in connection with Bark (above).

*Wallace-Hadrill, John M. *The Barbarian West, 400–1000.* New York: Harper & Row, Publishers, 1962.
: An intelligent condensation and popularization by England's leading authority on early-medieval Frankland. The account of the Carolingian Renaissance is particularly important.

Wallace-Hadrill, John M. *The Long-Haired Kings and Other Studies in Frankish History.* New York: Barnes & Noble, 1962.
: A collection of illuminating essays on the Merovingian period.

Asterisk (*) denotes paperback.

CHAPTER VIII
Carolingian Europe and the New Invasions

A. The Rise of the Carolingian Empire

THE SIGNIFICANCE OF THE CAROLINGIAN RENAISSANCE

In the course of the eighth century Western Christendom began to emerge as a coherent civilization. It did so under the aegis of the Carolingian Empire—a vast constellation of territories welded together by the Frankish king Charlemagne and his talented predecessors. Here for the first time the various cultural ingredients—classical, Christian, and Germanic—that went into the making of European civilization achieved a degree of synthesis. Charlemagne was a Germanic king who surrounded himself with Germanic warrior-aristocrats. But he also drew churchmen and classical scholars around him and took very seriously his role as protector and sustainer of the Western Church. Although his empire was fundamentally Germanic, its intellectual life, limited though it was, drew heavily from the classical-Christian tradition. The fusion of these cultural ingredients was evident in the life of the Carolingian court, in the rising vigor of the Carolingian Church, and in the person of Charlemagne himself.

Charlemagne's Frankland stood in sharp contrast to contemporary Byzantium and the Abbasid Empire of Islam. Baghdad and Constantinople were the centers of brilliant, opulent, mercantile civilizations. Charlemagne's Franks were a half-barbarized agrarian people struggling toward political and intellectual coherence. But eighth-century western Europeans were steadily moving toward a life of larger meaning for themselves and for those who came after them. For the first time it began to dawn on a few of them that they were a people apart, that they were *Europeans,* that they were the agents of a new, distinctive civilization with its roots in Athens and Jerusalem, Germany, and Rome, bound together—much as the Byzantines and Muslims were—by a common faith, a common scholarly language, and a common heritage.

The new Europe was spiritually and intellectually enlivened by the wide-ranging Benedictines, who disseminated a cultural tradition based on the Bible, the writings of the Latin Doctors and their contemporaries, and the surviving masterpieces of Latin literature. This evolving culture was bound together politically by a new dynasty of Frankish monarchs, the Carolingians.*

Carolingian Europe differed profoundly from the western Roman Empire of old. It was a land without large cities, thoroughly agrarian in its economic organization, with its culture centered on the monastery, the cathedral, and the perambulatory royal court rather than the forum. And although Charlemagne extended his authority into Italy, the center of his activities and his interests remained in northern Frankland. In a word, the new Europe no longer faced the Mediterranean; its axis had shifted northward.

AGRICULTURAL TECHNOLOGY

The relative brightness of the Age of Charlemagne was the product of creative processes that had been at work during the preceding dark centuries. From the economic standpoint the most interesting and significant of these processes was the gradual evolution of a new agrarian technology which increased the productivity of northern European farmlands beyond the level of the old Roman Empire.

The New Plow

By the opening of the eighth century the ineffective scratch plow of Roman times had been superseded throughout the northern districts of the barbarian West by a heavy compound plow with wheels, colter, plowshare, and moldboard, which cut deeply into the soil, pulverized it, and turned it aside into ridges and furrows. The development of this heavy plow was complex and gradual; the basic idea may perhaps have been brought into western Europe by the Slavs in the sixth or seventh century. Its introduction into the West opened up vast areas of rich, heavy soil in which the older scratch plow was ineffective, and accentuated the tendency toward dividing fields into long strips cultivated by the eight-ox teams which the heavy plow required. Peasants now pooled their oxen and their labor in order to exploit the new plow; in so doing they laid the foundation for the cooperative agricultural communities of medieval Europe with strong village councils to regulate the division of labor and resources. In these village communities the medieval peasantry learned the attitude of responsible, voluntary cooperation—an attitude that may well have contributed to the rise of capitalist enterprise many centuries later.

The Three-Field System

The upsurge in productivity brought about by the introduction of the heavy compound plow made possible a fundamental change in the method of rotating crops. By the Carolingian age parts of northern Europe were beginning to adopt the three-field system in place of the two-field system typical of Roman times. Formerly a typical farm had been divided into two fields, one of which was planted each year and allowed to lie fallow the second year. But it was found that the rich northern soils, newly opened by the heavy plow, did not require a full year's rest between crops. Instead, they were often divided into three fields, each of which underwent a three-year cycle of autumn planting, spring planting, and fallow. The shift from two fields to three had an important impact on the European economy, for it increased food production significantly and brought a degree of prosperity

---

* Whose family name is derived from that of their most illustrious representative—Charles the Great, or Charlemagne.

to northern Europe. It is possible that the heavy plow and the three-field system, which could not be employed efficiently in the light, dry soils of the Mediterranean South, contributed to the northward shift in the economic and cultural orientation of Carolingian Europe.

Mechanization

The Age of Charlemagne also profited from a trend toward mechanization. The water mill, which was used occasionally in antiquity for grinding grain, had now come into more widespread use and was often to be seen on Carolingian farms. During the centuries following Charlemagne's death the water mill was put to new uses—to power the rising textile industry of the eleventh century, and to drive triphammers in forges. Thus, the technological progress of Merovingian and Carolingian times continued into the centuries that followed. By 1000 the development of the horseshoe and a new, efficient horse collar, both apparently imported from Siberia or central Asia, made possible the very gradual replacement of the ox by the more energetic horse as the chief draught animal on the farms of northwestern Europe. And in the twelfth century the windmill made its debut in the European countryside. These new advances resulted in still greater productivity and underlay the rich, prosperous civilization of Northern Europe in the High Middle Ages (ca. 1050–1300). Slowly one of the chief economic bases of human slavery was being eroded as human power gave way more and more to animal and machine power.

Carolingian Europe gained much from the earlier phase of this drawn-out revolution in agrarian technology, but even so the peasants of the Carolingian age remained near the level of subsistence, owing in part to the rise of population along with productivity. During a great famine of 791, for example, the peasants were driven to cannibalism and were even reported to have eaten members of their own family. Conditions may have been improving, but only very gradually, and a single bad year could be disastrous.

POLITICAL AND RELIGIOUS-DEVELOPMENTS

Rise of the Carolingians

The dynasty of Clovis, the Merovingians, had declined over the centuries from blood-thirsty autocrats to crowned fools. By the later 600s all real power had passed to the aristocracy. Meanwhile, as a consequence of the Merovingian policy of dividing royal authority and crown lands among the sons of a deceased king, Frankland had split into several distinct districts, the most important of which were Neustria (Paris and northwestern France), Austrasia (the heavily Germanized northeast including the Rhinelands), and Burgundy in the southeast (see map, p. 364).

During the seventh century a great landholding family, known to historians as the Carolingians, rose to power in Austrasia. The Carolingians became "mayors" of the itinerant royal household; that is, they held the chief administrative post in the Austrasian government (such as it was) and made their office hereditary. As the Merovingians grew increasingly feeble and inept the Carolingians became the real masters of Austrasia. The Carolingian mayor increased his power by gathering around him a considerable number of trained warriors somewhat in the tradition of the old Germanic comitatus (see p. 314). These men became his vassals, placing themselves under his protection and maintenance and swearing fealty to him. Other nobles also had their private vassalic armies. But the Carolingians, with far the greatest number of followers, dominated the scene. In 687 a Carolingian mayor named Pepin of

Heristal led his Austrasian army to a decisive victory over the Neustrians at Tertry, and the Carolingians thenceforth were the leading family in all Frankland. With Neustria under their control they were able to dominate Burgundy, and when the Muslims moved into Gaul in the early 730s the Franks were able to unite against them under the able leadership of Pepin of Heristal's son, the vigorous Carolingian mayor Charles Martel.

Charles Martel ("The Hammer"): 714—741

This brilliant, ruthless warrior not only turned back the Muslims at the battle of Tours (732); he also won victory after vic-

356   Carolingian Europe and the New Invasions

Illuminations from the Flemish Hours of the Virgin *(ca. 1515):* LEFT, *the month of July;* ABOVE, *the month of September. Note two examples of medieval technological achievement: the windmill and the compound plow with moldboard.*

tory over Muslims and Christians alike, consolidating his power over the Franks and extending the boundaries of the Frankish state. Like the Adams family in American history, the Carolingians of the seventh and eighth centuries had the good fortune to produce exceedingly able men over several generations. Martel's father, Pepin of Heristal, had conquered Neustria; Martel himself defeated the Muslims and, indeed, almost everybody he faced. His son, Pepin the Short, gained the Frankish crown, and his grandson, Charlemagne, won an empire.

Surprisingly, the Carolingians followed the same policy of divided succession among male heirs that had so weakened the Merovingians. But here too Caro-

357   A. The Rise of the Carolingian Empire

lingian luck played a crucial role in history. For as it happened, the Carolingian mayors and later kings, over several generations, had only one long-surviving heir. Frankish unity was maintained not by policy but in spite of it. When Charles Martel died in 741 his lands and authority were divided among his two sons, Carloman and Pepin the Short. But Carloman ruled only six years, retiring to a Benedictine monastery in 747—leaving the field to his brother Pepin. Carloman represented a new kind of barbarian ruler, deeply affected by the spiritual currents of his age, whose piety foreshadowed that of numerous saint-kings of later centuries. Christian culture and Germanic political leadership were beginning to draw together.

Missions from Northumbria

The fusion of these two worlds was carried still further by Pepin the Short (741–68) who supported a Benedictine Christian revival in Frankland and consummated an alliance of far-reaching consequences between the Frankish monarchy and the papacy. By the time of Charles Martel's death in 741 English Benedictine monks had long been engaged in evangelical work among the heathen Germanic peoples east of the Rhine. The earliest of these missions were directed at the Frisians, a maritime people who were settled along the coast of the Netherlands. The first of the Benedictine evangelists were monks from Northumbria who brought to the Continent not only the strict organizational discipline and devotion to the papacy that had been characteristic of the Northumbrian Benedictines but also the peripatetic missionary fervor which the Celtic monks had contributed to the Northumbrian revival. So it was that Benedictine monks such as Wilfrid of Ripon and Willibrord left their Northumbrian homeland during the later 600s to evangelize the heathen Frisians. The transference to Frankland and Germany of the vital force of Northumbrian Christianity, with its vibrant culture, its Roman-Benedictine discipline, and its profound spiritual commitment was of immense significance in the development of Western civilization. Wilfrid of Ripon, Willibrord, and their devoted followers represent the first wave of a movement that was ultimately to infuse the Frankish empire of Charlemagne with the vibrant spiritual life that had developed in Anglo-Saxon England during the century following St. Augustine's mission. The dynamic thrust of Roman-Benedictine Christianity, having leapt from Rome to Kent and thence to remote Northumbria, was returning to the Continent at last.

Saint Boniface in Germany

The key figure in this cultural movement was St. Boniface, an English Benedictine from Wessex. Reared in Benedictine monasteries in southern England, Boniface left Wessex in 716 to do missionary work among the Frisians. From that time until his death in 754 he devoted himself above all other tasks to the tremendous challenge of Christianizing the heathen Germanic peoples. Boniface was a man of boundless energy and considerable learning, a wise and magnetic leader of men. He worked in close cooperation with both the papacy and the Anglo-Saxon church; a great number of his letters survive, many of which request support from his compatriots in Wessex and advice from Rome. On three occasions he visited Rome to confer with the pope, and from the beginning his work among the heathens was performed under papal commission. In 732 the papacy appointed him archbishop in Germany. Some years later he was given the episcopal see at

Mainz as his headquarters. Throughout his career he was a devoted representative of the Anglo-Saxon church, the Benedictine Rule, and the papacy. As he put it, he strove "to hold fast the Catholic faith and Unity, and to yield submission to the Church of Rome as long as life shall last for us."

Boniface also worked with the backing of the Frankish mayors—Charles Martel, Carloman, and Pepin the Short. Armed with the Christian faith and the Benedictine rule, and supported by England, Frankland, and Rome, Boniface labored among the Germanic tribes in Frisia, Thuringia, Hesse, and Bavaria. There he won converts, founded new Benedictine monasteries in the German wilderness, and erected the organizational framework of a disciplined German church. There were moments of discouragement, as when he wrote to an English abbot, "Have pity upon an old man tried and tossed on all sides by the waves of a German sea." Yet Boniface accomplished much, and the monasteries which he established—particularly the great house of Fulda in Hesse—were to become centers of learning and evangelism which played a great role in converting and civilizing the peoples of Germany.

Symbol of St. Mark from the Eternach Gospel, *which was designed about 690 for use by Willibrord in his effort to spread Christianity among the barbarians.*

Reform of the Frankish Church

During the decade following Charles Martel's death in 741 Boniface devoted much of his energy to Frankland itself, for the Frankish church of the early eighth century stood in desperate need of reform. On the whole it was corrupt, disorganized, and ignorant—the product of several centuries of Merovingian misrule. Many areas of Frankland had no priests at all; numerous Frankish peasants were scarcely removed from heathenism. Priests themselves are reported to have sacrificed animals to the gods and shared their homes with concubines. Charles Martel, although willing enough to support Boniface's missionary endeavors among the Germanic heathens, had no taste for ecclesiastical reforms within his own Frankish church. Indeed, he weakened the church by confiscating a considerable amount of ecclesiastical property and granting it to his military vassals. Carloman and Pepin, however, encouraged Boniface to work toward the reform of the Frankish church, and beginning in 742 he held a series of synods for that purpose. Working in close collaboration with the papacy, Boniface remodeled the Frankish ecclesiastical organization on the disciplined pattern of Anglo-Saxon England and papal Rome. He reformed Frankish monasteries along the lines of the Benedictine Rule, saw to the establishment of monastic schools, encouraged the appointment of dedicated prelates, and worked toward the development of an adequate parish system to bring the Gospel to the country folk. Thus Boniface laid the groundwork for both the new church in Germany and the reformed church in Frankland. In doing so, he served as one of the chief architects of the Carolingian cultural revival.

THE FRANCO-PAPAL ALLIANCE

Carolingian Motives

Boniface's introduction of Roman discipline and organization into the Frankish church was followed almost immediately by the consummation of a fateful political alliance between Rome and Frankland. It may well have been at Boniface's prompting that the Carolingian mayor Pepin the Short sought papal support for his seizure of the Frankish crown. Although the Merovingian monarchs retained the enormous prestige always enjoyed by a Germanic royal dynasty, they had long been shadowy, do-nothing kings. Even so, if the Carolingians hoped to replace the Merovingians on the Frankish throne, they would have to call upon the most potent spiritual sanction available to their age: papal consecration. In supporting Boniface and his fellow Benedictines the Carolingian mayors had fostered papal influence in the Frankish church. Now, seeking papal support for a dynastic revolution, Pepin the Short could reasonably expect a favorable response in Rome.

Papal Motives

For their part, the popes had been seeking a strong, loyal ally against the untrustworthy Byzantines and the aggressive Lombards who had long been contending for political supremacy in Italy. The Carolingians, with their policy of aid to the Benedictine missionaries and their support of Boniface's reform measures, must have seemed strong candidates for the role of papal champion. And by mid-eighth century a papal champion was desperately needed. Traditionally the papacy had followed the policy of turning to Byzantium for protection against the Lombards who, although they had by now adopted trinitarian Christianity, remained an ominous threat to papal independence. By 750 the popes could no longer depend on Byzantine protection for two reasons: (1) the Byzantine emperors had recently embraced a doctrine known as *iconoclasm* which the papacy regarded as heretical, and (2) Lombard aggression was rapidly becoming so effective that the Byzantine army could no longer be counted on to defend the papacy.

The iconoclastic controversy was the chief religious dispute of the Christian world in the eighth century. It was a conflict over the use in Christian worship of statues and pictures of Christ and the saints. These icons had gradually come to assume an important role in Christian worship. Strictly speaking, Christians might venerate them as symbols of the holy persons whom they represented, but in fact there was a strong tendency among the uneducated to worship the objects themselves. A line of reform emperors in Constantinople, beginning with Leo the Isaurian (717–41), sought to end the superstitious practice of worshiping images—vigorously fostered by the numerous monks of the Eastern empire—by banning icons altogether. This sweeping decree served the interests of the Byzantine emperors by weakening the power of the Eastern monasteries, which controlled far too much land and wealth for the empire's good, but it offended a great many Byzantines, image worshipers, and intelligent traditionalists alike. In the West little or no support was to be found for the policy of iconoclasm; the papacy in particular opposed it as heretical and contrary to the Christian tradition. Although it ultimately failed in the Byzantine Church, iconoclasm in the 750s was a vital issue and a storm center of controversy which aroused intense enmity between Rome and Constantinople.* The papacy was deeply apprehensive of depending on the troops of a heretical emperor for its defense.

Even without the iconoclastic controversy it was becoming increasingly doubtful that the papacy could count on the military power of Byzantium in Italy. For by 750 the Lombards were on the rampage once again, threatening not only Byzantine holdings but also the territories of the pope himself. In 751 the Lombards captured Ravenna, which had long served as the Byzantines' Italian capital, and the papal position in Italy became more precarious than ever. If Pepin the Short needed the support of the papacy, the papacy needed Pepin's support even more.

Pepin the Short:
Mayor, 741–751; King, 751–768

Accordingly the alliance was struck. Pepin sent messengers to Rome with the far from theoretical question, "Is it right that a powerless ruler should continue to bear the title of king?" The pope answered that by the authority of the Apostle Peter, Pepin was henceforth to be king of the Franks, and ordered that he should be

* That is, it failed in its extreme form. Eventually a compromise was reached that permitted flat representations of holy persons but not their representation in the round.

anointed into his royal office at Soissons by a papal representative. The anointing ceremony was duly performed in 751. It had the purpose of buttressing the new Carolingian dynasty with the strongest of spiritual sanctions. Not by mere force, but by the supernatural potency of the royal anointing was the new dynasty established on the Frankish throne. Appropriately, this ceremony—the symbolic junction of the power of Rome and Frankland—was performed by the aged Boniface.

With Pepin's coronation the last of the Merovingians were shorn of their long hair and packed off to a monastery. Three years thereafter Boniface, now nearing 80, returned to his missionary work in Frisia and met a martyr's death. In the same year, 754, the pope himself traveled northward to Frankland where he personally anointed Pepin and his two sons at the royal monastery of Saint-Denis, thereby conferring every spiritual sanction at his disposal upon the upstart Carolingian monarchy. At the same time he sought Pepin's military support against the Lombards.

Pepin obliged, leading his armies into Italy, defeating the Lombards, and donating a large portion of central Italy to the papacy. This "Donation of Pepin" was of lasting historical significance. It had the immediate effect of relieving the popes of the ominous Lombard pressure. In the long run, it became the nucleus of the Papal States, which were to remain a characteristic feature of Italian politics until the later nineteenth century. For the moment, the papacy had been rescued from its peril. It remained to be seen whether the popes could prevent their new champion from becoming their master.

Pepin the Short, like all successful monarchs of the Early Middle Ages, was an able general. As the first Carolingian king he followed in the warlike traditions of his father. Besides defeating the Lombards in Italy he drove the Muslims from Aqui-

361   A. The Rise of the Carolingian Empire

taine and maintained a domestic peace. He died in 768, leaving Frankland larger, more powerful, and better organized than he had found it.

Charlemagne (768–814)

Pepin was a talented monarch, but he was overshadowed by his even greater son. Charlemagne was a phenomenally successful military commander, a statesman of rare ability, a friend of learning, and a monarch possessed of a deep sense of responsibility for the welfare of the society over which he ruled. In this last respect he represents a tremendous advance over his Merovingian predecessors whose relationship to their state was that of a leech to his host.

The Man

Charlemagne towered over his contemporaries both figuratively and literally. He was 6'3½" tall, thick-necked and pot-bellied, yet imposing in appearance for all that. Thanks to his able biographer, Einhard, whose *Life of Charlemagne* was written a few years after the emperor's death, Charlemagne has come down to posterity as a three-dimensional figure. Einhard, who was dwarfish in stature, wrote enthusiastically of his oversized hero. The Roman historian Suetonius was Einhard's model, and he lifted whole passages from Suetonius's *Lives of the Twelve Caesars,* adapting many other phrases from the work to his own purposes. Yet there is much in Einhard's *Life* that represents his own appraisal of Charlemagne's deeds and character. Reared at the Monastery of Fulda, Einhard served for many years in Charlemagne's court and so gained an intimate knowledge of the emperor. Einhard's warm admiration for Charlemagne emerges clearly from the biography, yet the author was able to see Charlemagne's faults as well as his virtues:

Charlemagne: A later, idealized bust.

Charles was temperate in eating and particularly so in drinking, for he hated drunkenness in anybody, particularly in himself and those of his household. But he found it difficult to abstain from food, and often complained that fasts injured his health. . . . His meals usually consisted of four courses not counting the roast, which his huntsmen used to bring in on the spit. He was fonder of this than of any other dish. While at the table he listened to reading or music. The readings were stories and deeds of olden times; he was also fond of St. Augustine's books, and especially of the one entitled *The City of God.* So moderate was he in the use of wine and all sorts of drink that he rarely allowed himself more than three cups in the course of a meal.

Einhard provides a full account of Charlemagne's military and political career; but the most fascinating passages in the biography deal with the emperor's way of life and personal idiosyncrasies which reveal him as a human being rather than a shadowy hero of legend:

While he was dressing and putting on his shoes, he not only gave audience to his friends, but if the Count of the Household told him of any suit in which his judgment was necessary, he had the parties brought before him forthwith, considered the case, and gave his decision, just as if he were sitting on the judgment seat.

Einhard was also at pains to show Charlemagne's thirst for learning. He portrays the emperor as a fluent master of Latin, a student of Greek, a speaker of such skill that he might have passed for a teacher of rhetoric, a devotee of the liberal arts, and in particular a student of astronomy who learned to calculate the motions of the heavenly bodies. Einhard concludes this impressive discussion of Charlemagne's scholarship with a final tribute which unwittingly discloses the emperor's severe scholastic limitations:

He also tried to write, and used to keep tablets and blank pages in bed under his pillow so that in his leisure hours he might accustom his hand to form the letters; but as he did not begin his efforts at an early age but late in life, they met with poor success.

Charlemagne could be warm and talkative, but he could also be hard, cruel, and violent, and his subjects came to regard him with both admiration and fear. He was possessed of a strong, if superficial, piety that prompted him to build churches, collect relics, and struggle heroically for a Christian cultural revival in Frankland. But it did not prevent him from filling his court with concubines and other disreputable characters. In short

This contemporary illustration, which shows how the stirrup was used by Carolingian warriors, is from the Golden Psalter of St. Gall.

Charlemagne, despite his military and political genius, was a man of his age, in tune with its most progressive forces yet by no means removed from its barbaric past.

Military Career

Above all else Charlemagne was a warrior-king. He led his armies on yearly campaigns as a matter of course. When his magnates and their retainers assembled around him annually on the May Field the question was not whether to go to war but where to fight. Traditionally the Franks

363   A. The Rise of the Carolingian Empire

Italy and Spain

It was only gradually, however, that Charlemagne developed a coherent scheme of conquest built on a notion of Christian mission and addressed to the goal of unifying and systematically expanding the Christian West. At the behest of the papacy Charlemagne followed his father's footsteps into Italy. There he conquered the Lombards completely in 774, incorporated them into his growing state, and assumed for himself the Lombard crown. Thenceforth he employed the title, "King of the Franks and the Lombards."

Between 778 and 801 Charlemagne conducted a series of campaigns against the Spanish Muslims which met with only limited success. He did succeed in establishing a frontier district, the "Spanish March," on the Spanish side of the Pyrenees. In later generations the southern portion of Charlemagne's Spanish March evolved into the county of Barcelona which remained more receptive to the influence of French institutions and customs than any other district in Spain. A relatively minor military episode in Charlemagne's Spanish campaign of 778—an attack by a band of Christian Basques against the rearguard of Charlemagne's army as it was withdrawing across the Pyrenees into Frankland—became the inspiration for one of the great epic poems of the eleventh century: the *Song of Roland*. The unknown author or authors of the poem transformed the Basques into Muslims and made the battle an heroic struggle between the rival faiths. Charlemagne was portrayed as a godlike conqueror, phenomenally aged, and Roland, the warden of the Breton March and commander of the rearguard, acquired a fame in literature far out of proportion to his actual historical importance.

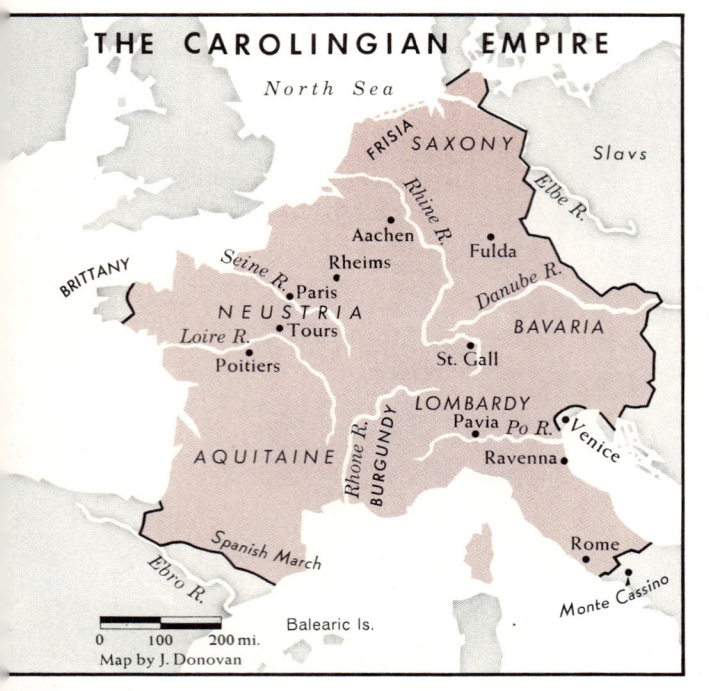

had fought on foot; but the epoch of Charles Martel and Pepin the Short had witnessed the rise of cavalry as the elite force in the Frankish army. This momentous shift, which amounted in effect to the birth of the medieval mounted knight, was perhaps associated with the coming of the stirrup to Frankland in the earlier 700s. For the stirrup gave stability to the mounted warrior and made possible the charge of cavalrymen with lances braced against their arms which was such an effective feature of later feudal warfare. In any case, the conquering armies of Charlemagne were built around a nucleus of highly trained horsemen. Such warriors were still something of a novelty in the age of Charlemagne, and under his masterful leadership they struck fear in their foes and acquired a reputation for invincibility.

Central Europe

Charlemagne devoted much of his strength to the expansion of his eastern frontier. In 787 he conquered and absorbed Bavaria, organizing its easternmost district into a forward defensive barrier against the Slavs. This East March or *Ostmark* became the nucleus of a new state later to be called Austria. In the 790s Charlemagne pushed still farther to the southeast, destroying the rich and predatory Avar state which had long tormented eastern Europe. For many generations the Avars had been enriching themselves on the plunder of their victims and on heavy tribute payments from Byzantium and elsewhere. Charlemagne had the good fortune to seize a substantial portion of the Avar treasure; it is reported that 15 four-ox wagons were required to transport the hoard of gold, silver, and precious garments back to Frankland. The loot of the Avars contributed significantly to the resources of Charlemagne's treasury and broadened the scope of his subsequent building program and patronage to scholars and churches. Indeed, it placed him on a financial footing comparable to that of the Byzantine emperors themselves.

Charlemagne's most prolonged military effort was directed against the heathen Saxons of northern Germany. With the twin goals of protecting the Frankish Rhinelands and bringing new souls into the Church, he campaigned for some 32 years (772–804), conquering the Saxons repeatedly and baptizing them by force, only to have them rebel when his armies withdrew. In a fit of savage exasperation he ordered the execution of 4500 unfaithful Saxons in a single bloody day in 782. At length however, Saxony submitted to the remorseless pressure of Charlemagne's soldiers and the Benedictine monks who followed in their wake. By about 800 Frankish control of Saxony was well established, and in subsequent decades Christianity seeped gradually into the Saxon soul. A century and a half later Christian Saxons were governing the most powerful state in Europe and were fostering a significant artistic and intellectual revival that was to enrich the culture of tenth-century Christendom.

CHARLEMAGNE'S EMPIRE

Imperial Coronation: A.D. 800

Charlemagne's armies, by incorporating the great territories of central Germany into the new civilization, had succeeded where the legions of Augustus and his successors had failed. No longer a mere Frankish king, Charlemagne, by 800, was the master of the West. A few small Christian states such as the principalities of southern Italy and the kingdoms of Anglo-Saxon England remained outside his jurisdiction, but with these relatively minor exceptions Charlemagne's political sway extended throughout Western Christendom. He was, in truth, an emperor, and on Christmas Day, 800, his immense accomplishment was given formal recognition when Pope Leo III placed the imperial crown upon his head and acclaimed him "Emperor of the Romans." From the standpoint of legal theory this dramatic act reconstituted the Roman Empire in the West after an interregnum of 324 years. In another sense it was the ultimate consummation of the Franco-Papal Alliance of 751.

The imperial coronation of Charlemagne is difficult to interpret and has evoked heated controversy among historians. According to Einhard, Pope Leo III took Charlemagne by surprise and bestowed upon him an unwanted dignity. Charlemagne had such an aversion to the titles of Emperor and Augustus, so Einhard reports, "that he declared he would not have set foot in the Church the day that they were conferred, although it was a great feast day, if he could have forseen the design of the pope."

Many modern historians have tended to be skeptical of this assertion. It has been argued that Charlemagne was too powerful—too firmly in control of events—to permit a coronation that he did not wish. It has been pointed out that scholars in Charlemagne's court, beguiled by the dream of empire, may well have urged their emperor on. Some historians have stressed the fact that Byzantium lacked an emperor in 800 and that Charlemagne disclosed his interest in the Roman imperial crown by engaging unsuccessfully in marriage negotiations with the Byzantine empress Irene. Conversely, it has recently been suggested that the coronation was largely a product of internal Roman politics during the years 799–800.* In any event, the acclamation that Charlegmagne received from the people of Rome immediately after his coronation had obviously been well researched. It was this ceremony of popular acclamation that had traditionally made a Roman emperor, and even if Charlemagne was not expecting the pope to crown him, he must have known that the populace was preparing to acclaim him.

Most likely Charlemagne's imperial coronation of 800, like the royal coronation of Pepin the Short in 751, represents a coalescence of papal and Carolingian interests. For some years Charlemagne had been attempting to attain a status comparable to that of the Byzantine emperors. In 794 he had abandoned the practice, traditional among Germanic kings, of traveling constantly with his court from estate to estate, and had established his permanent capital at Aachen in Austrasia. Here he sought, though vainly, to create a Constantinople of his own. Aachen was called "New Rome," and an impressive palace church was built in the Byzantine style—almost literally a poor man's Sancta Sophia. Even though Charlemagne's "Mary Church" at Aachen was a far cry from Justinian's masterpiece it was a marvel for its time and place and made a deep impression on contemporaries. Einhard describes it as a beautiful basilica adorned with gold and silver lamps, with rails and doors of solid brass, and with columns and marbles from Rome and Ravenna. It was evidently the product of a major effort on Charlemagne's part—an effort not only to create a beautiful church but also to ape the Byzantines. The coronation of 800 may well have been an expression of this same imitative policy.

The papacy, on the other hand, may well have regarded the coronation as an opportunity to regain some of the initiative it had lost to the all-powerful Charlemagne. To be sure, the Carolingians had been promoted from kings to emperors; but their empire thenceforth bore the stamp, "Made in Rome." In later years the popes would insist that what they gave they could also take away. If the papacy could make emperors it could also depose them. Indeed, it was only shortly before this that the papal chancery had produced a famous forged document called the "Donation of Constantine"* in which the first Christian emperor allegedly gave to the pope the imperial diadem and governance over Rome, Italy, and all The West. The pope is alleged to have returned the diadem but kept the power of governance. Later popes, drawing on the "Donation of Constantine," regarded the Holy Roman emperors as Stewards exercising political authority by delegation from the papacy, wielding their power in the interests of the Roman church. So convincing was this theory of papal supremacy in the eyes of the papacy that if justified the use of any documentation to support its case. The "Donation of Constantine," therefore, was not an effort to rewrite history but an attempt to buttress the papal position by manufacturing evidence for an event that

---

* See Geoffrey Barraclough, *The Medieval Papacy* (New York: Harcourt Brace Jovanovich, 1968), pp. 52–54.

* Probably sometime in the 740s.

Interior of the "Mary Church" at Aachen. The Byzantine arches and the structural formation are very similar to Justinian's Basilica of San Vitale at Ravenna.

had actually occurred, so the papacy imagined, but was unfortunately unrecorded.

Though Charlemagne always respected the papacy he was unwilling to cast himself in the subordinate role which papal theory demanded of him. He was careful to retain the title, "King of the Franks and the Lombards" alongside his new title of "Emperor"; when the time came to crown his son emperor, Charlemagne excluded the pope from the ceremony and did the honors himself. In these maneuvers we are witnessing the prologue to a long, bitter struggle over the correct relationship between empire and papacy—a struggle that reached its crescendo in the eleventh, twelfth, and thirteenth centuries. At stake was the mastery of Western Christendom.

But during the reign of Charlemagne the struggle remained latent for the most part. Charlemagne's power was unrivaled, and the popes were much too weak to oppose him seriously. Indeed, the warm Carolingian-papal relations of Pepin's day continued, and the papacy was nearly smothered in Charlemagne's affectionate embrace.

Carolingian Theocracy

At no time since has Europe been so nearly united as under Charlemagne. And never again would Western Christendom flirt so seriously with theocracy. The papal anointing of Pepin and Charlemagne gave the Carolingian monarchy a sacred, almost priestly quality with which Charlemagne merged his immense authority to govern not only the body politic but the imperial Church as well. The laws and regulations of his reign, which are known as *capitularies,* dealt with both ecclesiastical and secular matters. Although he did not claim to legislate on Church doctrine he felt a deep sense of responsibility for purifying and systematizing ecclesiastical discipline. He was a far greater force in the Carolingian Church than was the pope. He summoned a number of ecclesiastical synods and even presided over one of them. Indeed, the significant intellectual revival known as the "Carolingian Renaissance" was mostly a product of Charlemagne's concern for the welfare of the Church and the perpetuation of ecclesiastical culture.

The Carolingian Renaissance

The term "Carolingian Renaissance" can be misleading. Charlemagne's age produced no lofty abstract thought, no original philosophical or theological system, no Thomas Aquinas or Leonardo da Vinci. If we look for a "renaissance" in the ordinary sense of the word, we are bound to be disappointed. The intellectual task of the Carolingian age was far less exalted, far more rudimentary: to rescue continental culture from the pit of ignorance into which it was sinking.

As with so many other aspects of the era the Carolingian Renaissance bears the stamp of Charlemagne's will and initiative. It was he who saw the desperate need for schools in his kingdom and sought to provide them. There could be no question of establishing institutions of higher learning. None existed north of the Alps, and none would emerge until the High Middle Ages. It was for the Carolingians to build a system of primary and secondary education, and even this was an immensely difficult task. Frankland had no professional class of teachers either lay or clerical. The only hope for pedagogical reform lay with the Church, which had an almost exclusive monopoly on literacy. So Charlemagne tried to force the cathedrals and monasteries of his realm to operate schools which would preserve and disseminate the rudiments of classical-Christian culture. A capitulary of 789 commands that

In every episcopal See and in every monastery, instruction shall be given in the psalms, musical notation, chant, the computation of years and seasons, and grammar, and all books used shall be carefully corrected.

A curriculum of the sort described in this capitulary can hardly be described as intellectually sophisticated or demanding, yet many Carolingian monasteries and cathedrals fell considerably short of the modest standards that it sought to establish. Still, Charlemagne succeeded in improving vastly the quantity and quality of schooling in his empire. There was even an attempt to make village priests provide free instruction in reading and writing. Only a minute fraction of Charlemagne's subjects acquired literacy. But those few provided an all-important learned nucleus which kept knowledge alive and transmitted it to future generations. It was above all in the monastic schools that learning flourished—in houses such as Fulda, Tours, and Reichenau. During the turbulent generations following Charlemagne's death many of these monastic schools survived to become seedbeds of the far greater intellectual awakening of the eleventh and twelfth centuries. In sum, Charlemagne's pedagogical reforms insured that learning in Europe would never again descend to the pre-Carolingian level.

The Carolingian Scholars

As an integral part of his effort to raise the intellectual standards of his realm and sustain Christian culture, Charlemagne assembled scholars at his court from all over Europe. One such scholar was the emperor's biographer, Einhard, from eastern Frankland. Another was the poet-historian Paul the Deacon, of the great Italian Benedictine house of Monte Cassino. Paul the Deacon's *History of the Lombards* provides an invaluable account of that Germanic tribe and its settlement in Italy. From Spain came Theodulf, later bishop of Orleans and abbot of Fleury, a tireless supporter of Charlemagne's pedagogical reforms as well as a poet of considerable talent. The most important of these Carolingian scholars was the Northumbrian Alciun of York, the last significant mind to be produced by the Northumbrian Renaissance. Alcuin, along with his fellow countrymen of an earlier generation—Wilfred of Ripon, Willibrord, and Boniface—represents the vital connecting link between the Christian cultural life of seventh- and eighth-century England and the intellectual upsurge of Carolingian Frankland.

Alcuin performed the essential task of preparing an accurate new edition of the Bible purged of the scribal errors which had crept into it over the centuries, thereby saving Christian culture from the confusion arising from the corruption of its most fundamental text. For many years the chief scholar in Charlemagne's court school, Alcuin spent his final years as abbot of St. Martin of Tours. He was extraordinarily well educated for his period, and his approach to learning typified the whole philosophy of the Carolingian Renaissance: to produce accurate copies of important traditional texts, to encourage the establishment of schools, and in every way possible to cherish and transmit the classical-Christian cultural tradition (without, however, adding to it in any significant way). Alcuin and his fellow scholars were neither intellectual innovators nor men of conspicuous holiness. Drawn by Charlemagne's wealth and power and enriched by his patronage, they struggled to improve the scholarly level of the Carolingian Church; but they showed little concern for deepening its spiritual life or exploring uncharted regions of speculative thought. They had the talents and inclinations—and the limitations—of the schoolmaster. At best they were scholars and humanists; in no sense could they be described as philosophers or mystics.

Accordingly, Alcuin, Theodulf, Einhard, Paul the Deacon, and others like them purified and regularized the liturgy of the Church and encouraged the preaching of sermons. They carried on some of the monastic reforms begun by Boniface and saw to it that every important monastery had a school. It was a question not of producing new Platos and Augustines but of preserving literacy itself. A new, standardized script was developed—the Carolingian minuscule—which derived in part from the Irish and Northumbrian scripts of the previous century. Thenceforth the Carolingian minuscle superseded the often illegible scripts earlier employed on the Continent. Throughout the realm monks set about copying manuscripts on an unprecedented scale. If classical-Christian culture was advanced very little by these activities it was at least preserved. Above all, its base was broadened. In the task they set themselves, these Carolingian scholars were eminently successful.

Carolingian Renaissance after Charlemagne

It is characteristic of the powerful theocratic tendencies of the age that this significant cultural-pedagogical achievement was accomplished through royal rather than papal initiative. Germanic monarchy and classical-Christian culture had joined hands at last. With the breakdown of European unity after Charlemagne's death the momentary fusion of political and cultural energies dissolved; yet the intellectual revival continued. A deeply spiritual movement of monastic reform and moral regeneration began in Aquitaine under the leadership of the ardent and saintly Benedict of Aniane. Soon the influence of this movement took hold at the court of Charlemagne's son and successor, Louis the Pious. Louis gave St. Benedict of Aniane the privilege of visiting any monastery in the empire and tightening its discipline in whatever way he chose. And in 817 a significantly elaborated version of the old Benedictine Rule, based on the strict monastic regulations of Benedict of Aniane, was promulgated for all the monasteries of the empire and given the weight of imperial law. Benedict of Aniane's reform represents a marked shift from the spiritually superficial monastic regulations of Charlemagne's day to a deep concern for the Christ-centered life. The elaborated Benedictine Rule of 817 lost its status as imperial law on Louis the Pious's death in 840, but it remained an inspiration to subsequent monastic reform movements in the centuries that followed. Thenceforth the Benedictine life par excellence was based on Benedict of Aniane's modification of the original Rule.

While Carolingian spiritual life was deepening in the years after Charlemagne's death, Carolingian scholarship continued to flourish in the cathedral and monastic schools. A vigorous controversy over the question of free will and predestination testifies to the vitality of Carolingian thought in the early and middle decades of the ninth century. And in keeping with the Carolingian intellectual program of preserving the classical-Christian tradition, learned churchmen of the Carolingian Renaissance's "second generation" devoted themselves to the preparation of encyclopedic compilations of received knowledge, unoriginal but important none the less in the significant process of cultural transmission. For example, Raban Maur (d. 856), abbot of the great monastery of Fulda, provided an elaborate encyclopedia on the pattern of Isidore of Seville's *Etymologies,* entitled *De Universo*. He also carried forward the Carolingian pedagogical tradition by writing a handbook on the instruction of the clergy—*De Clericorum Institutione*—which had a significant influence on the operation of monastic schools.

John Scotus

The most interesting scholar in this "second generation" was the Irishman, John Scotus Erigena, who stands as the one original thinker of the whole Carolingian age. John Scotus, or John the Scot (the "Scots" in his day were inhabitants of Ireland rather than Scotland), served for years in the court of Charlemagne's grandson, Charles the Bald. Not only a brilliant speculative thinker, he was also a precocious wit, at least if we can give credence to the later legend of a dinner-table conversation between John the Scot and King Charles the Bald. The King, intending to needle his court scholar, asked the rhetorical question, "What is there that separates a Scot from a sot," to which John is alleged to have replied, "Only the dinner table."

John Scotus was a profound student of Neoplatonism and the only western European scholar of his age to master the Greek tongue. He translated into Latin an important Greek philosophical treatise, *On the Celestial Hierarchy,* written by an anonymous late-fifth-century Christian Neoplatonist known as the Pseudo-Dionysius. This author was incorrectly identified in the Middle Ages as Dionysius the Areopagite, the first-century Athenian philosopher who is described in the *Acts of the Apostles* as being converted to Christianity by St. Paul. He was further misidentified as St. Denis, evangelist of the Gauls and first bishop of Paris, who was decapitated by the pagans and in whose honor the great royal monastery of St. Denis was built. Accordingly, the writings of the Pseudo-Dionysius, even though tinged with pantheism, passed into the Middle Ages with the powerful credentials of an early Christian author who was a Pauline convert and a martyred missionary who brought Christianity to Gaul. In reality, the importance of the Pseudo-Dionysius lay in his providing a Christian dimension to the philosophical scheme of Plotinus and other pagan Neoplatonists. The unknowable and indescribable Neoplatonic god—the center and source of the concentric circles of reality—was identified with the God of the Christians. Such a god could not be approached intellectually but only by means of a mystical experience; hence, the Pseudo-Dionysius became an important source of inspiration to later Christian mystics.

Stimulated by the work of the Pseudo-Dionysius that he translated, John Scotus went on to write a highly original Neoplatonic treatise of his own, *On the Divisions of Nature,* which, in its blurred distinction between God and the created world, reflected the Neoplatonic tendency toward pantheism. The work was condemned as heretical in the thirteenth century but made little impact on contemporaries who lacked both the interest and the background to understand it. John Scotus is a lonely figure in intellectual history, without any immediate predecessors or successors. He founded no schools of thought and carried on no real philosophical dialogue with his contemporaries who were scholars, poets, and pedants rather than abstract thinkers. He figures as the supreme intellect in the West between St. Augustine and the philosophers of the High Middle Ages, yet being neither the direct product of earlier intellectual currents nor the cause of subsequent ones, he played a minor role in the evolution of thought. He remains, nevertheless, the one interesting philosopher of the Carolingian epoch.

Historical Significance of the Carolingian Renaissance

The intellectual revival instigated by Charlemagne reverberated down through subsequent generations. John Scotus' Neoplatonism may have been generally ignored and quickly forgotten. Yet in the monasteries and cathedrals of the ninth and tenth centuries, particularly in the German districts of Charlemagne's old empire, documents continued to be copied, schools continued to operate, and commentaries and epitomes of ancient texts continued to appear. By the eleventh century Europe was ready to build on her sturdy Carolingian foundations.

The Carolingian State

Charlemagne's empire was an ephemeral thing, arising from a chaotic past and disintegrating in the turbulent age that followed. It is far easier to understand why the empire broke up than to explain how such a vast, primitive, amorphous state was able to coalesce even briefly. The answer to this puzzle is to be found above all in the person of Charlemagne himself. It was Charlemagne who held his empire together, and he did so by the quality of his leadership and the strength of his personality. In an era of primitive roads and wretched communications he was obliged to depend heavily on the competence and loyalty of the counts, dukes, and margraves who administered his provinces. He kept some control over these magnates by sending pairs of inspectors known as *missi dominici* (envoys of the lord) from his court into the provinces to insure the implementation of his will. The missi dominici, consisting normally of one churchman and one layman, typified the theocratic trend of Charlemagne's age. They were moderately effective in binding the empire together, but only because they were received respectfully in the provinces as representatives of a fear-inspiring monarch. The allegiance of Charlemagne's counts and dukes was mostly a product of their respect for Charlemagne himself. They obeyed his commands and submitted to his capitularies not out of patriotism to his state but because of their devotion to his person. In sum, the administrative institutions of the Carolingian Empire were grossly inadequate to the needs of a great state. Beneath the imposing military and cultural veneer Carolingian Europe was still semi-barbaric. Alcuin was yielding to illusion when he told Charlemagne, "If your intentions are carried out, if may be that a new Athens will arise in Frankland, and an Athens fairer than of old, for our Athens, ennobled by the teachings of Christ, will surpass the wisdom of the Academy." Alcuin's vision was a pathetic mirage; the Carolingian state remained a land of rude, untutored warriors and peasants just emerging from barbarism.

Charlemagne's "Roman Empire" was a faint shadow of the Augustan state, yet one must admire this dogged Carolingian who could do so much with so little; who could make such an effort to transcend his own barbaric past; who as an adult struggled vainly to learn how to write and to master the subtleties of Augustine's *City of God*. The historian Christopher Dawson caught the spirit of Charlemagne's achievement perfectly when he wrote, "The unwieldy empire of Charles the Great did not long survive the death of its founder, and it never really attained the economic and social organization of a civilized state. But, for all that, it marks the first emergence of the European culture from the twilight of prenatal existence into the consciousness of active life."[1]

[1] Christopher Dawson, *The Making of Europe*, (New York: World Publishing Co., Meridian Books, 1957), p. 187.

B. The New Invasions

Tentative though it was, the economic and cultural revival under Charlemagne might conceivably have evolved in the direction of a prosperous, sophisticated civilization had it not been for the devastating new invasions that followed Charlemagne's death in 814. Until then the Carolingian realm had enjoyed relative peace. Intellectual life, although still rudimentary, was in the process of reawakening, and with the stimulus of the silver coinage which Charlemagne issued, commerce quickened. One historian has even suggested that under the bracing influence of Charlemagne's economic policy towns were beginning to grow and flourish once again. But these hopeful signs proved to be a false dawn. During the ninth and tenth centuries Europe was obliged to fight for its life against the triple thrust of alien invaders—the seminomadic Hungarians from the east, the piratical Saracens (Muslims) from the south, and the wide-ranging Vikings from the north. As a result, the maturing of a higher civilization was delayed in Europe for another two centuries.

THE LATER CAROLINGIANS

Louis the Pious (814–840)

It would be wrong to ascribe the political fragmentation of the Carolingian Empire entirely to these outside pressures. Charlemagne himself, in keeping with Frankish tradition, planned to divide his state among his several sons. As it happened, however, Charlemagne outlived all but one of them. The luck of the Carolingians was still running, and when the great conqueror died in 814 his realm passed intact to his remaining heir, Louis the Pious (see Table I).

Although Louis was by no means incompetent, his military and political talents were distinctly inferior to those of his father Charlemagne, his grandfather Pepin the Short, and his great-grandfather Charles Martel. Carolingian unity continued but Carolingian leadership showed signs of faltering. Louis the Pious was well named. He ran Charlemagne's minstrels and concubines out of the imperial court and replaced them with priests and monks. Far more than his hard-headed father, Louis committed himself to the dream of a unified Christian Empire—a City of God brought down to earth. Yet he was far less suited than Charlemagne to the Herculean task of maintaining unity and cohesion in the immense, heterogeneous empire which the Carolingians had won. He was the first of his line to conceive the notion of bequeathing supreme political authority to his eldest son and thereby making the unity of the kingdom a matter of policy rather than chance. Ironically, he turned out to be the last Carolingian to rule an undivided Frankish realm. His bold plan for a single succession was foiled by the ambitions of his younger sons who rebelled openly against him and plunged the empire into civil war.

Treaty of Verdun

When Louis the Pious's unhappy reign ended in 840 his three surviving sons struggled bitterly for the spoils. The eldest of the three, Lothar, claimed the indivisible imperial title and hegemony over the entire realm. The other two sons, Louis the German and Charles the Bald, fought to win independent royal authority in East and West Frankland respectively. In the end Lothar had to yield to the combined might of his younger brothers. The controversy was settled by the Treaty of Verdun in 843, which permanently divided the empire and foreshadowed the political structure of modern Europe. Lothar was permitted to keep the imperial title but was denied any superior jurisdiction over the realms of Louis the German and Charles the Bald. Louis ruled East Frankland, which became the nucleus of the modern German state. In a very real sense, he was Germany's first king. Charles the Bald became king of West

TABLE I
Carolingian Chronology

- 687: Pepin of Heristal, Carolingian mayor of Austrasia, defeats Neustria; Carolingian hegemony established.
- 714–741: Rule of Charles Martel.
- 732: Arabs defeated at Tours.
- 741–768: Rule of Pepin the Short.
- 751: Pepin crowned king of the Franks. Merovingian Dynasty ends.
- 754: Death of St. Boniface.
- 768–814: Reign of Charlemagne.
- 772–804: Charlemagne's Saxon Wars.
- 800: Charlemagne crowned Roman Emperor.
- 814–840: Reign of Louis the Pious.
- 843: Treaty of Verdun.

B. *The New Invasions*

PARTITION OF THE EMPIRE
TREATY OF VERDUN, 843

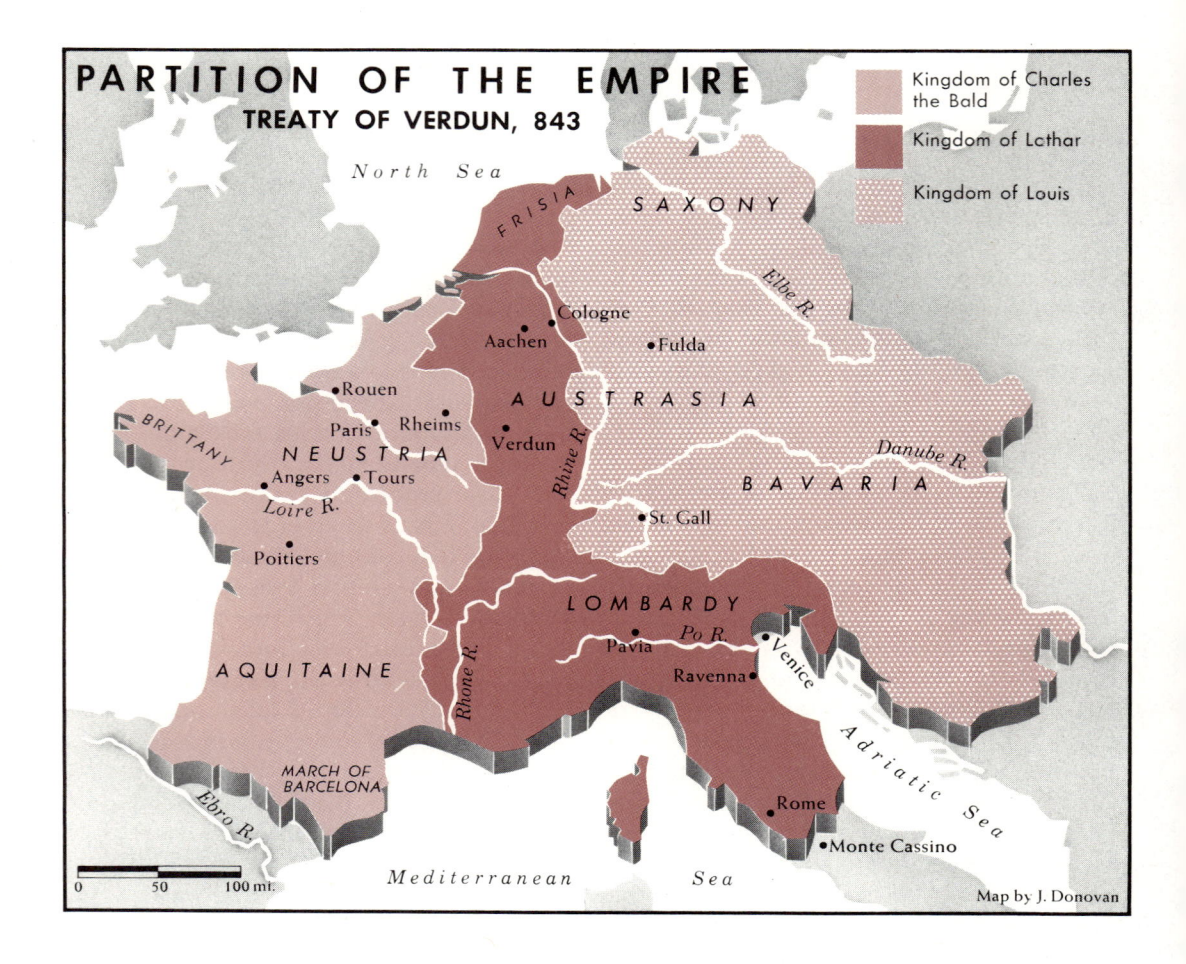

- Kingdom of Charles the Bald
- Kingdom of Lothar
- Kingdom of Louis

Frankland, which evolved into modern France. Lothar retained a long, narrow strip of territory which stretched for some thousand miles northward from Italy through Burgundy, Alsace, Lorraine, and the Netherlands, embracing considerable portions of western Germany and eastern France.* This Middle Kingdom included the two "imperial capitals"—Rome and Aachen—but its exposed frontiers were difficult to defend, and it was utterly lacking in unity. At Lothar's death in 855 it was subdivided among his three sons, one of whom inherited Carolingian Italy and the increasingly insignificant imperial title. From the ninth century to the twentieth, fragments of Lothar's middle kingdom have been the source of endless bitter territorial disputes between Germany and France.

The struggles among Charlemagne's grandsons occurred against a background of Viking, Hungarian, and Saracen invasions, which accelerated the tendency toward political fragmentation brought about by internal weaknesses. But even without the invasions, and without the Frankish tradition of divided succession, Charlemagne's huge, unwieldy empire could not have long remained intact once his iron hand had been removed from control. As it turned out, even the more modest political units arising from the Treaty of Verdun were too large—too far

* See map on this page.

374   Carolingian Europe and the New Invasions

removed from the desperate realities of the countryside—to cope successfully with the lightning raids of Viking shipmen or Hungarian horsemen. During the ninth and tenth centuries Carolingian leadership was visibly failing. The incapacity of the later Carolingians was nowhere better illustrated than in their names: Charles the Fat, Charles the Simple, Louis the Child, Louis the Blind.

SARACENS, MAGYARS, VIKINGS

Impact of the Invasions

The Saracens, Hungarians, and Vikings, who plundered the declining Carolingian state, were in part drawn by the growing political vacuum, and in part impelled by forces operating in their own homelands. Europe suffered much from their marauding, yet it was strong enough in the end to survive and absorb the invaders. And these invasions were the last that Western Christendom was destined to endure. From about A.D. 1000 to the present the West has had the unique opportunity of developing on its own, sheltered from alien attacks that have so disrupted other civilizations over the past millennium. As the historian Marc Bloch has said, "It is surely not unreasonable to think that this extraordinary immunity, of which we have shared the privilege with scarcely any people but the Japanese, was one of the fundamental factors of European civilization. . . ."[2]

Yet in the ninth and tenth centuries Europe's hard-pressed peoples had no way of knowing that the invasions would one day end. A Frankish historian of the mid-ninth century wrote, perhaps with a touch of melodramatic exaggeration, "The number of ships grows larger and larger; the great host of Northmen continually

[2] Marc Bloch, *Feudal Society*, trans. L. A. Manyon (Chicago: The University of Chicago Press, 1961), p. 56.

increases; on every hand Christians are the victims of massacres, looting, and incendiarism—clear proof of which will remain as long as the world itself endures. The Northmen capture every city they pass through, and none can withstand them." In southern Gaul people prayed for divine protection against the Saracens: "Eternal Trinity . . . deliver thy Christian people from the oppression of the pagans." To the north they prayed, "From the savage nation of the Northmen, which lays waste our realms, deliver us, O God." And in northern Italy: "Against the arrows of the Hungarians be thou our protector."

Saracens and Magyars

The Saracens of the ninth and tenth centuries, unlike their predecessors in the seventh and early eighth, came as brigands rather than conquerors and settlers. From their pirate nests in Africa, Spain, and the Mediterranean islands they preyed on shipping, plundered coastal cities, and sailed up rivers to carry their devastation far inland. Saracen bandit lairs were established on the southern coast of Gaul, from which the marauders conducted raids far and wide through the countryside and kidnapped pilgrims crossing the Alpine passes. Charlemagne had never possessed much of a navy, and his successors found themselves helpless to defend their coasts. In 846 Saracen brigands raided Rome itself, profaning its churches and stealing its treasures. As late as 982 a German king was severely defeated by Saracens in southern Italy; but by then the raids were tapering off. Southern Europe, now bristling with fortifications, had learned to defend itself and was even beginning to challenge Saracen domination of the western Mediterranean.

The Hungarians, or Magyars, fierce nomadic horsemen from the Asiatic steppes, settled in the land now known as Hungary. From the late 800s to 955 they terrorized Germany, northern Italy, and eastern Gaul. Hungarian raiding parties ranged across the land, seeking defenseless settlements to plunder, avoiding fortified towns, outriding and outmaneuvering the armies sent against them. In time, however, they became more sedentary, gave more attention to their farms, and lost much of their nomadic savagery. In 955 King Otto the Great of Germany crushed a large Hungarian army at the battle of Lechfeld and brought the raids to an end at last. Within another half-century, the Hungarians had adopted Christianity and were becoming integrated into the community of Christian Europe.

Vikings

The Vikings, or Norsemen, were the most fearsome invaders of all. These redoubtable warrior-seafarers came from Scandinavia, the very land that had, centuries before, disgorged many of the Germanic barbarians into Europe. Thus the ninth century Vikings and the Germanic invaders of Roman times had similar ethnic backgrounds. But to the ninth-century European—the product of countless Germanic-Celtic-Roman intermarriages, tamed by the Church and by centuries of settled life—the heathen Vikings seemed a hostile and alien people.

Then, as now, the Scandinavians were divided roughly into three groups: Danes, Swedes, and Norwegians. During the great age of Viking expansion in the ninth and tenth centuries the Danes, who were brought cheek to jowl with the Carolingian Empire by Charlemagne's conquest of Saxony, focused their attention on Frankland and England. The Norwegians raided and settled in Scotland, Ireland, and the North Atlantic. The Swedes concentrated on the East—the Baltic shores, Russia, and the Byzantine Empire. Yet the three Norse peoples had much in common, and the distinctions between them were by no means sharp. It is therefore proper to regard their raids, their astonishing explorations, and their far-flung commercial enterprises as a single great international movement.

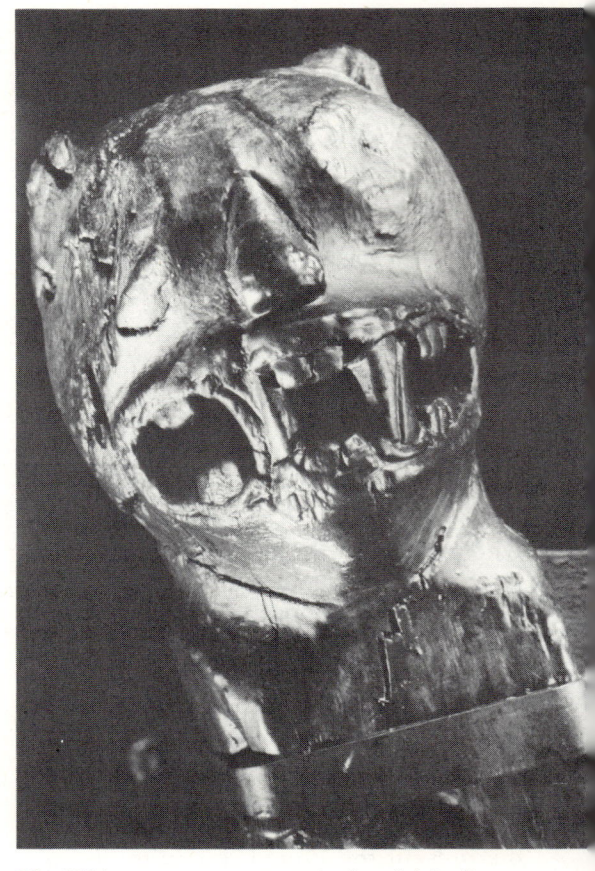

The Viking terror: cornerpost of a sleigh discovered in archaeological excavations at Gokstad, near Oslo.

Though the breakdown of Carolingian leadership doubtless acted as a magnet to Viking marauders, their raids on the West began as early as Charlemagne's age. The basic causes for their outward thrust must be sought in Scandinavia itself. Since pre-tenth-century Scandinavia is almost a closed book to historians, our explanations for the Viking outburst are little more than educated guesses. It is likely, however, that the Scandinavian population, once sharply reduced by the outward migrations of Roman times, had increased by the later 700s to a level which the primitive Norse agriculture was scarcely able to support. The pressure of overpopulation was probably aggravated by growing centralized royal power which cramped the more restless spirits and drove them to seek adventures and opportunities abroad. A third factor was the development of improved Viking ships, eminently seaworthy, propelled by both sail and oars, and capable of carrying crews of 40 to 100 warriors at speeds up to ten knots. In these longships the tall, muscular, reddish-haired Viking warriors struck the ports of Northern Europe. They sailed up rivers far into the interior, plundering the towns and monasteries of Frankland and England, sometimes stealing horses and riding across the countryside to spread their devastation still further.

The people of Europe were accustomed enough to warfare among their own nominally Christian warrior-nobility. But Christian barons tended to respect the sanctity of the monastaries, which, with their wealth, enticed the acquisitive Vikings and, with their near monopoly on literacy, produced almost all our information about the Viking raids. The monastic chroniclers of the time, accustomed to peace within their walls, doubtless exaggerated the violence of the Viking age and the size and ferocity of the Viking armies. Yet the Viking impact on northern France, England, and Russia was real, and it was lasting.

Attacks against England

England was the first to suffer from Viking attacks. About 789 three longships touched the Channel coast in Dorset and Vikings poured out of them to loot and sack a nearby town. Thenceforth the Anglo-Saxon kingdoms were tormented by incessant Viking raids. In 794 Norse brigands annihilated the Northumbrian monastery of Jarrow, where Bede had lived and died. Other great monastic centers of Northumbria suffered a similar devastation.

In 842 the Danes plundered London, and a few years thereafter they began to establish permanent winter bases in England which freed them from the necessity of returning to Scandinavia after the raiding season. By the later 800s they had turned from piracy to large-scale occupation and permanent settlement. One after another the Anglo-Saxon kingdoms were overrun until at length, in the 780s, only the southern kingdom of Wessex remained free of Danish control—and even Wessex came within a hair's breadth of falling to the Danes.

Attacks against the Continent

To mariners such as the Vikings the English Channel was a boulevard rather than a barrier, and their raiding parties attacked the English and Frankish shores indiscriminately. They established permanent bases at the mouths of great rivers and sailed up them to plunder defenseless monasteries and sack towns. Antwerp was ravaged in 837, Rouen in 841, Hamburg and Paris in 845, Charlemagne's old capital at Aachen in 881.

But if some Europeans were driven to helpless resignation others fought doggedly to protect their lands. King Alfred the Great of Wessex saved his kingdom from Danish conquest in the late 870s and began the task of rolling back the Danish armies in England. King Arnulf of East Frankland won a decisive victory over the Norsemen in 891 at the battle of the Dyle and thereby decreased the Viking pressure on Germany—although it was at this very moment that the Hungarian

as the Franks. They adopted French culture and the French language, yet retained much of their old energy. In the eleventh century Normandy was producing some of Europe's most vigorous warriors, Crusaders, administrators, and monks.

Ireland, Greenland, North America

France, England, and Germany formed only a part of the vast Viking world of the ninth and tenth centuries. By the mid-800s Norwegians and Danes had conquered the greater part of Ireland, and between 875 and 930 they settled remote Iceland. There a distinctive Norse culture arose which for several centuries remained only slightly affected by the main currents of Western civilization. In Iceland the magnificent oral tradition of the Norse saga flourished and was eventually committed to writing. The Icelandic Norsemen were perhaps the greatest sailors of all. They settled on the coast of Greenland in the late 900s, and established temporary settlements on the northern coasts of North America itself in the eleventh century, anticipating Columbus by half a millennium.

Russia

To the east Swedish Vikings overran Finland and penetrated far southward across European Russia to trade with Constantinople and Baghdad. The Byzantine emperors took pride in the tall Norse mercenaries who served in their imperial guard. In Russia a Swedish dynasty established itself at Novgorod in the later ninth century, ruling over the indigenous Slavic population. In the tenth century a Norse prince of Novgorod captured the south-Russian city of Kiev, which became the capital of the powerful, well-organized state of Kievan Russia. Deeply influenced by the culture of its subjects, the dynasty at Kiev became far more Slavic than Scan-

raids began. West Frankland continued to suffer for a time, but in about 911 King Charles the Simple created a friendly Viking buffer state in northern France by concluding a treaty with a Norse chieftain named Rolf. The Vikings in Rolf's band had been conducting raids from their settlement at the mouth of the Seine River. Charles, less simple than his name would imply, reasoned that if he could make Rolf his ally the Seine settlement might prove an effective barrier against further raids. Rolf became a Christian, married Charles the Simple's daughter, and recognized at least in some sense the superiority of the West Frankish monarchy. Thus his state acquired legitimacy in the eyes of Western Christendom. Expanding gradually under Rolf and his successors, it became known as the land of the Northmen, or "Normandy." Over the next century and a half the Normans became as good Christians

This scene depicts the visit of Princess Olga of Kiev to Constantinople in the tenth century. The princess was the first Russian ruler to embrace Christianity.

dinavian. Around the turn of the millennium, as we have already seen, Prince Vladimir of Kiev adopted Byzantine Christianity and submitted himself and his people to the Patriarch of Constantinople, thereby opening Russia to the influence of Byzantine culture (see p. 329).

Twilight of the Viking Age

The development of centralized monarchies in Denmark, Norway, and Sweden, which may well have been a factor in driving enterprising Norse seamen to seek their fortunes elsewhere, ultimately resulted in taming the Viking spirit. As Scandinavia became increasingly civilized its kings discouraged the activities of roaming independent warrior bands, and its social environment gave rise to a somewhat more humdrum, sedentary life. Far into the eleventh century England continued to face the attacks of Norsemen, but these invaders were no longer pirate bands; rather, they were royal armies led by Scandinavian kings. The nature of the Scandinavian threat had changed, and by the late eleventh century the threat had ceased altogether. Around the year 1000 Christianity was winning converts all across the Scandinavian world. In Iceland, in Russia—even in the kingdoms of Scandinavia itself—the Norsemen were adopting the religion of the monks who had once so feared them. Scandinavia was becoming a part of western European culture.

Even at the height of the invasions the Norsemen were by no means pure barbarians. They excelled at commerce as well as piracy. They were the greatest seafarers of the age. They introduced Europe to the art of ocean navigation and enlarged the horizons of Western Christendom, injecting a spirit of enterprise and cosmopolitanism into the conservative, parochial outlook of Carolingian civilization.

C. Europe Survives the Siege

RESPONSE TO THE INVASIONS: ENGLAND

The invasions of the ninth and tenth centuries wrought significant changes in the political and social organization of western Europe. Generally speaking, political authority tended to crumble into small local units as unwieldy royal armies failed to cope with the lightning raids. This was true in France, but it was less so in Germany, where the monarchy, after a period of relative weakness, underwent a spectacular recovery in the tenth century. In England, paradoxically, the hammerblows of the Danes had the ultimate result of unifying the several Anglo-Saxon states into a single kingdom.

In the later eighth century, on the eve of the Viking invasions, England was politically fragmented, as it had been ever since the Anglo-Saxon conquests. But over the centuries the several smaller kingdoms had gradually passed under the control of three larger ones: Northumbria in the north, Mercia in the Midlands, and Wessex in the south. The Danish attacks of the ninth century, by destroying the power of Wessex's rivals, cleared the field for the Wessex monarchy and thereby hastened the trend toward consolidation that was already underway. But if the Danes were doing the Wessex monarchy a favor, neither side was aware of it during the troubled years of the later ninth century. For a time it appeared that the Danes might conquer Wessex itself.

King Alfred

At the moment of crisis a remarkable leader rose to the Wessex throne: Alfred the Great (871–99). Alfred did everything in his power to save his kingdom from the Vikings. He fought ferocious battles against them. He even resorted to bribing them. In the winter of 878 the Danes, in a surprise attack, invaded Wessex and forced Alfred to take refuge, with a handful of companions, on the isle of Athelney in a remote swamp. Athelney was England's Valley Forge. In the following spring Alfred rallied his forces and smashed a Danish army at the battle of Edington. This victory turned the tide of the war; the Danish leader agreed to take up Christianity, to withdraw from the land, and to accept a "permanent" peace. Wessex was never again seriously threatened.

But other Danes under other leaders refused to honor the peace, and Alfred, in his later campaigns, conquered Kent and most of Mercia and captured London—even then England's greatest city. In the 880s a new peace treaty gave Wessex most of southern and southwestern England. The remainder of England—the "Danelaw"—remained hostile, but all non-Danish England was now united under King Alfred.

Like all successful leaders of the age, Alfred was an able warrior. But more than that, he was a brilliant, imaginative organizer who systematized military recruitment and founded the English navy, seeing clearly that Christian Europe could not hope to drive back the Vikings without challenging them on the seas. He filled his land with fortresses which served both as defensive strongholds and as places of sanctuary for the agrarian population in time of war. And gradually, as the Danish tide was rolled back, new fortresses were built to secure the territories newly reconquered. Alfred clarified and rationalized the laws of his people, enforced them strictly, and ruled with an authority such as no Anglo-Saxon king had exercised before his time.

Intellectual Revival

King Alfred was also a scholar and a patron of learning. His intellectual environment was even less promising than Charlemagne's. The great days of Bede, Boniface, and Alcuin were far in the past, and by Alfred's time, Latin—the key to classical Christian culture—was almost unknown in England. Like Charlemagne, Alfred gathered scholars from far and wide—England, Wales, the continent—and set them to work teaching Latin and translating Latin classics into the Anglo-Saxon language. Alfred himself participated in the work of translation, helping to render such works as Boethius's *Consolation of Philosophy*, Pope Gregory's *Pastoral Care*, and Bede's *Ecclesiastical History* into the native tongue. In his translation of Boethius, Alfred added a regretful comment of his own: "In those days one never heard of ships armed for war." And in his preface to the *Pastoral Care* he alluded with nostalgia to the days "before everything was ravaged and burned, when England's churches overflowed with treasures and books." Alfred's intellectual revival, even more than Charlemagne's, was a salvage operation rather than an outburst of originality. He was both modest and accurate when he described himself as one who wandered through a great forest collecting timber with which others could build.

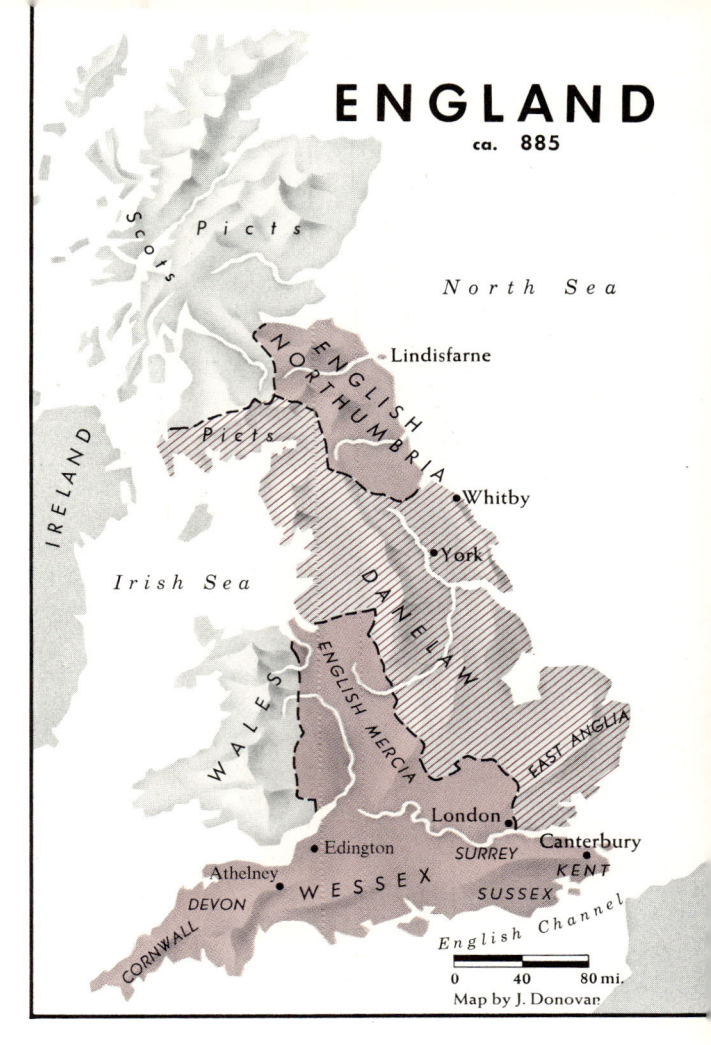

Alfred's task of reconquest was carried on by his able successors in the first half of the tenth century. By mid-century all England was in their hands, and the kings of Wessex had become the kings of England. Great numbers of Danish settlers still remained in northern and eastern England—the amalgamation of Danish and English customs required many generations—but the creative response of the Wessex kings

381   C. Europe Survives the Siege

The Alfred Jewel, a ninth-century ornament, two and a half inches long. Around its outer rim is the inscription "Alfred ordered me to be made." The rim, which terminates in a boar's head, encircles an enamel portrait of the king holding crossed scepters.

to the Danish threat had transformed and politically united the Anglo-Saxon world. Out of the agony of the invasions the English monarchy was born.

Renewal of the Danish Attacks

For a generation after the conquest of the Danelaw, from about 955 to 980, England enjoyed relative peace and prosperity. English flotillas patrolled the shores, the old fortresses began to evolve into commercial centers, and churchmen addressed themselves to the task of monastic reform. But the Danish inhabitants of northern and eastern England remained only half committed to the new English monarchy, and with the accession of an incompetent child-king, Ethelred the Unready, (978–1016), Danish invasions resumed.

The new invasions evolved into a campaign of conquest directed by the Danish monarchy. The English defense was characterized by incompetence, treason, and panic. In 991 Ethelred began paying a tribute to the Danes, known thereafter as "danegeld." In later years the danegeld evolved into a land tax which was exceedingly profitable to the English monarchy, but at the time it was a symbol of humiliation. In 1016 Ethelred fled the country altogether, and in the following year King Canute of Denmark became the monarch of England.

Canute (1017–1035)

Canute has been described as nearly a dwarf and nearly a genius. He conquered Norway as well as England, and joining these two lands to his kingdom of Denmark, he became the master of a huge empire centering on the North Sea. A product of the new civilizing forces at work in eleventh-century Scandinavia, Canute was no bloodthirsty Viking. He issued law codes, practiced Christianity, and kept the peace. Devoting much of his time to England, he cast himself as an English king in the old Wessex tradition. He respected and upheld the ancient customs of the land and gave generously to the monasteries. Despite his Danish background, he was a far better English monarch than Ethelred. His reign was a continuation of the past, and he added luster to the crown that Alfred's dynasty had forged. English religion and culture prospered as before: "Merry sang the monks of Ely as Canute the king rowed by."

Canute's Danish-Norwegian-English

empire was hopelessly disunited and failed to survive his death in 1035. When the last of his sons died in 1042 the English realm fell peacefully to Edward the Confessor, a member of the Old Wessex dynasty who had grown up in exile in Normandy.

The Aftermath

Though a poor general and a mediocre administrator, Edward the Confessor was a man of piety who won the support of his people despite his political ineptitude. His pious insistence on his own virginity (or possibly his impotence) ensured a disputed succession upon his death in 1066 and set the stage for the Norman Conquest. When William the Conqueror, duke of Normandy, invaded England and won its crown in 1066, he inherited a prosperous kingdom with strong, well-established political and legal traditions—a kingdom still divided by differences in custom but with a deep-seated respect for royal authority. Ethelred the Unready notwithstanding, the Wessex dynasty had done its work well. With the timber that Alfred collected, his successors had built an ample and sturdy edifice.

RESPONSE TO THE INVASIONS: FRENCH FEUDALISM

In England the invasions stimulated the trend toward royal unification; in France they encouraged a shattering of political authority into small local units. This paradox can be explained in part by the fact that France, unlike England, was far too large for the Vikings to conquer. Although many of them settled in Normandy, the chief Norse threat to France came in the form of plundering expeditions rather than large conquering armies. Distances were too great, communications too primitive, and the national territorial army too unwieldy for the king to take the lead in defending his realm. Military responsibility descended to local lords who alone could hope to protect the countryside from the swift Viking assaults. The French Carolingians became increasingly powerless until at length in 987 the crown passed to a new dynasty—the Capetians. During the twelfth and thirteenth centuries the Capetian family produced some of France's most illustrious kings, but for the time being the new dynasty was as powerless as the old one. After 987, as before, the nobles overshadowed the king. About all one can say of the French monarchy in these dark years is that it survived.

Benefice and Vassalage

The Viking Age witnessed the birth of feudalism in France. In a very real sense feudalism was a product of France's response to the invasions. Yet in another sense the Franks had long been drifting in a feudal direction. The roots of feudalism ran deep: one root was the honorable bond of fidelity and service of a warrior to his lord—which characterized the lord-vassal relationship of late-Merovingian and early-Carolingian times, and the still earlier comitatus of the Germanic barbarians. Another root was the late-Roman and early-medieval concept of land-holding in return for certain services to the person who granted the land. An estate granted to a tenant in return for service was known as a *benefice.*

Charles Martel took an important step toward feudalism by joining the institutions of benefice and vassalage. He undertook heavy confiscations of Church property and granted the appropriated estates to his military vassals. One reason for this step was the shortage of money in the Early Middle ages; it was almost impossible for a ruler to support his soldiers with wages. Often the vassals of an important Frankish lord were fed and sheltered in his household. Indeed, the "household knight" persisted throughout the feudal age. But as their military importance grew these warrior-vassals exhibited an ever-increasing hunger for land. Their lords were therefore under considerable pressure to grant them estates—benefices—in return for their loyalty and service.

This tendency was associated with a shift in Frankish military tactics. The Franks had originally been infantrymen, but gradually cavalry became increasingly important. The Frankish warrior par excellence became the armored, mounted knight, more effective than the infantrymen, but also far more expensive to support. The knight needed a fine mount, heavy armor and weapons, several attendants, and years of training. Hence the tendency for a lord to support his knightly vassals by granting them estates in return for their service. The knight did not, of course, labor on his own fields; rather he administered them and collected dues, chiefly in kind, from his peasants.

The Carolingian military vassal was typically a knight. As knightly tactics came more and more to dominate warfare, the custom of vassalage spread widely. Frankish magnates of Charlemagne's time had pledged their allegiance to their emperor and had thereby recognized that they were his vassals and he their lord. Moreover, these royal vassals had vassals of their own who owed primary allegiance to their immediate lords rather than to the emperor. Charlemagne himself approved of this practice of private lordship and encouraged the free men of his realm to become vassals of his magnates. In time of war these vassals of vassals (or subvassals) were expected to join their lords' contingents in the royal army. The disintegrative tendencies implicit in such an arrangement are obvious. Yet Charlemagne, lacking a coherent civil service or adequate funds to hire a professional army of his own, was obliged to depend on this potentially unstable hierarchy of authority and allegiance.

With the removal of Charlemagne's commanding personality, and under the pressure of the invasions, the rickety hierarchy began to crumble into its component parts. Charlemagne's old territorial officials, the dukes, counts, and margraves, backed by their own vassals, tended increasingly to usurp royal rights. They administered justice and collected taxes without regard for the royal will. In time they built castles and assumed all responsibility for the defense of their districts. Nominally these feudal magnates remained vassals of the kings of France, but they soon became too powerful to be coerced by the crown. Their authority was limited chiefly by the independence of their own vassals, who began to create subvassals or sub-subvassals of their own. At the height of the feudal age the lord-vassal relationship might run down through some ten or twenty levels; there was scarcely a vassal to be found who was not the lord of some still lower vassal.

The ultimate consequences of these developments have been described as "feudal anarchy." In a sense the term is well chosen but it should not mislead us into thinking of feudalism simply as a "bad thing." Given the instability of the Carolingian Empire and the vulnerability of France in the Viking era, feudalism emerges as a successful accommodation to the realities of the age. Roman Europe succumbed to barbarian invasions; feudal Europe survived its invaders and ultimately absorbed them.

The Fief

French feudalism reached its height in the tenth and eleventh centuries. Its key institution was the military benefice, the estate granted by a lord to his vassal in return for allegiance and service—primarily knightly military service. This military benefice was commonly known as a *fief* (rhyming with beef). It was a practical response to the requirements of local defense, the breakdown of central authority, and the scarcity of money which necessitated the paying for service in land rather than wages. A great lord would grant an estate—a fief—to his vassal. The vassal might then grant a part of the estate— another fief—to a vassal of his own. And so on and on, down and down, the process of enfeoffment went. The result was a hierarchically organized landed knightly aristocracy. Each knight gave homage and fealty—that is, pledged his personal allegiance—to his immediate lord; each lived off the labor and dues of a dependent peasantry which tilled the fields that his fief embraced; each administered a court and dispensed justice to those below him.

Feudalism Defined

Such were the essential ingredients of feudalism. The term is extremely difficult to define and has often been abused and misunderstood. The great French scholar Marc Bloch defined it in these words:

"A subject peasantry; widespread use of the service tenement (that is, the fief) instead of a salary, which was out of the question; the supremacy of a class of specialized warriors; ties of obedience and protection which bind man to man and, within the warrior class, assume the distinctive form called vassalage; fragmentation of authority—leading inevitably to disorder; and in the midst of all this, the survival of other forms of association, family and state . . . —such then seem to be the fundamental features of European feudalism."[3]

With this description in mind it may be helpful to emphasize some of the things

[3] Bloch, op. cit., p. 446.

Twelfth-century bronze seal, showing Raimon de Mondragon kneeling before the archbishop of Arles, his suzerain. This is an act of faith and homage.

that feudalism was not. It was not, for one thing, a universal and symmetrical system. Born in northern France in the Viking age, it took on many different forms as it spread across Europe. In northern France itself it varied widely from one region to another. It by no means encompassed all the land, for even at its height many landowners owed no feudal obligations and had no feudal ties. The feudal hierarchy, or feudal "pyramid," was riddled with ambiguities: a single vassal might hold several fiefs from several lords; a lord might receive a fief from his own vassal, thereby putting himself in the extraordinary position of being his vassal's vassal. The degree of confusion possible in feudalism is well illustrated by this twelfth-century act of enfeoffment:

I, John of Toul, affirm that I am the vassal of the Lady Beatrice, countess of Troyes, and of her son Theobald, count of Champagne, against every creature living or dead, excepting my allegiance to Lord Enjourand of Coucy, Lord John of Arcis, and the count of Grandpré. If it should happen that the count of Grandpré

385   C. Europe Survives the Siege

should be at war with the countess and count of Champagne in his own quarrel, I will aid the count of Grandpré in my own person, and will aid the count and countess of Champagne by sending them the knights whose services I owe them from the fief which I hold of them.

Feudalism was not, in its heyday, associated with the romantic knight errant, the many-turreted castle, or the lady fair. The knight of the ninth, tenth, and eleventh centuries was a rough-hewn warrior. His armor was simple, his horse was tough, his castle was a crude wooden tower atop an earthen mound, and his lady fair was any available wench. Chivalry developed after a time, but not until the foundations of the old feudal order were being eroded by the revival of commerce, royal government, and infantry tactics. Only then did the knight compensate for his declining usefulness by turning to elaborate armor, courtly phrases, and fairy-tale castles.

Feudalism was not exclusively a military institution. The vassal owed his lord not only military service but a variety of additional obligations as well. Among these were the duty to join his lord's retinue on tours of the countryside; to serve in his lord's court of justice; to feed, house, and entertain his lord and his lord's retinue on their all-too-frequent visits; to give money to his lord on a variety of specified occasions; to contribute to his lord's ransom should he be captured in battle. Early in its history the fief became hereditary. The lord, however, retained the right to confiscate it should his vassal die without hiers, to supervise and exploit it during a minority, and to exercise a power of veto over the marriage of a female fief-holder. In return for such rights as these the lord was obliged to protect and uphold the interests of his vassals. The very essence of feudalism was the notion of reciprocal rights and obligations, and the feudal outlook played a key role in steering medieval Europe away from autocracy.

Political Feudalism

Feudalism was both a military and a political system. With military responsibility went political power. As the central government of West Frankland demonstrated an ever-increasing incapacity to cope with the invasions or keep peace in the countryside, sovereignty tended to sink to the level of the greater feudal lords. Although nominally royal vassals, these magnates were powers unto themselves, ruling their own territories without royal interference and maintaining their own courts and administrative systems as well as their own armies. In the days of the Viking raids many of these magnates had extreme difficulty in controlling their own turbulent vassals; feudal tenants several steps down in the pyramid were often able to behave as though they had no real superiors. Subvassals with their own courts and armies were frequently in a position to defy their lords. Accordingly, it is hard to identify the real locus of political power in early feudal France. Sovereignty was spread up and down the aristocratic hierarchy, and a lord's real power depended on his military prowess, his ambition, and the firmness of his leadership.

Specialists in medieval history are inclined to limit "feudalism" to the network of rights and obligations existing among members of the knightly aristocracy—the holders of fiefs. Although resting on the labor of peasants, the feudal structure itself encompassed only the warrior class of lords and vassals. There was, in other words, a world of difference between a vassal and a serf. Beneath the level of the feudal warrior class, 80 or 90 percent of the population continued to labor on the land, producing the food that sustained society. Yet the peasants were scorned by the nobility as boors and louts, and were largely ignored by the chroniclers of the age.

The feudal chaos of the ninth and tenth

centuries, with its fragmentation of sovereign power and its incessant private wars, gradually gave way to a somewhat more orderly regime. Great territorial magnates such as the counts of Anjou and Flanders and the duke of Normandy extended their frontiers at the expense of weaker neighbors and tightened their control over their own vassals and subvassals. But not until the twelfth and thirteenth centuries did the French monarchs began to rise above the level of their greater magnates and assert real authority over the realm. The high noon of feudalism was a period of virtual eclipse for the French crown.

RESPONSE TO INVASIONS: GERMANY

"Tribal" Duchies

In England the invasions brought royal unification; in France, feudal particularism. The response of Germany differed from those of both England and France, owing to the special character of the invasions that Germany faced and the unique conditions prevailing in Germany itself. Although East Frankland (Germany) was subject to Viking attacks, the real threat came from the Hungarian horsemen of the East. When the late Carolingian kings of Germany proved incapable of coping with the Hungarian raids, real authority descended, as in France, to the great magnates of the realm. But these magnates were not the dukes and counts of Carolingian officialdom. Most of Germany had remained outside Frankish control until the Carolingian conquests of the eighth century, and the Frankish system of local administration was relatively ephemeral there. The ancient tribal consciousness of Saxons, Bavarians, and Swabians was still strong. In the critical decades of the late ninth and early tenth centuries ambitious noblemen exploited this tribal patriotism by grasping leadership over the old tribal districts. These men of the hour assumed the title of duke, and the regions that they ruled came to be known as tribal duchies.* The "tribal" dukes sought to dominate the local ecclesiastical organizations, to seize the royal Carolingian estates in their duchies, and to usurp royal powers. It was they who stood up to the Hungarian thrust.

In the early tenth century Germany was dominated by five tribal duchies: Saxony, Swabia, Bavaria, Franconia, and Lorraine. The first three had been incorporated only superficially into the Carolingian state, whereas the western duchies of Franconia and Lorraine were much more strongly Frankish in outlook and organization.

The five "tribal" dukes might well have become the masters of Germany. Their ambitions were frustrated by two closely related factors: (1) their failure to curb the Hungarians, and (2) the reinvigoration of the German monarchy under an able new dynasty. The Carolingian line came to an end in Germany in 911 with the death of King Louis the Child. He was succeeded first by the duke of Franconia and then, in 919, by the duke of Saxony—the first of an illustrious line of kings whose power was based on their domination of the powerful Saxon duchy.

Otto I

The Saxon kings struggled vigorously to assert their authority over the tribal duchies. With the duchy of Saxony under the authority of the monarchy, the Saxon kings quickly won direct control over Franconia as well. But the semi-independent dukes of the two southern duchies, Swabia and Bavaria, presented problems. The real victory of the Saxon monarchy occurred in the reign of the second and greatest of the Saxon kings, Otto I (936–73).

---
* Otherwise known as "stem duchies."

Otto I, or "Otto the Great," directed his considerable talents toward three goals: (1) the defense of Germany against the Hungarian invasions; (2) the establishment of royal power over the remaining tribal duchies; and (3) the extension of German royal control to the crumbling, unstable Middle Kingdom that the Treaty of Verdun had assigned to Emperor Lothar back in 843. We have already seen how this Middle Kingdom began to fall to pieces after Lothar's death. By the mid-tenth century it had become a political shambles. Parts of it had been taken over by Germany and France but its southern districts—Burgundy and Italy—retained a chaotic independence. The dukes of Swabia and Bavaria both had notions of seizing these territories. Otto the Great, in order to forestall the development of an unmanageable rival power to his south, led his armies into Italy in 951 and assumed the title "King of Italy."

From 951 onwards events developed rapidly. Otto the Great had to leave Italy in haste to put down a major uprising in Germany. His victory over the rebels enabled him to establish his power there more strongly than ever. In 955 he won the crucial battle of the age when he crushed a large Hungarian army at Lechfeld, bringing the Hungarian raids to an end at last. Lechfeld served as a vivid demonstration of royal power—a vindication of the monarch's claim that he, not the "tribal" dukes, was the true defender of Germany. With the Hungarians defeated, Germany's eastern frontier now lay open to the gradual penetration of German-Christian culture. The day of the tribal duchies was over; the monarchy was supreme. Otto the Great now towered over his contemporaries as the greatest monarch of the West and the most powerful ruler since Charlemagne. The invasions of Germany, which had begun by uplifting the tribal duchies, ended with the revival of royal authority.

Revival of the Empire

Not long after his victory at Lechfeld, Otto I turned his attention to still another crisis. Since his departure from Italy, a Lombard magnate had seized the Italian throne and was harassing the pope. In response to a papal appeal—which dovetailed with his own interests—Otto returned to Italy in force and recovered the Italian throne. In 962 the pope hailed Otto as Roman Emperor and placed the imperial crown on his head. It is this momentous event, rather than the coronation of Charlemagne in 800, that marks the true genesis of the medieval Holy Roman Empire. Although the events of 962 are reminiscent of 800, Otto's empire was vastly different from Charlemagne's. Above all, Otto and his imperial successors exercised no universal jurisdiction over France or the remainder of Western Christendom. The medieval Holy Roman Empire had its roots deep in the soil of Germany, and most of the emperors subordinated imperial interests to those of the German monarchy. From its advent in 962 to its long-delayed demise in the early nineteenth century the Holy Roman Empire remained fundamentally a German phenomenon.

The German orientation of Otto's empire is illustrated by the fact that neither he nor the majority of his successors over the next two centuries made any real effort to establish tight control over Italy. Only when they marched south of the Alps could they count on the obedience of the Italians; when they returned to Germany they left behind them no real administrative structure but depended almost solely on the fickle allegiance of certain Italian magnates and bishops. The German emperors were never successful in straddling the Alps.

In Germany conditions were quite different. There the coming of feudalism was delayed for more than a century after Otto's imperial coronation. The great magnates became vassals of the king but normally had no vassals of their own. The chief tool that Otto and his successors used in governing their state was the Church. In an era of a weak papacy the German kings dominated the churchmen within their realm and kept close control over important ecclesiastical appointments. Otto had successfully wrested control of the Church in the various tribal duchies from the defunct dukes, and in a very real sense the great bishops and abbots of Germany were the king's men. They made ideal royal lieutenants. They could not pass on their estates to heirs, and when a bishop or abbot died his successor was handpicked by the king. Thus the loyalty and political capacity of the king's administrator-churchmen was assured. After 962 the German monarchy was, on occasion, even successful in appointing popes. There would come a time when churchmen would rebel at such treatment; but in Otto's reign the time was still far off.

Otto's claims to proprietorship of the imperial Church were supported by both tradition and theory. Otto was regarded as more than a mere secular monarch. He was *rex et sacerdos,* king and priest, sanctified by the holy anointing ceremony which accompanied his coronation. He was the vicar of God—the living symbol of Christ the king—the "natural" leader of the Church in his empire. And in the closing years of his reign his actual political power over church and state came close to matching his exalted pretensions.

The Ottonian Renaissance

Otto's reign provided the impulse for an impressive intellectual revival which reached its culmination under his two successors, Otto II (973–83) and Otto III (983–1002). This "Ottonian Renaissance" produced a series of able administrators and scholars, the greatest of whom was the brilliant churchman Gerbert of Aurillac—later Pope Sylvester II (d. 1003). Gerbert visited Spain and returned with a comprehensive knowledge of Islamic science. With this event the infiltration of Arab thought into Western Christendom began.

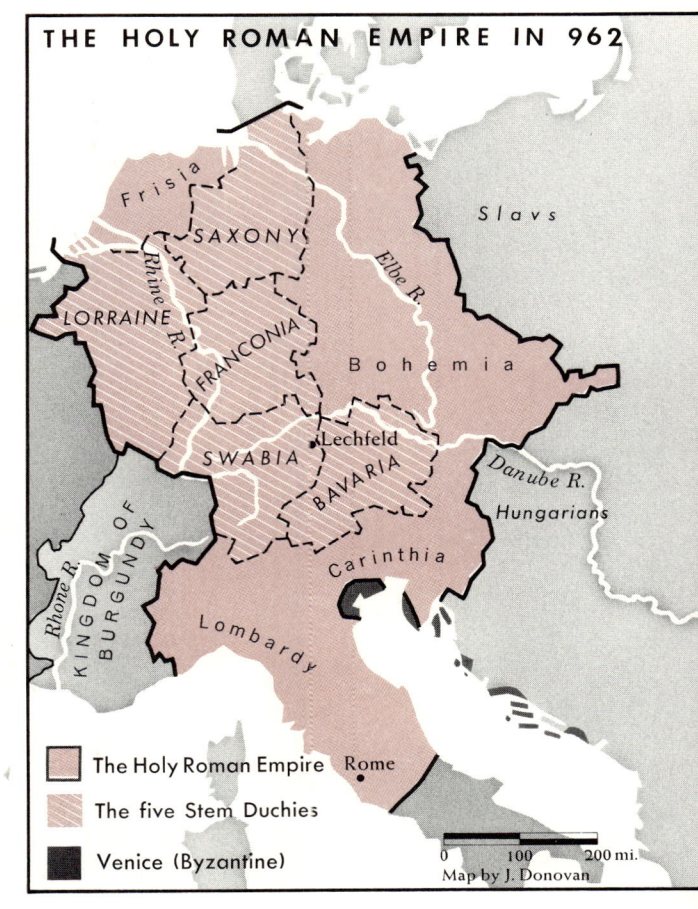

Gerbert had an encyclopedic, though unoriginal, mind. A master of classical literature, logic, mathematics, and science, he astonished his contemporaries by teaching the Greco-Arab doctrine that the earth was spherical. It was widely rumored that he was a wizard in league with the Devil—but the rumors were dampened by his elevation to the papacy. Ger-

Otto III from a contemporary manuscript illumination flanked by two warriors (right) and by a pair of ecclesiastics, holding the staff and orb, symbols of divinely inspired earthly power.

bert was no wizard but an advance agent of the intellectual awakening that Europe was about to undergo—a harbinger of the High Middle Ages.

Although successors of Otto the Great were no longer troubled by the tribal duchies or the Hungarians, they were obliged to cope with new problems and devise new solutions. In 1024 the Saxon dynasty died out and was replaced by a Franconian line known as the Salian dynasty (1024–1125). The "tribal" dukes gave way to a new, particularistic aristocracy whose impulse toward independence taxed the ingenuity of the emperors. Still, the early Salian kings were generally successful in maintaining their power. Working hand in glove with the German church, the Salians improved and expanded the royal administration and ultimately came to exercise even greater authority than Otto I. In the mid-eleventh century the strongest of the Salian emperors, Henry III (1039–56), ruled unrivaled over Germany and appointed popes as freely as he selected his own bishops. In 1050, at a time when France was still a mixup of feudal principalities and England, under Edward the Confessor, was relatively small and more-or-less isolated,

390   Carolingian Europe and the New Invasions

the German Emperor Henry III dominated central Europe and held the papacy in his palm.

EUROPE ON THE EVE OF THE HIGH MIDDLE AGES

During the centuries between the fall of the Roman Empire in the West and the great economic and cultural revival of the later eleventh century, the foundations were built on which Western civilization rose. Kingdoms were forming, distinctive customs and institutions were developing, and a classical-Christian intellectual tradition was gradually being absorbed, adapted, and broadened. At the bottom of the social order, the peasant had become firmly attached to the soil, hedged about with various obligations, and trained from childhood in a variety of traditional techniques.

The Organization of Agriculture

To discuss the typical medieval manor is as difficult as to discuss the typical American business. Medieval agrarian institutions were almost infinitely diverse; medieval agriculture exhibited countless variations. Nevertheless some features of agrarian life recur throughout much of the more fertile and heavily populated portions of northern Europe. Certain generalizations can be made about medieval agrarian institutions if we bear in mind that numerous exceptions to any of them can always be found.

Any discussion of medieval husbandry must begin by distinguishing between two fundamental institutions: the village and the manor. The village, the basic unit of the agrarian economy, consisted of a population nucleus ranging from about a dozen to several hundred peasant families living in a cluster. In some of the poorer or more isolated districts, peasant families lived in separate farms or hamlets; but village life was the norm in medieval agriculture.

The manor, on the other hand, was an artificial unit—a unit of jurisdiction and economic exploitation controlled by a single lord. The lord might be a king, a duke or count, a bishop or abbot, or a great baron, with numerous manors under his control. Or he might be a simple knight, at the bottom of the feudal pyramid, with only one or two manors at his disposal. The manor—the unit of jurisdiction—was often geographically identical with the village; but some manors embraced two or more villages, and, on occasion, a village might be divided into two or more manors. In any case the agrarian routine of plowing, planting, and harvesting was based on the village organization, whereas the peasants' dues, obligations, and legal and political subordination were based on the manor.

The Village

The ordinary village consisted of a grouping of peasants' huts surrounded by open fields. There would normally be either two or three such fields. Two was the traditional number but, as we have seen, the agrarian economy had been shifting in many districts of northern Europe from a two-field to a three-field system of rotation. The peasants of a three-field village would plant one field in the spring for fall harvesting, plant one field in the fall for early summer harvesting, and let the third field lie fallow throughout the year. The next year the fields would be rotated and the process repeated.

The arable lands surrounding the village were known as *open fields,* because they were unfenced. They were divided into strips about 220 yards long, separated from one another by furrows. Each peas-

391   C. Europe Survives the Siege

ant possessed several strips scattered throughout the fields, but the peasant community labored collectively, pooling their plows, their draught animals, and their toil. Collective husbandry was necessary because plows were scarce and had to be shared and because no one peasant owned sufficient oxen or horses to make up the team of eight beasts necessary to draw the heavy plow. The details of this collective process were usually worked out in the village council and were guided by immemorial custom.

The shape, contour, and method of cultivation of the open fields was determined by the topography of the region and the fertility of the soil and varied enormously from place to place. The strips themselves were products of the heavy plow and the necessity of reversing the eight-ox team as

392 Carolingian Europe and the New Invasions

Illuminations from the Flemish Hours of the Virgin *(ca. 1515):* LEFT, *the month of April,* ABOVE, *the month of November. These two miniatures illustrate the communal nature of medieval village life.*

seldom as possible. The length of the strips was determined by the distance a team could draw the plow without rest. A group of four strips, which constituted the normal day's work of a plow team, became the basis of our modern acre.

The open fields were fundamental to the village economy and, indeed, to the entire agrarian economic system of the Middle Ages. But there was more to the village community than the cluster of peasants' huts and the encircling fields. Besides his scattered strips in the fields, a peasant ordinarily had a small garden adjacent to his hut where vegetables and fruits could be raised and fowl kept to provide variety to his diet. The village also included a pasture where the plow animals might graze, and a meadow from which hay was cut to sustain the precious beasts over the winter. Some village communities kept sheep on their pasture as a source of cheese, milk, and wool. Certain districts, particularly in Flanders and northern England, took up sheep raising on a scale so large as almost to exclude the growing of grains.

Attached to most village communities was a wooded area from which fuel and building materials could be gathered. It also served as a forage for pigs, which provided most of the meat in the peasants' diet. There was commonly a stream or pond nearby which supplied the community with fish, a water mill for grinding grain, and a large oven which the community used for baking bread. By the eleventh century most village communities were organized as parishes. Each parish possessed a village church supervised by a priest who was drawn from the peasant class and had land of his own scattered among the strips of the open fields.

The village community has often been described as a closed system, economically self-sufficient, capable of sustaining the material and spiritual needs of the villagers without much contact with the outside world. From the foregoing discussion it should be clear enough why this was so. The economy of the Early Middle Ages, lacking a vigorous commercial life and a significant urban population, failed to provide villages with much incentive to produce beyond their immediate needs. There was only the most limited market for surplus grain. Accordingly, village life tended to be uneventful, tradition-bound, and circumscribed by the narrowest of horizons. On the other hand, gradual but profound changes were occurring in medieval civilization which eventually made a deep impact upon the village. The medieval innovations in agrarian technology significantly increased agricultural efficiency and productivity. Moreover the commercial and urban revival of the High Middle Ages provided an ever-expanding market for surplus grain. These developments in turn eroded village parochialism, freed the village economy from its self-sufficiency by incorporating it into a regional economic system, and provided enterprising peasants with a means of acquiring considerable money. They also encouraged a tremendous expansion of villages and fields through the clearing of forests and wilderness and the draining of marshes. Timeless though it might have seemed, the village economy was changing.

The Manor

Superimposed on the economic structure of the village was the political-juridical structure of the manor. The average peasant was bound to a manorial lord. A few agrarian laborers were outright slaves, but slavery was in decline throughout the Early Middle Ages and had practically disappeared by the end of the eleventh century. Some peasants were of free status, owing rents to their lord but little or nothing more. A few were landless laborers working for a wage. But the great middle stratum of the medieval peasantry consisted of serfs—men of unfree status, bound to the land like the Roman coloni and possessed of strips of their own in the open fields. They owed various dues to their manorial lord, chiefly in kind, and were normally expected to labor for a certain number of days per week—often three—on the lord's fields.

The lord drew his sustenance from the dues of his peasants and from the produce of his own fields. The lord's fields were strips scattered among the strips of the peasants, and were known collectively as the lord's demesne. Theoretically, then, the fields of the manor were divided into two categories: the lord's demesne (perhaps one-fourth to one-third of the total area) and the peasants' holdings. But in fact the demesne strips and the peasants' strips were intermixed. The demesne was worked by the peasants who also paid their lord a percentage of the produce of their own fields and rendered him fees for the use of the pasture, the woods, and the lord's mill and oven. Such were some of the more common peasant obligations on many manors. But such obligations were exceedingly diverse, varying from district to district and from manor to manor.

The lord also enjoyed significant political authority over his peasants—authority that flourished and grew in proportion to the disintegration of sovereign power which occurred in late Carolingian times. The administrative center of the manor was the manorial court, usually held in the lord's castle or manor house. Here a rough, custom-based justice was meted out, disputes settled, misdeeds punished, and obligations enforced. Since most lords possessed more than one manor, authority over individual manors was commonly exercised by an agent of the lord known as a bailiff or steward. It was he who supervised the manorial court, oversaw the farming of the demesne, and collected the peasants' dues. In addition to the peasants' agrarian obligations, the lord was also entitled to certain payments deriving from his political and personal authority over his tenants. He might levy a *tallage*—an arbitrary manorial tax which was theoretically unlimited in frequency and amount but was in fact circumscribed by custom. He was normally entitled to payments when a peasant's son inherited the holdings of his father, and when a peasant's daughter married outside the manor.

In general the serfs had no standing before the law. The lord was prevented from exploiting them arbitrarily only by the force of custom. But custom was strong in the Middle Ages and protected the serf in many different ways. He was by no means a chattel slave. He could not be sold, nor could his own hereditary fields be taken from him. After paying his manorial dues he was entitled to keep the produce of his own fields. Although hardly enviable, his situation could have been worse.

The Medieval Agrarian System: Conclusions

Medieval agrarian institutions were endlessly various, evolving as time passed and differing significantly from one place to another. In the eleventh century the manorial regime was only incompletely established in England and was scarcely evident at all in Scandinavia and in parts of northern Germany and southern France. Although the two-field system was common in Southern Europe and the three-field system in the north, many northern villages had only two fields. Others had four or five or even more, all subject to complex rotation arrangements. Vital, diverse, and on the whole healthy, medieval agriculture proved itself capable of expanding sufficiently to support the soaring new economy and the rich civilization of the High Middle Ages.

The Church

The existence of parish churches in the villages of the eleventh century illustrates the deeply significant fact that the long process of Christianizing Europe was by now far advanced. Whatever were the intellectual and moral shortcomings of the village priests, they were at least representatives of the international Church operating at the most immediate local levels throughout the European countryside. At a rather more elevated level was the work and influence of the Benedictines. They offered prayers to God, copied manuscripts, taught in their schools, supplied knights to secular armies, and served as prelates and counsellors under counts, dukes, and kings. While continuing their traditional spiritual activities they played, even more than in early Carolingian times, a major role in lay political life.

The greatest Benedictine house of the later tenth and earlier eleventh centuries was Cluny in Burgundy. Founded in 910 by the duke of Aquitaine, Cluny was free of local episcopal jurisdiction, subject to the pope alone, and blessed with a series of remarkably able and long-lived abbots. Cluny followed Benedict of Aniane's modifications of the original Benedictine Rule. Its monks, shunning field work, devoted themselves to an elaborate sequence of daily prayers and liturgical services, and a strict, godly life. This strictness was relative, falling short of the austere regimes of several of the more ascetic orders of the High Middle Ages. Yet the Cluniacs were successful in avoiding the abuses and corruption that flourished in many monasteries of their day. Richly endowed, holy, and seemingly incorruptible, Cluny became famous and widely admired. In time it began to acquire daughter houses. Gradually it became the nucleus of a great congregation of reform monasteries extending throughout Europe—all of them obedient to the abbot of Cluny. In the mid-eleventh century the Congregation of Cluny was both powerful and wealthy, and its new abbey church completed in the early twelfth century was the most splendid building of its time in all Europe. Cluny's high ideals were tempered by a sense of dignity—and perhaps also by a comfortable feeling of spiritual success and social acceptance. Enriched and supported by the lay aristocracy, it was by no means in radical opposition to secular society; rather it tended on the whole to uphold the social system of its day and to worship the Lord God without disparaging the lords of men.

Cluny's attitude typified that of the entire Church in the earlier eleventh century. As the lay world became more and more exposed to Christianity, as pious kings such as Edward the Confessor in England and Henry III in Germany demonstrated their concern for the welfare of their churches, the Church itself tended increasingly to come to terms with lay society. Through the ceremony of anointing, kings became virtual priest-kings. Indeed, contemporary political theory taught that the Church and the world were one—a single, God-oriented organism in which churchmen and lay lords each had appropriate roles to play.

Apart from Cluny, the monasteries and bishoprics of eleventh-century Europe were largely under lay control. They were dependent on lay patronage and were often entangled in the feudal system. Their prelates were appointed by lay lords in much the same way that village priests were chosen and controlled by manorial lords. Although not free, the Church was wealthy, respected, and comfortable, and few churchmen were inclined to challenge the situation. Those few, however, were to undertake in the later eleventh century a political-spiritual revolution which severely undermined the long established church-state entente.

Summary

By 1050 both England and Germany were comparatively stable, well-organized kingdoms. The French monarchy was still weak, but within another century it would be on its way toward dominating France. Meanwhile feudal principalities such as Normandy, Champagne, Flanders, and Anjou were well on the road to political coherence. Warfare was still endemic, but it was beginning to lessen as Europe moved toward political stability. Above all, the invasions were over—the siege had ended. Hungary and the Scandinavian world were being absorbed into

Western Christendom, and Islam was by now on the defensive. The return of prosperity, the increase in food production, the rise in population, the quickening of commerce, the intensification of intellectual activity, all betokened the coming of a new era. Western civilization was on the threshold of an immense creative surge.

Selected Readings

Barlow, Frank. *Edward the Confessor.* Berkeley and Los Angeles: University of California Press, 1970.

Barlow, who knows more than any other living person about Edward the Confessor, tells his story in a tart, sometimes mordant style. Barlow shows that Edward's sanctity was in large part a matter of posthumous reputation.

*Barraclough, Geoffrey. *The Origins of Modern Germany.* New York: G. P. Putnam's Sons, Capricorn Books, 1963.

A general account of German constitutional history that places particular emphasis on the medieval period. The interpretations of Otto I and Otto III are particularly valuable.

*Bloch, Marc. *Feudal Society.* Translated by L. A. Manyon. 2 vols. Chicago: The University of Chicago Press, 1961; originally published 1940.

A masterly work, challengingly written and boldly original in its conclusions. Bloch interprets feudalism in a broad sociological sense.

Bloch, Marc. *French Rural Society.* Translated by Janet Sondheimer. Berkeley and Los Angeles: University of California Press, 1966.

A seminal study of agrarian life and institutions in medieval and early-modern France. Originally published in French in 1931, this book has changed our ways of looking at history.

Boussard, Jacques. *The Civilization of Charlemagne.* New York: McGraw-Hill Book Co., 1968.

This important French work, which was immediately translated into English, is now the best single book in English on the age of Charlemagne.

*Brentano, Robert, ed. *The Early Middle Ages, 500–1000.* New York: Free Press, 1964.

Well-selected original sources of the period in English translation, with an excellent introduction.

*Duckett, Eleanor Shipley. *Alfred the Great: The King and His England.* Chicago: The University of Chicago Press, 1956.

"This is a very simple book," the author states. It is also short, sound, and exceptionally well written.

*Einhard. *Life of Charlemagne.* Translated by S. E. Turner. Ann Arbor, Mich.: University of Michigan Press, Ann Arbor Paperbacks, 1960.

A short, reasonably trustworthy biography by Charlemagne's secretary.

*Ganshof, F. L. *Feudalism.* Translated by P. Grierson. 2d ed. New York: Harper & Row, Publishers, 1961.

> *A short, somewhat technical, and authoritative survey of medieval feudal institutions.*

*Hill, Boyd H., ed. *The Rise of the First Reich: Germany in the Tenth Century.* New York: John Wiley & Sons, 1969.

> *Original sources and modern historians' interpretations in English translation. An invaluable window on the age of the Ottos.*

*Lewis, Archibald R. *Emerging Medieval Europe: A.D. 400–1000.* New York: Alfred A. Knopf, 1967.

> *A short survey stressing economic and social history.*

*Lewis, Archibald R., ed. *The Islamic World and the West: A.D. 622–1492.* New York: John Wiley & Sons, 1970.

> *Translated sources interwoven with modern historical studies.*

Lyon, H. R. *Anglo-Saxon England and the Norman Conquest.* New York: St. Martin's Press, 1963.

> *An authoritative work emphasizing economic and social history.*

*Painter, Sidney. *French Chivalry.* Ithaca, N.Y.: Cornell University Press, 1957.

> *Short, witty, and perceptive.*

Sawyer, P. H. *The Age of the Vikings.* New York: St. Martin's Press, 1962.

> *A rather technical, highly significant reappraisal of the Viking age.*

Stenton, F. M. *Anglo-Saxon England.* 2d ed. New York: Oxford University Press, 1947.

> *A massive masterpiece.*

*Stephenson, Carl. *Medieval Feudalism.* Ithaca, N. Y.: Cornell University Press, 1956.

> *Brief, semipopular, and lucid; a well-organized account, broader and less detailed than Ganshof's.*

*White, Lynn. *Medieval Technology and Social Change.* New York: Oxford University Press, 1962.

> *An important and provocative pioneering work, beautifully written and opulently annotated, which stresses the significance of technological progress in the development of medieval civilization.*

Asterisk (*) denotes paperback.

CHAPTER IX
The High Middle Ages: Economic, Territorial, and Religious Frontiers

A. Economic Frontiers

THE HIGH MIDDLE AGES: PERIODIZATION, CHARACTERISTICS

History, it has often been said, is a seamless web. But the human mind can only cope with the flow of historical reality by chopping it into chronological slices, forcing it into compartments of the historian's own making. In this sense every historical "period" is a kind of falsehood—an affront to the continuity of human development. Yet unless we concoct historical epochs, unless we invent ages, unless we tame the past with some relatively tidy chronological framework, we cannot make history intelligible to the human mind. Thus the historian speaks of "Classical Antiquity," "The Early Middle Ages," "The Renaissance," etc. These are all historiographic artifices, but they are necessary ones. Without them the past would have little meaning. But we should never forget that they are inventions of our own; we must never lose sight of their limitations.

The term *High Middle Ages* has been applied to the great cultural upsurge of the later eleventh, twelfth, and thirteenth centuries. Yet no spectacular event occurred in 1050 to signal the advent of the new era; no cataclysm occurred in 1300 to mark its end. The transition from Early Middle Ages to High Middle Ages was gradual and uneven. It might be argued that the High Middle Ages came to Germany as early as the tenth century under the Ottos, or that it was delayed in France until the twelfth century, when the Capetian monarchy rose from its torpor. Ever since the waning of the Viking, Hungarian, and Saracen invasions, many decades prior to 1050, Europe had been pulsing with new creative energy. Broadly speaking, though, the scope and intensity of the revival did not become evident until the later eleventh century. By the century's end, Europe's lively commerce and bustling towns, her intellectual vigor and political inventiveness, its military expansion, and its heightened religious enthusiasm left no doubt that vital new forces were at work—that Western Christendom had at last become a great creative civilization. As the historian might say, a new age had dawned.

The causes of cultural awakening such as occurred in the High Middle Ages are far too complex to be identified precisely or listed in order of importance. One essential element was the ending of the invasions and the increasing political stability that followed. We know that in the eleventh century Europe's population was beginning to increase significantly and that its food production was rising. Whether increased productivity led to increased population or vice-versa is difficult to say. But productivity could not have risen as it did without the revolutionary developments in agricultural technology: the three-field system which spread across much of northern Europe, the windmill, the water mill (by 1086 there were over 5000 water mills in England alone), the heavy, wheeled plow, the horseshoe and improved horse collar which transformed horses into efficient draught animals, and the tandem harness which made it possible to employ horses and oxen in large teams to draw plows or to pull heavy wagons. These and numerous related inventions came to the West gradually over the centuries, but they had a powerful cumulative influence on the economic boom of the High Middle Ages.

TOWNS AND COMMERCE

Nature of Medieval Towns

The rise in productivity and population was accompanied by a commercial revival and a general reawakening of urban life. In turn, the new towns became the foci of a brilliant, reinvigorated culture. The intimate human contacts arising from town life stimulated European thought and art. The cathedral and the university, perhaps the two greatest monuments of high medieval culture, were both urban phenomena; the Franciscan order, possibly the most dynamic monastic institution of the new age, devoted itself chiefly to evangelical work among the new urban population. Yet the towns were also, and above all, centers of commercial and industrial enterprise. The European economy in the High Middle Ages remained fundamentally agrarian, but the towns were the great economic and cultural catalysts of the era. In them God and mammon stood face to face and often worked hand in hand.

There had been towns in Europe ever since antiquity. The administrative-military town of the Roman Empire gave way in time to the far humbler cathedral town of the Early Middle Ages. But both had one crucial thing in common: both were economic parasites living off the blood, labor and taxes of the countryside; both—like modern government-

Seal of the town of Dunwich (thirteenth century). Many towns used commercial symbols on their seals.

400   The High Middle Ages

cities such as Washington, D.C., and Sacramento, California—consumed more than they produced. The towns of the High Middle Ages, on the other hand, represented something radically new to western Europe. With few exceptions, they were true commercial entities who earned their own way, living off the fruits of their merchant and industrial activities. Small, foul, disease-ridden, and often torn by internal conflict, they were nevertheless western Europe's first cities in the modern sense.

The new towns brought with them a new way of life and a new, urban class in which were merged such attitudes as acquisitiveness, piety, and civic pride. These last two qualities are memorialized to this day in the great urban cathedrals of the High Middle Ages. And civic pride could drive townsmen to the point of rhapsodic exaggeration. Medieval London, the metropolis of England, with a population of 35,000 or so, was no less crowded, foul, or riotous than other "large" cities of its time, yet the twelfth-century writer William Fitz Stephen could describe it in these enthusiastic words:

Among the noble and celebrated cities of the world, London, the capital of the kingdom of the English, is one which extends its glory farther than all the others and sends its wealth and merchandise more widely into distant lands. Higher than all the rest does it lift its head. It is happy in the healthiness of its air; in its observance of Christian practice; in the strength of its fortifications; in its natural situation; in the honor of its citizens; and in the modesty of its matrons. It is cheerful in its sports, and the fruitful mother of noble men.[1]

---

[1] William Fitz Stephen, "Description of the City of London (1170–1183)," in *English Historical Documents*, ed. David C. Douglas and George W. Greenaway, 12 vols. (London: Eyre & Spottiswoode, 1953), 2:956.

Commercial Growth of Towns

The commercial towns arose in rhythm with the upsurge of international commerce and the development of vigorous markets for local agrarian products. Often they began as suburbs of older cathedral towns or as humble settlements outside the walls of some of the many fortresses that had arisen in ninth- and tenth-century Europe. These fortresses were generally known by some form of the Germanic word *burgh,* and in time the term came to apply to the town itself rather than the fortress that spawned it. By the twelfth century a burgh, or *borough,* was an urban commercial center, inhabited by *burghers* or *burgesses,* who constituted a new class known later as the *bourgeoisie.*

In the later eleventh century towns were developing rapidly all over Europe. They were thickest in Flanders and northern Italy where the immense opportunities of international commerce were first exploited. The greatest Italian city of the age was Venice, long a Byzantine colony but now an independent republic, whose merchants carried on a lucrative trade with Constantinople and the East. Other Italian coastal towns—Genoa, Pisa, and Amalfi—soon followed Venice into the profitable markets of the eastern Mediterranean, and the ramifications of their far-flung trade brought vigorous new life to the towns of interior Italy, such as Milan and Florence. During the High Middle Ages the Muslims were virtually driven from the seas and Italian merchants dominated the Mediterranean.

Meanwhile the towns of Flanders were growing wealthy from the commerce of the North—from trade with northern France and the British Isles, the Rhineland and the shores of the Baltic Sea. Flanders itself was a great sheep-growing district; its towns became centers of woolen textile production. In time, the towns were processing more wool than Flemish sheep could supply so that from the twelfth century onward Flemish merchants began to import wool on a huge scale from England. By then Flanders was the great industrial center of northern Europe, and its textile industry the supreme manufacturing enterprise of the age.

Urban Privileges

The new urban class arose in a society that had heretofore been almost exclusively agrarian. The burgher class was drawn from vagabonds, runaway serfs, avaricious minor noblemen and, in general, the surplus of a mushrooming population. At an early date ambitious traders began to form themselves into merchant guilds in order to protect themselves against confiscatory tolls and other exactions levied by a hostile landed aristocracy. A town was almost always situated on the territories of some lord—sometimes a duke or even a king—and the merchants found that only by collective action could they win the privileges essential to their calling: personal freedom from serflike status, freedom of movement, freedom from inordinate tolls at every bridge or feudal boundary, the rights to own property in the town, to be judged by a town court, to execute commercial contracts, and to buy and sell freely. By the twelfth century, a number of lords, recognizing the economic advantages of having flourishing commercial centers on their lands, were issuing town charters which guaranteed many of these rights. Indeed, some farsighted lords began founding and chartering new towns on their own initiative.

At first the urban charters differed greatly from one another, but in time it became customary to pattern them after certain well-known models. The charter granted by King Henry I of England to Newcastle-on-Tyne, and that of the French king to the town of Lorris, were copied repeatedly throughout England and France. In effect these charters transformed the commercial communities into semiautonomous political and legal entities, each with its own local government, its own court, its own tax-collecting agencies, and its own customs. These urban communes paid well for their charters and continued to render regular taxes to their lord. But—and this is all-important—they did so as political units. Individual merchants were not normally subject to the harassments of their lords' agents. These townsmen enforced their own law in their own courts, collected their own taxes, and paid their dues to their lord in a lump sum. In short, they had won the invaluable privilege of handling their own affairs.

One should not conclude, however, that the medieval towns were even remotely democratic. It was the prosperous merchants and master craftsmen who profited chiefly from the charters, and it was they who came to control the town governments, ruling as narrow oligarchies over the towns' less exalted inhabitants. Some towns witnessed the beginnings of a significant split between large-scale producers and wage-earning workers. It can be said, in fact, that the medieval town was the birthplace of European capitalism. For as time progressed towns tended to become centers of industry as well as commerce. Manufacturing followed in the footsteps of trade. And although most industrial production took place in small shops rather than large factories, some enterprising businessmen employed considerable numbers of workers to produce goods, usually textiles—on a large scale. Normally, these workers did not labor in a factory but rather in their own shops or homes. Since the entrepreneur sent his raw materials out to his workers, rather than bringing the workers to the materials, this mode of production has been called the "putting-out system." As a direct antecedent of the factory system, it was a crucial phase in the early history of capitalism.

Craft Guilds

The more typical medieval manufacturer worked for himself in his own shop, producing his own goods and selling them directly to the public. As early as the eleventh century, these craftsmen were organizing themselves into craft guilds, as distinct from merchant guilds. In an effort to limit competition and protect their market, the craft guilds established strict admission requirements and stringent rules on prices, wages, standards of quality, and operating procedures. A young craftsman would learn his trade as an apprentice in the shop of a master craftsman. After a specified period, sometimes as long as seven years, he ended his

Glassblowing needed training and skill, and tended to be a specialty of certain districts. This drawing from Bohemia shows the process, from digging the raw material, sand, through the final examination and packing of the finished vessels.

403   A. Economic Frontiers

apprenticeship. With good luck and rich parents he might then become a master himself. But normally he had to work for some years as a day laborer—a journeyman—improving his skills and saving his money, until he was able to demonstrate sufficient craftsmanship to win guild membership and accumulate enough money to establish a shop of his own. Toward the end of the High Middle Ages, as prosperity waned and urban society crystalized, it became increasingly common for journeymen to spend their whole lives as wage earners, never becoming masters at all. Accordingly, the town became the scene of bitter class feeling which erupted from time to time into open conflict.

Commerce and Money Economy

There were many who made their fortunes in commerce and manufacturing. Europe was astir with new life; for a clever, enterprising man the possibilities were vast. In the twelfth and thirteenth centuries, merchants were moving continuously along the roads and rivers of Europe. Italians crossed the Alps bringing spices and luxury goods from the Near East and the Orient to the aristocracy of France and Germany. French, Flemish, and German merchants carried goods far and wide across the continent, "buying cheap and selling dear." To William Fitz Stephen's London "merchants from every nation under heaven delight to bring their trade by sea. The Arabian sends gold; the Sabean sends spice and incense; the Sythian brings arms; and from the rich, fat lands of Babylon comes palm oil. The Nile Valley sends precious stones; the men of Norway and Russia send furs and sables. Nor is China absent with purple silk. The French come with their wines." [2]

[2] Stephen in Douglas and Greenaway, op. cit., 2:959.

A series of annual fairs along the overland trade routes provided the long-distance merchants with excellent opportunities to sell their goods. As large-scale commerce grew, credit and banking grew along with it, and by the thirteenth century several banking families had amassed immense fortunes. It may seem paradoxical that the period which is often regarded as the supreme age of faith witnessed the rise of large-scale commerce and a money economy. Yet it was money that built the Gothic cathedrals and supported the Crusades, that financed the pious charities of St. Louis and gave substance to the magnificent religious culture of the thirteenth century—money and, of course, an ardent faith. In time, faith itself would fall victim to the acquisitive spirit which was evolving in the towns, but during the High Middle Ages the townsmen, by and large, exhibited a piety that was far more vibrant and intense than that of the peasantry and the aristocracy. Indeed, the powerful upsurge of lay piety among the European townsmen became a crucial factor in the evolution of medieval Christianity.

DECLINE OF FEUDALISM

Feudalism, based as it was on hereditary land tenure in return for service, was a characteristic product of a money-poor society which could not afford to pay wages to its warriors. With the rise of a money economy in Europe, the basic feudal relationship began to dissolve. The deep impact of feudal custom on the European mind is demonstrated by the various ingenious ways in which the aristocracy sought to adapt feudalism to the new economic realities. Indeed, during the eleventh and twelfth centuries the feudal system spread from France into England, Germany, and the Crusader States of the Holy Land. At the same time, however, kings and dukes were resorting increasingly to the hiring of mercenaries for warfare, and professional judges and civil servants for the administration of their realms. As the twelfth century progressed the feudal vassal was, oftener than not, asked to pay a tax in lieu of his personal service in the feudal army. With the income from this tax, which was sometimes called *scutage,* a monarch could hire professional warriors who were better trained, better disciplined, and more obedient than the landed knights. The feudal aristocracy retained its lands and much of its power for centuries to come, and even continued to produce warriors. But the knights of the new age expected to be paid. They no longer served at their own expense in return for their fiefs. Once the paying of taxes had replaced personal service as the vassal's primary obligation—and this was the case almost everywhere by the thirteenth century—feudalism had lost its soul.

EVOLUTION OF AGRARIAN LIFE

Changes in Peasant Life

The new social and economic conditions of the High Middle Ages wrought a profound transformation in the European countryside. Doubtless the most spectacular change was the immense expansion of arable land. The great primeval forest of northern Europe was reduced to isolated patches, swamps and marshes were drained, and extensive new territories were opened to cultivation. This prodigious clearing operation was stimulated by the soaring population and the rising money economy. Agricultural surpluses could now be sold to townsmen and thereby converted into cash. Consequently, the peasant was strongly motivated to produce as far in excess of the consumption level as he possibly could. Every new field that could be put into operation was likely to bring a profit.

A second change, no less significant than the first, was the elevation of the peasant's status. Slavery, which was rare in Carolingian times, had virtually disappeared from Europe by the eleventh century. The tillers of the land were chiefly freemen and serfs. Often the freeman owned his own small farm, but the serf was generally to be found on a manor. Normally, it will be remembered, the manor included the peasants' fields and the lord's fields (demesne) the produce of which went directly to the lord. Among the obligations which the serf normally owed his lord was labor service for a stipulated number of days on the lord's demesne. In Carolingian times, manorial lords had augmented the part-time serf labor on their demesne fields by using slaves. As slavery gradually died out, the lord was faced with a severe labor shortage on his demesne.

As a result of this problem, and in keeping with the trend toward transforming service obligations into money payments, the lords tended to abandon demesne farming altogether. They leased out their demesne fields to peasants and, in return for a fixed money payment, released their serfs from the traditional obligation of working part-time on the demesne. At about the same time they translated the serf's rent-in-kind from his own fields into a money rent. By freeing the serf of his labor obligation they transformed him, in effect, into a tenant farmer, thereby improving his status immensely. The obligations of the serf, like those of the feudal vassal, were gradually being placed on a fiscal basis.

The abandonment of demesne farming was a slow, uneven trend which progressed much more rapidly in some areas than in others. In thirteenth-century England, a countertrend developed whereby many lords successfully reclaimed and enlarged their demesnes. But on the continent the demesne gradually disappeared and, in quite a literal sense, the peasant inherited the earth.

When the lords transformed the dues and services of their serfs into fixed money rents, they failed to reckon with inflation. The booming economy of the High Middle Ages was accompanied by an upward spiral of prices and a concomitant decline in the purchasing power of money. Hence, the real value of the peasants' rents steadily diminished. Many lords of the later Middle Ages came to regret the bargains their ancestors had made, and endeavored to revise peasant rents upward.

Inflation ruined more than one lord, but it was a godsend to the medieval peasantry. The lords could do little to recoup their losses; indeed, they were often obliged to improve the condition of their peasants still more in order to keep them from fleeing to the towns or the newly cleared lands. The peasant was in demand, and the enterprising land developers who were turning woods and marshes into fields competed for his services. As a consequence, the High Middle Ages witnessed the elevation of innumerable peasants from servile status to freedom. Rural communes emerged—peasant villages whose lords had granted them charters closely paralleling those of townsmen. One should not idealize the lot of the thirteenth-century peasant—it was still impoverished and brutish by present standards—yet it compared very favorably with peasant life in the Roman Empire or the Early Middle Ages. The terrifying peasants' rebellions of Early Modern Europe were products of a later and different era when the expansion and prosperity of the High Middle Ages had given way to an epoch of recession and closed frontiers.

B. Territorial Frontiers

EUROPEAN EXPANSION

European frontiers were open and expanding in the High Middle Ages. The clearing of forests and draining of swamps represents the conquest of a great internal frontier. It is paralleled by an external expansion all along the periphery of Western Christendom which brought areas of the Arab, Byzantine, and Slavic worlds within the ballooning boundaries of European civilization and added wealth to the flourishing economy.

Western Europe had been expanding ever since Charles Martel repelled the Arabs in 732. Charlemagne had introduced Frankish government and Christianity into much of Germany and had established a Spanish bridgehead around Barcelona. The stabilization and conversion of Hungary and Scandinavia around the turn of the millennium pushed the limits of Western civilization far northward and eastward from the original Carolingian core. Now, in the eleventh, twelfth, and thirteenth centuries, the population boom produced multitudes of landless aristocratic younger sons who sought land and military glory on Christendom's frontiers. And the ever-proliferating European peasantry provided a potential labor force for the newly conquered lands. While the Christian warrior of the frontier was carving out new estates for himself, he was also

RECONQUEST OF SPAIN

1000 — Leon, Navarre, Barcelona, Caliphate of Cordova, France, Ebro R.

Muslim possessions / Christian conquests

1100 — Leon and Castile, Portugal, Aragon, Barcelona, Lisbon, Moorish States, Guadalquivir R., Balearic Is.

0 50 100 mi. Map by J. Donovan

1212 — Compostella, Leon, Navarre, Aragon, Saragossa, Catalonia, Portugal, Castile, Lisbon, Guadiana R., Toledo, Valencia, Cordova, Las Navas de Tolosa, Seville, Granada, Mediterranean Sea

1300 — Galicia, Navarre, Leon and Castile, Aragon, Barcelona, Portugal, Toledo, Valencia, Cordova, Seville, Granada, To Castile 1492

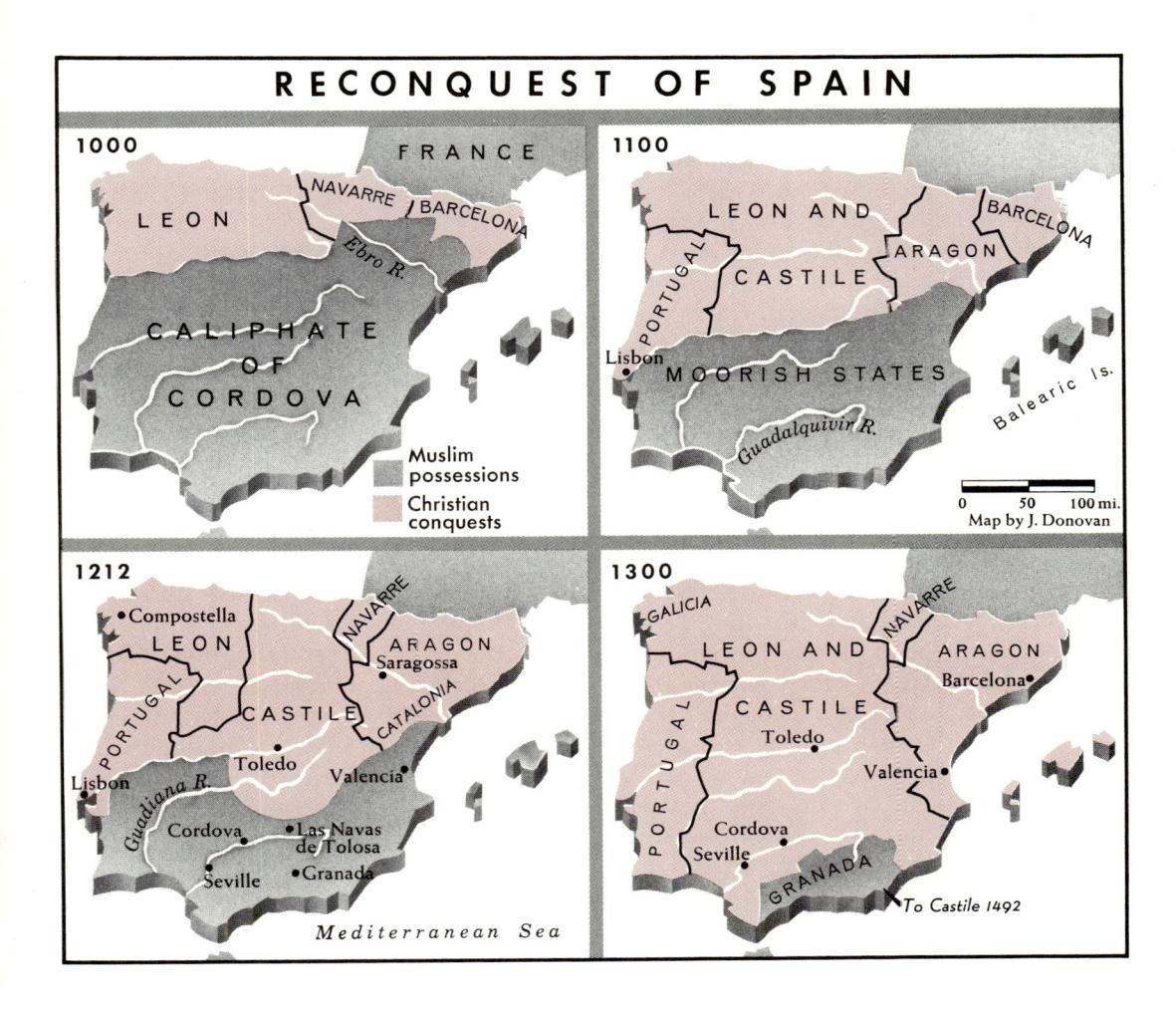

storing up treasures in heaven, for as a result of his aggressive militancy Christendom was everywhere expanding into Muslim Spain, Sicily, and Syria, and into great tracts of Slavic Eastern Europe. Land, gold, and eternal salvation—these were the alluring rewards of the medieval frontier.

SPAIN

Reconquest from the Moors

So it was that knightly adventurers from all over Christendom—and particularly from feudal France—flocked southwestward into Spain during the eleventh century to aid in the reconquest of the Iberian Peninsula from Islam. The powerful Moorish Caliphate of Cordova had broken up after 1002 into small, warring fragments, thereby providing the Christians with a superb opportunity. The Christians, however, were themselves divided into several kingdoms which consumed more energy fighting one another than fighting the Moors. Taking the lead in the reconquest, the Christian kingdom of Castile captured the great Muslim city of Toledo in 1085. In later years Toledo became a crucial contact point between

407   B. Territorial Frontiers

Islamic and Christian culture. Here Arab scientific and philosophical works were translated into Latin and then disseminated throughout Europe to challenge and invigorate the mind of the West.

Early in the twelfth century the Spanish Christian kingdom of Aragon contested the supremacy of Castile and undertook an offensive of its own against the Moors. In 1140 Aragon was strengthened by its unification with the county of Barcelona—the Spanish March of Charlemagne's time. During the greater part of the twelfth century Aragon, Castile, and the smaller Christian kingdoms exhausted themselves fighting one another and the reconquest stalled. But in 1212 Pope Innocent III proclaimed a crusade against the Spanish Muslims, and the king of Castile advanced from Toledo with a pan-Iberian army, winning a decisive victory over the Moors at the battle of Las Navas de Tolosa. Thereafter Moorish power was permanently crippled. Cordova itself fell to Castile in 1236, and by the later thirteenth century the Moors were confined to the small southern kingdom of Granada where they remained until 1492. Castile now dominated central Spain, and the work of re-Christianization proceeded apace as Christian peasants were imported en masse into the reconquered lands. Aragon, in the meantime, was conquering the Muslim islands of the western Mediterranean and establishing a powerful maritime empire.

Thus, the High Middle Ages witnessed the Christianization of nearly all the Iberian peninsula and its organization into two powerful Christian kingdoms and several weaker ones. The long crusade against the Muslims was the chief factor in the molding of Spanish life in the Middle Ages, and its ultimate result was to produce the intense blend of piety and patriotism which inspired the saints, soldiers, and *conquistadores* of Spain's sixteenth-century Golden Age.

SOUTHERN ITALY AND SICILY

The Normans in Southern Italy

The most vigorous and militant force in Europe's eleventh-century awakening was the warrior-aristocracy of Normandy—largely Viking in ancestry but now thoroughly adapted to French culture. These Norman knights, French in tongue, Christian in faith, feudal in social organization, plied their arms across the length and breadth of Europe: in the reconquest of Spain, on the Crusades to the Holy Land, on the battlefields of England and France, and in southern Italy and Sicily. Normandy itself was growing in prosperity and political centralization, and an ever-increasing population pressure drove the greedy and adventurous Norman warriors far and wide on distant enterprises. The impression which they made on contemporaries is suggested by a passage from an Italian chronicler:

The Normans are a cunning and revengeful people; eloquence and deceit seem to be their hereditary qualities. They can stoop to flatter, but unless curbed by the restraint of law they indulge in the licentiousness of nature and passion and, in their eager search for wealth and power, despise whatever they possess and seek whatever they desire. They delight in arms and horses, the luxury of dress, and the exercise of hawking and hunting, but on pressing occasions they can endure with incredible patience the inclemency of every climate and the toil and privation of a military life.

Early in the eleventh century the Normans began to try their luck in the chaotic politics of southern Italy. Here, Byzantine coastal cities—a legacy of Justinian's conquests—struggled with old Lombard principalities and rising seaport republics such as Naples and Amalfi. The great offshore island of Sicily was controlled by the Muslims—or rather it was divided among several mutually hostile Muslim princes who had been compounding the confusion of southern Italy by mounting raids against it. The whole area was a bewildering mixture of four peoples: Greek, Lombard, Latin-Italian, and Arab—and three major religions: Roman Catholic, Eastern Orthodox, and Islamic—in addition to which there existed an important and vigorous Jewish minority. It was, in short, a chaotic melting pot, politically unstable and, from the standpoint of the Normans, enormously promising.

First hiring themselves out as mercenaries to one side or another, the Norman adventurers quickly began to found states of their own. During the 1030s and 1040s a group of eight brothers, sons of a insignificant Norman Lord named Tancred d'Hauteville, began wandering into southern Italy and gradually assumed leadership in the movement of conquest. These eight d'Hauteville brothers illustrate vividly the dynamism engendered in Europe by the adventurous enterprises of landless younger sons of the north European nobility. For although they were nobodies in Normandy the d'Hauteville's rose to supreme power in southern Italy. In the early 1040s the district of Apulia was thrown into chaos by a Lombard insurrection against Byzantine control; when the dust had cleared, it was found that most of Apulia was dominated by neither Byzantines nor Lombards but by three of Tancred d'Hauteville's sons, bearing the formidable names: William Iron-Hand, Humphrey, and Drogo.

The papacy, fearing the ominous rise of Norman power to the south of the Papal States and spurred on by stories of Norman atrocities, mounted an army against the Normans and engaged them in battle at Civitate in 1053. The Normans defeated the army, captured the pope himself, and, after paying him due reverence, obliged him to confirm their conquests and become their lord—in short, to legitimize them. No longer freebooters, the Normans now enjoyed the status of respectable landholders and vassals of St. Peter.

Robert Guiscard

In the meantime the greatest of the d'Hauteville brothers, Robert Guiscard (the Cunning), had arrived in the area and had carved out a patrimony for himself in the southern province of Calabria. Robert was proud, ambitious, ruthless, calculating, and dishonest—possessed, in other words, of all the qualities of the successful empire builder. As master of Calabria he lived like a brigand, inviting distinguished guests to dinner and having them robbed. In 1054 he won control of Apulia and thereby rose to a position of dominance in Norman Italy. A treaty which he executed with the papacy in 1059 gave him the title, "By the grace of God and St. Peter, duke of Apulia, Calabria, and hereafter Sicily." This last phrase was in effect a papal license for Robert and his fellow Normans to direct their energies to the conquest of the Sicilian Muslims.

Robert Guiscard's newly-won duchy was wealthy and powerful by the standards of the age. It included an important center of medical studies at Salerno and several thriving commercial cities such as Amalfi which carried on an extensive trade with Africa, Arabia, and Constantinople. But the Normans, who "despise whatever they possess and seek whatever they desire," were not satisfied with dominion over Apulia and Calabria. In 1060 Guiscard, taking up the papal challenge, landed with a Norman army in Sicily. Shortly afterward he turned the enterprise over to his brother Roger, the youngest of the d'Hautevilles. In later years Guiscard, although hard pressed to suppress the incessant revolts of his Norman-Apulian nobles, found time to launch a major attack against Byzantine lands and to come to the papacy's rescue by driving a hostile Holy Roman emperor from Rome.* His death in 1085 terminated a career that reflected in full measure the limitless confidence, enterprise, and ambition of his age.

Conquest of Sicily

While Robert Guiscard was occupied in his farflung projects, his brother Roger was proceeding with the subjugation of Sicily. The Norman conquest of the island was difficult and prolonged, but in 1072 the rich Sicilian city of Palermo, with one of the finest harbors in the Mediterranean, fell to the Normans. By 1092 the conquest was completed and Roger d'Hauteville stood as undisputed master of Sicily.

By now the entire area of Sicily and southern Italy was in Norman hands, yet it remained for a time politically divided. Robert Guiscard's heterogeneous, rebellious state passed first to his son, then to his grandson who died without direct heirs in 1127. Under these two successors, southern Italy became ever more turbulent. Sicily, on the contrary, was much less prone to rebellion. Roger d'Hauteville wisely instituted a policy of toleration which placated the Sicilian Muslims and won their support for the new Norman dynasty. When Roger died in 1101 he passed on to his heirs a well-organized state and a sophisticated administration that combined Muslim, Byzantine, and feudal elements and was backed by an obedient Saracen army.

In 1105 Sicily passed to Roger d'Hauteville's son, Roger II or Roger the Great (d. 1154), a brilliant administrator and empire builder of a rather different type than Guiscard. Roger the Great was able, ambitious, tolerant, and cruel—less the adventurous feudal warrior than his predecessors had been, and far more sophisticated than they. In 1127 Roger undertook a campaign for the mastery of southern Italy, and by 1129 he assumed control of all the Norman domains, Apulia and Calabria as well as Sicily. In the following year he was elevated to royal status by papal coronation and the lands won by the Normans were fused into a kingdom.

The Kingdom of Sicily

Although Roger the Great's new realm embraced both Sicily and southern Italy it was called simply the Kingdom of Sicily; it would later be called the Kingdom of the Two Sicilies. Roger ruled strongly but tolerantly over the assorted peoples of his realm with their variety of faiths, customs, and languages. The Sicilian capital of Palermo, with its superb harbor and magnificent palace, its impressive public buildings and luxurious villas, was at once a great commercial center and a crucial point of cultural exchange. Known as the city of the threefold tongue, Palermo drew its administrators and scholars from the Latin, Byzantine, and Arabic cultural traditions.

The legal structure of the kingdom included elements from Justinian's *Corpus Juris* and subsequent Byzantine law, from Lombard law, and from Norman feudalism. The royal court, or *curia,* was the core of an efficient, centralized bureaucracy with special departments of justice and finance. The administration profited from the inclusion of an important non-noble professional class, devoted to the king and to the efficient execution of its duties. Drawing on the long experience of Byzantium and Islam, Roger's government was far in advance of most other states in Latin Christendom.

* See p. 446.

The Capella Palatina at Palermo; note the mosaics on the inside of the arches and on the floor.

The kingdom's splendid and varied architecture was similarly multicultural in inspiration. The Capella Palatina (palace church) at Palermo, built on a marble foundation and opulently decorated with mosaics, was a source of wonder and admiration and remains so to this day. Not far from the capital, the magnificent cathedral at Monreale, begun several decades after Roger's death, synthesizes Italian, Norman-French, Moslem, and Byzantine artistic traditions with wonderful

Mosaic of Christ from the cathedral at Monreale.

artistry. The nave of the cathedral is built on the pattern of the Italian basilica, but the building is enlivened with rich Islamic and Byzantine decorations. It contains a remarkable set of brass doors executed in the Byzantine style, and its interior sparkles with some 70,000 square feet of Byzantine mosaics. This remarkable structure, the cathedral church of the archbishop of Sicily, remains today in an excellent state of preservation. It epitomizes in stone the multiform civilization of twelfth-century Norman Sicily.

Under Roger and his successors the kingdom enjoyed a vital and diverse intellectual life. Its history was well chronicled by talented contemporary historians—in particular, Hugo Falcandus who produced an illuminating biography of Roger the Great. The Muslim scholar Idrisi, the greatest geographer of his age, contributed a comprehensive geographical work which drew from classical and Islamic sources. Characteristically, Idrisi dedicated his masterpiece to Roger the Great, and the work bears the title, "The Book of Roger." Sicily, like Spain, became a significant source of translations from Arabic and Greek into Latin. The Sicilian translators provided western European scholars with a steady stream of texts drawn from both classical Greek and Islamic sources, and these texts, together with those passing into Europe from Spain, served as the essential foundations for the impressive intellectual achievements of thirteenth-century Christendom.

In many ways Norman Sicily was western Europe's most interesting and fruitful frontier state. Having been carved out partially at Muslim expense, it was representative of twelfth-century Europe's advancing territorial frontier, and as a vibrant center of cultural interplay it demonstrated that the frontier was not only advancing but also open. Europe besieged had given way to a new Europe—buoyant, expanding, and exposed to the invigorating influences of surrounding civilizations. And nowhere was this stimulating cultural contact more intense than in Norman Sicily. East and West met in Roger the Great's glittering, sun-drenched realm, and worked creatively side by side to make his kingdom the most sophisticated European state of its day.

THE CRUSADES

Background and First Crusade

The Crusades to the Holy Land were the most spectacular and self-conscious acts of Western Christian expansionism in the High Middle Ages, although by no means the most lasting. They arose in response to a major political crisis in the Near East. During the eleventh century a new warlike tribe from Central Asia, the Seljuk Turks, had swept into Persia, taken up the Islamic faith, and turned the Abbasid caliphs of Baghdad into their pawns. In 1071 the Seljuk Turks had inflicted a nearly fatal blow on the Byzantine Empire, smashing a Byzantine army at the battle of Manzikert and seizing Asia Minor, the essential reservoir of Byzantine manpower.* Stories began filtering into the West of Turkish atrocities against Christian pilgrims to Jerusalem, and when the desperate Byzantine emperor, Alexius Comnenus, swallowed his pride and appealed to the West for help, Europe, under the leadership of a reinvigorated papacy, was only too glad to respond.

* For a discussion of the Seljuk Turks and the battle of Manzikert see p. 330.

The Crusades represented a fusion of three characteristic impulses of medieval man: sanctity, pugnacity, and greed. All three were essential. Without Christian idealism the Crusades would be inconceivable, yet the pious dream of liberating Jerusalem and the Holy Land from the infidel and reopening them to Christian pilgrims was reinforced mightily by the lure of new lands and unimaginable wealth. The Crusades provided a superb opportunity for the Christian warrior aristocracy to perform their knightly skills in the service of the Lord—and to make their fortunes in the bargain.

It was to Pope Urban II that Emperor Alexius Comnenus sent his envoys asking for military aid against the Turks, and Urban II, a masterful reform pope, was quick to grasp the opportunity. The Crusade presented many advantages to the Church. It enabled the papacy to put itself at the forefront of an immense popular movement and grasp the moral leadership of Europe. Moreover, the Church may well have seen in the Crusade a partial solution to the problem of endemic private warfare in Europe. The Church had long been trying to pacify the warrior nobility; through such principles as the "Truce of God" it had sought to outlaw warfare on holy days and during holy seasons. The Crusade promised to be a far more effective means of domestic pacification, drawing off warlike and restive members of the European nobility and turning their ferocity outward against the Muslims rather than inward against each other. Then, too, as a rescue mission to Byzantium, the Crusade opened the possibility of reuniting the Eastern and Western churches which had been in schism for more than a generation. Finally, Urban shared with many other Europeans of his day the beguiling dream of winning Jerusalem for Christendom.

Accordingly in 1095 Pope Urban summoned the European nobility to take up

Peter the Hermit preaching the First Crusade. His splinter group consisted of a wildly enthusiastic and undisciplined rabble.

the Cross and reconquer the Holy Land. He delivered a powerful address to the Frankish aristocracy at Clermont-Ferrand, calling upon them to emulate the brave deeds of their ancestors, to avenge the Turkish atrocities (which he described in gory detail), to win the Biblical "land of milk and honey" for Christendom and drive the infidel from the holy city of Jerusalem. Finally, he promised those who undertook the enterprise the highest of spiritual rewards: "Undertake this journey for the remission of your sins, with the assurance of the imperishable glory of the kingdom of Heaven."

The response was overwhelming. With shouts of "God wills it!" Frankish warriors poured into the crusading army. By 1096 the First Crusade was under way. A great international military force—with a large nucleus of feudal knights from central and southern France, Normandy, and Sicily—made their way across the Balkans and assembled at Constantinople. Altogether the warriors of the First Crusade numbered around twenty-five or thirty thousand, a relatively modest figure by modern standards but immense in the eyes of contemporaries. Emperor Alexius was gravely disturbed by the magnitude of the western European response. Having asked for a certain amount of military support, he had, as he put it, a new barbarian invasion on his hands. Cautious and apprehensive, he demanded and obtained from the Crusaders a promise of homage for all the lands they might conquer.

From the beginning there was friction between the Crusaders and the Byzantines. They differed in temperament and also in aim, for the Byzantines wished only to recapture the lost provinces of Asia Minor whereas the Crusaders were determined on nothing less than the conquest of the Holy Land. Alexius promised military aid, but it was never forthcoming, and not long after the Crusaders left Constantinople they broke with the Byzantines altogether. Hurling themselves southeastward across Asia Minor into Syria, they encountered and defeated Muslim forces, captured ancient Antioch after a long and complex siege, and in the summer of 1099 took Jerusalem itself. Urban, who had remained behind, died just before the news of Jerusalem's fall reached Rome.

The Crusaders celebrated their capture

414   The High Middle Ages

of Jerusalem by plundering the city and pitilessly slaughtering its inhabitants. As a contemporary eyewitness describes it,

> If you had been there you would have seen our feet colored to our ankles with the blood of the slain. But what more shall I relate? None of them were left alive; neither women nor children were spared. . . . Afterward, all, clergy and laymen, went to the Sepulcher of the Lord and His glorious temple, singing the ninth chant. With fitting humility they repeated prayers and made their offering at the holy places that they had long desired to visit.

With the capture of Jerusalem, after only three years of vigorous campaigning, the goal of the First Crusade had been achieved. No future crusade was to enjoy such success as the first, and during the two centuries that followed, the original conquests were gradually lost. For the moment, however, Europe rejoiced at the spectacular triumph of its Crusaders. Some of them returned to their homes and received heroes' welcomes. Others remained in Latin Syria to enjoy the fruits of their conquests. A long strip of territory along the eastern Mediterranean shore had been wrested from Islam and was now divided, according to feudal principles, among the Crusader knights. These warriors consolidated their conquests by erecting large and elaborate castles whose ruins still excite the admiration of travelers.

The conquered lands were organized into four Crusader States: the County of Edessa, the Principality of Antioch (under a dynasty of south-Italian Normans), the County of Tripolis, and the Kingdom of Jerusalem. This last was the most important of the four states, and the king of Jerusalem was theoretically the feudal overlord of all the crusader territories. In fact, however, he had difficulty enforcing his authority outside his own kingdom. Indeed, the feudal knights who settled in the Holy Land were far too proud and warlike for their own good, and the Crusader States were characterized from beginning by dangerous rivalries and dissensions.

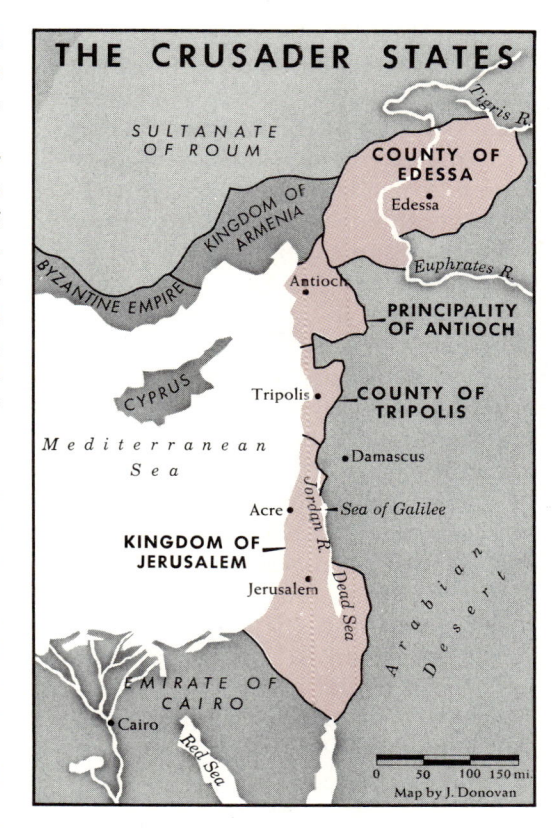

Second Crusade

Gradually over the years the Muslims began to reconquer their lost lands. In 1144 the County of Edessa fell before Islamic pressure, and the disaster gave rise to a renewal of crusading fervor in Europe. The renowned twelfth-century abbot, St. Bernard of Clairvaux, preached the crusade across Europe, and described the enthusiastic response to his preaching as nothing less than miraculous. The Second Crusade (1147–48) was led by King Louis

VII of France and Emperor Conrad III of Germany. Louis transported his army by sea while Conrad's forces took the land route. They met in Jerusalem and at once encountered friction with the established Christian residents who had learned to live alongside the Muslims, who imitated their dress and customs, and who lacked the zeal of the newly-arrived warriors. This contrast in mood between established residents and new crusaders was to be a recurring problem in the Holy Land.

Rather than moving on Edessa, the Crusaders decided to besiege the great inland caravan center of Damascus. It was a wise plan, in theory, for possession of Damascus would have added much to the strategic and commercial stability of the Crusader States, but Damascus proved impregnable and the siege failed. The Crusaders returned to Europe empty-handed, prompting St. Bernard to describe the campaign as "an abyss so deep that I must call him blessed who is not scandalized thereby."

The 1170s and 1180s witnessed the rise of a new, unified Islamic state centered in Egypt and galvanized by the skilled leadership of a Kurdish warrior-prince named Saladin. Chivalrous as well as able, Saladin at first engaged in a truce with the Crusader States, but the rise of his new principality was nevertheless an ominous threat to Latin Syria. The truce was broken by a Christian robber baron, a typical product of the feudal environment, who persisted in attacking Muslim caravans. Saladin now moved on Jerusalem, and in 1187 he captured it. Jerusalem was not to be retaken by a Christian army for the remainder of the Middle Ages.

Third Crusade

This new catastrophe resulted in still another major crusading effort. The Third Crusade (1189–92) was led by three of medieval Europe's most illustrious monarchs: Emperor Frederick Barbarossa of Germany, King Philip Augustus of France, and King Richard the Lion-Hearted of England.* Frederick Barbarossa had a long and successful career behind him as Holy Roman Emperor; Philip Augustus was later to become the architect of the great thirteenth-century Capetian monarchy in France; and Richard the Lion-Hearted was already a warrior of immense renown on the battlefields of Europe. Yet for all that, and notwithstanding the abundant growth of legend and romance that has sprung up around the Third Crusade, the enterprise can hardly be described as successful. Frederick Barbarossa never reached the Holy Land at all. He drowned while crossing a river in Asia Minor and the greater part of his army returned to Germany. Philip and Richard, who had been enemies at home, were hostile toward one another from the beginning. They joined forces in besieging and capturing the important coastal city of Acre, but shortly thereafter King Philip returned to France to plot against Richard. There followed a series of encounters between the forces of Saladin and Richard the Lion-Hearted during which the two chivalrous antagonists developed a degree of mutual admiration. Richard won several battles but failed to retake Jerusalem, and in the end he settled for a pact with Saladin, granting Christian pilgrims free access to the holy city. It was, all in all, a miserably disappointing conclusion to such an immense undertaking. As an ironic postscript, King Richard fell into hostile hands on his return journey and became the prisoner of Frederick Barbarossa's son, Emperor Henry VI, who released his royal captive only after England had paid the immense sum of 100,000 pounds—quite literally, a king's ransom.

* All three will be encountered in the next chapter.

Fourth Crusade

Within another decade Europe was ready for still another attempt on Jerusalem. Although lacking the distinguished royal leaders of the previous campaign, the Fourth Crusade (1201–4) had as its instigator the most powerful of the medieval popes: Innocent III. Like the First Crusade, it was led not by kings but by great feudal lords such as Baldwin IX, count of Flanders. It was, withal, the oddest of the Crusades. It never reached the Holy Land at all, yet in its own way it was spectacularly successful.

The Crusaders resolved to avoid the perils of overland travel by crossing to the Holy Land in Venetian ships. The doge of Venice, a Christian but also a man of business, demanded as payment for the service of his ships a sum of money greater than the Crusaders could afford. He agreed, however, to take what money the Crusaders had and to transport them to the Holy Land if in return they would do him an errand on the way. They were to capture for Venice the port of Zara which had recently come into the hands of the king of Hungary. Pope Innocent III was infuriated by this bargain which diverted the crusading army against a king who was not only a Christian but a papal vassal. The Crusaders were automatically excommunicated on their attacking Zara, and Innocent repudiated the entire enterprise.

Nevertheless, the warriors went doggedly ahead. Capturing Zara in 1202, they were then diverted still again, this time by a political dispute in Constantinople involving the succession to the Byzantine throne. One of the two claimants, having recently fled to the West, contacted the Crusaders and begged their support, promising them immense wealth, aid against the Muslims and reunion of the Eastern and Western churches under Rome. Rising to the challenge, the Crusaders moved on Constantinople. The emperor-in-residence panicked and fled to the city, and a delegation of citizens, realizing that further resistance was useless, opened Constantinople's gates to the Crusaders. Their imperial claimant was installed in power but was murdered shortly afterwards by one of his anti-Latin countrymen. Meanwhile the Crusaders had withdrawn from the city as a result of growing hostility and violence between Greeks and Latins. But now, having expended considerable effort in what was apparently a fruitless cause, they resolved to take the city for themselves, to elect a new Byzantine emperor from their own ranks, and to divide the Eastern Empire among them.

Accordingly, the Crusaders besieged Constantinople and took it by storm in 1204. The impregnable Byzantine capital had fallen at last to enemy conquerors; the Crusaders had succeeded where hordes of Muslims, Persians, and barbarians had failed. Count Baldwin IX of Flanders became emperor, and he and his heirs ruled in Constantinople for more than half a century. A nucleus of the old Byzantine state held out in Asia Minor, gathering its strength, until in 1261 the Latin empire was overthrown and Greek emperors reigned once again in Constantinople. But the Fourth Crusade had delivered a blow from which Byzantium never entirely recovered.

The wealth of Constantinople permanently diverted the warriors of the Fourth crusade from the Holy Land. The Eastern and Western churches were temporarily reunited, however. A Latin patriarch now sat in Constantinople, and a Latin hierarchy presided over a captive Greek church. Innocent III, who had absolved the Crusaders from excommunication after the fall of Zara and had excommunicated them anew for attacking Constantinople, readmitted them once again to communion when he realized the "great blessings" that had befallen Christendom by the capture of the schismatic city. The Crusaders, for their part, returned to Europe with immense booty from Constantinople—precious gems, money, and gold such as few of them had imagined, but the greatest prize of all was the immense store of relics which the Westerners liberated from the Byzantine capital and brought to their homeland. Bones, heads, and arms of saints, the crown of thorns, St. Thomas the Apostle's doubting finger, and many similar treasures passed into western Europe at this time. Perhaps more important, the West was given additional access to the intellectual legacy of Greek and Byzantine civilization. But the old hostility between Greeks and Latins was aggravated by the events of the Fourth Crusade into a virtually insurmountable wall of hatred.

Later Crusades

During the thirteenth century crusading fervor gradually waned. Crusades against the Muslim Near East were generally unsuccessful, and the papacy weakened the crusading ideal by calling for repeated crusades not only against the Muslims in the Holy Land but also against the Muslims in Spain, the Albigensian heretics of southern France, and even the Holy Roman emperor. In 1212 a visionary and ill-organized enterprise known as the "Children's Crusade" ended in disaster as thousands of boys and girls—gripped by religious fervor and convinced that the Mediterranean would dry up before them and provide them a miraculous pathway into the Holy Land—flocked into the ports of southern Europe. Many of them were obliged to abandon the enterprise and return home disillusioned; the remainder were sold into Muslim slavery.

The next major effort against the Muslims of the Near East, the Fifth Crusade (1217–1221), was directed not at the Holy Land but against the real center of Muslim power: Egypt. The Crusaders captured the important Egyptian port of Damietta in 1219 and refused a Muslim offer to trade Jerusalem for it. But dissension within the crusader ranks and an abortive attack against Cairo in which the Crusaders were caught between a Muslim army and the flooding Nile, resulted in military disaster, the abandonment of Damietta, and the failure of the Crusade.

Three additional crusades of importance were undertaken in the thirteenth century. The first of these, led by the brilliant emperor Frederick II, was at once the most fruitful and least edifying of the three. Frederick negotiated with the sultan of Egypt rather than fight him, and in 1229 obtained possession of Jerusalem by treaty. The triumph was ephemeral, however, for Jerusalem fell into Muslim hands once again in 1244. And because of the lack of fighting, Frederick II's crusade was never dignified by being given a number.

The Sixth and Seventh crusades were led by the saint-king of France, Louis IX. One was undertaken against Egypt in 1248, the other against Tunisia in 1270. Both failed, and the second cost St. Louis his life. Crusades continued to be organized and mounted in subsequent generations, but as the thirteenth century closed it was obvious that crusading enthusiasm was waning and the movement dying out. In 1291, the fall of Acre—the last Christian bridgehead on the Syrian coast—brought an end to the Crusader States in the Holy Land.

Significance of the Crusading Movement

Yet the Crusades were more than simply a splendid failure. During the greater part of the High Middle Ages Christian lords ruled portions of the Holy Land. Their activities caught the imagination of Europe and held it for two centuries, uniting Western Christendom in a single vast effort. At the same time European merchants established permanent bases in Syria and enormously enlarged their role in international commerce. Knights and barons who participated in the crusades broadened their perspective through contacts with other civilizations. The effect of such contacts in dissolving the provincial narrow-mindedness of the European nobility is incalculable.

The Crusades gave rise to several semimonastic orders of Christian warriors bound by monastic rules and dedicated to fighting the Muslims and advancing the crusading cause in every possible way. One such order was the Knights Hospitalers, which drew chiefly on the French for its membership. Another was the Knights Templars, an international brotherhood that acquired great wealth through pious gifts and intelligent estate management, and gradually became involved in far-flung banking activities. A third order, the Teutonic Knights, was composed chiefly of Germans. In the thirteenth century the Teutonic Knights transferred their activities from the Holy Land to northern Germany where they devoted themselves to the eastward thrust of German-Christian civilization against the Slavs. Orders of a similar sort arose on other frontiers of Western Christendom. The Knights of Santiago de Compostella, for example, were dedicated to fighting the Muslims in Spain and aiding in the Christian reconquest of the Iberian peninsula. These crusading orders, bridging as they did the two great medieval institutions of monasticism and knighthood, represented the ultimate synthesis of the military and the Christian life. They brought the Church into worldly affairs as never before.

THE GERMAN EASTWARD EXPANSION

Eastern Germany was still another of medieval Europe's expanding frontiers. The German eastward drive was not a product of active royal policy but rather a movement led by enterprising local aristocrats and, in particular, the dukes of Saxony. It was a slow movement with a great deal of momentum behind it which succeeded, over a long period between 1125 and 1350, in pushing the eastern boundary of Germany from the Elbe River past the Oder to the Vistula at Slavic expense. The gains were consolidated by the building of innumerable agrarian villages and a massive eastward migration of German peasants. Consequently, the new areas were not only conquered; they were in large part Christianized and permanently Germanized. As an indirect consequence of the movement, the Slavic kingdom of Poland was converted to Catholic Christianity and incorporated into the fabric of Western Christendom.

The later phases of the German push were spearheaded by the Teutonic Knights who penetrated temporarily far northward into Lithuania, Latvia, and Estonia, and even made an unsuccessful bid to conquer Russia. During the fourteenth and fifteenth centuries the Teutonic Knights lost many of their conquests, but much of the German expansion proved to be permanent. The epoch between 1125 and 1350 witnessed the conquest and Germanization of what ultimately became the eastern two-fifths of pre-World-War-II Germany.

In the later thirteenth and early fourteenth centuries European expansion was coming to an end. The internal frontiers of forest and swamp had by then been won, and the external frontiers were everywhere hardening, sometimes even receding as in the holy land. The closing

GERMAN SETTLEMENTS TO THE EAST 800–1400

- German before 800
- 800–1400
- Large minorities, 1400
- Small minorities, 1400

Map by J. Donovan

of the frontiers was accompanied by diminishing prosperity and a drying up of high medieval culture. For the brilliant cultural achievements of the High Middle Ages were products of a buoyant, expanding, frontier society, fired by a powerful faith, driven by immense ambitions, and captivated by a world in which, so it seemed, anything was possible (see Table I).

TABLE I

Chronology of the European Territorial Frontier Movement

SPAIN	SICILY	HOLY LAND
1002: Breakup of Caliphate of Cordova	ca. 1016: Norman infiltration begins	
	1060–91: Sicily conquered	
1085: Capture of Toledo	1085: Death of Robert Guiscard	1095: Calling of First Crusade
1140: Aragon unites with Catalonia	1130: Coronation of Roger the Great	1099: Crusaders take Jerusalem
	1154: Death of Roger the Great	
		1187: Crusaders lose Jerusalem
1212: Christian victory at Las Navas de Tolosa		1204: Crusaders take Constantinople
1236: Castile takes Cordova		1291: Crusaders driven from Holy Land

C. Religious Frontiers — THE CHURCH IN THE HIGH MIDDLE AGES

The expansion of civilization during the High Middle Ages has been viewed thus far as a series of advancing economic and territorial frontiers. In fact, however, frontiers of all sorts were being explored and extended. Scholars were pioneering in new intellectual frontiers, artists and writers were adding ever-new dimensions to Western culture. Administrators were pushing forward the art of government. And underlying all these phenomena—which will be explored in the next two chapters—was an intense deepening of the religious impulse which manifested itself in many different ways: in the rise of a vigorous papacy dedicated to reform and the creation of a Christian world order,* in the development of new forms of monasticism, in the rapid expansion of ecclesiastical administration and Church activities, in the intensification of lay piety, and in the growth of religious heterodoxy.

Medieval religion followed many different paths. It could be devoutly orthodox, it could be anticlerical, and it could be openly heretical. Yet its basic institutional expression was the Catholic Church, and the most obvious thing that the preponderant majority of Western Christians had in common was their Catholicism. Nationalism was scarcely yet alive, and the allegiance of Europeans tended to be either local or international. In the twelfth and thirteenth centuries the majority of Europeans were still intensely local

* See pp. 440–41.

in their outlook, only vaguely aware of what was going on beyond their immediate surroundings. But alongside their localism was an element of cosmopolitanism—a consciousness of belonging to the international commonwealth of Western Christendom, fragmented politically, but united culturally and spiritually by the Church.

The Church in the High Middle Ages was a powerful unifying influence. It had made notable progress since the half-heathen pre-Carolingian era. A flourishing parish system was by now spreading across the European countryside to bring the sacraments and a modicum of Christian instruction to the peasantry. New bishoprics and archbishoprics were formed, and old ones were becoming steadily more active. The papacy never completely succeeded in breaking the control of kings and secular lords over their local bishops, but by the twelfth century it was coming to exercise a very real authority over the European episcopacy, and the growing efficiency of the papal bureaucracy evoked the envy and imitation of the rising royal governments.

The Sacraments

The buoyancy of high medieval Europe is nowhere more evident than in the accelerating impact of Christian piety on European society. The sacraments of the Church introduced a significant religious dimension into the life of the typical European layman: his birth was sanctified by the sacrament of *baptism* in which he was cleansed of the taint of original sin and initiated into the Christian fellowship. At puberty, he received the sacrament of *confirmation* which reasserted his membership in the Church and gave him the additional grace to cope with the problems of adulthood. His wedding was dignified by the sacrament of *matrimony*. If he chose the calling of the ministry, he was spiritually transformed into a priest and "married" to the Church by the sacrament of *holy orders*. At his death, he received the sacrament of *extreme unction*, which prepared his soul for its journey into the next world. And throughout his life he could receive forgiveness from the damning consequences of mortal sin by repenting his past transgressions and humbly receiving the comforting sacrament of *penance*. Finally, he might partake regularly of the central sacrament of the Church—the *eucharist*—receiving the body of Christ into his own body by consuming the eucharistic bread. Thus, the church, through its seven sacraments, brought God's grace to all Christians, great and humble, at every critical juncture of their lives. The sacramental system, which only assumed final form in the High Middle Ages, was a source of immense comfort and reassurance: it brought hope of salvation not simply to the saintly elite but to the sinful majority; it made communion with God not merely the elusive goal of a few mystics but the periodic experience of all believers. And, of course, it established the Church as the essential intermediary between God and man.

Evolution of Piety

The ever-increasing scope of the Church, together with the rising vigor of the new age, resulted in a deepening of popular piety throughout Europe. The High Middle Ages witnessed a profound shift in religious attitude from the awe and mystery characteristic of earlier Christianity to a new emotionalism and dynamism. This shift is evident in ecclesiastical architecture, as the stolid, earthbound Romanesque style gave way in the later twelfth century to the tense, upward-reaching Gothic.* A parallel change is evi-

* See pp. 501–7.

dent in devotional practices as the divine Christ sitting in judgment gave way to the tragic figure of the human Christ suffering on the Cross for man's sins. And it was in the High Middle Ages that the Virgin Mary came into her own as the compassionate intercessor for hopelessly lost souls. No matter how sinful a person might be, he could be redeemed if only he won the sympathy of Mary, for what son could refuse the petition of his mother? Indeed, a legend of the age told of the devil complaining to God that the tenderhearted Queen of Heaven was cheating Hell of its most promising candidates. In this atmosphere of religious romanticism, Christianity became, as never before, a doctrine of love, hope, and compassion. The God of Justice became the merciful, suffering God who died in agony to atone for the sins of men and to bring them everlasting life.

Like all other human institutions, the medieval Church fell far short of its ideals. Corrupt churchmen were in evidence throughout the age, and certain historians have delighted in cataloguing instances of larcenous bishops, gluttonous priests, and licentious nuns. But cases such as these were clearly exceptional. The great shortcoming of the high-medieval Church was not gross corruption but rather a creeping complacency which resulted sometimes in a shallow, even mechanical attitude toward the Christian religious life. The medieval Church had more than its share of saints, but among much of the clergy the profundity of the Faith was often lost in the day-to-day affairs of the pastoral office and the management of far-flung estates.

THE CRISIS IN BENEDICTINISM

The drift toward complacency has been a recurring problem in Christian monasticism—as in most human institutions. Again and again, the lofty idealism of a monastic reform movement has been eroded and transformed by time and success until, at length, new reform movements arose in protest against the growing worldliness of the old ones. This cycle has been repeated countless times. Indeed, the sixth-century Benedictine movement was itself a protest against the excesses and inadequacies of earlier monasticism. St. Benedict had regarded his new order as a means of withdrawing from the world and devoting full time to communion with God. But Benedictinism, despite Benedict's ideal, quickly became involved in teaching, evangelism, and ecclesiastical reform, and by the tenth and eleventh centuries the whole Benedictine movement had become deeply immersed in worldly affairs. Benedictine monasteries controlled vast estates, supplied significant contingents of knights in their service to feudal armies, and worked closely with secular princes in affairs of state. Early in the tenth century the Cluniac movement, which was itself Benedictine in spirit and rule, arose as a protest against the worldliness and complacency of contemporary Benedictine monasticism,* but by the later eleventh century the Congregation of Cluny had come to terms with the secular establishment and was beginning to display traces of the very complacency against which it had originally rebelled. Prosperous, respected, and secure, Cluny was too content with its majestic abbeys and priories, its elaborate liturgical program, and its bounteous fields to give its wholehearted support to the radical transformation of Christian society for which many Christian reformers were now struggling.

St. Benedict had sought to create monastic sanctuaries in which Christians might retire from the evils and temptations of society, but the High Middle Ages

* See pp. 395–96.

witnessed an endeavor to sanctify society itself. The new goal, pioneered by the reform papacy of the eleventh century, was not *withdrawal* but *conversion*. Rather than making Christians safe from the world, the world would be made safe for Christianity. During the eleventh and twelfth centuries, these two contrary tendencies—withdrawal and conversion—both had a profound impact upon monastic reform.

In the opening decades of the High Middle Ages the Benedictine movement was showing signs of exhaustion. During the long, troubled centuries of the early Middle Ages, Benedictine teachers and missionaries, scribes and political advisors, had provided indispensable services to society. Benedictine monasteries had served as the spiritual and cultural foci of Christendom. But in the eleventh and twelfth centuries, the Benedictines saw their pedagogical monopoly broken by the rising cathedral schools and universities of the new towns. These urban schools produced increasing numbers of well-trained scholars who gradually superseded the Benedictine monks as scribes and advisers to princes. In other words, the urbanizing impulse of the High Middle Ages drastically diminished the traditional Benedictine contribution to society.

Still, the Benedictines retained their great landed wealth. The Benedictine monastery was scarcely the sanctuary from worldly concerns that St. Benedict had planned. Nor was it any longer the vital force it once had been in Christianizing the world. Twelfth-century Benedictinism followed neither the path of withdrawal nor the path of conversion, and even in the arena of secular affairs it was losing its grip. The Benedictine life was beginning to appear tarnished and unappealing to sensitive religious spirits caught up in the soaring piety of the new age.

THE NEW MONASTICISM

Carthusians

The monastic revolt against Benedictinism followed the two divergent roads of uncompromising withdrawal from society and ardent participation in the Christianization of society. The impulse toward withdrawal pervaded the Carthusian order which arose in eastern France in the later eleventh century and spread across Christendom in the twelfth. Isolated from the outside world, the Carthusians lived in small groups, worshiping together in communal chapels but otherwise living as hermits in individual cells. This austere order exists to this day and, unlike most monastic movements, its severe spirituality has seldom waned. Yet even in the spiritually-charged atmosphere of the twelfth century it was a small movement, offering a way of life for only a minority of heroically holy men. Too ascetic for the average Christian, the Carthusian order was much admired but seldom joined.

Cistercians

The greatest monastic order of the twelfth century, the Cistercian, managed for a time to be both austere and popular. The mother house of the order, Citeaux, was established by a little group of religious radicals in 1098 on a wild, remote site in eastern France. The Cistercian order grew slowly at first, then gradually acquired momentum. In 1115 it had four daughter houses; by the end of the century it had 500.

The success of the Cistercians demonstrates the immense appeal of the idea of withdrawal to the Christians of the twelfth century. Like Citeaux, the daughter houses were deliberately built in remote wilderness areas. The abbeys themselves were stark and primitive in contrast to the elaborate Cluniac architecture. Cistercian life was stark and primitive too—less severe than that of the Carthusians but far more so than that of the Cluniacs. The Cistercians sought to resurrect the strict, simple life of primitive Benedictinism, but in fact they were more austere than Benedict himself. The numerous Cistercian houses were bound together tightly, not by the authority of a central abbot as at Cluny, but by an annual council of all Cistercian abbots meeting at Citeaux. Without such centralized control it is unlikely that the individual houses could have clung for long to the harsh, ascetic ideals on which the order was founded.

Saint Bernard of Clairvaux

The key figure in twelfth-century Cistercianism was St. Bernard, who joined the community of Citeaux in 1112 and three years later became the founder and abbot of Clairvaux, one of Citeaux's earliest daughter houses. St. Bernard of Clairvaux was the leading Christian of his age—a profound mystic, a brilliant religious orator, and a crucial figure in the meteoric rise of the Cistercian order. His moral influence was so immense that he became Europe's leading arbiter of political and ecclesiastical disputes. He persuaded the king of France and the Holy Roman emperor to participate in the Second Crusade. And he persuaded Christendom to accept his candidate in the years following a hotly disputed papal election in 1130. On one occasion he even succeeded in reconciling the two great warring families of Germany, the Welfs and Hohenstaufens. He rebuked the pope himself: "Remember, first of all, that the Holy Roman Church, over which you hold sway, is the mother of churches, not their sovereign mistress—that you yourself are not the lord of bishops but one among them. . . ." And he took an uncompromising stand against one of the rising movements of his day: the attempt to reconcile the Catholic faith with human reason which was led by the brilliant twelfth-century philosopher, Peter Abelard. In the long run Bernard failed to halt the reconciliation of faith with reason, but he succeeded in making life miserable for Abelard and in securing the official condemnation of certain of Abelard's teachings.*

Above and beyond all his obvious talents as a leader and persuader of men, St. Bernard won the devotion and admiration of twelfth-century Europe through his reputation for sanctity. He was widely regarded as a saint in his own lifetime, and stories circulated far and wide of miracles that he performed. Pilgrims flocked to Clairvaux to be healed by his touch. This aspect of Bernard's reputation made his skillful preaching and diplomacy even more effective than it would otherwise have been. For here was a holy man, a miracle worker, who engaged in severe fasts, overworked himself to an extraordinary degree, wore coarse and humble clothing, and devoted himself totally to the service of God. By contemporary standards he was relatively tolerant: he opposed the persecution of Jews, and urged that heretics—"the little foxes that spoil the vines"—should be won over to the truth "not by force of arms but by force of argument." But if a heretic should prove immune from persuasion, "he should be driven away or even a restraint put upon his freedom, rather than that he should be allowed to spoil the vines." Such views were moderate and restrained, coming from an age when heresy was regarded as an affront to God and a grave threat to society, when a heretic preaching Albigensianism in the streets of Paris was approximately as popular as a Ku-Klux

* See p. 520.

C. Religious Frontiers

Klansman today preaching white supremacy on the campus of Yale.

St. Bernard impressed Europe deeply with his nobility of spirit and his genuine charity and humility. His religion was essentially Christ-oriented; Christ was at the center of his devotional life, with the Virgin Mary and the saints occupying important subordinate positions. Humble and prayerful though he was, he could also overawe men with his energy and iron will. On one occasion he commanded Duke William of Aquitaine to reinstate certain bishops whom the Duke had driven from their sees. When, after much persuasion, the Duke proved obdurate, St. Bernard celebrated a High Mass for him. Holding the consecrated host in his hands, Bernard advanced from the altar toward the Duke and said, "We have besought you, and you have spurned us. The united multitude of the servants of God, meeting you elsewhere, has entreated you and you have scorned them. Behold! Here comes to you the Virgin's Son, the Head and Lord of the Church which you persecute! Your Judge is here, at whose name every knee shall bow. . . . Your Judge is here, into whose hands your soul is to pass! Will you spurn him also? Will you scorn him as you have scorned his servants?" The Duke threw himself on the ground and submitted to Bernard's demands.

Bernard's career demonstrates vividly the essential paradox of Cistercianism. For although the Cistercians strove to dissociate themselves from the world, Bernard was drawn inexorably into the vortex of secular affairs. Indeed, as the twelfth century progressed, the entire Cistercian movement became increasingly worldly. Like the later Puritans, the Cistercians discovered that their twin virtues of austere living and hard work resulted in an embarrassing accumulation of wealth and a corrosion of their spiritual simplicity. Their efforts to clear fields around their remote abbeys placed them in the vanguard of the internal frontier movement. They became pioneers in scientific farming and introduced notable improvements in the breeding of horses, cattle, and sheep. The English Cistercians became the great wool producers of the realm. Altogether the Cistercians exerted a powerful, progressive influence on European husbandry and came to play a prominent role in the European economy. Economic success brought ever-increasing wealth to the order. Cistercian abbey churches became more elaborate and opulent, and the primitive austerity of Cistercian life was progressively relaxed. In later years there appeared new offshoots, such as the Trappists, which returned to the strict observance of original Cistercianism.

Monasticism in the World

The Cistercians had endeavored to withdraw from the world, but despite their goal they became a powerful force in twelfth-century Europe. At roughly the same time, other orders were being established with the deliberate aim of participating actively in society and working toward its regeneration. The Augustinian Canons, for example, submitted to the rigor of a rule, yet carried on normal ecclesiastical duties in the world, serving in parish churches and cathedrals. The fusion of monastic discipline and worldly activity culminated in the twelfth-century Crusading orders—the Knights Templars, the Knights Hospitalers, the Teutonic Knights, and similar groups—whose ideal was a synthesis of the monastic and the military life for the purpose of expanding the political frontiers of Western Christendom. These and other efforts to direct the spiritual vigor of monastic life toward the Christianization of society typify the bold visions and lofty hopes of the new, emotionally-charged religiosity that animated twelfth-century Europe.

As seen in this illuminated manuscript, open-air evangelism was practiced by both the clerics and the heretics.

HERESIES AND THE INQUISITION

Rise of Heresy

The surge of popular piety also raised serious problems for the Church and society, for it resulted in a flood of criticism against churchmen. It was not that churchmen had grown worse, but rather that laymen had begun to judge them by harsher standards. Popular dissatisfaction toward the workaday Church manifested itself in part in the rush toward the austere twelfth-century monastic orders. Yet the majority of Christians could not become monks, and for them, certain new heretical doctrines began to exert a powerful appeal.

The heresies of the High Middle Ages flourished particularly in the rising towns of southern Europe. The eleventh-century urban revolution had caught the Church unprepared; whereas the new towns were the real centers of the burgeoning lay piety, the Church, with its roots in the older agrarian feudal order, seemed unable to minister effectively to the vigorous and widely literate new burger class. Too often the urban bishops appeared as political oppressors and enemies of burghal independence rather than inspiring spiritual directors. Too often the Church failed to understand the townsmen's problems and aspirations or to anticipate their growing suspicion of ecclesiastical wealth and power. Although the vast majority of medieval townsmen remained loyal to the Church, a troublesome minority, particularly in the south, turned to new, anticlerical sects. In their denunciation of ecclesiastical wealth, these sects were doing nothing more than St. Bernard and the Cistercians had done. But many of the anticlerical sects crossed the line between orthodox reformism and heresy by preaching without episcopal or papal approval; far more important, they denied the exclusive right of the priesthood to perform sacraments.

Waldensians, Cathari, and the Inquisition

One such sect, the Waldensians, was founded by a merchant of Lyons named Peter Waldo who, around 1173, gave all his possessions to the poor and took up a life of apostolic poverty. He and his followers worked at first within the bounds of orthodoxy, but gradually their anticlericalism and their denial of special priestly powers earned them the condemnation of the Church. Similar groups, some orthodox, some heretical, arose in the communes of Lombardy and were known as the *Humiliati.* Naturally these groups proved exceedingly troublesome and embarrassing to the local ecclesiastical hierarchies, but generally they escaped downright condemnation unless they themselves took the step of denying the authority of the Church. Many of them did take that step, however, and by the thirteenth century heretical, anticlerical sects were spreading across northern Italy and southern France, and even into Spain and Germany.

The most popular and dangerous heresy in southern France was sponsored by a group known as the *Cathari* (the pure) or the Albigensians—after the town of Albi where they were particularly strong. The Albigensians represented a fusion of two traditions: (1) the anticlerical protest against ecclesiastical wealth and power, and (2) an exotic theology derived originally from Persian dualism. The Albigensians recognized two gods: the god of good who reigned over the universe of the spirit, and the god of evil who ruled the world of matter. The Old Testament God, as creator of the material universe, was their god of evil; Christ, who was believed to have been a purely spiritual being with a phantom body, was the god of good. Albigensian morality stressed a rigorous rejection of all material things—of physical appetites, wealth, worldly vanities, and sexual intercourse—in the hope of one day escaping from the prison of the body and ascending to the realm of pure spirit. In reality this severe ethic was practiced only by a small elite known as the *perfecti;* the rank and file normally begat children, and participated only vicariously in the rejection of the material world—by criticizing the affluence of the Church. Indeed, their opponents accused them of gross licentiousness, and it does seem to be true that certain Provençal noblemen were attracted to the new teaching by the opportunity of appropriating Church property in good conscience.

However this may be, Albigensianism was spreading rapidly as the thirteenth century dawned and was becoming an ominous threat to the unity of Christendom and the authority of the Church. Pope Innocent III, recognizing the gravity of the situation, tried with every means in his power to eradicate Albigensianism. At length, in 1208, he responded to the murder of a papal legate in southern France by summoning a crusade against the Albigensians. The Albigensian Crusade was a ruthless, savage affair which succeeded in its purpose but only at the cost of ravaging the vibrant civilization of southern France. The French monarchy intervened in the Crusade's final stages, brought it to a bloody conclusion, and thereby extended the sway of the Capetian kings to the Mediterranean. The Albigensian Crusade was an important event in the development of French royal power, and it succeeded in reversing the trend toward heresy in southern Europe. It also disclosed the brutality of which the Church was capable when sufficiently threatened.

In the years immediately following the Albigensian Crusade, there emerged an institution that will always stand as a grim symbol of the medieval Church at its worst: the Inquisition. The Christian persecution of heretics dates from the later fourth century, but it was not until the High Middle Ages that heterodox views presented a serious problem to European society. Traditionally, the problem of converting or punishing heretics was handled at the local level, but in 1233 the papacy established a permanent central tribunal for the purpose of standardizing procedures and increasing efficiency in the suppression of heresies. The methods of the Inquisition included the use of torture, secret testimony, conviction on the testimony of only two witnesses, the denial of legal counsel to the accused, and other procedures offensive to the Anglo-American legal tradition but not especially remarkable by standards of the times. Indeed, many of these procedures—including torture—were drawn from the customs of Roman law. In defense of the Inquisition it might be said that convicted heretics might escape death by renouncing their "errors," and that far from establishing a reign of terror, the Inquisition seems to have enjoyed popular support.

Some historians have adduced other arguments in an attempt to defend an indefensible institution. Let us say here merely that the Christian faith was far more important to the people of medieval Europe than national allegiance—that the medieval Church, with its elaborate charitable activities, its hospitals and universities, and its other social services, performed many of the functions of the modern state, and that therefore medieval heresy was analogous to modern treason. To the medieval Christian, heresy was a hateful, repugnant thing, an insult to Christ, and a source of contamination to others. Today, when political and economic doctrines are more important to most people than religious creeds, the closest parallels to medieval Waldensianism or Albigensianism are to be found in the Communist and Nazi parties in modern America, Zionism in Soviet Russia, and revisionist Marxism in Peking. In examining opposition to movements such as these, we can gain an inkling of the state of mind that produced the medieval Inquisition.

MENDICANTISM

The thirteenth-century church found an answer to the heretical drift which was far more compassionate and effective than the Inquisition. In the opening decades of the century two radically new orders emerged—the Dominican and the Franciscan—which were devoted to a life of poverty, preaching, and charitable deeds.

Rejecting the life of the cloister, they dedicated themselves to religious work in the world—particularly in the towns. Benedictines and Cistercians had traditionally taken vows of personal poverty, but the monastic orders themselves could and did acquire great corporate wealth. The Dominicans and Franciscans, on the contrary, were pledged to both personal and corporate poverty and were therefore known as mendicants (beggars). Capturing the imagination of thirteenth-century Christendom, they drained urban heterodoxy of much of its former support by demonstrating to the townsmen of Europe that Christian orthodoxy could be both relevant and compelling.

The Dominicans

St. Dominic (1170–1221), a well-educated Spaniard, spent his early manhood as an Augustinian canon at a cathedral in Castile. In his mid-thirties he traveled to Rome, met Pope Innocent III, and followed the pope's bidding to preach in southern France against the Albigensians. For the next decade, between 1205 and 1215, he worked among the heretics, leading an austere, humble life, and winning considerable renown for his eloquence and simplicity. For the most part the Albigensians seem to have been unaffected by Dominic's preaching; they respected him but did not follow him.

The Dominican Order evolved out of a small group of volunteers who joined Dominic in his work among the Albigensians. Gradually Dominic came to see the possibility of a far greater mission for his followers: to preach and win converts to the faith throughout the world. In 1215 Dominic's friend the bishop of Toulouse gave the group a church and a house in the city, and shortly thereafter the papacy recognized the Dominicans as a separate religious order and approved the Dominican rule. The congregation founded by Dominic was to be known as the Order of Friars Preachers. It assumed its permanent shape during the years between its formal establishment in 1216 and Dominic's death in 1221 by which time it had grown to include some 500 friars and 60 priories organized into eight provinces embracing the whole of western Europe. The Dominicans stood in the vanguard of the thirteenth-century upsurge of piety. Their order attracted men of imagination and unusual religious dedication, men who could not be satisfied with the enclosed and tradition-bound life of earlier monasticism but who were challenged by the austerity of the Dominican rule, the disciplined vitality of the order, and the stimulating goal of working toward the moral regeneration of society rather than withdrawing from the world.

The Dominican rule drew freely from the earlier rule of the Augustinian Canons which Dominic had known in his youth, but added new elements and provided a novel direction for the religious life. The order was to be headed by a minister-general, elected for life, and a legislative body that met annually and consisted sometimes of delegates from the Dominican provinces, sometimes of priors from all the Dominican houses. The friars themselves belonged not to a particular house or province but to the order, and their place of residence and activity was determined by the minister-general. Their life, strictly regulated and austere, included such rigors as regular midnight services, total abstinence from meat, frequent fasts, and prolonged periods of mandatory silence. And the entire order was strictly bound by the rule of poverty which Dominic had learned from his contemporary, St. Francis. Not only should poverty be the condition of individual Dominicans as it was of individual Benedictines, it was to be the condition of the order itself. The Dominican order was to have no possessions except churches and priories. It was to have no fixed incomes, no manors, but was to subsist through charitable gifts. It was, in short, a mendicant order.

The Dominican order expanded at a phenomenal rate during the course of the thirteenth century. Dominican friars carried their evangelical activities across Europe and beyond, into the Holy Land, Central Asia, Tartary, Tibet, and China. Joining the faculties of the rising universities they became the leading proponents of Aristotelian philosophy and included in their numbers such notable scholars as St. Albertus Magnus and St. Thomas Aquinas. Dominic himself had insisted that his followers acquire broad educations before undertaking their mission of preaching and that each Dominican priory include a school of theology. Within a few decades after his death his order included some of the foremost intellects of the age.

The Dominicans were, above all, preachers, and their particular mission was to preach among heretics and non-Christians. Their contact with heretics brought them into close involvement with the Inquisition, and in later years their reputation was darkened by the fact that they themselves became the leading inquisitors. The grand inquisitor of Spain, for example, was customarily a Dominican. They acquired the nickname *"Domini canes"*—hounds of God—by their willingness to supplement St. Dominic's policy of persuasion with the easier and crueler policy of force.

The Dominican order still flourishes. The rule of corporate poverty was softened increasingly and finally, in the fifteenth century, dropped altogether, for it was recognized that full-time scholars and teachers could not beg or do odd jobs or be in doubt as to the source of their next meal. But long after their original mendicant ideals were modified, the Dominicans remained faithful to their essential mission of championing Catholic orthodoxy by word and pen.

Saint Francis

Dominic's remarkable achievement was overshadowed by that of his contemporary, St. Francis (ca. 1182–1226)—a warm, appealing man who is widely regarded as Christianity's ideal saint. Francis was a product of the medieval urban revolution. He was the son of a wealthy cloth merchant of Assisi, a northern Italian town with an influential Albigensian minority. As a youth he was generous, high-spirited, and popular, and in time he became the leader of a boisterous but harmless teen-age gang. He was by no means dissolute but rather, as one writer has aptly expressed it, he "seems altogether to have been rather a festive figure."

In his early twenties St. Francis underwent a profound religious conversion that occurred in several steps. It began on the occasion of a banquet which he was giving for some of his friends. After the banquet Francis and his companions went into the town with torches, singing in the streets. Francis was crowned with garlands as king of the revellers, but after a time he disappeared and was found in a religious trance. Thereafter he devoted himself to solitude, prayer, and service to the poor. He went as a pilgrim to Rome where he is reported to have exchanged clothes with a beggar and spent the day begging with other beggars. Returning to Assisi, he encountered an impoverished leper and, notwithstanding his fear of leprosy, he gave the poor man all the money he was carrying and kissed his hand. Thenceforth he devoted himself to the service of lepers and hospitals.

To the confusion and consternation of his bourgeois father Francis now went about Assisi dressed in rags, giving to the poor. His former companions pelted him with mud, and his father, fearing that Francis's almsgiving would consume the family fortune, disinherited him. Francis left the family house gaily singing a

This painting of St. Francis, ascribed to the thirteenth-century Italian artist Cimabue (ca. 1240–1302), is taken from a series of frescoes in the upper church of St. Francis at Assisi. Modern restorations have probably changed Francis's features significantly.

French song and spent the next three years of his life in the environs of Assisi, living in abject poverty. He ministered to lepers and social outcasts and continued to embarrass his family by his unconventional behavior. It was at this time that he began to frequent a crumbling little chapel known as the Portiuncula. One day in the year 1209, while attending Mass there, he was struck by the words of the Gospel that the priest was reading: "Everywhere on your road preach and say, 'The kingdom of God is at hand.' Cure the sick, raise the dead, cleanse the lepers, drive out devils.

Freely have you received; freely give. Carry neither gold nor silver nor money in your girdles, nor bag, nor two coats, nor sandals, nor staff, for the workman is worthy of his hire."* Francis at once accepted this injunction as the basis of his vocation and immediately thereafter—even though a layman—began to preach to the poor.

Disciples now joined him, and when he had about a dozen followers he is said to have remarked, "Let us go to our Mother, the Holy Roman Church, and tell the pope what the Lord has begun to do through us and carry it out with his sanction." This may have been a naive approach to the masterful, aristocratic Pope Innocent III, yet when Francis came to Rome in 1210, Innocent sanctioned his work. Doubtless the pope saw in the Franciscan mission a possible orthodox counterpoise to the Waldensians, Albigensians, and other heretical groups who had been winning masses of converts from the Church by the example of their poverty and simplicity. For here was a man whose loyalty to Catholicism was beyond question and whose own artless simplicity of life might bring erring souls back into the Church. Already Innocent III had given his blessing to movements similar to that of Francis. An orthodox group of Humiliati had received his sanction in 1201, and in 1208 he permitted a converted Waldensian to found an order known as the "Poor Catholics," which was dedicated to lay preaching. In Francis's movement the pope must have seen still another opportunity to encourage a much-needed wave of radical reform within the orthodox framework. And it may well be that Francis's glowing spirituality appealed to the sanctity of Innocent himself, for the pope, even though a great man of affairs, was genuinely pious. However this may be, thirteenth-century Europe deserves some credit for embracing a movement that in many other ages would have been persecuted or ridiculed. Rome crucified Christ; high medieval Europe took Francis to its heart and made him a saint. But the hard edges of Franciscan religious austerity were blunted in the process.

Immediately after the papal interview Francis and his followers returned to the neighborhood of Assisi. They were given the Portiuncula as their own chapel, and over the years it continued to serve as the headquarters of the Franciscan movement. Around it the friars built huts of branches and twigs. The Portiuncula was a headquarters but not a home, for the friars were always on the move, wandering in pairs over the country, dressed in peasants' clothing, preaching, serving, and living in conscious imitation of the life of Christ. During the next decade the order expanded at a spectacular rate. Franciscans were soon to be found throughout northern Italy; by 1220 Franciscan missions were active in Germany, France, Spain, Hungary, and the Holy Land, and the friars numbered in the thousands. The captivating personality of Francis himself was doubtless a crucial factor in his order's popularity, but it also owed much to the fact that its ideals were singularly relevant to the highest religious aspirations of the age. Urban heresy lost some of its allure as the cheerful, devoted Franciscans began to pour into Europe's cities, preaching in the crowded streets and setting a living example of Christian sanctity.

The Franciscan ideal was based above all on the imitation of Christ. Fundamental to this ideal was the notion of poverty, both individual and corporate. The Franciscans subsisted by working and serving in return for their sustenance. Humility was also a part of the ideal; Francis named his followers the Friars Minor (little brothers). Preaching was an important part of their mission, and it answered an urgent need in the rising cities where the Church had hitherto re-

---

* Matt. 10:7–10.

sponded inadequately to the deepening religious hunger of townsmen. Perhaps most attractive of all was the quality of joyousness, akin to the joyousness that Francis had shown prior to his conversion, but directed now toward spiritual ends. Contemporaries referred to Francis affectionately as "God's own troubadour."

Pious men of other times have fled the world; the Albigensians renounced it as the epitome of evil. But Francis embraced it joyfully as the handiwork of God. In his "Song of Brother Sun" he expressed poetically his holy commitment to the physical universe:

> Praise be to Thee, my Lord, for all thy creatures,
> Above all Brother Sun
> Who brings us the day, and lends us his light;
> Beautiful is he, radiant with great splendor,
> And speaks to us of Thee, O most high.
> Praise to Thee, my Lord, for Sister Moon and for the stars;
> In heaven Thou hast set them, clear and precious and fair.
> Praise to Thee, my Lord, for Brother Wind.
> For air and clouds, for calm and all weather
> By which Thou supportest life in all Thy creatures.
> Praise to Thee, my Lord, for Sister Water
> Which is so helpful and humble, precious and pure.
> Praise to Thee, my Lord, for Brother Fire,
> By whom Thou lightest up the night.
> And fair is he, and gay and mighty and strong.
> Praise to Thee, my Lord, for our sister, Mother Earth,
> Who sustains and directs us,
> And brings forth varied fruits, and plants and flowers bright.
> . . . .
> Praise and bless my Lord, and give Him thanks,
> And serve Him with great humility.

Crisis and Aftermath

Early Franciscanism was too good to last. The order was becoming too large to retain its original disorganized simplicty. Francis was a saint rather than an administrator, and well before his death the movement was passing beyond his control. In 1219–20 he traveled to Egypt in an effort to convert its Muslim inhabitants —a hopeless task, but Francis was never dismayed by the impossible—and while he was away it became apparent that his order required a more coherent organization than he had seen fit to provide it. Many perplexing questions now arose: With thousands of friars invading the begging market, what would become of the common tramp? Would Europe's generosity be overstrained? Above all, how could these crowds of friars be expected to cleave to the ideal without an explicit rule and without Francis's personal presence to inspire and guide them? In short, could the Franciscan ideal be practical on a large scale? For the movement was proliferating at a remarkable rate. Besides the Friars Minor themselves, a Second Order was established—a female order directed by Francis's friend, St. Clare—known as the Poor Clares. And there was a peripheral group of part-time Franciscans, known as Tertiaries, who dedicated themselves to the Franciscan way while continuing their former careers in the world. The little band of Franciscan brothers had evolved into a multitude.

On his return from the Near East Francis prevailed on a powerful friend, Cardinal Hugolino—later Pope Gregory IX—to become the order's protector. On Hugolino's initiative a formal rule was drawn up in 1220 which provided a certain degree of administrative structure to

Mathematician monks; one is studying the globe and the other is copying a manuscript. As this miniature indicates, the traditional monkish "work of God" had been broadened in the thirteenth century under the influence of the mendicant friars to include a wide variety of scholarly and intellectual activities.

the order. A novitiate was established, lifetime vows were required, and the rule of absolute poverty was softened. In 1223 a shorter and somewhat laxer rule was instituted, and over the years and decades that followed, the movement continued to evolve from the ideal to the practical.

St. Francis himself withdrew more and more from involvement in the order's administration. At the meeting of the general chapter in 1220 he resigned his formal leadership of the movement with the words, "Lord, I give thee back this family that Thou didst entrust to me. Thou knowest, most sweet Jesus, that I have no more the power and the qualities to continue to take care of it." In 1224, St. Francis underwent a mystical experience atop Mt. Alverno in the Apennines, and legend has it that he received the *stigmata** on that occasion. It is not entirely clear how St. Francis reacted to the evolution of his order, but in his closing years his mysticism deepened, his health declined, and he kept much to himself. At his death in 1226 he was universally mourned, and the order which he had founded remained the most powerful and attractive religious movement of its age.

As Franciscanism became increasingly modified by the demands of practicality it also became increasingly rent with dissension. Some friars, wishing to draw on Francis's prestige without being bur-

---

* The stigmata, which have been attributed to several saints, consist in wounds or scars, supposedly of supernatural origin, that correspond to those sustained by Christ in his crucifixion.

C. Religious Frontiers

dened with his spiritual dedication, advocated an exceedingly lax interpretation of the Franciscan way. Others insisted on the strict imitation of Francis's life and struggled against its modification. These last, known in later years as "Spiritual Franciscans," sought to preserve the apostolic poverty and artless idealism of Francis himself, and by the fourteenth century they had become vigorously antipapal and anticlerical.

The majority of Franciscans, however, were willing to meet reality halfway. Although Francis had disparaged formal learnings as irrelevant to salvation, Franciscan friars began devoting themselves to scholarship and took their places alongside the Dominicans in the thirteenth- and fourteenth-century universities. Indeed, Franciscan scholars such as Roger Bacon in thirteenth-century England played a crucial role in the revival of scientific investigation, and the minister-general of the Franciscan order in the later thirteenth century, St. Bonaventure, was one of the most illustrious theologians of the age. The very weight and complexity of the Franciscan organization forced it to compromise its original ideal of corporate poverty. Although it neither acquired nor sought the immense landed wealth of the Benedictines or Cistercians, it soon possessed sufficient means to sustain its members. It is interesting to see how the minister-general Bonaventure, a holy man and also a brilliant philosopher, instituted and justified some of the changes that the order underwent in the thirteenth century. Although an intense admirer of St. Francis, Bonaventure was not himself a beggar by nature, nor a wandering minstrel, nor a day laborer, but a scholar-administrator burdened with the task of adapting a way of life designed for a dozen friars living in huts of twigs to an international order of many thousands. Contrary to Francis, Bonaventure encouraged scholarship as an aid to preaching and evangelism. St. Francis had urged his followers that "manual labor should be done with faith and devotion." Bonaventure, after demonstrating the superiority of contemplation to manual labor, concluded that Franciscans were under no compulsion to engage in physical work, although if any wished to do so he should by all means do it, "with faith and devotion."

Necessary though they were, these compromises robbed the Franciscan movement of a good measure of the radical idealism that Francis had instilled in it. In the progress from huts of twigs to halls of ivy something very precious was left behind. The Franciscans continued to serve society, but by the end of the thirteenth century they had ceased to inspire it.

THE PASSING OF THE HIGH MIDDLE AGES

The pattern of religious reform in the High Middle Ages is one of rhythmic ebb and flow. A reform movement is launched with high enthusiasm and lofty

---

TABLE II
Chronology of High Medieval Monasticism and Heterodoxy

910:	Founding of Cluny
1084:	Establishment of Carthusian Order
1098:	Establishment of Citeaux
1112–53:	Career of St. Bernard of Clairvaux as a Cistercian.
1128:	Original rule of the Knights Templars.
ca. 1173:	Beginning of the Waldensian sect.
1208:	Innocent III calls the Albigensian Crusade.
1210:	Innocent III authorizes the Francisan Order.
1216:	Dominican Rule sanctioned by the papacy.
1226:	Death of St. Francis.
1233:	Inquisition established.

purpose, it galvanizes society for a time, then succumbs gradually to complacency and gives way to a new and different wave of reform (see Table II). But with the passing of the High Middle Ages one can detect a gradual waning of spiritual vigor. The frontiers were closing as the fourteenth century dawned. Western political power was at an end in Constantinople and the Holy Land, and the Spanish reconquest had stalled. The economic boom was giving way to an epoch of depression, declining population, peasants' rebellions, and debilitating wars. And until the time of the Protestant Reformation, no new religious order was to attain the immense social impact of the thirteenth-century Franciscans and Dominicans. Popular piety remained strong, particularly in northern Europe where succeeding centuries witnessed a significant surge of mysticism. But in the south a more secular attitude was beginning to emerge. Young men no longer flocked into monastic orders; soldiers no longer rushed to crusades; papal excommunications no longer wrought their former terror. The electrifying appeal of a St. Bernard, a St. Dominic, and a St. Francis was a phenomenon peculiar to their age. By the fourteenth century, their age was passing.

Selected Readings

Douglas, David C. *The Norman Achievement.* Berkeley and Los Angeles: University of California Press, 1969.

An expert and readable comparative study of Norman activities in Normandy, Syria, Italy, Sicily, and England during the heroic age of Norman international enterprise, ca. 1050–1100.

*Guilbert of Nogent. *Self and Society in Medieval France.* Edited and translated by John F. Benton. New York: Harper & Row, Publishers, 1970.

The revealing autobiography of a twelfth-century abbot and scholar, to which the editor gives a Freudian twist in his provocative introduction.

*Heer, Frederick. *The Medieval World.* New York: New American Library of World Literature, Mentor Books, 1964.

The author contrasts twelfth-century expansion with thirteenth-century stabilization.

Knowles, David. *The Monastic Order in England.* 2d ed. New York: Cambridge University Press, 1963.

A splendid scholarly study of monasticism in England, from the mid-tenth century to 1216, that casts much light on continental monasticism as well.

Knowles, David. *The Religious Orders in England* 3 vols. New York: Cambridge University Press, 1948–59.

From the coming of the Friars to the Anglican Reformation.

*Leclerc, Jean. *The Love of Learning and the Desire for God.* Translated by Catherine Misrahi. New York: Fordham University Press, 1961.

The best short study of monasticism in English.

*Luchaire, Achille. *Social France at the Time of Philip Augustus.* New York: Harper & Row, Publishers, 1967 (originally published 1909).
> A vivid and rather grim recreation of northern French society and life ca. 1200.

*Pirenne, Henri. *Economic and Social History of Medieval Europe.* New York: Harcourt Brace Jovanovich, Harvest Books, 1956 (originally published 1933).
> A compact, richly interpretative survey by a great scholar.

Rorig, Fritz. *The Medieval Town.* Berkeley and Los Angeles: University of California Press, 1967.
> This study examines the relationships between commerce and town growth in central Europe.

*Runciman, Steven. *A History of the Crusades.* 3 vols. New York: Harper & Row, Publishers, 1964–67.
> This comprehensive and authoritative study was first published in 1951–54.

Sabatier, Paul. *St. Francis of Assisi.* New York: Charles Scribner's Sons, 1894.
> A warm and deeply sympathetic older work.

*Sherley-Price, Leo, trans. *The Little Flowers of St. Francis.* Baltimore: Penguin Books, 1959.
> A fascinating collection of sources relating to the life of St. Francis.

*Southern, Richard W. *The Making of the Middle Ages.* New Haven: Yale University Press, 1953.
> A sympathetic, thought-provoking treatment of the eleventh and twelfth centuries.

*Southern, Richard W. *Western Society and the Church in the Middle Ages.* Baltimore: Penguin Books, 1970.
> A masterful new survey and interpretation showing the interactions between the Church and the world from Carolingian times to the Reformation.

Villehardouin and de Joinville. *Memoirs of the Crusades.* Translated by Sir Frank Marzials. London: J. M. Dent & Son, Everyman's Library, 1908.
> Excellent contemporary accounts of the Fourth Crusade and the crusading exploits of St. Louis.

Asterisk (*) denotes paperback.

CHAPTER X
Church and State in the High Middle Ages

A. Empire and Papacy — THE BACKGROUND OF THE STRUGGLE

Papacy and Church in the Mid-Eleventh Century

The role of the papacy in the changing religious configurations of the High Middle Ages was scarcely touched upon in the previous chapter, for although it was fundamental to the spiritual development of the period it was also closely associated with the politics of empire and kingdom which is the central topic of this chapter. Therefore we must go back to the mid-eleventh century, the age when Cluny still stood in the vanguard of European monasticism, when Citeaux was yet an untouched wilderness and the mendicant movement lay in the distant future.

With the dawning of the High Middle Ages there emerged a newly invigorated papacy, dedicated to ecclesiastical reform and the spiritual regeneration of Christian society. Almost at once the reform papacy became involved in a struggle with the Holy Roman Empire—a tragic conflict that dominated European politics for more than two centuries. On the eve of the conflict, Germany was the mightiest monarchy in Western Christendom and the German king or Holy Roman Emperor held the papacy in his palm. By 1300 Germany was fragmented and the papacy, after 250 years of political prominence, was exhausted and on the brink of a prolonged decline.

Prior to the beginnings of papal reform in the mid-eleventh century, a chasm had existed between the papal theory of Christian society and the realities of the contemporary Church. The papal theory, with a venerable tradition running back to the fifth-century pope, Leo the Great,* envisaged a sanctified Christian commonwealth in which lords and kings accepted the spiritual direc-

* See pp. 302–3.

439

tion of priests and bishops who, in turn, submitted to the leadership of the papacy. The popes claimed to be the successors—the vicars—of St. Peter. Just as St. Peter was the chief of Christ's apostles, they argued, the pope was the monarch of the apostolic Church. And as eternal salvation was more important than earthly prosperity—as the soul was more important than the body—so the priestly power was greater than the power of secular lords, kings, and emperors. The properly ordered society, the truly Christian society, was one dominated by the Church which, in turn, was dominated by the pope. In the intellectual climate of the High Middle Ages this view had great pertinence and caught the imagination of many thoughtful men. It provided the papal monarchy with a persuasive justification.

The reality of mid-eleventh-century society was far different. Almost everywhere the Church was under the control of aristocratic lay proprietors. Petty lords appointed their priests; dukes and kings selected their bishops and abbots. As we have seen, the Holy Roman Emperors used churchmen extensively in the administration of Germany. In France, the Church provided warriors from its estates for the feudal armies, clerks for the feudal chanceries, and shrewd political advisers for the feudal princes. The Church played a vital role in the operation of tenth- and early-eleventh-century society but it was usually subordinate to the lay ruling class. Its spiritual and sacramental role was compromised by its secular administrative responsibilities. As was bound to happen under such conditions, the Church tended to neglect its sacred mission. From the lay standpoint it was an effective administrative tool, but from the spiritual standpoint it was inadequate and sometimes corrupt. Monasteries all too frequently ignored the strict Benedictine rule. Some priests had concubines, and many had wives, despite the canonical requirement of priestly celibacy. Lay lords often sold important ecclesiastical offices to the highest bidder, and the new prelate customarily recouped the expense of buying his office by exploiting his tenants and subordinates. This commerce in ecclesiastical appointments was known as *simony*. It was regarded by some contemporary reformers as the arch sin of the age.

Ecclesiastical corruption was nowhere more evident than in Rome itself. The papacy of the earlier eleventh century had fallen into the soiled hands of the Roman nobility and had become a prize disputed among the several leading aristocratic families of the city. In 1032 the prize fell to a young aristocratic libertine, who took the name of Benedict IX; his pontificate was scandalous even by contemporary Roman standards. Benedict sold the papacy, then changed his mind and reclaimed it. By 1046 his right to the papal throne was challenged by two other claimants; the papacy had fallen into a three-way schism.

Ecclesiastical Reform

Such were the conditions of the European Church as the mid-eleventh century approached. A Church dominated by lay proprietors had long existed in Europe and had long been accepted. But with the upsurge of lay piety that accompanied the opening of the High Middle Ages, the comfortable church-state relationship of the previous epoch seemed monstrously wrong to many sensitive spirits. This was the epoch in which Christians were beginning to join hermit groups such as the Carthusians; they would soon be flocking into the new, austere Cistercian order. Such men as these were responding to the spiritual awakening of their age by following the path of withdrawal from worldly society. Others chose the more novel and adventurous approach of *con-*

version and took up the task of reforming the Church and the world. The dream of sanctifying society, which was later to find such vivid expression in the career of St. Francis, was shared by many Christians of the High Middle Ages. During the second half of the eleventh century it manifested itself in a powerful movement of ecclesiastical reform which was beginning to make itself felt across the length and breadth of Western Christendom. At the heart of this movement was the reform papacy.

In general, the reformers fell into two groups: (1) a conservative group which sought to eliminate simony, enforce clerical celibacy, and improve the moral calibre of churchmen, but without challenging the Church's traditional subordination to the lay aristocracy—a subordination that had been sweetened by countless generous gifts of lands and powers to submissive prelates, and (2) a radical group which sought to demolish the tradition of lay control and to rebuild society on the pattern of the papal monarchy theory. The radical reformers struggled to establish an ideal Christian commonwealth in which laymen no longer appointed churchmen—in which kings deferred to bishops and a reformed papacy ruled the Church. The conservative reformers endeavored to heal society; the radicals were determined to overturn it.

Henry III and Leo IX

The Congregation of Cluny, firm in its spiritual rectitude yet at peace with the existing social order, was one of the chief centers of conservative reform in the eleventh century. Its ideals were shared by several of the more enlightened rulers of the age, among them Emperor Henry III, the powerful Salian monarch of Germany. Shocked by the antics of Pope Benedict IX and the three-way tug-of-war for the papal throne, Henry III intervened in Italy in 1046, arranged the deposition of Benedict and his two rivals, and drastically improved the quality of papal leadership by appointing the first of a series of reform popes. The ablest of these imperial appointees, Pope Leo IX (1049–54), carried on a vigorous campaign against simony and clerical marriage, holding yearly synods at Rome, sending legates far and wide to enforce reform, and traveling constantly himself to preside over local councils and depose guilty churchmen. Leo's reform pontificate opened dramatically when, at the Roman Synod of 1049, the bishop of Sutri was condemned for simony and promptly fell dead in the presence of the whole assembly—a victim, it was assumed, of the divine wrath.

Leo IX labored mightily for reform, and his pontificate constitutes the opening phase in the evolution of the high-medieval papacy. His concern for a secure territorial position in central Italy prompted him to lead an army against the enterprising Norman adventurer to the south, Robert Guiscard, but being defeated and captured at Civitate he was forced to recognize the Normans and give them the status of papal vassals.* His vigorous assertion of papal authority aggravated the long and deepening hostility between the churches of Rome and Constantinople, and in 1054 two of his legates placed a papal bull on the high altar of Sancta Sophia excommunicating the Eastern patriarch. More than anything else, Leo struggled to enforce canon law and to purge the Church of simony and incontinence. In all his enterprises, he could count on the general support of Emperor Henry III. In these early years empire and papacy worked hand in glove to raise the moral level of the European Church.

But however successful this reform movement might have been, there were

---

* See p. 409.

those who felt that it was not going far enough. The real evil, in the view of the radical reformers, was lay supremacy over the Church, and Henry III's domination of papal appointments, however well-intentioned, were the supreme examples of a profound social sin. A number of ardent reformers were to be found among the cardinals whom Pope Leo appointed and gathered around him. These new men, who dominated the reform papacy for the next several decades, came for the most part from monastic backgrounds. Many of them were deeply influenced by the strong piety surging throughout the towns of eleventh-century northern Italy, a piety that was stimulating the widespread revival of eremitic monasticism.

Damiani, Humbert, and Hildebrand

One such man was St. Peter Damiani, a leader of the northern-Italian eremitic movement before he was brought to Rome by Leo IX and made a cardinal. Zealous and saintly, Damiani was deeply respected by his contemporaries. He was a mystic and, like St. Bernard after him, a vigorous opponent of the growing tendency among Christian intellectuals to elucidate the Faith by reason and logic. Damiani served the reform papacy tirelessly, traveling far and wide to enforce the prohibitions against simony and incontinence and to reform the clergy. Yet he drew back from what seemed to him the irresponsible efforts of his more radical brethren to challenge and destroy the social order. Aflame with the new piety and deeply dedicated to the papacy, Damiani was nevertheless one of the less extreme of Leo IX's new cardinals.

The real leaders of the radical group were Humbert and Hildebrand. Both were cardinals under Leo; both had, like Damiani, left monastic lives to join the Roman curia. Humbert was a German from Lorraine, probably of aristocratic background, who used his subtle, well-trained intellect to support papal reform in its most radical form. He was one of Pope Leo's legates to Constantinople during the dispute with the Eastern Church, where his uncompromising attitudes on papal supremacy clashed with the equally intransigent views of the Eastern patriarch. Indeed, it was Humbert himself who instigated the schism of 1054 by laying a bull excommunicating the patriarch on the high altar of Sancta Sophia. A few years later Humbert produced a bitter, closely reasoned attack against the lay-dominated social order in the West, *Three Books Against the Simoniacs,* in which he extended the meaning of simony to include not merely the buying or selling of ecclesiastical offices but any instance of lay interference in clerical appointments. In Humbert's view the Church ought to be utterly free of lay control and supreme in European society.

Hildebrand, an Italian probably of humble origin, lacked the originality and intellectual depth of Humbert but had a remarkable ability to draw ideas from the minds of others and formulate them into a clearly articulated program. Intellectually, Hildebrand was a disciple of Humbert, but as a leader and man of action he was second to none. Contemporaries described him as a small, ugly, pot-bellied man, but they also recognized that a fire burned inside him—a holy or unholy fire depending on one's point of view, for Hildebrand was the most controversial figure of his age. Consumed by the ideal of a Christian society dominated by the Church and a Church dominated by the papacy, Hildebrand served with prodigious vigor and determination under Pope Leo IX and his successors. At length he became pope himself, taking the name Gregory VII (1073–85). His pontificate was to be one of the greatest and most tragic of the Middle Ages.

The Papal Election Decree

So long as Henry III lived, radicals such as Humbert and Hildebrand remained in the background. But in 1056 the emperor died in the prime of life, leaving behind him a six-year-old heir, Henry IV, and a weak regency government. Henry III's death was a catastrophe for the empire and a godsend to the radicals who longed to wrest the papacy from imperial control. At the death of Henry III's last papal appointee in 1057, the reform cardinals began electing popes of their own choosing. In 1059, under the influence of Cardinals Humbert and Hildebrand, they issued a daring declaration of independence known as the *Papal Election Decree,* which stated that thenceforth emperors and Roman laymen would merely give formal approval to the candidate whom the cardinals elected. In the years that followed, this revolutionary proclamation was challenged by both the empire and the Roman aristocracy, but in the end the cardinals won out. The papacy had broken free of lay control and was in the hands of the reformers. For now the cardinals elected the pope* and the pope appointed the cardinals. The Decree of 1059 created at the apex of the ecclesiastical hierarchy a reform oligarchy of the most exclusive sort.

THE INVESTITURE CONTROVERSY

The next step in the program of the radical reformers was infinitely more difficult. It involved nothing less than the annihilation of lay control over the entire Church.

---
* Strictly speaking, the Decree of 1059 provided that the pope should be elected not by all the cardinals but by the cardinal bishops alone. The other cardinals—cardinal priests and cardinal deacons—were empowered to participate in papal elections by a decree of the twelfth century.

At a time when the Church possessed untold wealth, including perhaps a third of the land in Europe, the total realization of such a goal would cripple secular power and revolutionize European society. Yet only by its realization, so the radical reformers believed, could a true Christian commonwealth be achieved.

Reform in Milan

One of the first arenas of conflict was the ancient city of Milan with its proud archbishopric, renowned since St. Ambrose's time. Milan was in the grip of the new commercial revival and, like many other Lombard towns of the eleventh century, was seething with activity. The Lombard towns of this era were, as a rule, dominated by their bishops—who were inclined to cooperate with the Holy Roman Empire—and by an élite group of landed noblemen. As a group, the Lombard bishops tended to ignore the new wave of reform, and some were themselves guilty of simony. Throughout Lombardy, and in Milan in particular, the rule of the nobles and episcopacy was being challenged by the growing lower classes of artisans, day workers, and peasants. In Milan and elsewhere, this revolutionary lower-class group was called, by its enemies, the *patarenes* (ragpickers). Hostile to the domination of the traditional ruling group and fired by the new piety, the patarenes made common cause with the reform papacy against their unreformed and oppressive masters. The reformers in Rome had no sympathy for the Lombard bishops and were especially antagonistic toward the archbishop of Milan who was, in effect, an imperial agent and who, by condoning simony and incontinence among his clergy, symbolized the old proprietary Church at its worst.

In 1059 Cardinal Peter Damiani journeyed to Milan to enforce reform. Backed by the patarenes and the authority of Rome, he humbled the archbishop and the higher clergy, made them confess their sins publicly, and wrung promises of amendment from them. Thus, the Milanese church, despite its traditional cooperation with the Empire and independence of Roman authority, was made to submit to the power of the papacy. Over the next 15 years struggle between the patarenes and the noble-ecclesiastical ruling group continued, and the city was torn by murder and mob violence. When, in 1072, the young Emperor Henry IV ordered the consecration of an antireformer as archbishop of Milan, he was at once faced with the combined wrath of the papacy and patarenes. The patarenes rioted and the pope excommunicated Henry's counselors. The most significant aspect of this entire affair is the way in which it typifies the close alliance between radical urban piety and papal reform. During the second half of the eleventh century the papacy managed to place itself at the forefront of the new piety and to draw upon the vital energy of the revolutionary social-spiritual movement that was sweeping across Europe. At odds with much of the traditional ecclesiastical establishment, the radical reformers in Rome were nevertheless in tune with the most vigorous spiritual forces of the age.

The Ban against Lay Investiture; Its Consequences

The struggle over lay control of ecclesiastical appointments broke out in earnest in 1075 when Hildebrand, now Pope Gregory VII, issued a proclamation banning lay investiture. Traditionally, a newly chosen bishop or abbot was invested by a lay lord with a ring and a pastoral staff, symbolic of his marriage to the Church and his duty toward his Christian flock. Gregory attacked this custom of lay investiture as the crucial symbol of lay authority over churchmen. Its prohibition was a challenge to the established social order. It threatened to compromise the authority of every ruler in Christendom, and none more than the Holy Roman Emperor himself, whose administrative system was particularly dependent on his control of the German church. By Gregory VII's time Henry IV had grown to vigorous manhood and was showing promise of becoming as strong a ruler as his father, Henry III. Refusing to accept the decree against lay investiture, Henry sent a

Thirteenth-century bishop. The episcopal ring and staff were traditionally conferred by lay lords against whose right of investiture medieval reformers struggled fiercely during the eleventh and twelfth centuries.

flaming letter of defiance to Gregory in which he asserted his right as a divinely appointed sovereign to lead the German church without papal interference and challenged Gregory's very right to the papal throne. The letter was addressed to Gregory under his previous name, "Hildebrand, not pope but false monk." It concluded with the dramatic words, "I, Henry, king by grace of God, with all my bishops, say to you: 'Come down, come down, and be damned throughout the ages.'"

Henry's letter was in effect a defense of the traditional social order of divinely ordained priest-kings ruling over a docile church. Gregory's view of society was vastly different: he denied the priestly qualities of kings and emperors, suggested that most of them were gangsters destined for Hell, and repudiated their right to question his status or his decrees. Emperors had no power to appoint churchmen, much less depose popes, but the pope, as the ultimate authority in Christendom, had the power to depose kings and emperors. Accordingly, Gregory responded to Henry's letter with a startling and unprecedented exercise of spiritual authority which was, nevertheless, perfectly in accord with his conception of Christian society: he excommunicated and deposed Henry. It was for the pope to judge whether or not the king was fit to rule, and Gregory had judged. His judgment was nothing less than revolutionary, however, for in banning lay investiture and deposing the king of Germany he was putting into practice the papal theory in its most radical form and striking at the very bedrock of the traditional order.

Canossa: Background and Aftermath

Radical though it was, the deposition was effective. Under the relatively calm surface of Salian monarchical authority in Germany, a powerful aristocratic opposition had long been gathering force. Subdued during the reign of Henry III, local and regional particularism asserted itself during the long regency following his death, and Henry IV, on reaching maturity, had much ground to recover. In 1075 he succeeded in stifling a long, bitter rebellion in Saxony and seemed to be on his way toward reasserting his father's power when the investiture controversy exploded. Gregory VII's excommunication and deposition—awesome spiritual sanctions to the minds of eleventh-century Christians—unleashed in Germany all the latent hostility that the centralizing policies of the Salian dynasty had evoked. Many Germans, churchmen and laymen alike, refused to serve an excommunicated sovereign. The German nobles took the revolutionary step of threatening to elect a new king in Henry's place, thereby challenging the ingrained German tradition of hereditary kingship with the counterdoctrine of elective monarchy. The elective principle, which crippled the later-medieval and early-modern German monarchy, had its real inception at this moment.

Desperate to keep his throne, Henry crossed the Alps into Italy to seek the pope's forgiveness. In January 1077, at the castle of Canossa in Tuscany, the two men met in what was perhaps medieval history's most dramatic encounter—Henry IV humble and barefoot in the snow, clothed in rough, penitential garments; Gregory VII torn between his conviction that Henry's change of heart was a mere political expedient and his priestly duty to forgive a repentant sinner. Finally, Gregory lifted Henry's excommunication and the monarch, promising to amend his ways, returned to Germany to rebuild his authority.

Down through the centuries Canossa has symbolized the ultimate royal degradation before the power of the Church.

Emperor Henry IV kneeling before the abbot of Cluny and Matilda, countess of Tuscany, at Canossa, imploring them to intercede for him with Pope Gregory VII.

Perhaps it was. But in the immediate political context it was a victory, and a badly needed one, for Henry IV. It did not prevent a group of German nobles from electing a rival king, nor did it restore the powerful centralized monarchy of Henry III; but it did save Henry IV's throne. Restored to communion, he was able to rally support, to check for a time the forces of princely particularism, and to defeat the rival king.

As his power waxed, Henry ignored his promises at Canossa and resumed his support of lay investiture. In 1080 Gregory excommunicated and deposed him a second time, only to find that these potent spiritual weapons were losing their strength through overuse. In the early 1080s Henry returned to Italy, this time with an army. Gregory summoned his vassal and ally, the Norman Robert Guiscard, to rescue him from his situation, but Robert's boisterous Normans, although they frightened Henry away, became involved in a destructive riot with the Roman townspeople. The commoners of Rome had always supported Gregory, but now they turned furiously against him and he was obliged, for his own protection, to accompany the Normans when they withdrew to the south. In 1085 Gregory died at Salerno, consumed by bitterness and a conviction of failure. His last words were these: "I have loved justice and hated iniquity; therefore I die in exile."

The Investiture Controversy after Gregory VII: The Concordat of Worms

Although Gregory VII failed to transform Europe into what he conceived to be a proper Christian society, his theory of papal monarchy retained its potency. The reform papacy soon fell into the able hands of Urban II (1088–99), a former prior of Cluny, who seized the moral leadership of Europe by calling the First Crusade. Urban steered a more moderate course than Gregory had done, yet he and his successors continued to harass the unlucky Henry, stirring up rebellions in Germany and eroding the power of the imperial government. In 1106 Henry died as unhappily as had Gregory. In the end Henry's own son and heir, Henry V, led an army of hostile nobles against his father. As Henry IV died, the German empire seemed to be collapsing around him.

Henry V (1106–25) enjoyed a happier reign than his father's, but only because he foresook his father's struggle to recover the fullness of imperial power as it had existed in the mid-eleventh century. The independence-minded aristocracy consolidated the gains it had made during the preceding era of chaos, and Henry V could do little about it.

Toward the end of his reign, Henry V worked out a compromise settlement with the Church which brought the Investiture Controversy to an end at last. Already the controversy had been settled by compromise in England and France where the church-state struggle had been considerably less bitter than in Germany. As time progressed both papacy and empire tended to draw back from the extreme positions they had taken during Gregory VII's pontificate, and in 1122 they reconciled their differences in the Corcordat of Worms. Henry agreed that the investiture ceremony would no longer be performed by laymen, but the pope conceded to the emperor the important privilege of bestowing on the new prelate the symbols of his *territorial* and *administrative* jurisdiction. Bishops and abbots were thenceforth to be elected according to the principles of canon law, by the monks of a monastery or the canons of a cathedral, but the emperor had the right to be present at such elections and to make the final decision in the event of a dispute. These reservations enabled the emperor to retain a considerable degree of de facto control over the appointment of important German churchmen. The reconciliation of royal control and canonical election is illustrated in a twelfth-century charter of King Henry II of England to the monks at Winchester: "I order you to hold a free election, but nevertheless I forbid you to elect anyone except Richard, my clerk, the archdeacon of Poitiers."

Consequences of the Investiture Controversy

There was no real victor in the Investiture Controversy. The Church had won its point—lay investiture was banned—but monarchs still exercised very real control over their churches. The theory of papal monarchy over a reconstituted Christian society remained unrealized, and the old tradition of peaceful cooperation between kings and prelates was badly shaken. The papacy, however noble its intentions, had become politicized as never before, and by asserting its authority in deeds and treatises it evoked hostile countertrends of royalist political propaganda and growing anticlericalism.

Still, the papal-imperial balance of power had changed radically since the mid-eleventh century. The papacy was now a mighty force in Europe, and the power of the emperor had declined sharply. During the chaotic half-century between the onset of the Investiture Controversy in 1075 and Henry V's death in 1125, feudalism came to Germany. In these decades of civil strife a powerful new aristocracy emerged. Ambitious landowners rose to great power, built castles, extended their estates, and usurped royal rights. They forced minor neighboring noblemen to become their vassals and, in some instances, forced free peasants to become their serfs. The monarchy was helpless to curb this ominous process of fragmentation.

The Investiture Controversy resulted in the crippling of imperial authority in northern Italy. The fierce patarene struggle of Milan was repeated throughout Lombardy, and in the anarchy wrought by the papal-imperial conflict the pro-imperial Lombard bishops lost the wide jurisdictional rights that they had formerly exercised over their cities and the surrounding countryside. Everywhere the pious and vigorously independent Lombard townsmen took up the cause of papal reform, rebelled against the control of nobles, bishops, and emperor alike, and established quasi-independent communes or city states. By 1125, Milan and her sister cities were free urban communes, and imperial authority in Lombardy had become virtually nominal.

In Germany and Italy alike, imperial power was receding before the whirlwind of local particularism, invigorated by the Investiture Controversy and the soaring popular piety of the age. Well before the Concordat of Worms, the decline of the medieval empire had begun.

THE AGE OF FREDERICK BARBAROSSA

Welfs and Hohenstaufens

The Salian dynasty died out with the passing of Henry V in 1125. During the next quarter century Germany reaped the harvest of princely particularism. The nobles disparaged the principle of hereditary royal succession and reverted to the elective principle that they had asserted at the time of Canossa. Their choice always fell to a man of royal blood but never to the most direct heir. In the turbulent decades between 1125 and 1152 a rivalry developed between two great families that had risen to power in the anarchic era of the Investiture Controversy: the Welfs of Saxony and the Hohenstaufens of Swabia. In 1152 the princes elected as king a powerful and talented Hohenstaufen, Frederick Barbarossa (the Red-Bearded), duke of Swabia, who took as his mission the revival and reconstruction of the German monarchy.

Policies of Frederick Barbarossa

Emperor Frederick Barbarossa recognized that the mighty imperial structure of Henry III was beyond recovery. His goal was to harness the new feudal forces of his age to the royal advantage. He actually encouraged the great princes of the realm to expand their power and privileges at the expense of the lesser lords, but at the same time he forced them to recognize his own feudal lordship over all the kingdom. In other words, he succeeded in establishing an effective lordship over the leading feudal magnates, making them his obedient vassals—his tenants-in-chief. He was the supreme overlord at the apex of the feudal pyramid.

Emperor Frederick Barbarossa, from a contemporary manuscript.

But as the sorry state of the early French monarchy well illustrates, feudal overlordship was an ephemeral thing if the royal overlord lacked the power and resources to support his position. Therefore, Frederick Barbarossa set about to increase his revenues and extend the territories under his direct authority. A strong feudal monarchy required a substantial territorial core under exclusive royal control—an extensive royal demesne to act as a counterweight to the great fiefs of the chief vassals of the realm. Frederick enlarged his demesne territories, most of which were concentrated in Swabia, by bringing many of the new monasteries and rising

449   A. Empire and Papacy

towns under imperial jurisdiction. The crux of his imaginative policy was the reassertion of imperial authority over the wealthy cities of Lombardy. With Lombardy under his control and its revenues pouring into the imperial treasury, no German lord could challenge him.

Barbarossa's Lombard policy earned him the hostility of the papacy which had always feared the consolidation of imperial power in Italy, and of the intensely independent Lombard cities, which were determined to give up as little of their wealth and autonomy as they possibly could. And should he become too deeply involved in Italy, Barbarossa exposed himself to rebellion on the part of the German aristocrats and high nobility—in particular, the Welf family which was vigorously represented at the time by Duke Henry the Lion of Saxony.

Hadrian IV and Arnold of Brescia

The papacy of the mid-twelfth century was having problems of its own. Pope Hadrian IV (1154–59), who was to become one of Frederick Barbarossa's most ardent foes, was faced at the beginning of his pontificate with the problem of maintaining the papacy's hold on Rome itself. A gifted man of humble origins, Hadrian IV was the one Englishman ever to occupy the papal throne. Rome was turbulent during his years, for the patarene movement had reached the Holy City and had turned violently antipapal. The revolutionary social forces that had earlier allied with the papacy in breaking the power of an archbishop in Milan were now challenging the pope's authority over Rome. In the 1140s the city was torn by a lower-class rebellion whose leaders struggled to drive out the pope and dreamed of reestablishing the ancient Roman Republic. Very quickly this anti-papal communal movement spread to other cities in the Papal States, and for a time the papacy itself was forced into exile.

Before long, the Roman rebellion fell under the leadership of Arnold of Brescia, a gifted scholar and spiritual revolutionary, whose goal it was to strip the Church of its wealth and secular authority. Suppressed by the Norman troops of Roger the Great in the 1140s, Arnold's revolution reasserted itself under Hadrian, and the pope was driven to the desperate expedient of placing Rome under interdict, ordering the suspension of church services throughout the city. The interdict proved an effective weapon; among other things, it severely curtailed the influx of pilgrims and thereby had an adverse effect on Rome's economy. The revolution collapsed and Arnold was driven from the city. Hadrian and Barbarossa joined forces to hunt him down, and, once he fell into their hands, he was hanged, burned, and thrown into the Tiber (1155). Thus, Arnold was emphatically eliminated and his relics were put out of the reach of any future admirers. But his movement persisted as an anti-clerical heresy—an early example of the opposition to ecclesiastical wealth and power that was soon to find expression among the Waldensians and Albigensians and, by implication, among the Franciscans.

The growing split between the papacy and the Roman townsmen was an ominous indication that papal leadership over urban reform movements was at an end. The papacy was no longer able to make common cause with the explosive forces of popular piety as it had done in the age of Gregory VII, but was now beginning to suppress them. Pope Hadrian actually had little choice but to defend himself in whatever way possible against Arnold of Brescia, yet, in laying Rome under interdict, he was following a path that would lead within a century to the Albigensian Crusade and the Inquisition. This schism between papal leadership and popular piety was a factor of no small importance in the ultimate downfall of the later medieval papacy.

Barbarossa and the Lombard League

Hadrian IV and Frederick Barbarossa first met on the occasion of the imperial coronation in Rome in 1155. The two men had collaborated against Arnold of Brescia, but thereafter they became enemies. At their initial encounter, Hadrian insisted that Frederick follow ancient tradition and lead the papal mule.* At first Frederick refused to humble himself in such a manner, but when it appeared that there would be no coronation at all he grudgingly submitted. This small conflict was symbolic of far greater ones, for Hadrian and his successors proved to be implacable opponents of Frederick's drive to win control of the Lombard cities.

The Lombard struggle reached its climax under the pontificate of Alexander III (1159–81), Hadrian's successor. Wise, shrewd, and learned, Alexander was the greatest pope of the twelfth century and Frederick Barbarossa's most formidable opponent. Whereas most of the early reform popes had been monks, Alexander and many of his successors were canon lawyers. Hildebrand himself had urged the study of canon law and the formulation of canonical collections in order to provide intellectual ammunition to support papal claims. During the later eleventh and twelfth centuries the study of canon law was pursued vigorously in northern Italian schools, particularly the great law school at Bologna, and a good number of twelfth and thirteenth century popes were products of these schools. Alexander III was one of the ablest of them.

---

* The tradition of the ceremonial mule-leading seems to have originated in the eighth-century forgery, the "Donation of Constantine."

Determined to prevent Frederick Barbarossa from establishing himself strongly in northern Italy, Alexander rallied the Lombard towns which had long been engaged in intercity warfare but now combined forces against the empire. They formed an association called the Lombard League and organized a powerful interurban army to oppose Frederick. The emperor had meanwhile thrown his support behind a rival claimant to the papal throne, and Alexander responded by excommunicating and deposing Frederick. There followed a prolonged struggle involving Alexander, Barbarossa, and the Lombard League, which ended in the total victory of the Lombard army at the battle of Legnano in 1176. Barbarossa submitted as graciously as he could, granting de facto independence to the Lombard cities in return for their admission of a vague imperial overlordship. Pope and emperor tearfully embraced; Barbarossa led Alexander's mule and promised to be a dutiful son of the Roman See.

Barbarossa's Triumph

Barbarossa had lost a battle, but he had by no means lost the war. Leaving Lombardy severely alone, he shifted his operations southward to Tuscany, establishing administrative control over this rich province immediately to the north of the Papal States. At the same time he arranged a fateful marriage between his son and the future heiress of the Norman Kingdom of southern Italy and Sicily—a marriage which ultimately brought that opulent kingdom within the imperial fold. The papacy had been outwitted and was in grave danger of being encircled and stifled by the empire. In 1180 Barbarossa consolidated his power in Germany by crushing the greatest and most hostile of his vassals, Henry the Lion, the Welf duke of Saxony. After Alexander III's death in

1181, the papacy ceased for a time to be a serious threat, and the far-sighted emperor was at the height of his power in 1190 when he died while leading his army toward the Holy Land on the Third Crusade.

Barbarossa had taken pains to circumvent the princely policy of elective monarchy by forcing the princes, prior to his death, to elect his son, Henry VI. In 1190 Henry succeeded to the German throne without difficulty, and in 1194 he made good his claim to the Kingdom of Sicily. The Papal States were now an island completely surrounded by Holy Roman Empire, and the papacy was powerless to alter the situation. The bounteous revenues of southern Italy and Sicily fattened the imperial purse. The territories under imperial rule had never been so extensive.

But for an age in which the emperor had to remain ever vigilant against the centrifugal forces of local particularism and, above all, against the ambitions of the great German vassals, the imperial frontiers had become dangerously overextended. It remained uncertain whether a single man could rule Italy and Germany concurrently. Whether Henry VI might have accomplished this task we shall never know, for he died prematurely in 1197 leaving as his heir his infant son, Frederick II. The problems the empire faced in 1197 would have taxed the ablest of leaders, yet at this crucial moment imperial leadership failed. The papacy had its opportunity.

The High Noon of the Medieval Papacy

During the twelfth century, the papacy lost much of its former zealous reform spirit as it evolved into a huge, complex administrative institution. Revenues flowed into its treasury from all the states of Western Christendom; bishops traveled vast distances to make their spiritual submission to the Roman pontiff; the papal curia served as a court of last appeal for an immense network of ecclesiastical courts. Papal authority over the European Church had increased immeasurably since the mid-eleventh century. As the dream of a papal monarchy came ever nearer realization, the traditional theory of papal supremacy over Christian society was increasingly magnified and elaborated by the canon lawyers. These subtle ecclesias-

A fourteenth-century symbolic fresco from the cathedral at Siena depicting the hierarchical organization and the goals of the Church during the High Middle Ages. The pope and the temporal sovereign sit side by side in representation of the ecclesiastical power supported by temporal rule. The religious orders and the afflicted, whom the Church aided, are in the foreground. At the pope's feet is a black and white dog representing the Dominican order, whose special duty it was to protect the faithful against the wolf of heresy.

tical scholars were beginning to dominate the papal curia and, like Alexander III, to occupy the papal throne itself.

Pontificate of Innocent III

Innocent III (1198–1216), the greatest of all the lawyer popes, came to power in the year following Emperor Henry VI's death. It was he who seized the opportunity offered by the succession of an infant to the throne of the overextended empire. Innocent was history's most powerful pope—a brilliant, astute diplomat, an imperious, self-confident aristocrat who, although genuinely pious, was distinctly aloof from the surging religious emotionalism of the humbler folk of his age. He had the wisdom and sensitivity to support the Franciscans, and the ruthlessness to mount the Albigensian Crusade.*

Animated by the theory of papal monarchy in its most uncompromising form, Innocent forced his will on the leading monarchs of Europe, playing off one king against another with consummate skill. In the course of a long struggle with King John of England over the appointment of an archbishop of Canterbury, Innocent laid John's entire kingdom under interdict, threatened to depose John himself, and asked King Philip Augustus of France to send an army against him. The struggle

* See pp. 428–29.

A dream of Innocent III, in which the pope sees St. Francis supporting the falling church of St. John Lateran. A predella by Giotto.

ended with John's complete submission, the installation of Innocent's man in the archbishopric of Canterbury, and the establishment of papal lordship over England.

Innocent had earlier clashed with Philip Augustus over the king's refusal to repudiate an uncanonical second marriage and return to his first wife. After laying France under interdict and excommunicating Philip, Innocent obtained his submission.* It has already been shown how Innocent instigated the Fourth Crusade, which was aimed at Jerusalem but ended in Constantinople, and how he mounted crusades against the Albigensians and the Spanish Moors. These diverse activities

---

* Philip Augustus's submission was less complete, however, than might have been wished. His controversial second wife had died—conveniently but naturally—and his reconciliation with his first wife was a mere formality.

454 Church and State in the High Middle Ages

illustrate the unprecedented political and moral sway which Innocent exercised over Christendom.

A mighty force in the secular politics of his age, Innocent also dominated the Church more completely than any of his predecessors had done. In 1215 he summoned a general Church council in Rome —the Fourth Lateran Council—which produced a remarkable quantity of significant ecclesiastical legislation: clerical habit was strictly regulated, a moratorium was declared on new religious orders, the ancient Germanic legal procedure of the ordeal[†] was condemned, fees for the administration of sacraments were forbidden, cathedral churches were ordered to maintain schools and to provide sermons at their chief services, and all Catholics were bound to receive the sacraments of penance and the eucharist at least once a year. The efficient organization of the Fourth Lateran Council, and the degree to which Pope Innocent dominated and directed it are clearly illustrated by the fact that the churchmen in attendance—more than 1200 bishops, abbots, and priests—produced their important new legislation in meetings that lasted a total of only three weeks. By contrast, the fifteenth-century Council of Basel met off and on for 18 years and the Council of Trent for 19.

The Disputed German Succession

The range of Innocent III's activities was seemingly boundless, but throughout his pontificate one political issue took precedence over all others: the problem of the German imperial succession. It was a marvellously complex problem which taxed even Pope Innocent's diplomatic skill. Involved were the questions of whether or not the kingdom of Sicily would remain in imperial hands, whether the imperial throne would pass to the Welfs or the Hohenstaufens, and whether an accommodation could be achieved between the traditionally hostile forces of papacy and empire. The German succession problem also touched the interests of the French and English monarchies: the Welf claimant, Otto of Brunswick, was a nephew of King John of England and could usually count on his support, whereas the Hohenstaufens enjoyed the friendship of the French king, Philip Augustus.

The direct Hohenstaufen heir was the infant Frederick, son of the late Henry VI. But since a child could hardly be expected to wage a successful fight for the throne in these turbulent years, the Hohenstaufen claim was taken up by Frederick's uncle, Philip of Swabia, brother of the former emperor. The young Frederick remained in Sicily while Philip of Swabia and the Welf, Otto of Brunswick, contended for the imperial throne. Innocent recognized the German princes' right to elect their own monarch but, as it happened, Philip and Otto had both been elected, each by a different group of German nobles. In the case of a disputed election such as this, Innocent claimed the right to intervene by virtue of the traditional papal privilege of crowning the emperor. He delayed his decision considerably, and in the meantime, civil war raged in Germany. At length he settled on Otto of Brunswick. Otto had promised to support the papal interests in Germany and to abandon almost entirely the policy of imperial control of the German church which had been spelled out in the Concordat of Worms of 1122. Further, a Welf emperor would have no claim on the Hohenstaufen kingdom of Sicily, and Otto's coronation would therefore realize the papal goal of separating the two realms.

Despite Innocent's decision, the civil war continued in Germany until, in 1208, Philip of Swabia died. Otto was crowned emperor in 1209, but now, having no rival

[†] See pp. 314–15.

A. Empire and Papacy

to oppose him, he repudiated his promises to Innocent, asserted his mastery over the German church, and even launched an invasion of southern Italy. Innocent responded to this breach of faith by deposing and anathematizing Otto and throwing his support behind the young Frederick. From the beginning, the kingdom of Sicily had been, at least nominally, a papal vassal state, and Innocent, as overlord, claimed the feudal privilege of guardianship over its minor king. Frederick, in other words, was Innocent's ward. Before undertaking to back Frederick, Innocent wrung a number of promises from him, making him swear to abdicate as king of Sicily and sever the Sicilian kingdom from the empire, to go on a crusade, to follow the spiritual direction of the papacy, and in general to confirm the promises that Otto of Brunswick had made and later repudiated.

Innocent's decision in favor of Frederick resulted in a revival of the Hohenstaufen cause in Germany and a renewal of the civil war. Innocent employed all his diplomatic skill and leverage to win over German nobles to Frederick's cause. He was supported in these maneuverings by King Philip Augustus of France, now on friendly terms with the papacy, traditionally sympathetic to the Hohenstaufens, and hostile to the English and their Welf allies.

The complex currents on international politics in Innocent's pontificate reached their climax and their resolution in 1214; King John invaded France from the west while Otto of Brunswick led a powerful army against Philip Augustus from the east—an army heavily subsidized by England and consisting of the combined forces of pro-Welf princes from Germany and the Low Countries. John's invasion bogged down and accomplished nothing; Otto's army met the forces of Philip Augustus in pitched battle at Bouvines and was decisively defeated. The battle of Bouvines of 1214 was an epoch-making engagement. Philip Augustus emerged as Europe's mightiest monarch, Otto's imperial dreams were demolished, and Frederick became emperor in fact as well as in theory. Bouvines was a triumph not only for Philip Augustus and Frederick but also for Innocent III. His ward was now emperor-elect and was pledged to sever the kingdom of Sicily from Germany and free the German Church of imperial control.

Germany itself was in a state of chaos. The solid achievements of Frederick Barbarossa, which might have served as the foundation for a powerful revival of imperial power, were compromised by the subsequent imperial involvement in the affairs of the Sicilian kingdom and were demolished by 19 years of civil strife during which the German princes usurped royal privileges and royal lands on a vast scale. By the time of Innocent's death the imperial authority that Barabarossa had achieved was almost beyond recovery.

Achievements of Innocent III—an Appraisal

The policies of Innocent III were everywhere triumphant. Yet Innocent, by the very range and breadth of his political activities, had involved the papacy in secular affairs to such a degree that its spiritual authority was becoming tarnished. Innocent had won his battles, but he had chosen a dangerous battlefield. His successors, lacking his skill and his luck, could do little to arrest the gradual decline of papal political authority during the middle and later decades of the thirteenth century and over the centuries that followed. For papal power was based ultimately on spiritual prestige, and the thirteenth-century popes, despite their piety, despite their continuing concern for ecclesiastical reform, were lawyers, administrators, and diplomats rather than charismatic spiritual leaders. The papacy was a mighty force in the world of the thirteenth century, but it was failing more and more to satisfy the spiritual hunger of devoted Christians. Piety remained strong, but many of the pious were coming to doubt that the papal government, with its vast wealth and bureaucratic efficiency, was indeed the true spiritual center of the apostolic Church and the citadel of Christ's kingdom on earth. The popes were doing what they had to do, and in playing the game of international politics they continued to dream of a regenerated Christian society led and inspired by the Church. But as time went on they dreamed less and plotted more, permitting their political means to overshadow their spiritual ends.

The impressive diplomatic success of Innocent III's pontificate ended abruptly with his death in 1216. Once Innocent was gone, his former ward, Frederick II, now a grown man, made it clear that he would ignore his promises as completely as Otto of Brunswick had earlier done. Frederick ruled exactly as he pleased, and as his reign progressed he became the medieval papacy's most ferocious adversary. In choosing Frederick and supporting his candidacy to the imperial throne, Innocent III had made a fearful miscalculation.

Frederick II (1211–1250)

Frederick II, whose Sicilian childhood exposed him to several faiths, grew up to be a brilliant, anticlerical skeptic, more concerned with his harem and his exotic menagerie than with his soul. He dazzled his contemporaries and earned the name *Stupor Mundi*, the "Wonder of the World." His vision of unifying all Italy and making it the nucleus of the empire won him the hatred of the papacy. Some churchmen regarded Frederick quite literally as the incarnate antichrist.

Frederick II was a talented, many-sided man—perhaps the most flamboyant product of an intensely creative age. He was a writer of considerable skill and an amateur scientist, curious about the world around him, but in some matters deeply superstitious. After much delay he kept his promise to lead a crusade (1228), but instead of fighting the Muslims he negotiated with them, and did so with such success that Jerusalem itself came into his hands for a time. The amicable spirit of Frederick's crusade against the infidel struck many churchmen as unholy, and its success infuriated them.

Sicily and Italy

Frederick II ruled his kingdom of Sicily in the autocratic but enlightened manner of a Renaissance despot, establishing a uniform legal code, tightening and broadening the centralized administrative system of his Norman-Sicilian predecessors, encouraging agriculture, industry, and commerce, abolishing interior tariffs and tolls, and founding a great university at Naples. He had promised Innocent III that he would cut Sicily off from his Empire, but he made no effort to keep his word. He had always preferred his urbane, sunny Sicilian homeland to the cold forests and gloomy castles of Germany. Although he tried to follow Frederick Barbarossa's policy of strengthening the royal demesne and enforcing the feudal obligations of his great German vassals, he did so half-heartedly. To him, Germany was important chiefly as a source of money and military strength with which to carry out his policy of bringing all Italy under his rule.

As it happened, this policy proved disastrous to the Holy Roman Empire. Frederick's aggressions in Italy evoked the opposition of a revived Lombard League and the implacable hostility of the papacy. He gave up lands and royal rights in Germany with an almost careless abandon in order to keep the peace with the German princes and win their support for his persistent but inconclusive Italian campaigns. In the end, he was even obliged to tax his beloved Sicily to the point of impoverishment in order to support his endless wars. Astute lawyer-popes such as Gregory IX and Innocent IV devoted all their diplomatic talents and spiritual sanctions to blocking Frederick's enterprises, building alliances to oppose him and hurling anathemas against him. In 1245 Innocent IV presided over a universal council of the Church at Lyons, which condemned and excommunicated the emperor. Frederick was deposed, a rival emperor was elected in his place, and a crusade was called to rid the empire of its ungodly tyrant. Revolts now broke out against Frederick throughout his empire. The royal estates in Germany slipped more and more from his grasp, and his Italian holdings were ridden with rebellion. Against this unhappy background Frederick II died in 1250.

THE DECLINE OF THE MEDIEVAL EMPIRE

Germany

In a very real sense, the hopes of the medieval empire died with him. His son succeeded him in Germany but died in 1254 after a brief and unsuccessful reign. For the next 19 years, Germany endured a crippling interregnum (1254–73) during which no recognized emperor held the throne. In 1273 a vastly weakened Holy Roman Empire reemerged with papal blessing under Rudolph of Habsburg, the first emperor of a family that was destined to play a crucial role in modern European history. Rudolph attempted to rebuild the shattered royal demesne and shore up the foundations of imperial rule, but it was much too late. The monarch's one hope had been to strengthen and extend the crown lands, gradually transforming them into the nucleus of a modern state. This was the policy on which the medieval French monarchy had risen to a position of dominance in France; it was the policy that Frederick Barbarossa had pursued so promisingly in Germany. But it aroused the unremitting opposition of the great German princes who had no desire to see their own rights and territories eaten away by royal expansion and would much prefer to extend their own principalities at the expense of the crown.

The civil strife during Innocent's pontificate, the Italian involvements of Frederick II, and the Interregnum of 1254–73 gave the princes their opportunity, and by 1273 the crown lands were hopelessly shrunken and disorganized. Germany was now drifting irreversibly toward the loose confederation of principalities and the anemic elective monarchy which characterized its constitutional structure from the fourteenth to the later nineteenth century. The tragic failure of the medieval empire doomed Germany to 600 years of agonizing disunity—a heritage which may well have contributed to her catastrophic career in the twentieth century.

Italy

Italy, too, emerged from the struggles of the High Middle Ages hopelessly fragmented. The Papal States, straddling the peninsula, were torn with unrest and disaffection, and the papacy had trouble maintaining its authority over the turbulent inhabitants of Rome itself. North of the Papal States, Tuscany and Lombardy had become a chaos of totally independent warring city-states—Florence, Siena, Venice, Milan, and many others—whose rivalries would form the political backdrop of the Italian Renaissance.

The kingdom of Sicily, established by the Normans and cherished by the Hohenstaufens, passed shortly after Frederick II's death to his illegitimate son, Manfred. The papacy, determined to rid

Italy of Hohenstaufen rule, bent all its energies toward securing Manfred's downfall. At length it offered the Sicilian crown to Charles of Anjou, a cadet member of the French royal house, with the intention that Charles should drive Manfred out of the Sicilian kingdom. Charles of Anjou—dour, cruel, and ambitious—defeated and killed Manfred in 1266 and established a new, French dynasty on the throne of the kingdom.

The inhabitants of the realm, particularly those on the island of Sicily, had become accustomed to Hohenstaufen rule and resented Charles of Anjou. They looked on his French soldiers as an army of occupation. When, on Easter Monday, 1282, a French soldier mishandled a young married woman on her way to evening services in Palermo, he was struck down, and on all sides was raised the cry "Death to the French!" The incident resulted in a spontaneous uprising and a general massacre of the French which quickly spread throughout the island. When the French retaliated, the Sicilians offered the crown to Peter III of Aragon, Manfred's son-in-law, who claimed the Hohenstaufen inheritance and led an army to Sicily.

There ensued a long, bloody, indecisive struggle known by the romantic name, "The War of the Sicilian Vespers." For 20 years, Charles of Anjou and his successors, backed by the French monarchy and the papacy, fought against the Sicilians and Aragonese. In the end, southern Italy remained Angevin and its kings ruled from Naples, while Sicily passed under the control of the kings of Aragon. The dispute between France and Aragon over southern Italy and Sicily persisted for generations and was an important factor in the politics of the Italian Renaissance. The chaotic strife of the thirteenth century destroyed the prosperity of the region. Once the wealthiest and most enlightened state in Italy, the kingdom of Sicily became backward, pauperized and divided —a victim of international politics and of the ruthless struggle between church and state.

THE PAPACY AFTER INNOCENT III

Signs of Weakness

To judge by the disintegration of the Holy Roman Empire in the thirteenth century, one might conclude that the papacy had won an overwhelming victory. But the victory was an empty one. For as popes like Innocent III, Gregory IX, and Innocent IV became increasingly involved in power politics, their spiritual role was more and more obscured. In the thirteenth century the papacy's international religious mission was being steadily subordinated to its local political interests. Slowly, almost imperceptibly, it was losing its hold on the heart of Europe. Papal excommunication, after several centuries of overuse—often for political purposes—was no longer the terrifying weapon it once had been. To call a crusade against Frederick II was doubtless an effective means of harassment, but the crusading ideal was debased in the process. The time would come when a pope would call a crusade and nobody would answer.

As the papacy became a great political power and a big business, it found itself in need of ever-increasing revenues. By the end of the thirteenth century the papal tax system was admirably efficient, with the result that the papacy acquired an unsavory reputation for greed. As one contemporary observer complained, the supreme pastor of Christendom was supposed to lead Christ's flock but not to fleece it. Ironically, the fiscal and political cast of the later medieval papacy came as a direct consequence of its earlier dream of becoming the spiritual dynamo of a reformed Christendom. Rising to prominence in the eleventh century upon the floodtide of the new popular piety, the papacy became in the twelfth and thirteenth centuries increasingly insensitive to the deep spiritual aspirations of European Christians as it became more and more absorbed in the external problems of political power.

Boniface VIII

The papacy humbled the Empire only to be humbled itself by the rising power of the new centralized monarchies of northern Europe. By the end of the thirteenth century a new concept of royal sovereignty was in the air. The kings of England and France were finding it increasingly difficult to tolerate the existence of a semi-independent, highly privileged, internationally controlled Church within their realms. By endeavouring to bring these ecclesiastical "states within states" under royal control, the two monarchies encountered vigorous papal opposition. The issue of papal versus royal control of the Church was an old one, but the ancient controversy now took on a new form. The growing monarchies of the late thirteenth century found themselves increasingly in need of money. This was particularly true after 1294 when England and France became locked in a series of costly wars. Both monarchies adopted the novel policy of systematically taxing the clergy of their realms, and Pope Boniface VIII (1294–1303) retaliated in 1296 with the papal bull *Clericis Laicos* that expressly forbade this practice. Once again, church and state were at an impasse.

Boniface VIII was another lawyer-pope —a man of ability but not of genius— proud and intransigent, with a vision of absolute papal power that transcended even the notions of Innocent III, but with a fatal blindness to the momentous implications of the new centralized monarchies of late thirteenth-century Europe. His great weakness was his inability

The collection of tithes on wine (fifteenth century). The Church's growing need for larger revenues during the High Middle Ages continuously thrust ecclesiastical functionaries deeper into the economic life of society with serious consequences for relations between the Church and the laity.

to bend his stupendous concepts of papal authority to the hard realities of contemporary European politics.

In King Philip the Fair* of France (1285–1314) Boniface had a powerful, ruthless antagonist. Philip ignored the papal bull prohibiting clerical taxation; he set his agents to work spreading scandalous rumors about the pope's morals and exerted financial pressure on Rome by cutting off all papal taxes from his French realm. Boniface was obliged to submit for the moment, and Philip taxed his clergy unopposed. But a vast influx of pilgrims into Rome in the Jubilee year of 1300 restored the pope's confidence. He withdrew his concession to Philip the Fair on clerical taxation and in 1302 issued the famous

---

* I. e., handsome; see pp. 487–88.

bull *Unam Sanctam,* which asserted the doctrine of papal monarchy in uncompromising terms: " . . . We declare, announce, affirm, and define that for every human creature, to be subject to the Roman pontiff is absolutely necessary for salvation."

Philip the Fair now summoned an assembly of the realm and accused Boniface of every imaginable crime from murder to black magic. A small French military expedition crossed into Italy in 1303 and took Boniface prisoner at his palace at Anagni with the intention of bringing him to France for trial. Anagni, the antithesis of Canossa, symbolized the humiliation of the medieval papacy. The French plan failed—Boniface was freed by local townsmen a few days after his capture—but the proud old Pope died shortly thereafter, outraged and chagrined that armed Frenchmen should have dared to lay hands on his person.

Decline

The great age of the medieval papacy was now at an end. In 1305 the cardinals elected the Frenchman Clement V (1305–14), who pursued a policy of cautious subservience to the French throne. Clement submitted on the question of clerical taxation, repudiated *Unam Sanctam,* and abandoned faction-ridden Rome for a new papal capital at Avignon on the Rhone. Here the popes remained for the next several generations, their independence often limited by the power of the French monarchy and their spiritual prestige continuing to decline. The town of Avignon belonged to the papacy, not to the French Crown, yet France's enemies could never be confident of the Avignon papacy's political objectivity. The French kings were strong, and they were nearby.

It is easy to criticize the inflexibility of a Boniface VIII or the limpness of a Clement V, but the waning of papal authority in

King Philip the Fair, from the Abbey of St. Denis.

461   A. Empire and Papacy

TABLE I
Chronology of the Papal-Imperial Conflict

1039–1056:	Reign of Henry III
1046:	Henry III deposes 3 rival popes. inaugurates papal reform movement.
1049–1054:	Pontificate of Leo IX
1056–1106:	Reign of Henry IV
1059:	Papal Election Decree
1073–1085:	Pontificate of Gregory VII
1075:	Gregory VII bans lay investiture.
1076:	Gregory VII excommunicates and deposes Henry IV.
1077:	Henry IV humbles himself at Canossa.
1080:	Second excommunication and deposition of Henry IV.
1088–1099:	Pontificate of Urban II
1106–1125:	Reign of Henry V
1122:	Concordat of Worms
1152–1190:	Reign of Frederick I, "Barbarossa"
1154–1159:	Pontificate of Hadrian IV
1155:	Execution of Arnold of Brescia
1159–1181:	Pontificate of Alexander III
1176:	Lombards defeat Barbarossa at Legnano.
1180:	Barbarossa defeats Duke Henry the Lion of Saxony.
1190–1197:	Reign of Henry VI
1194:	Henry VI becomes king of Sicily.
1198–1216:	Pontificate of Innocent III
1211–1250:	Reign of Frederick II
1214:	Philip Augustus defeats Otto of Brunswick at Bouvines.
1215:	Fourth Lateran Council
1227–1241:	Pontificate of Gregory IX
1243–1254:	Pontificate of Innocent IV
1245:	Council of Lyons
1254–1273:	Interregnum
1273–1291:	Reign of Rudolph of Habsburg
1282–1303:	War of the Sicilian Vespers
1294–1303:	Pontificate of Boniface VIII
1302:	Boniface VIII issues *Unam Sanctam*.
1305–1314:	Pontificate of Clement V. Papacy moves to Avignon.

the later Middle Ages did not result primarily from personal shortcomings. Rather it stemmed from an ever-widening gulf between papal government and the spiritual hunger of ordinary Christians, combined with the hostility to Catholic internationalism on the part of increasingly powerful centralized states such as England and France. It would be grossly unfair to describe the high medieval papacy as "corrupt." Between 1050 and 1300 men of good intentions and high purposes sat on the papal throne (see Table I). Not satisfied merely to chide the society of their day by innocuous moralizing from the sidelines, they plunged into the world and struggled to transform and sanctify it. Perhaps inevitably they soiled their hands.

B. England in the High Middle Ages

THE ANGLO-NORMAN MONARCHY

England and France

While empire and papacy were engaged in their drawn-out struggle, England and France were evolving into centralized states. Strong monarchy came earlier to England than to France, yet in the long run it was the English who were the more successful in imposing constitutional limitations on the crown. French royal absolutism and English parliamentary monarchy are both rooted in the High Middle Ages.

The Anglo-Saxon period of English history came to an end when Duke William of Normandy won the English crown with his victory at Hastings in 1066. In the centuries that followed, England was more closely tied to the continent than before; her rulers dominated both England and significant portions of France. As kings of England they were masterless, but they held their French territories as vassals of the king of France. England's territorial involvement in France continued from 1066 until the mid-sixteenth century. It was a source of cultural enrichment to the English, but it also led to centuries of hostility and warfare between the two monarchies.

The Anglo-Saxon Background

The English kingdom that William the Conqueror won was already centralized and well-governed by the standards of mid-eleventh-century Europe. Its kings enjoyed the direct allegiance of all their subjects. Its army was subject only to the commands of the king or his representatives; private armies and private war were virtually unknown. A royal council of nobles and household officials known as the *witenagemot* advised the king on important matters and approved the succession of new kings. The chief officers in the royal household were gradually coming to assume important administrative responsibilities: issuing writs that carried royal commands to local officials in the countryside, administering the royal treasury, and performing other governmental functions. Although the late-Saxon royal household was constantly on the move, traveling around England from one royal estate to another, the treasury had become fixed permanently at Winchester in Wessex.

England in 1066 had long been divided into regional units known as shires, each with its own shire court and administered by a royal officer called a "shire reeve", or sheriff. The sheriff presided over the shire court, the membership of which was drawn from important men of the district. The customs and procedures of the shire courts were rooted in the traditions of the locality rather than in royal mandates. In operation as in membership, the shire courts were local phenomena and are often described, quite accurately, as folk courts. The sheriff, too, was usually a local figure whose sympathies were apt to be divided between his native shire and the king. The subtle interplay between local initiative and royal authority—a significant characteristic of Anglo-Saxon government—persisted over the post-conquest centuries to give medieval England a political balance lacking in many contemporary states.

The English shires were subdivided into smaller administrative units known as hundreds—deriving perhaps from the early days of the barbarian invasions when such a district might provide settlements for a hundred warriors. Each hundred had its own court which handled less important cases than those brought to the shire courts. Like the shire courts, the hundred courts were local in membership and legal custom yet were presided over by royal officials. By 1066 a number of hundreds had passed into the hands of private lords—lay or ecclesiastical—in which case the royal official was replaced by an official of the lord.

The sheriff was responsible for administering the unique Anglo-Saxon land tax, the danegeld, which varied somewhat in amount but in most instances provided the crown with about 10 pounds from each hundred. It was also the sheriff's task to assemble the shire's contingent when the king summoned the army—the *fyrd*, as it was then called. Our evidence suggests that by 1066 it had become customary for each hundred to provide about twenty armed men for the fyrd and to supply their sustenance during their period of duty.

The Norman Conquest and Settlement

Such were some of the more important institutions which William the Conqueror inherited when he won the English crown. He came to England not as an open aggressor but as a legitimate claimant to the throne, related (distantly) to the Anglo-Saxon royal family and designated—so he claimed—by King Edward the Confessor who died childless early in 1066. On the Confessor's death, the witenagemot had chosen an able warrior, Earl Harold Godwinson of Wessex, to succeed him, but William had always regarded Harold as a usurper, and when Harold was killed at Hastings and his army put to flight, William took the position that he was passing into his rightful inheritance. Although another five years were required to put down the last vestiges of English resistance, William was crowned king of England in London on Christmas Day, 1066, and turned at once to the problem of governing his new realm.

Taking up his role as Edward the Con-

Edward the Confessor giving advice to Harold in a scene from the Bayeux Tapestry.

fessor's proper successor, William promised to preserve the laws and customs of Edward's day. Indeed, it was to his advantage to do so, since many of these customs were exceedingly beneficial to the monarchy. He maintained the danegeld, as well he might, continued to summon the fyrd whenever he needed it, perpetuated the folk courts of shire and hundred, and drew needed strength from the Anglo-Saxon custom of general allegiance to the Crown.

The Conqueror preserved much, but he also built energetically on the system that he inherited. The changes and additions that he introduced were products in part of the customs that he had known in Normandy, in part of his own creative imagination, and in part of his unique position as unquestioned master of a conquered land. If the government of Anglo-Saxon England was remarkably strong, the government of Norman England was far stronger, and its strength was, in some measure, a consequence of the political genius of William the Conqueror.

Establishment of Feudalism

In the years immediately following the conquest, William divided much of England among the leading warriors of his victorious army, thereby introducing into the kingdom a new, knightly, French-speaking aristocracy. He established a feudal regime in England more-or-less on the Norman pattern, but more rationally organized and more directly subordinate to the royal will. Most English estates, both lay and ecclesiastical, were transformed into fiefs, held by crown vassals in return for a specified number of mounted knights and various other feudal services. He was careful to reserve about one sixth of the lands of England for his own royal demesne, so that he and his successors would never be mere nominal overlords like the early Capetians and the later Hohenstaufens.

The Crown vassals, or tenants-in-chief, in order to raise the numerous knights required by the monarchy, subdivided portions of their fiefs into smaller fiefs and granted them to knightly subvassals. In other words, the process of subinfeudation proceeded in much the same way that it had centuries earlier on the continent. As a natural byproduct of the establishment of feudalism in England, scores of castles were quickly erected across the land by the king and his barons.

Feudalism in England was by no means accompanied by political disintegration as it had been in Carolingian Frankland. With the resources of their vast royal domain on which to draw, the Norman kings of England were firmly established at the apex of the feudal pyramid and were generally successful in keeping their vassals under tight rein. Their authoritative position in the Anglo-Norman feudal structure owed much to the centralizing traditions of the Anglo-Saxon monarchy. The new barons established feudal courts, as had been their custom in Normandy, but alongside these baronial courts there persisted the far older courts of shire and hundred. The new feudal army could be an effective force, but when it proved inadequate or when barons rebelled against the monarchy, the Old English fyrd could be summoned or mercenaries could be hired. Feudal particularism was attenuated by the Anglo-Saxon custom of general allegiance to the crown, which enabled the Norman kings to claim the direct and primary loyalty of every vassal and subvassal in the English feudal hierarchy. A knight's allegiance to his lord was now secondary to his allegiance to the crown. Private war between vassals was prohibited, and private castles could be built only by royal license. In brief, the new institution of feudalism was molded by the powerful Anglo-Saxon tradition of royal supremacy into something far more centralized—far less centrifugal—than the feudalism of the continent.

Anglo-Norman Administration

On the Conqueror's death, his kingdom passed in turn to his two sons, William II (1087–1100) and Henry I (1100–35). Both were strong, ruthless men, but Henry I was the abler of the two. A skillful general and brilliant legal and administrative innovator, Henry I rid England of rebellion and exploited the growing prosperity of his day by a policy of severe taxation. He was not a kindly man, but his was an age in which firmness and military skill were the chief requisites to successful rule and excessive geniality was a grave weakness. His great service to his English subjects was his pitiless enforcement of the peace.

The reigns of William the Conqueror and his sons witnessed a significant growth in royal administrative institutions. The unique survey of land holdings known as *Domesday Book*—the product of a comprehensive census of the realm undertaken by royal order in 1086—testifies to the administrative vigor of William the Conqueror. Between 1066 and 1135 royal administration became steadily more elaborate and efficient. By Henry I's reign, royal justices were traveling about England hearing cases in the shire courts, and thereby extending the king's jurisdiction far and wide across the land. The baronial courts and the ancient folk courts of the counties and hundreds continued to function. But the extension of royal jurisdiction under Henry I was the initial step in a long and significant process whereby folk justice and baronial justice were gradually overshadowed and finally superseded by the king's justice.

Administrative efficiency and royal centralization were the keynotes of Henry I's reign. Royal dues were collected systematically by local noblemen in the king's service—the sheriffs—who passed the money on to a remarkably effective accounting agency known as the exchequer. A powerful royal bureaucracy was gradually coming into being. The growing efficiency of the exchequer and the expansion of royal justice were both motivated chiefly by the king's desire for larger revenues. For the more cases the royal justices handled, the more fines went into the royal coffers; the more closely the sheriffs were supervised, the less likely it was that royal taxes would stick to their fingers. The Norman kings discovered that strong government was good business.

The Anglo-Norman church was ornamented by two leaders of exceptional ability: Lanfranc (d. 1089) and St. Anselm (d. 1109). Both were brilliant theologians, both, in different ways, were deeply involved in the politics of their day, and both were Italians who migrated to the great Benedictine monastery of Bec in Normandy.

William the Conqueror drew Lanfranc from Normandy to become archbishop of Canterbury and primate of the English church. William and Lanfranc were contemporaries of Hildebrand and could not help but become involved in the raging controversy over ecclesiastical reform. The king and the archbishop were both sympathetic to reform, but neither was receptive to the Gregorian notions of an independent church and a new social order. William was more than willing to work toward the reform of the Anglo-Norman church, and Lanfranc supported him vigorously, but when Gregory VII demanded that William become his vassal, the Conqueror flatly refused: "I have not consented to pay fealty nor will I now, because I never promised it, nor do I find that my predecessors ever paid it to your predecessors."

Gregory VII, preoccupied with his struggle against the Holy Roman emperor, could not afford to alienate William, who was, after all, friendly toward reform.

Accordingly, the specific issue of lay investiture did not emerge in England until after Gregory's death. It was raised by St. Anselm, who had followed Lanfranc to Bec and was chosen in 1093 to succeed him as archbishop of Canterbury. Lanfranc and William the Conqueror had worked in close cooperation with one another, but St. Anselm's relations with the Norman monarchy were turbulent. Already advanced in years when he reluctantly assumed the archbishopric, Anselm was the greatest theologian of his age and was, perhaps, the most profound philosopher that Western Christendom had produced since St. Augustine's time. He was also devoted to Gregorian notions of ecclesiastical independence, lay investiture, and papal monarchy.

These notions no Norman king could accept, and Anselm came into bitter conflict with both William II and Henry I. He spent much of his tenure as archbishop in exile, and it was not until 1107 that a compromise on the investiture issue was hammered out between Henry, the papacy, and himself. As in the later Concordat of Worms, the agreement of 1107 prohibited lay investiture as such, but permitted the king to retain a certain control over important ecclesiastical appointments. Ecclesiastical tenants-in-chief were to continue their traditional practice of rendering homage to the king. More important than the settlement itself is the fact that Anselm died two years thereafter, and Henry, rid at last of his troublesome saint, dominated the English church through pressure and patronage. Anselm had won a point, but the Church remained generally subservient to the Norman monarchy.

The Disputed Succession: Stephen and Matilda

Henry I's death in 1135 was followed by a period of unrest brought on by a disputed royal succession. Henry was survived by a daughter, Matilda, who was wed to Geoffrey Plantagenet, count of Anjou. Henry had arranged the marriage with the hope of healing the long rivalry between the two great powers of northern France: Normandy and Anjou. Shortly before Henry's death Matilda bore him two grandsons, the eldest of whom, Henry Plantagenet, was destined ultimately to inherit a vast territory including Anjou, Normandy, and England. But when the old King died, Henry Plantagenet was still an infant, and the English crown was seized by Henry I's nephew, Stephen of Blois (King of England 1135–54). For two turbulent decades Stephen and Matilda struggled for control of England while the English barons, often shifting their allegiance from one side to the other, threw up unlicensed castles and usurped royal rights. English churchmen and commoners, tormented by the endemic warfare of the period, looked back longingly toward the peaceful days of Henry I.

HENRY II

The Accession

During Stephen's troubled reign Henry Plantagenet grew to vigorous manhood and established control over Anjou and Normandy. A marriage with Eleanor of Aquitaine, the heiress of that large, heterogeneous southern duchy, extended still further the territories under his jurisdiction. And at King Stephen's death in 1154 Henry peacefully acquired the English throne and became King Henry II of England (1154–89). He now held sway over an immense constellation of territories north and south of the English Channel, which has been called the Angevin Empire. On the map, the Angevin Empire dwarfs the modest territory controlled by the King of France. But Henry II and his sons who succeeded him had difficulty in keeping order throughout their vast, diverse territories. The Angevin Empire was doubtless a source of power and prestige to the English monarchy, but it was also a burden.

Henry was an energetic, brilliant, exuberant man—short, burly, and redheaded. Named after his grandfather, he ruled in Henry I's imperious tradition and consciously imitated him. In many respects he was a creature of his age—a product of the great intellectual and cultural outburst of twelfth-century Europe. He was a literate monarch who consorted with scholars, encouraged the growth of towns, and presided over an age of economic boom. A chaos of feverish activity pervaded his court, which was constantly on the move and, in the opinion of one of Henry's court scholars, was "a perfect portrait of Hell."

Policies and Administration

Henry's chief goals were the preservation of the Angevin Empire, the strengthening of royal authority, and the increasing of his revenues. He began his reign by ordering the destruction of unlicensed baronial castles that had been thrown up during the previous anarchic period, and was cautious thereafter in permitting new private castles to be built. At once he began to recover the royal privileges that had been eroded during Stephen's reign and, in some cases, to expand them considerably. During the 35 years of his rule the royal administration grew steadily in complexity and effectiveness. The maturity of Henry's exchequer is illustrated not only by a series of annual financial accounts—known as *Pipe Rolls*—but also by a comprehensive detailed treatise on the exchequer's organization and methods—the *Dialogue of the Exchequer*—which was written by one of the king's financial officers. The royal secretarial office—the chancery—was similarly increasing in efficiency and scope. Indeed, the entire royal administration was growing more specialized, more professional, and more self-conscious. Separate administrative departments were evolving, and public records became fuller and more extensive. Many Englishmen were delighted at the return of peace and order; others were uneasy over the steady rise of "Big Government."

Throughout the twelfth century, commerce was becoming ever more vigorous and the circulation of money was rapidly increasing. Under the pressure of royal ambition and the growing money economy, the older feudal relationship of service in return for land was giving way to wage service. By the time of Henry II it had become commonplace for feudal tenants-in-chief to pay scutage to the crown in lieu of their military-service obligation. Dues from the royal demesne estates were being collected in coin rather than in kind, and royal troops, servants, and administrators customarily served for wages. These trends can be traced back to the reign of Henry I and beyond, but under Henry II they were accelerating. The feudal hierarchy remained powerful, but feudal obligations were being translated into fiscal terms. Both the economy and the administration were steadily increasing in complexity and sophistication.

Of necessity, the authority of the king and the efficiency of his central administrative system depended upon an effective local government and the maintenance of strong bonds between court and countryside. The two were linked under Henry II, as under Henry I, by the activities of sheriffs and itinerant royal justices. Henry II broadened the scope of these itinerant justices and increased their organizational efficiency, thereby making royal justice more available to ordinary Englishmen than ever before. Now, itinerant royal justices made periodic circuits of the countryside, bringing the king's law to considerable numbers of Englishmen who had previously been untouched by it.

The sheriffs were bound to enforce the king's orders which continued to issue from the chancery in the form of writs. It was also the sheriff's duty to collect royal dues and fines and to render a periodic accounting of them to the exchequer. Thus, the sheriffs were subordinated to the central administration and subjected to royal control. Nevertheless, most sheriffs were powerful local nobles with wide estates of their own and were by no means completely dependent on the royal favor. Many of them abused their power and displayed a degree of independence such as to challenge the king's authority. In 1170 Henry II ordered a searching investigation of his sheriffs' behavior—the Inquest of Sheriffs—and subsequently replaced most of them with new and more tractable men.

Expansion of Royal Justice

Henry II has been called the father of the English common law. Like his predecessors, he favored the extension of royal jurisdiction chiefly for its financial rewards to the crown, and in his quest for ever-greater judicial revenues he was able to advance the powers of the royal courts well beyond their former limits. His *Assize of Clarendon* of 1166 widened the scope of royal justice to include the indictment and prosecution of local criminals. It provided that regional inquest juries should meet periodically under royal auspices to identify and denounce notorious neighborhood criminals whose guilt or innocence was then to be determined by the ordeal of cold water.* The inquest jury was more akin to the modern grand jury than to the modern trial jury, for its duty was to investigate and indict rather than to judge guilt. Inquest juries had been used before: they were assembled under William the Conqueror to provide information for the Domesday survey; there is a reference to one such jury in the records of late Anglo-Saxon times, and bodies of a similar nature were employed in the administration of Carolingian Frankland. Never before, however, had they been used in such a systematic fashion.

Henry also extended royal jurisdiction over the vast, turbulent field of land disputes, employing local juries to determine the rightful possessors or heirs of disputed estates. The most important of Henry's "possessory assizes," the *Assize of Novel Disseisin*, was designed to curb local violence by providing a legal action against forcible dispossession of an estate. Regardless whether the plaintiff had a just

---

* See p. 315.

469   B. England in the High Middle Ages

claim to the estate in question, if he was driven from his land by force he was entitled to purchase a royal writ commanding the sheriff to assemble a jury to determine the facts of the case. If the jury concluded that the plaintiff had indeed been violently dispossessed, the sheriff, acting with full royal authority, would see that the estate in dispute was restored to the plaintiff. Another of the new legal actions provide by Henry II—the *Grand Assize*—used a similar procedure of purchased writ and jury to determine not whether the plaintiff had been dispossessed but whether he had, in fact, the best title to the land in question.

These and similar assizes carried the king's justice into an area that had formerly been dominated by the feudal courts which usually settled questions of land possession by the crude procedure of trial by combat. Previous kings had intervened in territorial quarrels, but never in a consistent, systematic way. Now, Englishmen learned to turn to Henry's courts for quick, modern, rational justice. Feudal law, with its archaic and time-consuming procedures, had little chance in the competition. Gradually the patchwork of local laws and customs which had so long divided England gave way to a uniform royal law—a *common law* by which all Englishmen were governed. The *political* unification of the tenth century was consummated by the *legal* unification under the Angevin kings.

The Controversy with Becket

Predictably, Henry II also sought to expand royal justice at the expense of the ecclesiastical courts. Since at least the reign of William the Conqueror, a separate system of ecclesiastical jurisdiction had been in effect, distinct from the various secular courts—local, feudal, and royal. The ecclesiastical court system can be regarded as one manifestation of the complex government of the international Church, which—as it grew steadily more elaborate—came increasingly into conflict with the proliferating governmental structures of England and other secular states. The two governments, royal and ecclesiastical, were both expanding in the twelfth century, and conflicts between them were bound to occur. The first great conflict centered on St. Anselm, the second on St. Thomas Becket.

In 1162 Henry sought to bring the English church under strict royal control by appointing to the archbishopric of Canterbury his chancellor and good friend, Thomas Becket. But in raising Becket to the primacy, Henry had misjudged his man. As chancellor, Becket was a devoted royal servant, but as archbishop of Canterbury he became a fervent defender of ecclesiastical independence and an implacable enemy of the king. Henry and Becket became locked in a furious quarrel over the issue of royal control of the English church. In 1164 Henry issued a list of pro-royal provisions relating to church-state relations known as the *Constitutions of Clarendon,* which, among other things, prohibited appeals to Rome without royal license and established a degree of royal control over the Church courts. Henry maintained that the Constitutions of Clarendon represented ancient custom; Becket regarded them as novel encroachments on the freedom of the Church.

At the heart of the quarrel was the issue of whether churchmen accused of crimes should be subject to royal jurisdiction after being found guilty and punished by Church courts. The king complained that "criminous clerks" were often given absurdly light punishments by the ecclesiastical tribunals. A murderer, for example, might simply be defrocked and released, and the Constitutions of Clarendon provided that such a person should then be remanded to a royal court for punishment. Becket replied that no man should be put

The dramatic impact of Becket's murder on the mind of medieval Europe is illustrated in this graphic illumination from a thirteenth-century psalter.

in double jeopardy. In essence, Henry was challenging the competence of an agency of the international Church, and Becket, as primate of England, felt bound to defend the ecclesiastical system against royal encroachment. Two worlds were in collision.

Henry turned on his archbishop, accusing him of various crimes against the kingdom, and Becket, denying the king's right to try an archbishop, fled England to seek papal support. Pope Alexander III, who was in the midst of his struggle with Frederick Barbarossa, could ill afford to alienate Henry; yet neither could he turn

471   B. England in the High Middle Ages

against such an ardent ecclesiastical champion as Becket. The great lawyer-pope was forced to equivocate—to encourage Becket without breaking with Henry—until at length in 1170, the king and his archbishop agreed to a truce. Most of the outstanding issues between them remained unsettled, but Becket was permitted to return peacefully to England and resume the archbishopric. At once, however, the two antagonists had another falling-out. Becket excommunicated a number of Henry's supporters; the king flew into a rage, and four overenthusiastic knights of the royal household went to Canterbury cathedral and murdered Becket at the high altar.

This dramatic crime made a deep impact on the age. Becket was regarded as a martyr; miracles were alleged to have occurred at his tomb, and he was quickly canonized. For the remainder of the Middle Ages, Canterbury was a major pilgrimage center and the cult of St. Thomas enjoyed immense popularity. Henry, who had not ordered the killing but whose anger had prompted it, suffered acute embarrassment. He was obliged to do penance by walking barefoot through the streets of Canterbury and submitting to a flogging by the Canterbury monks. But his campaign against the ecclesiastical courts was delayed only momentarily. Although forced to give in on specific matters such as royal jurisdiction over criminous clerks and unlicensed appeals to Rome, he obtained through indirection and maneuvering what he had failed to get through open conflict. He succeeded generally in arranging the appointment to high ecclesiastical offices of men friendly to the crown, and by the end of his reign royal justice had made significant inroads on the authority of the Church courts. The monarchy had succeeded in bringing the English church under tight rein. Here, as elsewhere, Henry was remarkably successful in steering England toward administrative and legal centralization.

The Angevin Empire

Throughout his reign Henry had to divide his time between England and the other territories of the Angevin Empire. Strictly speaking, these territories did not constitute an "empire" in any real sense of the word. For they were in fact a multitude of individual political units, each with its own customs and its own administrative structure, bound together by their allegiance to Henry Plantagenet. The French monarchy did what it could to break up this threatening configuration, encouraging rebellions on the part of Henry's dutiless sons and his estranged wife, Eleanor of Aquitaine. Henry put down the rebellions one by one, relegated Eleanor to comfortable imprisonment, and sought to placate his sons. It did little good. The rebellions persisted, and as Henry neared death in 1189 his two surviving sons, Richard and John, were in arms against him. In the end the aged monarch was outmaneuvered and defeated by his offspring and their French allies; he died with the statement, "Shame, shame on a conquered king."

RICHARD AND JOHN

Richard

Although Henry's final days were saddened by defeat, the Angevin Empire remained intact, passing into the capable hands of his eldest surviving son, Richard the Lion-Hearted (1189–99). This illustrious warrior-king devoted himself chiefly to two great projects: defending the Angevin Empire against the French crown and crusading against the Muslims. He was a superb general who not only won renown on the Third Crusade but also foiled every attempt of the French monarchy to reduce his continental territories. He was far less impressive as an administrator and, indeed, spent less than six months of his ten-year reign in England. During his protracted absences, the administrative system of Henry II proved its worth; it governed England more or less satisfactorily for ten kingless years. Meanwhile Richard was engaging in his romantic but fruitless adventures in the Holy Land, and campaigning along the frontiers of the Angevin Empire against the remorseless pressure of King Philip Augustus of France.

John and the Loss of the Angevin Empire

The fortunes of the Angevin Empire veered sharply with the accession of King John (1199–1216), Richard the Lion-Hearted's younger brother. John was an enigmatic figure—brilliant in certain respects, a master of administrative detail, but a suspicious and unscrupulous leader. He trusted nobody, and nobody trusted him. Consequently his subjects never supported him more than halfheartedly in moments of crisis.

In Philip Augustus of France (1180–1223) John had a shrewd, unremitting antagonist. Philip took full advantage of his position as feudal lord over John's continental possessions. In 1202 John was summoned to the French royal court to answer charges brought against him by one of his own Aquitainian vassals. When John refused to come, Philip Augustus declared his French lands forfeited and proceeded to invade Normandy. The duchy quickly fell into Philip's hands (1203–4) as John's demoralized vassals defected, one after another, and John himself fled to England. In the chaos that followed, Philip Augustus was able to wrest Anjou and most of the remaining continental possessions of the Angevin Empire from John's control. Only portions of distant Aquitaine retained their connection with the English monarchy. King John had sustained a monstrous political and military disaster.

For the next ten years John nursed his wounds and wove a dextrous web of alliances against King Philip in hopes of regaining his lost possessions. His careful plans were shattered by Philip's decisive victory over John's Flemish and German allies at the battle of Bouvines in 1214.* With Bouvines went John's last hope of reviving the Angevin Empire.

John and Innocent III

In the decade between the loss of Normandy and the catastrophe at Bouvines, John engaged in a bitter quarrel with Pope Innocent III. At stake was royal control over the appointment of an archbishop of Canterbury. According to canon law and established custom, a bishop or archbishop was to be elected by the canons of the cathedral chapter. The Investiture Controversy notwithstanding, such elections were commonly controlled by the king who would overawe the canons into electing the candidate of his choice. Canterbury differed from most other cathedrals in that a body of monks performed the functions that were ordinarily the responsibility of cathedral canons; it was the monks who customarily elected the archbishop, but they, no less than canons, were usually susceptible to royal control. In 1205, however, the monks of Canterbury declined to wait for royal instructions and elected one of their own number as archbishop, sending a delegation to Rome to obtain Pope Innocent's confirmation. Going personally to Canterbury, John forced the monks to hold another election and to select his own nominee. In the course of events several delegations went from England to Rome, and Innocent, keenly interested in the enforcement of proper canonical procedures,

* See p. 456.

quashed both elections. He ordered those Canterbury monks who were then in Rome—quite a number by this time—to hold still another election, and under papal influence they elected Stephen Langton, a learned Englishman who had spent some years as a scholar in Paris.

Furious that his own candidate should have been passed over, John refused to confirm Langton's appointment or to admit him into England. For the next six years, 1207–13, John held to his position while Innocent used every weapon at his disposal to make the king submit. England was laid under interdict; John retaliated by confiscating all ecclesiastical revenues. John was excommunicated, and Innocent even threatened to depose him. This threat, together with the danger of a projected French invasion of England with full papal backing, forced John to submit at last. In 1213 he accepted Stephen Langton as archbishop and, evidently on his own initiative, conceded to Innocent the overlordship of England. John would hold his kingdom thenceforth as a papal fief and would render a substantial annual tribute to Rome. Having lost the battle, John was anxious to transform his antagonist into a devoted friend, and his concession of the overlordship had precisely that effect.

Magna Carta

John had won the papal friendship, but many of his own barons were regarding him with increasing hatred and contempt. The Bouvines disaster of 1214, coming at the end of a long series of expensive and humiliating diplomatic failures, destroyed what remained of John's royal prestige. It paved the way for the English baronial uprising that culminated on the field of Runnymede in 1215 with the signing of *Magna Carta*. John's barons had good reason to oppose him. He had pushed the centralizing tendencies of his Norman and Angevin predecessors to new limits and was taxing his subjects as they had never been taxed before. The baronial reaction of 1215 was both a protest against John and an effort to reverse the trend toward royal authoritarianism of the past 150 years.

Magna Carta has been interpreted in contradictory ways: as the fountainhead of English constitutional monarchy, and as a reactionary, backward-looking document designed to favor the particularistic feudal aristocracy at the expense of the enlightened Angevin monarchy. In reality, Magna Carta was both feudal and constitutional, both backward-looking and forward-looking. Its more important clauses were designed to keep the king within the bounds of popular tradition and feudal custom. Royal taxes not sanctioned by custom, for example, were to be levied only by the common council of the kingdom. But implicit in the traditional feudal doctrine that the lord had to respect the rights of his vassals—and in the age-old Germanic notion that the monarch had to adhere to the customs of his people—was the constitutional principle of government under the law. In striving to make King John a good feudal lord, the barons in 1215 were moving uncertainly, perhaps unconsciously, toward constitutional monarchy. For this was the crucial moment when the English nobles were just beginning to represent a national viewpoint. In the past, baronial opposition to royal autocracy had taken the form of a selfish insistence on local aristocratic autonomy. But one finds in Magna Carta the notion that the king is bound by traditional legal limitations in his relations with all classes of free Englishmen. It would be misleading to lay too much stress on the underlying principles of this intensely practical document which was concerned primarily with correcting specific royal abuses of feudal custom, but it would be equally misleading to ignore the momentous implication in Magna Carta of an over-arching body of law which limited and circumscribed royal authority.

The chief constitutional problem in the years following Magna Carta was the question how an unwilling king might be forced to stay within the bounds of law. A series of royal promises was obviously insufficient to control an ambitious monarch who held all the machinery of the central government in his grasp. Magna Carta itself relied on a committee of 25 barons who were empowered, should the king violate the charter, to call upon the English people "to distrain and distress him in every possible way." Thus, the monarch was to be restrained by the crude sanction of baronial and popular rebellion—a desperate and unwieldy weapon against an unscrupulous king.

John himself seems to have had no intention of carrying out his promises. He repudiated Magna Carta at the first opportunity, with the full backing of his papal overlord, Innocent III. At his death in 1216 England was in the midst of a full-scale revolt. John's death ended the revolt, and the crown passed to his nine-year-old son, Henry III (1216-72) who was supervised during his minority by a baronial council. In the decades that followed, Magna Carta was reissued many times, but the great task of the new age was to create political institutions capable of limiting royal autocracy by some means short of rebellion. The ultimate solution to this problem was found in Parliament.

HENRY III AND EDWARD I

Henry III was a petulant, erratic monarch: pious without being holy, bookish without being wise. Surrounding himself with foreign favorites and intoxicated by grandiose, impractical foreign projects, he ignored the advice of his barons and gradually lost their confidence.

Beginnings of Parliament

Ever since its beginning, the English monarchy had customarily arrived at important decisions of policy with the advice of a royal council of nobles, prelates, and officials. In Anglo-Saxon times, this council was called the witenagemot; after 1066 it was known as the *curia regis*. Its composition had always been vague, and it had never possessed anything resembling a veto power over royal decisions. But many Englishmen, particularly among the upper classes, put much importance in the fact that royal policies were framed in consultation with the lay and ecclesiastical magnates.

Traditionally, English royal councils were of two types. Ordinary royal business was conducted in a small council consisting of the king's household officials and whatever barons happened to be at court at the time. But in moments of crisis, or when some important decision was pending, the kings supplemented their normal coterie of advisers by summoning the important noblemen and churchmen of the realm to meet as a great council. It was this great baronial council that eventually evolved into Parliament.

A key factor in the evolution from great council to Parliament was the trend in the thirteenth century toward including representatives of the county gentry and the townsmen alongside the great barons and prelates. This development resulted from the royal policy, particularly evident after Magna Carta, of summoning the great council for the purpose of obtaining approval for some uncustomary tax. As wealth gradually seeped downward into the sub-baronial classes, the king found it expedient to obtain the consent of these lesser orders to new royal taxes by summoning their representatives to the great council.

Henry III and the Barons

The vigorous baronial opposition to Henry III arose from the fact that he summoned the great council not for the purpose of consulting his magnates on policy matters but chiefly for the purpose of obtaining their consent to new taxes. The barons resented being asked to finance chimerical foreign schemes in which they had not been consulted and of which they disapproved. They might well have chosen as their motto, "No taxation without consultation." They responded to Henry's fiscal demands with increasing reluctance, until at last in 1258 the monarch's soaring debts brought on a financial crisis of major proportions. In order to obtain desperately needed financial support from his barons, King Henry submitted to a set of baronial limitations on royal power known as the *Provisions of Oxford.*

These Provisions went far beyond Magna Carta in providing machinery to force the king to govern according to good custom and in consultation with his magnates. The great council was to be summoned at least three times a year and was to include, along with its usual membership, 12 men "elected" by the "community"—in other words, chosen by the barons. These 12 were empowered to speak for the magnates in the great council, so that even if heavily outnumbered their authority would be great. The Provisions of Oxford also established a *Council of Fifteen,* chiefly baronial in composition, which shared with the king control over the royal administration. Specifically, the council was given authority over the exchequer and was empowered to appoint the chancellor and other high officers of state.

The Provisions of Oxford proved premature, and the governmental system that they established turned out to be unworkable because of baronial factionalism. Their importance lies in the fact that they disclose clearly the attitude of many mid-thirteenth-century barons toward the royal administration. These magnates had no thought of abolishing the enlightened administrative and legal achievements of the past two centuries or of weakening the central government. Their interests were national rather than parochial, and they sought to exert a degree of control over the royal administration rather than dismantle it. Most of them acted as they did, not on the basis of theoretical abstractions, but because they thought it necessary to curb an incompetent, arbitrary, spendthrift king.

With the failure of the Provisions, Henry resumed exclusive control over his government and returned to the arbitrary policies that his barons found so distasteful. At length, baronial discontent exploded into open rebellion. The barons, led by Simon de Montfort, defeated the royal army at Lewes in 1264 and captured Henry himself. For the next 15 months Simon ruled England in the king's name, sharing authority with two baronial colleagues and a committee of magnates similar to that of the Provisions of Oxford. The rule of Simon de Montfort and his committee was augmented periodically by meetings of the great council—now commonly called "parliaments." Simon's government was a product of the same philosophy that underlay the Provisions of Oxford, and like the government of the Provisions, it was weakened and ultimately brought to ruin by baronial factionalism.

In 1265 the monarchy rallied under the leadership of Henry's talented son, Edward. A baronial army was defeated at

Evesham, and Simon de Montfort's rebellion faltered and died.

Further Evolution of Parliament

But the effect of the uprising proved to be lasting. England had undergone an interesting experience in baronial government and, far more important, a significant step had been taken in the development of Parliament. Earlier in 1265 Simon de Montfort had summoned a great council—a parliament—which included for the first time all three of the classes that were to characterize the parliaments of the later Middle Ages. Simon de Montfort's parliament included, in addition to the barons, two knights from every shire and two burghers from every town. Simon's chief motive in summoning this parliament was probably to broaden the base of his rebellion, but in later years parliaments were summoned for many purposes: to sit as a high court of law, to advise the king on important matters of policy, to declare their support in moments of crisis, and to give their consent to the ever-increasing royal taxes.

The English Parliament was built on a sturdy foundation of local government, and all three of the major parliamentary orders—barons, burghers, and shire knights—brought with them a wealth of local political experience. The burghers in Parliament were usually veterans of town government. The shire knights had long been involved in the administration of the counties and the county courts. Intermediate between the baronial nobility and the peasantry, these men constituted a separate class—a country gentry—rooted to their shires and their ancestral estates, experienced in local government, and well suited to represent their counties in Parliament.

In 1272 Henry III was succeeded by his son, Edward I (1272–1307), a far wiser man than his father. Edward I was a monarch of strong will and independence, but he had the sagacity to take the barons into his confidence and he was successful by and large in winning their support. Although he, like his father, regarded parliaments chiefly as means of winning approval for new taxes, he used them for many other purposes as well. He summoned parliaments frequently and experimented endlessly in their composition. In the later years of his reign the inclusion of shire knights and townsmen became customary. It was not until the fourteenth century, however, that the knights and burghers began meeting separately from the barons, thereby giving birth to the great parliamentary division into Lords and Commons.

As the thirteenth century closed, the actual powers of parliaments remained vague and their composition was still fluid. At best, they might bargain discreetly with the king for concessions in return for financial aid. Still, a beginning had been made. The deep-rooted medieval concept of limited monarchy had given rise to an institution that would develop over the centuries into a keystone of representative government. There was nothing remotely democratic about the parliaments that Edward I summoned. He regarded them as instruments of royal policy and used them to aid and strengthen the monarchy rather than limit it. Yet ultimately, Parliament was to be the crucial institutional bridge between medieval feudalism and modern democracy.

Edward I

The reign of Edward I witnessed the culmination of many trends in English law and administration that had been developing throughout the High Middle Ages. Edward was a great systematizer, and in his hands the royal administrative struc-

Parliament of Edward I. The Prince of Wales sits at his left and the king of Scotland at his right. The smaller figures in the foreground are the secular nobility and the bishops and abbots.

ture and the common law acquired the shape and coherence that they were to retain in future centuries.

The four chief agencies of royal government under Edward I were the chancery, the exchequer, the council, and the household. Chancery and exchequer were by now both permanently established at Westminster. The chancery remained the royal secretarial office, and its chief officer, the chancellor, was the custodian of the great seal by which royal documents were authenticated. A staff of professional chancery clerks prepared the numerous letters and charters by which the king made his will known, and preserved copies of them for future reference. The exchequer, headed by a royal official known as the treasurer, continued to serve, as it had for nearly two centuries, as the king's accounting agency. By now it supervised the accounts not only of sheriffs but of many other local officials who were charged with collecting royal revenues.

Unlike the chancery and exchequer, the council and household accompanied the king on his endless travels. Since meetings of the great council were coming more and more to be referred to as "parliaments," the "council" in Edward's government is to be identified with the earlier "small council." It was a permanent group of varied and changing membership, consisting of judges, administrators, and magnates, who advised the king on routine matters. In the Provisions of Oxford the barons had endeavored to dominate the council, but in Edward's reign it was firmly under royal control. The household was a royal government in miniature, with its own writing clerks supervised by the keeper of the privy seal and its own financial office known as the "wardrobe." By means of his household administration the king could govern on the move, without the necessity of routing all his business through Westminster.

Royal government in the countryside continued to depend on sheriffs and itinerant justices, whose duties and responsibilities were defined and regularized as never before. But now other royal servants were working alongside them: coroners, who were charged with investigating felonies; keepers of the peace, whose duty it was to apprehend criminals; assessors, tax collectors, customs officials, and others—local men, for the most part, who were responsible for serving the king in their native districts.

The royal legal system was also taking permanent form. Cases of singular importance were brought before the king himself, sitting in Parliament or surrounded by his council. Less important cases were handled by the king's itinerant justices or by one of the three royal courts sitting at Westminster. These three were the courts of the *king's bench,* which heard cases of particular royal concern; *exchequer,* which, besides its fiscal responsibilities, heard cases touching on the royal revenues; and *common pleas,* which had jurisdiction over most remaining types of cases. These three courts were all staffed with highly trained professionals—lawyers or, in the case of the exchequer, experienced accountants. By Edward I's day the royal judicial system had come of age.

Like his predecessors, Edward worked toward the expansion of royal justice over private justice. From the beginning of his reign he issued numerous writs of *quo warranto* (by what warrant?), which obliged noblemen who claimed the right of private legal jurisdiction to prove their claims. They might do so either by producing royal charters granting such jurisdictional privileges or by demonstrating that they and their predecessors had exercised such rights since before the reign of Richard I. In 1290 Edward issued the statute of *Quo Warranto,* which quashed all private jurisdictions unsupported by royal charter, no matter how ancient such jurisdiction might be. By means of these policies, Edward eliminated a good number of private jurisdictional franchises, and, perhaps more important still, made it clear that all remaining private franchises were exercised through royal license and royal suffrance. The absolute supremacy of royal jurisdiction was at last established beyond question.

Edward's reign was marked by the appearance of a great many royal statutes—issued by the king in Parliament—which elaborated and systematized royal administrative and legal procedures in many different ways. Law had formerly been regarded as a matter of custom; the king might interpret or clarify it, but did not have the right to make a new law. As ancient Germanic tradition had it, the king was bound by the customs of his people. It is not always possible to distinguish between the act of clarifying or elab-

The medieval concern with the idea of justice helped to reinforce the policy of establishing a nationwide system of royal courts to supervise that of the feudal magistrates. This illumination from a fifteenth-century manuscript shows the court of the King's Bench. In the foreground are prisoners awaiting sentence.

480   Church and State in the High Middle Ages

orating old law and making new law, and many of Edward's predecessors had been lawmakers whether they admitted the fact or not. But only in the later thirteenth century did Englishmen begin to recognize that their government had the power to legislate. Even in Edward's day original legislation was such a novel and solemn affair that the king issued his statutes only with the approval of the "community of the realm" as expressed in his parliaments. Edward dominated his parliaments, and his statutes were unquestionably products of the royal initiative, but it is nevertheless significant that in his reign the role of parliaments in the making of law was clearly established. In the course of the fourteenth century, Parliament employed its power of approving royal taxes to win control of the legislative process itself.

Thus, Edward I was a crucial figure in the development of English law. He completed the great work of his predecessors in creating an effective and complex royal administrative system, bringing feudal justice under royal control, and building a comprehensive body of common law. More than that, he solidified the concept of original legislation and nurtured the developing institution of Parliament, thereby setting into motion forces that would have an immense impact on England's future.

Edward was also a skillful and ambitious warrior. He brought to a decisive end the centuries-long military struggle along the Welsh frontier by conquering Wales altogether in a whirlwind campaign of 1282–83. He granted his eldest son the title "Prince of Wales," which male heirs-apparent to the English throne have held to this day. By a ruthless exploitation of the traditional English overlordship over the Scottish realm he came very near to conquering Scotland and was foiled only by the dogged determination of the Scottish hero-king, Robert Bruce. His war with Philip IV of France was expensive and inconclusive, but it did succeed in preserving English lordship over Gascony which had been seriously threatened by French aggression. These wars gradually exhausted the royal treasury, and during the latter portion of his reign, Edward was faced with growing baronial and popular opposition to his expensive policies. But the king was able to ride out this opposition by making timely concessions: reissuing Magna Carta and recognizing Parliament's right to approve all extraordinary taxation. At his death in 1307, Edward left behind him a realm exhausted by his prodigious foreign and domestic activities but firmly under his control. Edward's England was still, in spirit, a feudal kingdom rather than a modern nation, but feudalism was waning and the initial steps toward nationhood had been taken.

The most significant of all Edward's contributions was, in the long run, his policy of developing Parliament into an integral organ of government. It is ironic, therefore, that King Edward looked upon Parliament as a source of strength to the crown and a useful instrument for raising the necessary revenues to support his far-flung projects. He would have been appalled to learn that his royal descendants would one day be figurehead kings and that Parliament was destined to rule England.

C. France in the High Middle Ages

THE CAPETIANS

Weakness of the First Capetians

When William of Normandy conquered England in 1066, the French monarchy exerted a feeble control over a small territory around Paris and Orleans known as the Île de France and was virtually powerless in the lands beyond. To be sure, the French kings had as their vassals great feudal magnates such as the dukes of Normandy and Aquitaine and the counts of Anjou, Flanders, and Champagne, but vassalage was a slender bond when the king lacked the power to enforce his lordship. In theory the anointed king of the French, with his priestly charisma, with the sovereign power traditionally associated with royalty, and with the supreme feudal overlordship, was a mighty figure. But in grim reality he was impotent to control his great vassals and unable to keep order even in the Île de France itself.

Since 987 the French crown had been held by the Capetian dynasty. The achievement of the Capetians in the first century or so of their rule was modest enough. Their one triumph was their success in keeping the crown within their own family. The Capetians had gained the throne originally by virtue of being elected by the magnates of the realm, but from the first they sought to purge the monarchy of its elective character and to make it hereditary. This they accomplished by managing to produce male heirs at the right moment and by arranging for the new heir to be crowned before the old king died. They may have been aided by the fact that the crown was not a sufficiently alluring prize to attract powerful usurpers.

Capetian Policy

In the early twelfth century the Capetians remained weaker than several of their own vassals. While vassal states such as Normandy and Anjou were becoming increasingly centralized, the Capetian Île de France was still ridden with fiercely insubordinate robber barons. If the Capetians were to realize the immense potential of their royal title they had three great tasks before them: (1) to master and pacify the Île de France; (2) to expand their political and economic base by bringing additional territories under direct royal authority; and (3) to make their lordship over the great vassals real rather than merely theoretical.

During the twelfth and thirteenth centuries a series of remarkably able Capetian kings pursued and achieved these goals. Their success was so complete that by the opening of the fourteenth century the Capetians controlled all France, either directly or indirectly, and had developed an efficient, sophisticated royal bureaucracy. They followed no hard and fast formula. Rather their success depended on a combination of luck and ingenuity—on their clever exploitation of the powers which, potentially, they had always possessed as kings and feudal overlords. They were surprisingly successful in avoiding the family squabbles that had at times paralyzed Germany and England. Unlike the German monarchs, they maintained comparatively good relations with the papacy. They had the enormous good fortune of an unbroken sequence of direct male heirs from 987 to 1328. Above all, they seldom overreached themselves: they avoided grandiose schemes and spectacular strokes of policy, preferring instead to pursue modest, realistic goals. They extended their power gradually and cautiously by favorable marriages, by confiscating the fiefs of vassals who died without heirs, and by dispossessing vassals who violated their feudal obligations toward the monarchy. Yet the majority of the Capetians had no desire to absorb the territories of all their vassals. Rather they sought to build a kingdom with a substantial core of royal domain lands surrounded by the fiefs of loyal, obedient magnates.

Philip I and Louis VI

The first Capetian to work seriously toward the consolidation of royal control in the Île de France was King Philip I (1060–1108), a bloated, repugnant man who grasped the essential fact that the Capetian monarchy had to make its home base secure before turning to loftier goals. Philip's realistic policy was pursued far more vigorously by his son, Louis VI, "the Fat" (1108–37). Year after year, Louis the Fat battled the petty brigand-lords of the Île de France, besieged their castles one after another, and at last reduced them to obedience. At his death in 1137 the Île de France was relatively orderly and prosperous, and the French monarchy was pulling abreast of its greater vassals.

Louis the Fat received invaluable assistance in the later part of his reign from Abbot Suger of the great royal abbey of Saint Denis. This talented statesman served as chief royal adviser from 1130 to 1151 and labored hard and effectively to extend the king's sway, to systematize the royal administration, and, incidentally, to augment the wealth and prestige of Saint Denis.

Louis VII

Suger provided an invaluable element of continuity between the reigns of Louis the Fat and his son, Louis VII (1137–80), who pursued his father's goals with less than his father's skill. Pious and gentle, Louis VII was, in the words of a contemporary observer, "a very Christian king, if somewhat simple-minded." When Abbot Suger died in 1151, Louis was left to face unaided a new and formidable threat to the French monarchy. The Angevin Empire was just then in the process of formation, and in 1154 the ominous configuration was completed when Henry Plantagenet, count of Anjou and duke of Normandy and Aquitaine, acceded to the English throne as King Henry II. Louis VII sought to embarrass his mighty vassal by encouraging Henry's sons to rebel, but his efforts were too halfhearted to be successful. Still, Louis's reign witnessed a significant extension of royal power. Indeed, as one historian has aptly said, it was under Louis VII that "the prestige of the French monarchy was decisively established."[1] The great vassals of the Crown, fearful of their powerful Angevin colleague and respectful of Louis's piety and impartiality, began for the first time to bring cases to the court of their royal overlord and to submit their disputes to his judgment. Churchmen and townsmen

[1] Robert Fawtier, *The Capetian Kings of France* (London: The Macmillan Co., 1960), p. 23.

alike sought his support in struggles with the nobility. These developments resulted not so much from royal initiative as from the fundamental trends of the age toward peace, order, and growing commercial activity. Frenchmen in increasing numbers were turning to their genial, unassuming monarch for succor and justice, and, little by little, Louis began to assume his rightful place as feudal suzerain and supreme sovereign of the realm.

PHILIP AUGUSTUS, LOUIS VIII, AND ST. LOUIS

Philip Augustus and the Angevin Empire

The French monarchy came of age under Louis VII's talented son, Philip II "Augustus" (1180–1223). By remorseless insistence on his feudal rights and by a policy of dextrous opportunism, Philip Augustus enlarged the royal territories enormously and, beyond the districts of direct royal jurisdiction, transformed the chaotic anarchy of the vassal states into an orderly hierarchy subordinate to the king.

Philip Augustus's great achievement was the destruction of the Angevin empire and the establishment of royal jurisdiction over Normandy, Anjou, and their dependencies. For two decades he plotted with dissatisfied members of the Angevin family against King Henry II and King Richard the Lion-Hearted, but it was not until the reign of King John (1199–1216) that his efforts bore fruit. Against John's notorious faithlessness and greed, Philip was able to play the role of the just lord rightfully punishing a disobedient vassal. And when Philip Augustus moved against Normandy in 1203–4, John's unpopularity played into his hands. The prize that Philip had sought so long was now won with surprising ease, and, once Normandy was conquered, John's remaining fiefs in northern France fell quickly. Ten years later, in 1214, Philip extinguished John's last hope of recovering the lost territories by winning his decisive victory over John's German allies at Bouvines.* Settling for good the question of Normandy and Anjou, Bouvines was also a turning point in the power balance between France and Germany in the High Middle Ages. Thereafter the waxing Capetian monarchy of France replaced the faltering kingdom of Germany as the great continental power in western Europe.

Capetian Government

Under Philip Augustus and his predecessors significant developments were occurring in the royal administrative system. The curia regis had assumed its place as the high feudal court of France and was proving an effective instrument for the assertion of royal rights over the dukes and counts. Hereditary noblemen who had traditionally served as local administrators in the royal territories were gradually replaced by salaried officials known as *baillis*. These new officials, whose functions were at once financial, judicial, military, and administrative, owed their positions to royal favor and were therefore fervently devoted to the interests of the crown. Throughout the thirteenth century the baillis worked tirelessly and often unscrupulously to erode the privileges of the feudal aristocracy and extend the royal sway. This intensely loyal and highly mobile bureaucracy, without local roots and without respect for feudal or local traditions, became in time a powerful instrument of royal absolutism. The baillis stood in sharp contrast to the local officials in England—the sheriffs and the shire knights—who were customarily drawn from the local gentry and whose

* See p. 456.

485   C. France in the High Middle Ages

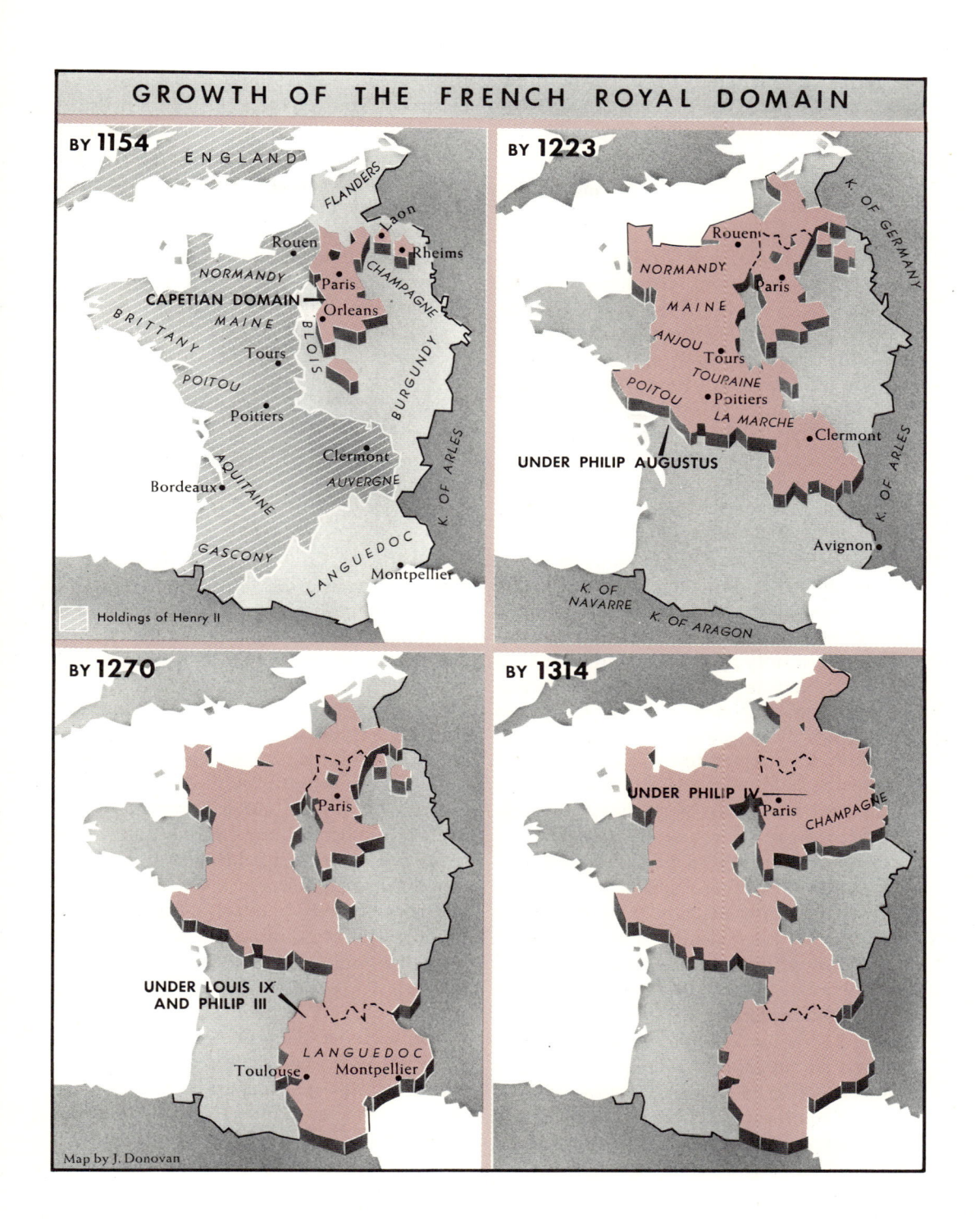

loyalties were divided between the monarch whom they served and the region and class from which they sprang.

Louis VIII

The closing years of Philip Augustus's reign were concurrent with the savage Albigensian Crusade in southern France, called by Philip's great contemporary, Pope Innocent III, against the supporters of the Albigensian heresy which was spreading rapidly through Languedoc and northern Italy.* Philip Augustus declined to participate personally in the crusade, but his son, Prince Louis, took an active part in it, and when the Prince succeeded to his father's throne in 1223 as Louis VIII (1223–26) he threw all the resources of the monarchy behind the southern campaign. The crusade succeeded in eliminating the Albigensian threat to Western Christendom but only by devastating large portions of southern France and exterminating the brilliant culture that had previously flourished there. Thenceforth southern France tended to be dominated by northern France, and the authority of the French monarchy was extended to the Mediterranean.

It may perhaps be surprising to discover that Louis VIII, who inherited a vastly expanded royal jurisdiction from his father and extended it still further himself, gave out about a third of the hard-won royal territories as fiefs to junior members of the Capetian family. These family fiefs, created out of the royal domain, are known as *appanages*. Their emergence should serve as a warning that the growth of the Capetian monarchy cannot be understood simply as a linear process of expanding the royal territories. The Capetians had no objection to vassals so long as they were obedient and subject to royal control. Indeed, given the limited transportation and communication facilities of twelfth and thirteenth-century France, the kingdom was far too large to be controlled directly by the monarchy. The new vassals, bound to the crown by strong family ties, played an essential role in the governance of the realm and strengthened rather than weakened the effectiveness of Capetian rule.

Character of St. Louis

Louis VIII died prematurely in 1226, leaving the land in the capable hands of his stern and pious Spanish widow, Blanche of Castile, who acted as regent for the boy-king Louis IX (1226–70), later St. Louis. Even after St. Louis came of age in 1234 he remained devoted to his mother, and Queen Blanche continued for years to be a dominant influence in the royal government.

St. Louis possessed both his mother's sanctity and his mother's firmness. Unlike some saint-kings, he was a strong monarch, obsessed with the obligation to rule justly and firmly and to promote moral rectitude throughout the kingdom of France. His sanctity, although thoroughly genuine, was perhaps too conventional. He persecuted heretics and crusaded against the Muslims. He once remarked that the only possible response for a Christian toward Jews who blasphemed was "to plunge his sword into their bellies as far as it would go." Still, in asserting these attitudes he was only mirroring the biases of his age. His reign was far different from that of Philip Augustus, for he oriented his life not toward political ends but toward what he conceived to be religious ends. He believed in war against the infidel, but he believed just as fervently in peace among Christian rulers. Accordingly, he arranged treaties with

---

* See pp. 428–29.

Henry III of England and with the king of Aragon which settled peacefully all outstanding disputes. He played the role of peacemaker among Christian princes and was even called upon to arbitrate between Henry and his barons. (He decided uncompromisingly in favor of royal authority, and the English barons were outraged.)

Administration and Cultural Life

St. Louis was content, in general, to maintain the royal rights established by his predecessors. His baillis and other officials were actually far more aggressive than he in extending the royal power. As one modern historian puts it, "in this reign monarchical progress was the complex result of the sanctity of a revered ruler, and the patient and obstinately aggressive policy of the king's servants." Indeed, St. Louis went to the length of establishing a system of itinerant royal inspectors—*enquêteurs*—who reported local grievances and helped keep the ambitious local officials in check.

In France under Louis IX medieval culture reached its climax. Town life flourished under St. Louis's rule, and in the towns magnificent Gothic cathedrals were being built. This was the great age of the medieval universities, and at the most distinguished university of the age, the University of Paris, some of the keenest intellects of medieval Europe—St. Bonaventure, St. Albertus Magnus, St. Thomas Aquinas—were assembled concurrently. The universities produced brilliant and subtle theologians, but they also produced learned and ambitious lawyers—men of a more secular cast who devoted their talents to the king and swelled the ranks of the royal bureaucracy. The Capetian government became steadily more complex, more efficient and, from the standpoint of the feudal nobility, more oppressive.

The corporate permanence of a great medieval university is symbolized by this fourteenth-century seal of the University of Paris.

PHILIP THE FAIR (1285–1314)

Philip III and Philip IV

St. Louis died in the midst of his second crusade. Under his successors the bureaucracy pursued its centralizing policies without restraint. The saint-king was succeeded by his inept son, Philip III (1270–85) and his frigid, unscrupulous grandson, Philip IV, "the Fair" or "the Handsome" (1285–1314). Philip the Fair was a mysterious, silent figure, conventionally pious, but with a flair for choosing able, aggressive and thoroughly unprincipled ministers—chiefly middle-class lawyers from southern France—who devoted themselves singlemindedly to the exaltation of the French monarchy.

Policies of the Reign

The reign of Philip the Fair was an age of unceasing royal aggression against the territories of neighboring states, against the papacy, and against the traditional privileges of the French nobility. Philip waged an indecisive war against King Edward I of England over Edward's remaining fiefs in southern France. He made a serious effort to absorb Flanders, imprisoning the Flemish count and ruling the district directly through a royal agent, but he was foiled by a bloody uprising of Flemish nobles and townsmen who won a stunning victory over him at the battle of Courtrai in 1302. He pursued a successful policy of nibbling aggression to the east against the Holy Roman Empire. He suppressed unscrupulously the rich crusading order of Knights Templars, ruined their reputation by an astonishingly modern campaign of vituperative propaganda, and confiscated their wealth. We have already seen how he struggled with Pope Boniface VIII, how his agents held Boniface captive for a brief time, and how he finally engineered the election of the pliable French Pope Clement V, who took up residence at Avignon.* Against his nobles he pursued a rigorously anti-feudal policy. He short-circuited the feudal hierarchy and demanded direct allegiance and obedience from all Frenchmen. All these activities were manifestations of the prevailing political philosophy of his reign: that the French king was by rights the secular and spiritual master of France and the dominating figure in western Europe. We encounter this same philosophy in ambitious French statesmen of succeeding centuries: in Cardinal Richelieu; in Louis XIV; and, stripped of its monarchical trappings, in Napoleon and De Gaulle.

Administrative Developments

Throughout the thirteenth century the French royal bureaucracy had been developing steadily. The royal revenues came to be handled by a special accounting bureau, roughly parallel to the English exchequer, called the *chambre des comtes.* The king's judicial business became the responsibility of a high court known as the *Parlement of Paris,* which was to play a highly significant political role in later centuries. Under Philip the Fair the bureaucracy became a refined and supple tool of the royal interest and its middle-class background and fanatical royalism gave the king a degree of independence from the nobility that was quite unknown in contemporary England.

Still, the king could not rule without a certain amount of support from his subjects. Philip's victory over the papacy on the issue of royal taxation of the clergy and his rape of the Knights Templars brought additional money into his treasury, but the soaring expenses of government and warfare forced him to seek ever-new sources of revenue and, as in England, to secure his subjects' approval of extraordinary taxation. But instead of summoning a great assembly—a parliament—for this purpose, he usually negotiated individually with various taxpaying groups.

The Estates General

Nevertheless it was under Philip the Fair that France's first great representative assemblies were summoned. Beginning in 1302, the *Estates General* was assembled from time to time, primarily for the purpose of giving formal support to the monarchy in moments of crisis—during the height of the struggle with Pope Boniface VIII, for example, or in the midst of the Knights Templars controversy. The assembly included members of the three great social classes, or "estates": the clergy, the nobility, and the townsmen. It continued to meet occasionally during the succeeding centuries, but it never became a real organ of government as did Parliament in England. Its failure resulted in

---

* See pp. 460–62.

part from a premature and unsuccessful bid for power during the fourteenth century in the midst of the Hundred Years' War. But even under Philip the Fair the Estates General lacked the potential of the contemporary parliaments of England. It had no real voice in royal taxation and was therefore not in a position to bargain with the king through increasing control of the purse strings. It was not, as in England, an evolutionary outgrowth of the royal council, but rather an entirely separate, exotic body. There was no real opportunity for the townsmen and the gentry to join ranks as in the English House of Commons; lacking the important responsibilities in local government which fell on the English shire knights, the knights of France remained an inarticulate and subordinate part of the aristocratic class. Above all, the French nobility and bourgeoisie lagged far behind the English in developing a national consciousness of a feeling of cohesion. Late-thirteenth-century France was too large, too heterogeneous, and too recently consolidated under royal authority for its inhabitants to have acquired a meaningful sense of identification as a people. Their outlook remained provincial. (See Table II.)

Yet despite the significant differences between the English Parliament and the French Estates General, the two institutions had much in common. Both were products of a European-wide evolution out of feudal monarchy and out of the vague but pervading medieval notion of government under the law or government by the consent of the realm. Similar representative institutions were emerging concurrently all over Western Christendom: in the Christian kingdoms of Spain, in Italy under Frederick II, in the rising principalities of Germany, and in innumerable counties, duchies, and communes across Europe. Of these many experiments only the English Parliament survives today. But Parliament was not merely the outgrowth of an isolated English experience; it was one particular expression of a broad and fundamental trend in medieval European civilization.

TABLE II

Chronology of the English and French Monarchies in the High Middle Ages

England
1066: Norman Conquest of England
1066–1087: Reign of William the Conqueror
1087–1100: Reign of William II
1100–1135: Reign of Henry I
1135–1154: Disputed succession: King Stephen
1154–1189: Reign of Henry II
1189–1199: Reign of Richard the Lion-Hearted
1199–1216: Reign of John
1203–1204: Loss of Normandy
1215: Magna Carta
1216–1272: Reign of Henry III
1258: Provisions of Oxford
1264–1265: Simon de Montfort's rebellion
1272–1303: Reign of Edward I

France
987–1328: Rule of the Capetian Dynasty
1060–1108: Reign of Philip I
1108–1137: Reign of Louis VI, "the Fat"
1137–1180: Reign of Louis VII
1180–1223: Reign of Philip II, "Augustus"
1214: Battle of Bouvines
1223–1226: Reign of Louis VIII
1226–1270: Reign of St. Louis IX
1270–1285: Reign of Philip III
1285–1314: Reign of Philip IV, "the Fair"

Selected Readings

Barraclough, Geoffrey. *Medieval Germany, 911–1250*. 2 vols. Oxford: Basil Blackwell & Mott, 1961.

Volume 1 is a valuable introductory essay by Barraclough; volume 2 consists of specialized studies by German scholars in English translation.

*Barraclough, Geoffrey. *The Medieval Papacy*. New York: Harcourt Brace Jovanovich, 1968.

A thoughtful, interpretative survey.

Brown, R. Allen. *The Normans and the Norman Conquest*. London: Constable & Co., 1969.

A well-written, slightly pro-Norman account of the conquest and its background and aftermath.

*Brooke, Christopher. *From Alfred to Henry III*. New York: Thomas Nelson, 1966 (originally published 1961).

Accurate, up-to-date, and interestingly written.

*Douglas, David. *William the Conqueror*. Berkeley and Los Angeles: University of California Press, 1964.

This beautifully written work of scholarship is the best account of William the Conqueror. Due attention is given to William's background and achievements in Normandy.

*Fawtier, Robert. *The Capetian Kings of France*. New York: St. Martin's Press, 1960.

A short, masterful treatment, highly recommended.

Heer, Friedrich. *The Holy Roman Empire*. New York: Praeger Publishers, 1968.

A brilliantly written study that defends the empire as a viable "federal" system.

*Hill, Bennett D. *Church and State in the Middle Ages*. New York: John Wiley & Sons, 1970.

Sources and modern interpretative essays on key church-state issues from the time of the New Testament to Pope Boniface VIII, including the controversies surrounding Gregory VII, Becket, and Innocent III.

*Hollister, C. Warren. *The Impact of the Norman Conquest*. New York: John Wiley & Sons, 1969.

A collection of diverse scholarly views and original sources relating to the question of the Norman Conquest's effect on history.

*Jones, Thomas M. *The Becket Controversy*. New York: John Wiley & Sons, 1970.

A well-organized and thoughtfully interpreted collection of contemporary accounts and later interpretations by historians of the eighteenth, nineteenth, and twentieth centuries, concluding with excerpts from three modern plays about Becket.

Kantorowicz, Ernst. *Frederick II*. New York: Frederick Ungar Publishing Co., 1957.

An excellent biography. Kantorowicz's conclusions should be compared with those of Barraclough in his Origins of Modern Germany (Capricorn Books).

*Kelly, Amy. *Eleanor of Aquitaine and the Four Kings.* New York: Random House, Vintage Books, 1957.
Sound and entertaining. The kings are Eleanor's two husbands, Louis III and Henry II, and her two sons, Richard and John.

Otto of Freising. *The Deeds of Frederick Barbarossa.* Translated by C. C. Mierow and R. Emery. New York: Columbia University Press, 1953.
A good example of medieval historical writing.

Poole, A. L. *From Domesday Book to Magna Carta: 1087–1216.* 2d ed. New York: Oxford University Press, 1955.
This book, like F. M. Stenton's Anglo-Saxon England, is a volume in the monumental Oxford History of England. Poole's volume, covering the period from 1087 to 1216, is more genial in style than many of its companions.

Powicke, F. M. *The Thirteenth Century: 1216–1307.* New York: Oxford University Press, 1953.
This volume of the Oxford History of England is full, authoritative, and highly detailed.

Russell, Jeffrey B. *A History of Medieval Christianity.* New York: Thomas Y. Crowell Co., 1968.
This compact survey interprets medieval Christianity as evolving dialectically between the two poles of charisma and law—"prophecy and order."

Tellenbach, Gerd. *Church, State and Christian Society at the Time of the Investiture Contest.* New York: Humanities Press, 1940.
The finest analysis of the Investiture Controversy in English.

Ullmann, Walter. *The Growth of Papal Government in the Middle Ages.* 2d ed. New York: Barnes & Noble, 1962.
An intellectual history of the medieval papal ideology.

Wilkinson, Bertie. *The Creation of the Medieval Parliament.* New York: John Wiley & Sons, 1971.
A stimulating, original essay illustrated by contemporary sources and excerpts from modern scholarly writings.

Asterisk (*) denotes paperback.

CHAPTER XI
Literature, Art, and Thought in the High Middle Ages

A. The Dynamics of High Medieval Culture: Literature and Art

Thirteenth-century Paris has been described as the Athens of medieval Europe. And despite all the obvious and fundamental differences that separate the golden age of Periclean Athens from the golden age of thirteenth-century France, these two epochs did have something in common. Both developed within the framework of traditional beliefs and customs which had long existed but were being challenged and transformed by powerful new forces—a new rationalism, a new art, a burgeoning of commerce, an expansion of frontiers, and an influx of ideas from other cultures. The socioreligious world of the Early Middle Ages, like the socioreligious world of the early Greek polis, was parochial and traditionbound. As the two cultures passed into their golden ages, the values of the past were assailed by new intellectual currents, and the old economic patterns were expanded and transformed. Yet, for a time, these dynamic new forces resulted in a heightened cultural expression of the old values. The Parthenon, dedicated to the venerable civic goddess Athena, and the Gothic cathedrals of Notre Dame (Our Lady) that were rising at Paris, Chartres, Reims, Amiens, and elsewhere, were all products of a new creativity harnessed to the service of an older ideology. In the long run, the new creative impulses would subvert the old ideologies, but for a time, both ancient Greece and medieval Europe achieved an elusive equilibrium between old and new. The results, in both cases, were spectacular.

Thus, twelfth and thirteenth-century Europe succeeded, by and large, in keeping its vibrant, audacious culture within the bounds of traditional Catholic Christianity. And the Christian world view gave form and orientation to the new creativity. Despite the intense dynamism of the period, it can still be called, with some semblance of accuracy, an Age of Faith.

Europe in the High Middle Ages underwent an artistic and intellectual awakening that affected every imaginable form of expression. Significant creative work was done in literature, architecture, sculpture, law, philosophy, political theory, even science. By the close of the period, the foundations of the Western cultural tradition were firmly established. The pages that follow will provide only a glimpse at the achievements of this fertile era.

LITERATURE

Latin Literature

The literature of the High Middle Ages was abundant and richly varied. Poetry was written both in the traditional Latin—the universal scholarly language of medieval Europe—and in the vernacular languages of ordinary speech that had long been evolving in the various districts of Christendom. Traditional Christian piety found expression in a series of somber and majestic Latin hymns, whose mood is illustrated—through the clouded glass of translation—by these excerpts from "Jerusalem the Golden" (twelfth century):

> *The world is very evil, the times are waxing late,*
> *Be sober and keep vigil; the judge is at the gate.*
> . . . . .
> *Brief life is here our portion; brief sorrow, short-lived care.*
> *The life that knows no ending, the tearless life, is there.*
> . . . .
> *Jerusalem the Golden, with milk and honey blessed,*
> *Beneath thy contemplation sink heart and voice oppressed.*
> *I know not, O I know not, what social joys are there,*
> *What radiancy of glory, what light beyond compare.*

At the opposite end of the medieval Latin spectrum one encounters poetry of quite a different sort, composed by young, wandering scholars and aging nonstudents. The deliberate sensuality and blasphemy of their poems is an expression of student rebelliousness against the ascetic ideals of their elders:

> *For on this my heart is set, when the hour is neigh me,*
> *Let me in the tavern die, with a tankard by me,*
> *While the angels, looking down, joyously sing o'er me. . . .*

One of these wandering-scholar poems is an elaborate and impudent expansion of the Apostles' Creed. The phrase from the Creed, "I believe in the Holy Ghost, the Holy [Catholic] Church . . ." is embroidered as follows:

> *I believe in wine that's fair to see,*
> *And in the tavern of my host*
> *More than in the Holy Ghost*
> *The tavern will my sweetheart be,*
> *And the Holy Church is not for me.*

These sentiments do not betoken a sweeping trend toward agnosticism. Rather, they are distinctively medieval expressions of the perennial student irreverence toward established institutions. A modern student activist shouting obscenities in a D.A.R. meeting would create much the same effect, though less cleverly.

Vernacular Literature; the Epic

For all its originality, the Latin poetry of the High Middle Ages was outstripped both in quantity and in variety of expres-

494   Literature, Art, and Thought in the High Middle Ages

sion by vernacular poetry. The drift toward emotionalism, which we have already noted in medieval piety, was closely paralleled by the evolution of vernacular literature from the martial epics of the eleventh century to the delicate and sensitive romances of the thirteenth. Influenced by the sophisticated, romanticism of the southern troubadour tradition, the bellicose spirit of northern France gradually softened.

In the eleventh and early twelfth centuries, heroic epics known as *chansons de geste* (songs of great deeds) were enormously popular among the feudal nobility of northern France. These chansons arose out of the earlier heroic tradition of the Teutonic north that had produced such moody and violent masterpieces as *Beowulf*. The hero Beowulf is a lonely figure who fights monsters, slays dragons, and pits his strength and courage against a wild, windswept wilderness. The chansons de geste reflect the somewhat more civilized and Christianized age of feudalism. Still warlike and heroic in mood, they often consisted of exaggerated accounts of events in the reign of Charlemagne. The most famous of all the chansons de geste, the *Song of Roland*, tells of a heroic, bloody battle between a horde of Muslims and the detached rearguard of Charlemagne's army as it was withdrawing from Spain. Like old-fashioned Westerns, the chansons de geste were packed with action, and their heroes tended to steer clear of sentimental entanglements with women. Warlike prowess, courage, and loyalty to one's lord and fellows-in-arms were the virtues stressed in these heroic epics. The battle descriptions, often characterized by gory realism, tell of Christian knights fighting with almost superhuman strength against fantastic odds. The heroes of the chansons are not only proud, loyal and skilled at arms, but also capable of experiencing deep emotions—weeping at the death of their comrades and appealing to God to receive the souls of the fallen. In short, the chansons de geste mirror the bellicose spirit and sense of military brotherhood that characterized the feudal knighthood of the eleventh-century Europe:

> *Turpin of Rheims, his horse beneath him slain,*
> *And with four lance wounds he himself in pain,*
> *Hastens to rise, brave lord, and stand erect.*
> *He looks on Roland, runs to him, and says*
> *Only one thing: "I am not beaten yet!*
> *True man fails not, while life in him is left."*
> *He draws Almace, his keen-edged steel-bright brand*
> *And strikes a thousand strokes amid the press.*
> . . . .
> *Count Roland never loved a recreant,*
> *Nor a false heart, nor yet a braggart jack,*
> *Nor knight that was not faithful to his lord.*
> *He cried to Turpin—churchman militant—*
> *"Sir, you're on foot, I'm on my horse's back.*
> *For love of you, here will I make my stand,*
> *And side by side we'll take both good and bad.*
> *I'll not leave you for any mortal man."*
> . . . .
> *Now Roland feels that he is nearing death;*
> *Out of his ears the brain is running forth.*
> *So for his peers he prays God call them all,*
> *And for himself St. Gabriel's aid implores.*

Roland's rear guard is slain to a man, but the Lord Charlemagne returns to avenge him, and a furious battle ensues:

> *Both French and Moors are fighting with a will.*
> *How many spears are shattered! lances split!*
> *Whoever saw those shields smashed all to bits,*
> *Heard the bright hauberks grind, the mail rings rip,*
> *Heard the harsh spear upon the helmet ring,*
> *Seen countless knights out of the saddle spilled,*
> *And all the earth with death and deathcries filled,*
> *Would long recall the face of suffering!*

The French are victorious, Charlemagne himself defeats the Moorish emir in single combat, and Roland is avenged:

> *The Muslims fly, God will not have them stay.*
> *All's done, all's won, the French have gained the day.*

The Lyric

During the middle and later twelfth century the martial spirit of northern French literature was gradually transformed by the influx of the romantic troubadour tradition of southern France. In Provence, Toulouse, and Aquitaine a rich, colorful culture had been developing in the eleventh and twelfth centuries, and out of this vivacious society came a lyric poetry of remarkable sensitivity and enduring value. The lyric poets of the south were known as *troubadours*. Many of them were court minstrels, but some, including Duke William IX of Aquitaine, were members of the upper nobility. Their poems were far more intimate and personal than the chansons de geste, and placed much greater emphasis upon romantic love. The wit, delicacy, and romanticism of the troubadour lyrics disclose a more genteel and sophisticated nobility than that of the feudal north—a nobility that preferred songs of love to songs of war. Indeed, medieval southern France, under the influence of Islamic courtly poetry and ideas, was the source of the romantic-love tradition of Western civilization. It was from southern France that Europe derived such concepts as the idealization of women, the importance of male gallantry and courtesy, and the impulse to embroider relations between man and woman with potent emotional overtones of eternal oneness, undying devotion, agony, and ecstacy. One of the favorite themes of the lyric poets was the hopeless love—the unrequited love from afar:

> *I die of wounds from blissful blows,*
> *And love's cruel stings dry out my flesh,*
> *My health is lost, my vigor goes,*
> *And nothing can my soul refresh.*
> *I never knew so sad a plight,*
> *It should not be, it is not right.*
> . . . .
> *I'll never hold her near to me*
> *My ardent joy she'll ever spurn,*
> *In her good grace I cannot be*
> *Nor even hope, but only yearn.*
> *She tells me nothing, false or true,*
> *And neither will she ever do.*

The author of these lines, Jaufré Rudel (fl. 1148), unhappily and hopelessly in love, finds consolation in his talents as a poet, of which he has an exceedingly high opinion. The poem concludes on a much more optimistic note:

> *Make no mistake, my song is fair,*
> *With fitting words and apt design.*
> *My messenger would never dare*
> *To cut it short or change a line.*
> . . . .
> *My song is fair, my song is good,*
> *'Twill bring delight, as well it should.*

Many such poems were written in southern France during the twelfth century. The recurring theme is the poet's passionate love for a lady. Occasionally, however, the pattern is reversed, as in the following lyric poem by the poetress Beatritz de Dia (fl. 1160):

> I live in grave anxiety
> For one fair knight who loved me so.
> It would have made him glad to know
> I loved him too—but silently.
> I was mistaken, now I'm sure,
> When I withheld myself from him.
> My grief is deep, my days are dim,
> And life itself has no allure.
>
> I wish my knight might sleep with me
> And hold me naked to his breast.
> And on my body take his rest,
> And grieve no more, but joyous be.
> My love for him surpasses all
> The loves that famous lovers knew.
> My soul is his, my body, too,
> My heart, my life, are at his call.
>
> My most beloved, dearest friend,
> When will you fall into my power?
> That I might lie with you an hour,
> And love you 'til my life should end!
> My heart is filled with passion's fire.
> My well-loved knight, I grant thee
>   grace,
> To hold me in my husband's place,
> And do the things I so desire.

Not all the lyric poems of southern France took love or life quite so seriously. In some, one encounters a refreshing lightness and wit. The following verses, by Duke William IX of Aquitaine (1071–1127), typify the vivacious spirit of the South and contrast sharply with the serious, heroic mood of the chansons de geste:

> I'll make some verses just for fun,
> Not of myself or anyone,
> Nor of great deeds that knights have
>   done
> Nor lovers true.
> I made them riding in the sun,
> My horse helped, too.
> When I was born, I'm not aware,
> I'm neither gay nor in despair,
> Nor stiff, nor loose, nor do I care,
> Nor wonder why.
> Since meeting an enchantress fair,
> Bewitched am I.
>
> Living for dreaming I mistake,
> I must be told when I'm awake,
> My mood is sad, my heart may break,
> Such grief I bear!
> But never mind, for heaven's sake,
> I just don't care.
>
> I'm sick to death, or so I fear,
> I cannot see, but only hear.
> I hope that there's a doctor near,
> No matter who.
> If he can heal me, I'll pay dear,
> If not, he's through.
>
> My lady fair is far away,
> Just who, or where, I cannot say,
> She tells me neither yea nor nay,
> Yet I'm not blue,
> So long as all those Normans stay
> Far from Poitou.
>
> My distant love I so adore,
> Though me she has no longing for,
> We've never met, and furthermore—
> To my disgrace—
> I've other loves, some three or four,
> To fill her place.
>
> This verse is done, as you can see,
> And by your leave, dispatched 'twill be
> To one who'll read it carefully
> In far Anjou.
> Its meaning he'd explain to me
> If he but knew.

These verses, only a brief sampling of the fascinating lyrics of southern France—and distorted by translation—may provide some feeling for the rich and delightful civilization that flourished there in the twelfth century and disintegrated with the savage horrors of the Albigensian Crusade.

497   A. High Medieval Culture: Literature and Art

The Romance

Midway through the twelfth century, the southern tradition of courtly love was brought northward to the court of Champagne and began to spread rapidly across France, England, and Germany. As its influence grew, the northern knights discovered that more was expected of them than loyalty to their lords and a life of carefree slaughter. They were now expected to be gentlemen as well—to be courtly in manner and urbane in speech, to exhibit delicate, refined behavior in feminine company, and to idolize some noble lady. Such, briefly, were the ideals of courtly love. Their impact on the actual behavior of knights was distinctly limited, but their effect on the literature of northern Europe was revolutionary. Out of the convergence of vernacular epic and vernacular lyric there emerged a new poetic form known as the romance.

Like the chanson de geste, the romance was a long narrative poem, but like the southern lyric, it was sentimental and imaginative. It was commonly based on some theme from the remote past: the Trojan War, Alexander the Great, and, above all, King Arthur—the half-legendary sixth-century British king. Arthur was transformed into an idealized twelfth-century monarch surrounded by charming ladies and chivalrous knights. His court at Camelot, as described by the late-twelfth-century French poet, Chrétien de Troyes, was a center of romantic love and refined religious sensitivity where knights worshipped their ladies, went on daring quests, and played out their chivalrous roles in a world of magic and fantasy.

In the chanson de geste the great moral imperative was loyalty to one's lord; in the romance it was love for one's lady. Several romances portray the old and new values in conflict. An important theme in both the Arthurian romances and the twelfth-century romance of *Tristan and Iseult* is a love affair between a vassal and his lord's wife. Love and feudal loyalty stand face to face, and love wins out. Tristan loves Iseult, the wife of his lord, King Mark of Cornwall. King Arthur's beloved knight Lancelot loves Arthur's wife, Guinevere. In both stories the lovers are ruined by their love, yet love they must—they have no choice—and although the conduct of Tristan and Lancelot would have been regarded by earlier standards as nothing less than treasonable, both men are presented sympathetically in the romances. Love destroys the lovers in the end, yet their destruction is romantic—even glorious. Tristan and Iseult die together,

Lancelot and Guinevere, an early depiction of the Arthurian legend. The widespread influence of this legend and its continuing popularity attest to its importance as one of the major literary creations of the Middle Ages.

and in their very death their love achieves its deepest consummation.

Alongside the theme of love in the medieval romances, and standing in sharp contrast to it, is the theme of Christian purity and dedication. The rough-hewn knight of old, having been taught to be courteous and loving, was now taught to be holy. Lancelot was trapped in the meshes of a lawless love, but his son, Galahad, became the prototype of the Christian knight—pure, holy, and chaste. And Perceval, another knight of the Arthurian circle, quested not for a lost loved one but for the Holy Grail of the Last Supper.

The romance flourished in twelfth- and thirteenth-century France and among the French-speaking nobility of England. It spread also into Italy and Spain, and became a crucial factor in the evolution of vernacular literature in Germany. The German poets, known as Minnesingers, were influenced by the French lyric and romance, but developed these literary forms along highly original lines. The Minnesingers produced their own deeply sensitive and mystical versions of the Arthurian stories which, in their exalted symbolism and profundity of emotion, surpass even the works of Chrétien de Troyes and his French contemporaries.

Aucassin et Nicolette; the Romance of the Rose

As the thirteenth century drew toward its close, the romance was becoming conventionalized and drained of inspiration. The love story of *Aucassin et Nicolette,* which achieved a degree of popularity, was actually a satirical romance in which the hero was much less heroic than heroes usually are, and a battle is depicted in which the opponents cast pieces of cheese at each other. Based on earlier Byzantine material, *Aucassin et Nicolette* makes mortal love take priority over salvation itself. Indeed, Aucassin is scornful of Heaven:

For into Paradise go only such people as these: There go those aged priests and elderly cripples and maimed ones who day and night stoop before altars and in the crypts beneath the churches; those who go around in worn-out cloaks and shabby old habits; who are naked and shoeless and full of sores; who are dying of hunger and of thirst, of cold and of misery. Such folks as these enter Paradise, and I will have nothing to do with them. I will go to Hell. For to Hell go the fair clerics and comely knights who are killed in tournaments and great wars, and the sturdy archer and the loyal vassal. I will go with them. There also go the fair and courteous ladies who have loving friends, two or three, together with their wedded lords. And there go the gold and silver, the ermine and all rich furs, the harpers and the minstrels, and the happy folk of the world. I will go with these, so long as I have Nicolette, my very sweet friend, at my side.

Another important product of thirteenth-century vernacular literature, the *Romance of the Rose,* was in fact not a romance in the ordinary sense but an allegory of the whole courtly love tradition in which the thoughts and emotions of the lover and his lady are personified in actual characters such as Love, Reason, Jealousy, and Fair-Welcome. Begun by William of Lorris as an idealization of courtly love, the *Romance of the Rose* was completed after William's death by Jean de Meun, a man of limited talent and bourgeois origin. Jean's contribution was long-winded and encyclopedic, and the poem as a whole lacks high literary distinction, yet it appealed to contemporaries and enjoyed a great vogue.

Fabliaux and Fables

Neither epic, lyric, nor romance had much appeal below the level of the landed aristocracy. The inhabitants of the rising towns had a vernacular literature all their own. From the bourgeoisie came the high medieval *fabliaux*, short satirical poems, filled with vigor and crude humor, which devoted themselves chiefly to ridiculing conventional morality. Priests and monks were portrayed as lechers, merchants' wives were easily and frequently seduced, and clever young men perpetually made fools of sober and stuffy merchants.

Medieval urban culture also produced the fable, or animal story, an allegory in the tradition of Aesop in which various stock characters in medieval society were presented as animals—thinly disguised. Most of the more popular fables dealt with Renard the Fox and were known collectively as the *Romance of Renard*. These tales constituted a ruthless parody of chivalric ideals in which the clever, unscrupulous Renard persistently outwitted King Lion and his loyal but stupid vassals. Thus, paradoxically, the medieval town, which produced such powerful waves of piety, was responsible for literary forms characterized chiefly by secularism, lasciviousness, and the ridiculing of customs and conventions. To balance the impression conveyed by the fabliaux and fables one most consider the great Romanesque and Gothic cathedrals, the *Song of Brother Sun* composed by that illustrious son of a medieval merchant, St. Francis of Assisi, and the deeply religious poetry of the Florentine Dante.

Dante

Vernacular poetry matured late in Italy, but in the works of Dante (1265–1321) it achieved its loftiest expression. Dante wrote on a wide variety of subjects, sometimes in Latin, more often in the Tuscan vernacular. He composed a series of lyric poems celebrating his love for the lady Beatrice, which are assembled, with prose commentaries, in his *Vita Nuova* ("The New Life"). Dante's lyrics reflect a more mystical and idealized love than that of the troubadours:

> A shining love comes from my lady's eyes,
> All that she looks on is made lovelier,
> And as she walks, men turn to gaze at her,
> Whoever meets her feels his heart arise.
> . . . .
> Humility, and hope that hopeth well,
> Come to the mind of one who hears her voice,
> And blessed is he who looks on her a while.
> Her beauty, when she gives her slightest smile
> One cannot paint in words, yet must rejoice
> In such a new and gracious miracle.

Firmly convinced of the literary potential of the Tuscan vernacular, Dante urged its use in his *De Vulgari Eloquentia*, which he wrote in Latin so as to appeal to scholars and writers who scorned the vulgar tongue. And he filled his own vernacular works with such grace and beauty as to convince by example those whom he could not persuade by argument. In his hands the Tuscan vernacular became the literary language of Italy.

Dante was no mere disembodied writer, but a man deeply immersed in the politics of his age. His experience brought him to the opinion that Italy's hope for peace lay in imperial domination and in divorcing the papacy from politics. Although futile and anachronistic in view of the Empire's impotence in Dante's time, these views were expressed forcefully in his great political essay, *On Monarchy*.

Dante's masterpiece was the *Divine Comedy*, written in the Tuscan vernacular. Abounding in allegory and symbolism, it encompasses in one majestic vision the entire universe of medieval man. Dante tells of his own journey through hell, purgatory, and paradise to the very presence of God. This device permits the poet to make devastating comments on past and contemporary history by placing all those of whom he disapproved—from local politicians to popes—in various levels of hell. Virgil, the archetype of ancient rationalism, is Dante's guide through hell and purgatory; the lady Beatrice, a symbol of purified love, guides him through the celestial spheres of paradise; and St. Bernard, the epitome of medieval sanctity, leads him to the threshold of God. The poem closes with Dante alone in the divine presence:

> Eternal Light, thou in thyself alone
> Abidest, and alone thine essence
>   knows,
> And loves, and smiles, self-knowing
>   and self-known. . . .
>   . . . .
> Here power failed to the high fantasy,
> But my desire and will were turned—as
>   one—
> And as a wheel that turneth evenly,
> By Holy Love, that moves the stars and
>   sun.

ARCHITECTURE AND SCULPTURE

The Romanesque Style

The High Middle Ages is one of the great epochs in the history of Western architecture. Stone churches, large and small, were built in prodigious numbers: in France alone, more stone was quarried during the High Middle Ages than by the pyramid and temple builders of ancient Egypt throughout its 3000-year history. But the real achievement of the medieval architects lay not in the immense scope of their activities but in the splendid originality of their aesthetic vision. Two great architectural styles dominated the age: the Romanesque style flourished in the eleventh century and early twelfth, and during the middle decades of the twelfth century gave way gradually to the Gothic style. From about 1150 to 1300 the greatest of the medieval Gothic cathedrals were built. Thereafter the Gothic builders, having exhausted the structural possibilities of their style, turned from basic innovation to decorative elaboration. But during the High Middle Ages Gothic architecture constituted one of humanity's most audacious and successful architectural experiments.

The evolution of high medieval architecture was shaped by two fundamental trends in medieval civilization. First, the great cathedrals were products of the urban revolution—of rising wealth, civic pride, and intense urban piety. Second, the evolution from Romanesque to Gothic parallels the shift in literature and piety toward emotional sensitivity and romanticism. Romanesque architecture, though characterized by an exceeding diversity of expression, tended toward the solemnity of earlier Christian piety and the uncompromising masculinity of the chansons de geste. Gothic architecture, on the other hand, is dramatic, upward-reaching, aspiring. To some historians the Gothic has seemed more feminine than the Romanesque, and it is true that a great many Gothic cathedrals were dedicated to Notre Dame.

The development from Romanesque to Gothic can be understood, too, as an evolution in the principles of structural engineering. The key architectural ingredient in the Romanesque churches was the round arch, which appears in their portals, their windows, their arcades, and the massive stone vaulting of their roofs. Romanesque roof design was based on various elaborations of the round arch, such as the barrel vault and the cross vault (see illustration). The immense downward and outward thrusts of these heavy stone roofs required massive pillars and thick supporting walls.

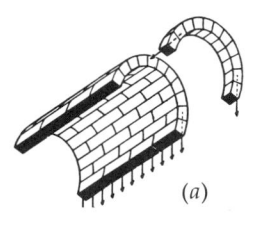

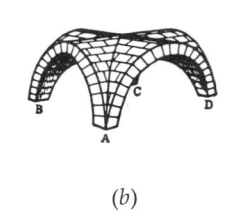

ABOVE:
Romanesque tympanum from the Cathedral of St. Lazare at Autun.

LEFT:
(a) *Barrel vault*
(b) *Cross vault*

BELOW:
"Adoration of the Magi," Romanesque cloister capital, Moissac, 1100.

RIGHT:
Romanesque nave capital, Anzy-le-Duc, late eleventh century.

RIGHT:
Detail of right portal, Vezelay, begun 1120.

BELOW:
Romanesque cloister capital, Moissac, 1100.

RIGHT: *Gothic interior: Bourges cathedral, begun 1195.*

BOTTOM RIGHT: *The flying buttresses of Reims cathedral.*

ABOVE: *Nave looking east (showing vault ribs), Notre-Dame in Paris, begun 1163.*

RIGHT: *Gothic exterior: Reims cathedral, 1211–90.*

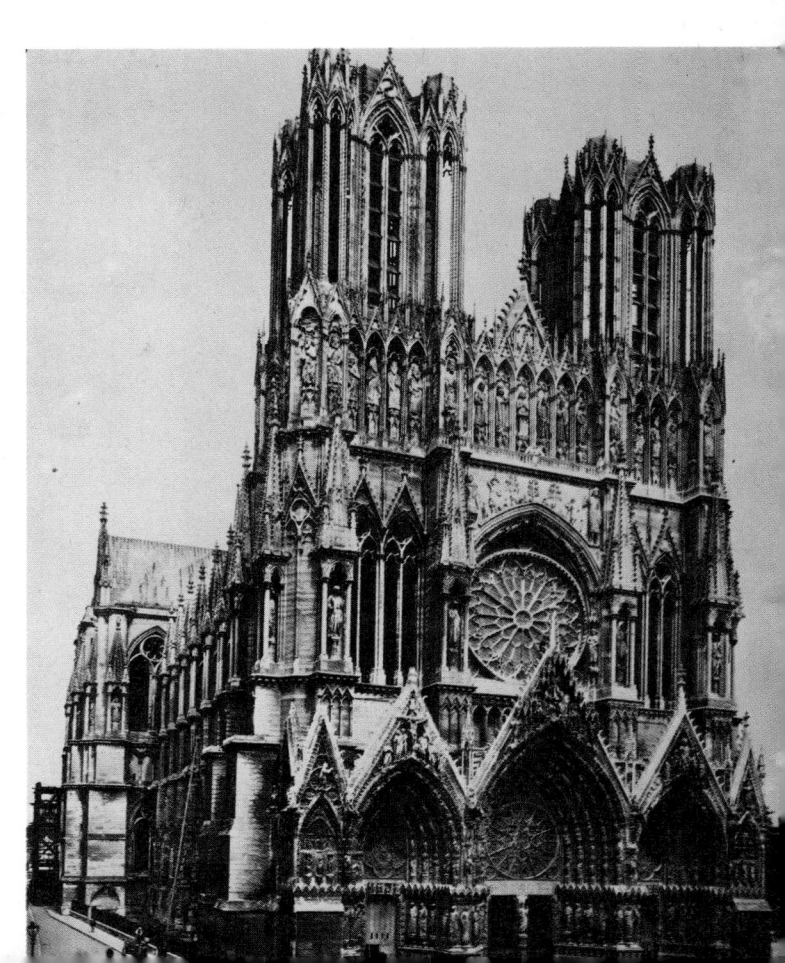

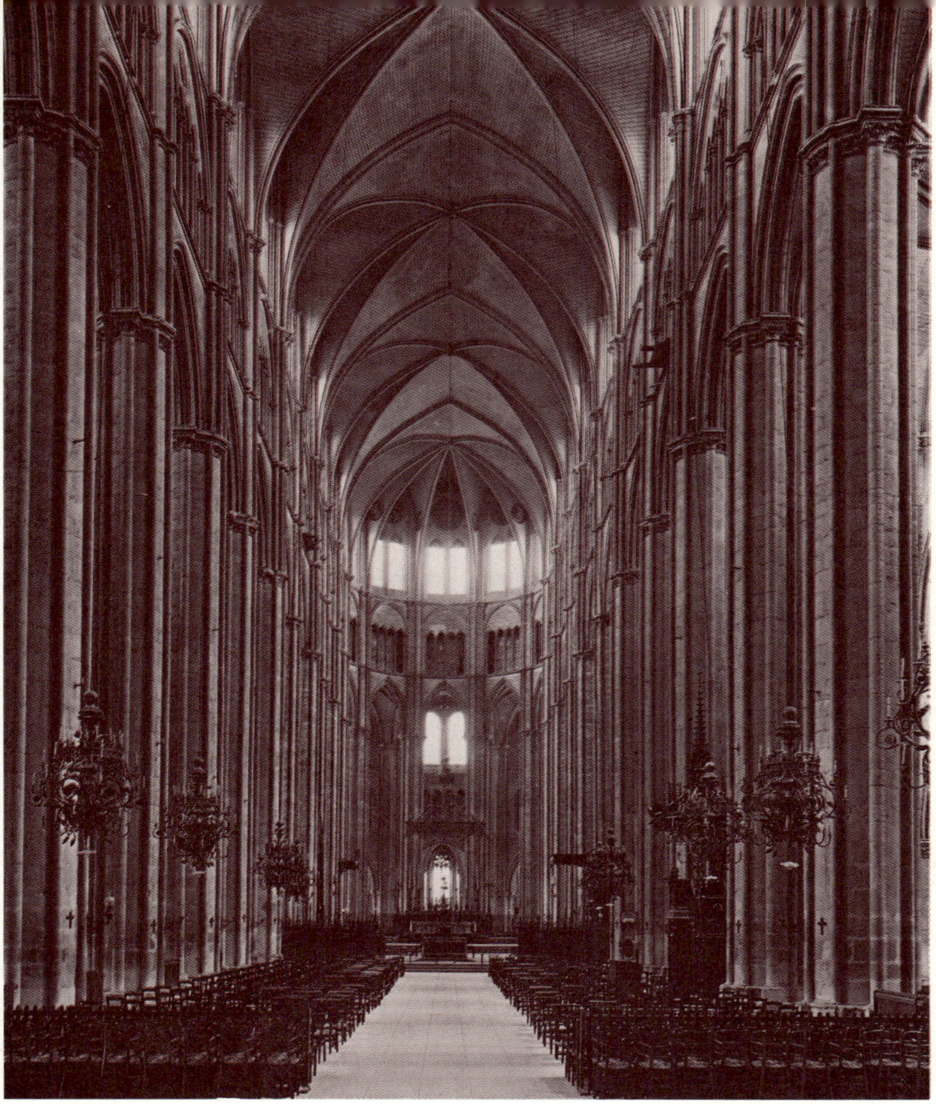

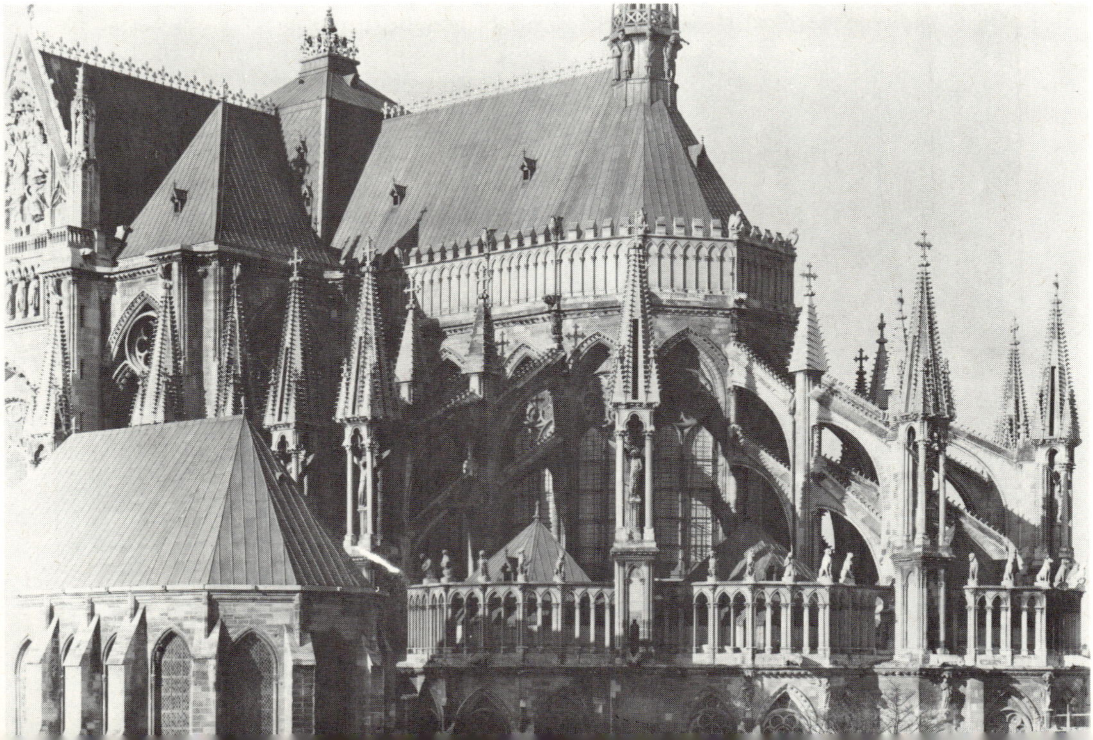

The great engineering achievement of the Romanesque architects was to replace flat wooden ceilings with stone vaulting, thereby creating buildings less susceptible to fire and more organic. In achieving this goal, the Romanesque builders constructed stone vaults far larger than ever before. The glittering mosaics and wooden roofs, which characterized the churches of late-Roman, Byzantine, and Carolingian times, gave way to the domination of stone as the key material in both Romanesque architecture and Romanesque sculpture. Indeed, the inventive, fantastic religious sculpture of the age—ornamenting the capitals of Romanesque columns and the semicircular areas between the lintels and round arches of the doors (the *tympana*)—were totally architectonic—completely fused into the structure of the church itself.

By the standards of the later Gothic style, the Romanesque interior is dark—characterized by heavy masses and relatively small windows. Graceful and richly decorated in southern Europe, the style tends to become increasingly severe as one moves northward. A church in the fully developed Romanesque style conveys a feeling of artistic unity and earthbound solidity. Its sturdy arches, vaults, and walls, and its somber, shadowy interior give the illusion of mystery and otherworldliness, yet suggest at the same time the steadfast might of the universal Church.

The Gothic Style

During the first half of the twelfth century new structural elements began to be employed in the building of Romanesque churches: first, ribs of stone that ran along the edges of the arched cross vaults and helped to support them; next, pointed

Gothic sculpture from the west portal of Reims' cathedral: The Visitation (early 1230s). The Virgin Mary and St. Elizabeth represent High-Gothic idealizations of beauty in the young girl and the elderly woman.

arches that permitted greater flexibility and height in the vaulting. By the middle of the century these novel features—vault rib and pointed arch—were providing the basis for an entirely new style of architecture, no longer Romanesque but Gothic. They were employed with such effect by Abbot Suger in his new abbey church of Saint-Denis near Paris around 1140 that Saint-Denis is regarded as the first true Gothic church.

French Gothic churches of the late twelfth century such as Notre Dame of Paris disclose the development of vault rib and pointed arch into a powerful, coherent style. During these exciting years, every decade brought new experiments and opened new possibilities in church building, yet Notre Dame of Paris and the churches of its period and region retain some of the heaviness and stolidity of the earlier Romanesque. Not until the thirteenth century were the full potentialities of Gothic architecture realized. The discovery of the vault rib and pointed arch, and of a third Gothic structural element—the flying buttress—made it possible to support weights and stresses in a totally new way. The traditional building, of roof supported by walls, was transformed into a radically new kind of building—a skeleton—in which the stone vault rested not on walls but on slender columns and graceful exterior supports. The walls became mere screens—structurally unnecessary and, with the passage of time, replaced increasingly by huge windows of stained glass which flooded the church interiors with light and color. For concurrent with the Gothic architectural revolution was the development, in twelfth- and thirteenth-century Europe, of the new art of stained-glass making. The glorious colored windows created in these two centuries, with episodes from the Bible and religious legend depicted in shimmering blues and glowing reds, have never been equalled.

The Gothic innovations of vault rib, pointed arch, and flying buttress created the breathtaking illusion of stone vaulting resting on walls of glass. The new churches rose upward in seeming defiance of gravity, losing their earthbound quality and reaching toward the heavens. By about the mid-thirteenth century all the structural possibilities of the Gothic skeleton design were fully realized, and in the towns of central and northern France there now rose churches of delicate, soaring stone with walls of lustrous glass. Never before in history had windows been so immense or buildings so lofty; and never since has European architecture been at once so assured and so daringly original.

Gothic sculpture, like Romanesque, was intimately related to architecture, yet the two styles differed markedly. Romanesque fantasy, exuberance, and distortion gave way to a serene, self-confident naturalism. Human figures were no longer crowded together on the capitals of pillars; often they stood as statues—great rows of them—in niches on the cathedral exteriors: saints, prophets, kings, and angels, Christ and the Virgin, depicted as tall slender figures, calm yet warmly human, or as lovely young women, placid and often smiling. The greatest Gothic churches of thirteenth-century France—Bourges, Chartres, Amiens, Reims, Sainte-Chapelle—are superb syntheses of many separate arts. The pictures in the glass, the sculpture, and the architecture of the buildings themselves are all fused and directed to a single end: the expression and illumination of a deep, vital faith.

B. The Dynamics of High Medieval Culture: Education, Medicine, and Law

THE RISE OF UNIVERSITIES

The University Defined

Like the Gothic cathedral, the university was a product of the medieval town. The urban revolution of the eleventh and twelfth centuries brought about the decline of the old monastic schools which had done so much to preserve culture over the previous centuries. They were superseded north of the Alps by cathedral schools located in the rising towns, and in Italy by semi-secular municipal schools. Both the cathedral schools and the municipal schools had long existed, but it was only in the eleventh century that they rose to great prominence. Many of these schools now became centers of higher learning of a sort that Europe had not known for centuries. Their enrollments increased steadily and their faculties grew until, in the twelfth century, some of them evolved into universities.

In the Middle Ages, *university* was a vague term. A university was simply a group of persons associated for any purpose. The word was commonly applied to the merchant guilds and craft guilds of the rising towns. A guild or university of students and scholars engaged in the pursuit of higher learning was given the more specific name, *studium generale*. When we speak of the medieval university, therefore, we are referring to an institution that would have been called a studium generale by a man of the thirteenth century. It differed from lesser schools in three significant respects: (1) the studium generale was open to students from many lands, not simply those from the surrounding districts; (2) the studium generale was a large school with a number of teachers rather than merely one omnicompetent master; (3) the studium generale offered both elementary and advanced curricula. It offered a basic program of instruction in the traditional "seven liberal arts": astronomy, geometry, arithmetic, music, grammar, rhetoric, and dialectic; and also instruction in one or more of the "higher" disciplines: theology, law, and medicine. Upon the successful completion of his liberal arts curriculum, the student could apply for a license to teach, but he might also wish to continue his studies by specializing in medicine, theology, or—most popular of all—civil or canon law. Legal training offered as its reward the promise of a lucrative administrative career in royal government or the Church.

Fundamentally, the medieval university was neither a campus nor a complex of buildings, but a guild—a privileged corporation of teachers, or sometimes of students. With its classes normally held in rented rooms, it was a highly mobile institution, and on more than one occasion, when a university was dissatisfied with local conditions it won important concessions from the townsmen simply by threatening to move elsewhere.

University Organization and Student Life

In the thirteenth century, flourishing universities were to be found at Paris, Bologna, Naples, Montpellier, Oxford, Cambridge, and elsewhere. Paris, Oxford, and a number of others were dominated by guilds of instructors in the liberal arts. Bologna, whose pattern was followed by other universities of southern Europe, was governed by a guild of students. The Bologna student guild managed to reduce the exorbitant local prices of food and lodgings by threatening to move collectively to another town, and established strict rules of conduct for the instructors. Professors had to begin and end their classes on time and to cover the prescribed curriculum; they could not leave town without special permission. It is important to point out that Bologna specialized in legal studies and that its pupils were older professional students for the most part—men who had completed their liberal arts curriculum and were determined to secure sufficient training for successful careers in law.

The students of the medieval universities were, on the whole, at least as exuberant and as riot-prone as students of American universities today. Their underlying hostility toward the surrounding towns often exploded into town-gown riots. New students were hazed unmercifully; unpopular professors were hissed, shouted down, and even pelted with stones. Most of the students were of relatively humble origin—from the towns or the ranks of the lesser nobility—but they were willing to spend their student days in poverty if necessary in order to acquire the new knowledge and prepare themselves for the rich social and economic rewards that awaited many graduates.

The differences between medieval and modern university life are obviously enormous, yet the modern university is a direct outgrowth of the institution that came into being in high medieval Europe. We owe to the medieval university the concept of a formal teaching license, the custom—unknown to antiquity—of group instruction, the idea of academic degrees, the notion of a liberal arts curriculum, the tradition of professors and students dressing in clerical garb (caps and gowns)

A sitting of the Doctors of the University of Paris (ca. fifteenth century). The formal organization and the ritual of medieval university life were to influence the academic traditions of the Western world down to our own time.

509   B. High Medieval Culture: Education, Medicine, Law

on commencement day, and numerous other customs of university life. Even the letters written by medieval students to their parents or guardians have a curiously modern ring:

> This is to inform you that I am studying at Oxford with the greatest diligence, but the matter of money stands greatly in the way of my promotion, as it is now two months since I spent the last of what you sent me. The city is expensive and makes many demands; I have to rent lodgings, buy necessities, and provide for many other things which I cannot now specify. [A fuller elaboration here would have been illuminating.] Wherefore I respectfully beg your paternity that by the promptings of divine pity you may assist me, so that I can complete what I have well begun. For you must know that without Ceres and Bacchus, Apollo grows cold.

MEDICINE AND LAW

Medicine

The chief medical school of medieval Europe was the University of Salerno. Here, in a land of vigorous cultural intermingling, scholars were able to draw from the medical heritage of Islam and Byzantium. In general, medieval medical scholarship was a bizarre medley of cautious observation, common sense, and gross superstition. In one instance we encounter the good advice that a person should eat and drink in moderation. But we are also instructed that onions will cure baldness, that the urine of a dog is an admirable cure for warts, and that all one must do to prevent a woman from conceiving is to bind her head with a red ribbon. Yet in the midst of this nonsense, important progress was being made in medical science. The writings of the great second-century scientist Galen, which constituted a synthesis of classical medical knowledge, were studied and digested, as were the important works of Arab students of medicine. And to this invaluable body of knowledge European scholars were now making their own original contributions on such subjects as the curative properties of plants and the anatomy of the human body. It is probable that both animal and human dissections were performed by the scholars of twelfth-century Salerno. These doctors, crude and primitive though their methods were, laid the foundations on which western European medical science was to rise.

Civil Law

Medieval legal scholarship addressed itself to two distinct bodies of material: civil law and canon law. The legal structure of early medieval society was largely Germanic in inspiration and custom-based, particularly in northern Europe, where Roman law had disappeared without a trace. Customary law remained strong throughout the High Middle Ages: it governed the relationships among the feudal aristocracy and determined the manorial obligations of the medieval peasantry. It limited the feudal prerogatives of kings, and underlay Magna Carta. But from the late eleventh century on, Roman law was studied in Bologna and other European universities. Christendom was now exposed to a distinctly different legal tradition—coherent and logical—which began to compete with Germanic law, to rationalize it, and in some instances to replace it.

The foundation of medieval Roman law was the *Corpus Juris Civilis* of Justinian, which was all but unknown in the West throughout most of the Early Middle Ages but reappeared at Bologna in the last quarter of the eleventh century. Italy remained the center of Roman legal studies throughout the High Middle Ages, for the traditions of Roman law had never entirely disappeared there, and the Italian peninsula therefore provided the most fertile soil for their revival. From Italy, the study of Roman law spread northward. A great school of law emerged at Montpellier in southern France, and others flourished at Orleans, Paris, and Oxford. But Bologna remained the foremost center of Roman legal studies. There, able scholars known as "glossators" wrote analytical commentaries on the *Corpus Juris,* elucidating difficult points and reconciling apparent contradictions. Later on they began to produce textbooks and important original treatises on the *Corpus* and to reorganize it into a coherent sequence of topics. Eventually such an extensive body of supplementary material existed that the glossators turned to the task of glossing the glosses—elucidating the elucidations. Around the mid-thirteenth century the work of the earlier glossators was brought to a climax with a comprehensive work by the Bolognese scholar Accursius—the *Glossa Ordinaria*—which was a composite synthesis of all previous commentaries on the *Corpus Juris.* Thereafter the *Glossa Ordinaria* became the authoritative supplement to the *Corpus Juris* in courts of Roman law.

The impact of the glossators was particularly strong in Italy and southern France where elements of Roman law had survived as local custom. By the thirteenth century Roman law was beginning to make a significant impact in the north as well, for by then civil lawyers trained in the Roman tradition were achieving an increasingly dominant role in the courts of France, Germany, and Spain. These men devoted themselves wholeheartedly to the royal service and used their legal training to exalt their monarchs in every possible way. Although the Roman legal tradition had originally contained a strong element of constitutionalism, it inherited from Justinian's age an autocratic cast which the court lawyers of the rising monarchies put to effective use. Thus as Roman law gained an increasingly firm hold in the states of continental Europe it tended to make their governments at once more systematic and more absolute. In France, for example, civil lawyers played an important part in the gradual transformation of the early Capetian feudal monarchy into the royal autocracy of later times. And the development and durability of the parliamentary regime in England owed much to the fact that a strong monarchy, founded on the principles of Germanic law with its custom-based limitations on royal authority, was already well established before Europe felt the full impact of the Roman law revival.

The enormous respect that medieval man had for the intellectual powers of the classic philosophers may be seen in this thirteenth-century illustration which credits Socrates with the power to foretell the sex of an unborn child.

Canon Law

Canon law developed alongside Roman law and derived a great deal from it. Methods of scholarship were similar in the two fields—commentaries and glosses were common to both—and the ecclesiastical courts borrowed much from the principles and procedures of Roman law. But whereas Roman law was based on the single authority of Justinian's *Corpus Juris,* canon law drew from many sources: the Bible, the writings of the ancient Church fathers, the canons of Church councils, and the decretals of popes. The *Corpus Juris,* although susceptible to endless commentary, was fundamentally complete in itself; popes and councils, on the other hand, continued to issue decrees, and canon law was therefore capable of unlimited development.

Canon law, like civil law, first became a serious scholarly discipline in eleventh-century Bologna and later spread to other major centers of learning. The study of canon law was strongly stimulated by the Investiture Controversy and subsequent church-state struggles, for the papacy looked to canon lawyers to support its claims with cogent, documented arguments and apt precedents. But the medieval scholars of canon law were far more than mere papal propagandists. They were grappling with the formidable problem of systematizing their sources, explaining what was unclear, reconciling what seemed contradictory—in other words, imposing order on the immense variety of dicta, opinions, and precedents upon which their discipline was based.

The essential goal of the canon lawyers was to assemble their diverse sources—their canons—into a single coherent work. It was up to them, in short, to accomplish the task that Justinian had performed for Roman law back in the sixth century. The civil lawyers had their *Corpus Juris Civilis;* it was up to the canon lawyers to create their own "Corpus Juris Canonici." The first attempts to produce comprehensive canonical collections date from the Early Middle Ages, but it was not until the eleventh-century revival at Bologna that serious scholarly standards were applied to the task. The definitive collection was completed around 1140 by the great Bolognese canon lawyer Gratian. Originally entitled *The Concordance of Discordant Canons,* Gratian's work is known to posterity as the *Decretum.*

Gratian not only brought together an immense body of canons from a bewildering variety of sources; he also framed them in a logical, topically organized scheme. Using scholarly methods that were just beginning to be employed by scholastic philosophers and logicians, he raised questions, quoted the relevant canons, endeavored to reconcile those that disagreed, and thereby arrived at firm conclusions. The result was an ordered body of general legal principles derived from particular passages from the Bible, the fathers, and papal and conciliar decrees. The *Decretum* became the authoritative text in ecclesiastical tribunals and the basis of all future study in canon law.

As time passed, and new decrees were issued, it became necessary to supplement Gratian's *Decretum* by collecting the canons issued subsequent to 1140. One such collection was made in 1234 under the direction of the lawyer-pope Gregory IX, another in the pontificate of Boniface VIII, and still others in later generations. Together, the *Decretum* and the supplementary collections were given the title *Corpus Juris Canonici,* and became the ecclesiastical equivalent of Justinian's *Corpus.* These two great compilations, ecclesiastical and civil, symbolize the parallel growth of medieval Europe's two supreme sources of administrative and jurisdictional authority: church and monarchy.

C. The Dynamics of High Medieval Culture: Philosophy and Science

PHILOSOPHY

Background of High Medieval Philosophy

It is only to be expected that an age which witnessed such sweeping economic and political changes and such vigorous creativity in religious and artistic expression would also achieve notable success in the realm of abstract thought. Medieval philosophy is richly variegated and marked by boundless curiosity and heated controversy. Although every important philosopher in the High Middle Ages was a churchman of one sort or another, ecclesiastical authority did not stifle speculation. Catholic orthodoxy, which hardened noticeably at the time of the Protestant Reformation, was still flexible in the twelfth and thirteenth centuries, and the philosophers of the age were far from being timid apologists for official dogmas. If some of them were impelled by conviction to provide the Catholic faith with a logical substructure, others asserted vigorously that reason does not lead to the truth of Christian revelation. And among those who sought to harmonize faith and reason there was sharp disagreement as to what form the logical substructure should take. All were believers—all were Catholics—but their doctrinal unanimity did not limit their diversity or curb their adventurous spirit.

The high medieval philosophers drew nourishment from five earlier sources: (1) From the Greeks they inherited the great philosophical systems of Plato and Aristotle. At first these two Greek masters were known in the West only through a handful of translations and commentaries dating from the late Roman times. By the thirteenth century, however, new and far more complete translations were coming into Christendom from Spain and Sicily, and Aristotelian philosophy became a matter of intense interest and controversy in Europe's universities. (2) From the Islamic world came a flood of Greek scientific and philosophical works that had long before been translated from Arabic and were now translated from Arabic into Latin. These works came into Europe accompanied by extensive commentaries and original writings of Arab philosophers and scientists, for the Arabs had come to grips with Greek learning long before the advent of the High Middle Ages. Islamic thought made its own distinctive contribution to European science; in philosophy it was important chiefly as an agency for the transmission and interpretation of Greek thought. (3) The early Church fathers, particularly the Latin Doctors, had been a dominant influence on the thought of the Early Middle Ages and their authority remained strong in the twelfth and thirteenth centuries. St. Augustine retained his singular significance and was, indeed, the chief vessel of Platonic and Neoplatonic thought in the medieval universities. No philosopher of the High Middle Ages could ignore him, and some of the most distinguished of them were conscious and devoted Augustinians. (4) The early medieval scholars themselves contributed significantly to the high medieval intellectual revival. Gregory the Great, Isidore of Seville, Bede, Alcuin, Raban Maur, John the Scot, and Gerbert of Aurillac were all studied seriously in the new universities. The original intellectual contributions of these men were less important, however, than the fact that they and their contemporaries had kept learning alive, fostered and perpetuated the classical tradition in Europe, and created an intellectual climate that made possible the reawakening of philosophical speculation in the eleventh century. Although stimulated by contacts with other civilizations, the intellectual surge of the High Middle Ages was fundamentally an internal phenomenon with roots in Ottonian, Carolingian, and pre-Carolingian Europe. (5) The high-medieval philosophers looked back beyond the scholars of the Early Middle Ages, beyond the fathers of the early Church, to the Hebrew and primitive Christian religious traditions as recorded in Scripture. Among medieval theologians the Bible, the chief written source of divine revelation, was the fundamental text and the ultimate authority.

Nature of Scholasticism

Such were the chief elements—Greek, Islamic, Patristic, early medieval, and scriptural—that underlay the thought of the scholastic philosophers. Narrowly defined, scholasticism is simply the philosophical movement associated with the high medieval schools—the cathedral and monastic schools, and later the universities. More basically it was a movement concerned above all with exploring the relationship between rationalism and theism—reason and revelation. All medieval scholastics were theists, all were committed, to some degree, to the life of reason. Many of them were immensely enthusiastic over the intellectual possibilities inherent in the careful application of Aristotelian logic to basic human and religious problems. Some believed that the syllogism was the master key to a thousand doors and that with sufficient methodological rigor, with sufficient exactness in the use of words, the potentialities of human reason were all but limitless.

The scholastics applied their logical method to a vast number of problems. They were concerned chiefly, however, with matters of basic significance to human existence: the nature of man, the purpose of human life, the existence and attributes of God, the fundamentals of human morality, the ethical imperatives of social and political life, the relationship between God and man. It would be hard to deny that these are the most profound sorts of questions that men can ask, although many philosophers of our own day are inclined to reject them as unanswerable. Perhaps they are, but the scholastics, standing near the beginning of Europe's long intellectual journey and lacking the modern sense of disillusionment, were determined to make the attempt.

Relationship of Faith and Reason

Among the diverse investigations and conflicting opinions of the medieval philosophers, three central issues deserve particular attention: (1) the degree of interrelationship between faith and reason; (2) the relative merits of the Platonic-Augustinian and the Aristotelian intellectual traditions; and (3) the reality of the Platonic archetypes, or, as they were called in the Middle Ages, "universals."

The issue of faith vs. reason was

perhaps the most far-reaching of the three. Ever since Tertullian in the third century, there had been Christian writers who insisted that God so transcended reason that any attempt to approach him intellectually was useless and, indeed, blasphemous. It was the mystic who knew God, not the theologian. Tertullian had posed the rhetorical questions,

What has Athens to do with Jerusalem? What concord is there between the Academy and the Church? . . . Let us have done with all attempts to produce a bastard Christianity of Stoic, Platonic, and dialectic composition! We desire no curious disputation after possessing Christ Jesus, no inquisition after enjoying the Gospel!

Tertullian had many followers in the Middle Ages. St. Peter Damiani, standing at the source of the new medieval piety, rejected the intellectual road to God in favor of the mystical. Damiani had insisted that God, whose power is limitless, cannot be bound or even approached by logic. He was followed in this view by such later mystics as St. Bernard, who denounced and hounded his brilliant rationalist contemporary Peter Abelard, and St. Francis, who regarded intellectual speculation as irrelevant and perhaps even dangerous to salvation. A later spiritual Franciscan, Jacopone da Todi, expressed the anti-intellectual position in verse:

> *Plato and Socrates may oft contend,*
> *And all the breath within their bodies spend,*
> *Engaged in disputations without end.*
> *What's that to me?*
> *For only with a pure and simple mind*
> *Can one the narrow path to heaven find,*
> *And greet the King; while lingers far behind,*
> *Philosophy.*

The contrary view was just as old. Third-century theologians such as Clement and Origen in the school of Alexandria had labored to provide Christianity with a sturdy philosophical foundation and did not hesitate to elucidate the faith by means of Greek—and particularly Platonic—thought. The fourth-century Latin Doctors, Ambrose, Jerome, and Augustine, had wrestled with the problem of whether a Christian might properly use elements from the pagan classical tradition in the service of the Faith, and all three ended with affirmative answers. As Augustine expressed it,

If those who are called philosophers, and especially the Platonists, have said aught that is true and in harmony with our faith, we must not only not shrink from it, but claim it for our own use from those who have unlawful possession of it.

Such is the viewpoint that underlies most of high medieval philosophy—that reason has a valuable role to play as a servant of revelation. St. Anselm, following Augustine, declared, "I believe so that I may know." Faith comes first, reason second; faith rules reason, but reason can perform the useful service of illuminating faith. Indeed, faith and reason are separate avenues to a single body of truth. By their very nature they cannot lead to contradictory conclusions, for truth is one. Should their conclusions ever *appear* to be contradictory, the philosopher can be assured that some flaw exists in his logic. Reason cannot err, but man's use of it can, and revelation must therefore be the criterion against which reason is measured.

This, in general, became the common position of later scholastic philosophers. The intellectual system of St. Thomas Aquinas was built on the conviction that reason and faith were harmonious. Even the arch-rationalist of the twelfth century, Peter Abelard, wrote: "I do not wish to be a philosopher if it means resisting St.

C. High Medieval Culture: Philosophy and Science

Paul; I do not wish to be Aristotle if it must separate me from Christ." Abelard believed that he could at once be a philosopher and a Christian, but his faith took first priority.

Among some medieval philosophers the priorities were reversed. Averroës, a profound Aristotelian Muslim of twelfth-century Spain, boldly asserted the superiority of reason over faith. He affirmed the truth of several propositions which were logical byproducts of Aristotle's philosophy but were directly contrary to Islamic and Christian doctrine. Averroës taught, for example, that the world had always existed and was therefore uncreated—that all human actions were determined—that there was no personal salvation. In the thirteenth century a Christian philosophical school known as Latin Averroism became active at the University of Paris and elsewhere. Latin Averroists such as Siger of Brabant took the position that reason and revelation led to radically contrary conclusions. As Christians they accepted the teachings of the Church as ultimate truth, but as scholars they insisted that the conclusions of Aristotle and Averroes, being logically air-tight, were "philosophically necessary." This position came to be called the doctrine of the "two-fold truth."

The Latin Averroists shared with anti-intellectuals such as Damiani the belief that reason did not lead to the truth of revelation; they shared with Anselm and Aquinas the conviction that ultimate truth was revealed truth. Yet unlike most scholastics they abandoned altogether the effort to harmonize reason and revelation, and unlike the anti-intellectuals they did not reject philosophy but made it their profession. As believers they conceded the supremacy of dogma; as philosophers they insisted on the supremacy of reason. And although Siger of Brabant and most of his contemporaries appear to have held this awkward position in full sincerity, some of their successors became outright religious skeptics and only paid the necessary lip service to Christian doctrine. The fourteenth-century Latin Averroist John of Jaudun, for example, never lost an opportunity to poke subtle fun at any Christian dogma that seemed to him contrary to reason. On the subject of the Creation, John points out that according to reason the world has always existed. He concludes—with tongue in cheek—that as Christians we must nevertheless believe that God created the world; "Let it be added that creation very seldom happens; there has been only one, and that was a very long time ago."

Platonism-Augustinianism versus Aristotelianism

Thus, medieval thought produced a diversity of views on the proper relationship of reason and revelation. The same is true of the other two issues that we are to consider: the rivalry between Platonism and Aristotelianism, and the controversy over universals. The conflict between the intellectual systems of Plato-Augustine and Aristotle did not emerge clearly until the thirteenth century when the full body of Aristotle's writings came into the West in Latin translations from Greek and Arabic. Until then, most efforts at applying reason to faith were based on the Platonic tradition transmuted and transmitted by Augustine to medieval Europe. St. Anselm, for example, was a dedicated Augustinian, as were many of his twelfth-century successors. The tradition was carried on brilliantly in the thirteenth century by the great Franciscan, St. Bonaventure. Many thoughtful Christians of the thirteenth century were deeply suspicious of the newly recovered Aristotelian writings, and the rise of Latin Averroism served to deepen their apprehensions. They regarded Aristotle as pagan in viewpoint and dangerous to the Faith. Other thirteenth-century intellectuals, such as St. Thomas Aquinas, were much too devoted to the goal of reconciling faith and reason to reject the works of a man whom they regarded as antiquity's greatest philosopher. St. Thomas sought to Christianize Aristotle much as Augustine had Christianized Plato and the Neoplatonists. In the middle decades of the thirteenth century, as high medieval philosophy was reaching its climax, the Platonic and Aristotelian traditions flourished side by side, and in the works of certain English scientific thinkers of the age they achieved a singularly fruitful fusion.

The Conflict over Universals

The contest between Platonism and Aristotelianism carried with it the seeds of yet another controversy: the argument over archetypes or universals. Plato had taught that terms such as "dog," "man," or "cat" not only described particular creatures but also had reality in themselves—that individual cats are imperfect reflections of a model cat, an archetypal or universal cat. Similarly, there are many examples of circles, squares, or triangles. Were we to measure these individual figures with sufficiently refined instruments we would discover that they were imperfect in one respect or another. No circle in this world is absolutely round. No square or triangle has perfectly straight sides. They are merely crude approximations of a perfect "idea." In "heaven," Plato would say, the perfect triangle exists. It is the source of the concept of triangularity that lurks in our minds and of all the imperfect triangles that we see in the physical world. The heavenly triangle is not only perfect but *real*. The earthly triangles are less real, less significant, and less worthy of our attention. To take still another example, we call certain acts "good" because they partake, imperfectly, of a universal good which exists in heaven. In short, these universals—cat, dog, circle, triangle, beauty, goodness, etc.—exist apart from the multitude of individual dogs, cats, circles, triangles, and beautiful and good things in this world. And the person who seeks knowledge ought to meditate on these universals rather than study the world of phenomena in which they are only imperfectly reflected.

St. Augustine accepted Plato's theory of universals but not without amendment. Augustine taught that the archetypes existed in the mind of God rather than in Plato's abstract "heaven." And whereas Plato had ascribed our knowledge of the universals to dim memories from a prenatal existence, Augustine maintained that God puts a knowledge of universals directly into our minds by a process of "divine illumination." Plato and Augustine agreed, however, that the universal existed apart from the particular and, indeed, was *more real* than the particular. In the High Middle Ages, those who followed the Platonic-Augustinian approach to universals were known as *realists*—they believed that universals were real.

The Aristotelian tradition brought with it another viewpoint on universals: they existed, to be sure, but only in the particular. Only by studying particular things in the world of phenomena could men gain a knowledge of universals. The human mind drew the universal from the particular by a process of abstraction. The universals were real, but in a sense less real—or at least less independently real—than Plato and Augustine believed. Accordingly, medieval philosophers who inclined toward the Aristotelian position have been called *moderate realists*.

Medieval philosophers were by no means confined to a choice between these two points of view. Several of them worked out subtle solutions of their own. As early as the eleventh century the philosopher Roscellinus declared that universals were not real at all. They were mere names that men gave to arbitrary classes of individual things. Reality was not to be found in universals but rather in the multiplicity and variety of objects which we can see, touch, and smell in the world around us. Those who followed Roscellinus in this view were known as *nominalists*—for them, the universals were *nomina*—"names." Nominalism remained in the intellectual background during the twelfth and thirteenth centuries but was revived in the fourteenth. Many churchmen regarded it as a dangerous doctrine, since its emphasis on the particular over the universal seemed to suggest that the Church was not, as Catholics believed, a single universal body but rather a vast accumulation of individual Christians.

St. Anselm

Having examined the great issues of high medieval philosophy—the relationship of reason to revelation, the relative validity of the Platonic-Augustinian and Aristotelian systems of thought, and the problem of universals—we shall now see how they developed in the minds of individual philosophers between the eleventh and fourteenth centuries.

The scholastic philosophers first made their appearance in the later eleventh century, products of the general reawakening that Europe was just then beginning to undergo. The earliest important figure in scholastic philosophy was St. Anselm (ca. 1034–1109), the Italian intellectual who came to Bec in Normandy and later, as archbishop of Canterbury, brought the Investiture Controversy into England. During his eventful career he found time to write profoundly on a variety of philosophical and theological subjects.

As an Augustinian, Anselm took the realist position on the problem of universals. It was from Augustine, too, that he derived his attitude on the relationship of faith and reason. He taught that faith must precede reason, but that reason could serve to illuminate faith. His conviction that reason and faith were compatible made him a singularly important pioneer in the development of high medieval rationalism. He worked out several proofs of God, and in his important theological treatise, *Cur Deus Homo,* subjected the doctrines of the incarnation and atonement to rigorous logical analysis.

Anselm's emphasis on reason, employed within the framework of a firm Christian conviction, set the stage for the significant philosophical developments of

LEFT: *The continuing influence of Augustine. These two fifteenth-century illustrations portray the admiration of later generations of the faithful for the great bishop of Hippo. In the portrait Augustine is wearing the dress of his order under his episcopal cape, surrounded by monks to whom he is giving the books of prayer. At his feet lies Aristotle, whose doctrine of the eternity of matter Augustine was believed to have satisfactorily refuted.*

ABOVE: *A miniature of Augustine's "City of God." The upper enclosure is inhabited by saints already received into heaven; the lower enclosures surround people who are either preparing themselves for the heavenly kingdom by exercising Christian virtues or excluding themselves from it by committing one of the seven capital sins.*

C. High Medieval Culture: Philosophy and Science

the following generations. With Anselm, Western Christendom regained at last the intellectual level of the fourth-century Latin Doctors.

Abelard

The twelfth-century philosophers, intoxicated by the seemingly limitless possibilities of reason and logic, advanced across new intellectual frontiers at the very time that their contemporaries were pushing forward the territorial frontiers of Europe. The most brilliant and audacious of these twelfth-century Christian rationalists was Peter Abelard (1079–1142), an immensely popular teacher, dazzling and egotistical, whose meteoric career ended in tragedy and defeat.

Abelard is perhaps best known for his love affair with the young Heloise, an affair that ended with Abelard's castration at the hands of thugs hired by Heloise's enraged uncle. The lovers then separated permanently, both taking monastic vows, and in later years Abelard wrote regretfully of the affair in his autobiographical *History of My Calamities*. There followed a touching correspondence between the two lovers in which Heloise, now an abbess, confessed her enduring love, and Abelard, writing almost as a father confessor, offered her spiritual consolation but nothing more. Abelard's autobiography and the correspondence with Heloise survive to this day, providing modern students with a tender, intimate picture of romance and pathos in a society far removed from our own.

Abelard was the supreme logician of the twelfth century. Writing several decades before the great influx of Aristotelian thought in Latin translation, he anticipated Aristotle's position on the question of universals by advocating a theory rather similar to Aristotle's moderate realism. Universals, Abelard believed, had no separate existence, but were derived from particular things by a process of abstraction. In a famous work entitled *Sic et Non* ("Yes and No"), Abelard collected opinions from the Bible, the Latin fathers, the councils of the Church, and the decrees of the papacy on a great variety of theological issues, demonstrating that these hallowed authorities often disagreed on important religious matters. Others before him had collected authoritative opinions on various theological and legal issues, but never so thoroughly or systematically. Abelard, in his *Sic et Non*, employed a method of inquiry that was developed and perfected by canon lawyers and philosophers over the next several generations. We have already seen how the canonist Gratian, in his *Decretum*, used the device of lining up conflicting authorities. But Abelard's successors sought to reconcile the contradictions and arrive at conclusions, whereas Abelard left many of the issues unresolved and thereby earned the enmity of his more conservative contemporaries. Abelard was a devoted Christian, if something of an intellectual show-off, but many regarded him as a dangerous skeptic. Thus he left himself open to attacks by men such as St. Bernard who were deeply hostile to the Christian rationalist movement which he so flamboyantly exemplified. The brilliant teacher was driven from one place to another. At length his opinions were condemned by an ecclesiastical council in 1141. He died at Cluny, on his way to Rome to appeal the condemnation, and the abbot of Cluny wrote a touching letter to Heloise describing his final days.

Peter Lombard and Hugh of Saint-Victor

But twelfth-century rationalism was far more than a one-man affair, and the persecution of Abelard failed to halt its growth. His student Peter Lombard (ca. 1100–60) produced an important theological text, the *Book of Sentences,* which set off conflicting opinions on the pattern of the *Sic et Non,* but which, like Gratian's *Decretum,* took the further step of reconciling the contradictory authorities. Lombard's *Book of Sentences* remained for centuries a fundamental text in schools of theology.

The Augustinian tradition was best represented in Abelard's time at the school of Saint-Victor in Paris, and in particular by the distinguished scholar, Hugh of Saint-Victor (d. 1141). Hugh was a Christian rationalist, but he believed that reason was only the first step in man's approach to God. Beyond reason lay mysticism, and God could not be circumscribed by logic alone. Hugh and his school emphasized the subordination of the material to the spiritual, and—drawing on the ancient tradition of Biblical allegory—interpreted the entire natural world as a vast multitude of symbols pointing to spiritual truths.

John of Salisbury

The intellectual mood of the twelfth century was one of immense excitement at the possibilities of logic or dialectic. In this atmosphere, the remaining liberal arts—and especially the study of humanistic disciplines such as Latin literature—began to lose out in the competition. Cathedral schools of northern France such as Chartres, Paris, and Laon were important centers of literary studies in the eleventh century and remained so throughout much of the twelfth. But as the century progressed, as more and more Aristotelian texts became available, and as the vision of rational solutions to the great questions became ever more captivating, the interest of students and scholars shifted increasingly from literature to logic. The accomplished twelfth-century English scholar, John of Salisbury (ca. 1115–80), was a student of Abelard's, a scholar of Greek, and a well-trained logician, but he was above all a humanist—a student of classical literature. He approved of dialectic but regretted that it was growing to the exclusion of all else; he complained that the schools were tending to produce narrow logicians rather than broadly educated men.

In his *Policraticus* (1159), John of Salisbury made a major contribution to medieval political philosophy. Drawing on the thought of Classical Antiquity and the Early Middle Ages, he stressed the divine nature of kingship but emphasized equally its responsibilities and limitations. The king drew his authority from God but was commissioned to rule for the good of his subjects rather than himself. He was bound to give his subjects peace and justice and to protect the Church. If he abused his commission and neglected his responsibilities he lost his divine authority, ceased to be a king, and became a tyrant. As such he forfeited his subjects' allegiance and was no longer their lawful ruler. Under extreme circumstances, and if all else failed, John of Salisbury recommended tyrannicide. A good Christian subject, although obliged to obey his king, might kill a tyrant. Apart from the highly original doctrine of tyrannicide, the views expressed in the *Policraticus* reflect the general political attitudes of the twelfth century—responsible limited monarchy and government in behalf of the governed. These theories, in turn, were idealizations of the actual feudal monarchies of the day which were deterred from autocracy by the power of the nobility, the authority of the Church, and ancient custom.

The New Translations

In the later twelfth and early thirteenth centuries the movement of Christian rationalism was powerfully reinforced by the arrival of vast quantities of Greek and

Arabic writings in Latin translation. Significant portions of the philosophical and scientific legacy of ancient Greece now became available to European scholars. Above all, the full Aristotelian corpus now came into the West through the labors of translators in Spain, Sicily, and the Latin Empire of Constantinople.

These translations were by no means fortuitous. They came in answer to a deep hunger on the part of Western thinkers for a fuller knowledge of the classical heritage in philosophy and science. The introduction of certain new Aristotelian works provoked a crisis in Western Christendom, for they contained implications that seemed hostile to the Faith. And with them, as we have seen, came the skeptical and intellectually impressive works of the Spaniard Averroës which gave rise to the doctrine of the "two-fold truth." For a time it seemed as though reason and revelation were sundered, and the Church reacted in panic by condemning certain of Aristotle's writings. It was one of the major goals of St. Thomas Aquinas to refute the Latin Averroists—to rescue Aristotle and, indeed, reason itself for Western Christianity.

The Shape of Thirteenth-Century Thought

The thirteenth century—the century of St. Thomas—differed sharply in spirit from the twelfth. The philosophers of the twelfth century were intellectual pioneers undertaking a great adventure, advancing across new frontiers into virgin soil. They were daring, original, and often radical; their mood was one of youthful exploration. The thirteenth century, although by no means lacking in intellectual originality, was preeminently an age of consolidation and synthesis. Its scholars digested the insights and conclusions of the past and cast them into great comprehensive systems of thought. The characteristic products of the age were encyclopedias and summas. Vincent of Beauvais (d. 1264), attempted in his *Speculum Majus* to bring together all knowledge of all imaginable subjects into one immense compendium. At a much higher level, theologians such as Alexander of Hales (d. 1245), Albertus Magnus (1193–1280), and Thomas Aquinas (1225–74) produced great systematic treatises on theology known as summas in which they gave majestic structure and unity to the theological speculations of theirs and past ages.

St. Bonaventure

The thought of Aristotle loomed large in the thirteenth-century schools, but the Platonic-Augustinian tradition was well represented, too. There was a tendency for the Dominican scholars to espouse Aristotle, and the Franciscans to follow Plato and Augustine. Thus, the outstanding thirteenth-century exponent of Platonism-Augustinianism was the Franciscan St. Bonaventure (1221–74), an Italian of humble origin who rose to become a cardinal of the Church and minister-general of the Franciscan order.

Bonaventure was at once a philosopher and a mystic. Following in the Augustinian tradition, he was a realist on the matter of universals and a rationalist who stressed the subordination of reason to faith. He accepted the nature symbolism of Hugh of Saint-Victor, and visualized the whole physical universe as a vast multitude of symbols pointing to God and glorifying Him. For example, he regarded everything in the natural world that could possibly be divided into three parts as a reflection of the Holy Trinity. Bonaventure's universe was eternally reaching upward toward the Divine Presence.

Bonaventure, like many of his intellectual predecessors and contemporaries, regarded the cosmos as an immense series of transparent concentric spheres. At its periphery, beyond the range of mortal eyes, were the nine spheres of angels. According to medieval theology, the angels were divided into nine ranks arranged hierarchically into three major groups, each containing three subgroups. Characteristically, Bonaventure interpreted these three angelic triads as multiple symbols of the Trinity. Inside the spheres of angels was the sphere of stars which whirled daily round the earth. Within the stellar sphere were the spheres of the planets, sun, and moon. Such, in essence, had been Plato's conception of the universe, and Bonaventure remained faithful to it.

At the center of all the celestial spheres was the earth itself, and on the earth was man—the ultimate reason for the physical universe. Man was a creature of immense dignity and importance—the lord of the earth, the master of all lower creatures. The cosmos was created for man—to sustain him and, through its myriad symbols, to lead him to God. Indeed, it was for man that God himself died on the cross.

Man was at the fulcrum of creation. His body gave him kinship with beasts; his soul gave him kinship with the angels. The human soul was created in the image of the Trinity, with three components: intellect, will, and memory. Man perceived the physical universe through his senses, but he knew the spiritual world—the world of universals—through the grace of divine illumination. The road to God and to truth, therefore, lay in introspection, mediation, and worship, not in observation and experiment.

Bonaventure's philosophy is not coldly intellectual but warm, emotional, and deeply spiritual. His discussion of God's attributes becomes a litany—an act of worship. His emphasis is less on knowledge than on love, and his entire system of thought was a kind of prayer in praise of God.

The New Aristotelianism; St. Albertus Magnus

While Bonaventure was bringing new dimensions to traditional Platonism-Augustinianism, several of his contemporaries were coming to grips with the great Aristotelian-Averroistic challenge to orthodox Christian rationalism. The conflicting intellectual currents of the age were brilliantly represented by philosophers and theologians on the faculty of the mid-century University of Paris—the Augustinian Bonaventure, the Latin Averroist Siger of Brabant, and the orthodox Aristotelians Albertus Magnus and Thomas Aquinas.

Albertus and his student, Thomas Aquinas, were both Dominicans, and both devoted themselves wholeheartedly to the reconciliation of reason and faith through the fusion of Aristotelianism and Christianity. They sought to confound the Latin Averroists by demonstrating that reason and revelation pointed to one truth, not two. A product of Germany, Albert Magnus was a scholar of widely ranging interests who made important contributions to natural science—especially biology—as well as to philosophy and theology. He was a master of Aristotelian philosophy and a summa writer, whose goal was to purge Aristotle of the heretical taint of Averroism and transform his philosophy into a powerful intellectual foundation for Christian orthodoxy. Albertus Magnus came near to realizing this audacious goal, but its full achievement was left to Albertus's gifted student Thomas Aquinas.

St. Thomas Aquinas

St. Thomas was born of a Norman-Italian noble family in 1225. His parents intended him to become a Benedictine, but in 1244 he shocked them by joining the radical new Dominican Order. He went to the University of Paris in 1245 and spent the remainder of his life traveling, teaching, and writing. Unlike Augustine he had no youthful follies to regret. Unlike Anselm, Bernard, and Bonaventure, he played no great role in the political affairs of his day. His biography is agonizingly dull except for an incident late in his life in which he abandoned his theological work, asserted that all his writings were worthless, and devoted his remaining days to mysticism. At his death, the priest who heard his final confession described it as being as innocent as that of a five-year-old child.

From the standpoint of intellectual history St. Thomas is a figure of singular interest and significance. In his copious writings—particularly his great comprehensive work, the *Summa Theologica*—he explored all the great questions of philosophy and theology, political theory and morality, using Aristotle's logical method and Aristotle's categories of thought but arriving at conclusions that were in complete harmony with the Christian faith. Like Abelard, St. Thomas assembled every possible argument, pro and con, on every subject that he discussed, but unlike Abelard he drew conclusions and defended them with cogent arguments. Few philosophers before or since have been so generous in presenting and exploring opinions contrary to their own, and none has been so systematic and exhaustive.

St. Thomas created a vast, unified intellectual system, ranging from God to the natural world, logically supported at every step. His theological writings have none of the fiery passion of St. Augustine, none of the literary elegance of Plato; rather, they have an *intellectual* elegance, an elegance of system and organization akin to that of Euclid. His *Summa Theologica* is organized into an immense series of separate sections, each section dealing with a particular philosophical question. In Part I of the *Summa*, for example, Question 2 takes up the problem of God's existence.

The *Question* is subdivided into three Articles: (1) "Whether God's existence is self-evident" (St. Thomas concludes that it is not); (2) "Whether it can be demonstrated that God exists" (St. Thomas concludes that it can be so demonstrated); and (3) "Whether God exists" (here St. Thomas propounds five separate proofs of God's existence).

In each article, St. Thomas takes up a specific problem and subjects it to rigorous formal analysis. First, he presents a series of *Objections* (*Objection 1, Objection 2*, etc.) in which he sets forth as effectively as he possibly can all the arguments *contrary* to his final conclusion. For example, Question 2, Article 3, "Whether God exists," begins with two *Objections* purporting to demonstrate that God does not exist. One of them runs as follows:

Objection 1. It seems that God does not exist, because if one of two contraries can be infinite, the other would be altogether destroyed. But the name "God" means that He is infinite goodness. Therefore, if God existed there would be no evil discoverable; but there is evil in the world. Therefore God does not exist.

After presenting the *Objections*, St. Thomas then turns to the second step in his analysis, the appeal to authority. This appeal is always introduced by the phrase, *On the contrary*, followed by a quotation from Scripture or from some authoritative patristic source that supports St. Thomas's own opinion on the subject. In the *Article* on God's existence the *Objections* are followed by the statement, "On the contrary, It is said in the person of God: 'I am Who I am' (Exod. 3:14)." Having cited his authority, St. Thomas next appeals to reason and subjects the problem to his own logical scrutiny, beginning always with the formula, *I answer that.* . . . for example, "I answer that, The existence of God can be proved in five ways" (followed by a presentation of the five proofs of the existence of God). Here is one:

The power of the Summa Theologica. *St. Thomas Aquinas, flanked by Plato and Aristotle, holds the* Summa *in his hands. The brilliant rays of its truth have struck down the heretical Averroës, who lies at St. Thomas's feet.*

The fifth way is taken from the governance of the world. We see that things which lack knowledge, such as natural bodies, act for an end, and this is evident from their acting always or nearly always in the same way, so as to obtain the best result. Hence it is clear that they achieve their end not only by chance but by design. Now whatever lacks knowledge cannot move toward an end unless it be directed by some being endowed with knowledge and intelligence, as the arrow is directed by the archer. Therefore some intelligent being

525 C. High Medieval Culture: Philosophy and Science

exists by whom all natural things are directed to their end; and this being we call God.

The analysis concludes with refutations of the earlier *Objections:*

Reply to Objection 1. As Augustine says, "Since God is the highest good, He would not allow any evil to exist in His works unless His omnipotence and goodness were such as to bring good even out of evil." This is part of the infinite goodness of God, that He should allow evil to exist, and out of it to produce good.

Having completed his analysis, St. Thomas then turns to the next *Article* or the next *Question* and subjects it to precisely the same process of inquiry: *Objections; On the contrary, I answer that; and Reply to Objections.* And as in Euclidian geometry, so in Thomistic theology, once a problem is settled the conclusion can be used in solving subsequent problems. Thus the system grows, problem by problem, step by step, as St. Thomas's wide-ranging mind takes up such matters as the nature of God, the attributes of God, the nature and destiny of man, human morality, law, and political theory. The result is an imposing, comprehensive intellectual edifice embracing all major theological issues.

As the Gothic cathedral was the artistic embodiment of the high medieval world, so the philosophy of Aquinas was its supreme intellectual expression. Both were based on clear and obvious principles of structure. St. Thomas shared with the cathedral builders the impulse to display rather than disguise the structural framework of his edifice. Like the boldly executed Gothic flying buttress, the Thomistic *Questions, Articles, and Objections* allowed no doubt as to what the builder was doing, where he was going, or how he was achieving his effects. The scholastics were nothing if not systematic—they loved to exhibit the underlying principles of their organization—and none carried this tendency farther than St. Thomas. It is not without reason that the *Summa Theologica* has been called a cathedral of thought.

As a devoted Christian and Aristotelian, Aquinas contended against both the Augustinians, who would reject Aristotle altogether, and the Latin Averroists, who would make a heretic of him. St. Thomas distinguished carefully between revelation and reason but endeavored to prove that they could never contradict one another. Since human reason was a valid avenue to truth, since Christian revelation was undoubtedly authoritative, and since truth was one, then philosophy and Christian doctrine had to be compatible and complementary. "For faith rests upon infallible truth, and therefore its contrary cannot be demonstrated." This was the essence of St. Thomas's philosophical position. This was the conviction that separated him so radically from the Latin Averroists.

As against the Augustinianism of St. Anselm, Hugh of Saint-Victor, and St. Bonaventure, Aquinas emphasized the reality of the physical world as a world of things rather than symbols. Embracing the moderate realism of Aristotle, he declared that universals were to be found in the world of phenomena and nowhere else—that knowledge came from observation and analysis, not from divine illumination. Whereas Augustine, following Plato, had emphasized the *duality* of matter and spirit, earth and heaven, body and soul, Aquinas emphasized the *unity* of God's creation. He asserted the unity of ideas and phenomena—the universal was not outside the particular but within it—and thus he shared with St. Francis and others the notion that the physical world was deeply significant in itself, that matter mattered. He affirmed the unity of intellectual knowledge and sensation, maintaining that knowledge is acquired by a gradual ascent from things to concepts, from the visible to the invisible world. He stressed the unity of man, declaring that a human being was not a soul using a body or a spirit imprisoned in flesh, as the Platonists suggested, but an inseparable composite of body and soul. The human body, although a source of temptation, was good in itself and was an essential part of man.

Likewise, the state, which previous Christian thinkers had commonly regarded as a necessary evil—an unfortunate but indispensable consequence of the Fall of Adam—was accepted by Aquinas as a good and natural outgrowth of man's social impulse. He echoed Aristotle's dictum that "Man is a political creature" and regarded the justly governed state as a fitting part of the Divine Order. Like John of Salisbury, St. Thomas insisted that kings must govern in their subjects' behalf and that a willful, unrestrained ruler who ignored God's moral imperatives was no king but a tyrant. Just as the human body could be corrupted by sin, the body politic could be corrupted by tyranny. But although the Christian must reject both sin and tyranny, he should nevertheless revere the body, the state, and indeed all physical creation as worthy products of God's will, inseparable from the world of the spirit, and essential ingredients in the unity of existence.

Such was the Thomistic vision. In binding together matter and spirit, the concrete and the abstract, body and soul, God and man, Aquinas was seeking to encompass the totality of being in a vast existential unity. At the center of this majestic system was God, the author of physical and spiritual creation, the maker of heaven and earth, who himself assumed human form and redeemed mankind on the cross, who discloses portions of the truth to man through revelation, permits him to discover other portions through the operation of his intellect, and will lead him into all truth through salvation. Ultimately, truth is God Himself, and it is man's destiny, upon reaching heaven, to stand unshielded in the divine presence—to love and to know. Thus the roads of St. Thomas, St. Bonaventure, St. Bernard, and Dante, although passing over very different terrain, arrived finally at the same destination. It is not so very surprising, after all, that in the end St. Thomas rejected the way of the philosopher for the way of the mystic.

Critics of St. Thomas: Duns Scotus

To this day there are men of keen intelligence who accept the philosophy of St. Thomas. On the other hand, many of his own thirteenth-century contemporaries rejected it in whole or in part, and it remained a source of intense controversy in the centuries that followed. Franciscan philosophers such as Bonaventure were particularly suspicious of the intellectual tour de force of this gifted Dominican. Bonaventure was a rationalist, but in a far more limited sense than was Aquinas, and Bonaventure's Franciscan successors came increasingly to the opinion that reason was of little or no use in probing metaphysical problems. The Scottish Franciscan Duns Scotus (d. 1308) undertook a rigorous and subtle critique of St. Thomas' theory of knowledge. Although he by no means rejected the possibility of supplementing and elucidating revealed truth through reason, he was more cautious in using it than Aquinas had been. Whereas St. Thomas is called "The Angelic Doctor," Duns Scotus is known as "The Subtle Doctor," and the almost tortured complexity of his thought prompted men in subsequent generations to describe anyone who bothered to follow Duns's arguments as a "dunce." The sobriquet is unfair, for Duns Scotus is an important and original figure in the development of late scholasticism. Nevertheless, one is tempted to draw a parallel between the intricacies of his intellectual system and the decorative elaboration of late-Gothic churches. A Christian rationalist of the most subtle kind, he nevertheless made the first move toward dismantling the Thomist synthesis and withdrawing reason from the realm of theology.

William of Ockham

In the field of philosophy, as in so many other areas, the synthesis and equilibrium of the High Middle Ages began to disintegrate with the coming of the fourteenth century. In the hands of the astute English Franciscan, William of Ockham (ca. 1300–49), reason and revelation were divorced altogether. Christian doctrine, Ockham said, could not be approached by reason at all but had to be accepted on faith. The Thomist synthesis was a mirage. Reason's province was the natural world and that alone. Thus, Ockham was a pietist on matters of faith—a firm Christian believer—but a man who employed his keen philosophical mind to emasculate reason and challenge the whole Christian rationalist position of the High Middle Ages. There was no metaphysics; there was no rational theology. God could neither be proved nor defined but only accepted. Reason could not be elevated beyond the world of the senses.

SCIENCE

Its Origins in the West

The Ockhamist position, with its duality of mysticism and empiricism, blazed two paths into the future: pietism uninhibited by reason and science uninhibited by revelation. In Ockham's time Western science was already well evolved. As far back as the later decades of the tenth century, Gerbert of Aurillac (Pope Sylvester II) had visited Moorish Spain, familiarized himself with Islamic thought, and made his own modest contributions to scientific knowledge.* Gerbert built a simple "planetarium" of balls, rods, and bands to illustrate the rotation of the stellar sphere and the motions of the planets. He introduced the abacus and Arabic numerals into the West and, following the Greeks and Arabs, he taught that the earth was round.

Islamic science continued thereafter to inspire western scholars, particularly in the late-eleventh and twelfth centuries when men such as Adelard of Bath (d. 1150) retraced Gerbert's pilgrimage into Islamic lands and returned with a new respect for scientific inquiry. Among the works that Adelard translated from Arabic into Latin were Euclid's *Elements* and an important Muslim work on arithmetic that used Arabic numerals. Through the labors of the twelfth-century translators, the great scientific works of Greece and Islam were made known in the West—Aristotle's *Physics,* Ptolemy's *Almagest,* Arabic books on algebra and medicine, and many others. And now Western scholars began to write scientific books of their own, such as Adelard of Bath's *Natural Questions*. Such works, however, were mere summaries of Greek and Arabic knowledge. The purely assimilative phase of western science continued until the thirteenth century when, particularly among the Franciscans, the first serious original work began.

Thirteenth-century Franciscans, anticipating the later duality of Ockham, were inclined toward both pietism and the investigation of nature. The mysticism of St. Bonaventure represents one pole of Franciscan thought; at the other stands a group of scientific thinkers, who, inspired perhaps by St. Francis's love of nature, applied their logical tools to the task of investigating the physical world. Thirteenth-century Oxford became the leading center of scientific work, and it was there that western European science came of age.

* See pp. 389–90.

528   *Literature, Art, and Thought in the High Middle Ages*

Robert Grosseteste

The key figure in the development of medieval science was the great English scholar, Robert Grosseteste (1168–1253), who, although not a Franciscan himself, was chief lecturer to the Franciscans at Oxford. Grosseteste was on intimate terms with Platonic and Neoplatonic philosophy, Aristotelian physics, and the rich scientific legacy of Islam. At bottom, he was a Platonist and an Augustinian, but he wrote important commentaries on the scientific works of Aristotle and was able to draw on both traditions. From Plato he derived the notion that mathematics is a basic key to understanding the physical universe; the fundamental importance of numbers is very much in keeping with the Platonic realist interpretation of universals, and Plato himself had once asserted that "God is a mathematician." From Aristotle he learned the importance of abstracting knowledge from the world of phenomena by means of observation and experiment. Thus, bridging the two traditions, Grosseteste brought together the mathematical and experimental components that together underlie the rise of modern science. More than that, drawing on the suggestive work of his Islamic predecessors he worked out a far more rigorous experimental procedure than is to be found in the pages of Aristotle. A pioneer in the development of scientific method, he outlined a system of observation, hypothesis, and experimental verification that was elaborated by his successors into the methodology that modern physical scientists still employ.

Like other pioneers, Grosseteste followed many false paths. He was better at formulating a scientific methodology than in applying it to specific problems, and his explanations of such phenomena as heat, light, color, comets, and rainbows were rejected in later centuries. But the experimental method which he formulated was to become in time a powerful intellectual tool. The problem of the rainbow, for example, was largely solved by the fourteenth-century scientist Theoderic of Freiburg, who employed a refined version of Grosseteste's experimental methodology. The great triumphs of European science lay far in the future, but with the work of Robert Grosseteste the basic scientific tool had been forged. Grosseteste's career illustrates not that science was born in the thirteenth century but rather that scientific thought evolved gradually from antiquity to modern times, and that the High Middle Ages contributed markedly to its development.

Roger Bacon

Grosseteste's work was carried further by his famous disciple, the Oxford Franciscan Roger Bacon (ca. 1214–94). The author of a fascinating body of scientific sense and nonsense, Roger Bacon was more an advocate of experimental science than a consistent practitioner of it. He dabbled in the mysteries of alchemy and astrology, and his boundless curiosity carried him along many strange roads. He led a turbulent life, at times enjoying the friendship of the papacy, at other times imprisoned by his own Franciscan order, which suspected him of practicing magic. Roger Bacon was critical of the deductive logic and metaphysical speculations that so intrigued his scholastic contemporaries: "Reasoning," he wrote, "does not illuminate these matters; experiments are required, conducted on a large scale, performed with instruments and by various necessary means."

At his best, Roger Bacon was almost prophetic:

Experimental science controls the conclusions of all other sciences. It reveals truths which reasoning from general principles would never have discovered. Finally, it starts us on the way to marvelous inventions which will change the face of the world.

One such marvelous invention, the telescope, was not to be invented for another three centuries, yet Roger Bacon described it in astonishing detail:

> We can give such figures to transparent bodies, and dispose them in such order with respect to the eye and the objects, that the rays will be refracted and bent toward any place we please, so that we will see the object near at hand or at a distance, under any angle we wish. And thus from an incredible distance we may read the smallest letters, and may number the smallest particles of dust and sand, by reason of the greatness of the angle under which we see them. . . . The sun, moon, and stars may be made to descend hither in appearance, and to be visible over the heads of our enemies, and many things of a like sort which persons unacquainted with such matters would refuse to believe.

The Medieval Intellectual Achievement

Thus the intense intellectual activity of the thirteenth century produced both the supreme synthesis of Christian rationalism in the philosophy of St. Thomas and the genesis of a new method of scientific inquiry in the thought of Robert Grosseteste and his successors. In the realm of the intellect, as in so many others, the thirteenth century was both synthetic and creative.

With the coming of the fourteenth century, the growth of scientific thought was accompanied by the gradual erosion of the Thomist synthesis. Universal systems such as that of St. Thomas have seldom been lasting, but for a few brief years Thomism represented, for many, the perfect fusion of intellect and belief. As such, it takes its place alongside the Gothic cathedral, the *Divine Comedy* of Dante, and the piety of St. Francis as a supreme and mature expression of high medieval culture.

CONCLUSION

The world of the High Middle Ages is described in some outworn textbooks as stagnant, gloomy, and monolithic. At the other extreme, it has been portrayed as an ideally constituted society, free of modern fears and tensions, where men of all classes could live happily and creatively, finding fulfillment in their service to the common good. In reality, the medieval era was neither of these things. It was an age of vitality, of striking contrasts, of dark fears and high hopes, of poverty that was often brutal yet gradually diminishing. Above all, it was an age in which Europeans awoke to the rich variety of possibilities that lay before them. A thirteenth-century poet, in his celebration of springtime, captured perfectly the spirit of this awakening:

> The earth's ablaze again
> With lustrous flowers.
> The fields are green again,
> The shadows, deep.
> Woods are in leaf again,
> And all the world
> Is filled with joy again.
> This long-dead land
> Now flames with life again.
> The passions surge,
> Love is reborn,
> And beauty wakes from sleep.

Selected Readings

*Anselm of Canterbury. *Trinity, Incarnation, and Redemption.* Edited and translated by Jasper Hopkins and H. W. Richardson. New York: Harper & Row, Publishers, 1970.
Theological letters and treatises by St. Anselm in new, scholarly translations.

*Brooke, Christopher. *The Twelfth-Century Renaissance.* New York: Harcourt Brace Jovanovich, 1969.
A beautifully illustrated, sensitively written essay on some of the key cultural figures of twelfth-century Europe.

*Dante Alighieri. *The Divine Comedy.* Edited and translated by Thomas Bergin. New York: Crofts Classics, 1955.
One of many available translations.

Flores, Angel. *An Anthology of Medieval Lyrics.* New York: Modern Library, 1962.
Skillful English translations of medieval lyric poems from France, Italy, Germany, and the Iberian peninsula.

*Haskins, C. H. *The Renaissance of the Twelfth Century.* New York: World Publishing Co., Meridian Books, 1957 (originally published 1927).
An epoch-making book, particularly strong in the area of Latin literature.

*Haskins, C. H. *The Rise of the Universities.* Ithaca, N.Y.: Cornell University Press, 1957 (originally published 1923).
Short, authoritative, and a pleasure to read.

*Hollister, C. Warren. *The Twelfth-Century Renaissance.* New York: John Wiley & Sons, 1969.
Excerpts and commentaries on Haskins's Renaissance of the Twelfth Century *followed by a selection of documents and pictures illustrating twelfth-century civilization.*

*Knowles, David. *The Evolution of Medieval Thought.* New York: Random House, Vintage Books, 1964.
A lucid survey of medieval intellectual history; sympathetic, judicious, and readable.

*Leff, Gordon. *Medieval Thought.* Baltimore: Penguin Books, 1958.
A good survey that emphasizes the development of metaphysics.

*Lewis, C. S. *The Allegory of Love: A Study in Medieval Tradition.* New York: Oxford University Press, 1958 (originally published 1936).
An illuminating, beautifully written study of courtly love and the medieval Romance.

*Panofsky, Erwin. *Gothic Architecture and Scholasticism.* New York: World Publishing Co., Meridian Books, 1957 (originally published 1951).
A challenging study that endeavors to demonstrate lines of connection between these two great medieval enterprises.

Pegis, Anton C., trans. *Introduction to St. Thomas Aquinas.* New York: Modern Library, 1948.
> *Intelligently chosen selections together with a stimulating introduction.*

Rashdall, Hastings. *The Universities of Europe in the Middle Ages.* 3 vols. Edited by F. M. Powicke and A. B. Emden. New York: Oxford University Press, 1936.
> *This is the great, definitive treatment of the subject.*

*Sayers, D. L., trans. *The Song of Roland.* Baltimore: Penguin Books, 1957.
> *A good, new translation of the famous medieval epic.*

Southern, R. W. *Medieval Humanism and Other Studies.* Oxford: Basil Blackwell & Mott, 1970.
> *A series of important related essays on medieval thought and life containing a fundamental reinterpretation of medieval humanism and its relationship to scholastic philosophy.*

Stoddard, Whitney. *Monastery and Cathedral in France.* Middletown, Conn.: Wesleyan University Press, 1966.
> *A superbly illustrated account of French Romanesque and Gothic art.*

*Ullmann, Walter. *A History of Political Thought: The Middle Ages.* Baltimore: Penguin Books, 1965.
> *A short, synthetic work that stresses the ideology of the papal monarchy and points to the medieval background of modern political thought.*

Asterisk (*) denotes paperback.

CHAPTER XII
The Renaissance: 1300—ca.1520

A. The Meaning of Renaissance

WHY WE USE THE WORD RENAISSANCE

"Renaissance" means rebirth. Its usage in the fourteenth and fifteenth centuries derives from Italian literary scholars who believed that the centuries following the Fall of Rome had been dominated by barbarians. By way of contrast, their own age marked a wonderful revival of classical learning and art. By 1435 Matteo Palmieri, a patriotic Florentine advocate of republican activism, was thanking God for having been "born in this new age, so full of hope and promise." This optimism rested not only on the recent attainments of the Italian city-states but also on a new way of looking at the past. Equating the urban civilization of antiquity with the civic revival of their own times, they provided later Western historians with the idea that a "medieval" period of darkness had followed the glories of the ancient world. Modern authors who have shared these Italians' disdain for the Middle Ages have extended the concept of rebirth to apply to almost all phases of human activity during this era. In 1860 the German-Swiss historian Jacob Burckhardt popularized this view in a famous book, *The Civilization of the Renaissance in Italy*. He believed that the Renaissance was a "golden age" of beauty and individualism, when esthetic considerations so dominated the minds of men that even making war or building a state became a work of art. "The Renaissance," his follower J. A. Symonds wrote, "was the liberation of the reason from a dungeon, the double discovery of the outer and the inner world."[1] Modern Protestant historians have extended this interpretation to include the claim that the Renaissance formulated a concept of elitist individualism that the Reformation, in making every man his own priest, subsequently democratized for the masses.

---

[1] Alfred Pearson, *A Short History of the Renaissance in Italy Taken from the Work of John Addington Symonds* (New York: Henry Holt & Co., 1894), p. 6.

Post-Reformation historians steeped in classical educations along lines first laid down by Renaissance scholars have also argued persistently that a new civilization —one no longer medieval, but recognizably modern—came into being during the fourteenth and fifteenth centuries. Their influence on historical writing has been so strong that even those who think that the modern world was not born so early usually use the term *Renaissance* in the same sense as a matter of convenience. But many historians reject it for northern Europe because they consider society there to have been essentially medieval until after the closing date for this chapter (ca. 1520).

The Rebirth Disputed

Nineteenth-century romantics who idolized the Middle Ages, as well as a good number of medievalists who admire that epoch, have tried to deny that a rebirth actually occurred and to prove that earlier significant rebirths occurred during the Middle Ages. Especially as science and technology rather than classical education appears to have become the touchstone of modernity, historians have attempted to disprove Burckhardt's interpretation. On close examination, they say, the break with the Middle Ages was not so sharp as Renaissance Italians and the Burckhardtian school thought. In fact, to assert that a rebirth occurred is to assert a false view of history, for men now know that one cannot break abruptly with the past. Medievalists have found a long train of predecessors for the alleged innovations of the Renaissance, and they have made their point: medieval ways and institutions had great staying power. For example, the aristocracy, which had dominated medieval institutions, proved resilient enough to overcome the challenge of the urban middle classes. But in order to prevail, the aristocracy had to adopt new ways and to rely on new, more authoritarian governments. Thus the Renaissance was an age of transition, and some of its changes anticipated more recent events.

In order to study that transition we shall examine in turn the changes that occurred in three important areas. First, we shall trace in some detail the major developments in learning and the arts—those parts of civilization that are the most pliable in men's hands, where changes are highly visible. It is only in this area that we can apply the concept of Renaissance without reservation. Scholars and artists self-consciously used classical models to express new attitudes toward learning, man, society, and nature. Second, we shall study the great secular institutions and activities, the Renaissance economies, societies, states, and politics. Changes in that area during the two centuries were gradual and, for the most part, slighter. Third, we shall examine the grave problems affecting the Church, for conditions leading to a religious explosion—the Reformation—were created during the Renaissance.

B. Cultural and Artistic Developments

LETTERS AND LEARNING

The revival of classical philosophy, law, and science had made substantial advances in the High Middle Ages; during the Renaissance, revival also spread to rhetoric, poetry, and especially to history. But whereas the medieval revival of classical studies had been undertaken by churchmen, the vastly broadened revival that took place during the Renaissance was mainly the work of laymen. In either case we call these scholars humanists because they were devoted to the humanities or liberal arts, especially the moral philosophy of the classics. Renaissance humanists propagated secular classical, moral, and esthetic standards as the code of an educated and social elite. The strongest lay influence, however, came not from humanists but from those officials of the territorial and dynastic states who were trained in law. Although their outlooks were not drastically different from earlier jurists trained in Roman law, their burgeoning numbers in positions of power enhanced their role in Renaissance society. It was these men who also censored the new printing press which, had it been free of political and religious controls, might have extensively democratized literary culture.

Vernacular Literature and Literary Naturalism

The cultural unity of medieval Europe rested on the use of a common language of learning, administration, and liturgy: ecclesiastical Latin. As we have seen in the previous chapter, certain dialects, or vernaculars—usually the language of political administration and the royal court—achieved literary stature as competitors with Latin in the thirteenth and fourteenth centuries. In the Spanish kingdoms Castilian—a blend of Germanic, Latin, and some Moorish elements—gained ascendancy as the language of affairs. English, a composite of Anglo-Saxon and Norman French as spoken in Middlesex, was required in the courts of law and used in most official documents by the middle of the fourteenth century.

The most influential late medieval vernacular was Parisian French. Although local dialects vied with it, as the language of the French court it became the literary pacesetter and the language of much commerce as well. Later, Tuscan—the spoken Latin of the northern Italian peninsula and the language of the most advanced commercial areas of the Middle Ages—began to set literary standards. German was slower to crystallize, but after the middle of the fourteenth century High Saxon was used by most local princely courts. Except for a temporary period of Czech religious and political agitation during the late fourteenth and fifteenth centuries, the Slavic and Ural-Altaic languages of eastern Europe failed to achieve literary status until the nineteenth century.

Early vernacular literatures incorporated the themes and content of oral traditions: from the courts of the French nobility came heroic epics, troubadour songs, and lyric poetry; from the townsmen came anticlerical tales, called *fabliaux*, often touched with barnyard bawdiness; from them too came secularized church dramas, didactic devotional tracts, and stories of cunning such as *Reynard the Fox.* Learned vernacular writers sought to popularize in poetry the science and theology of the universities, while popular writers drew upon peasant, bourgeois, and noble themes. Stirred by an interest in classical literature, such men as Dante (1265–1321), Petrarch, and Boccaccio developed local tongues—in this case Tuscan—into highly influential mediums of expression.

In the previous chapter we saw Dante's use of the vernacular as the climax of medieval poetry.* Dante's life span and works are often seen as bridging the Middle Ages and the Renaissance. His greatest work, *The Divine Comedy*, was medieval in that it was a religious allegory in which natural science (and many Florentine businessmen) were relegated to the inferno. But he put Pope Boniface VIII there too. Dante also gave expression to the notion that feminine beauty and goodness could exercise a regenerative influence. It was an idealized woman, Beatrice, who led him into paradise. But Beatrice was a symbol of a virtue, of holy rather than carnal love, that kindled Dante's hope, faith, charity, and assurance of his own salvation.

Dante's claim to fame was advertised, and the Tuscan tongue further developed, by Francesco Petrarch (1304–74) and Giovanni Boccaccio (1313–75). Although both were humanists dedicated to classical learning, their principal literary impact came from Petrarch's poetry and Boccaccio's *Decameron.* In the person of Laura, Petrarch continued Dante's theme of feminine inspiration, and it is to her that his sonnets are dedicated, lyrics that became classic models imitated in Italy and the rest of Europe. The uneasiness that Petrarch felt in breaking with older, more ascetic norms was not shared by his friend Boccaccio. The Paris-born illegitimate son of a Florentine merchant, Boccaccio witnessed the horrors of the Black Death, which provides the *Decameron*'s setting. Seven fashionable young men and women from Florence pass their time in a secluded refuge relating tales that Boccaccio culled from popular lore. Satirical, witty, full of situations involving the artful defenses of virtue and the more frequent yieldings to temptation, Boccaccio's "Human Comedy" set down the realism, actual or touched up, of Florence. In common with other bourgeois writers of the time, he pilloried the Church and the clergy for their hypocrisy. In one tale the idea of the equal validity of Christianity, Judaism, and Muhammadanism is introduced. In another a Jew returning from a trip to Rome is converted to Christianity on the grounds that any institution so degenerate at its core could have survived so long only with divine assistance. Like other urban anticlerics Boccaccio made no formal break with the Church; in fact, he later regretted the *Decameron*'s tone, which nevertheless struck popular fancy by artfully handling subjects more often discussed than written. Boccaccio's naturalistic tone found echo throughout Europe in the writings of Chaucer, Rabelais, and many others.

Italian, like other modern vernaculars, developed under the tutelage of classical Latin. However, after Boccaccio Italian humanists directed almost all of their energies into the rarefied field of classical letters, style, and antiquities, disdaining the vulgar tongue of commoners. Until

---

* See above, pp. 500–501.

close to the end of the Renaissance only a few gifted individuals, not many of them humanists, continued to write in polished Italian prose and verse. Meanwhile, as Italian society became more aristocratic, Northern feudal themes found expression in popular literature. When Italian of any influence reappeared in the early sixteenth century, it was dominated by crusading adventures, Italianized versions of the French *Song of Roland* (for example Ariosto's *Orlando Furioso*), and manuals of the art of being a proper courtier.

Italian served as a model for subsequent Northern vernacular naturalism. In the Middle English of London and the court Geoffrey Chaucer (1340–1400) drew on a busy life of public affairs, French and Italian literary contacts, and late medieval lore to produce *The Canterbury Tales*. Chaucer set his tale-tellers on a pilgrimage in the course of which some of them related episodes equaling Boccaccio in anticlericalism and naturalism; others defended matrimony and honorable clerks (clerics). Chaucer initiated the first tradition of vernacular English realism, a tradition that culminated in Shakespeare in the sixteenth century.

French chronicles and poetry tended toward chivalric and generally medieval subject matter. But secular elements of love, anticlericalism, and even the debunking of crusades and fraudulent relics were represented. After the Hundred Years' War, François Villon (1431?–63) left both a great and a small *Testament* of the world of thieves and harlots, of sickness and want, of death, dungeons, and the expectation of execution. A century later such lower-class naturalism had yielded to the aristocratic erudition of court and polished letters, represented by Margaret of Navarre and François Rabelais (1494?–1553).

Margaret, sister of Francis I and patron of French humanism, imitated Boccaccio's *Decameron*, but her tone was more mystical and moralizing. French vernacular literature reached its maturity in Rabelais, as much a child of humanism as of popular naturalism. German vernacular was represented by Sebastian Brant (1458–1521), who satirized social foibles in the *Ship of Fools*. He also pioneered the use of popular tracts which flooded Germany during the early Reformation. In Spain, where governments had first used a written version of the spoken language for administrative records, the emergence of a distinctly modern literary masterpiece was delayed until the early seventeenth century, when Cervantes's *Don Quixote* appeared.

The evolution of different local spoken languages into written literary vehicles increased the diversification of cultures. Political boundaries tended to become linguistic frontiers, while patriotic impulses helped shape the development of local language patterns. As rivals to ecclesiastical Latin—to which must be added the revival of classical Latin—vernacular languages threatened the hold of the Church on culture. And since the themes of works in these tongues were frequently naturalistic, they similarly threatened the standards of ideal and absolute values that the Church historically represented.

The Decline of Scholastic Universalism

The breakdown of medieval linguistic universalism also had parallels in academic thought. Thirteenth-century schoolmen headed by Thomas Aquinas had met the challenge of Aristotelian philosophy and science—much of it handed on to Europeans by the Arabs—by subordinating its natural reason to Christian revelation and the divine authority of the Church. Nevertheless Aquinas considered Aristotle to be "the philosopher" because he came so close to perfection in his use of

Theology lecture at the Sorbonne in Paris of the kind that repulsed humanists.

natural reason. The Thomists—Aquinas's followers—believed that ultimate reality consisted of universal concepts grasped by both reason and revelation; provided that proper premises—universals—were used, they could deduce from these the nature of particular things by means of logical syllogisms. As we saw in the preceding chapter, this method undergirded the Church's claims to universal obedience and the medieval idea of a single commonwealth of Christendom, but during the Renaissance both theory and practice were attacked by nominalist philosophers, Augustinian theologians, and empirical scientists.

Scholars working in the tradition of St. Augustine held that only knowledge of divine things secured in the pursuit of salvation constituted real wisdom; they never accepted Aquinas's "Aristotelianized" Christianity. In the universities, particularly among Franciscan teachers, *nominalist* scholastics followed the Augustinian tradition. They attacked Thomist universals as mere names (*nomina*) and found ultimate reality only in individual things. The most forceful fourteenth-century nominalist was William of Ockham. Like Augustine he denied that reason could either penetrate divine mysteries or demonstrate the dogmas of the Church. Reason, for example, could not uphold the doctrine of the Trinity, since reason required that there be either one or three gods. For Ockham the Trinity was a divine mystery; logic could not explain it. It had to be accepted on the basis of revelation, faith, and authority. Moreover, the sovereign will of God was not circumscribed by reason; God could save the wicked and damn the virtuous as he chose.

In theology, nominalists encouraged non-rational faith, mysticism, and unquestioned obedience to authority. But for the study of nature they advocated direct observation or experiment rather than deduction from given universal principles. At fourteenth-century Oxford and Paris this empirical approach to nature led to a rethinking of Aristotle's physics. Although the nominalists hardly dared deny that the universe was directed by spirits they nevertheless found Aristotle's explanation of motion untenable. Deficiencies and inadequacies in instruments, mathematics, and conceptual tools probably accounted for their failure to achieve a scientific revolution. But their conclusions were carried to Italy, where the soil for scientific advances proved to be more fertile; there the universities were not dominated by theology, nor had scholastic theology taken deep root. In addition, Archimedes' methods had been rediscovered, and manuscripts edited by humanists demonstrated that not all of the ancients had agreed with the Aristotelians. Professors at the Venetian university of Padua studied Aristotle without the theological trappings of supernatural causation that Thomists had added to his philosophy; they sought only natural causes for natural phenomena. Leonardo da Vinci—the foremost empirical scientist of the Italian Renaissance—and, later, Copernicus and Galileo were in intimate contact with this scientific tradition. Aided by significant advances in mathematics during the Renaissance the tradition bore fruit in the scientific revolution of the seventeenth century.

Italian natural scientists agreed with the nominalists that current religious doctrines could not be demonstrated empirically; hence they often agreed with the nominalists and Augustinians that reason was not a proper tool for theology. The nominalists, however, did not persist in their quest for an empirical science of nature; they abandoned it for a theology based on faith and revelation, engaging in complicated disputes with the Thomists and each other at stratospheric levels of abstraction. This, too, weakened the hold of scholastic universalism.*

Italian Humanism

Theological wrangling generated robust skepticism concerning the meaningfulness of all scholastic hairsplitting. This was especially true for laymen of the Italian city-states who came to find a better treatment of their personal problems in classical Roman and Greek texts than by academic philosophers and theologians. Urban rather than feudal, practical rather than metaphysical, Italian society first supported a corps of scholars devoted to the revival of ancient, pagan moral philosophy produced by similar societies of antiquity. Thus the range of its interests far exceeded the Christian humanism of the High Middle Ages.

Consistent with the belief that their age marked a new departure from the medieval past, the Italian humanists heralded a "revival of learning" held up in conscious opposition to scholasticism. Classical humanism rapidly became a movement whose contagiousness grew among the many educated laymen hungering for a secular, practical ethic. For them, neither the medieval monastic ideal nor the timeless, abstract philosophical doctrines of the scholastics seemed livable. Medieval scholars had also used the classics widely, but they had subordinated them to theology and scholastic philosophy or else had borrowed legal and scientific data from them as final, authoritative statements. Humanists whose manuscript discoveries

---

* But it should not be assumed that scholastic universalism was dead; rather, it continued to coexist with humanism in the universities. Revived during the religious controversies of the 1500s and disseminated more widely than ever by the new printing presses, it continued to thrive at least until the eighteenth century.

immensely expanded the body of available classical writings approached them with a different intent and purpose. The "revival of learning" was thus not so much the discovery of a new set of authorities as a different appreciation of the meaning and usage of pagan antiquity.

Generally recognized as the first to give classical studies a new turn was Petrarch (Petrarca), a notary living in the Florentine colony at papal Avignon. As a youth he broke from legal studies to take up the classics, and as an adult he spurned the "crazy and clamorous set of scholastics." In classical literature, especially in Cicero's writings, he found his model of literary style and moral philosophy. Noting that Cicero had been an active statesman forced against his will to become a reclusive Stoic philosopher, Petrarch turned his attention to "civic humanism." Here he made a lasting contribution to the moral philosophy of involvement in political affairs, for Cicero taught that the primary task of man is action in, and service to, the community. Henceforth Cicero became the object of the kind of enthusiasm previously directed toward Aristotle; but Petrarch was not himself a political activist. His enthusiasm for the ancients encouraged him to hunt down manuscripts for his library, to woo fame by writing a long Latin epic poem in imitation of Virgil, and to urge the recovery of Greek language and literature. His *Familiar Letters* and *Lives of Illustrious Men* displayed a new depth of classical scholarship and a preoccupation with historic personalities whose lives might serve as models for living in civic society.

Since Petrarch conceived of religion as moral philosophy rather than knowledge of doctrine, he saw no conflict between Cicero and Christ. But the quest for fame and the exaltation of ideal womanhood in his vernacular sonnets brought him into conscious conflict with traditional ascetic ideals. He set down the tensions generated by this conflict in his *Soul's Secret*, an imaginary exchange of letters with St. Augustine, who himself had abandoned classical wisdom for doctrinal and institutional Christianity. Petrarch agreed with the great otherworldly theologian on many points but insisted on living in one world at a time. "There is a certain justification of my way of life," he writes to Augustine.

"It may be only glory that we seek here, but I persuade myself that so long as we remain here, that is right. Another glory awaits us in heaven and he who reaches there will not wish even to think of earthly fame. So this is the natural order, that among mortals the care of things mortal should come first; to the transitory will then succeed the eternal; from the first to the second is the natural progression."[2]

Although Petrarch affirmed the value of contemplation, he praised civic activity more than anyone since Roman times. His successors, inflamed by his enthusiasm for classical studies, lent increasing emphasis to Augustine's "earthly city" as against his "heavenly" one.

It was Boccaccio who transmitted Cicero's civic humanism and standards of style to Florence, where they found their fullest development between 1375 and 1450. After Boccaccio's death, in 1375, prominent Florentines formed study groups to reexamine the classics. They collected libraries and manuscripts and, beginning with Coluccio Salutati (1331–1406), installed a succession of distinguished humanist chancellors. The development of republican Florentine humanism coincided with the victory of the woolen guild masters over the lower classes in 1382. It reached a peak shortly thereafter as Florence defended itself

[2] Quoted by James Harvey Robinson and Henry Winchester Rolfe, *Petrarch, The First Modern Scholar and Man of Letters* (New York: G. P. Putnam's Sons, 1914), p. 452.

against Milan, seat of an aggressive despotism. Rather surprisingly this venture of Florence into civic humanism did not particularly encourage businessmen or lower-class elements to exploit it in order to gain a higher place in society. Instead it served as a rationale for the Florentine elite to use their talents and leisure for the advancement of the commonweal of the republic. For the most part their ideals were culled from the study of classical history and moral philosophy. Preeminent among them was the development of the well-rounded man of universal accomplishments, strength of character in adversity, possession of fortune or luck's favor, and the ability to wield power.

Florentine civic humanism became most secular and utilitarian at the hands of Leonardo Bruni (1370–1444), a biographer of Cicero. As chancellor he promoted educational practices designed to create citizens rather than scholars. For patriotic purposes he wrote a legend-purged history of the city that looked for human political and economic causes for events of the past. However worthy such efforts were, civic humanists could flourish only in a republic; thus when Florence became a Medicean principality the institutional support for their ideology withered. Sixteenth-century Venice, whose leading families belatedly adopted humanism, preserved some aspects of its outlook. For the most part civic humanism was a transient phenomenon of the Renaissance confined to one city, Florence, and even there it lasted less than a century. Moreover in many parts of Italy classical humanists supported despots whose conquest of all Italy would presumably put an end to the peninsula's constant wars.

While activist republican humanism was running its course classical scholarship matured in method and achievement to the point where it became a potentially explosive cultural and intellectual force. Boccaccio contributed to a deeper knowledge by compiling biographies of famous men and women, a genealogy of the gods, and a classical geography. With all the enthusiasm of prospectors caught up in the fervor of a gold rush, traveling scholars combed monastic libraries and Eastern cities for manuscripts of classical Latin and Greek authors. Their energies were devoted variously to inscriptions, archaeology, architecture, and coinage. Visiting Eastern Orthodox church dignitaries taught Italians Greek philosophy, especially Platonic philosophy.* In addition to learning Latin and Greek in their ancient styles, humanist scholars, the better to cope with deviating texts and copyists' errors, developed historical philology and a respect for original sources. Unlike the scholastics, who used multiple allegorical meanings for passages picked out of historical context, they learned to rely upon a single literal, historical meaning within a specific context.

Enamored of the clarity and forcefulness of ancient expression as compared with contemporary "barbarous" Latin, the humanists became zealous advocates of pure classical style. But the implications of their method and knowledge reached much deeper than the mere training of stylists. The career of Lorenzo Valla (1405–57) illustrates this. As a young teacher, rhetorician, and philologist, he was employed in 1433 by King Alfonso of Naples who, like many other princes, was an enemy of the pope. Before he had long been at his job Valla conclusively demonstrated from internal evidence that the Donation of Constantine, a purported cession of central Italy to the papacy in the fourth century was in fact a fabrication of the ninth century. Retained thereafter by the hu-

---

* They also taught some northern Italian humanists the Greek language, but in southern Italy and Sicily a Greek-speaking populace had preserved a knowledge of that language throughout the Middle Ages. Thus the humanists' study of Greek was not entirely new.

manist pope Nicholas V as his secretary, Valla followed this exposé (which others had anticipated) with a demonstration that the Apostles' Creed originated in Nicene rather than apostolic times and that other popular authorities were similarly antedated or fraudulent. Having access to Vatican codices, he also treated the Bible as a historical document and called attention to numerous errors in the Latin Vulgate edition of the New Testament.

Valla's method of going to the sources undercut much traditional authority, and it epitomized the birth of a new sense of historical consciousness among the humanists. No longer were the ancients treated as timeless oracles. Rather, the humanists were aware of the span of time that separated them from the ancients. It was precisely that historical perspective which enabled them to enter into the thoughts of the ancients as living men trying to solve real human problems in the context of their own times. This new sense of historical perspective and the use of evidence introduced the novel idea of *anachronism*, something utterly foreign to most previous thought which had dealt with timeless universals and authority. To the idea of going back to pure sources was linked that of returning to a period of ecclesiastical or ethical purity as a standard or model. Long the practice of religious reformers, this primitivism soon became a revolutionary tactic of the Protestant Reformation. Historical consciousness was a real revolution of the Renaissance, but because its implications were too sensitive for so many cherished beliefs, it was centuries before they were followed up thoroughly. As a result numerous humanists and historians, instead of pursuing the new principles to their logical conclusions, put themselves to the composition of idylls and the depiction of Arcadias, or ideal country life, utterly detached from contemporaneous reality.

In addition to the employment of a revolutionary method, Italian humanists differed from traditional theologians and scholastics in posing a different set of significant questions. Most of them totally ignored metaphysics, formal theology, and preoccupation with death. Instead they were concerned with practical questions of human relationships. Language (rhetoric) was basic because it was the means of social communication, of moving and directing human will and actions. Because they ignored theology the humanists found no conflict between ancient pagan philosophers and Christianity. Although they taught rational restraint, they considered nature good and worthy of enjoyment and artistic imitation. Religion was seen to be a part of nature, therefore while all but a few denounced monasticism or monastic vows, rarely did the humanists break formally with the Church. They found divinity less in sacrament and priest than in wordly and classical beauty. To most Northern humanists as well as to later religious reformers, whether Catholic or Protestant, the esthetic, political, and social morality of the Italian humanists appeared pagan.

Whatever evaluation is made, the Italian humanists formulated a lay ethic rivaling the monastic ideal—which, it should be remembered, the Church never intended to apply to society as a whole. Moreover, the Renaissance papacy and hierarchy tended increasingly to accept classical humanism's standard of values. To the extent that they did, the Church's authority was undermined for all those who believed in the preeminence of doctrine and traditional ideals. Wherever doctrinal religion recovered ascendancy, classical studies were again subordinated to the role that they had played in the Middle Ages.

Italian humanists made their greatest impact as educators. If they were mistrustful of logic and abstract philosophy, they were downright scornful of law and science.* For these disciplines they substituted rhetoric, grammar, poetry, history, and purified classical languages. Mathematics, physical education, and music also received attention. The emphasis on classical languages and perfected style tended to make humanist scholarship a cult with high admission requirements, particularly as these scholars began to look down on vernacular languages. As late as the nineteenth—even the twentieth—century, classical education was a mark of achievement and status in Western countries.

Obviously not all products of humanist schools became scholars. The fact that humanism became a movement of general social importance is probably best explained by the availability of positions open to men trained in style and rhetorical persuasion. Most young men with classical educations found employment with states, prelates, or private patrons. Many were employed as the equivalent of modern press agents to present their employers' cases persuasively. As historians they frequently wrote commissioned and biased accounts, gracing their patrons' heroic deeds with impossible classical perorations.

The nature of patronage and of educational opportunities helped shape the course of late Italian humanism. The Church, the princes, and the aristocracy were the principal patrons. As republics declined, civic humanism waned or adjusted to courtly surroundings. In Florence Cosimo de' Medici founded a formal school of philosophy—the Platonic Academy—headed successively by Marsilio Ficino and Pico della Mirandola. Although both championed free will and the dignity of man, both also exalted the contemplative life above the active. Rising despotism and a feeling of helplessness in the face of foreign invasion after 1494 made faith in man's ability to use institutions for human improvement difficult to sustain.

In Florence the powerful popular preacher Savonarola (1452–98) tried to turn back the tide with a blend of civic democracy and Christian fundamentalism. Gaining a following among the Florentines when his prophecies of repeated disasters seemed to be fulfilled, he became the leading figure behind an attempt to restore Florentine republicanism when the Medici were driven out by an invading army in 1494. For four years his sermons steered the Florentine republic, whose citizens were moved to burn their immoral books and works of art. His puritanism and his attacks on Pope Alexander VI made him many enemies, however; in 1497 he was excommunicated by the pope, and in the following year the Florentine government executed him. After a short interlude, the Medici regained control over the city. Temporary as it was, Savonarola's career demonstrated how slight a hold the humanists had on Florence.* Witch-hunts during the fifteenth century exposed the same weakness. This humanistic elitism, with its requirements of wealth, leisure, and political participation in an oligarchic society, had confined the values of humanism to a narrow cult.

As defeated Florentine republicans became disillusioned cynics, the typical ideal that emerged from the Italian Renaissance was that of the refined, well-rounded courtier, witty in repartee, appreciative of feminine beauty, and adept

---

* Nevertheless they contributed heavily to the development of both science and law. Their emphasis on mathematics in the schools and their recovery of classical texts from antiquity aided the scientific revolution that culminated in the seventeenth century. Some of them—notably Valla—turned their critical philology to the historical understanding of legal texts with eventually revolutionary effects.

* The conversion of no less a humanist than Mirandola testifies to the persuasive power of this reformer, by whose message Michelangelo was also deeply affected.

Savonarola preaching, 1496.

at arms. Count Baldassare Castiglione (1478–1529), a product of the polished courts and diplomatic service of Milan, Mantua, and Urbino, gave definitive and much-imitated expression to the new courtly ideal of the secular, classically educated chivalric gentleman in *The Courtier*. Translated into northern tongues, his work more than any other of the Renaissance provided a ready definition of the all-accomplished gentleman, the universal man of polite courtly society that characterized the ideals of Europe's educated aristocracy in the following century.

Northern Humanism

By the end of the Renaissance the more aristocratic and religiously oriented parts of Europe outside Italy were receptive to the force of the contemplative, religious, and chivalric humanism that the Italians had evolved. But Northern humanism did not become a mere copy of Italian models —local traditions and the vagaries of individual humanists filtered and modified their impact; therefore Northern humanism had many different facets. In general it was less esthetic than Italian humanism; in particular, philology and the content of the classics were more subordinated to religion and metaphysics. Northern humanists were also less antagonistic toward scholasticism and the study and practice of Roman law.

In Spain tradition blunted the impact of secular humanism. There, philological and linguistic studies, which spread rapidly during the reign of Ferdinand and Isabella, were strictly subordinated to theology. This diluted brand of humanism culminated in the career of Cardinal Ximénes, Queen Isabella's confessor, head of the Spanish Inquisition, and regent on Ferdinand's death.* Ximénes was responsible for the founding and reform of several universities, notably Alcalá. The fa-

---
* See p. 579.

culties of these schools devoted a third of their instructional time to language and literature as auxiliaries to theology. Ximénes's crowning philological achievement was a Polyglot Bible. To facilitate textual comparison the Scriptures were presented in different early languages set up in parallel columns. Other Spanish humanists such as Juan Luis Vives (1492–1540) proved more receptive to the advanced doctrines of Eramus of Rotterdam. But under pressure of the Inquisition to conform to scholastic tradition, they either emigrated or were silenced. As political master of Italy during the Catholic Reformation, Spain also served to stifle Italian humanism.

Ultimately France, the hearth of medieval scholasticism, responded more creatively to Italian humanism, especially after the French invasion of Italy in 1494. The royal court of Francis I and especially of his sister, Magaret of Navarre, patronized the "new learning." Most of its early devotees sought a fusion of traditionalism, religious mysticism, and classical forms. Prominent among them were Lefèbvre d'Étaples; Guillaume Briçonnet, bishop of Meaux; and Guillaume Budé, all of whom flourished around the turn of the sixteenth century. They spurned secularism and devoted their energies to religion based on the classics and Scripture. In particular they deemphasized the sacraments and exalted conduct as the essence of Christianity. In phrases such as "salvation by faith alone," they seemed to anticipate a Protestant theme. In fact, their fundamental assumptions concerning human dignity and free will were quite different from the Augustinian premises of the depravity and bondage of the will held by Luther and Calvin.

Alongside this strain of French thought ran the secular naturalism of Francois Rabelais, physician and humanist who relished emancipation from the "thick Gothic night" of the Middle Ages. His *Gargantua and Pantagruel* pilloried scholasticism and proposed an ideal coeducational "monastic" system in which universal learning and disciplined willpower would set all the rules. Stoicism, which identified virtue with happiness and wisdom with prudence, was also widespread in French humanist circles.

German humanism had roots in a variety of institutions: the imperial court of the fifteenth century, the schools of the Brethren of the Common Life, and the elite families of the imperial cities. Colored by romantic cultural nationalism, this humanism refuted the Italian charge that Northern barbarians had ruined classical culture during the Middle Ages. Some German humanists upheld scholasticism and were trained in civil or canon law or both; most were primarily interested in religious reform. Although they usually conceived religion more as deeds than creeds, they rejected the "paganism" of the Italian Renaissance. The most accomplished German humanist was Johann Reuchlin (1455–1522), a jurist and professor who mastered not only Greek and Latin but also Hebrew literature. Influenced by Hebraic studies, especially the esoteric mystical interpretations of scriptures known as the *Kabbalah,* Reuchlin's works touched off a celebrated controversy with anti-Semitic traditionalists who indicted him (unsuccessfully) before the Inquisition. In his defense a small group of radical humanists under the leadership of Ulrich von Hutten* satirized the ignorance, credulity, and petty doctrinal preoccupations of Reuchlin's monkish opponents in the *Letters of Obscure Men,* two series of which appeared in 1515 and 1517. The Reuchlin affair was soon overshadowed by the creedal conflicts of the Reformation that fractured German humanism.

England also developed a strain of re-

---

* See pp. 615–16.

ligious humanism that drew inspiration from the late Italian Renaissance. John Colet returned from Italy to lecture after 1496 on the Scriptures, particularly the letters of St. Paul. Of greater fame was another English townsman, Thomas More (1478–1535), a lawyer and classically educated layman who served Henry VIII. An ascetic more devoted to redemptive religion than to the classics, More published a mocking satire on contemporary England, *Utopia*, which showed that non-Christian people could create a near-perfect society. In this and other writings, More advocated partial tolerance, a warm sympathy for the lower classes, and a concept of limited government. As an official, he did not always act in conformity to his theoretical views. Caught up by the religious controversies of the Reformation, he became an anti-Protestant polemicist. Ultimately he had to choose between loyalty to Henry VIII as head of the English church and loyalty to the Roman church. Preferring the latter, he became a martyr and was canonized in the twentieth century.

Erasmus

Far overshadowing the reputations and influence of all other contemporary Northern and Italian humanists, with most of whom he kept in some contact, was the cosmopolitan "prince of the humanists," Erasmus of Rotterdam (1467?–1536).

An orphaned illegitimate son of a priest educated at the Deventer school of the Brethren of the Common Life, Erasmus was sent by guardians to a monastery. Thereafter he became an episcopal secretary, a student of theology at the University of Paris, and a nomadic scholar. Attracted early by the classics and the works of Lorenzo Valla, he rejected contemporary scholasticism (but not Thomas Aquinas) and—with a papal dispensation—spent the remainder of his life outside cloister walls. A visit to England in 1500 yielded contacts that produced uninterrupted patronage as well as the friendship of Thomas More and John Colet, who encouraged him to follow a career of religious scholarship. When he returned to the continent he began a prolific publishing career, editing the early Church Fathers, beginning with St. Jerome, and a Greek edition of the New Testament. Textbook selections from the classics for purposes of style and reference, works of satirical criticism, personal letters, and paraphrases from the New Testament followed and attained wide popularity. They mostly dealt with literary history and a specific educational reform program and had very little to do with scholastic theology and philosophy.

Among Erasmus's publications were the *Adages*, a selection of classical quotations, and the *Colloquies*, a reader much used in schools. From inspired pagans who were thought to have anticipated Christianity he sought to gain knowledge of all that was known of the arts of war and peace, poetry, writing, speech, and science. "Good letters"—training in classical literature and moral philosophy—were essential to virtue, for love without knowledge he held to be blind. For Erasmus classical scholarship could never be an end in itself. Although he constantly revised his immense personal correspondence in order to achieve literary excellence, he chided "Ciceronian" stylistic purists and decried Italian "paganism." Indeed, he subordinated classical scholarship to a broad educational and religious reformation that was to be rooted in the New Testament and the early Fathers of the Church.

Although Erasmus wrote on theological subjects, he deemphasized ritual, doctrines, and external observances in favor of a Christian ethic defined by the letters

Erasmus *by Hans Holbein the Younger.*

of Paul and the Sermon on the Mount, which he described as "the philosophy of Christ." He worked to reform Christianity so that it might rest on texts, institutions, and practices purged of corruption. His "social gospel" involved a drastic social transformation, but his method was marked by gradualism and nonviolent education rather than by force. His publication of critical editions of the Greek New Testament was intended as the basis for vernacular translations that he hoped would eventually be read and sung by the simplest laymen, male and female alike. Most of his publishing efforts were devoted to the printing of the early Church Fathers' writings, which appealed to him not only because they represented primitive uncorrupted Christianity but also because they differed sharply from one another on doctrines that had become hardened orthodoxy in the medieval Church. Toward controverted or unverified dogmas, Erasmus was tolerantly skeptical; for the purposes of his classical moral Christianity, they were beside the point. In his first edition of the Greek New Testament, for example, he omitted, on literary and historical grounds, the proof text for the Trinity. He was supported by Pope Leo X, but he nevertheless lived in fear that an aggressive, intolerant doctrinal resurgence by "the monks" would turn to force and destroy his reform by education.

Founder of neither a church nor a state to perpetuate and circulate his writings, Erasmus became known to posterity primarily as a satirical critic who tried to take an independent course through the confessional wrangles of the early Reformation. Best known of his writings has been *The Praise of Folly*, a tract in which Folly, a laconic woman, twits the foibles of society, clergy, businessmen, and—so alive and honest was Erasmus's sense of humor—even scholars. More devastating was *Julius Excluded from Heaven,* an anonymous tract.* In it he depicts Julius II, the "warrior pope," boasting to St. Peter of his manipulation of Church councils and threatening to take heaven's gates by military storm if refused admission. In other writings Erasmus associated war with savagery and held that it should be prevented among Christians by arbitration between judicious princes—a rare lot, he said, for princes, like fools, needed only to be born! His satirical criticism extended to relics, indulgences, domination of clerical posts by nobles, pilgrimages, invocation of saints, and sundry other aspects of external popular piety then current. His satire and his pacific humor were intolerable to both doctrinal Protestants and traditionalist Catholics; for Erasmus they were a means of laughing his opponents out of

---

* Erasmus may not have written this, but contemporaries attributed it to him, and with good cause.

court, much preferable to reliance on force. The latter course he accurately predicted would lead to generations of religious warfare rather than to peace and unity under reformed institutions.

Always writing in Latin (with the exception of the Greek New Testament, to which was joined a fresh Latin translation), Erasmus believed in a cosmopolitan aristocracy of talent that should practice and develop a social as well as an individual moral gospel. To others he left the task of translating and implementing his humanistic reform program; however, after 1517 its fate became inextricably bound up with the confessional conflicts of the Reformation, a consequence that we shall consider in the following chapter.

Jurists and Political Theorists

Humanists have usually been considered the truest representatives of the Renaissance, but in their own day jurists and officials commanded more prestige. During the late Renaissance four concepts of the state were formulated: the Roman law—or absolutist—conception; the divine-right theory; the humanistic idealism of Erasmus; and the political realism of Machiavelli and Guicciardini.

The study of Roman law as preparation for service in governments and the Church was the surest path to power, fortune, and prestige. As secular governments curbed the jurisdiction of ecclesiastical canon law, Roman civil lawyers gained preeminent influence. For example, their foremost Renaissance teacher, Andrea Alciati (1492–1550) of Pavia, was renowned throughout western Europe.

Roman law in its late absolutist, or Justinian, form* was revived ca. 1100, when Irnerius of Bologna began teaching the subject to mature students. Townsmen

---

* See pp. 510–11.

found congenial its recognition of, and legal support for, absolute property rights (as distinct from feudal tenure and manorial rights of use) as well as contractual obligations basic to a commercial, capitalistic society. Other parts of the law were used by kings as a rationale for centralizing power in the hands of state officials rather than delegating it to feudal tenants.* In late imperial Rome the will of the prince (or council) had become law. Now in the late Renaissance, growing authoritarianism gave rise to comparable law, important for effecting the transition from decentralized feudalism to the centralized, absolute state of the late Renaissance. As oligarchies tightened and monarchs undermined the nobles' political power, existing authorities laid exclusive claim to the secret "mysteries of state."

Clergymen reinforced and extended Roman law absolutism with the doctrine of the divine right of kings: kings were accountable to God alone; resistance to them was a cardinal sin. As the pope had been exalted by many canonists, especially in the thirteenth and fourteenth centuries, divine-right princes were now exalted above the law and representative assemblies. Their courts, councils, and officials combined legislative, executive, and judicial functions; still, in practice, they shared authority with the Church. By the beginning of the sixteenth century, all wielders of power—magisterial, ecclesiastical, patrimonial—constituted a separate "estate," a privileged status group within the traditional social hierarchy. The members of this estate were too numerous and often too obscure to warrant mention by name here.

Quite different from the viewpoints of Roman lawyers and theological theorists of divine-right monarchy were those of the Erasmian humanists. For Thomas More and Erasmus, the ruler was neither

---

* Often, however, royal officials exploited these powers to benefit themselves rather than the ruler.

possessor of the kingdom nor above the law. Rather he was a steward subject to deposition by "freemen"—that is, by the aristocracy. In his *Institution of a Christian Prince* Erasmus subsumed politics under ethics as defined by the New Testament. The prince's first duty was to care for the commonweal of his subjects. He ought to tax the luxuries rather than the necessities of life and to promote peace, education, and the practical arts. In matters of taxation and peace Erasmus was advocating nothing less than a complete reversal of political trends then current. Although he wrote guides for existing rulers, his critiques of princes frankly implied republicanism.

The humanist concept of government existing for the commonweal was very widespread on the eve of the Reformation; but religious controversies restored the notion that Christian magistrates must secure the salvation of souls by enforcing doctrinal purity. Its enforcement need not, however, coincide with the mundane general welfare. Erasmian influences remained strongest in republican towns, the Low Countries, and in England. Although critics have tended to dismiss Erasmus's thought as an impracticable return to medieval political theory, more recently he has assumed the position of an intellectual godfather to the European Economic Community and to other attempts to secure international peace and cooperation.

The most significant approach to politics during the Renaissance was the realism of Machiavelli and Guicciardini. Niccolò Machiavelli (1469–1527) became one of the most celebrated political theorists of all history. Born into a prominent Florentine family and given a gentleman's education (which included the Roman classics), he entered public service in 1498 while Florence's rulers, the Medici, were in exile. After serving as secretary of the secret committee for military affairs, in the chancery, and on the highest council, he was sent as a diplomatic agent to France,

Germany, Switzerland, and various parts of Italy. His letters show that he was particularly impressed with Ferdinand of Spain, Cesare Borgia, Julius II, and the armed citizenry of the Swiss Confederation. When the Medici returned in 1512, he was recruiting peasant subjects for a citizens' army with which to recover rebellious Pisa.

This experience served him well, but it was his literary gifts, not his reputation as an administrator, that made Machiavelli famous. Politically suspect to the restored Medici, he spent the remainder of his life writing political commentaries, history, satirical drama, and even a piece of devotional literature. Apart from his *Art of War*, which advocated the restoration of a citizens' army, his most significant political works were *The Discourses on the First Ten Books of Titus Livy* and *The Prince*. His writing reflected secular humanism, but he included topics that most humanists omitted: conspiracies, assassinations, and the calculated use of terror. His announced intention was to create a science of statecraft based on classical learning. He tried to do for politics what others did for art, medicine, and jurisprudence: to clarify and codify the principles that antiquity, especially Rome, had followed. With instructive examples and maxims drawn from the repetitiveness of history--a record forever marked by the depravity of man—perhaps men could foresee events and prevent future errors. Many critics consider him the first empiricist in modern political science, although one not without his doctrinaire prejudices.

Machiavelli followed civic humanists in rejecting religious justification for the state. He conceived the state as having its own rules apart from social or individual morality and from divine or natural law. In a wicked world, moral rulers failed. Statebuilding required force, fraud, and deceit to advance security of the state; in both foreign and domestic policies

Niccolo Machiavelli.

"reason of state"—concern exclusively for the security of the state—should determine political action. Machiavelli's state is not irreligious, however. Princes and heads of republics should uphold religion, keep their people pious, and esteem miracles as the means of increasing their own authority and keeping the state well ordered and united. But ultimate human values should be concerned with the preservation and growth of the state. "I love my native city more than my own soul," wrote Machiavelli, thus chastizing the Church for making men soft, indolent, and unfit for battle. In common with most officials and diplomats of the time, he advocated state supremacy over the Church.

In Machiavelli's age, society was rigidly stratified and gentle birth highly honored, but he was an antiaristocratic advocate of a popular regime. In his scheme of things the heroic virtues would supplant gentility, for at all times force was decisive in human affairs. For extraordinary crises he advocated despotic tyranny. In *The Prince* we find the ideal nature of his autocrat: he is both feared and loved—but mostly feared. By concentrating cruelties in short periods and extending well-advertised liberality over longer times he maintains an aura of goodness. He kills opponents rather than confiscates their property, for heirs are grateful for the inheritance and not permanently alienated as dispossessed persons. He keeps the faith—when it serves his interest to do so.

The Prince lends itself to varying interpretations. In the seventeenth century men of such diverse political philosophies as the French monarchist Richelieu and the English Radical Republican Whig James Harrington found it congenial to their positions. The work is sometimes taken for Machiavelli's attempt to gain the favor of the Medici, sometimes for a sincere exposition of realistic politics. A few scholars have seen it as tongue-in-cheek satire. They argue that Machiavelli's republican contemporaries could not have sanctioned the despotic prince. Yet many Italian classical republicans did indeed approve of temporary tyrannies under unusual circumstances. Whatever its author may have intended, *The Prince* offered a rationale for power politics in a world of competing states. Often, however, Machiavelli was condemned as immoral by statesmen and clergy who nevertheless subordinated religion to secular rule and who approved Machiavellian tactics when these advanced their own religious viewpoint.

Equally pessimistic and cynical about human nature and the violent basis of all state power was Machiavelli's contemporary, Francesco Guicciardini (1483–1540), Florentine diplomat, professor of law, and civil servant. A partisan of the aristocratic Medicean clique, he was ousted when Florence fell to Spain in 1527. Spurning Machiavelli's classical maxims and precedents as unrealistic romanticism, Guicciardini nevertheless agreed that opportunism based on expediency was the most rational and desirable policy for the efficient state. When Italy collapsed before Northern conquerors, he advised each individual to enrich himself as best he could (whereas Machiavelli had held that seeking after wealth was evil). In retirement he penned histories of Florence and Italy that bristled with unmerciful psychological analyses of individuals and societies, writings that are more deserving of the label "scientific" than Machiavelli's writing. But until his unpublished history of Florence was brought to light in the nineteenth century, Guicciardini's influence was slight.

The Impact of Printing with Movable Type

All types of Renaissance letters and learning were profoundly affected by the major technological innovation of the era, the invention of the printing press. Heretofore all forms of thought and expression had been dependent on handwritten manuscripts and "books" printed with carved wooden blocks. But now editions or printings of a single work or broadside could easily go into thousands of copies, and governments could rapidly publicize laws and decrees and circulate instructions to their officials and subjects.

Technologically, printing brought together the skills and inventions of craftsmen—goldsmiths, silversmiths, metallurgists, paper makers—and artists who had developed oil-based paints suitable for pressurized application to paper. Transition from wood-block printing to movable type may have been developed simultaneously in two or more cities, but

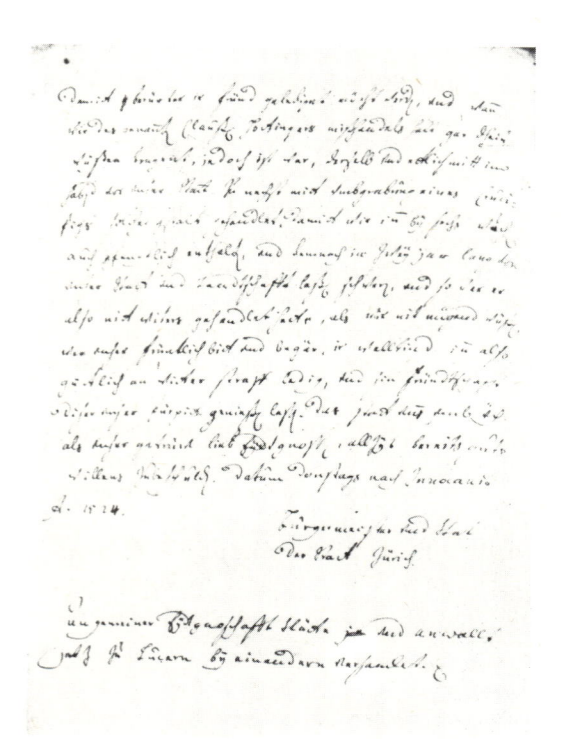

German handwriting and printing of the late Renaissance.

the first printing shop known to the book trade was that of Johann Gutenberg (whose contribution to the technology of printing is obscure). He set it up in Mainz, Germany, slightly before 1450. From Mainz printing establishments spread rapidly. By 1500 the Low Countries had at least 50, Venice and Paris more than 150. England had only two, but the number rapidly increased. Presses were also located in all the large towns of Spain and in some towns of eastern Europe outside Russia.

Mass-produced books implied the democratization of culture. Now, for example, the goal of Erasmus and Martin Luther to have biblical texts in the hands of the simplest layman was possible of achievement. But printing in itself extended neither literacy nor the amount of leisure available for reading and learning. Most early books* were traditional in content. The great majority of them were devotional works or treatises. Books on the art of dying, apocalyptic themes, and prophecy had greater circulation than reports of new geographical discoveries or business techniques, especially in Germany.

Churchmen and political authorities quickly realized the power of the press to influence public opinion—educated opinion. They moved early to control heresy and sedition, particularly after the religious schism of the sixteenth century. Where this control was weak, as in parts of pre-Reformation Germany, large numbers of popular tracts gave impetus to revolutionary social movements. Throughout Europe, including all of Germany after 1525, censorship became a function of

---

* Books produced before 1500 are called *incunabula*. Since printed books were considered inferior to fine manuscripts, printers tried to imitate as closely as possible the appearance of manuscript books.

government. Only in periods of tension did censorship break down (as in England during the 1640s, or in France during the religious wars of the second half of the sixteenth century), at which time large quantities of critical materials circulated in the vernacular. These periods were preludes to revolution.* Degrees of censorship varied in different times and places, but relative freedom of the press was primarily the work of nineteenth-century liberals. Where they failed to gain power, as in eastern Europe, political and ecclesiastical authorities have an unbroken record of control over the written word. Thus, although the invention of printing was able to revolutionize the means of communication, it could not of itself revolutionize modern culture.

THE FINE ARTS

Renaissance thinkers were self-consciously certain that their age had broken sharply with the medieval past. They could point not only to the revival of classical literature and philosophy but also to vast accomplishments in the fine arts. In his *Lives of the Painters, Sculptors, and Architects* Giorgio Vasari reveled in this decisive break even though progress might not continue into the future. He wrote of the "rebirth" of naturalism and classicism, describing how they gained ascendancy over post-Roman "barbarian" and Christian philosophies. Although his generalizations would not apply to many areas of fourteenth- and fifteenth-century life, his judgments on esthetic expression (he might have included literature) have been upheld. Without question, there was a "renaissance" in art.

---

* Two longer-term exceptions were the Dutch Republic after the seventeenth century and England's North American colonies during the eighteenth. English censorship was also relaxed after the revolution of 1688.

Late fifteenth-century printing press.

Gothic Realism

In its naturalism Renaissance art was partly an outgrowth of Gothic art. Medieval artists had used allegorical symbols, not seeking to imitate nature. But the same spirit of "naturalism" that came to prompt new forms of literature, new methods of philosophy, and new views of theology, also eventually worked changes in art. Gothic painters and sculptors began to portray individuals rather than types. In northern France of the thirteenth century they began to master the techniques of realistic detail, evident in the late statuary on the Cathedral of Chartres. At the Burgundian court, the Low Country sculptor Claus Sluter (d. 1406) achieved fleshlike verisimilitude with painted stone. The van Eyck brothers, especially Jan (1370?–1440), painted almost photographic altar pieces with oil paint, a new medium permitting greater detail. Although they achieved marked realism, northern Gothic artists, like the architects

Flemish realism: The Crucifixion *by Hubert van Eyck.*

of Gothic cathedrals, multiplied picturesque details without achieving consistency of form; nor did they master the portrayal of natural space. Despite the fact that lay patrons commissioned some works from them, these artists did mostly death and crucifixion scenes for traditional, didactic purposes.

This Gothic realism became universal during the Renaissance. It was the preeminent art form of the era, especially in northern Europe. Prior to 1500 only Italy produced a competing style; and there, too, the plastic arts were dominated by Gothic realism until the fifteenth century. But during the quattrocento (1400s) Italy became the heart of a scientific realism that displayed mastery of the rules of linear perspective, and Italian artists turned to classical expression.

Medieval Italian art owed much to Byzantine forms, particularly to the flat iconography of the Eastern church, which did not give the illusion of depth. But under French influence an Italian form of Gothic painting reached a peak that established norms in the wet plaster (fresco) paintings of Giotto (d. 1336). He transformed the style of Byzantine painting by arranging figures more naturally in space, foreshortening them to give the illusion of depth, and using expressive postures and gestures to indicate emotions. His themes were religious—the most famous of his works is the *Life of Christ* on the walls of the Arena Chapel at Padua—but he abandoned abstract symbolism to portray emotions of joy, sorrow, hope, and despair. According to a contemporary chronicler, Giotto's figures "live and breathe." His paintings could be valued apart from their religious content, and they constituted a model for such of his successors as Fra Angelico and Fra Lippo Lippi. Until the fifteenth century Italian Gothic painters strove for prettiness of detail and exactness of representation but had no formal rules of perspective.

Italian Gothic realism in fresco: Giotto's Kiss of Judas, *a detail from his* Life of Christ.

Scientific Naturalism and Classicism in Italy

When Italy's artists departed from the Gothic style they were influenced in their new directions both by scientific naturalism and by Roman classicism. Contemplating Roman ruins, architects were the first to turn to classical forms. Since Renaissance artists were not usually specialized—one and the same man was often shop-trained in sculpture, painting, goldsmithery, and architecture—boundaries between disciplines were fluid. Classical forms spread rapidly, first to sculpture, later to painting.

Science and classicism often merged in the careers of fifteenth-century artists. The work of Brunelleschi, architect and sculptor, is illustrative. He was the first both to work out mathematical laws of linear perspective and influentially to

555   B. *Cultural and Artistic Developments*

Brunelleschi's Dome, Cathedral of Florence.

Alberti, interior of S. Andrea at Mantua.

LEFT: *Naturalism and pathos:* Masaccio's Adam and Eve.

Classical realism at its peak: Donatello's David.

Leonardo's The Madonna of the Rocks.

TOP RIGHT: *Botticelli's return to mystical allegory:* The Birth of Venus.

BOTTOM RIGHT: *A page from Albrecht Dürer's scientific treatise on human proportions, 1528.*

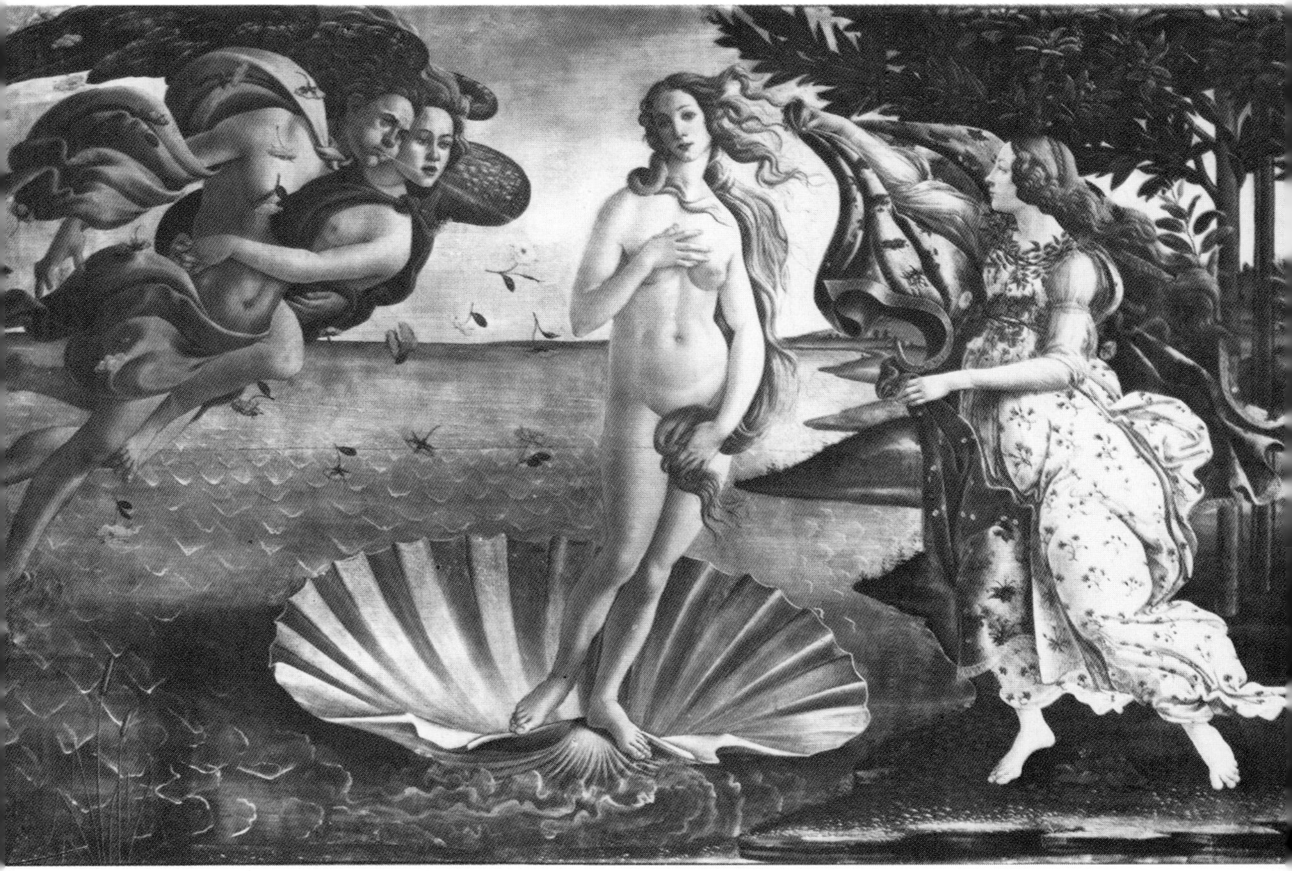

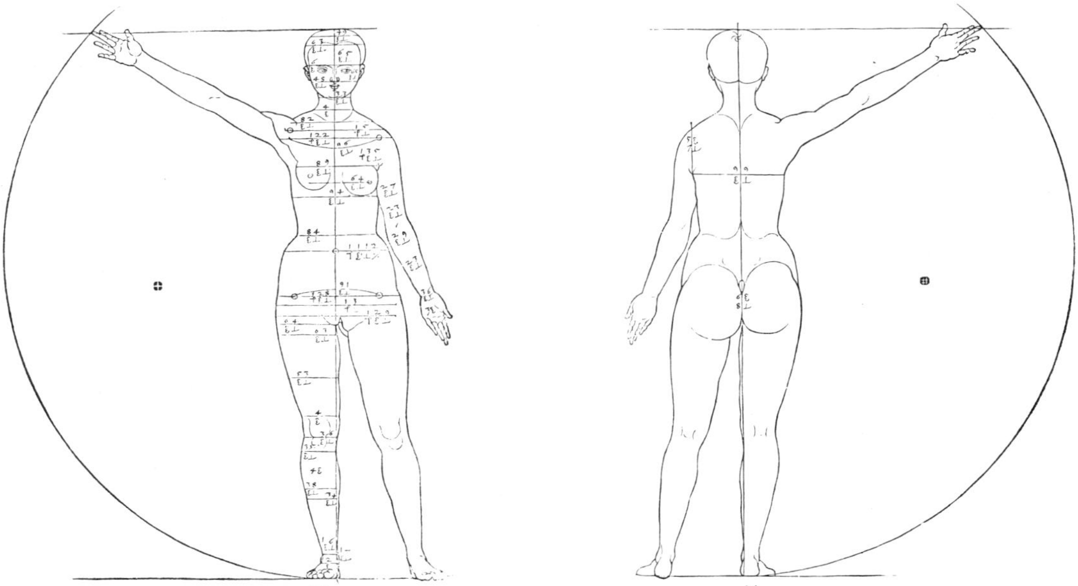

Religious naturalism and quizzical cherubs: **Sistine Madonna** *by Raphael.*

TOP RIGHT: *Realism and power:* **The Creation of Adam** (*Sistine Chapel*) *by Michelangelo.*

BOTTOM RIGHT: *Manneristic sensuousness: a nude by Titian.*

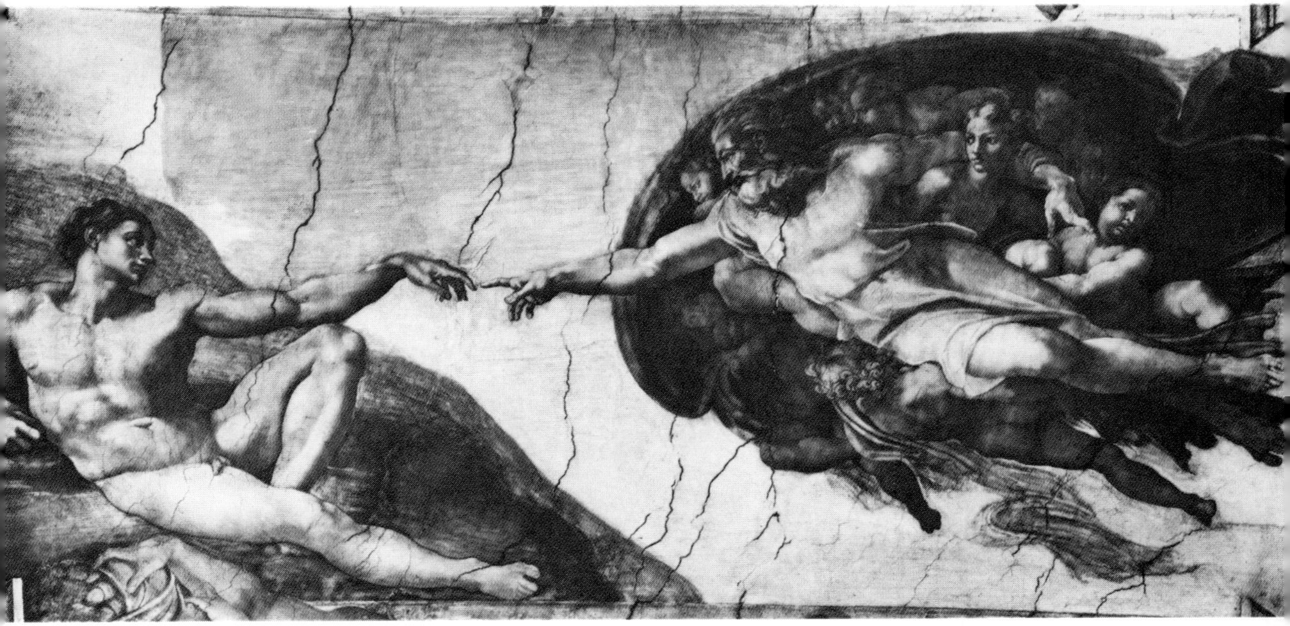

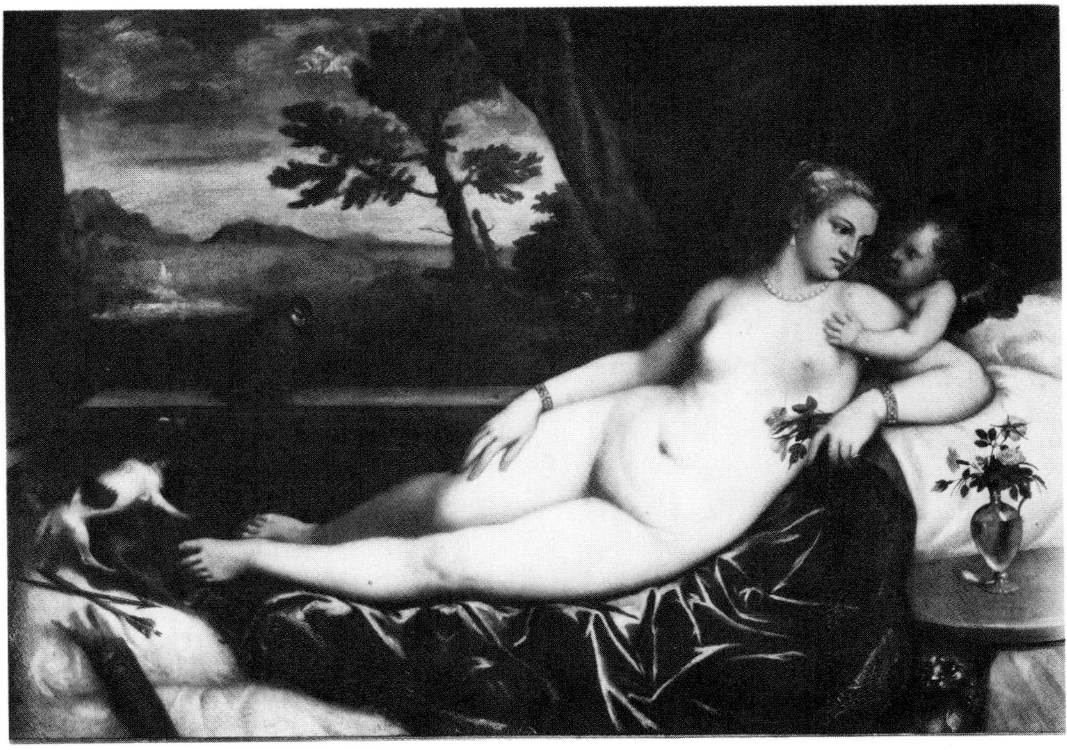

A giant to kill a giant: Michelangelo's David.

emulate classical styles of building. Disliking Gothic, he studied in Rome, a veritable museum of ancient, earthbound architecture. Commissioned to remodel Florence, he introduced round columns, rounded arches, pilasters, and domes. He refrained, however, from copying buildings of antiquity. Another architect and theorist, Leon Battista Alberti (1405–71), soon developed a more imitative classicism and proposed to make architecture a mathematical science of balance and proportion as well as the most utilitarian of the arts.

In 1401 Brunelleschi competed with Ghiberti, Jacopo della Quercia, and others for the commission to cast sculptured bronze doors for the Baptistery of Florence. Ghiberti won. He spent a decade executing the project, which Michelangelo later described as worthy of being the gates of paradise. Ghiberti put the biblical story of Isaac into a natural setting, using light and shade to give dramatic impressions of depth. His student, Donatello (d. 1466), who excelled in obtaining balance between scientific realism and classical models, cast a bronze *David* designed to stand alone in a garden. A combination of grace, reserve, mathematically conceived proportions, and naturalism, *David* was presumably chosen to kill the giant because of his natural perfection, not because of his piety. In another feat of symmetry and balance, Donatello cast at Padua one of the first equestrian statues since antiquity (*Gattamelata*). In this work, the movements of the horse and rider are in perfect harmony. Other sculptors, such as Verrocchio, equaled or surpassed Donatello in specific projects, but at his best Donatello came closer than any other to achieving perfection as it was then defined.

As an art for which no antique models survived, painting was slow to respond to classical stimulation. But Masaccio, who died in 1428 at the age of 27, introduced mathematical laws of perspective. He was realistic without being Gothic; imitating nature rather than his masters, he worked out the perspective of the human body. His figures exist in three-dimensional space, so that the viewer feels able to touch them. In the expressions of the two lifelike nudes, *Adam and Eve,* he portrayed the pathos of man's expulsion from the Garden of Eden. Before Masaccio, Florence had been the fountainhead of Renaissance sculpture and architecture. Now it also became the center of painting's "rebirth."

Realism in painting made the canvas a transparent windowpane with nature on the other side. "That picture is most praiseworthy," wrote Leonardo da Vinci, "which most clearly resembles the thing to be imitated."[3] No paintings better conformed to this dictum than his own. His service as a military and civil engineer for Cesare Borgia and others took precedence over his artistic work; so did his research into anatomy, physiology, botany, geology, and mechanics. But these pursuits were also closely related to his art. In whatever he did da Vinci sought to derive rational, mathematical laws from empirical reality. He noted hitherto unobserved color and line aberrations in ocular perception and combined these with the use of light and shade to secure a better illusion of perspective. His adherence to imitation was selective. He tempered his realism with a classical sense of decorum, carefully picking elements of ideal beauty from his environment. Classical repose and dramatic tension coexist in the few paintings he completed, which include *St. John the Baptist, St. Jerome, The Madonna of the Rocks,* and *The Last Supper.* Even when scientifically conceived, Italian realism was usually selective and strove for an ideal form.

Just as contemporary humanists sought

---

[3] Quoted by Erwin Panofsky, *Renaissance and Renascences in Western Art* (Copenhagen: Russack and Co., 1961), p. 162.

to describe a perfect literary style, so artists sought to temper realism with classical balance, harmony, proportion, and decorum. While Northern artists concentrated on desolate scenes of death and crucifixion, Italian artists, painting both secular and religious works, dealt with life, natural beauty, and the spectrum of human emotions. At the peak of classical realism man became the measure of all things; his dignity, perfection, or fame replaced metaphysical principles as the measure of values; his struggles with himself replaced the struggle between heaven and hell as the chief concern of artist and humanist; and the enjoyment of life, which art enhanced, was seen to be more divine than the contemplation of death and salvation. In tracts on architecture, sculpture, painting, mathematics, natural science, family life, law, and religion the civic humanist and universally accomplished Florentine Leon Battista Alberti summed up this blend of humanism and realism.

During the second half of the fifteenth century artists began to draw more on classical literature than on contemporary life. The realistic imitations of da Vinci and Alberti gave way to Greco-Roman gods, heroes, battles, and myths painted by such artists as Mantegna and Piero de Cosimo. Other painters such as Botticelli were influenced by the philosophy of Neoplatonism. His *Allegory of Spring* and *Birth of Venus* combine a command of scientific realism and a return to allegorical symbolism (classical rather than religious); both depict hierarchies of spirits, types of soul, and forms of love. Following Botticelli, artists of the High Renaissance no longer considered themselves recorders of external nature; rather they were creative geniuses inspired by divine spirit. Having developed the ability to reproduce nature in almost photographic detail, they began to look away from their immediate environment for new themes with which to experiment.

The High Renaissance

Idealized classical form rather than fidelity to nature as recorded by the senses characterized the art of the High Renaissance, a short period of two or three decades following 1500. Compared to the youthful realism of the previous century, High Renaissance art emphasized grandeur, perfection of form, and self-assurance. Artists now often worked in greater-than-life proportions, and were encouraged in this by the patronage of monarchs in Rome, northern Italy, and France—successful bidders for the greatest artistic skills. Increasingly art's purpose became one of glorifying these ruling patrons and attaining immortal fame for both them and the artist. By 1500 the major artists were no longer merely respected guildsmen but were highly rewarded individuals of great prestige and affluence who traveled from one court to another, at least until Spanish influence reduced the status of most of them.

The most ambitious patron of the High Renaissance was Pope Julius II, who called Bramante, Raphael, Michelangelo, and others to Rome. Bramante was a student of Roman architecture who brought principles of mathematics and physics to bear on his work. Julius commissioned him to build St. Peter's Basilica in the capital of Christendom, a grandiose project whose completion required more than a century. Raphael also worked on the design of St. Peter's, but his fame rests primarily on paintings of idealized madonnas—for example, his *Sistine Madonna*—and of various classical themes. His madonnas were generally more human than pious in appearance, but they conveyed an abstract humanity of grace and dignity rather than an individuality. Like other late Renaissance painters Raphael drew on philosophical and classical themes in the *School of Athens,* an assemblage of savants of the past, and in *Parnassus,* an anachronistic combination of classical antiquity, the classical present, and inventive imagination.

The crowning jewel of Julius's assemblage of talent was Michelangelo, a Florentine-trained sculptor. The pope set him to work from 1508 to 1512 on frescoes of the Sistine Chapel and later on the plans of St. Peter's. Working on his back for four years in order to paint 300 figures on the wet plaster of the Sistine Chapel ceiling, Michelangelo displayed both dependence on and independence of Florentine scientific naturalism. Departing from mathematical laws of perspective, he consciously used distortion to awake a heightened sense of perspective and to convey a feeling of power. Ideal beauty he found in the nude human form, which he used in his depictions of creation and of man's early biblical history. He included no crucifixion or judgment scenes until Pope Paul III pressed him into doing a wall on the chapel entitled the *Last Judgment* (1535–41).

Michelangelo was primarily a sculptor rather than a painter or architect. For the Medici he built tombs portraying the family head as a victor in greater-than-life size and flanked by symbolic figures whose meaning is debatable. His most classical work was *David,* a relaxed and serene but powerful giant who could self-assuredly kill his biblical opponent without miraculous intervention. For the tomb of Julius II he carved another giant, *Moses,* in a psychological state of restrained wrath. In sculpture, as in painting, Michelangelo relied on his own subjective standards and produced art for art's sake. But his inner tranquility was shaken by political and religious crises after 1527, and this is reflected in his art. Rome was sacked in 1527; Italy was conquered by the emperor in 1529; advocates of force replaced Catholic humanists at the papal court in 1541. As his optimistic world of the Renaissance crumbled, Michelangelo turned more and more to mysticism and pious resignation.

The full range of his work is impossible to classify under a single heading: his art styles chronicle successive changes from classical realism to subjective and imitative "mannerism" to, finally, the baroque.

In quantity of works and in grandeur of restrained style the High Renaissance far surpassed the early Italian Renaissance. It was no longer primarily a Florentine or even exclusively Italian phenomenon. Venice rivaled Rome as a center of High Renaissance art. There a school of painters developed whose members relied more on color and oil-painted texture than on light and shade. Founded by Giovanni Bellini (d. 1516) and his student Giorgione (d. 1510), this school was carried to its greatest heights by Titian (1477–1576). Like those of Michelangelo, his works, which run from larger-than-life religious frescoes to sensuous nudes, are too varied to be classifiable by either subject or technique. He helped introduce a new phase of Italian art: *Mannerism,* the imitation of individual masters and the distortion of classical techniques. At the very same time when Italian art began to influence all of Europe, its own foundations of classical and scientific realism were crumbling.

By 1500 an Italian journey had become a necessity for Northern men of culture and learning, and Italian artists were summoned to the Northern courts. Still, High Renaissance influence was uneven outside Italy. France proved receptive to both its art and its letters, but Spain and Germany remained primarily Gothic and religious in a doctrinal sense. Albrecht Dürer (1471–1528) of Nuremberg and Hans Holbein (d. 1543), primarily a portrait painter, utilized Italian techniques of perspective, but neither they nor other Northern artists would adopt the secular esthetic content of the Italian Renaissance. Symbolism and Mannerism eventually proved easier for them to absorb.* The

---

* The Low Countries produced their own humanistic art without classical standards of beauty.

North, inclusive of England, was also primarily responsible for the development of Renaissance music, which Italy and other countries adopted. Despite much concourse with Italy, Northern artists under continuing Gothic influences did not fully comprehend the language of Italian art and music until that language became baroque and metaphysical during the religious wars of the sixteenth and seventeenth centuries.

C. Socioeconomic, Political, and Religious Developments

ECONOMIC AND SOCIAL TRENDS

It used to be a natural assumption that Renaissance culture rested on a continued upsurge of the "commercial revolution" of the eleventh, twelfth, and thirteenth centuries. This economic growth contributed to the rise of towns and a money economy; to territorial expansion and centralizing states; to the erection of cathedrals and the establishment of universities; and to the elaboration of more secular, sophisticated levels of thought. Indeed it must be granted that Renaissance culture is inconceivable apart from this late medieval economic development. But recent economic studies conclusively demonstrate that this culture came not on the crest of growing prosperity but in the slough of a century-long depression. Since recovery was slow, uneven, and in many older commercial centers incomplete, contemporary historians are inclined to explain the Renaissance as a delayed phenomenon of "cultural lag" rather than as the cutting edge of a new, triumphant bourgeois world.

A Century of Depression

The commercial depression that extended from ca. 1350 to ca. 1450 may have been due in part to previous overexpansion, but famine, plague, war destruction, and domestic turmoil were the more likely causes.

Following a series of severe famines the Black Death (or bubonic plague) killed more than a quarter of Europe's population between 1348 and 1350; in Mediterranean towns the figure was as high as 35 to 65 percent. Thereafter the plague recurred generation after generation.* The decline in population retarded both commerce and industry. With fewer opportunities of profit, entrepreneurs became demoralized, and the rise of newly enriched merchants competing for positions of power and influence diminished. Old banking families such as the Bardi, Peruzzi, and Acciaiuoli of Florence were ruined by the depression. Financial power fell into the hands of a few great banking families or

---

* The bubonic plague did not cease to be a major urban killer in Europe until the eighteenth century.

Burial of plague victims at Tournai, 1349.

individuals including the Medici of Florence, the Fuggers of Augsburg, and Jacques Coeur of France. Such techniques as double-entry bookkeeping at least temporarily secured some of them against losses. Although outstanding as great "individualists" of the age, they commanded fewer total resources than had a greater number of earlier merchant capitalists. And these "few great" increasingly tied their resources to the foremost ruling dynasties and to the papacy.

Endless warfare also affected trade. In western Europe the Hundred Years' War (1338–1453) between France and England disturbed trade routes, laid waste to considerable parts of France, and led to feuds and dynastic civil war in England. Similarly, endemic warfare in Italy, Spain, Scandinavia, and eastern Europe disrupted trade and destroyed wealth. The invasion of eastern Europe by the Ottoman Turks made Eastern trade more difficult. In approximately 1340 the Mongol Empire, which had policed trade routes from Poland to Korea, began to disintegrate, and Europeans were barred from China by the nativist Ming dynasty. As trade and industry declined, Italian banks, including those of the Medici, often involved in financial military ventures, began to fail.

In the wake of depression and war, peasant and urban revolutions enveloped fourteenth-century Europe. Indeed, domestic disorders continued in some areas, notably Germany, until the sixteenth century. Had these revolts produced a more nearly egalitarian political order they might have contributed to a return of prosperity. But they failed, and the crushing tax burdens, which had in part stimulated the revolts and which the privileged classes escaped, continued to fall exclusively on the productive elements of society, stripping them of purchasing power.

Venice, although it escaped revolution, exemplified many mercantile difficulties of the late fifteenth century. Venetian merchants had dominated Far Eastern trade through the city's commercial empire in the eastern Mediterranean, where Arab caravan and sea routes terminated. But new Ottoman rulers raised the wholesale prices of Oriental spices and cottons by setting up royal monopolies. At the same time Portugal opened up a cheap, all-water transportation route to the Far East around Africa. Italian wars disrupted Venetian commerce as shipments of goods were often confiscated. As a result of these challenges, after 1496 Venetian merchant-nobles intensified their efforts to pursue safer investments. They found some outlets abroad, in England or Spain, but government bonds and real estate gained favor over commercial investment. In the early sixteenth century, war crises caused suspension of interest payments on bonds and deprived owners of the use and the revenues of their estates. Deforestation deprived Venice of necessary raw materials for building new ships, and, although it remained the major shipping and trading city of the Mediterranean, it steadily lost economic vitality and initiative.

The depression might have been arrested sooner had the period been rich in technical inventions. While it is true that earlier discoveries in commerce, industry, and agriculture continued to spread, few innovative changes revitalized basic production and exchange in the Renaissance. There were new industrial processes in paper making, silk throwing, cloth production, glass manufacture, metallurgy, and distilling, but none of these processes involved use of the new sources of motive power that characterized the later Industrial Revolution. The craft guilds, which preserved and transmitted industrial techniques, increased in number. Still, the Renaissance, like societies of the sixteenth, seventeenth, and eighteenth centuries, was as dependent as the Middle Ages on the power furnished by wind, water, animals, and humans. Except in Flanders and northern Italy urban commerce and industry occupied only a minute proportion of the population; the overwhelming majority remained peasants. Substantial changes in the pattern of agricultural production occurred in some areas supplying wool, wines, or garden produce for towns. For the most part, however, agricultural technology made few advances.

Partial Recovery

As we have noted, recovery from the depression was uneven. Some formerly thriving towns, especially those of eastern Europe, never recovered from the combination of misfortunes that befell them in the fourteenth and fifteenth centuries. Other towns, such as the German centers of Augsburg and Nuremberg, did not reach their former levels of population and economic activity until after 1450.

Substantial commercial expansion occurred in areas along the Atlantic seaboard thanks to the development of three-masted ships, capable of tacking against the wind, which made ocean voyages feasible although still exceedingly dangerous. The peoples along the Atlantic seaboard now secured geographic and economic advantages over the Italian and German cities that had previously dominated Europe's carrying trade. These ships, armed with weapons using gunpowder, were also to give seaboard peoples naval and military superiority over the offshore islands, Africa, the New World, and the Orient. Portugal, soon challenged by Spain and the Low Countries, took the lead in building a commercial empire using Atlantic trade routes to supply Negro slaves, sugar, ivory, gold, and herbs to new markets. Thus a commercial revolution was in the making that would transfer the hub of international trade to Antwerp in the sixteenth century, but it had little impact on most of fifteenth-century Europe. Throughout the greater part of the Renaissance period, commerce stagnated at a lower level than it had reached in the High Middle Ages.

Urban Revolutions and Reaction

Seen as a whole the Renaissance was marked by the unprecedented prominence of townsmen in affairs. Nevertheless the economic depression and the internal revolutions that followed in its wake undermined the long-term impact of these people as a class on government and society.

The rise of the medieval commercial towns had thrust revolutionary ingredients into the rural, chivalric, manorial, and ecclesiastically oriented society of the Middle Ages. Town life was built on formal legal equality, personal freedom, property ownership, and the goals of commerce. Dominated by merchant oligarchies, town governments overrode rural custom with legislation, taxes, and titled property and rent records. As long as prosperity lasted, the towns provided paths of social mobility upward for the newly enriched, the skilled, and the rural immigrant. Late medieval depression, however, reinforced previous tendencies in the towns to form rigid hierarchies of privilege and power and to restrict the opportunities of "out" groups. Town societies were dominated by cliques of families who intermarried and monopolized positions of power. To a great extent they adopted the social values of the traditional aristocracy in seeking status, coats of arms, luxury, country estates, and offices. Below these elite families were the guildmasters, who closed their ranks to all except their own descendants and who secured the power to forbid their journeymen and apprentices to organize. Below the guildmasters stood their disunited employees and the bulk of the town population, largely engaged in agriculture or marketing. Instead of providing a common front asserting "middle-class" over against rural aristocratic social ideals, the classes in Renaissance towns were caught up in internal conflicts that weakened their influence and invited authoritarian rule or hostile intervention.

Medieval town life had always been turbulent, but during the economic crises of the Renaissance, social and political tension flared into open revolution in almost every European town. Each revolt had its local peculiarities, but certain patterns were general. Masters of leading craft guilds and some merchants were excluded from power by the closing of patrician ranks, so when economic or military setbacks occurred, both craftsmen and merchants were likely to organize internal dissent, attack ruling oligarchies for mismanagement, and demand the right to fill certain town offices. Guild victories in turn led to restrictive trade laws, the proscription of patrician families, and the continued exclusion from power of the lower classes. Popular urban revolts, frequently joined by neighboring peasants, often followed. The fear of bloodshed by mobs was great, but both patricians and the new business elite were adept at using terror to secure the submission of the disunited lower classes.

Rarely did the masses secure more than momentary concessions, and rarely did these urban revolts result in increased autonomy or prosperity. Each victorious faction sought to strengthen its own position in (and sometimes against) the community and to maintain its power by securing outside help. Frightened by lower-class restiveness, urban patricians invited intervention by princes who grasped these discords as opportunities of appointing their own officials to key urban posts, of breaking town and guild charters, and of assuming responsibility for public peace. The towns of France, England, Spain, and the German states all lost their autonomy

Draper's market at Bologna, 1411.

to monarchs during the Renaissance. In Italy, where there were no princes to turn to, single-party or family tyrannies were set up. Both patricians and despots adopted the social outlook of the traditional aristocracy and sought either royal offices or aristocratic marriages and titles.

The continuing but unsuccessful popular resistance to aristocratic control is well illustrated by Florence, the heart of secular

Renaissance culture. With more than 90,000 people in 1300, it was one of the world's largest cities and both a commercial and an industrial center. Probably one-third of its population was employed as "barefoot" (*Ciompi*) wool workers by the masters of the leading craft guilds. In 1282 a revolution had given political rights to the 21 leading guilds and political dominance to the upper seven. To awe the old patricians the new oligarchy used extraordinary police measures and penalties. But financial and political crises after 1338 drove Florence into decline. An exceedingly expensive war to conquer Lucca failed. Edward III of England defaulted on large debts owed to the two leading banking families, the Bardi and the Peruzzi. Plagues that had begun in approximately 1340 and that had continued intermittently came to a climax in the Black Death of 1348. Following a plague and a three-year war against the papal states, in 1378 the Ciompi revolted for political and social rights. After only four years they were put down by a mercenary army hired by the great guildmasters; but the latter's restored oligarchical government was harassed by Milan's aggressive expansion southward into Tuscany.

Following successive military reverses the oligarchy was undermined and finally replaced in 1434 by the city's foremost banker, Cosimo de' Medici, who ruled the city effectively from behind a facade of traditional republican institutions. Under him Florence enjoyed a golden age of subsidized art and scholarship and of luxurious living by the upper classes; anomalously, it also suffered decline, as did the fortunes of the Medici. War, first with Milan as an ally of Venice, and then with Venice as an ally of Milan, failed to gain more than the negotiation of an uneasy "balance of power." In 1469, after a bland interlude under Piero de' Medici, Lorenzo the Magnificent took over the reins of the city and the family bank. When, a few years later, he allied himself with Milan and Venice to prevent the popes from consolidating the papal states, all Italy burst into arms again. Pressed by the failing resources of heavily indebted Florence, Lorenzo managed in 1480 to negotiate peace on the peninsula just as a Turkish expedition was landing at Otranto. Because of the death of the reigning sultan, however, Italy was spared a Turkish invasion. To save the Medici's fortunes after failure of the bank's branches in Bruges and London, Lorenzo established ties with the French royal family.* Similar ties were contracted with the highest Italian aristocratic families and the papacy. Lorenzo, for example, secured the appointment of his 14-year-old son, Giovanni (the future Pope Leo X), as cardinal in 1489.

The political glitter of Medicean Florence was the flicker of a dying candle for Italian republicanism; involving only the leading citizens and rigidly excluding the lower classes, it was always narrowly oligarchical, perhaps too narrowly based to last. During the French invasion of 1494–95, the Medici were driven out by a democratic and theocratic revolution led by Savonarola, under whom the Florentine republicans opposed both the papacy and the Medici oligarchs, until his execution in 1498. Subsequently (1512) the Medici family returned to power because of Giovanni's influence with an invading Spanish army. (He himself was to assume the papal crown in the following year.) Habsburg victories in Italy after 1527 destroyed all hope of reviving representative republican constitutional forms, except in Venice. The republican towns proved to be more resistant to invasion than the princely despotisms, but Florence itself became a hereditary duchy under a branch of the house of Medici after Spanish power in the peninsula became entrenched.

* Likely enough he also helped himself to public funds in Florence for the same purpose.

lower class majority and the ... subjects of ruling towns, this ... oligarchic republic to despotic ... made little difference. Both ... government resorted to heavy indirect taxes on foodstuffs and other common items of consumption, the poor being the most adversely affected. Political and economic organization was prohibited, and the prohibition was enforced. The republics differed from the despotisms primarily in giving, at least, some of the capitalists decisive influence over affairs.

Aristocratic Recovery and the Decline of the Peasantry

Although the Renaissance saw more government positions held by townsmen than before, its conclusion in most areas was marked by an aristocratic recovery. Monarchs acknowledged the importance of the wealthy bourgeoisie by employing them as officials and by drawing them into diets or parliaments. Instead of imposing urban social standards on the state, however, these officials usually used their talents to secure admission into the aristocracy, whose social traditions they aped. Even in Tudor England, where by reputation the middle classes were supposed to be of decisive influence, they were, in fact, supposed to keep their place well below the aristocracy. In short, the shifting of the most talented townsmen from business to royal service weakened the urban impact on early modern European institutions.

Despite its considerable recovery after approximately 1450, the traditional aristocracy was for a time demoralized by several important innovations. One was the new means of warfare with expensive firearms and mercenary infantry, which they could not afford. Another was the commutation of peasant obligations into fixed money payments whose value was cut by inflation. Still another was the competition of educated burghers for church and state offices. Even so, the aristocracy proved resilient enough to maintain its social dominance. In eastern Europe the ascendancy at this time of the aristocracy and the gentry (aristocratic untitled country squires) is unquestioned; they dominated peasants, townsmen, and kings. Elsewhere noblemen and gentry found compensation for their losses in tighter estate management, well-paying Church positions, and posts at princely courts—often sinecures. Titled nobles were exclusive; they made it difficult for commoners to marry into noble families or otherwise to gain noble status. At the same time they saw to it that their sons secured education sufficient to outbid lower-class competition for offices. Noblemen responded to the creation of infantry armies, financed by kings, by becoming royal officers.

In strong monarchical states the rulers helped the nobility to preserve this caste system. Although monarchs curbed the nobles' political powers, royal courts shared their social outlook and culture, bestowing grants and sinecures once their political rebelliousness was tamed. When kings employed commoners, they usually provided them with privileges or titles and expected them to act as aristocrats. Thus the traditional nobility, the gentry, and a new "service" aristocracy (particularly jurists drawn from the bourgeoisie but no longer part of it) proved to be the most dynamic elements of Renaissance society.

The lower urban and peasant classes, which constituted the bulk of the population, were even more unsuccessful than the bourgeoisie in their bid for social and political recognition. Peasant revolts were endemic during the Renaissance; but only in areas where town life remained active and expansive did the peasants' *legal* position improve. Here the bonds of serfdom disintegrated within a market economy.

Economically their gains, if any, were not so clear. New taxes, legal fees, and requisitions by new state officials for civil and military purposes—when added to traditional obligations to church and manorial lords—took the greater part of their income. And in eastern Europe (outside the Ottoman Empire) both the legal and the economic status of the peasant deteriorated as the German-Slavic frontier, which had been an area of relative freedom, became an area of nascent serfdom.

THE COURSE OF POLITICS

In the traditional view, Renaissance politics were a continuation and culmination of the efforts of medieval monarchs, aided by townsmen invoking the precepts of Roman law, to centralize their kingdoms into "national states." In certain instances this generalization has merit, particularly as it applies to England; but as an overall statement it is misleading. Political loyalties continued to be focused on local provinces that had their own oligarchical representative assemblies, not on the larger unit of nation-states. Despite the invention of the printing press, poor communications continued to retard the growth and effectiveness of central governments. It is true that courts and precepts styled on Roman law emerged prominently in the monarchical states and enhanced the power of the king. But they were in competition with the canon law administered by the Roman Catholic church. They also had to compete with local customary law, which buttressed the privileges of aristocracies and oligarchical townsmen and regulated daily life in the local villages.

With few exceptions royal politics were dominated by dynastic rather than national interests. The right to rule was passed on by inheritance from one ruler to another and was considered to be private: like the royal domain, it could be acquired and transferred. Usually dynasts sought to enlarge their territories by advantageous marriages of their children. However, their domains were often diminished by marriage portions given to daughters, division of inheritance among heirs, and grants of autonomy to princes of royal blood. The result of dynasticism was the personal union of disparate principalities under a single ruler, not the creation of nation-states.

Townsmen served as royal officials, often as aggressive centralizers. Yet, as we have seen, townsmen serving kings failed to make the monarchies after their own image. The social order that the monarchical states served was predominantly aristocratic and traditional.

Nothing better illustrates the hierarchy of the social order than the diets that Renaissance rulers began to call in almost every monarchy of western Europe. Summoned to get influential sectors of society to accept treaties, defy the pope, accept succession settlements, or impose taxes, their composition varied in detail but they were basically similar. Representatives of the clergy and the nobility made up the two highest orders; delegates from privileged towns represented the commoners; rarely was the peasantry—the mass of the population—represented at all. Deliberation was by order or estate, and each estate negotiated separately with the monarch, particularly when its privileges were at stake. In addition to some kingdomwide assemblies such as the English Parliament and the French Estates-General, each provincial part of the continental dynastic kingdoms often maintained its own diet as a guardian over local customs, law, and privileges. None of the diets—provincial or national—constituted a modern legislative assembly, at least not before the seventeenth century, when the English Parliament made that transition.

The most decisive political innovations occurred among the city-states of northern Italy, no one of which encompassed a modern "nation." As in the late Middle Ages, Lombardy and Tuscany served as laboratories for the creation of a territorially compact state subject to a uniform law and administrative system. Resting solely on secular power in their relationships with one another, these city states also developed the first modern system of diplomatic representation. Venice followed suit, creating the most renowned diplomatic corps of the late Renaissance. Although the kingdoms of Europe were incompletely consolidated, in most cases for three centuries or more, nevertheless they became ready converts to Italian-style diplomacy as the Renaissance came to an end.

The States of Italy: 1300–1527

Italy was a region of many different states. In the extreme south, Sicily—the former centralized, cosmopolitan, and secular imperial headquarters of the Holy Roman Emperor, Frederick II—claimed Naples. Naples was dominated by local feudal barons. Central and parts of northern Italy were controlled by the Papal States, which were in a permanent state of crisis. The popes' residence in Avignon for more than 70 years paralyzed government, and the states had to be reconquered to return them to loyalty to the pope, thereafter to remain an attractive area for mercenary captains bent on carving out states for themselves. The principal victim of the chaos and continued warfare was communal government.

Distinctly different in political evolution were the towns of the Tuscan and Lombard plains, where town life and Roman law had never completely disappeared. Beginning, like other medieval towns, as republican communes, the Lombard and Tuscan towns leagued together

ITALY, ca. 1490

Republics shown by diagonal lines

Map by J. Donovan

and, allied with the papacy, threw off the authority of the Holy Roman Emperor in the twelfth century. Titular imperial governors presided over several of their councils, but thenceforth they retained *de facto* independence. Bankers from Lombardy and Tuscany dominated financial affairs in late medieval courts, fairs, and the Crusades. Two cities, Florence and Venice, gave their stable units of money—the florin and the ducat—to the early modern commercial world.

The commercial rivalry of the various towns led to naval and land wars in which the stronger city-states swallowed their weaker neighbors. In Tuscany, Florence extended her territory to include, among others, Arezzo and Pisa (a port city that had previously reduced her neighbors to submission). In Lombardy, Milan under the Visconti—later under the Sforzas—was the principal expansionist state. Here republicanism gave way to a dynastic monarchy set up by a prominent captain of mercenary troops. Milan's territorial ambitions collided with those of Venice, which abandoned its aloofness from peninsular affairs in the fourteenth century to push its holdings landward for control of the commercial routes extending northward across the Alps.

By the middle of the fourteenth century Italy consisted principally of five major states locked in a relative equilibrium of power maintained by shifting alliances: Naples, the Papal States, Venice, Florence, and Milan.

Constant factional strife and turbulence affected constitutional development among ruling cities, with the exception of Venice.* Elsewhere factionalism that had social and economic roots was a major cause for the failure of Italian republicanism. When the Holy Roman Emperor was the principal enemy, the Ghibellines, or imperialists, were proscribed with their property confiscated. Where the Guelfs (Welfs), or papalists, triumphed, they formed one-party states; but their ruling factions, based on family groupings, were split apart by family rivalries. Newly rich families tried, by revolution if the need arose, to break into the ruling oligarchies. In Venice such efforts were curbed by the creation of a permanent committee of public safety, which preserved the old oligarchy in uneasy power. When Florentine guildsmen came to power in 1282 they proscribed, exiled, or executed their patrician foes. Warfare gave this factionalism another dimension, since military defeats were the most frequent causes for revolution and the outbreak of civil war. But victory also had its dangers: town councils, fearing to arm their own subjects, often hired mercenary troop captains to conduct wars on land. These captains, in Milan and other towns, seized power and set up hereditary dynastic tyrannies, marking a general trend away from oligarchical republican government.

Both republics and despotisms had established territorial states whose law and administration were sovereign within their borders. Establishment of that sovereignty required the eradication of both noble and clerical privileges and jurisdictions. Once the authority of the emperor was removed, the aristocracy, which tended to live in the towns and to engage in commerce, was brought under city law. Similarly the Church was more thoroughly subordinated to secular government in the Italian city-states than in any monarchy, even though the towns had achieved their independence as allies of the papacy. A Visconti of Milan once summed up his powers to an archbishop in this way: "Do you not know, you fool, that here I am pope and emperor and lord in all my lands, and that no one can do anything in my lands save I permit it—no, not even God."[4]

Considerations of power rather than legitimate family claims of succession regulated the relationships among the Italian city-states. Milan originated the practice of sending resident diplomatic agents to neighboring states. Their chief tasks were to acquire intelligence, to mask

---

* At the end of the thirteenth century the leading merchant-nobles consolidated their hold over Venetian affairs. Henceforth only those whose names were inscribed in genealogical "golden books" were eligible to participate in public affairs. Venice's stability under this narrow oligarchy excited the awe of aristocratic factions elsewhere, notably in Florence.

[4] Quoted by Denys Hay, *The Italian Renaissance in its Historical Background* (Cambridge: Cambridge University Press, 1961), p. 105.

aggressive intentions with pacific eloquence, and to secure allies. Other Italian states soon adopted the practice. Mercenary armies and diplomats were inspired by neither religious zeal nor modern nationalism, but solely by the desire to gain expansive domains and political power.

By the middle 1400s, the states of the whole peninsula had achieved a balance of power by means of constantly shifting alliances in which yesterday's enemy became tomorrow's ally. As each state strove to tip that balance in its own favor, allies were sought among the great monarchies, two of which, France and Spain, had conflicting claims to Naples and Milan. Once these giants intervened, however, no individual Italian state could turn them back. In the early sixteenth century the papacy shifted alliances to prevent dominance by either. But by 1527 the Spanish house of Habsburg was in effective control of the peninsula, except for Venice.

More than any other court the Spanish royal house of Habsburg developed an Italian type of diplomatic corps and supported it with immense resources. In this way the secular diplomacy of the Italian city states was grafted onto the foremost divine-right kingship of sixteenth-century Europe.

The Iberian Kingdoms

In contrast to northern Italy, Spain tended to favor the creation of an empire based on religious rather than secular goals. The country may have been divided among the contending kingdoms of Castile, Leon, and Aragon, but it was united in its long holy war, beginning in the tenth century, to drive out the Moors. After 1230, victory was facilitated by the union of Leon and Castile. Although the Moors continued to hold Granada, the Iberians dashed Moorish hopes of recovery in 1340, and finally achieved their aim in 1492 with the fall of Granada to the combined forces of Castile and Aragon. Reconquest proceeded in the guise of a holy war inspired by the legend of St. James (Santiago). Erroneously believed to be a brother of Christ who came to Spain, Santiago was considered the peculiar property of Iberian Christians, especially the Castilians. Crusading orders joined the secular clergy in obtaining vast lands, income, and local political powers as the frontiers were pushed southward and colonists settled on confiscated lands. Christian towns and nobles also obtained extensive grants of local authority and autonomy. Thus as the kingdoms of Portugal, Castile, and Aragon expanded territorially, they became administratively and legally decentralized.

Reconquest also bred the idea of a Christian ruling caste, to which Spaniards of rank high and low aspired. Even in the reconquered areas the Moors and Jews furnished most of the technical skills in finance, industry, agriculture, scholarship, and medicine. Rather than imitate the heretic's superior skills most of the conquerors relied on the sword or piety to secure positions of power. Probably no other people in Europe stigmatized manual labor so much as the Castilians. Especially among them honor, religious faith, and arms rather than knowledge and skills became the basis of an "individualism" based on gentle, or even simply Spanish, birth. For all its pious character this code cheerfully allowed defiance of authority and defrauding of the government at every opportunity. In the Middle Ages considerable tolerance, cultural exchange, and intermarriage occurred among Christians, Moors, and Jews. But as the Iberian Christians obtained unquestioned military ascendancy, they turned their sense of divine mission into a drive for empire, total uniformity, and "racial purity."

After military security against the Moors had been obtained, endless dy-

SPAIN AT THE TIME OF FERDINAND AND ISABELLA

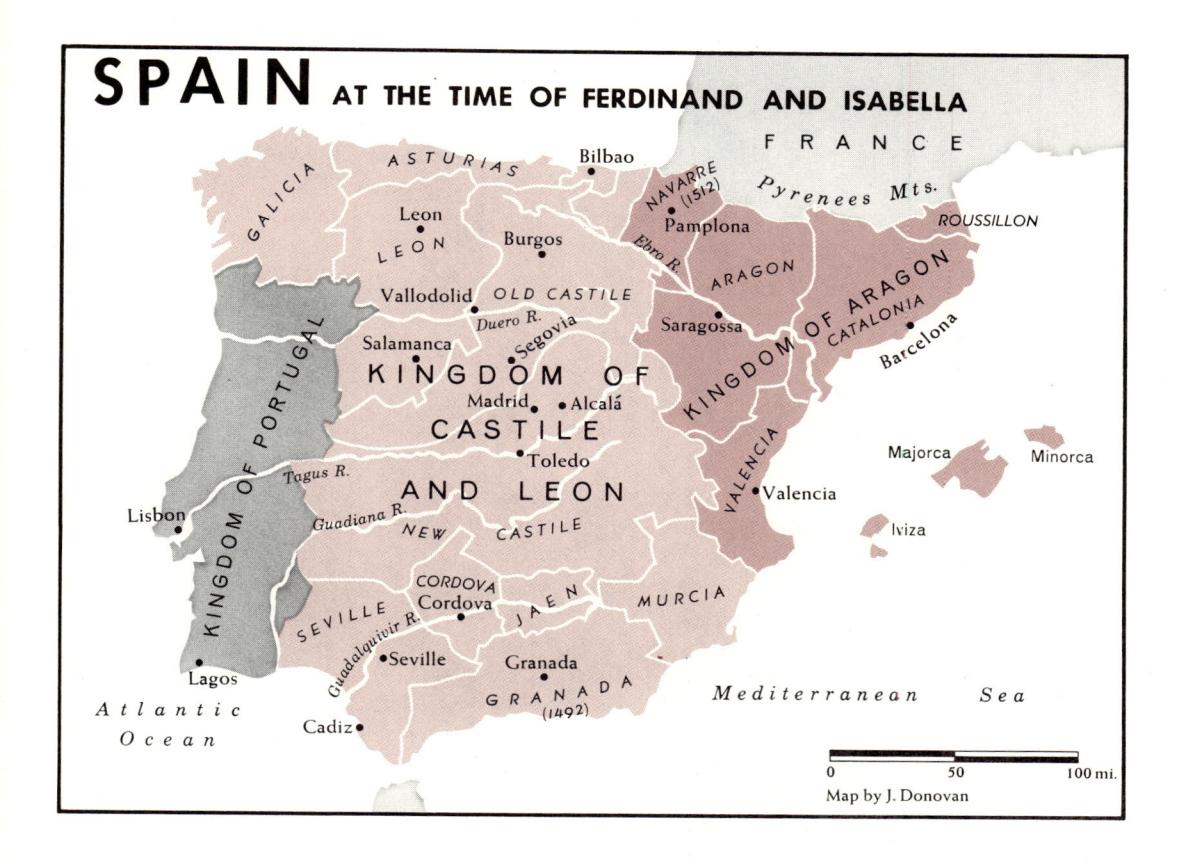

nastic feuds and civil wars broke out in the fourteenth and fifteenth centuries. Royal weakness provided an opportunity for local estates (*cortes*) to consolidate their power in Aragon, where the diets remained the watchdogs of noble, clerical, and urban privileges rather than legislative chambers responsive to the common welfare. Royal dominance in Castile was easier to maintain because the Castilian Cortes withered when the clergy and nobility ceased to attend. Even though leagues of townsmen usually fought for kingly order against noble lawlessness, the principal beneficiaries of the disorders were the nobles, who gained lands at the expense of the royal domains. Towns, under royal officials who severely taxed commerce, began to decline in the fourteenth century.

Ultimately the joint reign of Ferdinand of Aragon (1479–1516) and Isabella of Castile (1474–1504), husband and wife, produced order out of chaos through monarchical despotism. Even so, their kingdoms retained their separate identities and constitutions. These Catholic sovereigns enforced domestic peace and set up a system of royal councils, courts, and administration that overrode the political claims of towns, nobles, and clergy, with all towns in Castile coming under firm royal control by 1480. Gentry loyal to the crown (*hidalgos*) were placed in half the towns' offices, town leagues were broken up, and the guild system was spread throughout the kingdom under royal auspices. Ferdinand attempted similar measures in Aragon against fairly effective opposition by the local cortes. Individual townsmen continued to serve in the royal administration, especially as Roman-law jurists; but politically the towns' autonomy was broken and their future prosperity under-

C. Socioeconomic, Political, Religious Developments

St. Dominic Burning Books—*painted while the Spanish Inquisition was at its height.*

mined by royal taxation and social policies.

Ferdinand and Isabella also stripped the nobility of autonomous political power. Royal police enforced order, dueling and private warfare were forbidden, baronial castles were torn down, and the crown regained part of the lands previously seized from the royal domain. The monarchs relied on councils and courts rather than the cortes, which they seldom called. The Catholic sovereigns also attempted to abolish serfdom, but in Aragon success was limited to the abolition of a few practices such as noble rights to peasant brides. The crown also took over the patronage and income of the three great wealthy crusading orders, which the nobility had controlled. The nobles' political role was further diminished by the Crown's use of churchmen and townsmen as jurists and administrators. But these officials sought and were accorded privileges and status defined by noble social ideals.

Military changes also affected the nobility as Spanish infantrymen and artillery replaced feudal troop levies. Assembled in phalanxes of hollow squares called *tercios*, these troops made Spain dominant on the battlefields of Europe for a century and a half. The monarchs, however, had no intention of making war on the aristocracy as a social class. Except where potential political rivalry was involved the nobility retained and enlarged its wealth, privileges, and social importance. Once noblemen ceased to be a revolutionary danger, they dominated the court, which became the font of further privileges, sinecures, and appointments to high civil, military, and clerical posts.

In establishing royal control over the Roman Catholic church the monarchs removed another rival and made its structure serve their ends. In addition to gaining control of the crusading orders, the Crown dominated another ecclesiastical source of revenue and power, the Spanish Inquisition, established by a papal bull of 1478. Although its procedures were no worse than those of many other secular and clerical courts, the scope of its activity under Tomás Torquemada and Cardinal Ximénes earned it a well-deserved reputation as a secret terrorist agency. The Crown appointed the inquisitors and shared the confiscated property of its victims. Until Christian "deviationists" became suspect during the Reformation, the primary targets were converted and unconverted Jews and Moors.

Ferdinand and Isabella obtained the power to nominate, in addition to the inquisitors, all major ecclesiastics in Castile, Aragon, and Sicily. Not only did they reward loyal servants with ecclesiastical posts, but the state also took a portion of the tithes collected. Themselves technically exempt from secular taxation, the clergy of the wealthy Spanish church acted as zealous agents of the royal treasury. Having achieved their political and financial objectives, the sovereigns had no intention of further despoiling the church. Churchmen such as Cardinal Ximénes, Isabella's confessor and, later, regent on Ferdinand's death, held the most powerful positions in the monarchy. Clerical keepers of the royal conscience played a larger role in Spain than in any other European state.

Although the monarchy's rise to political ascendancy was aided by the towns, its economic policies were detrimental to both merchant capitalism and productive enterprise. Pressed for foreign exchange, which sales of wool would provide, Ferdinand and Isabella confirmed the privileges of the Mesta, a corporation of shepherds whose long sheep drives to and from summer pastures destroyed peasant agriculture. They also increased the *alcabala*, a tax on every commercial transaction. Maintenance of a large army and diplomatic corps increased taxes which, thanks to the exemption granted clergy and nobility, fell primarily on the commoners. In catering to popular prejudices the Inquisition harassed, or secured the expulsion of, the most productive economic groups, the Jews and the Moors. Lacking native capitalists after the Jews were expelled in 1492, the Crown relied for financial support on German and Italian bankers, who in turn secured control of many royal revenues. Internal economic policies favored the privileged, restrictive position of master guildsmen rather than merchant capitalists. Although the Crown's

C. Socioeconomic, Political, Religious Developments

treasury was supplemented by New World metals, most of the revenues for Spain's expansionist policies came from domestic sources. In the sixteenth century the strains of supporting a world empire proved too much for the domestic economy, while imports of bullion from the New World inflated domestic prices to the point that Spain could not compete successfully in foreign markets.

The first decades of the sixteenth century marked the reconciliation of the nobility with royal predominance. When the new Habsburg king, Charles I (1516-56), initially appointed Burgundians* to the highest posts in church and state and increased court expenses tenfold, Castilian nobles joined townsmen in revolt. When the nobles realized that their town allies were hostile to aristocratic privileges, however, they accepted Charles's promise that he would henceforth appoint only Spaniards to office. Thus the nobility again turned to the court as the protector of its privileges. As the Renaissance era drew to a close the nobles found the court lavish in providing the means of securing fortunes. Particularly fruitful for them were the burgeoning expansion of Spain (and Portugal) into the New World and the protracted Habsburg-Valois wars of the sixteenth century.†

England and France: The Hundred Years' War and After

As in Italy and the Iberian peninsula, the Renaissance period in England and France was marked by both internal and external conflicts, which led to the establishment of authoritarian governments that curbed domestic turmoil and directed aggressive energies outward. Unlike the Iberian and Italian peninsulas, however, England and France had had strong medieval monarchies.

After the Norman conquest of 1066 England had greater legal and economic unity than any other European kingdom. Edward I (1272-1307) reversed feudal decentralization by attaching nobles directly to the king and forbidding them to grant fiefs to underlings owing allegiance to themselves rather than to the monarch. Out of Edward's royal council evolved a Parliament that drew the aristocracy, townsmen, and clergy into the affairs of the entire kingdom. His successor Edward III (1327-77) humbled the barons and wielded an effective (though legally limited) political, judicial, and administrative authority in conjunction with Parliament.

Because English kings held large sections of France (as vassals of the French kings), English power was a constant threat to the security of the French throne, and over a period of 175 years feudal warfare had flared up intermittently between the French Capetians and their overmighty English royal vassals. When the direct male Capetian line died out in 1328, English kings claimed the French throne itself. Anglo-French conflicts went deeper, however, than feudal and dynastic rivalries. France supported Scotland, England's perennial enemy; it also sought to acquire Flanders, the principal market for English wool; and seamen of both countries engaged in piracy and coastal raids. War broke out in 1338 when the French king seized England's feudal property. Thereafter and sporadically for more than 100 years popular passions contributed to wanton destruction, pillage, and the killing of prisoners and noncombatants. Large parts of France were denuded of people and economic resources.

The opening phases of the Hundred Years' War demonstrated the superiority of English ships and the ability of yeomen armed with longbows to win battles such

---

* For Charles's ties to Burgundy see below, p. 585.
† For the Habsburg-Valois wars see below, pp. 608, 622.

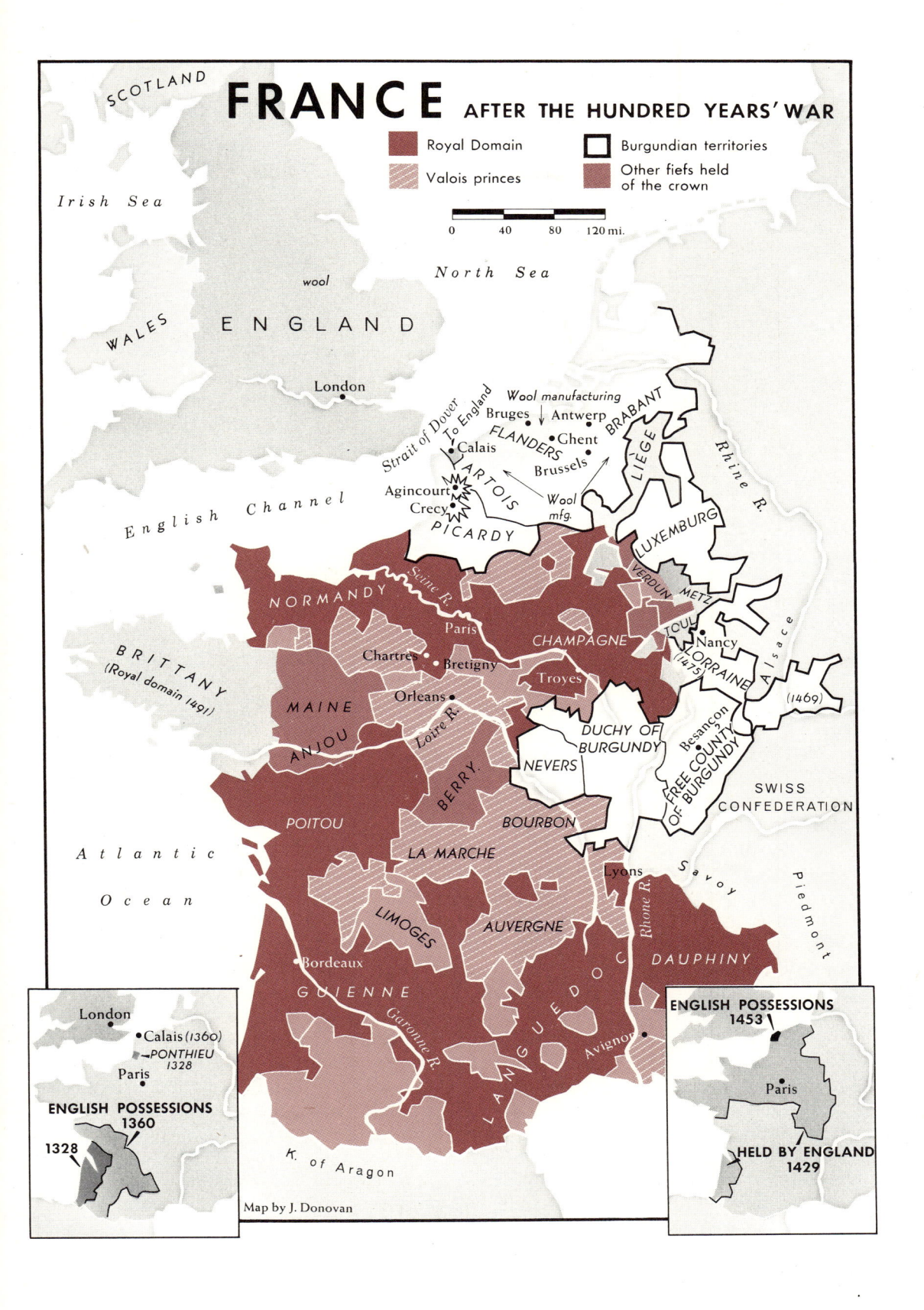

FRANCE AFTER THE HUNDRED YEARS' WAR

Early field gun and gunmaster.

as those of Crécy (1346), Poitiers (1356) and, later, Agincourt (1415). But sufficient resources to conquer and garrison France were lacking, and by the beginning of the fifteenth century France had recovered from early defeats. Henry V's new invasion after 1415 was successful, but it affected the new course of the war only temporarily. In 1428 the French rallied once again, this time under the leadership of Joan of Arc, whom the English burned at the stake in 1431. Finally in 1453 the English made peace, retaining only the port of Calais.

The Hundred Years' War left deep marks on France's constitutional and political development. At first the Estates General was brought into prominence. It represented the privileged clergy, nobles, and commoners who were called to vote taxes, ratify treaties, and deal with crises in which the Crown felt the need of support from its leading subjects. But later French kings undermined the Estates-General by collecting war taxes, maintaining a standing army independent of its control, and dealing with select groups of notables rather than the formal representatives of the kingdom. Until approximately 1440 Charles VII, financially assisted by Jacques Coeur, attempted to centralize the entire monarchical structure under royal authority. The king emerged from the war with independent tax powers, a small standing army, control over the French church and, for the period, a substantial bureaucracy. Before the end of the war, however, he was obliged to begin making concessions to local provinces and duchies. Local *parlements* (law courts) were established in many provinces; royal finances were decentralized; and laws were codified locally by estates or assemblies rather than by a national Estates General.

Charles's successor, Louis XI (1461–83), used force to suppress the nobility politically but compensated them with pensions and emoluments so that he became their principal benefactor socially and economically. French constitutional development after the Hundred Years' War was marked by tension between centralized royal authority and the provincial law courts and estates that upheld local autonomy. At the level of central government Louis and his immediate successors (Charles VIII, Louis XII, and Francis I) ignored the Estates General and ruled absolutely. Nevertheless French commoners found "government" and aristocracy to mean very much the same, for provincial authorities maintained their rights in vigorous local estates. Thus French absolutism was still far from absolute.

Because England was spared battle at home during the Hundred Years' War, it suffered less than France; hence its social, political, and constitutional development differed considerably from those of France.

Parliament, for example, retained control over finances, and in 1399 it even deposed a monarch who displayed absolutist tendencies. Instead of representing three estates separately as on the Continent, it evolved into a two-house body. Dissatisfied with their status, the lower clergy withdrew from the lower house, (the Commons); in that house knights and townsmen were joined together, significantly bridging a broad social gulf (an achievement that continental assemblies were never able to effect). The House of Lords represented the titled nobility and prelates. Together the houses of Parliament acted as both a court and a legislature—not a modern legislative body, yet the king's enactments in response to grievances presented by it gave its members a role in legislation that tended to make England a limited constitutional monarchy.

For administration in the counties English kings had no paid bureaucracy comparable to that of the French monarchy. They depended rather on newly created justices of the peace—paid by fees and drawn from prominent local families—who thereafter became the local governors of England, although they were subject to parliamentary statutes applicable to the whole kingdom.

Neither Parliament nor the justices of the peace represented the interests of either the peasantry or the lower urban classes. Following the Black Death, the Statute of Laborers (1351) charged justices of the peace with checking the wage increases that resulted from the shortage of labor. Angered by the egalitarian doctrines of anticlerical priests known as "Lollards" (see p. 595) and reacting to severe poll taxes, in 1381 the peasants and townsmen revolted. Disarmed by the king's false concessions to their demands, including emancipation from serfdom, the revolutionaries were easily suppressed; but their failure did not check the gradual release of English leaseholders from compulsory services, a process completed in the sixteenth century.

Hostile to the wealth of the Church, the revolt of 1381 was evidence of the strong antipapal and often anticlerical sentiments that led to state encroachment on the Church's independence during the Hundred Years' War. As early as 1279 the English Parliament had acted to curtail further transfers of property to the "dead hand" of the Church,* where they no longer produced revenues. But political conditions during the Hundred Years' War favored stronger measures, since the papacy at Avignon was considered a tool of French foreign policy. Until his Lollard followers became embroiled in the revolt of 1381, John Wycliffe (1320?–84) was allowed to attack the validity of sacramental rites performed by miscreant priests and to urge that the Church be stripped of its temporal wealth.† Parliament itself enacted laws that regulated papal appointments, although enforcement by the Crown was not always consistent. Additional laws restricted the papacy's legal jurisdiction and stopped feudal payments to the pope.

Following the Hundred Years' War England was plagued by feuds between private armies. Nobles had assembled bands of warriors under their "livery and maintenance" (i.e., under their colors and at their expense) in the course of the wars with Scotland and France during the fourteenth and fifteenth centuries. Finally these feuds merged in the dynastic Wars of the Roses,‡ from which the first Tudor monarch, Henry VII, emerged victorious in 1485. Fearful of further disorders, Henry established a popular absolutism

---

* Once acquired, property—acquired through wills and gifts—could not be alienated from Church hands; hence, its policy was called *mortmain*—the dead hand.

† For further discussion of Wycliffe and the reasons why secular officials and nobles were favorably disposed toward his doctrines see p. 595.

‡ The conflict is so named because the Lancastrians used the symbol of a red rose, the Yorkists a white rose.

Chivalric Burgundian shield.

favorable to the commercial interests and antagonistic to the nobility. His use of the court of Star Chamber (a court made up of certain councillors who met in secret and decided cases more or less arbitrarily), his administrative organization, and his taxation policies were extraordinarily effective in establishing order, removing potential competitors for the throne, and intimidating the old nobility, whose ranks had been thinned by the dynastic wars. Henry retained Parliament as part of the sovereign power of the state; before his reign it had already been reduced to an echo of whatever military faction was temporarily predominant. By working with Parliament, which represented the major vested interests of the kingdom, Henry wielded greater power than his French counterparts—even though Parliament continued to control taxation and deny the king a standing army. Thrust off the Continent by the Hundred Years' War, Englishmen applied their energies increasingly to commerce, industry, and mercantile expansion.

The Rise and Fall of Burgundy

The Hundred Years' War roused national passions in England and France, but the framework of politics remained decidedly dynastic, as the rise and fall of Burgundy vividly illustrates. After the last male Capetian duke of Burgundy died of the plague in 1361, the Valois king of France gave Burgundy as an autonomous dependency to a younger son, Philip the Bold, who also received Franche-Comté, a territory between France and the Swiss Confederation, as a fief from the Holy Roman Emperor. Philip immediately contracted an ambitious marriage with the heiress of Flanders—the most industrialized, most urbanized, and richest part of northern Europe. To prevent Flanders from falling to England, on which it was dependent economically for raw wool, the French monarch agreed to Burgundian control. Marriage alliances further extended Philip's control of the Low Countries from the Somme River to the Zuyder Zee. Thereafter a succession of Burgundian dukes played off France and England against each other in the Hundred Years' War. As the leading vassal-rivals of the Valois kings, they built up a dynastic state whose revenues were probably the largest in Europe.

When Henry V invaded France the Burgundian Duke, John the Fearless, secretly allied with the English forces and brought the archbishopric of Liège, a pioneer area in coal and iron production, under his control. His immediate successor, Philip the Good, openly allied with the English but denied them access to the Low Countries. By separate peace with the king of France at Arras in 1435, he secured royal recognition of his domain in the Low Countries. Philip brought all local principalities in that region directly or indirectly under his control and tried to acquire a royal title commensurate with his power. Burgundian expansion and its threat to the integrity of Louis XI's France reached their peak under Charles the Rash (1467–77). After almost securing royal recognition of Burgundian independence, Charles acquired rights to Alsace and then conquered Lorraine, which directly linked the Burgundian inheritance with the Low Countries. In 1474 he simultaneously allied with England and Aragon to reopen the Hundred Years' war. But instead of attacking France he pushed his troops eastward and southward along the Rhine.

Between 1475 and 1477, however, Charles's dreams of imperial grandeur rapidly faded. Deserted by Burgundy, England made a separate peace. Meanwhile Louis XI supported revolts in Alsace and Lorraine, and the Swiss and the Austrian Habsburgs joined the ranks of Burgundy's enemies. The empire retrieved Alsace, and in 1476 Charles was twice beaten roundly by Swiss pikemen. In 1477 he died in the siege of Nancy, in Lorraine, without leaving a male heir.

Territorial aggrandizement had proceeded more rapidly than political centralization. At Charles's death the duchy of Burgundy was still a personal union of disparate principalities; Louis XI of France thereupon reclaimed it and occupied Franche-Comté. To protect her inheritance Charles's daughter, Mary, married Maximilian, son of the Holy Roman Emperor. By this dynastic marriage Burgundy became the cradle of the greatest political coalition of the sixteenth century for, as part of an anti-French diplomatic maneuver, Philip the Handsome, son of Mary and Maximilian, married Joanna the Mad, daughter of Isabella and Ferdinand of Spain. Philip's and Joanna's son Charles in time inherited the Spanish throne as well as the Low Countries and in 1519 was elected to the imperial title. Thereafter the Burgundian inheritance* became part of the Habsburg Empire, but the continued existence of the Low Countries as a political entity separate from France and the

Burgundian defense of a besieged town.

---

* In 1493 France abandoned claims to the Netherlands and Franche-Comté to Maximilian by treaty; nevertheless, the French monarchy did not give up attempts at recovering Franche-Comté. Quarrels over the Burgundian inheritance became a major cause of the Habsburg-Valois wars of the sixteenth century.

empire remained as a monument to Burgundy's fleeting existence.

Socially and politically Burgundy was a mirror of the major conflicts of the Renaissance. Drawing revenues from the most advanced urban centers of northern Europe, its court effected a dazzling revival of chivalry. Under its great bourgeois administrators the court consumed immense revenues—and much borrowed money besides—for festive displays, ceremonies, and tournaments. Court etiquette became incredibly complicated and formalized. There was even a hierarchy of kitchen hands. The dukes collected libraries and patronized historians whose writings upheld chivalric values. The court was also the major patron of a Northern, "Gothic" Renaissance in sculpture, painting, drama, and poetry. Such genteel activity, however, did not prevent the dukes from practicing ruthless power politics. They also effectively utilized propaganda to appeal to the lower classes, established universities to train officials, and sponsored the codification of laws in local provinces. Thus a romantic chivalry and a realistic use of administrative power existed side by side.

Eventually this most flamboyant of princely courts collided head on with the social and political aspirations of urban guildsmen and the common people of Ghent, Ypres, and Bruges, already in revolt against the patrician oligarchies of merchants. French kings supported urban revolts in Flanders while Burgundian dukes aided French rebels. But in their own domains the dukes proceeded ruthlessly and successfully against democratic movements in the towns.

The Holy Roman Empire

Meanwhile the Holy Roman Empire continued to disintegrate into local clerical and secular principalities. Triumph of the more influential princes over the emperors, towns, and papacy was formalized by the Golden Bull of 1356, which remained the basic constitution of the empire until its dissolution in 1806. As declared in the bull, permanent right to elect the emperor was vested in three archbishoprics (Mainz, Cologne, and Trier) and four secular principalities (Saxony, Brandenburg, the Rhine Palatinate, and Bohemia), with the papacy excluded from elections. The bull forbad unauthorized leagues of towns, and until 1489 the imperial cities were not recognized as an estate within the Imperial Diet (Reichstag). On the other hand, the princes constituted a second "house" within the Reichstag. And the third "house," the Electors, whom the emperor had to consult on convening the Reichstag (as well as on other matters), imposed crippling checks on the imperial executive. Lacking administrative officials, taxes, and a fixed capital, the emperor had to depend on the resources of his inherited personal domains to govern imperial affairs.

During the fourteenth century the emperors drawn from the House of Luxembourg failed to check the tide of decentralization and the consolidation of local princely domains. Nor were the Habsburgs, who after 1438 held the imperial title, any more successful, despite their large holdings along the Danube. Authority in the German states centered on local principalities that, because of the absence of primogeniture and inheritance contracts, were divided and redivided among heirs. Thus hundreds of splintered principalities of Germany developed their own systems of officials and courts bringing the local towns, nobility, and churches under varying degrees of dependence.* Over all of these affairs, therefore, the empire had but little control.

During the fifteenth century the empire not only lost border territories but failed to maintain internal order as it had done

---

* Not all of the ecclesiastical states were thus fragmented, however.

586   The Renaissance: 1300–ca. 1520

THE EMPIRE AND CENTRAL EUROPE, ca. 1490

in the fourteenth century. As we have seen above, Italy had already escaped from imperial control. So had the forest cantons of the Swiss Confederation, whose infantry was more than a match for feudal knights unfamiliar with the mountainous terrain. They achieved almost complete independence in the fourteenth century. In standing off the aggressive designs of the emperor Switzerland remained a republican irritant both to him and to the German princes. On the eastern frontier German penetration (by the Teutonic Knights and colonists) was turned back. Indeed, during the 1420s the Bohemian Hussites* not only repulsed repeated crusades but also in turn ravaged large parts of eastern Germany. Throughout the long inactive reign of Frederick III (1440–93), the empire lost territory to Burgundy and on two occasions the Hungarian king seized Vienna. Internally German society remained as turbulent during the fourteenth century as the western kingdoms. The nobility persisted in waging private warfare and preying on commerce. In 1493 the emperor complained that "the nobility as well as the common man was in great poverty." Ever-new taxes only left the populace restive and left insolvent those governments that were overweighted with military expenditures.

Demands for reform were vocal and

* See p. 596.

587   C. Socioeconomic, Political, Religious Developments

widespread, but almost invariably they became muted in the din of conflict between the emperor and the princes. A Reichstag at Worms in 1495 tried to provide a constitutional "reformation" by banning private warfare and establishing an imperial high court. Reform was carried further in Cologne in 1512, when local "circles" were organized for defense and the emperor obtained an administrative council. In addition, monopolistic banking and trading companies in the imperial cities were dissolved, at least on paper.

But in practice all these reforms amounted to little. The ban on private warfare was enforced primarily against increasing revolts by townsmen, peasants, and imperial knights, while the major princes continued to fight dynastic battles with impunity. The trading companies were not in fact dissolved. And the court and council could not function effectively without an imperial army and tax system. Chronic differences between princes and emperor made cooperative efforts for reform difficult. The difficulty became especially acute after the Habsburgs secured the imperial election of Charles, already duke of Burgundy and king of Spain. When shortly after this triumph they dispossessed the duke of Wurttemberg (1520), princely tempers flared again. United by growing fears of Habsburg domination, the princes were able to score a resounding victory at the Diet of Worms (1521), where the question of constitutional reform was finally passed upon.*

The Eastern Frontiers

During the fourteenth and fifteenth centuries eastern Europe absorbed little of the culture of the West. Through royal courts, colonization, and commerce, Western sociopolitical institutions filtered into parts of the area—Poland-Lithuania, Bohemia, Hungary, Novgorod—but the vast distance that separated many areas of eastern Europe from the commercial centers of the West retarded the development of a flourishing town life. So did endemic warfare and the hostility of princes and noblemen. For the most part, therefore, the political and social life of eastern Europe was oriented away from the culture of the West. East of the Elbe River peasants began to lose their legal status as independent yeomen, and by the seventeenth century many had become formally bound to soil and master. The critical development for the political evolution of all eastern Europe was the rise of two aggressive, non-Western military autocracies, Muscovy and the Ottoman Empire.

Because of its great size the most striking state in eastern Europe during the Renaissance was the dynastic union of Poland-Lithuania. The dual kingdom extended from the Baltic to the Black Sea, and occasionally as far east as Moscow. Lithuania incorporated most of the medieval Russian state of Kiev. Twice Poland defeated the Teutonic Knights and eventually turned the order into a feudal dependency; but royal power was on the wane. With stubborn persistence nobles and gentry usurped the governing authority, crowded urban merchants out of the diets, and reduced the legal status of the peasantry.

Other strong monarchies in eastern Europe did not survive the Renaissance era. Serbia's empire was destroyed by the Turks and Hungarians in the fourteenth century. Bohemia emerged only briefly into prominence during the Hussite period* of the 1420s and 1430s when it was a center of popular revolution and military

---

* Although the Diet of Worms is most famous for the appearance there of Martin Luther, the outcome of his case before the Diet, as will be related in the next chapter, is inexplicable apart from the constitutional crisis of the Holy Roman Empire.

* For the Hussites see p. 596.

might. With the Turkish invasion of the Balkan peninsula after 1333, Hungary became a buffer state, a military frontier between Ottoman and Habsburg. It achieved a strong central government only under Matthias Corvinus, after whose death without an heir in 1490 the nobility regained most of its privileges.

On the far northeastern fringes of Europe the princes of Muscovy built a more lasting autocratic state, almost totally outside the reach of Western influence. The part of Kievan Russia that had not been incorporated into Lithuania fell under the suzerainty of the Mongol-led Tartars (1238) until Muscovite princes threw off the "Tartar yoke" and substituted their own authority for it. Under the Tartars these same princes had gained ascendency by collecting tribute and helping to suppress revolts. They also made Moscow the seat of the Russian Orthodox church. The latter's repudiation of both Rome and Constantinople as corrupt centers of Christianity made it easy to identify the divine mission of Moscow—the "Third Rome"—with the Muscovite state.

With full Church support Ivan III and Vasili III pushed Muscovite frontiers to the Baltic Sea and the Ural Mountains by purchase, treaty, and war. Noteworthy victims of their military autocracy were the city-states Novgorod (1478) and Pskov (1510), whose institutional and social developments had closely paralleled those of the city-states of Italy. The czars rooted out their republican institutions and exiled their leading citizens into remote areas. As a consequence Russia, lacking a native middle class, failed to develop a diet or parliament comparable to those of the Renaissance kingdoms of the West. Most Russians, in fact, remained peasants on the estates of the military aristocracy, and for the next two centuries the general trend was toward a uniform level of serfdom.

EXPANSION OF MUSCOVY TO 1533

Map by J. Donovan

Muscovite expansion cut off Western trade routes and more than ever isolated Russia from the West; but the other Eastern autocracy, the Ottoman Empire, thrust itself into Western affairs, invading by land and sea. Originally mercenaries of the Seljuk Turks from Asia Minor, the Ottomans took possession of Anatolia and turned it into a base for imperialism. Heading the government, the army, and the Church was the sultan, who relied on slaves as administrators and infantrymen. His military machine was further served by fief-holding cavalrymen and by the development of effective artillery. By 1333 the Ottomans had reached the Dardenelles; thereafter they moved into the Balkan peninsula, overrunning Greeks, Serbs, and Bulgarians. Thus they encircled Constantinople, whose empire had degenerated into feudal factions and civil war. In 1453 the old capital of the eastern

C. Socioeconomic, Political, Religious Developments

THE OTTOMAN ADVANCE

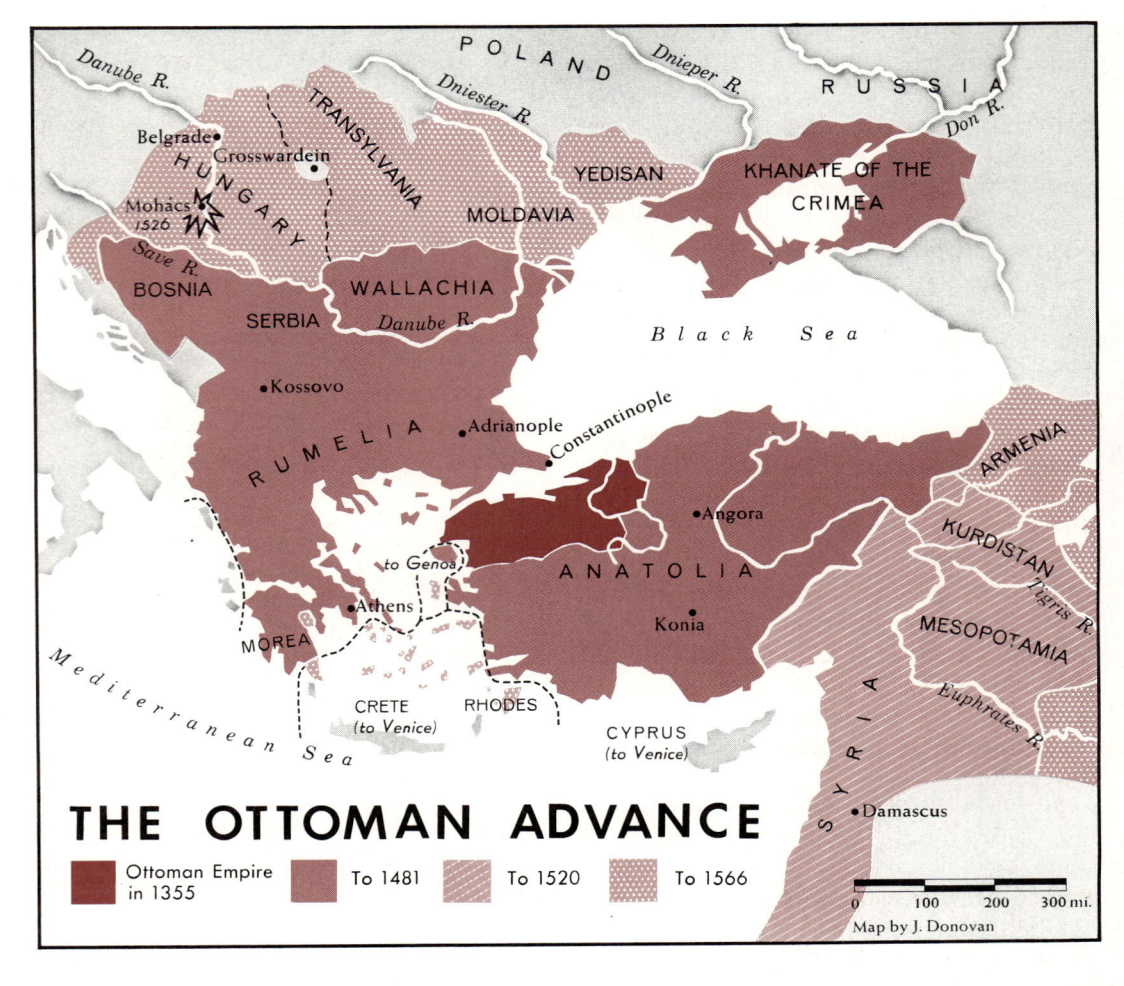

- Ottoman Empire in 1355
- To 1481
- To 1520
- To 1566

Map by J. Donovan

Roman Empire fell. Until 1480 the Turks pressed their advantage in the Balkans and in the eastern Mediterranean; then Europe received a respite for 40 years. But between 1515 and 1519 the Turks doubled their empire in the Near East by conquering Persia, Mesopotamia, Syria, and Egypt. These victories put the Ottomans in control of the overland trade to the Far East, a commercial advantage that was weakened, however, by Portugal's earlier establishment of a cheaper, all-water route to the Indies around Africa. At the end of the Renaissance the Ottoman Empire was poised to launch a new wave of invasions of Europe.

Ottoman expansion revived talk of crusades in Europe, but the crusading spirit against foreign infidels had been replaced by interest in dynastic conflicts and forceful maintenance of the social status quo. Venice salvaged part of her Mediterranean empire by coming to terms with the Turks. In 1494 Pope Alexander VI sought an alliance with the Turks against France, and in subsequent years France repeatedly allied with them against the Habsburgs. The renewed Turkish attacks after 1520 coincided with the outbreak of religious strife in Germany and the beginning of a long series of Habsburg-Valois conflicts. The impact of this new thrust had serious consequences that we shall consider in the following chapter.

The Territorial State

Eastern autocracies centralized their states by military conquest. More typical of the West was the growth of bureaucratic governments that partially daunted or displaced the feudal and ecclesiastical authorities, who were already their nominal subjects. Commerce encouraged consolidation by providing a taxable money economy, regular lines of communication, demands for secure trade routes, and economic problems too broad for local authorities. Privileged officials also gave impetus to centralization, but they often employed their increased powers for personal and family gain. More significant for the centralization of authority were the great problems of internal disorder and warfare that confronted every Western state. At some point during the Renaissance private warfare waged by feudal nobles or bands of mercenaries destroyed the internal security of every major state. Civil war shook nearly every town as the lower classes, aided by local peasants, rose against their oligarchical authorities. New taxes imposed on townsmen and peasants to meet the costs of modernized warfare (fought with mercenary troops and guns) commonly caused these revolts.

European responses to these problems varied, but they shared a common pattern in the emergence of authoritarian territorial states. The transition from feudal to national monarchy made the greatest advance in England. By limiting royal power Parliament made its extension over courts, church, towns, military forces, and taxation acceptable to, at least, the propertied classes. French centralization began later and was less complete. Royal officials encroached on the political prerogatives of church and nobility, and the kings relied on the officials rather than cooperate with the Estates General. By circumventing the latter's control of finance, French monarchs achieved absolute control of the army. In the provinces, however, their officials met with local vested interests that they could superintend but not control. Spanish centralization began still later. At the end of the fifteenth century royal absolutism emerged from feudal chaos in Castile, but other kingdoms of the peninsula successfully resisted royal discipline and incorporation into a single territorial unit. In the empire secular princes began to build territorial states, but their dynastic conflicts disrupted public order and weakened the empire's external security. A similar decentralization occurred in Italy, except that the local Italian states achieved unmatched compactness and administrative efficiency.

Everywhere except in the various political entities of northern Italy territorial authority was incompletely centralized— but all of these states legislated economic and social controls and curbed the autonomous power of the Church, the nobility, and the town corporations. This authoritarianism imposed some degree of order and social stability. In international affairs, however, internal consolidation was a prelude to dynastic warfare on an unprecedented scale. This consolidation and conflict naturally posed grave problems for the one institution in Europe whose claims to authority transcended the local territorial states—the Roman Catholic church.

CRISIS IN THE CHURCH

For the Roman Catholic church the Renaissance was a period of unprecedented crisis. Although its institutional machinery had never been more centrally organized, the areas of its jurisdiction and effective obedience were shrinking. Popular piety may not have been declining, but ecclesiastical influence on culture and secular activities clearly was. Part of the problem concerned the inability to meet the spiritual needs of a great many Europeans; another grew out of the old church-state disputes of the High Middle Ages.

The Papacy at Avignon

Medieval Church reformers had attempted to wrest control from secular rulers by concentrating authority in the papacy. In elaborating papal claims to spiritual and secular authority canon lawyers developed a full-blown theory of the pope's sovereignty. In the words of a leading fourteenth-century canon lawyer, "The pope is the wonder of the world. . . . He is neither God nor man, just as if he were neuter, he is between the two."[5] Renaissance monarchs were no more inclined than their predecessors to accept papal supremacy over the hierarchy, which included bishops and abbots with political as well as religious functions. In the medieval investiture struggle with the Holy Roman Emperor the papacy had won; but during the pontificate of Boniface VIII (1294–1303), himself a canon lawyer, the Church failed to make good its claims to the right of superintending secular rulers.

In 1296 Boniface forbade laymen to collect levies from the clergy and the clergy to pay them without the pope's authorization. Supported by a new institution—Parliament—Edward I frustrated Boniface by outlawing the clergy. Philip IV of France also defeated this enactment by forbidding the export of money and valuables from the kingdom. Philip and Boniface soon clashed again, however. After Philip's courts charged a bishop with blasphemy, heresy, and treason, Boniface called a council to reform the French government. Buoyed by a successful jubilee in Rome and a Flemish victory over France, Boniface issued a bull in 1302 (*Unam Sanctam*) in which he reaffirmed the old claim of papal supremacy in the most resounding language ever used by a pope. Infuriated, Philip responded with a boldness and brutality that indicated how little regard monarchs felt for the moral authority of the pope. In 1303 Philip assembled a meeting of clergy, nobles, and commons in Paris—France's first Estates General—to increase his support. Then Philip's henchman, the great lawyer Nogaret, went to Italy and invaded the little town of Anagni where the pope was staying, with the object of dragging him to France to depose him. The townspeople prevented that, but Boniface died soon after (1303).

Thereafter Philip secured a total victory, including the exoneration of Nogaret. In 1309 the pope (Clement V) moved the papal see to the little enclave of Avignon in southern France. Here French influence predominated until 1378, giving credence to the belief, in other kingdoms, that the papacy was in "Babylonian Captivity," subservient to the foreign policy of France.

During the years of the Babylonian Captivity the Avignon popes expanded the central administration of the Church, the Curia. The chancery, courts, and diplomatic service of the Church excelled those of all contemporary governments. Particularly elaborate was collection of the pope's revenue. Because some of the traditional sources of income such as tithes had fallen to lay collectors, other resources were developed. In addition to exacting various smaller obligations, the Curia levied a tax on the clergy's net income, which drew tremendous amounts from great prelates unprotected by their rulers. New offices were created and sold, and fees were set for dispensations, absolutions, legal cases, and document services. The sale of in-

---

[5] Johannes Andreae, *Glossa ad Proemium s. v. papa,* in *Clementis Papae Quinti Constitutiones* (Paris, 1601).

dulgences* also became a major source of income.

The Avignon papacy marked the Church's adjustment to a world of commercial wealth. To handle papal accounts the popes turned to the great banking houses whose services were necessary for the collection and disbursement of funds in diverse currencies. In the eyes of its critics the Avignon papacy was also seen to mark a period in which monetary concerns dominated papal policies. Finance took precedence over other administrative tasks which, due partly to the sale of offices and exemptions (simony), were often in disarray. Moreover, centralization of ecclesiastical courts inevitably led to conflicts between the secular states and the papacy over conflicting jurisdictions. Governments at odds with Avignon curtailed papal courts, taxes, land acquisition, and appointments. Some of them protected heretics who drew wide popular followings, and not a few pitted claims of divine-right kingship against papal claims of divine authority.

The Great Schism and the Conciliar Movement

In 1378 papal prestige and influence plunged further when part of the College of Cardinals seceded and elected a second pope. Thus arose the Great Schism, with rival popes at Rome and Avignon claiming divine sovereignty, exchanging anathemas, sponsoring polemical propaganda, erecting competing administrative and tax systems, and vying for support of local hierarchies. For the most part, foreign policy considerations determined alignment behind one or the other pope.

* In the fourteenth and fifteenth centuries indulgences were exemptions from temporal punishment of sins in purgatory granted by authority of papally sanctioned writs to penitents or persons representing the dead.

More than the Babylonian Captivity, the Great Schism invited total rejection of the ecclesiastical system and the subordination of local hierarchies to secular rulers.

Since each pope considered himself the only true Vicar of Christ and the apostolic successor to St. Peter, the schism seemed constitutionally insoluble without abandonment of the principle of papal sovereignty. One of the two popes would have to step down; but neither would. The two separate colleges of cardinals offered no solution, for each perpetuated its own line of popes.

To end the Great Schism such University of Paris scholars as Pierre d'Ailly and Jean de Gerson argued the doctrine of conciliarism, which held that Church councils, which princes as well as popes could summon, possessed authority equal to or greater than that of the pope. One recalls that many councils were held since the first ecumenical one at Nicaea in A.D. 325 in order to resolve fundamental problems. In 1409 a new council convened at Pisa. It debated the schism, the urgency of moral and administrative reform, and the spread of heresy. Dealing with the schism first, the council elected a new pope. But alas! Both existing popes denounced the council's authority and refused to give way. So now the Church had three successors to St. Peter, each claiming full papal powers.

Since Pisa resolved nothing, the Holy Roman Emperor Sigismund took the initiative in forcing another council at Constance (1414–18). The problems were still the same: schism, reform "in head and members," and the spreading heresy, especially the Hussite heresy in Bohemia. The dead Wycliffe was anathematized. The leaders of Bohemian dissent, John Hus and Jerome of Prague, were interrogated, condemned, and burned at the stake despite guarantees of safe conduct granted by the emperor. Instead of moderating Bohemian dissent, the executions spurred Bohemia into a national religious revolt.

On constitutional issues the Council of Constance was more assertive and successful than Pisa. In legislation that anticipated acts of the seventeenth-century English Parliament against divine-right kings, the council declared in the decree *Sacrosancta* (1415) that it possessed sovereignty directly delegated by Christ, whence its authority was superior to that of the contesting popes. In 1417 it decreed that regular councils should be held whether or not the pope convoked them. By persuasion and coercion it also secured the resignation of all three existing popes and the reestablishment of a single papal line under Martin V. The Great Schism ended, but Martin V promptly repudiated the conciliar movement that ended it by reaffirming papal sovereignty.

The hostility of the popes delayed any future conciliar action of significance until 1431, when churchmen assembled at Basel (1431–49). The theme of this convocation was the conflict between conciliar and papal powers. The delegates eventually voted to depose Eugenius IV and replace him with another head of the Church. Radicalism divided the council and made enforcement of its decisions impossible; nor could the council abrogate papal taxes or reform papal appointment procedures. Following the collapse of the crusades against the Hussites, the council was obliged to offer them concessions, which constituted a disastrous blow to the council's prestige.

Pope Eugenius outmaneuvered the embarrassed council by calling an official rival council at Ferrara and Florence (1438–45) and by negotiating a much-heralded but empty reunion with the Eastern Orthodox church (1439), whose sees were being overrun by the Turks. More significantly, Eugenius won monarchs away from their support of the council by negotiating concordats with them or by pragmatically sanctioning their curtailment of papal authority. In theory these agreements required that local Church posts be filled in the future by election; in practice they delivered control of ecclesiastical affairs to local rulers. Thus monarchical and papal authoritarianism joined hands for their mutual advantage.

Despite papal hostility the conciliar idea survived, but in 1460 Pius II threatened to excommunicate all who appealed to conciliar authority over the pope. Because any council attempting to reform the papacy would by necessity be subversive of papal sovereignty, reform by council was barred until after the Protestant Reformation made great progress, creating a new and greater crisis for the Church. On the other hand, the Renaissance popes were not free agents to carry out reforms even when they were so minded, for their hands were tied by vested ecclesiastical, noble, and monarchical interests serving the status quo.

Heresy, Mysticism, and Reform Agitation

Christian teachings had led Europeans to believe that the hallmark of the Church was spiritual purity and Christian solicitude. What they actually saw was something quite different. The vows of poverty, chastity, and obedience were violated with impunity. Wealth was visibly used for the self-gratification of high churchmen, but parishes were poor. Many prelates held several benefices at the same time (pluralism), enjoyed their extra incomes, but were rarely if ever seen in the benefices (absenteeism). Meanwhile poverty was the lot of the vicar who substituted for the absentee churchman. Nepotism, simony, and concubinage were openly practiced. The interests of the aristocracy and wealthy townsmen were given priority over those of the poor by bishops and abbots. Mendicant friars, such as the Spiritual Franciscans who held to apostolic poverty, stimulated popular dissatisfaction with the Church by their denunciations of the worldliness of the secular clergy. It should be understood that anticlericalism was a protest against the intolerable secularism of the clergy; it was not a sign of disbelief in Christianity.

The erosion of confidence in the Church revealed itself in many ways, but the causes were not altogether the worldliness of the clergy. The Black Death (1348–50) was a traumatic event, a spiritual crisis. Occurring during the Babylonian Captivity, the early years of the Hundred Years' War, and the general retrenchment of Europe, it seemed to some a terrible judgment on wayward Christianity. Millenarianism, self-flagellation, apocalyptic prophecy, social revolt, violence, and morbid preoccupation with death (such as the "dance of death" drawings, with their grinning skeletons) were some of the manifestations of a deep fear bordering on hysteria and a spiritual dislocation that endemic plagues only deepened. Here were ample psychological conditions for a diversity of religious expression. At the same time that humanism began to give expression to lay attitudes, a kind of religious epidemic swept Europe.

Of the major heresies of the Middle Ages, Albigensianism had been reduced to impotent fragments. But the Waldensians were still active in parts of France, Italy, and Germany. They proclaimed the priesthood of all believers, denied the efficacy of sacraments performed by priests in states of mortal sin, and used the Bible as authority in opposing the hierarchy's demand for obedience.

During the Hundred Years' War John Wycliffe of Oxford, a popular preacher, writer, and scholar who assisted in the preparation of the government's antipapal enactments of the 1350s, initiated a similar heretical movement in England. Wycliffe relied on the Bible for authority and, asserting the competence of inspired laymen to understand it, stimulated its translation into English (1380). Disdaining the hierarchical Church at Avignon, he taught that the true Church consisted of all who were predestined to salvation. He denied the miracle of the Mass, in which the priest transformed bread and wine into the flesh and blood of Christ, and from the exercise of which the priest secured his elevated status. In addition, he denounced the temporal possessions and temporal authority of churchmen. He also encouraged poor wandering priests, or "Lollards," to preach throughout the country.

Although Wycliffe taught absolute obedience to secular authority even when it was tyrannical, the royal court eventually had second thoughts about his religious orthodoxy and secured his retirement to a country estate. Wycliffe's teachings continued at Oxford, however, eventually permeating all classes of society. When they reached the lower classes through the Lollards, they became mixed with demands for secular and social reforms. The Peasants' Rebellion of 1381 involved religious radicalism, causing a conservative reaction to set in. A half-century of persecution by the authorities of church and state, during which the burning of heretics was first introduced in England, sufficed to extinguish organized Lollardy, whose ideas nevertheless lingered on until the outset of the English reformation; but as an organized movement, it had all but disappeared by the end of the Hundred Years' War.

Opposition to the affluence and secular power of the prelates, to the practice of simony, and to the sale of indulgences became general during the Renaissance. In Bohemia a heretical reform movement compounded of religious, political, and social grievances burst into widespread revolution. Religious criticism was mixed with a Czech cultural movement that emanated from Prague, the capital of Emperor Charles IV (1346–78). Dissatisfaction with ecclesiastical conditions came to a climax in the writings and teachings of John Hus (1369–1415).

A Czech of humble parentage, he became a professor at the new University of Prague as well as the queen's confessor. Drawing upon the teachings of Wycliffe and Czech predecessors, Hus and popular preachers using the Czech language attacked a host of religious malpractices. The reformers especially denounced simony, clerical immorality, scholastic philosophy, reverence of relics and saints, and the sale of indulgences. Accepting the challenge, the local archbishop excommunicated Hus and placed Prague under interdict. At first King Wenzel resisted the interdict and supported Hus, but the two disagreed over the sale of indulgences, in whose proceeds the king shared. After riots broke out in Prague, Hus retired to a country estate to write. In 1414 his case came before the Council of Constance, which stripped him of his imperial safe-conduct, condemned him for heresy, and handed him over to secular authorities to be burned at the stake.

Instead of ending the Bohemian heresy Hus's betrayal and execution fanned national and religious resistance to the Church and to the German emperor who inherited the Bohemian crown in 1419. Nobles and knights drew up a reform program; and the emperor was turned away from Prague's gates by force. Between 1420 and 1436 a series of Bohemian wars, at once civil and foreign, devastated central Europe as the Czechs turned back repeated German and papal crusades and raided neighboring territories. Internally, the Hussites split between moderate nobles and militant egalitarian radicals (Taborites) who sought the destruction of noble and clerical privileges as well as the abolition of all doctrine not to be found in the Bible. Although the Taborites were ultimately defeated, the Church was obliged to yield to doctrinal deviations that it could not stamp out by force of arms. Thus Bohemia became the first country to carry out a successful religious reformation.* Had the printing press then been available for the reformers' use, the Hussite movement might have spread to other parts of Europe as Luther's reformation did later.

No less critical of existing conditions in the Church, but uneasily trying to remain within it, were those who deemphasized the role of the priest as mediator between God and man. They exhorted fellow Christians to establish a direct relationship to God either through self-exertion (mysticism) or by divine direction (spiritualism). Both tendencies were old within monasticism. During the Renaissance their principal advocates among the clergy were the Spiritual Franciscans, a branch of the Order of St. Francis that held to apostolic poverty in imitation of Christ and his disciples. Their literal emphasis on poverty embarrassed the popes at Avignon, who condemned them as heretics. On the fringe of the controversies over apostolic poverty was the foremost Franciscan schoolman, William of Ockham, a nominalist philosopher. Protected after 1327 by the emperor, Ockham attacked the Avignon popes and undermined the theology of the late medieval sacramental system. His most telling attack was directed against the doctrine that human reason could fathom divine will and nature; the elaborate arguments he used to undermine rational philosophy were later adopted by many Protestant reformers of the sixteenth century. Ockham was excommunicated in 1328. Moved by the mass misery wrought by the Black Death, many of the Spiritual Franciscans became involved in social revolts, extreme practices such as self-flagellation, and predictions of the imminent end of the world.

More successful in avoiding official con-

---

* Memory of this reformation has largely lapsed, however, because it was completely undone during the 1620s, a victim of the Thirty Years' War.

demnation were the mystic Upper Rhenish "Friends of God" who produced a popular devotional treatise entitled *The German Theology*. In the Netherlands others formed lay brotherhoods called Brethren of the Common Life, founded in the wake of the Black Death by Gerard Groote (1340–84), a scholar-priest from a prominent Deventer family. The Brethren organized laymen of both sexes who dedicated themselves to devotions, education, and preaching in the vernacular without taking irrevocable vows. As mystics they held the complexities of scholastic theology in low esteem and emphasized a simple ethic of humble imitation of the life of Christ. The Brethren achieved great success in educating the townspeople of the lower Rhine, and Deventer became the center of Northern humanism and an important seat of publishing. One of its pupils was Erasmus, who, as we have seen, became the leading humanist of Renaissance Europe. Despite their criticism of the clergy, the Brethren escaped excommunication during the fifteenth century. In the early part of the Reformation many of the people influenced by them apparently became "Sacramentarians," that is, persons who denied any divine miracle in the sacraments. On the other hand Ignatius Loyola, founder of the Society of Jesus during the Catholic Reformation, was significantly influenced by their writings, especially by *The Imitation of Christ*, attributed to Thomas a Kempis.

The spread and influence of the Brethren of the Common Life was only one expression of general lay piety during the Renaissance. More than half of the books published in the first half-century after the invention of printing (1450–1500) were religious, usually devotional tracts. Rites of the Church, many of which would be considered superstitious today, permeated every aspect of life. Towns competed in building churches; and, since indulgences were often granted to those who visited sacred places, crowds thronged to shrines and relic collections. Also, in areas under interdict the clergy were compelled by the laity to continue services. But the Church hierarchy was unable or unwilling to accommodate new forms of piety. After its experience with the Franciscans it refused to authorize the foundation of new orders, and critics who might otherwise not have turned against the Church's authority were forced into heresy by official condemnation.

The Papacy of the High Renaissance

By 1450 the papacy had won a clear-cut victory over councils as the supreme authority in the Church, but it was clearly losing control over culture, the secular state, and the administrative power to effect reforms. Popular anticlericalism was a clear indication that the tutelage of clergymen, or at least the policies they pursued, were objectionable to large segments of the populace. Intervention by secular rulers to secure relief from papal authority was popularly approved. Even local prelates, especially those who owed their appointments to those rulers, offered little or no protest.

As we noted above in connection with humanism, clerical control of education and culture gradually passed, at least in part, into the hands of laymen. Wealthy patrons were commissioning secular works of art, and town schools and colleges of civil law and medicine were turning out educated laymen; thus the ranks of educated persons who were not clergymen swelled. Among the educated the cult of humanism developed a passion for the secular culture of classical antiquity. Few of these changes threatened the Church's existence, but they narrowed the scope of its accepted jurisdiction.

In the absence of ecclesiastical reform the papacy of the High Renaissance was powerless to check the erosion of its influ-

Julius II, detail from the Mass of Bolsena *by Raphael.*

ence. It did move, however, to regain its hold on culture and, at least in Italy, on political affairs. Popes and prelates became foremost patrons, and often even practitioners, of classical arts and letters. They sought to make humanism "safe" by drawing it into the service of religious education and scholarship. Many high churchmen became more concerned with esthetics, learning, and luxurious living than with religious doctrines and administration. Understandably, they alienated fundamentalists preoccupied with salvation, self-denial, and the traditional ideals of the Church. As social conservatives they also frustrated social as well as religious reform. Thus although the higher clergy came to terms with Renaissance arts and letters, they risked social and doctrinal revolts against their authority.

It was the tragedy of the papacy as a temporal state to be drawn into inescapable political situations that caused it to lose further prestige as a spiritual force. During the Great Schism noble families, mercenary captains, and nearby princes and republics carved up the Papal States into local domains or dependencies. With the restoration of a single line of popes in Rome the task of recovery began. Lacking reliable officials, Renaissance popes distributed offices among their own relatives, a nepotistic device that soon yielded fresh scandals. Alexander VI (1492–1503), for example, attempted to establish his son, Cesare Borgia, at the head of a conquered family principality. Military efforts to reconquer the Papal States reached their peak under Julius II (1503–13). This "warrior pope," a patron of Michelangelo, Bramante, and Raphael, personally led his troops in the field.

Invasion of Italy by France and Spain after 1494 further complicated papal politics. The popes, fearing domination of Italy and the papacy by either France or Spain, organized "holy leagues" against whichever was more threatening at the moment. Thus papal diplomacy became indistinguishable from the secular diplomacy of the Italian city-states, and its spiritual weapons of interdict and excommunication lost all effectiveness. Eventually the papacy failed to prevent the domination of the peninsula by Spain; thereafter papal fortunes were wed to the secular power of the Spanish Habsburgs, who superintended much of the Catholic Reformation of the sixteenth century. Meanwhile the expenses of war, papal patronage of the arts, and clerical luxury alienated non-Italians, on whom fell heavy financial burdens. Particularly roused were the Germans, who had little sympathy with the purposes to which papal revenues were being put.

Failure to effect reforms and a related contest for power between popes and cardinals continued to sap papal prestige. The foremost Italian townsman, Lorenzo de' Medici, was wont to refer to Rome as a moral "cesspool" even when actively seeking ecclesiastical preferments for his son Giovanni (the future Pope Leo X). Responsibility for this reputation was not, however, due to the popes alone. The Curia, especially the cardinals, had heavy vested interests in the status quo. These they sought to extend by wringing advance concessions or "capitulations" from candidates for the Holy See who were preferably older men with short prospective reigns. As papal electors the cardinals did not want to destroy papal sovereignty; they merely sought to use it for their own ends. Alexander VI fought back by creating 43 new cardinals, almost all from Italy and Spain, including five from his own family. But his successor, Julius II, was obliged to grant further financial and personal privileges to the cardinals. Leo X, pope when the Lutheran issue broke in Germany, let things rest as they were. His reform-minded successor, Adrian VI, the last non-Italian to sit on the papal throne, found resistance to reform too strong to overcome during his brief reign (1522–23). Papal tenure too short to master opposition and assert executive authority continued to be a source of administrative weakness throughout the sixteenth century.

THE LEGACY OF "THE RENAISSANCE STYLE"

Now that we have surveyed the developments of the fourteenth and fifteenth centuries, let us return to our question of departure: what is the legacy of the Renaissance for the modern world? Some historians claim that "the Renaissance style" subverted tradition and pervaded the Western World, bringing with it new concepts and institutions. Prominent among these were individualism, nationalism, capitalism, the rise of the bourgeoisie as a social class, the secularization and simplification of religion, classical standards of esthetics, and an optimistic, lusty enjoyment of life. The Renaissance did include all of these elements; but to cite them as *the* Renaissance style and to imply that they were ascendant is to underestimate the heavy weight of tradition—especially in eastern Europe, Germany, and Spain—that soon dominated Italy, the hearth of Renaissance secularism. Such a "style" could and did continue to flourish only in those countries where economic and political developments were auspicious (England, the Low Countries, France).

Seen as a whole, the Renaissance cannot be considered a solo of subsequent modernity. Composed and performed by diverse creators, it was a dissonant symphony of contradictory voices. Nor were its ideals always novel; often they accommodated rather than undermined chivalric tradition. The "universal man," for example, had become a gentleman. But his highest values continued to be medieval: military valor, honor, and the thirst for fame and glory.

Many would measure the Renaissance by the ideals of a few of its shining lights: Lorenzo de' Medici, Leonardo da Vinci, Erasmus. These men epitomized the ideals of the Renaissance, but they did not set the tone of the succeeding age, the Reformation. Still, the humanistic world view, Renaissance esthetics, and the new concepts of state and society survived the passions of the sixteenth century. Combined with new scientific discoveries, they inspired the secular thought of the Age of Reason, thus helping to shape the world view of modern man.

Selected Readings

*Bainton, Roland H. *Erasmus of Christendom.* New York: Charles Scribner's Sons, 1969.

> *The latest and best biography of Erasmus in English. With superb quotes, good illustrations, and an extensive bibliography, it pushes the ecumenical thesis of basic agreement between Erasmus and Luther too far.*

*Berenson, Bernard. *Italian Painters of the Renaissance.* New York: World Publishing Co., Meridian Books, 1957.

> *Vivid interpretations of individual painters, especially those who made of two-dimensional canvases "windowpanes" through which appeared the illusion of an external, objective reality.*

*Blunt, Anthony. *Artistic Theory in Italy 1450–1600.* London: Oxford University Press, 1962.

> *This sketches with illustrations the purposes for which art was intended from the Middle Ages through the Catholic Reformation.*

Bouwsma, William J. *Venice and the Defense of Republican Liberty: Renaissance Values in the Age of the Counter Reformation.* Berkeley: University of California Press, 1968.

> *An extended account of the role that civic consciousness played in Renaissance Venice and its points of collision with the papal monarchy.*

Brucker, Gene A. *Florentine Politics and Society 1343–1378.* Princeton: Princeton University Press, 1962.

> *This study portrays the factional turbulence of Renaissance town life within the machinery of a "one-party" state.*

*Burke, Peter. *The Renaissance Sense of the Past.* New York: St. Martin's Press, 1969.

> *A heavily documented account of the birth and growth of historical consciousness during the Renaissance.*

Burckhardt, Jacob. *The Civilization of the Renaissance in Italy.* Many editions in English.

A discovery of the spirit of the Renaissance in the union of the classics and the genius of the Italian people. An extremely influential, controversial, and romantic interpretation of the nineteenth century.

Bush, Douglas. *The Renaissance and English Humanism.* London: Oxford University Press, 1962.

These are lectures that emphasize the religious traditionalism in English humanism.

Carsten, Francis L. *The Origins of Prussia.* London: Oxford University Press, 1954.

This traces the transition of the German-Slavic frontier from freedom to serfdom. The account goes up to the seventeenth century.

Chabod, Federico. *Machiavelli and the Renaissance* Cambridge, Mass.: Harvard University Press, 1960.

Essays assessing Machiavelli's realism as a political reporter and theorist; they conclude with a keen analysis of what was new in the Renaissance.

Calmette, Joseph. *The Golden Age of Burgundy.* New York: W. W. Norton & Co., 1963.

A cultural and political account of Burgundy's blending of northern Europe's richest urban culture, dynastic aggrandizement, and sumptuous chivalric display at court.

*Cheyney, Edward P. *The Dawn of a New Era: 1250–1453.* Rise of Modern Europe Series. New York: Harper & Row, Publishers, 1962.

A comprehensive summary stressing the emergence of national cultures and concluding with an extensive annotated bibliography.

Ergang, Robert. *The Renaissance.* Princeton: D. Van Nostrand Co., 1967.

A new account, excellent in its treatment of literature, that demonstrates the perseverance of the Burckhardtian school.

*Ferguson, Wallace K. *Europe in Transition: 1300–1520.* Boston: Houghton Mifflin Co., 1962.

A new standard textbook account that makes the middle of the fifteenth century a turning point from depression and internal disorder to economic improvement and dynastic consolidation.

Ferguson, Wallace K. *The Renaissance in Historical Thought: Five Centuries of Interpretation.* Boston: Houghton Mifflin Co., 1948.

Chronicles changing attitudes toward the Renaissance, as informative of later generations as of the Renaissance itself.

Ferguson, Wallace K. et al. *The Renaissance: Six Essays.* New York: Harper & Row, Publishers, 1962.

Interpretative essays by representative authorities on politics, economics, art, literature, science, and religion.

Garin, Eugenio. *Italian Humanism, Philosophy, and Civic Life in the Renaissance.* Translated by Peter Munz. New York: Harper & Row, Publishers, 1965.

An English translation of an influential Italian work that traces the Italian

Renaissance up to the seventeenth century, placing considerable emphasis upon philosophy and science.

Gilbert, Felix. *Machiavelli and Guicciardini: Politics and History in Sixteenth-Century Florence.* Princeton: Princeton University Press, 1965.

This study contrasts subjects' political theory with humanist writing of history and relates it to the actual conditions of practical politics, including the partisan factions to which each belonged.

*Gilmore, Myron P. *The World of Humanism: 1453–1517.* Rise of Modern Europe Series. New York: Harper & Row, Publishers, 1962.

A general history of all Europe and its contacts with other civilizations.

Hay, Denys. *The Italian Renaissance in its Historical Background.* Cambridge: Cambridge University Press, 1961.

A readable survey based on the most recent scholarship.

*Hexter, J. H. *Reappraisals in History.* New York: Harper & Row, Publishers, 1961.

A collection of articles on early modern European history that provocatively challenges such commonly accepted clichés as "the rise of the middle class."

Huizinga, Johan. *The Waning of the Middle Ages.* Garden City: Doubleday & Co., 1954.

A perceptive cultural history (based on the Low Countries) that fails to find evidence of revolutionary changes during the Renaissance.

Leff, Gordon. *Heresy in the Later Middle Ages: The Relation of Heterodoxy to Dissent ca. 1250—ca. 1450.* 2 vols. New York: Barnes & Noble, 1967.

A brilliant account of the mystics and heretics of the Renaissance period with apt conclusions about the role official repression played in driving dissenters to extremes.

*Lucki, Emil. *History of the Renaissance 1350–1550.* Salt Lake City: University of Utah Press, 1963–65.

A textbook arranged according to subject in five small volumes, emphasizing continuity rather than change.

Mariéjol, J. H. *The Spain of Ferdinand and Isabella.* New Brunswick, N. J.: Rutgers University Press, 1961.

A translation of a nineteenth-century French account still fresh and valuable.

Martines, Lauro. *The Social World of the Florentine Humanists: 1390–1460.* London: Routledge and Kegan Paul, 1963.

A sociological investigation of the leading Florentine humanists and their family connections, placing them among the ruling elite.

Mattingly, Garrett. *Renaissance Diplomacy.* London: Jonathan Cape, 1955.

A masterful combination of institutional analysis and political events that traces the origin and spread of the sending of diplomatic envoys and characterizes Renaissance politics as dynastic rather than national.

*Mollat, G. *The Popes at Avignon: 1305–1378.* New York: Harper & Row, Publishers, 1965.

> *A detailed classical French account of the Church's "Babylonian Captivity" and the efforts of the papacy to recover the Papal States.*

*Perroy, Edouard. *The Hundred Years' War.* New York: G. P. Putnam's Sons, Capricorn Books, 1965.

> *An English translation of the best account of the war, including its social history as well as the military and political aspects.*

*Pirenne, Henri. *Early Democracies in the Low Countries.* New York: Harper & Row, Publishers, 1963.

> *An opinionated but rare treatment of conflicts leading to the loss of urban autonomy in the Low Countries.*

*Roover, Raymond de. *The Rise and Decline of the Medici Bank 1397–1494.* New York: Norton & Co., 1966.

> *Probably the best work in English on banking institutions, this account of the leading Renaissance bank is highly revealing with respect to economic trends and sources of wealth.*

Smith, Preserved. *Erasmus.* New York: Frederick Ungar Publishing Co., 1962.

> *A sympathetic biography of the "prince of the humanists," which finds in him roots of a twentieth-century nondogmatic religion.*

Taylor, Henry O. *Thought and Expression in the Sixteenth Century.* 2d rev. ed., vol. 1. New York: Frederick Ungar Publishing Co., 1959.

> *A literary history that, despite its title, begins with the early Italian humanists of the fourteenth century.*

Asterisk (*) denotes paperback.

CHAPTER XIII

The Confessional Age: The Reformation of the Sixteenth Century

A. The Protestant Reformation

Before an aggressive Catholic Reformation checked their progress, several churches successfully broke from Rome between 1520 and 1560. Their success tore Western religious unity further asunder and laid the basis for prolonged religious warfare in the following century. Their zealous rivalry produced a confessional age, which attempted to restore the primacy of revealed religion as the norm for society, government, and truth.

In the past, overt heresy within Christendom had been recurrent and heated, but force and persuasion had succeeded in preventing most heresies from causing lasting schisms.* Nevertheless, following 1054 the schism between the Greek Orthodox and Roman Catholic churches had become quite clear and almost irreparable. Also the Bohemian Hussites successfully wrested concessions from the Roman church in the fifteenth century, and remnants of the Waldensians managed to survive persecution by the Inquisition. But in the main schismatic threats had been checked by crusades and reforms. In the sixteenth century the papacy failed to check dissenting religious leaders, who were supported by many local princes and governments, from establishing rival organizations.

The religious schism of the 1500s has often been described as a simple rift between traditional Catholicism and emergent Protestantism. This is hardly satisfactory, for it obscures divisions and changes within Catholicism and attributes to the Protestant reformers a unity that they did not possess. Moreover it ignores other traditions—neither orthodox nor Protestant by sixteenth-century standards—such as the Erasmian humanists and the sectarians who

---

* Technically heresy is the belief in any doctrine contrary to that taught by the Church, whereas schism simply means visible separation from the ecclesiastical framework of the Church. The two need not go together, but the Roman Catholic church taught that schismatics would almost necessarily become heretics, since they had abandoned the infallible, true chruch.

605

Illustrations from a German tract of 1508, prophesying disasters to come.

broke away from the Protestant reformers. The intensity and passion with which these varied groups fought one another remind the modern student of the fierce conflicts between rival totalitarian and social ideologies of our own day. But to give exclusive emphasis to these differences, uppermost though they were in sixteenth-century minds, is to conceal their dependence on common authorities.

The founders of new religious movements in the sixteenth century were primarily theologians preoccupied with new interpretations of old authorities revered by their Roman Catholic opponents. For this reason the historian must consider divergent schools of theology as critically important. Harder to assess but everywhere present and equally critical were the religious passions of the common people. In addition to the ultimate terror of death, their lives were made doubly uncertain by new diseases, large-scale warfare, famine, and plague—scourges for the partial control of which they lacked the science and institutions of more recent, less religiously oriented men. Whether Catholic, Protestant, or sectarian Anabaptist, they sought solace in supernatural salvation along paths prescribed by revelation and tradition. Religious faith was the principal focus of their loyalties and concerns, and for it most were willing even to kill as instruments in the hands of God.

Thus theology and popular faith were constant ingredients of the Reformation era, but they alone do not satisfactorily explain the success or failure of specific religions in specific areas. Social, economic, and especially political movements became an inextricable part of both the religious controversies and their eventual outcomes. Except for sectarians of the radical left of the Reformation movement, religious thinkers of the sixteenth century did not conceive of a separate church and state. Indeed, most theologians used religious principles to buttress the existing order, for changes in the status quo inevitably meant changes in the administration, if not in the doctrine, of the Church.

THE HOLY ROMAN EMPIRE ca. 1520

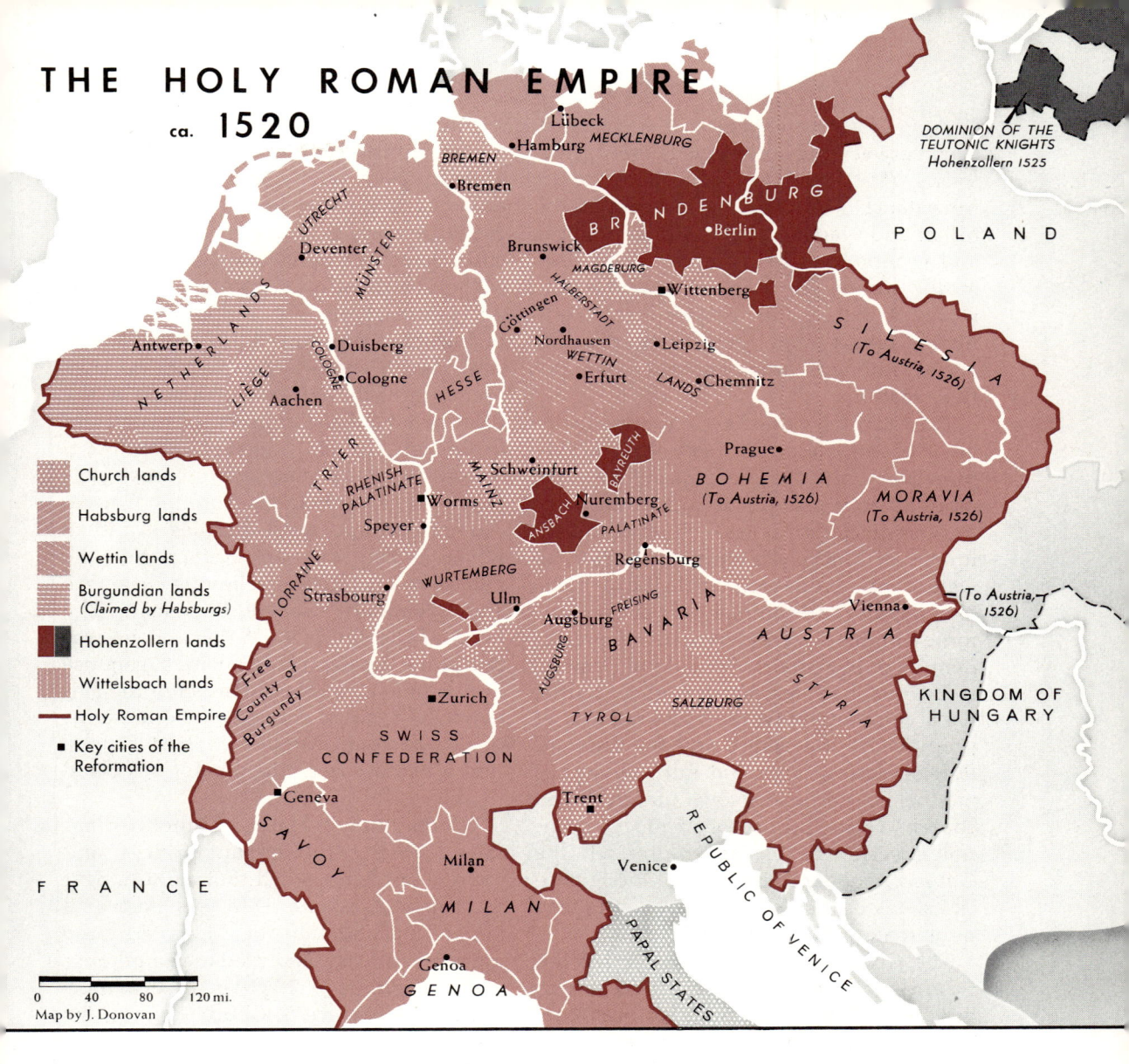

Legend:
- Church lands
- Habsburg lands
- Wettin lands
- Burgundian lands (Claimed by Habsburgs)
- Hohenzollern lands
- Wittelsbach lands
- Holy Roman Empire
- ■ Key cities of the Reformation

Scale: 0 – 40 – 80 – 120 mi.
Map by J. Donovan

Thus reform programs that supported the existing power structures, particularly "absolutist" princes and councils, received political and military support. By the same token, sectarians and humanists who opposed existing power structures suffered general persecution and frequently extirpation. International politics, such as the alliance of Catholic France with German Protestants in the 1530s, was also involved. How well a given government could suppress religious dissent depended on how much support it had. But when dissenters had foreign assistance, attempts to suppress them involved international as well as domestic conflict.

THE GERMAN REFORMATION

The Secular Background

Soon after Martin Luther sparked the theological dispute in Germany in 1517, eastern Europe was under attack by

A. The Protestant Reformation

Turkey. The empire was also engaged in wars between the houses of Habsburg and Valois (1521–59) over the Burgundian inheritance and over the possession of Milan and Naples. Also, various political and economic crises complicated its domestic affairs. The empire became a network of interaction between the conflicting religious, political, economic, and social interests that characterized the Reformation.

The Church exercised exceptionally great power under the Holy Roman Empire. Not only did the papacy draw far more revenues from it than the emperor, but certain clerical states—chiefly the electorates of Mainz, Cologne, and Trier, as well as numerous principalities of bishops, abbots, and commanders of the Teutonic Knights—were provocatively prominent in public affairs. Some local princes, it is true, had restricted clerical courts, papal appointments, the accumulation of property by the clergy, and the outward flow of clerical taxes. But until the Reformation more decisively subordinated church to state, the lack of an effective central government in the empire left the Church stronger there than in the territorial states of Italy or the more centralized monarchies of France and England.

The Church's immense power fed anticlerical movements at every level of society. At the imperial diets princes presented their grievances, or *gravamina*, against Rome and demanded redress through the imperial government. Popular feeling ran also against the clergy for failure to conform to its professed moral code. Guildsmen and merchants protested clerical exemptions from property taxes, excises, and tolls; they also naturally resented direct economic competition with privileged churchmen in milling, craft production, and retail sales. Especially in towns under clerical rulers revolts often led to armed attacks on the clergy.

The principal weakness of the German church, however, was not so much popular anticlericalism as the dynastic and economic ambitions of princely families. The same princes who complained vociferously of Roman power shared the proceeds from sales of indulgences and secured leading Church posts for members of their families, often young boys. Albert of Hohenzollern was appointed Archbishop of Mainz (his third major church post) even before he came of age. Members of the Wittelsbach family of the Palatinate held or administered bishoprics in Speyer, Utrecht, Freising, Naumburg, Regensburg, and many remunerative cloisters. But reaping spoils from the Church did not guarantee these families' loyalty to Rome. During the early Reformation the Palatinate wavered in religious allegiance and eventually became Protestant. The head of the house of Hohenzollern was one of the first German princes to espouse Lutheranism. Another member of the Hohenzollern family converted the holdings of the Teutonic Knights in East Prussia into a hereditary Lutheran fief of Poland in 1525.

Whether they remained Catholic or became Protestant, German princes and town councils extended their control over ecclesiastical affairs. This was part of a larger consolidation of local territorial governments that deprived the emperor as well as the pope of effective, direct authority. In the absence of Church reform, the secular governments reorganized monasteries, took control of schools, and enacted stringent laws governing lay and clerical morality.

In their striving for local autonomy, princes went much further than curbing the Church. Through newly established chanceries they worked to replace semiautonomous nobles with a new corps of paid officials. They also changed the composition of law courts by putting Roman law jurists (with incomes from salaries, fees, and bribes) on the benches. In the name of the "commonweal" (a universal but ambiguous slogan) lawyers and officials systematically overrode local custom. In effect, a legal-administrative revolution from above—of which the Reformation was but one part—was under way during the late fifteenth and early sixteenth centuries. Out of the changes came assurance of social privilege—but not political rights—for aristocrats. For chartered guildmasters and merchants came guarantees of monopoly. The peasantry and unprivileged townsmen had to bear the burden of supporting these social and economic advantages; for most of them, channels of appeal were closed. In peasant villages, for example, appointed officials replaced traditional assemblies and courts. These officials, whose decisions in practice were not subject to appeal, collected dues and services in the name of the prince.

Economic pressure from authoritarian governments was one of several factors intensifying social revolutionary movements that came to a climax in the "Peasants' Revolt" of 1524–26. Accelerating prices after 1450 depressed real wages. Population increase led to the division of estates into smaller parcels and jeopardized livelihood, especially after short harvests. English and Flemish competition made deep inroads in the German textile market at the expense of native producers. Small traders, lenders, and mine operators were supplanted by large monopolizing commercial and banking firms in Augsburg and Nuremberg. These firms, such as the Fuggers, Welsers, Hochstetters, and Peutingers, were supported by the emperor and the papacy. Meanwhile, upon the very people who could barely subsist the Church continued to lay heavy obligations. And almost intolerable governmental taxation—probably outweighing all other sources of economic strain—increased with endemic public disorder. Local governments tried to stabilize their shaking economic foundations by protective measures, while popular leaders sought to overcome German woes

A Bundschuh rebel, as pictured by a hostile tract of 1513.

by leading revolts against the Church and the princes, against landlord nobility in the country and patrician oligarchy in the cities.

These uncoordinated revolts of the fourteenth and fifteenth centuries continued into sixteenth-century Germany. In the towns there was conflict between guildsmen and patrician oligarchs. Revolutionaries accused officials of improper behavior, demanding an end to financial corruption, nepotism, and government by secret manipulation. They also sought to prevent the legal system from making justice too expensive for common people to obtain. Above all, they protested the increasing indirect taxation on items of consumption and commerce. Between 1509 and 1512 there were revolts in scores of towns.

At the same time, in the southern countryside, peasant uprisings occurred. These *Bundschuh* revolts (named after the thonged peasant boot which they adopted as their emblem) were sometimes directed toward a return to communal authority and old customs. The latter had certainly not been based on equality and justice, but many felt that it was a far easier kind of oppression to live under. Sometimes the revolutionaries aimed at establishing a standard of divine justice that would render serfdom unchristian. Nevertheless these revolts failed: the oppressed had access to no political lever with which to pry concessions from the ruling powers. Furthermore, their uprisings were disorganized and disconnected from one another. Of course, there had arisen among the privileged classes the fear that these eruptions would lead to a general revolution and to the establishment of a social order akin to that of Switzerland where villagers and townsmen had gained a greater degree of personal liberty. But not until the early Reformation did such fears coincide with actual developments. By then the revolutionaries were united in a general anticlerical feeling. After the emergence of Luther and the early reformers they were spurred on by a common conviction that their standard of justice was supported by God.

The Emergence of Luther

For a short time the different levels of German discontent were knit together by the activities and writings of Martin Luther (1483–1546) in Saxony and Ulrich Zwingli in Zurich. Although their main appeal was religious, their early attack on the status quo was sufficiently broad to bring together divergent, even contradictory, bodies of dissent under common slogans.

Born a younger son of a coppersmelting family of peasant stock, Luther grew up while his family's fortunes were rising. Educated in urban schools, he obtained a bachelor's and a master's degree in liberal arts at Erfurt University. At his parents' urging he began the study of Roman law, the most promising path to power and prestige. Fulfilling a vow taken in a moment of terror, young Martin suddenly switched his career, broke with his father, and joined an Augustinian cloister at Erfurt in 1505. His personal account of this decision, taken in the anguish of a search for religious identity, later endeared him to generations of German Protestants who were preoccupied with the question of the salvation of their souls. Zealous but dissatisfied as a monk, Luther was directed by his superiors to obtain a doctorate in theology at the new university founded at Wittenberg by Elector Frederick the Wise of Saxony. There, as a professor of theology, Luther resolved his personal longings for certainty of salvation in the course of preparing his lectures. More than a personal discovery, his solution formed the basis of a revolutionary assault on the hierarchy of the Roman Catholic church. It also led him to a career of religious reform that, without his intending it, brought him greater influence with the Elector than was enjoyed by any contemporary lawyer.

Despite Luther's rapid rise within monastic orders, he later reported that he experienced great anxiety and dissatisfaction with monastic rules as a religious way of life leading to salvation. Despairing of ever meriting through his own works, grace from an angry, incomprehensible, and predestining God, he found an escape from eternal damnation in St. Paul and St. Augustine. Salvation was not to be found in pious acts or ethical behavior but in a God-implanted faith that alone served to justify man. On his own, man remained immutably and impotently depraved. Authority for this doctrine of "faith alone" he found not in the papacy or tradition of the Church but in the Scriptures. Luther's changing subjective moods made him a volatile and sometimes inconsistent theologian; but he was confident that whatever position he took in a given situation represented faith in an objective, revealed creed that anyone not blinded by the Devil could find for himself in Scripture.

Luther began his career of reform with

Martin Luther *by Lucas Cranach the Elder.*

the curriculum of Wittenberg University. At the university he met and befriended Melanchthon, an accomplished classical scholar and nephew of Reuchlin. Melanchthon became Luther's lifetime ally and the systematizer of his doctrine. Together they excluded the traditional scholastic disciplines from Wittenberg's course of study, giving Luther a reputation for being an Erasmian. But his theology opposed that line of thought as much as it opposed scholasticism. Erasmians were concerned with replacing ignorance with reason and with encouraging men to behave ethically. Luther was preoccupied with religious justification and with opening people's hearts to the experience of faith. For him reason and ethics were helpful only under the direction of that faith; otherwise reason was the "Devil's harlot" and ethical conduct a lure to heresy.

The Wittenberg monk became a public figure when, on October 31, 1517, he posted his Ninety-Five Theses attacking abuses in the sale of indulgences. In neighboring territories the Dominican friar Johannes Tetzel was proclaiming an indulgence to raise money for Albert of Hohenzollern, who had become heavily indebted to the papacy and the Fuggers in the acquisition of the archbishopric of Mainz, his third major ecclesiastical post. Luther's ire was raised when pilgrims visiting Frederick the Wise's relic collection confronted him with Tetzel's indulgences, for he believed that writs of indulgence inculcated a false sense of religious salvation. Although Luther did not deny the principle of indulgences, his theses argued that only God could forgive sins; the pope could forgive only punishments he himself had imposed. Luther posted his theses for an academic debate that never took place, but they were translated, printed, and circulated throughout Germany. Unlike his earlier more radical attack on scholasticism, his theses against indulgences appealed to popular resentment against financial exactions from Rome, and their popularity threatened to dry up a fruitful source of papal revenue.

Luther did not attack the principle of indulgences as such until 1520, but in the meantime he attacked the Church in tracts and debates. He went so far as to call for a new general Church council, an excommunicable offense. Later he questioned the infallibility of past councils. Pope Leo X tried to curb Luther's attacks, but political complications—namely Leo's efforts to prevent the powerful Charles of Spain from becoming emperor in 1519—delayed decisive action. Meanwhile the monk ignored papal rulings. Finally in 1520 Leo X issued a papal bull excommunicating Luther and his associates.

Because Luther originally believed himself a loyal son of the Church, he had not foreseen conflict with the hierarchy. Yet since he placed Scripture above the authority of tradition, such conflict was inevitable, however unforeseen. Debating Johann Eck at Leipzig in 1519, Luther had declared both popes and councils fallible. He elaborated on this declaration in a series of tracts the following year. His *Address to the Christian Nobility of the German Nation* was directed to the princes, calling on them to reform the Church if clerics would not. Luther further argued for the "priesthood of all believers." With this principle (introduced earlier by Waldensians and others) he could justify state intervention: since princes were also priests, they could reform the Church. In the same tract he advocated congregational control over pastors and Church property. (This demand would later be repeated by the Peasants' Revolt and the Anabaptist movement.) He also called for reform in secular affairs. In *The Babylonian Capitivity of the Church*, written in Latin since it was addressed to the clergy, Luther argued that only baptism, the Liturgy of the Lord's Supper and, perhaps, penance were based on Scripture. (Later he decided that penance was not scriptural and therefore not a sacrament.) All other so-called sacraments had been added by papal antichrists and deserved destruction. A third tract, *On the Freedom of a Christian*, was intended for both the papacy and the general populace. In it Luther—who had already denounced the merit of all good works and the saving efficacy, by themselves, of sacraments, liturgies, acts of charity, and the like—developed more fully his concept of the efficacy of faith and God's grace as well as the priesthood of all believers. He set freedom apart from the secular world, defining it as wholly internal and spiritual.

Often considered Luther's primary reformation writings, these tracts established his emergence as an Old Testament type of prophet for Germans who felt oppressed by the papal yoke. In full rebellion against the secularization of the Renaissance Church and society, he operated in an apocalyptic framework: either the Church was to be reformed by itself or by the princes or the end of the world was at hand. Luther always opposed the use of violence to advance his gospel, but as a prophet he cared little for Erasmus's irenic secular wisdom of not provoking violent opposition, at least at first. He was fond of quoting Christ, who had "not come to preach peace, but the sword." On December 10, 1520, he defied authority by burning both the papal bull condemning him and collections of the canon law, the basis of the Church's legal system. Feeling that he had rediscovered the historical core of revelation, the unique work of God in Christ, Luther was prepared to court martyrdom even though he was to be plagued by self-doubts for the rest of his life. Luther expected God to secure the victory of His Gospel over its Roman foes, but at the same time he made the fullest use of humanist scholarship and the printing press to advance it and to discredit the papacy. A powerful penman in both Latin and the vernacular, he kept up a continuous output of tracts, treatises, commentaries, sermons, and letters for the rest of his life. His literary gifts, armed with his convictions, enabled him to grasp leadership of the German reformation. Other provincial reformers gained wide reputations, but it was Luther, a national hero of anti-Roman Germans, who was summoned to the Diet of Worms in 1521. Not only did he impress many of his contemporaries as a prophet; he has continued to inspire more literature, pro and con, than any other figure of modern times.

The Diet and Edict of Worms

So long as Church and state cooperated as in the past, excommunication and condemnation for heresy were preludes to secular outlawry and execution. Thus Luther's case, which popular agitation had made a major German issue, came before the first diet that the young Emperor Charles V attended. More was at stake than the fate of an individual condemned by the Church, for his case involved the question whether the German princes would continue to put secular force at the disposal of the Church.

For both ruler and assembly, Luther's hearing was secondary to more pressing problems. With the help of generous bribes and concessions to the princes, Charles had become emperor in 1519. Although he was now the greatest dynast Europe had yet beheld, his vast holdings were threatened by revolts in Spain and an imminent war with France and the Turks. Understandably, he was primarily concerned with securing tax grants and a new military organization for the empire. These the princes refused. Princes and emperor also clashed on the question of creating a central appellate court and an executive Regency Council to maintain order in Charles's absence. Both institutions were established, but the contest over control of them seriously weakened their authority. The Diet also enacted "antitrust" laws against the great southern German trading companies. These laws Charles would soon undermine, for they threatened the very interests that financed him as emperor.

This rivalry between the princes and the emperor was important for Luther's case. Charles backed the pope, but not all of the princes were prepared to enforce Luther's excommunication and brand him an outlaw; they were aggrieved with the papacy and fearful of Charles's power. They handed their grievances to Aleander, papal legate to the assembly, and de-

German lampoon depicting Luther with seven heads.

manded either a general or a German council to reform the Church. Some of them feared that suppression of Luther would provoke a general revolution. Even during the Diet, Worms, the scene of an anticlerical revolution only seven years before, seethed with discontent. Aleander feared for his life as Luther received a rousing welcome from the townsmen; still, he was able to secure the emperor's condemnation of the excommunicated monk. Together, emperor and legate were able to prevent him from arguing the details of his position. After some delegates had departed, they pushed through a proclamation—the Edict of Worms—outlawing Luther, his followers, and his books.

But this edict was to go generally unenforced. At Nuremberg the newly established Regency Council, nominally representing the emperor's authority, simply ignored the Edict while the emperor was preoccupied elsewhere. A few princes such as the rulers of ducal Saxony* and Bavaria did enforce it, but they did not begin to coordinate their efforts until the spring of 1524. Meanwhile Luther had been spirited away for safekeeping to Wartburg Castle by agents of Frederick the Wise. Under Frederick's protection Luther continued to work. He translated the New Testament into idiomatic German from Erasmus's Greek and Latin texts and continued to pen influential tracts. In one particularly powerful piece he appealed to monks and nuns to leave their cloisters. Luther's revolt was characterized by considerable personal courage, but for its success it depended on the simultaneous revolt of the German princes and city councils against the emperor and Rome.

Pamphlets, Agitation, and Revolts

Meanwhile, Luther's religious appeal had swept through Germany, gaining influential converts, especially among the clergy. Personal contacts and students supplemented the written word in converting such future Protestant leaders as Martin Bucer, who became the reformer of Strassbourg and an influence on Calvin's thought. Monks leaving their cloisters provided a constant flow of new recruits. Led by local clergymen and converts in city councils, numerous local towns began to introduce the Reformation and to depose Roman Catholic officials. In their rapid expansion, however, Luther's doctrines were popularized so that they meant different things to people with different religious or social grievances. The best evidence of this confusion is preserved in the popular tracts that circulated while the lines of confessional allegiance among the anti-Romanists were still fluid.

*Ruled by Duke George, a vociferous opponent of Luther, ducal Saxony was separate and distinct from Luther's electoral Saxony, ruled by Frederick the Wise.

In these tracts Luther was mistakenly identified with anticlerical causes more radical than he was prepared to support.

Luther and his followers took their cause directly to literate laymen with tracts printed in the German language. Between 1517 and 1525—when censorship confined discussion to government approved polemics—thousands of tracts circulated. Luther was most influential in setting their initial theme, but other writers, many of them anonymous, soon developed positions from which he rapidly backed away. In attributing German woes solely to clerical greed, sophistry, and obscurantism, he had kept religious reform separate from, although conjoined with, secular change. But fellow pamphleteers, such as Martin Bucer, combined social and religious reform in a "social gospel," an anticipated reorganization of society based on divine justice and Scriptural text. Many of them insisted that the Gospel was about brotherhood and justice, basic reform meaning the transformation not only of the Church but of society as well. Deep strains of antiintellectualism and utopianism ran through these writings, lifting people from the depths of despair to heights of exultant expectations. At the same time, some writers addressed themselves to the practical problem of achieving social and political as well as religious reforms.

The chief objects of their attack were the existing authorities, many of whom were prince-bishops and prince-abbots. On this issue Luther was ambiguous. He denounced clerical rule as illegitimate and castigated princes hostile to his Gospel, but he soon deferred to friendly princes, allowing them to take all initiative in introducing ecclesiastical changes. For those living under hostile rulers he gave no practical advice prior to his development of a doctrine of passive obedience. According to this, a Christian was obligated to obey the existing authorities even though they be infidels. But not all the reformers were so willing as Luther to accept the prevailing political and social system. An influential anonymous tract, probably written by Martin Bucer, went further in urging the peasants—whom these pamphlets venerated as superior in religious judgment to Roman prelates—to "use their flails" to coerce authorities into accepting reform without overt revolution. In Zurich, Ulrich Zwingli denounced tithes and called for resistance to ungodly governments. In Saxony Thomas Müntzer preached revolution against princes who barred the Gospel's path. To be sure all these positions had revolutionary implications, but there was no agreement on the path to reform, especially in territories ruled by clerical or aggressively Catholic princes.

After 1521 the slogans of the major reformers penetrated the lower classes. Often led by former monks, urban masses attacked the existing order and the partial reforms of the authorities who owed allegiance to Luther. They pressed for more stringent regulation of morality as well as for changes in rites and doctrine. Congregations in some places made faltering attempts to control pastors, properties, and alms; in widespread areas peasants began to withhold tithes, dues, and services.

In 1522 reform erupted into violence on a major scale with the revolt of the imperial knights led by Franz von Sickingen. Eclipsed in wealth by trading companies and in political power by princes, the knights desired to regain their old position of power and eminence serving directly under the emperor. Their leader Sickingen had commanded a mercenary army for the emperor in the Low Countries and terrorized towns and weak principalities by extorting indemnities. In so doing he could count on the sympathy of many provincial nobles restive under princely rule. Acting as publicist for the Knights' Revolt was Ulrich von Hutten, a nationalist humanist and pamphleteer who published Valla's *Donation of Constantine* in Germany in 1519. When Sickingen set out to seize the archiepiscopal electorate of Trier in 1522, Hutten portrayed the attack as a step toward religious reform, a characterization that Luther felt compelled to repudiate. But other rising leaders of the German Reformation accepted Hutten's judgment and applauded it. They collected at Sickingen's castle and supported him by siring anonymous popular tracts. Instead of assisting the revolt, however, the religious issue served to divide the dissident nobility. Nor was Hutten and Sickingen's circle of popular pamphleteers able to gain allies from the towns and peasantry. In 1523 Sickingen was surrounded in his castle by the princely armies of Saxony, Hesse, and the Palatinate. Their guns pierced his fortifications and mortally wounded him. Although some knights were to participate in the Peasants' Revolt of 1524–26, the Knights' Revolt collapsed, leaving the princes in control of southwestern Germany.

After a poor harvest in 1524, the condition of the peasant and urban lower classes of southwestern Germany was rife with deprivation and discontent. Their hostility, which clerical and secular rulers had nurtured by trying to enforce the Edict of Worms, spilled over into what is known in German history as the Great Peasants' War. Revolutionary townsmen of the major cities adopted articles condemning clerical and peasant economic competition. Most of these revolts, however, were inspired by a common program of reform, *The Twelve Articles of the German Peasantry*, which swept northward through the clerical states of central Germany. In 1525 they joined another center of revolt in Saxony. The Articles, written in the form of a contract to which local rebel "hosts" sought to secure their lords' assent, asserted that society and politics should rest on Scripture unadulterated by human invention and that congregations should have the right to elect and depose their own clergy. It would be further agreed that communal property seized illegally by present authorities should be returned. Common people would have hunting and fishing rights. Serfdom would be abolished. Tithes not mentioned in the Bible would be forgotten. And the legal system would be renovated.

Counting on divine assistance rather than overt revolution, the rebels sought to enforce these contracts by withholding dues, tithes, and services from the authorities. Thus deprived, governments collapsed, and large numbers of local nobles and churchmen signed the Articles. Townsmen, radical clergymen, and sometimes nobles joined the revolt and provided leadership. In Franconia such leaders drew up a formal military organization and proposed an abortive liberal constitution to be implemented by a parliamentary government. In place of princely absolutism, urban oligarchies, and the traditional social hierarchy, the peasant hosts universally proclaimed a society based on "Christian brotherhood"—a civic equality similar to the *fraternité* sought in the French Revolution of 1789.

The initiative taken by the rebellious lower classes, their demand for civic equality or brotherhood, and their ecclesiastical congregationalism collided squarely with the existing order. They also challenged the position of Luther and his followers, who were veering sharply toward authoritarian absolutism. Raising charges of anarchy and communism, local leagues of princes organized loyal nobles, townsmen, and mercenary troops into an aggressive counteroffensive determined to make sanguinary examples of those who dared to revolt. In meeting this counterattack, the rebels destroyed large numbers of castles and monasteries but seldom resorted to bloodshed. One by one the "peasant" hosts were isolated and annihilated, usually in flight from the point

Two armed peasants from a tract of 1524.

of confrontration with the princes' armies. Divine assistance was not forthcoming. In routing the "peasant" hosts the lords' armies seldom lost more than two or three men. Financing their expeditions as far as possible by booty and indemnities, the princes were believed by some contemporaries to have killed or executed 300,000 men; 100,000 would probably be closer to the truth. Only in Tirol, where peasants and townsmen had military strength and could fight on their own ground, were concessions retained. Elsewhere the "prewar" power structures were restored after indemnities and destruction were made good.

Roman Catholicism had made its first major recovery. The rebels had not only been soundly defeated but bitterly disillu-sioned. They had assumed (except in Saxony) that they were acting in accord with Luther's wishes, but in the closing days of the revolt Luther himself preached a crusade of extermination against them. Terrified by the anarchical implications of their uprising, he came to believe that they had perverted the spiritual Gospel for "fleshly" gain.* Already disillusioned with Rome, the rebels of 1525 were now

---

* Luther later took credit for the suppression of the revolt, even though his tract *Against the Robbing and Murdering Bands of Peasants* did not appear until the eve of the peasants' rout at Frankenhausen in Thuringia, one of the last encounters of the revolt. Similarly, he attributed the whole uprising to his archenemy in Saxony, Thomas Müntzer, an opinion that documentary evidence fails to substantiate.

disenchanted with Wittenberg. Many returned to Roman Catholicism. Others either resigned themselves to their lot or joined the burgeoning Anabaptist movement that swept across Germany from Switzerland on the heels of the revolt's suppression.

THE SHATTERING OF REFORMATION UNITY

Luther's premise that scriptural authority would produce a single, objectively revealed creed that every person could quickly discover for himself soon ran into trouble. Erasmian humanists abhorred his precipitate actions and repudiated his Augustinian predestinarian doctrines as subversive of morality. Radical Evangelicals and humanists opposed his social and political authoritarianism. The rebels of 1525 learned the hard way that they and Luther held different concepts of scriptural authority and Christian brotherhood. Reformers in southern German towns, such as Martin Bucer in Strassbourg and Oecolampadius in Basel, maintained varying degrees of independence from Luther's leadership; one of them, Ulrich Zwingli of Zurich, became an acknowledged leader of a rival creed and organization. Thus the common front against existing Catholicism soon dissolved into a number of competing creeds and organizations seeking consolidation and control over local areas.

Zwinglian Reform in Zurich

Ulrich Zwingli (1484–1531) became a public figure of reform in Zurich at about the same time that Luther became famous in Saxony. An outspoken opponent of indulgences, he also attacked dietary regulations and clerical celibacy in theory and practice. Nor did tithes and infant baptism escape his criticism—at first. A former chaplain attached to Swiss mercenary troops in Italy in 1515, he excoriated the ruling oligarchy of Zurich for selling the services of Swiss mercenaries to foreign powers. Theologically Zwingli had much in common with Luther, from whom he derived some of his doctrines. They agreed on the absolute sovereignty and inscrutability of God from whom fallen man was separated by a gulf unbridgeable except by divine grace. Although both affirmed the principle of biblical authority, Zwingli treated the Liturgy of the Lord's Supper as a memorial service rather than a supernatural sacrament. He also offended Luther's followers by justifying revolution.

Zwingli established a state church in Zurich, a republican state controlled largely by the guilds from whom Zwingli drew most of his political support. His urban republican reformation spread among the townsmen of southern Germany, and in this, too, he differed from and antagonized Luther, who leaned heavily on princely support and authoritarian urban governments. "Sacramentarians," as Zwinglians were called, were soon proscribed by Saxon laws. Thus both theologically and politically a basis for cooperative efforts between northern and southern reformers was lacking. Although Philip of Hesse, an energetic early Protestant prince, was able to bring Luther and Zwingli together at Marburg in 1529, Luther refused to discuss what he considered to be Zwingli's use of reason in matters of revelation. Shortly thereafter Zwingli was killed in a war between Zurich and the Swiss Catholic cantons that resisted Zwinglian proselytism. His mantle fell to Heinrich Bullinger, who eventually secured agreements with John Calvin rather than the Wittenbergers. Bullinger's many writings were also translated into English and exerted considerable influence upon the English reformation after 1558.

Sectarians and the Radical Reformation

Whatever their differences on other questions, both Luther and Zwingli, like the Roman Catholics they opposed, relied on coercion to secure their religious authority. Both set up established or state churches binding on all members of the political community. In Zurich the state church was directed by the city council, which heard debates and legislated new doctrine and rites. Working through it, Zwingli reinstated infant baptism and tithes and made state intervention in religious affairs common practice. Rejection of the state's authority in enforcing the Gospel was denounced by Zwingli as sedition and blasphemy.

Certain radical reformers soon proved "blasphemous" and "seditious." Like the Erasmian humanists, they insisted that doctrine must be judged by its adherents' behavior, that a creed was acceptable only if its observance meant living by New Testament ethics, and that the priesthood of all believers required voluntary religious participation and tolerance. In 1524 Conrad Grebel, a Zurich humanist, led a secession from Zwingli's ranks. He and his followers refused to obey government regulations concerning religion, thus following the example of Christians as recorded in the Acts of the Apostles. For example, they insisted that only adult or adolescent converts had the faith requisite for baptism and that converts baptized in older confessions had to be baptized a second time. Joined by other dissenters from established churches (whether Protestant or Catholic) they thus launched the Radical Reformation. Quite naturally, this was denounced by all established clergy—Protestant and Catholic—as sedition, heresy, and blasphemy. The very name applied to them—Anabaptists (rebaptizers)—reflects this animosity, for under the Justinian code rebaptism was a capital offense.

The Anabaptists found their model in the early persecuted Church recorded in the Acts; for them, the true Church was not an invisible body or the political community at large, but rather a voluntary association of baptized believers whose purity of conduct was maintained through admonition and expulsion. Their measure for both creed and society was the New Testament, especially the Sermon on the Mount. Most Anabaptists refused to take oaths and disavowed the taking of human life by any state or individual, although some, like the south German preacher Balthasar Hubmaier, defended the use of the sword. The ruling concerns of their common life were Christian brotherhood and the distribution of alms; they were not much preoccupied with distinctions of rank and sex. Those who fled to Bohemia for sanctuary practiced a form of consumption communism or communitarianism. Although humanists and persons of high social status occasionally joined or led their congregations, most Anabaptists were petty craftsmen and peasants. From the Anabaptist point of view the Reformation that relied on the state to enforce uniformity offered no improvement over the previous order: it still relied on compulsion rather than individual faith. Their ranks in Germany rapidly swelled after the suppression of the Peasants' Revolt, but Protestant and Catholic churchmen, viewing them as a revolutionary threat to established society, subjected them to bloody persecution. As their leadership fell, adversity tended to encourage their belief that the end of the world was at hand.

Until very recently historians have been content to recount Catholic and Protestant charges against Anabaptists as unimpeachable truth. According to this reading of history, the real spirit of Anabaptism was revealed by an action that occurred in the Westphalian episcopal city of Münster in 1534 and 1535. A few radicals who had fled from the terror of the Inquisition in the Low Countries and had taken over the city tried desperately to hold out against the bishop's army, which was reinforced by the troops of neighboring princes. In their desperation they made a drastic transition from New Testament pacifism to Old Testament theocracy: with Anabaptist leaders in charge, they invested the kingship in a tailor, introduced polygamy, and established a form of "war communism."*

When Münster fell the Anabaptist leaders were executed. Their remains were placed in a basket at the city's gates, where they stayed until the nineteenth century. After the Münster episode, Menno Simons led Anabaptists in the Low Countries back to the sober, pacific tradition that marked most of their history in the sixteenth century; one group of Anabaptists—the Dutch Mennonites, prominent in business and agriculture—obtained tolerance there in 1572. But elsewhere persecution continued. As a minimal penalty, Anabaptists were excluded from urban trades. At the maximum, many paid with their lives.

Other radicals were lumped together under the derogatory Anabaptist label. In the main they tried to reconstitute the early New Testament Church and to emphasize a humanitarian ethic. In Germany, Spain, Italy, and the Low Countries anti-Trinitarian biblicists (heavily influenced by Erasmus) tried to practice their beliefs. Those who survived fled to Poland or other pockets of temporary toleration. The German historian and former Lutheran pastor Sebastian Franck (1499–1542) developed an individualistic mysticism that emphasized personality rather than doctrine and that rejected all existing churches, including the Anabaptists, for being sectarian. However, these radical reformers of the sixteenth century were "hunted heretics," not founders of influential movements; not until after the fury of the religious wars was spent would they succeed at all in "reforming the Reformation."

The Consolidation of Lutheran Territorial Churches

While Charles V was proccupied with the Turks and wars with France, and while the Roman Catholic church was paralyzed by the princes' failure to support it, Lutheran princes and town councils took control of religious affairs. Charles V had decisively won over Francis I at Pavia in 1525, but just before the first Diet of Speyer (1526) the papacy, the northern Italian states, and Henry VIII of England joined with Francis to expel Charles's forces from Italy. At the same time, a Turkish army of 100,000 was moving into Hungary where it killed the king of Bohemia and Hungary and routed his forces at Mohács at the end of August 1526. This weakened Charles's influence over his German states, some of which had already become Lutheran. After the Peasants' Revolt several German princes prominent in its suppression—Landgrave Philip of Hesse, Elector John of Saxony, and Margrave Casimir of Brandenburg—had become converts to Lutheranism, finding it more effective than Catholicism in maintaining public order; and several imperial cities also adopted Lutheranism or a modification of it. The Diet of Speyer (1526), over which the emperor had little control, resolved to leave each prince free until a general council should be called to interpret the Edict of Worms subject to his readiness "to answer before God and His Imperial Majesty."

Philip of Hesse seized this opportunity to install Lutheran clergymen in his towns and to confiscate all church property and endowments. Under Luther's advice, he brushed aside proposals for a representative church structure and personally took all initiative in reforming the church,

---

* That is, all resources were commandeered for the common defense and support of the city.

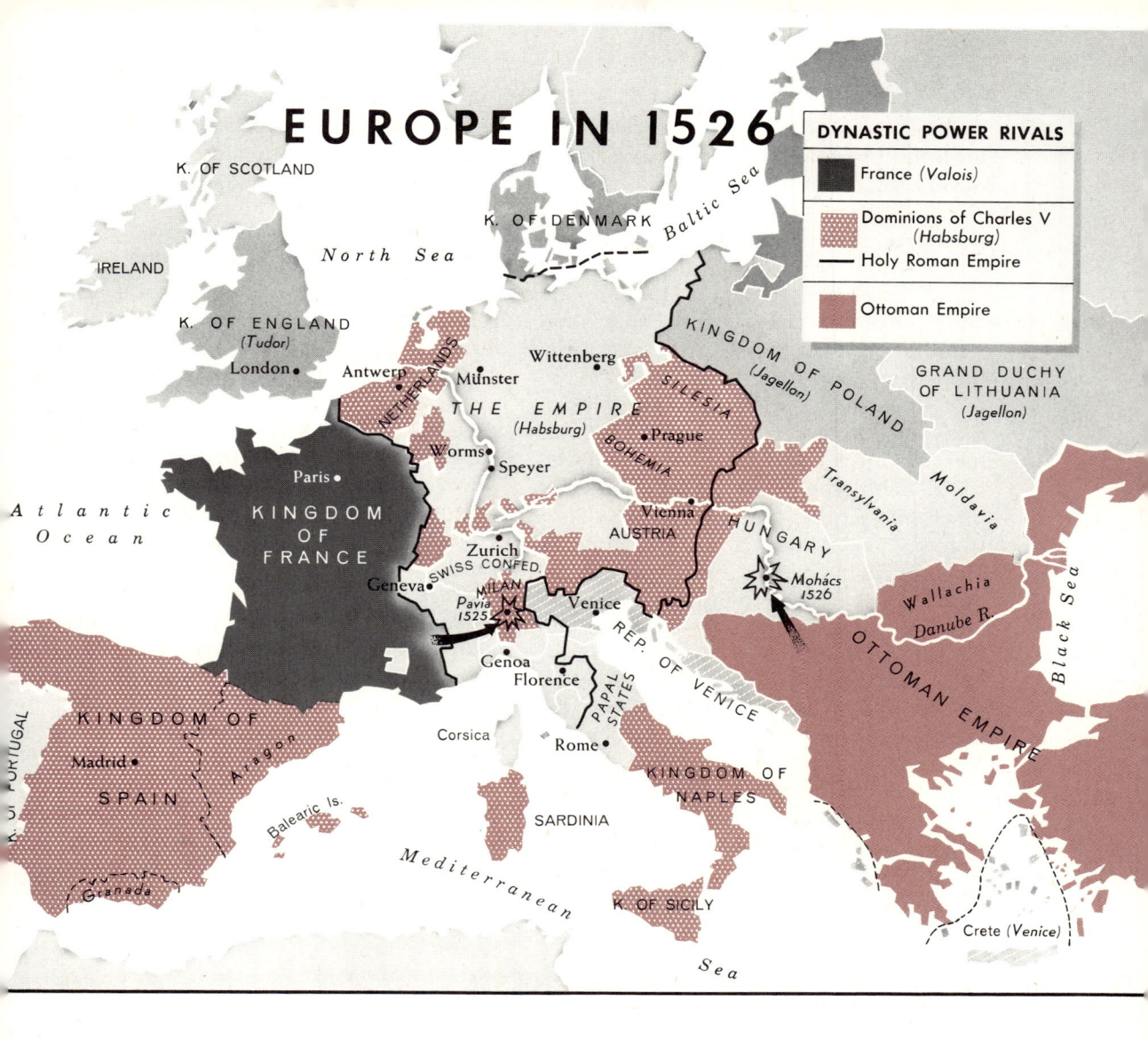

making minor concessions to townsmen and nobles in allowing them, for example, to retain their patronage in the appointment of local clergy. But to peasants nothing was conceded; they now had to pay the state all obligations previously owed the church and were forbidden to compete with urban guilds. Most former church incomes now went to Philip's treasury, and after a military attack against the Archbishop of Mainz in 1528, Philip seized control over all ecclesiastical jurisdictions. Cramped by Luther's passive attitude toward politics, Philip soon turned to Zwingli and Martin Bucer for theological advice. His precedent in establishing princely control over a territorial church was soon followed in Saxony, Brandenburg, Prussia, Denmark, Sweden, Wurttemberg, and other principalities. Everywhere the chief beneficiaries were the privileged orders of town and country and the "Christian magistracy"—usually a prince or king, considered by Lutherans as the father of an extended family. To him as head of the family—or to the city council—the Lutheran church taught passive obedience as the first requirement of piety, and the clergy relied on him to root out all remnants of Roman Catholicism as well as all new heresies, especially Anabaptism. New state-appointed clergy un-

621   A. The Protestant Reformation

dertook the strict enforcement of creedal uniformity in which only true believers could exhibit their religious faith. To dissenters—Zwinglians, Calvinists, Anabaptists, spiritualists, papists, and others—they applied various civil penalties, including corporal punishment and execution. The German and other reformations had substituted the Christian magistracy for the humanists' concept of a secular commonweal. Opposition to Lutheranism, in other words, had become a crime worse than murder.

The German magisterial reformers emphasized that their work was purely spiritual and uncorrupted by material motives. Most of their changes were confined to doctrine and liturgy: the number of sacraments was reduced to two—baptism and the Liturgy of the Lord's Supper; monasticism was suppressed; and in worship, but not in scholarship, the vernacular language was used. Also, to church services the reformers added more sermons and congregational singing. Otherwise they followed tradition. Luther, unlike Calvin and the radical sectarians, taught that only those traditions directly in conflict with Scripture should be abolished. The rest were to be retained.

For a generation these changes took place without imperial intervention, for the emperor was not strong enough to oppose them, fend off the Turks, and fight France all at the same time. Although he was at first content to seek a political compromise, nevertheless in 1529 and 1530, backed by alarmed Catholic princes (who were building their own territorial churches), he regained enough power to threaten the Lutherans. Having won a new war with Francis I in 1529, Charles secured an order from the second Diet of Speyer in the same year to halt all further innovations. The Lutheran princes and 14 imperial cities *protested* formally (hence, the name Protestant, which did not apply to the sectarians), but in vain.

In 1530 Charles V, freshly strengthened by the defeat of the Turks at Vienna, attended the Diet of Augsburg in person. Failing to get a compromise between the Lutherans (for whom Melanchthon drew up the conciliatory Augsburg Confession) and the Catholics, and profiting from the doctrinal divisions separating northern from southern Protestants, Charles ordered a return to the traditional faith. Led by Philip of Hesse, the Lutheran princes organized the League of Smalkald for defense against a Catholic League and the emperor. Hostilities were postponed, however: both sides entertained some hope of working together on common religious reforms. In 1532 a temporary truce was arranged, but in 1541 a final effort at religious reconciliation collapsed at Regensburg. From then on papal policy became more uncompromising and aggressive. Meanwhile German Protestantism, aided and supplied by Francis I, continued to expand by court revolutions, conversions, and the military conquests of Philip of Hesse.*

The emperor was again busy with foreign affairs. In 1536 a new Habsburg-Valois war broke out. At the same time, the Turks were still threatening Hungary and Charles's recent inheritance—central Europe. From 1542 to 1544 Charles warred against a French-Ottoman alliance. The peace concluded with France in 1544 at Crépy freed his hands to proceed against the Protestants, but not until 1546, after the first session of the Council of Trent had opened, was he able to launch a military and diplomatic offensive. In 1547 at the battle of Mühlberg he checked the superior Protestant forces, but his victory was temporary. Unable to secure ecclesiastical concessions from the pope or from the Council of Trent and failing in his own efforts to settle the German religious dis-

---

* Philip captured Wurttemberg, Brunswick, and other territories for the Reformation, but he embarrassed the cause by taking a second wife. Luther approved this secret bigamous marriage as preferable to divorce.

pute,* Charles was forced in 1552 to strike a truce with the Protestant princes, temporarily recognizing their territorial state churches. In the same year, war with France broke out again. In 1555, in the Peace of Augsburg, the Lutheran states forced Charles to tolerate their existence and grant them equal rights within the empire. Neither Calvinism, Anabaptism, nor any other religious group secured toleration.

Thus the German princes wrested religious autonomy from the German emperor. Exhausted and disillusioned with the task of ruling his vast dynastic empire, Charles retired as a private person to a monastery in 1556. He abdicated the Spanish crown to his son Philip and the eastern Habsburg lands to his brother Ferdinand, who became the new emperor. Relationships between Lutherans and Catholics in the empire remained tense but, strange to say, there followed the longest period of peace in Germany since the Reformation. The major German wars of religion did not break out until 1618.

ENGLAND SECEDES FROM ROME

The Reformation in England was quite different from the German experience because religious doctrine and popular protest movements had little to do with it; what doctrinal disputes there were concerned papal supremacy and the English translation of the Bible. The English Catholic clergy were not scandal-free, but popular resentment did not force England's secession from Rome; on the contrary, the only major popular protest movement was directed against the king's break with Rome. Initially the English reformation was mainly an act of state, a change of administration led by the king himself. Because papal authority in England had long

---

* See below, p. 643.

been checked by secular controls, this change seemed at first more an evolutionary mutation than a clean break with the past.

Henry VIII and the Succession Crisis

In 1509 Henry VIII inherited his father's throne, a well-stocked treasury, and an efficient administration. By then that administration had wrested obedience to the King and Parliament from the nobility. Fond of display, arbitrary in action, and ambitious beyond his means in foreign policy, Henry quickly drained the treasury surplus with few international gains to show for it. In domestic affairs he was mainly concerned with the growth of royal power, in which he was more successful. Within a few years he had won for the monarchy supreme control over both church and state.

The process of bringing church and state under a single head was initiated by Thomas Wolsey, Henry's lord chancellor from 1515 to 1529. Not only was he the chief governmental administrator and diplomat, but he also held important church positions throughout northern and western England and was the archbishop of York. The only absentee holder of many bishoprics in England, Wolsey also—with the king's assistance—became a cardinal and a papal legate. Although a favorite of the King, Wolsey was hated by nobles and churchmen for his enormous wealth and power. In 1526 he was given certain duties by the King that exceeded his capabilities and brought his downfall.

Of the children born to Henry and his queen, Catherine of Aragon, only his daughter—Mary—survived, whereas Henry wanted a male heir to prevent renewed dynastic civil war on his death. Furthermore, he had tired of Catherine and was transferring his favor to Anne Boleyn, the daughter of a recently elevated peer. He ordered Wolsey to secure a papal annulment of his long marriage, which itself had been effected under papal dispensation, since Catherine had first been the wife of Henry's older brother. Wolsey filed the plea for annulment in 1527, aware that such requests from monarchs had been granted before by the papacy. But the pope, Clement VII, was prisoner of Charles V, Catherine's nephew and a dominant force in Italian affairs and papal policy. Thus Wolsey's petition was denied. Henry, to whom the request was urgent for personal as well as dynastic reasons, stripped Wolsey of all authority in 1529 and set about getting the annulment on his own by intimidation.

Henry gained authorization from Parliament in 1529 to investigate the clergy; in 1531 he extorted a huge fine of £100,000 from the clergy for having accepted Wolsey (his own nominee) as legate. In 1532 he persuaded Parliament to abolish *annates*—payments to Rome approximately equal to the first year's income of a new bishop. (They were restored after the king became head of the Anglican church.) When these measures failed Henry named a new archbishop of Canterbury, Thomas Cranmer, a Cambridge scholar and an advocate of royal supremacy in all matters. In haste and secrecy Cranmer nullified Henry's marriage to Catherine and pronounced her daughter, Mary, illegitimate. Anne Boleyn, soon to be a mother, was proclaimed queen in 1533. In 1534 a succession act required that all subjects swear to the legitimacy of Henry's new marriage and made dissenters guilty of high treason. Still the King's problem was not solved: Anne also produced a daughter, Elizabeth. Following her in the marriage bed were Jane Seymour and a succession of new queens. Meanwhile the state church of England had become a permanent institution.

Secession from Rome was formalized in 1534 by the Act of Supremacy, which proclaimed the king head of the church; henceforth no authority outside England was recognized. Although no doctrinal issue except papal supremacy was at stake, Henry nevertheless enforced this administrative revolution with statutes of treason. The executions of Bishop John Fisher and Sir Thomas More served notice of the penalties that resistance, even merely oral resistance, entailed.

The Reformation Settlement of Henry VIII and Edward VI

Henry VIII's break from Rome proved to be a wedge with which to force further changes. In 1535 he commissioned Thomas Cromwell, who replaced Wolsey as lord chancellor, to investigate the cloisters. These monasteries were no longer playing a major social or economic role in society; rather, they served mainly as inns and centers of alms distribution. Cromwell gave an exaggerated account of their degeneration, submitting a detailed report on their assets and revenues. Parliament responded by ceding the smaller cloisters to the king, and monks, nuns, and other cloister workers were either transferred or sent home. A new centralized court administered this additional royal income and proceeded on its own to sequester further properties, and in 1539 Parliament sanctioned the dissolution of all cloisters. The redistribution of property that followed was more far-reaching than any other since the Norman Conquest. The recipients of this property, local gentry families and royal favorites, now had a vested interest in Henry's reformation that his Roman Catholic daughter, Mary, would later be unable to shake when she temporarily returned England to Roman jurisdiction (1553–58). Perhaps even more significant, the redistribution opened church lands to progressive economic exploitation. Historians frequently cite this as a crucial step toward England's emergence as the foremost commercial and

Henry VIII in Parliament.

industrial country of eighteenth-century Europe.

The English reformation catered for latent antipapal sentiments, but the dissolution of church holdings did not please the lower classes of the countryside. In northern England they joined with old believers in the Pilgrimage of Grace (1536) to petition the king to preserve the monasteries, resume papal jurisdiction, and abolish penalties of treason against opposing clergymen; they also sought to curb consolidation of so much power in the hands of the king. But the Pilgrimage of Grace, like other resistance to the king and Parliament, came to naught, and after its participants had disbanded voluntarily their leaders were condemned by the courts and executed.

In breaking with Rome, Henry VIII had no intention of bringing England into conformity with continental Protestant doctrines. He worked to repress the influence of William Tyndale, whose Protestant-oriented translation of the New Testament was nevertheless absorbed into the official English translation of the Bible. The Six Articles of Faith, passed by Parliament in 1539 and for which the king was primarily responsible, upheld clerical celibacy, private masses for the dead, auricular confession, and the transubstantiation of sacramental bread and wine into the body and blood of Christ—all of these being orthodox Roman Catholic positions. Lutherans were sent to the stake in the later part of Henry's reign, and his will affirmed the existence of purgatory and the validity of private masses for the dead. Nevertheless he did not cut off all Protestant growth, for his heir was reared in that tradition.

Henry was succeeded by Edward VI, a boy of ten whose regency was dominated until 1550 by his uncle, the earl of Hereford (then duke of Somerset), who allowed the English reformation to veer more toward continental Protestantism; he relaxed the heresy and treason laws and permitted the clergy to marry. In 1549 Parliament proclaimed an Act of Uniformity, introducing the first Book of Common Prayer. It failed to affirm transubstantiation, and it contained Protestant prayers by Archbishop Cranmer, one of the most influential men during the regency. Opposition to the Prayer Book arose in Devonshire and Oxfordshire, but the action of Protestant mobs in destroying relics and images indicated that Protestant doctrines were reaching into the consciousness of the general population.

Social Tension, Revolt, and Reaction

Somerset's government faced difficult economic and social problems rooted in the preceding reign. Despite income from the confiscation of the cloisters, Henry VIII had left the treasury empty and in debt. To meet financial needs, the regency continued and expanded expedients used by Henry: debasement of the coinage and further confiscation of church and corporate properties; it also expropriated chantries (special funds for private masses for the dead), other endowments, and guild welfare treasuries that were intended for both welfare and religious purposes. Henry's confiscations had struck primarily the old clergy, but these expropriations affected many laymen as well; funds were drained from the schools, poor relief, and the guilds. And promises to use the proceeds for schools and charity went unredeemed. The principal beneficiaries were the king's treasury and, as before, the gentry.

The people hurt worst by these confiscations and the debased money were already the victims of other social and economic miseries. Of these, enclosures of common lands for sheep pasturage and more profitable cultivation were the most detested because they revoked cottagers' and tenants' rights to common village lands. Peasants', and especially cottagers', tenure rights to village lands were replaced by terminable leases so that rents could be raised. Economic pressures on the poor were further increased as prices spiraled while wages remained fixed. Somerset sympathized with the plight of the lower classes and launched an investigation of enclosures, whose continuance he forbade. In Norfolk and nearby counties an estimated 16,000 peasants, participating in "Kett's Rebellion," rose up against the enclosures and plundered—but seldom killed—the gentry. Blamed for causing the abortive uprising, Somerset was displaced by the Earl of Warwick (later duke of Northumberland), who threw the weight of law and administration behind the gentry. Former heresy and treason laws were restored, and the gentry was allowed to determine tenants' needs as common lands were enclosed. Resistance by 40 or more peasants was defined as treason, by 12 to 39 as simply a felony.

Northumberland carried the Reformation still further toward Protestantism, but both his power and English Protestantism were jeopardized by the imminent succession of a Roman Catholic monarch—Mary. In 1552 a second Book of Common Prayer

Mary Tudor, *portrait by Antonio Moro.*

omitted references to the mass and the altar. The regency council then adopted a Protestant definition of faith in the Forty-Two Articles. The failing health of Edward VI made these changes tenuous, for Henry VIII's will designated Catherine of Aragon's daughter Mary—a fervent Catholic—as his heir. From Edward VI (but not from Parliament) Northumberland secured a new will passing the throne to Lady Jane (Grey) Dudley, a Tudor who had married Northumberland's son. However when Edward died in 1553, Mary eluded Northumberland's grasp and raised an army. In his desperate bid for power, Northumberland failed to command the loyalty necessary to precipitate a new dynastic war for the throne, and Mary became queen—with the intention of restoring Roman Catholicism.

Mary (1553—58) achieved gradual but only partial success in restoring Catholicism, and this success was in its turn jeopardized by a prospective Protestant successor, Elizabeth. While Mary's first parliament returned the religious question to the status quo at the end of Henry VIII's reign, it refused to persecute non-Catholics, to restore confiscated church properties, and to revert to papal authority. Against her will, the queen remained head of the English church until she could secure a more pliant parliament. She also failed to gain support for her alliance with Spain (sealed by her marriage to Philip II, the son of her cousin Charles) against France and the papacy. As a result, Mary lost much of her popularity, and England lost Calais, the last British foothold on the Continent. Finally, however, a parliament was returned that restored papal authority and enacted laws against the Protestant heretics. But under this persecution, which led more than 300 to the stake, Protestant resistance stiffened: its exiles to the Continent imbibed deeply of a more strident Protestantism, with which they returned after Mary's death in 1558, at which time the Catholic cause in England was lost. Her successor—Elizabeth, daughter of Anne Boleyn—was necessarily Anglican, for in Catholic eyes she was illegitimate. A single short reign by a Catholic monarch proved insufficient to reverse the English religious revolution.

THE CALVINIST REFORM

Except among the sectarians, most religious revolutionaries were not interested in missionary attempts to universalize their faith. Anglicanism was particularly a national religion. Lutheranism remained German, Scandinavian, and East European; its passive obedience to existing authorities appealed to the city governments and paternal courts of Eastern Europe, many of which adopted it. The reformation initiated by John Calvin (1509–64), however, constituted an aggressive "international" movement that threatened existing governments with armed revolution and Roman Catholicism with a "visible," disciplined, rival church whose ideal state-church relationship closely resembled the ideal church-state relationship which several medieval popes had dreamt of and worked toward but never fully realized. As militant Roman Catholics became aware, Calvin's combination of the moral zeal of the sectarians with the conscious use of political and military power in carrying out "the will of God" made Calvinism the most serious threat to the religious status quo of Europe during the sixteenth and seventeenth centuries.

John Calvin, Would-be Reformer of France

John Calvin, (Jean Cauvin) was born into a rising middle-class family of artisan ancestry in the French cathedral city of Noyon. His half-cleric, half-layman father was secretary for secular affairs to the bishop—the *seigneur* ("lord")—of the city. At an early age he was pointed by his father toward the priesthood, but he never became a priest, although he began drawing church revenues at the age of 12. Educated among the notables of Noyon, the boy went to the College of Montaigu in Paris. Among his classmates was Ignatius Loyola, later to found the Jesuit order. The rigorous rules of the college, which had repelled Erasmus, may have provided Calvin with a disciplinarian model for his later reorganization of Geneva.

After his father was charged with mishandling funds, Calvin, under parental direction, turned from Paris and the study of theology to Roman law at Orléans and Bourges. Both schools had come under the influence of humanist philology and historical interpretation of the Justinian code. Calvin pursued law only so long as his

John Calvin.

father lived; with the elder Calvin's death in 1531, he returned to Paris and the study of the classics. For these languages, and later Hebrew, he had the best teachers in France—teachers who also happened to be Protestant in outlook. His first book, a commercial failure, was a humanist commentary on Seneca's Stoicism, emphasizing morality and a sense of sin yet quite different in tone from the biblical and God-centered theology to which he devoted his life after 1533. Although his study of law was brief, marks of the legalist remained strong in his systematic theology and in his refutation of opponents.

Calvin was one of several in a circle of humanists patronized by the royal family and defended by them against the Sorbonne's indictments. Part of this group eventually abandoned humanism to adopt the pessimistic Protestant view of man's moral and religious capabilities. Unlike Luther, Calvin left few detailed personal reminiscences about his conversion to Protestantism. Probably it occurred in or before 1533, for in the following year he resigned his ecclesiastical sinecures. It is certain that he considered his conversion the work of a sovereign God who directed all of his subsequent actions and whose honor was at stake wherever he, Calvin, was criticized or contradicted. A second-generation reformer, Calvin never passed through a transient radical or liberal period during which he committed himself, as had Luther, to the freedom of the individual conscience.

Calvin's conversion came ten years after the first Protestant heretic had been burned in Paris at the instigation of the university, and it coincided with a new wave of suppression, precipitated by outbreaks of iconoclasm and the appearance of anti-Roman placards. Unsafe as a Protestant, Calvin wandered about France and then fled early in 1535 to Basel, a Protestant but humanist city. There he drafted the first edition of *The Institutes of the Christian Religion,* the most influential handbook of Protestant doctrine produced in the sixteenth century. To the *Institutes* Calvin appended a prefatory letter to Francis I in which he exonerated French Protestants from charges of anarchy and attributed such charges to malicious rumors. His plea failed to secure tolerance for French Protestants, but it projected its author, an exile, into leadership of the French Reformation. Before the *Institutes* appeared in print in Basel, Calvin wandered further to Italy, back to Noyon, and from there to Geneva en route to Strassbourg. Asked to remain in Geneva by William Farel, reformer of Berne and Geneva, Calvin thus acquired accidentally a very fortunate base for the implementation of his ideas.

The *Institutes,* repeatedly revised and enlarged and eventually published in French as well as Latin, contained few novelties, but its clarity and precision made it the cutting edge of expanding Protestantism. In asserting the absolute sovereignty of a predestining God and the total, immutable depravity of man, Calvin was in agreement with Luther, on whom he depended heavily. Pessimistic as to man, he was optimistic with respect to divine providence, individual predestination, and the revealed goal of history. Rather than conduce to gloom or uncertainty, predestination served to give the parishioner confidence of salvation by divine election and to stimulate a communal feeling of "God-chosedness." Men need not live as doomed reprobates predestined to eternal hell. In Calvin's system all aspects of life—economic activity, politics, worship services, and family relationships—were subordinated to the literal, absolute standard of scriptural revelation. All that was not sanctioned by Scripture was forbidden. Morality he defined as the advancement of the kingdom of God on earth or God's honor; if familial or humanitarian considerations conflicted with this objective, they were denounced as blasphemies. Calvin emphasized the progressive evolution of revelation from the Old Testament to the New; but Old Testament concepts undergirded his concept of politics and society and his justification for the use of force. In addition to denouncing works as a means of salvation, Calvin emphasized that love and charity originated from faith. But the boundaries of the religious brotherhood or commonweal were set by the boundaries of doctrinal orthodoxy. The toleration of blasphemers—those who impugned the honor of God by defying His revealed doctrine—he made tantamount to blasphemy itself.

For authority, Calvin used the Scripture, but he interpreted it more narrowly than Luther. Custom unsupported by the Word of God he rejected in principle, although not always in practice; the Church should be governed as the early Church was—by pastors, elders, and deacons whose duties were spelled out in the text. He agreed with Luther in reducing the sacraments to two, but he denied the effective physical presence of the body and blood of Christ in the Liturgy of the Lord's Supper, a denial that precipitated acrimonious exchanges with various Lutherans. In the same way, Calvin's scripturalism cut away more of the supernatural and magical tradition of Christianity than Luther's; but the parts of that tradition which he did retain, including belief in witchcraft, were rigidly enforced.

In theory, Calvin—like Luther—advocated the Christian's freedom from binding laws. But like Bucer, he reconstituted in practice both laws and enforcement procedures that regulated private life to the minutest degree. Although he did not impose celibacy, dietary regulations, or formal works of grace, Calvin tried to establish a universal monastic standard; thus all laymen were to take the sacrament weekly and submit themselves to daily sermons. Legislation of morals was equally stringent in Lutheran, Anglican, and Calvinist areas, but Calvin and his followers enforced their laws with particular zeal by threatening excommunication and sending teams of elders and clergymen into all homes annually to ferret out any religious or moral nonconformists.

Unlike the Anglican and Lutheran established churches, the Calvinist church was not subservient to secular authority. Calvinism adopted a system of synods representing clergy and elders. Through them the state was to serve as the handmaiden of the church, its primary task the prevention of blasphemy. Far from introducing a separation of church and state, Calvin sought to reassert the authority of the clergy and elders over the social and political order.

Politically a sharp difference separated Calvinism from the Anglican and Lutheran churches. Both of the latter taught obedience to the existing authorities as a matter of conscience. Declaring doctrinal orthodoxy the only legitimate basis of government, Calvin proselytized even when hostile secular governments forbad him to do so. Faced with royal suppression of his gospel in France, he abandoned the obedience originally offered to Francis I and justified resistance to that monarchy when it was led by the "lesser magistrates"—nobles, town councillors, and jurists. In France and other areas Calvin attracted powerful political forces of dissidence that potentially constituted alternate governments. Thus his followers laid the groundwork for the civil and international wars of the second half of the century.

The Holy Commonwealth of Geneva

Calvin never succeeded in converting more than a small minority of his French countrymen. But following his accidental appearance in Geneva—which he interpreted as an act of divine providence—he turned that city into his own religious kingdom.

A commercial city of about 13,000 people, Geneva had been in political turmoil for 20 years prior to Calvin's arrival. Nominally ruled by bishops (usually young boys from the neighboring house of Savoy), the city was striving to establish its independence from both bishop and Savoy. The first thrust toward that independence was engineered by William Farel, an iconoclastic French Puritan. Farel came to Geneva from Berne, where he had been part of a Protestant reformation in 1528 and had played a role in the expulsion of the prince-bishop of Lausanne. In Geneva he instigated disputations and riots that finally led to an official but precarious and unorganized Protestant reformation in 1535. Soon thereafter he convinced the city council to hire John Calvin as a teacher. Almost immediately, the youthful Calvin introduced a program of religious reorganization.

Calvin wanted to establish an autonomous church wielding the power of excommunication and moral censorship, but the ruling city council, which had become a closed oligarchy in the fifteenth century and assumed the bishop's former powers in 1535, resisted the French re-

View of Geneva.

former. In 1538 opponents of Calvin and Farel gained control of the city's executive offices. Farel left the city permanently for Neuchâtel; Calvin emigrated to Strassbourg. There, as pastor of the French refugee colony between 1538 and 1541, he observed Jakob Sturm's reformed educational system at work, became more familiar with Martin Bucer's liturgy and ecclesiastical discipline, and introduced the singing of psalms in service. Here also in a singularly unromantic union he married, upon Bucer's recommendation, the widow of a converted Anabaptist. Meanwhile his opponents in Geneva had discredited themselves by an unfortunate foreign policy, and the city fathers asked him to return and reorganize the church. Although Calvin was never to obtain all that he wanted from the councils, he did succeed in gaining a permanent and increasing hold on city affairs, both religious and secular.

The Ecclesiastical Ordinances enacted by the councils of Geneva in 1541 were basically his; but the city magistrates retained their right to confirm appointments of pastors, teachers, elders, and deacons, and only they could name the elders who met every Thursday with the "Venerable Company" of ministers. (The fate of citizens who breached either church doctrine or the city's moral code was decided at these meetings.) The councils also reduced Calvin's proposed weekly communion to four times a year, and they jealously guarded the city's authority in legal affairs by denying the clergy the power to pronounce civil penalties. Although the secular authorities retained these legal prerogatives, the clergy still gained considerable autonomy of action. And Calvin, who until 1559 was not a citizen, became, as the interpreter of the "Word of God," the city's most powerful political figure until his death.

Calvin's political power, absolute by 1555, derived from two sources: an unshakable belief in his own righteousness —accompanied by limitless zeal—and the numerical strength of his following. He was unalterably determined to overcome all obstacles to the execution of God's will, and all opponents, personal and political, he denounced as enemies of God. An influx of refugee pastors and other exiles contributed significantly to his following, which outnumbered that of the divided Genevan opposition.

In 1547 the elections went against Calvin. His supporters organized popular demonstrations and kept the new government under a continuous fire of criticism until they at last prevailed, whereupon leading men of the opposition were beheaded. Tortured and banished were theological critics who had attacked Calvin's predestination doctrine on the grounds that it made God a tyrant. In 1551 the Genevans countered Calvin's ascendancy by making a 25-year residency requirement for citizenship. Two years later, however, in the events that surrounded the case of Michael Servetus, Calvin routed and broke his opposition. "Holy terror" thus served to consolidate the reformer's position.

Michael Servetus (1511–53) was a Spanish physician and humanist scholar, who, following Erasmus's method of philological criticism, denied the doctrine of the Trinity on biblical grounds. Like the Anabaptists, he desired the restitution of the early Church, the exclusion of coercion from religion, and a humanitarian definition of Christian ethics. He lived under a pseudonym in France until his true identity was discovered. Then he was prosecuted by the Inquisition on the basis of evidence provided by one of Calvin's colleagues in Geneva. Escaping prison, Servetus made his way to Geneva for reasons unknown. Here he was recognized, taken into custody, and tried for heresy. He probably counted on aid from Calvin's foes, but the reformer successfully pressed the prosecution and used Servetus's heresy to discredit his opposition. In 1553, in an action approved by most of the Protestant clergy on the Continent, Servetus was burned at the stake. Protests came from Erasmian humanists such as Sebastian Castellio, but he, like Calvin's other opponents, was obliged to seek physical safety outside Geneva. The Holy Commonwealth, solicitous of the welfare of the disinherited as well as of the industrious within its communion, held out only destruction by divine wrath to those who challenged the authority or accuracy of its leading interpreter of Holy Writ.

The Calvinist International

Often identified as a forerunner of modern nationalism, Calvinism was in fact the most international of the major Protestant reformations. Although Calvinists in every area were preoccupied with the establishment of their own "New Jerusalem," common aims and coordination from Geneva held their efforts together at least so long as Calvin lived. Had he succeeded in becoming head of a successful French reformation, his church might have become identified politically with France; but as a religious body of refugees in Geneva, it was never connected with the foreign policy of a major state.

Calvinism varied only slightly from place to place. Its adherents accepted a common doctrine, performed the same liturgy, and organized their churches according to the Genevan model. Everywhere Calvin's *Institutes,* clarified and extended by his personal correspondence, were the guide. Missionaries and pastors were trained almost exclusively in Geneva, and their orthodoxy was assured before they were allowed to fill teaching or pastoral posts; in some instances the work of missionaries was kept under surveillance. Most of the Genevan students were from other lands, such as France, Scotland, England, and Germany. In 1559 the Genevan consistory—a court composed of ministers and lay elders—established a college headed by Theodore Beza, Calvin's eventual successor, to enlarge and systematize the training of the Calvinist clergy.

This uniform and well-controlled Calvinism spread widely in Europe. Only Spain and Spanish-dominated areas such as Italy were exempt from its impact. Penetrating the Swiss Confederacy, in 1549 the Calvinists reached an agreement with Heinrich Bullinger in Zurich; they also made inroads into Germany, especially the southern and Rhenish states. In 1580 the Lutheran evangelical churches res-

Anti-Reformation woodcut depicting Calvin, Luther, and Beza as its primary villains.

ponded to this "reformed" encroachment with the Formula of Concord, which made Calvinists heretics; however they failed to check the spread of Calvinism.

Under conditions of relative tolerance, Calvinist missionaries gained followings in Bohemia, Hungary, Poland, and Transylvania. Calvinism also grew in the Low Countries where it was less under Genevan control. Trained at Geneva, John Knox returned to Scotland and carried out a political and religious revolution there. Calvinist influences became perceptible also in England during and after the reign of Edward VI. Everywhere radical, armed Calvinist reformers were striving for total control over the machinery of state, and thus they precipitated violent reactions from kings and traditionalist religious opponents. Except where they were in full control or else too weak to challenge existing authority, the growth of their influence was the prelude to civil war. During the religious-political wars of the sixteenth century, the Calvinist clergy preached solidarity against the common Roman Catholic enemy, whose internationalism it rivaled.

634 Confessional Age: Reformation of the Sixteenth Century

B. The Humanist between Confessional Fronts

Men educated in the classics were involved on all sides of the Reformation, but the followers of Erasmus came to occupy a middle ground from which they mediated the violent extremes. After religious wars had taken heavy tolls, Erasmians gained influence on both sides; but at the outset they were despised all around. To traditional Catholics their appeals for reform were heresy. Their opposition to schism and vituperation also alienated them from the Protestants. In the midst of brutality and authoritarianism they and a few humane but powerless sectarians stood alone for diversity, tolerance, and for a humanitarianism that placed the commonweal above religious differences.

The Break between Luther and Erasmus

When the Reformation began, Protestant reformers were commonly identified with Erasmian critics of the Church; indeed, their criticisms coincided at many points, and such Protestants as Melanchthon and Zwingli were also humanist scholars of philology and Church history. Yet humanism and early Protestantism proved incompatible; the fundamental differences between them came to light in the irreparable break (1525) between Erasmus and Luther.

As early as 1517, Luther, for whom all wisdom consisted of knowing about sin, grace, and the revealed path to salvation, had complained that Erasmus was too secular and too preoccupied with human concerns. For his part, Erasmus feared that Luther's inflammatory popular writings could produce violence and counter-violence. To forestall tumult, Erasmus urged moderation on the reformers while he strove to prevent the traditionalists from indicting Luther for heresy without redressing his grievances. In 1520 Luther undercut Erasmus's mediation by attacking the sacraments and burning canon law. The humanist began to fear that the reformer would destroy the cause of peaceful reform and cultural renaissance in an abortive doctrinal and doctrinaire revolution.

As Luther and Erasmus became more familiar with each other's reform programs, they recognized gulfs between themselves that could not be bridged. Neither their temperaments nor their methods agreed. In Luther's theology of predestination the human will was totally without merit; free exercise of it led to sin. Without divine grace—that is, without professing Luther's creed—the doer of good works was doomed to eternal damnation. To Erasmus, preoccupied with ethics and the overcoming of ignorance and violence, Protestant denial of free will weakened man's sense of morality and made God a tyrant who kept men bound to evil. This quarrel pitted Luther the theologian against Erasmus the moralist. The moralist deemphasized the sacraments and was skeptical of the theologian's "revealed" and absolute dogmas. In 1525 the two exchanged polemical pamphlets on the nature of the human will. Erasmus upheld the dignity and capabilities of man; Luther asserted man's total immutable depravity and denied that he had a free will. As this quarrel grew heated, Erasmian humanists drew back from Luther. Melanchthon, who stayed with him, nevertheless retained enough confidence in human initiative to be denounced as a "crypto-Calvinist" in Saxony after Luther died in 1546.*

In adopting "Calvinism" as a derogatory synonym for Erasmus's philosophy, the Lutherans were greatly oversimplifying. Erasmians found Geneva no more hospitable than Wittenberg; as we have seen, Sebastian Castellio, among others, was obliged to flee Geneva for his life. Theodore Beza, Calvin's successor, frankly wrote that he preferred tyranny to religious individualism and that "the freedom of conscience is the devil's principle of faith"—it allowed everyone to chose his own path to hell. Eventually such humanists did influence Protestantism, especially in England, the Netherlands, and to a lesser extent in southern Germany. But the Protestants who opened themselves to humanist influence were not the major continental reformers of the sixteenth century.

The Expulsion of Humanists from Catholic Reform

Meanwhile Catholic traditionalists attacked Erasmus and his followers for

* This attack on Melanchthon was particularly inappropriate because Calvin denied human initiative even more systematically than did Luther.

aiding and abetting the Protestant enemy. Led by Girolamo Aleander, papal nuncio to the emperor, and the Spanish Dominicans, they argued that unconditional obedience was due to the papal church whatever its shortcomings, because it was commissioned by God. Nonconforming humanists and their books were burned in the Low Countries as early as 1522 and 1523, and Erasmus complained of being "stoned by both sides." Between the fronts of intolerant "integralist" Protestantism and militant Catholic traditionalists, Erasmians were caught in the crossfire of denunciation and physical jeopardy. Until aggressive conservatives gained control within the Roman church, however, most humanists retained some hope of effecting their kind of reformation within it. Their optimism soared briefly under Pope Adrian VI (1522–23), who conceded to the German diet at Nuremberg the necessity of drastic reform. Time was too short and resistance was too strong for Adrian, however; his successor, Clement VII—a Medici—dropped this approach.

The sacking of Rome in 1527 by the unpaid German troops of Charles V indicated how badly things were going for the traditionalists. Spanish humanists applauded it as a forerunner of reform, but their position became untenable when they came under heavy attack by the Inquisition. Of course, the pope could still have called a council had he not feared that he would lose papal prerogatives to any council he did not tightly control. A further force militating against this decision was the continuing conflict between Valois and Habsburg, the two leading Catholic dynasties.

In the absence of leadership from Rome or a general council, Catholic reform began at the local level; in fact, many small reform movements had existed before the Protestant Reformation began. Early in their history a struggle developed between advocates of persuasion and advocates of force: the Brethren of the Common Life advocated tolerance and humanitarian brotherhood; in Spain reformers led by Cardinal Ximénes often relied on coercion; in Italy some reformers followed the Venetian nobleman, Gasparo Contarini, an apostle of conciliation, while others supported Giovanni Pietro Caraffa—equally dedicated to changes, but by inquisitional methods. As both these men were appointed by Pope Paul III to successively higher posts, they came to epitomize the two conflicting trends in the Catholic Reformation.

Paul commissioned a body including cardinals Contarini and Caraffa to draw up a general proposal for regenerating the Church. In 1537 they returned their report. It so frankly indicted the clergy for avarice and irresponsibility in high places that when it leaked out German Protestants circulated it as propaganda for their own cause. Other cardinals and secular rulers, however, opposed the calling of a council to act on the report. So Contarini and Caraffa proceeded along their own rival paths of reform.

Contarini equated Christianity with freedom. He denied the theory of absolute papal authority and refused to exalt the papal monarch above canon law. He also pursued a course of conciliation with the Protestants. At the Imperial Diet of Regensburg (Ratisbon) in 1541, he followed a very liberal interpretation of Catholic dogma in order to seek agreements with Bucer and Melanchthon, the more flexible Protestant reformers. In so doing, he overrode Catholic traditionalists and exceeded his instructions from the pope. But he failed to reach a general agreement with the Protestants: the Colloquy of Regensburg—the last attempt to heal the religious schism—fell apart, and negotiators on both sides were denounced in their respective camps as heretics. Rapidly losing influence, Contarini died in 1542. His demise marked a milestone in the disappearance of Erasmian influence on the Catholic Reformation.

While Contarini was at Regensburg his rival reformer, Caraffa (who became Pope Paul IV in 1555), had helped institute the Roman Inquisition and an extensive *Index of Prohibited Books.* Although classical studies as well as humanist philology and educational techniques were used by subsequent reformers, particularly those in the Society of Jesus, it was symptomatic of the spirit of Catholic reform henceforth that all of Erasmus's writings appeared on the early *Index,* where most of them remained until the twentieth century.

The Continued Vitality of Humanism

Wherever rigid doctrinal orthodoxy was enforced as in Spain, most of Italy, Geneva, Scotland, and the German principalities, Erasmian humanism could survive only when expressed in nonverbal disciplines; talents not in accord with the prevailing creed were more safely expressed in music or painting. Though exceptional, pockets of toleration continued to exist. After 1555 the Austrian Habsburgs were influenced by Erasmian humanists, but their toleration aimed at an eventual restoration of religious unity. In other areas, notably France, England, and the Low Countries, latitudinarian religious policies* or toleration necessitated by religious pluralism left greater room for the continuation of the "Northern Renaissance." Most productive of new viewpoints within the humanist tradition were the French and the Dutch.

French humanists developed a notable secularization of thought and new methods for studying society. They laid

---

* Latitudinarians drew up vague creeds for state churches that were intended to encompass the beliefs of most of the population.

the basis for a political faction, the *politiques,* that shunned both the militant Calvinist and Catholic sides during the French wars of religion (1562–98) because they considered the commonweal or security of life more important than creedal orthodoxy. The most original of these humanists was Jean Bodin (1530–96), who is best known for developing the theory of the absolute sovereignty of the secular state. But he was no less significant for applying a comparative empirical approach to theology and law. In theology it led him to conclude that different religions share a common or natural core, an assumption that provided the basis for deism during the eighteenth-century Enlightenment. In law he denied the validity of the Justinian codes for all times and places; rather he considered them a composite of historical laws, applicable to specific conditions in the past and subject to such local influences as climate. Thus he undermined the revival of Roman law which had become basic to the legal systems of most European countries earlier in the sixteenth century. Bodin's empiricism resulted in a curious paradox: it led him to accept the testimony of women that they were witches and at the same time to argue for social reform based on accumulated knowledge. Bodin's method and his idea of progress, which Erasmus had developed, gained wide circulation during the Enlightenment of the eighteenth century when the Baron de Montesquieu mined his works for their content and methodology.

A parallel humanist evolution developed in the Netherlands. Dirck Coornhert (1522–90), for example, developed an ethical code based on religious sectarianism and the social philosophy of Cicero that had been so inspiring to the civic humanism of the Italian Renaissance. He too conceived of a natural religion whose rites and dogmas could vary from one environment to another. His humanism and denial of predestination attracted a following of Dutch burghers (the Arminians) who resisted the religious and political objectives of both orthodox Calvinists and the Spanish Inquisition. Although it was nominally a Calvinist movement, Arminianism itself was a humanistic religion, for it emphasized the compatibility of reason and faith, deemphasized dogmas and sacraments, and asserted some human initiative in achieving salvation.

Humanism was narrowed and restricted by the competing orthodoxies it tried to temper, reform, or stand against. After surviving the religious wars, it became a rallying point for many who were weary of fanaticism and violence in the late sixteenth and early seventeenth centuries.

C. The Catholic Reformation

By the middle of the sixteenth century Protestantism's rapid growth in northern Europe posed a graver crisis for Roman Catholicism than had the papal schism and heretical movements of the Renaissance. England, Scandinavia, numerous principalities and cities of the Holy Roman Empire, and parts of the Swiss Confederation had defected. Under the leadership of John Knox, a Geneva-trained Calvinist, Scotland followed in 1560. Tightly organized Calvinist minorities were forming in the Low Countries and in France. And in the empire the militant Calvinists were displacing the Lutherans in the territories along the Rhine, even Bavaria and Austria were

Woodcut showing the "true" Roman church surrounded by heretical devils.

eigns with the popular support to meet Protestantism by force. At the same time, the protracted Habsburg-Valois wars were temporarily suspended (1544) and terminated for more than half a century in 1559 by the Treaty of Cateau-Cambrésis. These lulls in warfare between the two major Catholic dynasties permitted Charles V to launch military and diplomatic offensives against German Protestants. They also gave Catholic leaders the confidence to attempt a general council, the Council of Trent (1545–47, 1551–52, 1562–63). Moreover the Treaty of Cateau-Cambrésis, which recognized Spanish dominance in Italy, was signed in the same year as that in which the last outspoken anti-Spanish pope, Paul IV, died. Thereafter the leading secular power in the Catholic Reformation and the model for its institutions and procedures was Habsburg Spain.

New Religious Orders

In medieval crises brought on by moral and administrative decay, the founding of new monastic orders had refurbished the Church's reputation and released its wasted energies. Such had been the origins of the Cluniacs, the Cistercians, and the mendicant Franciscans and Dominicans. New orders had been rejected during the Renaissance, but in the sixteenth century new orders and reform movements within existing ones again heralded fresh vigor in the Roman church.

At about the same time that Luther was becoming famous in Germany, reformers —clergy and lay aristocrats of diverse religious views—were organizing in Italy. They founded Oratories of the Divine Love—small societies dedicated to prayer, frequent reception of the sacraments, and acts of charity. Among their ranks were leading Catholic reformers of the following generation: Jacopo Sadoleto, Giovanni Pietro Caraffa (later Pope Paul IV), and

tottering in allegiance while their proximity to Protestant territories weakened Rome's control over the thought of their clergy. Only Spain, where a state-directed Reformation had already occurred, and—to a lesser degree—Italy, remained impervious to the Protestant onslaught.

Instead of submitting to a rout, the Roman Catholic church began to muster forces to check the Protestant tide and, in subsequent decades, to regain lost or wavering territories. Barriers to the foundation of new religious orders collapsed. Following the lead of the Society of Jesus a host of new orders emphasizing education, social welfare, and pastoral work labored to counteract heresy and inculcate piety. These were most effective in mobilizing the emotional religious passions of the masses behind tradition and ingrained patterns of religious life; and these passions provided Catholic sover-

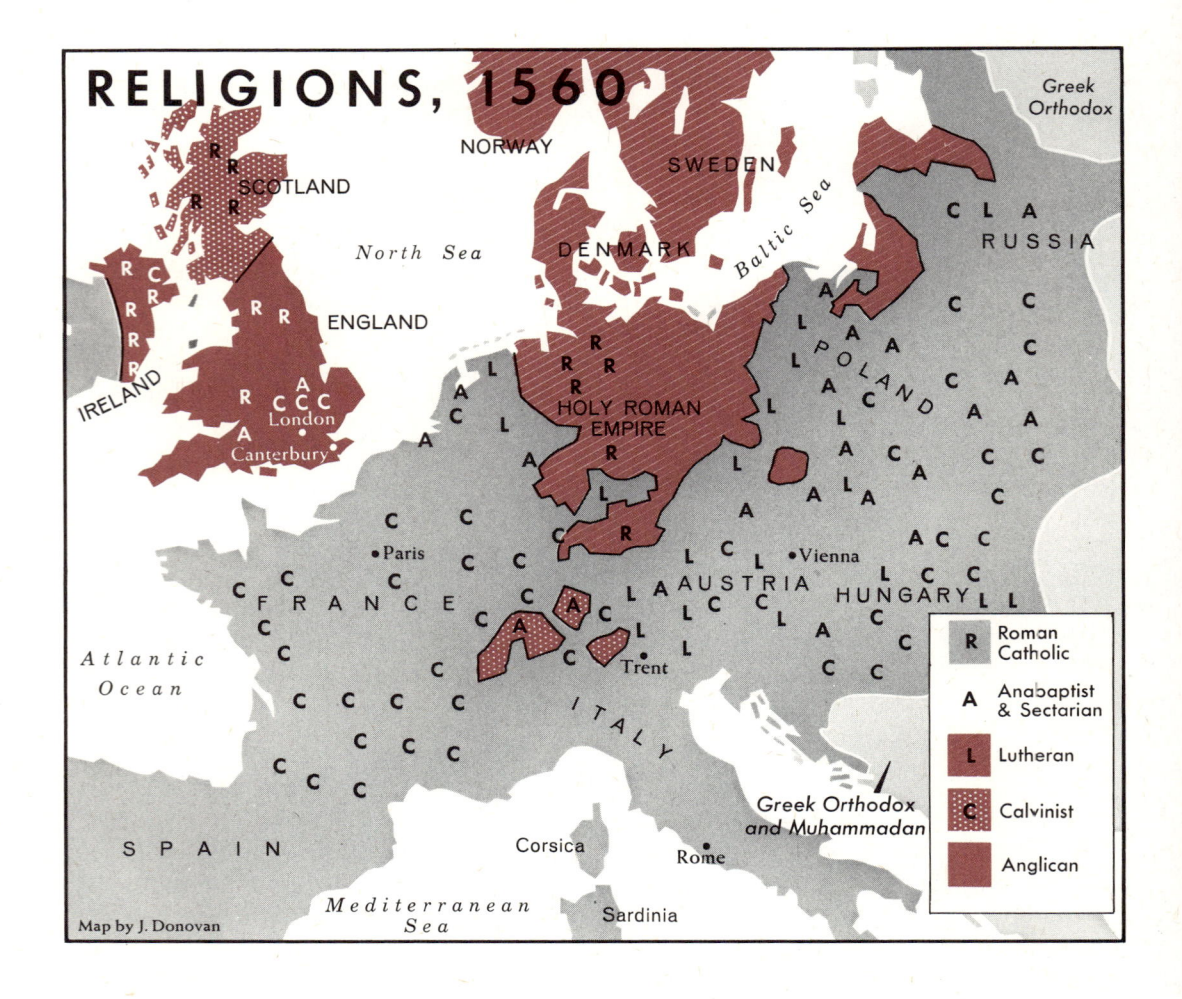

Gaetano di Thiene. Thiene founded another new order in 1524, the Theatines; like most of the orders that followed, it adjusted old ideals of monasticism to the needs of a new generation. These "clerks regular" did not withdraw from the world but combined methodical prayer with secular activism. Like the mendicant friars, they owed allegiance directly to the papacy, and their clerical members were bound by formal vows; but they were neither friars nor monks. Although they were exceedingly few in number, the Theatines (who took their name not from Thiene but from Caraffa's bishopric) enforced Caraffa's severe discipline against clerical neglect, concubinage, and other abuses by personal visitations and provided the papacy with more than 200 bishops during the remainder of the sixteenth century. In addition to the Theatines, Italy produced similar orders, including the Somaschi and the Barnabites. In both Italy and France, new women's orders, beginning with the Ursulines, were also organized to care for the poor and especially to teach the young.

Within the existing order, Franciscans began another influential reform movement, the Capuchins. As disappointed with their order as Luther was with his, they tried to go back to the purity of St. Francis rather than destroy the monastic tradition. In origin the Capuchins were the offspring of the Italian populace; their direct approach to the masses made them the principal agents in regaining and holding the loyalty of the Italian lower classes. In 1542 they were shaken by the desertion of their leading popular preacher and third vicar-general, Bernardino Ochino, to the Unitarians, but they recovered rapidly. In France, where the Spanish background of their Jesuit competitors was suspect, the Capuchins gained positions of power and influenced the court.

Far exceeding the other new orders in total efforts and effectiveness was the Society of Jesus, the "shock troops of the Counter Reformation," founded by a disabled Spanish soldier, Ignatius of Loyola (1491–1556). A young nobleman serving in the Habsburg-Valois wars, Loyola was wounded while campaigning in Navarre in 1521. While recuperating, he experienced a mystical religious conversion comparable in impact to Martin Luther's revelation of salvation by faith alone, and from chivalry he turned to "spiritual knighthood." In 1523 he set out on a pilgrimage via Rome and Venice to the Holy Land. Returned to Barcelona in 1524, he decided that he lacked sufficient education to be an efficient instrument of God. With the city's school children he attended grammar school; thereafter he attended the universities of Alcalá, Salamanca, and Paris. It was at Paris that he gathered around him ten disciples who became the Society's early nucleus. He demanded of them a disciplined will and unconditional obedience to higher authority. He strongly encouraged their higher education and urged that they foster the zeal to work (in the words of his personal motto) "to the greater glory of God."

After going to Rome, where their frequent religious observances had made them suspect, the Jesuit initiates received official papal approval as a new order on the recommendation of Cardinal Contarini in 1540. There they took permanent vows of poverty, chastity, and obedience to the papacy, and were commissioned soldiers of God to propagate doctrine and faith by public preaching, acts of charity, and especially public education. Until 1544 the order was limited to 60 members but, freed of this restriction, it expanded rapidly, especially in the Iberian kingdoms and their colonial empires. The Jesuits' zeal for missionary work proved as intense as that of the Franciscans and Dominicans. One of the original founders, Francis Xavier (1506–52), is credited with hundreds of thousands of converts in India, China, Malaya, and Japan.

The Jesuits did not limit their missionary efforts to the Iberian colonial empires; they also moved into those areas of Europe jeopardized by Protestantism. Many parts of western and southern Ger-

Ignatius of Loyola.

many were recovered for the Roman church by Peter Canisius of Nimwegen (1521–97). An educator and Jesuit administrator, he competed hard and effectively against Protestant preaching. Supported by the rulers of Bavaria and Poland during the second half of the century, the Jesuits almost totally restored religious conformity there by persuasion and force.

Among primitive peoples, the Jesuits usually secured little more than acceptance of the sacraments as a sign of conversion. But in Europe their goals were political and power-oriented as well as spiritual, and their methods, both admired and feared by their enemies, were highly sophisticated. Aside from pastoral work, Jesuits devoted great attention to higher education, founding colleges to train and indoctrinate the elite of both church and state. These colleges and their faculties became an integral part of the Catholic resurgence, enjoying reputations that attracted non-Catholics as well. More controversial were the strivings of Jesuit confessors to influence rulers' policies. The order was committed to papal supremacy in spiritual affairs, but nothing prevented its members from trying to influence secular events. In the eyes of its Protestant opponents, the Society of Jesus was a centralized papal conspiracy. The members persuaded receptive kings that their religious ends justified the use of political means. Thus a large Protestant literature denouncing Jesuit casuistry grew up during the religious wars. In itself, the heat of the Protestant reaction was a strong indication of the Jesuits' effectiveness.

The Council of Trent

Jesuit zeal and scholarship were not the only indication that the carefree days of the Renaissance papacy had come to an end. After disastrously long delays, prelates, theologians, canonists, generals of the mendicant orders, and papal legates assembled with other dignitaries of the Roman church at the city of Trent. This council faced the serious business of refuting Protestantism and purifying the Church of the abuses that had helped the Protestant influence to spread.

More than vested interest in the status quo had caused the council to be postponed until the eleventh hour. Although the pope and the Curia had surely feared that a general council would usurp their prerogatives, the wars between Francis I and Charles V had nevertheless made an ecumenical council impossible. Following the truce in 1544 the papacy entered into a military alliance with Charles under the terms of which a papal army was dispatched to help fight the German Protestants. It was hoped that the convening of the council would coincide with a military victory.

Politically the moment seemed auspicious for the council to enforce a religious settlement after the Protestants' defeat, but this strategy was frustrated by an incomplete military victory and by disagreement among the Catholics. Pope Paul III set highest priority on refuting Protestant doctrines. Fearing nothing more than rigid doctrinal proclamations that would make peace in Germany impossible, Charles V wanted immediate reform of abuses. Charles's political priorities alarmed the pope, and as their alliance expired, the pope withdrew the remnants of his army from Germany and approached France diplomatically. Meanwhile Charles also became disillusioned with the council because it followed papal leadership in promulgating uncompromisingly traditional religious doctrines before carrying out reforms.

From the start, legates instructed by the pope were in command of the council so that it did not become a threat to papal sovereignty. They secured the restriction of voting rights to the higher clergy, set the agenda, and reserved for the pope the exclusive right to promulgate, interpret, and execute the council's decrees. Opposition to the legates, although divided, was heated, and the council did not conform completely to papal wishes. Giving ear to the opinions that "only reform can save Germany for the Church,"[1] the assembled fathers agreed to deal simultaneously with doctrines and reforms. In practice, however, the council offended Charles V, for reform proposals were delayed by long debates and divisions, whereas rigid doctrinal decrees passed rapidly with near unanimity.

Rather than cataloging Catholic doctrine comprehensively, the doctrinal decrees uncompromisingly reaffirmed Catholic dogmas that unnamed Protestants had attacked. In opposition to Protestant reliance on scriptural authority alone—which no Protestant reformer maintained consistently for long—the council declared the parity of unbroken apostolic tradition with the Bible. It also affirmed the Church as the sole interpreter of Scripture and established prepublication censorship over all theological works. Repudiating the humanists' criterion of textual purity, the council approved only the Latin Vulgate edition of the Bible on the grounds that its long use by the Church established its authenticity. Another decree rejected the Protestant dogma that man was totally and immutably depraved as a result of original sin, to remedy the effects of which—concupiscence and death—Trent relied on the sacraments. The debate on original sin, the longest of the entire council, inexorably compelled participants to grapple with Luther's fundamental doctrine of unmerited salvation by faith alone. The council avoided rigid personal predestination and asserted the necessity of human free will to opt for salvation through the sacraments, which had to be supplemented by faith, love, hope, and good works. The emphasis on sacraments included a denunciation of Anabaptists as well as Protestants. Logically this position on original sin required another decree that affirmed the seven sacraments, the greater number of which Protestants had denounced as human inventions.

The council took major steps to restore the authority of bishops over their dioceses, and to produce a more competent clergy. In order to make clergymen capable of public preaching, bishops and monastic orders were required to provide them with instructors in theology. Another decree attacked the central problems of administrative disorder: absenteeism, pluralism—the holding of several church posts simultaneously—the use of offices as sinecures, and exemptions from episcopal visitation. With few exceptions the council ordered heavy penalties for absentee prelates. The price of this reorganization was not only greater clerical discipline; papal revenues derived from dispensations from the canon law also shrank. Meanwhile in other moves against the prelates' affluence, the pope suspended the sale of indulgences and reduced the sale of offices.

The first sessions terminated following Paul III's rift with Charles V. Dismayed by the council's doctrinal decrees and unable to prevent the pope's removal of the council to Bologna, where it ended, Charles in 1548 proclaimed a religious settlement for Germany on his own authority. This "Interim" permitted the continuance of married priests in their functions and the dispensation of Communion to the laity in both bread and wine until the council resumed. The Interim divided the German Protestants but failed to bridge the confessional gap in the empire.

Pope Julius III (1550–55) reassembled the council again in 1551–52. This time Protestant representatives were invited, but instead of contributing to conciliation, they demonstrated the breadth of the schism by insisting on the nullification of

---

[1] Quoted by Hubert Jedin, *A History of the Council of Trent*, vol. 2, *The First Session at Trent* (St. Louis: B. Herder Book Co., 1961), p. 36.

all previous actions. Little was accomplished also because Protestant forces, aided actively by France, defeated the emperor and threatened to overrun Trent itself. The council hastily disbanded. Subsequently the Peace of Augsburg (1555), which placed religious affairs in the hands of ruling German princes, provided a settlement the council had failed to reach.

The council did not reconvene until 1562. Caraffa, reigning as Pope Paul IV from 1555 to 1559, preferred autocratic rule as an instrument of reform. His successor, Pius IV, called the final assembly. It amplified and extended previous decisions, creating the basic legislation by which the Roman Catholic church has subsequently been governed. To curtail commercialization of religion the council forbade the sale of indulgences and regulated the cult of saints and the veneration of relics. Reacting against Renaissance naturalism, the fathers issued some puritanical decrees. As one result, second-rate artists painted loincloths on the frescoes of Michelangelo and other great Renaissance painters.

The council ordered the redistribution of parish incomes and dictated in detail the content of eduction in the seminaries. At the same time a host of dispensations and privileges were abolished; Spanish, French, and imperial bishops sought and were denied greater prerogatives for themselves. The fathers elaborated on the sacraments, especially holy orders and matrimony, and they espoused the teachings, though not the rationalism, of Thomas Aquinas, proclaiming him the authoritative interpreter of Christianity. To inculcate the approved doctrines, the council ordered that clerical and popular catechisms be prepared. The *breviary* (daily prayers of the priesthood), the official lives of the saints, and the *missal* (prayers of the Mass) were also to be revised. Charles Borromeo, archbishop of Milan and director of the final session at Trent, supervised these tasks.

The Implementation of Catholic Reform

To legislate reforms was one thing; to enforce them over the opposition of vested political and clerical interests was another. Catholic reform depended heavily on papal leadership, since the pope reserved for himself all rights of implementing the council's decrees. His power outside Italy, however, was narrowly circumscribed by the Catholic monarchs, whose predecessors had established a tradition of royal control over the local churches. Now they refused to let the papacy with its reform rulings encroach on their jurisdiction: they quite simply vetoed whatever rulings they wished not to adopt or tolerate. Thus the implementation of Catholic administrative reform depended on the policies of Catholic rulers, especially the Spanish Habsburgs, who commanded the most formidable military forces during the wars of religion.

In the decades after 1559 most of the popes made Catholic revival their primary concern. Pius IV began work on the Catechism, *Breviary,* and the *Missal,* projects which were completed under his successor, Pius V (1566–72). A former monk and inquisitor-general, Pius V applied the Inquisition rigorously and commanded a puritan standard of morality for Rome. The actions of these two popes made Rome a less attractive place for seekers of fortune and pleasure. Another noteworthy reformer-pope was Gregory XIII (1572–85), a canon lawyer who revised the canon law, encouraged the rapid growth of the Society of Jesus and its colleges, and issued the revised Gregorian calendar. The succession of reforming popes continued into the middle of the seventeenth century.

Catholic reformers relied heavily on persuasion, but the popes had at their disposal two instruments of coercion initiated by Cardinal Caraffa, the Roman

Didactic Reformation art: Detail from Seven Deadly Sins *by Hieronymous Bosch, an earlier Flemish artist (d. 1516). Bosch's works were widely reproduced, especially in Spain.*

Inquisition and the *Index of Prohibited Books.*

The Inquisition served as an extraordinary court for the extirpation of heresy.*

Proceedings were secret, torture was used on both the accused and the witnesses, and suspects were imprisoned without recourse to counsel or confrontation with witnesses. Although the Inquisition functioned as a confessional tribunal in which mercy was normally extended to those who confessed guilt and begged forgiveness, the inquisitor-generals were empowered to override the jurisdiction of local bishops, to pronounce judgments,

---

* The Roman Inquisition had a medieval predecessor founded in the thirteenth century to stamp out heresy on the Continent, but it fell into disuse during the Renaissance. In 1478 the papacy approved the establishment of the Spanish Inquisition, which Caraffa observed and admired, imitating it in the foundation of the Roman Inquisition in 1542.

and to turn the condemned over to the secular authorities for punishment. Since most secular governments preferred their own tribunals or autonomous inquisitions, the Roman Inquisition in practice functioned little outside Italy, where it played a heavy and controversial role. It succeeded in crushing heresy in the Italian cities, but in so doing it has since been held accountable for creating an atmosphere of intellectual stagnation. In this regard, however, it was scarcely more repressive than many secular tribunals.

Cardinal Caraffa's other innovation, the Index, initially banned all the works of Erasmus as well as those of the Protestant reformers. Under Caraffa's original orders, too, thousands of books were burned; this Index of 1559 established categories of prohibited offensive works: all the books of certain outlawed authors, anonymous heretical writings, works of specific printers, and all vernacular translations of the New Testament. The Council of Trent ordered a revision of the Index that led to its modification, but at the same time more efficient machinery for its enforcement was set up, including a system of prepublication censorship. The Index, a powerful tool of thought control during the Reformation, proved to be a lasting institution; however more recent revisions have restricted its scope—for example, no works of Erasmus appear in the latest compilation, and the list of specific works permission to read which has still to be secured is confined to matters relating solely to faith and morals. Recently, after the Second Vatican Council, all penalties relating to the Index were removed.

At the last meeting at Trent the major Catholic princes agreed to cooperate with reform under papal leadership, but no Catholic sovereign followed suit; and the kings retained their control over Church affairs. Occasionally some of them with subjects of differing faiths outrightly resisted Trent's decrees on doctrine. The Austrian Habsburgs, for example, attempted to maintain domestic peace by offering concessions to the Protestants. Similarly, the French house of Valois, which was on the threshhold of a long religious civil war, sought a more tolerant solution to doctrinal controversies than the final assembly at Trent provided.

Resistance to the doctrinal decrees was slight, however, compared to resistance to administrative decrees and to the Inquisition. For the monarchs to comply with these meant that they surrendered control over the higher clergy and would further lose their power to reward favorites with sinecures and ecclesiastical revenues. Their favorites, the local aristocracy, would in turn lose a major source of family income. Moreover, the local churches in both Catholic and Protestant kingdoms were beginning to espouse the principle of divine-right monarchy. Profiting from the doctrine drawn from the Epistle of St. Paul to the Romans, that he who resists constituted authority resists God himself,* rulers were adamant against returning to papal overlordship. No secular government, least of all the Most Catholic King of Spain, fully accepted the administrative reforms of the Council of Trent. Outside the clerical archbishoprics few German principalities ever adopted them, and the French church was not reformed administratively until the revolution of 1789.

Catholic resurgence was a reality, especially in producing a more highly educated clergy and in establishing a host of new orders engaged in social work as well as acts of piety. But the locus of power remained not in the papacy or Church councils but in the hands of secular rulers who had broken from Church control prior to the Reformation. For them religion was subordinate to the interests of power.

* "Let every person be subject to the governing authorities. For there is no authority except from God, and those that exist have been instituted by God. Therefore he who resists the authorities resists what God has appointed, and those who resist will incur judgment" (13: 1–3).

D. Eastern Europe and the Reformation

By the mid-1500s the Protestant Reformation had spread into Roman Catholic central Europe, where it became entangled in the political conflicts within Bohemia, Hungary, and Poland-Lithuania; but the Balkan countries, Greek Orthodox by tradition and ruled by Muhammadans, were impervious to its creeping influence. So was Muscovy, the only independent principality with an Orthodox population. Muscovite Orthodoxy, isolated from developments in the West by barriers of both geography and tradition, remained devoted to antiintellectualism, monasticism, and an authoritarian political state. Therefore the Reformation never went beyond western and central Europe.

Bohemia, Hungary, and Poland-Lithuania

At the beginning of the Protestant Reformation the borderlands of eastern Europe were governed by the Jagellon family. Under military pressure from both east and west, these rulers (who were failing to produce male heirs) lost extensive territory to neighboring kingdoms. They also yielded internal authority to aristocrats and gentry who, in the absence of central authority, exercised considerable "local option" in religious affairs. At Mohacs in 1526 the Turks killed Louis, the childless Jagellon king of Bohemia and Hungary, whereupon the Habsburgs took possession of his throne. They also had designs on Poland-Lithuania, the last surviving Jagellon state, which at this time was under attack from the east by Turks, Tartars, and Muscovites. Its leaders sought maximum internal unity to stand off the encircling threats, and in 1569 they effected the Union of Lublin. The state, once jointly governed by Polish and Lithuanian dynasts, now came under a single, elective kingship and a common diet, the latter dominated by the nobles and gentry. When the last Jagellon king died, factions of the nobility and the gentry competed with one another and with various foreign influences for the ruling power.

These conditions of political instability were conducive to religious dissent, which political power-seekers used for their own advantage. Supported by Lutherans, Calvinists, and anti-Trinitarians (Unitarians), they defied traditional authority then embodied in Sigismund I (1506–48). In vain he and his successors tried to suppress these heresies—their decrees went unacknowledged. A diet of 1556 demanded comprehensive religious reforms, and in 1573 Henry of Valois (temporarily king of Poland before becoming king of France) was obliged to extend religious toleration. Following 1550, soon after the rise of Calvinism in Poland, the Jesuits launched a Counter-Reformation. Sigismund III (1587–1632) utilized their services to almost wholly extirpate dissent from Polish religious life.

Events followed a somewhat similar course in Habsburg Bohemia, where first Lutheranism and then Calvinism became an important movement of political and religious revolt. There the native Hussite tradition was dominant although divided between conservative Utraquists, who had gained the Church's permission for extending Communion to the laity under species of both bread and wine (*utra* = L. "both"), and the more radical Czech Brethren, who had replaced revolutionary fervor with pacifist pietism. Persecution of the Czech Brethren between 1548 and 1552 failed to check religious dissent, and Maximilian II (1564–76) permitted extensive toleration.

Compared with Bohemia, which was neither invaded nor beset with civil war, Hungary's reformation was much more chaotic. After 1526 the Ottoman Turks held the eastern two-thirds of that kingdom, and the Habsburgs occupied the remainder. Against these two powers Transylvanian nobles led a movement for Hungarian autonomy. Denouncing the authority of the Church as well as of the state, they espoused Calvinism and Lutheranism, and after 1560 anti-Trinitarianism also became an important force in their revolt. In 1564 all three new religions were recognized as legally equal with Catholicism. Unlike the Roman resurgence in Poland and Bohemia, the Catholic Reformation in Habsburg Hungary never entirely suppressed religious dissent.

Greek Orthodoxy and the Turks

Several times in the sixteenth century Lutherans and Calvinists both sought active cooperation with the Greeks against Rome. One patriarch of Alexandria and Constantinople actually published a Calvinist-like confession of faith in Geneva in 1602, but he was thoroughly repudiated by official synods in the East. Differences between Greek Orthodoxy and the West, Catholic and Protestant, were deep-rooted. Protestant hopes of uniting with the East against Rome proved illusory.

For the continued schism splitting Orthodoxy from the West, not only different religious traditions but Turkish tolerance was responsible. When the Ottoman Turks conquered Asia Minor and the Balkans in the late fourteenth century they brought almost all Greek Orthodox peoples except the Muscovites under Muhammadan rule. But even the shock of conquest and government by the foreign infidel created no more than temporary ties between Eastern and Western Christianity. The sultans moved the Patriarch of Constantinople from Santa Sophia, which was converted to a mosque, and deposed refractory patriarchs; however they did not disestablish the popularly supported Greek Orthodox clergy. Instead they profited from selling high church offices to the highest bidder. By the sultan's religious toleration, political stability was fostered.

Nor did the common threat of renewed Turkish invasion in the sixteenth century heal splits within the West. Idealists and kings talked of, or even committed themselves to, joining crusades against the Ottoman power, but in fact most Europeans feared their own neighbors more than the infidel. Only once, in 1571, was an effective joint crusade launched under papal leadership, resulting in the naval victory of Lepanto. Even then the Venetians, whose territories were in jeopardy, were as wary of Spanish as of Ottoman predominance in the Mediterranean. Crusading zeal during the Reformation period was directed not so much toward the Turks as toward the Indian population of the New World, overrun by Spanish conquistadores.

The Ottomans, often as allies of Francis I, made repeated invasions along the

Panel of icons for Russian Orthodox services, Moscow, late fifteenth century.

Danube, distracting the German emperor and keeping him from working against domestic and religious uprisings. Their influence in eastern trade was considerable, too. They imposed tolls and transfer fees, all to the commercial advantage of the Atlantic seaboard states, whose traders had meanwhile opened all-sea routes to the Indies. After 1566 the efficiency of Ottoman rule declined—but up to then the Turks made a distinctive impact on events in western Europe.

Muscovy

With the expansion of Muscovy went extension of the Russian Orthodox church, which added monastic frontier colonies to its vast but taxed holdings. In its social organization the Duchy of Moscow had much in common with east-central Europe, and its subordination of religion to politics was paralleled in many countries in western Europe after the Reformation. But from the intellectual ferment of the Reformation, Muscovy was a world apart: while other heads of state were engaged in conflicts over the subtleties of theology, Ivan IV (the Terrible, 1533–84) was waging more primitive wars. Reared in a setting of palace violence, he was brought up to rule a society shamelessly dominated and exploited by the traditional aristocracy, the *boyars*. Although a literate and educated man, he monopolized and wielded power in a way that led exiles to portray him as a madman.

To keep the land-hungry nobility occupied while he broke their strength, Ivan contrived constant warfare. His forces conquered almost the whole of the Volga River Valley and the watersheds of the Don and Donetz rivers as well as the territory along the Ural Mountains. Against the Teutonic Knights of Livonia and their Polish protectors he loosed a "human sea" of warriors from 1558 to 1583.

To break the boyars' monopoly, Ivan established a special bodyguard, the *streltsy*, which he enlarged to garrison the cities. Suddenly in 1564 he opened a veritable war on the boyars, whom he accused of treason. He confiscated their estates and transferred them to new areas while the confiscated lands went into the hands of favorites directly dependent upon him. This redistribution of land and destruction of custom took place in about half of

D. Eastern Europe and the Reformation

the state—furthered by secret police, torture, and liberal application of the executioner's ax. In the other half of the duchy traditional practices were continued. Ivan also called Russia's first representative assembly, the *zemsky sobor,* two and one-half centuries after parliaments had appeared in western and central Europe; but thereafter Russian development did not follow the Western constitutional pattern.

E. The Reformation and the Modern World

The Reformation made only a shallow impact on eastern Europe, but it became a lasting part of the western European heritage. Until very recently, most Catholic and Protestant historians have identified heroes and culprits according to their doctrinal affiliations, and both sides have condemned the Erasmian humanists and the radical sectarians. In the nineteenth century as nationalism, industrial capitalism, secular science, and the idea of evolutionary progress came to influence Reformation historians, they began to abandon doctrinal polemics for assessments of the Reformation's contributions to the modern world.

Some Roman Catholic writers continued to denounce the "Protestant Revolt" as a catastrophic opening of society to further revolutions, schisms, and secularization. But secular and many Protestant historians began to discover the roots of the modern world in the Protestant Reformation. They portrayed the reformers as purveyors of individualism, tolerance, nationalism, and a capitalistic economy. Some historians, on the other hand, have been impressed with the reformers' traditionalism and have questioned the evidence on which the equations of Protestantism with progress have been based. Others, mainly "Neo-Orthodox" theologians, assert that the early reformers were spokesmen for an other-worldly religion based on pessimism about the earthly capabilities and future of man. Scholars studying sectarian movements that advocated and practiced tolerance and religious individualism have also raised doubts about the interpretation of major reformers as liberal nationalists. They point to reformers such as Luther who tried determinedly to stamp out the very views that have been attributed to him. The role of the Reformation in shaping the modern world is thus a matter of dispute. Because theological ways of thinking have declined, most twentieth-century Western peoples have difficulty projecting themselves into the arguments of the sixteenth century. But discussion of some consequences or alleged consequences of the Reformation should help us assess its controversial role in shaping the modern world.

Individualism

Since Luther proclaimed every man his own priest, the Protestant Reformation has been widely interpreted as a major step toward the recognition of individual judgment or conscience. In theory, the assertion of a direct relationship between man and God was a powerful fillip to the idea of individuality, for which past heretics had struggled in vain. Nothing was further from the reformers' minds, however, than the submission of divine revelation to private judgment or interpretation. For Holy Church they substituted Holy Writ, which each reformer in his own way held to be concretely and objectively revealed. To assert that the individual should take any initiative in his own salvation was to derogate the absolute sovereignty of God. Faith came from hearing or reading the Word, but its reception was a divine miracle for which the individual person was totally unworthy. Inwardly a person could believe what he would—faith could not be forced—but the honor of God required the magistrates to enforce external conformity, including church attendance and submission to the sacraments. For this reason mystics, sectarians, and humanitarian humanists accused the reformers of forcing dissenters to be hypocrites. In reality, Protestants of the sixteenth century adopted a new absolute authority; they found "freedom of conscience" quite compatible with the persecution of nonconformists.

The Catholic Reformation, especially the Council of Trent, had no such ambiguities as the "priesthood of all believers" to deal with. It categorically denounced religious individualism and substantially narrowed the tolerable range of diversity in thought. Like the Protestants, but to a lesser degree, the Catholic reformers also curbed individual expression in the arts.

Toleration

Expression of individual religious judgment was inseparable from the question of tolerance. Luther at first opposed the use of force and the burning of books to deal with religious dissent. But he came to equate religious dissent from his reformation with political rebellion and insisted that princes maintain uniformity. Soon he and other Protestant writers were trying to justify coercion and to reconcile it with the repeated assertion that a man could not be compelled to believe. Ultimately the Protestant Reformation contributed indirectly to tolerance in certain areas and circumstances, but its immediate impact was the creation of several intolerant creeds, each maintained by the force of local political authorities.

Because they believed in predestination—that a sovereign God had selected the elect and damned the rejected before earthly time began—the Protestant reformers, unlike the Roman inquisitors, could not justify persecution on the grounds that it could lead to the heretic's salvation. They found sufficient other bases for it, however. One was scriptural authority as interpreted by St. Augustine —a favorite theologian of the Protestants— who had sanctioned persecution of North African heretics. Another was the Protestants' concept of heresy: deviations from their own version of divine revelation could only be the work of Satan. Persecution of Satan's legions (the heretics) upheld the honor of God and protected the faithful who were incapable of recognizing the Devil's snares. Still another justification was political. The reformers shared the traditional Roman Catholic belief that no state divided in religion could survive and that it was the magistrate's commission from God—from whom all legitimate authority flowed—to maintain the morality and orthodoxy of his subjects. The alternative, they believed, was civil war. Until religiously pluralistic

Anti-Catholic intolerance of Henry VIII: the beheadings of John Fisher (cardinal-bishop of Rochester), Thomas More, and the Countess of Salisbury are included in one illustration.

states began to survive in peace and demonstrate that coexistence was possible—an expedient for the security of life and property—the secular premises of religious persecution went unchallenged except among sectarians, radical humanists, and state-church minorities too small to attempt a seizure of power.

Such sectarians as the Anabaptists advocated separation of church and state and the exclusion of force from religious affairs. They and the most avidly read publicist on behalf of toleration in the sixteenth century, Sebastian Castellio, shared the belief that, besides faith, Christianity required the imitation of Christ. They could not sanction the bloody acts of Old Testament kings whose precedent the reformers invoked against humanitarianism when doctrine was at stake. Where sectarians were numerous they pressured rulers into granting at least toleration and at most equal religious rights.

Erasmian humanists, on the other hand, were latitudinarians; regarding many contested dogmas as conflicts over nonessentials, they usually worked to make official creeds flexible enough to be acceptable to a majority of the population.

Eventually the Reformation tended in Protestant and religiously divided states to diminish the intolerance that it had initially generated. By substituting secular for clerical judges, state-church Protestantism turned religious disputes over to laymen, who were not as meticulous on the fine points of theology as the clerics, but who nevertheless dealt out harsh penalties to dissenters. However in both Catholic and Protestant states where nonconformist minorities were too large to be easily exterminated, jailed, or banished, expediency dictated compromise and limited toleration as alternatives to civil war. The religious diversity produced by the Reformation also produced some doctrinal relativity as reflected in the adage "orthodoxy is my doxy." But the establishment of toleration based on political—and sometimes commercial—expediency drastically altered the authoritarianism on which the Protestant reformers had based their politics. Rather than an outgrowth of Protestantism, toleration was more often the result of religious, civil, and international wars. People came to choose diversity over the devastation and turmoil of war.

Political Ramifications

Churchmen, Protestant and Catholic alike, usually sought the support of secular governments; thus they were invariably involved in politics and with political theory. To separate church and state was inconceivable to all except the radicals. Most Reformation thinkers were very much concerned to define the role of the magistrates in reforming the Church, and they devoted considerable thought to the problems of a ruler whose religion differed from that of the majority or sizable minorities of his subjects.

By attempting to restore the primacy of religion in affairs of state the Reformation inaugurated an era of "Christian princes." Rulers gained extensive additional powers by controlling or intervening in religious affairs. No religious reform succeeded without the direction, or at least the approval, of the government; and no government supported reform without acquiring more power for itself in the process. In the Protestant (non-Calvinist) states of the early Reformation princes held the main legislative and executive powers within the churches. The Peace of Augsburg (1555) recognized this state of affairs by legally authorizing them to make their states Catholic or Lutheran. Clergymen cast these reforming princes as Old Testament ruler-priests, agents of an inscrutable deity to whom alone they were accountable. This divine warrant did not give Protestant rulers absolute control over religious affairs, however: they were subject to Holy Writ. If they transgressed this limitation, Lutheran and Anglican divines sanctioned passive resistance against them. But as we have already seen, according to Romans XIII active resistance was no less than resistance to God.

Thus many Protestant churches encouraged the notion of divine-right kingship. Defending the old order, Roman Catholic spokesmen also advocated rule by divine right as well as timid obedience to constituted authority. But the aggressive Calvinists actively defied traditional governments, and by the middle of the sixteenth century they began to collide violently with Roman Catholics made desperate by the extent of their losses. Civil wars followed in France, the Netherlands, and England, exceeding all bounds of diplomacy and all conventional restraints on warfare. These conflicts, whose course will be sketched in the following chapter, were between factions that sought to impose their religious positions on a state by seizing the machinery of its government. In France, for example, Calvinists sanctioned revolution by "lesser magistrates," whereas Jesuits appealed democratically to the majority of the population. Both viewpoints reflected a broader appeal to people than was characteristic of the past, and to this degree the Reformation released forces that were "democratic" but not liberal in the sense of protecting individual rights or establishing constitutional processes for government by persuasion.

Because the Reformation focused political loyalties on divine-right kings or councils that acknowledged no earthly limitation, it has often been hailed as the forerunner of modern nationalism. In particular, Calvinist "New Jerusalems" resembled the fervent nationalist states of the last two centuries. A kind of nationalism did characterize the foreign policy of Spain and other governments that the Spanish Jesuits—who formulated and encouraged adherence to a theory of international law—tried in vain to influence. But irresponsible state sovereignty lodged in divine-right kings or in the magistrates of "God's chosen people" was not a distinct creation of the Reformation. It was probably more clearly enunciated in the messianism of czarist Russia: Ivan claimed that Muscovy was the "Third Rome," the only pure representative of Christianity on earth, with a world mission to perform. Certainly the Reformation coincided with the disruption of Western Christendom into individual states, each claiming a divine head equal in authority to the pope or else acting totally without reference to the papacy. But how far this disruption was the result of political forces already in operation before the Reformation, and how much the Protestant reformers were responsible for it, are moot questions. It is certain, however, that religious innovations contributed as often to irreconcilable divisions within existing states as they did to a new basis for national unity.

Social and Economic Repercussions

The Reformation was a revolution that stopped short of a general social upheaval. Apart from religious practices, the lives of the great majority of the population—the peasantry and the lower townsmen—were little changed. Only for the clergy—one of the two privileged medieval estates—was it a partial social revolution. Sectarian anticlericals were prevented from removing the clergy as officers of the state or as wards of noble patrons, but in resources and positions of power the Protestant clergy declined far more precipitously than the Catholic clergy. In Protestant states the economic power previously commanded by clergymen was transferred to secular governments and laymen. In some instances the transfer of property from the corporate "dead hand" of the Church to laymen contributed to more rapid economic development. According to some historical sociologists, Protestants, especially Calvinists and sectarians, made religious virtues of economic attitudes. Thus they stimulated the growth of capitalism and contributed to the transfer of the most active trading centers from Catholic to Protestant territories.

Protestants made drastic changes in the status and role of the clergy. They removed its prestige as unique agent in transforming the bread and wine into the body and blood of Christ in the Eucharist; they suppressed monasticism and discouraged clerical celibacy. In dress, social status, and political obligations, the Protestant clergy became less distinguishable from ordinary subjects. Their profession came to resemble most other occupations and, as in other fields, the sons began to follow the calling of their fathers. Exemptions of clergy from secular justice and from taxes, tolls, and guild regulations usually lapsed; clerical representation in territorial diets dwindled; courts staffed in part by clergymen still ruled on family affairs such as legitimacy, marriage, divorce, and wills, but they functioned only in special departments of government. Pastors were considered officials of the state as well as of the Church, but they seldom served as leading ministers or diplomatic representatives of princes. What is perhaps most significant, the higher clergy no longer received large revenues. Former obligations of peasants and townsmen to the Church were not canceled, but they were diverted to recipients other than prelates. Costly projects such as relief, education, and building now required *state* support or administration.

In some respects the Catholic Reformation took a course diametrically opposed to that of the Protestants; in others there were distinct similarities. The Council of Trent spurned all pleas for clerical marriage and legislated strict enforcement of clerical celibacy. It reasserted the role of the priest as sharply separated from that of the laity, and the prelates retained their political role as the first estate in the territorial diets. In most Roman Catholic states of the late Reformation, the Church regained its position as a major landholder, and monasticism flourished. The clergy generally lost their exemptions from civil penalties, but they retained more of their privileges than their Protestant counterparts. The Protestant and Catholic reformations paralleled one another in the gradual creation of an educated clergy charged with preaching, teaching, and pastoral care. Both also curtailed commercialized religion and the sale of offices.

According to some historians the Protestant reformers not only secularized society and weakened clerical influence over it but also played a major role in advancing modern capitalism. Noting apparent correlations of Protestant and nonconformist religion with individual and group business success, nineteenth- and twentieth-century historians and historical sociologists have sought an explanation of this association in the social ethic of Protestantism, Judaism, and such sectarian minorities as the Anabaptists, Quakers, Baptists, and Wesleyans. At the end of the nineteenth century Max Weber, a German sociologist, published a classic thesis, *The Protestant Ethic and the Spirit of Capitalism*, to demonstrate this connection. He argued that the positive attitude of Protestants, especially Calvinists and sectarians, toward hard work, self-denial, and the holiness of secular callings was *one* factor in the development of the spirit of capitalism. He defined that spirit not as the desire for unlimited accumulation of wealth but as the rational organization of men and material to produce recurrent profits. Paradoxically he found that the practice of ascetic otherworldliness, which repudiated the aristocracy's ostentatious displays of wealth, contributed to constructive social and individual economic success.

Weber's thesis is not immune from serious criticism in several details, and incautious popularizers have distorted his case by exaggeration. Therefore some qualification of the reckless associations of Protestantism and economic progress is in order. Before the Reformation capitalism flourished in Catholic Italy and Flanders. In the nineteenth century Catholic Belgium industrialized rapidly while a distinctly medieval economic organization persisted in large parts of Lutheran Germany. Furthermore the fact that Calvin sanctioned the taking of interest does not mean that he was a pioneer of an unregulated economy. The five percent interest which he approved was below rates already current. Finally, orthodox Calvinist sermons from seventeenth-century England and the Netherlands—the two areas of greatest economic development and the period from which Weber drew much of his evidence—indicate that capitalism eventually influenced Calvinist doctrines rather than vice versa.*

Nevertheless certain Protestant and sectarian practices had undeniable significance for economic growth where resources and other requisites were present. The creation of a literate laity is one case in point, although this was not achieved by all Protestants; the devotion of nonconformists (barred from aristocratic and royal favors) to productive economic activity and to the building of reputations for business integrity is another. The social attitudes of radical Protestantism helped to dissolve traditions

---

* More recently Weber's method has been used with equally ambiguous results to assert a Protestant, especially Calvinist, encouragement of science by emphasizing the idea of a divine universal order purged of much superstition. Consideration of the rise of scientific approaches to nature is deferred, however, to the following volume.

wherever they were maintained. But—as Weber, although unfortunately not all his popularizers, knew—these attitudes in themselves do not completely explain the complex interaction of material and human resources that increased per capita production and distribution. According to some historians, the major reason that Protestantism came to be associated with capitalism was that it was less hostile than rejuvenated Roman Catholicism to the needs of business.

As in other aspects of life, the Protestant assault on tradition, which varied widely from confession to confession, helped open the path to innovations that the reformers themselves did not intend or necessarily promote. The immediate sequel to the Reformation, however, was not the immediate blossoming of the modern world but rather a series of crises that challenged the very bases of Western civilization.

Selected Readings

*Bainton, Roland. *Here I Stand: A Life of Martin Luther.* Nashville: Abingdom Press, 1950.

   A leading critical but sympathetic biography with excellent bibliography. Unlike many biographies of Luther, it includes details of his later life.

*———. *The Travail of Religious Liberty.* New York: Harper & Row, Publishers, 1951.

   A series of biographical sketches treating victims and practitioners, Catholic and Protestant, of religious persecution. In effect it presents the Reformation as a highly intolerant age.

Brandi, Karl. *The Emperor Charles V.* London: Jonathan Cape, 1954.

   A lengthy standard political biography concerned mainly with Charles's government of the Holy Roman Empire.

Breen, Quirinus. *John Calvin: A Study in French Humanism.* 2d ed. Hamden, Conn.: Archon Books, 1968.

   An excellent study of Calvin's humanist background and the basis of his break with the humanists. It provides references to other biographies of Calvin and their points of view.

*Burns, Edward McNall. *The Counter-Reformation.* New York: Van Nostrand Reinhold Company, 1964.

   A recent short, critical account with major documents in an appendix.

Butterfield, Herbert. *The Whig Interpretation of History.* London: G. Bell & Sons, 1931.

   A devastating critique of nineteenth-century liberal-national history, which rebuts popular Protestant interpretations of the Reformation.

*Chadwick, Owen. *The Reformation.* Baltimore, Md.: Penguin Books, 1964.

   An excellent nonpartisan survey concentrating on religious developments; especially good for the Reformation's impact on the clergy as a social class.

*Dickens, A. G. *The Counter Reformation.* London: Thames & Hudson, 1968.

    A sympathetic account of the Catholic Reformation that finds saints among its mystics. Lucid and superbly illustrated, it exaggerates the cultural unity of a Europe confessionally divided.

―――. *Thomas Cromwell and the English Reformation.* London: English Universities Press, 1959.

    A political biography of the leading lay architect of the English Reformation.

*Elton, Geoffrey R. *Reformation Europe. 1517–1559.* New York: World Publishing Co., Meridian Books, 1964.

    One of the author's many works on the Reformation, emphasizing the role of politics in determining its outcome.

Evenett, H. Outram. *The Spirit of the Counter-Reformation.* Cambridge: Cambridge University Press, 1968.

    A series of sympathetic, insight-filled lectures that capture what was new and distinctive in the piety of the Catholic Reformation.

Franklin, Julian H. *Jean Bodin and the Sixteenth-Century Revolution in the Methodology of Law and History.* New York: Columbia University Press, 1963.

    This traces French humanist origins of new comparative and empirical methods in sixteenth-century studies of society. It is basic for understanding differences between humanist and religious approaches to society and politics.

Gelder, Herman Arend Enno van. *The Two Reformations of the 16th Century.* The Hague: Martinus Nijhoff, 1961.

    A development of the controversial thesis that the major reformation of the sixteenth century was not Protestant but humanist.

Grimm, Harold J. *The Reformation Era: 1500–1650.* 2d ed. New York: The Macmillan Co., 1965.

    A factual, standard textbook treating all aspects of the period.

Hillerbrand, Hans J., ed. *The Reformation: a Narrative History Related by Contemporary Observers and Participants.* New York: Harper & Row, Publishers, 1964.

    A collection of vivid sources related to major personalities and events.

Holborn, Hajo. *A History of Modern Germany.* Vol. 1, *The Reformation.* New York: Alfred A. Knopf, 1959.

    A definitive political, cultural, and religious history of Germany from about 1500 to 1648.

Hughes, Philip. *A Popular History of the Reformation.* Garden City, N.Y.: Doubleday & Co., 1960.

    A balanced summary by a Roman Catholic authority on the English Reformation.

Janelle, Pierre. *The Catholic Reformation.* Milwaukee: Bruce Publishing Co., 1949.

    A Catholic version that treats the Catholic Reformation as a spontaneous movement and omits reference to the Inquisition.

Jedin, Hubert. *A History of the Council of Trent.* 2 vols. St. Louis: B. Herder Book Co., 1957–61.

> *An exhaustive account of the Church councils of the Renaissance and Reformation by a German Catholic scholar. These volumes reach only the first session at Trent.*

Kidd, B. J. *The Counter-Reformation: 1550–1600.* London: Society for Promoting Christian Knowledge, 1958.

> *Emphatically Protestant, this reverses the interpretation of Janelle.*

*McNeil, John T. *The History and Character of Calvinism.* New York: Oxford University Press, 1957.

> *This sympathetically and comprehensively relates the origins, nature, and spread of Calvinism.*

*Mosse, George L. *The Reformation.* New York: Holt, Rinehart & Winston, 1953.

> *A short, balanced account of the entire Reformation; excellent as an introduction.*

Nelson, Benjamin N. *Idea of Usury.* Princeton, N.J.: Princeton University Press, 1949.

> *This restates the Weber-Tawney thesis for Calvinism by investigating the psychological background of prohibiting usury and provides rare detail on the anticapitalistic attitudes of the early German Reformation.*

Philips, Margaret Mann. *Erasmus and the Northern Renaissance.* London: Hodder and Stoughton, 1949.

> *This study presents Erasmus as the formulator of an independent religious and secular reform movement. Publication of Erasmus's later correspondence has forced modification of this interpretation—at least of the older Erasmus. (See Bainton listing in previous chapter.)*

*Ridley, Jasper. *Thomas Cranmer.* New York: Oxford University Press, 1962.

> *A definitive biography of the leading cleric of the English Reformation which finds his consistency in belief in the divine right of kings.*

Ritter, Gerhard. *Luther, His Life and Work.* New York: Harper & Row, Publishers, 1963.

> *This treats Luther in the role of a prophet of the Germans, breaking the bonds of medieval piety but not as a man who wished to secularize the world in any way.*

*Rupp, Gordon. *Luther's Progress to the Diet of Worms.* New York: Harper & Row, Publishers, 1964.

> *An appreciative sketch by a prominent English scholar on Luther.*

Schapiro, Jacob S. "Social Reform and the Reformation," Ph. D. dissertation, Columbia University, 1909.

> *The only collection in English of documents on the German Peasants' Revolt; it includes penetrating commentaries that find the origins of liberalism within the revolt rather than among the reformers.*

Tavard, Georges H. *Holy Writ or Holy Church: the Crisis of the Protestant Reformation.* New York: Harper & Row, Publishers, 1960.
> *A description of the differing bases of authority used by sixteenth-century Catholics and Protestants, tracing the origins of the latter.*

*Tawney, Richard H. *Religion and the Rise of Capitalism.* New York: New American Library, 1950. *Weber, Max. *The Protestant Ethic and the Spirit of Capitalism.* New York: Charles Scribner's Sons, 1958.
> *Both advance the classic thesis—in vulnerable form—that Protestants, especially Calvinists and sectarians, stimulated capitalism by fostering ascetic renunciation of luxury and dedication to secular work.*

Trevor-Roper, H. R. *Religion, the Reformation, and Social Change.* New York: Harper & Row, Publishers, 1968.
> *Two of these essays, one on witchcraft and one on the rise of capitalism, concern this chapter. The author provides the best rejoinder to Weber and Tawney thus far.*

Williams, George Hunston. *The Radical Reformation.* Philadelphia: The Westminster Press, 1962.
> *This makes heavy use of recently published documents on the Anabaptists and other sectarians to reevaluate the defamed radicals of the Reformation. Heavily theological in tone.*

Asterisk (*) denotes paperback.

CHAPTER XIV
The Century of Crises: 1560–1660

Facing new realities with old ideas, Europeans passed through a century of terrible crises from 1560 to 1660. It was not a simple matter for them to adjust to the new religious and political pluralism, the recent intellectual, spiritual, and social upheavals, and the enormous new geographical world. Their traditions and experiences had not taught them how to cope with ideological ferment on such a colossal scale, or how to form a new conception of the world that shattered their familiar biblical view of three continents inhabited by the three races of men, descendants of Shem, Ham, and Japheth. Europeans became global men for the first time, and immediately projected their internal conflicts on a world stage. As population growth outstripped subsistence at home, they fought for such of the world's wealth as could be fed into the engines of war to give an advantage to one side or another. Seething with religious hatreds, Europeans fought one bloody ideological war after another among themselves until they were forced by sheer exhaustion, after the Thirty Years' War (1618–48), to try to reorganize their civilization as a family of coexisting nations.

A. Empires and Mercantilism

EUROPE'S TERRITORIAL EXPANSION

From the time of the Crusades Europeans had been expanding territorially, but in the late Renaissance that expansion entered a new phase: states along the Atlantic seaboard had extended and consolidated their economic and political influences on overseas territories. Looking at developments from a worldwide perspective, we see that western Europe was rapidly emerging as the most dynamic and powerful area in the world. Not many people directly participated in this expansion, and only a few of these people appreciated its implications. Nevertheless, vast numbers of European villagers and townspeople were significantly affected in their economic and political life by the activities of merchants, seamen, officials, and intellectuals.

Why should European expansion have entered such a dazzling phase in the sixteenth century? The answer is partly that European technology and institutions were more advanced than those in other parts of the world. With superior arms and ships and with advanced knowledge of navigation and naval warfare, western Europeans could control the seas: their fleets could strike coastal targets at will and could retreat in relative safety; with this advantage they could dominate commerce. Where they were forced to strike out far beyond the range of their ships, their command was less sure. Their conquests on land often failed to equal their prowess on the sea. Still, Europeans did wrest vast territories from "less civilized" peoples who could not combat Western organization and technology. Strong, highly structured societies in Asia effectively barred European penetration, and climate and disease repulsed Western moves into the interior of Africa. On the African coast, however, the European triumphed, forcing the populations into slavery. In the New World he triumphed again, even more impressively, for the Indian had neither iron weapons, nor horses, nor extensive political organization. From him the European could take an entire virgin continent.

People from Europe seized control of the New World by more than sheer force of arms. Powerful commercial companies, officially backed by home governments, sold cheaply produced wares to primitive peoples who had almost no concept of economic organization and whose craving to acquire fascinating but economically useless gadgets like mirrors and equally fascinating but not so harmless products like alcohol hastened their subjection. Even more devastating were the white man's diseases such as smallpox or measles, which wracked many colonial peoples and destroyed their power to resist.

It seems, too, that European civilization had developed within it a strong drive for dominance. With conquerors and traders came missionaries to propagate the faith and education. Already convinced that they were sent by divine providence to subjugate and convert God's enemies, the Europeans saw in the natives' acceptance of Christianity certain proof that Western expansion had divine sanction. Missionaries like Bartolomé de Las Casas (1474–1566) had more humanitarian ideas, but all in all, the more advanced European societies were convinced of their superior right to dominate the globe.

Nevertheless, cultural exchange between Europe and the outside world was reciprocal. To the dependent populations of the New World, Europeans brought animals, crops, technology, learning, social and political institutions, the printing press, and religion. From overseas they gained wealth and adopted new products, some of which eventually had a profound impact on Europe. Spices, tea, chocolate, and tobacco became common consumption items even though they lacked the medicinal qualities claimed for them by their early promoters. The potato was a gift from the New World, and American plantations soon became the primary source of sugar. The consumption of both of these foods would increase over the centuries until they became vital to Europeans' survival. The New World also opened new horizons of experience: contact with other civilizations slowly eroded European parochialism and reinforced the idea that men could live in a state of nature under natural law without the sanctions of supernatural religion. However, before 1660 beliefs like these were confined to narrow intellectual circles.

Confrontation of Europeans and Indians in Mexico.

Portugal's Commercial Empire

At the end of the fifteenth century the kingdoms along the Atlantic seaboard were beginning to build worldwide empires. They had at their disposal the skills, knowledge, and financial resources of the Italians who had built Mediterranean empires during the High Middle Ages and the Renaissance. The first Atlantic explorations that led to durable overseas empires were made by the Portuguese. With a long history as a seafaring people, they ventured into Africa in the course of waging war against the Moors; once there, they established important trading contacts.

From 1418 until his death in 1460 Prince Henry ("the Navigator") sent out an expedition almost yearly. His policy plunged the royal family heavily into debt, but it also created for the Portuguese kingdom the most advanced geographical knowledge and the best navigational equipment of the times. At first Portuguese sailors sought to explore the western coast of Africa. Later, spurred on by reports of lucrative trade opportunities in India, Henry sent navigators to find a route eastward around Africa. The famous voyage of Vasco da Gama at the very end of the century proved that it was profitable as well as possible to trade with India by sea. With their new route to the East the Portuguese outflanked the Ottoman Turks who, by their monopolies and tolls, had until then frustrated Venetian trade with the Orient. In 1509 a Portuguese fleet defeated an Arabic and Egyptian fleet off Diu on the west coast of India, putting Portugal in a position to monopolize the spice trade with Europe. From Goa, their

A. Empires and Mercantilism

base in India, the Portuguese flung out a series of trading stations: Java and Sumatra (1511), the Moluccas (1512), Formosa (1542), Japan, and later Macao on the coast of China. The Portuguese empire in the Far East was strictly commercial; the only Portuguese who went to the colonies were traders rather than settlers. Spices were the main commodity of the empire, but the Portuguese did not even market the spices in Europe; rather they turned that business over to an Antwerp monopoly. In the vast Portuguese empire only Brazil—which was of little economic significance before the establishment of sugar plantations using African slaves—was to become a major colonial settlement to which the Portuguese emigrated in considerable numbers.

Spain's Bid for Colonial Wealth

Portuguese supremacy did not go long unchallenged. Da Gama had no sooner preempted the route around Africa than Castilian venturers embarked on their own imperial search. The voyage of the Genoese captain Christopher Columbus in 1492 was Spain's first bid in the overseas competion. Columbus, as everyone knows, was sailing west in the hope of finding a direct trade route to the Far East (hence, the name West Indies for the islands lying off the coast of the New World). The Spanish were still effectively cut off from the profitable Eastern trade, but the gold and silver they found in South America was compensation.

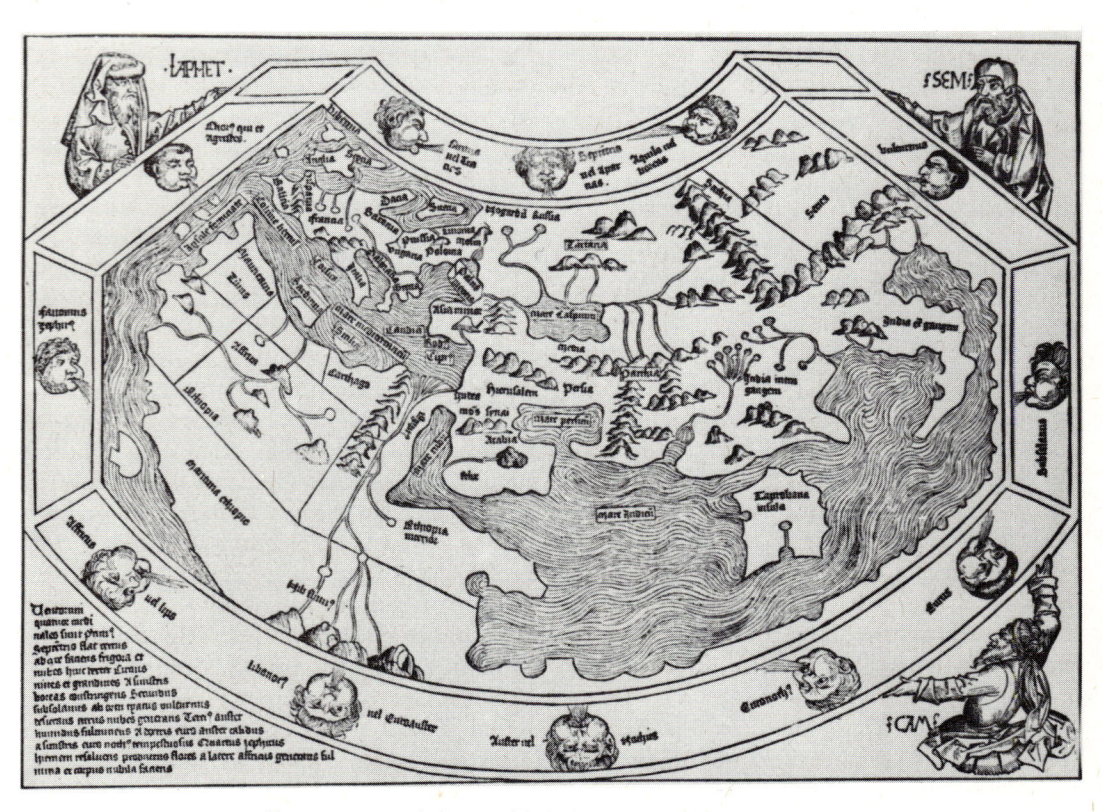

German map of the world, 1493.

664   *The Century of Crises: 1560–1660*

World map of 1529, reflecting the age of discovery.

Spanish conquerors and explorers fanned out from the West Indies to subjugate Aztec, Inca, and Central American Indians. The gold and, particularly, the silver mines yielded phenomenal wealth. In 1545 the richest mine of all, the Potosí mine in Peru, was brought into production; in 1600 precious metals constituted 90 percent of all European imports from Spanish America. Meanwhile Magellan's voyage around South America in 1519 had opened a route to the Far East, but the Pacific crossing was so hazardous that, except for trade with the western coast of South America, the new route was of little commercial value. Content to rule the Philippines (first settled in the reign of Philip II) indirectly through Mexico, the Habsburgs left the Portuguese commercial monopoly in the Far East undisturbed.

The Spanish tried, but largely failed, to transplant their institutions to American soil. By the end of the sixteenth century their New World colonies were in serious decline. Fortune-hunting noblemen were superb conquerors but inept administrators. When the rulers of Spain replaced Columbus, Pizzaro, Cortes, and other conquistadores with their own appointees, New World affairs passed into the hands of men who were seldom capable and usually uninterested. These royal appointees, who often bought their offices, made many mistakes. Castilians tried to harness Indian labor, but the natives died so rapidly from European diseases, such as smallpox, that by 1600 their population had dwindled from an estimated 11 million to 2 million. African slaves were imported, but they too were subject to disease. After 1576 the history of the Spanish Empire is a history of economic depression and the breakdown of order. Colonial officials lost control over the hinterlands of the empire to cattlemen on the continent and buccaneers on the islands who defied their authority. The buccaneers were particularly lawless: by selling provisions to foreign interlopers they undermined Spain's monopoly of commerce. By the early seventeenth century, when the flow of gold and silver from the colonies became a trickle, Europe began to feel the decline of Spain's empire in America.

A. Empires and Mercantilism

Empire Building by Northern Europeans

Meanwhile English and French explorers staked out claims to North America (Cabot for England, 1497–98, and Verrazano—also Italian—for France in 1524). They found scant riches, established no permanent colonies, and failed to find a new commercial route to the Far East. In the 1550s, however, Englishmen did succeed in opening Russia to western trade by sailing around Norway. In the same century the English also began to encroach on Spain's colonial trade—especially the profitable slave trade—eventually bringing on a prolonged Anglo-Spanish conflict. Throughout most of this century France was too occupied with civil wars to develop her imperialism; for both England and France the establishment of empires in the New World awaited the dawn of the seventeenth century.

At first the Dutch were far more successful empire builders than the English and the French. Like the Italians, they already had solid experience in fishing, shipping, banking, and manufacturing. When Phillip II of Spain acquired the poorly defended Portuguese empire in 1580, the Dutch (having revolted against the Habsburgs in 1566) were still at war with Spain. Soon they sought to establish a direct link with the Far East. By organizing the East India stock company they eliminated competition among themselves and, in the first years of the seventeenth century, outbid Portuguese merchants in the East Indies, Formosa, and Japan. Like the Portuguese before them, the Dutch monopolists carefully controlled supplies for the European spice market. They also dealt in silk, chinaware, sugar, coffee, tea, cocoa, precious metals, Japanese copper, and Indian cloth. Even more lucrative was the local Far Eastern carrying trade, which shipped cargoes from India around Malaya and the East Indies to Japan. East India Company officials like Jan Pieterszoon Coen ruthlessly eliminated native competitors and maintained an exclusive preserve closed to all other European shippers. The Eastern trade lured fortune hunters not only because it yielded a high return on investment but also because company employees could smuggle private cargoes of such prized commodities as opium and slaves. For a while Batavia (in what is now Indonesia) was the most profitable post in the Dutch commercial chain; but during the Thirty Years' War its richness was rivaled by trade centers in Persia, especially those that supplied Europe with silver. Australia, which was discovered by the East India Company in 1627, was a commercial disappointment.

By displacing the Portuguese in the Far East the Dutch accomplished considerably more than they did in competing with rivals in the Atlantic. The West India Company, for example, fell short of its primary objective, the seizure of Brazil. But, by searching for northwestern and northeastern passages to India, the Dutch added to man's store of knowledge about geography. In the course of their search they also secured a place for themselves in the Russian trade and founded a fur-trading settlement colony on the Hudson River.

Closer to home the Dutch were immensely successful. They displaced the Hanseatic League in the carrying trade from the Baltic Sea, and on the Mediterranean they dislodged the Italians. Still, overseas trade made only a small contribution to the general prosperity of the Netherlands, which depended on local trade in fish, Baltic grains, salt, Scandinavian timber, and French wine. Thriving Dutch commerce benefited from adopting advanced techniques in industry, finance, and technology. Especially rewarding was the development of an unarmed sailing ship called the flute (*fluit*) that required few men and offered little resistance to wind and water. By the end of the sixteenth century the Dutch merchant marine had an estimated 10,000 ships.

Sweden prospered from Dutch Baltic trade—the great Swedish export was naval stores—and participated for a brief time in the quest for overseas empire. Russia was a more persistent expansionist once her isolation was broken by contact with English and Dutch traders. From her contacts with the West she appropriated a technology for successful military expansion into Poland and Sweden. At the same time a major market for her furs opened in Europe. The Stroganov family built an enormous fortune from a fur company that sent Cossack trappers across Siberia, established villages, and opened mines.

Russia's eastern expansion produced no rivalry with the major imperial powers, but the other northern peoples' entry into the quest for colonies and overseas wealth intensified Europe's struggles for hegemony of power. These struggles continued to be primarily dynastic and religious, but economic warfare for commercial advantages was beginning to play an increasingly important role in them.

THE COURSE OF ECONOMIC CHANGE

The establishment of empires overseas was only one facet of Europe's radically changing economic shape in the sixteenth century; the astonishing growth in volume, variety, and value of its long-distance trade was another. Also, the centers of commerce were shifting, for states along the Atlantic seaboard now held the economic initiative and were speedily gaining control. The fruits of European economic expansion were, however, unevenly divided. Once the merchant fleets of Italy had been the greatest in Europe; now they were unable to compete on the high seas. Italians continued to engage in trade in the Mediterranean and on the coast, but by the 1550s it was clear that profits from the sea would go mainly to the Atlantic states. Spain and Portugal were in the ascendancy in the sixteenth century, but at the same time Antwerp and Lyons were beginning to rival the Italian city-states as centers of banking and exchange. Although bullion flowed directly to Spain and Portugal from the New World at first, the profits of imperial trade were ultimately reaped by others, notably the Dutch, English, and French. Near the end of the sixteenth century Antwerp and Lyons were crippled by religious and civil wars. After 1600, Amsterdam stood as the greatest commercial *entrepôt* of the Western world.

To characterize the century between 1560 and 1660 as an era only of expanding commercial wealth and capitalism is to oversimplify. As with most generalizations, the student of history must acknowledge important exceptions. First, eastern and southern Europe did not participate in this expansion. Italy, which had led the rest of Europe in industrial, agricultural, and financial techniques during the Renaissance, actually experienced a serious decline throughout this period. Capital flowed westward out of Italy, and in Italy itself investment was siphoned out of industry and commerce and diverted to baroque art and architecture, a spendthrift style of life in the courts of the aristocracy, and unprofitable—even wasteful—loans to the Habsburgs. Second, even in the maritime states—England and the Netherlands—commerce apparently entered a long period of general stagnation or decline during the Thirty Years' War, the effects of which were particularly severe in Germany. There the prosperity of commercial towns was throttled and technological innovation decreased. In eastern Europe the devastations of war served to bolster aristocratic domination of overwhelmingly agrarian societies. Eastern European social patterns became rigid, and the populations consisted almost ex-

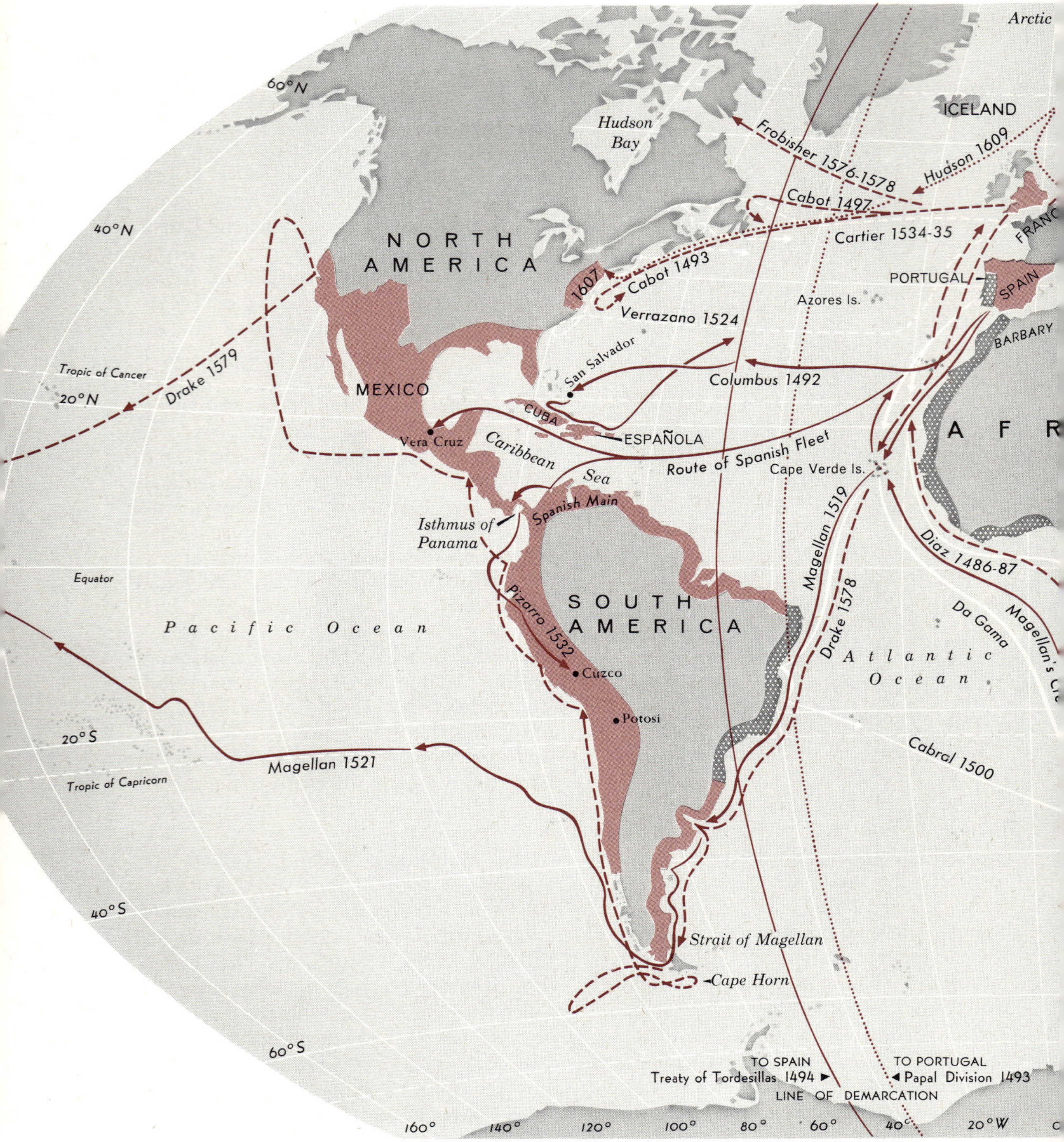

Arctic
60°N
Hudson Bay
ICELAND
Frobisher 1576-1578
Hudson 1609
Cabot 1497
40°N
NORTH AMERICA
Cartier 1534-35
1607
Cabot 1493
PORTUGAL
SPAIN
Verrazano 1524
Azores Is.
BARBARY
San Salvador
Tropic of Cancer
Drake 1579
Columbus 1492
20°N
MEXICO
CUBA
ESPAÑOLA
Vera Cruz
Caribbean Sea
Route of Spanish Fleet
Cape Verde Is.
Isthmus of Panama
Spanish Main
Magellan 1519
Diaz 1486-87
Equator
SOUTH AMERICA
Pizarro 1532
Drake 1578
Da Gama
Pacific Ocean
Atlantic Ocean
Cuzco
Potosi
20°S
Cabral 1500
Magellan 1521
Tropic of Capricorn
40°S
Strait of Magellan
Cape Horn
60°S
TO SPAIN
Treaty of Tordesillas 1494
TO PORTUGAL
Papal Division 1493
LINE OF DEMARCATION
160°
140°
120°
100°
80°
60°
40°
20°W

EXPLORATIONS
AND COLONIAL EMPIRES ca. 1450–ca. 1600

- Spanish
- Portuguese
- English
- Dutch
- French
- Russian

Map by J. Donovan

669   A. Empires and Mercantilism

clusively of lords and serfs. Lastly, we must recognize that the mere fact of commercial expansion in the maritime states did not assure the general prosperity of their populations. More and more men were becoming rich, but at the same time population increase mainly added to the number of the poor, who were particularly vulnerable to the effects of commercial crises, inflation, and famine. For all except the most favored peoples and classes this century was an era of stark scarcity. To provide for subsistence, trading opportunities, social stability, and military strength most territorial governments extended their regulation of economic activity.

Commercial Capitalism in the Netherlands and England

Italian merchants had been the first to develop techniques by which capital resources could be pooled and used to underwrite large-scale commercial ventures. During the sixteenth century merchants in the Dutch Netherlands and England adopted these techniques and improved on them. Banking institutions were particularly important, since it was through them that capital savings could be mobilized, foreign exchange provided, private loans negotiated, and notes issued. The Bank of Amsterdam, founded in 1609, rapidly became the model for banks in Sweden, Hamburg, and eventually, London. As the flow of money was organized and capital grew more plentiful, interest rates were lowered and also became stable. During the Middle Ages financial activities had been carried on at fairs; now they were replaced by the *bourses*, which were at once money markets and commodity exchanges. Here goods, public debts, and land—in the form of mortgages—would be represented by documents—pieces of paper that could circulate and become objects of speculation; in short, they could be treated like coinage. People of various classes rushed to put their savings into commercial ventures, and the hope of easy profit often drove men into manias of speculation. In the Netherlands between 1633 and 1637 tulip bulbs were the object of market speculation. Rather than cultivate the exotic oriental import, people invested huge sums in the bulb market. Before the inevitable bursting of the bubble, the craze had engulfed large numbers of both rich and poor. This was, however, an unusual instance. Investments in insurance—of cargoes, of lives, and against fire—were much more reliable.

One of the most significant commercial innovations during this period was the development of the joint-stock company, a method of conducting trade in which Dutch and English merchants soon excelled. The joint-stock company was an outgrowth of the regulated company, a trading organization that had devolved from the Middle Ages. The regulated company was a group of merchants who were usually granted a monopoly of trade in a specific area under a charter. The men who directed the company made arrangements for transportation and shipment, established rules of competition, and decided what the destination of cargoes would be. Within this loose framework the individual traders who were members of the company operated entirely on their own. During the sixteenth century the regulated company was the common means of overseas trade. The Merchant Adventurers, an old English company that sold unfinished cloth to the Low Countries, is a good example of a regulated company; the Muscovy Company, founded in 1554, the Eastland Company (1579), and the Levant Company (1581) are others. Out of the regulated company developed a more centralized business enterprise, the joint-stock company. Particularly well suited to enterprises that required heavy capital, the joint-stock company appeared first in mining. The investors in the joint-stock company did not participate as traders; rather they used their money to purchase shares in the company and, by virtue of their status as shareholders, elected directors who were responsible for managing paid company employees. The joint-stock company bore more resemblance to the corporation as we know it today than to the old regulated companies: shares could be converted to cash, and the death of a shareholder in no way disrupted the company's operations or affected its continuity as would death in a partnership. Naturally, the earliest joint-stock companies were rather crudely organized. At first, the capital invested as well as the profits realized on each specific venture were distributed among shareholders after each undertaking. The idea of continuity took a while to develop, but by 1660 managers of both great pioneer joint-stock ventures (the Dutch and English East India Companies, founded at the beginning of the seventeenth century) were controlling permanent aggregations of capital.

Joint-stock trading companies were often chartered with great powers to wage aggressive economic warfare for the expansion of trade. Grants of monopoly concentrated in the hands of company directors all of the state's economic power in specific areas, with the directors receiving legal and political power to exclude all competitors outside the company. Against foreign rivals they were empowered to wage war with their own ships and troops, and frequently they did this despite the fact that their home governments were at peace. Some of these chartered companies, such as the English East India Company, gained immense power in domestic politics and continued to function as colonial governments until the nineteenth century.

The Organization of Production

Local craftsmen following traditional methods continued to supply goods for local markets. But where production for distant markets served by trading companies was concerned—and in some branches of domestic industry as well—significant changes took place in business organization and technology.

Since the late Middle Ages the cloth dealers who met the needs of large markets had sought to employ cheap labor and evade the stringent quality controls imposed by the urban guildmasters. The usual method was to distribute raw materials among suburban and rural laborers who bought or rented their own hand-operated machines, although the word

Domestic carding, spinning, and weaving.

671   A. Empires and Mercantilism

machine is really too modern to apply to these rudimentary devices. After the various steps of production were completed, the entrepreneur (merchant-capitalist) collected the finished cloth and stored it in a *factory* for further shipment or sale. (Thus he was often known as a *factor.*) This method of organizing production revolved about the merchant-capitalist. His main role was to coordinate the various functions of production and distribution, his knowledge of market conditions being crucial for success. The "domestic system," which required that little fixed capital be tied up in productive machinery, allowed merchant-capitalists to adjust output to the demands of rapidly fluctuating markets. As the system was extended during the commercial expansion of the sixteenth century, a large and insecure class of laborers came into existence—men who lived on subsistence wages and who, since their labor could as easily be discarded as purchased, absorbed the shocks and dislocations inevitable in commercial depressions.

Occasionally the entrepreneurial system brought pieces of work together in some finishing process at a single place resembling a modern factory. But centralized production calling for heavy capitalization was required in only a few industries like mining, shipbuilding, cannon founding, and printing. In what we would call "heavy industry" privileged chartered companies or state ownership was common.

Institutional developments—the growth of banks, the rise of new commercial companies, the spread of entrepreneurial middlemen, and the appearance of heavy capitalization in some industries—were signs of an expanding economy. The capital accumulation required for economic growth in the sixteenth and seventeenth centuries has been explained by a variety of factors: profits from urban rents, military spending by governments, expanded markets offered by territorial states, increased commercial profits, and the influx of gold and silver from the New World. No one now ascribes the economic expansion of Europe to any single cause, for conditions varied from country to country and from generation to generation. Although no full-scale "industrial revolution" occurred in any part of Europe, it is now believed that technological innovations contributed significantly to economic growth in certain areas, notably England and the Low Countries.

These innovations included the introduction of hand-operated machines like the knit-stocking frame (invented in England in 1589) and the ribbon loom, which could weave several ribbons at

German mine water-pump linkage of the sixteenth century.

672 The Century of Crises: 1560–1660

once (invented in the Netherlands in 1621). More important in reducing production costs, especially in England, was the substitution of coal for firewood as a source of heat. Coal was inexpensive and readily available, while the scarcity of wood and charcoal made their prices soar. That coal could be used for smelting or transformed into energy was not discovered until the eighteenth century, but long before this, coal as a cheap fuel was exploited in brewing, distilling, sugar refining, glass making, soap making, and the production of salt, gunpowder, and alum. Apart from these developments, however, the most important mechanical means of converting inanimate energy was found in the sailing ship. In the century that we are considering this was so improved as to enable a mere handful of men to manage and direct a force equivalent to the power of many horses. The higher standard of living and the accumulation of wealth for investment in the Netherlands, England, and Sweden were due in no small part to the impressive proportion of the world's shipping fleet that was at the disposal of merchants in those countries.

Despite new developments in commerce and industry, agricultural expansion was still restrained by traditional techniques and the lack of new arable land. Productivity increased in England, in the Netherlands, and in the vicinity of commercial centers. Elsewhere output per acre was limited by the peasants' ignorance how to replenish the fertility of the soil by any means other than letting it lie fallow. Until seed grasses for hay were introduced the scarcity of forage dictated that few cattle could be kept alive over the winter, and in turn the scarcity of cattle meant a shortage of manure for fertilizer. Good weather brought mediocre harvests, and poor weather meant famine, soaring grain prices, starvation, and weakened resistance to disease. Food shortages were general in Italy and Spain. In 1599 and again during the 1630s importation of Baltic grains by Dutch merchants failed to stave off general famines, which were followed by the plague; in other parts of western Europe local famine was endemic. Grain shortages pushed food prices up, accounting for the bulk of consumer expenditures. Famine thus invariably reduced the sale of industrial products and threw workmen in the domestic industries out of work. The combination of war levies, war devastation, and plagues carried by armies produced a similar pattern in theaters of war.

The "Price Revolution"

Famines struck primarily at the lower classes, but a general inflation of prices penetrated all economic developments and cut across all social levels in the period from 1450 to ca. 1650. At first gradual, this acceleration of prices—often called the "price revolution"—was most rapid in western Europe between 1500 and 1600, during which time prices almost doubled. The timing and intensity of the price inflation varied from country to country and from product to product. In some places the price of grain, hay, and wood increased fifteenfold between 1500 and 1650. Generally the prices of industrial goods rose less than the costs of foodstuffs; this meant that the heaviest burden of the change fell on the poor.

Few contemporaries could offer a rational explanation of the inflation. However modern economic historians, working, we must realize, with incomplete and inaccurate data, attribute it to a shortage of products whose supply was inelastic or declining, combined with the influx of precious metals into the economic system. The population increase heightened the demand both for foodstuffs whose supply was limited because of the stagnation in agricultural productivity and for forestry products whose supply was shrinking.

Prices were inevitably driven upward. At the same time, the introduction of precious metals into the economy, first from the mines of central Europe, then from New Spain, doubled and then redoubled the amount of gold and silver in circulation. Because more money was avilable to buy the same amount of goods and services, prices soared.

The inflationary effects of new bullion supplies were further compounded by governments and speculators. Rulers had to cope with rising expenses while the real money value of the taxes they collected decreased. Generally they debased the value of their coinage, a measure that only further increased the money supply. New sources of silver bullion caused an imbalance in the traditional ratios of gold and silver, and this too unsettled monetary exchanges. In a process described by Sir Thomas Gresham (Elizabeth I's agent at the Antwerp exchange), hoarders and speculators gathered up "dear money."* Monetary confusion injured commerce as it disrupted exchanges and allowed informed speculators to reap quick profits.

Inflation affected various social classes in different ways, but in general it operated to reinforce the distinctions among classes. Hardest hit were the landless laborers whose wages lagged far behind prices. In 1630, according to a detailed study, the real wages of English building craftsmen were less than half what they had been in 1450. Some economic historians have concluded that the growing disparity between prices and wages contributed both to the profits of merchants and entrepreneurs and to the accumulation of industrial capital. But this result did not always follow. As usual, inflation benefited debtors and reduced the value of fixed incomes. Many petty nobles (*hidalgos* in Spain, *hobereaux* in France, *Rittern* in western Germany) who were bound by long-term rent contracts with their peasants eventually lost their estates to peasants and townsmen. These newly landless men, together with vagabonds, were ready recruits for mercenary armies. On the other hand, those English gentry who were able to raise their rents often prospered. East of the Elbe River, where local lords exploited their powers over the peasants, serf labor was used to produce market surpluses, but here prosperity was undermined by the wars of the seventeenth century. During the era of inflation the largest fortunes were, on the whole, amassed by merchants, courtiers, officials, lawyers, and commanders of mercenary troops.

State Economic Policies

The course of economic change created new problems for sixteenth- and seventeenth-century governments. Military expenditures were steadily increasing, but inflation depreciated tax revenues. Commercial expansion enriched some states, but for others it represented an unequal competition that only siphoned off their circulating coinage. As the domestic system spread, the class of insecure subsistence workers grew, and their demands threatened to undermine the traditional social order. Population increase and famine contributed to swell the ranks of the unemployed, vagrant poor, and brigands. In their efforts to secure order in society and to maintain the flow of tax revenues into the coffers of the state, early modern governments intervened directly and participated extensively in economic life.

Bullionism is the term often applied to the fiscal expedients and traditional protectionist measures used by governments that tried to keep coinage in circulation by regulating imports, exports, and exchange rates. Above all, it attempted to prevent the export of precious monetary metals like gold and silver. Often this effort led to

---

* A modern dictum has Gresham's law thus: "Bad money drives out good."

attempts to curtail the importation of expensive cloth, such as silk, by restricting its use to the nobility. Usually bullionists upheld the traditional social order by preserving the tax exemptions of the privileged nobility. They also responded to urban complaints about rural competition from domestic workers by instituting restrictive statewide guilds. For revenues kings were expected to support their governments from the royal domains instead of by taxes. To raise money they commonly sold offices, negotiated loans in expectation of future revenues, and granted—or sold—monopolies of such commodities as salt. By this procedure monopolists' profits were in effect shared with court and crown. Despite these measures, income seldom covered expenses. A few rulers—the dukes of Saxony and the Austrian Habsburgs—benefited from locally mined bullion, but no other European kingdoms had significant deposits of gold and silver ores within their own territories. The rest tried to make up for their deficiency of precious metals by legislation protecting their money supply or by gaining an empire.

Castile and Portugal followed bullionist economic policies exploiting their imperial resources and geographical advantages to amass great treasure from colonial mines and trade. But in both kingdoms taxation policies reflected the interests of court, church, and dynastic ambition rather than those of the productive classes. As bullion flowed in from the New World, Spanish prices rose and the kingdom's manufactured goods were priced out of the European markets. Since its wares could not compete at home or abroad, Spanish industry lagged. Thus despite the influx of bullion, Spanish industry did not accumulate capital but fell victim to cheaper imports from abroad. Spanish fiscal difficulties even dealt heavy blows to Italian, German, and Spanish bankers when the government defaulted on loans in 1557, 1575, 1607, 1627, 1647, and 1653.

Eventually the Iberian kingdoms saw their bullion and trade absorbed by other countries, and they finally came to depend on goods imported by Dutch merchants. Since bullionism failed in the Iberian kingdoms, it was discredited as a policy that could achieve self-sufficiency or economic growth. Its most resounding success—the discovery and import of precious metals from the New World—seemed to produce more problems than it solved.

In contrast to continental monarchies where royal officials set fiscal policies and supervised economic activities, Dutch policy was largely formulated and executed by a group of men who formed a merchant oligarchy. Merchants sought and obtained governmental assistance, yet they were subject to a minimum of restrictions on commerce and production. Provincial governments negotiated agreements that opened new markets, preserved old ones, and kept the North Sea open to their ships. Dutch mercantile interest groups, who preferred peace to war and naval warfare to war on land, secured monopoly trading charters and naval protection from the government. When war increased the power of the House of Orange supported by Dutch Calvinists who advocated war on land, the States-General banned trade with Spain and required that merchant ships be armed; but in practice merchants usually ignored such laws. They continued to profit from trade with the enemy. Since the Dutch Republic (the United Provinces)* depended on imported foodstuffs and raw materials, these goods were admitted duty-free, and the export of monetary metals was allowed as a normal part of trade. Thus Dutch mercantile policy and practice deviated significantly from the

---

* Comprising the seven northern provinces of the Burgundian inheritance, the United Provinces, or Dutch Republic, gained independence under a confederated government, the States General, in a revolt from Spain. See pp. 683–87.

A. *Empires and Mercantilism*

Dutch warships of the seventeenth century.

bullionism of its foes, and it prospered.

Instead of encouraging freer trade elsewhere, Dutch commercial dominance only provoked protectionist measures on the part of other states. On the Continent these measures were in most cases traditionalist, bullionist, and defensive. England and France, however, responded with policies that favored native merchants, native producers, and new industries over foreign competitors. The term mercantilism is the general label applied to the policies that aimed to gain power abroad and thus expand wealth at home. Mercantilists continued the bullionists' emphasis on protectionism but went much further in attempting to achieve self-sufficiency and a favorable balance of trade by stimulating native manufactures that would employ the poor, provide a surplus of foreign exchange, and provide tax revenues.

During Elizabeth I's reign, English trade contracted. There were periodic depressions that caused unemployment and food riots, to which the government responded by reforming the coinage and granting charters to new monopoly companies that proposed to exploit new markets. By such regulations as the Statute of Artificers (1563) the growth of the domestic system was checked, while such measures as the Poor Law (1601) represented an effort to provide relief and employment for the indigent and hungry who seemed to be growing more numerous. Elizabeth's leading counselor, Lord Burghley, encouraged English industry: patents were granted for new industries, searches for mineral deposits were sponsored, skilled artisans were imported from the Continent, and the production of gunpowder and naval stores was fostered.

After 1620 serious commercial depressions affected England's traditional export product—woolen cloth. These crises played a part in the formulation of mercantilist economic principles, which were expounded in such treatises as the *Discourse on England's Treasure by Forraigne*

Trade by Thomas Mun, a director of the East India Company. The Stuart governments tried to counter the depressions with relief measures; they also pressed commercial companies to buy up domestic cloth production so that employment would be maintained, but this policy did not succeed. In addition they continued to protect English markets and shipping against foreign competition and embarked on a program to expand the navy. Gradually English commerce and production adjusted as Englishmen learned to adopt new products for new markets. The process was facilitated because both the justices of the peace and the central government neglected to enforce traditional industrial regulations.

As the enforcement of domestic regulations grew lax, England was slowly establishing an empire in North America and the West Indies. In 1651 the empire was brought under a comprehensive navigation act that was designed to exclude Dutch competition. By 1660 a strengthened and expanding English fleet was engaged in a series of commercial wars with the Dutch.

French governments at the end of the sixteenth century and at the beginning of the seventeenth century also sponsored new industries and sought to protect native merchants from foreign competition. But the industrial regulations designed to maintain uniform standards of quality grew more and more rigid, and French economic policy, compared with that of England and the Dutch Republic was more explicitly directed to fill war treasuries. French officials could also exercise more initiative because they had direct authority from the crown and because French merchants were timid in taking the initiative in forming new companies. French entrepreneuers continued to be inhibited by social traditions stigmatizing commerce as less noble than investment in land, titles, offices, and state loans.

Economic policies, which varied from state to state, all shared certain fundamental assumptions that constituted the core of "mercantilist" thought. Mercantilists took it for granted that state intervention was necessary to secure prosperity and power, which they believed went hand in glove. They lived in an age of scarcity and thus readily assumed that the world's wealth was relatively static and that one state's gain was another's loss. Hence even in those states where merchant prosperity was identified with the general welfare, a powerful state—or at least a powerful navy—was considered indispensable to maintain and extend prosperity, for mercantilists considered power to be the source of plenty. Nevertheless in the continental monarchies state intervention during this period served to preserve the traditional framework of society more often than it advanced commerce and industry. The kind of mercantilism practiced in the continental monarchies often hewed to traditional bullionist regulations; their rulers did not yet subscribe to Thomas Mun's belief that expanding exports even with the export of bullion was the surest way to national prosperity.

B. Spain and the Religious Wars

THE DOMINANCE OF THE SPANISH HABSBURGS

Warfare lay at the heart of the crises of the century between 1560 and 1660. Commercial rivalry inspired few wars; the conflicts that wracked Europe were more often generated by issues of politics and religion. Religious hatreds fed international as well as dynastic civil strife, breeding militant ideologies whose zeal often overrode rational considerations of life, prosperity, and property. Almost all factional leaders were belligerent, but Philip of Spain wielded the preponderant power. He identified his own dynastic ambitions with God's will that all Europe be restored to Roman Catholicism, preferably under Spanish control.

Philip II's father, Emperor Charles V, had bequeathed to him a vast but scattered empire: the Spanish kingdoms, territory in Italy, the Low Countries, the so-called Free County of Burgundy, Spain's possessions in Central and South America, the West Indies, and a claim to the Philippine Islands. By 1560 French resistance to Habsburg dominance in Italy and the Low Countries had waned. The treaty of Cateau-Cambrésis of 1559 terminated a long series of wars and in effect ratified Philip's European hegemony. But his ambitions exceeded his far-flung empire. He wed Mary Tudor in order to bring England into the Catholic Habsburg orbit, but Mary failed to produce a male heir. Following Mary's death he courted Elizabeth Tudor—and suffered a further marital-diplomatic fiasco. Finally he married another Elizabeth, the daughter of the king of France. This connection with the house of Valois in 1559 gave him the opportunity of actively intervening in French affairs. But not until his fourth and last marriage, this time to his Habsburg cousin, Anne of Austria, did Philip succeed in begetting an heir to the throne (Philip III).* This marriage alliance also paved the way for renewed political cooperation with the Austrian branch of the Habsburg family.

In 1580 Philip came closest to satisfying his hunger for empire when he succeeded to the Portuguese throne. The childless king of Portugal had been killed while fighting the Moors in Africa, and, assisted by Castilian noblemen, Philip was able to make good his claim to the throne. He swore to maintain the Portuguese constitution and promised that the country would not be administered by Castile; the Portuguese were to govern themselves and to continue the direction of their commercial empire. But while Philip was technically only an administrator, the territories he "administered"— the Azores, the Canaries, the Madeiras, Cape Verde, posts on the eastern and western African coasts, and trading stations in Sumatra, Java, Ceylon, Burma, China, and Japan—comprised the second greatest world empire in the sixteenth century.

---

* Don Carlos, his son by his first wife (who was Portuguese), was demented. Philip kept him in confinement where he died under mysterious circumstances in 1568.

Bust of Philip II.

The Government of Philip II

Dynastic tradition legitimized Philip's enlargement of his empire; to maintain it he had the most powerful military machine in Europe; but the practical problems of ruling such extensive lands eventually overwhelmed him. He was unable to maintain communication with his far-flung outposts, and he could hardly pursue policies that served the conflicting interests of all his subjects.

Only in the kingdom of Castile and in the Castilian empire did Philip have an efficient bureaucracy that had the power to impose his will. Outside Castile he ruled through his viceroys and regents, who were obliged to bend to local customs and

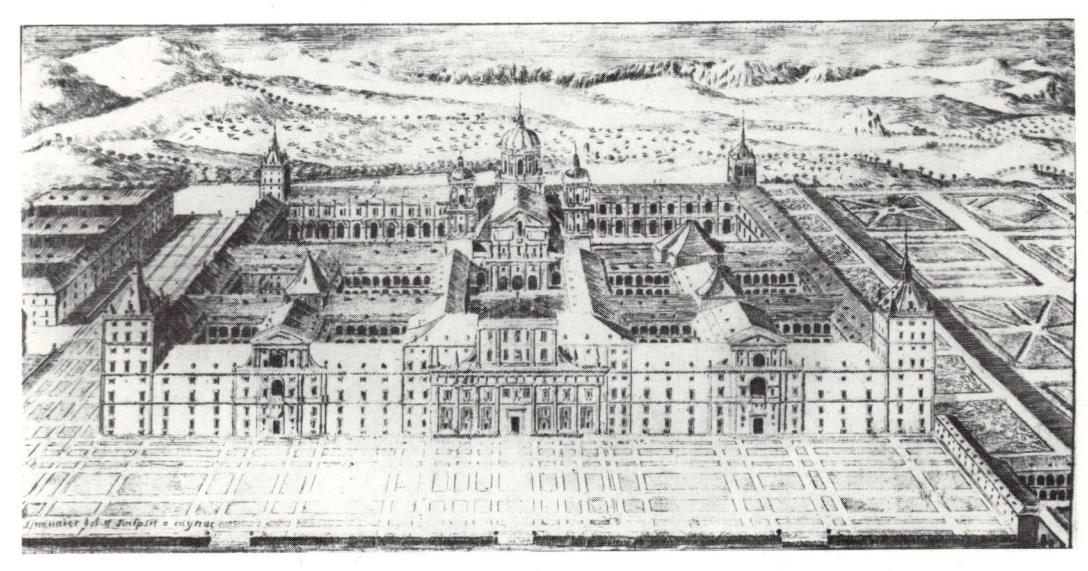

El Escorial.

representative assemblies. The Iberian kingdoms in no sense constituted a national "Spanish" state, for in neighboring Aragon Castilians were looked on as foreigners, just as they were in Portugal or in the Low Countries. Philip's empire was a federation of provinces and kingdoms united only by his person. In most of them a separate royal council sat in the capital, but no single council—not even the Supreme Tribunal of the Spanish Inquisition—was capable of exerting authority throughout the king's possessions.

In Castile various royal councils held nominal and legal jurisdiction over colonial trade (a Castilian monopoly), military matters, and other areas of government. The only link and coordination among them was the king, who directed their operations through his powerful royal secretaries. The secretaries dispensed patronage (as they had done under Charles V) and wielded more influence in formulating state policy than the council members. But real control of Castilian policy remained in Philip's hands.

Although suffering from gout and asthma, he was a dedicated and hard-working administrator. Often behaving more like a bureaucrat than a ruler, he applied a phenomenal memory to the minutest details of administrative and military affairs. From his permanent capital in Madrid he exercised close personal control, keeping court factions in check by arbitrary rule whenever he felt his power threatened. He used the magnificent Escorial Palace near the city only as a summer residence and to house dignitaries whom he summoned to court.

Philip had been educated by a bishop and was deeply devout. He placed full confidence in his confessors and theologians, all of whom were advocates of absolute monarchy: according to these clerical advisers he ruled by divine right and could be subject to no institutional checks. Although quick to curb local autonomy in the Low Countries and Aragon, in Castile his absolutism was tempered by solicitude for the Church and for the welfare of the provincial aristocrats, from whose ranks he drew most of his local officials and highest administrators. Traditionally Philip has been represented as a bigoted, humorless champion of the Cath-

Burning of heretics (auto-da-fé) by the Spanish Inquistion.

olic Reformation. He was always sensitive to the interests of the Church, and the Church in turn was sensitive to his, providing both substantial revenues and offices to which he could appoint his favorites. But he was not in any way a servant of the papal hierarchy: he ruled the Spanish church quite as authoritatively as Henry VIII ruled the Church of England. His proclamation of "one king, one faith" was perfectly in keeping with all other measures—fiscal, military, political—that he took to preserve the Habsburg power.

One institution was common to all Spanish lands under Philip's rule: the Inquisition. Designed to enforce religious conformity and obedience, it was superbly equipped to ferret out and destroy heretics. In 1559 arrests and burnings snuffed out the first signs of organized Protestantism. Then Philip took further measures to insulate his empire from Christian heresy: he had an enlarged Spanish edition of the *Index of Prohibited Books* published; he forbad his subjects to attend foreign universities; and he ordered all bookshops searched for subversive material.

Protestants, however, posed less of a threat to Philip's "one faith" than Jews and Moors. Spain had expelled unconverted Jews in 1492, but the converts who remained behind preserved their traditions. They, along with the converted Moors (*Moriscos*), were charged with responsibility for all heresy and evil. The Inquisition enforced a test of "blood purity" that barred them from admission to the state, the Church, and the professions. Numerically the Moriscos were far more significant than the Jews; they, too, defied the laws, retained their old traditions, and were hated for their refusal to assimilate completely. In addition they suffered the stigma of being identified with African pirates and Ottoman forces, who were engaged against Spanish power in the Mediterranean. In 1567, when Philip tried to enforce edicts against Moorish customs and the use of Arabic, the Moriscos in Granada revolted. The struggle, marked by savage atrocities and reprisals on both sides, ended in 1571 when the defeated rebels, 80,000 strong, were deported to Castile and dispersed among Castilian families. They remained there until 1609, when all Moriscos were expelled by Philip III.

Philip's religious policies were closely bound up with his financial measures. King and Church shared all property confiscated from "heretics" condemned by the Spanish Inquisition. By the end of the sixteenth century the Church controlled half the revenues of the kingdom, but from them it made substantial contributions to the crown. Philip accepted this state of affairs, thus proving that, despite grand theoretical statements of divine-right monarchy, social tradition and fiscal expedients played a determining role in his economic policy. Although the flow of bullion imported from America increased, Philip never established a firm structure of finance. Direct taxes levied on Castile were his main source of revenue, but because the aristocracy and clergy were exempt from direct taxation, almost the entire weight of the tax burden fell on peasants and townsmen. Only with the imposition of the *alcabala*—a tax of 10 (later 14) percent on every commercial transaction—as well as a heavy excise (*millones*) were the other social classes forced to contribute to the costs of the state. Still, revenues always failed to cover expenditures, and the monarchy negotiated new loans, debased the coinage, sold royal offices, and disposed of its shares in privileged monopolies.

Disaster ultimately overtook the Castilian economy. By raising prices the alcabala priced Spanish goods out of foreign and domestic markets. As the value of imports exceeded exports many times over, the crown encouraged the raising of merino sheep, hoping that the sale of wool would narrow the gap in foreign exchange. This it did, but the unbalanced extension of sheep pasturage also caused erosion of farm lands. And although the crown extended privileges to sheep raisers' guilds, there was no redress of grievances for the peasants whose crops were destroyed by sheep. Royal policy also diverted to court and Church the income that people might have invested in productive enterprise. The expenses of the court were a major drain on the king's treasury, but the bulk of his dwindling resources went to defend and extend his empire.

Defense of the Mediterranean

Philip is usually remembered as a militant foe of Protestantism, but for the first 20 years of his reign he was more concerned with Ottoman power on the Mediterranean Sea and with the Moriscos at home. Ottoman naval power was at peak strength under Suleiman the Magnificent (1520–66), whose navy was augmented in the west by corsairs operating from the rapacious pirate states of Tripoli and Algiers. When the peace treaty of 1559 deprived Suleiman of his French ally, Philip turned his newly built galleys against Tripoli—a premature effort in which he suffered serious defeat. After the papacy had helped subsidize more Spanish naval construction, Philip took the offensive again in 1565, at which time he drove the Turks from Malta. This victory broke Ottoman power in the western Mediterranean, but the Turks then invaded Cyprus, a Venetian possession. Determined to end Ottoman conquest, the papacy organized a huge fleet made up mainly of Spanish forces. Its victory at Lepanto in 1571 under Don Juan, a natural brother of Philip who was fresh from triumph over the Moriscos in Granada, was joyously celebrated, but the Turks persisted in Cyprus and continued to dominate the east. Both Spain and the Turks rebuilt and enlarged their navies after Lepanto, but there was to be no second encounter. In 1580 Philip negotiated a truce that proved to be lasting, although it did not put an end to African piracy. In the meantime his attention was diverted westward, where the Low Countries were in revolt and English and Dutch raiders were attacking his lines of communication and challenging his colonies in the Atlantic.

The Revolt of the Low Countries

The Low Countries constituted the 17 richest provinces of Philip's Burgundian territory. His father, Charles V, had crushed the independence of the towns and executed thousands of religious dissenters, but in the time of Philip the Low Countries still persisted in their defiance of Habsburg absolutism. Many of their provinces were highly urbanized, and among their prosperous towns was Antwerp, the greatest financial center and commercial *entrepôt* of Europe. The domestic textile industry flourished, particularly in Flanders. Literate and well-educated townsmen came under the influence of Erasmian humanism, radical sectarianism, and Protestantism. In the States General at Brussels the Low Countries boasted a representative body that possessed real vitality, although we must remember that only urban oligarchies and rural aristocracies were actually represented. This diet had a long established tradition of collecting taxes as well as voting them. Against royal encroachment it was ready to defend jealously the vested interests of its members, interests that included patronage and control of local church affairs.

Philip became ruler of the Low Countries in 1556. Three years later, when he took up residence in Spain, he appointed a regent—his natural sister, Margaret of Parma. She at once pressed for heavy new taxes and demanded ecclesiastical reorganization, measures that were fiercely resented by Dutch aristocrats as well as the urban oligarchs. The new taxes were intended to fall only on commoners, but from the very outset of her regency Margaret managed to alienate the leaders of society, some of whom were members of her own council of state.

The regency was determined to halt the spread of Calvinism and bring the Church under its control. This proved to be a thorny task. In the French-speaking Walloon provinces, Calvinist preachers set to organizing armed congregations; they were also successful in the larger towns where, by 1566, economic depression was breeding serious social discontent. Even the Inquisition, which operated through local bishops, failed to check the spreading Calvinism. When the nobility resisted all attempts to reorganize the Church, the regency, acting on its own authority, resorted to means of persecution more violent than those practiced by the Inquisition in Spain.

The nobles were hostile to radical Calvinism, but they were even more afraid of Habsburg absolutism. In 1566 they demonstrated unified opposition. Four hundred nobles—whom the regent called "beggars"—petitioned for a moderation of regency policy. They also demanded that royal edicts that encroached on the prerogatives of the States General be repealed. Margaret yielded and issued an order for moderation, but the Calvinists continued their iconoclasm. In 1567 Philip responded by sending the inflexible Duke of Alva with German, Italian, and Spanish mercenaries to reassert royal authority. When Margaret relinquished the regency, Alva reconstituted her council of state as a "council of blood," which set out brutally to reduce all opposition. Public preaching was ruled treasonous; also anyone who denied the king's power to abrogate all

Flemish protest in Biblical allegory: Pieter Brueghel the Elder, Massacre of the Innocents.

charters, laws, and privileges was declared a traitor. To define treason thus was to declare war on the aristocracy, and, indeed, two leaders of the aristocrats' resistance—the counts of Egmont and Hoorn—were executed by the council. Thereafter William of Orange, known as William the Silent, became disillusioned with pacific resistance and, until his assassination in 1584, led armed aristocratic resistance. William had a Lutheran upbringing, a Catholic education, and little sympathy for the fanaticism of his Calvinist coreligionists. He enunciated a policy of religious toleration in 1572, hoping to ease conflict and promote unity among the opponents of Spanish rule.

Actually Alva's government was more effective than William in uniting the opposition. When, in imitation of policies in Castile, it imposed taxes on commerce, the whole of the Low Countries, Catholic as well as Protestant, took up arms. William's troops were supplemented by "sea beggars"—privateers who disrupted Habsburg lines of communication at sea and seized coastal towns in Holland and Zeeland. Insurrection spread rapidly. In the same year, 1572, the sea beggars overturned local governments, pillaged churches, and established Calvinist dictatorships in one town after another. Alva's policy may be summed up in his own words. "It is far better," he wrote, "to preserve by war for God and the king, a kingdom that is impoverished and even ruined than, without war, preserve it entire for the benefit of the devil and his disciples, the heretics."[1] But with his program of terror Alva neither extirpated heresy, disarmed the nobility, nor impoverished the kingdom. In 1573 Philip replaced him with another general, Requesens, who was instructed to repeal the new taxes, dissolve the "council of blood," and proclaim a general amnesty.

Requesens set out to indulge the moderates and wage war to the death against the Calvinists. He succeeded with neither party. The Calvinists supported by southern refugees, gained control over Holland and Zeeland, the two richest provinces of the north. The moderates were effectively alienated in 1576 by the "Spanish Fury," in which Requesens's unpaid troops mutinied, pillaged Antwerp, raped women, and killed several thousand burghers. Delegates from the southern provinces met at Ghent immediately after the "Spanish Fury," and under the terms of a treaty known as the *Pacification of Ghent* the provinces united to expel Spanish troops and try to settle their religious differences by deferring them to a States General. Requesens died in 1576. Obliged to bow to the Pacification of Ghent, Spain's new governor-general, Don Juan of Austria, dispersed his troops.

But the rebels were soon divided again by religious strife. Calvinist refugees returning to Flanders after 1576 set up radical urban governments and persecuted Catholics, who in turn became more reconciled to Spain. In the south Calvinist centers fell one after another. In 1579 the schism within the rebels' ranks was ratified: Calvinists banded together in the Union of Utrecht, and Catholics formed their own League of Arras. With the rebels divided, Spanish troops under the Duke of Parma were able to reconquer the ten southern provinces. The northern provinces declared their independence in 1581, and, taking advantage of defensible terrain, maintained themselves as the United Provinces (Dutch Republic). Finally, in 1609, after the death of Philip II, the merchants of Holland negotiated a Twelve-Year Truce, but it did not recognize their independence. At the end of the truce the renewed Dutch war for independence merged with a larger struggle, the Thirty Years' War.

Economically the war affected each belligerent in a different way. Subject to Spanish taxation and crippled by Dutch control over the River Scheldt, its major artery of commerce, the southern ten provinces took long to recover. Many of its leading capitalists emigrated. Meanwhile the center of European finance and commerce shifted from Antwerp in the south to Amsterdam in Holland. Castile was drained of men and money, but Dutch pirates, privateers, and merchants prospered; they were beginning to build a commercial empire on the colonies and markets wrested from Portugal. Moreover, the merchants of Holland and Zeeland regained their war expenditures by selling foodstuffs and raw materials to the enemy in return for Spanish bullion. In short, while the southern Netherlands and Spain continued to suffer and their economies to stagnate, the seven United Provinces rapidly recovered from the worst effects of the "price revolution."

Although they were obliged to renew their struggle for independence between 1621 and 1648, the seven United Provinces had succeeded in escaping from the most formidable divine-right ruler in Europe. In their revolt the Dutch broke away from the tradition of "one king, one faith," and Holland—the name of the leading province which contemporaries applied to the whole United Provinces or Dutch Republic—became an enclave of relative lib-

---

[1] Quoted by John Lynch, *Spain under the Habsburgs*, vol. 1, *Empire and Absolutism, 1516–1598* (New York: Oxford University Press, 1964), p. 290. Philip made a similar statement, that he would prefer being king in a desert to being a lord of heretics.

DIVISION OF THE NETHERLANDS
1579-1609

erty in a sea of seventeenth-century absolutism. Instead of one monarch ruling through his court and councils, governing powers were partitioned among the local oligarchies in the various confederated provinces and a weak States General. Either the ruling oligarchy of the province of Holland or the House of Orange imposed unity, as each in turn predominated in a long contest for power. Although they had led the drive for independence, Calvinists constituted a minority, and a divided one at that. Orthodox Calvinists were counterbalanced by the merchants of Holland and Zeeland, whose religion was not dogmatic. As a result there emerged the first pluralistic society in western Europe, for it was obliged to tolerate religious and secular heterodoxy.

To justify their revolt against a God-anointed king, Dutch leaders appealed to their chartered rights and privileges, which princes, by contractual obligation, were bound to respect; otherwise they were released from obedience to the princes. This was an aristocratic rather than a democratic position; democratic ideas did make a hesitant appearance but were rapidly submerged when urban patricians and the landed aristocracy took over the direction of the revolt. Yet conflicts between those two classes went unresolved and prevented them from forming a solid alliance. Dutch society remained in their control, but they were too much divided to impose a new absolutism.

Philip II and Tudor England

The success of the Dutch revolt was partially due to Philip's logistical problems. He had to divert resources from the Duke of Parma's forces to his wars with England and to his involvement in the French civil war; meanwhile both England and France gave aid to the rebellious Low Countries. After Elizabeth restored Protestantism to England, Philip tried to recover his influence there by marrying the queen. Failing in that, he became increasingly hostile; his emissaries were implicated in a Catholic uprising in northern England in 1569, and on the Continent his government helped support Catholic colleges for training emigrés who were to bring about a Catholic restoration in England. But the King of Spain refrained from attempting to conquer England so long as Mary Queen of Scots was alive. Prospective ruler of a Catholic England, she was a Guise by birth and a Valois by marriage. Because Philip feared that her accession would lead to a coalition of England and France, he had no intention of conquering England for her benefit even though she was a Roman Catholic.

For Englishmen, Spain and Catholicism were the national enemies. Nationalism reached a peak of ferocity in 1570 when the pope excommunicated Elizabeth, declaring her deposed, and when Catholic plots to assassinate her and her leading counselors were exposed. When the "Sea Dogs" under Francis Drake and John Hawkins ran pirate raids against Spanish naval power, they were widely acclaimed. Eventually Elizabeth sanctioned their deeds. In 1585, when she sent troops to aid the Dutch Republic, she also publicly supported the Protestant rebels in the Low Countries whom for the past eight years she had assisted only covertly.

Once Mary Queen of Scots was executed, Philip had a Catholic martyr to avenge, and he decided that the best and most economical way to protect the coast, colonies, and shipping trade of Spain was to invade England. After many delays the "invincible" Armada was dispatched in 1588, consisting of 130 ships—an imposing number; but they were ill equipped. Philip's plan called for transporting troops from the Netherlands to conquer England, but he neglected to arrange for the shallow-draft vessels needed to transport them from the Dutch coast to the Armada for transport to England. While the Armada waited at anchor for troops that never came, an English fleet composed of private vessels and government warships attacked from the windward side. The outnumbered English effectively deployed fireships and artillery, breaking the elaborate but inflexible formations of the Armada. To return to Spain the Armada was forced to sail northward around Scotland, where the damaged fleet suffered severe losses from storms. England suffered no loss of ships, but about half of the Armada failed to return.

According to common accounts England emerged as mistress of the seas as a result of her defeat of the Armada. In fact no such rapid shift of power occurred. Philip received the bad news impassively and announced that he would build a still larger armada. And he did. New convoy tactics and increased naval construction made Spanish sea power stronger than ever before. Drake and Hawkins had predicted that Philip's supply of New World treasure would be cut off, but for the next 15 years bullion flowed to Spain at an unprecedented rate, and new fortifications of naval bases made them less vulnerable to piracy. Still, costs of defending the Spanish empire were prohibitive. In fact, neither Spain nor England possessed the technology or the requisite number of ships to command the whole Atlantic.

The defeat of the Armada had more significance in European politics. When it occurred, Spain appeared to be at the brink of global dominance; but it proved to spectators all over Europe that the Habsburgs were not omnipotent and that they had no special claim to the blessings of divine providence. Protestant England had escaped being made a Catholic kingdom within the Habsburg empire; no longer could Spain be seen as the instrument that would enforce a uniform Catholic peace on Europe. From the English victory over Spain, Henry III of France took courage and undertook the assassination of his rival, Henry of Guise, the leader of French Catholics who relied on Spanish support. Philip, however, continued to aid Catholic partisans against the Huguenots when their leader, Henry of Navarre, succeeded to the throne as Henry IV in 1589.

Although still unable to defeat his old enemies, Philip had committed himself to taking on new ones. Castile, still the strongest land power in Europe, was nevertheless entering a period of relative decline. Internal economic difficulties, the overcommitment of her resources, and the rise of powerful rivals all hastened the decay of Spanish supremacy.

The Reign of Philip III (1598–1621)

Monarchy, it has been observed, is a lottery; there is no guarantee that an heir will pursue the policies of his predecessor. When death seemed imminent, Philip lamented that "God who has given me so many kingdoms has not granted me a son fit to govern them." Unlike his diligent father, the sickly Philip III would not concern himself with affairs of state. For more than 20 years the real ruler of Spain was his royal favorite, the Duke of Lerma, who was a descendant of the great king Ferdinand I. In his time state offices were sold en masse for purposes of revenue, the coinage was debased, extravagant festivities marked even the most trivial social event at court, and public funds were embezzled in staggering amounts. Lerma himself accumulated a fortune of incredible size, much of it consisting of fines from the Moriscos, who were expelled in 1609. When his opponents finally insisted on an accounting, Lerma hastily secured a cardinal's hat and papal permission to leave the court, thus escaping punishment and avoiding restitution.

It is to Lerma's credit, however, that he concluded peace with England and the United Provinces. Philip II had already been forced to make peace with France in 1598. Before Spain and England came to terms there was one more encounter, when Castilian troops and ships joined an Irish uprising in 1601. The Spanish were again defeated, although more narrowly than in 1588. Under James I, England's militant policies against Spain were relaxed, and peace was negotiated in 1604. With the Dutch, however, full-scale hostilities on land and sea continued, and the Spanish suffered defeat off Gibraltar in 1607. But then Lerma found a Milanese general, Ambrose Spinola, who was able to drive back the forces of Maurice of Nassau, the son of William of Orange. In 1609 both sides agreed to a truce. By terminating these two wars and by checking French schemes of aggression (this was accomplished by intrigue in Henry IV's court), Lerma gave Spain the time she desperately needed to recuperate. The greatest test of Habsburg power, the Thirty Years' War, was still to come.

ELIZABETHAN ENGLAND

In the past, French rivalry had checked Habsburg ambition, but after 1560 French strength was drained by civil and religious wars. Meanwhile England, whose smaller population and limited resources hardly seemed to warrant such resistance, stepped into the breach to defy Spanish power, and Elizabeth reluctantly assumed the role of rallying Protestant Europe. Rivalry with Spain, which broke into naval warfare and brought the Armada, also profoundly affected English domestic affairs.

The Elizabethan Religious Settlement

Elizabeth had little of the religious fanatic in her, but religious questions were central to the political and diplomatic policies of her reign (1558–1603). Her policies concerning religion were tailored to fit political expediency. From her first parliament (1559) she sought only one measure to overturn Mary's restoration of Catholicism: the reassertion of royal supremacy over the English church. But many of her subjects took their religion far more seriously than that. A strong group in the House of Commons sympathized with the Marian exiles—those laymen and clergymen who had fled England under the persecution of "Bloody Mary." During their residence in Geneva and the cities of Germany these exiles had absorbed Protestant doctrines as well as techniques of propaganda. Their militant supporters in the House of Commons pressed for a return to the religious settlement of Edward VI, and they further demanded punitive measures against Catholics and retribution for past persecution. Elizabeth compromised: she agreed to both an act of royal supremacy and an act of uniformity which imposed a common prayer book on the whole kingdom. Nevertheless the prayer book that was finally published was theologically ambiguous enough to accommodate many diverse opinions. She resolutely refused to persecute nonconformists unless their actions were seditious or treasonable. This compromise between queen and Commons laid the basis for a middle way. What emerged in England was a state church whose strict hierarchy was traditional but whose doctrines were flexible and broad.

Most Englishmen, except for a number of Roman Catholics (and these were dwindling) and a vociferous Puritan minority, adjusted gradually to the Anglican settlement. Deep-rooted Catholic customs were perpetuated in some rural areas, particularly in the north. But without any institutions to rely on, Catholic teachings and ritual practices could now be preserved only in the households of devout gentlemen and lords. Calvinists, or Puritans, on the other hand, began to penetrate the power structure of the state, church, and society; they had partisans in the Queen's Privy Council itself. So long as she was sure of their political support, Elizabeth kept and used them within the church. The spread of Puritanism among the gentry was reflected in the House of Commons, where Puritans attacked what they considered popish survivals in the services authorized by the Elizabethan settlement, such as the wearing of vestments by ministers. They also criticized the queen's leniency toward Catholics, for they were not prepared to be tolerant. In what may be taken as a typical outburst, one of them declared in 1559 that "Maintainers of false religion ought to die by the sword."[2] The Puritans' political influence increased as they became outspoken patriots and vigorously denounced Spain. Eventually the queen came to oppose them. After 1574 she was convinced that they constituted a threat to the stability of the Church of England, and she took steps to limit their power and influence in the church hierarchy. During the latter part of her reign, clashes in the House of Commons between Elizabeth and the Puritans laid bare those issues that would later ignite the civil wars of the seventeenth century.

Society, Politics, and Constitutional Development

The gentry, whose power and influence grew during the sixteenth century, constituted one of the most important classes in Elizabethan society. They were landed gentlemen whose estates were a main source of income. Membership in this social class was extremely fluid: from below, their ranks absorbed yeomen, wealthy lawyers, officials, and merchants who purchased country estates; in their turn, the gentry—who had no titles—very much wanted to narrow the gap between themselves and the titled nobility.

[2] Quoted by John E. Neale, *Elizabeth I and Her Parliaments 1559–1581* (New York: St. Martin's Press, 1958), p. 117.

Although the nobles were forced to share their political and social power with the gentry, they retained tremendous prestige and influence and continued to represent the highest goals of social ambition. Still, some of the wealthiest men in England could be found among the merchants, particularly the narrow coterie of London merchant-bankers who were closely allied with crown and court.

The first half of the sixteenth century was an era of expanding commerce and urbanization. One city—London—dwarfed all other English towns as the center of trade, finance, and marketing. The line between wealth and poverty was drawn more sharply in England as commerce expanded, for as more men became rich, and as rich men grew more affluent, the lower classes became more numerous and in some cases poorer. Church and state subscribed to the social theory of a well-ordered hierarchical society in which each rank had its fixed place; but in reality men were always struggling in ruthless competition to move up the social ladder or to secure a stronghold near the top. Charity and private contributions to education relieved some of the friction between rich and poor, but at the end of Elizabeth's reign the greatest single financial and administrative problem facing English society was the growth of poverty. The Poor Law was one attempt to deal with it.

The Elizabethan Poor Law of 1601 was the last in a series of statutes directed toward regulating the economy and the social system of England. It made local parishes or districts responsible for providing for the destitute. These districts are good places with which to begin a study of Elizabethan government, for the success of all legislation eventually depended on local administration. Almost every traditional executive function of local government was filled by justices of the peace, many of whom were also members of the House of Commons, where they helped make the laws that they enforced in the counties. Administering the Poor Law became their largest single task. Recruited from the gentry to serve in their own neighborhoods, they set compulsory tax rates and appointed and supervised the overseers of the poor in each parish. They also served as judges and sheriffs, searched out and penalized Catholic recusants, set wages and prices, enforced craft and trade regulations, and maintained waterways. Many of the educated gentry also had some degree of legal training. Familiarity with the law helped them to secure their own lands as well as carry out their official functions. During the sixteenth century the law became an ever more fashionable and profitable pursuit. The gentry thus exerted enormous power, for fundamental to Elizabethan government was the fact that the queen could carry out only those policies that the gentry supported; to put it another way, the government had no chance of implementing any policies to which the gentry was opposed.

The central government under Elizabeth was little changed from the days of her father, Henry VIII. Her chief counselors—Burghley, Walsingham, and Leicester—made sure that the men appointed as lord lieutenants were usually peers or privy councillors. Since the lord lieutenant in each county nominally supervised administration, this system of appointment gave a semblance of unified central administration to the country; but because his jurisdiction conflicted with that of the justices of the peace, the lord lieutenant's actual power seldom extended beyond military recruitment and training.

During Elizabeth's reign the House of Commons expanded and developed new vigor. Although it could neither initiate legislation nor directly supervise the execution of laws, and although the speaker usually wielded considerable power on behalf of the crown, still, the Commons did initiate tax measures; and no such measure or any other bill could be passed without its assent. Since many new towns were chartered and privileged to send two burgesses to Parliament, the size of the Commons increased. Townsmen did not gain more power, however, for borough elections usually returned gentry to the House of Commons. These latter resided in the countryside and primarily looked after only their own interests. Still, Englishmen possessed more civil rights, and were subject to fewer taxes, than their counterparts living under the monarchies on the Continent. Parliament was representative of an important segment of society, and its continued vitality was in great part responsible for the notable cooperation between ruled and ruler in England. While static continental diets functioned as guardians of class privilege, the Parliament of England assumed an active role in the fiscal and political life of the nation.

On the issue of royal succession Elizabeth's government was perhaps most vulnerable. The sixteenth century was an era of dynastic as well as religious conflict, and the English throne, secured only by the life of a single woman, was a prime target for the Spanish Habsburgs and the French house of Guise. Constantly in fear of the confusion that might ensue if Elizabeth died without an heir, the House of Commons defied her orders to be silent on the subject of marriage and vociferously urged her to wed. But she insisted on remaining single. For as long as it was possible, she played her marital eligibility for all it was worth in the game of diplomacy, trusting to luck that on her death no crisis of internal succession would develop.

Elizabeth's Foreign Policy

In the Elizabethan era England ceased to be an insignificant factor in European affairs. Its strategic location, economic interests, and unsought role as the champion of

Protestantism thrust it into the power struggles of Europe. To subsequent generations the defeat of the Armada was dramatic evidence of English emergence; but at the same time it was mainly an act of defense. Until 1588 the English position in relation to Spanish power had been extremely precarious. Elizabeth could count on brilliant ministers such as William Cecil (Lord Burghley), who directed one of the most efficient intelligence services in Europe. Until the 1580s she successfully coped with coalitions of powerful foreign enemies without placing heavy strains on the economic resources of her kingdom.

The first major threat came from France and Scotland. Mary Stuart, Queen of Scotland and the wife of Francis II of France, ruled Scotland with the aid of her French mother, Mary of Guise. The queen, who was a Roman Catholic, also had strong claims to the English throne—claims that France strongly supported. Philip II, anxious to thwart Guise ambitions, tried to marry Elizabeth. Fearful of provoking either side, Elizabeth remained noncommittal. In 1559 Protestants in Scotland revolted against French rule. Although the leader of the revolt, John Knox, was a strict Calvinist (as well as the author of a polemic against women rulers), Elizabeth supported him. In 1560 Mary Stuart became a widow, and for a time thereafter—even though she remained Queen of Scotland—she posed a lesser threat to Elizabeth's throne.

Wanting to weaken the house of Guise, Elizabeth supported the Huguenots in the French civil wars between 1562 and 1564. England regained Calais, which it had lost under Mary Tudor, but the venture ended in disaster when the French united temporarily to expel the English. Meanwhile Mary Stuart married another claimant to the Tudor throne, Lord Darnley. Once more it appeared that she intended to displace Elizabeth; but instead (although James, the child of her marriage with Darnley, would eventually rule Scotland and England) Mary lost even her own throne. Darnley grew jealous of her affections for her royal secretary and had him murdered. The very next year (1567) Darnley himself was murdered. When the Queen then married Bothwell, another of her favorites who had been implicated in Darnley's death, the scandal that ensued forced her to seek refuge in England. There she was confined. Serving as the focus of Catholic plots against Elizabeth's life, she was compromised and eventually sacrificed to the executioneer's block in 1587.

The real foe of England was Spain. Elizabeth, however, was reluctant to become involved in a major war against this enemy. When the important English cloth trade with the Low Countries dictated that England support their revolt against Spain, Elizabeth offered herself as bait. By protracted but fruitless marriage negotiations with the younger brother of the king of France, she lured the house of Valois into supporting the Dutch revolt. But after 1584, when William of Orange was assassinated, the French deserted the rebels. Once Elizabeth had openly intervened on the Dutch side, England remained more or less in a state of war for the duration of her reign. Not until a Stuart attained the English throne would there be a settlement with Spain.

FRENCH CIVIL AND RELIGIOUS WARS

While England united under Elizabeth against Spain, France floundered in civil wars, of which there were eight between 1562 and 1598. Had a strong monarch been at the helm in France as long as Elizabeth ruled in England, these wars might have been avoided; instead, a succession of weak boy-kings undermined the power of the throne. The unsteady control of Catherine de' Medici over her royal sons and the extinction of the Valois male line subjected the kingdom to bitter feuds among aristocratic factions. Less avoidably, it allowed a Calvinist minority to establish an alliance with noble dissidents who were bidding for power.

Prelude to Religious Revolution

Between 1536 and 1559 French Calvinists (Huguenots) became strong enough to challenge the unreformed French church. Although Francis I considered them anarchists, his alliance with the German Protestants at first forced him to be lenient. After 1540, however, his government began to uproot heresy systematically. His more bigoted successor, Henry II (1547–59), established a special court in the Parlement of Paris, the *chambre ardente*, or "hot box," where summary justice was handed down to Protestants. The Huguenots defied persecution and even increased in numbers, especially in the southern provinces. At Paris in 1559 they held a clandestine "national synod," which drew up a uniform confession of faith. The Huguenot organization in effect provided an alternative government capable of raising money and troops.

Most of the early Huguenots were people of education but little political significance—workingmen, petty tradesmen, professionals, and regular clergy—who resignedly suffered martyrdom. They remained a small minority because Protestants never gained much support among the peasants, but after 1559 highly placed noblemen joined their ranks, compensating for their lack of broad popular support. When these powerful men flocked to the movement, resignation gave way to armed resistance, a course compatible with Calvinist doctrine. Thus Protestantism became involved in the power struggles at the top echelons of the French state. Its involvement further complicated family feuds, court rivalries, and what was after 1584 a three-cornered struggle among the houses of Valois, Bourbon, and Guise for possession of the French throne.

The First Seven Wars: 1562–1580

Calvinism grew into a significant political force at a time when the two oldest and most powerful feudal families were arrayed against each other. The Bourbon faction was headed by Anthony of Navarre, who held vast territories in south-central France. The Guise family from Lorraine, whose cardinal-patriarch administered the sees of Rheims, Metz, and Verdun (among other benefices) and the rich abbeys of St. Denis and Clery, led the other faction. Members of a third great family, the Montmorencys, divided their loyalties between Bourbon and Guise.

In 1560 the Huguenots plotted to seize the boy-king, Charles IX, a plot foiled by the court and attributed by the Guise family to the Bourbons and Montmorencys, against whom they swore vengeance. The Queen Mother, Catherine de' Medici, tried to bring peace by calling a religious colloquy and issuing an edict of toleration in 1562. The edict was very much limited and Catherine herself intended it to be temporary; but the Huguenots, for whom toleration was not enough, refused to cooperate. So did the Guise family, which was determined to enforce the doctrines of Trent by fire and sword. Local riots and killings expanded into general war in 1562 when Guise troops slaughtered a Huguenot congregation at Vassy. There followed a complicated series of seven wars punctuated by truces.

As a result of the first war the nobility gained religious toleration, which was anathema to the Guise family. From the second and third the Huguenots won liberty of conscience and four fortified towns, something still more detestable to the Guises. Worse still, the Huguenots' politi-

The Massacre of St. Bartholomew's Day *by Francois Dubois.*

cal spokesman, Admiral Coligny, was given a position of royal confidence. His influence with Charles IX led to the betrothal of the king's sister to Henry of Navarre, son of the leading Huguenot nobleman. This marriage pact threatened Catherine's sway over her son and brought her wrath down on Coligny's head. She plotted his assassination, but the plot miscarried; then she became involved in a conspiracy to kill several prominent Huguenot nobles, including Henry and Coligny. The murderers struck during Henry's marriage celebration on St. Bartholomew's Day, 1572, and assassination turned into massacre. Mob passion led to the slaughter of approximately 20,000 Huguenots in Paris and provincial towns. Coligny was killed, but Henry of Navarre escaped with his life by embracing Catholicism (a momentary conversion, however).

The massacre of St. Bartholomew's Day ravaged the Huguenots' leadership but their organization survived. Determined to root it out, Henry of Guise accepted Spanish aid, but again in vain. Royal treachery had alienated moderate Catholics from Catherine de' Medici. Moreover, she herself had lost enthusiasm for a Guise victory when she realized that the dashing Henry of Guise could be a dangerous rival to her son. Following the death of Charles IX and the accession of his younger brother, Henry III, Catherine arranged another truce in 1576, which put great sections of France under Guise administration but still contained a provision utterly unacceptable to ardent Catholics: except in the city of Paris, the Huguenots were again to enjoy religious toleration.

The "War of the Three Henrys": 1585–1589

Disaffected by these concessions to the Huguenots, zealous Catholics organized a Guise-led "Holy League" supported by

Spain and the papacy. Henry III tried to neutralize it as a threat to his power by becoming its head, but Henry of Guise was too domineering an ally. When the king's younger brother—the last direct male heir to the throne since it was obvious that Henry III would not beget a son—died in 1584, the Holy League proposed its own candidate for the throne to prevent its passing to Henry of Navarre, Bourbon leader of the Huguenots, who was next in line. In 1588 the League seized Paris and tried to depose Henry III. (The coup was coordinated with the Spanish Armada's attack on England.) But Henry III escaped and had Henry of Guise murdered. The Guise faction retaliated with a full-scale revolt, which Henry met by enlisting the aid of Henry of Navarre and the *politiques,* a powerful faction of moderates who eventually set the terms that ended the war.

Reacting against foreign intervention and appalled by the destruction of civil war, the politiques set the welfare of France above religious creed—as zealous religious partisans put it, "they preferred the safety of their country to the salvation of their souls." In Languedoc, a province about evenly divided between Catholics and Huguenots, the politiques found a spokesman in the royal governor, Henry of Montmorency-Damville. To prevent further atrocities and destruction, Montmorency enforced toleration; resorting to authoritarian, even despotic, means, he became the "uncrowned king of the south": neither side could hope to win the civil war without his support. After 1584 he threw his weight to the side of Henry of Navarre, who promised him high office in the future.

Henry of Navarre became King Henry IV in 1589 after Henry III was assassinated by a fanatical monk. In the north, especially Paris, Henry faced strong Spanish-supported Catholic opposition. Belatedly following Montmorency's advice, he removed his religious impediment; "Paris vaut bien une messe!" he is reported to have said.* He announced his (third) conversion to Roman Catholicism, entered the capital, and drove the Spanish troops back to the Netherlands.

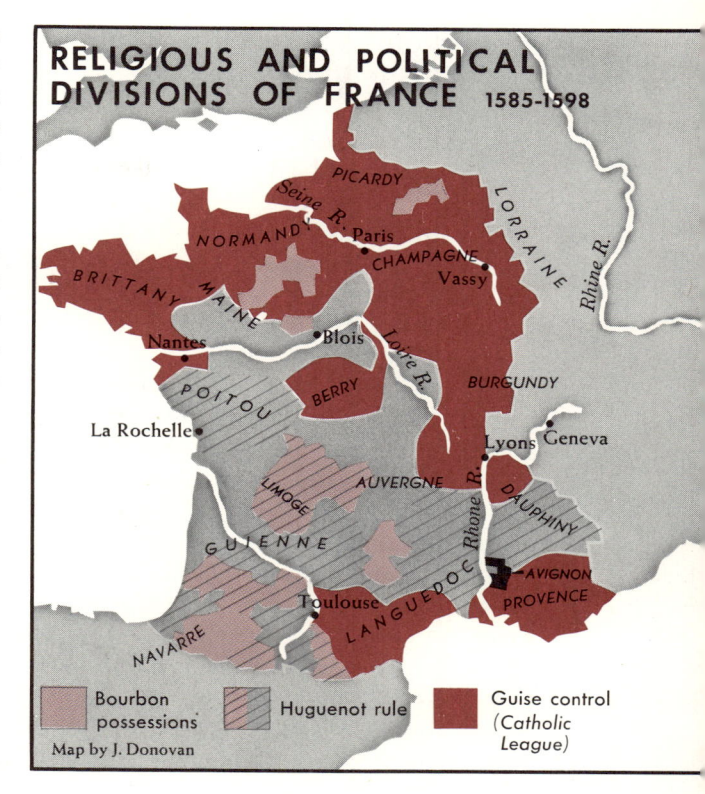

Continuing to follow politique guidance, Henry made toleration an official and enforceable policy when he issued the Edict of Nantes in 1598. One other concept had high priority in the politiques' program: the establishment of a strong national monarchy. Henry helped make that concept a political reality as he laid the foundation for subsequent Bourbon absolutism.

---

* "Paris is well worth a Mass."

B. *Spain and the Religious Wars*

Toleration, Absolutism, and Power

In order to take firm possession of his throne Henry had adopted Catholicism. Now, for the peace of the kingdom, he issued the Edict of Nantes, one of the most advanced programs of toleration of the sixteenth century. By its terms the Huguenots were granted freedom of conscience and were authorized to conduct private and extensive public worship; they could attend schools and universities, establish a limited number of colleges, and hold public office; and, to guarantee their security amid the Catholic majority, they were given complete control over 200 towns, including the seaport of La Rochelle. These walled towns were garrisoned at royal expense, and they boasted more troops than the king himself maintained. Later Cardinal Richelieu would sharply reduce this Protestant "state within a state"; but for the time being it set limits on Bourbon absolutism. By the end of the century the Huguenots had assumed an influential role in French affairs. Meanwhile their great antagonist, the Roman church, had been forced to sell many of its monastic lands (during the reigns of Charles IX and Henry III), and its power was waning.

Throughout the period of protracted civil wars men discussed the right of oligarchs, even of the masses, to resist heretical kings. Not surprisingly, the monarch and his advisors were all advocates of royal absolutism. Henry IV was in theory, and to a certain extent in practice, an absolute monarch. During his reign he convoked no meeting of the Estates General, and with huge sums of money he brought off Catholic leaders who pressed for feudal decentralization. His principal minister, the Duke of Sully, introduced a new official called the *intendant*, who was a direct agent of the crown in the provinces.

Henry IV, 1589–1610.

Nevertheless Henry's "absolutism" was a political compromise just as the Edict of Nantes was a religious one. Great lords lost their independence, but their pockets bulged with the king's gold, and institutions that preserved local privileges and autonomy were left intact. Sully cut court expenses and halted peculation of public funds, but as a financial expedient the king permitted some officials to transform their offices into hereditary property by the payment of a special tax, the *Paulette*. Thus many officials gained independence from their royal master. Rather than a political revolution, the Bourbon accession represented a restoration of royal power as it existed under Francis I in the early part of the century. Internal stability was not completely assured, however, and on occasion the kingdom was still rocked by the schemes of dissident court nobles who conspired with Spain.

With domestic peace and some government aid French peasants and tradesmen could recover from the extensive destruction of the wars. The Duke of Sully promoted agriculture, introduced new silk and glassware industries, and built highways and canals. Overseas Champlain was laying the basis for a French empire in Canada. As the economy rapidly recovered, taxes decreased and the royal treasury grew fat.

Although Henry chafed against Habsburg power, he delayed a show of force until 1609. Then he decided to intervene into a dynastic dispute between Brandenburg and the Palatinate over the Rhenish duchies of Cleves and Jülich. Had he moved an army into Germany, a general war would probably have begun, but in 1610 a fanatic's dagger ended both his life and the expedition. All three Henrys had died by assassination, the last of which postponed the confrontation of Habsburg with Bourbon until the middle of the Thirty Years' War. Meanwhile France was again ruled by a boy-king and his queen mother: Louis XIII and Marie de' Medici.

C. Four Decades of War and Revolution: 1618–1660

THE ERA OF THE THIRTY YEARS' WAR

At the beginning of the seventeenth century Europe had a respite from war and religious revolution. Philip III made peace with Spain's enemies. Henry IV pacified France and was assassinated before he could shatter the peace of Germany. But peace was too fragile to last; it was the prelude to the worst series of religious, civil, and dynastic wars of the entire century of crises.

Origins of the Thirty Years' War

The first of these conflicts, the Thirty Years' War (1618–48), originated in the domains of the German Habsburgs as a response to the Catholic Reformation. Unlike their Spanish cousins, the emperors after Charles V—Ferdinand, Maximilian II (1564–76)—tolerated or even sympathized with Lutheranism, and under their relaxed vigilance Lutherans and Calvinists made heavy inroads among upper townsmen and the nobility who were represented in the provincial diets. Then, in the latter part of Emperor Rudolf's reign (1576–1612) Habsburg leniency began to change toward intolerant rigor. Rudolf himself granted Bohemian Lutherans religious toleration, but his brothers were attempting to depose him. One of them—his successor, Matthias—entered into a family compact with the Spanish Habsburgs, who encouraged him to suppress the Protestants. When his heir-apparent, Ferdinand, the king of Bohemia who became Emperor Ferdinand II in 1619, openly imitated Spanish Catholic rule, the Protestant estates of Bohemia rebelled. In Prague Bohemian noblemen threw the emperor's representatives out of a palace window (the Second Defenestration of Prague), declared the throne vacant, and solicited aid from Protestants throughout Europe.

Mercenaries in hand-to-hand combat by Holbein.

The Bohemians primarily counted on assistance from the Protestant estates of the empire. As their new king they chose Frederick V of the Palatinate, the Calvinist head of a German Protestant league (the Protestant Union) and son-in-law of James I of England. German conditions, however, were not auspicious for substantial aid.

German Lutheranism had taken possession of many Catholic lands in northern Germany after the Peace of Augsburg (1555), but the tide turned in 1577 when a Lutheran was elected archbishop-elector of Cologne and was then deposed by the imperial high court. Thereafter Lutherans were preoccupied more with checking the inroads of radical Calvinism than with staying the progress of resurgent Catholicism. "Better popish than reformed" was their watchword as the Calvinists began to spread along the Rhine. In 1580 they drew up a strict common creed, the Formula of Concord, which branded Calvinists as heretics. After this, effective political cooperation between the two creeds became almost impossible. In 1609 they did join in a Protestant Union, in opposition to which the rival Catholic League soon formed, but the Union was paralyzed by conflict between Lutherans and Calvinists; only the Calvinists, who were not recognized by the Peace of Augsburg, actively supported it. Instead of coming to the aid of the Bohemians, Lutheran Saxony used the opportunity of the Bohemian revolt to seize part of the Bohemian crownlands (Lusatia).

From the outset the Bohemian revolt was an international affair, outside forces converging on Austria and Bohemia. Maximilian of Bavaria sent military assistance to the emperor, and Spanish troops and Catholic forces assembled by Poland and the papacy came to the aid of Ferdinand. Bohemia obtained aid from only a few small territories and from Bethlen Gabor, a rebel leader of Transylvania, whose forces twice beseiged Vienna before a Turkish attack disabled them. In 1620 troops of the Catholic League, commanded by Baron Tilly—the "monk in arms"—decisively defeated the Bohemians at the Battle of White Mountain, outside Prague. The army of Frederick V was routed in less than two hours.

After Frederick's hasty flight to Holland, the Habsburgs proceeded to wreak revenge on Bohemia, rooting out both the Hussite and Protestant reformations. They executed intellectuals and military leaders, banished some Protestant clergy, and condemned the rest to death. Habsburg dragoons enforced mass conversions of Bohemian Protestants to Catholicism. Refugees—prominent intellectuals among them—swarmed out of Bohemia in numbers that have been estimated from 30,000 to 150,000. About half of all land belonging to the nobility was confiscated and distributed among aristocrats of the Habsburg domains. This policy of redistribution created large landed estates—*latifundia*—worked by serfs, who had heavier duties imposed on them. The extent of the nobility's control over their lives is suggested by the name for their service obligations (Czech, *robota;* Ger. and Eng., *robot*). The men who directed the parceling out of lands, particularly Albert of Wallenstein, grew enormously rich. In 1627 the Habsburgs gave Bohemia a new constitution, which abolished the elective monarchy and placed Bohemian affairs under the direct supervision of the imperial Habsburg court—an arrangement that persisted for more than two centuries. Bohemia would suffer further from the Thirty Years' War when, in its last years, foraging troops again ravaged her countryside.

The collapse of Bohemia spelled doom for Austrian Protestantism. Austria was subjected to a rigorous counterreformation; between 1622 and 1628 Protestants throughout the Habsburg provinces were shorn of all their rights.

Spread of the Thirty Years' War

After the battle of White Mountain the seat of war moved to the Palatinate. Spanish troops under Spinola and Tilly's forces had systematically devastated Frederick V's home base by 1623. Meanwhile Spain gained possession of important passes through the Alps, a crucial advantage since renewal of the Dutch war of independence in 1621 threatened Spain's lines of communications at sea.

Renewal of the Dutch war was the next major extension of the conflict, carrying it beyond Europe to the colonial empires. Before the Spanish-Dutch truce expired, a revolution in the United Provinces brought to power Calvinists favoring war. The truce of 1609, negotiated by the Arminian lord advocate of Holland, Jan van Oldenbarneveldt, had never been popular with the Calvinists; it was the work of Arminian burghers who denied predestination and advocated a relatively tolerant state church. Calvinists considered it a weak-kneed heresy, and at the synod of Dortrecht (1618–19) they delivered the Arminians a serious theological defeat. Following the synod the victorious Calvinists executed Oldenbarneveldt and began preparations for the war which began again in 1621. When France joined the fray in 1635, the Calvinist-led United Provinces established a firm alliance with it in order to overcome the Habsburgs.

Between 1624 and 1629 Ferdinand II routed the German Protestants, gaining control over the empire more complete than any emperor had held for centuries. Tilly and Wallenstein (whose large private army was now paid by booty and run for profit) won victory after victory as Germany became one great theater of war. During the so-called Danish period,

1625–29, King Christian IV of Denmark led the Protestants to defeat at the hands of Tilly and Wallenstein, who went on to conquer Holstein and to occupy the German coast as far east as Stralsund, not far from the Polish border. Much to the discomfiture of the German princes, Ferdinand II made Wallenstein—a mere upstart—Duke of Mecklenburg. By 1629 Ferdinand was master enough of the empire to order the German Protestant princes, except Saxony, to return to the Roman church all the lands taken since the Peace of Augsburg in 1555.

Ferdinand was so successful that even his allies felt threatened. Just when his Catholic Reformation seemed to be at the crest of victory, the Pope, who had subsidized Ferdinand's armies, deserted him; and Bavaria, fearful that Ferdinand would suppress her autonomy, entered into negotiations with France and forced Wallenstein's dismissal, which Ferdinand accepted in an effort to keep the Catholic forces together. But while German affairs were still unsettled, the war suddenly entered a new phase: partly at French instigation, Gustavus Adolphus, king of Sweden, proceeded to invade Germany as the self-proclaimed deliverer of German Protestantism.

Swedish and French Intervention

Mercenary warfare allowed small states, if they had sufficient money, to become major military powers. Gustavus Adolphus ruled only about 1,500,000 people, but he successfully invaded the most populous area of Christendom. During his reign war became a successful business: he had an efficient conscription system, his army used revolutionary tactics involving the use of small firearms, and his country had an iron industry to produce artillery. These factors, in addition to heavy subsidies from Cardinal Richelieu of France and some from the Dutch, underlay his success in Germany.

The Swedish invasion of 1630 quickly turned the military situation about. In Saxony, near Leipzig, Gustavus Adolphus's forces met, and nearly annihilated, half of the imperial army under Tilly. Then he swung through the Church states along the Rhine and invaded Catholic Bavaria. To stop Gustavus the emperor restored Wallenstein and granted him extensive personal power. At Lützen (Saxony) in 1632 the Swedes defeated Wallenstein, but in the battle the "snow king" of Sweden was killed. Thereupon Bavaria was cleared of Swedish troops after the battle of Nördlingen in 1634; but Swedish troops remained on German soil for the remainder of the war. Meanwhile Wallenstein negotiated secretly with the Swedish and the French. For this Ferdinand deposed him and had him assassinated. The emperor then took charge of his own army and rapidly gained strength. Once again German Protestantism and the foreign policy of Richelieu, the cardinal architect of Bourbon French opposition to the Habsburgs, were in serious trouble.

Since 1624 Richelieu had been building up France's military and diplomatic power for the day that he could force a showdown with the Habsburgs. In 1635 that day arrived, whereupon he brought France directly into the Thirty Years' War. Central Europe continued to be the principal battleground, but the final phase of the war became a struggle between Habsburg and Bourbon for European hegemony.

The assassination of Henry IV had left France under the nine-year-old Louis XIII with Marie de' Medici as regent. Royal weakness was again the occasion for the nobles to reassert their powers and privileges. In 1614 they secured a summoning of the Estates General (it would be the last until 1789), but the Third Estate opposed the nobility and stalemated the meeting.

700   The Century of Crises: 1560–1660

Three of the many sides of Cardinal Richelieu—a triple portrait.

Louis XIII did not prove to be a strong ruler, but he made up for his deficiencies by making Cardinal Richelieu first minister in 1624. Richelieu was a *politique* whose ruling passion was to build the authority of the French monarchy at home and extend French influence abroad. In 1626 he destroyed the fortresses of the great nobles and removed them from positions of command in his new navy. In the meantime the Huguenots, who made common cause with the aristocracy, rebelled. By 1628 they were crushed and their political and military rights withdrawn; they retained only religious toleration under the Edict of Nantes. Richelieu further subordinated France to royal authority by extending the power of the *intendants,* bureaucrats who came from the middle class: gradually they assimilated the judicial and financial functions that had once belonged to the aristocratic governors of the provinces. Richelieu followed a typical mercantilist policy in building a navy, expanding the army, founding trading companies and colonies, and allowing the increasing burden of taxes and services to be laid on the nonprivileged classes. In addition, tax farmers abused their authority and kept about one-half of all the money collected. But Richelieu overlooked the need for reform in order to devote himself to immediate diplomatic and military tasks.

At first Richelieu believed that France was too weak to risk a direct assault on the Habsburgs and indeed French weakness was displayed both during the Huguenot revolt when Spain seized strategic Alpine passes, and again in 1635 when Spanish invaders nearly took Paris. Richelieu had had to content himself with aiding Protestant allies against the Habsburgs from 1624 to 1635. When France finally entered the war against the Habsburgs in 1635, however, his efforts to mobilize French resources soon began to pay dividends. While Gustavus Adolphus invaded Germany, French troops made major gains in Alsace. Richelieu died in 1642, but French strength continued to grow. In 1643, after the Dutch cut Spanish lines of communication with the Netherlands, French troops defeated the Spanish at Rocroi in the Spanish Netherlands, the first such victory over Spain in more than a century. Following victory at Rocroi so much of the Spanish Netherlands fell to France that the Dutch soon feared their French ally more than distant Spain.

In the German states and Bohemia the effect of active French participation in the Thirty Years' War was to prolong the war devastation for 13 more years.

The Outcome of the War in Central Europe

As Gustavus Adolphus had noted, the wars of Europe had all been rolled into one. Complexities of the war were so great that they baffled negotiators, who brought it to an end in the Peace of Westphalia in 1648. Peace in Germany was impossible until the two major outside belligerents, France and Spain, were weakened by exhaustion and revolution, nor could Germans unite to expel foreign invaders, for Protestants needed foreign troops to protect themselves against Catholics; and the princes needed them to maintain their "liberties" against the emperor. Since the papacy could not sanction concessions to heretical Protestants, the negotiators could not all meet at the same place. Protestants met at Osnabrück, Catholics at Münster. This separation, as well as slow communications between Westphalia and distant Spain, slowed the pace of the talks. Westphalia was the first general peace conference in history, and for it there was no body of accepted rules by which precedence and rank could be determined. Such was only one of the difficulties. Not until the alliance system broke down could meaningful talks get under way. This finally happened when Dutch fears of French expansion led to a separate peace between the United Provinces and Spain. By then both France and Spain, torn by internal revolution, were anxious to reduce their foreign commitments.

A compromise on the question of Church property and official recognition of Calvinism resolved the religious wars in Germany. Princes continued to maintain religious uniformity in their territories, but individual Lutheran, Catholic, or Calvinist dissenters were given certain rights to worship privately and to emigrate. After the Peace of Westphalia few princes changed the religion of their states; religious boundaries hardened into a pattern little disturbed until the mass migration of Germans after 1945. France and Sweden made sure that the German princes obtained almost complete sovereignty. Although the princes were not to make war on the emperor, France and other powers promptly began to organize leagues of German princes to challenge the emperor under the pretext of preserving German liberties.

Sweden, France, and France's protegé, Brandenburg, all left Westphalia with substantial territorial gains. France retained the Alsatian bishoprics of Metz, Toul, and Verdun as well as sovereign but vaguely

CENTRAL EUROPE AFTER 1648

Legend:
- Church lands
- Habsburg lands
- Wettin lands
- Hohenzollern lands
- Wittelsbach lands
- Holy Roman Empire
- Land ceded by Westphalia

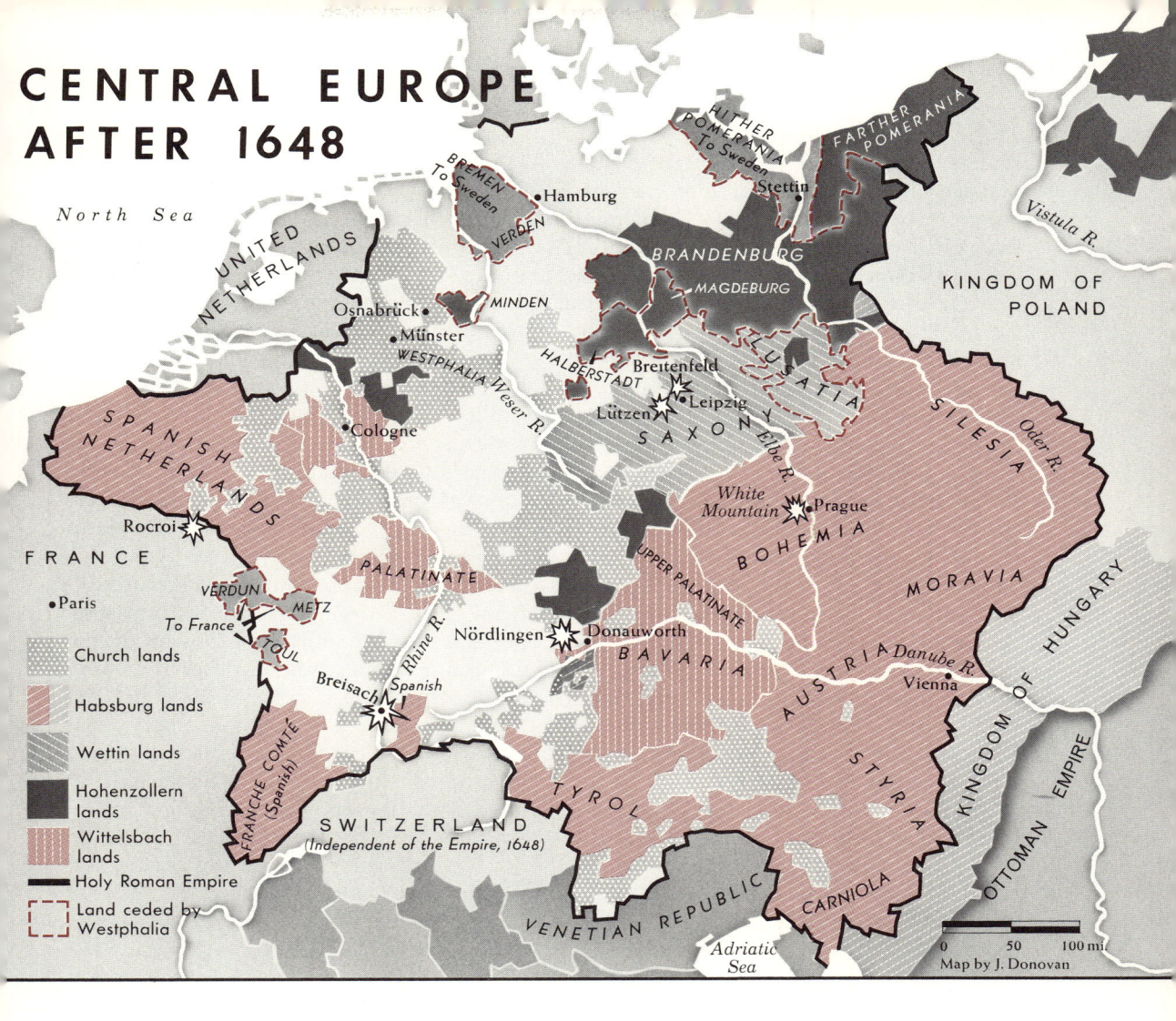

defined authority over all of Alsace. Sweden received Western (Hither) Pomerania and territory (towns, bishoprics, or islands) near the mouth of every major river flowing from the empire into the Baltic; these were remunerative toll stations. In their capacities as German princes, the rulers of both France and Sweden became members of the Imperial Diet. With French support the Hohenzollerns of Brandenburg increased their scattered holdings, gaining Eastern Pomerania, the bishoprics of Minden, Halberstadt, and Cammin, and inheritance rights to Magdeburg. The peace also recognized the independence of Switzerland and the United Provinces (the Dutch Republic).

Westphalia began the final breakup of the Holy Roman Empire and sealed the decline of the papacy as a force in international affairs. Although modified by subsequent treaties, it laid the foundation of the European state system that prevailed until the days of the French Revolution. Nationalists would eventually lament the fact that Westphalia divided Germany, but at its inception the treaty was generally hailed as a diplomatic success and a keystone of European order and peace.

703　　C. Four Decades of War and Revolution: 1618–1660

This settlement implied that states, no matter how they differed in might, were—at least in theory—equal members of a community of sovereign states. The medieval ideal of universal rule by pope and emperor thus gave way to a new order.

After hostilities were ended central Europe faced an immense task of reconstruction. Although we do not have accurate statistics, the empire as a whole probably lost one third of its population. Some areas in Saxony were barely touched; others, like Henneberg along the Main River, may have lost four-fifths of their people. Depopulation on this scale resulted not so much from military losses as from the plagues that swiftly followed armies and swept through the towns where civilians sought refuge from marauding troops. Under normal conditions human beings are generally able to recover from such losses within a generation, but conditions in postwar Germany were severely abnormal.

German nationalists later exaggerated the destructive effects of the war; but of the serious agrarian crisis that followed in its wake there can be no doubt. Shortages of money and labor led ruling aristocrats to force harsh servitude on lower-class youth and to appropriate much peasant land. Peasants were enserfed at a particularly rapid rate east of the Elbe, where fighting continued for some time. But the shrunken supply of money and workers does not alone account for Germany's failure to recover from the war: central Europe also lost its commercial initiative to the west, largely because its small individual states followed restrictive, protectionist policies of mercantilism. The petty German princelings, desperate for local self-sufficiency and revenues, put so many barriers in the way of commerce that continental trade became extremely difficult. Economically, Germany grew more parochial and sluggish than it had been in the Middle Ages.

War, Revolution, and Defeat in Habsburg Spain

The Thirty Years' War fatally drained the ebbing resources of the Spanish Habsburgs. And the Peace of Westphalia left Spain to fight alone against France in a war that would last for 11 more years.

At the Habsburg helm during the critical years 1621 to 1643 was the favorite of Philip IV, the Count of Olivares. His career and policies—save for their notable lack of success—ran strikingly parallel to those of Richelieu. Trained for the Church, Olivares became the most powerful minister in Spanish history. He began his career as a reformer, setting out to force officials to disgorge the fortunes that they had embezzled, curb the power of the Church, abolish taxes on necessities, and reduce the size and costs of the court. But the status quo put up too strong a resistance, and as a consequence he was able to accomplish little. Moreover he became an advocate of an aggressive foreign policy, and the war he favored forced him to double the very excises he considered ruinous to Castile.

Bled by the costs of defense and aggression, Castile faced imminent exhaustion of men and money. To save it and to distribute the financial burdens among other parts of the empire, Olivares sought to bring all the Iberian kingdoms under one law and to establish a common army. But the other kingdoms were too firmly wed to their own constitutions, administrations, and privileges to concur in these changes; in their provinces local *cortes* controlled finance, and troops could not be recruited for use outside their own borders. In 1626 Catalonia, Aragon, and Valencia rejected the common army. Valencia and Aragon voted money, but Catalonia, strategically situated on the French frontier, cited past violations of local laws by Castilian viceroys and refused to grant either men or money. Portugal, whose colony of Brazil was being defended by Philip against the Dutch, was no more cooperative.

The rejection by the other kingdoms of "Castilianization" forced Olivares to fall back on the inadequate resources of Castile. He resorted to radical manipulations of the coinage, stamp duties, sales of offices and titles, revival of old feudal obligations of the nobility, and confiscations of dwindling silver shipments from America. None of these exactions averted defeat: in 1638 the fall of Breisach cut land communications with the Spanish Netherlands, and in the following year, in a battle off the English coast, the Dutch destroyed much of the Spanish fleet and blocked Spain's sea communications with the Netherlands. In addition, Castile's colonial trade was faltering. And in 1640 the old foundations of empire gave way.

The first blow was the revolt of Catalonia, which was trapped in a general Mediterranean depression and prodded by tax demands by Olivares at the same time; Castilian exactions after 1637 for the defense of Catalonia against French invasion had offended all social classes. In 1640 revolutionaries killed the Castilian viceroy, proclaimed a republic, and solicited French assistance. Although the revolution lacked unity of purpose and leadership, Castile was unable to suppress it until 1652. When Olivares called on Portugal for assistance against Catalonia in 1640, the Portuguese nobility proclaimed the duke of Braganza king and initiated their own war for independence which, with French and English aid, they eventually secured. Olivares sought to make peace with France and the Netherlands as a way out of his difficulties, but they spurned his offers.

Confronted with two simultaneous revolutions, gyrating prices, and a flagging war effort, Philip IV (1621–65) dismissed Olivares in 1643 and took personal charge of the government. Crisis followed on crisis. In 1647 new revolts against the policies of Castilian viceroys broke out in Sicily and Naples; in that same year—and again in 1653—the treasury, unable to meet its obligations by any expedient, was forced into bankruptcy.

The most remarkable outcome of these crises was that the Habsburg dynasty survived them all. The Habsburgs' greatest asset was that their foes, foreign and internal, were at odds among themselves. In 1647 the United Provinces broke with France (a break largely manipulated by Spain); and at about the same time Catalonia also stopped taking aid from the French, feeling that its autonomy was more threatened by them than by the powers in Madrid. Rebellious forces in Iberia and Italy never broke out of their isolation to cooperate with one another for mutual gains, and class conflicts within the revolutionary ranks proved ultimately irresolvable. The rebel aristocrats were so frightened by the social and political radicalism of their commoner brethren that when Philip IV offered to restore their old privileges, they eagerly cooperated with him. One by one the isolated revolutions collapsed, except in Portugal. The house of Habsburg had survived by appealing to the traditionalism of the nobility; but such reverence for tradition also prevented reform, and the monarchy still tottered on the verge of financial collapse. Probably only a fourth of the tax moneys collected actually reached the treasury. The Peace of the Pyrenees with France (1659) came barely in time to save Philip IV from total insolvency.

Spain accepted the Pyrenees as a boundary, and thus abandoned Roussillon and part of Cerdagne to France; in the Low Countries it ceded Artois. The marriage of Maria Theresa of Spain to Louis XIV sealed the treaty—until the Habsburgs failed to pay her dowry and thus gave Louis an excuse to claim other Spanish lands. From that time onward Spain's role in Europe was limited to defensive efforts against Louis XIV's ex-

REVOLTS AGAINST PHILIP IV

Map by J. Donovan

pansionist policies. Spanish predominance had been superseded by French hegemony.

Mazarin, Revolution, and Peace in France

A major reason why France agreed to peace in 1648 and why Spain was able to hold out successfully so long alone against France was that France, too, was weakened by a revolution that had Spanish diplomatic support.

Both Louis XIII and his chief minister, Richelieu, died before the end of the Thirty Years' War (Richelieu in 1642, Louis in 1643); but French policy changed little. The new king, Louis XIV, was only five years old and the state was controlled by his first minister, Cardinal Mazarin. Handpicked by Richelieu as his successor, the Italian-born Mazarin was a Jesuit-educated international adventurer serving his apprenticeship in war and diplomacy under the papacy when Richelieu noticed him, took him into the French court, and secured for him a cardinal's hat. Mazarin's policies followed Richelieu's so closely that the epigram "the cardinal is not deceased, he has changed his age" was very apt.

But unlike Richelieu, Mazarin had no mature king to rely on. He compensated for this somewhat by becoming the queen mother's lover, but her support could not mitigate his widespread unpopularity: the French nobility and upper classes hated him. Not only was he a foreigner building a private fortune at state expense, but also he refused to recognize the aristocracy as tax exempt. Hostile satires (*Mazarinades*) began to circulate, especially when he bestowed state favors on his own family. What popularity he did enjoy derived mainly from his military feats, but even these proved self-defeating. His war policy—which was designed to conquer the whole of the Spanish Netherlands—only caused the Dutch to break with France. And when domestic revolts further strained his control, Mazarin was forced to accept the more moderate gains of the Peace of Westphalia.

In 1648 disaffected jurists of the Parlement (high law court) of Paris and members of royal councils initiated a revolution (the *Fronde*) against Mazarin. Borrowing from arguments used by the English parliamentarians against the Stuarts, the Fronde was a revolt against the whole financial-administrative system of Richelieu and Mazarin. Taxes were to be levied only with the consent of the high law court, extortions by tax farmers were to be investigated, and the land tax was to be reduced and levied solely for purposes of war. The *Frondeurs* also demanded abolition of the office of intendant, approval by the Parlement of all new offices created, and no imprisonment without trial for more than 24 hours. Although these demands might have held great appeal for the masses, the motives behind them were suspect. The leaders of the Fronde were primarily concerned with protecting ennobled officeholders from taxation and with freeing them from the supervision of administrative officials; but such aims were too narrow to sustain an effective revolt. The Frondeurs were thus unable to constitute themselves as a representative legislative assembly, and Mazarin undermined them with temporizing concessions and dissimulating intrigues. After a major victory in Artois (1648) he stormed Paris with veteran troops, and in 1649 stubborn resistance in the capital collapsed.

Mazarin's victory satisfied neither nobility nor populace, however. A new revolution, the Nobles' Fronde, broke out in 1649. Supported by Spain, it was aimed simply at overturning Mazarin. But Mazarin overturned it instead. By 1653 his foreign mercenaries had defeated the nobles, whereupon he renounced all his previous concessions to them and set about in earnest to realize the ambitions of Louis XIV to rule absolutely.

Before Mazarin died, in 1661, he negotiated the Peace of the Pyrenees and, by aligning German princes along the Rhine with French foreign policy, laid the groundwork for future French expansion. He also left Louis XIV the corps of officials who made the French monarchy a model of dynastic absolutism. An outstandingly efficient bureaucracy in the service of the crown was one legacy of the seventeenth-century crisis in France.

Crisis in Eastern Europe

The Swedish invasion of Germany from 1630 to 1648 was only one part of a larger and longer eastern power struggle, mainly instigated by Sweden's imperial ambitions, which was a contest for control of the territories adjoining the Baltic Sea. Between 1655 and 1660 all of Europe was concerned about its outcome. Sweden's rise to power in Europe was impressive, but she did not maintain for very long her role as a leading state. Gustavus Adolphus, until he invaded Germany in 1630, was fighting for the throne of Poland and the Baltic Sea coast. While Sweden was engaged in Germany, Russia tried and failed to conquer the Smolensk area from Poland and in 1634 renounced all claims to the Baltic littoral. After Westphalia, Sweden had bases in Germany (Pomerania was an especially vital one) from which to launch new assaults on Poland across Hohenzollern East Prussia.

The first link in the chain of events leading to general war in 1655 was a revolt of seminomadic Cossacks in the Ukraine against their Catholic Polish overlords in 1648. Defeated by Poland, the Cossacks sought Russian protection in 1653. Soon the Ukraine became part of the czars' empire. With the Cossack war chieftains on his side, the Romanov czar, Alexis (1645–1676), renewed war with Poland, captured Smolensk, and proceeded to invade Lithuania. Sweden resisted Russia's push to the Baltic and, taking advantage of

707   C. Four Decades of War and Revolution: 1618–1660

Poland's involvement in the east, invaded that country.

The Northern War (1655–60) soon involved most of Europe. At first the Swedish invasion of Poland was immensely successful. Soon, however, the Poles were antagonized by the invaders' aggressive Protestantism and their capacity for cruelty. Brandenburg, caught between Poland and Sweden, was obliged to become a Swedish ally in 1656. When Denmark entered the war against Sweden, Brandenburg, supported by the emperor, secretly switched sides in return for a promise of sovereignty over East Prussia, which the elector of Brandenburg had held previously as a fief of Poland. In order further to check Sweden, the emperor allied with Poland. Then Mazarin, who was locked in a diplomatic battle with the emperor, prompted the western maritime states—England and the United Provinces—to intervene also. Wanting to establish a balance of power in the northeast, Mazarin secured an international peace conference at Oliva, near Danzig. By the Treaty of Oliva (1660) Sweden lost her wartime conquests with the exception of Livonia (now part of Latvia and Estonia), and the Baltic was opened to the ships of all states.

The peace terms of Oliva proved transitory, but the Northern War left lasting marks on the societies of the Baltic states. Like the Thirty Years' War, it provoked an agrarian crisis that helped to rivet the status of serfdom onto the peasants of east-central Europe; it also cleared new ground in which authoritarianism could take root. The principality of Brandenburg, for example, was so dismayed at its vulnerability to foreign invaders that Frederick William "the Great Elector" had little trouble building a standing army and instituting a military despotism there. The outstanding exception to the despotic social order that took root in the wake of these wars was Sweden, but it, too, passed through a revolutionary crisis after the Thirty Years' War. Gustavus Adolphus's successor, the erratic Queen Christina, ceded a major portion of the royal domain to the nobility and created a horde of new nobles who claimed state office as an aristocratic privilege. Meanwhile the nobles sought powers commensurate with the German and Polish lords with whom they had made contact in Sweden's new acquisitions along the Baltic. In 1650 a social-constitutional crisis rocked Sweden. Unlike peasants and townsmen in Poland and Germany, the Swedish commoner had well-established legal rights and sent representatives to a diet that possessed considerable vitality. The nobles made impressive gains in power, but the lower orders in the diet—in coalition with lower-ranking officials—were able to check them. In this respect, Swedish social and constitutional development resembled that of England more than the rest of the Continent.

STUART ENGLAND

By and large, England remained aloof from the struggles on the Continent, but it had its own religious revolution, its own civil wars. As on the Continent, the major source of those conflicts was the growth of a revolutionary Calvinist movement that championed the rights of Parliament and the courts against the absolutist claims of the monarchy.

Stuart Kings and Parliaments

The aspirations of James I were probably no more despotic than those of Elizabeth, but his insistence on proclaiming the principle of divine-right kingship quickly brought him into conflict with Parliament and the common-law courts. Elizabeth had always managed the House of Commons very diplomatically, but James departed from this policy and asserted that its members owed him obedience as a matter of right and principle—

an obedience that he claimed from all his subjects. Parliament was not amenable to this approach and was particularly recalcitrant in meeting the king's demands for taxes to cover the mounting expenses of the state. In order to raise money, therefore, James was forced back on other expedients: he sold titles and honors wholesale to wealthy men desirous of buying prestige, liquidated large portions of the royal domain, and established and sold monopolies in consumer items. None of these schemes satisfied the financial needs of the state, and all of them detracted from royal prestige and weakened the power of the Crown. The massive sale of titles cheapened the status of men who already had them and weakened their attachment to the Crown. To sell lands from the royal domain was bad economic policy; it meant that the king was living on his capital and transferring his economic power to his wealthier subjects. The monopolies antagonized merchants who were excluded from them and alienated the ordinary consumers who had to pay higher prices. And Parliament was hostile to measures that were designed to circumvent parliamentary control over finance; the Parliament that met in 1614 persisted in discussing constitutional issues rather than voting supplies, and it finally provoked James to dissolve it.

Between 1611 and 1621 James called Parliament only once—in 1614. But a serious depression in the cloth trade from 1620 to 1624 so strained the already flagging royal revenues that James was forced in 1624 to seek new grants of taxes. The House of Commons not only failed to comply, but reasserted some of its ancient prerogatives. In that same year Parliament attacked trading company monopolies, which many independent merchants held responsible for the depression. Now Parliament was no longer staging a defensive struggle against the king; it was claiming the right to initiate legislation and to appoint committees to supervise the execution of the laws it enacted. Although the concept of the modern legislative assembly was yet only dimly perceived, Parliament was gradually assuming the character of a legislature that could call on some degree of popular support. But just as on the Continent in the seventeenth century—where diets defended only the privileges of the aristocracy—so in England at that time popular support meant mostly support from the wealthier classes of society. In the face of his rebellious legislature James I denounced men who presumed "to meddle with anything concerning our government mysteries of state," and at one point he even arrested the leaders of the House of Commons. Nevertheless, he did make some concessions to Parliament.

Although the reign of his successor, Charles I, would end at the executioner's block, it appeared to open auspiciously. As a young prince Charles had opposed his father's pro-Spanish foreign policy, an attitude that gained him considerable popularity. But once on the throne, he soon came into conflict with the same institutions and doctrines that had confronted James. When Charles requested money, Parliament proceeded to proclaim its rights anew and to attack his favorite minister. In his desperate search for new forms of revenue, the king exacted forced loans from his subjects and revived archaic feudal dues. In 1628 Parliament firmly responded with the Petition of Right, a landmark in the history of constitutional government. It declared that no taxation should be levied without parliamentary consent, that no troops should be billeted in private homes, that martial law should not be imposed in peacetime, and that no man should be imprisoned without the cause being shown. As it reaffirmed personal liberty, attacked royal control over a standing army, and claimed the right of Parliament to approve taxation, the Petition of Right significantly challenged the fundamental bases of royal absolutism.

The struggle against the king had religious as well as political roots. English Calvinists had produced a talented and articulate group of propagandists who used the press and pulpit to fullest advantage. The increasing strength of Puritanism was further reflected in the membership of the House of Commons. Puritanism was a social doctrine as well as a religious creed: it established an aristocracy of the predestined elect—"the Godly people"—who were known by their moral code and their religious devotion. Puritan doctrines placed a high premium on individual thought and action and set commitments derived from personal experience above rulings handed down from church hierarchies, and moral responsibility counted for more than formal religious observance. In rituals and traditions of priestly privilege—whether Roman Catholic or Anglican—Puritans saw the embodiment of the devil and superstitious idolatry. They identified their enemies as God's enemies, deserving bitter invective, persecution and, ultimately, death. They were doing God's work and it was his will that they reach their goal. They did not conspire—as Royalists later accused them of doing—to create a revolution. But as they tried to achieve the reforms dictated by their consciences, they followed a course that led, gradually but inexorably, to the overthrow of the monarchy. Certainly James I had never shown a readiness to conciliate them. "If you aim at a Scottish presbytery," he said to them, "it agreeth as well with monarchy as God with the devil." But although harsh measures were taken against the more Puritan clergy and against Separatists, who wanted to break away from the official church, James interfered very little with the religious lives of his subjects. Charles I, however, yielding to Archbishop William Laud, followed quite another policy. By 1629, Laud, whose beliefs seemed to border on Catholicism, had gained substantial influence in Charles's court. He began, through the ecclesiastical court of High Commission (a Tudor creation), to restrict and penalize Puritan practices. After 1630 it seemed all too apparent to Puritans that royal policy offered them only the choices of emigration, conformity, or struggle. Some did emigrate; but eventually most of them took to arms.

In 1629, when the House of Commons disobeyed Charles's command and discussed religious issues, the king locked the chamber and arrested eight of its leaders. Charles then ruled without Parliament from 1629 to 1641, but the conflict did not abate. The Puritans were eager for the king to intervene in the continental religious struggle, but Charles's financial difficulties dictated caution. He was forced to follow a weak and very unpopular foreign policy. At the same time, the laws against Catholics were only casually enforced, which infuriated Puritans who were themselves under legal pressure to conform. But it was the king's attempt to institute an Anglican prayer book and establish an episcopal hierarchy in his Calvinist kingdom of Scotland that finally brought an end to his financial independence of Parliament. The Scottish Presbyterians rose and invaded England in 1640, and Charles was forced to summon a new Parliament. Many Puritans were returned as members, and the body (which has come to be called the Short Parliament) proved so obstreperous that the king hastily dissolved it. Continued pressure from Scotland, however, forced him to call another a few months later. The first session of this "Long Parliament" lasted almost a year, a period of unmatched significance in English legislative history.

Although members of the Long Parliament claimed that the measures they were enacting were merely restoring the old fundamental laws of England, the Long Parliament stripped the king of some of his traditional powers, and some of its enactments did represent constitutional innovations. Charles was forced to assent to an act that authorized Parliament to meet once every three years whether or not summoned by the Crown (the Triennial Act). He was also made to abolish such unpopular prerogative courts as High Commission and Star Chamber and to eliminate all feudal revenue measures. His two closest ministers, Strafford and Archbishop Laud, were impeached; a parliamentary statute was passed demanding Strafford's execution, and the King assented to it. Despite all his concessions, a majority of the members of the House of Commons did not trust Charles with control of the army. The situation came to a head in October 1641 when there was a revolt in Ireland. Parliament voted—by a narrow majority—to assume command of the militia, an act that precipitated civil war, the first that England had known since the Wars of the Roses in the fifteenth century and her last to date.

The Civil Wars

In every English county there was a contest for loyalty between the king and the revolutionary parliamentarians. Opposing armed camps of Roundheads (parliamentarians) and Cavaliers (royalists) were slowly and reluctantly formed, and war preparations were interspersed with negotiations. While parliamentary and royalist agents jockeyed for control of arms and men, some counties tried to remain neutral. Alliances shifted. Some parliamentarians who had previously opposed the king and voted against him joined Charles now that the choice was between revolution and loyalty to the Crown. The first campaigns of the civil war were half-hearted and inconclusive. Until 1642 the conflict was confined to the members of the ruling aristocracy who feuded among themselves, but once the conflict developed into full-scale hostility, the door was opened to the more radical Puritan minorities to take control of the parliamentary movement and armies.

Heretofore religious opposition to the royalist Cavaliers had been led by Presbyterians who wanted to abolish the bishops replacing them with a synodal type of Calvinist government of the Scottish variety. Their opposition to the crown was not unanimous or zealous, for most of them were prepared to support the king provided that he introduced the church reforms that they desired. The radical Puritans, however, would go much further. Paramount among these were the so-called Independents (Separatists or Congregationalists) who demanded autonomy for their religious congregations and advocated toleration of at least other Puritan sects. These aims could only be achieved by defeating both the king and the conservative Presbyterians. As the Independent Oliver Cromwell emerged as the leader of the radical Puritans, the civil war began in earnest.

Ever since the seventeenth century men have offered various explanations of the civil wars, and historians still argue about how and why loyalties were divided into warring factions. Royalists attributed the wars to a Puritan conspiracy directed against the rich and the well born. Thomas Hobbes, the political philosopher who formulated a theory of secular absolutism, laid the Puritan revolution that caused the civil wars at the feet of men of the universities and the pulpits whom we would nowadays characterize as "alienated intellectuals." In the nineteenth century historians were dedicated to a "Whig interpretation" whose heroes were the Puritans and parliamentarians. They presented the Roundheads as crusaders who successfully defended the constitutional liberty of Englishmen against Stuart despotism at the same time that they established the foundations for English commercial and imperial power. Recent interpretations of the English civil wars, however, have looked to social factors in an attempt to explain political alignment. No longer are the parliamentarians and the Stuart kings seen solely in terms of black and white. Some historians believe that Stuart social policy was socially useful and that the men who opposed the Stuart kings in Parliament were primarily defending their own class and economic interests. For Marxists, the English civil war represents one stage in the development of capitalism, the "bourgeois revolution," or the phenomenon by which an emerging capitalism frees itself of feudal restraints.

Because in England the ownership of land was the foundation on which all social prestige and, hence, political power was based, the role of the gentry in the upheavals of seventeenth-century England has been subject to intense scrutiny. The term "gentry" itself, although essential, is often misleading, and historians have not been able to agree among themselves what sort of men the term should include. It is not surprising therefore that the role of the gentry should have engendered fierce controversy. One school has held that the gentry as a class was growing rich because its members applied business techniques to farming; they were engaging in a form of capitalist agriculture and—at the expense of a declining nobility—were accumulating land and the political power that went with it. This interpretation has it that the revolutionary civil wars were caused to a large extent by these members of the rising gentry, who were eager to grasp and exercise social and political power commensurate with their economic wealth. Other historians, however, have come to completely opposite conclusions. They believe that the civil wars were brought about by the efforts of a gentry whose fortunes were declining, and they maintain that the radical Independents of the revolution were the men who, because they were in fact losing their lands, turned in desperation against the Stuart kings. Still other historians are convinced by solid evidence that the gentry maintained its status quo and preserved a relatively comfortable position in society, but that great fortunes were made by lawyers, merchants, and courtiers who naturally invested their money in land. This academic battle, which has been described as a "storm over the gentry,"[3] is not likely to abate, for our knowledge of early seventeenth-century economic history is too meager to be conclusive. One thing, however, is certain: every major faction of the revolution drew its leadership from men of the gentry. How then can we say which factors determined an individual's loyalty? Whether a man chose the side of the king or of Parliament, his decision was probably influenced by his religious feelings and his connections—or lack of connections—at court.

Owing to the structure of economic life in early seventeenth-century England, men who had friends at court were likely to prosper from favors. It was only natural, therefore, that merchants and members of the gentry who had no or only weak court connections blamed their economic difficulties on the court, on the monopolies, and finally on the Crown itself. Small producers, who were suffering from a slump in the export trade of woolen goods, voiced the same kinds of complaint; also, tradesmen in the towns were exposed to radical religion and participated to a marked degree in the Puritan movement.

Religious affiliation was also crucial in defining loyalties, for in the past only Anglicans stood to prosper from court connections and favors. Since the established episcopal church was the main agent of social control, conflict raged over what structure the English church would assume. Should the church be dominated by bishops appointed by the king, should it be organized on the basis of presbyteries under the control of men of substance, or—the most radical suggestion of all—should it consist of independent democratic congregations? These were questions that aroused religious dispute; they also stirred up social conflict. Men of wealth feared that the demands of the lower classes for religious equality were only a prelude to demands for political,

[3] J. H. Hexter, *Reappraisals in History* (New York: Harper & Row, Publishers, 1961), pp. 117–62.

and eventually economic, equality. Nor were these forebodings completely unjustified.

When Oliver Cromwell took command of what would become the nucleus of the national army—the "New Model"—he picked his men for their fighting zeal, a quality that apparently went hand in glove with radical religious views. Under Cromwell and his men the war became an enthusiastic crusade to defeat "papist" royalists and secure toleration for sectarian Puritans. Cromwell's army, "Ironsides," backed by the resources of the wealthier southeastern part of England (now taxed by excises never conceded to Stuart kings), destroyed the main Cavalier army at the decisive battle of Naseby in 1645. The Royalist cause was crushed and Charles I surrendered to the Scots, who delivered him as a prisoner to the parliamentarians.

Once the king was defeated the Puritans in Parliament set about the religious and political reconstruction of the nation, a task that was at once complicated by the sharp disputes that arose between conservative Presbyterians and more radical Independents. The Independents drew their support from the victorious army whose members were every day growing more vociferous in their demands. Parliament sought to disband the army, leaving the soldiers' pay in arrears. Led by Cromwell, the army seized power in 1647. It looked as though Presbyterian intolerance had been defeated, but the army itself was divided between the Independents (represented by Cromwell) and more radical sectarians who demanded reforms much more democratic than any Cromwell and his associates envisaged.

The relative freedom of thought and expression permitted under the earlier Cromwellian government was fully exploited by political and social reformers. After 1643 debate became fiercer, and in the years that followed thousands of pamphlets appeared. The Independents soon found themselves challenged by a sectarian movement that was growing more and more radical. One of the most extreme radical sects—the Diggers—claimed the right of every man to use the common lands of England, and they attempted to

Oliver Cromwell, a contemporary portrait.

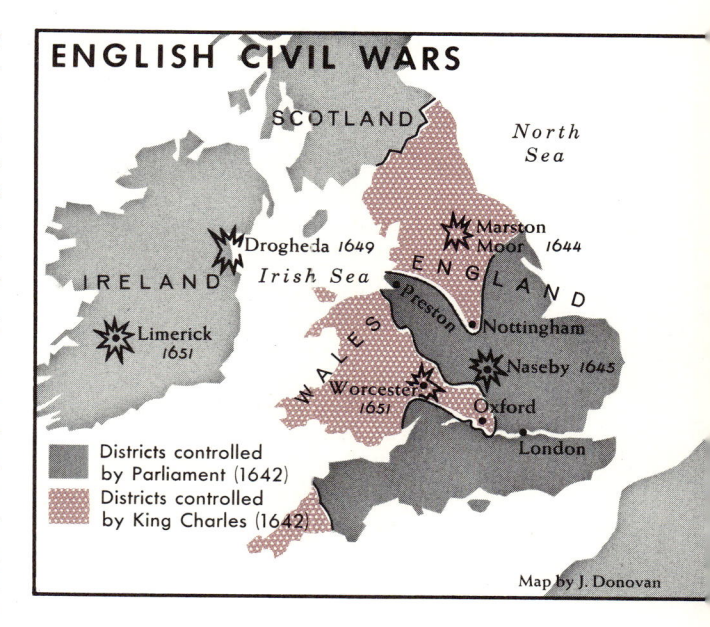

C. Four Decades of War and Revolution: 1618–1660

found a communal society. Another sect, known as the Fifth Monarchy Men, believed that the final day of judgment was at hand. A larger, less radical, and more significant group was the Levellers—a name given them by their opponents, who feared that the extension of the franchise they advocated (by no means universal manhood suffrage) would lead to an assault on property rights and the ultimate leveling of all social distinctions. Twentieth-century historians have paid considerable attention to the Levellers, who are often cited—with much justification—as representing the first modern democratic political movement. The Levellers based their political programs on the doctrine of natural rights. They demanded legal equality, a written constitution, annual parliaments, a single-chamber legislature, separation of church and state, the abolition of tithes and excise taxes, and intensive reform of common law that among other things would do away with imprisonment for debt, arbitrary imprisonment, and compulsory self-incrimination. The Levellers were a small minority, and even within the army they had no real opportunity of achieving their objectives. Although Cromwell and his Independents were willing to assent to part of this program, they saw in the most advanced of the Levellers' ideas a threat to public order and an attack on the rights of property. Cromwell finally turned against them and the Leveller leader, John Lilburne, acknowledged political defeat when he joined the Quakers. The Quakers, who were not originally pacifists, were another group that had appeared during the civil war to "reform the Reformation." Later they adopted the technique of nonviolence to achieve humanitarian reform. None of the more radical groups was sufficiently organized or powerful to influence the course of events.

Rather it was Cromwell's army that took the lead in crushing the resurgence of royalism that culminated in the second civil war (1648). Fearful of army radicalism, Presbyterian parliamentarians in 1647 offered to restore Charles I in return for a temporary establishment of a Presbyterian church. The army forestalled this alliance by taking custody over the king, but he escaped and negotiated a treaty with the Scots recognizing Presbyterianism. As the Scots invaded England, royalists and some Presbyterians rallied to the royalist cause. Under Cromwell's leadership the army united against the counterrevolutionary coalition decisively defeating the Scots at Preston in 1648. Thereafter the army purged Parliament of its Presbyterian members, leaving it—the "Rump"—with only members who supported the army. One of the Rump's first actions was to try Charles Stuart for treason; in 1649 he was executed under conditions that made him a popular martyr of the royalist cause.

The Commonwealth and the Protectorate

The Rump promptly abolished the monarchy and the House of Lords, proclaiming the sovereignty of the people represented solely by the commons. This action inaugurated the Commonwealth, an experiment in republican government, but the real power of the state was in the hands of the parliamentary commander, Oliver Cromwell, who accepted his victories as evidence that he was now the chosen instrument by which England would become a truly "Godly" society. (That England was also becoming a Protestant imperial power seemed equally a part of divine providence.) Before the end of 1649 Cromwell began the suppression of Ireland, where a royalist-Catholic faction was strong, with calculated military terror, and in 1650 he put down Scottish royalist opposition with his stunning victory at Dunbar. Both Scotland and Ireland were united with England. Under the Commonwealth the Navigation Act of 1651, designed to remove the Dutch from the English carrying trade, was passed, and England conducted a naval war against the Dutch Republic.

But despite his foreign and military successes, Cromwell failed to unify England behind him. When the Rump refused to disband, Cromwell cleared the house with troops, declaring Parliament dissolved. It was replaced by a parliament picked by the council of the army from nominations submitted by Independent congregations. The inexperience and radicalism of this "Barebones Parliament," which set out to disestablish the existing tithe-supported church and made marriage a civil contract, so disappointed Cromwell and his fellow officers that they drew up a new constitution for England, the Instrument of Government of 1653.

The Instrument of Government (England's last written constitution) represents an effort to separate and balance the central powers of government. Thus it did not terminate the tension between the executive and Parliament which England had experienced under the Stuarts. Cromwell rejected the crown for himself, preferring to take the title of Protector, but like the Stuarts whose mantle he spurned he dismissed Parliament for its encroachments on executive powers. The army began again to determine what elected members were eligible to sit, and soon a new house of lords was created to counterbalance the commons' power.

By 1655 real power was lodged in the hands of major generals in command of eleven military districts into which the country was divided, but even with military rule Cromwell was never able to force Englishmen to accept toleration and Puritanism. Instead there was a strong reaction in favor of restoring the son of the martyred Charles I. Cromwell died in 1658 leaving his son Richard as his designated successor, but Richard was completely ineffectual. Control over the army fell to General George Monck who reestablished the Long Parliament of 1640, returning to it those expelled Presbyterians who were still alive. Under his direction the Crown was restored to Charles II. Although a Stuart was once again on the throne, the Crown was stripped of extraordinary prerogative courts, extraparliamentary powers of raising revenue, feudal rights, and rule by royal edict. These were the positive constitutional gains produced by the revolutionary epoch that closed in 1660.

England under Cromwell had experimented with a variety of constitutional systems, but even military rule under a republic did not expunge traditional monarchist sentiment. The failure of the army also meant the failure of Puritanism. As a spiritual force Puritanism continued to survive in England, but, as in the Netherlands, Puritans did not succeed in imposing their political will on the nation. Under the restored Stuarts the Puritans were effectively excluded from political life. Never again would they attempt to overthrow the government in hope of achieving their aims; never again would England know religious fanaticism so strong or pass through a crisis so deep that it would result in civil war.

D. The Art and Literature of Crisis

THE AGE OF THE BAROQUE

In a climate of conflict the Renaissance ideals of art and literature were unable to flourish. Humanists and artists of the Italian Renaissance had emulated a classical tradition, aiming at perfect form and style, proportion, naturalism, tempered emotion, and decorous serenity. Italians continued to maintain their artistic and literary preeminence while their own states fell to despots and foreign invaders and while religious controversies set the rest of Europe ablaze. But the model of classical simplicity was supplanted by the colossal grandeur, metaphysical allegory, and emotional subjectivity we characterize as baroque. Traditional classicism and naturalism retained a hold in Venice and spread, except where they were banned by Puritan sentiments, through the mercantile states of northwestern Europe.

Baroque became a pejorative term, connoting extremely ornate and gaudy works. Baroque artists retained classical themes, but adapted them to portray power, spirit, suffering, emotion, and sensuality, the measure of individuality in this kind of art being the extent to which its creator had pressed the rules of classicism. To view most Renaissance works with maximum effect, the eye rests on definite planes and within fixed boundaries. But the baroque characteristically required a visual sweep which knew no bounds and suggested something beyond. In both art and literature baroque artists revived the use of allegory and metaphysical symbolism that had been dominant in the Middle Ages and subdued by the classical realism of the early Italian Renaissance.

Baroque art was a product of the militant Catholic Reformation. It first appeared in Italy, from which base missionaries and armed forces were operating to reinstitute the Catholic faith in Europe. Italian-trained artists went to capitals as far apart as London and Moscow, but they were not always warmly welcomed; populations whose main concern was commerce were unresponsive. Anglicans, German Lutherans, and followers of the Russian Orthodox faith could disregard doctrinal content and yet be moved by the emotional religious quality of the baroque style. But Calvinists were often distinctly hostile. Outside Italy the baroque had its greatest appeal in Habsburg Europe; there Crown, nobility, and Church exploited it to celebrate victories, exalt noble families, and satisfy the emotional hunger of a people beset by war, famine, epidemics, and oppression by a rigid social hierarchy. Baroque art flourished in Spain, Portugal, southern Germany, Flanders, Bohemia, Hungary, Poland, and, to a lesser extent, France. The Iberian kingdoms carried it to their American colonies, where some of its most exotic expressions can still be found today.

Sculpture and Architecture

The most versatile and influential baroque artist was Giovanni Bernini (1598–1680). After 1629 he was the architect of St. Peter's in Rome. Together with his famous contemporary, Borromini, he worked under papal patronage to make Rome the fittingly ornate capital of a rejuvenated Catholicism. Bernini grew famous as the only worthy successor of Michelangelo. Louis XIV, the English court, and other high powers sought him out for commissions; and he was paid a personal visit by the pope. Although he thought his genius lay in painting, Bernini is best known today for such architecture as the Plaza and Colonnade of St. Peter's and such sculptures as *Daphne and Apollo, Bust of Louis XIV*, and the *Ecstasy of St. Theresa*. He also drew plans to rebuild the Louvre in Paris, but royal ministers rejected them as too expensive. Most of his career was spent in Rome, where he and his large staff of assistants were employed by a series of pontiffs.

Bernini and his Italian contemporaries profoundly influenced architecture and sculpture in Catholic Europe, particularly churches, palaces, and villas that were usually as large as funds permitted—the churches to provide in addition to services and rituals an imposing setting for elaborate decorations and large numbers of worshippers, the palaces and villas to accommodate lavish parties in addition to opera and ballet performances. In the case of the Escorial—the vast structure Philip II built near Madrid (it included a royal palace, a church, a mausoleum, a college, and a monastery)—baroque architecture was a means of exalting the nobility of an entire kingdom. Before Louis XIV created Versailles the Escorial was the outstanding example of monumental and sumptuous construction. Baroque buildings were characterized by curved exterior walls with recesses, twisted columns, massive facades, and ornate (and sometimes grotesque) statuary both inside and out. The rooms were often oval-shaped, and interiors were heavily laden with paintings, tapestries, and massive carved decorations. Ceilings sometimes took on the appearance of infinite sky, an impression that floating figures were designed to convey. Statuary, including altar pieces (Bernini's *Ecstasy of St. Theresa* was designed as such), expressed movement and dynamic emotion. Twisted figures were shown in diagonal positions, and the figures were partially shrouded in blowing drapery to magnify the sense of grandeur or movement.

Not all statuary and architecture in Catholic countries were baroque, and the baroque influence outside Catholic boundaries was limited. Traditional classicism and simple functionalism predominated in England, the United Provinces and, to some degree, in France. In classical architecture the simple lines and pillars of the Venetian architect Andrea Palladio (1518–1580) were widely imitated.

Painting

Baroque painting reflected the same emotionalism found in baroque statuary, and techniques were as parallel as the different media allowed. Baroque painters covered a wide range of subjects. They frequently portrayed the great religious themes (saints and martyrs were particularly popular), mythological episodes, and grotesque or disfigured persons from the lower classes. Mysterious or eerie lighting effects often gave their works an otherworldly aura. The plethora of canvasses produced in the baroque era defies any attempt to discuss individual examples. We shall limit our study here to representative groups. Italians of Rome and Venice produced most of the baroque art of the seventeenth century, but important baroque painters also appeared in Spain during the reign of Philip IV (El Greco, Velásquez, Murillo, José Ribera), and in Flanders (Rubens and Van Dyck). Classicism and realism were intermingled with the baroque in France by Poussin, Lorrain, and the Le Nain brothers.

That baroque techniques also penetrated the Dutch provinces is demonstrated by the later works of Rembrandt van Rijn (1606–69), the greatest of the Northern masters. He was not alone in portraying religious themes infused with anguish, pity, or passion. But as he became more drawn to these themes—after his famous *Night Watch* of 1641—his commissions declined, and he (and other painters), long dependent on a highly competitive market, fell into poverty. Perhaps as many as 2000 painters were working in the Netherlands. Most of them employed some baroque techniques, but they catered to urban middle-class patrons who preferred art that was less gaudy and not so metaphysical. The works of Hobbema, van Ruisdael, Vermeer, and Hals were painstakingly realistic. Baroque art had little opportunity of flourishing in the Netherlands, for its religious and social requisites were lacking. A landowning aristocracy did not dominate society, nor did the Dutch have a monarch bent on glory and grandeur. And Catholicism, which provided the imagery and emotional content in baroque works, was not a force in the Netherlands. England and the German states produced no notable painters during the heyday of the baroque, and their major commissions went to foreign artists.

Bernini's Ecstasy of St. Theresa.

Bernini's colonnade at St. Peter's.

An example of Borromini's work in Rome: S. Carlo alle Quattro Fontane.

Music

Italian composers, like other Italian artists, were leaders in their medium in the seventeenth century. Their achievements were rivaled only by the chorale, a notable Protestant contribution. Their chief creations, the oratorio and the opera, both partook of the baroque spirit, having originated in the Renaissance when drama was first set to music—oratorios in the church, and opera on the secular stage. The oratorio remained almost exclusively a Catholic form of music until George Friedrich Handel (1685–1759) popularized it in England. The opera, too, thrived best where other baroque art flourished, notably in Italy at the hands of Claudio Mon-

Dutch baroque: Rembrandt's Night Watch.

LEFT: *Eerie otherworldliness: El Greco's* View of Toledo.

teverdi, a composer of madrigals exploring new departures in harmony whose first great opera *Orfeo* was performed in Mantua in 1607. Italians attended opera with gusto, but it was also applauded in a few Protestant courts. Eventually Italy lost its lead to Vienna and Versailles. The Habsburg emperors were ardent devotees, as was Louis XIV, who awarded a monopoly of operatic production to Jean Baptiste Lully. At Versailles the opera, and the ballet that complemented it, were cherished by the monarchy as symbols of prestige, and Lully encouraged his royal master to identify himself and members of his court with the gods and goddesses portrayed on the stage.

Italians also pioneered in developing

721   D. The Art and Literature of Crisis

new instruments, particularly the church organ and the violin, but of all the arts music proved to be the one most capable of transcending the boundaries of religious confessions. Those instruments were especially congenial to the genius of Heinrich Schütz (1585–1672). Born in Germany and trained in Italy, he played and composed some of the finest baroque music of the period. Baroque organ music eventually culminated in the towering genius of John Sebastian Bach, a fellow German and a contemporary of Handel. As Lutheran choir director at Leipzig, Bach brought the baroque traditions of the seventeenth and eighteenth centuries to a climax in preludes, fugues, and choral preludes, also in over 200 cantatas secular and sacred. The elderly Bach outlived the popularity of the tradition he represented, but later musicians regarded him as their greatest teacher, and his works are still being mined for musical themes today.

Literature

The baroque literature of the century between 1560 and 1660 is ornate, dramatic, and tense. Baroque writers, playwrights, and poets were influenced by chivalric romance of the late Renaissance, elaborate treatises on courtly behavior, classical mythology, and the Judeo-Christian religious tradition revived during the Reformation. They repudiated the skeptical humanism and robust earthiness of writers like Montaigne, Cervantes, and Shakespeare. Baroque writers saw life governed by two irreconcilable bodies of law: strict secular laws of vengeance and personal honor, and absolute moral laws of obedience to divine commands. Running through their works were themes of violent conflict: in politics, between the rewards and penalties of power; in morality, between the norms of society and the teaching of religion; in art, between the rigid formal rules to which they bowed and the ornateness and complexity of expression that often led them to pile words on words in great profusion. The best examples of baroque literature are the works of the Spanish poets and dramatists like Góngora (1561–1627), Lope de Vega (1562–1635), Calderón de la Barca (1600–81), and the priest-dramatist Tirso de Molina (1571–1648). Unlike *Don Quixote,* which was written at the beginning of the seventeenth century as a satire on the lingering traditions of Spanish chivalry, their works have seldom been translated, owing to their ponderous formal style, emphasis on aristocratic virtues and dilemmas, and complicated allusions to classical mythology and geography. They are therefore little appreciated today.

To some degree baroque forms did appear in England, France, and the Low Countries. Although his particular genius defies any simplified labeling, Shakespeare shares the emotionalism of the baroque writers and often seems to echo their conclusion that secular life is only an empty illusion. For Macbeth life is "a tale/Told by an idiot, full of sound and fury,/Signifying nothing"; and in *The Tempest* Prospero tells us that

> *We are such stuff*
> *As dreams are made on, and our little*
>   *life*
> *Is rounded with a sleep.*

The dominant literary and artistic form developing in northern and western Europe, however, was a neoclassicism adapted to meet the needs of aristocratic society in those areas. Neoclassicists uncovered and tried to honor the formal canons of simplicity, serenity, conciseness, emotional restraint, and brevity that had defined the classical tradition. They sponsored campaigns to standardize the spelling and form of vernacular languages and were supported in such efforts by royal literary societies. But these campaigns were only beginnings, and neoclassicism would not really flower until after the century of crises.

E. The Roots of Crisis

RELIGIOUS, MILITARY, AND ECONOMIC TURMOIL

No century of human history has been without crises; however in examining the period between 1560 and 1660, we are forced to the conclusion that few centuries have had simultaneous crises in so many different compartments of human experience. This century was an age of ideological warfare and revolution, of power politics, incredible corruption, famine, inflation, plague, judicial torture, and spreading bondage. Its barbarity has gone unsurpassed until our own day.

The most conspicuous cause of upheaval was an interlocked combination of religious, political, and social discontent. Minorities—ardent Catholics and revolutionary Calvinists—were determined to impose their views by force. The Catholic Reformation became identified with the imposition of absolutist society based on a hierarchy of ranks. Revolutionary Calvinism combined with the dissident nobility that tried to thwart that absolutism by vesting power in parliaments, courts, and councils. The Calvinists also recruited lower-class townsmen pinched by the price revolution. Again and again the outcome was civil war, which was then caught up in the diplomacy of dynastic power politics.

In these wars religious hatreds inspired the use of unrestrained force and represented an important threat to life, property, and domestic tranquility. No government launched a purely religious crusade, but religious ideologies nurtured militancy and were used to justify duplicity and atrocities. Kings, clerics, and laymen cited precedents from the Old Testament to sanction acts of extreme barbarity, taking their victories as proof that divine providence was on their side. Finally, religious differences seriously affected international diplomacy, thwarting negotiations between states whose rivalries were primarily dynastic.

In addition to these obvious roots of disorder, historians now look to concrete social and technical data to understand the depth of this period's crises more fully.

One area of such investigation has been the changing nature of warfare. In 1560 wars were fought by armies of mercenary infantry supplemented by artillery and cavalry. Societies already unable to provide adequate subsistence for the bulk of their populations found that the costs of supplying and equipping mercenary armies could not be sustained by public revenues. Troops were paid through the captains who had recruited them, but armies also maintained themselves by foraging the countryside, imposing taxes and services on peasants under their control, extorting indemnities from towns, seizing booty, and holding prisoners for ransom. Discipline was casual and armies led by the incentive of plunder were often as destructive of friendly as of enemy territory. In the early seventeenth century the Dutch and the Swedish challenged the traditional mode of warfare, effecting what has been called "the military revolution." Maurice of Nassau, the son of William the Silent, and Gustavus Adolphus replaced massed squares of infantry with thin lines of men using firearms; they enforced discipline by increasing the number of officers, establishing regular pay, and introducing distinctive uniforms; and they applied scientific skills and knowledge to the building of fortifications and the use of artillery. Their enemies were unable to imitate these changes immediately; instead, they further increased the size of their traditional armies. Thus the deleterious influence of mercenary warfare only deepened in many areas.

Another line of inquiry has sought to throw light on the underlying economic weakness of the century of crises. Agriculture and commerce were unable to support the growing population, and colonial products and imports from the "new lands" of eastern Europe did not provide sufficient relief. War, famine, plague, and what is so far an unaccountable decline in the birthrate reduced or at least stabilized the European population in the first half of the seventeenth century. But there could be no basic solution to the age-old subsistence problem until agricultural and industrial technology improved drastically—something that did not begin to happen to a sufficient extent until the eighteenth century.

RENAISSANCE COURTS

Some historians believe that military, religious, and economic explanations cannot satisfactorily account for either the prevalence of religious civil wars or the epidemic of revolutions that swept through the monarchies of Europe as the Thirty Years' War came to a close. They have suggested that states where top-heavy "Renaissance courts" were still to be found suffered from inherent weaknesses that religious conflict and warfare simply increased. The Renaissance court consisted of favorites and noble magnates who clustered about the monarch and who were, to a large extent, maintained by him. The court nobles relinquished their old feudal political rights, but in compensation they were given remunerative posts in the army, diplomatic corps, church, and administration—posts whose powers they exploited for personal and family gain. The cost of their maintenance consumed a large portion of royal revenues even though the bulk of their income came from fees, services, church obligations, monopolies, tolls, bribes, and embezzlement of funds ostensibly collected for public purposes. And they rivaled the king as dispensers of favors and vied with the monarch in determining state policy. Only a very strong king who personally controlled a loyal bureaucracy could triumph over factional intrigues that characterized court life. For the king who was weak, or whose courtiers allied with foreign kings or discontented domestic factions, court politics were dangerous. Further, the fiscal expedients to which kings were driven only served to provoke domestic opposition that often developed into revolution. To raise money kings sold titles, honors and offices. This large-scale "lay simony" cheapened the prestige of the nobility and effectively alienated the older aristocracy and officials. Monarchs endangered their security even more by trying to channel the profits from taxes, patronage, and legal fees out of the hands of local aristocrats and into the royal treasury. Every major revolution and religious civil war during the century involved either factions that competed for power at court or entrenched privileged bodies that resisted all efforts of economic and social reform.

WITCHCRAFT: TRADITION REAFFIRMED

To understand these crises, contemporaries had only their own immediate experiences, intuitive feelings, and traditions to draw on in order to explain and confront the dilemmas of their age. Many of them, especially the clergy, were swept away by the worst witch-craze in European history. Indeed, the Protestant Reformation had done nothing to diminish the late medieval belief in compacts between Satan and witches and in conspiracies of Satan's legions against those of God; and the religious wars did much to further such beliefs. Trials and executions of witches flourished, especially during the first half of the seventeenth century. Between 1623 and 1631 the Catholic bishop of Würzburg in Germany is alone reported to have had 900 persons burned as witches. Protestant countries took their toll, too, on a smaller scale. Skeptics, largely Erasmian humanists, were persecuted by both sides. The witch-craze would not die until a new cosmology, a new world view in which embattled spirits no longer played a conspicuous part, was accepted. Such a revolution was underway. Copernicus had already offered part of the basis for it in 1543, but for a century it remained confined to narrow intellectual circles that were themselves embattled with the weight of tradition.

ABSOLUTISM AND THE SEARCH FOR SECURITY

Meanwhile a few contemporaries developed new political and religious ideologies as a response to the breakdown of the old order. Led by Jean Bodin (who had a fair understanding of the causes of inflation but who also believed in witchcraft!), the *politiques* in France formulated the notion of a secular state sovereignty and proposed that the sovereign state, responsible to the commonweal, tolerate religious dissent too strong to be crushed without civil war. The Arminian humanist Hugo Grotius, who wrote in the United

A contemporary woodcut illustrating the treatment of witches.

E. The Roots of Crisis

Provinces during the Thirty Years' War, outlined a theoretical system of international politics independent of theology, and for this he is credited with having founded the science of international law. Under his system the sovereign state, in its own self-interest, had to accept rational restraints on the conduct of war.

The often disastrous interaction of religion and power politics had helped discredit Reformation doctrines in certain religious circles. Partly as a consequence of this, pietists in Germany and Quakers in England, as well as many other sectarian groups, cultivated religions that set personal morality above formal creeds. Many Roman Catholic reformers such as St. Vincent de Paul (1580–1660) also attached new importance to humanitarian social reform.

Before these humanitarians, the new scientists, and their humanistic popularizers provided alternative ways of thinking, the main response of contemporary people to the crises of the seventeenth century was to establish greater state absolutism. Rulers sought to achieve security from invasion and tried both to eliminate warfare conducted for private profit and to control all military forces within their realms. By 1660 European monarchs had generally adopted disciplined standing armies (although at sea private warfare was still accepted as a normal means of conducting hostilities). The same rulers attempted to control the economy and society by mercantilistic regulations. In their attempt to discipline all aspects of life that had become chaotic during the century of crises they also sought to control the arts, bringing them under the canons of neoclassicism. Religion, too, became a matter of state. Uniformity was the goal, and fanaticism of any kind became suspect. Although the maritime states—England and the Dutch Republic—charted different courses, the immediate sequel of the century of crises for most countries was an age of absolutism.

Selected Readings

Ashley, Maurice. *The Greatness of Oliver Cromwell.* London: Hodder & Stoughton, 1957.

An outstanding apologetic biography by the leading English authority on Cromwell's career.

Ashton, Trevor, ed. *Crisis in Europe: 1560–1660.* New York: Basic Books, 1965.

Articles from Past and Present, *an English journal of "scientific history." The contributors agree that a general crisis existed, but they fail to find a single common cause.*

*Burckhardt, Carl J. *Richelieu: His Rise to Power.* Rev. ed. New York: Random House, Vintage Books, 1964.

An interpretation in political psychology that finds Richelieu's centralized absolutism a prototype of modern democratic society—a controversial thesis useful for its material on court intrigue.

Cipolla, Carlo M. "The Decline of Italy." *Economic History Review*, 2d series, V (1952–53): 178–87.

One of many recent articles in that journal, whose conclusions sharply modify older general histories of early modern Europe.

*Clark, George N. *The Seventeenth Century.* 2d ed. New York: Oxford University Press, 1961.
> *Perceptive analytical chapters arranged by subject and particularly useful for early modern institutions.*

Clough, Shepard B. *The Economic Development of Western Civilization.* New York: McGraw-Hill Book Co., 1959.
> *Several chapters incorporating recent research are pertinent to this period.*

Davies, D. W. *A Primer of Dutch Seventeenth-Century Overseas Trade.* The Hague: Martinus Nijhoff, 1961.
> *A basic discussion of the commerce of Europe's dominant trading state.*

*Elliott, J. H. *Europe Divided: 1559–1598.* New York: Harper & Row, Publishers, 1968.
> *A panoramic survey of the religious wars of the sixteenth century, good for showing the interconnections between different conflicts.*

*———. *Imperial Spain: 1469–1716.* New York: St. Martin's Press, 1964. Lynch, John. *Spain Under the Habsburgs.* Vol. 1, *Empire and Absolutism: 1516–1598.* New York: Oxford University Press, 1964.
> *Two recent in-depth accounts of Spanish institutions and policies by recognized authorities.*

*Friedrich, Carl J. *The Age of the Baroque: 1610–1660.* Rise of Modern Europe Series. New York: Harper & Row, Publishers, 1962.
> *An excellent factual account that finds baroque art the prevailing symptom of the era's tensions.*

*Geyl, Pieter. *The Revolt of the Netherlands.* New York: Barnes and Noble, 1958. ———. *The Netherlands in the 17th Century: 1609–1648.* Rev. ed., vol. 1. New York: Barnes & Noble, 1961.
> *These replace the classic account of the Dutch Republic by John L. Motley with a fundamental reevaluation and deemphasis of the role of Calvinism in determining the outcome of the Dutch revolt.*

Hamilton, Earl J. *American Treasure and the Price Revolution in Spain: 1501–1650.* Cambridge, Mass.: Harvard University Press, 1934.
> *This study demonstrates that inflation was related to bullion imports, but in this and other writings Hamilton exaggerates the role of bullion in producing the "price revolution" and economic growth.*

Heckscher, Eli F. *Mercantilism.* 2d ed., 2 vols. New York: The Macmillan Co., 1955.
> *A much-criticized attack on mercantilism; however, it provides basic facts on economic policies and conditions in the continental monarchies.*

Lea, Henry C. *A History of the Inquisition of Spain.* 4 vols. New York: The Macmillan Co., 1906–7.
> *A heavily documented indictment of the Spanish Inquisition; volume 4 pertains to this period.*

Mattingly, Garrett. *The Armada.* Boston: Houghton Mifflin Co., 1959.

> Good literature and excellent history, assessing the significance of England's naval victory over Spain.

Merriam, Roger B. *Six Contemporaneous Revolutions.* Oxford: Clarendon Press, 1938.

> A study of the revolutions at the end of the Thirty Years' War; a pioneer in the comparative history of revolutions.

Mosse, George L. *The Holy Pretense.* Oxford: Basil Blackwell & Mott, 1957.

> This demonstrates that English Puritans condemned Machiavelli's principles but implemented them under religious terms.

Neale, John E. *The Age of Catherine de' Medici.* London: Jonathan Cape, 1943.

> A particularly valuable study of Calvinism as an international revolutionary movement.

———. *Elizabeth I and Her Parliaments: 1559–1581.* New York: St. Martin's Press, 1958.

> This outlines Elizabeth's relations with Puritans in Parliament and the compromises behind the "Elizabethan Settlement."

*Neff, John U. *Industry and Government in France and England: 1540–1640.* Ithaca, N.Y.: Cornell University Press, 1957.

> A comparative history of mercantilist industrial regulations and their enforcement, emphasizing England's lack of a centralized bureaucracy as a major factor in the decline of English mercantilism.

*Ogg, David. *Europe in the Seventeenth Century.* 8th ed. New York: The Macmillan Co., 1962.

> An old but useful survey that does not consider England part of Europe.

Palm, Franklin C. *Politics and Religion in Sixteenth-Century France.* Boston: Ginn and Co., 1927.

> A political biography of Montmorency-Damville, a leader of the politiques.

Redlich, Fritz. *De Praeda Militari: Looting and Booty: 1500–1815.* Wiesbaden: Franz Steiner Verlag, 1956.

> Legal study that provides reasons why mercenary warfare was economically deleterious.

Reynolds, Robert L. *Europe Emerges: Transition Toward an Industrial Worldwide Society: 600–1750.* Madison, Wis: University of Wisconsin Press, 1961.

> Basic for the expansion of early modern Europe, Europeans' advantages over non-Europeans, and economic policies.

Roberts, Michael. *The Military Revolution: 1560–1660.* Belfast: Boyd, 1956.

> A lecture on military adoption of firearms, new tactics, and discipline by the foremost biographer of Gustavus Adolphus.

Rowse, Alfred L. *The England of Elizabeth: The Structure of Society.* New York: The Macmillan Co., 1950.

> An exceedingly well-written social history.

Simpson, Alan. *The Wealth of the Gentry: 1540–1660.* Chicago: The University of Chicago Press, 1961.
> *A most definitive attack on Tawney's thesis that the gentry was rising economically. Simpson finds that the law and officeholding were more remunerative than agriculture.*

*Steinberg, S. H. *The Thirty Years' War and the Conflict for European Hegemony: 1600–1660.* New York: W. W. Norton & Co., 1966.
> *A revisionist survey that puts the Thirty Years' War in the context of a general European struggle for power and attacks older German views of its effects on the empire.*

*Stone, Lawrence. *The Crisis of the Aristocracy: 1558–1641.* Abr. ed. London: Oxford University Press, 1967.
> *A thorough social and economic analysis of the English aristocracy before the civil wars.*

Supple, B. E. *Commercial Crisis and Change in England: 1600–1642.* Cambridge: Cambridge University Press, 1959.
> *This study derives "mercantilism" from government efforts to remedy specific commercial crises rather than from an ideology of power.*

Tapié, Victor-L. *The Age of Grandeur: Baroque Art and Architecture.* New York: Grove Press, 1960.
> *A stimulating art history that relates baroque artistic tastes to the social, political, and religious milieu of the Catholic Reformation.*

Tawney, Richard H. *The Agrarian Problem in the Sixteenth Century.* London: Longmans, Green & Co., 1912.
> *One of several works in which Tawney presents economic arguments for the rise of the English gentry.*

Trevor-Roper, Hugh, ed. *The Age of Expansion; Europe and the World: 1559–1660.* New York: McGraw-Hill Book Co., 1968.
> *A profusely illustrated folio volume with well-written summary sections written by experts.*

Unwin, G. *Industrial Organization in the Sixteenth and Seventeenth Centuries.* Oxford: Clarendon Press, 1904.
> *An old but useful analysis based on England.*

Wedgwood, Cicely V. *Richelieu and the French Monarchy.* London: English Universities Press, 1949.
> *A useful short political biography.*

———. *The Thirty Years' War.* London: Jonathan Cape, 1938.
> *A standard English account from the emperor's point of view, now under revisionist attack.*

Wernham, R. B. *The Counter-Reformation and Price Revolution: 1559–1610.* The New Cambridge Modern History, vol. 3. Cambridge: Cambridge University Press, 1968.
> *A reference work incorporating the latest scholarship on political and economic topics.*

Asterisk (*) denotes paperback.

Credit List for Volume I

PROLOGUE.—11: Mas-Art Reference Bureau.

I.—22: Marburg-Art Reference Bureau. 23: Marburg-Art Reference Bureau. 26: Art Reference Bureau. 27: Cliché des Musées Nationaux, Louvre. 28: Art Reference Bureau. 30: Alinari-Art Reference Bureau. 31: Herbert Links/Black Star. 32: George Holton/Photo Researchers. 36: The Metropolitan Museum of Art, contribution from Henry Walters and the Rogers Fund, 1916. 40: Marburg-Art Reference Bureau. 41: Art Reference Bureau. 48: Iraq Museum. 52: Marburg-Art Reference Bureau. 53: The University Museum. 55: The Oriental Institute, University of Chicago. 56: Art Reference Bureau. 59: Cliché des Musées Nationaux, Louvre.

II.—74: Marburg-Art Reference Bureau. 76: Marburg-Art Reference Bureau. 80: Oriental Institute, University of Chicago. 87: Yale University Art Gallery. 89: Cliché des Musées Nationaux, Louvre.

III.—102: Marburg-Art Reference Bureau. 104: Both Alison Frantz. 105: Alison Frantz. 111: Alison Frantz. 114: Hirmer Fotoarchiv, Munich. 115: The Metropolitan Museum of Art, Rogers Fund, 1950. 124: Wadsworth Atheneum, Hartford. 129: Museum of Fine Arts, Boston. 134: Ashmolean Museum, Oxford. 135: Staatliche Museen, Berlin. 136: The Metropolitan Museum of Art, Rogers Fund, 1914. 139: Alinari-Art Reference Bureau.

IV.—148: Alinari-Art Reference Bureau. 152: Alinari-Art Reference Bureau. 157: Vatican Museum. 162 (left): Alison Frantz; (below): Alinari-Art Reference Bureau. 163: Alinari-Art Reference Bureau. 164: Both Alinari-Art Reference Bureau. 165: Alinari-Art Reference Bureau. 168 (top): Camera Press-Pix; (bottom): Alison Frantz. 169 (top): Alinari-Art Reference Bureau; (bottom): Greek National Tourist Office. 175: Vatican Museum. 184: The Art Museum, Princeton University. 188 (top): Staatliche Museen, Berlin; (bottom): Alinari-Art Reference Bureau. 189: The Metropolitan Museum of Art, Rogers Fund, 1909. 190: Both Alinari-Art Reference Bureau. 191: Hirmer Fotoarchiv, Munich.

V.—198: Alinari-Art Reference Bureau. 208: John G. Ross/Photo Researchers. 210: Vatican Museum. 218: Alinari-Art Reference Bureau.

220: Staatliche Antikensammlungen, Munich. 227: Both Alinari-Art Reference Bureau. 229: Alinari-Art Reference Bureau. 232: Alinari-Art Reference Bureau. 242: Alinari-Art Reference Bureau.

VI.–249: Alinari-Art Reference Bureau. 250: Roger-Viollet. 260: Alinari-Art Reference Bureau. 261: Alinari-Art Reference Bureau. 266: Alinari-Art Reference Bureau. 269: Giraudon. 276: Both Alinari-Art Reference Bureau. 277: Both Alinari-Art Reference Bureau. 278: Louis Renault/Photo Researchers. 280: Both Alinari-Art Reference Bureau. 282: All Alinari-Art Reference Bureau. 284: Deutschen Archaeologischen Institute, Rome. 296: Alinari-Art Reference Bureau.

VII.–310: Alinari-Art Reference Bureau. 317: Bayerische Staatsbibliothek, Munich. 322 (top): Erich Lessing/Magnum Photos; (bottom): Alinari-Art Reference Bureau. 323: Both Alinari-Art Reference Bureau. 324: Alinari-Art Reference Bureau. 325: Alinari-Art Reference Bureau. 335: British Museum. 336: Vatican Museum. 343: Smithsonian Institution, Freer Gallery of Art, Washington, D.C. 349: Anderson-Art Reference Bureau.

VIII.–356: The Pierpont Morgan Library. 357: The Pierpont Morgan Library. 359: Nicole Bourgeois, Paris. 362: Marburg-Art Reference Bureau. 363: Art Reference Bureau. 367: Marburg-Art Reference Bureau. 376: Universitetets Oldsaksamling, Oslo. 379: Biblioteca Nacional, Madrid. 382: Ashmolean Museum, Oxford. 385: Nicole Bourgeois, Paris. 390: Bayerische Staatsbibliothek, Munich. 392: The Pierpont Morgan Library. 393: The Pierpont Morgan Library.

IX.–400: New York Public Library Picture Collection. 403: British Museum. 411: Alinari-Art Reference Bureau. 412: Alinari-Art Reference Bureau. 414: Bibliothèque de l'Arsenal. 427: Fitzwilliam Museum, Cambridge. 432: Alinari-Art Reference Bureau. 435: Bibliothèque Nationale, Paris.

X.–444: Historical Pictures Service. 446: Vatican Library. 449: New York Public Library Picture Collection. 453: Siena Cathedral. 454: The Granger Collection. 460: Historical Pictures Service. 461: Art Reference Bureau. 464: Marburg-Art Reference Bureau. 471: Walters Art Gallery, Baltimore. 477: The Granger Collection. 480: The Granger Collection. 487: Imperial Library, Paris.

XI.–498: Bibliothèque Nationale, Paris. 502: Both Marburg-Art Reference Bureau. 503: All Marburg-Art Reference Bureau. 504 (top): Alinari-Art Reference Bureau; (bottom): Marburg-Art Reference Bureau. 505: Both Marburg-Art Reference Bureau. 506: Marburg-Art Reference Bureau. 509: Historical Pictures Service. 511: The Bodleian Library, Oxford. 518: Campani Museum. 519: St. Geneviève Library. 525: Alinari-Art Reference Bureau.

XII.–538: Historical Pictures Service. 544: The Metropolitan Museum of Art, Dick Fund, 1925. 547: Cliché des Musées Nationaux, Louvre. 550: The Granger Collection. 552: Johann Jakob Simmler Collection—City Library of Zurich. 553: Historical Pictures Service. 554: The Metropolitan Museum of Art, Fletcher Fund, 1933. 555: Alinari-Art Reference Bureau. 556: Both Alinari-Art Reference Bureau. 557: Both Alinari-Art Reference Bureau.

558: Cliché des Musées Nationaux, Louvre. 559 (top): Alinari-Art Reference Bureau; (bottom): Huntington Library, San Marino, California. 560: Staatliche Kunstsammlungen, Dresden. 561: Both Alinari-Art Reference Bureau. 562: Alinari-Art Reference Bureau. 567: Brussels Library. 570: Alinari-Art Reference Bureau. 578: Museo del Prado, Madrid. 582: Historical Pictures Service. 584: Historical Pictures Service. 585: Historical Pictures Service. 598: Vatican Museum.

XIII.–606: Both Bayerische Staatsbibliothek, Munich. 609: Staatsbibliothek der Stiftung Preubischer Kulturbesitz, Marburg. 611: The Granger Collection. 614: Bettmann Archives. 617: Crozer Theological Library. 625: Historical Pictures Service. 627: Museo del Prado, Madrid. 629: Bibliothèque publique et universitaire, Geneva. 632: Bibliothèque publique et universitaire, Geneva. 634: Bettmann Archives. 639: Historical Pictures Service. 641: Bettmann Archives. 645: Museo del Prado, Madrid. 649: Walters Art Gallery, Baltimore, 652: Historical Pictures Service.

XIV.–663: American Museum of Natural History. 664: Historical Pictures Service. 665: Historical Pictures Service. 671: The National Library of Wales. 672: The Huntington Library, San Marino, California. 676: The Metropolitan Museum of Art, Dick Fund, 1925. 679: The Metropolitan Museum of Art, Bequest of Annie C. Kane, 1926. 680: Prints Division, New York Public Library. 681: Historical Pictures Service. 684: Kunsthistoriches Museum. Vienna. 694: Propriété du Musée cantonal des beaux-arts à Lausanne. 696: Musuem of Fine Arts, Boston, Gift of Gordon Abbott and George P. Gardner. 698: Kuperstichkabinett, Basel. 701: The National Gallery, London. 713: Essex Institute Collection. 718 (top): Alinari-Art Reference Bureau; (bottom): New York Public Library Picture Collection. 719: Alinari-Art Reference Bureau. 720: The Metropolitan Museum of Art, Bequest of Mrs. H. O. Havemeyer, 1929. 721: Copyright Fotocommissie Rijksmuseum, Amsterdam. 725: New York Public Library Picture Collection.

Index

Aachen, 366-367, 374, 378
Aaron, 84, 87
Abbasids, 305, 346-347, 413
Abelard, Peter, 425, 515, 520-521
Abraham, leadership of Hebrews by, 83
Absolutism, beginnings in Castile, 591, 680; Henry IV (France) and, 696-697; Louis XIV and, 706-707; Petition of Right and, 709; as quest for security, 726; Reformation and, 607, 616, 653; Roman law and, 548-549; Stuart kings of England and, 708-709
Academica (Cicero), 240
Academy, Plato's 151
Achaea, 225
Achaean League, 177, 217
Achaeans, 107; commerce of, 109; see also Mycenaeans, Hellenes
Acharnians, The, (Aristophanes), 157
Acre, 416, 418
Acropolis, 166-169
Act of Supremacy (1534), 624
Actium, battle of (31 B.C.), 236
Adelard of Bath, 528
Adrian VI (Pope), 599, 636
Adrianople, battle of (A.D. 378), 288
Aediles, 203
Aegean World, sea routes and ports, 107
Aegina, 138
Aeneas, 255-258
Aeneid, The, 253-258
Aequi, 200-201
Aeschylus, 114, 130, 154-156
Aetolian League, 177, 217
Africa, Europeans in, 568, 662-663; Roman protectorate in, 224
Against Heresies (Irenaeus), 301
Agamemnon (Aeschylus), 154-155; in Aristotle's *Poetics,* 153

Agamemnon, tomb of, 108
Agincourt, battle of (1415), 582
Agricola (Tacitus), 275
Agriculture, Egypt and, 23; prehistoric revolution in, 10-11; Middle Ages and, 391-395, 400, 405-406; open field system, 391-392; Renaissance and, 568; in the 16th and 17th centuries, 673
Agrigentum, 128, 211
Ahmos, 37
Ahura-Mazda, 303
Akhenaton, 40-41
Akkad, 45-47; cultural borrowings by Assyrians from, 71; see also Mesopotamia
Alaric, 288
Alberti, Leon Battista, 556, 563, 564
Albigensians (Cathari), 418, 425, 428-429, 431, 450; crusade against (1208), 428-429; decline of, 595; Innocent III and, 453, 486
Alcabala, 682
Alcaeus, 128, 133
Alciati, Andrea, 548
Alcuin, 340, 369, 372, 381, 514
Aleander, Girolamo, 613-614, 636
Alexander III, (Pope), 451, 453, 471
Alexander VI (Pope), 543, 590, 598, 599
Alexander the Great, 175-176; division of Empire of, 176-177
Alexandria, 183
Alexis (Tsar of Russia), 707
Alexius I (Byzantine Emperor), 413-414
Alfred the Great (King of England), 378, 380-382
Allia, battle of (390 B.C.), 201
Alphabet, Aramaeans, spreading of by, 69; Phoenician, adapted to

Greek language, 129; Phoenicians, development of by, 68-69
Altamira cave art, 9
Alva, duke of, 683-684
Amarna, see Tell el Amarna
Amenhotep IV, see Akhenaton
Amiens Cathedral, 493, 507
Amon-Re, 30
Amores (Ovid), 261
Amorites, 49, 58-60; see also Babylonians, Mesopotamia, *Pax Babylonica*
Amsterdam, 667, 685; bank of, 670
Anabaptists, 612, 618, 619, 621-623, 643, 652
Anabasis (Xenophon), 160
Anagni, 461
Anatolia, 127; see also Anatolian Peninsula
Anatolian Peninsula, Assyrian colonies on, 71; Hittite civilization on, 67; Persian subjugation of, 78; Sea People's invasion of, 67
Anaxagoras, 145-146
Anaximander, 131; Lydian influences on, 70
Anaximenes, 131; Lydian influences on, 70
Ancient Near East, cultural collapse in, 79; three major epochs in, 70
Andronicus, Livius see Livius Andronicus
Angevin Empire, 467-468, 472-473, 483
Anglican Church, and civil wars, 710, 711, 712; under Henry VIII and Edward VI, 624, 625, 626-627; under Elizabeth I, 689
Anglo-Saxon England, 463-466; Alfred and, 380-382; end of, 463-465; institutions of, 463-465

733

Annales (Ennius), 216
Annales (literary genre), 207
Annales (Tacitus), 275
Anticlericalism, 583, 595, 597, 608, 610, 654
Antigone (Sophocles), 156
Antigonus, 176
Antioch, 183
Antiochus III (ruler of Syria), 217, 219
Antiochus IV, 290
Antisemitsm, 545
Antitrinitarianism, 620, 647, 648; see also Arianism
Antonius Pius, 271
Antony, Mark, 228, 232, 235-236, 240
Antwerp, 378, 568, 664, 667, 683, 685
Apella (Assembly), 124
Aphrodite, 114
Apocalypse, belief in, 595, 596, 613, 619
Apollo, 109, 113, 114, 187; cult of, 119
Apologetics, Christian, 300
Apology (Justin Martyr), 300
Apostles, twelve chosen by Jesus, 292; work in spreading Christianity, 294-296
Apostolic grace, 301
Appian Way, 209
Appius Claudius, 209
Apulia, 212
Aqueducts, Roman, 209
Aquinas, St. Thomas, 537-538, 546, 644; see also St. Thomas Aquinas
Aragon, 408, 576, 577, 579, 680, 704; see also Spain
Aramaeans, 66, 69
Aramaic, 69
Arch, 501, 506-507
Archimedes of Syracuse, 182, 539
Architecture, Assyrian, 73-74; Byzantine, 324-325; Egyptian, 27-28; Gothic, 504-507; Greek, 166-167; medieval, 501-507; Mesopotamian, 54; Persian, 80; Roman, 275-283; Romanesque, 501-506
Archons (executive officers), 117, 120
Areopagus, Council of, 117, 118; Council of Elders, 120
Ares, 114
Argos, 138, 173
Arianism, 303, 309, 311, 316-318
Aristarchus of Samos, 181
Aristides "The Just," 170
Aristides the Sophist, 271
Aristo, 537
Aristocracy, *see* Nobility and Gentry
Aristophanes, 156-157
Aristotle, 126, 151-153, 513-514, 537, 539, 540; Aquinas and, 523-528; Grosseteste and, 529; medieval thought and, 513-530; works of, 153
Arius, 303
Ark, 88
Armada, 687-688, 692
Armenia, 270
Arminianism, 638, 699, 725
Army, Byzantine, 320; Charlemagne and, 363-364; feudalism and, 383-386; fyrd in England, 463, 465; *see also* Warfare
Arnold of Brescia, 450
Ars Amatoria (Ovid), 262
Art, in age of baroque, 715-722; Assyrian, 73-74, 80; Byzantine, 322-326; in Crete, 103-105; Cro-Magnon man and, 9-10; in Egypt, 26-28, 35, 39; Gothic, 422, 504-507; Gothic realism, 553-554; Greek, 134-135, 161-169, 186-187; High Renaissance, 564-566; Italian Renaissance, 553, 554, 555-556; in Mesopotamia, 54-55; Mycenaean, 106, 108; Persian, 80; Roman, 208-209, 275-283, 321, 324-326; in Sicily (twelfth century), 410-411
Artemis, 114
Arthur, King, 498
Artificers, Statute of (1563), 676
Ashurbanipal, 72
Ashurnasirpal II, conquest of, 72; *see also* Assyrians
Asia, European penetration of, 662, 678
Asia Minor, control by Caesar, 233
Assembly, 112
Assembly, Roman, *see Comita Curiata*
Assize of Clarendon, 469
Assur, 72, 74
Assyrians, 80; Anatolian settlements of, 71; architecture of, 73-74; conquests of, 71-72, 90; cultural heritage of, 71; decline of, 73; early settlements of, 71; empire of, 76; literature of, 74; origins of, 71; religion of, 74; revolts against, 72, 76
Astronomy, 181-182; Mesopotamian work in, 56; Persian work in, 82
Athanasius, Bishop of Alexandria, 303
Athelney, 380
Athena, 114, 119, 187
Athena, of the Parthenon (Phidias), 161, 167
Athena Nike, shrine, 167
Athenian culture, 145-174; history, 158-160, (*see also* Herodotus, Thucydides, Xenophon); philosophy, 145-153, (*see also* Anaxagorus, Democritus, Protagorus, Sophism, Socrates, Plato, Aristotle); literature, 154-160, (*see also* Tragedy, Euripides, Aeschylus, Sophocles, Aristophanes); poetry, 157-158, (*see also* Pindar)
Athenian society, 117-122
Athens, 109, 117, 145, 217; citizenship requirements, 171; Cleisthenes' rule in, 120-122; dominance of, 170-171; in Mycenaean times, 109; Pisistratus' rule in, 119-120; social classes of, 117-118; Sparta contrasted with, 122-126
Aton, 40-41
Attalus Philadelphus, 177
Attica, 109
Aucassin and Nicolette, 499
Augsburg, 568, 609; Diet of, 622; Peace of, 623, 644, 653, 698
Augustinian tradition, 538, 539, 545, 610; *see also* St. Augustine
Augustus, 248-265; boundaries of his empire, 252; genius of, 247-248; law under, 248-250; literature under rule of, 253-265; morality under, 251; paternalistic rule of, 251-253; provinces under, 251; social classes under, 251-252; succession of, 265; successors of, 267; Virgil's relationship to, 253
Australia, discovery of (1627), 666
Austrasia, 355, 366
Avars, 327-328, 365
Averroës, 516, 522
Avignon, papacy at, 461, 488, 540, 575, 583, 592-594, 595, 596

Ba, 29
Baal, Hebrew rejection of, 84, 90
Babylon, 72, 176
Babylonia, 77; Kassite conquest of, 60
"Babylonian Captivity", 592-593, 595
Babylonians, 58-60; subjugation of Assyrians by, 72; *see also* Amorites, Mesopotamia, *Pax Babylonica*
Bach, John Sebastian, 722
Bacon, Roger, 436, 529-530
Baghdad, in Middle Ages, 346-348; Swedish Vikings and, 378
Baillis, French official, 484-485
Baldwin IX, 417
Banking, Bardi and Peruzzi families and, 571; Fuggers and, 567, 571; High Middle Ages, 404; the

Medici and, 567, 571; papacy and, 593; in the seventeenth century, 670-671
"Barbarians" (non-Greeks), 115
Baroque, age of, 715-722; Calvinists and, 716; literature, 722; music, 720-722; painting, 717-721; sculpture and architecture, 716-717
Bartholomew's Day Massacre of, 694
Basel, Council of, 355, 594
Basil II (Byzantine Emperor), 329
Basilicas, Hellenistic, 187
Bavaria, 365, 419, 614, 698, 700
"Bell Beaker" people, 196
Bellicum Punicum (Naevius), 215
Bellini, Giovanni, 565
Bellum Catilinarium (Sallust), 240
Bellum Jugurthinum (Sallust), 240-241
Belshazzar, 77
Benedict of Aniane, 370, 396
Benedict IX (Pope), 440-441
Benedictine Rule, 370
Beotia, 126
Bernini, Giovanni, 716-718
Beza, Theodore, 633, 634
Bible, Anti-trinitarians and, 620, 633; Anabaptists and, 619-620; Bucer and, 615; Calvin and, 622, 630; Council of Trent and, 643; heretics and, 596; humanists and, 542, 546, 547; Luther and, 552, 610, 612, 614, 618, 622; Peasant's Revolt and, 616; Protestants and, 651; translated in England, 595, 623; Ximénes and, 545; Zwingli and, 618; *see also* Vulgate Bible
Black Death, 536, 566, 571, 583, 595, 596
Blanche of Castile, 486
Boccaccio, Giovanni, 536, 537, 540, 541
Bodin, Jean, 638, 725
Boethius, 316, 381
Bohemia, 588, 619, 634; Empire and, 586, 587; Hussites in, 588, 595-596; revolt against Habsburgs, 697-699; in 16th century, 647, 648; in Thiry Years' War, 697-699, 702
Boleyn, Anne, 623-624
Bologna, 196; center of Roman legal scholarship, 451, 509-510
Boniface VIII (Pope), 460-461, 488, 536, 592
Borgia, Cesare, 550, 563, 598
Borromini, 716, 719
Bosch, Hieronymous, 645
Botticelli, Sandro, 559, 564
Bourbon Dynasty, 693, 700; *see also* Henry IV, Louis XIII, and Louis XIV

Bourgeoisie, a new class, 401; in France in High Middle Ages, 488-489
Bouvines, battle of (1214), 456, 473, 484
Bramante, 564, 599
Brandenburg, *see* Hohenzollern, House of
Brant, Sebastian, 537
Brazil, 664, 666, 704
Brethren of the Common Life, 545, 546, 597
Brunelleschi, Filippo, 555, 556, 563
Bruni, Leonardo, 541
Brutus, Marcus, 233, 235-236
Bucer, Martin, 614, 615, 618, 621, 637; John Calvin and, 632
Budé, Guillaume, 545
Bullinger, Heinrich, 618, 633
Bullionism, 674, 675
Bundschuh revolts, 609-610
Burckhardt, Jacob, 533, 534
Bureaucracy, *baillis* in France under Capetians, 484-485; in Byzantium, 320; Charlemagne and, 371-372; under Edward I, 478-481; in Elizabethan England, 690; in France under Louis XIV, 696, 707; growth of, under Ferdinand and Isabella, 577; under Henry II, 468-469; Norman England and, 466-467; Papal, 422, 592-593, 643; under Philip II, 679-681; Renaissance courts and, 724; in territorial states, 591
Burghley, Lord, 676, 692
Burgundy, 356, 396; becomes part of Habsburg Empire, 585, 608; origins in Hundred Years' War, 584; rise and fall of, 584-586
Byzantine Empire, Crusades and, 413-418; culture in, 321-326; government in, 319-320; heresy in, 320-321; reign of Justinian, 326-327; Seljuk Turks and, 413; Swedish invasion of, 372
Byzantium, 127; influence on Italian art, 554

Cabot, John, 666
Caesar, Julius, 228, 230-235; writings of, 239-240
Caesar, Octavius, *see* Octavian
Caesaropapism, 309, 319; and Justinian, 326-327; and the Western Church, 340
Calais, 582, 628, 692
Calendar, Egypt's construction of, 24; Gregorian, 234; Julian, 234
Calf-bearer, 161
Caligula, 266
Callicrates, 167
Callimachus, 183-184

Calvin, John, France and, 545, 628-629, 633; *Institutes of the Christian Religion,* 630, 633; Luther and, 629, 630, 631; reform by, 628-634; Zwinglians and, 618
Calvinism, civil wars and, 634, 653; dissident nobles and, 723; in France, 693-696, 701; under the German Habsburgs, 622, 638, 697-698, 702; internationalism of, 633-634; in the Netherlands, 683, 684, 685, 687, 699; in Scotland, 634, 710; spread of, 633-634, 647, 648; in Stuart England, 710-715
Canaan, *see* Palestine
Canaanites, 68
Canon law, 451, 511-512; papal sovereignty and, 592
Canossa, 445-456, 448, 461
Canute (King of England), 382
Capetian Dynasty, 416, 429, 482-489; end of, 580; rise of, 383
Capitalism, in the Netherlands and England (1550-1660), 670-671; organization of production and, 671-673; Protestantism and, 654-656; in Spain, 682; *see also* Banking, Domestic System, Commerce, Industry, and Mercantilism
Capitularies, 368
Capua, 212-213
Capuan Venus, 186
Capuchins, 640-641
Caracalla, Baths of, 281
Caraffa, Giovanni Pietro, *see* Paul IV
Cardinals, College of, 599
Carloman, 358, 359
Carolingian Empire, 353-354; Charles Martel in, 356; rise of 356-358
Carolingian miniscule, 369
"Carolingian Renaissance," 368-371
Carthage, 69, 172, 209-213, 217, 219; in *Aeneid,* 255
Carthaginians, Sicilian, 202
Carthusians, 424, 440
Cassiodorus, 317
Cassius, 232, 235
Castellio, Sebastian, 633, 636, 652
Castiglione, Count Baldassare, 544
Castile, 407-408, 576-580, 675, 682, 704-705; *see also* Spain
Catalonia, revolt against Spain, 704-705
Cateau-Cambrésis, Treaty of, 639, 678
Cathedral, 501-507; schools, 508,

526; *see also* Architecture
Catherine of Aragon, 623-624
Catherine de Medici, 692, 693, 694
Catiline, Sergius, 231, 240
Cato, M. Porcius, 217, 221
Catullus, 238-239
Cavaliers, 711
Celts, Balkan, 175
Censors, 203
Censorship, 535, 552-553, 615, 643
Centuriae, 203
Cervantes, Saavedra, 537, 722
Chaeronea, battle of (338 B.C.), 174-175
Chalcis, 127
Chaldeans, 76-77, 90; Aramaic origins of, 69, 76-77; revolts against Assyria by, 72, 76
Champlain, Samuel de, 697
Chansons de geste, 495-498, 501
Charlemagne, 353-354, 362-370, 371; army of, 384; coronation of (800), 365-366
Charles I (King of England), civil wars and, 711-714; Parliament and, 709-711; Puritans and, 710
Charles II (King of England), 715
Charles IV (Holy Roman Emperor), 595
Charles (I of Spain, V of Empire), Council of Trent and, 622-623, 642-644; division of empire, 623, 678; heirs of, 623, 697; Henry VIII and, 624; Low Countries and, 683; Lutherans and, 613, 620, 622-623, 639; made Holy Roman Emperor, 612, 613; sack of Rome and, 636; Spanish nobility and, 580; Valois and, *see* Habsburg-Valois Wars
Charles IX (King of France), 693, 694, 696
Charles of Anjou, 459
Charles the Bald, 370, 373
Charles, Duke of Burgundy, 585, 588
Charles Martel, 345, 356, 358, 406
Charles the Rash (Burgundy), 585
Chartres Cathedral, 493, 507, 521, 553
Chaucer, Geoffrey, 536-537
"Children's Crusade" (1212), 418
China, 567, 678
Chivalry, in Burgundy, 586; Ignatius of Loyola and, 641; in Renaissance, 544, 600
Choephori (Aeschylus), 155
Christian IV (Denmark), 700
Christian Doctrine, 298-299
Christianity, 243, 290-304; Anglo-Saxon England and, 339-340; Benedictines and, 338-339; Clovis and, 318-319; Constantine's conversion to, 287, 308, 320; fourth century conversion to, 308, 320; heresy in High Middle Ages and, 427-428; Iberian peninsula and, 408-409; Normandy and, 378; Pauline, 297; Poland converted to, 419; as Roman administrative problem, 274; Roman Empire and, 308-309; Roman persecution of, 299-300; roots of, 290; Russia and, 329, 378; Scandinavia accepts, 378-379
Christina (Queen of Sweden), 708
Church, Albigensians and, 428-429; at beginning of Middle Ages, 333-334; in Carolingian times, 359-360; Catholic Reformation, 597, 638-646, 723; Charlemagne and, 367-368; early organization and government of, 301-302; in the eleventh century, 395-396; England and, 583; France and, 592; under Ferdinand and Isabella, 579; in the Holy Roman Empire, 608; lay lords (mid-eleventh century) and, 440; under Otto I, 389; Peasants' Revolt and, 617-618; property of, secularization, 620, 626, 696; St. Francis and, 430-434; territorial states and, 583, 591, 608
Church, Roman Catholic, adjustment to commercial economy, 593; baroque art and, 716; canon law, 573, 592; corruption of during Renaissance, 594-595, 637; crises during Renaissance, 591-599; Papal States, 574
Church Councils, 299, 455, 458
Church and state, advocates of separation of, 606, 619, 652; conflicts, 592-593, 608; established churches, 608, 619, 632, 620-623, 681-683, 726; implementation of Catholic reform and, 644-646; Protestantism and, 608, 628, 631, 653
Cicero, M. Tullius, 228, 230-231, 235, 236, 240, 540, 541, 546, 638
Cimbri, 225
Cistercians, 424-426, 440
City of God, 289, 312-313, 372
City-state, beginning of, 112
Civitate, battle of (1053), 410, 441
Classics, *see* Humanism
Claudius, 266
Clement V (Pope), 461, 488
Clement VII (Pope), 624, 636
Cleopatra, 44, 233, 236
Clouds, The, (Aristophanes), 157
Clovis (Merovingian king), 317-318, 333-334, 335
Cluny, 396, 423, 425, 439, 441
Coal, 673

Coeur, Jacques, 567, 582
Colet, John, 546
Coligny, Gaspard de, 694
Cologne, electorate of, 586, 608, 698
Colonization, Greek, 127-128
Colosseum, 268, 281
Columbus, Christopher, 664, 665
Comitatus, 314, 355, 383
Comitia Centuriata, 204
Comitia Curiata, 202, 204
Comitia Tributa, 212
Commerce, Aramaeans and, 69; Baghdad and, 346; Baltic, 662, 667, 708; under Charlemagne, 372; colonial, 662-667; depression in the Renaissance, 566-567; depression in 17th century England, 676, 709; in the Dutch empire, 666-667; Eastern Empire and, 319; Egypt and, 23, 35, 39; England and Low Countries, 580, 692; Greek colonization, 127-128; invention of money, 69; Mecca and, 341; in Mesopotamia, 58; Ottoman Turks and, 663; partial recovery in Renaissance, 568-569; Phoenician trade routes and, 68; Portugese commercial empire, 663-664; in sixteenth century, 665-667, 670-671, 690; Thirty Year's War and, 704; trade routes in Hellenistic age, 179; Vikings and, 379
Commercial and economic trends, 1560-1660, 667-671; in High Middle Ages, 400-404, 566; in Renaissance, 566-569; in sixteenth century, 661-677
Commodus, 272
Commonwealth, 714-715
Communication, effect of invention of printing press on, 551-553; significance of Crusades on, 418-419
Conciliar Movement, 593-594; Luther and, 612
Concilium Plebis, 204-205
Concord, Formula of, 634, 698
Conquistadores, 648, 665
Conrad III (Emperor), 416
Consolation of Philosophy, 316, 381
Constance, Council of (1414-1417), 593-594
Constantine (Roman Emperor), 287-288, 308-309, 320; acceptance of Christianity, 287
Constantine, Arch of, 281
Constantinople, 287; in Charlemagne's time, 353; fall of, 589; Muslim attack, 328; Sancta Sophia in, 322; Swedish Vikings and, 379; Venice and, 401

Constitution of Clarendon, 470
Consualia, 207
Consuls, 202-203
Contarini, Gasparo, 637, 641
Coornhert, Dirck, 638
Copernicus, 539, 725
Cordova, 348, 407-408
Corinth, 126, 138, 173, 219
Corpus Juris Civilis, 326-327, 510-512
Corsica, 211-212
Cortes, Spanish Estates, 577-578
Cossacks, 707
Council of Five Hundred, 120
Council of Four Hundred, 118
Councils, and the papacy, 455, 458
Courtrai, battle of, 488
Cranmer, Thomas, 624, 626
Crassus, Marcus Licinius, 228-232
Crécy, battle of, 582
Cretan culture, 99-108
Crete, 99-105; civilization of, 99-108; economic structure of, 101-102; geography of, 99; language of, 105; migrations to, 100; religion of, 102
Croesus, King, 71-72; *see also* Lydians
Cro-Magnon Man, art of, 11; characteristics of, 9; place in evolutionary scale, 7
Cromwell, Oliver, 711-715
Cromwell, Richard, 715
Cromwell, Thomas, 624
Crusader States, 404, 415-416
Crusades, against the heretics, 596, 605; attempts to crusade against the Ottoman Turks, 590, 648, 661; background and First Crusade (1095-1098), 413; Pope Urban II and First Crusade, 413; capture of Jerusalem, 414-415; Second Crusade (1147-1148), 415-416; Spain and, 576, 579; Third Crusade (1189-1192), 416; Fourth Crusade (1201-1204), 417-418; later Crusades, 418; significance of, 418-419
Crypteia (Secret Police), 124
Culture, in Anglo-Saxon England, 381-384; Athenian, 117-122, 145ff; Byzantine, 321-326; in Carolingian Renaissance, 368-371; Cretan, 99-108; Eastern Europe and, 588; European influence on New World, 662; German tribes and, 313-314; high medieval and Greek compared, 493-494; Hittites and, 67-68; Impact of printing press on, 551-553; Norse and European, 378-379; Ottonian Renaissance and, 389-390; Roman, 200ff, 207-209, 215-216, 231-244, 253ff, significance of the

Crusades and, 418-419
Cumae, 127
Curiae, 202
Curia Regis, 475
Cyclades, 110
Cylinder seal, 55
Cynoscephalae, battle of (197 B.C.), 218, 219
Cyprus, 127
Cyrene, 128
Cyrus, 136; conquests of, 78; empire of, 78; *see also* Persians

Dacia (Rumania), 270
Damascus, 72, 296, 343-344, 416
Damietta, 418
"Danegeld," 382, 463, 465
"Danelaw," 381
Dante, 500-501, 527, 530, 536
Darius, 136-138; conquests of, 78
Darnley, Lord, 692
David (King of Israel), 88, 95
Dead Sea Scrolls, 291
Delian confederacy, 170
Delos, 119
Delphi, 117, 135
Delphic charioteer, 161
Demeter, 102, 114, 130
Democracy, medieval towns and, 401; Parliament and, 475-476; theory of rise of, 316
Democritus, 146-147, 180, 238
Demosthenes, 174
Demotic writing, in Egypt, 25
De Natura Deorum (Cicero), 240
Denmark, 378-379, 382, 699, 700, 707
De Oratore (Cicero), 240
De Rerum Natura (Lucretius), 181, 236-238
Despotism, Italian Renaissance, 575; *see also* Machiavelli
Dido, 255-257
Diocletian, 309, 320; complete authoritarianism established by, 286-287
Diplomacy, age of crisis and, 723; in Italian city-states, 575-576, 599; at Westphalia, 702
Discobulus (Myron), 161
Disease, 327, 662, 665, 673; *see also* Black Death
Divine Comedy, 500-501
Divine Right of Kings, 549, 593, 621-622, 708
Domesday Book, 466
Domestic (Entrepreneurial) System, 671-673, 674, 676
Dominican Order, 429-431, 639, 641
Domitian, 274, 300
Donatello, 557, 563
"Donation of Constantine," 366; Valla and, 541, 616

"Donation of Pepin," 361
Dorians, 107, 109; invasion of Mycenae by, 109
Dortrecht, Synod of, 699
Draco, 117
Drake, Francis, 687-688
Durer, Albrecht, 559, 565
Dutch, Republic, break with absolutism, 685-687; East India Company, 665, 671; establishment of, 683-687; empire of, 665; English Navigation Act of 1651 and, 714; France during Thirty Years' War and, 702; independence recognized, 703
Dynasticism, 573, 608, 691

Earth, age of, 5
Eastern Europe, during the Reformation, 647-650; seventeenth-century crisis in, 667
East India Company, (English), 671; Thomas Mun in, 677; (Dutch), 665, 666, 671
East Indies, 663-664, 666
East March, 365
Ecclesia (Assembly), 117
Eclogues or *Bucolics* (Virgil), 253-254
Economy, under Charlemagne's influence, 372; course of European (1560-1660), 667-677; depression in Spain, 682; depression in Spanish colonies, 665; Hellenistic economic expansion, 178-179; in High Middle Ages, 399-404; in Renaissance, 566-569; Roman, 220-224, 243-244, 283-284; in sixth and seventh centuries, 333-334; in twelfth century England, 468-469; in sixteenth century Europe, 661-677; village economy in Early Middle Ages, 392-393
Edington, battle of (878), 380
Education, Benedictine power and, 424; cathedral schools and, 507; in Charlemagnes' time, 368, 370-371; and the Council of Trent, 644; impact of the Benedictines on, 338-339; Louis IX and, 487; Loyola, the Jesuits, and, 642; Renaissance humanists and, 542-543, 544-545; of the Renaissance aristocracy, 572; in Renaissance Spain, 544-545; St. Dominic and, 431; St. Francis and, 433-434; *studium generale,* 508; universities in eleventh and twelfth centuries, 508-510
Edward I (King of England), 383, 478-481, 488, 580, 592
Edward III (King of England),

737   Index

571, 580
Edward VI (King of England), 626-627; and Calvinsim, 634; social tensions and revolts in the reign of, 626-627
Edward the Confessor (King of England), 383, 390, 396, 464, 478-481, 488
Egypt, 336, 347, 434; Akhenaton, 40-42; Amarna period of, 40; Architecture of, 27; *Ba,* 29; Caesar in, 233; center of Muslim power during the Crusades, 418-419; Cleopatra, 44, 233, 236; conquered by Turks, 590; conquest of, 44; control of by Alexander, 175; divisions of, 18; dynastic periods of, 42-43; early settlements in, 17-18; Eighteenth Dynasty, imperial conquest of, 37-40; *Eisodus* of Hebrews into, 85-86; Empire period, 27-45; exodus of Hebrews from, 86, 87; "Fertile Crescent," 65; First Dynasty, 20-21; First Intermediate Period, 33-34; geography of, 19; Hatshepsut, 38; hieroglyphics, 25, 81; Horus, 31, 32, 44; Hyksos, 36-37; *Ka,* 29; Khufu, tomb of, 27, 32; Ma'at, 29, 34, 40; metaphysical foundation of, 21-22; Middle Kingdom, 34-36; monarchies of, 22-23; Nile, 22. Nineteenth Dynasty, 42-45; nomes, 18; Old Kingdom, 22-33; Osiris, 31, 32; periods of, 20-21; Persian conquest of, 78. pharaoh, concepts of 22-23; pharaohs of, 42-43, (*see also* main entry and particular dynasty); pre-dynastic history of, 17-20; Ptah, 29-30; pyramids in, 31-32; Ramses II, 42-43, 44; Ramses III, 44; *Re,* 22; religion of, 18, 28-31, 40-42; Sait period, 44; Sea Peoples, invasions of, 67, 68; Second Intermediate Period, 36-37; Sumerian contributions to culture of, 19; Thebes, 39; Thutmose III, 38; Tutankhamon, 41; wars against Hittites, 67; writing, 25; Zoser, 31
Einhard, 362-363, 365, 369
Eleanor of Aquitaine, 467, 472
Electra (Sophocles), 156
Eleusinian cult, 130
Eleusis, 130
El Greco, 717, 721
Elizabeth I (Queen of England), 624, 689-692, 708; Armada and, 687-688; government under, 691; Mary Stuart and, 687; religion and, 689-690; Philip II and, 687-688
Enclosures, in England, 626

England, break with absolutism, 726; under Alfred the Great, 380-382; at end of Anglo-Saxon period, 463; Benedictine monks and, 338-340; the Church and, 583, 623-628; civil wars of, 711-714; commerce of, 580, 584, 676, 692, 709; Comonwealth and Protectorate, 714-715; divine-right kingship and, 708-709; under Elizabeth I, 689-692; influence of Erasmus on, 549; feudalism in, 465-466; Germanic tribes in, 316, 332-333; Henry IV and Gregory VII and, 445-447; Henry VIII and the succession crisis, 623-625; Hundred Years' War in, 580, 582-583; James I and, 708-709; John of Salisbury and, 521; Investiture Controversy in, 466-467; medieval agrarian system in, 395; beginnings and evolution of Parliament, 475-481, 580, 584; Philip II (Spain) and, 687-688; beginnings of Protestantism and, 626; Reformation and, 623-628; in the Renaissance, 580-584; sixteenth-century exploration of, 666; in the seventeenth century, 708-715; Viking invasions in, 377; conquest of Wales by, 481; War of the Roses in, 583
English Common Law, development under Henry II, 469-470; under Edward I, 479
Epicureanism in Roman Republic, 241-242
Epicurus, 180-181, 236
Epigram (literary genre), 183-184
Episcopos ("overseer" or bishop), 301
Equites, 214, 218, 222-223, 225-226
Erasmian humanists, 605; conflict with Protestants, 611-612, 613, 618, 635-636; expelled from Catholic Reform, 545, 636-637; influence of, 549, 637-638, 650, 683; rejection of witchcraft by, 725
Erasmus, Desiderius, 545, 546-549, 552, 600, 633; conflict with conservative Catholics, 636-637; conflict with Luther, 635-636; influence on the Netherlands, 549, 683; political theory and, 549; Reformation and, 611-612
Eratosthenes, 182
Erechtheum, 167
Eretria, 127
Escorial palace, 680, 716
Essenes, 293
Estates-General (France), during Hundred Years' War, 582; Francis

I and, 582; Henry IV and, 696; meeting of 1614, 700-701; origins of, 488-489, 592
Ethelbert (King of Kent), 339
Etruria, 196, 212
Etruscans, 197-199, 200, 208
Etymologies, 332-333
Euclid, 182
Eugenius IV (Pope), 594
Eupatridae, 117, 154
Euripides, 114, 156
Europe in 600 A.D., 332-334; in the eleventh century, 396-397; in High Middle Ages, 399-400; at end of High Middle Ages, 493-494
European Economic Community, 549
Evans, Sir Arthur, views of Cretans and Mycenaean languages, 105, 108
Ezekiel, prophecies of, 93

Fabius Maximus, Q., 212
Fabliaux, 499-500
Famine, 566, 673
Farel, William, 631-632
Fatima, 344
Ferdinand I (Holy Roman Emperor) succeeds Charles V, 623, 697
Ferdinand II (Holy Roman Emperor), 697, 699, 700
Ferdinand and Isabella (Spain), 544, 550, 585, 688
Fertile Crescent, 65; cultural amalgamation in, 79, 80; *see also* Egypt and Ancient Near East
Feudal law, 465-466; Magna Carta and, 474-475
Feudalism, benefice in, 383-384; decline of, 404; definition of, 385-386; establishment of in England, 465-466; fief in, 384-385; height of, in France, 386; homage and fealty in, 384-385; Magna Carta and, 474-475; vassalage in, 383-384
Ficino, Marsilio, 543
Firemaking, discovery of, 8
Flaccus, Quintus Horatius, *see* Horace
Flaminius, 212, 218, 219
Flanders, 568, 580, 584, 586, 683; *see also* Burbundy
Fly buttress, 448-507
Florence, center of civic humanism, 540-541; civil strife in, 570, 571; in eleventh century, 401; extension of power of, 574; Guicciardini, Machiavelli and, 549-551; Renaissance in, 536, 540-541, 556, 556-557, 562, 563, 565, 567, 594; Savonarola

and, 543
Folk moot, 196
Fourth Lateran Council (1215), 455
France, birth of feudalism in, 483-487; Calvin and, 628; cathedrals in, 501-507; under the Capetians, 482-489; government in, 582, 677, 701, 706-707; Hapsburg-Valois Wars and, 580, 585, 590, 608, 615, 620, 622, 623, 636, 639, 642; Hundred Years' War and, John I invades (1214); 473, 580-582; under Mazarin, 706-707; religious and civil wars in sixteenth century, 692-697; under Richelieu, 700-702; sixteenth century exploration by, 666, 697; Spanish Bourbons, war with, 699, 700-702, 704, 705-706; Thirty Years' War and, 699, 700-702.
Francis I (King of France), 400, 430-434, 453, 528-529, 545, 582, 620, 622, 631, 648, 693, 696
Franciscan movement, 596, 597, 639-641
Franconia, 387, 390, 419
Frederick I, surnamed Barbarossa (German Emperor), 416, 448-452, 458, 471
Frederick II (German Emperor), 418, 452, 456-459, 489
Frederick III (Holy Roman Emperor), 587
Frederick the Wise (Saxony), 610, 614, 612
Frederick V (King of Bohemia), 698-699
Frederick William, the Great Elector, 708
Fronde, 706-707
Fugger family, 567, 609, 612

Gabor, Bethlen, 698
Galen, 275, 510
Galilee, 291
Galileo, 275, 539
Gama, Vasco da, 663, 664
Gaul, 198, 201-202, 212, 231; attacked by Vikings, 378; defeat of Muslims under Charles Martel, 345, 356; Frankish kingdom of, 316-317; invasions by Saracens and Magyars in ninth century, 375-376; under Merovingians, 332-334
Geneva, 631-634
Gentes, 196-202
Gentry, 572, 577, 626, 674, 690, 712
Geographical discovery, 568, 661-667
Geologic ages, table of, 7
Georgics (Virgil), 183, 254
Gerbert of Aurillac, 389-390, 514, 528
Germanic law, 314-316, 511
Germania, 275, 314
Germanic Tribes, 313-316; infiltration of Roman Empire by, 287
Germany, feudalism and, 447-448; Henry IV and Investiture Controversy, 443-447; Hungarian invasions and, 387-389; Interregnum and, 458; medieval expansion of, 419-420; Otto I and, 387-389; *see also* Holy Roman Empire
Ghiberti, Lorenzo, 563
Gilgamesh, 51; Assyrian modification of, 71
Giotto, Giovanni, 555
Glacial record, table of, 7
Glaucia, C. Servilius, 225
Glossa Ordinaria, 511
Gnosticism: 298, 299; influence on Christian doctrine, 298; influence of on Rome, 215
Golden Bull, 586
Gothic architecture, 422, 504-507
Gothic art, 422, 504-507
Gothic realism, 553-554, 586
Gothic Wars, 327
Government, in Burgundy, 586; in Byzantium, 320; under Charlemagne, 371; in the Church, 592-593; economic policies of, 674-677; in England, 580, 591; in England in 1066, 463; in France, 582, 591; German barbarians and, 332-333; in the Holy Roman Empire, 587-588, 613-614; in medieval towns, 402; under the Merovingians, 333-334; under Otto I, 338; political authority of lords in Early Middle Ages, 394-395; representative governments in England and France, 408-409; in Spain, 577-580, 591; in territorial states, 591; in twelfth century Sicily, 408-409
Gracchus, Gaius, 223
Gracchus, Tiberius Sempronius, 222
Granada, 576, 682
Grand Assize, 470
Granicus River, battle of (334 B.C.), 175
Gratian, 512, 520-521
Great Peasants' War, 616-618
Great Schism, 593-594
Grebel, Conrad, 619
Greece, age of colonization, 127-128; commercial relations of, 128-129; Cretan heritage of, 107-109; disunity in, 114-116; language of, 129; Lydians, influence of, on, 70; migrations into, 106; out of, 110; Mycenaean origins of, 109-111; sea trade of, 112; settlements in Italy, 197-198; social classes in, 117-119, 126-127; "tyranny", 129
Greek civilization, architecture in, 161 ff; aristocratic control in, 126-127; Athenian society in, 117-122; athletics in, 135-136; drama in, 154 ff; Greek mind, 130, 145 ff; Hellenic phase of, 100 ff; Hellenistic phase of, 174 ff; history as a discipline, 158-160; Ionian Renaissance in, 110-112; Mycenaean phase of, 106-110; mythology in, 102-103; philosophy, 130; poetry, 133-134, 157-158; potterymaking, 134; religion in, 112-114, 130; sculpture, 161-166; Spartan society in, 122-126; "tyranny" in, 129
Greek Fire, 345
Greek literature, study of, 539, 540, 541; New Testament, 545, 546-548; philosophy, 541
Greek Orthodox Church, 302
Greek Orthodoxy, reunion with West, 1439, 594; schism with West, 605; and the Turks, 647, 648-649
Greek Tragedy, 154-156
Gregory VII (Pope), 442-447, 450, 466-467
Gregory IX (Pope), 434-435, 458-459
Gregory of Tours, 332
Gregory the Great (Pope Gregory I), 332, 337-339, 381, 514
Gregory XIII (Pope), 644
Grimaldi Man, 7
Groote, Gerard, 597
Grotius, Hugo, 725-726
Grosseteste, Robert, 529
Guicciardini, Francesco, 549, 551
Guilds, craft, 569, 571, 579, 608, 609, 671-673, 675; in medieval towns, 403-404; 508
Guiscard, Robert, 409-410, 441, 446
Guise, Henry Duke of, 688, 695
Guise, House of, 687, 692-694
Gustavus Adolphus (King of Sweden), 700, 702, 707, 708
Gutenberg, Johann, 551-552

Habsburg, House of, as emperors, 586-587; Burgundy and, 585; France in Thirty Years' War and, 700-702; (Habsburg) loans to, 667; Rudolf of, 697; rivalry with Bourbons, 699, 700-702, 704, 705-706; Spanish Habsburg, 576, 678-689
Habsburg, Rudolph of, 458
Habsburg-Valois Wars, 580-585, 590, 608, 615, 620, 622-623, 636, 639, 642
Hades, 114, 130
Hadrian (Roman Emperor), 270

739 Index

Hadrian IV (Pope), 450-451
Hagia Triada, 103
Hals, Franz, 717
Hamilcar, 212
Hammurabi, 59; code of, 59-60, 71
Handel, Georg Friedrich, 720
Hannibal, 212-213
Hanseatic League, 666
Harrington, James, 551
Harun-al-Rashid, 346
Hastings, battle of,(1066), 463
Hatshepsut, 38
Hatti, see Hittites
Hauteville Dynasty, 409-412
Hawkins, John, 687-688
Hebrews, Assyrians and, 90; Babylonian captivity of, 77, 79, 90, 91-93; Chaldean destruction of, 90; conquests of Canaan by, 88; Egyptian oppression of, 85-86; *Eisodus* of, 85; Exodus of, 87-88; law of, 93; Messiah concept of, 95; nationhood of, 88-89; origins and migrations of, 66, 83; Palestine, life in, 83, 86; patriarchs of, 83-84; Persian rule over, 79, 90; political decline of, 89-90; power politics of, 89; prophecies about, 90-93; struggle against Philistines of, 88; "suffering servant" concept of, 95; Ten Commandments, 88; unification of under Saul, 88; Zoroastrian influences on, 94-95; see also Israelites, Jews
Hebrews, the book of, 300
Hegira, 342
Heidelberg Man, 6
Heliaea (popular courts), 118, 171
Hellas, 106; "School of," 145;
Hellenes, 106
Hellenics (Xenophon), 160
Hellenistic Age, art styles in, 186-187, 188-191; characteristics of, 177-187; cynicism in, 179; drama in, 184-185; economic conditions in, 178-179; Epicureanism in, 180-181; history, writing of, 185-186; literature in, 183-185; philosophy in, 179-181; religion in, 187; science in, 181-183; skepticism in, 180; stoicism in, 180; trade routes in, 179; women in, 178
Hellespont, 138
Heloise, 520
Helots (serfs), 124-125
Henry I (King of England), 402, 466-467
Henry II (King of England), 447, 467-472, 483-484
Henry II (King of France), 693
Henry III (Valois), 688
Henry III (King of England), 475-478, 487
Henry III (German Emperor), 390-391, 396; and reform of papacy, 441-442
Henry III, assassination of Henry of Guise, 688, 695; as King of France, 694, 695-697; as King of Poland, 647
Henry IV (Bourbon, King of France), 688, 694, 689, 695, 696, 700
Henry IV (German Emperor), 443-447; deposition of, 445
Henry V (German Emperor), 447-448
Henry VI (German Emperor), 416, 452, 455
Henry the Lion, 450-451
Henry VII (King of England), 583-584
Henry VIII (King of England), 546, 623-628
Hera, 113, 114
Hera of Samos, 161
Heraclitus, 132, 180
Heraclius, 327-328
Heresy, 450; in Byzantium, 320-321; definition, 605; in fourth century, 308-309; Louis IX and, 486; Philip II and, 681-682; Reformation and, 635; rise of, 427-428; St. Dominic and, 430; spread of, 595-597
Hermes (Praxiteles), 166
Herodotus, 158-159
Heroides (Ovid), 262
Hesiod, 126
Hesse, see Philipof Hesse
Hieratic writing, 25
Hiero (King of Syracuse), 182
Hieroglyphic writing, 25
High Renaissance, 564-566, 597-599
Hildebrand, see Gregory VII
Hipparchus, 182
Hippias, 148
Hippocrates, 182-183
Hippolytus (Euripides), 156
Histories (Tacitus), 275
History, as collective memory of mankind, 3-4; definition of, 1-2; not a science, 2-3; purposes of studying, 304; "use of", see purposes of studying; study of, 535, 536, 543; writing of, 541; writing of as an art, 2-3
History of Animals (Aristotle), 153
History of Rome, The, (Livy), 262-264
Hittites, under Assyrians, 71-72; city-states established by, 67; culture of, 67-68; decline of, 109; invasion of Babylonia by, 66; legal system of, 68; New Empire of, 67; Old Empire of, 67; struggle with Hurrians, 66
Hobbes, Thomas, 711
Hohenstaufen Dynasty, 425, 448, 455-456, 459
Hohenzollern, House of (Brandenburg), 608, 620, 621, 697, 702-703, 707, 708
Holbein, Hans, 565
Holland, see Netherlands
Holy leagues, 599, 694-695
Holy Roman Empire, during the Renaissance, 584, 586-588; economic decline of, 667; Investiture Controversy and, 443-447; Italy and, 574, 575; origin of, 389; Protestant Reformation in, 607-618; Rudolph of Hapsburg and, 458-459; Thirty Years' War and, 697-704
Homer, epics of, 111-112; model for Virgil, 254
Hominids, varieties of, 5-6
Homo habilis, see reference to on Table I, p. 7
Homo sapiens, age and characteristics of, 7
Honorius, 288
Horace, 215, 251, 258-261
Horatian Laws, 205
Hortensian Law, 205
Horus, 30, 44
Hospitallers, 419, 426
House of Commons, Elizabeth I and, 689, 691; Stuarts and, 709-711
House of Lords, 583, 714
Huguenots, see Calvinism, in France
Humanism, and the arts, 555, 563-564; in Byzantium, 330; civic, 540-543; definition of, 535; Deventer, center of, in Northern Europe, 597; Dutch, 638; English, 545-546; Erasmus, leading humanist of Renaissance, 546-548; expression of lay attitude by, 595; German, 545, 615-616; Italian, 536, 539-544; Northern, 544-548, 637-638; Reformation and, 542, 613, 638; Renaissance papacy and, 542, 597-599; Spanish, 544-545; see also Erasmian Humanists
Humanitarianism, 547, 662, 726
Humbert, 442
Hundred Years' War, 567, 580-582, 583, 584, 585, 595
Hungary, 387-389, 396, 406; after 1333, 588; settlement of, 487-489; in sixteenth century, 634, 647, 648, 699; Turkish invasion of, 620, 622

740   Index

Hurrians, Assyrian subjugation of, 71-72; cultural background of, 66; first migrations of, 66; Kingdom of Mittani, rulers of, 66; struggle against Hittites by, 66
Hus, John, 593, 596
Hussites, 587-588, 593-594, 596, 605, 648
Hutten, Ulrich von, 545, 615-616
Hyksos, 36-37

Iceland, 378-379
Iconoclasm, 360-361; iconoclastic controversy, 360-361
Ictinus, 167
Ideas, Platonic theory of, 150
Ides of March, 235
Indrisi, 412
Idyll (literary genre), 184
Ignatius (Bishop of Antioch), 300
Iliad, 111, 113, 114
Ilyria, 217
Imperial Expansion, European, 661-667
Independents (Separatists), 710, 711, 712, 713, 714, 715
Index of Prohibited Books, 645, 681
India, 663, 666; Alexander the Great in, 175-176; Persian conquests in, 78
Indians (American), 662, 665
Individualism, 173-174; and the Reformation, 533, 651; and the Renaissance, 599
Indo-Europeans, 198; appearance of, 65; *see also* Aramaeans, Hebrews, Hittites, Hurrians, Lydians, Philistines, Phrygians, Phoenicians
Indulgences, 593, 595, 596, 612, 644
Industry, in the Netherlands, 683; organization of, 671-673; during Price Revolution, 675; textile, 571, 683; *see also* Technology
Innocent III (Pope), 453-457; the Albigensians and, 453-454; instigates Fourth Crusade, 417, 454; quarrel with King John of England, 453-454, 473-474; St. Dominic and, 430; St. Francis and, 433
Inquisition, 428-429; Medieval, 605; in the Netherlands, 619-620, 683; under Philip II, 638, 681-682; Roman, 637, 644-646; in Spain, 450; and Servetus, 633; in Spain, 544, 579, 638, 680
Instrument of Government, 715
Invasions, 400; after Charlemagne's death, 372-379; renewal of in tenth century England, 380-382
Investiture Controversy, 441-448, 466-467; canon law and, 511-512
Ionia, 110
Ionian Greek culture, 106

Iphigenia at Aulis (Euripides), 156
Iranians, *see* Persians
Ireland, 711; Cromwell and, 714; the early Middle Ages, 334-335; Norse invasions, 378; Uprising of 1601, 688-689
Irenaeus (Bishop of Lyons), 301
"Ironsides," 713
Isaac, 85
Isabella (Queen of Spain), *see* Ferdinand and Isabella
Isidore of Seville, 332-333, 514
Isaiah (first), 91-92
Isaiah (second), prophecies of, 92-93; Zoroastrian borrowings by, 94
Ishtar, 74
Isis, cult of the goddess, 187, 308; in Rome, 215, 243
Islam, 342; background and origins of, 340-341; conquests of, 343-344; culture of, 348-349; Seljuk Turks and, 413; Spain and, 407-408; spread of, 343-344; Tours (battle of) and, 345, 356
Issus, battle of (333 B.C.), 175
Italian Peninsula, migrant groups in, 195-198
Italici, 196, 207
Italy, and baroque arts, 716, 717; cathedrals in 501-507; Charlemagne and 363; collapse of Ostrogothic Kingdom in, 316-317; consequences of Investiture Controversy in, 447-448; decline in seventeenth century, 667; invaded by Otto I, 387-389; Normans in Southern Italy and, 409-411; Ostrogoths in, 314; Renaissance in, 533, 544; Saracen and Magyar invasions of, 375-376; States of during the Renaissance, 574-576; under Theodoric, 316-317
Ivan III, the Great, 589
Ivan IV, the Terrible, 649

Jacob, 83
Jagellon Dynasty, 647
James I (King of England), 692, 698, 708-709, 710; Parliament and, 708, 709; peace with Spain, 689; Puritans and, 710
Japan, 664, 666
Java, 664
Java Man, 6
Jeremiah, 92-93
Jericho, 85-86
Jerusalem, capture of by Chaldeans, 77; capture of in 1187, 416; Crusader State, 415
Jesuits, *see* Society of Jesus
Jesus of Nazareth, 292, 294
Jews, 290-297; Islam and, 342; Sicily and, 409; St. Louis and, 486; in Spain, 576, 579, 681; *see also* Hebrews
Joan of Arc, 582

Job, Book of, 94
John (King of England), 455-456, 472-475, 484
John of Jaudun, 516
John of Salisbury, 449, 521
Joint-stock company, 666, 670-671
Joseph, 83, 85
Joshua, 86
Jove in *Aeneid,* 255-256
Juan, Don, 682, 685
Judah, 90
Judaism, 536, 545, 655
Judas, 294
Jugurtha, 224
Julius II (Pope), 548, 550, 564, 599
Juno, 254, 255
Jupiter (or Jove), 208
Justices of the peace, 583, 677, 690
Justin Martyr, 300-301
Justinian (Byzantine Emperor), 288, 322, 326-327, 511
Justinian codes, 619, 628, 638, *see also* Roman Law
Juvenal, 274

Ka, 29
Kadesh, battle at, 67
Kassites, 36, 60
Kett's Rebellion (England), 626
Khayyam, Omar, 349
Khufu (Cheops), 27, 32
Kidinnu, 181
Kiev, 329, 378, 589
Knight, 383-386
Knights, The (Aristophanes), 157
Knights' Revolt (Germany), 615, 616
Knossos, 101, 108-109; *see also* Crete
Knox, John, 634, 638, 692
Koine, 176
Koran, 342-343, 350

Laconia (or Lacedaemonia), 122
Lanfranc, 466
Langton, Stephen, 474
Language, Alfred (England) and, 380-382; alphabet, 69; of Aramaeans, 69; in Byzantium, 326-327; in Crete, 105; of Greeks, 108; Latin and vernacular literature in High Middle Ages, 521-522; Persian, 81; translations in High Middle Ages, 521-522
Laocoon, 186
Las Casas, Bartholome de, 662
Latifundia, 205, 213, 220
Latin, literature, study of 541; *see also* Humanism
Latin League, 201-202
Latins, 196

Latium, 196-200
Laud, William, 710, 711
Lavinia, 254, 257
Law, see Canon law; English Common Law; Feudal law; Germanic law; and Roman law
Lawyers, in Louis IX's time, 487
Lechfeld, battle of (955), 376, 388
Lefebvre d'Etaples, 545
Legnano, battle of (1176), 451
Lemnian Athena, 161
Leo I (Pope), 288, 439
Leo III (Pope), 365-366
Leo IX, 441-442
Leo X (Pope), 548, 571, 599, 612
Lepanto, Battle of, 682
Lepidus, M. Aemilius, 236
Lerma, Duke of, 688
Levellers, 714
Lewes, battle of, 476
Licinian-Sextian Laws, 205
Ligurians, 195-196
Lilybaeum (Marsala), 211
Linear *A,* 105
Linear *B,* 105, 108
Literature, Assyrian, 74-75; Athenian, 154, 160; in Crete, 105; in Egypt, 25-27; *fabliaux,* 499-500; Golden Age of Rome, 252-265; Greek poetry, 133-134; 157-158; in Hellenistic Age, 183-187; Homer, 111, 254; medieval, 494-501; medieval romance, 498-499; in Mesopotamia, 50-52; Roman, 207, 215-216; Silver Age of Rome, 273-275
Lithuania, see Poland
Lives, Plutarch's, 275
Lives of the Caesars, (Suetonius), 274-275
Livy, 200, 262-264
Livy, Titus, 550
Lollards, 583-595
Lombard, Peter, 520-521
Lombards, 328, 334, 338, 360-361, 364, 408-409
London, 380, 401, 404, 670, 690, 716
Long Parliament, 710
Lorraine, 374
Lothar, 373-374, 388
Louis VI (King of France), 483
Louis VII (King of France), 415-416, 483-484
Louis VIII (King of France), 486
Louis IX (King of France), 404, 418, 486-487
Louis the German, 373
Louis the Pious, 370, 373
Louis XI (King of France), 582, 585
Louis XIII (King of France), 697
Louis XIV (King of France), 705-707; bureaucracy of, 707; marries Maria Theresa, 705; patron of baroque, 716, 717, 721

Low Countries, *see* Netherlands and Dutch Republic
Loyola, Ignatius of, 597, 628, 641
Lucretius, 181, 236-238
Lully, Jean, 721
Luther, break with Erasmus, 635-636; emergence of, 607, 610-614; Saxon reformer, 611-613, 620-622; theology of, 545; Zwingli and, 618
Lutheranism, baroque art and, 716; in Bohemia, 648; Calvinism and, 634, 638; under German Hapsburgs, 608, 697; Peace of Augsburg and, 623, 698; Persecution of, in England, 626; Philip of Hesse and, 620-621, after Westphalia, 698
Lyceum, Aristotle's, 151
Lycurgan Constitution, 125
Lycurgus, 123-124
Lydia, 110, 127; Croesus, king of, 70
Lydians, early migrations of, 66, 69; founding of empire by, 69; invention of money by, 69-70
Lysistrata (Aristophanes), 157

Ma'at, 29, 34, 40
Maccabean revolt, 290-291
Macedonia, 78, 172, 174-175, 217, 219, 225
Macedonian Wars, *see* Table, 217
Machiavelli, Niccolo, 549-551
Maecenas, 254
Magellan, Ferdinand, 665
Magna Carta, 474-475
Magna Graecia, 128
Magnesia, battle of (189 B.C.), 218
Magyars, 375-376
Mainz, 551-552; 586, 608, 621
Manfred (King of Sicily), 458-459
Manichaeism, 311; threat to early Christianity, 303-304
Mankind, five ages of (Hesiod), 126-127
Mannerism, 565
Manzikert, battle of (1071), 330, 413
Marathon, battle of (490 B.C.), 78, 137-138, 154
Marcellus, 253, 257-258
Marcus Aurelius, 271-272
Margaret of Navarre, 537, 545
Margaret of Parma, 683
Marian exiles, 689
Marie de'Medici, 700
Marius, Gaius, 225-226, 227-228; depicted by Sallust, 241
Mars, 208
Martial, 183-274
Martin V (Pope), 594
Martyrdom, Christian, 296, 297-298, 300
Mary I (Queen of England), 623, 624, 627-628, 689, 692
Mary, Queen of Scots (Stuart), 687-692
Masaccio, 557, 563

Massilia (Marseilles), 128
Mathematics, 541, 543, 563
Matthias (Emperor of Germany), 697
Maxmilian I (Holy Roman Emperor), 585
Maximilian II (Holy Roman Emperor), 597, 648
Mazarin, Jules, 706-707
Mecca, 341-342
Medea (Euripides), 156
Medes, 72, 76-77, 81
Medici, and banking, 567, 571; and Machiavelli, 549-550; and Michelangelo, 565
Medici, Cosimo de', 543, 571
Medici, Lorenzo de', 571, 599, 600
Medina, 342-343
Meditations (Marcus Aurelius), 271
Megara, 126, 127, 138
Meggido, battle of, 38
Melanchthon, Philip, 611, 622, 635, 636, 637
Menaechmi (Plautus), 216
Menander, 183, 184-185, 216
Mennonites, 620
Mercantilism, in the Dutch Republic, 675-676; in England and France, 676-677, 714; in Germany after Thirty Years' War, 704; as part of absolutism, 677, under Richelieu, 701
Merovingian Dynasty, 333-334, 355, 361
Mesopatamia, settlement of, 45-47; Amorites, conquerors of, 58-60; architecture of, 54-55, 73-74; Babylonian rule of, 58-60; chart of stages of culture in, 11; city-state system in, 47; class structure in, 58; Mesopotamia, conquered by the Turks, 590; Jericho, 11; growth of villages in, 47-48; inter-city strife in, 48; invention of writing in, 19; language in, 53-54; literature of, 50-52; Lugal-Zaggesi, rule of, 48; mathematics of, 56-57; medicine in, 56-57; Neolithic revolution in, 46; peoples of, 45ff; political life in, 49; religion in, 49-50; Sargon the Great, empire of, 46 (chart), 48; science of, 55-57; sculpture of, 54-55; Sumer, settlement of, 45-47; trade in, 58
Messana(Messina), 128, 209-211
Messenia, 124
Metamorphoses (Ovid), 262
Metaurus River, battle of, 213
Metics (residents of foreign birth), 171
Mexico, 665
Micah, 92

Michelangelo Buonarrotti, 543, 561, 562, 564, 565
Milan, 541, 571, 574, 575, 576, 608
Miletus, 127, 137, 140, 171
Military revolution, 724
Milvian Bridge, battle of (A.D. 312), 308
Mining, 665, 671, 672, 674, 675
Minnesingers, 499
Missi dominici, 371
Missionary activities, 628, 662
Mithraism, 243, 303
Mithras, 303, 308
Mithridates (King of Pontus), 226-229, 230
Mohacs, Battle of, 620, 647
Monarchy, Church of England and, 470-472; English birth of, 381-382; in tenth century Germany, 388; Investiture Controversy and, 441-448; limited, 314, 326; Louis VII and, 483-484; Magna Carta and, 474-475; weakness of (under Capetians), 482-483
Monasticism, 302; Benedict of Aniane and, 370; Benedictinism and, 423-424; under Charlemagne, 370; Cluny, 396, 423; in Early Middle Ages, 337-340; and Catholic Reformation, 639-642; Luther and, 610; in Ireland, 334-335; Mysticism and, 596; St. Benedict and, 337; St. Boniface and, 358-360; rejection by humanists, 539-540, 542; St. Anthony and, 337; suppression by Protestants, 624-625, 654
Money, coined, 69, 128
Monophysitism, 320-321, 326, 343
Monopolies, under bullionism and mercantilism 675-677; in Dutch Empire 666; in the Holy Roman Empire 588, 613; in Portuguese trade, 663; in Spain, 682; in Spanish colonies, 665, 680; in Stuart England, 708, 709, 711
Montaigne, Michel, 722
Monte Cassino, 302, 337, 369
Montesquieu, Baron de, 638
Monteverdi, Claudio, 720-721
Montmorencys, 693, 695
Moors, Spain and, 407-408, 454, 576, 579, 681-682; Portugaland, 663
More, Sir Thomas, 546, 549, 624
Moriscoes (Spanish Moors), 681-682, 688
Moscow, 716; *see also* Muscovy
Moses, 84, 86-88
Muhammad, 341-344, 350
Muhammadanism, 536, 648
Mun, Thomas, 677
Munster, 619-620, 702
Muntzer, Thomas, 615, 617
Muscovy, 588, 589, 647, 649-650
Music, Baroque, 720-721; in humanist education, 543; in Lutheran services, 622

Muslims, attack against Constantinople, 328; conquest of Byzantine North Africa, 328; conquest of Persia, 343; defeated by Charles Martel, 345; Frederick II and, 457; in Spain, 334; spread of, 343-344
Mycale, 140
Mycenaeans, 101, 105, 106-110; *see also* Acheans, Greeks
Myron, 161
Mysticism, 596-597

Naevius, 215
Nahum, 73
Nantes, Edict of 1598), 695-696
Naples, 541, 574, 576, 608
Narbonensis, 225
Naseby Battle of (1645), 713
Nationalism, 421; in England, 687; Magna Carta and, 474-475; Reformation and, 653; Renaissance politics and, 573
Naturalism, Hellenistic style, 186-187
Navarre, *see* Bourbon, House of
Navigation Act of, 1651, 714; Portugal and improvements in navigation, 663
Naxos, 128, 170
Neanderthal Man, 6-7
Nebuchadnezzar, 70, 77, 90
Nemesis (retributive justice), 114, 156
Neoclassicism, 722
Neoplatonism, 308
Nero, 266, 300
Nerva, 284
Netherlands, baroque art in, 717; commercial dominance in 16th & 17th centuries 666-667; Elizabeth I and, 687-688; empire building of, 666; financial activities of, 670-671; influence of Erasmus on, 683; mercantilism in, 675-676; revolt against Philip II, 683-687, 688; Spanish Netherlands, 685, 702; Thirty Years' War and, 699
Neustria, 355
"New Model" army, 713
New Testament, 299
New World, 568, 580, 662, 665, 666, 675
Nicaea, Council of (325), 303, 309, 542, 593
Nike of Samothrace (Winged Victory), 186-187
Nineveh, 72-77
Nobility, in Bohemia, 699; in Burgundy, 586; in England, 623, 690; in France, 582, 702, 706; in the Holy Roman Empire, 615-616; in Muscovy, 649-650; private warfare by, 583, 591; in Spain, 577-580; in the Renaissance, 534, 543-544, 572, 575, 583, 584, 589; Renaissance courts and, 724; in revolt of Netherlands, 683-685; in Sweden, 708
Nobles' *Fronde,* 707
Nominalism, 517-518, 538-539, 596
Nordlingen, Battle of (1634), 700
Norman Conquest of England, 463-465
Normandy, 378, 383, 396, 408, 463-465
Normans, 330; conquest of England, 463-465; conquest of Sicily, 409-411, 446
North Africa, 333; conquered by Justinian, 327; falls to Muslims, 328; Vandal Kingdom of, 316, 327-328
Northern Renaissance, in Burgundy, 553-554; in England, 545-546; in France, 545; in Holy Roman Empire, 545; in Spain, 544-545
Northern War (1655-1660), 707
Northumberland, Duke of, 626-627
Northumbria, 339-340, 380; invaded by Vikings, 377-378; St. Bede in, 339-340; sends monks to Frankland, 358
Norway, 379, 404; conquered by Canute, 382
Notre Dame of Paris, 493, 507
Nous, 146
Novi homines, 205
Numidia, 224, 233
Nuremberg, 568, 609

Ockham, William of, 538, 596
Octavian, 228, 235-236, 244, 247-248; *see also* Augustus
Odyssey, 111-112, 114
Oedipus at Colonus (Sophocles), 156
Oedipus Rex (Sophocles), 156; in Aristotle's *Poetics,* 153
Oldenbarneveldt, Janvan, 699
Oliva, Treaty of, 707-708
Olivares, Count of, 704-705
Olympic games, 117, 135
On the Civil Wars (Julius Caesar), 239
On the Gallic Wars (Julius Caesar), 239-240
On the Nature of Things (Lucretius), 181, 236-238
Optimates, 226
Orators, Cicero, 240; Demosthenes, 174
"Ordeal," 314-315, 455, 469
Oresteia (Aeschylus), 154-156
Origen of Alexandria, 310, 515
Orphic cult, 130, 132
Osiris, 30-31
Ostracism, 122

743 Index

Ostrogothic Italy, 314-317
Otto of Brunswick, 455-457
Otto the Great, 387-389
Ottoman Empire, 589-590; alliance with France, 590; and German Reformation, 620, 622; invasion of Eastern Europe, 567, 588, 594, 607-608; Turks outflanked by Portuguese, 663; and Philip II, 682-683; Venetian trade and, 568
Ottonian kingship, 389
Ottonian Renaissance, 389-390
Ovid, 261-262
Oxford University, 509, 529; science at, 539; Wycliffe at, 595

"Pacification of Ghent" (1576), 685
Padua, University of, 539, 554, 563
Palatinate, Electorate of, 608, 616, 697, 698-699
Palestine, 83, 86-87, 88
Palladio, Andrea, 717
Palmieri, Matteo, 533
Panhellenic League, 138
Pantheon, 281, 283
Papacy, at Avignon, 540, 574, 592-594; Baroque art and, 716, 718; Charlemagne and, 366-368; conciliar movement and, 593-594; and Council of Trent, 642-643; Crusades and, 413-419; Frederick Barbarossa and, 448-450; in tenth and eleventh century Germany, 389; Gregory VII and, 442-447; Great Schism, 593-594, 598; heresy, mysticism, and reform agitation in the Renaissance, 594-597; in the High Renaissance, 597-599; "holy leagues" and, 599, 694-695; holy Roman Empire and, 599; iconoclastic controversy and, 360-361; impact of reform on revenues of, 643; Innocent III and, 453-457; Investiture Controversy and, 441-447; Normandy and, 409; papal decline, 456-457, 459, 462; papal states, 598-599; Pepin the short and, 358-359; reform in the High Middle Ages, 440-441; support of Benedictines by, 337; in the thirteenth century, 459-460; in the twelfth century, 452-453
Papal Election Decree (1059), 443
Papal states, 452, 458
Paradoxia (Cicero), 240
Paris, 552, 695
Paris, University of, 487, 509, 523, 538, 539, 546, 628, 629, 641
Parlement of Paris, 488, 693, 706
Parliament, beginnings of, 474-476; compared with Estates-General, 488-489; Charles I and, 709-711, 714; civil wars and, 594; under Edward I, 580; under Elizabeth I, 689, 691, 708; French *Fronde* and, 706;

Henry VII and, 584; James I and, 708-709; during Hundred Years' War, 580, 582-583, 584, 591; Reformation and, 624-625, 626; in seventeenth century, 573, 708-715; under Edward I, 477-481
Parma, Duke of, 685, 687
Parmenides, 132, 180
Parthenon, 161, 166, 167, 493
Parthia, 234, 270
Particularism, 447-448; feudal (in France), 383-385; Henry IV (Germany) and, 452, 455; in Holy Roman Empire in 14th and 15th centuries, 586; in sixteenth century, 608
Pastoral (literary genre), 184
Patarenes, 443-444, 450
Paterfamilias, 196, 207, 214
Patricians, Roman, 204-205
Paul the Deacon, 369
Paul III (Pope), 565, 637, 642, 643
Paul IV (Pope), 637, 639, 640, 644
Pax Babylonica, 58-60, 65
Pax Romana, 244, 265-284, 290
Peace of Westphalia, 703-704
Peasants in Charlemagne's time, 354-355; under feudalism, 386, 391-395, 405-406
Peasants and Calvinism in France, 693; decline at end of Renaissance, 572-573; in Eastern Europe, 588; Great Peasants' War, 616-618; in Habsburg Bohemia, 699; in Holy Roman Empire, 609-704; revolt in England 595, 626; revolts during Renaissance, 567; Roman law and, 609
Peasants' Revolt (1524-26), 609, 612, 616-618, 620
Peking Man, age and characteristics of, 6
Peloponnese, 122
Peloponnesian League, 126
Peloponnesian War, 170-173; history of, by Thucydides, 159; in Xenophon's *Hellenics,* 160
Penates, 207
Pepin of Heristal, 357
Pepin the Short, 357-359, 361-362; coronation of, 361, 366
Pergamum, 177, 183, 186, 213, 217
Pericles, 122, 147, 149, 166, 170-171
Persecution, religious, 618, 619-620, 622, 626, 633, 651-653, 683, 690, 693, 710
Persephone (Core), 114, 130
Perseus of Macedonia, 218
Persia: conquests by, under Cyrus, 78; under Darius, 78; conquests of Egypt by, 78; empire of, 78-79; fall of, 82; in Peloponnesian War, 172-173; rule over non-Persian peoples by, 79
Persians: architecture of, 80; art of,

80; astronomy of, 82; language of, 81; origins of, 78; religion of, 81-82; roads built by, 79; settlements at Persian Gulf by, 78
Persian Wars, 78-79, 82, 136-141; history of (Herodotus), 159; *see also* Greece
Perspective, linear, 563
Petition or Right (1628), 709
Petrarch, Francesco, 536, 540
Petrine Doctrine, 593
Pharisees, 293-294
Phidias, 161-166, 167
Philip I (King of France), 483
Philip II, Augustus (King of France), 416, 452, 473, 484
Philip II (King of Spain), Accession, 623; Armada and, 687-688; attempts to expand empire, 678-680; Escorial and, 680; government of, 679-682; Inquisition and, 682; Requesens and, 685; revolt in Low Countries, 683-686; England and, 628, 687-688, 692; war with Turks, 682-683
Philip III (King of Spain), 688-689, 697
Philip IV, the Fair (King of France), 460-461, 481, 487-489, 592
Philip IV (King of Spain), literature in the reign of, 722; painting in reign of, 717; revolts and, 705-706; Thirty Years' War and, 697, 702, 704-706
Philip V (Macedonia), 212-213, 217-218
Philip the Bold (Burgundy), 584
Philip the Good (Burgundy), 585
Philip of Hesse, 616, 618, 620, 622
Philip of Macedon, 175
Philip of Swabia, 455
Philippi, battle of (42 B.C.), 236; Horace in, 258-259
Philippines, 665
Philistines, 66, 88
Philosophy: Athenian, 145-153; in Greek civilization, 130-133; Hellenistic, 179-181; Roman, 241-243
Phoenicians: alphabet, development of, 69; Assyrian conquest of, 72; Canaanite origins of, 68; colonies of, 69; sea trade of, 68; settlements of, 68
Phrygia, 127
Phrygians, 66
Pico della Mirandola, 543
Pilate, Pontius, 294
Pilgrimage of Grace, 625
Pindar, 158
Piracy, 683, 685, 687-688
Pisa, Council of, 593
Pisistratus, 119-120

Pius II (Pope), 594
Pius IV (Pope), 644
Pius V (Pope), 644
Plantagenets, 467
Plataea, 140
Plataea, battle of (479 B.C.), 170
Plato, 126, 149-151, 173, 312; in medieval thought, 369, 513-518, 522
Platonic Academy (Florence), 543
Plebeians, Roman, 204-205
Plebiscita, 205
Pliny the Younger, 273-274
Plotinus, 308
Pluralism, and absenteeism in the Church, 594
Plutarch, 275
Plutarch's *Lives,* 185, 275
Poitiers, battle of (1356), 582
Poland, converted to Christianity, 419; invaded by Russia, 707; in Northern War, 707-708; in sixteenth century, 634, 647, 698; union with Lithuania, 596-647; war with Sweden, 707
Policraticus, 521
Polis (city-state), 115-116, 171, 177-178
Political theory, Aquinas and, 526-527; Calvin and, 631; caesaropapism, 309; Dante and, 500-501; divine right of kings, 621, 653-654; Edward I and, 481; Henry II (England) and, 467-469; John of Salisbury and, 521; Lutheran doctrine of passive obedience, 621, 653; Machiavelli and, 549-551; in medieval England and France, 488-489; Philip IV (France) and, 488; Reformation and, 725-726; representative government and, 475-488; Roman law and, 510; Greek, 118, 123-124, 149-151, 153; Hebrew law, 88; Mesepotamian, 149
Politics (Aristotle), 153
Politiques, 638, 695, 701, 725
Polybius, 185-186, 200
Polycarp (Bishop of Smyrna), 300
Polyclitus, 166
Pompey the Great, 228-233
Pontifex Maximus, 203, 207
Pontus, 177, 217, 226
Poor Clares, 434
Poor Law (1601), 676, 690
Populares, 224-225
Population, colonial, 665; decrease in early Renaissance, 566; effects of Thirty Years' War, 704; in eleventh century Europe, 400; and "Price Revolution," 673-674; recovery during Renaissance, 568; in seventeenth century, 661, 724; Vikings and, 376
Portugal, Brazil and, 664; commercial empire in 16th century, 568, 663-664-675, 678; independence movement, 705; Olivares and, 705; origins, 576; Philip II succeeds to throne, 678
Poseidon, 108, 114
Po Valley, 196, 198, 212, 233
Praetors, 203, 270
Praxiteles, 166
Prehistory: chronological chart of, 11; domestication of plants in, 10; species of man in, 5-7, tools and tool making in, 7-10; towns of, 10-11
Preliterate culture; chronological stages of, 13; food gathering stage of, 7-10; food producing stage of, 10-11; relationship of race to culture in, 8-9; religious concepts of, 8; transition from savagery to barbarism in, 10; see "Geologic Ages"
Presbyterians, 710-715
"Price Revolution", 609, 626, 673-674, 685, 723
Prince Henry, "the Navigator", 663
Princeps, role of, 232
Princeps Senatus, 250
Printing in Deventer, 597; early printed works, 552, 597; and English civil wars, 552, 713; impact on governments, 573; impact on Reformation, 596, 612-613; invention of, 551-553
Propylaea, 167
Protagoras, 147
Protectorate (England), 715
Protestantism, in Austria, 699; in Bohemia, 699; in eastern Europe, 648; Elizabeth I as champion of, 691-692; growth of, 638, 647; influence of, 533; origins of term, 622; in Spain, 681
Protestant Union (Empire), 698
Provisions of Oxford, 476
Ptah, 29-30
Ptolemy, 177, 275, 349, 528
Ptolemy, Claudius, 181
Ptolemy, co-ruler of Egypt with Cleopatra, 233
Ptolemy V, ruler of Egypt, 217
Punic Wars, 186, 208, 209-213
Puritanism, 426; in the Catholic Reformation, 644; Savonarola and, 543; spread of in England, 689-690, 710-715; see also Calvinism
Pydna, battle of (168 B.C.), 218, 219
Pylos (or Pylus), 108, 109
Pyramids, 31-32, 501
Pyrenees, Peace of, 705, 707
Pyrrhic wars, 210
Pyrrhus, 202, 212
Pythagoras, 131, 132

Quaestors, 203
Quakers, 655, 714, 726

Rabelais, Francois, 536, 537, 545

Ramses II, 42
Ramses III, 44
Raphael, Sanzio, 560, 564-565
Re, 22
Reformation, Anabaptists and, 619-620; Catholic Reformation, 638-646; Calvin and, 628-634; Eastern Europe and, 647-650; England and, 623-628; German and Luther, 607-618; Renaissance and, 642, 613, 636, 638; Zwingli and, 618-619
Regensburg, Diet and Colloquy of, 637
Regulated companies, 670-671
Reims Cathedral, 493, 507
Rembrandt van Rijn, 717
Renaissance, 399; artistic developments of, 553-566; commercial depression during period of, 566-569; literature of, 535-537; meaning of, 533; religious developments of, 591-599; see also Northern Renaissance
Representative Assemblies, in Muscovy, 650; in the Netherlands, 683; in Poland-Lithuania, 647; during the Renaissance, 573
Republicanism, 540, 543, 550-551, 571, 587, 589, 618, 705
Requesens, 685
Reuchlin, Johann, 545, 611
Revolution of 509 (B.C.), 199, 202, 248
Revolutions, *Fronde* in France, 706-707; Netherlands, 683-687; in the Renaissance, 567; in Spain under Philip IV, 704-706; see also Towns, Peasants, Nobility
Rhetoric, 173-174
Rhodes, 183-217
Richard I, the Lion-Hearted (King of England), 416, 472-473, 484
Richelieu, Armand Jean du Plessis, Duke of, 551, 696, 700-702
Roads, Roman, 208-209
Rocroi, Battle of (1643), 702
Roger the Great (Sicily), 410-412, 450
Rolf, 378
Roman Catholicism, in Elizabethan England, 689; in Stuart England, 710, 711; see also Church
Romance, medieval, 498-499
Romance of Renard, 500
Romance of the Rose, 499
Roman culture; architecture in Silver age, 275-283; arts in Early Republic, 208-209; Augustan Age of literature, 253-265; Early Republic, 200-209; Late Republic, 236-243; literature, in Early Republic, 207; literature in Late Republic, 236-241; literature of

745   Index

the Republic, 215-216; literature of the Silver Age, 273-275; philosophy in Late Republic, 241-243; religion in Early Republic, 207-208; religion in Late Republic, 241-243; religions in the Republic, 214, 215; science in Silver Age, 275; sculpture in Silver Age, 283; Silver Age, 273-284
Roman Empire, 247-290; Christianity and, 300, 302, 308-309; cosmopolitanism in, 269-270; division into western and eastern "empires," 283-284; 285-286; militarization in, 285; paternalism in, 251; rulers, see Table, 267; social classes in, 251-252
Romanesque architecture, 501-506
Roman law, 270, 314, 327, 544-549, 573, 574, 608-609, 610, 628, 638; Byzantium and, 327; Caesar and, 233-234; Inquisition and, 428-429; Justinian and, 327; Law of Twelve Tables, 205; Medieval Europe and, 510-511; Renaissance and, 548
Roman Republic: class struggles, 204-205, 221; economic conditions in, 220, 243-244; militarization of life in late days of, 214; political institutions of, 202-204; territorial expansion in Early Republic, 200-202; wars, chronological table, 217
Roman World, birth of imperialism in, 209-213; disintegration of, 285-288
Rome, fall of, 288-289; legacy of, 289-290; Visigothic sack of (410), 312, 327
Roundheads, 711
Rubicon River, 232
Rule of St. Benedict, 317-318
Rumolo family, 199
Rump, 714-715
Russia, 329, 404; attempts by Teutonic Knights to invade, 419; expansion of, 589, 649, 667, 707; invaded by Swedes, 376-377, 378-379; in the sixteenth century, 647, 649-650, 666; lack of printing presses, 552; Orthodox religion, 589

Sabines, 200, 201
"Sacramentarians", 597, 618
Sacraments, 442, 612, 613, 622, 626, 643; in Bohemia, 648; Council of Trent and, 643; Calvin and, 630; humanists and, 542, 545, 636; Luther and, 622; mystics and, 596; Wycliffe and, 583, 595
Sadducees, 293
St. Albertus Magnus, 431, 487, 522-523
St. Ambrose, 310-311, 443, 515
St. Anselm, 466-468, 470, 515, 518-520
St. Anthony, 302, 337
St. Augustine of Hippo, 289, 303, 311-313, 369, 372, 513-520, 538, 540, 610, 618, 651
St. Bartholomew's Day, Massacre of, 694
St. Basil of Caesarea, 302
St. Bede the Venerable, 339-340, 377, 381, 514
St. Benedict of Nursia, 302, 317, 337, 423-424
St. Bernard of Clairvaux, 415, 425-426, 437, 443, 515, 527
St. Bonaventure, 436, 487, 515, 522-523, 527
St. Boniface, 340, 358-360, 381
St. Denis, Church of, 361, 507
St. Dominic, 430-431, 437
St. Francis of Assisi, 430-434, 437, 515, 528, 530, 596, 640
St. Louis, see Louis IX (King of France)
St. Mark, Cathedral of, 325
St. Patrick, 334
St. Peter Damiani, 442-443, 515
St. Jerome, 310-311, 317, 515, 546
St. Paul, 295-297
St. Peter, 294, 295-296, 301, 440
St. Peter's, Rome, 564, 718
St. Simeon Stylites, 337
St. Thomas Aquinas, 312, 431, 487, 515, 522-528, 530
St. Thomas Becket, 470-472
Saladin, 416
Salamis, Bay of, 140
Salamis, victory at, 154
Salerno, University of, 409, 510
Salian Dynasty, 390
Sallust, 240-241
Salutati, Coluccio, 540
Samnites, 196-201
Sancta Sophia, 322, 326
Sanhedrin, 293-294
Sappho, 133
Saracens, 374-376
Sardinia, 211, 212
Sargon the Great, 48; see also Mesopotamia
Sargon II, 72; see also Assyrians
Saturnalia, 207
Saul, 88
Saul of Tarsus, 296-297
Savonarola, Girolamo, 543, 571
Saxony, 365, 376, 419, 610, 614, 618, 620, 621, 636, 698, 704; Welfs of, 448
Scholasticism, 514, 537-539, 544, 545, 596; Luther's attack on, 611
"School of Hellas", 145, 154
Schutz, Heinrich, 722
Science: 539, 543, 600; Albertus Magnus and, 523; ancient Greek science, translations of, 521-522; ancient Near East and, 55-57, 82; Greek, 131, 132, 146, 153; medicine in Egypt, 24-25; Hellenistic, 181-183; medicine in High Middle Ages, 510; Mesopotamian, 55-57; Otto Nian Rennaissance and, 389-398, Persian, 82; Roger Bacon and, 529; Roman, 275; Salerno, medical studies at, 409; Zoroastrianism and, 82
Scipio Africanus, 212-213, 218
Scipio Publius, 212-213
Scotland, 580, 634, 638, 710, 714; Irish monks in, 335, 376
Scotus, Duns, 527-528
Scotus, John, 370-371, 514
Scribes, 293
Scripture, see Bible
Scutage, 405
Sea Peoples, 67, 68, 109
Seleucus, 176-177
Senacharib, 72
Senate, Roman, 202, 205, 221, 233
Senatus consultum ultimum (the "last decree"), 223, 232
Seneca, 273, 629
Separatists (Independents), 710, 711, 713
Serfdom, easing of in West, 572, 583; English peasants revolt against, 583; in eastern Europe, 573, 588, 589, 674, 699, 708; in Holy Roman Empire, 610, 616, 704; Spanish attempts to abolish, 578-579
Serfs, 391-395, 405-406
Sermon on the Mount, 292
Sertorius, defeat of, 229
Servetus, Michael, 633
Severus, L. Septimius, 273, 285
Shakespeare, William, 537, 722
Sheep, and enclosures in England, 626; in Spain, 579, 682
Sheriffs, 463, 466, 469
Shi'ism, 344
Shires, 465; courts in, 465, 469-470
Siberia, 667
Sic et non, 520-521
Sicilian Vespers, 458-459
Sicily, 128, 197, 209-211, 225; conquest by Normans, 408-410; Frederick II, 457; Henry VI and, 452; Innocent III and, 455-456; War of Sicilian Vespers in, 458-459
Sickingen, Franz von, 615-616
Sigismund (Emperor), 593
Siger of Brabant, 516, 523
Simon de Montfort, 476-477
Simons, Menno, 620
Simony, 440-441, 443, 593, 594, 596
Skepticism, 180
Slavery, 219; in eleventh century, 405
Slave trade and slavery, 568, 662, 664, 665, 666

746 Index

Sleeping Hermaphrodite, 187
Sluter, Claus, 559
Social War, Roman, 225-226
Society, Athenian, 117-122; Augustus and social classes, 251-252; Greek, 117-126; in Mesopotamia, 49-57; in mid-eleventh century, 440; Roman, 200-209, 220-236, 253-605, 273-285; Spartan, 122-126; women in Hellenistic society, 178; effects of European expansion on, 662; under Elizabeth I, 690-691; in the period 1560-1660, 669-677; Reformation and, 654-655; Renaissance, 569-573; in Spain under Ferdinand and Isabella, 577-579; in Stuart England, 711-713
Society of Jesus, 597, 637, 639, 641-642, 644
Socrates, 147-149, 157, 173
Socratic Method, 148-149
Solomon, 88-89
Solon, 118
Somerset, Duke of, 626
Song of Roland, 364, 495-496
Sophism, 147-148
Sophocles, 114, 147, 156, 167
Sophrosyne, 147, 153, 178
South America, 664-665
Spain, Carthaginian control, 212; Charlemagne in, 364; insurgents in, 224; in Middle Ages, 407, 408; reconquest from Moors, 407-408; Roman control, 213, 233; commercial expansion in New World, 664-667; under Ferdinand and Isabella, 577-580; industrial depression in, 675; inquisition in, 544, 579, 638, 680; Italy and, 599; reconquest, 576-577; dominance of Spanish Habsburgs, 678-697; war with France, (1635-1659), 702, 704-706; war with Netherlands, 683-687; "Spanish Fury", 685; Visigoths in, 316, 328, 333-334
Spanish March, 364, 408
Sparta, 120, 122-126, 138, 145, 170-173, 217
Spartacus, 229
Spartans, 122-126; early settlements of, 122; political life of, 123-124; social structure of, 124-125; hegemony, 125-126; in Persian war, 139-141; Peloponnesian War, 170-173
Speyer Diet of, (1526), 620, (1529), 622
Spiritual Franciscans, 596
Star Chamber, 584, 711
Stephen, first Christian martyr, 296
Stesichorus, 130, 133
Stoicism, 180; and Calvin, 629; in the Renaissance, 545; in Roman Republic, 241-242
Strassbourg, 614, 632

Studium generale, 508
Suetonius, 274-275
Sufism, 347-348
Suger, Abbot, 483, 507
Suleiman the Magnificent, 682
Sulla, L. Cornelius, 225-228, *passim*
Sully, Duke of, 696-697
Sumatra, 664
Sumer, 45-49; *see also* Mesopotamia
Swabia, 419; Hohenstaufens of, 448
Sweden, 376-380, 621, 670, 700; constitutional crisis of 1650, 708; and Northern War (1655-1660), 707-708; and Thirty Years' War, 700, 703, 707; trade of, 667, 670
Swiss Confederacy, 550, 584, 585, 587, 610, 618, 619, 633, 703
Synod of Whitby (664), 339
Syracuse, 172, 209
Syria, 127, 217

Taborites, 596
Tacitus, 275, 300, 314
Taras (Taranto), 128
Tarquins, 199
Tartars, 589, 647
Taxation, as cause of lower-class unrest, 591, 609; in Castile, 579-580, 682; of the clergy by the Church, 592-593; of the clergy by the state, 592, 624; of the peasantry, 573; in France under Richelieu and Mazarin, 701, 706; James I and *Paulette* in France, 696; Spanish in Netherlands, 683-684; Petition of Right and, 709; Philip II and, 682; in Spain during Thirty Years' War, 704-705
Taxes, consent to (in England), 475-476; John I (England) and, 474-475; papal, 460-461; Philip IV (France) and, 488-489
Technology, advantages of over non-Europeans, 662; 1560-1650, 666-667, 672-673; in Renaissance, 568
Tell el Amarna, 66
Templars, 419, 426; Philip IV (France) and, 488
Ten Commandments, 88
"Ten lost tribes," 72, 90
Territorial states, general, 591; Italy, 574
Tertullian, 515
Tetzel, Johannes, 612
Teutonic Knights, 419, 426, 587, 608
Teutonic tribes, 272
Teutons, 225
Thalassocracy, Cretan, 108
Thales, 70
Thales of Miletus, 131
Theatines, 640
Thebes (Egypt), 39
Thebes (Greece), 138, 175, 176
Themistocles, 122, 138-140
Theocracy, 367-368

Theodoric the Great, 316-317, 326
Theodosius (Roman Emperor), 288, 302, 309
Theognis, 113, 133
Thermopylae, 140
Theseus, 102
Thespis, 133-134
Thessaly, 138
Thetes (lowest citizen class), 118
Thiene, Gaetano di, 640
"The Thirty" (of Athens), 160
Thirty Years' War (1618-1648), 661, 667, 685, 697-707, 708
Tholos Tombs, 108
Thrace, 78, 127, 175
Thrasymachos, 148
Thucydides, 159-160, 171-173, 240, 241
Thutmose III, 38
Tiberius, 255-266
Tiber River, 197, 199
Tiglath-Pileser I, 71-72
Tilly, Count of, 699-700
Timocracy, 118
Tiryns, 108
Titian, 561, 565
Titus, Arch of, 281
Toleration, by Austrian Habsburgs, 637, 648, 697; Brethren of Common Life and, 637; Calvin and, 630; Castellio and, 633, 636, 652; Charles I and, 710; Oliver Cromwell and, 715; Edict of Nantes, 695-696; Erasmus and, 548, 635; Independents and, 711; Medieval Spain, 576; More and, 546; Netherlands, 620, 684, 687; Peace of Augsburg and, 653; Peace of Westphalia and, 702; Reformation and, 651-653; Rejection by Beza, 636; by House of Valois, 646, 647, 693, 694; Turkish, 648
Tours, battle of (732), 345, 356, 406
Towns, architecture and, 504-507; at end of Roman Empire, 331; growth of (in Middle Ages), 400-402; government of, 402; craft guilds in, 402-403; heresies in, 428; Lombard towns and Frederick Barbarossa, 451; papal relationship with, 450; Mesopotamian villages, 47; prehistoric, 11; Roman urbanization, 199; in Elizabethan England, 691; in Renaissance culture, 566, 569, 599; revolutions of, in Renaissance, 569-572, 609-610; Spanish towns in 14th century, 577; vernacular literature in, 494-495, 500-501
Trajan, 268-270
Trajan, Column of, 281

747   Index

Trappists, 426
Trebizon, 127
Trent, Council of, 455, 622, 639, 642-644, 646
Tribunes, Roman, 204-205
Triennial Act, 710-711
Trier, Electorate of, 586, 608, 616
Trinity, doctrine of, 303
Tristan and Iseult, medieval romance, 498
Triumvirate, First, 231
Triumvirate, Second, 236
Trojans, 109; in the *Aeneid,* 254
Troubadours, 496-497
Troy, 109, 215
Turks, *see* Ottoman Empire
Tutankhamon, 41
Tyndale, William, 625
Tyrannicide, 521

Umayyads, 344-347
Umbrians, 196
Unam Sanctam, 461
United Provinces, *see* Dutch Republic
Universals, conflict over, in medieval thought, 514, 516-518, 520
Universities, medieval, 508-510
Urban II, 413, 447

Valla, Lorenzo, 541-542, 546
Valois Dynasty, civil wars and, 693-695; Burgundy and, 584; Elizabeth I and, 692; end of, 693; Hundred Years' War and, 580-582; Philip II and, 687, Scotland and, 687; *see also* Habsburg-Valois wars
Van Eyck, Jan, 553
Vasari, Giorgio, 533
Vassalage, 483-484, 465
Vault, 501, 506-507
Veii, 201
Venice, 401, 541, 565, 567-568, 571, 574, 590, 663, 682, 716
Venus Genetrix, 234
Verdun, Treaty of (843), 373-374, 388
Vermeer, Jan, 717
Vernacular Literature, 535-537; Czech, 535; English, 535; French, 535; German, 535, 613, 614-615; Reformation and, 614-615; Spanish, 535, 537; Tuscan, 535, 540
Verrazano, Giovanni de, 666
Versailles, 717, 721
Vespasian, 267-268, 281

Vikings, 329, 272, 276-380
Villon, Francois, 537
Vincent of Beauvais, 522
Vinci, Leonardo da, 539, 558, 563, 600
Virgil, 183, 200, 215, 253-258, 261, 540
Visigoths, 314, 333-334; conquer Byzantine southern Spain, 328; Justinian and, 327
Vives, Juan Luis, 545
Volsci, 200, 201, 263-264
Vulgate Bible, 311; Council of Trent and, 643; Erasmus and, 547, 548; Valla and, 542

Waldensianism, 428, 450, 595, 605
Waldo, Peter, 428
Wallenstein, Albert of, 699, 700
Wales, 381; conquest of, by Edward I, 481
Warfare, Anglo-Dutch war, 677; Armada, 687-688; Assyrian innovations, 75-76; civil wars in England, 711-714; civil wars in France, 693-695; civil wars and Reformation, 653; and crises, 723, 726; effects on Renaissance commerce, 567; under feudalism, 405; Frankish military tactics, 383-384; Habsburg-Valois wars, 580, 585, 590, 608, 615, 620, 622, 623, 636, 639, 642; Hundred Years' War, 580, 582; Hussite wars, 596; ideological, 723; impact on nobility, 579; invention of stirrup, 364; in Peasants' Revolt, 616-617; by Philip II, 682-688; Russia and, 649; rise of calvary under Charlemagne, 364; in seventeenth century, 726; and society, 667-668; as source of Renaissance despotism, 575; superiority over non-Europeans in, 662; Vikings and, 376-380
War of the Roses, 583, 711
Weber, Max, 655
Welfs, 425, 448, 450-451, 455-456
Wergeld, 314
Wessex, 380-382, 463
West Indies, 664, 665, 666, 677
Westphalia, Peace of, (1648), 702-704, 706
White Mountain, battle of, (1620), 699
William the Conqueror, 383, 463-466, 482
William of Lorris, 499
William of Ockham, 528

William II (England), 466-467
William IX of Auitaine, 426, 296-297
William the Silent (of Orange), 684, 689
Willibord, 358, 369
Windmill, development of, 355
Witchcraft, Calvin and, 631; in Renaissance Florence, 543; in sixteenth and seventeenth centuries, 638, 725
Wittenberg University, 610, 611
Wolsey, Thomas, 623, 624
Works and Days (Hesiod), 126-127
Worms, Concordat of (1122), 447-448, 455, 467
Worms, Diet of, (1495), 588; (1521), 588, 613-614
Worms, Edict of, 614, 616, 620
Wycliffe, John, 583, 593, 595, 596

Xavier, Francis, 641
Xenophanes, 131-132
Xenophon, 160
Xerxes, 138-140, 170
Ximenes, Cardinal, 544-545, 579, 637

Yahweh, 83-84, 86, 88, 90, 91, 92, 93, 94; covenants with Hebrews of, 83-84, 87, 88; Ten Commandments of, 88
"Year of the Four Emperors", 266-267; *see* Table of Roman Rulers, 267
Youth, training of Spartan, 125

Zama, battle of (202 B.C.), 213, 215, 217
Zeno, 180
Zeus, 102, 108, 113, 114, 130, 187
Zeus (Phidias), 161
Zoroastrianism, astronomy and, 82; ethical teachings of, 81; founding of, 81; influence on Hebrews of, 94-95; and Mithraism, 303; monotheism in, 81; mythology of, 81; and Orthodox Judaism, 291; in Rome, 215; writings about, 81-82
Zoser, 31
Zurich, 618-619
Zwingli, Ulrich, 610, 615, 618-619, 621, 622, 635